WITHDRAWN

NORTH DAKOTA
STATE UNIVERSITY
SEP 2 8 1983
SERIALS DEPT.
LIBRARY

The Bowker Annual

THE BOWKER ANNUAL
OF LIBRARY & BOOK TRADE INFORMATION

28TH EDITION · 1983

Compiled & Edited by
JOANNE O'HARE

Consulting Editor
Frank L. Schick

Sponsored by
The Council of National Library
& Information Associations, Inc.

R. R. BOWKER COMPANY
NEW YORK & LONDON

Published by R. R. Bowker Company
1180 Avenue of the Americas, New York, N.Y. 10036
Copyright © 1983 by Xerox Corporation
All rights reserved
International Standard Book Number 0-8352-1680-2
International Standard Serial Number 0068-0540
Library of Congress Catalog Card Number 55-12434
Printed and bound in the United States of America

No copyright is claimed for articles in this volume prepared by U.S. Government employees as part of their official duties. Such articles are in the public domain and can be reproduced at will.

Contents

Preface xi

PART 1
REPORTS FROM THE FIELD

NEWS REPORTS

LJ News Report, 1982. *Karl Nyren* 3

SLJ News Report, 1982. *Bertha M. Cheatham* 23

PW News Report, 1982. *John F. Baker* 31

SPECIAL REPORTS

The New Federalism: How It Is Changing the Library Profession
in the United States. *Patricia W. Berger* 36

Public Sector/Private Sector Interaction in Providing Library and Information
Services. *Toni Carbo Bearman* and *Douglas S. Price* 42

Professional Services Provided to Libraries and Information Centers by Private
Sector Organizations. *William A. Creager* and *Donald W. King* 48

The New Copyright Law: A Five-Year Review. *Nancy H. Marshall* 55

Library Networking in the United States, 1982. *Glyn T. Evans* 70

The Use of Microcomputers in Elementary and Secondary School Libraries.
Blanche Woolls 76

FEDERAL AGENCIES

The National Commission on Libraries and Information Science.
Toni Carbo Bearman and Douglas S. Price 81

The Copyright Office: Developments in 1982. *Victor W. Marton* 84

Federal Library Committee. *James P. Riley* 89

National Technical Information Service. *Ted Ryerson* and *Ruth S. Smith* ... 93

Educational Resources Information Center (ERIC). *Ted Brandhorst* 98

FEDERAL LIBRARIES

The Library of Congress. *James W. McClung* 105

National Library of Medicine. *Robert B. Mehnert* 112

National Agricultural Library. *Eugene M. Farkas* 117

The Presidential Libraries of the National Archives and Records Service.
David S. Van Tassel 120

NATIONAL ASSOCIATIONS

American Booksellers Association. *G. Roysce Smith* 124
American Library Association. *Carol A. Nemeyer* 127
American National Standards Committee Z39 and International Organization for Standardization Technical Committee 46.
Patricia W. Berger and *Robert W. Frase* 135
Association of American Library Schools. *Charles D. Patterson* 140
Association of American Publishers. *Jane Lippe-Fine* 143
Information Industry Association. *Fred S. Rosenau* 151
Society of American Archivists.
Ann Morgan Campbell and *Deborah Risteen* 156
Special Libraries Association. *Richard E. Griffin* 160

PART 2
LEGISLATION, FUNDING, AND GRANTS

Legislation Affecting Librarianship in 1982.
Eileen D. Cooke and *Carol C. Henderson* 167
Legislation Affecting Publishing in 1982. *AAP Washington Staff* 178
Legislation Affecting the Information Industry in 1982.
Robert S. Willard 184

FUNDING PROGRAMS AND GRANT-MAKING AGENCIES

Council on Library Resources, Inc. *Jane A. Rosenberg* 194
Library Services and Construction Act 203
Higher Education Act, Title II-A, College Library Resources.
Beth Phillips Fine 214
Higher Education Act, Title II-B, Library Career Training.
Frank A. Stevens and *Janice Owens* 216
Higher Education Act, Title II-B, Library Research and Demonstration Program. *Yvonne B. Carter* 221
Higher Education Act, Title II-C, Strengthening Research Library Resources.
Louise V. Sutherland and *Janice Owens* 224
Education Consolidation and Improvement Act of 1981, Chapter 2.
Phyllis Land 231
National Endowment for the Humanities Support for Libraries, 1982. 236
National Historical Publications and Records Commission 240
National Science Foundation Support for Research in Information Science and Technology. *Edward C. Weiss* 244

PART 3
LIBRARY EDUCATION, PLACEMENT, AND SALARIES

Recent Developments in Library Education. *Herbert S. White* 257
Education in Conservation of Library Materials. *Josephine Riss Fang* 260
Guide to Library Placement Sources. *Margaret Myers* 264
Placements and Salaries, 1981: Still Holding.
    Carol L. Learmont and *Stephen Van Houten* 279
Sex, Salaries, and Library Support, 1981.
    Kathleen M. Heim and *Carolyn Kacena* 294
Accredited Library Schools 309
Library Scholarship Sources 312
Library Scholarship and Award Recipients, 1982 314

PART 4
RESEARCH AND STATISTICS

LIBRARY RESEARCH AND STATISTICS
Research on Libraries and Librarianship in 1982. *Mary Jo Lynch* 323
U.S. Public Library Statistics in Series: A Bibliography and Subject
    Index. *Herbert Goldhor* 327
Characteristics of the U.S. Population Served by Libraries, 1982
    W. Vance Grant 335
Number of Libraries in the United States and Canada 337
Public and Academic Library Acquisition Expenditures 339
Urban-Suburban Public Library Statistics, 1980–1981. *Joseph Green* 344
NCES Survey of Private School Library Media Centers, 1979.
    Milbrey L. Jones 352
Library Buildings in 1982.
    Bette-Lee Fox, Ann Burns, and *Deborah Waithe* 356

BOOK TRADE RESEARCH AND STATISTICS
Book Title Output and Average Prices: 1982 Preliminary Figures.
    Chandler B. Grannis 371
Book Sales Statistics: Highlights from AAP Annual Survey, 1981.
    Chandler B. Grannis 380
U.S. Consumer Expenditures on Books, 1981. *John P. Dessauer* 382
Prices of U.S. and Foreign Published Materials. *Nelson A. Piper* 385
Number of Book Outlets in the United States and Canada 403
Book Review Media Statistics 405

PART 5
INTERNATIONAL REPORTS AND STATISTICS

INTERNATIONAL REPORTS
Frankfurt Book Fair, 1982. *Herbert R. Lottman* 409
The IFLA Conference, 1982. *Russell Shank* and *Jean E. Lowrie* 416
The Vatican Library and Archives. *Silvio A. Bedini* 419
Library and Information Services in Cyprus. *John F. Harvey* 428

INTERNATIONAL STATISTICS
International Standards Criteria for Price Indexes for Library Materials.
  Frederick C. Lynden 436
U.S. Book Exports and Imports and International Title Output
  Chandler B. Grannis 440
British Book Production, 1982 445

PART 6
REFERENCE INFORMATION

BIBLIOGRAPHIES
The Librarian's Bookshelf. *Jo-Ann Michalak* 453
Basic Publications for the Publisher and the Book Trade.
  Margaret M. Spier 465

DISTINGUISHED BOOKS
Literary Prizes, 1982 473
Notable Books of 1982 489
Best Young Adult Books of 1982 490
Best Children's Books of 1982 492
Best Sellers of 1982: Hardcover Fiction and Nonfiction.
  Daisy Maryles 495

PART 7
DIRECTORY OF ORGANIZATIONS

DIRECTORY OF LIBRARY AND RELATED ORGANIZATIONS
National Library and Information-Industry Associations,
United States and Canada 505
State, Provincial, and Regional Library Associations 578
State Library Agencies 591

State School Library Media Associations 595
State Supervisors of School Library Media Services 603
International Library Associations 607
Foreign Library Associations 618

DIRECTORY OF BOOK TRADE AND RELATED ORGANIZATIONS
Book Trade Associations, United States and Canada 630
International and Foreign Book Trade Associations 636

CALENDAR, 1983–1984. 644

INDEX 649

DIRECTORY OF U.S. AND CANADIAN LIBRARIES 681

Preface

Now in its 28th edition, *The Bowker Annual* continues to serve as a one-stop source of diverse information for and about libraries, the book trade, and the information industry. It is both an annual review of major events, trends, and developments in these fields and a compact handbook of current reference and directory information.

Of particular interest in the 1983 edition are several special reports in Part 1 that focus on the impact of recent political, economic, and technological developments on the library, publishing, and information worlds. In "The New Federalism: How It Is Changing the Library Profession in the United States," Patricia Berger examines the implications to the profession of two major policy issues advanced by the Reagan administration, including efforts of the U.S. Office of Personnel Management to revise the classification and qualification standards for government library personnel and of the U.S. Office of Management and Budget to encourage the use of private contractors, rather than federal employees, to perform a variety of commercial services, including library operations.

Toni Carbo Bearman and Douglas Price identify key issues in the ongoing debate over the principles of government involvement in information activities in "Public Sector/Private Sector Interaction in Providing Library and Information Services." In a related special report, "Professional Services Provided to Libraries and Information Centers by Private Sector Organizations," William Creager and Donald King survey the rise of, and outlook for, private companies in the field. Supporting articles on national information activities appear in the Federal Agencies and Federal Libraries sections of Part 1, including reports from two major federal clearinghouses—the National Technical Information Service (NTIS) and the Educational Resources Information Center (ERIC).

A special report by Nancy Marshall, "The New Copyright Law: A Five-Year Review," provides a detailed overview of the implementation of the new copyright law with particular emphasis on the controversial issue of library photocopying. A separate report in the Federal Agencies section describes the activities of the Copyright Office in 1982. In the area of technology, there are special reports by Glyn Evans on recent developments in library networking and by Blanche Woolls on the use of microcomputers in elementary and secondary schools.

A number of other themes emerge from the 1983 contents, as well. Library education is the subject of three articles, including, in Part 1, a report from the Association of American Library Schools, and, in Part 3, an overview of recent developments in library education by Herbert White and an article on education in conservation of library materials by Josephine Fang. Archives are discussed in Part 1 in an article on the Presidential Libraries of the National Archives and Records Service and in a report from the Society of American Archivists; a report on the funding programs of the National Historical Publications and Records Commission appears in Part 4.

Additional articles of special interest this year include, in Part 2, a report by Phyllis Land on the Education Consolidation and Improvement Act of 1981, Chapter 2, which surveys the gains and losses to date in federal funding to school libraries under the new state block-grant distribution system. Part 4 features a bibliography and subject index of U.S. public library statistics in series by Herbert Goldhor and a summary of the latest survey of private school library media centers from the National Center for Education Statistics (NCES).

International coverage in Part 5 includes Russell Shank and Jean Lowrie's report on the 1982 Montreal conference of the International Federation of Library Associations and Institutions (IFLA); a description of library and information services in Cyprus; and a report on the development of international standards criteria for library material price indexes. In recognition of the exhibit of artworks from the Vatican Museum traveling to major U.S. museums in 1983, a detailed article on the history and holdings of the Vatican Library and Archives is also included.

Finally, the 1983 *Bowker Annual* continues its comprehensive series of statistical articles and reports on book trade activity, including pricing, output, sales, and consumer and library expenditures.

Special acknowledgment is due to all contributors who provided articles and information to this edition of the *Annual*. In addition, the editor wishes to thank Filomena Simora for her special assistance in preparing this book.

Part 1
Reports from the Field

News Reports

LJ NEWS REPORT, 1982

Karl Nyren
Senior Editor, *Library Journal*

The main themes in the library news of 1982 were funding, automation, and networking and the impact of a fast-changing world on the people who operate libraries. Public and academic libraries both faced pressures for leaner, more productive operations. Both were engrossed with automation, many moving from the first-generation circulation systems into integrated library systems, experimenting with microcomputers, and working on computer literacy. Both were concerned with the fast coalescing networks and seeing the first concerted moves to bring them and all other types of libraries into resource-sharing programs. The impact of all this and other pressures was seen in the news of library personnel: demands for new staff expertise; the continuing growth in the number of volunteers, consultants, and nonlibrarian specialists; new assaults on both professional status and equality for women; and the efforts of libraries, associations, and library schools to respond to the new pressures.

Public library buildings continued to spring up, nourished by a stable stream of local funding in both prosperous and impoverished communities; both academic and public buildings were influenced by the need for greater efficiencies, resulting in energy saving design of new buildings, increased remodeling and reuse of older structures, and access for the handicapped. [For a detailed report on library building in 1982, see Part 4—*Ed.*]

Copyright was back in the news, as the fragile detente between libraries and publishers began to crumble. Publishers won court decisions over two special libraries and announced at year's end their intention to go after academic libraries. A copyright study by King Research, Inc., assessing five years under the present copyright legislation, backed industry charges of widespread violations, but was angrily attacked by librarians as heavily slanted and contradictory. [See the five-year review of the new copyright law in the Special Reports section of Part 1, as well as the annual report from the Copyright Office in the Federal Agencies section of Part 1—*Ed.*]

Adult programming in public libraries reached new heights of imagination and energy, with great efforts going into humanities-related, ethnic, literacy, and community information programs. Perhaps for the first time in recent years, this kind of library activity has come into question. Lowell Martin was the most eminent, but not the only, librarian doubting the public library's role in all these areas, many of which might be better handled by other agencies, allowing the public library's energies to go back into the provision of library materials and the dissemination of useful information not readily available at other agencies.

Security became a more pressing need than ever, dramatized by the conviction of book thief James Shinn and the destruction by arson of the Hollywood branch of the Los Angeles Public Library. Book detection systems are now accepted as necessities in

Note: Adapted from *Library Journal*, January 15, 1983.

most libraries, but no such remedy has been found for the massive mutilation of periodical and book materials by college and university students and even graduate researchers.

Prices continued to rise for most things libraries buy; a welcome exception was building construction, where contractors are lean and hungry. Books kept climbing in price, as did periodicals, and a new pricing policy adopted by some book publishers was attacked by librarians: the freight-pass-through practice of adding a freight charge to the price of every book was seen as an underhanded way of increasing prices. The sometimes astronomical price increases in government publications were assailed as one element in an overall administration policy of reducing the flow of information from government to the public.

Following is a detailed look at the major stories appearing in *Library Journal* and *LJ/SLJ Hotline* in 1982.

LIBRARY FUNDING

Federal funding for the nation's libraries and for services they depend on continued to shrink in 1982, and the situation threatened to get worse in the coming year. Only with a struggle were Library Services and Construction Act (LSCA) funds for this year protected, and as this is being written, the postelection return of Congress promises another battle and either another year's grace or the end of the Library Services and Construction Act. [See Part 2 for reports on LSCA and other federally funded programs in 1982—*Ed.*]

More fears are raised by the administration's desire to scuttle revenue sharing, which a 1982 study shows to have been a lot more useful to libraries than had been expected: It has built libraries, provided them with automation, and in many cases has been allocated to the day-to-day operations of libraries. In the latter case, loss of revenue sharing could pose a threat of disaster.

Slashing of archives funding has directly cut services to library users by throttling the flow of interloan traffic between the National Archives and the nation's libraries. Cancellation of thousands of government publications for lack of profitability, steep price increases on government publications, and reduction of efforts to apprise libraries and the public of new publications, all reduced services relied on by libraries. In the case of the GOP, cancellation of unprofitable titles may, as claimed, have rid the system of unneeded deadwood, but the sole criterion—profitability—provides little assurance to librarians that this kind of weeding is healthy. The announced intention of the Government Printing Office (GPO) to close most of its bookstores—again on a profitability basis—threatened still another reduction in service to the end user. GPO's novel solution to its budget deficit, furloughing its employees, was in keeping with its position that they constitute a vastly overpaid bureaucracy, but was at variance with the stance of the Joint Committee on Printing, which opposed the furloughs. It was at variance also with the District Court order that forbade the furlough remedy for GPO finances.

Unexpected support for new federal initiatives in education came from the Office of Technology Assessment (OTA), which in a September release predicted a greater demand for the understanding of technology and questioned whether either traditional institutions or profit-making suppliers of educational services will be able to meet the challenge. New federal action, said OTA, may be required to ensure that the benefits of education in technology are accessible to a wide range of people.

Eileen Cooke, director of the Washington office of the American Library Association, made an appeal on behalf of LSCA early in the year, urging that its cancellation would "not be a trimming of fat . . . but would deprive the disadvantaged and hinder the sharing of library resources."

A spreading concern for the effects of federal withdrawal of support from its own information agencies and the linkage of this withdrawal with the nation's industrial and social health is being voiced anew today, as it was after the first Sputnik. Today, concern is roused by embarrassing technological failures in areas such as automobile building, space suit design, and the construction of main battle tanks.

An editorial in the May 28 issue of *Science* spoke up in defense of two major recipients of federal funding: the National Library of Medicine and the National Technical Information Service. Both agencies have been eyed by critics for their presence in a niche that private industry might occupy. *Science* detailed their roles in the economy and pointed out that both are self-supporting, vital to the nation, and the source of services all too likely to degrade, if taken over by private enterprise concerned only with the mining of profits from them.

The threatened withdrawal of federal support had repercussions on the state and federal levels of library support at a time when state budgets were beginning to stagger under the blows dealt by the depression. For years the library community has been working for a federal-state-local funding structure that would unburden the local taxpayer, and with some success. But the current attack on government has proved the funding partnership to be a fragile structure. On the other hand, local funding has shown surprising stability.

Volatile State of the States

State funding of libraries, according to the Urban Library Council, rose in the past year by 9 percent. The third annual report from the states, following up on the White House Conference on Library and Information Services, comes to a similar optimistic conclusion; its survey notes nine states with increased funding to libraries or state agencies and ten states with new legislation to aid automation projects or cooperation. But within that broad picture there were four distinct streams of news reports: on pressures for new state library aid coming from librarians, trustees, associations, and Friends; on the question of life after LSCA; on the new priorities being identified at the state level; and finally, the roll call of victories and defeats.

Increased vitality at the state level was apparent in 1983: in the lawsuit brought by seven states to oppose the administration's impoundment of LSCA funds; in New York's creation of a new advisory committee to watchdog the block grant program that is expected to follow categorical funding; and in Wisconsin's and Wyoming's decisions to put the last of their LSCA funds into a statewide automated network.

This clear-cut stand on priorities was matched by Alaska's declaration of its priorities for state support: networks, books, and buildings; by Connecticut's decision to fund all in-library transactions serving nonresidents and its support of statutory funding for its regional Cooperating Library Service Units; by Maine's increase in state support for service to the blind and the handicapped; and by Nevada's (unsuccessful) referendum for a $10 million state contribution to public library construction.

It was also matched by Mississippi's increased funding for the placement of professional librarians in public libraries and Oklahoma's ground-breaking move to set priorities for a state pickup of lapsed federal funding: Lawmakers decided to replace at least 85 percent of Title I and III LSCA funds, because they ranked library programs under these LSCA titles fourth on their priority list—right after school lunches and venereal disease control and right ahead of the free milk program and school breakfasts. Before a state budget crisis struck, South Carolina awarded its libraries a $100,000 transfusion for book buying. Books were also the objects of largesse in Wyoming, where the state doubled the materials budget of the University of Wyoming, and although Wyoming declined to pick up LSCA programs per se, it provided the funding for a statewide multitype automation project.

Pressures for state aid drew support from on high in Pennsylvania, West Virginia, and California. Pennsylvania's Governor Thornburgh rewarded a well-organized campaign for state aid with his support and signature on new funding legislation. Governor Rockefeller stumped West Virginia in support of library funding increases, and in California, one of Jerry Brown's last acts in office was to sign a bill providing $23 million in new state funding and establishing state responsibility for basic public library service. A well-organized campaign had brought the measure through the legislature and laid it on the desk of the governor two years in a row; the second time around, the governor signed it.

The story of how politicking boosted state aid in Virginia was told in the June issue of *LJ* in "Libraries Are Nobody's Little Sister" by Dean Burgess. A vigorous petition drive in Arkansas sought unsuccessfully to lift a 40-year-old mill limit barrier on local library support. New York's highly capable library lobby organized an effective campaign for state funding of public library construction; at this writing its fate is still unknown, but if it is turned down, it will be back next year, on the theory that the lawmakers will be familiar with it and that much more susceptible to pressure.

There were losses at the state level; budget setbacks in Michigan, Ohio, and New Jersey threatened state and local services. New Mexico voters turned down an ambitious project to build a state network around the Online Computer Library Center (OCLC). Minnesota reported its funding as firm in 1982, but trouble is expected in the coming year. California libraries have enemies as well as friends in high places: One measure before the legislature would chop $5 million from the support of library systems and the state library—at a time when the probable loss of LSCA funding of multitype system administration threatens plans for resource sharing. Weakening state level funding in New England forced a scuttling of the New England Library Board.

Among the victories: Alabama reported state aid up 25 percent, although it was cut 10 percent in mid-December; Mississippi librarians beat back an attempt to cut state funding; the Oklahoma Department of Libraries gained $1 million, with which it will add staff, increase archival materials, and set up a materials preservation lab. Oklahoma libraries have powerful friends too: Governor Nigh issued a proclamation in November honoring the director of the Oklahoma Department of Libraries with a Robert L. Clark day.

Local Library Funding

Stability was the dominant—and surprising—characteristic of local library support in 1983; although there were individual setbacks reported, the depression did not seem to directly hurt public or academic libraries. An Indiana study made the prediction that library expenditures over the next ten years would increase at a stable rate of 28 percent, with new technology translating this into better service. Kansas libraries profited generally by statewide property valuation increases and Ohio urban libraries were prosperous; the Chicago Public Library reported a good year and the Denver Public Library, which had been reduced to charging fees to nonresidents for use of the library, found new, broader-based funding from counties and the state. Another urban library threatened with poverty, the San Francisco Public Library, followed the advice of Lowell Martin and reorganized its branch system; the resulting publicity helped win generous new funding. Hennepin County, Minnesota, awarded its library another big increase: 13 percent on top of the previous year's 11.3 percent. Right in the heart of Proposition 13 country, California's Kern County Library reported a boom year, thanks partly to the oil being pumped out of the ground there, but also to money-saving measures, automation, volunteers, and a pool of part-time workers.

The Jackson George Regional Library System in Pascagoula, Mississippi, posted a 26 percent budget increase that gave librarians parity with teachers for the first time. Prosperous Houston gave its public library a 34 percent boost, and the University of Houston a $2 million increase. The Jackson District Library in Michigan, in an area listed among the top ten for unemployment, was thriving fiscally and busy, with a branch addition and a new branch building in the works.

Broad and deep public support for libraries was reflected in municipal decisions to maintain their library budgets in a generally lean year; in many cases the voters directly mandated this generosity. On several occasions an angry electorate squelched administrations planning to cut back on library support. This happened in Broward County, Florida; Greenville County, South Carolina; Baltimore; San Francisco; and most dramatically in Mount Holly, New Jersey, which turned its city council out of office and elected a pro-library slate.

Voters ordered library increases or continued support in Toledo-Lucas County, Ohio; Oklahoma County, Oklahoma (first increase since 1965); Seminole County, Florida (for new branches); and Birmingham, Alabama (a 76 percent "yes" vote for a fat budget increase).

Two stories underlined the affection people have for libraries: In Shirley, New York, a poor community, in a depression year, built a big new library. The bipartisan nature of library support was demonstrated by the Amway organization, which is known for arch conservatism and opposition to government spending. Amway urged the many and far-flung members of its sales organization to give their support and their votes to public libraries seeking funding.

All was not sunshine in 1982, however. New York's Buffalo and Erie County Library lost 40 staff positions; the Newark Public Library, suddenly losing state funding, is facing layoff of a third of its staff. New York Public, which had apparently weathered a long period of scarcity and was restoring lost services, found itself torpedoed by a sudden crisis in New York City finances. In Paterson, New Jersey, last spring, the library and its seven branches were threatened with closing and at year's end the whole library was probably to be closed for two or more weeks for lack of funds.

The Seattle Public Library's straitened circumstances were forcing it to turn away unanswered some 1,300 calls a day; and in prosperous Shaker Heights, Ohio, the voters gave no support to a bond issue that would have tripled library space.

There are fears that the current depression will eventually get to libraries; but an article in the November 15 *LJ* pointed out that libraries are faring better today than they were in the depths of the Great Depression 50 years ago: Marcia Pankake, in "New Growth in a 'No Growth' Era," charted the recovery that libraries made from that low point in their fortunes and urged new growth through better administration and resource sharing.

Many libraries are seeking greater productivity by automating, by using volunteers, and by replacing full-time staff with substitutes or part-timers in busy hours. The public library in Westboro, Massachusetts, reported that it had been able to move into a new, larger building with increased circulation, but without any increase in its expenditures. Expenses are being cut in new and old buildings by energy saving through solar heat, insulation, computerized energy management, relamping with more efficient fixtures, and other tactics.

The search for alternative sources of revenue found libraries taking a new interest in fund raising. Two interesting variations were reported by academic libraries: The

University of California, Berkeley, may be the first state-supported, public university to engage a full-time, professional fund raiser. The University of Texas at Austin formed a new library support group, the Swante Palm Associates, named after the library's first benefactor. Members pay from $10 to $1,000 to belong and share in social events and other privileges. To encourage the search for alternate means of funding, ALA and the Gale Research Company announced a new award to honor creative approaches to funding.

Fund raising by public libraries produced the usual crop of inventive and even bizarre efforts. These included a celebrity shoe auction in Pawtucket, Rhode Island; a celebrity book auction in Coos Bay, Oregon; belly dancing in Columbus, Ohio; chain letters in Corpus Christi, Texas; a pennies-from-heaven project in Hershey, Pennsylvania, whereby banks matched and donated to the library all pennies turned in; sales of a clever poster and glassware by the New York Public Library; book sales ranging from Brooklyn's Books-for-Bucks sale to a blockbuster in Boston at which the collection of the famed Brattle Book Shop was sold to benefit the Boston Public Library; and a phone-a-thon in Providence, Rhode Island.

That old standby, the book sale, is being institutionalized by some libraries today; both the Baltimore County Public Library and the Prince George's County Memorial Library in Maryland have established bookstores, where library discards, periodicals, records, and other wares are sold.

An alternative funding strategy sure to be disapproved by librarians, but not by some administrators, is contracting out library operations to a private, for-profit firm. The Learning Resources Corporation of America, a Washington area-based firm, has already had experience in operation of government and special libraries and recently announced its availability to public and academic libraries, promising superior administration and money savings.

NYU's Carleton Rochelle, in an October 1 *LJ* article, "Telematics—2001 A.D.," predicted that the public library will wither away and its functions will be taken over by the private sector. Throughout 1982 widespread public debate on the roles of public and private sectors in library and information services raged, with private sector supporters taking heart from the administration's evident bias in their favor. The debate promises to continue into 1983 unabated, with the opposing viewpoints becoming ever more sharply polarized, but with the long term effect on local library funding not at all clear.

NETWORKS AND NETWORKING

This was a year of continued growth for OCLC, Research Libraries Information Network (RLIN), Washington Library Network (WLN), and University of Toronto Library Automation System (UTLAS). All except WLN experienced problems: OCLC service earlier in the year was the source of many user complaints, as the system strained to accommodate an ever-increasing number of terminals. It had technical problems with a new terminal and had to go back to Beehives It had the problems of moving its operations to its big, new building in Dublin, Ohio, where it is fighting an unfavorable local tax decision that threatens to create a severe drain on its finances. [For an in-depth report on these and other developments in library networking in 1982, see the Special Reports section of Part 1—*Ed.*]

The RLIN network was in a crisis situation early in 1983; its director, Edward Shaw, resigned after a highly critical consultant's report by William and Carolyn Arms of the Kiewit Computer Center at Dartmouth. The Arms team was called in to appraise RLIN, after a series of simultaneous head crashes destroyed 20 percent of the data base and brought RLIN processing to a halt. The catastrophe, which was linked to RLIN's sharing of a new computer with Stanford, forced a shakeup at RLIN. Shaw was replaced by Richard McCoy, who was chosen for his background in business and automated communications. The system began to recover swiftly after another computer was provided to handle the load.

The UTLAS system came close to losing the support of the University of Toronto, but the university increased, instead of cancelling, its loan, enabling the deficit-ridden network to acquire needed space and equipment. The possibility was raised of the university selling UTLAS, once it achieved profitability.

The turmoil of the past year included replacement of chief executive officers at RLIN and UTLAS. Only WLN seemed to be untouched by problems brought on by coping with growth and the development of new subsystems. Yet it too continued to grow slowly and to develop new products and services.

To some extent, all utilities are in competition with each other, but their most serious competition may come from another quarter: new, distributed systems that provide most of the functions the giants promise, without the telecommunications costs that go with a centralized network. Besides waiting impatiently for RLIN and OCLC to interface their systems, and to develop their own distributed systems, librarians are looking at alternatives such as the Carlyle system, which proposes to set up regional computing facilities for library clients: the minicomputer-based VTLS (Virginia Tech Library System) or the Integrated Library System developed at the National Library of Medicine.

Besides their large data bases, the utilities continue to offer new subsystems: OCLC's Interlibrary Loan Subsystem is revolutionizing resource sharing and greatly increasing interloan traffic among libraries large and small. RLIN now has an interloan subsystem in place. OCLC is offering the Total Library System developed at Claremont Colleges and promising a still more advanced system, the Local Library System, which is piloting at the Five Colleges consortium in Amherst, Massachusetts. A new "cluster" arrangement enables smaller libraries to access OCLC as a group, greatly increasing the number of potential clients.

Regional Networks

The regional networks, set up originally to broker OCLC services, probably must develop and market new technology products and services, if they are to become anything more than bookkeepers and system-use trainers for OCLC. The fragile nature of these systems was apparent in 1982, with NELINET (New England Library Network) retreating to a minimal operation and letting go its top administrative and technical people.

MIDLNET (Midwest Region Library Network) is expected to be disbanded after trying unsuccessfully to fill a new role as coordinator of other regional systems. PNBC (the Pacific Northwest Bibliographic Center) was another casualty; its staff has been laid off and some of its functions are being taken over by the University of Washington Libraries, which was PNBC's chief resource and benevolent landlord. BCR (the Bibliographic Center for Research, Rocky Mountain Region) is reported by its new executive director, JoAn S. Segal, to have been almost on the financial rocks last year, but to be recovering under financial and administrative reorganization; it is cutting overhead costs by moving to smaller quarters.

The healthiest of the group appear to be AMIGOS, SOLINET (Southeastern Library Network) and SUNY/OCLC (State University of New York/Online Computer Library Center); in 1982 AMIGOS extended its operations in Mexico and announced its availability beyond its original boundaries: the states contiguous with Texas. It is offering magtape services to other regionals, with BCR (Bibliographic Center for Research) announced as a client. AMIGOS is moving into a new area, one envisioned by regional networks for years: managing the automation of a member library, Southwestern University in Georgetown, Texas.

SOLINET, which changed leadership in 1982 (Frank Grisham replaced Lee Handley as CEO), provided its clients with new subject searching access to their data bases, and after a pilot trial, announced it will go ahead with its ambitious project to establish a regional data base, the LAMBDA system. Success in this pioneering venture will realize still another of the goals that the regional networks have envisioned, but have as yet not attained. Not all network clients agree that regionals should be developing new roles and products; a Mississippi critic, writing in that state library association's Automation Network Round Table newsletter, criticized SOLINET roundly for "expending efforts which could be used to solve problems which are known to exist at the present time . . . before trying to offer new services and create new capabilities, it would seem more advantageous to enhance the quality of products and services already supposedly available."

SUNY/OCLC, the regional that appears to be identified most closely with OCLC, sees its future today in marketing the distributed library systems created by OCLC and in expanding the use of the OCLC system. It has a new membership group recently formed to promote the use of the system in reference and other public service work.

Besides their inherent vulnerability as OCLC brokers, the regionals have potential competition from a growing number of state systems and even from smaller groupings. The Tri-State Library Cooperative, located at Rosemont College in Pennsylvania, in the area served by PALINET, offers network services on a cash-and-carry basis, providing document location, bibliographic verification, and reference services on a per-transaction fee basis—with no requirement for membership or other red tape. It serves 29 libraries in this way, with its main resource being an OCLC connection.

The rapid evolution of technology holds out to individual states, groups of libraries, and even individual libraries the attractive prospect of having their own independent systems capable of doing what the regionals and even the utilities are doing today; this poses still another threat to regional networks.

There were some signs in 1982 of the networks joining forces. BCR agreed to exchange services with WILS, the Wisconsin Interlibrary Loan System, swapping interlibrary loan service for document delivery. AMIGOS, as noted above, offers magtape services to other networks. And the network directors, according to a report in *Ohionetwork*, are moving toward taking a more active role in OCLC policy decisions and in addressing problems from a united front.

State Networks

The past year has been one of yeasty ferment for state level networking, with individual libraries participating far more vocally in planning than they did in the development of regional networks. A tour of state networking stories in 1982 finds Connecticut developing its network with the state library at the head of a number of regional groupings. These groupings are held together by the circulation systems adopted by each, and coordination statewide is encouraged by such state-funded mechanisms as document delivery (Connecticar), universal borrowing privileges (Connecticard), and reimbursement for interlibrary loan transactions.

Colorado is going a similar route, linking circulation systems, including CLSI (Computer Library Services, Inc.), DataPhase, and a UNIVAC-based system, and providing incentives for the coordination of collection development.

Iowa brought in Becker & Hayes to draw up a plan for an IOWANET, a coherent document that appeared to represent the state of the art in network thinking; it sparked furious opposition from a library community that wants a network that will leave already in-place library structures undisturbed and will build on those structures.

Massachusetts has the majority of its library resources in its big Eastern Regional Library System, which is provided with networking services by the automated system developed for the Boston Public Library. This system could have been extended to the state's two other regional systems, Central and Western, but they chose last year to automate with a DataPhase system.

New York has been moving toward the development of a state networking strategy that would coordinate the public library systems and the 3Rs systems that link academic and special libraries, creating nine new systems, including in each two public library systems and one 3Rs system. Stiff opposition has been voiced by the public library systems, which fear a loss of the autonomy they have enjoyed for 20 years.

Virginia came out strongly in 1982 for an evolutionary approach to networking, opting for autonomy and independence from the utilities; one likely course for the state to take would be adoption of the Virginia Tech Library System, a highly flexible distributed system designed to run on Hewlett Packard minicomputers.

West Virginia has gone that way already under the firm leadership of the State Library Commission, which is providing strong incentives to the state's regional groupings to adopt the VTLS and participate in an evolutionary development that will culminate in a coordinated statewide network.

Texas libraries are weighing their network options: membership-based regional library systems with their own boards of directors and independent of the major resource centers that now dominate systems—or a multitype system organization with public library systems permitted to admit school, public, and special libraries, if their member public libraries approve.

California has possibly the most unusual state networking organization: CLASS (California Library Authority for Systems and Services) is a unique agency, which has become a vendor of system services and products, not only to California libraries, but to libraries anywhere—even abroad. Illinois, with its state-library-based ILLINET, may have the most stable organization yet, and one that can coexist with the entrenched and powerful public library systems, as they take in school, academic, and special libraries to create a multitype library system.

Design Renaissance

The bewildering variety of state and regional library organizations points up a phenomenon that bids fair to make the late 1970s and the 1980s a high point in library history. A high degree of consensus in the library world has apparently made possible widespread and creative fashioning of institutions and institutional behavior, ranging from the multitude of local cooperative activities through the maze of state and regional network building and perhaps culminating in the creation of a class of supra-institutions to perform functions necessary but beyond the scope of existing institutions.

These include OCLC and the other utilities, the regional and state networks, CLENE (Continuing Library Education Network), the Urban Libraries Council, the National Commission on Libraries and Information Science, the upcoming crop of new regional materials preservation centers, and a veritable host of consortia organized in more or less formal structures.

The private sector has participated in this creation of new structures and agencies to fill library needs. Examples are the serials systems developed by Faxon; the specialized research expertise developed by King Research, Inc.; the machine-readable data bases of bibliographic information created by firms like Baker & Taylor, Brodart, and Autographics; the consultant firms like RMG Consultants and Joseph Matthews Associates; and the whole new world of research tools represented by the online data base services created by both public and private agencies.

The current wave of institutional creativity is not the first to have blessed the library world; another era saw the creation of USBE (the United States Book Exchange then, now the Universal Serials and Book Exchange); the Center for Research Libraries; the library associations; the Greenaway Plan; and the specialized publishers and vendors of library equipment and supplies. It is interesting that in many cases, these older, still existent supra-institutions have taken on new life in today's stimulating environment for innovation.

But it is out among the grass roots that one sees the source of this energetic behavior: a boundless enthusiasm for cooperation and resource sharing that manifests itself in dozens of ways uniquely responsive to local needs. A partial calling of the roll would turn up a new school library processing consortium in northeastern Ohio; small Milwaukee libraries sharing an OCLC terminal; Connecticut libraries pooling their orders with two vendors to gain better discounts; a cooperative project in Maryland to serve the small-scale farmer; a new metropolitan library authority being planned in Iowa; a free exchange of photocopies for interloan service in the New York City area; a public library and an Air Force library sharing access to their collections in Solano County, California.

In Manatee County, Florida, a library is joining forces with a museum and other community agencies to create a "discovery place" for children; libraries are bartering services in Bellingham, Washington; eight California libraries are joining to get a shared Geac circulation system; and informal cooperatives have been established in both northern and central Illinois with little or no formal staff, but the ability to identify and accomplish tasks of value to all.

The concept of networking, it would appear, is coming back to an identification with its roots in traditional library cooperation and in what amounts to almost a congenital predisposition for resource sharing and for actions with grass-roots validation.

AUTOMATION

In 1982 little doubt remained about the need of libraries for automation, although debate continued on the question of whether automation is something that can be tamed and put to work in libraries for the purposes of librarianship and library service, or whether it represents the victorious first wave of the "information society," which libraries had better hasten to swear allegiance to or vanish with the dinosaurs.

Richard de Gennaro made a strong case for the first position in "Libraries, Technology, and the Information Marketplace" in the June 1 issue of *LJ*. He predicted that the new technology will not vastly change libraries, but that it will be adapted by them and the changes will be gradual. It would be a mistake, he said, to rush to identify with an overarching "information society."

In a similar vein, Michael E. D. Koenig, in "The Information Controllability Explosion" (*LJ*, November 1), was optimistic about the future of libraries vis-a-vis automation and the private sector, but warned that libraries must keep up with the powerful new tools for harnessing the information explosion or they will find others doing the job.

The October 1 *LJ* juxtaposed Carleton Rochell of New York University, predicting doom for the public library (because of new technology), and Connie Tiffany of the Iowa City Public Library, with an upbeat account of how one city library has embraced new technology and new materials to imbue its services with new vitality.

A cautionary note was sounded by Margaret Beckman of Guelph University in the November 1 *LJ*. In "Online Catalogs and Library Users," she warns that automation must be in the service primarily of users, not of librarians—and not seized upon as a means of perpetuating traditional ways of librarianship, a caveat to bear in mind in relation to the foregoing points of view.

Data Bases Online

Hardly a week seems to go by without the reference librarian being alerted to new data bases available to bestow seven league boots upon the librarian, calling for a stream of (usually) very expensive decisions—or perhaps raising yet again the basic question of whether or not to buy into online services. In the past year, the reference librarian has been tempted by an online *Books in Print* from Bowker, new AV health data bases from BRS, a data base on DIALOG of microcomputer publications and programs, the *Toronto Globe & Mail* from the New York Times Information Service, Mathfile from BRS, a Superindex of Science and Reference Books from DIALOG, the full text of the *Encyclopaedia Britannica* online from Mead Data Central—the list grows daily with items that demand new expertise in both selection and use.

There was an RLIN terminal to be seen in action on a reference desk at the University of Pennsylvania this year, and the Chicago Public Library early in the year was exploring teletext as a means of coping with heavy telephone reference traffic. Online reference service was launched for dazzled library users at King County in Seattle and several other libraries, all of whom had to wrestle with the question of how to pay the online bills. New York State funded a program to subsidize the access to medical data bases, using a voucher system; the Elk Grove Public Library in Illinois was charging fees for public use of DIALOG; and the questions, economic and moral, posed by fees were aired thoroughly but inconclusively at countless library meetings.

At year's end, a polarization appeared to be developing and hardening. One side wants to treat information and related library services as commodities that are properly owned and deployed to earn profits. The other side has a vision of society entering an exciting new period of growth—fueled by widespread access to information freely available to everyone everywhere—the analogy to the pre-OPEC days of great economic growth has been suggested, and those who inveigh against the "bugaboo of free information" or the "iron curtain of free information" are cast in the role of an information OPEC.

Automation Systems

In the past year, libraries have moved from a preoccupation with automated circulation to the new problems of the next step—integrated library systems. There was great interest in the many systems on the market, both brand new ones and upgraded versions of older, established systems.

Libraries looking for new systems had no shortage of opportunities for comparison shopping. CLSI, they heard, was upgrading its system with multiprocessors and its book acquisition module was piloting at the Providence Public Library, which was planning to use CLSI for statewide resource sharing.

DataPhase, besides making a successful incursion into the Australian library market, was chosen to automate four cooperating library systems in Illinois. The Public Library of Columbus and Franklin County chose the VTLS (Virginia Tech Library System) to replace its first generation automation. The Canadian firm, Easy Data Systems, came over the border to automate the public library in Everett, Washington, and the Exxon headquarters in New York. Another Canadian, Geac, was chosen by the University of Houston to replace its first-generation mix of three different systems for circulation, acquisition, and interfacing with OCLC. OCLC was pressing ahead with development and pilot testing of its Local Library System, a distributed system aiming at the same market of online catalogs, circulation, and other integrated functions.

Palm Springs, however, went its own way with a locally based UNIVAC system; the University of Minnesota announced its own system was on the market; and in what may be the first of a host of little stand-alone systems, a library-developed Apple program for creating catalog cards was offered for $50 from the Clinton-Essex-Franklin Library System in New York.

Periodicals systems were arriving on the market one after another in 1982: Faxon announced new subsystems for its LINX system; and a new turnkey serials control system, Meta-Micro Serials Control System, was installed at the Valero Energy Corporation in San Antonio, Texas, its first customer.

Interface technology offered new options to libraries wishing to cooperate or to plan statewide or regional networks. Colorado was able to call on this technology to plan a network that will link libraries using CLSI, DataPhase, and UNIVAC hardware and software.

Microcomputers

The marvelous little micros charmed librarians out of their socks in 1982; hardly a library meeting went by without a session on micros for avid learners. In a June 1 *LJ* article, Don R. Swanson hailed the micros as offering an alternative to large bureaucracies and centralized systems and the burdens these inflict. The micros, he said, give individual librarians a new role in defining the future.

Early in the year, a survey by the Pacific Northwest Bibliographic Center found widespread and varied use of the micros. During the course of the year, these uses included an Apple scheduling pages in Fairport, N.Y.; a TRS 80 acting as an OCLC terminal; Gaylord micros doing serials control and file management; acquisition work being done at Western Maryland College on a Radio Shack micro; and Montana replacing its statewide teletype network with micros that were expected to pay back their cost in two years as well as speed up interloan communications.

Computer literacy swept the land with the help of the ubiquitous micros. A brief listing shows the states of Ohio and New York laying out substantial sums to promote computer literacy, especially in rural areas. The National Science Foundation offered libraries a chance to vie for grant support to become a "Computertown USA" and act as a center for compulit. The Cloqu Minnesota Public Library was one of many lending micros for this purpose. In Lorain, Ohio, community development funds bought micros—on the grounds that deprived populations need special help in gaining access to new technology. And still another deprived group, the "rehabilitation community" of the disabled, their famlies, and teachers, was the target of a pioneering micro program at the Rockville Library in Montgomery County, Maryland.

Microcomputers in Columbus, Ohio, are being considered for a highly ambitious plan that would marry them and videodisc technology to find a new way to teach literacy. In San Bernardino, California, the library reports "tremendous response" to its microcomputer-accessed job information. [For a report on the use of microcomputers in elementary and secondary school libraries, see the Special Reports section of Part 1—*Ed.*]

LIBRARY PERSONNEL

The people who staff libraries made news in several areas: Professional status was under fire; volunteers were ubiquitous; Friends groups continued to grow in number and force; sightings of consultants and nonlibrarian specialists were up; and alternate careers lured many out of libraries and provided new opportunities for library school graduates. Staff development at all levels was a strong preoccupation of both conference meetings and library personnel programs, and the shadow of privatization fell on this area as well as on other areas of library services and administration.

Professional Status

At year's end, the scuttlebutt from Washington had it that despite all the efforts to change the mind of the Office of Personnel Management, downgrading of the status of professional librarians in federal service would be effected early in 1983. Library spokespersons representing associations and federal libraries tried in vain to get changes in the draft of new personnel standards, handicapped by obstructionist tactics that made their task nearly impossible. [For a report on "The New Federalism: How It Is Changing the Library Profession in the United States," see the Special Reports section of Part 1—*Ed.*]

In mid-November, one lawmaker, Geraldine Ferraro (D-N.Y.) spoke up in outrage at the fact that librarianship, the only female-dominated profession in the federal service, is the only profession to be downgraded in this way. Too late, said one critic of the attempt to turn OPM around, as library leaders tried to bring their case to the White House, where growing concern over the loss of support among voters might have brought a respite from the curiously hostile actions of OPM.

The only other reported attempt at downgrading the profession occurred in Australia, where early in the year librarians were on strike against such action by academic libraries.

Professional status inched up in Massachusetts, where legislation signed by Governor King gave public librarians new status vis-a-vis library boards and municipal authorities: A new requirement of formal, written personnel policies and stipulation of due process for librarians who are threatened with dismissal protects librarians acting in correct professional manner from pressure by employers.

Volunteers consolidated their position in libraries last year; more and more libraries relied on them, admitting frankly that they save money (just as only in recent months has it been admitted that automation can and should save money). The spread of volunteers was documented dramatically in the response to a questionnaire sent out to libraries by Alice Sizer Warner, who was writing a sequel to the 1977 *LJ* Special Report on the subject, which provided timely documentation of the then-new expansion of volunteer programs, most then in their infancy. Warner's *Volunteers in Libraries II* was assembled by winnowing a veritable flood of reports, documents, and materials created for volunteer programs.

In the news pages of *LJ* and *LJ/SLJ Hotline* further change and maturing of the volunteer movement has been chronicled. As noted in the People section, two big urban public libraries appointed professional managers of their volunteer programs in 1982; a course on volunteer management offered by the University of Colorado, Boulder, was advertised specifically as "not for beginners" in the management of volunteers; and a clearinghouse was set up in Maryland to standardize statewide practice in volunteer staffing.

Some changes were noted in the makeup of the volunteer force: Involuntary volunteers, assigned to public service by courts, were reported. Retired librarians provided the reinforcement of their know-how in San Bernardino, California. The arrival of microcomputers in libraries attracted eager volunteers able to help others acquire computer literacy.

Volunteers in Arlington Heights, Illinois, under the leadership of a full-time coordinator, go far beyond the routine scut work assignments that librarians formerly—

and grudgingly—conceded they could handle. The 29 at this library perform a wide range of special tasks calling for skills in cataloging, moderating discussion groups, giving book talks, repairing 8mm films, and other responsible functions. It is still customary to consider the monetary value of volunteer work at the minimum wage level, but recognition is growing for the possibility that a given volunteer's work may be worth considerably more than the minimum wage—that work is no less valuable for being given free.

The current depression has had at least one unexpected repercussion on volunteers. A report from a high unemployment area of Michigan says that wives in the volunteer staff had to stay home and keep peace because their unemployed husbands were hanging around the house. Their places at the library were being taken, however, by their grown sons, who are also out of work and want to get out of the house.

Women in Libraries

The slow progress that has been made in improving the status of women in libraries, and of librarianship itself as a female-dominated profession, suffered a probable net loss in 1982. In San Diego, where pressure has been strong for "comparable worth" increases in library salaries, librarians won an 18 percent raise—but it was officially attributed to increased productivity. In Long Beach, California, a library staff did win an admitted comparable worth increase of 5 percent.

But two threats faced women in 1982: the depression, which made it financially difficult for libraries or their funding agencies to institute more liberal personnel programs, and the Reagan administration, which is generally perceived as inimical to progress in women's rights—and perceived as specifically on the attack against women in the current attempt by the Office of Personnel Management to downgrade the status of federal library professionals.

A look back over *LJ* stories on women's rights gives some assurance that setbacks may be temporary: a decade ago attorney Barbara Ringer forced the Library of Congress to abandon the discriminatory practices that had denied her the post of Register of Copyrights. Her victory led LC to adopt an affirmative action program for women and minorities, which became a model for other institutions. In 1979, the St. Paul (Minnesota) Public Library was successful in revising civil service titles to eliminate bias; active campaigns against discrimination also were going on at Temple University, the San Diego Public Library, and the Seattle Public Library—in the latter case with the backing of a militant union. In 1981, Canadian librarians in federal government positions won a landmark settlement of $2.3 million in a suit based on the principle of "equal pay for equal work."

One *LJ* story in 1982 sounded a note of optimism along the lines of a Virginia Slims advertisement: A Radcliffe College exhibit unearthed a grisly tale, recalling that just before Christmas in 1929, Harvard President Lowell fired the Widener Library's 19 cleaning women rather than give them a raise.

Friends

True to past performance, "Friends of the Library" groups continue to increase their activities in a time when libraries are threatened. One report early in 1982 found Friends groups up 50 percent in number since the White House conference. News items about Friends were mostly about fund-raising affairs and budget campaign support action. But there were unusual projects reported: The Friends of the San Francisco Public Library were at one point last year beating the bushes to find a rent-free home for the library's business branch. The august Folger Shakespeare Library Friends staged an elaborate Victorian garden party. The Chicago Public Library gave a literary arts ball with lions like Norman Mailer roaring for the library. What may be the most highly developed

Friends group going, the Friends of the Free Library of Philadelphia, with a full-time staff and an elaborate program of cultural activities, kept a spotlight on the library as a focus of the city's cultural life.

Consultants

Consultants are becoming a more common sight in libraries and seem to be increasingly recognized as an efficient way to acquire specialized expertise for a short time. Traditionally, consultants have been elder statesmen of the library field. This kind of consultant was epitomized in 1982 by Lowell Martin, who was called in by the ailing public libraries of San Francisco and Philadelphia to guide them through drastic program reductions.

Only recently have consultant groups or firms come on the scene, providing expertise in a range of library specialties: administration, automation, collection development, and other areas. Members of these firms tend to be librarians of good reputation with identifiable track records in their own libraries or regions; HBW Associates of Dallas is a good example.

Individual librarians sometimes amass a powerful reputation in a specialty and come to exert real leadership in the field. One such is Richard Boss, who is responsible for the excellent technical writing in the *Library Systems Newsletter*. He also provides technical expertise to individual clients and is a strong force for enlightenment as a speaker to library groups. Other outstanding specialist consultants include Maurice J. Freedman, Westchester Library System, New York; Joseph Matthews of Grass Valley, California (automation); and Frank Hemphill of the Baltimore County Public Library of Towson, Maryland, who specializes in building design.

Consultants from outside the library community are being called on more frequently for expertise in automation, administration, public relations, telecommunications, and system design. The nonlibrarian consultant has apparently survived the skepticism aroused by the ill-fated Conant Report on library education; in January 1982, three articles in the *Journal of Education for Librarianship* condemned the report to oblivion and closed the story. Later in the year a firm now familiar to librarians as well as the general information community, King Research, Inc., won a contract to chart the future of library education and specifically to identify the skills librarians need in an increasingly technological library environment. King was also engaged to work with Drexel on defining the right blend of technology and traditional library education. [See the report by Donald King and William Creager on the services provided by private companies to libraries and information centers in the Special Reports section of Part 1—*Ed.*] The University of Pittsburgh has been active and successful in handling consultant jobs abroad. Its latest coup is a contract with Saudi Arabia to design a library for the naval forces.

Consultants as a group are being nurtured by the field: The Association of Research Libraries offers training programs in its member libraries and the Special Libraries Association this year ran a well-attended workshop on consulting. Finally, there is a new General Consultants Discussion Group, which was formed at ALA/Philadelphia last year and, at this writing, is scheduled to meet in San Antonio during ALA midwinter. The focus appears to be on the full-time consultant employed on a permanent basis by the state agency or the library system headquarters, but the specialist nature of their work makes the line between the independent and the staff consultant a fine one.

Alternate Careers

The 1982 Allerton Institute at the University of Illinois annually chooses a topic that thereby is unofficially designated a mainstream concern of librarians (if it wasn't already so recognized); in 1982, the topic was Alternate Careers for Librarians. The interest in alternate careers took fire in 1980 with a book by Betty Carol Sellen, *What Else Can You Do with a Library Degree?* (Neal Schuman) and a series of workshops she conducted on the subject. News stories in the past year noted a number of individual migrations from the field or reported on the activities of earlier migrants.

Publishing is a likely haven for the librarian; in 1982 a former librarian, Jessica L. Milstead, was named vice president at Newsbank; Gail Schlacter, who left the library at the University of California, Davis, in 1981, was a vice president at ABC Clio Press in 1982. Peter Doiron, former editor of *Choice* and a librarian, turned up last year as a specialist in out-of-print acquisitions, serving libraries on an annual retainer basis. Jean Peters, former director of the R. R. Bowker Library, has moved up to become manager of research and development, Bowker Book Division. In 1982 she won the Special Libraries Association Fannie Simon Award for "outstanding contributions in the fields of publishing and librarianship."

Alfred Freund, director of the Ramapo Catskill Library System in Middletown, New York, acquired a great deal of fast expertise in microcomputers, which led to his conducting workshops on the subject both for his library system members and other library groups around the state. He went rather quickly from that to setting up an independent microcomputer consulting firm (but stayed in his library position). Fast learners elsewhere in the country probably have similar opportunities.

Reference service for pay has been well established in the case of FIND/SVP, which expanded its for-profit operations recently to include brokering of online searches. One Illinois library system found it cost-effective to farm out a large number of very difficult reference questions to a private reference service. Barry Porter left the position of Iowa State Librarian to join a for-profit firm, Carl Gaumer's Reference Service.

Librarianship is—in some cases—a subset of public administration. For varying reasons, librarians were promoted last year to higher municipal administrative roles, sometimes keeping the direction of the library, sometimes not. Joseph Sakey, director of the Cambridge, Massachusetts, Public Library, became the city's CATV Commissioner. In Monrovia, California, John L. Lustig moved up, as did Joseph Ruef in Windsor, California, and Barbara Campbell in Santa Clara County, California, who became the acting director of the environmental management agency. In San Rafael, California, Vaughn Stratford climbed from library director to director of library and cultural affairs, and in Pasadena, Texas, Roman Bohachevsky left the library to become the city's group administrator in charge of municipal records, data processing, purchasing, planning, and personnel.

Moving up in government by a different route—politics—were two librarians noted earlier in this report, Major Owens and Cynthia E. Jackson, two New York librarians who were elected to state and national legislative offices. A third librarian to go this route was Bobby Junkins, director of the Gadsden, Alabama, Public Library, who was elected to the Alabama state legislature.

Library Education

This has been a period of great uncertainty for many library schools. The SUNY-Geneseo library school shut down after 75 years; the school at the University of Missouri-Columbia was saved only by an "outpouring of support" from alumni and librarians of the state; the University of Minnesota school was similarly threatened, but in August, George d'Elia was named director and a university task force was assigned to study the feasibility of a restructuring to place greater emphasis on information processing. [For an overview of recent developments in library education, see the report by Herbert S. White in Part 3—*Ed.*]

It was a year of searching self-study—and study by their parent universities—for the Columbia and University of Texas at Austin schools, both of which were holding up action on appointment of library school heads, while the mission and direction of the school was being debated. The acting dean at Austin is Ronald E. Wyllys, a library automation and systems specialist.

Rutgers followed the direction already taken by the University of Pittsburgh: a merger, in this case, to create a new School of Communication, Information, and Library Studies. It looks now as though most library science schools will move to encompass new technology and information science. It is worth noting that the Association of American Library Schools will change its name in 1983 to the Association for Library and Information Science Education. [See the report on the recent activities of the association, in the National Associations section of Part 1—*Ed.*]

The only completely sunny report received from the library schools came from Texas Woman's University where Brooke Sheldon, incoming ALA president, is dean. TWU announced that it is planning for expansion in the fall of 1983, with new facilities, furniture, and equipment doing double duty as a display laboratory for library interiors planning.

Library Staff Development

The Association of Research Libraries, reporting on a survey of its members, said that efforts at professional staff development in its member libraries have intensified. Reasons for this included a need for greater productivity and for expertise in new technology. These reasons and others were concerns of many libraries and library associations in 1982; West Virginia ran another of its annual statewide campaigns to meet staff development needs with its "Learning in a Plain Brown Wrapper," financed by the state library commission.

Both public and academic librarians were offered specialized training for today's specialized needs in automation, microcomputers, preservation, and security, to name a few. Colorado, for example, brought in consultant Brigitte Kenney to provide an in-service training program in automation as a step toward statewide automation and networking. Kentucky had a similar one in 1982.

The new technologies were much in evidence in staff development programs: Indiana University was training library aides with the help of the PLATO system. The University of South Carolina School of Librarianship was starting to offer home courses by video, and at least one firm was offering training tapes to be used on videorecorders.

Staff development at the managerial level was also a strong concern. The Special Libraries Association announced a new training program for middle managers, a certificate program taking a hefty 75 hours to complete. A collection development institute presented by ALA's Resources and Technical Services Division was announced for 1983 in Boston. The Graduate Library School at the University of Chicago launched a program of management internships at participating area libraries. The University of Iowa announced a new fellowship in networking.

Also, Dade County, Florida, reported that its library managers, as well as other county managerial personnel, are required to take extensive managerial training. In Louisiana, a library management workshop was cosponsored by the state association, the state library, the Louisiana State University library school, and the Governmental Services Institute.

It came as something of a welcome relief during this stampede into the arms of the computer and the management experts to hear from Dick Ostrander that the Yakima Valley Library in Washington had put on a two-day staff development program that focused on books, book selection, and publishing. The Oakland Public Library, in an unusual approach to staff development, brought in humanities scholars to address the staff on social and ethical concerns. Further and welcome assurance that the past is not completely dead came from the University of Alabama Graduate School of Library Service, announcing a new book arts specialization.

Libraries and Unions

Library union news was sparse in 1983, but there were a few notable stories. The Library of Congress and union representatives achieved such a solid stalemate in talks last fall that it came as good news that they had agreed on a procedure for talking about resuming talks. A long simmering feud between the director of the Pawtucket, Rhode Island, Public Library and the union representing his staff resulted in the director's firing.

At the Detroit Public Library, however, a library racked by adversity and a union were able to agree on wage concessions that helped the library make ends meet and staved off the loss of six more staff members.

Temple University librarians also reached amicable agreement, with management winning a ten-month year (they were trying for nine) but making concessions on their salary goals.

Placements and Salaries

The October 1, 1982, *LJ* reported on the annual survey of library school placements in the previous year. [This report is reprinted in Part 3—*Ed.*] It found little change, with the average beginning librarian drawing a salary of $15,633 and the number of new graduates about the same as last year. Most schools reported "no difficulty" in placing graduates, only two admitting "some" and four reporting "major" difficulty—a slight improvement over the previous year. The schools say they still are short of people with science, mathematics, or engineering backgrounds; they also are looking for people interested in cataloging and work with children.

An interesting finding came from a survey of Illinois public libraries: Fringe benefits (expressed as a percentage of base salary) were only averaging 10 percent in the libraries; industry in the state is providing as much as 50 percent in fringe benefits.

LIBRARY PEOPLE OF 1983

A sample of noteworthy appointments: Don Foos is the new director of the new Master of Library and Information Science program at the University of Arkansas at Little Rock; Kaye Gapen is the dean of the University of Alabama Libraries; Marilyn Gell Mason was appointed director of the Atlanta Public Library; Eleanor Hashim was confirmed as member and new chairperson of the National Commission on Libraries and Information Science; Herbert Biblo is the new director of the Long Island (New York) Library Resources Council; Frank Grisham is the executive director of SOLINET; Bart Kane is the new State Librarian of Hawaii; Nancy Kellum-Rose is director of the Woodland, California, Public Library; James H. Fish is the director of the Springfield City Library, Massachusetts; Miles Jackson is the dean of the University of Hawaii Graduate School of Library Studies; Philip E. Leinbach is the university librarian of Tulane University (Louisiana); the new president of the Research Libraries Group is Richard W. McCoy; Maurice J. (Mitch) Freedman is the new executive director of the Westchester (New York) Library System; JoAn S. Segal is the executive director of the Bibliographic Center for Research, Rocky Mountain Region; Ben Wakashige is library director, University of Albuquerque; and Ann Woodsworth has been chosen associate provost and director of university libraries at the University of Pittsburgh.

Unusual new jobs: Susan Grover is the first full-time volunteer coordinator at the Providence (Rhode Island) Public Library; Linda Katsouleas is the volunteer programs director of the Los Angeles Public Library; Anne Lipow was named to the new post of library education chief at the University of California, Berkeley; Major R. Owens, who began his public service career as a librarian in Brooklyn, has moved up from New York State senator to become a member of the U.S. House of Representatives; and another New York City librarian, Cynthia E. Jackson of the Queens Borough Public Library, was elected to the New York State Assembly.

Fictional people: *LJ* was gulled by someone into printing the news of the appointment of Nouleigh Rhee Furbished, purportedly the new Conservation and Preservation Officer at NELINET, having been lured away from Houghton Library at Harvard.

Retirements and resignations: Susanna Alexander, associate state librarian, Missouri; John Anderson, director of the Tucson Public Library; Forrest Carhart, director of METRO (New York City); Paul B. Kebabian, university librarian, University of Vermont; and Lawrence E. Wikander, college librarian, Williams College, Massachusetts. Lawrence Eaton was dismissed from his post as director of the Pawtucket Public Library, Rhode Island; and Arial Stephens was removed from his position as director of the Charlotte and Mecklenburg County Library, Virginia.

Obituaries: three former Librarians of Congress: Luther Evans, Archibald MacLeish, and L. Quincy Mumford; Meredith Bloss, former director of the New Haven Public Library; Charles E. Dalrymple, former director of the Lincoln City Library, Nebraska; Harold Lancour, founding dean of the University of Pittsburgh library school; Harold Roth, library consultant; Jesse Shera, former dean of the Case Western Reserve School of Library Science; and Frederick Wezeman, professor emeritus, University of Iowa, School of Library Science.

LIBRARY ASSOCIATIONS

It was a financially shaky year for the American Library Association; at year's end, it was committed to a cutback of some 9 percent to erase a $200,000-plus deficit blamed on membership losses, empty rental space in the new building, and shrinking publishing profits. ALA's feisty divisions, however, are in the black. ALA's plight was mirrored in that of the (British) Library Association, which earlier in the year was facing austerity and a $200,000 deficit. The Medical Library Association was successful on a second try at a dues increase, which is expected to restore financial stability. The Special Libraries Association is healthy financially and is working toward a major expansion of its headquarters space, as well as vigorously pursuing new income from continuing education programs.

The uneasy truce between ALA and its divisions—and between divisions and state chapters—continues. There was much debate in 1982 on the need to limit the mushrooming number of library association conferences, and state library associations warily eyed possible encroachments on their turf by ALA divisions. The New York Library Association officially came out in favor of a curb on ALA meetings, and an *LJ* editorial, "Too Many Meetings?" drew extensive correspondence.

By design or not, ALA appears to be moving toward a federation structure, in which the secretariat would function as an umbrella organization for membership groups—both its own and any others that might come in as clients of its association services. The sweeping reorganization of ALA in the late 1960s was motivated by a desire to make the organization more democratic, more under the control of the general membership. The strengthening of the powers of the paid staff was one means of loosening the old boy/old girl network's grip on the association reins, but its effect has been to hand much of the power over to the staff and the offices established to effect membership priorities.

The September 1 editorial of *LJ*, "The Wedgeworth Decade," reviewed the pivotal role played by Executive Director Robert Wedgeworth. It found that after ten years of his forceful administration, ALA is bigger and richer, but fragmented and in financial straits. Unity, it concluded, is the issue for the 1980s.

Herbert White, dean of the Indiana University School of Library and Information Science, argued for federation in a May 1 *LJ* article, "An American Federation of Library Associations: The Time Has Come." He envisioned such a structure as an aid to both small and large groups wishing to meet and spend their meeting time focusing on their own concerns. [Part 3 includes a report by Herbert S. White on recent developments in library education—*Ed.*]

ALA and Legislation

The broad legislative program of ALA is this year almost diametrically opposed to the Reagan administration's stated aims and actions, with the exception of the administration's support for library cooperation and for research library collections. It is pressing for lower postal and telecommunication rates; reasonable pricing of government documents; a strengthened government documents depository system; better funding for the National Archives and Records Service and the National Historical Publications and Records Commission (NHPRC); a national access policy on government information; continued funding for LSCA, HEA, and the Educational Consolidation and Improvement Act; better funding for the Library of Congress, the National Commission on Libraries and Information Science, National Agricultural Library, and the National Library of Medicine; retention of the threatened Department of Education; and the creation of a National Library and Information Services Act to fund cooperation, literacy, urban and rural libraries, library construction, and outreach programs. Also on the ALA agenda are standards for school libraries, funding for academic and research libraries, a National Library Service for the Deaf, a tax break on gifts to libraries, and aid to library education. [See the reports on the effects of 1982 legislation on librarianship and the publishing and information industries in Part 2—*Ed.*]

PRESERVATION AND CONSERVATION

Headlining the news in this area last year were the mass deacidification tests conducted by the Library of Congress, the funding of a Johns Hopkins University study to develop a preservation strategy for the nation's libraries, and a number of state and university library initiatives, which seem to indicate that preservation has indeed become firmly entrenched in nationwide library planning.

The Library of Congress deacidifcation tests indicate that protection for the masses of books threatened with certain destruction in a very few years may be achieved for as little as $5 a volume by mass deacidification techniques.

In 1982, Johns Hopkins University received a grant of $185,000 from the National Endowment for the Humanities, signaling that agency's satisfaction that a sufficient level of consensus in the research library community had been achieved to make planning of an overall strategy feasible. Funding for preservation microfilming has been available for the last few years to research libraries, through the Higher Education Act, II-C, Strengthening Research Library Resources program, which also supports collection development and development of access tools. Critics of the program, which has given research libraries over $28 million in five years, see a want of coordination in the HEA program, with grants being doled out on an almost ad hoc basis. The Johns Hopkins study holds out hope that coordination and cooperation are going to be possible in the area of preservation.

Individual libraries and library agencies reported intensified activities in 1982: Harvard's new preservation fund was up to $250,000; the Morris Library at the University of Southern Illinois was awarded a federal grant to set up a cooperative conservation program for Illinois, utilizing the state network, ILLINET, to provide the linkage necessary for communications and assistance. A midwestern cooperative conservation program was found to be a need by a National Endowment for the Humanities study, and when the state of Oklahoma raised the funding of the state library by $1 million in 1982, a slice of that increase was earmarked for a preservation laboratory to serve the needs of the state's libraries.

The University of California at Berkeley's General Library has had an ambitious program going since 1980; a report last year mentioned establishment of a conservation department with several programs, including a "brittle books" component, preservation microfilming, and participation in cooperative conservation endeavors.

The University of Texas at Austin emerged in 1982 as a prime focus of preservation activity and training, with the "phase preservation" techniques introduced by UTA's Donald Etherington, who learned the approach at the Library of Congress. UTA takes a long view, starting now with staff training, which will take years to complete.

[For a report on the conservation training program at Simmons College, see the article by Josephine Riss Fang in Part 3—*Ed.*]

SLJ NEWS REPORT, 1982

Bertha M. Cheatham
Associate Editor, *School Library Journal*

Two years into the decade of the eighties, technology has taken a giant step forward. Youngsters are absorbed in playing arcade games by the hour; they rush to use microcomputers both during and after school. Despite budget cuts and the lack of support staff, librarians are keeping in the forefront of this technology and are soaking up as much information about computers as they can in the race towards the twenty-first century.

School administrators are using the block grant funds to equip schools with microcomputers. The consolidation of what was formerly the Elementary and Secondary Education Act amounts to $455 million, of which up to $175 million may be spent on microcomputers and courseware in 1982—an impressive increase over the $120 million in federal funds spent in the 1981–1982 school year. That year, librarians were wary of block grants; this year, it's a wait-and-see situation, with librarians making concerted efforts to get involved in the budgeting of expenditures. Because funds are allocated on a per-pupil basis, small school districts and nonpublic schools will benefit under the consolidation.

One caveat, as stated by Fred M. Hechinger, staff writer of the *New York Times*, the Educational Product Information Exchange (EPIE), the Microcomputer Research

Note: Adapted from *School Library Journal*, January 1983, where the article was entitled "1982 & Libraries: The News in Review."

Center at Teacher's College of Columbia University, and others, is that computer software may be "boring and pedagogically flawed." They say that programs produced to secure a fast buck in a mushrooming market are no more than drill exercises, are directed to one main curriculum area, do not introduce higher skills, and provide inadequate responses. Another criticism is that teachers are unprepared to use microcomputers effectively. In his April 30 column Hechinger writes, "Many experts have high hopes that the computer may usher in a very new day for education. But they fear that, without rapid improvements in current practices, teachers will let the machines gather dust, thus repeating what happened to earlier technology, such as teaching machines and language laboratories in the 1950s and even to educational films and television. The challenge, as seen by critics of present developments, is to insure that the educational computer will not be a robot without a brain."

Approximately 130,000 computers are now in the nation's 82,000 public schools. This figure will rise dramatically if Congress approves a bill proposed by Steven Jobs, the 27-year-old chairman of Apple Computer, and Rep. Pete Stark (D-Calif.), to permit manufacturers to donate one computer to every school in the country, with the provision that the manufacturers are allowed a tax write-off. Today's youth will be tomorrow's computer owners, and this bill, if passed, could have far-reaching implications.

In the near future college students will be required to purchase personal computers; Drexel University and Clarkson College are both moving in this direction. IBM is now designing an instrument that can be toted to class to be used, among other things, for instant access to library holdings, take-home exams via computers, and monitoring home telephone calls. And, to test the use of computers in elementary education, IBM has loaned computers using voice outputs and color graphics to evaluate the reading and writing skills of 10,000 kindergarten and first-grade students.

Librarians have discovered that the best way to compete with arcade games is to have micros available in the library. Santa Clara County Public Library has sent out a computer van equipped with 15 personal computers for class visitations; more than 8,000 students were reached by this fun "teaching tool."

PROFESSIONAL CONCERNS

The new technology, either directly or indirectly, has led to changes in professional association programs for members and in library school graduate programs. After surveying its membership, the board of directors of the National Audio-Visual Association (NAVA) voted in October to change its name to the International Communications Industries Association, but will retain the familiar acronym, which has served it well for 35 years. The new name was arrived at to "better reflect the scope of all the technologies" now in NAVA's membership.

A number of library schools have either changed their names to incorporate information sciences, or diminished programs due to several factors: budget stringencies, decreased enrollments, and new emphases on management, communications, and technology. The factors have also resulted in course changes, particularly in a diminution of children's literature courses and other areas of preparation for this services area. ALA's Committee on Accreditation is expected to investigate this matter.

Changes put into effect this year include

1. In April, Indiana University's School of Library and Information Science announced three dual masters programs: an MLS-MPA (master of public affairs); an MLS-MA (with the School of Journalism); an MLS-MA (with the History and Philosophy of Science Department). With this expansion it is expected that graduates will be able to enter a variety of specialized library and information positions in the public and private job markets.

2. Declining enrollment and financial setbacks led to the shutdown of SUNY-Geneseo's School of Library and Information Science (N.Y.) in 1982—a library school that was founded in 1907. The eight staff members teaching a total of 30 full- and 50 part-time students are out of jobs at the end of the school term.
3. The Educational Media Librarianship Program at the Matthew A. Baxter School of Information and Library Science, Case Western Reserve University, Cleveland, was suspended indefinitely at the end of the 1981–1982 school year. Professor John Rowell, who took early retirement at the end of the summer 1982 session, attributed this to cutbacks in government funding and to a nationwide trend, especially in his state, "to assign certified educational media specialists to classrooms and to replace them in the media centers with paraprofessionals." This is also the case in New York State, where it is estimated that more than 1,500 librarians have been released or vacancies not filled.
4. Because only nine students were left in the library media technology program at the Montgomery County Community College in Blue Bell, Pennsylvania, the program was dropped, and a weapons training program established in its place. The reasons cited were the lack of jobs in elementary schools and more positions available in the security field.

[For an overview of recent developments in library education in the United States, see the article by Herbert S. White in Part 3—*Ed.*]

365 DAYS IN MAINE

Most of the titles named in a recent PBS "Crisis to Crisis" program, "Books on Trial," are well known to children's and school librarians. The camera followed the people involved in the banning by a school board of *365 Days*, which received national attention in 1981. The book was pulled off the shelves of the Woodland High School Library (Baileyville, Maine) after a parent complained about the language used by author Dr. Ronald Glasser.

All the disparate elements of book-banning issues were brought into focus: A teacher said the matter quickly blew out of proportion; she really didn't believe the board would ban the book—"It came as a surprise!" A minister felt that children should not be exposed to the language used by Glasser in his description of young soldiers he had treated in a burns ward. Before 1982 was over, *365 Days* had received so much attention that more than 4,000 copies were sold in Maine, and the book went to a third printing.

The case was resolved in February 1982, when Judge Conrad Cyr ruled that there was no evidence that the book's "coarse language" would harm students and ordered the book restored to the school library.

SUPPORT LACKING

Maine librarians were highly critical of the American Library Association's lack of involvement in the Baileyville case. When Judith Krug, executive director of the Freedom to Read Foundation, was approached by Michael Scheck, a defendant, he was told not to use an ACLU lawyer, that the foundation would file an *amicus curiae* if the case went to a hearing, and that $1,000 would be sent to assist in the defense. Scheck appointed attorney Ron Coles, of the Maine CLU, and did the groundwork for the suit.

Before the suit was heard, Cole called Krug, who said that FRF had invested thousands of dollars in other cases, that she had consulted with the board, and that he was on his own. Cole believed she didn't consider the situation important.

ALA's Office of Intellectual Freedom claimed that approximately 1,000 censorship attempts occur every year, a highly speculative estimate in view of the number of censorship cases erupting in 1982. This claim was also refuted in Kenneth I. Taylor's article "Are School Censorship Cases Really Increasing?" (*School Library Media Quarterly*, Fall 1982).

Librarians' and educators' concerns about ALA's reports of the escalation of censorship incidents resulted in surveys, some published in state and library journals.

State associations that have conducted surveys to ascertain the extent of censorship on the state level have come up with little evidence. In *Idaho Libraries* (Summer 1982), Tom Tursky, associate professor of English at Boise State University, says, "Despite media stories of book burnings spreading across the nation, Idaho has remained lamentably unfashionable and nonflammable. In the last decade . . . there have been no apparent statewide campaigns by groups or individuals to censor books in Idaho public libraries—Moral Majority, Mormons, Catholics, John Birch Society, radical feminist groups, Eagle Forum, or conservative Democrats and Republicans notwithstanding."

In Illinois, Bernice B. Seiferth, professor of education at Southern Illinois University, published "The Holy War of Censorship" in the September 1982 issue of *Illinois Libraries*. Her survey of 96 Illinois high schools did not turn up evidence that outside groups were exerting pressure on the schools or that dictionaries were being removed.

Minnesota's CLU conducted a survey that showed that more challenges to materials are being made. A total of 88 out of the 235 high schools responding had experienced challenges; 52 percent kept the materials on the shelves, 48 percent either removed the books in question or restricted their circulation. Maine's CLU called this "appalling."

Following up his 1977 survey of libraries, Lee Burress, English professor at the University of Wisconsin at Stevens Point, found only a 4 percent increase in book challenges, according to reports in the national press. According to his recent survey, which was sponsored by the Committee against Censorship and the National Council of Teachers of English, *Go Ask Alice* was the most frequently censored book in high school libraries (a very interesting finding, since the anonymous Alice's "diary" about her drug addiction and eventual suicide has been around since 1971 and should be old news to today's teens).

Others include *The Catcher in the Rye* (which holds the all-time record—it came in second as the most censored book); *Our Bodies, Ourselves; Forever; Of Mice and Men; A Hero Ain't Nothin' but a Sandwich; My Darling, My Hamburger; Slaughterhouse-Five; The Grapes of Wrath;* and *Huckleberry Finn*. Burress notes that the majority of the reported challenges came from the Northeast.

WHO IS BANNING WHAT?

Other brushfires involving books used in the curriculum and libraries making the news this year were the following:

1. The Richford (Vt.) High School retained Steinbeck's *The Grapes of Wrath* in the curriculum after parents urged the school board to ban it on religious grounds.
2. In Polk County, Florida, a review committee voted to keep Vonnegut's *Slaughterhouse-Five* in the Lakeland High School curriculum despite vocal and persistent critics, but a review committee at neighboring Lake Gibbon High School voted 3-2 to remove it.
3. *Huckleberry Finn* is back in the news—in Spring, Texas, where black parents wanted it removed from the curriculum and in Fairfax County, Virginia, where John H. Wallace, a black administrative assistant at the Mark Twain Intermediate School and chair of its human relations committee, called the book "poison

... racist trash." Both complaints were about Twain's depiction of blacks. The title was retained in both schools.
4. In Minot (N. Dak.), the school board banned *Newsweek* from ninth- and tenth-grade social studies classes because, in the words of one member, "it was too liberal." And, because of a complaint, students in Indian River County (Fla.) cannot borrow Dale Carlson's *Loving Sex for Both Sexes* (Watts, 1979); it can be borrowed by parents in person and must be enclosed in a sealed envelope when they pick it up.
5. A 1981 controversy in the Tampa-Hillsborough County (Fla.) Public Library System, which erupted over Peter Mayle's *Where Did I Come From?* (Lyle Stuart, 1973) and five other sex education books, was resolved when the books were moved to the adult section. The complaint resulted in a long power struggle between the Tampa City Council and the Hillsborough County Commission over who controlled the library system. This was settled in July, when agreement was reached to establish a joint public library board.

WHO'S IN CHARGE?

Perhaps the most crucial and troubling question administrators must face—how much control a local school board can exert over book selection—is the basic issue in complaints involving books on library shelves. This issue was the basis of the six-year battle between five former students of the Island Trees (N.Y.) High School and the school board, which had removed nine books from the high school library. The students claimed that their First Amendment rights were abridged by the board, which had ordered the books removed because they were "anti-American, anti-Christian, anti-Semitic, and just plain filthy."

The case went to the Supreme Court on appeal after being dismissed by a district court judge. After a one-hour hearing, the Court, in a 5-4 vote, ordered the case to trial. The majority of the justices held that "local school boards may not remove books from school library shelves simply because they dislike the ideas contained in those books and seek by their removal to prescribe what shall be orthodox in politics, nationalism, religion, or other matters of opinion."

To avoid a long and costly trial (which their lawyer said would turn into a "zoo"), the Island Trees Union Free School Board voted 6-1 to restore the books. But they threw in a clinker—they required librarians to send written notification to parents that their child had checked out one of these books.

Although the Court's decision does not settle the issue of a school board's authority, Steven Pico, a student who filed the complaint and is now working for the National Coalition against Censorship, feels that it was a "clear victory for the First Amendment."

TEXTBOOKS ON TRIAL

There is no simple solution for textbook publishers. This year some school administrators and boards refused to buy textbooks that were amended or rewritten to suit state review boards. In Texas, State Commissioner of Education Raymond Bynum bucked his review committee's recommendation to reject five health books containing references to venereal disease. In fact, Bynum, who originally told the publishers of the health books (for grades 4-8) to delete all references to VD on his staff's recommendation, then actually read the books and, in the face of harsh criticism, admitted his mistake. He found that the books did not provide *enough* information on VD and other formerly taboo subjects for elementary school students and plans to ask textbook publishers to give children more facts about sexually transmitted diseases.

New York City's Board of Education also made news when it complained that three textbooks were unsuitable for the high school curriculum and banned them from use because they contained inadequate treatments of Darwin's theory of evolution. In rejecting the textbooks, the New York school system became one of the first major textbook buyers to serve notice that they will not accept unbalanced texts.

CRIMINAL STATUTES CAUSE ALARM

If textbook publishers had cause for alarm, trade publishers found the passage of child pornography laws equally alarming. When the U.S. Supreme Court upheld a New York criminal statute that prohibits the production or promotion of material in which sexual conduct by children under 16 is portrayed, regardless of whether the material is obscene, St. Martin's Press reacted by halting the publication of *Show Me!* Said Thomas McCormack, president of St. Martin's, "Since there is a jail sentence involved, I feel I have to protect my editors and salespeople by cancelling the book." He feels that the law is an "improper construction of the First Amendment," and has promised to republish *Show Me!* if the state appeals court finds the law unconstitutional. Almost 150,000 copies of *Show Me!* have been sold since it first appeared in 1975. It has been challenged in the courts of Massachusetts, New Hampshire, and Oklahoma.

Pressure from librarians led to the revision of a similar ordinance in Illinois. In December, the Cook County Board of Commissioners changed the measure to allow the distribution of educational and art materials. The original statute had defined sexual content, in part, as [any] "exhibition of post-pubertal human genitals or pubic areas." The librarians, who had threatened to sue, charged that the law as written could cause the exclusion of anthropological, medical, and health books, as well as art reproductions with pictures of naked children. The revision prohibits only "lewd" exhibitions. Conviction could lead to fines of up to $500 or imprisonment for up to six months of anyone caught producing, selling, or distributing "any performance or matter which depicts sexual conduct and has a child as one of its participants or portrayed observers."

James Coyne, member of the Illinois Library Association, was not completely satisfied with the revision: "We [members of the Illinois Library Association] would be much happier for our staffs if it clearly ruled out prosecution for our libraries. It does not, and it could get expensive."

EDUCATION—FUTURE DIRECTIONS

By the year 2050, the U.S. population is expected to hit a high of 308.9 million. The current population is estimated a 232 million. In 1990, increased enrollment from 27,613,000 to 30,298,000 is projected for grades 1-8. A decline in secondary school enrollment is predicted during the same period.

These statistics may signal the end of a steady decline in school enrollments over a 13-year period—or at least a shift in the age level population in schools—and it may mean an end to school closings due to the falling birth rate. The past year saw some western states initiating public school kindergarten programs because of a 1977 rise in the birth rate. Another factor stabilizing schools was the lack of mobility of families caught in the economic crunch, as well as a lower dropout rate due to a tighter job market.

In his two years in office, President Ronald Reagan has paid little attention to education in his efforts to step up the arms race. He did, however, establish a National Commission on Excellence in Education to bring attention to the quality of education.

His threat to abolish the Department of Education was not carried out, although the School Media Resources Branch in the Office of Libraries and Learning Technologies, which advised librarians on organizing and conducting programs under Title IV-B, was dismantled early in the year. [Reports on the various library programs administered by the Office of Libraries and Learning Technologies in 1982 are included in Part 2—*Ed.*]

Reagan's attempt to trim down the education budget has not resulted in tremendous savings. Terrell H. Bell, secretary of education, said when he took office that the budget for the department was $14.9 billion, and despite his goal to cut the budget by $10 million, it stands at $14.7 billion. Because of the forward funding of appropriations, the true level of cuts in spending cannot be assessed until 1983.

Bell, referring to the "teacher problem," a growing shortage of brighter teachers who elect to enter other fields, has proposed a system in which teachers will be offered more incentives in terms of pay, recognition, and promotion to higher ranks. The Commission on Excellence he appointed is expected to issue its report in March 1983.

FUNDING: PLUS AND MINUS

Once again public libraries, particularly those in large urban areas, had to cope with dwindling budgets, but the picture is not totally grim. New Jersey was hard-hit because of a substantial cut in state aid; Newark Public Library laid off 89 employees, cut salaries, cut children's service hours in branches, and took other measures to keep operating in the face of a $600,000 shortfall. Despite a healthy budget, Buffalo & Erie County Library (N.Y.) had to resort to branch closings and staff cutbacks due to increased costs. The San Francisco Public Library may go the route of library "supermarkets" and eliminate ten branches if it chooses to follow the recommendations made by Lowell Martin in a study of the system. Usage has dropped; funds are low.

On the brighter side, California's 168 public libraries will receive a boost in 1983 as a result of the passage of a bill authorizing $23 million in state funding assistance. And the Metropolitan Library System in Oklahoma County won an increase in tax revenue that added $1.9 million to the library system's budget—a 79 percent increase in its operating budget. The Oklahoma Department of Libraries was granted $1 million more for libraries in 1983. Houston Public Library's budget was increased 35 percent.

PROFESSIONAL ASSOCIATIONS IN 1982

Association for Educational Communications and Technology

The Association for Educational Communications and Technology was strapped with a deficit of more than $250,000 this year. Members became aware of this shortfall at AECT's annual convention in Dallas, where the board of directors took decisive action to turn the state of the association around. Meeting in closed session, they voted not to renew Executive Director Howard B. Hitchens's contract. He had held that position for 13 years.

AECT's hopes for pulling out of the deficit now rest on the COMMTEX International Exposition (with 800 booths sold and hotel rooms filled), Project BEST (funded by the Department of Education to disseminate information through networks), and increased membership (the year-old Division of School Media Specialists is now AECT's second largest division).

American Library Association

The American Library Association, under the leadership of President Betty Stone, had a productive year: ALA adopted a national library symbol, and a U.S. postage stamp honoring American libraries was released. ALA ended its three-year boycott of Chicago (because Illinois had not ratified the Equal Rights Amendment), when the deadline for ERA's ratification expired June 30.

Late in the year, it was revealed that ALA had a serious cash-flow problem resulting in a deficit of over $200,000: Membership has leveled off and the space ALA owns in the new headquarters building is not yet fully rented. In a special session, the executive board voted to borrow $95,000 from the Endowment Fund, to be paid back in five years. In addition, $100,000 will be cut from expenditures to make up the deficit and balance the budget.

After six years of debate and negotiations, the ALA Council adopted the operating agreement in June. This document defines the relationship between ALA and its membership divisions; now divisions are free to publish, set their own dues and fees, plan and conduct conferences, and plan continuing education activities.

The acceptance of the agreement puts to rest the question of whether divisions can hold conferences away from ALA. The American Association of School Librarians (AASL), which completed its second (financially successful) national conference in Houston in October, and the Association of College and Research Libraries have both held national conferences. Although the agreement limits such outside conferences to every two years, some members still disapprove because they feel this may weaken ALA by causing fragmentation. ALA chapters fear their own conferences will be diminished by ALA division conferences held on their territory.

[For further information on the 1982 activities of ALA, see the annual report from the association in the National Associations section of Part 1—*Ed.*]

ALA's DIVISIONS

American Association of School Librarians

As already reported, AASL is moving forward with its plans to hold national conferences. The Houston conference attracted almost 3,000 registrants. However, conference planning may have taken attention away from a crucial issue, which at year's end remained unresolved: When and by whom will the new school library media standards be rewritten?

Association of Library Services for Children

The Association of Library Services for Children is undergoing changes under the direction of its newly appointed executive director, Ann Carlson Weeks, whose predecessor, Mary Jane Anderson, resigned in June. Marilyn Kaye was named editor of *Top of the News*, replacing Audrey Eaglen.

Young Adult Services Division

The Young Adult Services Division published *Young Adults Deserve the Best: Competencies for Librarians Serving Youth*, a document that will strengthen its service area. Having accomplished this, YASD has drawn up a list of goals to pursue in 1983.

COPYRIGHT CONCERNS

The copyright law was another issue in debate—specifically, ALA's reaction to the 1982 *King Research Report on Photocopying in Libraries* issued early in the year. The report points out violations of copyright law by libraries; ALA contends that the report unfairly singles out library practices while neglecting to focus as much attention on publishing practices, and that it fails to quantify the amount of photocopying from foreign and public domain materials, which are not covered by the law. ALA's response to the King report, sent to David Ladd, Register of Copyrights, stated: "It may be time for those 'silent' publishers and users of copyrighted materials to work together to find mutually acceptable ways of insuring greater technological control of their publications while providing access to information through the nation's most precious storehouses of knowledge—libraries."

ALA contends that the copyright law, mainly Section 107 (fair use), is working. On the other hand, publishers represented by the Association of American Publishers (AAP) maintain that the copyright law is *not* working and call for stiffer penalties for violators. AAP is asking that the law be revised, citing "huge amounts" of illegal photocopying taking place in libraries.

[There are two separate reports on the new copyright law in Part 1—a five-year review in the Special Reports section and a report from the Copyright Office on developments in 1982 in the Federal Agencies section—*Ed.*]

THE YEAR AHEAD

Economists predict another stretch of hard times in 1983, with inflation and unemployment rising and a federal administration that is unable to ease the economic policies that create these conditions. ALA President Carol Nemeyer offered good advice in her inaugural address, when she urged librarians to join together to proclaim, "loudly and clearly . . . the full worth of librarians and libraries."

PW NEWS REPORT, 1982

John F. Baker
Editor-in-Chief, *Publishers Weekly*

The year 1982 was by no means a banner year for the publishing industry. Punished, like most businesses, by the continuing high interest rates—which made borrowing for capital investment prohibitive in most cases—and sorely beset by a depressed economy that made even the comparatively moderate prices of books seem out of the reach of many former book buyers, publishers found it a year for belt-tightening and consolidation.

Final sales figures for the year, as estimated by John Dessauer, showed trade sales in 1982 down over 1981 (itself hardly a banner year) by .6 percent in dollars and 3 percent in units. Broken down further, this reflected an 8.2 percent dollar decline in adult hardcover books and a 10.4 percent decline in units. Trade paperbacks fared much better, with a 15.5 percent increase in dollars and a 4.7 percent rise in units. For the book industry as a whole, including professional, religious, mail order, scholarly, and textbook publishers, 1982 showed a 4.5 percent increase in dollars (largely reflecting higher prices, and just about even with the rate of inflation) and virtually flat unit sales (.3 percent up).

Note: Adapted from *Publishers Weekly*, March 11, 1983, where the article was entitled "1982: The Year in Publishing."

THE PAPERBACK HOUSES

Nowhere was this flatness more apparent than in the paperback industry, where no less than four mass market houses either disappeared altogether or found their lines, and identities, absorbed into other houses. Newhouse Publications took over the Fawcett line from CBS and folded it into Ballantine; Popular Library, CBS's other paperback arm, went to Warner Books, hungry for strong backlist; the Playboy paperback operations were absorbed into Berkley/Jove, a division of Putnam; and Putnam also bought faltering Grosset & Dunlap, along with its paperback arms, Ace and Tempo.

Even among the surviving major paperback houses it was a tough year. They had begun pruning their purchases from hardcover houses in previous years, but the habit of paying extravagantly for major hardcover bestsellers died hard, and in 1982 the legacy of that habit hung around the necks of many like an albatross. The keenness of their distress was eloquently voiced at the Association of American Publishers divisional meetings in November, when Pocket Books president Ronald Busch declared: "There's a huge fire burning in the paperback business." He went on to note the loss of four houses in 1982 and predicted that within the next six months "at least one more house and possibly three will be gone." He candidly admitted that his own firm had lost $1 million on its publication of John Irving's bestselling *The Hotel New Hampshire* and named a number of other books, bought for large sums, that would mean certain losses for their publishers.

HARDCOVER PUBLISHING

There were a number of shifts in hardcover publishing in 1982 as well, though none on the scale of the paperback thinning. Doubleday continued to make adjustments in its relationships with Dell and the latter's hardcover imprints, Dial and Delacorte. The Dial juvenile line was sold to Dutton, the Delacorte sales force was abandoned as a separate sales entity and taken over by Doubleday, and two successful editors who had their own imprints with Delacorte, Seymour Lawrence and Eleanor Friede, were asked to take them elsewhere. Later it was announced that Doubleday would also manufacture most Dial and Delacorte books. At a time when most houses were shrinking both lists and staff, a Nashville-based Bible publisher, the Thomas Nelson Company, proved sufficiently bullish on the prospects of New York-based secular trade publishing to buy two such houses during the year: the old family owned house of Dodd, Mead—whose last president, S. Phelps Platt, Jr., retired—and the much newer Everest House, launched five years ago under the aegis of the Worldwide Church of God by Lewis Gillenson, who became head of both of them. The comparatively new house of Congdon & Lattès lost Lattès, its French partner, and became Congdon & Weed with new American backing (including that of Peter Weed, from Dodd, Mead). Late in the year Esquire, Inc., which once owned *Esquire* magazine and has become a major educational publisher with its Education Group, bought the Follett Publishing Company, the leading publisher of basal social studies texts.

PERSONNEL CHANGES

As usual there were a number of top-level personnel shifts, the most surprising of which was perhaps the dismissal of Robert Wyatt from Avon, where he had been editorial director for many years; he quickly found a berth as editor-at-large at Ballantine. Fawcett's publisher Leona Nevler also found a new home at Ballantine as executive editor. Betty Prashker, one of Doubleday's top editors, left to become editor-in-chief for Crown in another surprise move, and later in the year former Viking president Thomas Guinzburg joined Doubleday as senior consulting editor. Joseph Kanon left Coward, McCann & Geoghegan (which lost its last name some time after the departure of Jack Geoghegan) to become editor-in-chief at Dutton. Berkley president Victor Temkin went to Los Angeles to direct a new Consumer Products Group at MCA, his company's parent. Houghton Mifflin, which has become increasingly interested in electronic software, acquired a new president, Richard Young, from Polaroid Corporation, specifically to help coordinate electronic publishing activities. Marvin Brown, president and treasurer at Atheneum, went to New American Library at year's end to become its president.

PUBLISHERS TRIM COSTS

Not only people were moving; publishing houses, finding the rents demanded for midtown Manhattan office space more and more onerous, have been looking further afield in 1982—though none generally as far afield as Harcourt Brace Jovanovich, which moved most of its operations to Orlando, Florida, and San Diego, California. Viking, too, moved at the end of the year from its expensive Madison Avenue offices to less glamorous Twenty-third Street, the R. R. Bowker Company will move from the Avenue of the Americas to East Forty-second Street in 1983, and Little, Brown's New York office is leaving midtown Manhattan for offices further downtown.

Changing premises was just one of the more drastic ways in which publishers tried to cope with the economy in 1982. Others included financial maneuverings—both Harper & Row and Macmillan bought back large quantities of their own stock (Harper acting on behalf of its profit-sharing and pension-plan beneficiaries); attempts to become more potent in the marketplace by means of special marketing techniques—special sales departments, concentrating on sales through outlets other than bookstores and library outlets, have been mushrooming in the past couple of years; greater attention to subsidiary rights, including foreign sales, TV and movie options (which more and more publishers are trying to retain and then sell), and even electronic software; working increasingly with outside suppliers like book packagers and independent publicists for many of the functions formerly performed by in-house staff; and working hard to cut back on such fixed (and ever-rising) costs as printing, production, and transportation, by going to shorter runs, batch printing, a reduced range of book sizes and formats, and consolidated shipments.

AUTHOR/PUBLISHER RELATIONS

The relationship between authors and publishers, which had shown distinct strains in 1981, as manifested strongly in the angry American Writers Congress of that year, seemed to have improved marginally in 1981. One of the factors that helped to ameliorate it was undoubtedly the surprising development of many publishers agreeing to cover their authors with comprehensive liability insurance intended mainly to cover them against possible libel suits. This was a move pioneered by Viking, after extensive discussions with authors' representatives, and in the course of the year a number of other major publishers followed suit. The move to establish a National Writers Union to agitate for higher (and prompter) royalty payments, quicker response to manuscripts, and a host of other concessions from publishers seemed to have bogged down somewhat in organizational disputes; in any case the militancy of the drive seemed likely to be blunted by the very general impression in 1982, of publishers and agents alike, that it was becoming more and more difficult to find strong, publishable manuscripts.

COPYRIGHT

The vexed question of photocopying, long a bone of contention among publishers, librarians, and academic institutions, came very much to center stage in the course of the year. Urged on by the Association of American Publishers (AAP), suits were launched against a number of alleged offenders: Two giant corporations, Squibb and American Cyanamid, agreed out of court to cease and desist from the practice of photocopying without royalty payments; Gnomon, a large photocopying service, was successfully sued; and late in the year a number of publishers took New York University and several of its faculty to court, as an example of widespread alleged abuses in the academic world. AAP also decided to toughen up its position on the copyright law, in the wake of a report that showed that photocopying by libraries and their customers was widespread, much of it in contravention of the existing law. It declared that existing law "has failed to be readily enforceable as written, and has suffered from a failure to be fairly interpreted as written." Meanwhile the American Library Association claimed that the majority of libraries were in "overwhelming compliance" with the act's limitations on photocopying and asserted that the law required no change.

Another issue of considerable import to publishers is the manufacturing clause of the Copyright Act, which denies U.S. copyright protection to American authors whose works are printed or bound abroad. The clause had originally been scheduled to die in 1982, and the Copyright Office recommended that it be allowed to do so. It became involved in fiercely partisan politics, however, and in rapid succession a bill to extend the clause for another four years (seen as a protectionist gesture toward the American printing industry) was voted by Congress and vetoed, surprisingly, by President Reagan, who then promptly had his veto overruled.

[See the five-year review of the new copyright law in the Special Reports section of Part 1; also see the annual report from the Copyright Office in the Federal Agencies section of Part 1—*Ed.*]

BOOKSELLING

Among publishers themselves, 1982 seemed to have been a much less litigious year than usual. By far the most significant case of the year involved a fight with booksellers. The Northern California Booksellers Association took Avon—and later Bantam as well—to court, alleging that they gave preferential sales terms, including extra discounts, to the chain bookstores and were therefore acting in restraint of trade. Avon moved for dismissal of the suit, but that motion was denied, and the discovery process was still under way as of the end of the year. The case became more than just a faceoff between independent booksellers and publishers when, at the American Booksellers Association (ABA) meeting in Anaheim in May, it proved to be a divisive issue within the ABA itself. The ABA Board, despite earnest entreaties from the Northern California group, declined not only to help support the suit financially (its lawyers said it was "unwinnable" and might in fact be hazardous to the association) but even to give moral support in the form of an endorsement. As a result of the heightened feelings this stand aroused, the ABA Board only narrowly averted a motion of no confidence, and incoming president Donald Laing noted somberly that he was aware that the board lacked the confidence of half the membership.

Things were, in fact, difficult for independent booksellers and apparently getting more so. The ABA, as it admitted, had considerable financial problems itself; and early in the year it introduced a study showing that in the four years preceding 1980 the net profits of book retailers had declined, and that half of the stores responding to a survey were not profitable judged by a "reasonable" standard of performance. Reports of business failures were also common, and booksellers were among them; a report in late 1982 showed that they had been going out of business at an increasing rate during 1980 and 1981. Most booksellers with whom *PW* spoke during the course of the year seemed to feel, with the publishers, that from spring through early fall was a particularly depressed time for book sales in 1982. By the time the magazine's annual Christmas sales survey was conducted, however, in the first week of December, booksellers seemed somewhat more cheerful: About half of the 35 retailers polled around the country found their seasonal sales ahead of 1981, and only four said they had slipped from the level of the previous holiday season.

In its own attempt to lighten the distribution burdens of publishers and booksellers alike, ABA director G. Roysce Smith came up with an ambitious scheme for a Booksellers Clearing House (BCH), a strongly systems-oriented operation that would embrace order placement, payment, and collection, simplifying existing procedures by means of extensive consolidation of orders to publishers from BCH and of shipments from BCH to booksellers. The scheme is still to be decided upon by the full ABA Board, and a survey of publishers and booksellers by *PW* indicated considerable skepticism as to whether something on so large a scale could be managed by the association.

The American Book Awards (successor to the old National Book Awards) has been going through a series of shifts, in emphasis and presentation, of late, and after this year's Carnegie Hall ceremony an age-old argument resumed between those who felt that the awards should be purely a cultural occasion and those who wished to stress their commercial nature in an attempt to sell more books. After a meeting late in the year, it was resolved that the 1983 awards would be held in conjunction with the American Booksellers Association convention in Dallas, Texas, thus assuring widespread bookseller attention as well as extensive press and even TV coverage. Shortly afterwards, however, this decision was reversed, the organizers claiming lack of time to prepare adequately, and the 1983 awards seemed somewhat in limbo.

It was, in sum, a year in which the problems of publishers, compounded by those of the economy at large, took a greater share of publishers' attention than usual, and tended to overshadow the product itself. But it was also a year in which everyone in publishing had at last become intensely aware of the difficulties of pricing, economical production, effective distribution, and well-planned marketing and were making determined efforts to resolve them. For many, particularly among the middle-range paperback houses, it looked as though 1983 could be a make-or-break year.

Special Reports

THE NEW FEDERALISM: HOW IT IS CHANGING THE LIBRARY PROFESSION IN THE UNITED STATES

Patricia W. Berger
*Chief, Library and Information Services Division,
National Bureau of Standards*

The federal government is one of the country's largest employers of library and information center workers. In October 1980, more than 3,300 librarians, 3,500 library technicians, and 1,300 technical information specialists worked in federal libraries and information centers located in government agencies both in the United States and abroad. Because of the size and pervasiveness of this work force, government decisions about the status of federal librarians and the programs they operate tend to have ripple effects on the library community at large. Sometimes standards set by the federal government become baselines by which state and local governments measure their own programs. For example, it is not unusual for state library standards to be modeled along federal guidelines. For this reason, the revision of two documents that could generate major changes in present staffing patterns of federal libraries—Circular A-76 of the Office of Management and Budget (OMB) of the Executive Office of the President and the 1966 classification and qualification standards for librarians, library technicians, and information specialists of the Office of Personnel Management (OPM)—were of interest and concern to a broad range of people, including librarians (in and out of government), library educators, legislators, and information brokers.

In March 1979, the Office of Management and Budget issued a fourth revision of its Circular Number A-76. In it, OMB reiterated that it is the policy of the U.S. government "not (to) compete with its citizens" but to "rely on competitive private enterprise to supply the (commercial and industrial) products and services it needs."[1] OMB directed executive agencies to stop using federal employees to produce "commercial and industrial products and services"; instead, agencies were told to obtain them through contracts with private organizations and businesses. OMB listed 98 commercial and industrial activities, ranging from "art and graphic services" to "financial auditing," that ought not to be staffed by federal employees but should instead be purchased via contracts with private-sector institutions. "Library operation" is included in that list.[2]

During 1979, the Office of Personnel Management (formerly the Civil Service Commission) began revising its 1966 classification and qualification standards for librarians, library technicians, and information specialists. OPM's personnel standards stipulate educational and experience requirements and compensation levels (not salaries—only Congress sets salaries) for the many occupations that make up the federal work force. OPM began its work on the library-information service series (GS-1400) revisions by conducting preliminary fact-finding meetings and discussions with a limited number of professional and paraprofessional library workers.

Throughout 1981 and 1982, both of these efforts were continued and intensified.

OMB undertook a protracted reevaluation and rewrite effort of its Circular A-76, which lasted until late fall 1982. In December 1981, OPM circulated for public comment drafts of its proposed new standards for federal library workers.[3]

OPM PERSONNEL STANDARDS

From the first, the OPM proposals met with criticism from librarians, library educators, state library officials, and library-information science associations throughout the country. In the months that followed, OPM received more than 500 letters of protest and concern from members of the library community. On three separate occasions, members of the community furnished OPM suggestions, comments, proposed rewrites, and data for improving three separate versions of the drafts OPM prepared.[4,5] In addition, well over 100 letters from representatives and senators asked Donald Devine, the director of OPM, to respond to complaints and questions raised by constituents about the proposed standards. Only rarely in recent times has the library-information science community exhibited such widespread agreement on the merits and demerits of a single issue.

By early 1983, OPM had modified its position on only one issue. In June 1982, after several Democratic and Republican members of Congress had questioned OPM's proposal to deprofessionalize a major segment of federal librarians, OPM reversed that position and announced that bibliographers, indexers, catalogers, acquisitions librarians, systems librarians, and reference-information service librarians and specialists would indeed be covered by a new professional series, one that it had initially proposed to cover only library managers. Although OPM's reversal on this matter was important, as of late January 1983, no compromise had been reached on five additional, equally crucial issues:

1. OPM does not consider the master of library science degree to be the basic educational requirement for professional work in a library. A chief hallmark of all other professional series in federal service is recognition of a formal, basic educational requirement that *must* be met by all members of the profession. The proposed new standards would require only a baccalaureate that includes six undergraduate courses in "library-information service" in order to qualify for an entry-level professional job in a federal library. The library community has furnished OPM data showing that accredited baccalaureate programs for librarians (other than school librarians) do not exist today (and have not existed for 30 years).

2. Certain categories of nonprofessional on-the-job library experience are considered adequate to qualify for professional library work and are, therefore, substitutable for the formal education described earlier. However, OPM will not provide a test or some similar instrument by which the merits of paraprofessional experience in lieu of education could be measured.[6]

3. OPM asserts that because the semester-hour requirements leading to the master's degree in library science have been reduced since the library standards were last revised (1966), today's MLS is less valuable to the federal government than are the master's degrees of other professions. Therefore, OPM would bring librarians holding the master's degree into federal service at a level of pay lower than the comparable level accorded similarly educated professionals in other fields. The library community has provided OPM data to prove that semester-hour requirements for the MLS have not changed in 30 years, nor were they or are they markedly different from those of other professions. Meanwhile, the standards

for another professional series published during 1982 did not reduce the level of pay for beginning professionals holding master's degrees based on 30 to 36 semester hours of work.
4. Calibrations of the duties, responsibilities, and assignments for federal librarians are designated at lower levels of compensation than are comparable calibrations in either OPM's Primary Standard (used to measure the accuracy and adequacy of all OPM occupational standards) or OPM's standards for other professions. Although executive agencies of the federal government, the American Library Association, and Local 2910 of the American Federation of State, County, and Municipal Employees have called these discrepancies to OPM's attention, the same or similar ones reappear in subsequent revisions of the drafts.
5. Certain classification criteria have been omitted, specifically those that lead to assignments at the top step of the middle level of federal service. As a result, the promotional ladder provided by the standards will end at a point so low as to diminish seriously the chances for federal librarians to be considered for top positions in federal service. In contrast, classification standards published by OPM in 1982 for two other professions did include criteria at the top step of the middle level.

In effect, OPM's proposed new standards for the federal library-information service work force describe librarianship as a profession in name only. The differences that divide OPM and the library community remain unresolved, despite repeated attempts by the library community to rationalize them.

OMB CIRCULAR A-76

In early January 1983, OMB released a first draft of the proposed fifth revision of Circular A-76. Originally scheduled for publication in August 1982, the draft was delayed for an additional four months.[7] Although it is too early to state how the document might look when it is published in final form, certain elements of this first draft are worth highlighting:
1. The government reaffirms its intention to "rely on private enterprise to provide commercial goods and services" and not to "carry on any activity . . . if the product or service can be procured more economically from the private sector."[8]
2. A "private commercial source" is defined as any "non-Federal activity located in the United States, its territories and possessions, the District of Columbia, or the Commonwealth of Puerto Rico."[9] Thus, it would appear that a college or university, as well as a state or local government could qualify as a "private commercial source," as could foreign firms and their subsidiaries.
3. The "Circular does not authorize the establishment of an employer-employee relationship between the Government and individual contract personnel." Nor shall it be used "to avoid personnel ceilings or salary limitations."[10]
4. *All* agencies in the executive branch of government are directed either to justify continuing commercial activities "in-house" or else convert them "to contract performance" no later than September 30, 1984.[11]
5. If a contract price "is less than the in-house estimate (of personnel costs) by 10 percent then award a contract."[12]
6. Cost comparisons between a governmental activity and a commercial source for the same activity are valid only if "both Government and commercial cost esti-

mates (are) based on the same scope of work and standards of performance."[13] This suggests that if the government cannot require the MLS of federal librarians, it cannot require it of contractor librarians either.

"Library services and facility operation" are one of 108 commercial activities listed in the draft fifth revision.[14]

CONGRESSIONAL REACTIONS

Throughout 1982, the OPM standards and the current (fourth) version of OMB's Circular A-76, plus its rumored revisions, generated congressional interest and action. On September 30, 1982, the chairpersons of three subcommittees of the House Committee on the Post Office and Civil Service convened one of a series of hearings on the question of pay equity between male- and female-dominated professions. During the course of that session, OPM Director Donald Devine described in some detail the development and implementation procedures OPM uses to establish occupational standards for the federal work force. Testifying for the American Library Association, both the author and Elizabeth W. Stone, 1981-1982 president of the American Library Association, described the compensation-level implications for librarians if OPM's proposed standards for federal library and information service workers were to become final without further modification.[15] Some weeks later, Representative Geraldine A. Ferraro (D-N.Y.) and Devine exchanged letters about OPM's development and review processes for the proposed library-information service standards. Then on December 10, 1982, Representatives Ferraro, Patricia Schroeder (D-Colo.), and Rose Mary Okar (D-Ohio) wrote the comptroller general of the United States to request that the General Accounting Office:

> undertake an evaluation of OPM's "position classification system . . . to determine if it contains sex bias," because "there can be no doubt that . . . the same kind of wage discrimination which exists in the private sector exists in the Federal sector."[16]

On December 21, 1982, Representative Ferraro wrote Devine that she had "asked GAO to expedite its review" of sex bias in the proposed library-information service (LIS) standard. She strongly urged Devine to "delay developing final (LIS) standards until GAO completes its review."[17] As of January 1983, OPM had not agreed to Ferraro's request for a delay in publication.

In OMB's Circular A-76, contracting-out was restricted in health-care facilities run by the Veterans Administration by Sec. 4.09(a) of the Veterans Compensation, Education and Employment Amendments of 1982 Act [PL 97-306 (H.R. 6782); October 14, 1982]. In addition, PL 97-377, which funds most executive agencies of the government through September 30, 1983, includes the following:

> *Sec. 502* No part of any appropriation contained in this Act shall be expended by any executive agency as referred to in the Office of Federal Procurement Policy Act (41 U.S.C. 401 et seq.) pursuant to any obligation for services by contract unless such executive agency has awarded and entered into such contract in full compliance with such act and regulations promulgated thereunder.[18]
>
> *Sec. 120* Notwithstanding any other provision of this joint resolution, none of the funds made available to the General Services Administration under this Act shall be obligated or expended . . . for the procurement by contract of any service, which, before such date, was performed by individuals as employees of the General Services Administration in any position described in Section 3310 of title 5, United States Code.[19]

OUTLOOK FOR THE FUTURE

As of the end of 1982, both OPM's standards and OMB's revision of Circular A-76 were very much in dispute and still under scrutiny and review. Therefore, one can only speculate about their ultimate effects on the long-term health and prosperity of librarianship in the United States, if the final versions are not substantially different from those circulating in early 1983:

1. Both OPM's draft standards and OMB's Circular A-76 rewrite stress products produced, not the intellectual skills and special knowledge that distinguish the library profession today. Should either or both documents be published in their present form, measures of library service will derive from the quantities of things produced or controlled, not the quality of services or products offered.

2. Since public institutions at all levels frequently emulate federal practice, there is reason to believe that OPM's proposed new standards for library employees will affect librarians and the institutions and the publics they serve in all sectors of our society. If OPM does not recognize that the MLS meets *the* basic educational requirements of our profession, on the one hand, and accepts an unmeasurable, unvalidated trade-off between education and paraprofessional experience, on the other, librarianship will be dealt a double blow.

3. If levels of pay for federal librarians are reduced, either because of the new OPM standards or because of the migration of lower paid private-sector contractor library workers into federal jobs, then pay equity between librarians and their peers in other professions will be even less achievable than it is today.

For many years, librarianship has been a female-dominated profession that has been compensated at levels lower than those of male-dominated professions. This has been true in all sectors of our society. Indeed, in the federal government today, librarians and archivists remain at the bottom of OPM's compensation scale for all professionals in federal service. Of the 13 professional series OPM lists in the 1980 edition of its *Occupations of Federal White-Collar Workers*, none is paid a lower average salary by the government than are librarians and archivists; their average is 11 percent below that for all professions in the work force.[20]

4. Should there be an erosion or denial of a necessary educational foundation for librarianship and an increase in the disparities between the levels of responsibility and pay for librarians and those of other professions, OPM could find that the library-information service series ought to be reclassified as a nonprofessional occupation more nearly resembling the administrative, technical, or clerical occupations. Were such a reclassification to occur, it would be binding on all librarians and information specialists who work for the government, whether on the federal rolls or under government contract.

5. Throughout 1982, OPM's proposed standards united the entire library community. OMB's Circular A-76 may have just the opposite effect. Although it is difficult to predict just who will be on what side of which fence, it seems likely that major differences between federal librarians and their "commercial" colleagues over A-76 issues will develop.

Commenting on a similar phenomenon of conflicting needs between the large corporations and their smaller entrepreneurial colleagues, Kotkin and Gevirtz observed that "with economic circumstances pushing them to the wall, a major schism is widening between the ... entrepreneurs and the corporate bureaucrats ... (which) could alter the shape of American politics."[21] Should economic circumstances cause a similar schism between librarians in and out of government to develop, the shape of American librarianship may undergo significant redirection in the years ahead.

In January 1983, President Ronald Reagan told an audience in Chicago that the

United States is "suffering the structural problems of an industrial society being transformed into more of a service and information society."[22] At this juncture, it appears that federal librarians are perceived as part of the country's "structural problems," not as major contributors to the solutions of those difficulties, much less as essential members of an evolving information society. Whether or not this assessment of their relative worth is accurate remains to be seen—the jury is still out at the moment.

NOTES

1. U.S. Office of Management and Budget, "Policies for Acquiring Commercial or Industrial Products and Services Needed by the Government," OMB Circular No. A-76 Revised, Transmittal Memorandum No. 4, (Washington, D.C., March 29, 1979), p. 1.
2. Ibid., p. 4, Attachment A.
3. U.S. Office of Personnel Management, "Tentative Standards for Bibliographic-Information Analysis Series, GS-1409 (Classification and Qualification); Library-Information Service Management Series, GS-1410 (Classification and Qualification); Library-Information Service Assistant Series, GS-1411 (Classification and Qualification); Grade-Level Evaluation Guide for Professional Positions Providing Information Services" (Washington, D.C., December 8, 1981).
4. _____, "Position Qualification and Classification Standards for Library-Information Service Series (GS-1410) and Library Information Service Assistance Series (GS-1411)" (Washington, D.C., n.d.). Released for limited reading sessions in OPM's offices during August–September 1982.
5. _____, "Proposed Final Standards for Library-Information Service Series, GS-1410 (Classification and Qualification)" (Washington, D.C., November 12, 1982).
6. Statement by Paul A. Katz, then assistant director for standards development, U.S. Office of Personnel Management, to a joint meeting of the Federal Librarians Roundtable, American Library Association; the District of Columbia Chapter, Special Libraries Association; and the District of Columbia Library Association, held at the Library of Congress, January 4, 1983.
7. U.S. Office of Management and Budget, "Performance of Commercial Activities" (Washington, D.C., January 6, 1983). Supplement. Proposed revisions to OMB Circular No. A-76. Invitation for Public Comment. Revisions to Circular (not Supplement) published in the *Federal Register*, January 12, 1983, pp. 1376–1379.
8. Ibid., p. 1.
9. Ibid., p. 2.
10. Ibid., p. 3.
11. Ibid., p. 5.
12. Ibid., Supplement, part 1, Chapter 1, p. 6.
13. Ibid., Supplement, part 1, Chapter 2, p. 11.
14. Ibid., Attachment A, p. 3.
15. U.S. House of Representatives, Committee on Post Office and Civil Service, hearing on pay equity, convened September 30, 1982.
16. Letter, Representatives Geraldine A. Ferraro, Patricia Schroeder, and Mary Rose Okar to the Hon. Charles A. Bowsher, comptroller general of the United States, December 10, 1982.
17. Letter, Representative Geraldine A. Ferraro to the Hon. Donald J. Devine, director, Office of Personnel Management, December 21, 1982.
18. U.S. Congress PL 97-377, December 21, 1982. Continuing Appropriations for Fiscal Year 1983. 96 STAT. 1904.
19. Ibid., 96 STAT. 1913.
20. U.S. Office of Personnel Management, *Occupations of Federal White-Collar Workers*, October 31, 1980. (Washington, D.C.: U.S. Government Printing Office, 1981), pp. 42–44.
21. Joel Kotkin and Don Gevirtz, "Why Entrepreneurs Trust No Politician," *Washington Post*, January 16, 1983, p. B1.
22. Lou Cannon, "Reagan & Co.," *Washington Post*, January 24, 1983, p. A3.

PUBLIC SECTOR/PRIVATE SECTOR INTERACTION IN PROVIDING LIBRARY AND INFORMATION SERVICES

National Commission on Libraries and Information Science
1717 K St. N.W., Suite 601
Washington, DC 20036

Toni Carbo Bearman
Executive Director

Douglas S. Price
Deputy Director

There should be little need in this publication to belabor the point that the United States is becoming—if, in fact, it has not already become—an information society. With the burgeoning of the information component of the gross national product and the proliferation of modes and media for transmitting information, it is becoming more important and, at the same time, more difficult to achieve the ideal expressed in the 1975 program document of the National Commission on Libraries and Information Science (NCLIS):

> To eventually provide every individual in the United States with equal opportunity of access to that part of the total information resource which will satisfy the individual's educational, working, cultural and leisure-time needs and interests, regardless of the individual's location, social or physical condition or level of intellectual achievement.[1]

The information citizens need to cope with an increasingly complex society has already outstripped both the ability of our delivery systems to transmit it and that of the citizens—even some better educated ones—to use it. Promoting greater interaction between the public and private sectors in improving the delivery of information is only one facet—albeit a very important one—of the task of reducing the growing gap between the "information rich" and the "information poor." Because the question of public/private sector interaction clearly falls within the mandate of NCLIS and because there was great interest in addressing it throughout all segments of the community, NCLIS commissioned a task force to examine the interaction between the sectors.

CONTEXT

The question "What is the debate?" is most often answered by a statement to the effect that the debate is about the respective roles of the public and private sectors in providing library and information services. This simplistic answer only raises more questions. How do you define the public sector? The private sector? For that matter, how do you define library services or information? None of these questions can be answered easily; however, some points can be made to clarify the framework of the debate.

Information: What Is It?

In the first place, one can never define information as a stand-alone term. It is as generic a term as any in the language and encompasses everything from traffic signs to encyclopedias to tax records. It ranges in complexity from "No Left Turn" to statistical compilations of census data and mathematical models of the earth's atmosphere.

Strictly speaking, one should never speak of information without qualifying it with one or more modifiers, such as bibliographic information, statistical information, personal information, or information products.

A subset of the general discussion is the continuing debate about whether information is a resource or a commodity. One side of this debate argues that information is a unique and valuable resource that is not consumed (and may, in fact, be enhanced) by use. As a resource, it should be nurtured, preserved, managed, and made available—usually for a price. The other side argues that information, like gold or hog bellies, is a commodity to be traded, taxed, and sold. One's position in this debate bears directly on one's position with respect to the roles of the public and private sectors.

Another contribution to the muddy waters is the common failure to make adequate distinction among cost, price, and value of information. The determination of *costs* is a basic economic decision needed for effective management. The *pricing* of products and services, although clearly related to economic concerns, may also be a political decision, especially in the public sector. Determining the *value* of a product or service may extend far beyond economic questions to philosophical considerations of quality or ethical issues, such as the notion of "public good."

Not only are these three distinctly different attributes, but even individually they are extremely hard to quantify. For example, it is relatively easy to determine the cost of an information product or service, but it is far more difficult to determine the cost of creating the information in the first place. Setting prices is considerably more complicated. The private entrepreneur must set the price high enough to cover costs and provide a return on investment, but not so high as to be beyond the reach of the intended market or drive that market to competitors. The government information provider has to consider whether its responsibility to the public requires it to produce and disseminate information at a price of zero, a price below cost, a price to recover full cost (whatever that is), or at a sliding scale to subsidize some users, for example. None of these decisions is easy.

The picture becomes even fuzzier when one considers value. How does one quantify the value of a piece of information? The same piece of information may be utterly worthless in one environment and in another, inestimably valuable. Recently, Taylor[2] and King et al.[3] have made considerable progress in obtaining an indication of the value of information products and services by applying statistical methods and the value-added concept, but these efforts, although extremely useful, are limited in that they can be applied only to relatively large numbers. Also, value extends beyond economic value to include less quantifiable attributes, such as the value of the arts to society. The foregoing difficulties can be attributed to a number of peculiar characteristics of information, which have been listed by Cleveland:

1. Information is lifelike [It exists only in the human mind].
2. Information is expandable [The more it is used, the more there is of it].
3. Information is compressible [It can be summarized].
4. Information is substitutable [It can replace other resources].
5. Information is transportable [At the speed of light].
6. Information is diffusive [It always leaks].
7. Information is shareable [If one transfers information to another, both have it].[4]

These characteristics make information unlike any other resource or commodity known to society. Furthermore, the pace at which it has come to dominate the economy is considerably faster than we have ever before encountered. All of these phenomena make it imperative that we reexamine—and perhaps restructure—our concepts and practices in such fields as accounting, capital formation, political economy, law, education, psychology, and sociology.

The Stakeholders

The public sector/private sector debate is no simple dichotomy between large homogeneous sets of players. There are at least three major components (public, private not-for-profit, and private for-profit); each of these is further subdivided into many subsets and the boundaries between them are, at best, indistinct.

For example, the public sector is divided into at least federal, state, and local governments; the not-for-profit sector includes universities, professional societies, and research institutes such as Battelle; and the for-profit sector includes some information services, publishers, and in-house corporate libraries. Each of these is further subdivided into many different kinds of organizations, and the boundaries between even the major components are virtually impossible to define. Is a contractor that is operating an information service for the federal government a part of the government sector or of the for-profit sector? How does one classify the university presses, with the publishers or the universities? As Oettinger pointed out, any two organizations "are found on the same side of some issues as commonly as on opposing sides in others."[5]

Nor can we ignore the ultimate users. They are—or at least, ought to be—the *raison d'être* for the entire information chain, because more often than not, the users of information are also its creators. Users are found in every one of the sectors and subsectors, and their concerns are frequently very different from those of their fellows. The multiplicity of different positions is staggering. When NCLIS established the Conference on Resolution of Copyright Issues (which became known as the "upstairs-downstairs" group), at least 40 different constituencies were sufficiently concerned to foot the bill for their representatives to participate. Nevertheless, while the debate can probably never be settled completely, ameliorative action to reduce the tensions among the sectors can and should be taken. This is what NCLIS set out to do.

THE TASK FORCE

During 1975, an ad hoc task group of NCLIS commissioners met to consider the topic "The Aversion of Conflict between the Public and Private Information Sectors." The September 1975 interim report of this group recommended a fact-finding effort by a Public/Private Sectors Task Force. This report was updated in 1976 by another commissioner, Colonel Andrew A. Aines, who affirmed the continuing need for such an effort, but because of NCLIS's other priorities and budget constraints, it was not until 1979 that the task force actually began its work.

Organization and Operation

Selecting and soliciting participation of the members of the task force was a difficult, time-consuming process. The commission had specified that there be equal representation of the public, the private not-for-profit, and the private for-profit sectors. In an attempt to provide for representation of at least some of the subsectors, the number of participants was set at 21, nearly 50 percent larger than most NCLIS task forces. The commission had also specified that the members of the task force should be of the highest caliber possible and that participation by alternates, rather than selected principals, was to be discouraged.

Scores of names were screened to select candidates in each sector; these were ranked and contacted in turn. When the roster was finally complete, Dean Robert M.

Hayes of the Graduate School of Library and Information Science, University of California, Los Angeles, who had been selected as chairperson, convened the first meeting of the task force in June 1979.

The purpose of the task force was "to make a significant contribution to the delineation of the proper roles of government and private organizations with respect to the generation and dissemination of scientific, technical, business and other information." At the first meeting, the task force agreed:

1. To work principally through subcommittees.
2. To undertake a Delphi study among the members.
3. To limit the focus to the functional, information-related aspects of dissemination and distribution.
4. To focus on federal government operations.

This last point is made clear in the statement of objectives: "The Task Force is to focus its attention on policies concerning federal governmental decisions on the dissemination and distribution of information held by the government and produced as a result of government action."

The task force was originally scheduled to complete its work in four meetings over a period of one year. In fact, the effort extended over eight meetings and more than two years. Nevertheless, attendance at the meetings was very high.

The Results

The task force produced 7 principles for guiding interaction between the public and private sectors and 27 recommendations for implementing these principles. What is remarkable, considering the diversity of backgrounds, is that the task force was unanimous—or nearly so—on all 7 principles and voted overwhelmingly in support of all but 2 of the 27 recommendations.

Because it is important that the principles and recommendations be evaluated only in the context of the entire report, they will not be listed here. The findings, however, are summarized below.

In general, the principles and recommendations are:

1. In favor of open access to information generated by the federal government.
2. In favor of reliance upon libraries and private-sector organizations (both for-profit and not-for-profit) to make readily available information that can be distributed by the federal government.
3. In favor of a leadership role for government, rather than a management role.
4. In favor of limiting direct government intervention in the marketplace.

COMMUNITY RESPONSE

Early in March 1982, the task force report was published and more than 3,000 copies were distributed to government agencies and officials, members of Congress, librarians, professional and trade associations, and many other individuals and groups.[6] The frontispiece of the report and the accompanying news release requested comments from any and all interested parties.

Meetings, panel discussions, and open forums on the report have been held by the American Library Association, the Association of Research Libraries, the Network Advisory Committee of the Library of Congress, the Federal Information Managers, METRONET, and many others. At this writing, the American Society for Information

Science is undertaking an extensive review. In addition, NCLIS has received comments from many individuals throughout the country. All of these are being carefully reviewed as they are received and will be reflected in future actions insofar as possible.

Summary of Comments

Almost without exception, the report has been praised as a valuable contribution to the furtherance of public sector/private sector cooperation. McDonald has characterized it as "the single most comprehensive distillation of the issues surrounding the public sector/private sector roles in information services ever attempted."[7] Evans has stated that: "A record of the conditions and perspectives of a broad spectrum of the information community at the start of the 9th decade of the century such as that provided by this document is a valuable and permanent contribution to society."[8]

Although, in general, the principles in the report have been supported as a group, there have been criticisms of individual principles and recommendations. Constructive criticisms of the report have focused principally on those areas that the task force, for lack of time and resources, omitted from consideration. Some of these are international issues; state and local government roles; specific recommendations regarding scientific and technical information; definitions of "information"; and serious speculation on developing information technologies and their effects on society and on the interrelationships among the sectors. Other criticisms include the lack of data supporting the task force's conclusions and the general nature of the principles and recommendations.

Suggested Guidelines for Cost Recovery and Pricing

Consideration of the report has prompted Horton to propose for discussion cost recovery and pricing policy based on a pyramidal construct of information categories analogous to Abraham Maslow's hierarchy of needs.

Maslow's Hierarchy of Needs	*Hierarchy of Information Needs*
Self-actualization/fulfillment	Edifying information
Ego needs	Enriching information
Social needs	Enlightening information
Security needs	Helping information
Biological/physiological needs	Coping information

Based on these information categories, which are admittedly vulnerable to criticism, Horton proposes the following pricing policies:

Information Category	*Public Sector Pricing*	*Private Sector Pricing*
Coping information	Free	Less than fully competitive and possibly subsidized
Helping information	Less than full cost recovery	Competitive
Enlightening information	Full cost recovery	Fully competitive
Enriching information	Less than fully competitive marketplace pricing	Fully competitive

Information Category	Public Sector Pricing	Private Sector Pricing
Edifying information	Fully competitive marketplace pricing	Fully competitive

These suggestions are followed by extensive lists of specific examples. Horton emphasizes that his proposal is intended solely as a basis for discussion throughout the community.[9]

NEXT STEPS

The principles and recommendations can serve as a springboard for the development of uniform guidelines for federal involvement in the production and distribution of information products and services. Before the principles and recommendations can serve as guidelines, however, they must be subjected more fully to the test of real-life circumstances—something that the task force was unable to do within the limits of its resources. The principles and recommendations, if they were to become government policy, would have a major impact on existing, planned, or proposed library and information services funded by the federal government, as well as on related activities in the private sector. The commission wants to ensure that, to the maximum extent possible, the implications and potential impacts of these principles and recommendations are known and that their effects will be supportive of the public interest. To this end, NCLIS will initiate a study during 1983 to obtain a more complete understanding of the implications and potential effects that the principles and recommendations would have on services to users and on government and private-sector activities, if they were to be adopted.

NOTES

1. *Toward a National Program for Library and Information Services: Goals for Action* (Washington, D.C.: U.S. National Commission on Libraries and Information Science, 1975).
2. Robert S. Taylor, *Value Added Processes in the Information Life Cycle* (Syracuse, N.Y.: Syracuse University, School of Information Studies, 1981).
3. Donald W. King, Jose Marie Griffiths, Nancy K. Roderer, and Robert R. V. Wiederkehr, *The Value of the Energy Data Base* (Rockville, Md.: King Research, 1982).
4. Harlan Cleveland, "Information as a Resource," paper presented at the METRONET Conference, Minneapolis, Minn., 1982.
5. Anthony G. Oettinger, *Elements of Information Resources Policy: Library and Other Information Services* (Cambridge, Mass.: Harvard University, Program on Information Technologies and Public Policy, 1976).
6. *Public Sector/Private Sector Interaction in Providing Information Services* (Washington, D.C.: U.S. National Commission on Libraries and Information Science, 1982).
7. Dennis D. McDonald, "Public Sector/Private Sector Interaction in Information Services," in *Annual Review of Information Science and Technology*, ed. Martha E. Williams (White Plains, N.Y.: Knowledge Industry Publications, 1982).
8. Glyn T. Evans, "Public Sector/Private Sector Interaction in Providing Information Service," discussion paper presented to the Network Advisory Committee, Washington, D.C., 1982.
9. Forest Woody Horton, "The Public-Private Sector Role Controversy in Producing and Distributing Information Goods and Services," unpublished paper, Washington, D.C., 1982.

PROFESSIONAL SERVICES PROVIDED TO LIBRARIES AND INFORMATION CENTERS BY PRIVATE SECTOR ORGANIZATIONS

William A. Creager

*Chairman, Board of Directors
Capital Systems Group, Inc.*

Donald W. King

President, King Research, Inc.

There is little question that society is rapidly entering an information age.[1,2] In 1950, approximately 17 percent of the work force was engaged in information-related activities; the current proportion is thought to be nearly 60 percent.[3,4] In 1982, the number of hard-core information professionals who organize or process information on behalf of others, manage information units, teach information workers, or are engaged in information research or technology is estimated at nearly 2 million persons.[5] The growth in information production and use has pervaded all facets of our lives, including our personal lives, work, and the governing of our society. Librarians and other information professionals have played an essential role by providing access to information in all these areas. In 1982 there are estimated to be 131,100 librarians in the United States[6] in public libraries (31,100), academic and school libraries (81,400), and libraries in the workplace (18,600). The 7.5 percent increase in the number of librarians, from 126,400 in 1978, partially reflects such indicators as the five-year growth in the U.S. population (4.2 percent), the decline in the number of students (−3.3 percent), and increases in the number of scientists and engineers (16 percent). Nearly 3,000 government libraries and approximately 200 information centers serve scientists and engineers in our nation.[7,8]

Since the end of World War II, private-sector corporations and nonprofit organizations have provided an increasing number of professional services to libraries and information centers, including nearly all of the operational, user-related, and management-support functions performed by libraries and information centers. Among the many reasons why private organizations are becoming such an essential part of library functions are the following:

1. Dramatic increases in the volume of information materials available to and desired by library and information center patrons;
2. Deteriorating budgets that have required libraries to seek and use nontraditional methods for operating their facilities and serving their patrons;
3. A large influx of federal government resources; and
4. The advent of new technology into information transfer processes.

This article attempts to identify the trends and future for library and information centers and how events have led to their increased use of the professional services of private-sector organizations.

A HISTORICAL PERSPECTIVE

By the end of World War II, libraries and other information organizations were charged with the control and management of a vast amount of new, documented information resulting from government-sponsored research and development and from the acquisition of documents from Germany and other nations. Since that time, a succession of events—including the cold war, Sputnik, and continued massive federal and private-sector research and development efforts—has sustained a level of information creation and documentation far beyond anything experienced previously. The amount of scientific and technical literature published, for example, has more than doubled since 1965, i.e., there has been more information published since 1965 than during all of history prior to that time![9]

Not only were librarians and information centers required to provide access to this published literature but they were also charged with providing such materials as technical report literature, audiovisual materials, cartographic information, and computer tapes. Fortunately, as necessity is the mother of invention, new concepts and techniques to control and manage information and documentation began to develop in the late 1940s and early 1950s, and these, coupled with the new technology of the 1960s and 1970s, would profoundly change the way information is organized and how libraries and information centers would function.

As the libraries and information centers within the federal government were the first ones to experience the rapid buildup of new materials, they were also the first to create new documentation systems to manage, control, and store the information. The Library of Congress developed Spindex and MARC tapes for books, and the Atomic Energy Commission (Department of Energy) and Department of Defense developed indexing procedures for handling the masses of new materials. Private organizations not only participated in developing these new systems and procedures under contract but also took versions of the software and systems and developed marketable services and products.

Thus, a new demand was created by the federal government for professional services provided by private-sector organizations.* Documentation, Inc., played a major role in the development of new indexing concepts, new retrieval techniques, and the design and operation of information facilities, under contracts from the Air Force and NASA, among others. General Electric and Computer Sciences Corporation participated in the development of the MEDLARS system under contract to the National Library of Medicine. Information Dynamics Corporation engineered the first major application of microfiche in the United States for NASA's Scientific and Technical Information facility. Many of the mission-oriented information centers and clearinghouses created by the Department of Defense and other agencies have been operated under contract by private information service organizations, including Informatics, Capital Systems Group, and Leasco. By 1980, about 40 percent of the nearly 200 federally funded information centers were entirely operated by such private organizations, and many of the remaining 60 percent contracted out at least a portion of their operations.[10] For example, abstracting and indexing services are provided by such companies as Dataflow, Herner and Company, and Aspen Systems Corporation.

In addition, private-sector organizations provided extensive professional management support services. Herner and Company and others performed studies of information use and of journal coverage by abstracting services for agencies such as the Atomic Energy Commission and the National Institutes of Health. Westat (predecessor of King Research) carried out extensive studies of marketing, document reproduction, ordering, and pricing patterns for the National Technical Information Service and other federal information centers. In addition, nonprofit organizations such as Battelle Memorial Institute, System Development Corporation, and Denver Research Institute conducted user studies and provided other management support services.

*Examples of private-sector organizations are given throughout the text. It is emphasized that not all such organizations could be listed; the authors apologize to those that are not mentioned.

One of the most significant contributions that the federal government made to the information transfer community was to support a number of nonprofit abstracting and indexing services and scientific and professional society publishers in the 1960s. In particular, such organizations as Chemical Abstracts Service, BIOSIS, the American Institute of Physics, the American Psychological Association, and Engineering Index, Inc., received large infusions of grant funds. These funds were used for research into, and development of, machine-readable bibliographic data bases that, combined with computer searching software partially developed under federal funding, have led to such rapidly growing bibliographic search services as Lockheed's DIALOG (an enhancement of the NASA RECON System), System Development Corporation's ORBIT (developed from the National Library of Medicine's MEDLARS), BRS (also developed from NLM's systems), and Mead Data Central (derived partially from an Air Force system).

An important outgrowth of federal involvement was the development and enhancement of the MARC catalog tapes at the Library of Congress. OCLC, a nonprofit organization, first used these tapes as an information utility to serve Ohio colleges and universities. It grew to a national and now international system with more than 3,000 organizational participants. Other services, such as the Research Library Information Network (RLIN), the Washington Library Network, and many other regional networks were beneficiaries of the MARC tape development of the Library of Congress.

Other companies have also gained from research and development originated within the federal government. For example, an integrated library automation system, partially developed at the National Library of Medicine, is being sold throughout the country by two companies, Online Computer Systems, Inc., and AVATAR.

Meanwhile, several commercial firms that provide professional services or products to libraries and information services have developed and flourished without government support. Such firms include the Institute for Scientific Information (ISI), which provides tables of contents of current journals (*Current Contents*) as a reference tool and sells copies of journal articles as well as other information services and products. The Congressional Information Service provides information derived from congressional records and other government sources. Subscription services and book jobbing are also provided by such organizations as FAXON, EBSCO, and Baker and Taylor.

In addition, during the 1970s, a number of research, evaluation, and planning studies of libraries and information centers were conducted by such companies as King Research, Inc., Metrics, Inc., Capital Systems Group, Inc., and Cuadra Associates, Inc. Many of the studies were performed under contracts or grants from the federal government (e.g., LSCA funding to states). Beyond this, nonprofit groups such as Battelle and Franklin Institute also performed a number of studies, as did library and information science departments at such universities and colleges as the University of Pittsburgh, Simmons College, Drexel University, and Syracuse University. Hundreds of doctoral theses were partially funded by government and foundation grants.

Probably the most significant factor that has led to private-sector involvement in providing professional services to libraries and information centers has been the severe constraints imposed on library budgets over the past five years. The world economy, federal and other government budget cutbacks, and community-level tax rebellions have all resulted in fewer funds available to manage information resources. Yet libraries and information centers are pressured to (1) provide more types of materials (e.g., technical reports, audiovisuals, cartographic materials, computer tapes, etc.), (2) maintain exponentially growing stores of materials, and (3) provide additional services such as online bibliographic searching and referral services.

The operational and user demands on libraries have, therefore, not diminished; in fact, they are still increasing. The information age has become more than a slogan. People are indeed acquiring and creating information for occupational, educational, and recreational use at an ever-increasing rate. At the same time, revolutionary changes in communications and computer technology are rapidly changing the ways in which people acquire information and communicate it—changes that augur a profound impact on libraries and other information organizations.

THE FUTURE OUTLOOK

Although new technologies seemed to be the answer to economic problems, some disappointments occurred in their application during the 1970s. For example, microform technology did not achieve its promise, because it was soon discovered that the prices necessary to cover fixed publisher costs (i.e., prerun costs, including editing, redacting, marketing, and composition) were the same for microform as for paperform issues and that, therefore, there was not a sufficiently large price differential to warrant buying microform instead of paperform, which was easier to read, transport, and copy.

Other new technologies in computing and communications resulted in a number of organizations providing automated library systems for supporting operational functions. Table 1 lists some of these professional services and the systems that they actually provide (or plan to make available in the future). Contrary to the belief of some, there is at this time no fully integrated library automation system commercially available. Furthermore, it must be emphasized that, although these systems often provide for substantial improvements in performance and reductions in cost, they do not necessarily lead to reduced budgets, because the librarians they replace are often reassigned elsewhere in the library.

Tight library budgets have resulted in other actions that generate new or expanded business opportunities for private-sector organizations. Many libraries have begun to recognize that frequently used services and products should be handled in-house, and that infrequently used ones can best be provided by outside organizations or by sharing resources. Cost models that have been developed clearly show that library services can be optimized using such approaches, depending on the amount of activity in a given library.[11,12,13] Some observations, comments, and speculations concerning professional services provided by private sector organizations are given below.

Acquisition services will probably continue a shift that has already been observed. More libraries are expected to utilize subscription agencies and book jobbers as they recognize that this approach is often the most cost-effective way to obtain materials. Certain libraries, such as some federal libraries, are almost forced into using such services because of purchasing red tape. On the other hand, libraries are expected to order fewer journal subscriptions and fewer books as budgets continue to remain tight.

Document processing services will continue to shift from cataloging services acquired from information service organizations to in-house personnel using OCLC and other automated cataloging utilities. One dilemma that will need to be resolved concerns the many services that are provided on dedicated terminals or microcomputers, such as OCLC, subscription agents, and library operational support services such as Data Phase. Libraries may be forced to make decisions as to which dedicated equipment to acquire and/or which services to employ. (However, this situation is beginning to improve, as the information services seek to expand their customer bases, by providing terminal emulation software for intelligent terminals and microcomputers or by expanding their networks to accept dial-up terminal input.) Pricing strategies by OCLC and the other services will dictate this trend to a large degree in the future.[14] It is also likely

TABLE 1 AUTOMATED LIBRARY SYSTEMS AND THEIR APPLICATIONS

	Library Operation Support Function				
Source	Acquisitions	Serials Controls	Online Catalog	Online Interface with OCLC	Circulation
Bibliographic Utilities & Associated Systems					
OCLC	Yes	Ordering and check-in; claiming, 1982?	Somewhat	NA	NA
OCLC/Claremont	Yes	Ordering and check-in	Yes	Yes	Yes
UTLAS/LCMS	Summer 1982	1983	Yes	NA	Yes
WLN/BLIS	Yes	Ordering	Yes	(Tape only)	1983
Vendor-Supplied Systems					
Advanced Data Management	Late 1982	Fall 1982	Yes	NA	Yes
Carlyle	NA	NA	Yes	(Tape only)	Yes
Class	NA	Ordering, check-in, claiming, routing	NA	NA	NA
Cincinnati Electronics	Late 1982	Summer 1983	Early 1983	Yes	Yes
CLSI	Summer 1982	1983	Yes	Yes	Yes
Data Phase	Fall 1982	Ordering: Fall 1982	Yes	Yes	Yes
Gaylord	Summer 1982	Summer 1982	NA	Yes	Yes
GEAC	Yes; to be reworked, late 1982	Check-in	Yes	(Tape only)	Summer 1983
ILS	198?	Check-in	Yes	Yes	Yes
Inforonics	On-order file, 1983	Some; acquisition, 1984	Yes	(Tape only)	Summer 1983
Ringgold	Yes	Ordering	198?	Yes	Yes
Sigma Data	Yes	Ordering	Yes	Fall 1982	Yes

NA = Not applicable.
Source: Janine Reid, Paula Strain, Arthur Linsley, Jose-Marie Griffiths, and Vernon E. Palmour, "Integration of New Technology in Army Libraries," submitted to the U.S. Army Management Office (Gaithersburg, Md.: DAMANS and Associates with King Research, Inc., July 1982) and Jose-Marie Griffiths and Donald W. King, "North Carolina Library Networking Feasibility Study," prepared for the Division of State Library, North Carolina Department of Cultural Resources, (Rockville, Md.: King Research, Inc., August 1982).

that a number of technical processing centers will be operated by private-sector organizations that will provide all services to those libraries without sufficient activity to justify in-house equipment or services. Whether such technical processing services will be run by groups of libraries or provided by private-sector organizations remains to be seen.

Many libraries, corporate and academic facilities in particular, are expected to continue their increased use of *data base searching,* resulting in greater expenditures in this sector of the information services industry. *Reference services* will undoubtedly continue to expand exponentially.[15] Systems are likely to be more user friendly.

During the 1970s, a new private-sector industry—information brokers—came into being to fill a vacuum created by library economies and some resistance to new technology in libraries. Several hundred small broker firms, such as Information on Demand, InfoQuest, and Find/SVP, provided reference searching. However, as libraries have acquired their own terminals, the growth of these services has begun to level off. It is very difficult to say how the relative activity levels and contributions of data base producers, vendors, brokers, libraries, and end users will shake down. Some data base producers (e.g., ISI) are (or are considering) distributing their data bases directly rather than providing them through vendors. A major problem in pricing multiple products from single data bases must be addressed and high baud terminals will perturb those pricing strategies that use connect time as the principal price component.[16] Economic evidence suggests that there is an opportunity for turnkey systems that will serve high-use libraries by direct downloading of data base segments from vendor systems.[17] Licensing or some other agreements would have to be made in order to compensate the vendors and the data base producers for their value-added services.

It is believed that *physical access services* by private-sector organizations may expand considerably. At the same time, *document delivery services* continue to gain in popularity and strength as more libraries accept such services as an alternative to acquiring infrequently used journal subscriptions or utilizing interlibrary loan systems. Libraries, because of pressures to allocate their budgets to alternative functions, are beginning to reduce their acquisitions and holdings to include only frequently used items and rely more on interlibrary loan or acquisition of separate copies of articles or technical reports through private-sector organizations such as Information on Demand and InfoQuest.[18,19,20] The increased amount of data base searching will also be another factor that results in the expanded use of information brokers for document acquisition and delivery. Evidence suggests that many libraries could easily reduce their holdings by 20 to 30 percent and rely on alternative resources, even when there is a charge for interlibrary loans or documents delivered by private-sector organizations.[21] In the future, there may even be a single source for such copies of articles provided by a private-sector organization(s). As electronic distribution becomes a reality, this possibility will become more likely.

Systems development is one area where an increase in activity is expected. Microcomputer technology has reached a point where automation is now within the practical reach of almost all libraries. Both hardware and software now exist to support many library functions, including serials management, cataloging, indexing, bibliography, and circulation, as well as the more general activities of word processing, list maintenance, and message communication. But the speed at which the field is developing and the vast number of choices available will lead most prudent librarians to seek expert advice in defining their system requirements, selecting system components, and preparing their staff for system changes and the use of new technology.

The demand for *studies* for library and information program planning and evaluation will probably remain the same overall. Reduced demands for such studies at the federal level will probably be offset by increases in the need for assistance at the state and local levels (partially through LSCA funding), among nongovernment libraries, and information networks and consortia.

Facilities management (utilized mainly by federal information organizations) has undergone both change and reductions in the past several years. The operation of information clearinghouses and the provision of on-site staffing services for libraries and information programs have been areas of federal procurement where heavy preference for small businesses and minority firms has resulted in substantial changes within the industry itself. Many new firms have entered the business; some established firms have lost their market share. In the past two years, some such clearinghouses and other projects have been eliminated; many others have experienced budget reductions. It is expected that federal funding for such services will continue to decline. On the other hand, a new firm called Library Resources Corporation of America has been formed for the stated purpose of providing library facility management services to all kinds of libraries, including federal libraries.

Looking beyond the next two to three years, a substantially brighter environment can be seen for libraries and private-sector information organizations that serve them, driven in large part by the following factors:

1. An ever-increasing demand for personal, educational, occupational and governmental information.
2. The transformation of many libraries, whereby traditional activities are replaced by new ones and the types of materials and information provided are different.
3. Broader acceptance of the value of information, translating into higher prices for information and information services based on value rather than on costs.
4. A dramatic increase in the demand for document acquisition and delivery services, as data base searches continue to lead users to relevant documents and as libraries conclude that interlibrary lending and direct acquisition are uneconomical alternatives.
5. A rapidly growing demand for systems development support, as libraries and other information organizations begin to adopt high technology solutions to the tasks of managing and communicating information.
6. The growing importance of technology as a sector of the economy of the United States and other developed nations, sustaining a parallel demand for scientific and technical information.
7. A shift of media from print to electronic means for both communicating and storing information, thus creating a demand for studies and systems development to accommodate these changes within the library community.

Regardless of the authors' prescience (or lack of it) it is almost certain that what libraries do and how they utilize professional service organizations will be quite different by the end of this decade. It is equally certain that libraries will remain vital elements in our system of information collection and usage and that they will draw increasingly on specialized service organizations to carry out their functions in the most cost-effective way possible.

NOTES

1. Fritz Machlup, *The Production and Distribution of Knowledge in the U.S.* (Princeton, N.J.: Princeton University Press, 1962).
2. Daniel Bell, *The Coming of Post-Industrial Society* (New York: Basic Books, 1973).
3. John Naisbitt, *Megatrends: Ten New Directions Transforming Our Lives* (New York: Warner Books, 1982).
4. Michael Rubin and Elizabeth Taylor, "The U.S. Information Sector and GNP: An Input-Output Study," *Information Processing and Management* 17, No. 4 (1981):163–213.
5. Anthony Debons, Donald W. King, Una Mansfield, and Donald L. Shirey, *The Information Professional: Survey of an Emerging Field* (New York: Marcel Dekker, November 1981).
6. Nancy K. Roderer, Ellen Sweet, Nancy A. VanHouse, and Michael D. Cooper, "Library Human Resources: A Study of Supply and Demand," draft submitted to the National Center for Education Statistics, Office of Libraries and Learning Technology (Rockville, Md.: King Research, Inc., January 1983).
7. King Research, Inc., "Survey of Federal Libraries, FY 1978," prepared for the Federal Library Committee of the Library of Congress (Rockville, Md.: King Research, Inc., December 1982).

8. Donald W. King and Dennis D. McDonald, "Federal and Non-Federal Relationships in Providing Scientific and Technical Information: Policies, Arrangements, Flow of Funds and User Charges," prepared for the National Science Foundation (Rockville, Md.: King Research, Inc., 1980).
9. Donald W. King, Dennis D. McDonald, and Nancy K. Roderer, *Scientific Journals in the United States: Their Production, Use, and Economics* (Stroudsburg, Pa.: Hutchinson Ross Publishing Co., 1981).
10. King et al., "Federal and Non-Federal Relationships. . . ."
11. Jose Marie Griffiths and Donald W. King, "North Carolina Library Networking Feasibility Study," prepared for the Division of State Library, North Carolina Department of Cultural Resources (Rockville, Md.: King Research, Inc., August 1982).
12. Vernon E. Palmour, Marcia C. Bellassai, and Robert R. V. Weiderkehr, "Costs of Owning, Borrowing, and Disposing of Periodical Publications," prepared for the National Commission on New Technological Uses of Copyrighted Works (Arlington, Va.: Public Research Institute, October 1977).
13. Nancy K. Roderer, Donald W. King, Robert R. V. Weiderkehr, and Harriet Lais-Gabbert, "Evaluation of Online Bibliographic Systems," prepared for the National Science Foundation, Division of Information Science (Rockville, Md.: King Research, Inc., September 1981).
14. Griffiths and King, "North Carolina Library."
15. Martha E. Williams, "Database and Online Statistics for 1979," *Bulletin of the American Society for Information Science* 7, No. 2 (December 1980):27-29.
16. Donald W. King, "A Potential Pitfall in the Economics of Information Products and Services," *Bulletin of the American Society for Information Science* 3, No. 5 (June 1977):39-40.
17. _____, "Marketing Secondary Information Products and Services," *Journal of the American Society for Information Science* 33, No. 3 (May 1982):168-174.
18. Allen Kent et al., "A Cost-Benefit Model of Some Critical Library Operations in Terms of Use of Materials," prepared for the National Science Foundation, Division of Science Information (University of Pittsburgh, April 1978).
19. Palmour et al., "Costs of Owning."
20. King et al., *Scientific Journals in the United States.*
21. Ibid.

THE NEW COPYRIGHT LAW: A FIVE-YEAR REVIEW

Nancy H. Marshall

Associate Director of Libraries, University of Wisconsin-Madison, and Chair, Copyright Subcommittee/ALA Legislation Committee

Nearly 20 years of effort to revise the U.S. copyright laws came to an end on October 19, 1976, when President Gerald R. Ford signed PL 94-553, to become effective January 1, 1978. The last decade preceding passage of the Copyright Act of 1976 saw increasingly heated debate between users and proprietors (librarians and publishers) over several proposed revisions; the issue that most seriously divided these naturally symbiotic parties—and does to this day—is that of photocopying (as covered by Section 108 of the copyright law, Reproduction by Libraries and Archives). A closer look at the issues, events, and activities of the past five years may assist in gaining a perspective on why, in an otherwise mutually compatible existence, the struggle between librarians and publishers over the copyright law continues.

1978/1979 AND A GLANCE AT THE PAST

When January 1, 1978 finally arrived, for many it came almost as an anticlimax. In the 14 months preceding January 1978, each of the major stakeholders—the Copyright Office, library associations, and publisher/author groups—engaged in educational programming and extensive planning for implementation of the new law. So much effort had gone into preparing for the effective date of implementation that, when the new year dawned, the transition for most appeared generally smooth.

Preparation for the New Law

The Copyright Office, under the skilled leadership of then Register of Copyrights Barbara Ringer, had established a Revision Coordinating Committee "to oversee the development and coordination for implementing the new law." The office also had established a special telephone information service and published its *General Guide to the Copyright Act of 1976*.[1] The Register prescribed by regulation the language and specifications for the "Display Warning of Copyright" and the "Order Warning of Copyright" required by Sections 108(d)(2) and 108(e)(2), respectively.

All of the library associations very seriously and systematically carried out their responsibility to help librarians understand the law and know the mechanisms of complying with it, publishing useful guides for their respective constituencies. The American Library Association (ALA) devoted the May 1977 issue of its *American Libraries* to copyright. ALA also prepared the *Librarian's Copyright Kit: What You Must Know Now*, a packet of 11 items that provided a thorough knowledge of the copyright law and its implementation.

The Interlibrary Loan Committee of the Reference and Adult Services Division of ALA did yeoman work. It revised the ALA Interlibrary Loan Form to include a space for copyright representation, suggested language for the "warning notice" required by Section 108(f)(1) to be on unsupervised reproducing equipment and the "Notice of Copyright" required by Section 108(a)(3) to appear on reproduced works, and recommended guidelines for the maintenance of records of interlibrary photocopying requests. These latter activities went through a review and concurrence process within the Ad Hoc Committee on Copyright Law Practice and Implementation of the Council of National Library and Information Associations (CNLIA), which represents the interests of the American Association of Law Libraries (AALL), American Library Association, Association of Research Libraries (ARL), Medical Library Association (MLA), Music Library Association (MuLA), and Special Libraries Association (SLA).

The Association of American Publishers (AAP), in cooperation with the Authors' League of America, the Information Industry Association, and some scientific societies and user organizations, established the Copyright Clearance Center, Inc. (CCC), as a centralized collection center for payments of royalties and licensing fees by institutions. The National Technical Information Service and commercial firms such as the Institute for Scientific Information and University Microfilms greatly increased the quantity and range of separate journal articles available for sale as an alternative to library photocopying. The prices of the separates include royalty payments to the copyright proprietor.

Despite the extensive educational processes undertaken by all concerned parties, problems of interpretation continued to arise, and many questions raised during development of the law remained unresolved, regarding "a" notice of copyright versus "the" notice of copyright; library reserves; copying of materials in the library's own collection; the relationship between Sections 107 (fair use) and 108; copying of articles from journal issues more than five years old; photocopying under Section 108 in for-profit organizations; the meaning of "fair price" and "reasonable effort"; "systematic" reproduction; compliance boxes on the interlibrary loan form; and multiple photocopying.

CONTU Report

The National Commission on New Technological Uses of Copyrighted Works (CONTU), which sponsored a number of studies on photocopying that significantly increased knowledge of how periodicals and journal literature are used,[2] completed its work and submitted its final report in July 1978.[3]

In its final report, CONTU concluded that it would not recommend changes in the provisions of the Copyright Act of 1976 affecting photocopying. In support of that decision, the final report cited the exhaustive debates that preceded enactment; the content of the law; the existence of guidelines supported by representatives of users, publishers, and authors; the evidence of the first few months that both government and private organizations were adapting photocopying activities to the requirements of the new law; and the lack of evidence that there was any immediate, measurable crisis in the publication of periodical journal literature, that journals for which there is a significant demand were going out of existence because of photocopying, or that the procedure for obtaining authorization for photocopies not covered under Section 107 or 108 imposed unacceptable burdens on individuals or organizations wishing to copy. The final report stated that "at present no persuasive evidence exists that the provisions of the Copyright Act of 1976 affecting photocopying are inadequate to serve the dual purposes of copyright: to reward creators of and facilitate public access to works of authorship."[4]

The only exception made to this was a recommendation to amend the 1976 act to provide specific guidance to organizations engaged in photocopying for profit and their customers. In its final report, CONTU recommended that Congress "require the posting of a notice in commercial copying organizations, both to describe that copying which in most cases would not constitute fair use and to warn prospective customers of the liability they might incur for copying in violation of the copyright law."[5]

Five-Year Review

Since the issue of library reproduction of copyrighted works had been the central focus of the major disagreements between librarians and publishers during development of the legislation, librarians were instrumental in seeing that Subsection 108(i), providing for a five-year review of the library reproduction provisions, was incorporated in the new law. The overriding objective and intent of the Congress in support of the five-year review was that of "balancing" the needs of users with the interests of copyright proprietors.[6]

The Register took as her first step in this review process the appointment in early 1978 of Ivan R. Bender as consultant to the Copyright Office. Soon thereafter, representatives of libraries/users and copyright proprietors/authors were invited to separate meetings to begin substantive discussions on the review issues. By the end of the second meeting, each group recognized the need for a joint advisory committee and agreed to suggest five members. Appointed to the Section 108(i) Advisory Committee were James Barsky, Academic Press; Charles Butts, Houghton Mifflin; J. Christopher Burns, *Washington Post*; Efren Gonzalez, Bristol-Myers Products; Irwin Karp, The Authors' League of America; Madeline Henderson, National Bureau of Standards; Rita Lerner, American Institute of Physics; Nancy Marshall, University of Wisconsin-Madison; August Steinhilber, National School Boards Association; and Alfred Sumberg, American Association of University Professors. Members of the Copyright Office Planning Group were Barbara Ringer, Register of Copyrights; Waldo H. Moore, assistant Register of Copyrights for Registration; Ivan Bender, consultant; Jon Baumgarten, general counsel; Richard Glasgow, assistant general counsel; Lewis Flacks, special legal assistant to the Register; Michael Keplinger, special legal assistant to the Register; Marlene Morrisey, special assistant to the Register; and Robert Stevens, chief, Cataloging Division.

The first meeting of the Register of Copyrights Advisory Committee on the Five-Year Review, held on December 19, 1978, was largely exploratory and informational. The advisory committee, representative of all interests involved, was asked to advise the Register on the preparation of certain aspects of the necessary surveys so that the report to Congress would offer a clear idea of how the law was working, its strengths, and any recommendations for modification that might be needed. The committee assisted the Copyright Office in working out the Request for Proposal for a contractual study that was aimed at acquiring the statistical data for the report, identification of appropriate issues and questions to be addressed, as well as reviewing the responses and serving as liaisons between the Copyright Office and interested organizations. Interested parties were urged to collect adequate data to substantiate their positions, and librarians were advised to monitor carefully the impact of the new law on user access to copyrighted works.

The advisory committee was in general agreement that the issues of the review could be distilled into two broad areas of investigation: (1) the impact of the law on access to and flow of information to users, and (2) the economic impact of the law on users, libraries, and copyright owners. Herein, ideally, would the assessment of "balance" be made.

ALA Copyright Subcommittee

In spring 1978, the ALA took the first steps to fulfill its role and responsibility to the library community relevant to the five-year review. With the passage of the law, it was appropriate that the focus of the Copyright Subcommittee of the ALA Legislation Committee change from monitoring the *development* of the new law to monitoring the *implementation* of the new law. The charge to the subcommittee, chaired by Nancy H. Marshall, University of Wisconsin-Madison, was: "To set up and implement a mechanism for monitoring the new copyright law, in preparation for the five-year review by the Register of Copyrights. To determine the kinds of data that should be collected for the review and how best to collect them. To serve as liaison with ALA divisions and other units and other library organizations, to receive information, serve as a sounding board and relay information to the Legislation Committee on the various aspects of the copyright law, which are unsettled or on which there is general lack of understanding among librarians."[7]

In an effort to carry out its responsibilities, the subcommittee set up a network of liaisons with representatives of all ALA divisions and other ALA units, as well as with state library associations. The subcommittee was vitally interested in the two-way communication that this structure afforded. For their part, the liaisons' role was twofold: (1) to alert the subcommittee to copyright concerns of constituencies and (2) to act as a link between the subcommittee, ALA divisions and units, and the library and user communities.

Off-Air Taping

Left unresolved with the passage of the 1976 copyright law was the issue of off-air taping of broadcast audiovisual works by educational institutions. At the time the House Judiciary Subcommittee on Courts, Civil Liberties, and the Administration of

Justice chaired by Representative Robert W. Kastenmeier (D-Wis.) wrote its 1976 conference report, it simply expressed the belief that the fair use doctrine had some application to off-air taping, took note of the unfinished state of the negotiations among the parties, and encouraged the parties to continue to attempt to resolve their differences under the leadership of the Register of Copyrights.[8]

In July 1977, the Copyright Office and the Ford Foundation sponsored a Conference on Video Recording for Educational Uses, at Arlie House in Virginia, at which a wide range of interested parties were brought together for a discussion of the issues. No substantive negotiations took place. Then on March 2, 1979, Representative Kastenmeier, with the assistance of the Copyright Office, convened a meeting in an attempt to find a nonlegislative solution as to what constitutes fair use for broadcast audiovisual works. Testimony was given by 20 different groups divided equally among proprietor and user interests.

Subsequent to this meeting, Kastenmeier, in consultation with the Copyright Office, asked 19 people representing a cross section of affected groups to constitute an ad hoc negotiating committee to develop guidelines on fair use for off-air taping for educational purposes. Kastenmeier was concerned that a procedure be developed that both protected the legitimate rights of producers and also facilitated the educational process through reasonable fair use standards. Eileen D. Cooke, director of the ALA Washington Office, and Leonard Wasser, of the Writers Guild of America East, co-chaired the negotiating team. The committee met continuously throughout 1979, 1980, and into 1981, when guidelines were finally agreed upon by all affected parties.

1980/1981

If 1978/1979 were years of study, implementation, development of procedures, informal data gathering, and living with the law, 1980/1981 can be characterized as years of continued education and communication for library constituencies, litigation and resolution on the part of copyright proprietors, and action on the part of the Copyright Office under its mandate for review of Section 108.

Library and Education Associations

At the January 1980 ALA midwinter meeting in Chicago, the ALA Copyright Subcommittee prepared a *Resolution on Data Needed for the Copyright Five-Year Review*, which urged the Copyright Office to request that copyright proprietors provide statistical data for the five-year review describing the economic impact on authors and proprietors of the library reproduction provisions of the Copyright Act, just as libraries would be asked to provide statistical data. This resolution was adopted by the ALA Council on January 24, 1980.[9] At the 1980 annual conference in New York, several ALA units with copyright responsibility cosponsored a program entitled "Copyright: The Rights of Creators and the Interests of Users," with Barbara A. Ringer, long-time Register of Copyrights until her retirement in May 1980; Ivan R. Bender, now vice president and general counsel of Films, Inc., and former consultant to the Copyright Office on the five-year review; and Elwood K. Gannett, director of publishing services, Institute of Electrical and Electronics Engineers (IEEE).

The Ad Hoc Committee on Copyright Law, a long-standing coalition of Washington-based nonprofit organizations representing education, libraries, and scholars, filed an *amicus curiae* brief in 1980 in the case of *Encyclopaedia Britannica Educational Corporation v. Board of Cooperative Educational Services (BOCES)* of Erie County, New York. The concern to which the brief was addressed was the maintenance of the full scope of the fair use doctrine as embodied in the Copyright Act of 1976.[10] Another action taken by the ad hoc committee was a request to the newly appointed Register of Copyrights, David Ladd, that the Copyright Office refuse to register a copyright when publications carry exaggerated statements of copyright restrictions that could readily cause a scholar, teacher, or librarian to refrain from exercising his or her rights in making or obtaining a copy of material required for successful research or teaching. Ladd's response indicated that the Copyright Office had no control over these exaggerated warnings, as they are not themselves elements of the copyright notice even though they stand near the notice.

In an effort to begin to explore possible new approaches to the differences between publishers and librarians on copyright, an ALA delegation of librarians met with publishers in May 1981 prior to the opening of the AAP annual meeting in Key Biscayne, Florida. No specific commitments were made by either side, but there was agreement to give further thought and discussion to several copyright issues, particularly photocopying, which continued to be unresolved between the parties.

In September 1981, the ad hoc negotiating committee of educational users and copyright proprietors transmitted to Representative Kastenmeier the final *Guidelines for Off-Air Recording of Broadcast Programming for Educational Purposes*. In the narrowest application, the guidelines are merely an agreement among the organizations represented on the negotiating committee: The users generally agree to limit their activities to those delineated, and the proprietors agree not to sue the users who stay within those limits. It is probably safe, however, to apply these guidelines to the entire community of users and proprietors, including those groups not directly represented on the negotiating committee, who qualify as nonprofit educational institutions.

The Washington-based ad hoc committee of nonprofit organizations (mentioned previously) issued an advisory statement regarding these guidelines for the organizations that it represents. In part, its statement says:

> From the point of view of educators generally, it is recognized that there are likely to be instances in which adherence to the letter of these guidelines would interfere with legitimate needs of educational procedures. In pursuit of those needs, particular educators may deem uses beyond the guidelines to be appropriate, fair, and within the law. It must also be recognized, however, that individual copyright owners, for their part, are not constrained by these guidelines to refrain from a claim of infringement in what they consider to be unfair application of the agreed upon guidelines. . . . The Ad Hoc Committee alerts its membership that the guidelines contained in the agreement *only* apply to copyrighted materials. Programs that are not copyrighted do not enjoy the protection of the guidelines. They may be copied in toto and kept literally forever. Similarly, the Ad Hoc Committee urges all of its members to be on the alert and to report any instances where a copyright proprietor tries to restrict the application of these guidelines.

In early 1982, ALA distributed the guidelines and advisory statement in a booklet that addressed 30 questions librarians ask on the subject of off-air taping.[11]

Computer Software

When Congress enacted the 1976 Copyright Act, it left in legal limbo a specific protection for the multimillion-dollar computer software industry. CONTU, in its final report, recommended such legislation, and the Computer Software Copyright Act was passed by Congress in November 1980, amending Title 17 of the United States Code.[12]

The legislation is aimed at protecting the rights of individuals and corporations engaged in the development, sale, and leasing of computer programs, the sets of instructions that direct computers in performing automated tasks with the assistance of mathematical formulas called algorithms. Under the legislation, the instructions are copyrightable but not the algorithms on which a computer program is based because the formulas are considered "ideas" not covered by copyright law.

Copyright Proprietors

Basic Books, Inc. v. *Gnomon Corporation*, the first copyright infringement action against a commercial copying concern under the Section 107 fair use provisions of the Copyright Act was initiated by the AAP on behalf of seven publishers in February 1980. The suit alleged that Gnomon had infringed the publishers' copyrights by engaging in "massive" photocopying of "substantial portions" of textbooks, general trade books, and journal articles published by them and many other firms at Gnomon's branches near universities in New Haven, Connecticut, Cambridge, Massachusetts, Ithaca, New York, and State College, Pennsylvania.[13] In April 1980, the lawsuit ended in a consent decree substantially limiting Gnomon's activities, which said it had accepted only because the corporation could not afford a protracted legal fight.

The consent decree prohibits Gnomon from making more than one copy of any published work for any person, either at the same time or at different times. But multiple copies (more than one) are allowed for a requestor who surrenders an original written permission for the copies, or for a faculty member who certifies compliance with the classroom copying guidelines. Gnomon is responsible for all copying done on its premises, must keep all permissions, authorizations, and certifications for one year, and must provide the publishers access to its premises to ascertain compliance.

In 1980, the AAP also stated that publishers would increase their efforts to force colleges and universities and libraries in for-profit institutions to comply with copying restrictions. The library community does not accept the AAP assumption that institutions are not complying with the law and sees the AAP's statement as an attempt to discredit widespread library compliance. Robert Wedgeworth, executive director of ALA, spoke to this issue in his "State of the Association" address at the ALA 1980 annual conference in New York: "One problem we thought had quieted down now looms more ominously, with the mandated five-year review of Section 108 of the new copyright law approaching. Publishers once again are assailing librarians with unfounded allegations. In response, ALA will accelerate its copyright education programs in 1980–81. We shall not let certain publishing interests win through intimidation what they could not win through the courts and Congress."[14]

Of considerable concern to library associations were copyright proprietor statements such as the following from 1980 issues of *Information World* and *AAP Newsletter*, respectively: "Librarians contend that most of their copying is within the law and that, therefore, it is not necessary to keep records on most of it"[15] and "If publishers fail to make a major effort to defend Section 108, they will strengthen the argument of librarians that the section should be removed from the law in 1983, on the grounds that the publishers have not sought to enforce it."[16] The position of the library associations is that librarians have always been advised to keep records for copyright purposes, and that they have never entertained the notion of recommending removal of Section 108.

In contrast to the above statements, the AAP Copyright Committee, in recognition of the natural alliance of libraries and publishers in disseminating literary material, passed a resolution in June 1980 that the AAP Board of Directors appoint a special representative to consider the question of improving access to authorized photocopies and the role of AAP in connection therewith.[17] The special representative was charged with considering possible solutions such as broadening the coverage of the CCC to include chapters and sections of books, changing the CCC system from a transactional to a blanket fee basis (similar to ASCAP), or creating a wholly new and comprehensive permissions-payment clearinghouse for all copyrighted materials. Although this AAP action was welcomed as a step in the right direction, the library community continued to assert its right under the law in the areas of fair use and library reproduction of copyrighted works.

On October 19, 1981, the Ninth Circuit Court of Appeals in San Francisco overturned the December 1979 court decision in the controversial *Betamax* case—*Universal City Studios* v. *SONY Corporation of America*—and ruled that taping a television program in the home violates a producer's copyright, for which the manufacturers of such recording equipment are liable. Immediately, legislation was introduced in Congress to exempt home use or private noncommercial recording of copyrighted works on video recorders from copyright infringement. Of major concern to the library community is the court's view and conclusion that ". . . the mass copying of the sort involved in this case precludes an application of fair use." The court's decision further states: "We hold that, particularly in the context of new technology, there is a danger to including the sort of copying involved in *Williams & Wilkins Co.* v. *United States* within the scope of the fair use doctrine. New technology, which makes possible the mass reproduction of copyrighted material (effectively taking control of access from the author) places a strain upon the fair use doctrine."[18] Thus, the court's decision could affect photocopying practices not clearly within the confines of Section 108. The Ninth Circuit Court's view also threatens to deprive the 1976 Copyright Act of any flexibility in dealing with new technologies. The library community remains concerned with the possible broad implications of the decision, particularly its effect on the doctrine of fair use.

In response to this concern, both ALA and the Washington-based educational coalition filed *amicus curiae* briefs on the side of SONY Corporation. Testimony was given on behalf of ALA and the coalition in August 1982 at a hearing held by Representative Kastenmeier on proposed legislation, and the Supreme Court heard oral arguments in the case early in 1983, with a decision on whether to uphold the Ninth Circuit Court's decision expected in the spring. The AAP and Authors' League of America filed separate briefs supporting the lower-court ruling.

In 1981, David Waite, president of the Copyright Clearance Center, reported that CCC would distribute 45 percent of 1980 earnings versus 40 percent in 1979 and 30 percent in 1978; CCC collected more than $300,000 in 1980, up from $59,000 in 1978.

The CCC also initiated a new program in 1981, called the Document Delivery Awareness Program, to help identify information brokers who comply with the U.S. copyright law. The program includes a quarterly publication, *Guide to CCC-Participating Document Delivery Services*, which began with the November/December 1981 issue. Document suppliers who have accounts with CCC and provide authorized copies (either under direct photocopy-license agreements with publishers or through the CCC Photocopy Permissions Service) are given free space in each issue to advertise and promote their businesses. The audience for the *Guide* is high-volume photocopy end users participating in the program, who will receive updated issues without charge.

In 1982, the CCC initiated two new services, the Large Industrial Users Assistance Program to "assist large industrial firms to establish policies to prevent copyright infringement," and an Annual Authorizations Service, which will allow heavy users to pay a flat fee rather than using the transaction-based pay-as-you-copy system. Large industrial users who wish to take advantage of the flat fee will be required to participate in an audit of actual copying, after which annual use-level projections will be made for each publication in the sample. This method theoretically will enable the CCC to distribute royalties in direct proportion to the photocopy usage of each publication.

Most libraries, however, continue to find it unnecessary to register or report to the CCC as most library photocopying, as substantiated by the King surveys, falls legitimately under Section 108 provisions of the law.

Copyright Office

King Research Study. The Copyright Office awarded a contract in the fall of 1980 to King Research, Inc., of Rockville, Maryland, to do a survey of libraries, publishers, and users to determine whether Section 108 had achieved a balancing of the rights of creators of copyrighted works and the needs of users who receive or make copies. The 108(i) Advisory Committee met twice in early 1981 to assist both the Copyright Office and King Research in the development of the questionnaires to be used to gather the needed data. By the end of 1981, the data had been gathered and analyzed by King Research, and the final report of the contractor was scheduled to be submitted to the Register not later than March 1, 1982.

The survey of libraries collected background data from 500 public, academic, federal, and special libraries regarding the reproduction of copyrighted works by the library staff, on unsupervised machines, and on copying machines elsewhere in the surveyed institution. The 500 sample libraries surveyed were asked to provide information regarding the number of photocopying machines, photocopying revenue, reserve operations, photocopying permission requests, royalty payments, interlibrary borrowing and lending, patron access, network activities, computerized data base activities, record keeping practices, replacement of lost, stolen, or mutilated materials, out-of-print materials, audiovisual materials, and fair use policies. In addition, 200 of the 500 sample libraries were asked to participate in on-site monitoring of photocopying activities during three periods in March, June, and September 1981 (one-third of the 200 in each period), filling out two kinds of forms, similar to those used by King in its 1977 library photocopying study: an interlibrary loan request log and a photocopying request log. The response rate of the library community was 71 percent.

The publisher survey, conducted in April–July 1981, sampled 150 publishers from each of the following three categories: books, scholarly and scientific journals, and general audience periodicals. Major areas covered included birth and mortality rates, copying royalty revenue to publishers, copying royalty disbursements to authors, membership in the CCC, proportion of works in the CCC, individual versus institutional subscription prices, permission requests granted or denied, and journal reprint/tearsheet distribution plans. The response rate of the publishing community was 51 percent.

Users were surveyed on-site by trained survey personnel in 25 libraries (distributed among types) in five widely dispersed geographic areas. A total of 1,250 library user responses were gathered using two questionnaire forms: one for interviewing users of unsupervised copying machines and one for library patrons who were returning library materials. Users were surveyed in March–May 1981.

Hearings. During 1980 and 1981, the Copyright Office held a series of six regional hearings to gather information concerning the effect of the new law in further preparation for the five-year review. The 1980 hearings were held in Chicago on January 19, in conjunction with the annual midwinter meeting of the ALA; on March 26 in Houston, at the time of the annual conference of the American Chemical Society; in Washington, D.C., during the annual meetings of the Special Libraries Association (June 11) and the Medical Library Association (June 19); and on October 8, in Anaheim, California, in conjunction with the annual meeting of the American Society for Information Science. The sixth and final hearing was held on January 28–29, 1981, in New York City.

More than 50 librarians, publishers, lawyers, educators, and others concerned with the photocopying of copyrighted materials testified before the Copyright Office panel on their experiences under the new law and the problems they perceived as a result of the law. The Copyright Office was particularly interested in receiving comments and testimony on such issues as

1. The extent to which Section 108 may have altered library procedures and its effect on public access to information
2. Its effect on established patterns in the publishing industry and the relationship among authors, libraries, and library users
3. Its effect upon the type and amount of copying performed by the library on its own behalf or on behalf of users and any changes experienced by publishers and authors in the number of requests from libraries to reproduce works
4. The manner in which the CCC has affected libraries, users, and publishers, and the effect of a National Periodicals Center should it be created
5. The impact, if any, of Section 108 on reproduction of nonprint materials
6. The effect of the CONTU guidelines on library practices
7. Views concerning the relationship between Section 107 (fair use) and Section 108 (reproduction by libraries and archives)
8. Treatment of foreign copyrighted works and requests from foreign libraries
9. Identification of problems and suggestions for their resolution.

Testimony by the library community indicated that librarians are living with the law fairly well, although some difficulties had arisen in areas such as academic library reserve collections, interpretation of the classroom copying guidelines, and the extra record keeping required by the interlibrary loan guidelines.

At the final hearing in January 1981, Robert Wedgeworth, executive director of the ALA, summarized the position of the association on a number of key issues:

1. There is no evidence that the law, in most cases, is failing to balance adequately the interests of creators and users of copyrighted materials.
2. Most photocopying done by or in libraries falls within the protections of fair use and of Section 108 of the law.
3. There is no evidence of a causal link between any reductions in library periodical subscriptions and library photocopying practices.
4. Libraries may utilize rights under both Sections 107 and 108 to contribute to the widest possible dissemination of information to the public and to fulfill their traditional role in society as lenders and facilitators of such information.
5. Librarians are complying with the law, and any lack of use of the CCC does not indicate the contrary but merely reflects the fact that most photocopying done in libraries is within the bounds of Sections 107 and 108.
6. Publishers should not view librarians as the "enemy" in a war over photocopy profits. Libraries do not reduce the size of their collections because of the availability of photocopies. Indeed, reliance on networking to substitute for a subscription to a periodical is not only illegal but is inefficient and expensive as well. Every library strives to be as comprehensive in its collection development area as it can be. The availability of photocopies for the occasional user interested in an unusual field makes possible the kind of access to information so important to our society's very foundation.
7. Because the purpose of the copyright law in rewarding publishers and authors is to stimulate creation and dissemination of intellectual works, statutory pro-

visions should not be interpreted to impede dissemination and access if the stimulus to creation is not thereby augmented. It is doubtful that authors would in any way benefit from any further restriction on access to information in photocopied form.
8. Librarians are neither administratively equipped, nor should they be required, to police their patrons' photocopying activities.
9. The CONTU guidelines are useful, but they do not carry the force of law. The guidelines do not purport to set maximum limits on library photocopying practices but strive only to establish a safe harbor. They should not be allowed to become firm rules that may cause librarians to deny unnecessarily their patrons' rights.
10. No new restrictions are needed at this time. Certainly no changes in the law or additional guidelines should be considered prior to the completion of the five-year review and the compilation of data and other evidence clearly demonstrating a need for such restrictions. If anything, a clarification of the unique applicability of the Section 107 fair use factors to address the special concerns of college and university library patrons would be justified.

Although librarians and publishers seemed as far apart as ever on the issue of library photocopying, Wedgeworth called for both groups to come together to discuss the electronic distribution of copyrighted materials. Instead of condemning libraries, Wedgeworth testified that publishers and authors should "join librarians in planning how the electronic networks can be structured to support publishing and authorship, while providing users with greater access to published works through libraries and other agencies."[19]

Further Attempts at Dialogue. In September 1981, the Register initiated discussions between producers and users of copyrighted material, in an attempt to get the parties to agree on issues that are still unresolved before the report to Congress on the subject required by January 1, 1983. A second meeting was scheduled for November with representatives of library associations, authors, publishers, and selected other interested parties but was canceled by the Register because of a misunderstanding between AAP and the Copyright Office. AAP believed that the Copyright Office had misrepresented its position to the invited participants regarding the initiation of litigation by AAP while the discussions were being held. With this misunderstanding cleared up, a series of discussions were scheduled for 1982.

1982 AND A LOOK AT THE FUTURE

Library and Educational Associations

College and University Photocopying. In March 1982, a "Model Policy Concerning College and University Photocopying for Classroom, Research and Library Reserve Use," prepared by ALA legal counsel Mary Hutchings Reed of the law firm Sidley and Austin, was issued.[20] The policy, written with the advice and assistance of the Copyright Subcommittee of ALA's Legislation Committee, the Association of College and Research Libraries (ACRL) Copyright Committee, the Association of Research Libraries (ARL), other academic librarians, and copyright attorneys, outlines fair use rights in the academic environment for classroom teaching, research activities, and library services. Intended for the guidance of academic librarians, faculty, researchers, scholars, administrators, and legal counsel, it points out the need for those constituencies to understand the safeguards that were written into the law and its legislative history to protect and guarantee their rights of access to information as they carry out their responsibilities in the higher education context. The publishing community has criticized the "Model Policy" as not reflecting all of the criteria incorporated in the "Classroom Guidelines" accompanying Section 107. Because those guidelines were negotiated primarily for elementary and secondary educational uses, they are seen by the library community as inappropriate in the higher education environment for which the "Model Policy" was specifically developed.

A milestone of sorts was reached during the ALA annual conference in Philadelphia in July 1982, when, for the first time at the invitation of the ALA Copyright Subcommittee, the AAP Copyright Committee held a joint meeting. The agenda items discussed included still unresolved issues between librarians and publishers, as well as current litigations. Although no agreements were reached, the informal meeting provided the opportunity for the two groups to interact on a face-to-face basis and opened the door for possible future discussions of mutual interest and concern.

In 1982, ALA issued an update to its *Librarian's Copyright Kit*, first released in 1978, which included several new items.

CNLIA. During 1982, the Council of National Library and Information Associations Committee on Copyright Law Practice and Implementation (ad hoc) met bimonthly to discuss current copyright concerns, exchange information, and develop strategies. The committee's major work during 1982 centered around the upcoming five-year review, including the King Research, Inc., report published in May 1982; meetings of librarians and copyright proprietors under the auspices of the Copyright Office; and litigations by the publishers against for-profit organizations and others.

Copyright Proprietors

Association of American Publishers. On behalf of specific publishers, the AAP coordinated and financed three lawsuits charging unauthorized photocopying practices. Similar out-of-court settlements were reached with two for-profit corporations, American Cyanamid Company and E. R. Squibb & Sons, Inc. Both agreements involve the corporation's registration with the CCC, as well as procedures for reporting and paying fees for the photocopying of journals and other materials registered with the CCC; payments for reproduced copies on attended central copying facilities and unattended/unsupervised machines, as well as copies received from outside sources unless the source has already paid a photocopying fee; and the corporation's right to alter or discontinue its part of the agreement should the copyright law be changed or should any court decision on copying practices by a comparable company be rendered that would benefit the corporation.

The significant difference in the Squibb settlement is that it recognizes a percentage (6 percent) of the total copies made as fair use or nonreportable photocopying that the company has the right to exclude from reporting and payment to the CCC. It is important to note that the copyright law does not prohibit photocopying by for-profit organizations and that the legislative history of the law plainly indicates that neither Section 107 (fair use) nor Section 108 (reproduction by libraries and archives) is intended to apply solely to not-for-profit organizations. In the absence of full details from the parties involved in the litigation, it is not possible to determine all the factors behind the settlement.

In December 1982, AAP, on behalf of nine publishers, filed suit against New York University, ten of its faculty members, and an off-campus commercial copy center, charging copyright infringement by copying books or parts of books and using them as classroom texts. The suit also seeks to demonstrate that academic institutions need policies governing the use of copyrighted materials. The final resolution of this litigation will be of major significance to the rights and responsibilities of all segments of the higher education community.

BOCES Case. The long-awaited decision in the 1977 case filed by Encyclopaedia Britannica Educational Corporation, Learning Corporation of America, and Time-Life Films, Inc., against the Erie County (New York) Board of Cooperative Educational Services (BOCES) and ten individuals was handed down in June 1982 by Judge John T. Curtin of the New York Federal District Court. The court upheld the firms' contention that off-air taping practices such as those undertaken by BOCES were in violation of the U.S. copyright law and not fair use. In addition to awarding monetary damages, the court issued a permanent injunction against the defendant from copying works of the plaintiffs and also ordered the erasure of the videotapes of the plaintiffs' motion pictures that were deemed infringed. This decision, as well as the adoption by Congress of the *Guidelines for Off-Air Recording of Broadcast Programming for Educational Purposes*, gives the educational community a clearer understanding of their rights and responsibilities in the area of off-air videotaping.

Copyright Office

Five-Year Review. Work on the first five-year review of the copyright law of 1978 continued in 1982, and its intensity increased for Copyright Office staff as the January 3, 1983, deadline for the Register of Copyrights report to Congress rapidly approached.

In May 1982, King Research, Inc. issued *Libraries, Publishers, and Photocopying: Final Report of Surveys Conducted for the U.S. Copyright Office*, a 200-page document, consisting of a wealth of information in more than 90 statistical tables.[21] Comments on this report, as well as on a series of questions posed for the hearings, were to be submitted to the Copyright Office by August 1, 1982, when the final comment period for the Section 108(i) review was closed.

The consensus of the library and educational communities as reflected in the 30 comments filed, including individual comments by all the CNLIA library associations, publisher associations, author associations, and individual librarians, publishers, and unaffiliated interested parties, is that the intended statutory balancing has been achieved. The data reveal that there was an overall decrease in all library photocopying of 16 percent between 1976 and 1981; mean gross sales by all publishers increased 31 percent, in constant dollars, between 1976 and 1980, with a 59 percent increase in scholarly, scientific, and technical journal sales; and less than 2 percent of users reported that libraries had refused to make photocopies for them, with less than 7 percent indicating interlibrary loan requests had been refused. The library community also recommended that, based on the data, no changes in the law were necessary or warranted. The only exception to this was a joint proposal for revisions of Section 108 from the Music Library Association and the Music Publishers' Association that would permit the rights of reproduction granted in Subsection (e) with respect to musical works, provided the library first undertakes a diligent search for the copyright owner, which, if unsuccessful, allows reproduction in accordance with Subsection (e), or if successful prohibits reproduction without the approval of the copyright owner.

As a result of its analysis of the report, the ALA, in consultation with ARL, has issued a fact sheet, "Scholarly Journal Publishing and Library Photocopying: Economic Issues Bearing on Copyright," which confirms that authors of scholarly journal articles more often than not pay to be published, that scholarly journal publishing is in healthy shape, that libraries pay more for journals than individual subscribers, that libraries maintain journal expenditures despite price increases, and that interlibrary loan does not substitute for subscriptions.

The publishing community claims that the King report shows that the intended statutory balancing has not been achieved, that libraries are making "massive multiple copies" in violation of the law, that libraries, particularly special libraries, are guilty of systematic and unauthorized copying, that the CONTU guidelines are not working, that AAP's previous "overly generous" position was "too lenient," and that the copyright law needs to be amended. AAP has recommended statutory changes in Section 108 to require that a photocopy include "*the* notice of copyright," in Section 504 to increase statutory damages, and a new section 511, called the "umbrella statute," which would create new limitations, including the requirement of advance permission for reproduction, entry of a work in a qualified licensing system such as the CCC, and the registration of a user with a qualified licensing system as a protection against possible infringement litigation.

Photocopying Discussion Group. During all of 1982, under the auspices of the Copyright Office, a group of invitees from the library, publishing, and author communities were meeting to address unresolved issues. Discussions were focused on a change in the wording of the copyright statement now stamped on all photocopies made by a library for a patron or another library, the inclusion of the statutory notice of copyright with all photocopies made for users by a library, use by libraries of the copyright compliance boxes on the national interlibrary loan request form, photocopying for purposes of academic reserve, and a definition of systematic photocopying. Proposals and counterproposals were made by the groups party to the discussions but no joint agreements were reached.

In an effort to resolve some of these issues, librarians representing the American Library Association, Association of Research Libraries, Special Libraries Association, and Medical Library Association issued a statement in October 1982 in which they agreed to encourage use by the library community of a revised statement to appear on all photocopies and inclusion of the statutory notice of copyright with photocopied material under certain conditions. In addition, the ALA Copyright Subcommittee will investigate how librarians use the copyright compliance boxes on the interlibrary loan request form and determine if the current instructions give librarians sufficient guidance in making a decision on which box to check. A renewed call to begin a new series of discussions with copyright proprietors to focus on the future and new technologies, first proposed in 1981 by library associations, is made in the statement.

New Technologies

Library of Congress. In June 1982, the Library of Congress held a conference on "Preservation and New Technology," focusing on the future use of new technology, such as optical disk storage of information, which, among other issues, poses many copyright questions for librarians and publishers. Revisions in the copyright law, which until 1976 had remained essentially unchanged for more than 65 years, may be frequently necessary in the future in order to meet the difficult problems implicit in the new technology. Optical disk technology will allow rapid access to full text through terminals, with the capability to copy and to distribute. Questions of user fees, royalty payments, selection of materials to be converted to optical disk, and control of copying and distribution all need to be addressed in terms of copyright.

In addition to the optical disk, other new technologies, including video disks, fiber optics, satellite transmissions, and computer software and data bases, will impact on copyright laws. As originally and severally proposed by the library associations, all interested parties must address these issues so that five years from now we do not find ourselves in the same adversarial position as we presently do over photocopying issues.

CONCLUSIONS

As 1982 drew to a close, two major events on the near horizon held center stage in the copyright arena: the Register's report for the five-year review and the Supreme Court's review of the SONY Betamax decision. Each of these promised to be a landmark document.

The Register's report issued on January 6, 1983,[22] is a source of disbelief to the library community, based on the statistical data provided in the King report and library experience over the past five years; but it is a source of delight to the copyright proprietors as it supports their views of the photocopying world. Only time will tell whether Congress will decide to tackle copyright again after only five years of respite from the issues that were then and still remain divisive and unresolved.

If past is prologue, the road will continue to be rocky as the respective communities devote much of their time, energies, and funds to protecting the rights of their constituents under the law.

NOTES

1. Marybeth Peters. *General Guide to the Copyright Act of 1976*. U.S. Copyright Office, Washington, D.C., 1978.
2. King Research, *Library Photocopying in the United States*, 1977 PB 278-300 (the study originally suggested by the Conference on the Resolution of Copyright); V. Palmour, M. Ballassai, and R. Wiederkehr, *Costs of Owning, Borrowing, and Disposing of Periodical Publications*, 1977 PB 274-821; B. Fry, H. White, and E. Johnson, *Survey of Publishers Practices and Current Attitudes on Authorized Journal Article Copying and Licensing*, 1977 PB 271-033; M. Breslow, A. Ferguson, and L. Haverkamp, *An Analysis of Computer and Photocopying Issues from the Point of View of the General Public and the Ultimate Consumers*, 1977.
3. National Commission on New Technological Uses of Copyrighted Works (CONTU). *Final Report*. Washington, D.C., July 31, 1978.
4. *Ibid.*, p. 120.
5. *Ibid.*, p. 123.
6. 17 U.S.C. 108. Limitations on Exclusive Rights: Reproduction by Libraries and Archives: "(i) Five years from the effective date of this Act, and at five-year intervals thereafter, the Register of Copyrights, after consulting with representatives of authors, book and periodical publishers, and other owners of copyrighted materials, and with representatives of library users and librarians, shall submit to the Congress a report setting forth the extent to which this section has achieved the intended statutory balancing of the rights of creators, and the needs of users. The report should also describe any problems that may have arisen, and present legislative or other recommendations, if warranted."
7. Memorandum dated May 8, 1978, from Ella Gaines Yates, chair, and Eileen D. Cooke, staff liaison, to the ALA Legislation Committee.
8. House Committee on the Judiciary Report 94-1476, September 3, 1976, pp. 71-72.
9. *Resolution on Data Needed for the Copyright Five-Year Review*. ALA Copyright Subcommittee, January 1980.
10. Michael H. Cardozo, Attorney for Ad Hoc Committee on Copyright Law: Brief *amicus curiae* (June 1980) in the U.S. District Court for the Western District of New York (CIV-77-560), in the case of *Encyclopaedia Brittanica Educational Corp.* v. *Erie County Board of Cooperative Educational Services*.
11. *Guidelines for Off-Air Taping of Copyrighted Programs for Educational Use: 30 Questions Librarians Ask*. American Library Association, Washington Office, January 1982. The *Guidelines* may also be found in H.R. 97-495 accompanying H.R. 3530, May 10, 1982.
12. 17 U.S.C. 117. Limitations on exclusive rights: Computer Programs.

> Notwithstanding the provisions of section 106, it is not an infringement for the owner of a copy of a computer program to make or authorize the making of another copy or adaptation of that computer program provided:
>
> (1) that such a new copy or adaptation is created as an essential step in the utilization of the computer program in conjunction with a machine and that it is used in no other manner, or
>
> (2) that such new copy or adaptation is for archival purposes only and that all archival copies are destroyed in the event that continued possession of the computer program should cease to be rightful.

Any exact copies prepared in accordance with the provisions of this section may be leased, sold, or otherwise transferred, along with the copy from which such copies were prepared, only as part of the lease, sale, or other transfer of all rights in the program. Adaptations so prepared may be transferred only with the authorization of the copyright owner.
13. *Basic Books, Inc. et al. v. The Gnomon Corp.*, U.S. District Court, District of Connecticut, CIV 80-36, February 5, 1980.
14. Robert Wedgeworth, ALA Executive Director, "State of the Association" address to ALA Council, Annual Conference, New York, June 30, 1980.
15. Carol A. Risher. "Assessing the Act," *Information World* (April 1980).
16. "Copymills, For-Profit Libraries Warned of Possible AAP Litigation." *AAP Newsletter* 15, No. 6 (October 3, 1980): 1.
17. Association of American Publishers, Copyright Committee, Resolution adopted by Board June 18, 1980.
18. *Universal City Studios, Inc. v. Sony Corp. of America*, 659 F.2d 953, 9th Circuit, Central District of California, 1981.
19. Robert Wedgeworth, in hearing testimony before Copyright Office panel, New York, New York, January 28, 1981.
20. *Model Policy Concerning College and University Photocopying for Classroom, Research and Library Reserve Use.* American Library Association, Washington Office, March 1982.
21. Dennis D. McDonald et al. *Libraries, Publishers, and Photocopying: Final Report of Surveys Conducted for the United States Copyright Office.* King Research, Inc., Rockville, Maryland, May 1982.
22. *Report of the Register of Copyrights-Library Reproduction of Copyrighted Works (17 U.S.C. 108).* U.S. Copyright Office, Library of Congress, January 1983.

LIBRARY NETWORKING IN THE UNITED STATES, 1982

Glyn T. Evans

Director, Library Services, State University of New York
Director, SUNY/OCLC Network

The year 1982 was an interesting one in library networking—one in which the players took a deep breath. Some tendencies that were obvious in earlier years were muted. Major efforts and successes were consolidatory in nature, rather than dazzling breakthroughs—the base camp established, not the peak conquered. An annual report such as this is deceptive in its view of time: Projects come to completion that may have started years before; others may start and fail within the year under report. The field is also very volatile and difficult to control in an overview, as Henriette Avram and Susan Martin noted in their reports on library networking (in the 1982 and 1983 editions of *The Bowker Annual* respectively). Nonetheless, some trends, some milestones, can be noted.

MAJOR DEVELOPMENTS

OCLC and RLG/RLIN Stabilize Operations

During the year, both the Online Computer Library Center (OCLC) and the Research Libraries Group (RLG/RLIN) successfully stabilized their operations through hardware and software development. In the case of OCLC, problems were caused by the move, from Columbus, Ohio, to the newly built headquarters in Dublin, Ohio, of 48 minicomputers, which are communications and data base processors, seven large Sigma 9 mainframes, and 74 disc drives housing the data base, plus many miles of cables and plugs. OCLC sought to maintain constant service by moving one computer at a time, linking it to the online system, then another, and so on. There was little, if any, comparable experience in the data processing world to advise and design such a move. Little wonder that there were problems with system performance, which tried everyone's patience and lost income.

OCLC also had severe problems with its Ramtek 110 terminal, introduced in 1981. Manufacture of the terminal was suspended, and OCLC ordered more OCLC Model 105 terminals from Beehive Electronics. A moratorium on growth (i.e., no more terminals, libraries, subsystems, or enhancements added to the system) was imposed by OCLC in March 1982, while engineers and systems staff fought to stabilize the system. The moratorium on new terminals and libraries was lifted in October 1982, and for the remaining months of the year OCLC linked 75 new terminals a month to the system to catch up on the backlog. In December, the system seemed to have weathered that growth storm well, and installation continued into the new year. OCLC still, cautiously, would not give a date for the installation of system enhancements, even though some, such as the extremely desirable serials claiming, have been written and tested since fall 1981.

RLG was equally successful in stabilizing its systems, after a period of poor operational performance. In 1982, a new IBM 3081 Model D mainframe computer dedicated totally to the RLIN network (in the past, RLIN had shared a Stanford University IBM computer) was installed and dramatically improved the system service and stability. The RLIN network serves fewer users and supports fewer terminals than OCLC, but its subject search capability and the other selective data bases available cause a heavy demand on the system.

New OCLC User Categories

A second significant development was that a way was found to bridge the gap between RLG and OCLC. As RLG had grown, some research libraries, preferring the RLIN service, found that they were unable to access data online. In 1980, the Council on Library Resources funded a major study by Battelle Institutes to review the bibliographic and technical problems of interfacing the four major bibliographic sources (LC, WLN, OCLC, and RLIN).[1] Little action was taken on the results of the study, which were not without controversy.

In January 1982, however, OCLC announced that it would establish two new categories of users: A partial user could use any of the subsystems except cataloging; a tape-loading user of the catalog subsystem could load tapes from another source (e.g., RLG) onto the online catalog, be a member of OCLC, and use any or all of the subsystems.[2] Most of the RLG libraries that had left OCLC had decided to use the tape-loading service by the end of the year. The University of Minnesota RLIN tapes were the first to be loaded, in November 1982. This is only a stopgap solution, of course. Work is continuing within the Council on Library Resources Bibliographic Service Development Program (BSDP) on the technical interfaces that would lead to the realization of a national online library network.

Online Public Access Catalogs

Another significant development in 1982 was the awakening of interest in a large community in the need for an online public access catalog of library holdings. Here, again, work had been underway for some time in a number of locations. The widest ranging research effort was initiated by BSDP. The Council on Library Resources (CLR), OCLC, and RLG brought together a number of groups that had experience with online user-oriented library catalogs for a conference at Dartmouth in fall 1980. One result was a study of user behavior and expectations, in which the participants were RLG, OCLC, J. Matthews and Associates, the University of California, UTLAS (Toronto), and the Library of Congress. Information from user interviews and reviews of existing catalog performance were gathered.

At a crowded meeting at the ALA annual conference in Philadelphia, reports were made of the preliminary results. Some 10,000 survey questionnaires from both users and nonusers of online catalogs were reviewed. Satisfaction levels were quite high: 93 percent of users reported that they were satisfied; 47 percent claimed to have found what they were looking for in the online catalog. OCLC published a reworking of its contribution to the CLR study by Charles R. Hildreth under the title *Online Public Access Catalogs: The User Interface.*[3]

BSDP also held an important meeting in June on the problems of improving subject access in online public access catalogs. Twenty-three representatives of networks, research libraries, abstracting and indexing services, and other agencies were invited; the papers will be published in 1983.

Other activities in the online public access catalog were the development of the University of Minnesota system (Mankato State University has replaced its card catalogs with terminals), and Carlyle Systems is offering an online catalog service based on the MELVYL system at the University of California. Another straw in the wind is the increasing interest in libraries of all types to complete retrospective conversions of their records into machine-readable form. Some have circulation and COM (computer output microfilm) catalogs in mind, of course, but once the data are converted they can be used for an online catalog, too. Demand is so great that OCLC and AMIGOS (Dallas, Texas) have established units that undertake conversions into OCLC, and a significant part of the OCLC online catalog action is retrospective conversion of records.

Personnel Changes

The year 1982 was also remarkable for the number of changes in the leadership of networks. Edward Shaw resigned from the presidency of RLG in June 1982, and Pat Battin, vice president and university librarian at Columbia University was acting president during the six-month search for a successor. In December, it was announced that Richard McCoy would take up the appointment as president in January 1983. At OCLC, Rowland Brown's appointment, originally for two years, extended beyond 1982. In the regional networks affiliated with OCLC, there were changes of leadership at Bibliographic Center for Research (BCR), CAPCON (Washington, D.C.), NELINET (New England), and SOLINET (Atlanta). These followed two changes in 1981. The tempo of these changes is indicative of the political, fiscal, and technical uncertainties of network directing.

Regional and Statewide Networks

These uncertainties make all the more welcome a trend within the OCLC network toward the strengthening of relationships between the regional networks and OCLC. A joint statement on mutual relationships and tenets was agreed upon in 1982, and generally groups have worked together in a close, receptive atmosphere. Given the wide range of missions, interests, and structures that exist among the networks, this is not an insignificant development.

The year 1982 also saw two developments in the structure of regional networking. In the first place, two of the networks affiliated with OCLC decided to suspend those relationships in 1983. Both MIDLNET and FAUL are phasing out that segment of their operations, and the libraries are joining other regional networks. CAPCON was established as a separate entity, parting amicably with its founder organization, the Consortium of D.C. Universities. At the same time the Association for Library Information (AFLI), a new network, drawing its members from Pittsburgh Regional Library Center (PRLC) and OHIONET, became affiliated with OCLC.

The other development is a growing interest in statewide networks, initiated in some cases by the state library agency. North Carolina commissioned a report from King Research, Inc., which concluded that the state should continue its use of the OCLC system for cataloging and other services. A report commissioned by the state of Ohio from James Rush Associates proposed an interlibrary loan message system for small public libraries that would evolve into a bibliographic system managed by Compuserve. This proposal caused some controversy because of its potential effect on OHIONET and the existing regional library systems.[4] A proposal to establish a statewide network affiliated with OCLC in Missouri, where libraries presently are linked to OCLC through MIDLNET and Bibliographic Centers for Research (BCR), is under discussion in that state.

Minicomputer-Based Systems

The trend for libraries, primarily public libraries, to use minicomputer-based library systems developed by commercial vendors to establish local resource sharing networks continued in 1982. Data Phase, for example, announced the use of its Tandem computer-based ALIS II/E system for the C/W MARS (Central/Western Massachusetts Automated Resource Sharing) Network, which is expected to link 28 public, academic, and special libraries in 1983.[5] Services will include acquisitions, cataloging, and circulation. Another example is Boulder (Colorado) Public Library, which has been awarded a grant to develop a telecommunication link between Data Phase, CLSI, and UNIVAC and the five Denver metropolitan public libraries.[6]

For some time, both OCLC and RLIN have recognized the need to devolve certain processes from the main central computers by establishing distributed systems. In 1982, RLG announced the receipt of a $250,000 grant to begin research on a distributed system, and OCLC made announcements regarding two regional circulation systems that it has been developing since 1979.

Beginning in 1982, OCLC will market the Claremont Total Library System (TLS), a Hewlett-Packard 3000-based service that links with the OCLC Online Catalog System to provide local circulation, acquisitions, and catalog maintenance services.

The Local Library System (LLS), a distributed system developed internally by OCLC, will be field-tested by five libraries, including the University of Akron and SUNY Brockport, while it is housed at OCLC headquarters. Its purposes are to provide comprehensive integrated services to libraries on a local level, including circulation in the first phase, and eventually reference services, acquisitions, and public access catalogs. According to an agreement signed in May 1983, the first regional installation of the system is anticipated for 1983 at The Five Colleges, Inc. (Massachusetts).

The major difference between the RLG/RLIN and OCLC distributed systems, on the one hand, and the local minibased system, on the other, is that in the first case the local systems will retain a link with a major national data base. As one looks toward the future of library networking, it is difficult to underestimate the significance of the RLG and OCLC distributed system development.

In another interesting development, SOLINET announced that the first phase of the LAMBDA Patron Access Module (PAM) is operational in some test libraries throughout the Southeast. With PAM, the data base (drawn from OCLC distribution tape records) can be easily accessed using the keyword-in-title form of subject access.

PAM will eventually be expanded to provide author and subject searching through a more refined LAMBDA inquiry module, which is under development.[7]

A technical trend of similar potential significance is the growing use of microcomputers both in linked networks of their own and as terminals to interface with the bibliographic networks. The Wankesha County Library System, Wisconsin, for example, has established an interlibrary loan (ILL) network using an Apple computer,[8] and a proposal to link micros into an ILL network is being developed by PALINET and PRLC in Pennsylvania. One can expect that the evolution of microcomputer technology will lead to quite startling developments in downloading capability to library terminals from networks and data base services, with far more local flexibility in service for libraries using the networks.

Optical-Disk Technology

In August 1982, the Library of Congress announced its plans for a Catalog Distribution Service (CDS) DEMAND System, the first computerized system to store images on optical disks and reproduce them in facsimile quality using high-resolution laser printing.[9] In December 1982, the library awarded two optical disk development contracts, one to create five analog optical disk productions of films, videotapes, photographs, and graphics and the second to develop archival-quality document storage of 500,000 pages of frequently used periodicals, with rapid access, image display, and reproduction of single or multiple copies of pages or whole documents.[10] The high-resolution display (2,200 lines per screen) will be supported by LC's existing computer indexing and abstracting systems. Image reproduction will be either through terminal printer attachments or batch offline. Seven work stations for system access will be distributed throughout the library's three buildings. The implications of this work for library networking are as far-reaching and exciting as the work initiated by the Library of Congress 20 years ago on machine-readable cataloging data, which led to the MARC formats and are an essential component of the contemporary library network.

OTHER DEVELOPMENTS

In addition to the major shifts in network development described thus far, there were a number of events in 1982 that will exert an influence on library networks in future years, even though they may have had relatively little immediate effect.

The Telecommunications Competition and Deregulation Act of 1981, which led to the restructure of AT&T, will have a powerful effect on the telecommunication charges of networks, particularly interstate networks. The library and networking community tended to support the companion bill, Telecommunications Act of 1981, introduced by Representative Wirth on December 10, 1981, which was eventually withdrawn in 1982; however, it may be reintroduced in another form sometime in the future. It is not possible yet to discern the fate of proposals from within the library community for a library rate for communications. Clearly, high telecommunications tariffs will accelerate the efforts to develop distributed processing.

OCLC decided in December 1982 to copyright its data base, claiming that its action recognizes the growing value to the information community of the unique, international resource created by OCLC and its members. OCLC expects that this action will ensure both the integrity of the data base and its appropriate and responsible use in keeping with the mutual rights and obligations of its members.[11] It is a little early to know the full impact of this action and whether or not RLIN, WLN, or other networks will follow suit.

The Library of Congress Network Advisory Committee (NAC) met during the year to discuss future planning of document delivery, including public policy versus for-profit service methods, the needs for data collection, and evaluation procedures. Network Planning Paper No. 7 was published, containing the papers of the March NAC meeting, at which ADONIS, a project for the electronic delivery of documents, was presented.[12]

The Network Development Office completed the planning of the applications section of the Linked Authority System Project (LASP), and implementation of the telecommunications specifications Linked System Project: Standard Network Interconnection (LSP:SNI) began in 1982. LSP-Authority Implementation will enable institutions to participate in building a nationwide Name Authority File Service.

INCOLSA, in studying the relationship between the Library of Congress Name Authority Cooperative (NACO) Project and the need for additional headings for individual states, is discussing suggestions taht Indiana libraries pool their efforts to expand entries made to NACO. In another aspect of authority control work, the Library of Congress continued to hold institutes on authority control in different regions of the United States.

The Library of Congress and NCLIS jointly sponsored a study, on behalf of the Federal Library Committee, on government library resources. The result of the study, *Toward a Federal Library and Information Services Network: A Proposal*, was published in 1982.[13]

A number of interesting service initiatives were reported in 1982 by the regional networks affiliated with OCLC, which are responsible for direct network development for their members in all 50 states and also provide services other than OCLC. The SOLINET LAMDA development reported earlier in this paper (under "Minicomputer-Based Systems") is one of the initiatives. OHIONET reports progress in the development of its Library Machine, a minibased local library system for circulation, an online catalog, and other services, which will exist in two versions, for large and small libraries.[14] OCLC distribution tapes are the source of the data base. The test implementation will be at Toledo-Lucas County Public Library sometime in 1983.

Regional networks also have been active in the area of interlibrary loan, perhaps the most tangible example of local resource sharing. Bibliographic Center for Research (BCR) announced the development of a BCR interlibrary loan code, and BCR and Wisconsin Interlibrary Services (WILS) report a joint ILL request transmission service using the California Library Authority for Systems and Services (CLASS) On-Tyme II Electronic Mail System. SUNY/OCLC reported the development of SOLID Service, a 24-hour point-to-point document delivery service for SUNY/OCLC participants in New York State.

Interlibrary loan also attracted attention within the larger networks. RLG/RLIN announced its improved ILL message system in 1982,[15] and OCLC made it possible for local interlibrary loan policies to be recorded in its online Name-Address Directory (NAD), obviously facilitating the generation of ILL requests at the terminal. Universal Serials and Book Exchange (USBE), which became an OCLC participant in 1982, is converting its holdings into the OCLC data base and will accept requests for duplicate materials from its store via the OCLC ILL subsystem. The Center for Research Libraries (CRL), another OCLC member that is converting its data base into OCLC, is having discussions with OCLC on the possibilities of developing electronic document transmission through the network. With the continuing expansion of OCLC Europe, intriguing visions are generated of an improved international ILL mechanism.

SUMMARY

After a decade of fairly hectic activity both nationally and locally, network relationships are starting to stabilize. Smaller networks are relinquishing some of their services to larger units, and larger networks are consolidating their services and financial bases. Development is continuing technically at all levels and politically at the state level. There appears to be less tension and more cooperation among the players, although entrepreneurship is, thank goodness, by no means dead. The wellspring of initiative and imagination that created the network revolution is not dry.

Libraries accept networks as an essential service component, and for the moment the demand for network service is greater than the supply. The next two or three years should see libraries and networks become actively involved with distributed systems, microcomputers, electronic document delivery, optical-disk technology, and the administrative issues of data base copyright and telecommunications—a new set of experiences.

NOTES

1. Donald A. Smalley et al., *Linking the Bibliographic Utilities: Benefits and Costs* (Columbus, Ohio: Battelle Columbus Laboratories, 1980).
2. *OCLC Newsletter*, no. 140 (March 1982).
3. Charles R. Hildreth, *Online Public Access Catalogs: The User Interface.* (Columbus, Ohio: OCLC, 1982).
4. *OHIONETWORK* 4, no. 10 (October 1982), and 4, no. 11 (December 1982).
5. *Passwords: News from Dataphase Systems* 2, no. 3 (Winter 1982).
6. *Library Journal*, May 1, 1982, p. 846.
7. *Library Journal*, November 15, 1982, p. 2126.
8. *Small Computers in Libraries* 2, no. 12 (December 1982).
9. *Library of Congress Information Bulletin* 41, No. 34 (1982), p. 246.
10. *News from the Library of Congress*, PR82-118, December 7, 1982.
11. *OCLC Newsletter*, no. 144 (December 1982).
12. *Document Delivery—Background Papers Commissioned by the Network Advisory Committee.* Library of Congress Network Planning Paper No. 7 (Washington, D.C.: L.C. Cataloging Distribution Service, 1982).
13. *Toward a Federal Library and Information Services Network: A Proposal* (Stock No. 030-000-00038-9). (Washington, D.C.: Superintendent of Documents, U.S. Government Printing Office, 1982).
14. *OHIONETWORK* 4, no. 3 (March 1982).
15. *Library Journal*, November 15, 1982, p. 2126.

THE USE OF MICROCOMPUTERS IN ELEMENTARY AND SECONDARY SCHOOL LIBRARIES

Blanche Woolls

Professor, Department of Library Science,
School of Library and Information Science, University of Pittsburgh

The evolution from the mainframe computer to the microcomputer can be traced through the replacement of the vacuum tube by the transistor. Originally marketed to the business community, this new form of an existing technology has expanded the potential for teaching computer literacy from the vocational-technical school or the college and university setting to the elementary and secondary school. When white-collar residents who worked in the computer-based or computer-related industries demanded that schools teaching their children keep up with the computer industry, educators began purchasing microcomputers.

A recent report from the National Center for Education Statistics (NCES), "Instructional Use of Computers in Public Schools" (NCES 82-245, September 7, 1982), shows that, in Spring 1982, 24,000 computer terminals (connected to remote central processors) and 96,000 microcomputers were available to students. This is an increase from 22,000 terminals and 31,000 microcomputers in Fall 1980. A total of 29,000 public schools have at least one computer and 80 percent of these are microcomputers only. Fifteen percent have both microcomputers and terminals and 5 percent have terminals only. However, although school districts have been purchasing large numbers of microcomputers, until very recently the potential for their application was not fully utilized by most school administrators, teachers, or library media specialists.

SUPPORT FROM THE STATES

One of the first states to support microcomputer technology in the schools was Minnesota. The Minnesota Educational Computing Consortium (MECC) was created to provide instructional computing support for activities from elementary schools through the university. In 1978, a statewide contract established by MECC with one manufacturer permitted schools to purchase microcomputers at a reduced price. In three years some 3,000 microcomputers were purchased using this bid price. An additional 1,000 computers were selected from other manufacturers. MECC has also developed quality microcomputer courseware for a wide variety of classroom uses and further has provided the necessary training for staff. Ten teacher trainers have presented workshops, classes, and conferences to 300 school districts each year.

The technology initiatives of the governor and the secretary of education in another state, Pennsylvania, have promoted an extensive awareness program which has been in place for over three years. One Pennsylvania Department of Education (PDE) consultant has presented over 300 workshops with microcomputer shows for school administrators, the directors and staff of instructional materials centers, media specialists, and school librarians. The length of the workshops has varied and the expertise needed to participate has gradually increased. Trainers have been carefully prepared to return to their school districts or regional areas and duplicate the in-service and staff development programs. The success of the technology initiatives was demonstrated in Fall 1982 when block grant funding of $800,000 was allocated for $4,000 technology proposals from individual classroom teachers and other educators. The response to this Request for Proposal was overwhelming. Over 2,000 teachers, media specialists, and school librarians sent in their proposed projects.

Illinois has initiated programs which are applicable to other states. The Illinois Department of Education has a state repository for Computer-Assisted Instruction (CAI) programs for Apple II and TRS 80 Model III microcomputers. The Lyons Township high school district in LaGrange and Western Springs has an ongoing computer literacy program. The superintendent of the district, in an effort to reduce the literacy gap, purchased 220 computers for 3,800 high school students and their 275 teachers. All teachers in this district were given a four-day literacy course. These teachers then taught computer literacy to their students.

The Beltway Project, started in ten schools in the area near the Washington, D.C. beltway, was to test the potential of the microcomputer and the videodisc. Renamed Videodisc and Microcomputers (VIM) and expanded in 1982 to 45 additional sites all over the nation, this project now offers an electronic mailbox interconnection and interactive computer videodisc system. The American Institute for Research is providing national coordination and evaluation of the use of both microcomputers and interactive videodisc systems.

But not all states and school districts have achieved high levels of microcomputer use. The administration in one large metropolitan school system has declared a halt to the purchase of more microcomputers until those currently stored in closets or sitting idle in corners of classrooms can be activated for use by trained students and teachers. Still other districts have resisted the first rush to purchase. School personnel are waiting for additional funding, or until they are convinced of the best system to purchase, or until they can buy the "ultimate" system. These, however, would seem to be the exceptions.

THE INSTRUCTIONAL USES OF COMPUTERS

A study by the Center for Social Organization of Schools of the Johns Hopkins University (Henry Jay Becker, "Microcomputers in the Classroom—Dreams and Realities," Grant No. NIE-G-80-0113, Report No. 319, January 1982) places the instructional uses of computers into six headings:

1. For *Drill and Practice* by students after principles are taught by the teacher in more traditional ways.
2. For *Tutorial Dialog* to present information to students, diagnose misunderstandings, and provide remedial instructive communication and individually designed practice.
3. For *Management of Instruction* to provide the teacher with automatic reporting of individual student performance and appropriate assignment of skill levels.
4. For *Simulation and Model-Building* microcomputer programs to demonstrate the consequences of a system of assumptions, or the consequences of varying an assumption, usually in conjunction with instruction in science or social studies.
5. For *Teaching Computer-related Information Skills* to students and having them apply such skills as typing, editing text, and retrieving information from microcomputer systems.
6. For *Teaching Computer Programming* to students to have them solve problems that are a part of their mathematics curriculum or simply for the understanding of programming itself.

Table 1 taken from the NCES report cited earlier shows the major educational uses of microcomputers (by grade level) in the United States during the 1981–1982 school year.

TABLE 1 MAJOR USES OF MICROCOMPUTERS FOR INSTRUCTION IN THE UNITED STATES, 1981–1982 SCHOOL YEAR

Grade Level	No. of Schools with Micros	Compensatory and Remedial	Basic Skills	Learning Enrichment	Computer Literacy	Computer Science
Total	27,501	3,910	5,103	5,174	9,055	6,237
			(In percents)			
% of Total	100%	14%	19%	19%	33%	23%
Elementary	11,050	18	29	21	29	7
Jr. high	5,774	20	11	19	30	10
Sr. high	9,504	6	12	18	39	49
Combined and other	1,173	19	6	4	34	15

*Numbers may not add up to 100%—some schools reported more than one major use; others reported no major use.

THE SCHOOL LIBRARY MEDIA CENTER

Microcomputers as an Educational Tool

Microcomputers that are placed in the library media center under the responsibility of the school library media specialist become just another type of audiovisual technology scheduled for use in the center, for distribution to individual classrooms, for students and teachers to use at home, or for any necessary maintenance. (As repair services for hardware are being expanded to include repair of microcomputers, many districts and regions are purchasing hardware from a single manufacturer.) Microcomputer software, integrated with the existing book and audiovisual media collection, becomes another potential learning material for the school, and is selected along with all of the other instructional materials.

Media center staff become responsible for computer awareness programs and computer literacy campaigns. Selection, maintenance, integration, and adapting of the software also are new responsibilities. Staff may assist teachers who wish to use commercially available authoring programs to design learning packages. Some media specialists learn to program; others use the programming skills of students or teachers.

Microcomputers for Management Purposes

Use of the microcomputer in school libraries for management was started by library media specialists who had an interest in programming and an awareness of the potential of the microcomputer to accomplish clerical tasks. One of the first such applications was to write programs for a circulation system. Still other school library media specialists have been able to adapt commercially developed data management programs for use. Two elementary school library media specialists in Colorado have adapted an Ohio Scientific Incorporated (OSI) program to circulate audiovisual media, generate bibliographies of materials, and maintain equipment inventories, including costs and maintenance and repair schedules.

A recent study completed for the Department of Education (Woolls, 1982) described several administrative uses of the microcomputer. Microcomputers are used heavily to generate overdues and to keep circulation statistics. Locally written (often by students) and commercially tailored programs have been in place for some time. Many generate overdue lists, letters to parents, and invoices for materials to be replaced. Commercial systems are currently available which will handle about 500 circulations per week and 1,000 overdues per month.

One school librarian in Florida has a circulation program that includes statistics for all print and nonprint materials, production requests, and media center equipment requests. The microcomputer in this high school is also used to provide a readability index to materials, which is added to the shelf lists of all books, texts, and tests.

In one county in Maryland, the microcomputer not only books films but also generates circulation labels to send prints to the requesting schools. (The 2,500-print collection requires a hard disc to handle the data.) The microcomputer also is used to keep a record, by Dewey number and by school, of all acquisitions, as well as to generate a computerized list of "approved" materials for purchase.

Another management use of the microcomputer is to control special segments of a collection. A DB Master program on an Apple II generates bibliographies of the professional collection. These bibliographies, being kept current and handily revised, have increased awareness and access to this previously little-used collection. For another special segment, the paperback collection, accession numbers are used to identify books for a catalog of 2,000 paperback books. The microcomputer creates author and title labels for cards and pockets and keeps an inventory record. All overdues of paperbacks are also on the microcomputer.

In New York, "shoe-string" project grants from the New York State Education Agency have encouraged the use of microcomputers for the development of union lists of serials or other resources. Electronic mail with microcomputers is being tested with three school library pilot projects. A few library media specialists in this state have prepared library skills lessons as well as independent study courses, special bibliographies, and audiovisual catalogs on their microcomputers. One Board of Cooperative Educational Services (BOCES) is testing the potential of the microcomputer for film booking (2,200-film collection) by experimenting with computer management of preview films (approximately 600 per year).

In Wisconsin, microcomputers have been used with limited success for the production of catalog cards. Data storage is limited unless a hard disc is added to the system.

PROBLEMS IN THE USE OF MICROCOMPUTERS

One of the major problems with the placement of microcomputers in the school media center is the lack of training for school library media specialists. Certainly programs offered by state departments of education, local school districts, and professional associations have addressed the problem of computer literacy. One innovative program initiated by the Florida Department of Education in cooperation with the Florida Association of Media Educators (FAME) has presented workshops for media personnel during FAME conferences and at other times during the school year.

Among the many limitations of microcomputers are the small storage capacity of cassettes and floppy discs as well as such technological limitations as the slow response of the cassette and the problems of downloading if the tape is not completely rewound. Human limitations include resistance to change in general and technology in particular. Computers often require the use of numbers to identify program statements, and many persons reassign their math phobias to this technology. Also, until the typing skills that are required to manipulate the microcomputer are learned, input of data or responses to computer-generated questions can be very slow. (This may be overcome eventually with the refinement of programs for touch sensitive television screens.) Some persons fear that the availability of the microcomputer may encourage unnecessary storage of data. Others will attempt to network several microcomputers when the original purchase should have been the minicomputer.

But, in spite of the many problems that can arise in the use of microcomputers in elementary and secondary school library media centers, microcomputers appear to be the technology for the 80s. The microcomputer offers great potential for education and for administration. It is the first type of technology since the typewriter and the telephone (excluding videotapes of library orientation programs) that can reduce the clerical workload of media center staff. When reduced funding and smaller school populations lead to reductions in the professional staff, the knowledge and use of the microcomputer may be the *raison d'etre* for maintaining the library media specialist's position in the school.

Federal Agencies

THE NATIONAL COMMISSION ON LIBRARIES AND INFORMATION SCIENCE

1717 K St. N.W., Suite 601, Washington, DC 20036
202-653-6252

Toni Carbo Bearman
Executive Director

Douglas S. Price
Deputy Director

The National Commission on Libraries and Information Science (NCLIS) was established by PL 91-345 in 1970 as a permanent, independent agency in the executive branch, reporting directly to both the president and Congress. The commission has four major roles: (1) to serve as a "resident expert" for both the executive and legislative branches; (2) to be an "honest broker," bringing together agencies in both branches to focus on problems of common interest; (3) to serve as a forum for the entire library/information community, including both the public and private sectors; and (4) to be a catalyst to help get programs implemented. The commission's primary role is to advise Executive Branch agencies and Congress.

During 1982, NCLIS continued to work closely with Congress to develop new library legislation. NCLIS reviewed testimony received in oversight hearings held by the Subcommittee on Postsecondary Education of the Committee on Education and Labor (House of Representatives), on the Library Services and Construction Act (LSCA), resolutions from the White House Conference on Library and Information Services, and the opinions of professionals representing broad areas of the library/information community. Draft amendments to LSCA will be based, in large part, on concerns expressed by our community.

TASK FORCE REPORTS

Several of the commission's task forces completed their work during the year, and the report of the Public Sector/Private Sector Task Force, *Public Sector/Private Sector Interaction in Providing Information Services*, was published and widely disseminated with a request for reaction and response from persons and organizations throughout the library/information community. [For a summary of the *Public Sector/Private Sector* report, see the Special Reports section of Part 1 of this volume.—*Ed.*] The commission received the reports of the task forces on The Role of the Special Library in Nationwide Networks and Cooperative Programs (jointly sponsored by the Special Library Association), on Community Information and Referral (CI&R), and on Library and Information Services to Cultural Minorities. The first of these will be published jointly by NCLIS and the Special Libraries Association (SLA), and the other two by NCLIS early in 1983.

Two surveys performed by the SLA-NCLIS task force disproved the widely held notion that special libraries do not participate actively in networks; approximately half do. Of the 50 percent that do not participate in networking, perhaps half are deterred by lack of information. Among the recommendations included in the report are those for the collection and dissemination of better and more frequent statistics on special library networking activities and for efforts to educate executives of companies and other organizations in which special libraries are located on the benefits of networking. Also recommended are efforts to remove legal and regulatory barriers, as well as network policy and administrative barriers.

The CI&R task force report includes recommendations for: educating all parties—librarians, legislators, and the general public—about CI&R; provisions for CI&R in library legislation at all levels (federal, state, and local); extensive promotional efforts; and research on the impact of CI&R on users and on the application of automation to CI&R.

The report of the Cultural Minorities task force includes 42 recommendations aimed at: determining the library and information service needs of cultural minorities; changing library personnel policies and improving the education of library professionals; improving services and programs; improving the availability of cultural minority specific materials and resources; and funding library programs for minorities.

The commission also received the report of the Intergovernmental Library Cooperation Project, a study sponsored by NCLIS together with the Library of Congress and the Federal Library Committee, on federal libraries and resource sharing. (For more information on this project, see Section 4 of the 1982 edition of the *Bowker Annual*.)

NATIONAL RURAL INFORMATION SERVICES DEVELOPMENT PROGRAM

The commission continued to work with the Department of Agriculture, the Intermountain Rural Community Learning/Information Service project, and others on a National Rural Information Services Development Program. NCLIS's role in this largely state, local, and private-sector effort has been to assist the library, agricultural extension, and information communities, as well as the federal government, in removing barriers to more effective dissemination of information services to rural areas. As a part of this effort, NCLIS arranged and co-sponsored an exhibit of a model rural information center at the Fourth General Assembly of the World Future Society, and coordinated arrangements for a joint congressional hearing on the changing information needs of rural America, where nearly half of the population now lives. One of the witnesses at the hearing was 12-year-old Jason Hardman, who, frustrated by lack of access to library resources in his hometown of Elsinore, Utah, established a public library for the community on his own.

WHCOLIS-RELATED ACTIVITIES

NCLIS has continued its liaison with the White House Conference on Library and Information Services Taskforce (WHCOLIST), which promotes the implementation of resolutions adopted by the 1979 White House Conference. At the third annual meeting of WHCOLIST in Atlanta, Georgia, it was reported that since the previous meeting, 19 states had increased aid to libraries, 21 states had acted to heighten public awareness, and 14 states had expanded library services. The delegates voted in favor of support for the recently adopted national library logo, support for an International Year of Libraries, and a recommendation to amend the "Apple Bill" to include public, as well as school libraries.

ANNUAL REPORT

The *NCLIS Annual Report, 1980-81*, published in 1982, includes an extensive summary of the history of NCLIS (and of its predecessor, the National Advisory Commission on Libraries) and its accomplishments during the first ten years. It also includes as appendixes a summary of its 1975 Program Document, a bibliography of its publications, a list of the White House Conference resolutions, a bibliography of the White House Conference publications, and the recommended *Elements of a National Library and Information Services Program*. This document (available from NCLIS) will be a valuable reference tool for many years.

INTERNATIONAL ACTIVITIES

NCLIS continued its involvement in the international community not only by paying one-half of the U.S. national dues to the International Federation of Library Associations and Institutions (IFLA), but by holding its first commission meeting outside the United States in Montreal, in conjunction with the IFLA conference. In addition, at the request of the American Library Association (ALA), NCLIS has agreed to become the Secretariat for the U.S. National Committee for the UNESCO General Information Program (UNESCO/PGI). Under this agreement, the principal role of NCLIS will be to act as a conduit and focal point for the flow of information among the U.S. National Committee, the UNESCO/PGI, and the Department of State.

OTHER ACTIVITIES

On October 1, 1982, Miss Elinor Hashim, Supervisor of Reference and Technical Services at Perkin-Elmer Corporation, Norwalk, Connecticut, since 1981, was confirmed as the commission's third chairperson. Miss Hashim has worked in public libraries in Connecticut since 1968. From 1956 to 1968 she was employed at the United Technologies Research Center in East Hartford. From 1976 to 1982, Miss Hashim served as chairperson of the Connecticut State Library Board. She is a past president of the New England Library Association, has been active in the American Library Association, serving as a member of the council since 1980, and is also a member of the Special Libraries Association.

During 1982, NCLIS continued its activities as advisor to the executive and legislative branches of the federal government on matters related to library and information policy and programs. In addition to the regular informal meetings of representatives of agency publishing programs, the commission provided advice and assistance to: the Office of Information and Regulatory Affairs in the Office of Management and Budget on implementation of the Paperwork Reduction Act; the Office of Technology Assessment on a planned study of technology in libraries; and the Executive Office of the President in planning for the 1983 White House Conference on Productivity. NCLIS also arranged for the National Center for Education Statistics to meet with members of the Chief Officers of State Library Agencies (COSLA) and representatives of other library and information associations in order to identify statistical needs and improve the collection and dissemination of statistical information.

NEW PROGRAMS AND PROJECTS

In July 1980, the commission initiated a planning process that has resulted in the identification of the major program areas that it will support during 1983 and for the next several years. In one program area, the commission will examine the impact of information technology on various segments of the population. An exciting aspect of this area is the new partnership NCLIS has entered into with International Business Machines, Inc. Two IBM librarians will work with the commission in examining both the anticipated information environment of 1985 and the impact of technology on various segments of the population. They will also help to identify those qualities that make technology more useful and acceptable and will participate in the development of better and more effective mechanisms of communication with major libraries, information centers, and key library and information associations.

IBM and NCLIS also are working together in a cooperative project with the Drexel University School of Library and Information Science to develop a program that will encourage bright young students entering the information field by providing an opportunity for work experience in industry.

In another new program area, the commission will seek ways for libraries to take the leadership in providing library/information services to meet the changing needs of their communities. The commission will focus first on the library/information needs of rural residents and senior citizens.

THE COPYRIGHT OFFICE: DEVELOPMENTS IN 1982

Library of Congress, Washington, DC 20559
202-287-8700

Victor W. Marton

Supervisor, Information and Reference Division

The federal copyright law preempts virtually all state common law and statutory law equivalent to copyright and establishes a single federal system of copyright for all works, published or unpublished. Copyright protection begins from the moment a work is fixed in some tangible medium of expression and in most instances lasts for the life of the author plus 50 years after the author's death. The existence of copyright in a work therefore is not contingent upon registration in the Copyright Office.

All works protected by copyright are eligible for registration in the Copyright Office. Registration is voluntary, but it is a prerequisite to the initiation of an infringement suit. Other advantages are attached to registration, and in the fiscal year ending September 30, 1982, some 468,149 registrations were made.

Even though registration is voluntary, the law contains a mandatory deposit requirement for all works published in the United States with a notice of copyright. In 1982, the Deposits and Acquisitions Section of the Copyright Office obtained many new acquisitions for the collections of the Library of Congress. With severe reductions in funds available for acquisitions, the enforcement of the mandatory deposit requirement is an increasingly important source of materials for the Library of Congress.

The Licensing Division of the Copyright Office administers the compulsory licensing systems for secondary transmissions by cable television and for public performance of music on jukeboxes. In calendar year 1982, the office collected and invested in interest-bearing accounts more than $2 million from jukebox license fee receipts. This money is distributed to copyright owners by the Copyright Royalty Tribunal. The office also reported that more than $29 million dollars in cable royalty fees, collected in calendar year 1981, was available for distribution by the Copyright Royalty Tribunal.

The Copyright Office also maintains a national copyright information service, the Information and Reference Division, which responded to a record number of requests from visitors and by correspondence in 1982. Answers to questions, informational circulars, copies of the law, copies of regulations, and application forms may be obtained free of charge by writing to the Copyright Office, Library of Congress, Washington, DC 20559, or by calling 202-287-8700 between 8:30 A.M. and 5:00 P.M. (eastern standard time) on weekdays. The office also has an application forms hot line, 202-287-9100, which tape records requests 24 hours a day.

SPECIAL PROJECTS

The Copyright Office has the responsibility to report to Congress on a number of diverse topics. Three of these reports have been delivered: one on performance rights in sound recordings; one on voluntary licensing agreements that were made concerning the use of nondramatic literary works by public broadcast stations; and another on the effect of the phaseout of the manufacturing clause (Section 601 of Title 17 of the United States Code) on the U.S. book manufacturing and printing industries.

Section 108(i) Report

During FY 1982, the Copyright Office completed several projects in preparation for its report to Congress in January 1983, on whether or not Section 108 of the Copyright Act has achieved the intended statutory balance between the rights of creators and the needs of users of copyrighted works. There were several significant developments during FY 1982 that bear upon the preparation of the report: the receipt and preliminary evaluation of the results of several statistical surveys conducted by King Research Inc.; the formation of a group representing librarians, publishers, and authors, which met on several occasions to discuss the effects of Section 108 on areas of common concern; and the closing of the public record created by the public hearings on these matters.

The King Report, prepared under contract to the Copyright Office, was designed to examine those aspects of library, user, and publisher photocopying-related behavior that might lend themselves to objective measurement and statistical analysis. To that end, three surveys of libraries and their employees, two of library users, and one of publishers were carried out. An advisory committee of experts familiar with the issues aided the Copyright Office and King Research in preparing the overall plan for the surveys and some of the detailed questions that were asked. The surveys, as might be expected, generated a large quantity of data, which will be a major component of the report to Congress. The results of the King Report were announced in the *Federal Register*, so that interested persons could contribute their interpretation of the data to the evaluation of the effectiveness of Section 108.

At the conclusion of FY 1982, the staff of the Copyright Office had begun to work on the first draft of its report to Congress.

LEGISLATIVE DEVELOPMENTS

FY 1982 was a year of substantial congressional activity in the copyright field. Several proposals involved matters that might be considered part of the unfinished business of copyright revision; others reflected new concerns emanating from experience under the new law.

The so-called manufacturing clause, which has been a part of American copyright law since 1891, provides that certain nondramatic literary works in the English language by U.S. citizens or domiciliaries must be manufactured in the United States or Canada to have full copyright protection. The new copyright statute, as originally enacted, provided that this provision would expire July 1, 1982, unless the law was amended. At the request of Congress, the Copyright Office prepared a report on this provision, which concluded that the manufacturing clause should be allowed to expire and that, if the U.S. printing industry needed protection, other remedies such as subsidies, duties, import quotas, or tax credits would be more appropriate. After extensive hearings, Congress enacted a bill on June 30, 1982, to retain the provision for another four years in order to protect jobs in the U.S. printing and book manufacturing industries. President Ronald Reagan vetoed the bill, but on July 13, Congress overrode the veto, extending the manufacturing clause until July 1, 1986.

Several bills were introduced in the Ninety-seventh Congress to strengthen the laws and increase the deterrent against record, tape, and motion picture piracy and counterfeiting. After hearings in the summer of 1981, the House Subcommittee on Courts, Civil Liberties, and the Administration of Justice reported H.R. 3530 with amendments to the House Judiciary Committee. The Senate passed S. 691 with amendments on December 1, 1981. The Senate version was passed by the House, and President Reagan approved the bill on May 24, 1982.

Other copyright-related bills considered by Congress included proposals to clarify the existing exemption in Section 111(a)(3) of the copyright law governing secondary transmissions made by passive carriers (S. 2881); to establish royalties on both the recording devices and blank tapes used to make copies of audio and video recordings (H.R. 5705, S. 1758); to effect the Nairobi Protocol to the Florence Agreement on the importation of educational, scientific, or cultural materials (H.R. 6093); to provide greater protection for computer software (H.R. 6983); and to amend the Internal Revenue Code of 1954 by removing certain limitations on charitable contributions of literary, musical, or artistic expressions or similar intellectual property (H.R. 6662).

Hearings also were held on proposals to retain the compulsory license covering certain secondary transmissions made by cable television systems with a limited form of syndicated program exclusivity (H.R. 3560, H.R. 5949); to exempt home videorecorders from copyright liability whenever copies were made for private noncommercial use (H.R. 4783, H.R. 4794, S. 1758); and to amend the definition of a "work made for hire" as it presently appears in the copyright law (S. 2033).

COPYRIGHT OFFICE REGULATIONS

Several important points concerning the registration of renewal claims were clarified by the regulation that became final in December 1981, superseding the interim rule on renewals. It makes clear the effect of failure to renew on a timely basis, the relationship of renewal requirements to the provisions of the law that implement the Universal Copyright Convention, the meaning of "posthumous works," the practice with respect to multiple renewal claims, and the identity of proper renewal claimants. The rule also ends the practice of accepting renewal applications by telephone.

After accepting public comments, the Copyright Office amended a proposed regulation on the manner and place of affixation of the notice of copyright on copies of published works and adopted a final version in December. It provides examples of where the notice should be placed on many kinds of copyrightable works.

To provide a mechanism for the Library of Congress to acquire copies of unpublished transmission programs in accordance with Section 407(e) of the copyright law, a proposed rule was published and a public hearing was held on March 24, 1982. The proposed rule sets forth standards under which the Library of Congress could make videotapes off the air of unpublished transmission programs and also could demand copies from owners of the transmission rights. In addition, the proposal states rules for the disposition and use of copies acquired under the regulation for the registration of claims to copyright and for other purposes. A number of witnesses presented their views at the public hearing. These statements, together with the written comments that were received, will be considered in adopting a final regulation.

On September 11, 1980, the Federal Communications Commission removed the cable television distant signal limitations and syndicated program exclusivity rules from its regulations. Because the commission's actions had an immediate impact on the responsibilities of cable systems under the copyright compulsory license, the Copyright Office decided to issue interim regulations concerning this impact. The interim regulations, adopted on May 20, 1982, proposed revisions to the Statement-of-Account forms relating to computations of distant signal equivalents and logging of programming carried on a part-time basis.

On June 9, 1982 the Copyright Office amended its regulations to reflect the new fees for recordation and certification of coin-operated phonorecord players in accordance with the final ruling of the Copyright Royalty Tribunal. The new schedule calls for payment of $25 per jukebox per year in 1982 and 1983 and $50 per jukebox per year thereafter, with the fees subject to a cost of living adjustment on January 1, 1987.

On August 24, 1982, the Copyright Office published amendments to its Freedom of Information Act and Privacy Act regulations. The changes generally were of a technical housekeeping nature, reflecting the current address and telephone numbers of the Copyright Office and the present organizational structure. The two substantive changes are a specific prohibition of the disclosure of the Copyright Office mailing lists and a clarification that some of the Copyright Office systems of records are not public records.

INTERNATIONAL DEVELOPMENTS

In 1982, international copyright concerns continued to center on issues that first emerged in the early 1970s: accommodating copyright to the needs of developing countries; folklore protection; and the impact of new technologies (cable television, videorecording, satellites, and computers) on authors' rights.

At its November 1981 meeting in Geneva, the Intergovernmental Copyright Committee of the Universal Copyright Convention examined the problem of protection in member states for U.S. government works that are in the public domain in the United States. The discussion by the committee revealed a wide divergence of views on this issue. In the final analysis, the extent to which U.S. government agencies may exercise foreign copyrights in their works under the UCC can be determined only on a country-to-country basis.

At the end of October 1981, a group made up principally of ethnologists and folklore specialists met to refine earlier draft model statutory provisions to be recommended to national legislatures, in an effort to develop international recommendations for the protection of folklore. The draft recommendations will be submitted to the scrutiny of the governmental copyright officials of Berne and UCC member states in 1983. The thrust of these provisions is toward some form of comprehensive licensing at the national level, to achieve two purposes: to ensure authenticity of works incorporating material expressions of folklore and to provide remuneration derived from the commercial exploitation of such folklore derivative works for the indigenous communities historically associated with the particular folklore motif used. A central problem is to protect indigenous materials containing folkloric elements in a way that does not inhibit modern creation. Also important is the problem of identifying protectible subject matter and fixing ethnic authorship for purposes of remuneration.

The study of problems arising from the use of copyrighted works in electronic computers, which the World Intellectual Property Organization (WIPO) and UNESCO have been pursuing, was also reviewed at the Geneva meetings. Again, the program was formative. The Committee of Governmental Experts had examined the copyright computer uses issue in December 1980 but was unable, in the limited time available, to formulate detailed preliminary recommendations for national lawmakers. As a result, the draft recommendation, completed by the secretariats and officers of the Governmental Experts meeting, was only recently circulated to states for their comment. Discussions at the Intergovernmental and Berne Executive Committee meeting revealed the view that the division of computer proprietary rights and liabilities questions into two groups—that is, use of works in computers and protection of software—was somewhat artificial. Inquiry into computer software protection has been conducted principally within the framework of the Paris Union for Protection of Industrial Property. A number of delegations, stressing the relationship between software protection and copyright for data bases, urged that the mandate of the Governmental Experts studying computer uses be expanded to include copyright protection of computer software. In fact, the distinction between computer uses and software protection will in all probability be maintained for the time being. The software protection issues that arise out of consideration of computer use of copyrighted works will doubtlessly be noted at the Governmental Experts' meetings, but the topic will not be systematically analyzed nor made a part of the group's recommendations.

Between 1973 and 1977, WIPO and UNESCO provided a forum for preliminary examination of copyright problems created by cable television. With cable a relatively new service and national legislation in Berne and UCC states either untested or otherwise undeveloped, relatively little could be settled by 1977. However, in 1980, with cable television growing rapidly in Europe, and the new U.S. copyright law in force, the copyright issues first considered in 1973 had a more concrete basis. In that year, WIPO convened a series of meetings of independent experts, intended to develop recommendations to national legislatures for treatment of cable television copyright obligations and privileges. In May 1982, the Association Litteraire et Artistique Internationale (ALAI), one of the world's oldest and most prestigious associations of authors and artists, held an international symposium on cable television, the purpose of which was to distill common principles from state practices. Copyright specialists from Europe, North America, and Japan contributed papers on national copyright measures applicable to cable.

The complex problem of copyright in works created by employee-authors was first raised in the context of the creation of computer-assisted works in 1979. In September 1982, a Working Group of Experts met in Geneva to begin analysis of the legal treatment of employee-authors on a broad basis rather than limited to computer contexts. The three sponsoring international organizations, WIPO, UNESCO, and the International Labor Organization, commissioned detailed studies of the copyright status of employee-authors under three legal traditions: Anglo-Saxon, Continental, and Socialist.

[See the five-year review of the new copyright law in the Special Reports section of Part 1—*Ed.*]

FEDERAL LIBRARY COMMITTEE

Library of Congress, Adams Bldg., Rm 1023,
Washington, DC 20540

James P. Riley
Executive Director

Serving to provide the government and the nation at large with more efficient and effective information services, the Federal Library Committee (FLC) works to achieve better use of federal library resources and facilities and to provide more effective planning, development, and operation of federal libraries and information centers.

Many commercial information services used by federal libraries, particularly automated information services, offer economies of scale, such as lower rates to high-volume users, which are attainable to many agencies only by pooling resources and consolidating certain administrative functions. The Federal Library Committee offers such centralized, cooperative services to all federal library and information centers through its Federal Library and Information Network (FEDLINK). The FLC office provides coordination and cooperation with nonfederal libraries and information centers as well, through such varied activities as contracting with network offices to assist federal libraries in the field, participating in the planning and presentation of training programs, and serving as federal representatives and consultants to networks, library organizations and associations, and the information community.

FEDERAL LIBRARY AND INFORMATION NETWORK (FEDLINK)

During FY 1982, the FEDLINK membership grew to more than 425 libraries and information centers nationwide (an increase of 16 percent over the previous year), cooperating on 16 online data base services. There were 760 interagency agreements during the year, resulting in $10,800,000 worth of service (a 30 percent increase over FY 1981).

Before the end of the year, operational effectiveness was improved through the use of the WANG VS Minicomputer Word Processing/Data Processing System in the handling of fiscal accounts. Analysis also was done in other operational areas to determine whether they could be handled more efficiently with the WANG system.

The WANG VS Minicomputer system was upgraded in 1982 with an additional disk drive and two terminals. The disk drive provides a safety factor in the event that a drive should fail and additional storage space be needed for development of additional applications. The terminals add one more clerical work station and provide for a separate operator's console so that programming can be conducted without disruption.

In an effort to improve communications with the membership, the FLC investigated the use of electronic mail and hosted several demonstrations to determine cost and effectiveness. However, it was decided that each agency would have to make its own decision on whether to use electronic mail systems, and that it would not be possible for the FEDLINK network to install one system for all to use.

Online Bibliographic Data Base Services

The online cataloging service, which FLC shares with the Online Computer Library Center (OCLC), has grown from some 325 federal libraries and information centers in FY 1981 to more than 360 in FY 1982. The federal records added to the OCLC data base thus far consist of approximately 3,800,000 logical records; the number is growing at a rate of 60,000 logical records a month. These federal records are available to the membership for the production of customized products such as Computer Output Microfilm/fiche (COM), book catalogs, accessions lists, regional union catalogs, special awareness bibliographies, and members' circulation and acquisitions systems through FLC contracts with Blackwell North America and Informatics. These output tape processing contracts have allowed more federal libraries to extract records from the FLC/FEDLINK OCLC master tape data base. In addition to shared cataloging, FEDLINK members are participating in the interlibrary loan service and some are using the acquisitions and serial control subsystems.

Contracts to train FEDLINK members located outside the Mid-Atlantic region in the use of OCLC subsystems were continued with the Bibliographical Center for Research in Denver, the Wisconsin Library Consortium, the Midwest Region Library Network, and the AMIGOS Bibliographic Council in Dallas.

To offer members alternative or additional online cataloging and related services, contracts were continued with the Washington (State) Library Network, the Research Library Group for subject access to its Research Libraries Information Network, and Sigma Data Computing Corporation in Washington, D.C.

Online Information Retrieval Services

A consolidated request for waivers from GSA for the Teleprocessing Services Program and for the Delegation of Procurement Authority was obtained for the bibliographic services mentioned above and for ten online retrieval services: Bibliographic Retrieval Services (BRS); Lockheed, DIALOG; System Development Corporation, ORBIT; Mead Data Central (MDC), LEXIS/NEXIS; New York Times, INFOBANK; Legislate, Inc., LEGI-SLATE; West Publishing Company, WESTLAW; Dow Jones News/Retrieval; Participation Systems, Inc., POLITECHS/EIES; and Institute for Scientific Information (ISI).

Shared Retrieval Services

To support shared retrieval services, vendor contracts were continued with BRS, DIALOG, MDC, and West. Twenty-two member agreements were processed allowing members to load their own user-defined data files on a vendor's system to retrieve information using the full range of search capabilities of the system.

Shared Acquisitions Services

FLC continued its shared acquisitions services program with Sigma Data Computing Corporation, which operates a minicomputer system, DATALIB, allowing federal participants to share a common data base. Four members participated in this service in FY 1982.

Tape Processing

The tape processing contracts with Blackwell North America and Informatics were continued in FY 1982. Seventeen agencies used the contracts for the processing of FLC/FEDLINK OCLC and in-house tapes to produce various products and services.

FLC CONSULTATION SERVICE

During the year, the FLC office provided consultation services for the following agencies: Department of Treasury, Joint U.S.-Saudi Arabia Economic Commission; Department of Army, Training and Doctrine Command, Ft. Leavenworth, Kansas, and

White Sands, New Mexico; Department of the Interior; Federal Reserve Bank, Atlanta, Georgia; National Security Agency; and the National Oceanic and Atmospheric Administration. Consultation was primarily in the automation of libraries and information services and in telecommunications—definition of the requirements and writing specifications of automated systems, technical review of proposals, and evaluation of automated systems.

MICROCOMPUTER PROGRAM

As a result of a survey of the FLC/FEDLINK membership, regarding the desirability of a list of services, which included microcomputer support, the office undertook a project with the following two major objectives: (1) to demonstrate library applications of microcomputers; and (2) to develop microcomputer systems for small federal libraries.

An Apple II Plus microcomputer was installed in the FLC office to demonstrate the microcomputer capabilities of this popular computer. The Apple will eventually be used for educational programs on microcomputers as well as to evaluate commercially available software for word processing, budget preparation, and library automation functions. It will also be used experimentally to develop training programs for some of the educational services currently offered by the office, e.g., MARC tagging, OCLC terminal use, and introduction to OCLC services.

A second microcomputer was installed, the BMC if800, which will be used to develop a stand-alone work station for small federal libraries, those with a collection of 8,000 titles or less.

NATIONAL OCEANIC AND ATMOSPHERIC ADMINISTRATION (NOAA), AUTOMATED LIBRARY AND INFORMATION SYSTEM (ALIS)

The development of the Automated Library and Information System (ALIS) to provide the National Oceanic and Atmospheric Administration (NOAA) library system with the capability of automated catalog maintenance (interfacing with the OCLC cataloging system), acquisitions, serials control, authority control, and online information retrieval continued under the administrative and technical assistance of the FLC office. In September 1982, the contractor, Systems Control, Inc., Palo Alto, California, shipped the computer hardware to the NOAA library in Rockville, Maryland, for installation and implementation of the cataloging, authority control, OCLC interface, and information retrieval subsystems.

OPM TENTATIVE STANDARDS FOR LIBRARIANS

On December 7, 1981, the Office of Personnel Management (OPM) issued tentative standards for the library and information series. The FLC office distributed the tentative standards to all FLC members and other federal agency libraries. FLC held meetings on the standards on January 12 and 20, 1982, and FLC members participated in meetings on the standards with the American Library Association, the Special Libraries Association, and the Federal Librarians Round Table. FLC requested and was granted an extension of time for its review of and response to the standards, which was submitted to OPM on April 21, 1982, and included a copy of each FLC member's response.

During the last quarter of the fiscal year, OPM completed its revision of the tentative standards based on responses it received from federal personnel offices, the FLC and other agency librarians, library associations, and federal unions. At a number of brief meetings in September, FLC members reviewed the revised standards with the OPM staff; and, at the end of the month a marked copy of the revised standards containing FLC comments and recommended changes was submitted to OPM.

[See the report on "The New Federalism: How It Is Changing the Library Profession in the United States" in the Special Reports section of Part 1—*Ed.*]

INTERGOVERNMENTAL LIBRARY COOPERATION PROJECT

The final report of the Intergovernmental Library Cooperation Project, jointly sponsored by the National Commission on Libraries and Information Science and the Library of Congress, was completed and published in 1982. The report may be purchased from the Superintendent of Documents, U.S. Government Printing Office, Washington, D.C. 20402 (Stock No. 030-000-00138-9), $6.

The objective of the study was to determine ways to improve the coordination of resources and services among federal libraries, and between federal and nonfederal libraries, to meet national, state, and local needs. The study recommends the establishment of a federal multitype library service network to enhance resource sharing and document delivery among federal libraries and in the nonfederal library and information community as well. An organizing and planning committee of the FLC was appointed to study the report and consider its recommendations.

SURVEY OF FEDERAL LIBRARIES

The survey of federal libraries conducted in cooperation with the Learning Resources Branch of the National Center for Education Statistics, which will update the findings of the Survey of Federal Libraries, FY 1972, is nearing completion and will be available through ERIC, the Educational Resources Information Center in 1983. The data collected in the survey on the size of collections, staff, and budgets of individual federal libraries should assist those planning for library services in the legislative and executive branches of the government, as well as administrators of libraries.

INTERAGENCY PANEL FOR THE ASSESSMENT OF THE NATIONAL AGRICULTURAL LIBRARY

The FLC was represented on the Department of Agriculture, Interagency "Blue Ribbon" Panel for the assessment of the National Agricultural Library (NAL) by its executive director. The final report submitted to the secretary of agriculture recommended that the NAL serve as the nation's chief information resource for agriculture and allied sciences, providing its products and services to agencies of the USDA, to public and private organizations, and to individuals. It further recommended that the NAL coordinate a national network of public and private agricultural libraries and information centers, including libraries of land-grant colleges and universities, state-supported colleges and universities, and other public and private sector organizations involved in agricultural information. The final report, *Assessment of the National Agricultural Library: Final Report to the Secretary*, prepared by the Interagency Panel, has been published by the Department of Agriculture.

NATIONAL TECHNICAL INFORMATION SERVICE

U.S. Department of Commerce
5285 Port Royal Rd., Springfield, VA 22161
703-487-4600

Ted Ryerson
Chief, Office of Policy and Plans

Ruth S. Smith
Chief, Office of Customer Services

The National Technical Information Service (NTIS), an agency of the U.S. Department of Commerce, is the central clearinghouse for specialized business, economic, scientific, and social information, resulting principally from government-sponsored research. Each agency of the U.S. government is obliged by law to make available to the public and private sectors the unclassified, nonproprietary information it gathers and the knowledge it produces. Through interagency agreements, NTIS acts as agent for the public announcement and sale of agency research results and gathers information from other sources, such as state and local governments, foreign governments, and some nongovernment sources. Taken as a whole, these sources provide authoritative and timely information on almost every conceivable subject, and their information is used continually as a reference source for decision makers, policymakers and problem solvers.

BACKGROUND

For more than 35 years, NTIS and its predecessor organizations have served as a focal point for the collection, announcement, and dissemination of unclassified U.S. government-sponsored research and development reports and translations of foreign technical literature to the scientific, technical, and industrial communities. Its evolution can be summarized as follows:

1. An executive order established the Publication Board (PB) in 1945 to collect and declassify World War II technical data for dissemination to industry.
2. The U.S. Department of Commerce established the Office of Technical Services (OTS) in 1946 to consolidate the activities of the board and other organizations.
3. PL 81-776, enacted in 1950, directed the Commerce Department to set up and maintain a national clearinghouse for scientific and technical information to be implemented through the Office of Technical Services (OTS).
4. The Federal Council for Science and Technology recommended expansion of the department's clearinghouse function in 1964. The Clearinghouse for Federal Scientific and Technical Information (CFSTI) was organized on the foundations of OTS.
5. On September 2, 1970, the National Technical Information Service (NTIS) was established as a primary operating unit of the U.S. Department of Commerce. The order abolished CFSTI and transferred its functions to NTIS with full authority to establish and monitor a clearinghouse of scientific, technical, and engineering information and to assist operating units in the dissemination of business

and statistical information. The provisions of Title 15, United States Code 1151–1157, obligates NTIS to recover its costs and be self-sustaining through the sale of its products and services.

PURPOSE

The basic mission of NTIS is to collect, organize, announce and disseminate research publications containing scientific and technical information produced or funded by federal, state, and local government sources to (1) permit wider use of government-sponsored research and technology and (2) help increase productivity and innovation in the United States. To accomplish this, NTIS organizes these information products for easy access and promotes them by publishing news bulletins and catalogs, by exhibits and speeches, by mail promotion, and by other public and private mechanisms, such as marketing dealers. NTIS directs its services to private businesses and industry, individuals, colleges and universities, libraries, federal agencies, state and local governments, and international customers.

SCOPE

NTIS was founded to provide bibliographic control and physical availability for a class of documents rather than for a subject area. Because research reports as a class cover many different subjects, the NTIS coverage is very broad and its vast data base contains information on almost any conceivable subject. The scope of the NTIS collection is indicated by the diversity of its many acquisition sources.

The NTIS report collection includes more than 1.3 million titles from more than 450 sources—federal, state, and local governments, foreign governments, and some nongovernment organizations. A large percentage of the reports come from the National Aeronautics and Space Administration (NASA), the Department of Defense (DOD), and the Department of Energy (DOE). Other contributors are the Departments of Commerce and Health and Human Services and more than 200 federal agencies, as well as a growing number of foreign sources.

Each day approximately 270 new reports are processed into the system, adding some 70,000 reports to the collection annually. Roughly 15 percent of these are translations or original-language reports from foreign sources.

NTIS BIBLIOGRAPHIC DATA BASE

The NTIS Bibliographic Data Base, which began in 1964, is a composite of information from a number of sources. Some federal agencies, when they send their reports to NTIS, also send the bibliographic tapes. Because they use a compatible COSATI-based indexing system, these tapes can be merged into the NTIS Bibliographic Data Base. Documents received from other sources are assigned PB numbers and are indexed at NTIS.

The following thesauri are used by the major agencies that contribute indexing records to the NTIS Bibliographic Data Base:

DTIC Retrieval and Indexing Terminology (Defense Technical Information Center, May 1979. AD-A068500)

Energy Information Data Base: Subject Thesaurus (Department of Energy, October 1979. DOE/TIC-7000R4)

NASA Thesaurus. Volume 1: *Alphabetical Listing.* Volume 2: *Access Vocabulary* (National Aeronautics and Space Administration, 1976. vol. 1: N76-17992; vol. 2: N76-17993)

Thesaurus of Engineering and Scientific Terms (American Association of Engineering Societies, 1969; used by NTIS)

The NTIS Bibliographic Data Base is available for online searching through the following commercial services: DIALOG Information Services, SDC Search Service, and Bibliographic Retrieval Services (BRS). Custom online searches, tailored to individual needs, can be ordered from NTIS. In addition, published searches are available on more than 3,500 timely and topical subjects. These normally are updated annually.

The original purpose of the data base was to produce printed products more efficiently. Today a number of current awareness products are produced from the NTIS Bibliographic Data Base. Some of these are as follows:

Abstract Newsletters: published weekly in 26 different subject areas to announce new reports by subject.

Government Reports Announcements & Index (GRA&I): issued biweekly, primarily for librarians and others wanting all the announcements in one volume. The index is cumulated annually.

Title Index: on microfiche, is available as a current subscription, as well as a retrospective file. This contains keyword cross-references.

DOCUMENT DISTRIBUTION

Through its many awareness services, NTIS fills orders for about 23,000 individual items daily. Each year it supplies some 100,000 customers with about 6 million research reports, which generally are available in both paper copy and microfiche. All distribution is on a cost-recovery basis.

Three basic options are offered for ordering individual documents: rush, premium, and regular service. With rush service, documents are virtually hand-carried through the system; it costs an additional $10 per document, or $6 if the document is picked up at NTIS. Premium service provides priority handling in the regular processing cycle; it costs an additional $3.50 per document and is sent by first-class mail. Regular service is used when normal processing is adequate; delivery is by third- or fourth-class mail but an additional $3 per document may be paid for first-class delivery.

Automatic delivery of new reports can be arranged through a standing order service called Selected Research in Microfiche (SRIM). This specialized packaging service automatically provides subscribers with full text microfiche copies of research reports in the special interest subject areas they select. NTIS analysts help subscribers choose from among 500 different subject categories and 200,000 unique descriptive terms. For example, if a subscriber's area of interest is "energy" or "energy use, supply and demand," the subscriber would receive about 140 complete report texts over a 12-month period at about one-fourth the cost of individually purchased texts. The reports are sorted automatically and distributed to subscribers every two weeks as a standing order service.

Many federal agencies and some nonprofit organizations use NTIS as the public promoter and sales agent for their periodicals. More than 20,000 subscribers buy copies of more than 70 different periodicals sold by NTIS. These subscriptions range in subject matter from solar energy bibliographies, to monthly energy statistics, to the Environmental Protection Agency's quarterly bibliography.

OTHER SERVICES

Data Bases

NTIS also makes available government-generated machine-readable data products and the related computer software that is available to process the data. There has been a phenomenal increase in both the number and types of machine-readable data bases established by and for the U.S. government primarily for its own use. At the same time, the many users and potential users are finding that machine-readable data gathered, organized, and presented for one purpose can be reorganized, reformatted, and used just as effectively for other purposes. They are also finding that a number of data bases, or parts of data bases, can be merged into more comprehensive data bases that allow for new and more extensive analyses and correlations. Today NTIS has become the central source for more than 1,200 government-developed software programs and data bases (both bibliographic and statistical) from more than 100 government sources.

STRN Series

The responsibility for assigning American National Standard Technical Report Numbers (STRN) series codes was given to NTIS by the American National Standards Institute (ANSI), to bring order and consistency into a previously uncontrolled and chaotic bibliographic field. More than 300 public and private organizations nationwide have adopted the practice of using the STRN and have registered with NTIS for a unique report series code.

Patents and Patent Applications

NTIS is a central source for information on all new U.S. government-owned patents and patent applications. Cooperating agencies submit their new inventions to NTIS when patent applications are filed with the U.S. Patent and Trademark Office and again when the patents are issued. Patent licenses are granted at NTIS for development by industry of products based on the government-developed and government-owned inventions. The availability of licensable government technology is brought to customers' attention by a special abstract newsletter, *Government Inventions for Licensing*.

CUFT

The Center for the Utilization of Federal Technology (CUFT) is coordinated by NTIS. It was established by the Stevenson-Wydler Technology Innovation Act of 1980. Under this law, agencies are required to provide short "technology assessment" reports on completed (or nearly completed) projects having potential for use by the private sector or by local governments. When received, these summaries will be included in NTIS *Tech Notes*, which are one- or two-page briefs of applied technology from a variety of sources.

Marketing Services

Special technology groups use NTIS as the national marketing coordinator for making their products and services publicly available. These include the Infrared Information and Analysis Center, Electromagnetic Compatability Analysis Center, Machinability Data Center, Chemical Propulsion Information Agency, Technology Application Center, Thermophysical & Electronic Properties Information Analysis Center, Metals and Ceramics Information Center, Nuclear Safety Information Center, Plastics Technical Evaluation Center, Energetic Materials Division (Army Armament R&D Command), Non-Destructive Testing Information Analysis Center, Reliability Analysis

Center, Toxicology Information Response Center, and Mechanical Properties Data Center.

International Information Exchange

The National Technical Information Service, as the central source for scientific and technical information sponsored by the U.S. government, plays a key role in the international exchange of information. NTIS increasingly has become the lead agency within the federal establishment responsible for participation in bilateral, regional, and worldwide activities involving technology transfer and information. This has come about because of the growing recognition of the importance of technical information in the conduct of U.S. business overseas and in the conduct of U.S. international relations.

1. There are more than 300,000 reports based on foreign technology in the NTIS collection.
2. Some 20 percent of the authors represented in the NTIS collection of more than a million titles are sponsored by foreign organizations.
3. Approximately 20 percent of current annual acquisitions are from foreign sources.
4. More than 40 nations contribute information items to the NTIS Bibliographic Data Base.
5. NTIS has bilateral agreements with foreign government, regional, or private information organizations in some 40 countries, which stimulate the international exchange of information through local sales services and the acquisition of new information.

Foreign acquisitions are concentrated in areas of particular interest to U.S. industry. An abstract of every report acquired is published in NTIS newsletters and journals. The complete texts are also available from NTIS. Foreign-language materials judged by U.S. industry to be of particular importance are translated into English.

Several other new programs are expected to spur industrial innovations in the United States. Specific actions to aid the development and commercialization of new U.S. products and processes will emphasize an increased flow of foreign technical information to the United States. In support of these programs, it is NTIS's objective to provide its customers with much of the important foreign technical information available.

IN CONCLUSION

Thus, NTIS plays an important role in the technology transfer process. For the librarian or information specialist, NTIS is a source of verification and guide to government research reports, software programs, data bases, and patent information; for the manager it can go a long way in helping to solve the problems of funding and autonomy; and for the researcher it is a valuable source of information and, at the same time, a stimulus for innovation and productivity.

EDUCATIONAL RESOURCES INFORMATION CENTER (ERIC)

4833 Rugby Ave., Suite 301, Bethesda, MD 20814
301-656-9723

Ted Brandhorst

Director, ERIC Processing and Reference Facility

The Educational Resources Information Center, or ERIC as it is commonly referred to, was begun in 1965 by the Office of Education in an attempt to achieve bibliographic control over the technical report literature being generated by research efforts in education. In August 1972, when the National Institute of Education (NIE) inherited the research functions from the Office of Education, it also inherited the dissemination functions, and ERIC was, therefore, placed organizationally within NIE. In May 1980, NIE (and ERIC) became part of the new U.S. Department of Education. Over the years, ERIC has become the de facto U.S. national system for bibliographic control of the non-book literature of education.

MISSION AND OBJECTIVES

ERIC's mission is to bring the English-language literature of education to the attention of the educational community and to make it as easily accessible by this community as possible, so that improvements in the educational process can be facilitated. For this purpose, the educational community is broadly defined to include researchers, teachers, administrators, policy makers, librarians, counselors, students, and those members of the general public pursuing an educational interest.

To accomplish this broad mission, ERIC has established a number of specific ongoing objectives:

1. *Bibliographic control.* ERIC will establish procedures for the achievement of bibliographic control over English-language documents and journal articles dealing with education in all its aspects. Documents include research reports, project descriptions, evaluations, bibliographies, curriculum guides, speeches, dissertations, conference proceedings and papers, and many other types of material produced for all educational levels. Journal articles include not only those appearing in journals devoted to education, but also those dealing with education that appear in non-education journals. (Currently over 700 journals are covered by ERIC.)
2. *Announcement to the educational community.* The material placed under bibliographic control by ERIC will be announced to the user community on a timely basis and will be indexed for easy access. ERIC will not simply collect without announcement.
3. *Availability of documents in full text.* The material announced to the user community will be obtainable in full text. ERIC will not simply announce material for which no availability can be determined.
4. *Permanent archive.* Material announced by ERIC will be available indefinitely, since even information that eventually becomes obsolete can have value as a historical record, and to prevent replication.
5. *Computerized retrievability.* The ERIC database will be accessible to the users

by computerized techniques as well as by manual techniques. The ERIC database is very large and manual searches can be onerous and time-consuming. For this reason, computerized access and the sophisticated searching techniques that can be applied in that mode must be available. At the same time, since not all users have access to computers or computer terminals, manual access must continue to be provided.
6. *Information analysis, synthesis, and reduction.* Within its limited resources, ERIC will attempt to aid the users in coping with the large volume of information by performing and publishing analyses that, in effect, reduce many documents to one "Information Analysis Product" by summarizing the content of the many documents.
7. *Reference and user services.* ERIC will guide the user in the use of the ERIC database and its related products and, in those instances where ERIC cannot itself provide the information required or perform the service required, will refer the user to an appropriate source.
8. *Service to all levels of user.* ERIC will attempt to serve all levels of user, including the researcher in the laboratory, the administrator in the office, and the teacher in the classroom.
9. *Wide dissemination.* ERIC will attempt to disseminate its information as widely as possible, for the benefit of as many users as possible.
10. *Low cost.* ERIC will attempt to achieve its objectives at the lowest cost to the government. It will also attempt to provide its products and services at the lowest possible cost to the user commensurate with a quality product. This objective will require a judicious use of government, non-profit, and for-profit components.

ORGANIZATIONAL OVERVIEW

From an organizational perspective, ERIC is a network of decentralized but interlocking organizations, each with specific responsibilities and each performing specific functions. Such an organizational structure permits ERIC to better interface with the educational community, but it presents very real operational problems, particularly in the area of coordination of efforts, which must be solved by a variety of tools, procedures, and management controls.

The organizations that make up ERIC include a central office (establishing policy for, funding, and monitoring the entire system); 16 subject-specialized "clearinghouses" (collecting and analyzing the literature and producing information products); a central editorial and computer facility (maintaining the data base and preparing the abstract journal *Resources in Education*, as well as other products); a central "ERIC Document Reproduction Service" (preparing microfiche and document reproductions); a commercial publisher (publishing *Current Index to Journals in Education*, the *ERIC Thesaurus*, and other ERIC publications). Full names and addresses for all the components of ERIC appear in the list that follows.

THE ORGANIZATIONS THAT MAKE UP ERIC

National Institute of Education *(Central ERIC)*
Dissemination and Improvement of Practice
  Program
Washington, DC 20208
Tel: 202-254-5500

Clearinghouses

Adult, Career, and Vocational Education
Ohio State Univ.
1960 Kenny Rd., Columbus, OH 43210
Tel: 614-486-3655

Counseling and Personnel Services
Univ. of Michigan
2108 School of Education Bldg., Ann Arbor, MI 48109
Tel: 313-764-9492

Educational Management
Univ. of Oregon
Eugene, OR 97403
Tel: 503-686-5043

Elementary and Early Childhood
Univ. of Illinois
805 W. Pennsylvania Ave., Urbana, IL 61801
Tel: 217-333-1386

Handicapped and Gifted Children
Council for Exceptional Children
1920 Association Drive, Reston, VA 22091
Tel: 703-620-3660

Higher Education
George Washington Univ.
One Dupont Circle, Suite 630, Washington, DC 20036
Tel: 202-296-2597

Information Resources
Syracuse Univ.
School of Education, 130 Huntington Hall, Syracuse, NY 13210
Tel: 315-423-3640

Junior Colleges
Univ. of California
96 Powell Lib. Bldg., Los Angeles, CA 90024
Tel: 213-825-3831

Languages and Linguistics
Center for Applied Linguistics
3520 Prospect St. N.W., Washington, DC 20007
Tel: 202-298-9292

Reading and Communication Skills
National Council of Teachers of English
1111 Kenyon Rd., Urbana, IL 61801
Tel: 217-328-3870

Rural Education and Small Schools
New Mexico State Univ.
Box 3AP, Las Cruces, NM 88003
Tel: 505-646-2623

Science, Mathematics, and Environmental Education
Ohio State Univ.
1200 Chambers Rd., 3rd Fl., Columbus, OH 43212
Tel: 614-422-6717

Social Studies/Social Science Education
855 Broadway, Boulder, CO 80302
Tel: 303-492-8434

Teacher Education
American Association of Colleges for Teacher Education
One Dupont Circle N.W., Suite 610, Washington, DC 20036
Tel: 202-293-2450

Tests, Measurement, and Evaluation
Educational Testing Service
Rosedale Rd., Princeton, NJ 08540
Tel: 609-921-9000 ext. 2176

Urban Education
Teachers College, Columbia Univ.
Box 40, 525 W. 120th St., New York, NY 10027
Tel: 212-678-3437

Support Organizations

ERIC Document Reproduction Service (*EDRS*)
Computer Microfilm International Corporation (CMIC)
3030 N. Fairfax Drive, Suite 200, Arlington, VA 22201
Tel: 703-841-1212

ERIC Processing and Reference Facility
ORI, Inc., Information Systems Division
4833 Rugby Ave., Suite 301, Bethesda, MD 20814
Tel: 301-656-9723

Oryx Press
2214 North Central Ave. at Encanto, Phoenix, AZ 85004
Tel: 602-254-6156

PRODUCTS AND SERVICES

The information available from ERIC is disseminated in a variety of products. Inaugurated in November 1966, and still the cornerstone of the system, is the monthly abstract journal *Resources in Education* (*RIE*), which announces the document literature and assigns each document an "ED" accession number. In January 1969, *RIE* was joined by its sister abstract journal *Current Index to Journals in Education* (*CIJE*), which announces the journal article literature and assigns each article an "EJ" accession number. The ERIC data base is currently composed of the material from these two separate files. Many of the other ERIC products and services that are listed below are closely related to this fundamental data base.

Product	Source
Abstract Journals *Resources in Education* (*RIE*)	U.S. Government Printing Office (GPO), Washington, DC 20402 ($70/year)
Current Index to Journals in Education (*CIJE*)	Oryx Press ($115/year)
Microfiche 4″ × 6″ microfiche of documents announced in *RIE*. Available on subscription or on demand. Back collections available.	ERIC Document Reproduction Service (EDRS). Annual Subscriptions: Approx. $2000 (approx. 15,000 fiche) Titles $0.97 (1–5 fiche)
Magnetic Tapes (ERICTAPES) Computer-compatible tapes containing the contents of *RIE* and *CIJE* and the related authority files and inverted files. Available on subscription or on demand.	ERIC Facility (Write for price list)
Information Analysis Products State-of-the-art reports; interpretive summaries; syntheses; etc. Mini-files of these products on microfiche, together with printed index, are also available from EDRS.	Specific ERIC Clearinghouses
Computer Searches Complex searches by computer of the ERIC files, negotiated with the supplier and provided to the user in the form of printouts.	Please consult *Directory of ERIC Search Services* (over 500 locations, geographically arranged); available from ERIC Facility.
Online access, searching, retrieval from ERIC files via computer terminal.	Online vendors: BRS, DIALOG, SDC. See online retrieval panel for addresses.
ERICTOOLS Various printed indexes and other tools produced for the benefit of those working closely with the ERIC files, e.g., *Title Index, Report Number Index, Contract/Grant Number Index*, etc.	ERIC Facility (write for price list)
Thesaurus of ERIC Descriptors The master list of approved Descriptors (index terms) used by the ERIC system, with a complete cross-reference structure and rotated and hierarchical displays.	Oryx Press ($35)

Product	Source
Computer-Output-Microform (COM)	
Cumulative title and author indexes for *RIE*.	EDRS (write for price list)
Descriptor and identifier usage reports for both *RIE* and *CIJE*.	
RIE resume cumulations from 1966 to present.	
Document Reproductions	
Paper copy reproductions of documents anounced in *RIE*.	ERIC Document Reproduction Service (EDRS) ($2.15 for first 25 pages and $1.75 for each additional 1-25 page increment)
Paper copy reproductions of journal articles announced in *CIJE*.	University Microfilms International, Article Reprint Service, 300 N. Zeeb Rd., Ann Arbor, MI 48106
	Institute for Scientific Information, Original Article Tear Sheet Service, 325 Chestnut St., Philadelphia, PA 19106
	(Several journal article copy services exist of which the above are major examples)

Document Delivery

ERIC is notable among information systems in providing for the availability of reproductions of the documents and journal articles announced in its abstract journals *RIE* and *CIJE*.

ERIC obtains permission from authors and producers to reproduce approximately 95 percent of the documents currently being announced in *RIE*. This means that in a monthly issue announcing 1,500 documents, some 1,425 documents are microfilmed and made available to users in either microfiche or paper copy reproductions. Alternative availability instructions are always cited for the small number of items ERIC cannot make available.

The document delivery arm of ERIC is the ERIC Document Reproduction Service (EDRS). EDRS sells subscriptions to the total set of ERIC microfiche at a rate of 9.3¢ per fiche card. EDRS also sells microfiche copies and paper copies of documents on an on-demand basis. On-demand microfiche cost $0.97 per title (up to 5 fiche cards) and $0.20 for each additional fiche card required. On-demand paper copies cost $2.15 for 1 to 25 pages and $1.75 for each additional 25 pages required. For current prices, the most recent edition of *RIE* should always be consulted.

It is more difficult to provide copies of the journal articles announced in *CIJE* because of copyright restrictions on the original journals. However, several organizations provide reprint services and have made arrangements to reimburse the original publishers appropriately. Among these are: (1) University Microfilms International (Article Reprint Service) and (2) Institute for Scientific Information (Original Article Tear Sheet Service).

For those journals that do not permit reprints, it may be necessary to consult an original issue of the journal in a local university or public library. Some service organizations maintain relatively complete collections of the journals indexed by *CIJE*.

Microfiche

Microfiche of the documents announced in *Resources in Education* may be obtained on a monthly subscription basis from the ERIC Document Reproduction Service (EDRS). When purchased in this way, the price is a very economical 9.3¢ per microfiche card. For the period 1966 through 1981, the total ERIC microfiche collection consists of 270,795 microfiche cards, priced at $25,275.98.

Complete collections of ERIC microfiche are currently being subscribed to by approximately 700 organizations. In addition, there are several organizations which, while not currently subscribers, have substantial ERIC microfiche collections in their possession. All such organizations are listed in the biennial *Directory of ERIC Microfiche Collections*. This reference tool is arranged geographically in order to facilitate referral of users to the closest possible microfiche service point. Each entry in the directory provides the address, telephone number, contact person, collection status, services provided, and access hours.

Online Retrieval

The ERIC data base (both *RIE* and *CIJE* components) can be searched online by computer via all three of the major vendors of online retrieval services: DIALOG Information Services, System Development Corporation (SDC), and Bibliographic Retrieval Services (BRS).

ERIC was one of the very first bibliographic data bases to take advantage of this advanced technology and remains File #1, for example, among the many files offered by DIALOG.

Individuals and organizations wishing to search ERIC online need only (1) a computer terminal (that can link by phone with the online vendor's computer); and (2) an open purchase order with one or more vendors (you pay only for what you use).

Search Services

The ERIC data base (consisting of both *RIE* and *CIJE* data) is one of the most widely searched and heavily used bibliographic data bases in the world today. Approximately 50 organizations all over the world (including all the major online vendors) purchase the ERIC tapes and provide computerized access to them. Via these primary sources, several hundred service centers that provide computer searches of ERIC to various classes of users can be identified. The *Directory of ERIC Search Services*, a biennial compilation, attempts to identify these sources and to provide complete entries describing the address, telephone number, contact person, population served, price, turnaround time, services provided, files accessed, how to submit an inquiry, and search system used. The 1981 *Directory* lists over 500 service points. It is estimated that over 250,000 computer searches are made of the ERIC file each year by these service centers.

Question-Answering Services

In the course of a year, all the ERIC components combined answer more than 100,000 written and telephoned inquiries from users. Many of these inquiries are requests involving identification of specific documents and can be answered fairly rapidly and simply. This type of request is best directed to the ERIC Processing and Reference Facility (the ERIC Facility).

Many other requests, however, involve some level of subject expertise in the development of a customized response. Within the ERIC system, subject expertise resides primarily within the various specialized ERIC clearinghouses, which will accept questions in their subject areas. Clearinghouse scopes can usually be determined from their names; however, there is a flyer available from the ERIC Facility that contains detailed scope notes for each clearinghouse. For inquiries involving computer searches, cost recovery is normally sought. Referrals to other organizations where computer searches or other information services may be purchased are also made, as appropriate.

Information Analysis

In addition to collecting the literature of education for announcement in *RIE* and *CIJE*, the ERIC clearinghouses analyze and synthesize the literature into research reviews, knowledge syntheses, state-of-the art studies, interpretive studies on topics of high current interest, and many similar documents designed to compress the vast amount of information available and to meet the needs of ERIC users. These products constitute new contributions to the literature by ERIC.

ERIC information analysis products are published by the individual ERIC clearinghouses responsible for producing them. As long as stocks last, original copies are usually available directly from the responsible clearinghouse. In addition, information analysis products are generally announced in *RIE*. When announced in *RIE*, they are contained in all ERIC microfiche collections and may be ordered in microfiche or paper copy from: ERIC Document Reproduction Service (EDRS), P.O. Box 190, Arlington, VA 22210. Full ordering details and current prices are to be found in *RIE*.

Periodically, ERIC prepares bibliographies of its information analysis products and other major publications. These may be obtained by writing to the ERIC Facility. Through 1981, ERIC has published 3,835 information analysis products.

CURRENT STATUS AND FUTURE OUTLOOK

With level budgeting for most of the past decade, ERIC has managed to keep its basic operations going, but has been unable to expand its coverage to include other types of educational resources or to make various capital (mostly equipment) improvements that would enhance its internal technical capabilities. With less than $5 million a year, at the present time ERIC funds its entire network of 16 clearinghouses and various commercial support groups. Several of the commercial arrangements are at no cost to the government, with the commercial organization permitted to make use of the ERIC data, selling it to the public at a price low enough to encourage dissemination, but sufficient to support the providing of the service itself: e.g., the ERIC Document Reproduction Service (currently operated by CMIC, Inc.) and the three major vendors of online retrieval against large bibliographic files (currently BRS, DIALOG, and SDC). It is only through such symbiotic uses of the commercial sector that ERIC can achieve its dissemination objectives given the erosion of its level budget when adjusted for inflation.

Despite these handicaps, ERIC has built a substantial data base (about a half million items through 1982), with an excellent reputation, and has gradually brought the data base to the attention of the very large and diverse educational community. Recent studies estimate that over the past five years 1.25 million individuals have received some training in the use of ERIC.

With the future of the National Institute of Education and the entire Department of Education being debated by the administration as of this writing, it is difficult to predict what will happen to ERIC in the decade of the 80s. It is believed, however, that over the last 20 years ERIC has become an information fixture in the lives of hundreds of thousands, if not millions, of educators and students who have come to depend on ERIC's unique data base to assess the current state-of-the-art and to avoid duplication of effort. This substantial constituency among the country's largest professional community, coupled with ERIC's frugal budget, will, it is hoped, lead to its continued survival and evolutionary improvement.

Federal Libraries

THE LIBRARY OF CONGRESS

Washington, DC 20540
202-287-5000

James W. McClung
Public Information Specialist

In 1982, the Library of Congress accomplished several major goals and targeted several new ones that will become the focus of the Library's attention in the years to come. The first large-scale mass deacidification test of books was completed successfully, and the first contracts let to explore the application of optical disk technology to the Library's collections. The development and further refinement of collections development guidelines and the expansion of the project to inventory the collections went hand in hand with the exploration of a new preservation and retrieval system. Beginning in 1983, the *National Union Catalog* will be published only in microfiche and will be produced from an automated data base, ending nearly 30 years of manual production of the printed catalog. In 1982, 99 percent of the staff scheduled to move into the Madison Building had done so, bringing nearly to completion the occupancy project begun three years before. The Law Library of the Library of Congress, its oldest separately established department, celebrated its one hundred fiftieth anniversary in 1982 with an exhibit of some of its treasures and of a pictorial history of its development and with a reception at which Associate Justice Byron R. White of the U.S. Supreme Court and American Bar Association president Morris Harrell were honored guests. The Library was also active during the year in its preparation and coordination of a response to the U.S. Office of Personnel Management (OPM) proposal to revise the qualifications and position classification standards for librarians, library technicians, and technical information specialists. OPM subsequently dropped the proposal to divide the series into professional and nonprofessional categories and, by the end of the fiscal year, agreed to revise the proposed criteria for writing job descriptions for librarians in order to make them more in keeping with traditional standards. [See the report on "The New Federalism: How It Is Changing the Library Profession in the United States" in the Special Reports section of Part 1—*Ed.*]

PRESERVATION

The Library conducted the first large-scale test of its mass paper deacidification process in the fall of 1982. Using a large vacuum chamber originally designed to test satellites destined for outer space, the Library put 5,000 books through a week-long DEZ (diethyl zinc) deacidification treatment that is aimed at extending the life of book paper and other valuable papers for at least four times their anticipated current life span of 25 to 100 years.

The pilot project was beset with technical challenges. Quite apart from the initial challenges in the design of the project, the extreme volatility of DEZ presented unique shipping problems that were finally solved. In addition to items from the Library of Congress, six other organizations were invited to submit materials for the project so that they could also evaluate the process. They were the Yale University Library, Stanford University Library, the U.S. National Archives and Records Service, New York Public Library, Columbia University Library, and Northeast Document Conservation Center.

A second significant achievement in 1982 was the awarding of contracts to Teknekron Controls, Inc., and SONY Video Communications Products Company for the development of an optical disk-based image preservation and retrieval system. The research and development to be conducted by these companies will determine whether or not it will be feasible to capture the image of original documents in digital format and store these images in a random fashion for display on a video display terminal at a later date. Additional requirements include small-volume printing on remote printers and large-volume batch printing on a centrally located printer. Items from a number of collections, totaling about 854,800 images per year, have been selected to be used in the pilot project.

A special all-day conference in June on "Preservation and New Technology" attracted an invited audience of more than 60 representatives of university and private publishing houses, foundations, and libraries. Participants heard about and discussed the problems of lack of space and the physical deterioration of printed materials and the solutions to these problems devised by both publishers and libraries. They also dealt with the implications of these solutions—electronic or other compact storage and retrieval of information—for publishers and librarians in the areas of copyright law, cost, censorship, and reference service.

Several major works from the Library's Presevation Office were published in 1982. They represent the first publications of the National Preservation Program and a continuing contribution to a cooperative national preservation effort. (They are for sale from the Superintendent of Documents, U.S. Government Printing Office, Washington, DC 20402, for the prices indicated.)

Boxes for the Protection of Rare Books: Their Design and Construction (Stock No. 030-000-001-249; $18) is a comprehensive review of several conservation techniques developed at the Library and is intended to serve as a standard reference tool in the field. It is the outgrowth of the "Workshop Notes" used in the Restoration Office as in-house instructional material. *Matting and Hinging of Works of Art on Paper* (Stock No. 030-000-00134-6; $2.75) thoroughly reviews the conservation techniques that are used at the Library and is directed to practicing paper conservators, custodians, and curators who wish to utilize the latest methods for matting and hinging important works of art on paper. *Bookbinding and the Conservation of Books* (Stock No. 030-000-00126-0; $27) approaches conservation by examining the meaning and usage of many terms, expressions, and names pertinent to the field. The definitions were drawn from the most authoritative sources available and supplemented by the lengthy professional experience of the authors. It provides a history of the craft of bookbinding, the materials used, and acknowledges many notable binders.

JAMES MADISON MEMORIAL BUILDING

On December 7, 1979, the first Library unit to occupy space in the Madison Building was relocated to new quarters there. On December 7, 1982, the new Performing Arts Reading Room (formerly the Music Reading Room) opened in the new building, and as of that date 3,364 staff members—99 percent of the final projected occupancy—had been relocated.

In addition to the Music Division, the Library's collections of prints, photographs, serials, and government publications were transferred to the Madison Building in 1982.

The new Newspaper and Current Periodical Room reopened in May and the Prints and Photographs Reading Room in September. All three of the new reading rooms offer expanded and enhanced facilities to provide better service to readers.

At year's end, the move of the Motion Picture, Broadcasting and Recorded Sound Division was scheduled for early 1983. The division will occupy new listening facilities in the Performing Arts Reading Room as well as a new Motion Picture Reading Room and a small theater.

All remaining administrative and support offices scheduled for relocation to the Madison Building were also moved in 1982. Thus, with only the one division left to move, the Madison Building—more than 25 years in conception, design, and construction—is now a fully operational reality.

In December, the building's Assembly Room was renamed the L. Quincy Mumford Room in memory of the former Librarian of Congress (1954-1974) who died in August.

NATIONAL LIBRARY SERVICE FOR THE BLIND AND PHYSICALLY HANDICAPPED (NLS/BPH)

The circulation of braille and recorded books and magazines through the services of this Library program grew to a record 18 million pieces to 668,000 readers by the end of fiscal year 1982. Program emphasis during the year was on increased response to consumer needs, on the application of ALA public service standards to network agencies, and the application of quality control standards to production systems.

The evaluation of consumer response to NLS/BPH programs addressed the design, conduct, and analysis of effective reader surveys. The evaluation also studied such topics as how to organize and use consumer advisory committees and included the preparation of procedures manuals for use by library staff in working with consumers. The cassette-braille evaluation, which had lasted two years, was completed. The main findings are a high reader acceptability of the cassette-braille concept, a need for greater reliability of the braille-display system, and a need for significant cost reductions of the equipment. The evaluation also made specific suggestions for design improvements.

A review of regional libraries and multi-state centers based on the American Library Association's *Standards of Service for the Library of Congress Network of Libraries for the Blind and Physically Handicapped* was completed. The 56 regional libraries, four multi-state centers, and NLS/BPH itself were evaluated against the standards, and a written report was submitted to each agency with a copy to its administering agency. A separate summary report analyzing how the network is meeting the standards was submitted to NLS/BPH.

NLS/BPH continued to refine operating procedures, specifications, and testing techniques to improve the quality and timeliness of delivery of books, magazines, and equipment. Major evaluations continue in the areas of braille usage and high-speed production of braille on demand. Continued efforts in these areas are required to reduce costs and improve delivery performance. NLS also refined its inspection procedures for cassette books to provide for the first time a comprehensive assessment of all copies duplicated and shipped. An outgoing inspection program for cassette books was implemented at all manufacturers and a new crosstalk requirement for duplication was developed. Reporting procedures were developed for manufacturers, who now report monthly on cassette books and equipment warranty returns, lot inspections, and related items.

"The Sound and Touch of Reading," a 20-minute audiovisual program about the talking book program, was completed and is available on loan to network libraries and other agencies. A companion print publication, *An Introduction to the National Library Service for the Blind and Physically Handicapped*, was also completed. A permanent exhibit, "Braille, Bebop, and Bach," was installed at the Kennedy Center Library for the Performing Arts. A demonstration collection of selected music scores, books about music, and other recorded and braille reading materials about the arts, plus reference materials, accompanies the exhibit.

STAFF, BUDGET, AND SERVICES

At the end of FY 1982, there were 5,245 persons in the Library's employ, up slightly from 1981. The size of the Library staff has remained relatively unchanged over the past half decade.

For the present fiscal year, the Library has an operating budget of $215,179,000 authorized by PL 97-276, which funds Library operations through September 30, 1983. A total of $5,071,000 was approved for the architect of the Capitol for the structural and mechanical care of the Library buildings. One item covered by this appropriation is the continuing installation of automatic sprinklers in the bookstacks of both the Library's older buildings to help alleviate existing fire and safety hazards. Work on this project, several years in the planning, actually got under way in August and is expected to be completed in 18 months.

In FY 1982, direct reference services—via telephone, correspondence, or visit in person—totaled 1,350,000 requests. The Law Library Reading Room saw a better than 24 percent increase in in-person requests in its new Madison Building facility over FY 1981. More than 2,873,000 volumes or items were circulated inside the Library, and more than 118,000 outside the Library. The Congressional Research Service (CRS) responded in 1982 more than 430,000 times to the legislative, oversight, and representational needs of the Congress, clearing 45,600 requests—an all-time high—in August, normally one of the slower months for congressional activity. Record numbers of CRS products were distributed to congressional staff again in 1982. More than 2,150,000 people visited the Library buildings in FY 1982.

The Library conducted its second annual Cooperative Reference Exchange, part of the continuing effort to develop and extend services to the national library community, in September. Twenty-six senior reference staff members and managers from 23 states, from Maine to Louisiana, and including several in the West and Midwest, attended this year's week-long orientation.

Cultural services during 1982 included the Library's first Summer Chamber Festival—a series of five concerts by a dozen young musicians from around the world who were in residence at the Library during June—and, in observance of Scandinavia Today, a series of three chamber concerts, an evening of Scandinavian poetry, a lecture during National Children's Book Week by Swedish author Astrid Lindgren, and a symposium on children's books with four Scandinavian experts, all held during the fall. From September 30 to October 1, the Library held the first in a series of international symposia celebrating the one hundredth anniversary of the birth of José Ortega y Gasset.

The Center for the Book in 1982 completed its third and opened its fourth season of a cooperative project with CBS Television to prepare "Read More About It" announcements to be aired at the conclusion of selected CBS specials. The announcements suggest two or three good books on the subject of the special that are drawn from longer lists prepared by Library bibliographers. The lists are also published before the telecasts in library and book trade publications and distributed to libraries and bookstores. In May, the center and the National Endowment for the Arts (NEA) cosponsored a symposium celebrating the establishment of the NEA Small Press Collections in the Library's Rare

Book and Special Collections Division. "Books Make a Difference," a cooperative project of the Center for the Book to interview people throughout the United States about books that shaped their lives, was the subject of a special poster session at the 1982 ALA annual conference and inspired a national contest for students cosponsored by the center and by the editors of *Read*, a student magazine published by Xerox Educational Publications. In 1982, the center celebrated an Irish autumn with lectures by former Irish national librarian Alf MacLochlainn and Dan H. Laurence, literary and dramatic advisor to the estate of Bernard Shaw. The Library also marked the centenary of the birth of James Joyce with a lecture by Richard Ellmann early in 1982.

The American Folklife Center completed its first study called for by legislative mandate—the *Cultural Conservation Report*—and submitted it to the president and the Congress in December. The culmination of a year-long effort, the report addressed the significant omission of "important areas of the life of ethnic, occupational, religious, and regional groups in the United States from the protection afforded by existing historic preservation laws."

The center's Federal Cylinder Project, now into its third year, continued to duplicate cylinders on tape, to locate other cylinders held by U.S. government agencies, to identify and catalog materials on previously duplicated cylinders, and to plan the project's catalog publication program. A new task initiated by the center in 1982 is the Ethnic Heritage and Language Schools Project, which will document the history and status of such institutions.

In 1982, the center sponsored a symposium on the marketing of phonograph records of American folk expression, published *Ethnic Recordings in American: A Neglected Heritage* (based on a 1977 conference, the work is available from GPO; Stock No. 030-001-00098-2; $13), and issued a new two-record, long-playing album, *Children of the Heav'nly King: Religious Expression in the Central Blue Ridge* (available for $14 from the Library of Congress, Motion Picture, Broadcasting and Recorded Sound Division, Washington, DC 20540). Center programs during the year included six outdoor summer concerts offering music from Ireland, the Appalachian region, Africa, Japan, and Mexico, and winter events on British folk music, Easter egg decorating, Halloween, and wheat weaving.

A major project of the center in cooperation with other Library offices over the past several years has been the preparation for "The American Cowboy," a major exhibition scheduled to open at the Library on March 26, 1983. For that project, the center is cooperating on the production of a video disk that will incorporate materials created during its documentary project in Paradise Valley, Nevada.

COLLECTIONS

Although the Library's collections grew at a somewhat slower rate than over the past four years, the total number of items in its holdings at the end of FY 1982 nonetheless approached the 80 million mark. The rate of acquisition of microforms remained high.

A unified collections development effort continued to be a focus of Librarywide concern in 1982 and will remain so in the years to come. In addition to acquisitions, the Collections Development Office emphasized the control, preservation, custody, and management of the collections. The trend toward more integrated collections development policies is both accelerating and becoming more compelling. What the Library acquires and how these materials are handled at the time of receipt and in following years can no longer be treated as separate and unrelated functions. It is to be expected that the imperatives of space, preservation, and the new technologies that are transforming Library operations will in the next two decades underscore the need for such integrated policies.

Specific activities in support of this effort have included new acquisitions guidelines for materials in clinical medicine and technical agriculture, revised guidelines for acquisitions of microforms, especially in light of GPO's decision to issue a higher percentage of its publications in microform, and an accelerated replacement of long runs of bound serials. The project to conduct a comprehensive inventory of the collections got a boost with congressional authorization to create 20 new temporary jobs for this purpose. Perhaps the first comprehensive inventory of all the general collections in the Library's history, the project not only will count the collections for the obvious purposes of an itemized inventory of what is accounted for and what is missing, but also will examine the collections systematically for preservation purposes (including restoration and replacement by microfilm) and for errors in shelflisting, cataloging, or labeling, will weed the collections of nonessential volumes, and will recommend replacement of lost volumes. The pilot project begun in 1979 inventoried works in philosophy and religion, the auxiliary sciences of history, and some American history. The formal inventory has completed a review of works in naval science, and a review of political science, military science, and medicine is under way.

Notable gifts to the Library in FY 1982 included Manuscript Division acquisitions of oral histories conducted by the former members of Congress, the records of ERAmerica, and papers of author and editor Norman Podhoretz, former U.S. Secretary of Education Shirley Hufstedler, journalist John Osborne, author James Michener, and former Librarian of Congress Archibald MacLeish, who died in April 1982. The MacLeish manuscripts include an outstanding group of 22 letters from Ernest Hemingway, written in the 1930s. The Music Division acquired manuscripts of Erich Korngold, Ferde Grofé, Mendelssohn, and Brahms. A special effort was concentrated on the acquisition and preservation of Brahms material in anticipation of the international Brahms conference to be held at the Library of Congress in May 1983. The Library's prints, photographic, rare book, map, recorded sound, and motion picture collections also benefited from a number of gifts in 1982.

Once again, legislation was introduced in the Ninety-seventh Congress to restore a tax deduction for the donation of self-generated manuscripts and artwork materials to libraries, museums, and other nonprofit institutions equal to the fair market value of the materials donated. Since the deduction was disallowed by the Tax Reform Act of 1969, the Library of Congress and other libraries have been largely unable to attract significant gifts of such materials.

Enhancements to the retrieval systems and the growth of the Library's data bases continued to improve reader and staff access to the collections and information about them. The new Nitrate Film Control System, put into operation in October, is an online inventory control and tracking system for this most important Library collection.

CATALOGING AND NETWORKING

Following analysis of a 1981 survey, the Library announced that it will begin production of the *National Union Catalog* (*NUC*) in microfiche in 1983. An online system, inaugurated in 1982 to input records contributed to the *NUC* by the Library of Congress and some 1,500 other reporting institutions, will be used to produce the catalog in a register/index format. It will consist of four registers—*Books, U.S. Books, Audiovisual Materials,* and *Cartographic Materials*—each having a name, title, subject, and series index; the *Cartographic Materials* catalog will also have a geographic classification index. These COM (computer output microform) publications, produced by means of software developed by the National Library of Canada, will be sold by the Cataloging Distribution Service, Library of Congress, Attn: *NUC* Desk, Washington, DC 20541. The publication of the registers will be continuous rather than cumulative and will thus avoid the problems of the expensive paper edition of the previous *NUC*. The indexes will be cumulative.

In August 1982, the Cataloging Distribution Service (CDS) dedicated the DEMAND System, an optical disk-based storage, preservation, and printing system that allows CDS to access and reproduce on demand more than 5.5 million catalog cards in hundreds of different languages that are not in machine-readable form. Together with CARDS, the system for the on-demand production of cards from machine-readable records, DEMAND means the prompt fulfillment of libraries' orders for catalog cards without the necessity of maintaining a large inventory of stock. The CDS Customer Information Management System (CIMS), which became operational in December 1981, has also improved service to Library customers. CIMS has dramatically facilitated the processing of orders (no backlogs), claims (declining backlogs), and the accuracy and control of order-filling activities.

An important step forward in the cataloging of microforms, an ever growing and more important part of the Library's collections, was achieved in mid-1982 when the processing staff of the Microform Reading Room began online cataloging of these publications. The new online name authority file also became operational in 1982, and the Name Authority Cooperative Project (NACO) processed nearly 26,000 authority records contributed by 24 participating libraries, a more than 100 percent increase over 1981.

The Network Development Office continued to analyze the Library's role in the international exchange of MARC (machine-readable cataloging) information in 1982. Specifications for the conversion of records in the US MARC format into the UNIMARC (international MARC) format have been prepared, and the Library expects to be able to distribute its MARC data in the UNIMARC format in the coming year. Specifications were also prepared for the conversion of British MARC records into the US MARC format with the expectation that the Library will be able to distribute these through its MARC Distribution Service. At year's end, the number of records in the MARC Books data base had exceeded 1,600,000, and projects to implement or develop online cataloging of other types of material continued apace.

During the year, Library staff members compiled cataloging manuals for graphic materials and for manuscripts and archival materials to supplement the new *Anglo-American Cataloguing Rules*. A new guide, *Standard Citation Forms*, for rare book catalogers, appeared at year's end. They are all for sale from the Cataloging Distribution Service.

OTHER PUBLICATIONS AND EXHIBITS

Publications and exhibitions represent an important facet of the Library's continuing effort to share its resources with a larger public. In addition to those described elsewhere in this report, several bibliographies and guides and exhibits of representative items from virtually every type of Library collection constituted a significant contribution to public awareness of the Library of Congress. (Publications, except where noted otherwise, are available from the Superintendent of Documents, U.S. Government Printing Office, Washington, DC 20402.)

Pickaxe and Pencil: References for the Study of the WPA (Stock No. 030-000-00137-1; $6) is an 87-page bibliography of books and articles, both contemporary and from the period, describing the various programs of the Work Projects Administration.

Volume 8 of *Letters of Delegates to Congress, 1774-1789*, covering the period September 19, 1777-January 31, 1778, continues the projected 25-volume publication documenting comprehensively this important point in American history (volume 8, Stock No. 030-000-00119-2; $17.50), and volume 1 of *Musical Instruments in the Dayton C. Miller Flute Collection at the Library of Congress, A Catalog* (Stock No. 030-000-00135-4; $15) launches a projected seven-volume publication to describe and illustrate the collection of more than 1,600 flutes and other woodwind instruments left to the Library in 1941. *Literary Recordings: A Checklist of the Archive of Recorded Poetry and Literature in the Library of Congress* (Stock No. 030-001-00084-2; $8.50) describes another important collection, as does *Radio Broadcasts in the Library of Congress, 1924-1941* (Stock No. 030-000-00139-7; $10). Other valuable new publications included *Maps and Charts of North America and the West Indies, 1750-1789* (Stock No. 030-004-00020-5; $17), *The Canon Law Collection of the Library of Congress* (Stock No. 030-000-00123-1; $11), and *Vietnamese Holdings in the Library of Congress* (Stock No. 030-000-00136-2; $13).

Other new publications (available from the Library of Congress, Information Office, Box A, Washington, DC 20540, for the price indicated plus $2 per order for shipping and handling) included the first full-color *Guide to the Library of Congress* ($5.95) in the institution's 182-year history and *The 1812 Catalogue of the Library of Congress: A Facsimile* ($15). Free publications included reports on manuscripts and rare books in the series, Library of Congress Acquisitions, and the first bibliographies in two new series, Mideast Directions and Hispanic Focus. Persons interested in these and other Library publications should write to the Library of Congress, Central Services Division, Washington, DC 20540, for a free copy of *Library of Congress Publications in Print*, of *Library of Congress Selected Publications, 1982*, or of the *Card and Gift Catalog, 1982-1983*.

Major exhibitions in 1982 included the annual display of the prize-winning work of the White House News Photographers Association (which will become a traveling exhibit), portrait photography of Bern Schwartz on view at the Performing Arts Library in the Kennedy Center, and "A Nation of Readers," a project supported by the Book-of-the-Month Club, Inc., to show examples of works that reflect the history of reading in the United States. Other new exhibits included "Currier and Ives Revisited," "Bird's Eye Views: Panoramic Maps of North American Cities," and "Levine, Osborn, and Sorel," cartoons from the Caroline and Erwin Swann Memorial Exhibit of Satire and Caricature.

NATIONAL LIBRARY OF MEDICINE

8600 Rockville Pike, Bethesda, MD 20209
301-496-6308

Robert B. Mehnert
Public Information Officer

The National Library of Medicine (NLM) was the subject of two important studies issued by offices of the U.S. Congress in 1982. Their scope is suggested by the titles: "National Library of Medicine's Medical Literature Analysis and Retrieval System," by the General Accounting Office, and "MEDLARS and Health Information Policy," by the

Office of Technology Assessment. The studies were requested by members of the Congress responding to the concerns expressed by some in the information industry that NLM's computer-based retrieval services (MEDLARS/MEDLINE) are in unfair competition with information services of the commercial sector.

The report by the General Accounting Office (GAO), released in April, reviewed the capital and operating costs for MEDLARS and its associated products and services, the percentage of costs recovered through user charges, patterns of domestic use of the system, and the legality and propriety of NLM's cost-recovery policies. The study made two recommendations to modify slightly the way computer time and offline page charges are calculated. The needed changes have already been made to implement these recommendations; as a result the library has increased its rate of cost-recovery for online access and tape use from 95 to 100 percent. A third recommendation by the GAO is that NLM should "assess charges which would recover the full costs of providing service to those users not directly involved in health-related activities." This recommendation will receive further study. It would be difficult to identify these users because some, such as law firms and information brokers, that do not appear to be involved in health-related activities, may in fact be providing vital health-related information services to their clients.

These recommendations notwithstanding, the GAO study leaves no doubt that fundamentally the library's present practices are appropriate. The report concludes: "NLM's pricing policy for establishing user charges to recover those costs associated with accessing the MEDLARS data bases appears consistent with existing statutes and regulations. In addition, the methods NLM used to identify MEDLARS-related costs and determine its user charges seem reasonable."

The Office of Technology Assessment (OTA) released its report in September. The study was conducted by OTA analysts guided by 20 experts from the health community and from the information community, both public and private, for-profit and not-for-profit. The resulting 150-page report explored in some detail the development and current status of MEDLARS and the conditions under which MEDLARS-delivered services and products are made available to the biomedical community. Between the preface, which announced prospectively that "in most respects MEDLARS is an efficient system for disseminating health-related bibliographic information," and the last chapter, which concluded that "the creation of MEDLINE by the Library seems to be warranted by NLM's extensive collection of biomedical materials, by its legislative mandate, and on economic grounds," is an extensive collection of data and information on which these statements are based.

A third, broader study, *Public Sector/Private Sector Interaction in Providing Information Services*, by an independent task force of the National Commission on Libraries and Information Science (NCLIS), also has important implications for the NLM. This report calls on the federal government to "take a leadership role in creating a framework which would facilitate the development and foster the use of information products and services." Another of its principles states that "the Federal Government should actively use existing mechanisms, such as the libraries of the country, as primary channels for making governmentally distributable information available to the public." These injunctions have no more apposite illustration than the Regional Medical Library Network and the online bibliographic retrieval network, both developed under the leadership of NLM and using existing local, state, and regional institutions to provide coordinated information services to health professionals. [A summary of the *Public Sector/Private Sector* report appears in the Special Reports section of Part 1 of this volume—*Ed.*]

NETWORK SERVICES

The subject of the GAO and OTA studies—MEDLARS and its associated products and services—continues to enjoy widespread acceptance by the health community. The number of U.S. institutions with online access to NLM's data bases has grown to 1,850. Actual searches reached a new high of two and a quarter million in fiscal year 1982. These figures do not include foreign use of the system or the considerable volume of searching done by subscribers of Lockheed DIALOG and Bibliographic Retrieval Services, Inc. (BRS), both of which mount several of NLM's data bases on their extensive retrieval systems.

The acquisition this year of a new computer system (IBM 3033 multi-processor) has doubled the library's processing capacity and has led to several important changes in the MEDLARS online services. In December NLM announced that all MEDLINE backfiles were available for online search and retrieval. Previously, files of older references (back to 1966) were accessible only through offline prints. The new computers also made it possible to discontinue the arrangement with the State University of New York at Albany through which reliable backup and supplementary computer services had been supplied to the network for almost ten years. Adequate computing capacity is now ensured well into the mid 1980s, even allowing for parallel development and testing of third-generation MEDLARS enhancements while coping with day-to-day service workloads.

The extensive reconfiguration of the Regional Medical Library Network, announced in 1981, will be completed early in 1983. This year was devoted to the considerable task of soliciting and reviewing proposals from major health-science libraries seeking to serve as Regional Medical Libraries. The thoughtful planning that went into it should do much to ease the transition from eleven U.S. regions to seven and to ensure that document delivery and other vital information services continue uninterrupted.

LIBRARY OPERATIONS

An important indicator of how well the NLM is discharging its responsibilities as a "library's library" is the fulfillment rate for providing interlibrary loans. (See Table 1.) These figures remained high in 1982, for both original materials and photocopies, at 83 percent and 89 percent respectively. The great majority of these requests were filled within four days of receipt. This is the fifth year that the number of requests has declined, a trend that may reflect the greater availability of local and regional locator tools, the increasing number and efficiency of consortia meeting local and regional needs, and the recent trend toward imposing fees for interlibrary loans in the network. Whatever the reasons, it re-

TABLE 1   SELECTED STATISTICS, 1982*

Collection (printed and audiovisual)	3,044,400
Serial titles received	23,700
Articles indexed for MEDLARS	305,200
Titles cataloged	30,000
Circulation requests filled	340,800
For interlibrary loan	178,200
For readers	162,600
Computerized searches (U.S., all data bases)	2,251,700
Online	1,680,000
Offline	571,700

*For the year ending September 30, 1982.

mains true that NLM receives primarily requests for materials that are difficult to fill or unavailable elsewhere.

When NLM closed its card catalog in 1981, a public-access catalog was planned as the long-term alternative. This year staff completed a study to compare the performance of two prototype online catalog systems developed at the library: CITE (Current Information Transfer in English) and ILS (Integrated Library System). NLM patrons who used the system were asked to provide information detailing their experience and eliciting their reaction to being confronted with a terminal rather than a traditional card catalog. A concurrent project, to put into machine-readable form all pre-1965 catalog records, is nearing completion. Thus, it is expected that when the permanent public-access online catalog is installed in 1983 it will allow rapid and convenient searching of all catalog records for the library's collections.

A new unit, the Audiovisual Resources Section, was formed within the Reference Services Division. Its functions, largely transferred from the National Medical Audiovisual Center, are to handle reference inquiries about audiovisual materials, lend films and videocassettes, develop an archival film program, and operate a Learning Resource Center for patrons.

The development continues of MEDLARS III, an enhanced automation sytem to improve both internal processing of the literature at NLM and bibliographic services to the entire network. By the end of the year, an invitation for competitive bidding was issued to the commercial sector to design, develop, and implement the system. It is expected that a contract will be awarded in 1983. Meanwhile, several interim improvements have already been implemented, including a "front-end cataloging" system whereby catalogers are able to input catalog data directly online. A similar system for indexers is under development.

A signal event in 1982 was the publication of *A History of the National Library of Medicine: The Nation's Treasury of Medical Knowledge*. Compiled by Wyndham D. Miles, Ph.D., of the History of Medicine Division, this 500-page casebound and illustrated work traces the library's development from the early nineteenth century through its development as an international biomedical information center.

LISTER HILL NATIONAL CENTER FOR BIOMEDICAL COMMUNICATIONS

The Lister Hill Center, the research and development component of the library, explores the application of advanced computer and communications technology to improving the organization, dissemination, and utilization of biomedical information. This year saw continued progress on a number of important projects begun earlier:

The Knowledge Base Research Program has the goal of finding new ways to structure medical knowledge, to organize it, and to represent it in the computer in ways that can be responsive to the information needs of health-care professionals. The current emphasis in this program is on representing medical knowledge in the computer—compiling specific vocabularies for different medical areas and developing methods for logically and physically restructuring the information for the computer.

The Electronic Document Storage and Retrieval Program addresses a major mission of the NLM, namely, to provide for archival storage of the biomedical literature. The immediate objective is to develop a prototype system to demonstrate the feasibility of such features as scanning, storage, retrieval, and reproduction of black and white (two-tone) materials from books and journals. A looseleaf scanning capability has been developed and a bound-volume scanner will be completed in 1983. Hardware interfaces have been developed to link the various subsystems, including the hardcopy (paper), softcopy (screen), and dual-mode hardcopy/softcopy devices. Software is being developed for the system controller to exercise supervision and control over the entire system.

The Integrated Library System (ILS) is a computer-based system to handle the main functions of libraries. Successive versions of the ILS have been made available through the National Technical Information Service and it is now operational in a number of libraries, medical and nonmedical. Since the project is nearing the completion of its R & D phases, NLM is planning for an orderly transition of the ILS to the user community.

Under a pending reorganization, the functions of NLM's National Medical Audiovisual Center (NMAC) will be integrated with those of the Lister Hill Center. Until then, NMAC continues its functions within a structure of three branches and the Learning Resources Laboratory. A fourth branch, the Materials Utilization Branch, was transferred to Library Operations as the Audiovisual Resource Section in 1982. Among the activities continuing in 1982 were a series of studies and evaluations (for example, of the online public access catalog and the film and videocassette loan program), training in audiovisual instruction techniques through workshops in Bethesda and at field sites, the production of slides, videotapes, audiotapes, and other audiovisual and graphic materials, and the development of experimental computer-based education materials using microcomputers and optical video-discs.

TOXICOLOGY INFORMATION PROGRAM

This is the fifteenth year since the Toxicology Information Program (TIP) was established at the National Library of Medicine in response to the recommendation of the President's Science Advisory Committee. The objectives of the program are to create computerized toxicology data bases and to provide toxicology information products and services to the scientific community.

A new project, begun in 1982, is to develop the Hazardous Substances Information Services, a system that would efficiently provide toxicology and related information to health officials responsible for assessing the hazards from chemicals present in waste disposal sites or major accidental spills. One approach will be to enhance existing data bases like NLM's Toxicology Data Bank with additional factual data on hazardous chemicals.

TIP continues to provide a variety of data bases through the library's online network: TOXLINE (toxicology information online), CHEMLINE (chemical dictionary online), RTECS (Registry of Toxic Effects of Chemical Substances), and TDB (Toxicology Data Bank). Several publications (in addition to the monthly *TOX-TIPS*) made their appearance in 1982: two bibliographies on the health effects of environmental chemicals and the proceedings of the Symposium on Information Transfer in Toxicology, sponsored by TIP in 1981.

GRANT PROGRAMS

The Medical Library Assistance Act is the legislation under which the library provides support for improving health-science library resources and services, conducting research to improve biomedical communications, training health information personnel, publishing critical reviews and other works on important health topics, and the Regional Medical Library Network. In Fiscal Year 1982 the library made 110 grants and contracts under the act's authorities, for a total of $7.5 million (a 25 percent reduction from the previous year). Congress is presently considering legislation to renew the act for three years.

NATIONAL AGRICULTURAL LIBRARY

U.S. Dept. of Agriculture
Beltsville, MD 20705

Eugene M. Farkas

Head, Educational Resources Staff

The National Agricultural Library (NAL), marking its twentieth year as a national institution, received renewed support in 1982 for development and coordination of a nationwide network of public and private agricultural libraries and information centers. A recommendation for immediate planning of the network was made to the U.S. secretary of agriculture by an interagency federal panel following an extensive study of NAL management, operations, programs, and resources.

The panel report also proposed that an advisory council to the agriculture secretary be created to provide policy direction for the NAL, with members appointed from the library information and agricultural science communities. Other recommendations called for the broadening of the library's present 1.7 million volume collection to include more foreign materials and specialized subject areas, greater activity in international agriculture programs, and increased user fees.

HIGHLIGHTS OF NAL'S 1982 ACTIVITIES

The National Agricultural Library's ongoing programs and activities benefited during the year from the introduction of new systems and equipment, from satellites to computers, in a continuing effort to increase the speed, efficiency, and effectiveness with which agricultural information is transmitted into and out of the library's collection.

The electronic telecommunications capabilities necessary to support the projected information network were demonstrated in a number of projects. Cataloging data in computerized electronic form were sent from Iowa State University to a NAL computer at Beltsville, Maryland, and literature searches done at Beltsville were transmitted via satellite to U.S. Department of Agriculture (USDA) scientists in Saudi Arabia. The library was the receiving station for an American Library Association teleconference transmitted live from Denver, Colorado, via satellite. It also sponsored a comprehensive exhibit on aerospace remote sensing, a joint project of the Agriculture Department and the National Aeronautics and Space Administration (NASA).

Science Symposium

The impact of rapidly advancing communications technology on agricultural research was the focus of a symposium attended by more than 130 scientists, librarians, technical information specialists, and educators from across the country. Sponsored by the NAL, the Agricultural History Society, and the Associates NAL, Inc., the symposium featured speeches and discussions on the utility of information in agricultural research, its economic impact, and the role of the communications media. The future of computers in libraries and current cooperative efforts between land-grant and forestry institution libraries were other discussion topics. A computer fair featured data base demonstrations.

Rural Libraries

The NAL is participating in a major new initiative to provide agricultural information to rural Americans through the public library system. Initially, it cooperated with the Congressional Research Service in a hearing on computer-based information services in agriculture. A new program has now been launched with the Federal Extension Service to provide computer-based information to rural information centers to be set up and staffed by county librarians and extension agents.

To strengthen communications and cooperative projects among agricultural agencies and institutions at all levels, the NAL is a primary supporter of an extensive national electronic mail network linking an increasing number of state research and educational institutions with the library and other USDA agencies, including the Extension Service, Cooperative State Research Service, Economic Research Service, and the Forest Service. It is also assisting the department in the establishment of an information technology center where the latest computer technology will be demonstrated to agricultural managers working to modernize communications in the office and on the farm.

Land Tenure, Tropical Soils

Library resources and services continued to expand to meet the escalating information needs of agricultural communications and the general public. Both the collection and AGRICOLA, the NAL's bibliographic data base, were enhanced by the addition of two new adjunct files. The large international collection of the Land Tenure Center of the University of Wisconsin was made available to library users through a cooperative agreement to provide machine-readable records of the center's monographic holdings and indexed journal literature—currently 15,000 hardbound publications and 22,000 pamphlets and research reports. A tropical soils file consisting of 15,000 bibliographic entries is scheduled for mounting in early 1983. This file will also represent holdings at two land-grant institutions.

State Extension Publications

An increasing number of state 4-H and adult extension publications are being added to this high-interest subfile. Progress was made in developing programs and procedures to handle the remote offline input of such data to AGRICOLA from multistate records prepared by the Iowa Cooperative Extension Service Program. The NAL plans to extend the offline input procedures to other institutions and files.

New Publications

A landmark reference work, *The Guide to Sources of Agricultural and Biological Research*, was made available to scientists, librarians, and writers as the result of a three-year project sponsored by the National Agricultural Library. A 735-page volume with 5,779 citations covering the last 25 years, the *Guide* is based on reference collections of numerous research libraries around the world. The new book also includes material on the use of online data base files. The work was issued by the University of California in cooperation with the NAL. *International Directory of Animal Health and Disease Data Banks* and *Guidelines for the Preparation of Bibliographies* were other significant publications.

Education and Training

The online training program continued to expand in its second year in response to increased demand from librarians, technical information specialists, and scientists. A total of 15 workshops were conducted in the Washington, D.C., area and six land-grant institutions across the country. Two hundred and twenty-two persons from 32 states and 3 nations were instructed in the use of bibliographic and computerized research information systems. In addition to the basic and advanced level workshops, a third or introductory level was added, with research scientists and technicians learning how to search the AGRICOLA data base, the library's master bibliographic file. In cooperation with the Extension Service and other public and private groups, further expansion of the program to include additional data bases and new audiences was explored pursuant to recommendations made in the recent report of the interagency panel on the NAL.

International Agriculture

The NAL arranged with the National Technical Information Service for U.S. distribution of the tapes produced by AGRIS, the international bibliographic data base of the United Nations Food and Agriculture Organization (FAO). The library also is working with the National Library of Medicine (NLM) to include relevant AGRIS records in its TOXLINE data base. AGRIS may be available online in 1983 in the United States through commercial vendors. As the designated U.S. center for FAO activity, the NAL also sends monthly AGRICOLA tapes to Vienna, Austria, for incorporation of U.S. records in the AGRIS data base. The international AGROVOC vocabulary is being reviewed, and ways of putting it up for online access and maintenance are being studied.

Aquaculture

The development of a national aquaculture information service received substantial assistance from the NAL. In addition to a comprehensive bibliography, several directories—of research projects, key contacts, and information sources—are in preparation. A comprehensive, concise overview on aquaculture was published in the library's Agricultural Issues series. An exhibit on aquaculture was displayed in cooperation with the Smithsonian Institution.

Self-Guided Tour for Visitors

A 20-minute self-guided walking tour of the public areas of the National Agricultural Library Building at Beltsville, Maryland, is now being provided to visitors for the first time. The tape-recorded orientation describes the history, services, and operations of the library for those who have an interest in or wish to use the facilities. More than 1,000 visitors from the United States and abroad visited the library in fiscal year 1982. Countries represented included the People's Republic of China, the Netherlands, Germany, France, Great Britain, Brazil, Spain, and Canada. Land-grant university library directors, state extension specialists, college student groups, and librarians from the private industry were among those briefed on NAL resources and services and given tours of the facility.

NAL OFFICERS

Richard A. Farley, director; Samuel T. Waters, associate director; Eugene M. Farkas, head, Educational Resources Division; Richard A. Farley, acting chief, Information Access Division; Joseph R. Judy, chief, Information Systems Division; Wallace C. Olsen, chief, Field and Special Programs Division; Leslie A. Kulp, chief, Resource Development Division.

THE PRESIDENTIAL LIBRARIES OF THE NATIONAL ARCHIVES AND RECORDS SERVICE

Washington, DC 20408
202-523-3073

David S. Van Tassel

Archivist, Office of Presidential Libraries
National Archives and Records Service

The idea for the presidential library in its present form began when a dramatic increase in the volume of presidential papers during the New Deal era led President Franklin Roosevelt to look for new ways of caring for his papers after his presidency. Until that time, presidential papers, which were considered the private property of the president and his heirs, were either donated or sold to the United States government or to institutions outside the federal government or simply dispersed or destroyed.

On December 10, 1938, President Roosevelt announced his plan for an institution for preserving his papers and other historical materials and those of his associates. He proposed that the building be financed by popular subscription, that it be built on land donated from the Roosevelt estate at Hyde Park, and that it then be turned over to the Archivist of the United States to be administered at government expense. A joint resolution of Congress "to provide for the establishment and maintenance of the Franklin D. Roosevelt Library" was approved by President Roosevelt on July 18, 1939, in substantially the form he had proposed. The government accepted the completed building on July 4, 1940, and on June 30, 1941, the library opened its doors to the public.

In 1955, Congress passed and President Dwight Eisenhower signed PL 84-373, popularly known as the Presidential Libraries Act. Patterned after the joint resolution of 1939 that established the Roosevelt Library, the act authorizes the administrator of general services to accept for deposit the papers and other historical materials of a president or former president of the United States, together with the papers of other persons relating to or contemporary with him. It also permits the administrator to accept—or enter into an agreement to use—land, buildings, and equipment offered to the government as a presidential archival depository.

Presidential records created after January 20, 1981, will become the property of the United States under provisions of the Presidential Records Act of 1978. The establishment of presidential libraries in accordance with the act will likely remain the most effective means of administering these large and complex bodies of historical evidence.

THE PRESIDENTIAL LIBRARIES SYSTEM

Seven presidential libraries, including the Roosevelt Library, are part of the Presidential Libraries system administered by the National Archives and Records Service (NARS) of the General Services Administration.

The Harry S. Truman Library in Independence, Missouri, was built and furnished by the Harry S. Truman Library, Inc., through small contributions from many individuals and organizations. The library was dedicated and accepted as part of the national archival system in 1957.

The Dwight D. Eisenhower Library building was constructed by the Eisenhower Presidential Library Commission, with funds from a nationwide fund-raising drive, and was dedicated in 1962. That same year, on August 10, Herbert Hoover's eighty-eighth birthday, the Herbert Hoover Presidential Library, financed by the Herbert Hoover Library Corporation and constructed in West Branch, Iowa, was dedicated.

The John F. Kennedy Library Corporation began raising funds for the Kennedy Library by public subscription shortly after the president's death, but construction was long delayed. The building was completed and opened in 1979 on a site adjacent to the Columbia Point campus of the University of Massachusetts in Boston.

The University of Texas constructed the Lyndon B. Johnson Library on its Austin campus and dedicated it in 1971.

The Gerald R. Ford Library was constructed by the University of Michigan in Ann Arbor and opened in 1980. The Ford Museum, located in Grand Rapids but administered as part of the Ford Library, was opened to the public in 1981.

In addition to the fully operating libraries, NARS administers the Nixon Presidential Materials Project, in Alexandria, Virginia, and the Carter Presidential Materials Project in Atlanta, Georgia.

Richard Nixon's presidential historical materials are preserved and administered under provisions of the Presidential Recordings and Materials Preservation Act of 1974, which provides for government custody and control of materials created by the Nixon administration. The act requires GSA to process archivally the Nixon materials for eventual public access. NARS expects the first major bodies of textual materials to be ready for public access during 1983.

Carter Project archivists are processing President Jimmy Carter's papers in temporary quarters in Atlanta to ensure early public access to these materials in accordance with Carter's wishes. The Carter Library is now in the planning stages and will be located in Atlanta.

THE LIBRARIES' HOLDINGS

A president's White House papers form the core of the holdings of a presidential library. In addition to these materials, presidential libraries hold other manuscript materials accumulated by the president prior to and after his term of office. Personal papers of the president's associates, including cabinet officers and other high officials of his administration, and of his friends are also among presidential library holdings. Harry Hopkins, Henry Morgenthau, Jr., Dean Acheson, Walter Bedell Smith, Robert Kennedy, John Foster Dulles, and Drew Pearson are among the prominent public figures whose papers are in a presidential library.

The seven operating libraries and the two papers projects hold approximately 200 million pages of presidential and personal papers, more than half of which were created by the presidents and their staffs while in office. These materials constitute a nearly inexhaustible resource for the study of all aspects of presidents and the presidency for over five decades.

In addition to the paper records of the presidency, new technologies have augmented the historical record in the custody of the presidential libraries. The libraries hold more than 3 million still photographs, 10 million feet of motion picture film, and tens of thousands of hours of audiotape and videotape. Recent presidential administrations have also created computerized records, which will likely change the nature of research methods at future presidential libraries.

Oral history programs, undertaken by individual libraries, produce oral memoirs, which supplement manuscript collections. The libraries also hold the many gifts that the presidents receive from private citizens and foreign governments, as well as personal memorabilia of the presidents and their families. These three-dimensional objects have proved to be an aid in the scholarly understanding of the president and his era.

Through acquisition of books on the president and his administration and complete bibliographic information on this and related subjects, each library serves as a research center for the study of the presidency.

USE OF THE LIBRARIES

Information from presidential library holdings has become available to every American. Writers and historians have based many well-received studies on presidential library holdings, including several that have won Pulitzer, Bancroft, and Parkman prizes. More than 500 books have been based on Roosevelt Library holdings alone. Research performed at presidential libraries also has served as the basis for many textbooks. Millions of Americans have been exposed to television programs, motion pictures, and plays that have used information or copies of audiovisual holdings in the libraries. These include programs such as the ABC productions of "Eleanor and Franklin" and "Johnnie We Hardly Knew Ye," James Whitmore's one-man drama "Give 'em Hell, Harry," and the NBC series "Backstairs at the White House," as well as documentaries on recent periods or events in American history, including the Great Depression, World War II, the cold war, and the Cuban missile crisis. Copies of selected documents preserved in presidential libraries also have been incorporated into other libraries and research collections through microfilm and letterpress publication and are thereby available for use by those who may never have the opportunity to visit a presidential library.

During FY 1982, archivists at the libraries responded to more than 40,000 oral inquiries (in person or by telephone) and 12,000 mail inquiries during the year, and more than 2,500 researchers made a total of 8,235 visits to the presidential libraries.

Presidential Library Museums

Although presidential libraries originally were established primarily to serve researchers, over time they have responded to wide interest and have developed successful programs for the general public. Each presidential library presents exhibits relating to the president's life and times, significant themes of American history, and other topics specific to individual presidents. The exhibits include significant documents, still photographs, motion pictures and sound recordings, presidential memorabilia, and other materials from the libraries' holdings. In the period 1962-1982, more than 22 million visitors toured the presidential library museums, including more than 1.6 million during 1982.

Presidential library museums hold about 200,000 items gathered from many sources. A large portion of the museum holdings consists of the gifts that were given to the presidents by both the American people and foreign dignitaries. These gifts range from the humble (the Declaration of Independence done with alphabet soup characters) to the opulent (Greek antiquities, fine jewelry, and Persian rugs). Each museum has its own character, derived from the career and interests of each president. The Roosevelt Library exhibits FDR's many personal collections—of stamps, naval prints, and political items. The Hoover Library contains hundreds of meticulously hand-embroidered flour sacks, given in thanks to President Herbert Hoover by the beneficiaries of his European relief work after the First World War. The Eisenhower Museum chronicles the general's military career in a series of exhibits. The Johnson Library contains a notable collection of original political cartoons of LBJ. This personal "stamp" on each museum is also carried through the larger theme of each museum, as the exhibits seek to educate visitors about how the presidency works, in both its mundane and historic aspects, and how individual "style" contributes to the making and executing of the president's policies.

Recognizing their roles as educational institutions, presidential libraries encourage schools to use their museums as a supplement to classroom instruction. In recent years, more than 50,000 students have toured the Johnson Library museum in school groups, for example. Libraries have developed educational packages of documents and educational games to assist in the interpretation of the museums, as well as special tours for the blind and the handicapped.

Educational Programs and Scholarly Conferences

Each presidential library participates in the cultural affairs of the community in which it is located and serves as a center for educational activities. Presidential libraries work with educators in their regions and with civic groups to encourage use of the libraries and understanding of the historical study of the presidency. Several libraries hold seminars for teachers and professors to acquaint them with library resources. The Eisenhower Library has conducted workshops for students from the Topeka public schools. The Kennedy Library has worked with teachers to develop from library holdings packets of materials for classroom use and has also produced an educational film on presidential decision-making, *A Stroke of the Pen*, which encourages critical review of the complex elements of presidential decisions. The Truman Library has worked with local public schools to develop programs for students to use the resources of the library to assist in teaching American history and government.

Presidential libraries have benefited from the establishment of organizations of private individuals and associates of the president dedicated to supporting and supplementing the libraries' educational and research programs. These support groups sponsor symposia at the libraries, provide grants-in-aid to researchers using library resources, pay for special exhibits, and fund oral history programs.

Conferences and symposia form an important part of the program of the presidential libraries. In 1982, the libraries hosted several such events. The Herbert Hoover Library sponsored a conference of scholars on "The Social Philosophy of Herbert Hoover and Contemporary America." The Franklin D. Roosevelt Library was the site of the Armand Hammer Conference on Peace and Human Rights. Former President Gerald R. Ford participated in a conference titled "The Press and the Presidency" at the Ford Museum. The Dwight D. Eisenhower Library commemorated Eisenhower's role in the formation of NATO through a conference titled "Leadership in NATO." The John F. Kennedy Library hosted a series of lectures and discussions of contemporary political and social issues featuring local scholars and political figures, as well as individuals of national stature.

FUTURE OUTLOOK

With the geometric increase in the volume of paper records generated by American presidents and their staffs, presidential libraries are moving into the computer age. Recent advances in technology suggest that a portion of future presidential records will be maintained in electronic form. By the end of this decade, presidential libraries may be linked by a telecommunications network, which will permit researchers at one library to query another library through the computer. Some documents may also be available via the telecommunications system. Automation will permit the staffs of the libraries to serve their clientele with greater efficiency.

National Associations

AMERICAN BOOKSELLERS ASSOCIATION

122 East 42nd St., New York, NY 10168
212-867-9060

G. Roysce Smith
Executive Director

The American Booksellers Association (ABA), Inc., was organized in 1900 to bring together for their mutual benefit bookstores of all sizes and philosophies in one organization. On December 31, 1982, the association recorded 3,858 main stores and 695 branch stores as regular members. Publishers, wholesalers, sidelines manufacturers, and suppliers of goods and services are accepted as associate members, of which there were 656.

The ABA achieves its purposes in many ways—through publications, workshops and seminars, liaison with other segments of the industry, surveys and studies, national and regional meetings, and other related activities. It is governed by an elected board of 4 officers, 15 directors, and the immediate past president. Current officers, who will serve through May 30, 1984, are as follows: president, Donald Laing, Boulder Bookstore, Boulder, Colorado; vice president, Jean Wilson, The Book Shop, Boise, Idaho; treasurer, Jerry N. Showalter, Newcomb Hall Bookstore, University of Virginia, Charlottesville, Virginia; and secretary, Jo Ann McGreevy, New York University Book Centers, New York, New York.

The board employs a staff of 25, including G. Roysce Smith, executive director; Robert D. Hale, associate executive director; and Victoria Stanley, assistant director.

PUBLICATIONS

The ABA Book Buyer's Handbook, revised annually, lists publishers' addresses, key personnel, and the terms under which publishers do business with booksellers, e.g., discounts, co-op ad policies, and returns policies. It also contains a useful collection of supplementary information in its 575 pages. Edited by Mary Ann Tennenhouse, it is an indispensable bookselling tool. It is available only to ABA bookseller members. A copy of each of ABA's publications is sent free of cost to all bookseller members, and unless otherwise noted, to associate members. These publications are also available to nonmembers at established rates.

American Bookseller, the ABA's monthly trade magazine, began publication in September 1977. Edited by Ginger Curwen, the magazine addresses itself to the day-to-day challenges and problems of retail bookselling. Such topics as merchandising and promotion, inventory control, bookseller/publisher relations, computers, sidelines, and children's books are featured regularly in articles; media tie-ins, activities of the ABA, and those of regional bookseller associations are also covered each month in regular departments.

ABA Newswire, a weekly publication first issued in February 1973, lists advance information on author tours, book reviews, and advertising and promotion. The author listings include lectures as well as television, radio, and in-store appearances. Booksellers and librarians find this a valuable aid in ensuring that they have books on hand when demand is greatest. Also included are front page news briefs on matters of vital interest to retail booksellers. Barbara Livingston is the editor of *Newswire.*

The *ABA Basic Book List* is traditionally issued annually. A highly selective list of titles chosen by a committee of booksellers and based on actual sales records of member stores, it is intended as a guide for the neophyte bookseller or the established bookseller who may want to review what others find saleable. It is edited by Mary Ann Tennenhouse, as is the *ABA Sidelines Directory*, which contains brief articles by booksellers about sidelines and lists sources for both sidelines and store supplies and fixtures.

A Manual on Bookselling, a comprehensive textbook about establishing and maintaining a bookstore, now has over 20,000 copies in print of the third revised edition, which was published in 1980. A copy is supplied free of cost by ABA to each member store, and a trade edition for resale is published by Harmony Books, an imprint of Crown Publishers. A fourth edition is tentatively planned for 1985 publication.

In response to booksellers' growing interest in computers, ABA recently published the *ABA Evaluation of Computer Hardware & Software Vendors*, an analysis intended to guide booksellers through the perplexing maze of available computer ware. It was sent free of charge to bookstore members only (but is available to nonmembers), and is a follow-up to *ABA Computer Specifications for Independent Bookstores*, published in 1981.

WORKSHOPS AND SEMINARS

A major function of ABA is promoting professional competence through continuing bookseller education. While part of this goal can be attained through publications and through national meetings, ABA is committed to a series of highly successful training sessions, which provide more intensive advice and participation for those attending. The Booksellers School, now in its seventeenth year, is sponsored jointly by the ABA and the National Association of College Stores (NACS). Nearly 6,000 established and aspiring booksellers have attended the school. Five schools are scheduled for 1983, with three geared to experienced booksellers, one to prospective booksellers, and one for a combined audience. The basic schools will be held in Nashville, Tennessee (March); Colorado Springs, Colorado (April); and Cambridge, Massachusetts (May). A school for prospective booksellers will be held in Chicago, Illinois (March); and a combined school is tentatively scheduled for the fall on the West Coast.

BOOK PROMOTION

The ABA and the AAP (Association of American Publishers) teamed up this past year to launch a Category Paperback Bestseller List program which would highlight bestselling backlist titles for booksellers, consumers, and media. The Give-A-Book Certificate program, a national program in which book certificates could be purchased in any bookstore and redeemed in any other bookstore, was finally abandoned after a touch-and-go existence for the past six years. While it was hoped that the program would aid American readers in the way that Book Tokens have in Britain, the program suffered from insufficient advertising to the public and perhaps too, the very size of the country was a determining factor.

Along with other organizations in the book industry, ABA has been active in its support of the American Book Awards, now entering its fourth year. ABA also cooperates with other programs designed to develop and increase readership including those of The Center for the Book, the Children's Book Council, and "New York Is Book Country."

CONVENTIONS AND REGIONAL MEETINGS

Due in part to the dramatic growth of regional booksellers associations across the country, the ABA no longer sponsors regional meetings during the year. At the close of 1982, ABA records showed 21 regional associations, 7 of which sponsored regional trade shows in the previous fall. While the regional associations are not branches of nor sponsored by ABA, ABA does offer them assistance and support.

The annual ABA Convention continues to be a major event in the international book world. The 1982 Convention & Trade Exhibit was held in Anaheim, California, from May 29 to June 1. Some 17,000 booksellers, exhibitors, wholesalers, authors, and other members of the book industry were in attendance.

Authors addressing the convention included Anita Lobel, Paula Danziger, Lloyd Alexander, Jessica Savitch, Elizabeth Forsythe Hailey, Theodore White, Ntozake Shange, Calvin Trillin, and Jimmy Carter. Another 100 authors met booksellers in the autograph areas and at parties.

The 1983 Convention will be held in Dallas, Texas, from June 4 to 7.

CRITICAL ISSUES IN BOOKSELLING

The sluggish state of the economy was the major concern for retail booksellers in 1982 as they saw their own small margins shaved by double-digit inflation, and watched a number of well-known publishing houses merge or go up for sale.

Booksellers' net profits showed a decline in the third consecutive bookstore financial survey conducted in 1981 by the American Booksellers Association. The 1977 survey of ABA member stores revealed that one-half of the responding stores were not profitable when judged by a reasonable standard of financial performance. According to the 1981 survey, the number of non-profitable stores increased slightly since 1977, due to a decline in gross margin, which can be attributed to rising transportation costs and the deteriorating ability of stores to control expenses.

Unsurprisingly then, publishers' terms to retail booksellers were a prime focus of the year. Happily, 1982 saw many changes in terms which had remained static for years. One policy, dubbed "freight pass-through" even enabled the retailer to pass along some of the freight costs to the customers. Still some booksellers felt these changes were insufficient and did not address the central issue. The Northern California Booksellers Association, in conjunction with Cody's Books in Berkeley, California, and The Bookplate in San Francisco, California, filed an antitrust suit against Hearst Books in April 1982, charging the company with discriminatory pricing practices which, they claim, violate the Robinson-Patman Act. Bantam Books was added to the suit as a co-defendant in November.

The proliferation of proposed censorship legislation and attempts at book banning was another major concern to booksellers in 1982. In conjunction with the Media Coalition, the ABA supported a number of briefs as friends of the court. Sparked by the tremendous interest shown in an exhibit of banned books at the 1982 ABA Convention in Anaheim, California, the ABA sponsored with the National Association of College Stores a national Banned Books Week, September 5-11, and provided its members with posters, sample press releases, and a list of more than 500 banned books. The response was overwhelmingly enthusiastic. Booksellers with banned book displays became instant authorities for local media, and large and small newspapers devoted editorials to the problem of censorship.

At the close of the year, ABA was working on a different concept which it hoped would solve the distribution problems that have long plagued the industry. The concept is that of an order and fulfillment book service which would streamline current methods of shipping, order, and payment, would give the booksellers the advantage of added discount and reduced paperwork, and would give the publisher the advantage of consolidating order input and collection procedures. It is tentatively called Booksellers Clearing House, and thorough exploration of the concept is planned for 1983.

AMERICAN LIBRARY ASSOCIATION

50 E. Huron St., Chicago, IL 60611
312-944-6780

Carol A. Nemeyer

President

The American Library Association (ALA), the oldest and largest library association in the world, enjoyed a total of 38,330 members in 1982, including librarians, libraries, library trustees, authors, illustrators, members of the book trade, information scientists, Friends of the Library, and businesses in the United States, Canada, and 70 other countries. ALA's membership represents all types of libraries—state, public, school, academic and special libraries—serving persons in government, commerce, the armed services, hospitals, prisons, and other institutions. Many ALA members actively participate in its 850 divisions, round tables, committees, task forces, and other voluntary units.

With the theme for 1982-1983 "Library Connections" focusing on public awareness, ALA President Elizabeth W. Stone (1981-1982) set a goal to develop a national library symbol (as recommended by the 1979 White House Conference on Library and Information Services). A presidential task force considered the work already done on library symbols in the United States and other countries and recommended that ALA endorse for nationwide use the symbol developed by the Western Maryland Public Libraries—a white stylized graphic of a book reader on a blue background, designed by Ralph DeVore. The symbol was approved by ALA Council at the 1982 annual conference and was displayed by thousands of conference-goers on T-shirts, balloons, stickers, tote bags, buttons, and other promotional items. A Library Symbol Implementation Group, chaired by Robert Garen (Detroit Public Library), was named to work in 1982-1983 with local, state, and national associations, Friends groups, and individual libraries to promote use of the symbol on library signs appearing on streets, highways, campuses, and buildings and on library newsletters, posters, library cards, and other materials.

Many other year-long activities culminated at the association's 101st annual conference in Philadelphia, July 10-15. Libraries gained national recognition through the U.S. Postal Service's issuance of a first-class commemorative stamp honoring "America's Libraries." The First Day of Issue ceremony was held during an ALA membership meeting. The publication *68 Great Ideas: The Library Awareness Handbook* was debuted at the President's Program, representing the completion of a search for a library awareness idea—a search that elicited more than 200 marketing, public relations, and publicity ideas from America's libraries.

By meeting in Philadelphia, ALA returned to the city of its birth, where in 1876 such library luminaries as Melvil Dewey and Justin Winsor issued a call to librarians to form a professional organization. Ninety men and 13 women came from as far west as Chicago and as far east as England to organize the association and elect its officers. Some 106 years later, 13,000 people came to the City of Brotherly Love to attend 2,100 meetings and workshops and more than 700 exhibits. Barbara Bush (wife of the vice-president), Isaac Asimov, Herman Kahn, Judith Martin, Joyce Carol Oates, Susan Stamberg, and Cal Thomas were among the featured speakers; poster sessions premiered; and ALA Council adopted an operating agreement to define better the fiscal and administrative policies between ALA and its divisions. Council voted to end the boycott of Chicago as a conference site but reaffirmed ALA's support for Equal Rights Amendment passage.

The prospect of a deficit ALA budget for 1982-1983 was of special concern to the executive board; meeting in special session in December, the board approved a plan to reduce expenditures, increase revenues, and transfer $95,000 from ALA's endowment fund to reduce the deficit carried forward into the 1982-1983 year. The board voted to repay the endowment within five years and projected a balanced budget by August 1984. Executive Director Robert Wedgeworth reported that the association will continue to develop new revenue sources through its publishing and membership services and outside activities under development. He expressed confidence in ALA's strength in the midst of a faltering national economy and asked for cooperation in making the budget adjustments work.

The American Library Association's prime objective is to promote and to improve library and information services to the public. Current priorities, as adopted by the ALA Council, are access to information, legislation/funding, intellectual freedom, public awareness, and personnel resources.

ACCESS TO INFORMATION

Access to information for blind and physically handicapped individuals received special emphasis during 1982, the National Year of Disabled Persons. The Association of Specialized and Cooperative Library Agencies (ASCLA), a division of ALA, extended the term of the International Year of Disabled Persons Committee to continue ALA's special efforts to make librarians and consumers aware of the need and methods by which to reach this special clientele.

In Philadelphia, ALA units sponsored preconference and conference programs on serving deaf and hearing-impaired youth and their parents and on service to elderly and hard-of-hearing persons. Special attention is being given to improve meeting-room accommodations for disabled persons attending and participating in ALA conferences.

ASCLA helped to develop a brief guide to library service for deaf and hearing-impaired persons and published *Occasional Paper No. 1: Library Services to Developmentally Disabled Children and Adults*. ASCLA also completed and published the results of its three-year study on the adequacy of federal prison libraries.

The ALA unit specifically charged with increasing access to information for everyone is the Office of Library Outreach Services (OLOS). OLOS continued its work on adult literacy. A two-day postconference in Philadelphia brought together librarians working on library literacy programs to share experiences, information, and ideas. OLOS coordinates the activities of the Coalition for Literacy, which was formed to develop with the Advertising Council a three-year multimedia campaign to combat adult illiteracy in the United States. A brochure describing the newly formed coalition was developed and is being distributed. Press coverage in the *Washington Post*, the *Kiplinger Newsletter*, the *Christian Science Monitor*, and the *New York Times* generated interest in the coalition, its goals, objectives, and membership.

To meet the needs of the growing number of U.S. residents fluent in a language other than English, OLOS collaborated with the Center for Applied Linguistics in Washington, D.C., to identify state library agencies and public libraries concerned with English as a second language for adult Indochinese refugees, and the Young Adult Services Division (YASD) produced a new Spanish-language booklist, "Libros a tu gusto."

The measure for good library service is the ability to connect library users with the information they need, when they need it. The Reference and Subscription Books Review Committee (RSBRC)—a group of 50 volunteer members of ALA who evaluate encyclopedias, dictionaries, directories, atlases, indexes, and bibliographies to assist librarians and others in selecting such materials—is seeking ways to distribute effectively its findings directly to individual consumers. In 1982, RSBRC expanded its coverage to include reference works in microform and computer formats. An Association of American School Librarians (AASL) preconference in Philadelphia provided school media specialists with information about sharing library skills with students to increase their access to materials.

New technologies applied to library service are creating new means to connect users with information. *Financing Online Search Services in Publicly Supported Libraries* documents the results of the Office for Research's spring 1981 survey. The study, reflecting ALA's concern that fees for online searches are limiting access to information, shows that although most libraries do impose some charges, users are not generally required to bear the full cost of the search service. Teleconference services, online catalogs, programming, microcomputers, cable television, and interactive video all were subjects of conference programs and workshops held during the year. The interdivisional Catalog Form, Function, and Use Committee was organized at the 1982 midwinter meeting to discuss standards for online catalogs, user education, and the Council on Library Resources public access catalog survey.

In Washington, ALA was particularly concerned by Reagan administration actions to restrict government publication and information dissemination activities. In June, the Washington office published a January–June 1982 chronology, updating the 1981 chronology that first documented this trend toward limiting citizen access to government information.

LEGISLATION/FUNDING

Legislation and funding continued to receive close attention, especially when the president proposed in his 1983 budget the elimination of all federal library programs. The ALA Washington office stepped up efforts in 1982 to work with chapter legislative networks to determine the effect of zero funding on library services and to make Congress more aware of these impacts through testimony at hearings and constituent contacts.

Faced with the zero budget, more than 300 library supporters came to Washington on April 20 for the National Library Week Legislative Day sponsored by ALA and the District of Columbia Library Association. The administration held back or impounded almost $20 million in Library Services and Construction Act (LSCA) funds, but a major campaign by ALA and a lawsuit by ten states finally got the funds released. As Christmas approached, Congress was in the process of continuing current levels of funding for library programs, thus firmly rejecting the zero budget.

Conference programs on "Growing in Hard Ground," "The Role of the Trustee in Fund Raising," "Planning for Austerity," and "Stretching Dollars" made real ALA's drive to equip its members to face hard times with inventiveness and optimism. At the inaugural banquet for the new ALA president, librarians were invited to "compose . . . a new library declaration of interdependence. Loudly and clearly," said the new president, "we should proclaim the importance of libraries and librarians. If we care enough and have the guts we can make and strengthen a variety of connections with each other and with others who are, could, or should be influential in making libraries even stronger than they are now."

ALA members did join together in 1982 to hold hearings on the present and future of LSCA, to discuss how public information policies are developed and how librarians can be more influential, to improve grant proposal writing, to seek funds for public programs in the humanities, to discuss lobbying and the involvement of librarians and youth, and to testify before congressional committees and regulatory agencies on the Telecommunications Act of 1981.

ALA Publishing Services updated the popular *ALA Librarians Copyright Kit*; the Association of College and Research Libraries (ACRL) Legislation Committee compiled the ACRL *Legislative Policy and General Guide to Legislative Action; School Library Media Quarterly* introduced a new column, "Issues Alert," dealing with legislation; and the Library Administration and Management Association (LAMA) published *Facilities Funding Finesse*, detailing various approaches to financing a new library facility.

INTELLECTUAL FREEDOM

Since the 1980 revision of the Library Bill of Rights, the Intellectual Freedom Committee has been systematically revising and updating ALA's intellectual freedom policies. This review was completed in 1982 with the retention of the current Policy on Confidentiality of Library Records and with ALA Council approval of a new policy, Diversity in Collection Development. This policy replaces Racism, Sexism and Other -Isms in Library Materials. The new statement reaffirms the obligation of librarians to develop diverse collections representing all points of view, no matter how unpopular or offensive to members of the community or to librarians themselves. With the completion of this revision process, the Office for Intellectual Freedom (OIF) plans to proceed quickly to publish a new edition of the *ALA Intellectual Freedom Manual*.

Censorship in America's public schools was a burning issue in 1982. At the National School Board Association's 1982 conference, a 22-member panel of educators, librarians, school administrators, authors, publishers, federal judges, parents, Moral Majority leaders, and elected school board members discussed how books get into classrooms and libraries and how they are sometimes removed. A videotape of the discussion, *Censorship or Selection: Choosing Books for Public Schools*, was shown at the Philadelphia conference and is available with a discussion guide from OIF. Another recent OIF publication, *Coalition Building*, includes basic, practical information on how to start a coalition, sample coalition documents, and an up-to-date directory of such groups.

For the Freedom to Read Foundation, 1982 was a year of unparalleled promise and peril for those concerned with the future of intellectual freedom and the right to read. The promise was evident on June 25, when the U.S. Supreme Court rendered its decision in *Board of Education, Island Trees Union Free School District No. 26 et al. v. Pico et al.*, the most significant case to date involving the removal of books from a library. In its plurality opinion, the high court stated that the First Amendment's guarantee of freedom of speech limits the discretion of public school officials to remove books that they consider inappropriate from school libraries. The reasoning in Justice William Brennan's opinion for the plurality closely followed that of the *amicus curiae* brief filed by the Foundation for the American Library Association and the New York Library Association. The Court's decision to remand for trial was badly fragmented, however, and left many issues unresolved. The Court failed to set clear limits to the power of school boards to remove books, and it failed to resolve the serious question of appropriate procedures for school boards to follow in reviewing challenged materials.

In yet another Supreme Court case, *People* v. *Ferber*, the Court upheld the constitutionality of the law prohibiting the distribution of nonobscene materials showing children engaged in sexual activity and remanded the case for trial. In the remanded trial, the New York State Court of Appeals decided that the state's penal laws directed against child pornography do not violate the right of free expression under the New York constitution. The constitutional result of this decision is to add child pornography to those categories of "speech" not deserving of First Amendment protection, along with obscenity, defamation, and language that incites violence. The Court's ruling expressly declined to address the arguments of the Freedom to Read Foundation's brief that the law could be used to ban worthwhile materials, including medical and other instructional films. Disseminating serious works containing nonobscene sexual depictions of children becomes an increasingly high-risk proposition.

LIBRARY AWARENESS

The year 1982 was a banner year for library awareness. More and more librarians realize that to secure favorable legislation and adequate funding more people must know about libraries and their services. Betty Stone carried the awareness theme through her 1981–1982 presidential year, and this emphasis will be continued in 1983 with plans to repeat the successful poster sessions in Los Angeles and by adding another dimension, that of strengthening the links between libraries and corporate America—for it is good business to become strong library allies. The nation's first Business Council for Libraries is now being organized.

The President's Program on "Marketing: The Key to Surviving and Thriving" at the 1982 midwinter meeting was grist for the first national teleconference from an ALA meeting. Beamed from Denver to a network of 62 libraries in 30 states, the program was viewed by more than 3,000 librarians, library trustees, and city officials, who phoned in questions to expert panelists during the telecast.

ALA's Public Information Office (PIO) was awarded a Silver Anvil in 1982 by the Public Relations Society of America for its excellence in marketing programs. This year's National Library Week campaign was well received in all kinds of libraries across the country. Large die-cut posters of a jogging shoe, a pencil, and a rainbow-colored "library" illustrated the theme "A word to the wise—library." Many libraries that filed activity reports with PIO applauded the appropriateness of the theme and graphics for all age levels and for all library users. Columbia Pictures helped develop the 1982 READ poster, which featured Aileen Quinn as Little Orphan Annie, with Annie's dog Sandy on the steps of Daddy Warbucks' mansion.

Bold public service ads developed by ALA were run in 20 national publications, including *Woman's Day, New Yorker, Harper's Magazine,* and *Newsweek.* ALA provided information for major library stories in *Writer's Digest,* the *New York Times, Town & Country,* and *Communication World.* Local newspaper coverage of library activities and concerns was evident nationwide: The Philadelphia conference received daily coverage, with stories picked up by wire services for national syndication.

Several ALA units focused on public awareness, especially on librarians building positive public images. ALA units also developed bibliographies to accompany television programs, most notably an ABC special on Albert Speer, Nickolodean's new series on biographies of famous people, and a new public television series "Reading Rainbow."

The National Library Week theme for April 1983 is an enthusiastic "Go for it! Use your library." Quality clip art, posters, bookmarks, and postcards will help libraries promote their services all year long.

PERSONNEL RESOURCES

The Office for Library Personnel Resources (OLPR) is the primary ALA unit established to carry out programs related to personnel utilization, staff welfare, education, and career visibility and development. During 1982, OLPR launched a new publications series, Topics in Personnel (T.I.P.). T.I.P. kits are information packets on current personnel issues seen from both the viewpoint of employers and staff. The first kits in the series deal with unionization and collective bargaining, pay equity, equal employment opportunity, and quality of work life. T.I.P. kits are available from OLPR.

In January 1982 the ALA Office for Research and OLPR conducted a major survey of salaries earned by academic and public librarians in particular positions by geographic area. The results published in *The ALA Survey of Librarian Salaries* include data on scheduled starting and maximum salaries and salary ranges currently being paid for each of 13 full-time professional positions in 4 geographic regions.

ALA, along with many other organizations and the federal library community, worked throughout 1982 to monitor and protest the new classification and qualification standards for federal librarians proposed by the U.S. Office of Personnel Management in December 1981. The Federal Librarians Round Table, ALA Washington office, and OLPR were the ALA groups most involved. An ad hoc steering committee, chaired by Ellen Cook and guided by Betty Stone, submitted a 95-page ALA response to OPM in April 1982 and reviewed and commented on a revised OPM draft in September 1982. By mid-November, however, when a third draft was reviewed, it still generated strong opposition from federal librarians, the federal agencies and departments that employ them, and from the library community. Bipartisan congressional support helped to achieve some improvements in the draft standards. In a letter to OPM, Betty Stone reaffirmed ALA's objections to both the inequities of the proposed standards and the procedures followed in revision. Previous to the second review, OPM had announced plans to publish the standards in early 1983. At the year's end, the matter remained unresolved.

ALA presented testimony on this serious problem and on general pay equity issues affecting librarians at the U.S. House Post Office and Civil Service Committee hearings on pay equity in September. The Committee on the Status of Women in Librarianship represented ALA at the annual business meeting of the National Committee on Pay Equity, a coalition of women's groups, civil rights organizations, and educational and professional associations.

[See the report on "The New Federalism: How It Is Changing the Library Profession in the United States" in the Special Reports section of Part 1—*Ed.*]

CONTINUING EDUCATION ACTIVITIES

Continuing education opportunities were offered throughout 1982, in addition to preconferences and regular ALA conference programming.

The Association of College and Research Libraries (ACRL) sponsored continuing education courses in conjunction with the ALA annual conference in 1982 and at the 1983 midwinter meeting in San Antonio. Supervisory skills, time management, bibliographic instruction, survey research methods, publishing, map librarianship, and public relations were among the topics treated. The Bibliographic Instruction Section (BIS) won the Bailey K. Howard-J. Morris Jones Award for "Bringing Workshops to the Members." Efforts will be made to make these workshops available at the state level.

A "Workshop on Library Leadership," developed by the American Library Trustee Association (ALTA), was presented in April in cooperation with the Minnesota Library Trustees Association and Minnesota Office of Public Libraries and Interlibrary Cooperation. The workshop was aimed at helping library trustees learn more about their roles and responsibilities in the areas of public awareness, planning, legislation, policymaking, money, and advocacy. This workshop was designed as a model, and all states were encouraged to send an official observer.

ASCLA's Continuing Education Committee conducted a needs assessment in cooperation with the Multitype Library Cooperation Section to determine members' information needs. ASCLA's Bibliotherapy Committee published an introductory guide to bibliotherapy to define terms, describe major activities in the field, and list bibliotherapy organizations and educational opportunities.

Microcomputers in libraries was the focus for the Library and Information Technology Association (LITA) institute held in November in Wisconsin. The workshop covered such topics as availability and evaluation of software and hardware, cost models, trends for the future, and programming. An exhibit by vendors and manufacturers also was included. [For a report on "The Use of Microcomputers in Elementary and Secondary School Libraries," see the Special Reports section of Part 1—*Ed.*]

OLPR offered workshops on resume writing and job hunting in conjunciton with its conference placement center and continued to seek ways to expand its career development services. In May, OLPR conducted a workshop for the Illinois Library Association on assessing managerial skills.

Although the Public Library Association (PLA) Planning Process workshops were completed in 1981, PLA continued to offer consulting services and materials to state groups. *Public Libraries*, the PLA journal, started a new column, "Keep on Learning," to focus on the design and implementation of effective staff development and continuing education experiences.

After a round of successful 1981 workshops on AACR 2, the Resources and Technical Services Division (RTSD) offered intensive training at institutes in Washington, D.C., and Boston. An Authorities Institute was presented in cooperation with the Library of Congress and the Council of Regional Groups in San Francisco and New Orleans, and RTSD/LC/CRG and the Illinois Library Association presented an institute on Library of Congress subject headings in October.

In December 1981, YASD published *Cheap CE—Providing Continuing Education with Limited Resources: A Practical Guide*. This booklet presents suggestions for each step involved in providing quality continuing education, emphasizing young adult services.

In each issue, *American Libraries* continued to publish the "Datebook" section listing continuing education workshops and conferences. The journal's LEADS department remains the profession's largest clearinghouse for personnel resources. LEADS provided some 30,000 lines of classified job announcements in 1982, increased the listings of consultants by approximately 20 percent, and published 22 pages of continuing education announcements.

In its annual *Financial Assistance for Library Education* directory, the Standing Committee on Library Education (SCOLE) continued listing scholarships available for continuing education. At the annual Library Education Assembly it focused attention on competencies for library and information science education.

HIGHLIGHTS

The ALA Committee on Accreditation (COA) reviewed self-study applications from 12 library education programs and scheduled reaccreditation visits to 11 schools. Accreditation actions in 1982, including action on programs visited in late 1981, resulted in the reaccreditation of ten programs, initial accreditation for one program, and withdrawal of accreditation from one program. Two open meetings of the COA were held at ALA conferences to target future attention on matters of particular interest to library educators. Interviews and orientation sessions were held for new site visitors who will join in the accreditation process in the future. In October 1982 there were 69 accredited library education programs, 7 in Canada and 62 in the United States. [For a report on "Recent Developments in Library Education," see Part 3—*Ed.*]

AASL's second national conference, "'82 a New Emphasis," was held in Houston, October 21–24, 1982. There were 8 workshops, 24 forums, and 55 concurrent program sessions related to 7 major issues: legislation and funding, networking and resource sharing, freedom and access, expectations and public relations, professionalism and environment, curriculum, and technology. Both PLA and LITA are planning national conferences in 1983.

The ALA publication of *Output Measures for Public Libraries: A Manual of Standardized Procedures* was a big step toward assisting public libraries to measure the effectiveness of their efforts to serve the public. A 13-minute videotape, *Measure for Measure*, was developed to introduce the new performance measures to library staff and trustees. The long-awaited "The Public Library: Democracy's Resource—A Statement of Principles" was adopted by the PLA board of directors in Philadelphia. The document is a foundation statement for trustees, citizens, officials, and librarians who want or need a brief summary of the reasons why the public library has been and will continue to be an important institution in our society.

The ALA executive board approved an Information Service and Data Base Development Project to improve ALA's information services to the library profession through the headquarters library and by creating an ALA data base.

The Books and Pamphlets unit of ALA Publishing Services published 35 books and grossed more than $1.6 million in 1982. *Booklist/RSBR* contributed a like amount and continued to improve editorially by reviewing more books, possibly earlier than most other book review journals. ALA negotiated agreements for *Booklist/RSBR* to be the review source for two Teletext programs, Viewdata and Keycom. *Openers*, the quarterly library newspaper published by PIO, will provide feature articles for the programs.

STAFF CHANGES

Donald E. Stewart, associate executive director for ALA Publishing Services since 1974, retired in 1982. ALA published more than 240 new titles during the years 1974–1982 under Stewart's general direction. Gary Facente, former vice-president and editorial director of Follett Publishing Company, was appointed to direct ALA's publishing program.

In August a new ALSC executive director, Ann Carlson Weeks, was appointed to succeed Mary Jane Anderson. Since joining the staff in 1974, Anderson had developed joint activities with related organizations and agencies, expanding ALSC publications and fostering international relationships. Weeks, who recently earned a Ph.D. in library science from the University of Pittsburgh, has served as consultant to the New York State Education Department.

Rebecca Dixon is the new editor of *Choice*, the ACRL review journal. Dixon was director of the library services division at the Center for the Study of Youth Development, Boys Town, Nebraska; prior to that she was head librarian at the Institute for Sex Research, Indiana University, Bloomington. Richard D. Johnson had served as interim editor of *Choice* for a year while on leave as director of libraries at State University College, Oneonta, New York.

AMERICAN NATIONAL STANDARDS COMMITTEE Z39: LIBRARY AND INFORMATION SCIENCES AND RELATED PUBLISHING PRACTICES AND INTERNATIONAL ORGANIZATION FOR STANDARDIZATION TECHNICAL COMMITTEE 46—DOCUMENTATION

U.S. Department of Commerce, National Bureau of Standards,
Library E-106, Washington, DC 20234
301-921-3241

Patricia W. Berger

Chair

Robert W. Frase

*Executive Director**

The American National Standards Committee Z39: Library and Information Sciences and Related Publishing Practices has the principal responsibility in the United States for developing and promoting technical standards for information systems, products, and services. Committee Z39 was established in 1939 by the American Standards Association, predecessor of the American National Standards Institute (ANSI). The Council of National Library and Information Associations serves as the Z39 secretariat and is responsible to ANSI for the work of Z39.

The American National Standards, developed and promulgated by Z39 and published by ANSI, are intended to benefit both producers and consumers of information. Although compliance with Z39 standards is voluntary, Z39 encourages their adoption when appropriate in library, publishing, document delivery, information dissemination, and information- and data-handling systems.

Z39 also participates in the development of international technical standards

---

**Note:* On November 29, 1982, Robert W. Frase, Z39 executive director since October 1978, retired and was succeeded by Patricia R. Harris.

for libraries, documentation and information centers, indexing and abstracting services, and the publishing industry through its membership in the International Organization for Standardization, Technical Committee 46: Documentation.

MEMBERSHIP

Z39 has three classes of members: full voting members, nonvoting information members, and honorary members.

There were 52 *voting members* at the end of 1982—associations, organizations, and companies from fields within the scope of Z39 that are interested and willing to participate in Z39 activities. Voting members pay annual dues related to their budgets for activities within the Z39 scope.

The 63 *information members* at the close of 1982 consisted of non-U.S. associations or organizations and government agencies that have an interest in the activities of Z39 and U.S. associations or organizations that wish to maintain a liaison with Z39 without actively participating in its activities. They receive a variety of information and, on request, copies of standards that are in the process of development. An annual membership fee is charged.

Honorary members (at present four) are appointed by the Z39 Executive Council in recognition of their contributions to national or international technical standardization.

ORGANIZATIONAL CHANGES

On September 1, 1982, a revision of the ANSI Procedures for the Development and Coordination of American National Standards came into effect. Under these revised procedures, American National Standards Institute committees and their secretariats must take steps to become accredited under one of three methods, a report of intentions must be provided to ANSI by September 1, 1983, and the transaction must be completed by September 1, 1984.

After being incorporated as a nonprofit organization under the laws of the District of Columbia, for which application has been filed, Z39 intends to apply to become an accredited organization, responsible directly to ANSI without an intervening secretariat.

OFFICERS AND COMMITTEES

As of December 31, 1982, the officers of Z39 (with terms expiring June 30, 1983) were Patricia W. Berger, chairperson and Sandra K. Paul, vice chairperson. Members of the Executive Council (terms ending June 30, 1983) are Sally H. McCallum (libraries) and W. Theodore Brandhorst (information services). A vacancy exists for publishing. Councillors whose terms expire on June 30, 1984, are Linda K. Bartley (libraries), James E. Rush (information services), and Karl F. Heuman (publishing). Councillors whose terms expire on June 30, 1985, are Larry X. Besant (libraries), M. Lynne Neufeld (information services), and Seldon W. Terrant (publishing). John G. Lorenz is the Z39 treasurer by appointment.

The chairpersons of Executive Council committees were Sandra K. Paul (program), Seldon W. Terrant (finance), Larry X. Besant (membership), Linda K. Bartley (publicity) and Patricia W. Berger (international).

The standards under development at the end of 1982 were (with the Z39 subcommittee and the chairperson in parentheses) *Romanization of Yiddish* (SC 5, Herbert C. Zafren, Hebrew Union College), *Library Statistics* (SC 7, Katherine Emerson, University of Massachusetts), *Serial Claim Form* (SC 42, Lois N. Upham, University of Southern Mississippi), *Abbreviation of Titles of Periodicals* (SC A, Robert S. Tannehill, Jr., Chemical Abstracts Service), *Language Codes* (SC C, S. Arlene Schwartz, Illinois State Library), *Computer-to-Computer Protocol* (SC D, David C. Hartmann, MITRE Corporation), *Serial Holdings Statements at the Detailed Level* (SC E, Susan Brynteson, University of Delaware), *Standard Terms, Abbreviations and Symbols for Use in Interactive Information Retrieval* (SC G, Pauline Atherton Cochrane, Syracuse University), *Patent Data Element Identification and Application Numbering* (SC H, Philip J. Pollick, Chemical Abstracts Service), *Price Indexes for Library Materials* (SC I, Fred C. Lynden, Brown University Library), *Bibliographic Data Source File Identification* (SC J, W. Theodore Brandhorst, ERIC Processing and Reference Facility), *Basic Criteria for Indexes* (SC K, Jessica L. Milstead, News Bank, Inc.), *Romanization* (SC L, Charles W. Husbands, Harvard University), *Coded Character Sets for Bibliographic Information Interchange* (SC N, Charles T. Payne, University of Chicago Library), *Guidelines for Format and Production of Scientific and Technical Reports* (SC P, Astor V. Kane, NTIS), *Periodicals: Format and Arrangement* (SC Q, Ed Barnas, John Wiley & Sons), *Environmental Conditions for Storage of Paper-Based Materials* (SC R, Paul Banks, Columbia University School of Library Science), *Permanent Paper for Library Materials* (SC S, Gay Walker, Yale University Library), *Standard Order Form for the Purchase of Multiple Titles* (SC T, Peter Jacobs, Professional Media Service Corporation), *Standard Format for Computerized Book Ordering* (SC U, Ernest Muro, Baker & Taylor Company), *Standard Identification Numbers for Libraries, Library Items and Library Patrons* (SC V, Paul Lagueux, Council on Library Resources), *Item Location and Holdings Statement* (SC W, Stephen Davis, Library of Congress), *Revision of Z39.10 (1977) Directories of Libraries and Information Centers* (SC X, Scott Bruntjen, Pittsburgh Regional Library Center), *Guidelines for Format and Publishing of Standards and Specifications* (SC Y, chairperson not yet appointed), *Eye-legible Information on Microfilm Leaders and Trailers and Information on Containers of Processed Microfilms* (SC Z, Louis C. Willard, Princeton Theological Seminary), and *Interlibrary Loan Form* (SC AA, Olive James, Library of Congress).

STATUS OF Z39 PUBLISHED STANDARDS

Published Standard Reaffirmed

Z39.8-1977 Compiling Book Publishing Statistics

Published Standards in Process of Revision or Reaffirmation

Z39.1-1977 Periodicals: Format and Arrangement
Z39.4-1968 (R1974) Basic Criteria for Indexes
Z39.5-1969 (R1974) Abbreviation of Titles and Periodicals
Z39.6-1965 (R1977) Trade Catalogs
Z39.7-1968 (R1974) Library Statistics
Z39.10-1971 (R1977) Directories of Libraries & Information Centers
Z39.11-1972 (R1978) System for the Romanization of Japanese
Z39.12-1972 (R1978) System for the Romanization of Arabic
Z39.18-1974 Guidelines for Format & Production of Scientific Technical Reports
Z39.20-1974 Criteria for Price Indexes for Library Materials
Z39.23-1974 Technical Report Number (STRN)
Z39.24-1976 System for the Romanization of Slavic Cyrillic Characters
Z39.27-1976 Structure for the Identification of Countries of the World for Information Interchange
Z39.29-1977 Bibliographic References

Z39.31-1976 Format for Scientific & Technical Translations
Z39.33-1977 Development of Identification Codes for Use by the Bibliographic Community
Z39.34-1977 Synoptics

Other Published Standards

Z39.2-1979 Bibliographic Information Interchange on Magnetic Tape
Z39.9-1979 International Standard Serial Numbering
Z39.13-1979 Describing Books in Advertisements, Catalogs, Promotional Materials, and Book Jackets
Z39.14-1979 Writing Abstracts
*Z39.15-1980 Title Leaves of a Book
*Z39.16-1979 Preparation of Scientific Papers for Written or Oral Presentation
*Z39.19-1980 Guidelines for Thesaurus Structure, Construction & Use
*Z39.21-1980 Book Numbering
*Z39.22-1981 Proof Characters
*Z39.26-1981 Advertising of Micropublications
*Z39.30-1982 Order Form for Single Titles of Library Materials in 3-Inch by 5-Inch Format
*Z39.32-1981 Information on Microfiche Headings
Z39.35-1979 System for the Romanization of Lao, Khmer, and Pali
Z39.37-1979 System for the Romanization of Armenian
Z39.39-1979 Compiling Newspaper and Periodical Publishing Statistics
Z39.40-1979 Compiling U.S. Microfilm Publishing Statistics
*Z39.41-1979 Book Spine Formats
*Z39.42-1980 Serial Holding Statements at the Summary Level
*Z39.43-1980 Identification Code for the Book Industry

FUNDING

The year 1982 was the first year of Z39 self-financing by mandatory membership fees on a graduated scale. The fees in 1981 were on a voluntary basis. A number of member organizations resigned because of the introduction of membership fees, but a few new members were added and the income raised was sufficient to carry out the Z39 program. The 1983 fee scale will be somewhat lower than in 1982 in several categories, and in 1984 the number of categories in the fee scale will be increased from five to six.

PUBLICITY AND EXHIBITS

The Z39 publicity campaign was continued and intensified in 1982. Exhibits staffed by volunteers were staged at the American Library Association annual conference in Philadelphia (plus a poster session); the National Federation of Abstracting and Information Services annual conference in Arlington, Virginia; the Special Libraries Association annual conference in Detroit; and the American Society for Information Science annual meeting in Columbus, Ohio. Materials on Z39 were also made available for a number of smaller, less formal meetings of member organizations. The free mailing list of the quarterly newsletter, *The Voice of Z39* (which will be issued only three times a year beginning in 1983), was substantially increased. In addition to the regular annual reports in the *Bowker Annual* and the *ALA Yearbook*, a major report on technical standards for libraries, information services, and publishing was published in the Fall 1982, issue of *Library Trends*, with James E. Rush as issue editor.

*These standards include Library of Congress Cataloging-in-Publication data.

INTERNATIONAL STANDARDIZATION ACTIVITIES

Z39 participates in the development of international standards for libraries, documentation and information centers, indexing and abstracting services, and the publishing industry through ANSI membership in the International Organization for Standardization, Technical Committee 46: Documentation (ISO/TC 46). ISO/TC 46 is one of 1,940 technical bodies within ISO engaged in developing international standards to facilitate the exchange of goods and services and to foster mutual cooperation in intellectual, scientific, technological, and economic activities. Since its establishment in 1947, TC 46 has produced 29 ISO standards.

The plenary assembly, which meets every two years, is the governing body of TC 46. Delegates to the assembly represent member bodies (national standards organizations) that participate in the work of TC 46. The secretariat of TC 46, which is held by the Deutsches Institut für Normung (DIN), is responsible to the ISO council and to the members of the technical committee for TC 46 activities. An elected steering committee, on which the United States presently serves, assists the secretariat to plan and program the work of TC 46 and its subcommittees and working groups between meetings of the plenary assembly. The next plenary assembly will be held in Vienna, Austria, May 16-18, 1983.

Z39 comments and votes on TC 46 proposals many times each year at various stages in the development or revision of ISO standards: on subcommittee drafts; on draft proposals (DPs), through ANSI; and on draft international standards (DISs), through ANSI. There is frequently a close relationship between U.S. and international standards. Two of the standards are the same, *Bibliographic Information Interchange on Magnetic Tape* (Z39.9 and ISO 3297) and the *International Standard Book Number* (Z39.2 and ISO 2108). Several American National Standards are being used by TC 46 as a basis for developing ISO Standards: Z39.20 *Criteria for Price Indexes for Library Materials*, Z39.32 *Information on Microfiche Headings*, and Z39.34 *Synoptics*. In other cases, Z39 standards are based on ISO/TC 46 standards. At present, the following published Z39 standards are being revised to conform more closely to subsequent revisions of the ISO standards on which they are based: Z39.5 (Reaffirmed 1974) *Abbreviations of Titles and Periodicals* (ISO/4) and Z39.27 (1976) *Structure for the Identification of Countries of the World for Information Interchange* (ISO/2166). The international maintenance committee for ISO/2166 will be meeting in Washington, D.C., in April 1983.

ISO/TC 46 published standards in English and French are sold in the United States by the American National Standards Institute, 1430 Broadway, New York, New York 10018. In addition to the individual ISO/TC 46 published standards, ANSI also has for sale *ISO Standards Handbook I—Information Transfer* (second ed., 1982), which contains the texts of ISO/TC 46 and related ISO standards covering the fields of bibliographic references and descriptions, abstracts and indexing, presentation of documents, conversion of written languages, document copying, microforms, bibliographic control, libraries and information systems, mechanization and automation in documentation, classifications and controlled language for information storage and retrieval, and terminology principles.

ASSOCIATION OF AMERICAN LIBRARY SCHOOLS

c/o The Executive Secretary, 471 Park Lane, State College, PA 16801
814-238-0254

Charles D. Patterson
Editor, *Journal of Education for Librarianship*

The Association of American Library Schools, Inc. (AALS) is a not-for-profit corporation which was organized in 1915 and has as its objective "to promote excellence in education for library and information science as a means of increasing the effectiveness of library and information services."[1] To achieve this objective, the association has specific goals which are: "(a) To provide a forum for the active interchange of ideas and information among library educators, and to promote research related to teaching and to library and information science. (b) To formulate and promulgate positions on matters related to library education. (c) To cooperate with other organizations in matters of mutual interest."[2] These are the basic and overall principles which have effectively governed and given direction to the activities of the AALS since its founding.

ORGANIZATION AND MEMBERSHIP

The affairs of the association are guided and regulated by a board of directors, which includes the president, the president-elect, and the most recent past president (each serving a one-year term); the secretary-treasurer and the public relations officer (each serving a three-year term); and three directors, the latter occupying overlapping terms each of which is three years. Serving in ex-officio capacity on the board are the executive secretary of the association and the editor of the *Journal of Education for Librarianship*, the official publication of the AALS. The executive secretary is the director of the association's headquarters and also currently serves as assistant editor of the *Journal*.

The standing committees are very important in accomplishing the mission of the association. These are the Conference Planning, Communications and Public Relations, Continuing Education, Governmental Relations, International Library Education, Library Education Statistics, Membership, Nominating, Organization and Bylaws, Research, Resolutions, and Tellers. There are also a number of interest groups that provide personal members a forum for interaction in such areas as continuing education, curriculum, international library education, library history, online education, research, teaching methods, and women in librarianship.

The association offers five membership categories including personal members, associate personal members, institutional members, associate institutional members, and international affiliate institutional members. Consolidated total members in all categories as of April 1982, were 566 personal and 102 institutional, including all of the 62 library and information science education programs in the United States, and seven in Canada, which are accredited by the Committee on Accreditation of the American Library Association (ALA).

ANNUAL CONFERENCES, WORKSHOPS, AND PRE-CONFERENCES

Before its formal organization and as early as 1907, there were those teachers concerned with library education who met to share and discuss mutual problems. These meetings took place at the same time as the annual conference of the ALA or during its midwinter meeting. Although sometimes meeting in two different geographical locations, the AALS has, in recent years, established a pattern of holding its annual conference just prior to and at the same place as the ALA mid-winter meeting.

In keeping with its stated objective "to promote excellence in education for library and information service, . . ." the association selects a pertinent and timely theme that becomes the focal point of each of its annual conferences. Thus, as a direct result of the 1979 White House Conference on Library and Information Service, at which the AALS was officially represented, the theme for the 1980 Austin, Texas, conference directed its attention to an examination of the major issues, recommendations, and implications for library and information science education that emerged from the White House Conference.

Although once a mandatory degree requirement, the integration of field experience as an integral part of library education, had, through the years, been deleted from the curricula of most library education programs. Recent years, however, have shown this to be an important and necessary aspect of the education of those preparing to enter the information profession. Subsequently, the nature and role of field experience became the major theme of the 1981 annual conference in Washington, D.C., and many degree programs once again have internships or field work as a requirement.

Returning to the overall objective of the association, the themes for the next two conferences were directed "Towards Quality in Graduate Library Education" with the 1982 Denver, Colorado, meeting devoted to "Identifying Concerns to Achieve Excellence" and the 1983 San Antonio, Texas, conference to "Promoting and Achieving Excellence."

Another important part of the annual conference are workshops and pre-conferences. In recent years, these have been offered on a variety of diversified and significant topics and themes, including continuing education, the use of microcomputers, library and information science education in the Americas, and educating the prospective information entrepreneur. The results of many of these conferences and activities have been in evidence through subsequent publications of the association.

PUBLICATIONS

The *Journal of Education for Librarianship*, established in 1960, is the official and refereed publication of the association and appears five times each year with one issue containing a directory of the association membership and the association's bylaws. This scholarly journal, with a circulation of 2,000, is received by libraries and individuals in 83 countries throughout the world and is a major voice reporting research, events and activities in library and information science education. Although the *Journal* is the major publication of the association, there are, arising out of workshops, pre-conferences, and committee work, as well as issues and trends continually forming in the myriad activities of the world of information, other significant and worthwhile publications issued by the association. Although of primary interest to educationists, these publications are also sought by those in allied professions as well. Some of these recent publications are: *In-Basket Simulation Technique: A Sourcebook*, by Martha Jane Zachert; *Library and Information Science Education in the Americas: Present and Future*, edited by William V. Jackson; and *Library Education Statistical Report*, by AALS, now in its third year of publication. *Information Needs of the 80's*, edited by Robert D. Stueart—an outgrowth of the 1979 White House Conference on Library and Information Service—was sponsored by the association and published by JAI Press, Inc. In addition, the association has issued position statements, position papers, and reports on "The Role of Graduate Programs in Library and Information Science in Higher Education," "The Accreditation Process," "Implications of the White House Conference on Library and

Information Services for Library Education," "OPM Tentative Standards for GS1409, GS1410, and GS1411 Series," directed toward librarians and information workers in the employment of the federal government; "Standards for Development of 6th Year Programs"; and a statement entitled "Continuing Library and Information Science Education," which is a vital area of ongoing concern to all involved in education.

RESEARCH ACTIVITIES

Research continues to be an important and integral part of AALS activities. Established six years ago, the $2,500 Research Grant Award program provides incentive to personal members of the association to engage in scholarly pursuits. (Research resulting from the award may appear in the *Journal*.) In addition to the award program, the association also sponsors its Research Paper Competition, which is not limited to the field of library and information science education, but is broadened to include all aspects of information service. A third research activity consists of the research reports sessions that are held each year during the conference of the association. These sessions provide a forum whereby quality research activities of the AALS personal members are presented for the benefit of the entire organization and the profession at large.

RELATIONS WITH OTHER ORGANIZATIONS

AALS has long recognized the need for and benefits to be derived through interaction with other professions and organizations whose objectives may fall within or apart from those of library and information science education. These forms of liaison and other means of cooperation have become particularly important during the past decade, which has witnessed notable and astounding advancements in technology and a decline in federal support for library and information services. There is a critical need for traditional library schools to adjust the curricula of the various degree programs and for graduates of these programs to consider employment possibilities beyond those ordinarily associated with librarianship. AALS' ties with the ALA and its Standing Committee on Library Education (SCOLE), with the International Federation of Library Associations and Institutions (IFLA) in which it has held membership for many years, and with other library-related organizations have been long and fruitful. A recent example of cooperation with IFLA was the role AALS played in the 1982 Montreal, Canada, pre-conference entitled "Education for Research—Research for Education," and AALS is already represented on the planning committee for the 1985 New York City IFLA conference.

Another and equally beneficial form of communication with other organizations is of more recent origin. Following a pattern established in New York in 1980, the association sponsored in Philadelphia, Pennsylvania, in July 1982, a third meeting of the group that has come to be known as the Information Organization Heads, so named because the president, executive director, or executive secretary acts as the representative of the organization. Those associations presently represented are The American Society for Information Science, American Library Association, Association for Educational Communication and Technology, Association of Research Libraries, the Federal Library Committee, American Association of Law Librarians, Special Libraries Association, and the Medical Library Association. These meetings are extremely helpful to better understanding and appreciation of the work of these professional groups. Common areas of interest under discussion among the Information Organization Heads continue to center on accreditation, internships and field work, scholarships, and legislative concerns. Additional meetings are planned for future conferences of the association.

In May 1982, the association co-sponsored, with the Information Institute of the International Academy, a highly successful conference on "Education for Information

Management" held in Santa Barbara, California. Drawing a limited and select number of participants from business, education, and the information industry, the conference heard many provocative and pertinent issues raised and discussed in an effort to provide guidance and direction in the education of information management professionals.

In the light of the benefits to be gained through cooperation and interaction with organizations representing various disciplines, and in response to the multifaceted and fluid needs of a world so dependent on information, in 1982 the board of directors of the association proposed to the membership the possibility of changing the name of the association to the Association for Library and Information Science Education. This name more adequately embraces and describes the educational objectives and activities of the organization and places equal emphasis on *information science*, which has become prominent in recent years. This name change has been approved by the membership and will become effective sometime in 1983.

SUMMARY

Since its founding, the AALS has been an involved and viable organization that has effectively served its members in their endeavor to improve the quality of and the standards for the education of the library and information service professional. Cognizant of its important role in a burgeoning information society, the association has, through its own programs and by cooperation with other groups, been the leading advocate for library and information science education both in the United States and abroad. It will continue its efforts to identify and solve problems concerning education so that the information professional is better prepared to serve the needs of information communities in all environments and at all levels. As the centennial of library education in America will take place in 1987, the association has already begun planning for an appropriate observance of this important occasion.

[For a report on recent developments in library education, see Part 3—*Ed.*]

NOTES

1. AALS Bylaws, Article I, Section 2. *Journal of Education for Librarianship.* Directory Issue, 1982, p. 75.
2. Ibid.

ASSOCIATION OF AMERICAN PUBLISHERS

One Park Ave., New York, NY 10016
212-689-8920

2005 Massachusetts Ave. N.W., Washington, DC 20036
202-232-3335

Jane Lippe-Fine
Staff Director, Public Relations

The Association of American Publishers, the major voice of the book publishing industry in the United States, was founded in 1970 as the result of the merger of the American Book Publishers Council and the American Educational Publishers Institute.

AAP members—some 350 companies representing all regions of the United States—publish the great majority of printed materials sold to American schools, colleges, libraries, and bookstores and by direct mail to homes. Member firms publish hardcover and paperback books—textbooks, general trade, reference, religious, technical, scientific, medical, professional, and scholarly books—and journals. They also produce a range of other educational materials, including classroom periodicals, maps, globes, films and filmstrips, audio and videotapes, records, slides, transparencies, test materials, looseleaf services, and computer software learning packages.

AAP operates under an organizational plan that ensures central direction of association affairs and gives important initiatives to the seven AAP divisions, each covering a major product line or distinct method of distribution of the industry. Marketing, promotion, research projects, and relations with other associations regarding mutual problems are central features of divisional programs. Each AAP division annually elects a chairperson and establishes core committees to plan and implement independent projects.

Association policies are established by an elected 29-member board of directors. AAP President Townsend Hoopes, chief operating officer, is responsible for managing AAP within the framework of basic policies set by the board. Approximately 40 professional and nonprofessional personnel staff AAP's two offices, in New York and Washington.

1982 ACTIVITIES

At the AAP annual meeting in May 1982, incoming chairman Alexander J. Burke, Jr. (McGraw-Hill), announced several objectives for the year: to find ways to revitalize the institutional book markets of this country; to increase AAP initiatives in Washington; and to explore the potential for computer application to help publishers expand book markets.

In 1982, AAP vigorously continued its efforts in copyright enforcement. In November, AAP reached an amicable settlement in its dispute with E. R. Squibb & Sons, Inc., related to the photocopying of certain scientific journals. In December, nine publishers filed suit for copyright infringement against New York University, nine of its faculty members, and an off-campus copy center. This is the first AAP suit directed specifically at a university.

In Washington, AAP continued to provide active representation for the industry in testimony before congressional committees, liaison with allied organizations, monitoring of federal and congressional activities, and friend-of-the-court briefs filed in U.S. Supreme Court cases involving publishing or related activities.

The third American Book Awards were presented in 1982, honoring 90 hardcover and paperback nominees in the literary category and 19 winners for literary excellence. The program was chaired by Thomas H. Guinzburg.

Divisions

General Publishing Division

The General Publishing Division (GPD), chaired by Jeremiah Kaplan (Macmillan), represents 145 publishers of fiction, nonfiction, children's literature, and religious and reference books. It also frequently works cooperatively with publishers of professional and scholarly books and with mass market paperback publishers within AAP. The division's programs focus on three key objectives: broadening the audience for books, strengthening relationships with librarians and booksellers for the solution of common problems, and improving the management and marketing skills of publishers.

Among the activities the division supports is the American Book Awards program, a major recipient of divisional funds, as well as contributed services and materials, in its effort to call public attention to the best of American books. The program is also supported by authors, agents, booksellers, wholesalers, and librarians.

With the cooperation of the American Booksellers Association (ABA), members of the division serve as faculty members at schools for booksellers and promote the marketing of books through special activities for booksellers. Other educational initiatives and programs designed to enhance the effectiveness of book promotion efforts are under development. Active liaison with librarians is maintained through joint committees with the American Library Association and the Special Libraries Association. A group of smaller publishers within the GPD plans programs and publications of particular interest to the growing number of smaller publishers within all AAP Divisions.

Mass Market Paperback Division

The Mass Market Paperback Division, chaired by Howard Kaminsky (Warner Books), directs its efforts primarily toward the promotion of the paperback book as an integral tool for both educational and recreational readers in America today. As it continues to explore new approaches to the marketing, production, and distribution of the paperback, the division takes on such serious problems as the illegal sale of stripped books and the question of release date rights in the open market.

This division remains in close contact with booksellers throughout the United States through its liaison with the American Booksellers Association. It has joined efforts with the ABA to sponsor the Category Bestseller Program and the Mass Paperback Fiche Service, and also collaborates with the National Association of College Stores to produce the monthly list of Campus Paperback Bestsellers. The division serves as the official representative for the mass market paperback industry at the annual meetings of both the American Booksellers Association and the National Association of College Stores. It also works closely with the ABA and AAP's General Publishing Division in support of the American Book Awards program, now in its fourth year of operation under the auspices of the AAP.

The division has just completed its third year of support for the Rack Clearance Center (RCC), which serves as a clearinghouse, processing reimbursement claims for the installation of racks in retail outlets where mass paperback books are sold. The RCC receives claims from wholesalers and rack manufacturers, assesses them for accuracy, and ensures that appropriate backup papers are supplied. In 1981–1982, there was a 30 percent increase in the number of claims processed by RCC over the previous year.

College Division

The College Division, chaired by James Levy (Scott, Foresman), is directly concerned with all aspects of the marketing, production, and distribution of textbooks to the postsecondary education field. It pays special attention to maintaining good relations between the publishing industry and college faculty, bookstore managers, and college students. To develop and maintain strong relations with college students, the division has established the AAP Student Service, a public relations program featuring a series of publications directed to college students. They include *How to Get the Most Out of Your Textbook, How to Prepare for Examinations, How to Improve Your Reading Skills, How to Build Your Writing Skills, How to Get the Most Out of a College Education, How to Read Technical Textbooks,* and *How to Succeed in College: A Guide for the Non-Traditional Student.* The division has developed several publications directed to college faculty, including *LINKS* and *An Author's Guide to Academic Publishing.*

The College Division maintains close contact with college bookstores through the NACS-College Division Liaison Committee and operates the AAP College Textbook Publishers Fiche Service, started by the division and NACS in 1980. College bookstores can subscribe to the service for a nominal fee; in return, they are provided with microfiches (updated monthly) of about 40,000 textbook titles available from more than three dozen leading textbook publishers. The Liaison Committee also publishes a booklet for college bookstore managers, *Textbook Questions and Answers*, and each spring it cosponsors an Advanced Financial Management Seminar for college store managers.

The College Division Marketing Committee sponsored a "Rely on Your Textbook" advertising campaign with posters and news releases appearing in campus newspapers and college bookstores. The Marketing Committee is currently sponsoring a campaign addressed to college freshmen, entitled "Textbooks: An Investment in Your Future." Another important part of the division's public relations program is its sponsorship of a series of panels at various academic association annual meetings. Recently, the division sponsored a series of AAP panels at the NACS regional meetings. Past programs have dealt with such subjects as "The Copyright Law and the Teacher" and "How the New Technology Affects the Academic World."

The College Division has been alerted to the serious implications of the illegal copy/mill activities. Presently, in cooperation with the Copyright Committee, litigation is underway to combat this problem.

Professional and Scholarly Publishing Division

The Professional and Scholarly Publishing Division (PSP), chaired by William Begell (Hemisphere), is primarily concerned with production, marketing, and distribution of technical, scientific, medical, and scholarly books and journals. Essentially, although not exclusively, many of these publications are for the practicing engineer, scientist, and businessperson. The division monitors relevant government activity and policies, levels of funding, and related matters. It provides for a continuous exchange of information and experience through seminars in journal publishing, marketing, sales, new technology, and copyright and maintains relations with other professional associations, including the International Group of Scientific, Technical and Medical Publishers, government agencies, and industrial research groups. Professional societies and university presses play an integral role in divisional activities.

In 1980, an experimental committee of looseleaf publishers was added to the division and, accordingly, the annual PSP Awards program was expanded to include their publications. The Government Relations Committee continued to monitor the course of various pieces of legislation and participated in developing AAP's position on them. The PSP Marketing Committee is developing a presentation on selling professional books for the American Booksellers Association Convention and other booksellers' meetings; it is also developing a booth for the ABA convention. The PSP Journals and Marketing committees conducted an extensive program of seminars and workshops. Other standing committees are concerned with statistics and public relations.

School Division

The School Division, chaired by Robert C. Bowen (McGraw-Hill), is concerned with the production, marketing, and distribution of textbooks and other instructional materials for kindergarten through twelfth grade. It works to improve instructional programs and to increase levels of funding. It also sponsors seminars and conferences on topics of interest to educators and publishers.

The School Division retains legislative advocates in key states to monitor legislative activities and to represent the interests of educational publishers at education conferences. The division also maintains contact with state boards of education and members of state legislatures in the 22 adoption states, as well as selected open territory states.

In September 1982, the division sponsored a joint reading conference with the Center for the Study of Reading, University of Illinois, in Rye, New York, and cosponsored sessions at the convention of the International Reading Association and the National Council of Teachers of English, among others. It also sponsored the second annual Education Research Awards Competition (1982-1983) to provide grants to graduate students in education.

Division committees work to acquaint parents, educators, and others with some of the concerns of educational publishers through meetings and publications such as the *Parent's Guide to More Effective Schools, Textbook Publishers and the Censorship Controversy* and *Standardized Testing: How a Textbook Is Made.* Public service ads and radio spots are also part of the grass-roots public information campaign of the division.

Standing committees of the division include Communication, Social Issues in Education, Research, Statistics, Test, Textbook Specification, Order Flow Improvement, and selected state committees.

International Division

The International Division, chaired by Paul S. Feffer (Feffer & Simons, Inc.), was formed in response to the rising importance of foreign markets for U.S. books. It focuses on those issues that affect the marketing of books to other countries and the ever-growing complexities of the international marketplace. The division represents the entire spectrum of publishing in both size of firm and product line.

Among the division's priorities are improving trade relations with the Third World; developing the professional skills of members through seminars and workshops; developing strong relationships with U.S. government agencies (U.S. Information Agency and the State and Commerce departments) interested in promoting the book abroad through national fairs and exhibits; promoting respect for international copyright; developing international sales statistics; and promoting attendance and active participation at international book fairs. Continuing its efforts to combat piracy around the world, the division collects and disseminates information in cooperation with the International Publishers Association and lends support to members in their individual efforts. The division's annual meeting included reports on major world book fairs and markets.

Direct Marketing/Book Club Division

The Direct Marketing/Book Club Division is actively concerned with the marketing and distribution of books through direct response and book clubs. The division works closely with the AAP Postal Committee to study the effects of new postal rates and regulations and to monitor new postal developments. The division's Marketing Committee sponsors seminars during the year. Issues of concern are privacy legislation, copyright, and improved statistical programs. Merrill Vopni (Prentice-Hall, Inc.) is division chairperson; Arthur Heydendael (Meredith Corporation) is division vice chairperson.

Core Committees

Core activities include matters related to copyright, new technology, freedom to read, postal rates and regulations, statistical surveys, book distribution, public information, press relations, communications, international freedom to publish, and education for publishing.

The Copyright Committee

The Copyright Committee, chaired by Allan Wittman (Macmillan), safeguards and promotes the proprietary rights of authors and publishers domestically and internationally. Closely monitoring copyright activity in the United States and abroad, the committee prepares congressional testimony for appropriate AAP spokespersons, assigns representatives to attend national and international copyright meetings, and sponsors seminars on copyright matters.

The Copyright Committee plays an active role in disseminating information about the copyright law. It provides speakers to address publisher, librarian, and educator groups and prepares and distributes printed information. Three times a year the committee publishes the *AAP Copyright Circle*, an open forum on copyright issues of concern to publishers. More than 4,500 copies of its publication *Photocopying by Academic, Public and Non-Profit Research Libraries* have been distributed.

The Copyright Committee maintains liaison with the U.S. Copyright Office and informs publishers of new and proposed regulations that relate to their activities. It participates in negotiations concerning copyright-related policy to be followed by users of copyrighted material and also maintains an active copyright enforcement campaign. In the past year, AAP coordinated law suits against American Cyanamid, E. R. Squibb & Sons, and New York University, its faculty, and an off-campus copy shop for their photocopying activities. The former two suits resulted in settlements.

[See the five-year review of the new copyright law in the Special Reports section of Part 1; also see the annual report from the Copyright Office in the Federal Agencies section of Part 1—*Ed.*]

The New Technology Committee

The New Technology Committee was created in 1981 to meet the need expressed by member publishers to monitor the new technologies—the new means of distributing published information and the new products, i.e., online data bases, computer programs, videodiscs, videotapes, teletexts, and videotexts. Functioning as an information clearinghouse, the committee publishes a monthly column on technologies that affect the publishing business and sponsors workshops and seminars to assist publishers in gaining the knowledge required to enter these fields. Robert Badger (John Wiley & Sons) chairs this committee.

The Freedom to Read Committee

The Freedom to Read Committee (chaired by Brooks Thomas, Harper & Row president) is concerned with protecting freedoms guaranteed by the First Amendment. In addition to a major educational role, the committee analyzes individual cases of attempted censorship by Congress, state legislatures, federal, state, or muncipal governments, local school boards, or any other institution. Its actions may take the form of a legal brief in support of a position against censorship, testimony before appropriate legislative committees, or public statements and communications protesting any attempt to limit freedom of communication. The committee works closely with other organizations that support its goals.

The principal 1982 activity of the AAP Freedom to Read Committee was to organize, obtain funding for, and conduct a three-hour seminar on public school and school library book censorship pressures. Supported by grants from five foundations and produced for videotaping by Media and Society Seminars of Columbia University, the discussion was held in Atlanta in April at the convention of the National School Boards Association. The 22 seminar participants included authors Judy Blume and Kurt Vonnegut, plus judges, attorneys, librarians, teachers and school administrators, publishers, a student, and two representatives of the Moral Majority. A one-hour videotape with accompanying discussion guide was produced and marketed by AAP along with the seminar cosponsor, the American Library Association Intellectual Freedom Committee. The videotape was shown at the ALA annual conference in Philadelphia, with veteran producer Fred W. Friendly serving as moderator for the ensuing, lively question-and-answer period.

At the AAP annual meeting in May in Marco Island, Florida, the committee sponsored an address by Ithiel deSola Pool of MIT on First Amendment implications of electronic publishing.

Through the committee, AAP intervened as *amicus curiae* in the much-discussed Island Trees school library book removal case. The committee welcomed the general tone of the Supreme Court plurality holding in the case that, under the First Amendment, local school boards do not have unlimited authority to "purge" library books with which they disagree.

The committee intervened less successfully in a protracted case challenging the constitutionality (on account of alleged overbreadth) of a New York statute dealing with child pornography. Ultimately the statute was upheld in both the U.S. Supreme Court and the New York State Court of Appeals, although two members of New York State's highest court also expressed concern at the law's potential overbreadth. AAP, through the Intellectual Freedom Committee, testified before a U.S. Senate Judiciary subcommittee considering federal legislation to implement the Supreme Court decision.

The Postal Committee

The Postal Committee monitors the activities of the U.S. Postal Service, the Postal Rate Commission, and congressional committees responsible for postal matters. It presents the publisher's point of view to those in policymaking positions through direct testimony, by economic analyses of proposed postal programs, and through a variety of other means. Leo Albert (Prentice-Hall) chairs the committee.

The International Freedom to Publish Committee

The International Freedom to Publish Committee is the only body formed by a major group of publishers in any country for the specific purpose of protecting and expanding the freedom of written communication. The committee monitors the general status of freedom to publish and discusses problems of restriction with the U.S. government, other governments, and international organizations. When appropriate, it makes recommendations to these organizations and issues public statements.

During the year the committee investigated violations of free expression in Argentina, China, Cuba, Czechoslovakia, Haiti, Indonesia, Iran, Poland, South Africa, the USSR, and Yugoslavia. In September 1981, the committee organized the Third Moscow Book Fair Reception in Exile, which was held at the New York Public Library and honored Soviet writers in exile as well as those silenced by prison or other forms of persecution in the USSR. Committee members have testified at congressional hearings dealing with free expression and have maintained contact with persecuted writers and publishers in repressive countries and with emigre writers from those countries. John Macrae III (E. P. Dutton) is chairman.

The Book Distribution Task Force

The Book Distribution Task Force, created in 1976, continued its efforts to stimulate the development and implementation of more efficient distribution systems for all book publishers. In 1982 it attempted to make publishers and others on its mailing list aware of distribution-related technology in the publication of bulletins on the following topics: the 1981 International Distribution Specialists Meeting; implementation of the International Standard Book Number viewed from the publisher, bookseller, and wholesaler perspectives; the Standard Address Number viewed from those same perspectives; and the results of the Computer Hardware and Software Survey conducted in 1981.

The task force represented the AAP at the 1982 International Distribution Specialists Meeting in Frankfurt, which was organized by the German book trade, and will assume responsibility for planning the 1983 meeting. It also represented the AAP at three meetings of the Network Advisory Committee to the Library of Congress concerned with document delivery and one concerned with the National Commission on Libraries and Information Service report on public and private sector interface. [See the summary of this report in the Special Reports section of Part 1—*Ed.*] The task force reviewed all newly proposed national standards, as well as older standards up for review by American National Standards Committee Z39, distributing them to individual members for comment, as appropriate.

In June 1982, Robert J. R. Follett (Follett Corporation) completed his year as chairman of this core committee. At the time of this writing, the committee is being reorganized and will take on, as its first challenge, the development of experiments that will test some of the theories for improved distribution that appeared in *Book Distribution in the United States: Issues and Perceptions*, a study conducted by Arther Andersen & Company for the Book Industry Study Group, Inc.

The Education for Publishing Program

The Education for Publishing Program, implemented by AAP in 1978 after a three-year study of the education and training needs of the book publishing industry, works to promote and advance the continuing education of employees already in the industry; to attract, prepare, and educate new talent to enter the industry; and to inform the public about the book publishing industry. This mission is being carried out by guiding educational and training institutions in providing authoritative and useful courses on book publishing; initiating and sponsoring professional development courses on book publishing for industry employees; and by providing career and other information about the industry. Andrew H. Neilly, Jr. (John Wiley & Sons), chairs the Education for Publishing Committee.

The Publishing Education Information Service

A Publishing Education Information Service, established in 1979, acts as a research, referral, and communication resource for publishers, educators, and students seeking information about book publishing. The Stephen Greene Memorial Library contains a collection of more than 300 books, 40 periodicals, and archival material dealing with the industry. The library is staffed by a professional librarian and is open by appointment.

AWARDS

On April 27, 1982, under AAP auspices, the third American Book Awards were presented to 19 books at a ceremony at New York City's Carnegie Hall. The National Medal for Literature, endowed by the Guinzburg Fund in honor of Harold K. Guinzburg, founder of Viking Press, was presented to John Cheever. The medal, administered under the Book Awards aegis, carries a $15,000 cash prize. The Special Award of Recognition went to William Shawn and *The New Yorker*.

The seventh annual Curtis G. Benjamin Award for Creative Publishing was presented during the AAP annual meeting in May. The association administers this award on behalf of its founders. This year's recipient, Ian Ballantine, founder of Bantam Books, was praised for a career "marked by energy, creativity, and a total involvement in the publishing process."

The Professional and Scholarly Publishing Division completed the sixth year of its awards program, recognizing the best books and journals in its field; the program was expanded to include looseleaf publications and other media.

LIAISON WITH OTHER ASSOCIATIONS

The AAP has effective working relations with a large number of professional associations and agencies with allied interests. These include the American Booksellers Association, Association of American University Presses, Book Industry Study Group, Book Manufacturers Institute, Children's Book Council, Council of the Great Cities Schools, Information Industry Association, International Publishers Association, International Reading Association, National Association of College Stores, National Council of Teachers of English, National Education Association, P.E.N. American Center, Publishers Publicity Association, Publishers Library Marketing Group, Special Libraries Association, and UNESCO.

PUBLICATIONS

Although some AAP publications are circulated to members only, many are available to nonmembers.

The *AAP Newsletter* provides a periodic report to members on issues of concern to the publishing industry. The *Capital Letter*, issued monthly, offers news of federal government actions relating to the book community. Newsletters are prepared by the College, International, School, General Publishing, Mass Market Paperback, and Professional and Scholarly Publishing divisions and the Copyright Committee. Periodic bulletins are published by the Book Distribution Task Force.

The AAP also publishes industry statistics on sales and operating expenses and a report on compensation and personnel practices in the industry. The annual *AAP Exhibits Directory* lists about 600 book fairs and association meetings. The International Division publishes an annual *Profiles of International Book Fairs*. A publications list is available from AAP on request.

INFORMATION INDUSTRY ASSOCIATION

316 Pennsylvania Ave. S.E., Suite 400,
Washington, DC 20003
202-544-1969

Fred S. Rosenau

Director, Marketing and Publications

As a trade association, the Information Industry Association (IIA) (1) represents those organizations that are engaged in the intellectual property business, using any and all communications media and delivery mechanisms, and (2) promotes the purchase and use of information for the benefit of business people and consumers all over the world.

The IIA's 175 member firms provide information on such topics as business, science, technology, government, education and training, and entertainment. These organizations produce, distribute, retail, manage, and process information products and services in the following ways:

Producers acquire, edit, and process information, then deliver it in such forms as electronically accessible data bases, journals, books, and microforms.

Distributors provide value-added information based on their own data bases or those of others, using delivery services such as online, videotex, and teletext.

Retailers provide customized access to information sources, both traditional and electronic.

Managers operate clearinghouse or management information services.

Processors provide users with computer processing and communications capabilities that facilitate the delivery of private and public data and information sources.

Given that configuration of the IIA membership, which is growing both in numbers and in scope of services, where does the association find itself at the opening of 1983?

THE ANNUAL CONFERENCE

The IIA fourteenth annual conference, held at Walt Disney World in November 1982, in conjunction with the opening of the Experimental Prototype Community of Tomorrow, generated an enthusiastic response among the hundreds of executives who participated actively over a four-day period. Building on that experience, IIA planners are already developing programs and exhibits for the 1983 annual convention, which will be held at New York City's World Trade Center, November 7-9, under the banner "The Information Industry Talks with Wall Street—Wall Street Talks with the Information Industry." For the first time, this fifteenth annual convention and exposition will be jointly sponsored—by the Financial Analysts Federation and the New York Society of Security Analysts.

BUSINESS OF INFORMATION REPORT, 1983

One of the many highlights of that major meeting will be a firsthand report on, and analysis of, the *Business of Information Report, 1983*, based on survey data collected during 1983 by the A. C. Nielsen Company under contract to the IIA. This eagerly awaited publication will include trend analysis data that will be built upon the first industry survey conducted in 1979, the results of which were published by the IIA in 1980. This second survey will measure the current size and future directions of the industry in terms of profitability, types of firms, growth levels, product lines, markets served, foreign sales, number of employees, new areas of opportunity, and more. Charter participants in the survey will have an opportunity to obtain the final report at special presurvey prices, prior to publication late in 1983.

An IIA survey planning committee identified the following economic activities as generating information business revenues and thus, without question, falling within the survey universe:

Electronic data base production

Electronic data base distribution

Market research (if not simply custom work)

Information retailing (data base searching, document fulfillment)

Directory publishing (nonadvertising-based)

Custom management of data base or information facilities

Also included within the survey universe are media/format-independent businesses—those that package information in several formats or for delivery via several media. The sine qua non of the information industry is the fact that information companies recognize that their basic product is information content—its production, management, distribution, and marketing. In the bustling "information age," it is easy to observe a contagion spreading through the intellectual property universe as broadcasting, cable television, book publishing, news publishing, and hardware and communications companies begin to formulate, test, and implement a media/format-independent information business strategy in one degree or another.

OTHER PUBLICATIONS

Details on member companies and their products and services are provided in the IIA annual directory, *Information Sources, 1983–84*, released early in 1983 after the previous edition was sold out early in the fall of 1982. With a growing membership in a dynamic industry, the IIA has seen a much wider demand for its directory among business firms, information centers, libraries, and decision makers across the nation. It expects to be able to supply adequate inventory for the current edition.

The year 1982 heralded the appearance of the IIA's monumental four-volume set *Understanding U.S. Information Policy: The Infostructure Handbook*, edited by Forest Woody Horton, Jr. Its components included:

The Information Policy Primer, containing nearly 150 policy-building blocks, together with a preview of the 20 sections that appear in the three main volumes

The Resources for the Information Economy (Vol. I), embracing three major areas that affect delivery and use of information: information-handling technologies, productivity, and information management

The Participants in the Information Marketplace (Vol. II), spanning three major categories of competition: property concepts, the government's role in the marketplace, and international "players"

The Assets of the Information Society (Vol. III), analyzing three major areas that shape significant aspects of the economic, social, and political "information age" environment: public interests, knowledge centers, and the future

Before the end of 1982, a second printing was required. Reviewers' comments included: "Certainly any library worth its salt must invest in this set. . . . The broad grasp of the field evident here and the very useful means of organizing a great deal of information should prove useful to a wide variety of audiences. Highly recommended." [*Communication Booknotes*, September/October 1982 (Book of the Month)]

The IIA continued publication, for members only, of its weekly Information Industry newsletter, popularly known as *Friday Memo*. At the same time, the IIA staff launched a series of special publications in limited quantities. Two were ready in 1982: *Strategic Market Planning* and *The Information Industry: The Outlook for the 1980s*. Early in 1983 two others will become available: *Proven Techniques for Increasing Database Use* and *Business Realities in the Information Industry*. These publications are offered to nonmembers as well as members. An industry calendar for 1983 also is being distributed to members; it will be sold to nonmembers while supplies remain.

ORGANIZATION AND NEW OFFICERS

The IIA is now organized into three councils: Business Operations, chaired by Haines Gaffner, LINK Resources; Public Policy, chaired by William Giglio, McGraw-Hill; and Future Technology & Innovation, chaired by Daniel Sullivan, Frost & Sullivan. These councils carry on the day-to-day work of the association's membership—planning and conducting workshops and seminars, developing programs and exhibits for the annual convention, making budget recommendations to the board of directors, and so on.

Roy Campbell, senior vice president of product planning and research at Dun & Bradstreet Credit Services, is the 1983 chairman of the IIA board of directors. The chairman-elect is Norman Wellen, president and managing director of Business International Corporation. Robert November of ITT Communications Operations and Information Services is IIA's treasurer for 1983, and the board secretary is Peter Marx of Chase Econometrics/Interactive Data Corporation. The executive committee includes all of the foregoing officers, as well as the immediate past chairman, Thomas A. Grogan of McGraw-Hill. New members elected to the board include Lois Granick (director of Psyc-INFO), James Holly (executive vice president and general manager of Times Mirror Videotex Services), Peter Genereaux (president of DTSS Incorporated), and Paul Massa (president of Congressional Information Service). Daniel Carter of Texas Instruments and Alan Spoon of the Washington Post Company were selected by the board to serve in an advisory capacity in order to reflect the interests of two nonvoting membership categories, associate and affiliate members.

The board created a full complement of committees to carry on its work between the regularly scheduled board meetings: Executive (chaired by Roy Campbell), Audit (chaired by Robert Asleson of International Thomson Information), Compensation (chaired by Roy Campbell), Finance (chaired by Robert November), Membership (chaired by Peter Marx), Nominating (chaired by Thomas A Grogan), Planning (chaired by Norman Wellen), Publications (chaired by Elizabeth Eddison of Warner-Eddison Associates), and Communications.

1982 AWARDS

At its annual conference in Florida in late 1982, the IIA conferred its Hall of Fame Award on Roger K. Summit, president of DIALOG Information Services, Inc. The annual award recognizes an individual who has made a significant contribution to enhance the industry's integrity—a single achievement or an overall contribution. Previous awards had gone to Carlos Cuadra (Cuadra Associates), John Rothman (New York Times Information Services), William T. Knox (NTIS), Eugene Garfield (Institute for Scientific Information), Eugene Power (University Microfilms), and Mortimer Taube (Documentation, Inc.).

At the same time, the IIA honored two individuals for their long-term services to the industry: Ben H. Weil, formerly of Exxon Research Corporation, and Morton David Goldberg, Esq., partner in the New York law firm of Schwab Goldberg Price & Dannay. The Honorary Professional Member Award carries with it lifelong membership in the IIA.

Distinguished Service Awards, recognizing the unique contributions made by the recipients to the association, were received by Herbert R. Brinberg, president of Aspen Systems Corporation; J. Christopher Burns, former senior vice president of the *Minneapolis Star & Tribune;* Peter Marx; and Daniel Sullivan.

Significant Service Awards for "providing the benefits" that association members receive were given to Peter Genereaux, William Giglio, Lois Granick, James Kollegger (president of EIC/Intelligence), Georgette Semick (vice president for government services at Aspen Systems Corporation), Kurt Steele (vice president and associate general counsel of McGraw-Hill), and Charles Tower (vice president for government affairs of Dun & Bradstreet Corporation).

1983 SEMINARS AND WORKSHOPS

The IIA councils have scheduled a wide array of seminars and workshops for 1983, following the theme of the February 1983 meeting, "Moving and Marketing Information for Profit: Today, Tomorrow & Beyond," which was held in Boca Raton, Florida. One of the highlights of this schedule is the IIA midyear meeting planned for mid-May in Chicago; it takes as its theme "So You Want to Be a Profitable Database Publisher." A workshop focusing on fundamentals will be conducted for nonmembers on the day preceding the conference. Information about IIA conferences, workshops, seminars, and publications is available on request from the IIA office in Washington, D.C.

ACTIVITIES OF LOCAL CHAPTERS

IIA members in various metropolitan areas have begun to form local chapters to advance the business of information in their own regions. A New England chapter, led by Ted West of Cambridge Research Institute, held two meetings in 1982, culminating in a data base workshop in Cambridge, Massachusetts, in September. A Washington, D.C., chapter, spanning the entire national capital region, is being organized under the leadership of Jeff Emerson of Informatics, Inc.; it cooperated in conducted a two-day gathering on Capitol Hill that enabled member participants to meet new members of Congress and to show how their firms' informational capabilities meet the needs of private-sector government relations personnel. Chapter activities are also being planned for New York City, California, and the Midwest. No chapter bureaucracy is anticipated for planning and carrying out half-day, business-oriented gatherings. The IIA staff has prepared a draft "Local Meeting Handbook" to give help and guidance to these local groups.

MIDYEAR REPORT FROM THE PRESIDENT

In a midyear action report to the IIA membership, Paul G. Zurkowski, president of the association, said:

> It is now more vital than ever to report what the Association membership is doing as the information world continues to grow dramatically. This Report shows us at the center of that tremendous growth, as a commanding presence, influencing public and private sectors at key levels.
>
> The values of membership in the Information Industry Association have increased significantly within the last six months. They have matured in terms of the knowledge that is available and shared broadly for profit and strategy, articulated by three important action councils:
>
> Business Operations
>
> Public Policy
>
> Future Technology & Innovation
>
> These three councils champion new and changing methods, products, and legal resources for the information content world, to exploit emerging market options fairly and in the public interest. They work to distill the knowledge that takes us all more productively and securely into the future—the future we create ourselves.
>
> The hallmark of our community of information executives is that they share related objectives and experiences within the information industry. Our membership includes some of the largest corporations in America, as well as some of the smallest. Each member seeks to position its product or service within the mainstream of demonstrated Information Age trends and developments. Association workshops and meetings bring members together and regularly support dynamic interaction, delineating new and secure avenues for corporate

development and refinement. Such participation truly promotes progress: members anticipate industry growth and innovation more effectively.

Together we influence—and actually sculpt—the shape of our life and business, built upon knowledge, sustained by information and its dissemination, serving industry, academia, and government.

So we salute our 175 members and charge others in the Information Industry to take maximum advantage of the forum dynamic of the Information Industry Association. Membership is indeed a call to all for more knowledge—for profit, strategy, and continued growth.

SOCIETY OF AMERICAN ARCHIVISTS

330 S. Wells St., Suite 810, Chicago, IL 60606
312-922-0140

Ann Morgan Campbell
Executive Director

Deborah Risteen
Managing Editor

It was not until 1909, at the Conference of Archivists (a section of the Public Archives Commission of the American Historical Association), that individuals responsible for the care of original source materials first met as a formal organization. The conference served the fledgling profession well for more than 25 years, but the rapid growth in the archival profession during the 1920s and 1930s, brought on by an increased interest in history and by the establishment of the National Archives, created a demand for a separate professional organization outside the American Historical Association. In 1935 members of the Conference of Archivists made plans for the establishment of the Society of American Archivists.

The Society of American Archivists (SAA) was formally organized in Providence, Rhode Island, in December 1936. The mission of the new organization was to "promote sound principles of archival economy and to facilitate cooperation among archivists and archival agencies." Membership in the society was open to all "who are or who have been engaged in the custody or administration of archives or historical manuscripts or who, because of experience or qualifications, are recognized as competent in archival economy." Those present shared the hope that the new organization would prosper along with the profession. The initial membership drive reflected a keen interest in the new group, with more than 225 individuals and 18 institutions becoming charter members.

The Society of American Archivists has grown substantially since 1936, with especially rapid growth from 1976 to 1980, sparked by the U.S. bicentennial and the publication of Alex Haley's *Roots*, which generated tremendous interest in genealogical research. The society's present membership of 3,500 includes persons serving government (federal, state, and local), academic institutions, businesses, churches, and professional associations. Although SAA's geographic base is the United States and Canada, members in 60 other countries make SAA an international organization.

The society serves the archival profession in a number of ways. Through its publications program, annual meetings, workshops, professional affinity groups (PAGs), standing committees, and task forces, SAA provides a means for contact, communication, and cooperation among archivists and archival institutions. The society advances professional education and training, offers job placement services, supports research dealing with major archival problems, and represents archivists in areas involving related professions.

PUBLICATIONS PROGRAM

Certainly the most visible and recognizable facet of the work of the Society of American Archivists has been and continues to be its publications program. The society's quarterly journal, *The American Archivist*, has been published since 1938 and is recognized as the voice of the archival profession in the United States. Its articles on archival theory and practice, its reviews of writings on archives and the management of records, its extensive news and technical notes, and its reports on archival activities abroad have made the journal the major source of information on the archival field in North America.

In addition to the journal, the society publishes the bimonthly *SAA Newsletter*, which contains important archives-related news items; reports on SAA activities; listings of employment opportunities; announcements of grants awarded, upcoming meetings and workshops, and employment transitions; and guidelines and reports prepared by the society's committees, task forces, and professional affinity groups.

In recent years SAA has expanded its publications program beyond the journal and newsletter to include more than 40 manuals, directories, bibliographies, and other resource materials on archival topics. These include the ten-volume Basic Manual series, which covers appraisal and accession, arrangement and description, reference and access, security, surveys, exhibits, automated access, maps and cartographic records, public programs, and reprography; other manuals on business, religious, and museum archives; several compilations of forms used in archival work; volumes of selected articles and essays; bibliographies; directories of state, college and university, and business archives; and a series of Problems in Archives kits on such topics as starting an archives; finding employment as an archivist, developing a brochure, and disaster planning. Publications on conservation of archival materials, administration of photographic collections, and machine-readable records are currently being developed.

MEETINGS

Each year the society sponsors an annual meeting where archivists gather to discuss their common concerns and to plan activities for the coming year. This meeting features concurrent workshops, seminars, and sessions on topics of interest to all areas of the profession. In addition, the annual meeting is the occasion for various social events and tours of archival institutions and historical sites in the convention city.

The society also sponsors workshops and seminars on a wide range of archival topics. These range in length from two to five days and are held throughout the country. Future workshops will deal with starting an archives, business archives, management of archives, administration of photographic collections, oral history, introduction to archives, and archival conservation.

VOLUNTEER GROUPS

Much of the work of SAA is carried out by volunteer groups. Professional affinity groups, both by archival function and type of institution, were established to provide SAA members with the opportunity to meet and work with others of similar backgrounds. The functional PAGs are concerned with acquisition, aural and graphic records, conservation, description, oral history, and reference, access, and outreach. Institutional

PAGs represent archivists from businesses, colleges and universities, government records repositories, manuscript repositories, religious archives, and theme collections. Standing committees of the society concentrate on areas of long-term concern to the profession, such as information exchange, education, and international archival affairs. Task forces are created to make recommendations on specific issues, such as copyright, national information systems, minorities in the profession, and standard reporting practice. These groups have produced guidelines, reports, directories, and proposals for action, which have increased the skills of and the communication among archivists and have defined more clearly many of the issues facing the profession today.

SURVEY OF THE ARCHIVAL PROFESSION

In 1982, the society conducted a survey of the archival profession in the United States. Some 1,717 people responded from all 50 states, the District of Columbia, and Puerto Rico. The typical respondent was a middle-aged, white female with a master's degree and archival training from a professional workshop. This typical archivist has 4-15 years of archival experience and works in an archives with fewer than three employees. The average salary for the typical archival employee was just over $21,400. In a similar survey in 1979, the average salary was $17,136. Although the profession is still young, the 1982 survey showed that it has aged substantially since 1979. Over half the respondents were under 40, but the percentage fell from 60 percent in 1979 to 52 percent in 1982. Only 30 percent were over 50, but only 22 percent were in that bracket in 1979. More than 60 percent reported fewer than seven years of archival experience, and barely 10 percent had been in the profession for more than 15 years.

The average salary for archivists working for the federal government was the highest, $29,538. It was followed by the salaries for business archivists ($24,540), state archivists ($21,136), college and university archivists ($21,128), archivists for local government ($20,355), and religious archivists ($16,388).

ARCHIVAL ISSUES OF 1982

Archives and the Economy

The year 1982 was bad for the economy of the United States; budget cuts, layoffs, and high interest rates dominated the headlines. Archival institutions were not immune to the effects of this recession. In an informal poll conducted at SAA's 1982 annual meeting, 53 percent of those responding reported that their institutions had been adversely affected by the economy during the previous year.

Archival programs also felt the impact of uncertainty over appropriations for the National Endowment for the Humanities (NEH) and the National Historical Publications and Records Commission (NHPRC), two major sources of grant funding for archival projects. Early in the year it appeared that NEH funds would be cut severely and that funds for NHPRC would be eliminated entirely. NHPRC was forced to suspend awarding grants for several months, but at year's end it seemed that both NEH and NHPRC would have grant money available in 1983.

The National Archives and Records Service was also a victim of the budget ax in 1982. Approximately 230 National Archives staff members were RIFed (reduction in force) early in 1982, the result of a 16 percent cut in the archives' budget. Proposed appropriations for FY 1983 could result in even more layoffs.

National Archives Independence

A long-sought legislative goal of the archival profession moved closer to realization in 1982, when a bill providing for the independence of the National Archives from the General Services Administration (HR 6894) was introduced in the House of Representatives by Jack Brooks (D-Tex.). Brooks, chairman of the House Government Operations Committee, believed that both GSA and the archives would benefit from the proposed split. "Administrators past and present," he said, "have either ignored the Archives or meddled in its affairs without full understanding of its needs or purposes." The Brooks bill is a companion to S.1421, which was introduced in the Senate by Thomas Eagleton (D-Mo.) and Charles Mathias (R-Md.) in 1981.

National Information System

In 1981, SAA took up the challenge of promoting a national information system for archives and manuscript collections, which meets the diverse requirements of archival institutions and their clienteles. The society received two grants from the National Endowment for the Humanities to support the work of SAA's National Information Systems Task Force. The first grant funded a study of the descriptive elements employed in archives and manuscript repositories and paid for several task force meetings. The second grant provided funds to draft standard definitions of archival descriptive elements and to design a format to facilitate the exchange of archival information among repositories. These tasks were completed in 1982, and the society established a standing committee on archival information exchange to oversee the implementation of task force recommendations. Due to the work of the task force, a national information system, providing intellectual access to the nation's archival and manuscript resources and a means for repositories to disseminate and exchange information, is on the horizon.

Institutional Evaluation

Since 1977, SAA has been working to develop a program for evaluating archival institutions. In 1980, the society's Task Force on Institutional Evaluation prepared detailed self-study and site visit questionnaires, which were tested at six institutions with the help of a grant from the Council on Library Resources. These test cases led to further refinement of the documents, and in 1982 SAA published *Evaluation of Archival Institutions: Services, Principles and Guide to Self-Study*, which is designed to help archivists define standards and articulate measurable performance criteria. When fully operational, the institutional evaluation program will have three levels at which institutions can participate: (1) *Data collection* involves gathering data from individual archival repositories, which will then be used to provide an overview of archival institutions in general; (2) *Self-assessment* makes use of the guide to self-study outlined in *Evaluation of Archival Institutions;* and (3) *Peer review* involves a site visit by experienced archivists and a written report assessing strengths and weaknesses and making recommendations for improvement. Information on participation in the institutional evaluation program is available from SAA headquarters.

Tribal Archives

The Consortium for Native American Archives was awarded a grant of $190,757 from the National Endowment for the Humanities in 1982 to support a two-year program to assist Native Americans in the development of tribal archives. The program was developed by a consortium of organizations, including the American Association for State and Local History, the American Indian Library Association, Cultures and Arts of Native Americans, the National Anthropological Archives and the Office of Museum Programs of the Smithsonian Institution, the North American Indian Museum Association, and the Society of American Archivists. The program has three main components: (1) regional tribal archival conferences designed to raise the awareness of the Native American community concerning the value and importance of tribal archives; (2) production of a slide-tape program addressing the basic concepts of archival development; and (3) development of the manual "Tribal Archives: An Introduction."

Archives in China

In April and May, members of the Society of American Archivists on a study tour visited seven archives of the People's Republic of China. The archives were the First Historical Archives and the Imperial Records Storehouse in Beijing; the Kong Family Archives (Confucian Archives) in QuFu; the Shandong Provincial Archives in Jinan; the Second Historical Archives of Nanjing; the Shanghai Municipal Archives; and the Guangdong Provincial Archives in Guangzhou. For a report of the tour and information on archives in China, see the article by the trip's linguistic and cultural adviser, William W. Moss, in *The American Archivist*, Fall 1982.

SPECIAL LIBRARIES ASSOCIATION

235 Park Ave. S., New York, NY 10003
212-477-9250

Richard E. Griffin

Associate Executive Director

The Special Libraries Association (SLA) is the second largest library association in North America and the third largest in the world. In 1982, SLA's membership increased by 3 percent to 11,500, and two new chapters were formed, the Western Canada Chapter and the Fairfield County (Connecticut) Chapter, bringing the number of SLA chapters in North America and Europe to 54. The association also has 29 subject-related divisions and 24 student groups.

In 1982, as in the two preceding years, income generated by association programs far exceeded expenses. The annual conferences, continuing education program, publications program, mailing list service, interest income, and sound fiscal planning have been largely responsible for keeping the association well in the black. Members have benefited directly from the surpluses through improved and expanded membership services. Other beneficiaries have been the association's reserve fund, building fund, computer fund, and special programs fund.

One of the hard realities of association management is that income from member dues rarely covers the cost of services provided to the members. In SLA's case, dues income comprises only 73 percent of the cost of member services. Should any or all of SLA's income-producing programs fall on bad times, the association would be forced either to deplete its reserves in order to maintain the status quo or to reduce membership services in order to balance the budget. The association's leadership is confident that it will not have to choose between either of these drastic actions, as long as creative programming continues and prudent fiscal policies are followed.

Rather than attempting to summarize all of the complex and varied events that shaped SLA's course in 1982, this report highlights instead several key issues and concerns that SLA members and their elected representatives discussed, debated, and took action on during the year. Of the five issues selected for inclusion, the first three (long-range planning, public relations, and the building program) are good examples of how SLA is dealing with matters that have profound implications for the association's internal structure, organization, and future direction; and the last two (occupational standards for federal librarians and copyright) reflect SLA's proactive involvement with external issues that are facing the entire library profession.

KEY ISSUES IN 1982

Long-Range Planning

At the Association's 1981 winter meeting, the board of directors responded to the urging of SLA chapters and divisions for an association-wide long-range planning effort by establishing a Special Committee on Long-Range Planning. The purpose of the special committee was the selection of a plan for the association's long-range goals. The special committee presented its final report to the SLA board in June 1982, and in somewhat modified form, its recommendations were accepted.

In the summer and fall of 1982, a Delphi Inquiry of the board of directors identified priority issues of the long-range plan. At SLA's 1982 fall meeting, the last phase of the Delphi Inquiry resulted in agreement of board members on the association's six highest priorities. These priorities are subject to change and further refinement by the membership before the final long-range plan is drafted in mid-1983:

1. Reinforce and expand continuing education programs to (1) reflect the needs and desires of members; (2) assist members in developing skills to handle technological and economic changes occurring in library and information management; (3) train members to market information services; (4) provide for midcareer upgrading and retraining; and (5) develop or improve management skills.
2. Develop a strong public relations program for image creation, promotion, and interpretation of the special librarian and the information profession to the general public and to specific corporate, business, and government leaders.
3. Review the finances of the association and its constituent parts and develop a plan for maintaining a strong financial base.
4. Reappraise membership services with the specific goal of encouraging greater membership involvement. Also, identify and evaluate conference alternatives that would permit wider membership participation.
5. Develop curriculum objectives for graduate library and information management education and become a full participant in the graduate library education accreditation process.
6. Develop a plan and mechanism with full chapter and division involvement to improve chapter and division programming.

If the timetable for establishment of the association's long-range plan remains on schedule, the plan will be in place no later than October 1983.

Public Relations

In 1981, SLA President George Ginader appointed a Public Relations Task Force in response to a recommendation of the association's Chapter and Division cabinets for a stronger association-wide public relations effort. The task force's charge was to study the need for a public relations program and to make recommendations to the SLA board of directors for appropriate action. The task force completed its assignment in January 1982. Its report clearly indicates that there is a need to enhance the image of special librarians and the way special libraries are perceived by their users and the general public.

Acting on the task force's recommendation, the board of directors created a new staff position for a public relations professional. Funds for both program and salary have been authorized in SLA's 1983 budget. It is expected that the public relations program will begin operation in mid-1983.

The most extensive exposure SLA received in the media in 1982 was totally unexpected and absolutely free. This all came about as a consequence of the national and international interest generated by the first Detroit Grand Prix auto race, which was literally superimposed on the first two days of the SLA conference and on all of the preconference activities. Both before and during the conference, reporters had a field day pitting the stereotypes of librarians and race car drivers against each other in their news stories. SLA was not only covered daily by the Detroit press and television news but by *Sports Illustrated* and the *Wall Street Journal* as well. This provided SLA and conference attendees with several excellent opportunities to counter and respond to the frequently inaccurate depictions of librarians in the media.

Building Program

A definite move toward acquiring a new home for SLA was taken in June 1981, when the board of directors authorized Executive Director Dave Bender to begin a search in the New York City area for a building to purchase for the relocation of the association's headquarters. The board took this action because space at the present association office is inadequate for the staff, equipment, and materials needed to provide quality services for SLA's growing membership. The staff occupies overcrowded offices, and there is a severe shortage of short-term storage space. Under these conditions, staff performance is compromised, and plans for new or expanded membership services and programs cannot be implemented.

The board's decision to purchase property was also influenced by purely economic factors. The purchase of a building is essential to protect SLA from the inflationary spiral that is expected to result in more than a 300 percent rent increase when the association's lease expires (1987). SLA's only hedge against this and other increasing costs is the purchase of a building with adequate space for present and anticipated future needs, as well as additional space that can be leased to tenants. The income generated from the rental space will enable the association to improve its reserve fund position and cash flow and thus allow for the expansion of membership services. At the association's 1982 winter meeting, the board reaffirmed its commitment to purchase a new headquarters building by authorizing the appointment of a building inspection committee and establishing a building fund.

The building fund, the largest fund-raising project ever undertaken by SLA, has a goal of $500,000. To achieve the goal, the support of individual members and SLA chapters and divisions is crucial. The association is also soliciting contributions from its corporate friends. To launch this fund-raising effort, the board allocated $10,000 of the 1981 general fund surplus to the building fund, and it is anticipated that a similar or larger amount will be allocated from the 1982 surplus.

As 1982 drew to a close, more than 50 buildings, most of them in Manhattan, had been inspected. For a variety of reasons, none was deemed suitable. In 1983 the search for an SLA building will continue in earnest and may be broadened somewhat to include more properties in other New York City boroughs and suburban communities.

Occupational Standards for Federal Librarians

SLA has been watching closely activities at the U.S. Office of Personnel Management (OPM) relative to the drafting and adoption of revised occupational standards for librarians employed by the federal government. These standards are of concern to SLA members because their implementation will affect the professional status of 2,500 SLA members who are employed in federal government agencies and in U.S. military installations throughout the world. Furthermore, the standards in their final form will set a precedent for subsequent revision of occupational standards in every other sector of the library profession.

Among the many changes proposed in the December 1981 version of the tentative standards, SLA members took particular exception to the demotion of library specialists to a nonprofessional category, the overall lessening of minimum educational requirements for entry-level positions, and the downgrading of salary levels. On instructions from the SLA board, the association staff solicited comments on the standards from the membership, and the staff incorporated these comments into the SLA testimony that was submitted to OPM in March 1982. The testimony recommended: (1) the recombining of library specialist positions and library managers positions into a single professional series and (2) the holding of OPM-chaired hearings in all ten federal regions, so that the preparers of the standards could reflect in their next draft a more universal view of the range and complexity of federal library and information service positions.

SLA continued to monitor OPM activities associated with the review process during the months following the submission of the association's testimony. In June, the association staff was informed by another library association that OPM was receptive to some of the library community's objections. Likewise, a report received by the staff from OPM in August indicated that there was interest at OPM in SLA's testimony and that several of the association's concerns were being addressed.

When rewritten standards, ominously entitled "Final Standards," were issued by OPM in November 1982, SLA members were pleased to see that library specialists and managers were recombined into the same occupational series; however, members were displeased that the lower educational requirements and entry-level salaries had not been removed. A further matter of concern was the inadequate time period (30 days) OPM gave for response to the rewritten standards.

As a result of OPM's apparent haste to publish the "Final Standards" without the incorporation of further revisions, SLA's Government Relations Committee has prepared a fact sheet for publication in the *SpeciaList*. The fact sheet urges SLA members (1) to write to their senators and representatives to request OPM not to publish the "Final Standards" as they now exist, and (2) to request of OPM the establishment of an OPM-chaired task force for the resolution of all deficiencies and pay equity problems in the standards.

The "Final Standards" and the recommendations in the fact sheet are priority items for discussion among association leaders and members at the SLA winter meeting in January 1983. SLA will continue to keep abreast of this issue until the concerns of the library community are adequately addressed by OPM.

[See the report on "The New Federalism: How It Is Changing the Library Profession in the United States" in the Special Reports section of Part 1—*Ed.*]

Photocopying and Copyright

In 1982, a core group of publishers commenced civil actions against two major U.S. corporations for alleged copyright infringement arising out of their internal photocopying practices. Both suits were subsequently withdrawn as a result of out-of-court settlements. While the capitulation of these corporations to the demands of the publishers is distressing to special librarians, SLA has made an effort to remind its members that such settlements do not change the rights and privileges that the copyright law grants to the private sector users of information.

In the May 1982 issue of the *SpeciaList*, Efren Gonzalez, chairman of SLA's Copyright Law Implementation Committee, wrote:

> It is well known that lawsuits are frequently settled for reasons unrelated to the merits of the claim—for example, to avoid the direct and indirect expenses of litigation. . . . In any event, the fact that a suit was brought and settled does not alter the law. Sections 107 and 108 are not by their terms limited to not-for-profit organizations. The legislative history of the Copyright Law as contained in the House Report plainly indicates that neither Section 107 nor Section 108 are intended to be solely available to photocopying within not-for-profit organizations and, depending upon the facts and circumstances, photocopying in for-profit organizations may be possible under Section 107 or Section 108.

To reassert that the copyright law is alive and well in special libraries, the SLA Copyright Law Implementation Committee will offer in 1983 a seminar on the copyright law for special librarians and their employers' legal advisers. Among the many topics to be addressed at the seminar, permissible library photocopying under Section 108 and fair-use photocopying under Section 107 will receive special attention.

[See the five-year review of the copyright law in the Special Reports section of Part 1, as well as the annual report from the Copyright Office in the Federal Agencies section of Part 1—*Ed.*]

THE YEAR AHEAD

All the events and issues mentioned in this report will continue to influence SLA's activities and programs in 1983 and subsequent years. There is, in addition, a special occasion, SLA's seventy-fifth anniversary, around which a series of major events is being planned for 1983 and 1984. SLA will officially observe its seventy-fifth anniversary in 1984. The association year 1983-1984 has been designated as the anniversary year, and plans are under way for several commemorative programs and activities, many of which will begin in mid-1983. The anniversary celebration will culminate with gala festivities at the 1984 annual conference in New York (June 9-14). The SLA board of directors and staff hope that other library associations and organizations can join with it at that time to mark this milestone in SLA's history.

Part 2
Legislation, Funding, and Grants

LEGISLATION AFFECTING LIBRARIANSHIP IN 1982

Eileen D. Cooke
Director, Washington Office, American Library Association

Carol C. Henderson
Deputy Director, Washington Office, American Library Association

One had to blink to be sure it wasn't 1973—as in that year under President Richard Nixon, the president proposed to eliminate federal library programs and impound Library Services and Construction Act funds. As in 1973, it required a lawsuit by several states to get the LSCA funds released; and again as in 1973 Congress firmly rejected President Ronald Reagan's zero budget for libraries.

Congress spent most of the year trying to get its own budget in place. It was late December, three months into FY 1983 and near the end of a lame-duck session, before legislators provided funding for the full year in a continuing resolution. Most federal library programs were funded at the previous year's level, although the research library program received a slight increase and the school block grant a small cut.

In July, the library postage rate actually decreased and a commemorative stamp honoring "America's Libraries" was issued. Federal publication and information collection and dissemination programs were cut back. There were several copyright developments, and on a number of issues action was not completed before the Ninety-seventh Congress adjourned.

Federal librarians and library groups continued to protest both the substance and the revision process of the proposed new standards, which would downgrade federal library and information positions. Although a second public review of a new draft had been secured, the proposed standards were still unsatisfactory to all concerned, and the outcome was still in doubt as the year ended.

[For a report on "The New Federalism: How It Is Changing the Library Profession in the United States," see the Special Reports section of Part 1—*Ed.*]

FUNDING, FY 1982

As 1982 began, there was only a temporary funding measure in place through March 31. President Reagan's FY 1983 budget also contained requests to rescind $19,710,000 of Library Services and Construction Act funding, all funds ($1,920,000) for the Higher Education Act, Title II-A college library program, $480,000 of HEA, II-C research libraries funding, and $13,440,000 from the school block grant.

Most library programs proposed for rescission were included in a rescission message to Congress dated February 5, the same date on which the General Accounting Office first confirmed that the administration was impounding LSCA funds (see below under "LSCA Impoundment"). If Congress does not agree to a rescission request within 45 working days, the funds must be released. For the February 5 requests, this period expired April 23 without congressional action. Without changing any of the funding levels, Congress approved and the president signed on March 31 a continuing resolution (PL 97-161) extending funding for library and education programs through September 30, the end of FY 1982 (see Table 1).

Controversies over priorities caused a real tug-of-war between Congress and the president over two supplemental FY 1982 appropriations measures, which also affected

TABLE 1 APPROPRIATIONS FOR LIBRARY AND RELATED PROGRAMS, FY 1983

Appropriation (in thousands)

Library Programs	FY 1982 Appropriations	FY 1983 Budget	FY 1983 House	FY 1983 Senate	FY 1983 Appropriations
Education Consolidation and Improvement Act Chapter 2 (including school libraries)	$ 483,840	$ 433,000	$ 483,840	$ 475,000	$ 479,420
GPO Superintendent of Documents	27,423	28,889	27,291	27,291	27,291
Higher Education Act Title II	8,560	0	8,560	8,800	8,800
Title II-A: College Libraries	1,920	0	1,920	1,920	1,920
Title II-B: Training and Research	880	0	880	880	880
Title II-C: Research Libraries	5,760	0	5,760	6,000	6,000
Library of Congress	206,623	223,760	215,179	215,179	215,179
Library Services and Construction Act	71,520	0	71,520	71,520	71,520
Title I: Public Library Services	60,000	0	60,000	60,000	60,000
Title III: Interlibrary Cooperation	11,520	0	11,520	11,520	11,520
Medical Library Assistance Act	7,500	7,500	7,500	7,500	7,500
National Agricultural Library	8,750	9,016	8,849	8,849	8,849
National Commission on Libraries and Information Science	674	0	674	674	674
National Library of Medicine	37,535	38,543	38,543	38,543	38,543
Library-Related Programs					
Adult Education Act	86,400	—*	95,000	95,000	95,000
Bilingual Education	138,057	94,534	138,057	138,057	138,057
Corporation for Public Broadcasting†	130,000	85,000	130,000	130,000	130,000
ECIA, Chapter I (ESEA I Disadvantaged Children)	3,033,969	1,942,000	3,033,969	3,200,000	3,160,394
Education for Handicapped Children (state grants)	931,008	—*	962,428	970,000	970,000
HEA Title I-B: Education Outreach	0	0	0	0	0
III: Developing Institutions	134,416	129,600	129,600	129,600	129,600
IV-C: College Work Study	528,000	397,500	528,000	550,000	540,000
VI: International Education	19,200	8,767	20,000	21,000	21,000
Indian Education Act	77,852	51,119	65,519	66,216	67,247
National Archives and Records Service	79,403	85,293	84,644	83,000	83,000
National Center for Education Statistics	8,589	8,747	8,589	8,589	8,589
National Endowment for the Arts	143,456	100,875	143,875	143,875	143,875
National Endowment for the Humanities	130,560	96,000	130,560	130,060	130,060
National Historical Publications and Records Commission	2,500	0	3,000	3,000	3,000
National Institute of Education	53,389	53,645	53,389	55,614	55,614
Postsecondary Education Improvement Fund	11,520	11,900	11,520	11,900	11,710
Public Telecommunications Facilities	18,000	0	15,000	15,000	15,000
Women's Education Equity	5,760	0	5,760	5,760	5,760

*Included in block grant proposals for Vocational and Adult Education or Special Education.
†CPB funded two years in advance.

postal subsidies and National Archives' funding. After vetoing two earlier versions as too costly, President Reagan signed on July 18 HR 6685 (PL 97-216), a pared-down version of the FY 1982 urgent supplemental appropriation bill. It included $42 million in additional postal subsidy, which resulted in a reduction of the Library Rate from phased rate Step 14 to Step 13 (see below under "Postal Matters"), as it was before July 6. PL 97-216 also included a provision repealing language enacted during the reconciliation process in 1981, which applied any shortfall in revenue foregone first to the third-class nonprofit rate, thus helping to protect other subsidized rates, such as the library rate and free matter for the blind.

In the paring-down process, $6.5 million in additional funding for the National Archives and Records Service (NARS) recommended by the Senate was lost, but $4.1 million was included in the final supplemental appropriations bill (HR 6863) for FY 1982. This bill became law (PL 97-257) September 10, when Congress mustered the two-thirds vote necessary to override President Reagan's veto. The president characterized the measure as a budget buster with "excessive and unwarranted spending increases," but in fact the disagreement was over priorities. The bill was almost $2 billion below the president's budget, but had less for defense and more for domestic programs than he recommended. In addition to increased pay supplementals for most agencies, the bill included $39 million in additional revenue foregone postal subsidy for preferred rate mailers. Of the $4.1 million in additional funding for NARS, $1.5 million was for the National Historical Publications and Records Commission, and $600,000 was for preservation of House and Senate historical records. This brought the total for NHPRC grant programs to $2.5 million for FY 1982.

FUNDING, FY 1983

Congressional Budget

Before appropriating funds for specific programs, Congress must determine the total amount it intends to spend through its own budget process. The process was a difficult one again this year, as negotiations with President Reagan to revise his own budget dragged on and ultimately failed. Finally House and Senate budget committees developed their own budgets, but in the end the nominally Democratic House again passed a hastily drafted Republican package, which passed after eight previous budget plans had failed.

The process proved a veritable rollercoaster ride for library supporters. After suing over impounded LSCA funds, then getting them released, librarians found one budget plan, which almost passed, would have reinstated all the current year cuts Congress had rejected. An amendment drafted by Representative Paul Simon (D–Ill.) adding education and library funds passed overwhelmingly, but the vehicle to which it was attached was defeated. Then librarians and users were outraged and House members from all points on the political spectrum were embarrassed to discover that their final budget alternative eliminated free mailing for the blind and doubled the library postal rate. That budget plan passed, but part of the damage was repaired in conference, and the Simon amendment experience did influence the outcome for education and library programs. The final outcome (S. Con. Res. 92) assumed library programs would be continued at the FY 1982 levels.

Administration Budget

President Reagan's FY 1983 budget proposed to eliminate the Library Services and Construction Act, all Higher Education Act Title II library programs, and the National Commission on Libraries and Information Science. In addition, the Education

Consolidation and Improvement Act, Chapter 2 school block grant (which includes the former school library resources program), would be cut by $50,840,000.

Announced as part of the budget was a "new federalism initiative," in which the school block grant would be among 44 programs turned back to the states. Negotiations between administration and state officials on the details of the initiative broke down, and implementing legislation was never submitted to Congress. The budget also proposed to downgrade the Education Department to a Foundation for Education Assistance, but finding little support, the administration did not submit implementing legislation on this plan either.

Library Programs

The congressional budget process delayed the development of appropriations bills, so library programs were funded through continuing resolutions. The first was a temporary one through December 17. Finally on December 21 at the end of a lame-duck session, a further continuing resolution was signed into law (PL 97-377), covering the entire 1983 fiscal year (through September 30, 1983).

The continuing resolution, PL 97-377, provided funding for all of FY 1983 at the previous year's rate for the Library Services and Construction Act ($60,000,000 for Title I public library services, $11,520,000 for Title III interlibrary cooperation), the Higher Education Act, Title II-A college library program ($1,920,000) and the HEA, II-B training and research program ($880,000). For the HEA, II-C research library program there was a slight increase, from $5,760,000 to $6,000,000. For the Education Consolidation and Improvement Act, Chapter 2 school block grant, there was a decrease, from $483,840,000 to $479,420,000. The National Commission on Libraries and Information Science was funded at the FY 1982 level of $674,000.

These levels represent a significant demonstration of congressional support for a federal role in library services, considering that President Reagan's budget for all these programs except the school block grant was zero. A significant influence on congressional support was the data provided by 16 witnesses at a March 10 oversight hearing by the House Postsecondary Education Subcommittee on the impact of the proposed zero budget on library services. For instance, many multitype library cooperatives and resource-sharing arrangements are heavily dependent on LSCA III funds. As state and local budgets are squeezed, there are no funds to fill gaps left by federal funding cuts.

The House version of the continuing resolution was tied to HR 7205, the L-HHS-ED Appropriations Bill for FY 1983, as it passed the House 330-70 on December 1 with amounts for library programs at FY 1982 levels. The Senate version was tied to HR 7205 as reported by the Senate Appropriations Committee (S. Rept. 97-680) on December 8. The Senate committee bill made two changes in library programs—a $240,000 increase in the HEA II-C research library program initiated by committee Chairman Mark Hatfield (R–Oreg.) and a cut of $8,840,000 in the school block grant. Conferees on the continuing resolution accepted the II-C increase and split the difference on the school block grant cut. The Senate Appropriations Committee warned that future funding of the HEA, II-A college library program "may depend upon the establishment of a needs criteria so that only the most deserving institutions would receive an award sufficient to provide a meaningful supplement to the library materials budget."

The earlier FY 1983 continuing resolution (PL 97-276) provided funding for the legislative branch for the entire fiscal year. The Library of Congress received $215,179,-000, less than the $223,760,000 requested but higher than the previous year's $206,623,-000. Seven of the 54 additional positions requested were allowed. The Senate Appropriations Committee expressed concern over the deterioration of the library's collections of paper-based materials and noted that a process has been developed and patented by

LC to halt this deterioration. Congress provided $350,000 to treat up to 50,000 books in LC's mass deacidification program.

Several changes were made in the International Exchange Program involving the exchange of government publications with foreign governments. GPO's Superintendent of Documents, rather than the Smithsonian Institution, will be the agency responsible for distributing publications. The issuing agencies, which must participate, will be charged for the costs of printing, binding, and distribution and will determine which publications are eligible. Classified and confidential publications, as well as those with no public interest or educational value, are exempted. The Library of Congress will continue to coordinate the mutual exchange aspects of the program and maintain the foreign publications received.

For distributing government documents, the Superintendent of Documents in the Government Printing Office received $27,291,000, slightly less than the previous year and the amount requested. The National Agricultural Library was funded at $8,849,000, a bit above 1982 but less than requested. The National Library of Medicine received the requested amount of $46,043,000, of which $7,500,000 was for the Medical Library Assistance Act.

The National Archives and Records Service received $86,000,000, of which $3 million was earmarked for the grant programs of the National Historical Publications and Records Commission. This is slightly higher than the budget request and the previous year. During House floor debate on HR 7158, Representative William Dannemeyer (R-Calif.) attempted to raise a point of order against an appropriation for NHPRC and was prevented from doing so only by a parliamentary technicality. NHPRC grant programs are technically without authorization, but the continuing resolution provided general authority for the activities and programs funded under its terms.

The president requested a 27 percent cut for the National Endowment for the Humanities and a 30 percent cut for the National Endowment for the Arts. Congress disagreed and gave the Endowments essentially level funding—a marginal increase for NEA at $143,875,000 and a marginal decrease for NEH at $130,060,000, with the $500,000 cut to come from administrative costs rather than grant funds. Table 1 shows funding details for these and other library-related programs.

COPYRIGHT

The "Guidelines for Off-Air Taping of Copyrighted Programs for Educational Use" became part of the legislative history of the 1976 copyright law with its publication in a House Judiciary Committee report issued April 29. The report (H. Rept. 97-495) accompanied legislation (PL 97-495) passed by Congress to strengthen criminal penalties against record, tape, and film piracy and counterfeiting for commercial use.

Over President Reagan's veto, the manufacturing clause (Section 601) of the copyright law was extended for four years. The 1976 law would have eliminated the clause on July 1, 1982. The manufacturing clause is essentially a nontariff protective device for the U.S. printing industry, which provides that certain nondramatic literary material in the English language must be manufactured either in the United States or Canada in order to enjoy full U.S. copyright protection.

In preparation for the first five-year review of Section 108 of the Copyright Law (Title 17 USC), which was due to Congress January 3, 1983, the Register of Copyrights invited written final comments to nine questions published in the May 26 *Federal Register* (pp. 23061ff.). The subject of the report is the extent to which the law has achieved the intended balance between the rights of creators and the needs of users of copyrighted works that are reproduced by certain libraries and archives. At the same time, availability of the King Research, Inc., report, *Libraries, Publishers, and Photocopying: Final Report of Surveys Conducted for the U.S. Copyright Office*, was announced and comments invited.

Library associations generally felt that the King Report demonstrated overwhelming compliance with the law by librarians and described a healthy, viable scholarly journal publishing industry. They contended that the intended balance had been achieved, and that no amendments to the law were necessary at this time.

Hearings were held in the House on bills dealing with home recording of copyrighted works. Librarians and educators testified in opposition to a compulsory royalty tax on audio and video recorders and blank tapes, because of the many education- and library-related uses of the tapes and equipment, which have nothing to do with taping copyrighted broadcast programs off the air.

Congress took no action on any of the measures, but its interest in the matter stemmed from the October 19, 1981, decision by the Ninth Circuit Court of Appeals in San Francisco. That decision overturned a lower court decision in the controversial *Betamax* case and ruled that taping a television show in the home violates a producer's copyright, and that manufacturers of recording equipment are liable for such infringement. The Sony Corporation, makers and distributors of copying equipment, have taken the suit, brought by Universal City Studios and Walt Disney Productions, to the Supreme Court, which was scheduled to hear oral arguments on January 18, 1983.

In August, the American Library Association filed an *amicus curiae* brief urging the Supreme Court to reverse the Ninth Circuit Court's decision. The ALA brief contended that the circuit court's finding that only "productive" uses of copyrighted materials could be fair use has enormous consequences for librarians and library users, threatens to deprive libraries of their fair use rights, undermines their ability to serve their patrons adequately, and restricts the public's access to information.

[For a five-year review of the new copyright law, see the Special Reports section of Part 1; also see the annual report from the Copyright Office in the Federal Agencies section of Part 1—*Ed.*]

ECIA CHAPTER 2 BLOCK GRANT

The Department of Education issued revised final regulations for the school block grant (Chapter 2 of the Education Consolidation and Improvement Act of 1981) in the November 19 *Federal Register* (pp. 52368–52386). The original final regulations published July 29 (*FR*, pp. 32884–32900) were disapproved by Congress on August 10 because of the secretary of education's determination that the General Education Provisions Act (GEPA) did not apply to ECIA Chapters 1 and 2. The new final regulations state that the secretary has reconsidered and, except for some provisions of GEPA that are superseded by ECIA, adopts the interpretation that GEPA is applicable to Chapter 2 and will administer the block grant accordingly—thus retaining such GEPA provisions as advance funding, automatic extension, paperwork control, and prohibition against federal control of education, including selection of library resources.

Congress passed technical amendments (HR 7336) to the block grant, clarifying certain fiscal requirements for future audit purposes, and added citizenship education (PL 97-313) to the list of purposes for which block grant funds could be spent. [See the report on ECIA Chapter 2 later in Part 2—*Ed.*]

FLORENCE AGREEMENT—NAIROBI PROTOCOL

Both House and Senate gave final approval on December 21 to a tariff measure (HR 4566) that included implementation of the Nairobi Protocol to the Florence Agreement on the Importation of Educational, Scientific and Cultural Materials. Called the

Nairobi Protocol after the location of the negotiations, it would extend duty-free status to audiovisual and microform materials, whether educational or not, and to products for the blind and other handicapped persons. On September 30, the Senate had unanimously ratified the protocol as a treaty (Treaty Doc. 97-2). Ratification and implementation of the protocol follow up on a recommendation of the White House Conference on Library and Information Services. Remaining steps not yet completed at this writing include the president's signature and the deposit of the U.S. instrument of ratification.

GOVERNMENT INFORMATION POLICIES

On October 6, 1982, the Office of Management and Budget released a list of more than 2,000 government publications—one out of every six—targeted for termination or consolidation into other publications. This initiative, together with 4,500 other cost reductions proposed for an additional 2,300 publications, is expected to produce cost savings "of more than one-third of all federal publications." According to OMB 82-25, "Reform '88: Elimination, Consolidation and Cost Reduction of Government Publications," 16 percent of all government publications will be discontinued. This amounts to 70 million copies, one-twelfth of the 850 million copies printed, and is part of ". . . the Reagan Administration's continuing drive to eliminate costly, redundant and superfluous publications. . . ." Each federal agency will be reviewing its publications for increased user fees. OMB emphasized that "the cutback will not affect needed and necessary printed materials that should be available to the public. Use, not abuse, is the key phrase of this program as we evaluate the importance and use of each publication." Similar savings are expected in the years 1983 to 1985.

The OMB initiative, together with other examples of cutbacks in the collection, publication, and dissemination of information by the federal government, caused librarians concern, as did a September 8 *Federal Register* (pp. 39515-39530) notice by OMB regarding proposed regulations for the information collection provisions of the Paperwork Reduction Act of 1980. The assumption throughout was that federal data collection is a burden on the public, with little recognition given to the benefits to the public that are derived from accurate, nonbiased and timely statistics.

LSCA IMPOUNDMENT

Despite the lawsuit involving ten states and three adverse General Accounting Office opinions, the Reagan administration managed to impound for six months $19,710,000 in Library Services and Construction Act funds provided by Congress for FY 1982. The funds were finally released on April 26, after the period for congressional consideration of the administration's request to rescind the funds had expired.

The lawsuit sought a court order compelling the administration to end its illegal impoundment of library funds and to distribute to the states the full amount appropriated by Congress for this purpose. Prepared by the New York Attorney General's office, the suit was filed in Federal District Court in Washington, D.C., on March 5, with the states of California, Florida, Kentucky, Maryland, Ohio, and Oklahoma as coplaintiffs. The states of Maine, Alabama, and Connecticut later joined as intervenors. On May 4, the federal government moved to dismiss the suit.

Although a rescission request was not submitted until February, the administration had been releasing less than Congress approved for LSCA since October 1981. Under the continuing resolution (PL 97-92) in effect for the first half of FY 1982, and later extended through September 30 (PL 97-161), Congress funded LSCA at the rate of $71,520,000 (Title I at $60,000,000; Title III at $11,520,000), but the administration released funds only at the September budget request level of $51,810,000 (I, $41,250,000; III, $10,560,000). The rescission request for the lower amount submitted to Congress on February

5, the same day GAO sent a legal memorandum to Representative Peter Peyser (D-N.Y.) stated that the withholding of LSCA funds was illegal impoundment.

A second and third GAO opinion confirmed the first and characterized LSCA as a mandatory spending statute, for which the administration lacked the authority to request rescissions. Despite GAO's findings and a March 29 hearing by a House Budget Committee task force, the administration continued to withhold the funds until the 45-day rescission period ended on April 23.

MEDICAL LIBRARIES

The House passed and a Senate committee approved reauthorization of the Medical Library Assistance Act, but because Congress failed to complete the process, MLAA is technically without authorization. However, the continuing resolution (PL 97-377) for FY 1983 provided general authority for the activities and programs funded under its terms. In addition, the conference report (H. Rept. 97-980) on the continuing resolution specifically referred to the MLAA portion of the statute (Public Health Service Act, Title III, Part J) in providing $46,043,000 for the National Library of Medicine, of which $7,500,000 was for MLAA.

NCLIS APPOINTMENTS

On December 21, the Senate confirmed the nominations of John Juergensmeyer, Byron Leeds, Jerald Newman, and Julia Li Wu as members of the National Commission on Libraries and Information Science. On October 1, the Senate had confirmed Elinor Hashim as NCLIS chairperson. The five were first nominated by President Reagan in November 1981—Hashim and Leeds for terms expiring July 19, 1986, the other three to replace commissioners (Joan Gross, Clara Jones, and Frances Naftalin) who were being removed before the expiration of their terms. On July 19, 1982, the terms of the three appointments in question expired, and on August 5, the president resubmitted the three nominations for terms expiring July 19, 1987.

On April 27, the House Postsecondary Education Subcommittee held an oversight hearing to investigate the administration's attempt to remove three commissioners prematurely. Frederick Burkhardt, NCLIS chairman emeritus, pointed out that the five-year staggered terms were established by statute specifically to insulate commissioners, who advise both the president and Congress, from shifting political winds. The Senate Labor and Human Resources Committee delayed action on the nominations until the disputed terms had expired, and for the first time in NCLIS history, held a hearing on the nominations on December 9.

POSTAL MATTERS

Supplemental funding for FY 1982 increased the amount of money available to support subsidized postage rates, and reduced rates took effect July 28. For phased rates, this meant a return to Step 13, which was in effect prior to July 6. A 2-pound package sent fourth-class library rate dropped from 47¢ to 42¢. For FY 1983, a temporary funding measure maintained the lower rates, but the final continuing resolution pegged the subsidy at Step 14, which means that the 2-pound library rate package would go up to 47¢ again in January 1983. The $789 million in subsidy required for Step 14 contrasted sharply with the amount recommended by the president ($500 million) and by Congress's own budget ($400 million).

The first commemorative stamp honoring "America's Libraries" was issued by the U.S. Postal Service July 13. The first day of issue ceremony for the 20¢ stamp took place at the American Library Association's annual conference in Philadelphia.

STANDARDS FOR FEDERAL LIBRARY/INFORMATION POSITIONS

A proposed revision of the classification/qualification standards for library and information positions in the federal government was issued by the U.S. Office of Personnel Management in December 1981. The proposed standards generated lengthy and detailed responses from federal agencies, federal library groups, and professional associations, because they reduced entry grade levels and devalued librarians' educational qualifications. The revision was expected to compromise the quality of federal library and information services and have far-reaching implications for the profession. Important questions about pay equity and fairness to a female-dominated profession were raised, as standards for male-dominated fields such as accounting had been quite recently revised without depreciating those professions.

OPM turned down requests for a public review of a second draft, but in September allowed closed-door reading sessions at OPM for a limited number of groups, who found a much revised but still very unsatisfactory document. Inequities in the proposed standards were explored in September by three subcommittees of the House Post Office and Civil Service Committee at hearings on pay equity for women, with testimony from OPM Director Donald Devine and the American Library Association.

The hearings were followed by national publicity and increased congressional concern. Finally, OPM released a third draft for a brief public review with comments due by December 15, the date the standards were to be transmitted to the OPM director for final action. As the year ended, the controversy had not been resolved, but there was a congressional request to delay development of final standards until the General Accounting Office reviewed the substance and procedure used in the proposed revision as part of a major pay equity study.

OTHER LEGISLATIVE AND REGULATORY ACTIVITY

Two pending tax measures of interest to librarians did not receive final approval. A bill (HR 5573) to provide a tax deduction to corporations for donations of new computers to schools for use in educating students passed the House easily in September and was amended by the Senate Finance Committee to include libraries and museums as eligible recipients, but was never brought to the Senate floor. The Senate Finance Committee also approved restoration of a tax deduction (HR 1524) for donations of literary, musical, or artistic compositions by their creators to charitable institutions such as libraries. The deduction was lost to authors and artists in a 1969 tax reform measure with a consequent decline in donations of contemporary manuscripts to libraries. The Senate briefly considered the deduction as an amendment to the gasoline tax bill in the last days of the session, but did not vote on the amendment.

Librarians also monitored closely various telecommunications developments. Cable television legislation (S. 2172) was approved by a Senate committee but not passed. Revision of the common carrier provisions of the Communications Act of 1934 passed the Senate (S. 898) in October 1981, but a House bill (HR 5158) was dropped in July 1982 in committee, when its provisions became too controversial after the Justice Department announced a proposed settlement in the pending antitrust suit against American Telephone and Telegraph. The settlement involved divestiture of the local exchange service and access functions of the 22 Bell operating companies and would permit AT&T to enter unregulated markets. The settlement was approved in August by a U.S. District Court judge, and the restructuring of the Bell system will take effect in 1984. All these changes in the communications industry and the degree of federal regulation will affect the rates and conditions under which libraries use telecommunications. Table 2 shows the status of legislation of interest to librarians.

TABLE 2 STATUS OF LEGISLATION OF INTEREST TO LIBRARIANS
(97th Congress, 2nd Session, Convened January 25, 1982, Adjourned December 23, 1982. Chart Date: January 13, 1983)

Legislation	House Introduced	House Hearings	House Reported by Subcommittee	House Committee Report Number	House Floor Action	Senate Introduced	Senate Hearings	Senate Reported by Subcommittee	Senate Committee Report Number	Senate Floor Action	Conference Report	Final Passage	Public Law
Congressional Budget Ceilings	HConRes 352	X		597	X	SConRes 92	X		385	X	614	X	
Copyright—home video taping	HR 5250, 5705	X				S 1758	X						
Copyright manufacturing clause	HR 6198	X		575	X	S 1880			none	X	none	X	PL 97-215
Copyright Piracy Act	HR 3530		X	495	X	S 691			274	X	none	X	PL 97-180
ECIA Regs.—Res. of Disapproval	HConRes 388			701	X	SConRes 115				X			
ECIA Technical Amendments	HR 7336	X			X	HR 7336	X			X	none	X	Pocket Vetoed
Florence Protocol	HR 6093	X		977	X	HR 4566			564	X	989	X	PL 97-446
Foreign-language program assistance	HR 3231	X	X	316		S 1817							
Freedom of Information Act Amendments	HR 4805	X				S 1730	X	X	690				
Information Science and Technology Act	HR 3137	X											
Job Training Partnership Act	HR 5320	X	X	537	X	S 2036	X		469	X	889	X	PL 97-300
Medical Library Assistance Act	HR 6457	X	X	791	X	S 2311	X		461				
National Archives—Independent Agency	HR 6894					S 1421	X						
NHPRC Extension						S 2501							
National Library and Information Services Act						S 1431							
NTIS & NBS Authorization	HR 5726			501	X	S 2271			337	X	none	X	PL 97-286

176 / LEGISLATION, FUNDING, AND GRANTS

Taxation—Manuscript donations	HR 6662, etc.						
Taxation—Computer Equipment Contribution	HR 5573	X	X	836	X	HR 1524	X	643
Taxation—Thor Power Tool ruling	HR 1016, 1936					S2281	X	647
Telecommunications—Cable TV						S 578	X	
Telecommunications Competition and Deregulation	HR 5158	X	X			S 2172	X	518
						S 898	X	170
Appropriations								
Urgent Supplemental Approp. FY 1982	HR 6685			none	X	HR 6685	X	none	X	PL 97-216
Supplemental Appropriations FY 1982	HR 6863			673	X	HR 6863		516	X	747	X	PL 97-257
Continuing Resolution FY 1983	HJRes 631		X	959	X	HJRes 631		none	X	980	X	PL 97-377
Agriculture, FY 1983	HR 7072	X		800	X	HR 7072	X	566	X	957	X	PL 97-370
Commerce, State Department, FY 1983	HR 6957	X	X	721	X	S 2956	X	584		
HUD, Independent Agencies, FY 1983	HR 6956	X	X	720	X	HR 6956	X	549	X	891	X	PL 97-272
Interior, FY 1983	HR 7356	X	X	942	X	HR 7356	X	none	X	978	X	PL 97-394
Labor-HHS-Education, FY 1983	HR 7205	X	X	894	X	HR 7205	X	680		
Legislative, FY 1983	HR 7073	X	X	801		S 2939	X	573		
Treasury, Postal, FY 1983	HR 7158	X	X	854	X	S 2916	X	547		

For bills, reports, and laws write to: House and Senate Documentation Rooms, U.S. Capitol, Washington, D.C. 20515 and 20510, respectively.

LEGISLATION AFFECTING PUBLISHING IN 1982

AAP Washington Staff*

For the fourth straight year, there was no individual appropriation bill passed for the agency that funds education and library programs; yet it did not suffer under funding by the stopgap continuing resolution—the message was "keep on spending as you have."

A seemingly foolproof giveaway, a bill to provide schools with free computers and their benefactors with an extra tax deduction, appeared to be sliding easily through the Ninety-seventh Congress, when a Washington newspaper editorial attacked it as special interest legislation, a senator threatened to filibuster it, and a notable lack of enthusiasm from the White House left it dangling—unpassed—at the hectic time of adjournment.

A four-year extension of the protective manufacturing clause in the 1976 Copyright Law, opposed by publishers but favored by printers and their unions as a jobs measure, passed both houses of Congress overwhelmingly just before a June 30 deadline. It was vetoed by President Ronald Reagan as contravening administration trade policies, but then repassed over his veto by both houses in mid-July.

The continuing philosophical and partisan split between House and Senate, plus the winding down of the White House–congressional honeymoon, led to some stalemated legislation, such as the perennial recodification of federal criminal laws (some with First Amendment ramifications) and proposed new curbs on the federal Freedom of Information Act. The latter survived without sweeping amendments, but continued to be nibbled away by the granting of single-agency exemptions tucked away in other legislation.

In addition to the manufacturing clause extension, publishing suffered another legislative setback in 1982; over the opposition of the writing and publishing communities, Congress overwhelmingly enacted an excessively broad measure that, in its effort to protect the identity of covert intelligence agents, threatened to expose legitimate writers and reporters to prosecution for pursuing their normal investigative activities.

The year 1982 was an unusual legislative year for book publishing.

EDUCATION AND LIBRARY FUNDING PROGRAMS

If 1981 funding for federal education and library programs were compared with the night, 1982 would be a bright dawn—far from a full, sunshiny day, but clearly a bright dawn.

The second session of the Ninety-seventh Congress chose to ignore the president's requests for sharp reductions in FY 1982 and FY 1983 education and library spending. Although Congress reduced FY 1982 Department of Education spending slightly to $14.7 billion form FY 1981's $14.9 billion, by the time the year drew to a close, Congress had increased the department's funding for FY 1983 (October 1, 1982 to September 30, 1983) to $15 billion. Although this is little more than holding one's own, in a year of record federal deficits and unprecedented requests for slashes in education spending, it was considered a victory.

*The Association of American Publishers' (AAP) general Washington staff includes Richard P. Kleeman, Roy H. Millenson, Judith Platt, Diane Rennert, and Carol A. Risher, all of whom contributed to this article.

Underscoring the bipartisan support for education is the fact that the FY 1983 Education Department appropriation bill approved by the Democratic House of Representatives asked for $15.011 billion, while the Republican Senate's measure called for $15.018 billion. The difference was compromised at $15,011,145,000 (an increase of $5.11 billion over the budget), with increases over the previous year for compensatory education for the disadvantaged, elementary-secondary impact aid, education for the handicapped, vocational and adult education, college student aid, research libraries, and the National Institute of Education. Among the programs suffering losses were elhi block grants and departmental management, salaries, and expenses.

In addition, neither the Democrat-controlled House nor the Republican-controlled Senate approved any of the president's requests for rescissions (impoundments) of Department of Education programs. And, giving further emphasis to their support for education, senators and representatives in September joined in overriding the president's veto of the FY 1982 Supplemental Appropriations Bill, which, among other things, contained $148 million for education of disadvantaged children and $217 million for college student aid.

In other funding legislation, Congress appropriated $30 million for FY 1983 National Science Foundation (NSF) science and engineering education activities, twice the budget request and almost 50 percent more than FY 1982 funding. The increase is expected to be applied to precollege teacher training, public understanding of and research in science education, undergraduate science education, and enhanced opportunities for minorities in the sciences.

As it has done in previous years, AAP testified in support of needed education and library program funding. "Both guns and books," the AAP told House and Senate appropriation committees, "must stock any effective arsenal of democracy."

In other areas, the House of Representatives approved by a heavy 323–62 margin the Computer Equipment Contribution Act, the so-called Apple bill, providing for increased corporate tax deductions for donations of computers for educational purposes to elementary and secondary schools. The Senate Finance Committee reported the bill just before the election recess on October 1, making several changes, including adding libraries and museums as eligible recipients. However, the Senate failed to approve the bill during the brief postelection lame-duck session, thus making it necessary to reintroduce the measure in 1983.

The National Agricultural Library received a fiscal year 1983 appropriation of $8,849,000, up $99,000 from the previous year but $167,000 less than the president's budget request. The National Library of Medicine was also increased, receiving $46.043 million (the budget request), up from 1982's $40.035 million.

The new Education Consolidation and Improvement Act (ECIA), PL 97-35, which superseded the Elementary and Secondary Education Act (ESEA) and consolidated many elhi programs, went into effect on July 1 for the 1982-1983 school year. At this writing it is still too early to assess the effects of the new statute.

Final regulations on Chapters 1 and 2 of the ECIA issued on November 19 contained revisions advocated by AAP. The Department of Education now acknowledges that both programs are covered by the General Education Provisions Act (GEPA), which, among other provisions, prohibits federal control over the selection by assisted schools and colleges of library resources, textbooks, and other instructional materials, as well as barring federal "direction, supervision, or control" over curriculum. [See the report on ECIA Chapter 2 later in Part 2—*Ed.*]

Along the same lines, the Job Partnership Training Act, PL 97-300, contains a provision initiated by AAP that bars federal "direction, supervision, or control" over curriculum and the selection of library resources, textbooks, or other printed or published instructional materials by any educational institution or school system receiving funds under the bill. The new statute replaces the CETA employment training program.

Legislation passed the House but failed to pass the Senate restoring the fair market value tax deduction for donations of literary, musical, and artistic works by their creators to charitable institutions and libraries. Both AAP and the American Library Association supported the measure.

POSTAL AFFAIRS

Postal Rate Increase

Postmaster General William Bolger has stated frequently that he hoped to hold off on an overall rate increase until early 1984. As of September 1982, the United States Postal Service (USPS) was running a surplus of $612 million. Some of the factors that contributed to the surplus include a higher than expected mail volume, lower inflation, and fuel and energy savings of approximately $17 million under budget. It appears that a new rate increase request will be forthcoming in early 1983 with implementation in early 1984.

International rates, however, may increase as much as 10 to 20 percent in the first half of 1983. USPS may do this without going before the Postal Rate Commission. This rate increase is not to be confused with any rate increase resulting from the Universal Postal Union Conference (UPU), which is held every five years to set international rates between countries.

Revenue Foregone Appropriations

Since the advent of the Reagan administration, postal funding has been a hard-fought, seesaw adventure. The administration has consistently called for drastic reductions in revenue foregone, which allows the phasing of certain nonprofit rates, including the Library Rate and rates for classroom periodicals. Under current law, revenue foregone enables the Postal Service to maintain preferential rates for these classes of mail until 1987.

AAP, working with a broadened nonprofit coalition in 1982, launched an intensive effort to ensure that appropriations were forthcoming to continue the phasing schedule. The coalition argued that since the administration has called upon the private sector and charitable organizations to pick up the slack of reduced federal spending, it is unduly hampering such activity by calling for drastically increased postal rates for these groups.

Initial actions in 1982 by the House and Senate appropriations committees pegged phasing appropriations at $708 million for FY 1982. This would mean that phased rates would have gone from present Step 13 to Step 14 on October 1, 1982. However, under a continuing resolution adopted by the Congress prior to its recess for the November 1982 elections, funding was pegged to continue at Step 13, at $880 million. Final action taken by the Congress during the lame-duck session appropriated $789 million, thus mandating an increase to Step 14 to be effective on January 8, 1983.

Mail Fraud Legislation

In fall 1982, the House Post Office and Civil Service Committee reported out a scaled-down version of the original Senate-passed Mail Fraud bill. This legislation is an attempt to strengthen the Postal Service's mail fraud enforcement powers. After extensive hearings in the House, at which AAP testified, enforcement powers in the original bill were reduced to prevent infringement of constitutional rights.

AAP proposed incorporating the mirror-image concept currently adhered to by the Federal Trade Commission and welcomed its acceptance. Mirror-image provides that if an advertisement accurately reflects the contents of the book it is promoting, it cannot be subject to mail fraud proceedings. However, time ran out at the end of the session and the Senate and House bills were never reconciled. AAP will be working in the new Congress to have the measure reintroduced.

Repeal of the Private Express Statutes

Proposals for the repeal or modification of the private express statutes have been around for a long time but are presently receiving renewed interest because of administration backing. Congress has traditionally resisted efforts to repeal the statutes, which ensure a monopoly on first-class mail, because of the fear of reduced service and higher rates. Publishers and other mailers tied to USPS could suffer significantly if mail volume declined, as USPS fixed costs would have to be spread over fewer units of mail, thus requiring more frequent rate increases.

Supreme Court Case

The Supreme Court undertook to review the proper interpretation of the postal rate-making statutes. On one side of the litigation are the National Association of Greeting Card Publishers and United Parcel Service, which believe the statute calls for a rigid cost-accounting type of rate setting. On the other side, the solicitor general of the Justice Department argues in behalf of the Postal Service's more discretionary approach. AAP and most other parties support the USPS interpretation, which was endorsed by the Second Circuit Court of Appeals. A decision is expected in early 1983. Whatever the outcome, it is considered likely that parties dissatisfied with the decision may seek legislative relief.

Service Standards

Certain service standards for USPS that were written into the budget reconciliation act in 1981 may be subject to further examination in the new Congress. One mandated USPS to continue six-day delivery until September 30, 1984, and the other prohibited implementation of the nine-digit zip code before October 1, 1983.

Postal Reorganization Amendments

Two subcommittees of the House Post Office and Civil Service Committee conducted joint and extensive hearings in 1982 on the impact of the Postal Reorganization Act of 1970, a decade after it became law. AAP testified along with other major mail users.

A reorganization bill was scheduled to be introduced early in the new Congress. Some of the issues that were to be discussed include rate and classification matters, changes in the Postal Rate Commission, electronic mail, labor relations, and a host of miscellaneous provisions. AAP will play an active role during formulation of this legislation.

COPYRIGHT

The manufacturing clause, scheduled to disappear on July 1, 1982, received a reprieve in active legislative maneuvers during 1982. The late Congressman John Ashbrook (R–Ohio) had introduced H.R. 3940, a bill to retain in the copyright law the requirement that, as a condition of copyright protection in the United States, books be manufactured in the United States or Canada. Multiple hearings were held before the Judiciary Subcommittee and in March, when the bill was reported out of committee, the unlimited extension was modified to a four-year extension. The Ways and Means Subcommittee on Trade asserted jurisdiction in May and held hearings. Although the members also supported the compromise four-year extension provision, they requested the U.S. International Trade Commission to make a study of the trade implications of removing the clause. The ITC study is due July 1, 1983.

The House approved the four-year extension following a heated debate on June 15. The Senate passed the bill on June 30. The president vetoed the bill, leading the publishing industry to a short-lived euphoria that ended July 13, when both houses of Congress overrode the veto. Hence, until July 1, 1986, nondramatic literary works in English by American authors must be printed in the United States in order to be eligible for protection under the U.S. copyright law.

In August, the Authors League of America and Irwin Karp, its general counsel, filed suit against the Register of Copyrights, the secretary of the treasury, and the commissioner of customs, alleging that the manufacturing requirement is unconstitutional and violates both the First and Fifth amendments. The AAP joined the suit in December as an intervenor in support of Karp and the league.

Copyright Office Undertakes Study on Formalities

In February, the Copyright Office awarded a $262,869 contract to King Research, Inc., of Rockville, Maryland, to undertake a cost-benefit study of the effect of copyright office procedures, recordation, and registration requirements on the motion picture and textile industries. The study, to be completed by January 1, 1984, will also compare the U.S. copyright system with the systems in use in nations with fewer formalities. Among the formalities to be reviewed are the use of the copyright notice, the registration of claims, the recording of transfers of ownership, and the deposit of works to enhance the collection of the Library of Congress.

Betamax

In direct response to the Ninth Circuit Court of Appeals opinion that home videotaping is a violation of the copyright law, bills were introduced in both the House and Senate to change the law. The bills would have exempted home taping of television, radio, and audio recordings from copyright liability but would have provided a royalty payment on the sale of blank tapes and recording devices to compensate copyright owners. Although 1982 saw considerable activity in this arena, the Ninety-seventh Congress ended without enacting any legislation.

On June 14, 1982, the Supreme Court granted the petitions of *certiorari* and consented to review the *Betamax* case. Briefs were filed in September and October and oral argument was held January 18, 1983.

Five-Year Review

The Copyright Act of 1976 requires the Register of Copyright to prepare reviews of the effectiveness of the law in achieving the intended statutory balancing of the rights of creators with the needs of users. The first of these five-year reports is due January 3, 1983. As part of the review process, hearings were conducted, comments were solicited, and King Research was commissioned to do a comprehensive study on library photocopying. The King Report was provided to the Copyright Office in June 1982, and 40 groups, including AAP, filed comments on the study.

[A five-year review of the new copyright law is included in the Special Reports section of Part 1—*Ed.*]

Work for Hire

On October 1, the Senate Judiciary Committee convened a hearing on S. 2044, a bill introduced by Senate Thad Cochran (R-Miss.) to amend the work for hire provisions of the copyright law. Although the hearing was held, no further action occurred during the Ninety-seventh Congress.

FIRST AMENDMENT LEGISLATION

Differences between the two houses of Congress and between Congress and the White House resulted in the stalemate of much legislation with First Amendment implications. Thus, despite some committee activity on the perennial recodification and amendment of the federal criminal code, the measure wound up stymied between a conservative version, approved in Senate committee late in 1981 but never brought to the Senate floor, and the resolute House predilection for piecemeal, rather than omnibus, revision of criminal laws.

A coalition of the writing and publishing communities was unable, however, to stem the momentum of the bill to punish those who publicly expose the identity of covert intelligence agents. In statements on this bill, the coalition, of which AAP was a part, supported the objective of protecting intelligence agents but termed the bill unconstitutionally broad: As overwhelmingly passed by both houses, it did not require "intent to impair or impede" U.S. foreign intelligence to establish criminality but merely "reason to believe" that publication of an agent's identity would result in such harm. Also passed over in the rush to enact this legislation was the fact that public identification of a covert agent would be a crime even if the information were obtained from unclassified or public sources. The measure was signed by the president, with considerable fanfare, at CIA headquarters in Virginia. (In a subsequent published interview, a CIA spokesperson said the act "is not designed to prevent legitimate reporting on the intelligence community or intelligence abuses. It's strictly designed to counteract a few individuals who have made their careers out of publishing long lists of intelligence officers." The act, according to this spokesperson, will be used "only in very special circumstances.")

Controversial proposed changes in the federal Freedom of Information Act, approved by the Senate Judiciary Committee in somewhat moderated form and reported just as the Ninety-seventh Congress drew to a close, must be resubmitted and considered anew in the Ninety-eighth. Even if the Senate had approved this joint initiative of the Reagan administration and Senator Orrin Hatch (R-Utah), Senate Constitution Subcommittee chairperson, it would have faced tough sledding in the House. This probably will prove even more true in the new Congress, whose newly elected, expanded Democrat majority is expected to intensify resistance to any major weakening of public information legislation.

Late in the second session of the Ninety-seventh Congress, legislation surfaced that resulted from a June decision of the U.S. Supreme Court (*New York* v. *Ferber*). The decision held that sexually explicit depictions of minors need not be legally obscene to lose First Amendment protection. The legislation introduced by Senators Specter and Grassley (Pennsylvania and Iowa Republicans, respectively) was designed to implement that decision in federal criminal law. In December 1982, AAP testified on the legislation (which must be reintroduced in 1983), supporting the general objective of combating sexual exploitation of minors but urging the application of a test as to whether materials considered for prosecution "taken as a whole, (lack) literary, artistic, scientific or educational value." Otherwise, AAP cautioned, the legislation, in its attempt to suppress child pornography, might "sweep within (its) grasp a variety of serious works deserving of wide availability and unrestricted dissemination."

A nonlegislative act of the Reagan administration, over which Congress was virtually powerless to do more than criticize (which a House committee did), was the issuance of an executive order on national security information. In effect, this order turned on its head the formerly applied test of when to classify government information: Where previously there had been a balancing of the need to classify against the public's right to know, the 1982 executive order empowered federal officials to classify "if there is reasonable doubt about the need to classify."

LEGISLATION AFFECTING THE INFORMATION INDUSTRY IN 1982

Robert S. Willard

Vice President, Government Relations
Information Industry Association

The second year of the administration of Ronald Reagan showed signs of wear in the relationship between the White House and Congress. Although the president was still successful in getting much of the legislation he wanted during the second session of the Ninety-seventh Congress, such legislation did not always contain every provision he had requested. Furthermore, his margin of victory was lessened, principally in the House of Representatives, where straying Democrats who had pushed through the president's tax and spending reduction packages in 1981 now began to return to the folds of their party. The wisdom of their return was evident after the November midyear election; the mainstream Democrats significantly increased their numbers, probably to the point where they can derail any efforts of the Republicans and conservative Democrats whose coalition had been so successful in the first session of the Ninety-seventh Congress.

Furthermore, some of President Reagan's legislative efforts in 1982 had to be devoted to undoing parts of the prior year's efforts. The purity of supply side economics (which posits that reduction in taxes leads to more money in the hands of business and consumers, which will stimulate economic growth) had to be tainted by the reality of projected deficits of staggering and unprecedented dimensions. Reluctantly, the president supported a nearly $100 billion (over three years) tax increase, which was euphemistically packaged as the "Tax Equity and Fiscal Responsibility Act." The president also found it necessary to seek a $71 billion (in four years) increase in the federal tax on gasoline. Ostensibly sought to fund improvements in the "infrastructure," i.e., roads, bridges, tunnels, harbors, etc., this increase was seen by many as a means to create public jobs, many of which had been eliminated the prior year, and to reduce the level of unemployment, which had climbed past 10 percent during the year.

With the attention of the government focused on tax and spending issues, and with the attention of individual legislators directed toward their own employment problems (i.e., reelection), Congress did not pass a great deal of legislation of any type. De-

Note: The opinions expressed in this article are those of the author and do not necessarily represent those of the Information Industry Association.

spite the crescendo of attention to information issues in the world at large, perhaps best typified by *Time* magazine's selection of the computer as the "Machine of the Year" in place of its traditional "Man of the Year," Congress passed few information-related bills. Of course, as in past years, there were numerous information policy bills introduced, perhaps as high as 15 percent of the more than 13,000 bills introduced during the Ninety-seventh Congress. But very few of these were the subject of any attention at all, and only a handful made it to the president's desk to be signed into law.

It is not surprising that there is such a paucity of information-related legislation enacted, however. In general, the Ninety-seventh Congress did not produce record numbers of new laws. Partly, this may be attributed to the general conservative theory that less government is better government. It may also be ascribed, at least in part, to the institutional friction that develops when a different party controls each house and the traditional conflict between Congress and the White House. During 1982, Congress passed and the president signed 328 public laws, considerably below the 426 and 410 public laws produced by the second sessions of the Ninety-sixth and Ninety-fifth Congresses, respectively. (Notably, for all three Congresses, 65 to 70 percent of their total public laws were passed in the second session.)

Furthermore, the number 328 may be misleading. Anyone scanning a list of the public laws (for example, see page D22ff. of the *Congressional Record*, January 25, 1983) may justifiably wonder how Congress accomplishes anything substantive with all the time it spends on matters designating special days, weeks, months, and years, or naming federal buildings in someone's honor, or authorizing the award of gold medals. Nor were information concerns ignored in this congressional well-wishing. The following special observations were added to our calendars by Congress in 1982: National Newspaper Carrier Appreciation Day (PL 97-294), National Closed-Caption Television Month (PL 97-419), and National Children and Television Week (PL 97-443). Congress was still unsuccessful, despite Senate passage, in designating James Madison's birthday as Freedom of Information Day!

This article cannot attempt to describe all the information-related legislation that was introduced; it will, however, discuss some bills that did not become law. Such bills are significant to the information industry, and their introduction in the Ninety-seventh Congress may be a precursor of more extensive treatment by future Congresses. Legislation will be classified in one of five categories: (1) proposals that mandate or encourage the government to become involved in the information marketplace; (2) measures aimed at protecting the economic value of information resources; (3) government rules affecting the transport of information or communications; (4) legislative items that address civil liberty issues in the information arena, such as privacy and First Amendment rights; and (5) proposals that may be an incentive or an impediment to flows of information.

GOVERNMENT COMPETITION

In 1982, the National Commission on Libraries and Information Science published the report of a task force that had been grappling with the complex issue of what are the appropriate roles of the public and private sector in the provision of government information. This subject has long concerned the Information Industry Association, which argues that the dynamism of a private-sector, market-driven mechanism is the most efficient and effective device for ensuring the widest availability of information. The government, IIA argues, when it enters the information marketplace, should do so most cautiously in order not to upset the supply and demand relationships that provide the signals for the working of the marketplace. Although a summary of the NCLIS task force report would be beyond the scope of this article, it can be stated that the report will serve as a critical benchmark for Congress if that body decides to seek legislative treatment of the issue. [A summary of the task force report is included in the Special Reports section of Part 1—*Ed.*]

Congress did not turn its attention to this subject in any significant way during 1982. Earlier legislative imbroglios, such as the proposal to start a National Periodical Center or the request for funding a Worldwide Information and Trade System, were not repeated in the second session of the Ninety-seventh Congress. For the most part, Congress (to the extent it paid any attention to the subject) tended to deal with the subject of competition generically rather than through specific examples.

House and Senate joint resolutions had been introduced the year before, expressing the sense of Congress that it is the general policy of the government to rely on competitive private industry to provide the products and services it needs. In 1982 a proposed law was introduced in the Senate by John East (R-N.C.) that would establish a policy of promoting public-sector procurement of goods and services from profit-making business concerns; the bill also used the threat of withholding federal funds in order to extend this policy to state and local governments.

The East bill died with the end of the Ninety-seventh Congress. Like so many previous measures (either proposed or enacted) dealing with reliance on the private sector, this bill failed to differentiate between those products and services the government needs for itself (such as paper clips, cruise missiles, and trash collections on government installations) and those that the government provides to the public (such as medical screening tests, consumer literature, and trash collection from private facilities). East and his philosophical compatriots would argue that both should be provided by contracting with the private sector. However, in the latter case, there is often no reason for government involvement at all. There are municipalities where the government neither collects trash itself nor contracts with private collectors to do so; instead, individual consumers engage private collectors from a number of competitive services. The competition not only acts to keep prices low; it also provides dissatisfied clients an alternative for better service.

This theory—that sometimes the government need take no action, yet socially beneficial tasks will be accomplished—is the thrust of one bill that focuses squarely on information issues. Introduced in 1981 by Glenn English (D-Okla.), the bill, H.R. 4758, was the subject of hearings in 1982; it would have prevented federal agencies from vending telecommunications and automatic data processing services. The bill was originally focused on electronic funds transfer (as offered by the Federal Reserve Bank) and electronic mail (U.S. Postal Service). In both cases, the bill's sponsor felt that the public would be better served if these information services were provided by competitive private enterprise. At the hearings, additional witnesses (including the author) testified that the same concept held true in relation to information *content* services, i.e., that information dissemination functions such as those provided by the National Library of Medicine, the International Trade Administration, and the National Institute of Mental Health could have a deleterious effect on the development of competitive private-sector offerings.

English's bill, which did not go any farther in 1982, wisely recognized that there will still be times when the government must provide information services, and English was careful to provide an exception to the general prohibition of the bill. However, further recognizing marketplace ramifications, his bill requires full cost pricing of government-provided services to prevent predatory pricing that would drive or freeze out private-sector involvement in the marketplace. A similar sensitivity to pricing appears in a bill sponsored by Senator Orrin Hatch (R-Utah). S. 1730, the Freedom of Information Reform Act, allows agencies to charge fair value fees or royalties, in addition to processing fees, if the information requested under the act contains commercially valuable technological information acquired by the government at substantial public cost. The bill was reported out of committee in the waning days of the Ninety-seventh Congress, but it did not reach Senate debate, nor would it have been successful in the House. The pricing policy obviously raises serious questions. Price could be used as a means to bar access to information that an agency finds embarrassing, not necessarily commercially valuable. Furthermore, there is the tenet that if the government paid for information, it should be available to the public at a reasonable cost. On the other hand, a commercial vendor who has invested in developing an information system that could be replicated by information owned by the government does not want to see "instant competition" spring up with the tremendous price advantage that could come from buying information from the government at the cost of reproduction. This issue is sure to be before Congress again.

PROPRIETARY RIGHTS

Congress paid a significant amount of attention to copyright issues in 1982, especially as infringing activities came more into the realm of consumer issues. Although no legislation ultimately moved, both the House and Senate judiciary committees devoted a great deal of attention to legislative proposals to address home videotaping of copyrighted materials. Some argued for a blanket exemption for private home recording or for including such taping in the category of "fair use" copying, whereas others (principally the creators of the copyrighted presentations) sought a compulsory license provision that would permit copying but would impose a royalty fee that would be added to the price of recording machines and blank tapes. The issue engaged, on either side, some of the best known names in the legal community. (Frequently the media paid more attention to the lobbying activity than to any serious discussion of the issues involved.) Despite the intensive efforts, however, much of the wind went out of the sails when the Supreme Court agreed to review the original litigation that sparked the legislation and scheduled the presentation of oral argument for early 1983. The Court's decision may not be known until midyear, but it seems certain that a decision either way will spur the losing side to push with greater urgency for legislation that will change the Court's action. [For a five-year review of the new copyright law by Nancy H. Marshall, see the Special Reports section of Part 1—*Ed.*]

Congress did pass a few bills in the area of proprietary rights—i.e., patent, trademark, and copyright—although much was in administrative areas such as collecting fees or elevating the position in the Commerce Department hierarchy of the commissioner of patents. One substantive new law, the Piracy and Counterfeiting Amendments Act (PL 97-180), significantly increased criminal penalties for piracy in the area of records, tapes, and audiovisual material. Attempts by the Information Industry Association and other computer-related associations to amend this bill to protect also software and data bases from piracy were rejected shortly before final passage of the legislation because hearings on the legislation had not examined such proposals. However, toward the end of 1982, legislation specifically addressed to the issue of software piracy (H.R. 6420) was introduced by Representative Barney Frank (D-Mass.).

One amendment to the Copyright Act that became law generated a great deal of attention, although arguably the issue was one more of trade protectionism than of proprietary rights. The manufacturing clause of the Copyright Act, which links copyright protection of certain categories of work to their being produced in the United States or Canada, was scheduled to expire on July 1, 1982. In an eleventh-hour action the Senate passed and sent to the president a four-year extension of this clause. President Reagan, claiming that the printing industry was now robust and no longer needed the protection provided by the manufacturing clause, vetoed the bill. In a surprise move, Congress, returning from its Independence Day recess, voted to override the veto and the extension became law less than two weeks after the clause had lapsed. Notably, this veto override was the first time Congress voted to override a Reagan veto; out of 13 vetoes in the second session of the Ninety-seventh Congress, only one other was overridden.

A copyright proposal that received considerable attention during 1982 was a fragile compromise in the television area involving creators of program material, broadcasters, and cable television operators. H.R. 5949, the Cable Television Copyright Act Amendments, was introduced by Representative Robert Kastenmeier (D-Wis.) after extensive consultation with the affected industries. The bill, which dealt with what signals cable companies could, could not, and must carry, and more importantly, how much cable companies would have to pay for the rights to retransmit, passed the House in September. When the bill reached the Senate, however, it was referred to three committees; before the year was over, the compromise was unravelling and the legislation died in the Senate committees.

The proprietary aspects of new computer technology also absorbed the attention of some members of Congress during 1982, but, like the cable copyright bill, went nowhere. In addition to the software piracy act cited earlier, the House also had introduced H.R. 6983, a software protection bill (promoted by the Association of Data Processing Service Organizations, ADAPSO, and introduced by Representative Kastenmeier). One noteworthy feature of this bill was its recognition of the coexistence of (federal) copyright protection and (state) trade secret protection; some argue that current law is murky on this point (toward the end of 1982, the Supreme Court refused to hear a case on this subject). Also introduced in the House was an updated version of legislation introduced in earlier Congresses that would explicitly provide copyright protection to computer silicon chips, the near microscopic circuitry on which so much of today's information technology is built.

Finally, although not a copyright bill, H.R. 3970, introduced by Representative Bill Nelson (D-Fla.), recognizes the proprietary value of information. Originally introduced in the Ninety-fifth Congress by (now retired) Senator Abe Ribicoff (D-Conn.), the Federal Computer Systems Protection was introduced in the House in 1981 and was the subject of hearings in the fall of 1982. This bill, among other provisions, would make unauthorized access of information in a broad class of computers a federal crime. Nelson, as a state legislator, was successful in seeing a version of the Ribicoff bill through the Florida legislature, but the U.S. Congress has been reluctant to move the federal version. Some early critics felt the bill was too expansive in its claim of federal jurisdiction, arguing that pocket calculators (and later, personal computers) would be included under the law, and that a computer operator who kept a church mailing list on a computer, or who printed out a popular novelty calendar, without permission, would be a federal criminal. Although these particular points seem to have been remedied in the latest version of the bill, no groundswell appears to be advancing the prospects of Nelson's bill.

COMMUNICATIONS

Perhaps no aspect of information policy received more attention during 1982 than did telecommunications. For, if January 1 marked the beginning of a new year, January 8, 1982, marked a beginning of a new age. On that date, the Justice Department and the American Telephone & Telegraph Company announced the settlement of the eight-year-old government antitrust suit against AT&T, and AT&T announced how, as a condition of the settlement, it was going to divest itself of a great proportion of the Bell system. The operating companies that provide local telephone service to the vast majority of Americans would become independent entities, and the remaining AT&T would provide long-distance service and telecommunications equipment without the competitive strictures of an agreement signed by Bell and the U.S. government in 1956 settling an earlier antitrust complaint.

When this announcement was made, Congress already had before it major legislation dealing with telephone (more formally, common carrier) issues. Since June 1978, each Congress had grappled with rewriting all or at least part of the Communications Act of 1934, the basic charter for U.S. telecommunications. Although surprisingly elastic, this law, nearly 50 years old, was showing signs of strain when trying to accommodate some contemporary technological realities (such as the often cited blurring of the boundary between communications and computer processing). By January 1982, the Senate had already passed a comprehensive revision of Title II of the Communications Act, the part dealing with common carriers, and a similar, but appreciably different, bill (H.R. 5158) had been introduced in the House by Representative Tim Wirth (D-Colo.) just one month earlier.

But both these bills dealt with a predivestiture AT&T. Wirth, who chairs the House Telecommunications Subcommittee, prepared a series of amendments that would tailor H.R. 5158 to address some of the shortcomings he saw in the settlement; he successfully included these amendments in the bill, which was approved overwhelmingly by his subcommittee. When the bill was taken up by the full committee (on Energy and Commerce), experienced vote counters predicted that Wirth had the votes to bring the bill out of committee to the floor of the House.

However, AT&T had decided that the bill contained provisions that were unacceptable to it. While supporting the concept of some legislative action in the communications area, AT&T launched a massive lobbying campaign against Wirth's bill, arguing that "H.R. 5158 is the wrong number!" Despite the presence of enough votes on the committee, a small coterie of Bell supporters, ably led by Representative Tom Corcoran (R-Ill.), used a battery of dilatory legislative weapons to delay action on the bill. They engaged in such actions as insisting on reading the full bill and every amendment and demanding recorded votes even when amendments were noncontroversial and had received a unanimous voice vote.

Meanwhile, AT&T, in an unprecedented step, requested its millions of stockholders and its nearly 1 million employees (and, in at least one part of the country, its customers) to write to Congress in opposition to Wirth's bill. With this outpouring of opinion and a crowded legislative agenda facing the Commerce Committee, Wirth reluctantly withdrew the bill from further consideration, and prospects for communications legislation in the Ninety-seventh Congress died in midsummer.

However, many of the objectives of the Wirth legislation were attained anyhow that same summer. Under a procedure agreed upon by the Justice Department and AT&T, U.S. District Court Judge Harold Greene sought public comment and oral briefings before entering the settlement agreement into force. Following this fact finding, Judge Greene enumerated a number of changes that he wanted before signing the settlement. Of special importance to information publishers was a restriction on AT&T's ability to sell information electronically over communications facilities it owns. This provision was one that had been sought by the American Newspaper Publishers Association and that had been supported by the Information Industry Association in material submitted to Wirth. Indeed, Wirth had been a proponent of such a proscription in both his own bill, H.R. 5158, and in an amendment he had offered to similar legislation in the Ninety-sixth Congress. With very little discussion, both AT&T and the Justice Department accepted the judge's changes and started in motion a stream of events that will culminate in a divested Bell System in early 1984.

Congress was also unsuccessful in passing legislation dealing with international aspects of telecommunications. Following the successful passage of the Communications Act Title II rewrite, the Senate Commerce Committee was able to turn attention to a bill introduced by Barry Goldwater (R-Ariz.), the International Telecommunications Competition and Deregulation Act (S. 2469), which sought to inject into the international arena the same degree of free market competition that was being encouraged domestically. The bill also would have formalized a coordination mechanism within the Executive branch to deal with international information and communications matters. Although reported by the committee in late November, the bill received no further action by the Senate.

Despite the inability of Congress to pass major telecommunications legislation, a number of new laws touched on communications issues. The budget reconciliation act (PL 97-253), for example, trimmed the membership of the Federal Communications Commission from seven to five, effective in July 1983. Congress also passed a number of changes, mostly technical in nature, that became PL 97-259. Included in this statute is a requirement for the National Telecommunications and Information Administration to "conduct a comprehensive study of the long-range international telecommunications and information goals of the United States," along with the policies and strategies related to these goals.

Finally, in the area of communications is a small bill that was approved in the waning days of the Ninety-seventh Congress, mandating electromagnetic characteristics for telephones subject to FCC regulation. PL 97-410 seeks to guarantee the ability of hearing-impaired individuals to use hearing aids with most phones on the nationwide network.

CIVIL LIBERTIES

The most controversial legislation to be enacted in the area of First Amendment freedoms was H.R. 4, the Intelligence Identities Act of 1982 (PL 97-200). This bill, which was widely criticized by reporter and publisher organizations, establishes heavy penalties (up to $50,000 fine and/or ten years' imprisonment) for intentional disclosure of information identifying covert agents of the United States. Although the more severe penalties apply to those who had legitimate access to classified material, penalties are also set for individuals who discern the names of such agents from open material and disseminate their discovery publicly. Many observers characterize this as a restraint on the freedom to publish, especially in light of the fact that unclassified material is the source of the information. Others point out the legitimate needs for national security and the requirements—both strategic and on a human level—to provide a level of security to those agents of the United States who are endangering their lives to provide valuable intelligence to the national security establishment.

Conflicting rights characterize the issues in this particular category of information policy legislation. The right to privacy, for example, is often balanced off against some advantage the individual receives in exchange for the surrender of some personal information. One trades medical history information to gain insurance protection; another provides financial background information to ensure access to financial credit. Such sacrifices are tolerated in the knowledge that the provider of the desired service would be unwilling to offer the service unless some information was available to eliminate or, at least reduce, the risk. Sometimes the need to make the trade is more apparent than in others. Three bills passed by Congress in 1982 authorize the establishment of national personal information systems, and in each case a benefit, either to the individual involved or to society at large (or both), appears to exist. The rightness of each system, as in all of these balancing issues, lies in the eye of the beholder.

Least controversial of these new systems is authorized in the Missing Children Act (PL 97-292), which, according to one senator, meant that federal authorities would be able to retain the same degree of information on missing individuals (especially children) that they were already authorized to keep on stolen automobiles. This law also authorized the retention of information to assist in the identification of deceased individuals. Another national information system containing personal information is required by PL 97-364, which deals with alcohol traffic safety programs. Title II, known as the National Driver Register Act, authorizes the secretary of transportation to set up a system that would contain and relay data from participating states concerning drivers with bad records. One obvious objective is to prevent the issuance of a license by one state to a driver whose license had been revoked or suspended for cause by another state.

PL 97-365, the Debt Collection Act, specifically authorizes federal agencies to reveal personal information, generally protected under the federal government's Privacy Act, to consumer reporting agencies when the individual whose record is being disclosed has an outstanding debt to the U.S. government. Moreover, it requires that any person applying for federal loan programs must furnish a taxpayer identifier number at the time of application. The law also allows the usually sacrosanct tax records of the Internal Revenue Service to be tapped to provide a mailing address for a taxpayer against whom there is a federal claim.

Both these latter two laws required technical or conforming amendments to be made to the federal Privacy Act, but no major attempt to change the privacy laws of the country occurred in 1982, despite a large number of privacy bills having been introduced. Furthermore, despite the administration's assignment of a high level of priority, no change took place in the Freedom of Information Act in 1982 either.

REGULATION OF INFORMATION FLOWS

The second session of the Ninety-seventh Congress had before it a host of bills dealing with how the government could encourage or impede flows of information and the growth of information technology. Very few of these, however, became law. Nevertheless, it is worth reviewing some of them, because they give a sense of what some of the more information-sensitive legislators are concerned with; many are likely to receive further consideration in future Congresses.

One of the most far-reaching bills, in terms of government organizational response to the issues of the information age, received little attention at all in 1982. Introduced the year before by Representative George Brown (D-Calif.), the Information Science and Technology Act (H.R. 3137) would establish a national institute and create a presidential adviser to deal with information issues. During 1982, the only apparent action on the bill was the issuance by the House Science and Technology Committee of a report on the prior year's hearing.

A handful of bills was introduced with the general objective of increasing knowledge of computers and related technology. For example, S. Con. Res. 130, which was an expression of the sense of Congress with respect to scientific and technological superiority of the communications and electronics industry in the United States, was passed in the final weeks of Congress's 1982 session. This resolution, which did not require the signature of the president, supported the establishment of a Science Center for Communications and Electronics on unused federal land in Georgia. In a similar vein, George Miller (D-Calif.) introduced the Electronic and Computer Technician Vocational Education Incentive Grants Act, which would provide funds to states for electronic and computer technician training. A third bill, introduced in 1981, was Thomas Downey's (D-N.Y.) effort to establish a Computers in Education program.

Two novel ideas in the area of personal computers proposed to use the tax system to provide appropriate incentives to increase computer literacy. The proposal receiving more attention in the media was the Technology Education Act, introduced by Pete Stark (D-Calif.) in the House and John Danforth (R-Mo.) in the Senate. Popularly known as the "Apple bill," because it was conceived and actively pushed by the chairman of the Apple Computer Corporation, it would have liberalized the charitable deduction for the contribution of personal computers to primary and secondary schools. The other bill, with the not particularly pertinent name the "Family Opportunity Act," would have allowed a $100 tax credit per family member for the purchase of a personal computer up to 50 percent of the cost of the computer. This bill, introduced by Newt Gingrich (R-Ga.), did not move at all in 1982, but the Apple bill did pass the House in September. The Senate, which did report the bill out of the Finance Committee, failed to take any further action, partially due perhaps to the lack of any enthusiastic support on the part of other manufacturers of personal computers.

Congress paid attention to some international information issues. There was a flurry of action, principally in the context of the communications legislation, to provide some protection to domestic markets against foreign suppliers who may not have had markets in their countries open to U.S. suppliers. This concept went under terms such as "reciprocity" or "equal market access." In the absence of any clear administration position on the issue, no legislation became highly visible in 1982. Congress did, however, look at the issue of trade in services, such as telecommunications and information, in foreign countries, and the Senate passed Daniel Inouye's (D-Hawaii) Services Industries Development Act, which included in its purposes promoting the competitiveness of U.S. services and promoting the sale of U.S. services abroad. Also, as mentioned earlier, Congress directed the administration to prepare a study on telecommunications and information goals in the world marketplace, in the Communications Act amendments.

U.S. participation in international organizations having to do with information was questioned by the Congress in the Department of State Authorization Act (PL 97-241). Specifically, Congress expressed concern over the United Nations Educational, Scientific and Cultural Organization's (UNESCO) "efforts to regulate news content and to formulate rules and regulations for the operation of the world press." The president was required to report to Congress on U.S. participation in UNESCO; funding for such participation would be cut off if UNESCO took action that would have collided with the traditional U.S. concept of a free press.

This same authorization bill required the secretary of state to report to Congress on the status of scientific exchanges with the Soviet Union, including an "assessment of the equality or inequality of value of the information exchanged." Coincidentally, this bill also restored the name "U.S. Information Agency" to the organization President Jimmy Carter had named the International Communication Agency in 1977.

CONCLUSION

Although the record of Congress was lackluster in terms of generating information-related law during 1982, a broad range of provocative and promising issues began to be considered. Many observers voiced concern over the inability of Congress to accomplish even its basic work. For the second year in a row, and despite its return for a lame duck session following the general elections, Congress was unable to complete all of the funding bills required to run the government and instead restored to the contrivance of the continuing resolution to appropriate FY 1983 funding. So it is not surprising that Congress would not be able to turn attention to information issues. Nevertheless some of the most complex policy (and political) questions are going to be raised by the emergence of new information technologies. Congress—as an institution and as a collection of individual members—is going to have to increase the attention it pays to this area.

Funding Programs and Grant-Making Agencies

COUNCIL ON LIBRARY RESOURCES, INC.

1785 Massachusetts Ave. N.W., Washington, DC 20036
202-483-7474

Jane A. Rosenberg
Program Associate

The Council on Library Resources, Inc. (CLR), is a privately operated foundation established in 1956 by the Ford Foundation. Currently supported by a number of foundations, the CLR attempts to assist libraries, especially academic and research libraries, in solving problems and in reducing obstacles to information access. In pursuit of its objectives, the council awards grants to individuals and institutions to carry out projects in several areas: bibliographic services; professional education, training, and research; library operations and services; and library resources and their preservation. Two major programs also are currently maintained by the council: the Bibliographic Service Development Program (BSDP) and the Professional Education and Training for Research Librarianship Program (PETREL). Within these programs, the CLR provides funding for specific projects and for research related to the program objectives. In establishing its programs and constructing its agenda, the council depends heavily on the advice and assistance of research librarians, library educators, university officials, and other qualified persons. Such individuals assist program efforts as members of task forces and committees, as well as providing ongoing counsel.

In 1982, a special committee of the CLR board of directors was established to consider ways in which the council might be most useful to the library and scholarly communities during the decade ahead. Program adjustments that reflect the committee's observations and recommendations, and subsequent board discussions, are under way in the following areas, which will equally claim CLR attention during the years immediately ahead: the national aspects of collection development and preservation, bibliographic service for library users, access to documents and information, library management, technology, and professional education.

The board of directors of the council consists of 18 individuals affiliated with academic institutions, research libraries, and businesses. The officers are Whitney North Seymour, chairman; Louis B. Wright, vice chairman; Warren J. Haas, president; and Mary Agnes Thompson, secretary and treasurer. The council's headquarters has always been in Washington, D.C., but in 1982 the CLR offices moved from One Dupont Circle to the nearby National Trust headquarters building on Massachusetts Avenue.

BIBLIOGRAPHIC SERVICE DEVELOPMENT PROGRAM (BSDP)

Established in 1978, the BSDP is supported by seven major foundations and the National Endowment for the Humanities. Focused on helping to ensure access to a comprehensive set of bibliographic record data bases and on controlling costs of bibliographic processes in libraries, BSDP made substantial progress in a number of program areas during the year, especially in projects to evaluate online public access catalogs and to link bibliographic computer systems. Preparatory work for another program area, subject access, also has begun. During FY 1982, more than 40 BSDP grants were active, and funding of nearly $2 million was administered through the program. As a guide to the wide-ranging efforts to improve bibliographic services, the projects are described under broad topical headings.

Standards and Guides

Recognizing the need for consistent and dependable methods of accomplishing agreed-upon tasks, the BSDP has devoted much effort to help develop codes, protocols, and standards. Grants have been made to the Research Libraries Group (RLG), the Washington Library Network (WLN), and the Library of Congress (LC) to develop the Standard Network Interconnection (SNI), a standard means of linking computer systems. The SNI consists of a set of telecommunication protocols, based on existing telecommunication standards, that can be used to enable one computer system to communicate with another. A supplementary grant has been made to Northwestern University to assist in the coordination of protocol development activities with similar activities in Canada.

The council also continues to assist Committee Z-39 of the American National Standards Institute (ANSI) with grants for specific projects. Current support is for standards related to holdings information in bibliographic records, telecommunications protocols, and book paper quality.

The International Standards Organization (ISO) sponsors several working groups that are preparing for the use of standard character sets for non-Roman foreign languages. Such work is a necessary preliminary step toward eventual conversion of bibliographic records in these languages to machine-readable form. The BSDP supported travel expenses for a Library of Congress staff member to attend a Paris meeting of the ISO's Working Group on Character Sets.

Finally, the Pittsburgh Regional Library Center has been developing a prototype system for recording and communicating serials subscription cancellations via an online union list.

Linking Bibliographic Data Bases: The Linked Systems Project (LSP)

The goal of the LSP is to develop, coordinate, and link the bibliographic and computer systems of the Washington Library Network, the Library of Congress, and the Research Libraries Group so that they can exchange bibliographic records and other information. In effect, these links will provide the technical environment required to implement a national bibliographic record service. The project involves (1) the development of computer-to-computer protocols, as mentioned under "Standards and Guides," above; (2) the design of software to translate the languages of individual computer systems into the language of the telecommunication links; and (3) the test of the links. The participants will perform the test by exchanging authority records, utilizing the work of the council's task force on a Name Authority File Service (NAFS).

During the first two phases of the LSP, participants conducted an assessment of the feasibility of linking systems and defined a plan for accomplishing the work. RLG and WLN received assistance to make the changes in their authority systems that were necessary for a computer exchange of information. Plans also were made for the hardware and software for the link, and the telecommunications system itself was analyzed.

At the same time, the NAFS task force was developing guidelines for a national name authority file service. The task force will be hosted by the Library of Congress, with a number of institutions contributing records to the file. Those involved in the authorities work have incorporated the revised NAFS task force requirements into their specifications for the LSP. The specifications include software to translate commands from each system into the language of the telecommunications link and back again into system language.

Bibliographic Products

Major bibliographic record data bases built during the 1970s are now available to library users in the form of online public access catalogs. However, many questions about the catalogs and how they are used have yet to be answered. The BSDP has mounted a two-year project, in which the following groups are cooperating to evaluate online catalogs: J. Matthews & Associates, OCLC, Inc., the Research Libraries Group, the University of California, Division of Library Automation, and the Library of Congress.

During the first phase of the project, participants designed and tested questionnaires and other tools for data collection. Northwestern University Library, Stanford University Library, and Dartmouth College Library received grants to cover the costs of participation in these planning activities and for data collection activities. OCLC, Inc., received funding to support training activities for interviewers and data collection personnel. The University of California, Division of Library Automation, has received a BSDP grant to carry out machine analysis of the data collected by all participants, mostly during April and May 1982. One major report based on project research has been published: Charles Hildreth's *Online Public Access Catalogs: The User Interface* (Dublin, Ohio: OCLC, Inc., 1982).

Early results of the online catalog investigation are influencing another BSDP initiative, the investigation of subject access. Nearly two-thirds of the users of the catalogs begin their efforts with a subject search—a greater number than in card catalog use studies. The council has contracted with Pauline Atherton Cochrane to develop a plan to enhance the cross-reference structure of the *Library of Congress Subject Headings*, as one means of helping users find subject-related material more easily. The BSDP organized a meeting of 23 specialists in subject access to consider additional improvements to the existing systems for locating subjects. Participants have drafted recommendations for improvements, which include both short- and long-term projects.

Several other BSDP projects involve the use of bibliographic products. Victor Rosenberg, University of Michigan School of Library Science, is developing computer programs to extract and reformat bibliographic records from shared cataloging services data bases. Donald Cook, University of Toronto, has received funding to assess the differences in *Anglo-American Cataloging Rules (AACR-II)* applications in four national libraries: the National Library of Australia, the British Library, the National Library of Canada, and the Library of Congress. A final report has been received from Martha Williams, University of Illinois Coordinated Science Laboratory, on her project to compile statistics on the MARC data base. The report includes an analysis of changes in record length, field tags, and field lengths over an eight-year period (1973–1981). It also describes relationships among selected fields within the records.

Access to Bibliographic Data

Several BSDP projects concentrate on evaluating use of machine-readable data bases and on the addition of new capabilities for locating and delivering information. During the past year, support was provided for three meetings of the Network Advisory

Committee to the Library of Congress. The meetings focused on resource sharing and the need to improve delivery of information, as a direct response to improvements in locating material through online bibliographic data bases.

In 1980, the council provided funds to the LC Cataloging in Publication Division (CIP) to evaluate the effectiveness and impact of its program. *CIP Survey Final Report*, which appeared in May 1982, includes a description of the survey (conducted among libraries of all types), the results of the inquiry, and recommendations for future CIP activities.

One of two projects that focus on additions to existing data bases is the Association of Research Libraries Microform Project, which was funded for a two-year period beginning in March 1981. During the first year of the project, a survey was conducted to obtain information on libraries' current cataloging efforts, existing catalog records, and other activities related to cataloging microform series. At Rutgers University another project to build an international inventory of machine-readable texts in the humanities is receiving BSDP support. The data on existing texts will be gathered from responses to a questionnaire, and the information will be input as a specific data base in the Research Libraries Information Network (RLIN).

Conversion of Serials (CONSER)

CONSER is a cooperative effort among libraries to build a data base of bibliographic records for serial publications. Several projects relating to this effort are receiving council support. The Boston Theological Institute project to add unique titles in religion and theology to the CONSER data base is partially funded by CLR, and the council continues to support participation by the National Library of Canada in CONSER by providing funds to cover the U.S. telecommunication costs. In August 1981, the BSDP also provided funds for participants to travel to an Association of Research Libraries–National Federation of Abstracting and Indexing Services meeting to develop a detailed operational plan for adding information to the CONSER data base. The group has developed a proposal to input information on the indexing and abstracting services that include titles in the CONSER data base; the information would be added to the records for each title covered.

PROFESSIONAL EDUCATION, TRAINING, AND RESEARCH

The council's Professional Education and Training for Research Librarianship Program (PETREL) entered its second year in FY 1982. Four major projects, including three professional education programs, have been funded under this program. Other activities aimed at improving education and training and providing opportunities for professional growth also have received support. In June 1982, the PETREL Advisory Committee invited library school deans, library directors, and personnel officers to a two-day meeting to discuss the place of internships in professional education and to consider other topics pertaining to careers in librarianship. A forthcoming program report will include the substance of the June discussions. [For a report on "Recent Developments in Library Education," see Part 3—*Ed.*]

Professional Education Programs

In 1981, the University of Michigan School of Library Science was awarded a two-year grant to recruit highly qualified graduates of liberal arts and sciences programs to the profession of research librarianship and to develop a special curriculum for basic professional education in that area. The first class of four students completed the program in 1982, and a second six-member class began work in September 1982.

A program to advance working professionals' knowledge of management theory and practice and to prepare them for senior management positions in research libraries has begun at the University of Chicago Graduate Library School. Chicago has received a two-year grant for the program, and six students have been recruited for the initial year.

The Graduate School of Library and Information Science at the University of California, Los Angeles, received funding to operate a Senior Fellows Program for three years, beginning in August 1982. The program is intended to provide individuals who have assumed major administrative responsibilities in libraries with an intensive educational experience to enhance their management skills and to give them a chance to work with leading library educators. An initial six-week session is followed by one-year individual research projects, with occasional meetings to discuss progress.

In December 1981, a five-day conference, "Universities, Information, Technology, and Academic Libraries: The Next Twenty Years," was hosted by the Graduate School of Library and Information Science, University of California, Los Angeles. Forty-nine invited participants from libraries, library schools, university administration, and associations met to discuss predicted changes in academic institutions and the implications for research libraries. The conference, funded by CLR, was intended to provide an extraordinary educational opportunity for a selected group of professionals both inside and outside librarianship. Another goal of the conference was to help the profession identify the areas that require research and development assistance in the immediate future.

Research Support

As the year ended, a new PETREL project was launched, providing research support for joint projects by faculty members and librarians. Those whose projects are funded will receive small grants to cover the incremental costs of research.

In addition to this new project, several other efforts funded under the PETREL program continued. A report titled *MLA's Role in the Educational Process for Health Sciences Librarians* was completed for the Medical Library Association with council assistance, and at C. W. Post Center, Long Island University, faculty members continued their project to prepare to teach introductory information science courses in the library school. Jovana J. Brown of Evergreen State College received a CLR grant to study the British Library Research and Development Department funding of academic library research in Great Britain.

ACADEMIC LIBRARY MANAGEMENT INTERN PROGRAM

This CLR program was suspended during FY 1982 pending its evaluation by CLR staff, program participants, and others. For the program review, the council received comments from interns and library directors on their experiences with the program and opinions about its lasting value. Based on the positive response of the participants, the council made preparations during the spring of 1982 to select a 1983–1984 class of interns and to resume the program.

LIBRARY OPERATIONS AND SERVICES

The CLR maintains a strong interest in research library operations, including management, services, and economic matters. Another concern—and one that is receiving more of both librarians' and users' attention—is access to library resources. Helping to improve existing systems for delivering information and materials and supporting inquiries into major questions about locating and using materials are current council concerns.

In October 1981, a council-supported meeting convened by the Association of Research Libraries and the Research Libraries Group, Inc., was held to explore questions related to research library economics and financing. A report of the discussions, *The Economics of Research Libraries*, has been issued. Another cooperative project, which involves the council and the Association of American Universities (AAU), is ongoing. In 1981, the two organizations sponsored a meeting of 12 university officials, librarians, and foundation executives to discuss major issues facing research libraries. Task forces were named to address specific topics, and by early 1982 the groups had finished their research and discussions. Plans are under way to implement their findings and recommendations.

Since 1970, the council has provided support for the Association of Research Libraries' Office of Management Studies (OMS). In 1978, the OMS consolidated its assisted self-study programs in the Academic Library Program, funded by the council through a grant from the Carnegie Corporation (and others). This funding has helped the OMS develop and operate several types of self-study programs in which library staff members examine current conditions and needs and recommend changes in library programs and activities. As part of the program, the OMS implemented a Consultant Training Program to provide a selected number of librarians with the skills and experience to assist libraries' self-study efforts and training programs. During 1980 and 1981, 40 librarians completed the two-week training workshop and began working with OMS staff on self-study and training projects. A third class of trainees was selected in June 1982.

Several projects to enhance the library's role in the instructional process and to improve communication between librarians and faculty members are in progress. Following the recommendations of participants at an April 1981 meeting organized by the Association of Research Libraries and the American Association for the Advancement of the Humanities, the council funded the distribution of a bimonthly newsletter, *Library Issues*, to faculty at three institutions: the University of Colorado, University of North Carolina, Chapel Hill, and Princeton University. Another project aimed at improving faculty-library communication and understanding, scheduled to begin in 1983, is the University of Michigan study of faculty attitudes toward locating and obtaining materials held in storage. Improvements in both physical delivery systems and in bibliographic access are planned.

In the College Library Program, now in its last two years of operation, Ball State University, the University of Evansville, St. Olaf College, and Johnson C. Smith University submitted final reports on their project activities. The program has provided funding for selected libraries to institute or improve bibliographic instruction and other course-related activities. Another ongoing effort to bring faculty members and librarians together to facilitate instruction is the series of conferences on bibliographic instruction held at Ball State University. CLR grants have provided funding for the sixth and seventh conferences, held in April 1982 and planned for April 1983, respectively.

Two projects in the specialized fields of archives and records administration have received council support. The Society of American Archivists (SAA) is conducting a project to establish a self-study and evaluation process for archival agencies, with CLR assistance. Six institutions have tested the study process and accompanying documentation, and project coordinators have revised the materials in preparation for final SAA approval and publication. Another project focuses on the procedures and methods used to acquire, preserve, and make accessible government records. The council invited representatives of a number of interested institutions and associations to a June 1982 meeting to consider ways to address these concerns. The group has endorsed a major effort to find solutions to problems that concern archives and their users, and funding is being sought to support the work of a planned committee on government records.

LIBRARY RESOURCES AND THEIR PRESERVATION

Helping to ensure the availability of collections and information resources needed to support library use is the continuing focus of this area of the council's program. Preservation of materials is one subject to which the council has long devoted special attention. The CLR Committee on Production Guidelines for Book Longevity has been working for two years to help librarians, publishers, and others evaluate more carefully the materials used in book manufacturing. The goal is to prevent at least some future preservation problems. During FY 1982, the committee surveyed publishers' use of acid-free paper and produced an interim report on binding titled *Longevity in Book Binding*. Another attempt to gain a better understanding of how books have been constructed is the project by John Sharpe III (Duke University) and Guy Petherbridge to gather information on Byzantine bindings dating from the twelfth through the sixteenth centuries. Their research concentrates on a selected group of manuscripts, attempting to construct a profile of the features of traditional Greek bookbinding.

[For a report on "Education in Conservation of Library Materials," by Josephine Riss Fang see Part 3—*Ed.*]

Collection use and assessment projects also received council attention during 1981 and 1982. Four members of the Cooperative College Library Center in Atlanta—Atlanta College of Art, Dillard University, Tougaloo College, and Tuskegee Institute—are testing a collection assessment manual for small academic libraries. The ARL Office of Management Studies is coordinating the study, and the manual, when completed, will be available from ARL. Research on the use of library materials is being conducted by Paul Metz, of Virginia Polytechnic Institute and Virginia State University. Metz has received CLR funding to conduct a 13-month study of the status and disciplinary affiliation of users of library materials. His work is intended to extend earlier library use studies and to supplement bibliometric research on literature use.

Support continues for several projects related to the production of resources and guides for librarians and users. Since 1975, CLR has supported a regular column in *Choice* magazine, which provides evaluations of new periodicals and serials. The second edition of Robert Downs's *British and Irish Library Resources* was published in 1981. Downs received CLR assistance for travel to Great Britain to do research for the book. Finally, Wayne Wiegand, University of Kentucky, continued the project to produce essays on 15 prominent academic library leaders. The *Journal of Academic Librarianship* has published several of the essays, and a book-length collection of all the contributions is currently being prepared.

INTERNATIONAL PROGRAMS

CLR support for international activities is directed, for the most part, to projects similar to those described above. In past years, the Exxon Education Foundation has provided two general support grants for international programs; in 1981, a third grant was received from the foundation. Much of CLR funding is channeled through international organizations such as the International Federation of Library Associations and Institutions (IFLA). In early 1982, *The IFLA International Study of Copyright of Bibliographic Records in Machine Readable Form* was completed with the aid of a CLR grant. The report recommends bilateral exchange agreements among national bibliographic agencies as the most feasible current mechanism for governing the exchange of machine-readable bibliographic data. Another CLR-supported IFLA study, *Copyright and Library Materials for the Handicapped*, by Françoise Hébert and Wanda Noël, was made ready for publication with the help of a 1982 supplementary grant from the council.

The IFLA International Office for Universal Bibliographic Control received council assistance to organize an international meeting, held in August 1982, to consider the standards for, and the implementation of, cataloging in publication programs. It also is coordinating a review of the International Standard Bibliographic Descriptions that have been in use for five years. The CLR grant also provides support, in the form of consultant assistance from the director of the office, for developing countries attempting to establish national bibliographic services.

The council supported the publication of Thomas Wadlow's *The Disposition of Government Records*, a records management manual for third world countries that was published in 1981. The manual was the subject of discussion at an international seminar organized by the International Council on Archives and the National Archives of India, in October 1981, and jointly supported by CLR and the government of India. Archivists from India, Nepal, Pakistan, Malaysia, Sri Lanka, and Iraq attended the meeting. The proceedings have been published under the title *Disposition of Government Records: Proceedings of the International Seminar*.

Several additional projects have received CLR support. The International Association of School Librarianship was given a small grant, on the occasion of its tenth anniversary, to help expand programs. Forest Press, publisher of the *Dewey Decimal Classification*, continues work on the Arabic edition of the schedules. The text is nearly complete and it is currently being reviewed.

During FY 1982, several travel grants provided opportunities for professional activity that would not otherwise have been available. IFLA received a grant to enable an executive board member to attend the UNESCO/IFLA Congress on the Universal Availability of Publications in Paris, in May 1982. Two senior staff members of the National Library of China (Beijing) received assistance for an intensive six-month study and training period at the Library of Congress. Rutherford D. Rogers, chair of the Programme Management Committee of IFLA, received funding to attend meetings of the committee. CLR also supported the direct travel costs for a Library of Congress representative to attend the British Lending Library-United Kingdom Serials Group conference on resource sharing (April 1981).

CLR-SUPPORTED PROJECTS, FY 1982

NEW GRANTS AND CONTRACTS

American Association for the Advancement of the Humanities	
Distribution of *Library Issues* to ARL libraries	$ 2,500
Association of Research Libraries	
Collection assessment for small academic libraries	
Atlanta College of Art	$ 2,000
Dillard University	$ 2,000
Tougaloo College	$ 2,000
Tuskegee Institute	$ 2,000
Jovana J. Brown	
Study of the funding of academic library research in Britain	$ 5,000

C. Donald Cook
  Study of forms of *AACR2* catalog headings used by national
    libraries $ 15,000
Duke University
  Research on Byzantine bindings $ 7,500
Earlham College
  Seventh Conference on Bibliographic Instruction $ 7,500
International Association of School Librarianship $ 750
  Program expansion
International Federation of Library Associations and Institutions
  Report on copyright and materials for the handicapped $ 5,000
  International study of cataloging in publication $ 5,000
  Review of international standard bibliographic descriptions $ 15,000
  Travel funds for IFLA representative to international congress on UAP $ 1,500
University of Michigan
  Study of the relationship between bibliographic access to stored
    materials and faculty attitude and use $ 56,747
Virginia Polytechnic Institute and State University
  Research on use of library materials $ 7,000

BIBLIOGRAPHIC SERVICE DEVELOPMENT PROGRAM (BSDP)

Association of Research Libraries
  Planning for CONSER abstracting and indexing coverage $ 2,500
Boston Theological Institute
  Increasing access to theological journal literature $ 3,431
Pauline Cochrane
  Developing an improved entry vocabulary for Library of Congress
    subject headings $ 14,310
Council of National Library and Information Associations
  Support of American National Standards Committee Z-39 $ 10,000
Library of Congress
  Joint project for authorities implementation $221,998
  Travel grant for LC representative to International Standards
    Organization meeting $ 1,100
Northwestern University
  Canadian interface—application level protocol $ 4,500
OCLC, Inc.
  Participant in joint project to evaluate online public access catalogs $164,000
  Pilot test of online public access catalog evaluation tools $ 16,100
The Research Libraries Group
  Joint project for authorities implementation $342,528
  Joint project for Standard Network Interconnection $395,000
Rutgers University
  Inventory of machine-readable texts in the humanities $ 14,166
University of Michigan
  System for creating and maintaining bibliographies $ 7,500
University of Toronto Library Automation Systems
  Online public access catalog evaluation $ 20,160
Washington Library Network
  Joint project for authorities implementation $323,347
  Joint project for Standard Network Interconnection $330,000

PROFESSIONAL EDUCATION AND TRAINING FOR RESEARCH
LIBRARIANSHIP (PETREL)

Lauren Kelly	
Senior fellows program	$ 4,500
University of California	
Senior fellows program, 1983–1984	$127,000

COUNCIL ON LIBRARY RESOURCES PUBLICATIONS
(Free on Request)

Twenty-sixth Annual Report (Washington, D.C., 1982)
CLR Recent Developments (newsletter; irregular)

LIBRARY SERVICES AND CONSTRUCTION ACT

State and Public Library Services Branch Staff*

*Division of Library Programs,
Office of Libraries and Learning Technologies, ED*

During the past 25 years, more than $1.2 billion of LSCA funds have been used to provide increased access to public library and information services in areas where services were inadequate and for special populations. These funds have assisted the states in extending public library services to nearly every feasible area of the nation and in improving access for various target groups, including the disadvantaged, those with limited English-speaking ability, the elderly, the state institutionalized, and the blind and physically handicapped. Moreover, these funds have improved the ability of states to extend services through cooperative resource sharing and networking of libraries.

Some of the history of LSCA is documented in a report commissioned by the U.S. Department of Education, *The Library Services and Construction Act: An Historical Overview from the Viewpoint of Major Participants*, which was prepared under the direction of Dean Edward Holley, University of North Carolina School of Library Science, and will be published by JAI Press, Greenwich, Connecticut, in 1983. Along with the report, there are also five videotapes that document the recollections of those involved in the development and support of LSCA legislation.

For FY 1982, $60 million in LSCA funds was released for Public Library Services (Title I) and $11,520,000 for Interlibrary Cooperation (Title III). FY 1981 funding levels were the same, with the addition of more than $1.7 million transferred under the LSCA Title II authority from the Appalachian Regional Commission for construction of public libraries.

To qualify for Title I funding, states and communities must match the federal contribution. The matching ratio, which is set on the basis of the state's per capita income, must be at least 34 percent and can go as high as 66 percent of the program costs.

To participate in both Titles I and III, states must have a basic state plan and comprehensive program, setting forth the state's priorities, procedures, and specific activities to meet the library and information needs of the people on a three- to five-year basis.

*This report on the Library Services and Construction Act was written by Adrienne Chute, Nathan Cohen, Clarence Fogelstrom, Dorothy Kittel, Evaline Neff, Gladys Pendergraph, Trish Skaptason, and Robert Klassen, branch chief.

In addition, an annual program that describes all projects must be submitted to the U.S. Department of Education. All these qualifying documents are developed by the state library administrative agency in consultation with the branch program officer and with the assistance of a statewide advisory council. The annual reports submitted by the states to the branch at the end of the year provide the data from which analyses and descriptions are made for the following year. Detailed reports compiled by the branch are available to readers on request.

TITLE I—PUBLIC LIBRARY SERVICES

The legislative mandate of the Public Library Services Program is to

1. Extend public library services to geographic areas and groups of persons without library services and to improve services in areas and for groups that may have inadequate public library services.
2. Establish, expand, and operate programs and projects to provide library services to the disadvantaged, the state institutionalized, the physically handicapped, and those who have limited English-speaking ability.
3. Improve and strengthen state library administrative agencies; strengthen metropolitan public libraries that serve as national or regional resource centers.
4. Support and expand services of Major Urban Resource Libraries (MURLs). (The Major Urban Resource Library provision is effective when the appropriation exceeds $60 million.)

Table 1 gives a breakdown of the funding and population served by the Public Library Services Program.

Services to the Disadvantaged

Public library service to disadvantaged persons is one of the general priorities for which a significant amount of LSCA funds has been committed in the past. But there is also an identifiable trend that indicates sharply decreasing investments in projects for the disadvantaged as generally defined in LSCA. An analysis of funds expended in FY 1981 on the disadvantaged appears in Table 2. In FY 1981, the total amount (local, federal, and state) reported spent on the disadvantaged was $12.8 million (including $6.6 million in federal funds), representing 260 projects at a cost of $49,167 per project.

Some of the trends found in the distribution and impact of these funds are the following:

1. States have shown an increased reluctance to begin new disadvantaged projects. Ninety percent of the LSCA program dollars designated for the disadvantaged

TABLE 1   LSCA TITLE I, PUBLIC LIBRARY SERVICES, FUNDS AND POPULATIONS SERVED, FY 1981 (in thousands)

	Federal Funds	Number Served
Disadvantaged	$6,614	2,967
Limited English-speaking	2,505	1,990
Institutionalized	2,739	833
Physically handicapped	3,579	450
Aging	557	758

LIBRARY SERVICES AND CONSTRUCTION ACT / 205

TABLE 2 LSCA TITLE I, PROGRAM EXPENDITURES, DOLLARS SPENT ON DISADVANTAGED CATEGORIES AND TARGET GROUPS, FY 1981

Category/Target Group	Federal $	State and/or Local $	Total $	% of All Disadvantaged $	Average $/Project	Number of Projects	% of All Disadvantaged Projects	Number of States with Projects	Number of People Served
Socioeconomically disadvantaged	4,497,336	5,614,043	10,111,379	79.1	103,486	155	59.6	NA	2,605,859
All disadvantaged (includes blacks and whites who are poor)	4,099,368	5,574,260	9,673,628	75.7	NA	133	51.1	36	2,519,701
Unemployed	397,968	39,783	437,751	3.4	19,897	22	8.5	10	86,158
Educationally disadvantaged	1,875,231	522,415	2,397,646	18.8	30,739	78	30	NA	306,322
Children of socioeconomically disadvantaged adults	219,193	13,077	232,270	1.8	12,903	18	6.9	11	91,906
Preschoolers of socioeconomically disadvantaged adults	214,252	313,887	528,139	4.1	44,012	12	4.6	7	20,046
Those in need of adult education or coping skills	846,366	27,787	874,153	6.8	54,634	16	6.2	9	155,407
Developmentally disabled	14,644	0	14,644	.1	7,322	2	.8	2	413
Literacy	580,776	167,664	748,440	6.0	24,948	30	11.5	15	38,550
Culturally disadvantaged	241,313	33,178	274,491	2.1	10,166	27	10.4	NA	63,509
Young adults	236,362	33,090	269,452	2.1	11,715	23	8.8	13	56,421
Mentally ill	0	88	88	0	88	1	0.4	1	36
Deinstitutionalized	1,000	0	1,000	0	1,000	1	0.4	1	150
Drug abusers	3,951	0	3,951	0	1,976	2	0.8	2	6,902

was spent on the 64 percent of the disadvantaged projects that were continuing (rather than new) projects.
2. According to selected socioeconomic indicators, Alaska, Connecticut, the District of Columbia, Massachusetts, and Tennessee reached more than 50 percent of their disadvantaged populations under the LSCA program. On the other hand, 12 states spent no LSCA program funds on the disadvantaged.
3. New England led the nation in the percentage of its disadvantaged population reached, and the South Atlantic region had the largest commitment of LSCA Title I funds to the disadvantaged.
4. Approximately 32 million Americans lived below the $9,287 poverty line. The LSCA program reached 2.5 million of these people with innovative public library services.
5. Of the approximately 23 million functionally illiterate, LSCA program funds reached 40,000.
6. Of the 44.7 million who have never graduated from high school, LSCA public library service projects reached nearly 200,000.
7. Nearly 3 million disadvantaged persons were reached by all of these programs.

Services to the Physically Handicapped

LSCA defines services to the physically handicapped as "the providing of library services, through public or other nonprofit libraries, agencies, or organizations, to physically handicapped persons (including the blind and other visually handicapped) certified by competent authorities as unable to read or to use conventional printed materials as a result of physical limitations." In practice, library services to the disabled are of a broader nature and encompass the entire handicapped community including parents, relatives, teachers, and others who are involved with the handicapped. One of the most significant outcomes of the LSCA priority is increased public awareness of needs and problems of the disabled and fostering some new approaches to service.

According to FY 1981 reports, $3.6 million in LSCA funds was coupled with state and local expenditures totaling $12.4 million in support of library projects serving about 450,000 handicapped persons, of whom 314,000 were legally blind.

In FY 1981, all states funded special programs for the handicapped. Only four states did not combine state funds with LSCA funds for this purpose. In general, the states provide services on a statewide basis through a regional library for the blind and physically handicapped, which serves as a distribution center for audio recorded materials and playback equipment available from the National Library Services (NLS) of the Library of Congress. Because NLS makes no cash grants to the states, operating funds for the regional libraries come from federal (LSCA), state, and occasionally local sources. Several states contract with a neighboring state to provide all or some of the services to their residents. In addition, many states use LSCA funds to reach persons whose disabilities prevent them from coming to a library by funding projects at the local level.

Some of the trends represented in the FY 1981 projects are
1. More libraries are automating their circulation systems.
2. The number of readers and the circulation of materials are increasing.
3. More and greater efforts are being made to publicize services, especially during this International Year of Disabled Persons.
4. More libraries are providing services to the deaf (28 projects in 16 states), installing teletypewriters and conducting workshops in sign language.
5. Radio reading services are provided by 12 states.

Services to the Institutionalized

One of the priorities of LSCA is to establish and maintain library services to those who are inmates, patients, or residents of penal institutions, reformatories, residential training schools, orphanages, and hospitals operated or substantially supported by the state. In FY 1981, $2.7 million in LSCA funds and $13.9 million in combined state and local funds were used in projects to reach persons living in state institutions with library services.

The following are some of the trends represented in the FY 1981 projects:

1. As more institutions have established libraries (and not just paperback collections or donations from local service clubs), cooperative public library arrangements are flourishing, bringing expanded services to those in state institutionalized settings as well as to those in halfway houses and group homes.
2. More projects in mental health and rehabilitation institutions are using multimedia materials, including toys, sensory boards, and coping skills packets (how to get a job, how to use public transportation, how to order in a restaurant).
3. There are more reports of cooperation among institutional libraries (e.g., correctional institutions and mental rehabilitation centers) within the state.
4. The increase in prerelease and similar programs being run or coordinated by the institutional library staff results in many more cooperative projects with local public libraries and appears to have brought increased recognition within the correctional community of the significance of the library in working with and coordinating prerelease information programs.
5. Due to overcrowding and the budget crunch, many states indicate that programs supported by LSCA funds over the last decade are being threatened as never before, with states holding spending to the exact level required to earn federal funds. Although most states had been increasing their level of expenditures in this area since 1971, there was a definite leveling off in many states in 1981.

Services to Persons of Limited English-Speaking Ability

The Education Amendments of 1974 required the states under Title I of LSCA to add a priority for library services to areas of high concentrations of persons of limited English-speaking ability. In FY 1981, more than $2.5 million in LSCA funds was augmented by $1.7 million of state and local funds supporting projects in 24 states and territories, serving nearly 2 million persons of limited English-speaking ability.

Sixty-eight percent of the funds was used to provide cultural and library services to the Hispanic population. In addition, some of the multilingual projects may have included Hispanics, but state reports do not prorate services to various ethnic groups. Thirty-five languages were covered in the language programs provided by libraries: Albanian, Native American dialects, Arabic, Armenian, Bengali, Cambodian, Catalan, Chamorro, Chinese, Filipino, Finnish, French, German, Greek, Gujarati, Hindi, Hmong, Hungarian, Icelandic, Italian, Japanese, Korean, Laotian, Marathi, Micronesian, Persian, Polish, Portuguese, Russian, Samoan, Spanish, Thai, Urdu, Vietnamese, and Yiddish.

Varied services include

1. Information and referral programs via telephone.
2. Books, magazines, and audiovisual materials in foreign languages, with some in both the foreign language and English.
3. Storytelling for children in foreign languages, both live and recorded for telephone Dial-a-Story programs.

4. Cultural programs featuring non-English-speaking authors and artists whose works are available for loan or are on exhibit at libraries.
5. Outreach programs to deliver library materials and information to migrant camps and community centers.
6. Training for library personnel in providing services to bilingual communities.
7. English-as-a-second-language classes.
8. Information programs featuring specialists and community leaders on such practical topics as securing employment.
9. Publications such as directories, brochures, and pamphlets in foreign languages and English providing sources of information useful to ethnic groups.

Services to the Aging

LSCA was amended in 1973 to include a new Title IV for Older Reader Services. However, this title was never funded, because public libraries were funding programs for the aging under the more general Title I mandate to bring library service to the unserved. In FY 1981, more than $550,000 in LSCA funds, combined with approximately $65,000 in nonfederal funds, was used in support of 78 projects to provide special library services to more than 750,000 persons over age 65. Some trends in these services are noted here:

1. State and local funding for projects serving the aging dropped 92 percent from FY 1979. There was a corresponding drop of 97 percent in LSCA funds invested in such programs during the same period.
2. The most common new services are large print materials and film programs, mostly for nursing home residents.
3. Although projects are considered successful, reports indicate that the local library will not be able to pick up funding when the grant runs out.

Major Urban Resource Libraries

MURL program activity concluded its third and perhaps final year of operation in FY 1981 with $2.5 million designated above the $60 million LSCA appropriation. For all three years, in 169 cities with populations over 100,000, libraries that met the state library's criteria for the value of their collections were eligible to share in these funds, if they were able to demonstrate the extent to which the needs of users were being met and that their library collections served a defined region in the state. MURL expenditures for FY 1979 to FY 1981 are listed in Table 3. Expenditures for FY 1981 will not

TABLE 3 LSCA TITLE I, PUBLIC LIBRARY SERVICES, TOTAL AMOUNT PAID TO MAJOR URBAN RESOURCE LIBRARIES (MURL)*

Fiscal Year	Federal	State	Local
1979	$1,666,225	$ 15,264	$ 187,673
1980	1,722,990	18,138	497,883
1981 (est.)	1,776,609	678,724	502,593
Total	$5,165,824	$712,126	$1,187,673

*Figures updated from Table 3 in *The Bowker Annual, 1982*, p. 218.

be revised until after the FY 1982 annual reports have been received, since 20 states have elected to carry over their FY 1981 MURL funds.

The amendments of 1970 to the LSCA required state library administrative agencies to place a greater emphasis on strengthening metropolitan public libraries that serve as national or regional resource centers. The support for these libraries continues to be significant. Selected highlights are noted below:

Arizona

The Phoenix Public Library will share with the other libraries of the state, through the Channeled Arizona Information Network, materials that can be temporarily supplied or made available through photocopying without disenfranchising its own user constituency. A minimum of 55 percent of the interlibrary loan requests received by the library will be filled. Title requests from the Arizona State Library Extension Service will be processed within 48 hours of receipt. A minimum of 2,500 pages will be photocopied for libraries in Arizona.

Tucson Public Library will provide all users, regardless of geographic location or economic status, access to the facilities of the Tucson Public Library System, the University of Arizona system, and specialized sources of information such as the Arizona-Sonora Desert Museum and the Arizona State Museum. A minimum of 85 percent of requests received will be satisfactorily answered. Extensive use will be made of the latest online technologies for the retrieval of information. Responses to requests for information, particularly from remote areas, will be accompanied by supporting documentation. The network will be available to any county, regional, or community college library in the state upon referral from the library extension service. The project will serve as a functional model for the development of an information network within the state.

Maryland

The Enoch Pratt Free Library (Baltimore) continued its project to electronically inspect films distributed throughout the state by the State Library Resource Center Audiovisual Department. By the end of the project year, 23,300 films were inspected. The project improved information access for the 850,000 to 1 million viewers of these films by screening out and designating for repair films that were in poor condition.

Nebraska

Lincoln City Libraries received requests for 4,260 items and were able to answer 61 percent of these requests; of the 1,922 requests received by the Omaha Public Library 62 percent were answered.

In coordination with the Nebraska Library Commission, the Omaha Public Library agreed to establish an automated online reference service. In return, the commission provided funds for search equipment, for training at the Bibliographical Center for Research, for access fees to the data bases, and for actual searches. Despite a delay in the implementation of the program, the state of Nebraska anticipates extensive benefits from the reference service.

Lincoln City Libraries received funds for two projects: (1) to prepare its periodicals for inclusion in the Nebraska Union List of Serial Titles (NEULIST) and (2) to install and implement the operation of OCLC cataloging facilities and membership in NEBASE. The commission agreed to provide the terminal profile, training, and start-up expenses. Omaha Public Library had already agreed to become part of NEBASE; with the inclusion of Lincoln, the largest public libraries in the state have become members of the network facility.

North Carolina

Subgrants of $6,000 each were awarded to five libraries:

1. The Public Library of Charlotte and Mecklenburg County purchased replacement copies of books no longer available in its collection as reflected in interlibrary loan requests, both from patrons and from other libraries.
2. Durham County Library purchased replacement copies of significant nonfiction titles that were found to be missing at inventory time and that were considered likely targets for interlibrary loan requests.
3. Greensboro Public Library strengthened its collection of business books covering a range of subject fields of general interest.
4. The public library in Raleigh spent 50 percent of its grant on fiction, generally in the areas of foreign authors in translation and fiction by women authors. The 50 percent going to nonfiction was targeted to specific titles that had previously been borrowed on interlibrary loan.
5. The public library in Winston-Salem purchased 21 16mm films. The library's film collection is heavily used by other public libraries in the same Council of Government region as Forsyth County. Last year, Forsyth loaned 352 films to those libraries; the films were viewed by 44,981 people.

TITLE II—PUBLIC LIBRARY CONSTRUCTION

During the six-year period from FY 1976 to FY 1981, when there were no appropriations, 55 construction projects were administered under the Title II authority, utilizing $10.1 million of transfer funds from other federal programs. Federal funds for the 55 projects represented 40 percent of the total cost of the projects, and state and local funds represented 60 percent. Of the 55 projects, 46 were funded from the Appalachian Regional Development Act program in the amount of $8.6 million. In FY 1981, the ten projects listed in Table 4 received $1,653,963 in federal funds under Title II authority. All of these funds were from the Appalachian Regional Development Act program.

TITLE III—INTERLIBRARY COOPERATION

Funds for Title III were first authorized in FY 1967. Over the 15-year period from 1967 to 1981, amounts appropriated and made available to the states totaled $56.5 million, or 27.21 percent of the amount authorized. With a little more than one-quarter of the amount appropriated, the states have made rapid strides toward achieving the objectives enunciated by Congress when Title III was added to LSCA, as the FY 1981 South Carolina LSCA annual report testifies:

> An important aspect of LSCA has been the encouragement of interlibrary cooperation. Title III programs have helped build an active library network which promotes communications, bibliographic access, interlibrary loan, in-service training, and planning. The resulting coordination of library resources helps eliminate expensive duplication of materials and makes the State's library resources available to all South Carolinians.

FY 1981 marked the year of the largest appropriation for Title III in its 15-year history, $12 million. Not all of this amount was expended in FY 1981; some will be expended as carry-over in FY 1982. The states reported expenditures of over $8 million in FY 1981 funds and in FY 1980 carry-over funds for Title III activities.

It should be noted that although matching funds are not required in the Title III programs, states reported expenditures of $12.6 million in state and other funds to supplement the federal funds. Of this $12.6 million, California reported expenditures of

TABLE 4 PUBLIC LIBRARY CONSTRUCTION PROJECTS ADMINISTERED UNDER THE LIBRARY SERVICES AND CONSTRUCTION ACT, TITLE II, WITH APPALACHIAN REGIONAL DEVELOPMENT ACT FUNDS, FY 1981

Name and Location of Project	Federal ARDA	Local/State	Total
Brent-Centreville Public Library			
Brent, Alabama	$ 300,000	$ 100,000	$ 400,000
Leeds Public Library			
Leeds, Alabama	44,933	11,234	56,167
Lumpkin County Library			
Dahlonega, Georgia	100,000	459,440	559,440
Douglas County Public Library			
Douglasville, Georgia	300,000	1,001,592	1,301,592
Clemmons Branch Library, Forsyth County Public Library System			
Clemmons, North Carolina	100,000	527,000	627,000
Charles H. Stone Memorial Library			
Pilot Mountain, North Carolina	135,000	165,000	300,000
Rutherford County Library			
Spindale, North Carolina	104,150	160,300	264,450
Carroll County Public Library			
Hillsville, Virginia	267,400	82,600	350,000
Bath County Branch, Rockbridge Regional Library			
Warm Springs, Virginia	177,480	83,520	261,000
Clay County Public Library			
Clay, West Virginia	125,000	330,000	455,000
Total	$1,653,963	$2,920,686	$4,574,649

$8,300,000; New York, $2,077,391; and Minnesota, $1,096,688. In the other states, expenditures ranged from $67,335 by North Dakota to $275,000 by New Mexico.

The information that follows is based on the FY 1981 LSCA annual reports from the 50 states, the District of Columbia and the outlying territories. The full scope and range of the states' cooperative interlibrary activities are not included in this report; only those activities supported in whole or in part with Title III funds are included. (Table 5 lists the types of activities reported by the states.) These activities are rarely discrete projects, but are elements of a larger project, which, in turn, may be an element of still a more comprehensive activity. For example, the use of computers and automation to produce union catalogs and serials lists frequently involves participation in multistate organizations and continuing education for staff development.

Alabama

Two multitype library cooperative pilot projects were funded in Alabama, one in a 10-county region with 30 public libraries, 6 academic libraries, 20 school systems, and 10 special libraries; the other in a 2-county region having 13 public libraries, 9 academic libraries, 18 school systems, and 15 special libraries. Representatives from each participating library met in a general assembly and elected a board of trustees. Within a few months of planning, each system had hired a professional librarian to act as executive director. Various committees made up of member librarians developed goals and objectives to meet the specific designs of the original planning document produced by the Alabama Public Library Services agency. During FY 1981, pilot projects included

TABLE 5 LSCA TITLE III, INTERLIBRARY COOPERATION
TYPES OF ACTIVITIES

Type of Activity	Number of States Reporting
Interlibrary loan and reference networks	40
Computerized lists and catalogs	27
Multistate cooperation	24
Continuing education and staff development	22
In-state regional cooperation	16
Planning and evaluation studies	15
Production of directories and statistical reports	8
Production of catalogs of nonprint materials	4
Cooperation ordering and processing	4
Cooperation between school and public libraries	3

the completion of preliminary plans, the establishment of an office, and the development of multitype library cooperative systems.

The two statewide resource centers, Birmingham Public Library and the Alabama Public Library Service in Montgomery, continued to provide specialized reference and interlibrary loan services.

California

Napa City-County Library and Napa Community College, in the second year of their project, reported the following accomplishments:

1. Collection development coordination that realized considerable savings in periodical subscriptions.
2. New computerized ordering procedures and centralized, coordinated cataloging provided to the college by the county library.
3. Daily delivery and materials exchange between libraries.
4. Access by both the public and students to the services and collections of the two libraries.
5. Coordinated planning between the libraries and with the overall college program.
6. Shared programs, orientation, and public relations activities, as well as shared training for staff.

The success of the project can be measured by increased college library use, an increased college library budget, the decision to link the college to the holdings information of the public library with a computer terminal, the placement of the college media center under the supervision of the college librarian, and above all, the continuation by the college of two LSCA-funded professional library positions.

Indiana

Activities in the state of Indiana included:

1. The purchase of six additional terminals (to be delivered in FY 1982), to expand use of the OCLC system, and of word processing equipment, to facilitate the efficient production of written communications and for the manipulation of two major files, address and OCLC invoicing files.
2. Initiation of the OCLC automated union list of serials service.
3. Libraries with holdings reported in the printed union list were profiled and authorized.

4. Twenty-seven libraries have contracted through INCOLSA for information retrieval services. Training in online searching and management of online search services was provided by two vendors (DIALOG and BRS) and by INCOLSA staff.
5. James E. Rush Associates, Inc., was retained to prepare a plan for statewide services to include automated circulation, online catalogs, and other uses of the data bases. The study recommendations are being used toward further planning.

Massachusetts

In the state of Massachusetts, LSCA supported

1. Cataloging via OCLC of nonprint materials in five member libraries of the Worcester Area Cooperating Libraries. Of the 1,868 nonprint items cataloged since January 1981, 152 required original cataloging.
2. A contract with RMG Consultants, Inc., Chicago, to develop methods for members of the Central and Western Massachusetts Library Systems to determine the costs of manual circulation systems and of an appropriate automated system and to teach the librarians how to analyze the cost comparisons. As a result of the project, the librarians determined that a single automated system with on-line and real-time capabilities to link and share the materials resources (4 million volumes) of both public and academic libraries in the two regions was financially and technically feasible. This project enabled the librarian participants to develop a high level of understanding and technical expertise concerning automation.
3. A study by the Boston Library Consortium to determine the feasibility of eliminating or consolidating serials subscriptions and holdings. A use study manual has been developed and is being revised, as new knowledge is gained during the course of the project.

Mississippi

In the state of Mississippi, the operation of an outgoing WATS line, which links colleges, junior colleges, and public libraries, was continued as a base for an interlibrary loan network. The first edition of the *MS Union Catalog* (the second COM Catalog) was distributed containing the nonfiction holdings of the Mississippi Library Commission and of libraries that are members of the Mississippi processing centers via OCLC/SOLINET through December 1979. There was also a partial retrospective conversion of the Jackson Metropolitan Library System to all public, college, and special libraries in the state. Three workshops were sponsored on the policies and procedures manual of the Information Services Department, designed to aid Mississippi libraries in making more efficient use of the reference services offered by the library commission.

New York

In FY 1981, New York State supported five union serials lists projects with the expectation that they would become components in a statewide union list. Three positions in the interlibrary loan unit of the state library were funded to search and retrieve materials. NYSILL conducted 4,500 data base searches initiated by 22 public library systems; increased the number of data bases available to 62; and conducted 6 training sessions throughout the state for approximately 600 librarians. System administered projects included school-public library resource sharing; interlibrary delivery service; and production of nonprint media union lists.

Wyoming

A Continuing Education Recognition System for librarians was established in Wyoming in conjunction with the Wyoming Department of Education, and the Health Sciences Information Network (HSIN) was integrated into the Wyoming library in-

formation system. Two agreements also were developed, by which
1. County library systems could join HSIN as basic units and would have access to the network for health science professionals and lay persons.
2. The state library would provide telephone credit card numbers to the HSIN headquarters at the University of Wyoming and to consortia coordinators at community college libraries. The consortia coordinators use the credit card to call the HSIN for information and documents; the HSIN staff uses the card to contact the regional library of medicine located at the University of Nebraska Medical School.

HIGHER EDUCATION ACT, TITLE II-A, COLLEGE LIBRARY RESOURCES

Beth Phillips Fine

Education Program Specialist, Division of Library Programs,
Office of Library and Learning Technologies,
Office of Educational Research and Improvement, Department of Education

The College Library Resources Program under Title II-A of the Higher Education Act of 1965, as amended, awards discretionary grants to improve the library resources of eligible institutions of higher education and certain other eligible library agencies. Since 1966, an average of 2,500 institutions of higher education have participated annually, and more than 40,000 awards for basic, supplemental, and special purpose grants exceeding $195 million have been made.

In FY 1981, Congress reauthorized the Title II-A program until FY 1985 by enacting the Education Amendments of 1980. This legislation established a Resource Development Grant, which replaces the basic grant in assisting the institution in its acquisition of library materials, including books, periodicals, documents, magnetic tapes, phonograph records, audiovisual materials, and other related library materials. Institutions are also encouraged to use grant funds to pursue eligible networking activities for the purpose of resource sharing. Eligible networking costs include, but are not limited to, user fees, membership fees, and transaction expenses.

Funding is based on eligibility and fulfillment of the maintenance of effort requirement. Eligible applicants include public and nonprofit private institutions of higher education, as well as nonprofit library institutions whose primary function is to provide library and information services to students, faculty, and researchers of higher education on a formal cooperative basis. In addition, combinations of institutions of higher education may also apply. Members of eligible combinations of institutions of higher education may choose to allow the combination to apply on their behalf, relinquishing their option to apply for their own grants. If an eligible combination applies successfully on behalf of its members, as well as for its own grant, the grant award will equal the standard grant amount multiplied by the number of members plus the combination's award. The Associated Colleges of Kansas and the Western Oregon Regional Telecommunications Network (WORT) applied on behalf of their members.

The maintenance of effort requirement asks for consistency between the institution's proposed budget for library materials expenditures and its two-year average of spending prior to the year of application. It may be calculated through actual expenditures or average annual expenditures per full-time equivalent student. Waiver of the maintenance of effort requirement is limited to "very unusual circumstances."

The Title II-C Strengthening Research Library Resources Program assists major research libraries in the collection, preservation, and dissemination of research materials. Although institutions may apply for assistance under both programs, the legislation prohibits an institution from receiving funding from both Titles II-A and II-C in the same fiscal year.

In FY 1982 each successful applicant received an award of $840. Grantees are found in every state, the District of Columbia, Guam, Puerto Rico, the Virgin Islands, and the Trust Territories. Approximately $1.9 million was awarded to a total of 2,280 institutions of higher education, including 34 nonprofit library institutions and 29 combinations of institutions of higher education.

Notification of grant awards was made on June 11, 1982, with the monies to be used during the grant period of October 1, 1982 through September 30, 1983. (See Table 1 for the number of awards and funding by state. Table 2 traces the funding history of Title II-A from FY 1966 to date.)

TABLE 1   HEA, TITLE II-A, COLLEGE LIBRARY RESOURCES, FY 1982

State or Area	No. of Grants	1982 Obligations	State or Area	No. of Grants	1982 Obligations
Alabama	46	$ 38,640	Nevada	6	$ 5,040
Alaska	10	8,400	New Hampshire	22	18,480
Arizona	26	21,840	New Jersey	40	33,600
Arkansas	22	18,480	New Mexico	12	10,080
California	165	138,600	New York	189	158,760
Colorado	29	26,040	North Carolina	90	75,600
Connecticut	37	31,080	North Dakota	11	9,240
Delaware	11	9,240	Ohio	91	76,440
District of Columbia	10	8,400	Oklahoma	26	21,840
Florida	65	54,600	Oregon	27	27,720
Georgia	55	46,200	Pennsylvania	127	106,680
Hawaii	12	10,080	Rhode Island	13	10,920
Idaho	6	5,040	South Carolina	49	41,160
Illinois	96	80,640	South Dakota	17	14,280
Indiana	49	41,160	Tennessee	46	38,640
Iowa	47	39,480	Texas	95	79,800
Kansas	33	32,760	Utah	8	6,720
Kentucky	33	27,720	Vermont	20	16,800
Louisiana	22	18,480	Virginia	63	52,920
Maine	18	15,120	Washington	42	35,280
Maryland	31	26,880	West Virginia	22	18,480
Massachusetts	85	71,400	Wisconsin	68	57,120
Michigan	69	57,960	Wyoming	5	4,200
Minnesota	49	41,160	Guam	1	840
Mississippi	32	26,880	Puerto Rico	29	24,360
Missouri	46	38,640	Trust Territories	2	1,680
Montana	17	14,280	Virgin Islands	2	1,680
Nebraska	21	17,640			
			Total	2,265	$1,915,200

TABLE 2   HEA, TITLE II-A, COLLEGE LIBRARY RESOURCES, FY 1966-1982

FY	Appropriation	Basic	Supplemental	Special Purpose	Obligations
1966	$10,000,000	1,830	—	—	$ 8,400,000
1967	25,000,000	1,983	1,266	132	24,500,000
1968	25,000,000	2,111	1,524	60	24,500,000
1969	25,000,000	2,224	1,747	77	24,900,000
1970	12,500,000	2,201	1,783	—	9,816,000
1971	9,900,000	548	531	115	9,900,000
1972	11,000,000	504	494	21	10,993,000
1973	12,500,000	2,061	—	65	12,500,000
1974	9,975,000	2,377	—	—	9,960,000
1975	9,975,000	2,569	—	—	9,957,416
1976	9,975,000	2,560	—	—	9,958,754
1977	9,975,000	2,600	—	—	9,946,484
1978	9,975,000	2,568	—	—	9,963,611
1979	9,975,000	2,520	—	—	9,903,201
1980	4,988,000	2,595	—	—	4,926,970
1981	2,988,000	2,471	—	—	2,977,400
1982	1,920,000	2,265	—	—	1,915,200

HIGHER EDUCATION ACT, TITLE II-B, LIBRARY CAREER TRAINING

Frank A. Stevens

*Chief, Library Education, Research and Resources Branch,
Division of Library Programs,
Office of Libraries and Learning Technologies, Department of Education*

Janice Owens

Education Technician, Library Education, Research and Resources Branch

Title II-B (Library Career Training) of the Higher Education Act of 1965, as amended (20 U.S.C. 1021, 1032), authorizes a program of federal financial assistance to institutions of higher education and other library organizations and agencies to assist in training persons in librarianship and to establish, develop, and expand programs of library and information science, including new techniques of information transfer and communication technology. Grants are made for fellowships and traineeships at the associate, bachelor, master, postmaster, and doctoral levels for training in librarianship. Grants may also be used to assist in covering the costs of institutes or courses of training or study to upgrade the competencies of persons serving in all types of libraries, information centers, or instructional materials centers offering library and information services, and those serving as educators.

PROGRAM REDIRECTION

In FY 1974, the Title II-B Training Program Regulations were revised primarily for the purpose of establishing the evaluation criteria and the corresponding point-scoring system governing the selection and rejection of proposals. On May 17, 1974, the regulations were published in final form in the *Federal Register* (45 CFR 132). In the April 3, 1980, *Federal Register*, proposed revisions in program selection criteria were published to reflect the requirements of the Education Division General Administrative Requirements (EDGAR), which mandated the inclusion of certain standard criteria in all discretionary programs. On October 3, 1980, Title II-B was reauthorized by the Education Amendments of 1980 (PL 96-374), with no major changes other than to introduce a new program goal, "new techniques of information transfer and communication technology." However, as it was incumbent upon the Department of Education to revise the program regulations to reflect both the statutory change and the EDGAR general selection criteria, a new set of program regulations was published in the *Federal Register* on December 24, 1980 (pp. 85422-85428). These regulations, which had been rewritten only for brevity and clarity, later underwent a more thorough and exhaustive revision and were published on March 5, 1982, in the *Federal Register* (pp. 9786-9793).

The revised regulations, which are part of the application package that is provided upon request to all interested parties at the time of the annual program announcement, eliminate program priorities, but define program objectives more carefully to include the statutorily mandated emphasis on information acquisition and transfer (and communication technology). The program criteria have been revised to conform with EDGAR and to simplify special program criteria. The point system for all categories of training has been standardized, and several old definitions either have been redefined or deleted and new ones added. Participant eligibility has been simplified.

HOW TO APPLY

Announcement of the closing date for receipt of applications is published each year in the *Federal Register*. Application packages and further information on the Title II-B Library Career Training Program are available on request from: Frank A. Stevens, Office of Libraries and Learning Technologies, 400 Maryland Avenue S.W., Washington, D.C. 20202-3320.

FELLOWSHIP PROGRAM

The entire FY 1982 appropriation of $640,000 was awarded for fellowships. Thirty-three library and information science education programs received 74 fellowship awards (13 doctoral, 2 postmaster, 56 master, and 3 associate). The order of priorities for fellowship training levels in FY 1982 was as follows: master's, doctoral, postmaster's, associate of arts, and baccalaurate. Stipend levels varied, depending on the level of study and length of program, within a range of $1,750 to $6,000 per fellow plus dependency allowance as permitted. Additionally, grantee institutions received an institutional allowance equal to the amount of stipend per fellow. Table 1 shows the institutions to which fellowship grants were awarded in academic year 1982. (A more detailed analysis of these awards is contained in a booklet available upon request from the Office of Libraries and Learning Technologies.) Table 2 reviews the fellowship program since it began in 1966.

The selection of persons as fellowship recipients is, and has been throughout the history of the program, the responsibility of the grantee institution. However, such selection and program operation must be consistent with the grant application on which award of funds is based.

Key factors given substantial consideration in the review process are the extent to which the fellowship program award will increase opportunities for members of underrepresented groups to enter the library profession and to advance professionally and the extent to which the fellowship program award can prepare librarians to work more

TABLE 1 HEA, TITLE II-B, LIBRARY CAREER TRAINING ACADEMIC YEAR 1982-1983

Institution	Project Director	No.	Level	Amount
Arizona				
Arizona State University (Tempe)	Marina McIsaac	2	M	$16,000
California				
California State University (Los Angeles)	Marilyn Greenberg	1	M	8,000
University of California, Berkeley	Michael Buckland	1	M	8,000
University of California, Los Angeles	Dorothy Anderson	1	M	8,000
Colorado				
University of Denver	Camilla Chavez	5	M (3) PM (2)	48,000
District of Columbia				
Catholic University	Elizabeth Stone	4	M	32,000
University of D.C.	Edith Griffin	3	A	10,500
Florida				
Florida State University (Tallahassee)	Harold Goldstein	3	M (1) D (2)	32,000
Georgia				
Atlanta University	Lorene Brown	2	M	16,000
Illinois				
University of Chicago	W. Boyd Rayward	1	M	8,000
University of Illinois (Urbana)	Charles Davis	4	M (2) D (2)	40,000
Indiana				
Ball State University (Muncie)	Patricia Beilke	2	M	16,000
Indiana University (Bloomington)	Herbert White	1	M	8,000
Iowa				
University of Iowa (Iowa City)	Carl Orgren	1	M	8,000
Kentucky				
University of Kentucky (Lexington)	Timothy Sineath	1	M	8,000
Maryland				
University of Maryland (College Park)	Michael Reynolds	4	M	32,000
Massachusetts				
Simmons College (Boston)	Ching-chih Chen	2	D	24,000
Michigan				
University of Michigan (Ann Arbor)	Russell Bidlack	4	M (2) D (2)	40,000
Missouri				
University of Missouri (Columbia)	Mary Lenox	2	M	16,000
New Jersey				
Rutgers University (New Brunswick)	Betty Turock	2	M	16,000
New York				
Columbia University (New York)	Ellis Mount	2	M	16,000
CUNY, Queens College (Flushing)	David Cohen	2	M	16,000
Pratt Institute (Brooklyn)	Rhoda Garoogian	1	M	8,000
St. John's University (Jamaica)	Jovian Lang	2	M	16,000

TABLE 1   HEA, TITLE II-B, LIBRARY CAREER TRAINING
ACADEMIC YEAR 1982-1983 (cont.)

Institution	Project Director	No.	Level	Amount
North Carolina				
North Carolina Central University (Durham)	Annette Phinazee	2	M	$16,000
Pennsylvania				
Drexel University (Philadelphia)	Guy Garrison	1	M	8,000
University of Pittsburgh	Patricia Pond	2	M (1) D (1)	20,000
Texas				
North Texas State University (Denton)	Kenneth Ferstl	4	M (3) D (1)	36,000
Texas Woman's University (Denton)	Brooke Sheldon	3	M (2) D (1)	28,000
University of Texas (Austin)	C. G. Sparks	2	M	16,000
Wisconsin				
University of Wisconsin-Madison	Jane Robbins-Carter	2	D	24,000
University of Wisconsin-Milwaukee	Mohammed Aman	2	M	16,000
University of Wisconsin-Oshkosh	Norma Jones	2	M	16,000

responsively with the underserved and develop viable alternatives to traditional library service patterns.

In 1982, the recruitment efforts of 33 institutions were directed toward the following groups:

Number of Institutions	Recruitment Category
1	Asians
6	Blacks
11	Economically disadvantaged
3	Handicapped
5	Hispanic
21	Minorities
6	Native Americans
7	Women

Nineteen of the 33 institutions indicated 2 or more recruitment categories, while 14 indicated one. Examples of program objectives for FY 1982 were increase number of blacks and other minorities in the profession, provide training for women to advance to management positions, and train for service to the underserved, the economically disadvantaged, and the handicapped in the use of computer technology in libraries.

INSTITUTE PROGRAM

The Institute Program provides long- and short-term training and retraining opportunities for librarians, media specialists, information scientists, and those persons desiring to enter these professions. Many institutes have given experienced practition-

TABLE 2 LIBRARY EDUCATION FELLOWSHIP/TRAINEESHIP PROGRAM, ACADEMIC YEAR 1966–1982

		Fellowships/Traineeships						
Academic Year	Institutions	Doctoral	Postmaster	Master	Bachelor	Associate	Total	FY
1966/67	24	52	25	62	—	—	139	1966
1967/68	38	116	58	327	—	—	501	1967
1968/69	51	168	47	494	—	—	709	1968
1969/70	56	193	30	379	—	—	602	1969
1970/71	48	171	15	200	+ 20[a]	—	406	1970
1971/72	20	116	6	—	+ 20[a]	—	142	1971
1972/73	15	39	3	+ 20[a]	—	—	62	1972
1973/74	34	21	4	145 + 14[a]	—	20	204	1973
1974/75	50	21	3	168 + 3[a]	—	5	200	1974
1975/76	22	27	6	94	—	—	127	1975
1976/77	12	5	3	43	—	—	51	1976
1977/78	37	18	3	134	—	5	160	1977
1978/79	33	25	9	139	10	5	188	1978
1979/80	36	19	4	134	2	3	162	1979
1980/81	32	17	5	72	—	7	101	1980
1981/82	34	13	2	59	—	5	79	1981
1982/83	33	13	2	56	—	3	74	1982
Total		1,034	225	2,506 + 37[a]	12 + 40[a]	53	3,907	

[a]Indicates traineeships.

ers the opportunity to update and advance their skills in a given subject. Institute programs have been supported since FY 1968 under the Higher Education Act of 1965 and since FY 1973 under further amendments included in the Education Amendments of 1972. In FY 1971, the program was redirected to allow it to focus on certain critical and priority areas.

1. To attract minority and/or economically deprived persons in librarianship as professionals and paraprofessionals.
2. To train professionals in service to the disadvantaged, including the aged and the handicapped.
3. To present alternatives for recruitment, training, and utilization of library personnel and management.
4. To foster and develop innovative practice to reform and revitalize the traditional system of library and information service.
5. To retrain librarians to master new skills needed to support key areas, such as the Right to Read campaign, drug abuse education, management (planning, evaluation, and needs assessment), human relations and social interaction, service to the institutionalized, community learning center programs, service to foster the quality of life, intellectual freedom, and institute planning.
6. To train those who teach other trainers.
7. To train library trustees, school administrators, and other persons with administrative, supervisory, and advisory responsibility for library, media, and information services, such as members of boards of education and state advisory councils.
8. To train and retrain persons in law librarianship.

However, due to the limited appropriation in FY 1982, no institute or traineeship applications were requested. Table 3 is a history of the institute awards.

TABLE 3 LIBRARY TRAINING INSTITUTE PROGRAM ENROLLMENT DATA, ACADEMIC YEAR 1968-1979

Academic Year	Participants	Institutes	FY
1968/69	2,084	66	1968
1969/70	3,101	91	1969
1970/71	1,347	46	1970
1971/72	1,557	38	1971
1972/73	684	17	1972
1973/74	1,301 + 45[a]	26 + 3[a]	1973
1974/75	1,339 + 35[a]	30 + 2[a]	1974
1975/76	1,244 + 35[a]	26 + 2[a]	1975
1976/77	120	5	1976
1977/78	802 + 112[a]	22 + 3[a]	1977
1978/79	1,101 + 100[a]	24 + 1[a]	1978
1979/80	1,081	24	1979
Total	16,088	426	

[a]Traineeship program.

HIGHER EDUCATION ACT, TITLE II-B, LIBRARY RESEARCH AND DEMONSTRATION PROGRAM

Yvonne B. Carter

*Program Officer, Division of Library Programs,
Office of Libraries and Learning Technologies,
Office of Educational Research and Improvement,
Department of Education*

The Library Research and Demonstration Program of the Office of Libraries and Learning Technologies (OLLT) is authorized to award and administer grants and contracts for research and demonstration projects related to the improvement of libraries, training in librarianship, and information technology and for the dissemination of information derived from these projects. On July 20, 1981, new grant regulations for this program were published in the *Federal Register* (p. 37484), with such significant changes as the expansion of the program to include the promotion of economic and efficient information delivery and cooperative efforts related to librarianship, the support of developmental projects, and the improvement of information technology. The grant regulations also expand program eligibility to include profit-making organizations, agencies, and institutions.

Since late 1980, the Library Research and Demonstration Program has awarded only contracts. It will continue to do so during FY 1983, if funds are available. The projects described below include projects funded or completed in 1982, as well as updates on two projects that were funded in previous years. All project reports are available through the Educational Research Information Center (ERIC). Announcement of availability appears in ERIC's monthly *Resources in Education*, together with an abstract, the price of the report in hard copy or microfiche, and order instructions. (Table 1 provides additional information on these projects.)

PROJECTS COMPLETED IN FY 1982

In February 1982, the results of the Library and Information Science Research Agenda for the 1980s project, conducted by Cuadra Associates, became available. A major activity of the project was a colloquium convened by the Department of Education on December 2, 1981, to which the presidents of 15 major library and information science organizations were invited to review the project results and to help develop a means of disseminating the Research Agenda and translating it into action. The study will assist the Office of Libraries and Learning Technologies in planning to meet the most vital research needs of the library and information services community.

A contract awarded to Simmons College to conduct Phase II of a project concerned with consumer information needs also was completed in FY 1982. (Phase I, completed in an earlier fiscal year, determined the information needs and searching patterns of members of New England households.) Phase II, which included a comprehensive survey of 620 library networks, developed typologies for both library and nonlibrary networks and conducted in-depth case studies of nine networks (five library and four nonlibrary). An assessment model, containing 13 areas to consider in developing criteria for effectiveness, was developed and field-tested. The report contains many implications for improving library services (especially in public libraries) to meet consumer information needs.

Between July and October 1981, contracts were awarded for ten commissioned papers to discuss relevant library issues. Two papers were prepared for the White House

TABLE 1 HEA, TITLE II-B, LIBRARY RESEARCH AND DEMONSTRATION, FY 1967-1982

FY	Obligation	No. of Projects
1967	$ 3,381,052	38
1968	2,020,942	21
1969	2,986,264	39
1970	2,160,622	30
1971	2,170,274	18
1972	2,748,953	31
1973	1,784,741	24
1974	1,418,433	20
1975	999,338	19
1976	999,918	19
1977	995,193	18
1978	998,904	17
1979	980,563	12
1980	319,877	4
1981	239,954	12
1982	243,438	1
Total	$24,448,466	323

Conference on Aging: "Libraries: Aids to Life Satisfaction for Older Women" and "Public Library Services for Aging in the Eighties." The other eight papers were completed in 1982.

1. In "State Education Agency Responsibilities and Services for School Library Media Programs," Nina Nix Martin reviews and summarizes the literature of the past decade. She also describes the case studies that she conducted in nine departments of education.
2. Blanche Woolls and others also conducted nine case studies to determine the use of technology in administering school library media programs. The findings are reported in "The Use of Technology in the Administration Function of School Library Media Programs." [See the report by Blanche Woolls on "The Use of Microcomputers in Elementary and Secondary School Libraries" in the Special Reports section of Part 1—*Ed.*]
3. In "The Federal Role in Library Networking," Marilyn Gell Mason discusses research and development, planning and policy, financial support, and network operation and management.
4. In "New Technology and the Public Library," Jose Marie Griffith and Don King cite a number of trends affecting the traditional role of libraries.
5. In "Public Library Finance," Marilyn Gell Mason reviews recent developments in public library finance and identifies municipal libraries that have been successful in income maintenance.
6. Abigail Dahl-Hansen Studdiford, using primary source materials, compiled a "Historical Review of Projects Funded under Title II-C of the Higher Education Act of 1965: Strengthening Research Library Resources, 1978-1981."
7. In "Academic Library Resource Sharing through Bibliographic Utility Program Participation," Mary Kane Trochim discusses bibliographic utilities and interlibrary loan at six selected academic institutions.
8. In "The Changing Institutional Role of the Public Library," Donald Foos describes a number of public library programs and how new technology is affecting the delivery of information in each case.

PROJECT FUNDED IN 1983

In 1983, the Office of Libraries and Learning Technologies awarded one contract. The amount of $243,438 was awarded to King Research, Inc. (6000 Executive Blvd., Rockville, MD 20852) to identify the present and future competencies needed by library and information science professionals—"New Directions in Library and Information Science Education."

REQUESTS FOR CONTRACTS (RFC)

During FY 1983, OLLT will conduct directed contract research in the area of library and information science research and demonstration. Requests for Contracts (RFC) that describe the work to be done will be prepared for public response. Announcements of opportunities to offer proposals are published in the *Commerce Business Daily*, the publication in which all U.S. government solicitations are advertised. Forty-five to 60 days are usually provided for response to an RFC. The *Commerce Business Daily* provides information on how to obtain the RFC, which in turn provides all the information an offerer needs to prepare a proposal for consideration by OLLT and the Department of Education.

HIGHER EDUCATION ACT, TITLE II-C, STRENGTHENING RESEARCH LIBRARY RESOURCES

Louise V. Sutherland

Program Officer, HEA, II-C, Library Education Research and Resources Branch, Division of Library Programs, Office of Libraries and Learning Technologies, Office of Educational Research and Improvement, Department of Education

Janice Owens

Education Technician, Library Education, Research and Resources Branch

The Education Amendments of 1976 created a Part C of the Higher Education Act of 1965, entitled Strengthening Research Library Resources. Its specific purpose was to promote quality research and education throughout the United States by providing financial assistance to major research libraries. In authorizing the program, Congress recognized that the expansion of educational and research programs, together with the rapid increase in the production of recorded knowledge, was placing unprecedented demands upon these libraries by requiring programs and services beyond the financial capabilities of the individual and collective library budgets. Furthermore, the nation's major research libraries were acknowledged as essential elements to advanced and professional education and research. Major research libraries were defined as those public or private nonprofit institutions with collections that make a significant contribution to higher education and research, that are broadly based with national or international significance for research, that are unique in nature and contain material not widely available, that are in substantial demand by researchers and scholars not connected with the institution, and that are available to qualified users. The legislation directed the (then) commissioner of education to establish criteria designed to achieve regional balance in the allocation of funds. Also, it limited the number of institutions receiving grants to 150. These amendments authorized funds for three years—FY 1977, 1978, and 1979—and were signed into law by President Gerald Ford on October 12, 1976. However, no funds were appropriated for the program until FY 1978.

The program was reauthorized by the Higher Education Amendments of 1980 with some modifications. The requirement that limited the number of beneficiaries to 150 was dropped, and the requirement that there must be regional balance in the allocation of funds was reworded to instruct the secretary of education, in making grants, to endeavor to achieve broad and equitable geographical distribution throughout the nation. These modifications are reflected in the revised program regulations, which appeared in final form in the *Federal Register* on August 13, 1982.

During the five years of program operation, 429 applications have been received. Of these, 133 were funded, benefiting 169 institutions. A total of $28,752,264 has been awarded to further the purposes of the II-C program. Table 1 gives a summary of the program's funding for the years 1977 to 1983.

GRANTS IN FY 1982

As shown in Table 2, in FY 1982, 79 applications were received, requesting a total of $16,526,159. The 35 top-ranking applicants were funded using the entire amount ap-

TABLE 1 HEA, TITLE II-C, STRENGTHENING RESEARCH LIBRARY RESOURCES, SUMMARY OF PROGRAM FUNDING, 1977-1983

Fiscal Year	Authorization	Budget Request	Appropriation	Awarded
1977	$10,000,000	0	0	0
1978	$15,000,000	$5,000,000	$5,000,000	$4,999,996
1979	$20,000,000	$5,000,000	$6,000,000	$6,000,000
1980	$20,000,000	$6,000,000	$6,000,000	$5,992,268
1981	$10,000,000	$7,000,000	$6,000,000	$6,000,000
1982	$ 6,000,000	$6,000,000	$5,760,000	$5,760,000
1983	$ 6,000,000	0		

propriated ($5,760,000), with the average grant being $165,000. Four of these proposals were jointly sponsored, directly benefiting five additional institutions and making a total of 40 institutions overall benefiting in FY 1982. Four of these proposals were noncompeting continuations. Thirty of the recipients were institutions of higher education, two were independent research libraries, two were museums, and one was a public library. Nine applicants were funded for the first time, sending $1,402,573, or 24 percent of FY 1982 monies, to new institutions:

Institution	Amount
Massachusetts Institute of Technology	$240,743
Ohio University	115,999
Rice University	82,858
SUNY at Buffalo	104,063
University of California, Davis	104,999
University of Cincinnati	394,151
University of Minnesota	66,309
University of Nebraska	90,000
University of Oklahoma	203,451

Bibliographic control and access, which emerged as the major activity in the first year of the program with 57 percent of the funds, continued to receive the major portion, with 70 percent of the funds earmarked for this activity. Preservation projects accounted

TABLE 2 HEA, TITLE II-C, STRENGTHENING RESEARCH LIBRARY RESOURCES, APPLICATIONS, FY 1982

Type of Library	No. Received	No. Funded
Institutions of higher education	64	30
Independent research libraries	6	2
Public libraries	4	1
State libraries	1	0
Museums	3	2
Other	1	0
Total	79	35*

*Three of these proposals are jointly sponsored, directly benefiting five additional institutions.

for 27 percent of the funds, with only 3 percent going for collection development. All of the projects in the HEA Title II-C, Strengthening Research Library Resources program were funded for one year only. (See Tables 3 and 4.)

TABLE 3 ANALYSIS OF FY 1982 GRANT AWARDS BY MAJOR ACTIVITY, HEA, TITLE II-C, STRENGTHENING RESEARCH LIBRARY RESOURCES*

Institution	Bibliographic Control	Preservation	Collection Development
American Museum of Natural History	$125,929	—	—
Boston Public Library	—	$158,139	—
Brown University	$158,882	$ 9,744	—
Center for Research Libraries	$230,011	—	—
Folger Shakespeare Library	$ 45,011	$ 43,337	$ 20,642
Harvard University	$ 54,516	$234,469	—
Indiana University	$167,516	—	—
Massachusetts Institute of Technology	$226,793	$ 13,950	—
New York Botanical Garden	$225,042	—	—
Northwestern University	$ 51,254	—	$ 3,850
Ohio State University	$ 39,022	—	$ 61,995
Ohio University	$115,999	—	—
Princeton University	$ 60,631	$ 49,369	—
Rice University	$ 82,858	—	—
Southern Illinois University	$ 55,027	$ 34,979	—
Stanford University	$231,030	—	—
State University of New York at Buffalo	$104,063	—	—
University of California, Berkeley	$120,457	$ 21,218	$ 15,622
University of California, Davis	$ 45,577	$ 59,422	—
University of Cincinnati	$ 22,685	$371,466	—
University of Illinois	$124,036	—	$ 17,337
University of Kansas	$119,300	$ 29,200	—
University of Michigan	$ 72,677	$ 61,224	—
University of Minnesota	$ 66,309	—	—
University of Nebraska	$ 20,051	$ 19,890	$ 50,059
University of North Carolina	$339,007	—	—
University of Oklahoma	$203,451	—	—
University of Pennsylvania	$ 70,642	$ 38,156	—
University of South Carolina	$132,736	—	—
University of Texas	—	$130,893	$ 26,688
University of Utah	$119,680	—	—
University of Washington	$ 64,198	$185,802	—
University of Wisconsin	—	$ 60,000	—
Vanderbilt University	$148,159	—	—
Yale University	$400,000	—	—
Total	$4,042,549	$1,521,258	$196,193

*The nature of the Title II-C program is such that the grants do not conveniently break down into detailed categories of program activities. Furthermore, some grants include more than one activity. Therefore, the following table analyzes each grant by the amount of funding for three general program activities: bibliographic control, preservation, and collection development.

TABLE 4   PROJECTS FUNDED UNDER HEA, II-C, STRENGTHENING RESEARCH LIBRARY RESOURCES PROGRAM, FY 1982

Institution and Project Director	Grant Award	Project Description
American Museum of Natural History Nina J. Root	$125,929	To catalog scientific and historical photographic collections and to disseminate cataloging and subject information about them.
Boston Public Library Philip J. McNiff	158,139	To continue for a second year the preservation of deteriorating research materials in the special collections.
Brown University Merrily E. Taylor	168,626	To continue the cataloging of rare books from the John Carter Brown Collection and the cataloging and preservation of the John Hay Sheet Music Collection.
Center for Research Libraries Donald B. Simpson	230,011	To convert to machine-readable form, using the OCLC online cataloging system, the catalog records for all of its currently received serial titles, with the exception of those not in English.
Folger Shakespeare Library Philip A. Knachel	108,990	To provide bibliographic support for the English 18th-Century Short Title Catalog, prepare a bibliographic guide to and perform conservation work on original drawings and watercolors in the theater history collection, and acquire microform series in the fields of Renaissance English and European civilization.
Harvard University Oscar Handlin	288,985	To identify fragile collections of ephemera, increase the accessibility of selected collections by improved arrangement and listing or indexing where needed, and microfilm these collections.
Indiana University Elaine Sloan	167,516	To provide machine-readable bibliographic records for the microprint set *Three Centuries of English and American Plays, 1500–1830*.
Massachusetts Institute of Technology Jay K. Lucker	240,743	To increase the availability of research materials focused on technology and its impact on society by adding 38,000 records onto the OCLC data base, arranging, describing, and cataloging ten manuscript collections, and preserving deteriorating items.
New York Botanical Garden Charles R. Long	225,042	To enable the libraries of the New York Botanical Garden and the Missouri Botanical Garden to enter onto the OCLC data base full bibliographic records and/or locations for over 38,000 titles of plant science literature.
Northwestern University Scott Bennett	55,104	To strengthen and organize an extensive collection of environmental impact statements required by the National Environmental Policy Act of 1969.

TABLE 4 PROJECTS FUNDED UNDER HEA, II-C, STRENGTHENING RESEARCH LIBRARY RESOURCES PROGRAM, FY 1982 (cont.)

Institution and Project Director	Grant Award	Project Description
Ohio State University William J. Studer	$101,017	To strengthen and improve nationwide bibliographic access to its extensive collection of American fiction.
Ohio University Hwa-Wei Lee	115,999	To provide for cataloging and inputting onto the OCLC data base over 8,000 retrospective titles in the backlog of the Southeast Asia Collection.
Princeton University Dorothy Pearson	110,000	To conserve, catalog, and enter onto the RLIN data base 670 rare books in women's history and 732 Edwardian novels.
Rice University Nancy Boothe Parker	82,858	To prepare printed guides to the collections of Julian Huxley papers and the Johnson Space Center History Archive. The latter will also be entered onto a NASA-owned data base.
Southern Illinois University Kenneth Peterson	90,006	To continue for a second year the microfilming of designated collections within the Library of Living Philosophers and publish a guide to the philosophy collections.
Stanford University David Webber	231,030	To continue a project to create and input onto the RLIN data base bibliographic records for approximately 7,000 titles of *Early American Imprints: Second Series, 1806–1810.*
State University of New York (SUNY) at Buffalo Saktidas Roy	$104,063	To make its unique collection of research material on twentieth-century English-language poetry more accessible by contributing full bibliographic descriptions of monographic holdings to the OCLC national data base and developing bibliographic tools for providing access to nonmonographic resource materials in the poetry collection.
University of California, Berkeley Joseph A. Rosenthal	157,297	To review, conserve, and enrich three significant slavic and East European collections.
University of California, Davis Bernard Kreissman	104,999	To provide for the preservation of unique items of the Higgins Library of Agricultural Technology and to make it more accessible by contributing records onto the RLIN national data base.
University of Cincinnati Cecily Johns	394,151	To begin a retrospective conversion of the bibliographic records of the Burnam Classical Library into machine-readable form for further distribution through the OCLC data base and preservation microfilming of a large collection of rare and important scholarly materials now in a state of deterioration.

TABLE 4   PROJECTS FUNDED UNDER HEA, II-C, STRENGTHENING RESEARCH LIBRARY RESOURCES PROGRAM, FY 1982 (cont.)

Institution and Project Director	Grant Award	Project Description
University of Illinois, Urbana-Champaign Nancy Anderson	$141,373	To continue for a second year the establishment of a document delivery and reference system for mathematics at the same time as the American Mathematical Society makes available its online data base MATHFILE.
University of Kansas Ellen H. Brow	148,500	To catalog 6,000 valuable Central American titles, preserve fragile items within the collection, and enter cataloged items onto the OCLC data base.
University of Michigan Richard M. Dougherty	133,901	To microfilm, conserve, and place onto the RLIN data base American social science imprints published between 1876 and 1900.
University of Minnesota Elred Smith	66,309	To catalog University of Minnesota Library's dime novel collection, which is the largest in the world. This project will provide for the cataloging of 21 Street and Smith dime novel series, which cover the major dime novel subgenres.
University of Nebraska-Lincoln Gerald Rudolph	90,000	To assemble, preserve, and make accessible an exhaustive collection of early American railroad business history materials.
University of North Carolina, Chapel Hill James Govan	339,007	To develop a control system for a local online access network linking the library collections of Duke University, North Carolina State University, and University of North Carolina at Chapel Hill.
University of Oklahoma John Ezell	203,451	To catalog and input bibliographic records for 45,000 volumes of the western history collections onto RLIN and OCLC.
University of Pennsylvania Richard De Gennaro	108,798	To provide full cataloging onto the RLIN data base for 12,000 seventeenth- and eighteenth-century volumes in the rare book collection and to rebind and conserve volumes as required.
University of South Carolina Kenneth E. Toombs	132,736	To continue the online cataloging of the Fox Movietonews newsfilm collection.
University of Texas Harold Billings	157,581	To preserve through microfilming unique materials from the Benson Latin American Collection and to acquire energy-related Latin American scientific and technical publications.
University of Utah Roger K. Hanson	119,680	To continue for a second year the cataloging of the microformset *Early American Imprints, 1801–1819*.
University of Washington Gary L. Menges	250,000	To preserve and make accessible collections of Pacific Northwest newspapers and maps.

TABLE 4   PROJECTS FUNDED UNDER HEA, II-C, STRENGTHENING RESEARCH LIBRARY RESOURCES PROGRAM, FY 1982 (cont.)

Institution and Project Director	Grant Award	Project Description
University of Wisconsin-Madison Joseph H. Treyz	$ 60,000	To preserve through microfilming and bring under bibliographic control rare materials from the Germanic collection.
Vanderbilt University James D. Phelps, Jr.	148,159	To catalog the 20,000 volumes in the Pascal Pia collection and input the bibliographic records onto the SOLINET/OCLC data base.
Yale University Lawrence Dowler	400,000	To enter onto the RLIN data base bibliographic information describing the approximately 18,000 manuscript collections of Cornell, Stanford, and Yale universities.

NEW REGULATIONS PUBLISHED

Final regulations for the II-C program were published in the *Federal Register* on August 13, 1982, and became effective September 27, 1982. The major change in the program brought about by these regulations is found in Subpart D, How Does the Secretary Make a Grant?, which establishes new procedures for evaluating applications, using two sets of criteria. The first set will be applied by a panel of experts in determining the applicant's significance as a major research library, using such measures as the resources and funds made available to support research projects in the past year; evidence of recognition by the research community; the size and the comprehensiveness of the collection; the number and nature of special collections; the number of loans made outside the primary clientele; the demands for materials; formal, cooperative agreements for resources sharing with other information services; and active membership in a major computer-based bibliographic data base.

All applicants scoring at least 65 of 100 possible points on institutional significance under the first set of criteria will have their proposals evaluated strictly on the quality of the project by a second panel of experts using the second set of criteria. Points of consideration under this set include clarity of the project proposal; concise decription of the project; evidence of adequate planning; the need for the project; the size of the intended audience; effective plan of management; the effective use of personnel to achieve each objective; the quality of key personnel; adequacy and cost-effectiveness of budget; the quality of the evaluation plan; and the institutional commitment to the project. The separation of the criteria to evaluate significance as a major research library from the criteria to evaluate the quality of the proposed project is intended to enable smaller institutions to compete successfully with the larger institutions that in the past may have received funding chiefly on the basis of institutional strength. The change was made in an effort to be responsive to the needs and wishes of the library community.

After evaluating the applicants according to the quality of the projects, the secretary of education determines whether or not the most highly rated applications are broadly and equitably distributed. Other applications may be selected for funding if doing so would improve the geographical distribution of projects. Before selecting other applications, consideration will be given to the geographical distribution of projects during the preceding five fiscal years and the impact on the needs of the research community. However, in awarding grants the secretary of education will be guided as much as possible, consistent with the intent of Congress to achieve a broad and equitable distribution of awards, by the quality of the projects.

ADDITIONAL INFORMATION

In order to respond to requests from libraries and other members of the public for information about the projects funded in FY 1982, the Department of Education, on request, will make available in abstract form descriptions of the goals and activities of each project, together with several tables that summarize the funding record of the Title II-C program from FY 1978 through FY 1982. Similar information is available on projects funded in previous years. Requests should be addressed to Frank A. Stevens, Library Education Research and Resources Branch, Division of Library Programs, 400 Maryland Avenue S.W. (ROB-3, Room 3124), Washington, DC 20202.

EDUCATION CONSOLIDATION AND IMPROVEMENT ACT OF 1981, CHAPTER 2

Phyllis Land

*Director, Division of Federal Resources and School Improvement,
Indiana Department of Public Instruction*

The Education Consolidation and Improvement Act of 1981, which consolidates 33 previous education programs into a single authorization, is part of the Omnibus Budget Reconciliation Act of 1981—Title V (Education Programs), Subtitle D (Elementary and Secondary Education Bloc Grant), Chapter 2. Among the programs consolidated by ECIA, Chapter 2, is Title IV-B of the Elementary and Secondary Education Act, Instructional Materials and School Library Resources, under which school library media programs in public and private nonprofit schools received funding for purchase of instructional equipment and materials, textbooks, and other school library resources.

The authorization for ECIA-2 provides that Congress appropriate sums necessary to carry out the purpose of the act for each fiscal year through September 30, 1987. For the 1983 fiscal year, the appropriation was $483,840,000; the FY 1984 appropriation, passed with the 1983 budget in December 1982, is $479,420,000. From the sums appropriated, the secretary of education shall reserve no more than 6 percent to carry out discretionary programs, such as the Inexpensive Book Distribution program (as carried out through Reading Is Fundamental), the Arts in Education program, and the Alcohol and Drug Abuse Education program, which must be funded at their FY 1981 levels. Any remaining funds may be used for projects formerly funded under the National Diffusion Network or for research, teacher training, demonstrations, and technical assistance as they relate to the purposes of the Education Block Grant. One percent of the appropriation is reserved for payments to Guam, American Samoa, the Virgin Islands, the Trust Territory of the Pacific Islands, and the Northern Mariana Islands, to be allotted by the secretary in accordance with their needs. All other sums are awarded to the 50 states, the District of Columbia, and Puerto Rico on the basis of school age population, except that no state shall receive less than an amount equal to 5 percent of the funds reserved for states (Table 1).

The Department of Education issued revised final regulations for ECIA Chapter 2 in the November 19, 1982, *Federal Register*. The original final regulations, published in the July 29, 1982, *Federal Register*, were subsequently disapproved by Congress, because of the secretary of education's determination that the General Education Provisions Act (GEPA) did not apply to ECIA, Chapters 1 and 2. The revised regulations recognize that GEPA is applicable to Chapter 2 and that provisions such as advanced funding, automatic extension, paperwork control, and prohibition against federal control of education are retained.

The secretary of education makes funds available to the states, when a state application is on file and when the governor has appointed an advisory committee that is broadly representative of the educational interests and the general public, including representatives of the following areas: (1) public and private elementary and secondary school children; (2) classroom teachers; (3) parents of elementary and secondary school children; (4) local boards of education; (5) local and regional school administrators; (6) institutions of higher education; and (7) the state legislature.

In the Department of Education, ECIA, Chapter 2 is administered by the Division of Educational Support Services. The act provides that the state educational agency shall be responsible for the administration and supervision of programs assisted under ECIA, Chapter 2. Up to 20 percent of a state's allotment may be reserved for state use, leaving at least 80 percent to be allocated to local education agencies on the basis of an approved formula. The act allows each state to develop its own specific criteria for distribution of funds, as long as one of the criteria is the relative enrollments of public and nonpublic schools within the local school districts and that provision is made to provide higher per pupil allocations to the local education agencies that have the greatest numbers or percentages of children whose education imposes a higher than average cost per child. States most often include children from low income families in the high cost category. Also included are children living in sparsely populated school districts, children identified as gifted, and children for whom English is a second language. Once a local educational agency receives notice of its allocation, it has complete discretion as to how it chooses to expend the funds for Chapter 2 purposes.

Chapter 2 authorized activities are assigned to three subchapters.

Subchapter A—Basic Skills Development

1. State leadership and support services, including planning, research and development of materials, information dissemination, technical assistance, and programs involving parents and volunteers.
2. School-level programs, including diagnostic assessment, establishment of learning goals, training for teachers and support personnel, activities to involve parents, testing and evaluation.

Subchapter B—Educational Improvement and Support Services

1. Acquisition and utilization of school library resources, textbooks, instructional equipment, and other materials for instructional purposes.
2. Improvement in local educational practice.
3. State leadership and support services.
4. Addressing problems caused by concentrations of minority children.

TABLE 1   ALLOCATIONS UNDER EDUCATION CONSOLIDATION AND IMPROVEMENT ACT, CHAPTER 2, BY STATE

State	Dollar Amount*
U.S. Total	$437,472,000
Alabama	7,633,794
Alaska	2,187,360
Arizona	5,098,409
Arkansas	4,373,524
California	41,291,513
Colorado	5,222,993
Connecticut	5,626,052
Delaware	2,187,360
Florida	15,925,153
Georgia	10,864,739
Hawaii	2,187,360
Idaho	2,187,360
Illinois	21,163,055
Indiana	10,582,427
Iowa	5,330,630
Kansas	4,129,340
Kentucky	7,057,930
Louisiana	8,545,996
Maine	2,187,360
Maryland	7,896,680
Massachusetts	10,173,811
Michigan	18,231,651
Minnesota	7,629,692
Mississippi	5,283,644
Missouri	8,895,073
Montana	2,187,360
Nebraska	2,861,216
Nevada	2,187,360
New Hampshire	2,187,360
New Jersey	13,484,913
New Mexico	2,665,553
New York	31,340,642
North Carolina	11,047,452
North Dakota	2,187,360
Ohio	20,354,591
Oklahoma	5,484,556
Oregon	4,631,497
Pennsylvania	20,966,545
Rhode Island	2,187,360
South Carolina	6,203,609
South Dakota	2,187,360
Tennessee	8,574,919
Texas	27,672,973
Utah	3,088,955
Vermont	2,187,360
Virginia	9,824,822
Washington	7,348,288
West Virginia	3,652,768
Wisconsin	8,919,130
Wyoming	2,187,360
District of Columbia	2,187,360
Puerto Rico	7,766,406
Outlying areas	4,704,000

*Actual allotments reflect additional cents in some cases.

234 / FUNDING PROGRAMS AND GRANT-MAKING AGENCIES

TABLE 2 EDUCATION CONSOLIDATION AND IMPROVEMENT ACT, CHAPTER 2, 1981 APPROPRIATIONS

Program	Appropriations (in thousands of dollars)	Program	Appropriations (in thousands of dollars)
Subchapter A		*Subchapter C (cont.)*	
Basic Skills/Basic Skills Improvement (ESEA, Title II)	25,650	Consumers Education (ESEA, Title III-E)	1,356
Math (Special Program)	—	Ethnic Heritage (ESEA, Title IX)	2,250
Subtotal	$ 25,650	Gifted and Talented (ESEA, Title IX-A)	5,652
		Law-Related Education (ESEA, Title III-G)	1,000
Subchapter B		Metric Education (ESEA, Title III-B)	1,380
Emergency School Aid Act Title VI	149,209	PUSH for Excellence (ESEA, Title III-A)	825
Improving Local Educational Practice (ESEA, Title IV-C)	66,130	Academic & Vocational Education for Juvenile Delinquents	—
Pre-College Science Teacher Training (NSF Act)	1,875	Arts as Part of Curriculum	—
School Libraries and Instructional Resources (ESEA, Title IV-B)	161,000	Discretionary Programs for Gifted and Talented	—
		Educational Proficiency	—
Strengthening State Educational Agency Management (ESEA, Title V-B)	42,075	ESEA, Title III	—
Teacher Centers (HEA, Part A, Sec. 532)	9,100	Establish and Administer Proficiency Exams	—
Comprehensive Guidance, Counseling and Testing (ESEA, Title IV-D)	—	Identify and Encourage Educational Needs of Students with High Performance Capability	—
Instructional Equipment & Materials for Academic Subjects	—	In-School Partnership with Parents	—
Isolated or Minority Students	—	Population Education	—
Teacher Training and In-Service Staff Development	—	Preparation for Employment (Youth Employment)	—
Teacher Corps (HEA, Part A, Sec. 532)	22,500	Preschool Partnership with Parents	—
Subtotal	$451,889	Safe Schools	—
		Subtotal	32,471
Subchapter C			
Special Projects Arts in Education (ESEA, Title III-C)	$ 1,125	*Secretary's Discretionary Fund*	
		Alcohol and Drug Abuse (ADAEA)	2,850
Biomedical and Medical Sciences for the Disadvantaged (ESEA, Title III-L)	3,000	Arts in Education (ESEA, Title III-C)	2,025
		Basic Skills (Reading Is Fundamental)	5,850
Career Education Incentive Act	10,000	Educational Television Programming	6,000
Cities in Schools (ESEA, Title III-A)	2,745	Special Initiatives	8,750
Community Schools (ESEA, Title VIII)	3,138	Subtotal	25,475
		Grand Total	$535,485

TABLE 3   STATE SPENDING PATTERNS FOR ECIA, CHAPTER 2 FUNDS

State	Subchapter A	Subchapter B	Subchapter C	Materials & Equipment
Georgia	14.4%	79.1%	6.5%	49.7%
Indiana	8.5	85	6.5	65.4
Maine	7.4	85.5	7.1	53.3
New Mexico	12.5	81	6.5	69
Ohio	7.5	81.6	10.9	55
West Virginia	0	97.6	2.4	57.2

5. Guidance, counseling, and testing.
6. Improved management of educational programs.
7. Teacher training and staff development.
8. Assistance for schools undergoing desegregation.

Subchapter C—Special Projects

1. Special projects, including metric education, arts in education, in-school and preschool partnership programs, consumer education, employment preparation and work experience, education about the environment, health, the law, and population, programs for youth offenders, and biomedical career education for the disadvantaged.
2. Community schools.
3. Additional programs, including gifted and talented, educational proficiency standards, safe schools, ethnic heritage studies, and programs involving training and advisory services under Title IV, Civil Rights Acts.

The appropriation for the new ECIA-2 was $51,645 less than the combined previous year total of the programs that were consolidated (see Table 2). It should be noted that the FY 1982 Instructional Materials and School Library Resources program was the largest single program folded into the block grant. A preliminary examination of the first year spending patterns indicates that many local school districts have elected to spend the entire allocation on materials and equipment. Preliminary indications also reveal that in many local education agencies, the school library media staffs have major involvement in ECIA-2 funded programs, that large urban school districts with the greatest cuts in federal funds spent a sizable percentage of the allotments for continued projects that had been funded by the Emergency School Aid Act, and that gifted and talented programs received the biggest share of Subchapter C—Special Project funds.

A survey of more than half of the states shows that there is definitely a national trend in the way ECIA-2 monies are being spent. In the 28 states polled,* only one— Delaware—did not spend the largest portion of the funds for former ESEA Title IV-B purposes. (The states included in Table 3 represent the prevailing pattern.) Of the 27 states that reported large expenditures in materials and equipment, all except Mississippi reported microcomputer hardware as the largest single expenditure. In the case of Iowa, almost two-thirds of the local education monies (over $2 million) were spent for microcomputers. It was apparent from the survey responses that nonpublic schools have access to more federal dollars under ECIA-2 than under previous programs and that

*States contacted for ECIA information used in preparation of this paper: Alabama, Arkansas, Arizona, Delaware, Florida, Georgia, Indiana, Illinois, Iowa, Kentucky, Maine, Maryland, Michigan, Mississippi, Nebraska, New Mexico, New York, North Carolina, North Dakota, Ohio, Pennsylvania, South Carolina, South Dakota, Tennessee, Utah, Virginia, Washington, West Virginia.

the nonpublic schools are expending an extremely high percentage of the funds on materials and equipment.

Since the beginning of the Elementary and Secondary Education Act, Title II, state-level supervisors of library and media services have been paid with federal funds. In five of the states surveyed, those state positions either have been eliminated or the number of positions have been decreased. In three of the states surveyed, the chief administrator of ECIA, Chapter 2 previously worked as the library/media supervisor, or the administration of Chapter 2 falls within the section responsible for the state media program.

NATIONAL ENDOWMENT FOR THE HUMANITIES SUPPORT FOR LIBRARIES, 1982

Washington, DC 20506
202-724-0256

The National Endowment for the Humanities (NEH), an independent federal grant-making agency created by Congress in 1965, supports research, education, and public understanding in the humanities through grants to organizations, institutions, and individuals. According to the legislation that established the Endowment, the term "humanities" includes, but is not limited to, the study of archaeology, ethics, history, the history and criticism of the arts, the theory of the arts, jurisprudence, language (both modern and classical), linguistics, literature, philosophy, comparative religion, and those aspects of the social sciences that have humanistic content and employ humanistic methods.

The Endowment's grant-making operations are conducted through five major divisions. (1) The Division of Research Programs provides support for group projects of research in the humanities, for research resources, for the preparation of important research tools, for the editing of significant texts in the humanities, and for the publication of scholarship in the humanities. (2) The Division of Fellowships and Seminars, through several programs, provides stipends that enable individual scholars, teachers, and members of nonacademic professions to study areas of the humanities that may be directly and fruitfully related to the work they characteristically perform. (3) The Division of Education Programs supports projects and programs through which institutions endeavor to renew and strengthen the impact of teaching in the humanities at all levels. (4) The Division of General Programs (combining Public and Special Programs) was recently reorganized into three major units: Museums and Historical Organizations, Media, and Special Projects. Special Projects (consisting of Youth Programs and Program Development) is designed to fund projects in the humanities that are addressed to general audiences. It is particularly interested in proposals that do not fall into the categories established by other divisional programs at the Endowment. (Libraries are encouraged to submit proposals that foster public understanding and appreciation of the humanities; application should be made to Program Development in the Office of Special Projects.) (5) Finally, the Division of State Programs makes grants to citizens' committees in each state to provide support for local humanities projects, primarily directed toward general audiences.

Other projects are eligible for support through the Office of Planning and Policy Assessment and through the Office of Challenge Grants.

CATEGORIES OF SUPPORT

The NEH seeks to cooperate with libraries in strengthening the general public's knowledge and use of the humanities through its various programs. These programs are described below.

Division of General Programs

The Program Development Section awards grants for projects that draw upon those library resources in the humanities that are designed to serve general audiences. The specific goals of Program Development are to strengthen programs that stimulate and respond to public interest in the humanities; to enhance the ability of library staff to plan and implement these programs; and to increase the public's use of a library's existing humanities resources. Librarians are encouraged to replicate, combine formats, or create entirely new and imaginative approaches to humanities programming. Following is a list of project ideas that are eligible for support.

1. Programs on humanities themes that draw on the library's book, magazine, audiovisual, and staff resources. The theme must be directly related to the humanities disciplines or provide a humanities perspective on a topic or theme.
2. Projects involving work with community groups and humanities scholars to plan and present programs for the public, using and publicizing the library's humanities resources. Such projects could include humanities workshops for community leaders or the preparation of special print materials or displays on library holdings.
3. Projects to increase the use of humanities resources by planning programs in conjunction with television programs or exhibitions developed by other community institutions.
4. Projects that strengthen professional staff expertise in the humanities as well as provide humanities programming for the public. These could include workshops on the humanities disciplines, reference training, or programming ideas in preparation for a public humanities program.
5. Projects to produce "packaged" programs that would include specially prepared humanities materials, scholars and experts in the humanities as speakers, and special activities designed for use in local public libraries.
6. Projects to produce educational programs for the public on humanities topics or issues of interest to the community.

Any nonprofit library may apply. Libraries may submit proposals individually or in cooperation with other community organizations. Academic and school libraries are also eligible if the proposed project is open to the general public.

Division of Education Programs

Libraries may receive grants directly or be part of a large university effort to develop new curricula or educational materials, or otherwise to strengthen their teaching of the humanities. Grants directly to libraries are usually in support of humanities institutes in which scholars use the library's resources as part of a program of study with experts on the theme of the institute and simultaneous development of new curricula for the participant's home institution. The Folger Shakespeare Library and the Newberry Library are recent grantees.

Division of Fellowships and Seminars

Through its program of Fellowships at Centers for Advanced Study, this division provides funds to independent research libraries for stipends to resident scholars. In 1982, the Newberry Library, the Huntington Library, and the American Antiquarian Society were among the centers that housed NEH fellows.

Division of Research Programs

The Research Resources Program focuses on making raw research materials more accessible to scholars. It meets this goal through projects that address national problems in the archival and library field, through projects that serve as models in systems development and library automation, and through processing grants that are used to catalog, inventory, or otherwise gain bibliographic control of significant research collections.

The Research Resources Program also helps to develop collections by providing funds either to microfilm materials in foreign repositories, so that they will be available in the United States, or to collect data through oral history techniques. Responsibility for applications to prepare bibliographies, indexes, guides to various kinds of source materials, and similar finding aids has been transferred from the Research Tools Program to the Research Resources Program. The latter also has a small additional amount of funding available to support projects in the area of conservation and preservation that will benefit more than a single institution.

The Publications Program assists presses and publishing houses with the costs of publishing scholarly books in the humanities.

Office of Challenge Grants

Libraries are eligible for support within the Endowment's program of challenge grants, now in the sixth year of funding. By inviting libraries to appeal to a broader funding public, challenge grants assist institutions to increase capital support and thereby improve the quality of humanities activities, humanities collections, and the long-term financial stability of the institutions. To receive each federal dollar, a challenge grant recipient must raise three dollars from non-federal funding sources. Both federal and non-federal funds may apply to a variety of expenditures supporting the humanities: acquisitions, conservation, renovation, development (both programmatic and financial), equipment, and other managerial or program expenses related to the humanities.

Office of Planning and Policy Assessment

Through the Planning and Assessment Studies Program, the Endowment awards, on a competitive basis, a small number of grants each year to compile supplemental information, to analyze important policy issues, or to develop analytical tools for monitoring trends and studying programs in the humanities.

The program's broad areas of concern include the humanities labor force, funding patterns in the humanities, the financial status of humanities institutions, and trends in the demand for and use of humanities resources. Grant-supported studies in these areas generally fall into the following categories: humanities data bases, policy studies, and analytical tools.

Division of State Programs

The Endowment annually makes grants to state humanities councils in all 50 states, plus the District of Columbia and Puerto Rico. The state councils, in turn, award "regrants" to institutions and organizations within each state according to guidelines and application deadlines determined by each council. Most grants are for projects that promote public understanding and appreciation of the humanities. Guidelines and application deadlines may be obtained by contacting the appropriate state council direclty.

STATE HUMANITIES COUNCILS

The Committee for the Humanities in Alabama
Box A-40, Birmingham-Southern College, Birmingham, AL 35254

Alaska Humanities Forum
429 D St., Rm. 312, Loussac Sogn Bldg., Anchorage, AK 99501

Arizona Humanities Council
First Interstate Bank Plaza, 100 W. Washington, Suite 1290, Phoenix, AZ 85003

Arkansas Endowment for the Humanities
The Remmel Bldg., Suite 102, 1010 W. Third St., Little Rock, AR 72201

California Council for the Humanities
312 Sutter St., Suite 601, San Francisco, CA 94108

Colorado Humanities Program
601 Broadway, Suite 307, Denver, CO 80203

Connecticut Humanities Council
195 Church St., Wesleyan Station, Middletown, CT 06457

Delaware Humanities Forum
2600 Pennsylvania Ave., Wilmington, DE 19806

D.C. Community Humanities Council
1341 G St. N.W., Suite 620, Washington, DC 20005

Florida Endowment for the Humanities
LET 468, Univ. of South Florida, Tampa, FL 33620

Georgia Endowment for the Humanities
1589 Clifton Rd. N.E., Emory Univ., Atlanta, GA 30322

Hawaii Committee for the Humanities
2615 South King St., Suite 211, Honolulu, HI 96826

The Association for the Humanities in Idaho
1409 W. Washington St., Boise, ID 83702

Illinois Humanities Council
201 W. Springfield Ave., Suite 205, Champaign, IL 61820
also
67 E. Madison, Suite 1410, Chicago, IL 60603

Indiana Committee for the Humanities
4200 Northwestern Ave., Indianapolis, IN 46208

Iowa Humanities Board
Oakdale Campus, Univ. of Iowa, Iowa City, IA 52242

Kansas Committee for the Humanities
112 W. Sixth St., Suite 509, Topeka, KS 66603

Kentucky Humanities Council, Inc.
Ligon House, Univ. of Kentucky, Lexington, KY 40508

Louisiana Committee for the Humanities
1215 Prytania St., Suite 535, New Orleans, LA 70130

Maine Humanities Council
Box 7202, Portland, ME 04112

The Maryland Committee for the Humanities
516 N. Charles St., #304–305, Baltimore, MD 21201

Massachusetts Foundation for the Humanities and Public Policy
237 E. Whitmore Admin. Bldg., Univ. of Massachusetts, Amherst, MA 01003

Michigan Council for the Humanities
Nisbet Bldg., Suite 30, 1407 S. Harrison Rd., East Lansing, MI 48824

Minnesota Humanities Commission
LL 85 Metro Square, St. Paul, MN 55101

Mississippi Committee for Humanities, Inc.
3825 Ridgewood Rd., Rm. 111, Jackson, MS 39211

Missouri State Committee for the Humanities
Loberg Bldg., Suite 204, 11425 Dorsett Rd., Maryland Heights, MO 63043

Montana Committee for the Humanities
Box 8036, Hellgate Station, Missoula, MT 59807

Nebraska Committee for the Humanities
Cooper Plaza, Suite 405, 211 N. 12 St., Lincoln, NE 68508

Nevada Humanities Committee
Box 8065, Reno, NV 89507

240 / FUNDING PROGRAMS AND GRANT-MAKING AGENCIES

New Hampshire Council for the Humanities
112 S. State St., Concord, NH 03301

New Jersey Committee for the Humanities
73 Easton Ave., New Brunswick, NJ 08903

New Mexico Humanities Council
1712 Las Lomas N.E., Univ. of New Mexico, Albuquerque, NM 87131

New York Council for the Humanities
33 W. 42 St., New York, NY 10036

North Carolina Humanities Committee
112 Foust Bldg., Univ. of North Carolina-Greensboro, Greensboro, NC 27412

North Dakota Humanities Council
Box 2191, Bismarck, ND 58502

The Ohio Humanities Council
760 Pleasant Ridge Ave., Columbus, OH 43209

Oklahoma Humanities Committee
Executive Terrace Bldg., 2809 Northwest Expressway, Suite 500, Oklahoma City, OK 73112

Oregon Committee for the Humanities
418 S.W. Washington, Rm. 410, Portland, OR 97204

Pennsylvania Humanities Council
401 N. Broad St., Philadelphia, PA 19108

Fundacion Puertorriquena de las Humanidades
Box S-4307, Old San Juan, PR 00904

Rhode Island Committee for the Humanities
463 Broadway, Providence, RI 02909

South Carolina Committee for the Humanities
17 Calendar Court, Suite 6, Columbia, SC 29206

South Dakota Committee on the Humanities
University Station, Box 35, Brookings, SD 57007

Tennessee Committee for the Humanities
1001 18 Ave. S., Nashville, TN 37212

Texas Committee for the Humanities
1604 Nueces, Austin, TX 78701

Utah Endowment for the Humanities
10 W. Broadway, Broadway Bldg., Suite 900, Salt Lake City, UT 84101

Vermont Council on the Humanities and Public Issues
Grant House, Box 58, Hyde Park, VT 05655

Virginia Foundation for the Humanities and Public Policy
One-B W. Range, Univ. of Virginia, Charlottesville, VA 22903

Washington Commission for the Humanities
Olympia, WA 98505

The Humanities Foundation of West Virginia
Box 204, Institute, WV 25112

Wisconsin Humanities Committee
716 Langdon St., Madison, WI 53706

Wyoming Council for the Humanities
Box 3274, University Station, Laramie, WY 82701

NATIONAL HISTORICAL PUBLICATIONS AND RECORDS COMMISSION

General Services Administration
National Archives
Washington, DC 20408
202-724-1083

In 1934, Congress established the National Historical Publications Commission to make plans, estimates, and recommendations for the publication of important historical documents and to work with various public and private institutions in gathering, annotating, and publishing papers and records of national historical significance. By the enactment, in 1964, of PL 88-383, the commission was given the authority to recommend federal grants for these purposes. A records program was added in 1974 (PL 93-

356), and the commission became the National Historical Publications and Records Commission (NHPRC), with authority to assist agencies and institutions in all states and territories in gathering, arranging, describing, and preserving significant papers and records. The commission's grants for both the publications and records programs usually require the contribution of nonfederal funds in a matching or cost-sharing plan.

Representation on the commission is fixed by law to include a member of the federal judiciary, one member from each house of Congress, two presidential appointees, the Librarian of Congress or an alternate, the secretary of defense or an alternate, the secretary of state or an alternate, and two members each of the American Historical Association, the Organization of American Historians, the American Association for State and Local History, and the Society of American Archivists. The Archivist of the United States serves as chairperson.

PUBLICATIONS PROGRAM

In FY 1981 and 1982, many of the commission's publications grants went to help support continuing projects such as *The Papers of Andrew Jackson* ($15,000 grant to the University of Tennessee), *The Papers of John Muir* ($10,000 to the University of the Pacific), *Freedmen in Southern Society, 1861-67* ($83,000 to the University of Maryland), *The Correspondence of James K. Polk* ($40,059 to Vanderbilt University), and *The Papers of Thomas Jefferson* ($66,000 to Princeton University).

Volumes from commission-sponsored projects that were published during the two years include volumes 3 and 4 of *Lafayette in the Age of the American Revolution* (Cornell University Press), volume 1 of *The Papers of General George C. Marshall* (Johns Hopkins University Press), volume 2 of *The Frederick Douglass Papers* (Yale University Press), and volumes 35-38 of *The Papers of Woodrow Wilson* (Princeton University Press). Professor C. Vann Woodward's edition of *Mary Chesnut's Civil War*, a one-volume project completed in 1981, won the Pulitzer Prize for history. Among microform publications completed were *The Papers of the Women's Trade Union League* (131 reels, Radcliffe College) and *Black Abolitionist Papers, 1830-1865* (17 reels, Florida State University).

Grants to new publication projects included $18,900 to Transylvania University for a two-volume book edition of the papers of Constantine Rafinesque, one of the pioneers of natural history in the United States, and $18,483 to West Virginia University for a one-volume book edition of the correspondence of Mary Harris ("Mother") Jones, labor leader and one of the original organizers of the United Mine Workers union.

In all, during FY year 1981, the commission provided 83 grants, averaging $24,096 each, to publication projects at universities, historical societies, libraries, and state and federal agencies from New England to California. In 1982, there were 50 grants, averaging $15,000 each. These included a number of subvention grants to university and other nonprofit presses to help publish the editions sponsored by the commission.

The commission also is involved in a number of related activities. In addition to participating in a committee to promote higher quality book production standards, the commission continues to offer editing fellowships (with private gift funds) and conducts an annual historical editing institute, as well as occasional conferences of editors. Its research staff continues to provide reference materials from the National Archives, the Library of Congress, and other institutions to commission-supported projects and to offer guidance on a wide range of research questions.

RECORDS PROGRAM

The records grant program supports a variety of activities relating to preservation of historical records and their preparation for use by researchers. Survey and accession, appraisal, arrangement and description, preparation of guides and other finding aids, microfilming, and archival training are among the items that regularly appear in proposals to the commission. The records program does not at this time support projects relating to newspapers, rare books, published items (except where these are incidental parts of collections of historical records), or oral history interviews or transcriptions. Emphasis is on the information in records rather than on the artifact value; thus microfilming or other means of copying fragile records is usually preferred to the much more expensive restoration of individual documents.

The commission strongly endorses standard archival techniques, especially in the arrangement and description of historical records, and has supported several projects that foster the awareness of these techniques, including the Basic Manual series of the Society of American Archivists and H. G. Jones's *Local Government Records: An Introduction to Their Management, Preservation and Use*. Finally, the commission has supported several workshops on archival techniques and on conservation methods.

To carry out the historical records program, the commission relies heavily on the advice of State Historical Records Advisory Boards, made up of archivists, historical program administrators, and others interested in historical records within the state. These advisory boards, chaired by a historical records coordinator, develop priorities and review records grant proposals from the states prior to commission consideration. The head of the state's archival program is usually the state coordinator; the director of the state-funded historical society, where one exists, is also a member of the board. Many advisory boards, which have been appointed in every state except Maine, have placed local needs, especially local government records programs, among their highest priorities. State records are also often a high priority.

Although the commission wishes to respond as effectively to the needs of small and local repositories as it does to large ones, it hopes that small repositories will consider forming cooperative projects when possible. Often a cooperative program involving several institutions with common problems can be cost-effective and can more readily justify the level of resources necessary to support a professional approach.

In FY 1981, the commission recommended 93 records grants, totaling $2 million, for projects in 39 states. The average grant was $21,505. In 1982, there were 16 grants, totaling $250,000, for projects in 15 states and Puerto Rico; the average grant was $15,625. Grants were made to colleges and universities; private historical societies, museums, and archives; state agencies; cities and counties; public and special libraries; and other institutions. Many projects received reduced outright grants or offers of reduced grants conditional upon increased nonfederal funding.

The following grants are representative of those recommended during 1981 and 1982:

Detroit Public Library, Detroit, Mich.: $2,955 for consultation to develop an archives and records program for the records of the city of Detroit.

Flower of the Dragon, Santa Rosa, Calif.: $37,223 to locate an appropriate repository for the records of Vietnam War veterans and to survey Vietnam veterans and veterans' organizations to identify the archival materials that document the war from the veterans' perspective.

Newport News Public Library System, Newport News, Va.: $8,237 to assist in processing the records of the Old Dominion Land Company. The company was used by its owner, railroad magnate and financier Collis P. Huntington, to purchase land for the Atlantic terminus of a continental railway system and for developing the city of Newport News and the surrounding area.

New Hampshire Historical Society, Concord, N.H.: $29,185 to arrange and describe a portion of its manuscript collections, which contains materials on New Hampshire's social, political, and economic history.

Alabama Space and Rocket Center, Huntsville, Ala.: $2,500 for consultation in planning an archival program. The center's holdings include papers of Wernher von Braun and others who were instrumental in the development of rocketry in the United States and abroad from the beginning of space flight to the late 1970s.

Kansas State Historical Society, Topeka, Kan.: $64,054 to conduct a pilot survey of local government records in five representative counties, to develop model retention and disposition schedules, to prepare records manuals, and to offer workshops to help local officials apply the model schedules.

University of Connecticut, Storrs, Conn.: $41,803 to develop a comprehensive archival program for the statewide university system.

Ohio Historical Society, Columbus, Ohio: $3,750 to complete the preparation of a municipal records manual and to conduct a series of records management workshops for municipal officials and employees.

Merrimack Valley Textile Museum, North Andover, Mass.: $16,860 for the second and final year of the museum's project to arrange and describe its collections, which relate to the American textile industry.

Chicago Historical Society, Chicago, Ill.: $43,025 to arrange and describe the records of Holabird and Root, a major Chicago architectural firm, 1880–1940.

American Association for State and Local History, Nashville, Tenn.: $18,566 to study and report on the management, preservation, and use of local government records.

Twenty-seven states around the country also received a total of $596,033 for needs assessment; these grants will be administered by the State Historical Records Advisory Boards and will be used to assess statewide records needs and to draft recommendations. Similar grants for the remaining states are planned for 1983.

PUBLICATIONS OF THE COMMISSION

Annotation (newsletter)

Annual Report

Fact Sheet: The National Historical Publications and Records Commission and Its Work

Publications Catalog, 1976

Report to the President, 1978

Publications Program Guidelines and Procedures: Applications and Grants

Subvention Program Guidelines

Records Program Guidelines and Procedures: Applications and Grants

Suggestions for Records Program Applicants

The State Historical Records Coordinator and the State Historical Records Advisory Board: Suggested Roles and Procedures

Microform Guidelines

Directory of Archives and Manuscript Repositories in the United States

NATIONAL SCIENCE FOUNDATION SUPPORT FOR RESEARCH IN INFORMATION SCIENCE AND TECHNOLOGY

1800 G St. N.W., Washington, DC 20550
202-357-9572

Edward C. Weiss

Division of Information Science and Technology

The National Science Foundation (NSF), an independent agency of the federal government, was established by Congress in 1950 to promote the progress of science. Through its Division of Information Science and Technology (IST), NSF supports basic and applied research in information science under three related programs. The objectives of the division are to increase understanding of the properties and structure of information and information transfer; to contribute to the body of scientific and technical knowledge that can be applied in the design of information systems; and to improve understanding of the economic impact and other effects of information science and technology.

The Information Science Program is concerned with increasing the fundamental knowledge necessary for understanding information processes. Information science deals with the study of information as idealized organization or structure, as well as with its many facets, such as measures, storage, manipulation, retrieval, coding, and interpretation. Research is also directed toward biological systems because these are capable of complex information processing that contemporary artificial systems cannot accomplish. Human information processes, such as the extraction of meaning from text, complex object identification, language processing, and associative memory, are being investigated.

The Information Technology Program supports research to expand the scientific base for information system design. It provides a vehicle for translating the results of basic research into useful applications, as well as for the refinement and testing of theory. Information technology is usually understood to include the technologies of information storage, processing, transmission, input, and output. This program is not directly concerned with the development of such technologies, but focuses instead on the application of technologies to systems capable of augmenting human intellectual activities, and on research on the relationship of system design parameters to the abilities, limitations, and purposes of human users.

The Information Impact Program supports research that contributes to understanding both the impact of information production, distribution, and use, and the increasingly pervasive applications of advanced information technology. Information is a major consumer good and an element in the production of all goods and services. Much interest centers on its unusual economic properties as a commodity, on its exchange, and on the complex phenomena to which it gives rise. There is interest also in how the accessibility and availability of information channels affect patterns of communication, processes of decision making, and interpersonal transactions.

In order to enhance the development of information science and contribute to the scientific vitality of the field, IST has established Special Research Initiation Awards for New Investigators as part of its program of research support. These awards are offered only to principal investigators who have earned a doctoral degree within the last five years in a field related to information science, including the information, computer, cognitive, and mathematical sciences, linguistics, and electrical engineering.

SUBMISSION AND REVIEW OF PROPOSALS

Proposals may be submitted by academic institutions, by nonprofit and profit-making organizations, or by groups of such organizations. Joint proposals that bring a coordinated range of expertise and research skills to bear on complex problems are particularly encouraged. In the selection of projects to be supported, preference is given to research that is fundamental and general, and to applied research concerned with scientific and technical information rather than, for example, business information or mass communication. The development of hardware is beyond the scope of this program, as are projects to develop, implement, or evaluate information systems except for the purpose of generalizations beyond the particular information systems involved.

A program announcement, *Research in Information Science*, NSF 81-34, which also provides information on how to submit a proposal, is available from the Division of Information Science and Technology. Potential applicants are encouraged to discuss their research ideas with IST staff, either in person or by letter or telephone.

Except for proposals for Special Research Initiation Awards, for which the deadlines are the first Wednesday in August and the first Wednesday in February of any given year, research proposals may be submitted at any time. Review generally requires six to eight months, and proposed activities should be scheduled with that in mind. Proposals are reviewed by NSF staff and outside reviewers selected for their knowledge and expertise in topics addressed by the proposals. The award of NSF grants is discretionary. In general, projects are supported in order of merit to the extent permitted by available funds. The principal criteria by which a research proposal is evaluated are (1) the technical adequacy of the investigators and their institutional base; (2) the adequacy of the research design; (3) the scientific significance of the proposed project; (4) its utility or relevance; and (5) its implications for the scientific potential of the field.

The foundation plans to award approximately $5.4 million for information science research in FY 1983.

DISSEMINATION OF RESULTS

NSF encourages grantees and contractors to present their research results at appropriate professional meetings and to publish in scientific journals. Copies of final technical reports are made available through the National Technical Information Service of the U.S. Department of Commerce. In addition, summaries of awards are available through the Smithsonian Science Information Exchange. Annual lists of awards and bibliographies of reports from completed projects are available from IST.

Tables 1 and 2 list the research grants funded by IST in FY 1982. Table 3 lists the Small Business Innovation Research Awards administered by IST in FY 1982, but actually funded by the Division of Industrial Science and Technological Innovation (ISTI). Table 4 lists those awards funded jointly by IST and other NSF divisions, including the Division of Behavioral and Neural Sciences (BNS), the Division of Chemistry (CHE), the Division of Mathematical and Computer Sciences (MCS), and the Division of Social and Economic Sciences (SES).

TABLE 1   DIVISION OF INFORMATION SCIENCE AND TECHNOLOGY: AWARDS, FY 1982

Institution	Principal Investigator	Proposal Title	Duration (Months)*	Expiration Date	Amount
Information Science Program					
Battelle Columbus	R. T. Niehoff	The Impact of Subject Switching—An Assessment	16	10/31/83	$144,000
Boston University	S. C. Salveter	Verbs in Databases (Information Science)	24	2/28/85	129,980
Brandeis University	R. Jackendoff and J. Grimshaw	Information Structure of a Natural Language Lexicon	12	10/31/83	24,238
Brandeis University	R. Jackendoff and J. Grimshaw	Information Structure of a Natural Language Lexicon (Information Science)	NA	10/31/83	20,809
Columbia University	C. D. Parsons	Text Constructed from Informational Units	20	2/29/84	265,986
Massachusetts Institute of Technology	D. H. Klatt	Auditory Information Processing and Speech Perception	18	9/30/84	132,500
Massachusetts Institute of Technology	R. S. Marcus	Investigation of Models for Enhanced Information Retrieval through Computer-Mediated Assistance	12	8/31/83	97,445
Massachusetts Institute of Technology	S. Ullman and L. Vaina	A Functional Representation of Visual Information (Information Science)	26	2/28/85	151,183
New York University	J. Falmagne	Assessment and Measurement of Knowledge—Theory and Algorithms	30	2/28/85	193,839
New York University	N. Sager	Computable Models of Time and Quantity in Natural Language Data	NA	6/30/84	110,818
Rutgers University	C. Schmidt	Information Processing Analysis of Human Understanding of Action Sequences and Computational Traces (Information Science)	12	10/31/83	91,885
Southern Methodist University	C. M. Eastman	Performance of Multikey Information Search Algorithms (Information Science)	12	2/29/84	17,644
SRI International	D. E. Walker	Natural Language Access to Text (Information Science)	12	1/31/84	88,032

NATIONAL SCIENCE FOUNDATION / 247

Institution	Investigator	Title	Months	End Date	Amount
University of California	J. Pearl and N. Dalkey	Studies in the Organization of Information Structures	18	3/31/84	36,898
University of California	R. H. Granger	Judgmental Inference in Understanding Textual Information (Information Science)	12	12/31/83	64,158
University of California	R. Wilensky	Evaluating a Knowledge Representation for Planning and Natural Language Understanding (Information Science)	NA	5/31/84	73,184
University of Illinois	D. L. Waltz	Understanding Natural Language Scene and Event Descriptions: Cognitive Universals and Computer Programs Based on Combined AI and Linguistics Methodologies	36	4/30/85	267,407
University of Illinois	M. E. Williams	Comparative Analyses of Online Retrieval Interfaces (Information Science)	30	7/31/85	250,003
University of Maryland	M. L. Brodie	Symposium on Conceptual Modelling: Perspectives from Artificial Intelligence, Databases and Programming Languages; May 26-28, 1982, College Park, Maryland	12	1/31/83	40,339
University of Massachusetts	W. B. Croft	A Framework for User-Oriented Adaptive Document Retrieval Systems	24	6/30/84	121,240
University of Massachusetts	E. W. Rissland	Conference on Intelligent User Interfaces: October 19-22, 1982; Woodstock, Vermont (Information Science)	12	8/31/83	28,818
University of Rochester	J. F. Allen	Extended User-System Dialogues for Complex Information Retrieval (Information Science)	24	2/28/85	199,930
University of Texas	R. F. Simmons	Query Logic for a Text-Knowledge Base (Information Science)	24	11/30/84	70,693
University of Vermont	S. J. Hegner	Representation of Information and Ease of Update: A General Theory of Relational Data Base Normalization (Information Science)	24	12/31/84	25,162
University of Washington	R. W. Ritchie	Toward Automated Natural Language Processing: Phrase Linking Grammars for Syntax and Semantics (Information Science)	12	10/31/83	70,538 (MCS) 15,323 (MCS) 15,323

TABLE 1 DIVISION OF INFORMATION SCIENCE AND TECHNOLOGY: AWARDS, FY 1982 (cont.)

Institution	Principal Investigator	Proposal Title	Duration (Months)*	Expiration Date	Amount
Information Science Program (cont.)					
Yale University	R. C. Schank	Information Models for Reconstructive Memory and Learning	12	11/30/83	80,950
Information Impact Program					
Carnegie-Mellon University	S. B. Kiesler	Computer-Mediated Communication (Information Science)	24	2/28/85	149,923
Columbia University	E. M. Noam	Technical Innovation in Established Cable Television Systems in Comparison with Developments in the State of the Art (Information Science)	9	10/31/83	9,978
Georgia State University	S. E. Harris	Organizational Impacts of Local Information Network Technology (Information Science)	6	3/31/83	47,119
Massachusetts Institute of Technology	I. D. Pool	A Workshop on Measurement of Communications and Information (Information Science), Summer of 1982, Cambridge, Massachusetts	3	12/31/82	29,326
National Planning Assn.	N. E. Terleckyj	Growth of the Communication Sector and Productivity of the American Economy	12	5/31/83	53,707
New York University	M. C. Elton	Behavioral Research on Broadcast Teletext (Information Science)	5	2/28/83	59,910
New York University	F. Machlup	Information Science: An Analysis of Methodological Issues and Interdisciplinary Relationships	9	10/31/82	18,820
Northwestern University	D. G. Saari	Information Theory of Equilibrium Processes and of Regulatory Systems	24	8/31/84	46,592
Princeton University	W. J. Baumol	Productivity Growth and Scientific and Technical Information (Information Science)	24	11/30/84	128,259

| University of Minnesota | J. Ettema | The Home Information Utility: Individual-Level Basis of Societal-Level Impact (Information Science) | 9 | 11/30/83 | 54,403 |

Information Technology Program

Carnegie-Mellon University	M. G. Morgan	Experimental Analysis of Factors in the Design of Information Systems for Modelling Engineering/Economic Decisions	NA	6/30/83	8,723
Louisiana State University	D. H. Kraft	Group Travel to the Fifth International Information Retrieval Conference: West Berlin, May 1982	6	9/30/82	10,000
Massachusetts Institute of Technology	J. F. Reintjes	Advanced Technologies for Electronic Transfer of Text and Graphics (Information Science)	24	12/31/84	149,545
National Academy of Sciences	C. G. Carter	Partial Support of the Numerical Data Advisory Board	12	5/31/83	30,169
Stanford University	D. E. Knuth	Theoretical Basis for the Development of Document Preparation Systems (Information Science)	12	11/30/83	153,961
University of California	J. Pearl	Research on Computer-Based Systems for Problem Structuring	12	4/30/83	77,806

*NA = Not Applicable.

250 / FUNDING PROGRAMS AND GRANT-MAKING AGENCIES

TABLE 2 IST SPECIAL RESEARCH INITIATION AWARDS (BY PROGRAM), FY 1982

Institution	Principal Investigator	Proposal Title	Duration (Months)	Expiration Date	Amount
Information Science Program					
Boston University	M. F. Delaney	Representation and Utilization of Non-Textual (Chemical Spectral) Information	12	9/30/83	$ 33,000
SRI International	R. A. Amsler	Experimental Research on Knowledge Representations for Lexical Disambiguation of Full-Text Sources (Information Science)	24	1/13/85	129,951
SUNY at Stony Brook	M. A. Jones	Inducing Lexical Definitions for Word-Based Parsers	24	1/31/85	74,757
University of California	R. Reichman	Discourse Models for Extended Person-Computer Interaction	24	8/31/84	92,840
University of Illinois	G. Dejong	Explanatory Schema Acquisition	24	6/30/84	116,855
University of Illinois	L. C. Smith	Development of a Taxonomy of Representations in Information Retrieval System Design (Information Science)	12	1/31/84	29,960
University of Rochester	S. L. Small	Distributed Information Processing Models of Language Interpretation (Information Science)	24	2/28/85	113,606
Information Technology Program					
University of Pennsylvania	T. W. Finin	A Knowledge Based Approach to Intelligent Interactive Help Systems	24	12/31/84	99,544
Information Impact Program					
Carnegie-Mellon University	C. Spatt	Models of Information in Industrial Organization (Information Science)	12	3/31/84	25,000
New York University	R. N. Langlois	Information Science and Economic Theory	12	5/31/83	38,609
New York University	M. H. Olson	Pilot Testing of Distributed Work Environment Organization and Technology (Information Science)	3	3/31/83	18,648
Northwestern University	P. Milgrom	On the Role of Information in a Productive Organization (Information Science)	24	2/28/85	38,822

Ohio State University	R. A. Jensen	Informational Aspects of the Adoption and Diffusion of Innovation (Information Science)	15	3/31/84	39,771
University of Michigan	L. E. Blume	The Demand for Information by Rational Agents and the Market for Information	24	12/31/84	54,645
University of Pennsylvania	D. Sappington	Optimal Incentive Schemes Under Asymmetric Information (Information Science)	12	2/29/84	25,655

TABLE 3 SMALL BUSINESS INNOVATION RESEARCH AWARDS, FY 1982*

Institution	Principal Investigator	Proposal Title	Duration (Months)	Expiration Date	Amount
Information Technology Program					
Aerodyne Research Inc.	H. H. Caulfield	Synthetic Holographic Computer Output (Information Science)	6	4/15/83	(ISTI) $29,945
Continuous Learning Corp.	K. C. Cohen	Adaptive Referencing—A New Approach to Design of the Interface Between an Access System and Its User (Information Science)	6	4/15/83	(ISTI) 29,890
Relational Technology, Inc.	R. Kooi	Managing Text as Data (Information Science)	6	4/15/82	(ISTI) 29,786
Transtech International Corp.	G. Y. Wang	Computer Input and Output of Chinese Ideograms (Information Science)	6	4/15/83	(ISTI) 30,000

*Although the Small Business Innovation Research Awards are administered by the Division of Information Science and Technology (IST), they are actually funded by the Division of Industrial Science and Technological Innovation (ISTI).

TABLE 4 AWARDS FUNDED JOINTLY BY IST AND OTHER NSF DIVISIONS, FY 1982

Institution	Principal Investigator	Proposal Title	Duration (Months)	Expiration Date	Amount
Brown University	J. A. Anderson	Cognitive Applications of Matrix Memory Models	12	9/30/83	13,045 (BNS) 19,567 32,612
California Institute of Technology	L. Wilde and A. Schwartz	Intervening in Markets on the Basis of Imperfect Information: An Information Theoretic Approach	24	1/31/84	49,000 (SES) 49,980 98,980
Duke University	A. Biermann	Voice Interactive Computer Systems	12	6/30/83	54,000 (MCS) 54,041 108,041
Massachusetts Institute of Technology	W. A. Richards	Natural Computation and Control (Computer Research)	12	12/31/83	130,000 (MCS) 165,716 (MCS) 150,000 445,716
North Carolina State University	R. D. Rodman	Voice Interactive Computer Systems	12	6/30/82	16,500 (MCS) 16,743 33,243

Institution	PI	Title	Months	End Date	Amount
Pennsylvania State University	P. C. Jurs	Computer Assisted Studies of Structure-Property Relationships	12	11/30/83	11,500 (CHE) 34,500 46,000
Princeton University	C. Shapiro	Signals of Product Quality	24	12/31/84	8,000 (SES) 12,833 20,833
Stanford University	J. R. Perry	Computational Aspects of Situation Semantics (Computer Science)	24	12/31/84	23,067 (MCS) 23,128 (MCS) 23,068 69,263
University of California–Irvine	K. L. Kraemer	Longitudinal Study of Computer Technology and Impact in Cities	24	9/30/84	65,572 (SES) 120,000 185,572
University of Minnesota	L. Hurwicz	Comparison and Analysis of Systems and Techniques of Economic Organizations	12	12/31/83	19,190 (SES) 19,191 38,381
University of Wisconsin	K. J. Barwise	Computational Aspects of Situation Semantics (Computer Research)	24	12/31/84	17,536 (MCS) 17,537 (MCS) 17,536 52,609

Part 3
Library Education, Placement, and Salaries

RECENT DEVELOPMENTS IN LIBRARY EDUCATION

Herbert S. White

*Dean, School of Library and Information Science,
Indiana University, Bloomington, IN 47405*

There is little doubt that library education programs, caught between generally decreasing enrollments, reduced institutional support, and a reduction in federal programs to provide student financial aid, on the one hand, and increasing pressures to provide greater and more diverse educational experience, on the other hand, have been caught in a severe crunch between resources and expectations.

Some of the magnitude of the reduction in enrollment can be seen from the simple fact that in the five-year period since 1975–1976, average full-time enrollment in accredited programs decreased 37.5 percent, and average total enrollment (including part-time students) decreased 30.5 percent, while the number of accredited programs increased by 5, particularly early in the period. It is not easy to pinpoint reasons for the decline in the number of students. Part of it may be attributable to the general decline in post-baccalaureate students, as these are particularly susceptible to changes in financial aid support levels. Part of it may be due to the still commonly held view that there is a surplus of library school graduates, even though placement rates are reported as high, and even though the most pessimistic surveys conclude that the level of retirements will require new recruits at least at the level presently being produced, despite possible retrenchments. Part of the problem is undoubtedly the continuing low starting salaries, which cause us to lose some of the best and brightest of potential recruits to other graduate academic programs with greater remuneration and perhaps greater prestige. [For the most recent available statistics on placements and salaries, see the report by Learmont and Van Houten, "Placements and Salaries, 1981: Holding the Line," later in Part 3—*Ed.*]

CHANGES IN THE EDUCATION PROGRAMS

Library education programs continue to be (and possibly will always be) plagued by the perhaps contradictory pressures to provide general levels of education, largely perceived by faculty as pre-professional preparation, as opposed to the expectation that specific job skills be taught, to prepare graduates for productive activity upon assumption of the first professional job. Putting these concerns in terms of an adversary relationship is both simplistic and unfair, and there has in the past several years been a very worthwhile increase in communication between library educators and library administrators, particularly in academic and large public libraries. Concerns about the identification of preparation necessary for first professional positions is also at least part of the motivation behind a contract awarded by the Department of Education to King Research, Inc., a contract that will examine a large number of questions but will also consider the ramifications of competency-based educational criteria. These questions in turn are related to legal issues that have arisen concerning skill validation and the appropriateness of formal educational job qualifications as contrasted to job experience.

Library education programs are undergoing substantial changes in recognition of shifting emphases. Although no two schools are taking the same approach, areas of increased concentration can perhaps be broken down as follows: (1) the evaluation and application of computer technology, involving considerably more student exposure to data base access and online searching, and hands-on experience with microcomputers for library applications; (2) library management principles and concerns, including budgeting, planning, cost justifications, personnel supervision, and communication; (3) networking and resource sharing, including regional, national, and international cooperative systems and the legal and ethical implications of cooperative acquisition and photocopying; and (4) intellectual freedom and the dangers of group or individual censorship to the library's policies and activities.

After substantial increases in both the number and accreditation of library education programs in the early and mid 1970s, the number appears now to have stabilized at approximately the present level of 62 U.S. and 7 Canadian programs accredited for graduate education, generally at the masters level. Only the University of North Carolina at Greensboro represents a new first-time accredited program during the past several years. Two schools have been removed at least temporarily from the list of accredited programs and a number have had their accreditation extended only conditionally for a period of two years. (However, application for re-accreditation or removal of condition is a continuing process, and interested individuals are urged to keep in touch with the list of accredited programs published by the American Library Association on a semiannual basis.) As part of a general review and tightening within the higher education process, a number of library education programs are currently being evaluated by their own institutions, and it is expected that this process will continue and even accelerate. However, as of the date of this writing, only one program, that at the State University of New York at Geneseo, has been officially targeted for discontinuance. The program at the University of Missouri at Columbia was able to gain reversal of an initial judgment to that effect.

CHANGES IN THE STUDENT BODY

The last few years have also seen a substantial change in the character of the student body. Reports from library schools indicate for this program, as for many other educational programs, an increase in students returning to the job market, many of them after other careers or time spent at home. A large number of these are older students, with a greater maturity and somewhat different value systems. There also has been an increase in the percentage of part-time students, individuals with job or home responsibilities lacking some of the geographical flexibility of full-time students resident on the campus. Part of this change is undoubtedly caused by increases in tuition costs and a reduction of financial aid programs. Schools of library education are attempting to respond to these needs in a variety of approaches, including a sharp increase in evening and weekend courses, the removal of courses from the school campus to large metropolitan areas, and the use of such tools as television with two-way radio communication to bring appropriate courses to students in their own localities.

There has also been an increased interest in two perhaps contradictory areas. One involves a substantial increase in continuing education programs, offered through post-masters degree or certificate programs, through workshops and conferences, and in conjunction with professional associations and their programs. These activities recognize the changes that have taken place in the profession, since many present practitioners attended classes, and attempt to provide opportunities particularly in areas of technological development and management skills. Success of these programs has been mixed. Where they have been underwritten and supported at the university or governmental level to assure low registration fees, attendance has been encouraging. However, to the extent to which these activities are expected to be self-supporting, their success is largely dependent on the acceptance by professionals and particularly by their employers of the premise that such continuing education activity is an integral part of any profession, and that such activity must be both financially supported and demanded for promotion, tenure, and even job retention.

Simultaneously with this increased emphasis on continuing education has come an awakened concern for library and information science education at the undergraduate level. Such educational programs have always been in existence, but up to now their primary emphasis has been in unaccredited education programs, which have understandable difficulty attracting graduate students. The last few years have seen a sharp increase in the development of undergraduate degree programs at major library schools, not necessarily in librarianship but perhaps in such areas as information technology or information practice. According to reports from these institutions, these undergraduate programs, which frequently emphasize technology, have been successful both in attracting students and in placing their graduates in jobs, frequently in the private sector of the economy. What is less clear, and probably needs to be investigated, is the relationship between the jobs that these individuals are presumably qualified to fill and those that ought to require formal library education at the graduate level, and the possible concern that this could represent a dilution and cheapening of the professional job market. [See the report on "The New Federalism: How It Is Changing the Library Profession in the United States" in the Special Reports section of Part 1—*Ed.*]

IMPLICATIONS FOR LIBRARY EDUCATORS

There is little doubt that the pressures that affect all of academia at present and will during at least most of the 1980s will have serious implications for library education. Most library education programs are small; some are barely noticed within their institutions. Some of them will face the threat of elimination, of curtailment, or of a redirection of effort. It will be a particular challenge to library education to maintain and even improve quality in the face of these pressures. An acknowledgement of the new directions in library practice that education must reflect requires increasing investment in expensive technology and an offering of more and specialized courses. Faculties are already small and are getting smaller. According to statistics compiled for the Association of American Library Schools, about half of the presently accredited library education programs now have fewer than ten full-time faculty members, a figure that may be particularly disturbing when it is realized both that complexity of library education is growing, and that accredited education programs are assumed to be both the larger and more significant ones.

The need to update the competencies of library educators has accelerated programs to provide continuing education for teachers as well as practitioners, and at least some of these activities have been supported by grant funds from foundations and government agencies. To the extent to which faculty members may be somewhat isolated from the mainstream of library activities, an active program of interchange between library educators and library practitioners, in which particularly the former are given the opportunity to return to advanced operational settings, is particularly desirable. The reverse of this situation, of practitioners teaching in library education programs, already exists to a considerable extent, particularly for specialized courses.

Although there are now more than 25 institutions offering library education at the doctoral level, the number of students has been seriously impacted by the elimination of fellowship funds that stimulated higher education in the latter 1960s and early 1970s. We know from demographic data that many library educators are nearing retirement age, and the development of new junior faculty with interests and aptitudes for both teaching and research is essential. Without these candidates, positions may be badly filled, remain unfilled, or offer the temptation of elimination. Research into fundamental questions of library education is sorely required. The contract to King Research, Inc., provides an opportunity to examine one area, but there are many others. The recent study designed to identify and rank research priorities for the library profession in the 1980s failed to list library education as a high priority, and this is unfortunate, particularly if it suggests a lack of primary concern on the part of practitioners. To the extent to which none of the other identified priorities have as yet been funded it could be argued that this does not really matter, anyway. However, it is important that practitioners and educators establish a closer link, recognize their interdependence, and take steps to protect and upgrade both the quality of library education and the continuing review of its development.

IN CONCLUSION

The last several years have been both exciting and dangerous ones for library education, and the 1980s certainly promise only an acceleration in this direction. Dynamic and positive changes are certainly needed and called for. Hopefully, through a recognition of the fundamental importance of this area for the profession, and through an insistence on and a reward of high quality and achievement, progress will be made.

EDUCATION IN CONSERVATION OF LIBRARY MATERIALS

Josephine Riss Fang

*Professor, Graduate School of Library and Information Science,
Simmons College, Boston, MA 02115*

The inclusion of conservation training in library school programs is a fairly recent development in the United States. In 1978, the National Conservation Advisory Council recommended that "the highest priority should be to increase the awareness of librarians and archivists about various aspects of conserving the materials in their custody. The training of conservation administrators, who must be equipped to deal with organizational, administrative, and bibliographic control matters and at the same time administer the technical and craft aspects of an institution's conservation program, may become a specialty within library science or archives management requiring intensive courses in conservation." (*Report of the Study Committee on Libraries and Archives: National Needs in Libraries and Archives Conservation.* Washington, D.C.: National Conservation Advisory Council, 1978, pp. 45–46.)

In the fourth edition of the *Preservation Education Directory* (1981), Susan Swartzburg and Susan White found that 85 percent of the accredited library schools are now offering courses, units, or workshops on various aspects of preservation. This statistic reflects the growing awareness within the profession that librarians are responsible for the care as well as the development of their collections and that these two professional responsibilities go hand-in-hand. The *Directory* gives brief descriptions of courses offered and reveals the great variety of approaches to conservation training that do exist.

Note: This article is adapted from a paper presented at the forty-eighth General Conference of the International Federation of Library Associations & Institutions (IFLA), held in Montreal, Canada, in August 1982. [For a report on the 1982 IFLA conference, see Part 5—*Ed.*]

Three library schools offer specialized programs in conservation made up of several different courses: Columbia University, School of Library Service; Catholic University, School of Library and Information Science; and University of Maryland, College of Library and Information Services. At 20 other library schools, separate courses in conservation are taught as part of the regular curriculum. Another 37 library schools teach conservation within other courses. There also are 25 colleges and universities that offer courses on, or courses including, conservation training in nonlibrary school programs.

THE SIMMONS COLLEGE EXPERIENCE

At the Graduate School of Library and Information Science at Simmons College in Boston, Massachusetts, a course has been offered jointly with the Northeast Document Conservation Center (NEDCC) of Andover, Massachusetts, since summer 1981. In 1969, George Cunha, former curator of the Boston Athenaeum, invited the students in technical services classes at Simmons College to visit his conservation workshop and observe his staff at their various activities. These field trips became a popular part of the technical services course. When the New England Document Conservation Center (later renamed the Northeast Document Conservation Center) was created in 1973, as the first regional conservation center in the United States (and still the only one in existence), with George Cunha as its first director, field trips were made instead to the larger and better equipped facilities.

It soon became apparent that there was a need for and interest in a more structured and in-depth conservation experience. The leadership role of the Library of Congress Preservation Office, the abundance of conservation literature (e.g., the 1981 issue of *Library Trends*, which has become a required text for the students), the new program at Columbia University under Paul Banks, and the appearance of the first serial publication on conservation for librarians, *CAN (Conservation Administration News)* to all were factors that combined to justify the need for a separate course, not just one class session and one field trip. In 1976, Simmons began to offer continuing education institutes in conservation, together with George Cunha and the NEDCC staff. More and more alumni and students began to request a separate course; with the help of Cunha, a course outline and proposal were prepared and presented to the faculty and administration. The course finally was offered in summer 1981.

The new course, "Conservation Management for Libraries and Archives," is described as a basic course in the fundamentals of preventive and restorative conservation for librarians and archivists. Its objectives are (1) to provide participants with the necessary information to plan and establish in-house programs of preventive maintenance in their own institutions in order to minimize damage to collections; (2) to provide participants with sufficient knowledge in the theory and techniques of physical treatment to enable them to supervise effectively their institutions' preservation microfilming programs and commercial binding requirements; and (3) to enable participants to collaborate on a one-to-one basis with professional conservators and restorers in plans for the salvage and rehabilitation of the more seriously damaged books, documents, prints, broadsides, and other research materials in libraries and archives.

The course is taught with the cooperation of the staff of the Northeast Document Conservation Center, particularly Ann Russell, director (by the time the course was announced, George Cunha had relocated to Kentucky); Shirley Ogden, associate conservator; and Mildred O'Connell, field service director. The course includes two visits to the NEDCC, where Mary Todd Glaser (senior conservator) explains the work of the paper laboratory; Sherelyn Ogden, book restoration; Gary Albright (assistant conservator), photographic conservation; and Andrew P. Raymond (archivist and records specialist), conservation microfilming. Two hands-on sessions, both demonstration and practice, deal with surface cleaning, proper handling of library material, testing paper for acidity, testing for solubility of inks, paste making, mending with Japanese tissue, mending with heat-set tissue, polyester encapsulation, and the demonstration of making phase boxes.

Some of the topics covered in lectures and audiovisual presentations include a historical survey; information sources; the nature of library and archival materials; the deterioration of library and archival material; preventive maintenance (environmental control, housekeeping and storage, safe in-house procedures); and repair and restoration (paper, hand binding, and restoration binding). At a session with a commercial binder, students learn to evaluate the different types of bindings. Other topics include surveying an institution for conservation needs; disaster and disaster control; budgeting for conservation; sources for funding; national and international conservation planning; and new developments in library and archives conservation (such as the use of new technology by the Library of Congress and the Canadian Conservation Institute).

The students are given an extensive bibliography with recommended readings and a package prepared by the Northeast Document Conservation Center with useful mimeographed materials and recent publications, such as the newly revised *Standards for Library Binding* of the Library Binding Institute (1982). They are expected to do extensive readings on their own and to carry out one project of their choice or to prepare a research paper. At the end of each semester, the course is reevaluated, bearing in mind students' evaluations and incorporating new developments in the field.

CONTINUING EDUCATION PROGRAMS

In addition to the formal professional library education programs in conservation, there is a great need for continuing education for practicing professionals to keep them informed of new developments in the field. Library schools continue to play an active role in this area. At Simmons College, for example, a number of institutes on various aspects of conservation have been offered.

Professional associations at the national level offer further educational opportunities. For instance, the Society of American Archivists held extensive sessions on conservation at its meeting in Boston in October 1982. It also conducts separate workshops. Regional, state, and local professional groups have been inviting conservators to conduct one- and two-day workshops. (Some large institutions arrange similar workshops for their staff.) An increasing number of professional conferences include the topic as part of continuing professional awareness and education, and two annual national conferences on conservation have been held under the auspices of Meckler Communications, the publishers of *Microform Review*, with the third conference scheduled for February 1983 in Philadelphia. (The 1981 Allerton Park Institute also was devoted to this topic.)

With the support of foundations, major academic and research libraries are becoming increasingly involved in conservation awareness. For example, Harvard University arranged an International Preservation Microfilming Conference in Fall 1981, and the Association of Research Libraries has issued a number of publications that provide practical guidelines for conservation management. Further support is provided through the work and publications of the very active and successful Preservation Section of the Resources and Technical Services Division of the American Library Association, which was founded in 1980 and is steadily growing.

THE FUTURE OUTLOOK

The students who took the Simmons course will use their knowledge as practicing professionals and as library/archive administrators. Some will go on to acquire further experience. All will be better equipped to work in the library/archival profession. We are hopeful that a new generation of professionals will not only be well versed in computer applications to library processes and information services but will also be equipped to take measures to arrest the deterioration of our heritage.

But library schools must do more than merely fill current professional needs. They must continue their efforts, so that not just 85 percent, but *all*, of the library and information science programs in the United States will include courses in conservation and preservation as an integral component of professional education and so that no one graduates without at least some basic knowledge and awareness of available resources. In cooperation with professional conservators, they must take the initiative to plan and anticipate future developments. Research should be encouraged and supported at educational institutions, both in the practical and theoretical aspects of conservation and collection management and to develop educational guidelines. We live in challenging times, and educators must prepare librarians and information scientists for the decisions they will have to make.

BIBLIOGRAPHY

Banks, Paul N. *A Selective Bibliography on the Conservation of Research Materials*. Chicago: Newberry Library, 1981.

Buchanan, Sally. "Recent Developments in Library Conservation in the United States." In *Bowker Annual 1982*, pp. 61-68. New York: R. R. Bowker Co., 1982.

Darling, Pamela W., and Sherelyn Ogden. "From Problems Perceived to Programs in Practice: The Preservation of Library Resources in the U.S.A., 1936-1980." *Library Resources and Technical Services* 25 (January/March 1981): 9-29.

Gwinn, Nancy E. "CLR and Preservation." *College Research Libraries* (March 1981): 104-126.

"The Library Looks to the Future: 'Preservation and New Technology.'" *Library of Congress Information Bulletin*, July 16, 1982, pp. 205-207, 211-212.

Lundeen, Gerald, ed. "Conservation of Library Materials." *Library Trends* 30 (Fall 1981).

McCrank, Lawrence J. "Conservation and Collection Management: Educational Problems and Opportunities." *Journal of Education for Librarianship* 22 (1981): 20-43.

Patterson, Robert H. "Preservation of Library Materials," In *ALA Yearbook 1982*, pp. 212-214. Chicago: American Library Association, 1982.

Swartzburg, Susan C., and Susan B. White, eds. *Preservation Education Directory: Educational Opportunities in the Preservation of Library Materials, 1981*. Chicago: American Library Association, Resources and Technical Services Division, 1981.

The Systems and Procedures Exchange Center (SPEC) of the Association of Research Libraries, Office of Management Studies, Washington, D.C., has published the following SPEC Kits and Flyers on preservation: *Preservation of Library Materials* (no. 35, 1977); *Theft Detection Policies* (no. 37, 1977); *Planning for Preservation* (no. 66, 1980); *Preparing for Emergencies and Disasters* (no. 69, 1980); *Basic Preservation Procedures* (no. 70, 1981).

GUIDE TO LIBRARY PLACEMENT SOURCES

Margaret Myers
*Director, Office for Library Personnel Resources,
American Library Association*

This year's guide updates the listing in the 1982 *Bowker Annual* with the addition of new services and the latest information on previously listed services. The sources listed primarily give assistance in obtaining professional positions; a few indicate assistance for paraprofessionals, which as a group tend to be recruited through local sources.

GENERAL SOURCES OF LIBRARY JOBS

Library Literature. Classified ads of library vacancies and positions wanted are carried in many of the national, regional, and state library journals and newsletters. Members of associations can sometimes list "position wanted" ads free of charge in their membership publications. Listings of positions available are regularly found in *American Libraries, Catholic Library World, Chronicle of Higher Education, College & Research Libraries Newsletter, Journal of Academic Librarianship, Library Journal, LJ/SLJ Hotline,* and *Wilson Library Bulletin.* State and regional library association newsletters, state library journals, foreign library periodicals, and other types of periodicals carrying such ads are listed in later sections.

Newspapers. The *New York Times* in its Sunday Week in Review section carries a special listing of available jobs for librarians in addition to the regular classifieds. Local newspapers, particularly the larger city Sunday editions, often carry job vacancy listings in libraries, both professional and paraprofessional.

LIBRARY JOBLINES

Library joblines or job "hotlines" give recorded telephone messages of job openings in a specific geographical area. Most tapes are changed once a week on Friday afternoon, although individual listings may sometimes be carried for several weeks. Although the information is fairly brief and the cost of calling is borne by the individual job seeker, a jobline provides a more quick and up-to-date listing of vacancies than is usually possible with printed listings or journal ads.

Most joblines only carry listings for their state or region although some occasionally will accept out-of-state positions if there is room on the tape. While a few will list technician and other paraprofessional positions, the majority are for professional jobs only. If, when calling the joblines, one finds that the telephone keeps ringing without any answer, this usually will mean that the tape is being changed or that there are no new jobs at that time.

The classified section of *American Libraries* carries jobline numbers in each issue. The joblines that are presently in operation are: *American Society for Information Science,* 202-659-1737; *Arizona State Library/JAM,* 602-278-1327; *Association of College and Research Libraries,* 312-944-6795; *British Columbia Library Association,* 604-263-0014 (B.C. listings only); *California Library Association,* 916-443-1222 for northern California and 213-629-5627 for southern California (identical lists); *California Media*

Note: The author wishes to acknowledge the assistance of Sandra Raeside, OLPR administrative assistant, in compiling the information for this article.

and Library Educators Association, 415-697-8832; Colorado State Library, 303-866-2210 (Colorado listings only, includes paraprofessional); (Delaware jobs are listed on the New Jersey and Pennsylvania joblines); Florida State Library, 904-488-5232 (in-state listings only); Illinois Library Job Hotline, 312-828-0930 (co-sponsored by the Special Libraries Association Illinois Chapter and Illinois Library Association—all types of jobs listed); Maryland Library Association, 301-685-5760; Metropolitan Washington Council of Governments (D.C.), 202-223-2272; Midwest Federation of Library Associations, 517-487-5617 (co-sponsored by six state library associations—Illinois, Indiana, Michigan, Minnesota, Ohio, and Wisconsin; also includes paraprofessional and out-of-state if room on tape); Mountain Plains Library Association, 605-624-2511 (includes listings for the states of Kansas, Nebraska, Nevada, North and South Dakota, Utah, and Wyoming; updated on Thursdays); Nebraska, 402-471-2045 (during regular business hours); New England Library Board, 617-738-3148; New Jersey Library Association/State Library, 609-695-2121; New York Library Association, 212-227-8483; North Carolina State Library, 919-733-6410 (professional jobs in N.C. only); Oklahoma Jobline, 405-521-4202 (5:00 PM to 8:00 AM, Monday thru Friday and all weekend); Oregon Library Association, 503-585-2232 (co-sponsored by Oregon Educational Media Association); Pacific Northwest Library Association, 206-543-2890 (Alaska, Alberta, British Columbia, Idaho, Montana, Oregon, and Washington; includes both professional and paraprofessional and other library-related jobs); Pennsylvania Cooperative Jobline, 717-234-4646 (co-sponsored by the Pennsylvania Library Association, Pennsylvania Learning Resources Association, Pittsburgh Regional Library Center, Special Libraries Association—Philadelphia Chapter, Medical Library Association—Philadelphia and Pittsburgh groups, American Society for Information Science—Delaware Valley Chapter, Pennsylvania School Librarians Association, and West Virginia Library Association; also accepts paraprofessional out-of-state listings); Special Libraries Association, New York Chapter, 212-753-7247; Special Libraries Association, San Francisco Bay Chapter, 415-968-9748; Special Libraries Association, Southern California Chapter, 213-795-2145; Texas Library Association Job Hotline, 713-782-0570 (4:00 PM Friday to 8:30 AM Monday); Texas State Library Jobline, 512-475-0408 (Texas listings only); University of South Carolina College of Librarianship, 803-777-8443; Virginia Library Association Jobline, 804-355-0384.

Those joblines that accept vacancy listings from employers by telephone are: ACRL, 312-944-6780; ASIS, 202-659-3644; Arizona, 602-269-2535; California, 916-447-8541; District of Columbia, 202-223-6800, ext. 458; Florida, 904-487-2651; Illinois, 312-644-1896; New Jersey, 609-292-6237; New York, 212-227-8032; New York/SLA, 212-790-0639; North Carolina, 919-733-2570; Oklahoma, 405-521-2502; Pennsylvania, 717-233-3113; San Francisco/SLA, 408-277-3784; Southern California/SLA, 213-356-6329; Texas, 512-475-4110; Virginia, 804-257-1101.

The joblines to which employers must submit job listings in writing are: British Columbia Library Association, P.O. Box 46378, Station G, Vancouver, B.C. V6R 4G6, Canada; California media and Library Educators Association, 1575 Old Bayshore Hwy., Suite 204, Burlingame, CA 94010; Colorado State Library Jobline, 1362 Lincoln, Denver, CO 80203; Illinois Library Job Hotline, Illinois Library Association, 425 N. Michigan Ave., Suite 1304, Chicago, IL 60611 ($20 fee/2 weeks); Maryland Library Association, 115 W. Franklin St., Baltimore, MD 21201; Mountain Plains Library Association, c/o I.D. Weeks Library, University of South Dakota, Vermillion, SD 57069; Nebraska Job Hotline, Library Commission, 1420 P St., Lincoln, NE 68508; New England Library Jobline, c/o James Matarazzo, GSLIS, Simmons College, 300 The Fenway, Boston, MA 02115; Oregon Library Association JOBLINE, Oregon State Library, Salem, OR

97310; *PNLA Jobline*, c/o Pacific Northwest Bibliographic Center, University of Washington, 253 Suzzalo Library FM-25, Seattle, WA 98195; *Texas Library Association Job Hotline*, 8989 Westheimer, Suite 108, Houston, TX 77063; *University of South Carolina, College of Librarianship*, Placement, Columbia, SC 29208 (no geographical restrictions).

For the *Midwest Federation Jobline*, employers should send listings to their own state association executive secretary, who will refer these to the Michigan Library Association where the recording equipment is housed. There is a $5 fee to be paid by the employer for each listing. Paraprofessional positions are also accepted.

SPECIALIZED LIBRARY ASSOCIATIONS AND GROUPS

American Association of Law Libraries, 53 W. Jackson Blvd., Chicago, IL 60604, 312-939-4764. Placement service is available without charge. Lists of openings and personnel available are published several times per year in a newsletter distributed to membership. Applicants are referred to placement officers for employment counseling.

American Libraries, c/o Beverly Goldberg, 50 E. Huron St., Chicago, IL 60611. "Career LEADS EXPRESS" provides early notice (advance galleys) of some 40 to 60 "Positions Open" to be published in the next issue of *American Libraries*. Galleys are sent about the seventeenth of each month; they do not include editorial corrections and late changes as they appear in the regular *AL* "LEADS" section, but do include some "Late Job Notices." For each month, send $2 check made out to *AL* EXPRESS, self-addressed, standard business-size envelope (4 × 9), and 20¢ postage on envelope.

American Libraries, Consultants Keyword Clearinghouse (CKC), an *AL* service that helps match professionals offering library/information expertise with institutions seeking it. Published quarterly, *CKC* appears in the "Career LEADS" section of the January, April, June, and October issues of *AL*. Rates: $4/line (classified); $40/inch (display). Inquiries should be made to Beverly Goldberg, LEADS Editor, *American Libraries*, 50 E. Huron St., Chicago, IL 60611, 312-944-6780, ext. 326.

American Library Association, Office for Library Personnel Resources, 50 E. Huron St., Chicago, IL 60611, 312-944-6780. A placement service is provided at each Annual Conference (June or July) and Midwinter Meeting (January). Applicant or employer registration forms can be filled out prior to each conference. A pilot project at the 1983 ALA Midwinter Meeting offered job and applicant listings for sale after the conference. OLPR will be evaluating this type of expanded service for future conferences, which would especially benefit those who are not in attendance at the meetings. Handouts on interviewing, preparing a résumé, and other job-seeking information are available from the ALA Office for Library Personnel Resources.

American Library Association, American Indian Libraries Newsletter, 50 E. Huron St., Chicago, IL 60611, 312-944-6780. Periodic newsletter lists job openings, especially those oriented toward Indian library services and minority librarian recruitment. For subscription information write to above address attention OLOS (Office of Library Outreach Services).

American Library Association, Association of College and Research Libraries, Fast Job Listing Service, 50 E. Huron St., Chicago, IL 60611, 312-944-6780. Monthly circular lists job openings received in ACRL office during previous four weeks (supplements listings that appear in *C&RL News*). $10 to ACRL members (indicate ALA/ACRL membership number); $15 to nonmembers. Renewable each six months. Jobline recorded telephone message updated each Friday lists current job openings. Tel. 312-944-6795. Employers who wish to have a listing for two weeks should send check for $30 (ACRL members) or $35 (non-ACRL members).

American Library Association (ALA) Black Caucus, c/o Dean Lorene B. Brown, Atlanta University School of Library and Information Studies, Atlanta, GA 30314. Although not a placement service, the Black Caucus does maintain a data bank of black librarians, and employers do request information on possible candidates. The *Black Caucus Newsletter* publishes some job openings ($10 membership fee). Contact Edna F. Reid, P.O. Box 2145, Capitol Plaza Branch, Hyattsville, MD 20784.

ALA Social Responsibilities Round Table, Rhode Island Affiliate, c/o Mary Frances Cooper, Providence Public Library, 150 Empire St., Providence, RI 02903. "SRRT Jobline," which appears monthly in *RILA Bulletin,* lists positions in southeast New England, including paraprofessional and part-time jobs. Job seekers desiring copy of most recent monthly "Jobline," send self-addressed, stamped envelope. Groups of envelopes may also be sent. To post a notice, contact Lucinda Manning, 150 Empire St., Providence, RI 02903.

American Society for Information Science, 1010 16th St. N.W., 2nd Floor, Washington, DC 20036, 202-659-3644. There is an active placement service operated at ASIS Annual Meetings (usually October) and Mid-Year Meetings (usually May). All conference attendees (both ASIS members and nonmembers), as well as ASIS members who cannot attend the conference, are eligible to use the service to list or find jobs. Job listings are also accepted from employers who cannot attend the conference, interviews are arranged, and special seminars are given. During the rest of the year, current job openings are listed on the ASIS JOBLINE. Seventeen of the ASIS chapters have placement officers who also assist members in finding jobs.

The ASIS JOBLINE (202-659-1737) operates 24 hours a day, 7 days a week. Brief descriptions—including contact information—of current job openings around the country are recorded biweekly. New jobs are listed first, starting with overseas or West Coast jobs and ending with jobs in the Washington, D.C., area. Thereafter, jobs still available from the preceding recording are listed.

Art Libraries Society/ North America (ARLIS/NA), c/o Executive Secretary, 3775 Bear Creek Circle, Tucson, AZ 85749. Art librarian and slide curator jobs are listed in the *Art Documentation* (5 times a year).

Associated Information Managers, 316 Pennsylvania Ave. S.E., Suite 400, Washington, DC 20003, 202-544-2892. AIM Career Clearinghouse lists positions open and wanted on a biweekly basis in conjunction with the AIM *Network*. Position applicants send résumé and cover letter to AIM, which forwards materials to employers. Open to AIM members only. Employers may list positions free of charge.

Association for Educational Communication & Technology, Placement Service, 1126 16th St. N.W., Washington, DC 20036, 202-466-4780. Positions available are listed in the association publication, *Instructional Innovator,* by code number and state. Responses to ads are forwarded by the association to the appropriate employer. A referral service is also available at no charge to AECT members only. A placement center operates at the annual conference, free to all conference registrants.

Catholic Library Association, 461 W. Lancaster Ave., Haverford, PA 19041, 215-649-5250. Personal and institutional members of CLA are given free space (35 words) to advertise for jobs or to list job openings in *Catholic Library World* (10/year). Others may advertise at $1 per printed line.

Council of Library/ Media Technical Assistants, c/o Cynthia Clark, 3841 N. Calle Barranco, Tucson, AZ 85715. *COLT Newsletter* appears 11 times a year and will accept listings for library/media technical assistant positions. However, correspondence relating to jobs cannot be handled.

Information Exchange System for Minority Personnel (IESMP, Inc.), P.O. Box

668, Fort Valley, GA 31030, 912-825-7645. Nonprofit organization designed to recruit minority librarians for EEO/AA employers. *Informer*, quarterly newsletter. Write for membership categories, services, and fees.

Medical Library Association, 919 N. Michigan Ave., Suite 3208, Chicago, IL 60611, 312-266-2456. Monthly *MLA News* lists positions wanted and positions available in its "Employment Opportunities" column (up to 20 free lines for MLA members, plus $2 for each additional line; $3 per line for nonmembers). MLA members may request advance mailings of "Employment Opportunities" at no charge for six months; this service is available to nonmembers for a prepaid fee of $25. Also offers placement service at annual conference each summer.

Music Library Association, Placement Director, Ida Reed, Music and Art Department, Carnegie Library of Pittsburgh, Pittsburgh, PA 15213. Registration fee of $7 per year (September through August). MLA members who register receive the *Job List*.

The National Registry for Librarians, formerly housed in the Illinois State Job Service at 40 W. Adams St., Chicago, IL 60603 is no longer in operation. Referral service will still be carried out through state and local job service offices but no independent registry will be maintained for librarians.

Online, Inc., c/o Jean-Paul Emard, 11 Tannery Lane, Weston, CT 06883, 203-227-8466. The "Jobline" column is no longer carried in the *Online* or *Database* magazines. Position openings in the online field are now available through DIALOG in an online file as part of the *Online* "Chronicle."

Reforma, National Association of Spanish-Speaking Librarians in the United States. Editor, Luis Herrera, El Paso Public Library, 501 N. Oregon, El Paso, TX 79901. Quarterly newsletter invites listings, especially for bilingual and minority librarians. In addition, job descriptions will be matched and sent to those who submit résumé and job qualifications to Reforma Jobline at above address (members free; nonmember fee $10/year for job-matching service). For listing of Spanish-speaking/Spanish-surnamed professionals, request: *Quien Es Quien: A Who's Who of Spanish-Heritage Librarians in the U.S.* (rev. ed., 1981) for $5.50 from Mexican American Studies, College of Arts & Sciences, University of Arizona, Tucson, AZ 85721. The *Amoxcalli* quarterly newsletter of the Reforma El Paso Chapter lists job openings also. Contact chapter at P.O. Box 2064, El Paso, TX 79951.

Society of American Archivists, 330 S. Wells, Suite 810, Chicago, IL 60606, 312-922-0140. The *SAA Newsletter* is sent (to members only) six times annually and lists jobs and applicants, as well as details of professional meetings and courses in archival administration. The *Employment Bulletin*, which alternates with the *Newsletter*, is sent to members who pay a $10 subscription fee.

Special Libraries Association, 235 Park Ave. S., New York, NY 10003, 212-477-9250. In addition to the Conference Employment Clearing House, the SpeciaLine (a jobline), is in operation 24 hours a day, seven days a week (212-460-9716). Most SLA chapters also have employment chairpersons who act as referral persons for employers and job seekers. The official newsletter of the association, *SpeciaList*, carries classified advertising 12 times a year.

Theresa M. Burke Employment Agency, 25 W. 39th St., New York, NY 10018, 212-398-9250. A licensed professional employment agency which has specialized for over 30 years in the recruitment of library and information personnel for academic, public, and special libraries. Staffed by employment counselors who have training and experience in both library service and personnel recruitment. Presently the majority of openings are in special libraries in the northeast and require subject backgrounds and/or specific kinds of experience. Fees are paid by the employer.

STATE LIBRARY AGENCIES

In addition to the joblines mentioned previously, there are lists of job openings issued by some of the state library agencies for their geographical areas. These include: Indiana (monthly, on request); Iowa (*Joblist*, monthly); Kentucky (monthly, on request); Maine (on request); Minnesota (*Position Openings in Minnesota and Adjoining States*, semimonthly, sent to public and academic libraries); Mississippi (job vacancy list, monthly); Ohio (*Library Opportunities in Ohio*, monthly, sent to accredited library education programs and interested individuals upon request); and Texas (*Texas Placement News*, bimonthly, free).

On occasion when vacancy postings are available, they will be listed in state library newsletters or journals such as: Alabama (*Cottonboll*, bimonthly); Indiana (*Focus on Indiana Libraries*); Louisiana (*Library Communique*, monthly); Massachusetts (*Massachusetts Position Vacancies*, monthly, sent to all public libraries in-state and to interested individuals on a one-time basis); Missouri (*Show-Me Libraries*, monthly); Nebraska (*Overtones*, 13 times/year); New Hampshire (*Granite State Libraries*, bimonthly); New Mexico (*Hitchhiker*, weekly newsletter); Utah (*Horsefeathers*, monthly); Virginia (*News*, irregular); and Wyoming (*Outrider*, monthly).

Many state library agencies will refer applicants informally when vacancies are known to exist, but do not have formal placement services. The following states primarily make referrals to public libraries only: Alabama, Georgia, Idaho, Louisiana, South Carolina (institutional also), Tennessee, Vermont, and Virginia. Those who refer applicants to all types of libraries are Delaware, Florida, Maine, Maryland, Massachusetts, Mississippi, Missouri, Montana, Nebraska, Nevada (largely public and academic), New Hampshire, New Mexico, North Dakota, Ohio, Rhode Island, South Dakota, Utah, West Virginia (public, academic, special), and Wyoming. A bulletin board in the Connecticut State Library posts library vacancies for all types of libraries.

The Missouri State Library offers a formal placement service, matching interests and qualifications of registered job applicants with positions available in Missouri libraries. Addresses of the state agencies are found in the *Bowker Annual* or *American Library Directory*.

STATE AND REGIONAL LIBRARY ASSOCIATIONS

State and regional library associations will often make referrals, run ads in association newsletters, or operate a placement service at annual conferences, in addition to the joblines sponsored by some groups. Referral of applicants when jobs are known is done by the following associations: Arkansas, Delaware (for Delaware listings, also call the New Jersey or Pennsylvania joblines), Hawaii, Louisiana, Michigan, Nevada, Pennsylvania, South Dakota, Tennessee, Texas, and Wisconsin. Although listings are infrequent, job vacancies are placed in the following association newsletters or journals when available: Alabama (*Alabama Librarian*, 10 times a year); Alaska (*Sourdough*, 4 times a year); Arkansas (*Arkansas LA Newsletter*, 8 times a year); Connecticut (*Connecticut Libraries*, 11 times a year); District of Columbia (*Intercom*, 11 times a year); Georgia (*Georgia Librarian*, 4 times a year); Indiana (*Focus on Indiana Libraries*, 10 times a year; *Indiana Libraries: A Quarterly Journal*); Iowa (*Catalyst*, 6 times a year); Kansas (*KLA Newsletter*, 3 times a year); Minnesota (*MLA Newsletter*, 10 issues/year); Mountain Plains (*MPLA Newsletter*, bimonthly, lists vacancies and position-wanted ads for individual and institutional members or area library school students); Nevada (*Highroller*, 4 times a year); New Hampshire (*NHLA Newsletter*, 6 times a year; *Granite State Libraries*); New Jersey (*New Jersey Libraries*, 4 times per year); New Mexico (shares notices via State Library's *Hitchhiker*, weekly); New York (*NYLA Bulletin*, 10 times a year); Oregon (*Oregon Library News*, monthly); Rhode Island (*RILA Bulletin*, monthly); South Dakota (*Bookmarks*, bimonthly); Vermont (*VLA News*, 10 issues/year); Virginia (*Virginia Librarian*, bimonthly); and Wyoming (*Roundup*, quarterly). The *Southeastern Librarian* lists jobs in that geographical area.

At their annual conference the following associations have indicated some type of placement service although it may only consist of bulletin board postings: Alabama, Connecticut, Illinois, Indiana, Kansas, Louisiana, Maryland, Missouri, Mountain Plains, New Jersey, New York, Pennsylvania, South Dakota, Texas, and Vermont.

Those associations that have no placement service at this time are Minnesota, Mississippi, Montana, Nebraska, New Mexico, North Dakota, Pacific Northwest, Tennessee, and Wyoming. [State and regional association addresses are found in Part 7 of this edition of *The Bowker Annual*—Ed.]

LIBRARY EDUCATION PROGRAMS

Library education programs offer some type of service for their current students as well as alumni. Of the universities with ALA-accredited programs, the following handle placement activities through the library school: Alberta, Atlanta, British Columbia, Columbia, Dalhousie, Denver, Drexel, Emory, Geneseo, Hawaii, Illinois, Long Island, Louisiana, McGill, Michigan, Minnesota, Missouri, Pittsburgh, Pratt, Rosary, Queens, Rutgers, Tennessee, Texas-Austin, Toronto, Western Ontario, and Wisconsin-Madison.

Those at which placement is handled through the central university placement center are Case Western, North Carolina, Peabody/Vanderbilt, Southern California, and UCLA. However, in most cases, faculty in the library school will still do informal counseling regarding job seeking.

In some schools, the placement services are handled in a cooperative manner; in most cases the university placement center sends out credentials while the library school posts or compiles the job listings. Schools utilizing both sources include Alabama, Albany, Arizona, Ball State, Brigham Young, Buffalo, California-Berkeley, Catholic, Chicago, Clarion State, Denver, Florida State, Geneseo, Indiana, Iowa, Kent, Kentucky, Maryland, Mississippi, Montreal, North Carolina-Greensboro, North Carolina Central, North Texas, Northern Illinois, Oklahoma, Peabody/Vanderbilt, Pratt, Queens, Rhode Island, St. John's, San Jose, Simmons, South Carolina, South Florida, Southern Connecticut, Southern Mississippi, Syracuse, Tennessee, Texas Woman's, UCLA, Washington, Wayne State, Western Michigan, and Wisconsin-Milwaukee.

In sending out placement credentials, schools vary as to whether they distribute these free, charge a general registration fee, or request a fee for each file or credentials sent out.

In addition to job vacancy postings, some schools issue a printed listing of positions open which is distributed primarily to students and alumni and only occasionally available to others. The following schools issue listings free to students and alumni *only* unless indicated otherwise: Albany (weekly to Albany graduates registered with Placement Office); Brigham Young; California-Berkeley (if registered, alumni receive 10/year out-of-state listings for a $45 fee; also a jobline, tel. 415-642-1716 to list positions); Case Western (alumni $10 for 6 lists); Clarion State (free to students and alumni); Dalhousie ($5/year for students, alumni, and others); Denver (alumni $8/year, biweekly); Drexel (free in office; by mail to students and alumni who supply self-addressed stamped envelopes—12 for 6 months); Geneseo (free in office; by mail only to students and alumni who send self-addressed stamped envelopes); Illinois (free in office; 8 issues by mail for $2 and 8 self-addressed, stamped no. 10 envelopes to alumni, $4 and 8 SASEs to non-alumni); Indiana (free for one year following graduation; alumni and others may send self-addressed stamped envelopes); Iowa (weekly, $5/4 months for registered students and alumni); Long Island (issues printed job list monthly); Michigan (free for one year following graduation, all other graduates, $10/year, 24 issues); Minnesota (if 37-cent self-addressed envelopes are supplied); Missouri (Library Vacancy Roster, triweekly printout, 50¢ an issue, with minimum of 5 issues, to anyone); North Carolina (available by mail to alumni and students who pay $15 referral fee); North Texas State ($5/6 months, students and alumni); Oklahoma (supplied off campus on request); Peabody/Vanderbilt (students and alumni if registered for fee); Pittsburgh (others for $3/6 months); Pratt (alumni—weekly during spring, fall, and summer sessions; others—renew every 3 months); Rhode Island (monthly, $3/year); Rosary (every 2 weeks, $15/year for alumni); Rutgers (subscription $4/6 months, $8/year—twice a month to anyone); Southern Connecticut (printed listing twice a month, free in office, mailed to students/alumni free); Texas-Austin (bimonthly placement bulletin free to alumni and students); UCLA (alumni—every 2 weeks by request—renew every 3 months); Western Michigan ($10/26 weeks to anyone—issued by University Placement Services); Wisconsin-Madison (subscription $6/year for 12 issues, to anyone, price increase for 1983 probable); Western Ontario sends notices of available positions as they are received to graduates on the school's placement mailing list.

Those schools that post job vacancy notices for review but do not issue printed lists include Alabama, Albany, Alberta, Arizona, Atlanta, Ball State, British Columbia, Buffalo, Catholic, Chicago, Emory, Florida State, Hawaii, Kent, Louisiana, Maryland, McGill, Montreal, North Carolina-Greensboro, North Carolina Central, Northern Illinois, Oklahoma, Peabody/Vanderbilt, Queens, St. John's, San Jose, Simmons, South Carolina, South Florida, Southern California, Southern Mississippi, Syracuse, Tennessee, Texas Woman's, Toronto, Washington, Wayne State, Western Michigan, Western Ontario, and Wisconsin-Milwaukee.

A number of schools are providing job hunting seminars and short courses or are more actively trying to help graduates obtain positions. Most schools will offer at least an annual or semiannual discussion on placement often with outside speakers representing different types of libraries or recent graduates relating experiences. Some additional programs offered by schools include Albany (alumni/student career day, career possibilities colloquium series; sessions on résumé writing, interviewing, job counseling; computer-based placement file); Arizona (job hunting, résumé writing workshops); Atlanta (seminar on résumé writing); Ball State (job hunting, résumé writing, videotaped job interview role playing sessions); Brigham Young (students write résumé which is critiqued in basic administration class); British Columbia ("Employment Week" in spring term with employers invited to interview); Buffalo (assists laid-off local employees; sends list of graduates to major libraries in the United States; operates a selective dissemination of information [SDI] service; résumé seminar and follow-up critique, strategy sessions for conference job seeking; "Put a Buffalo in Your Library" buttons); California-Berkeley (career awareness workshops on résumés, interview and job search; also provides a career planning and information workbook for entering students); Case Western (résumé writing, interviewing skills, including videotape critique, job counseling; alumni as well as current graduates); Chicago (workshop on career opportunities, résumé writing and interviewing skills); Columbia (alumni/student career day; sessions on résumé writing, interviewing, individual and group job counseling during the spring); Dalhousie (sessions on job searching, etc., with critiquing of résumés); Denver (résumé writing in administration course, interview workshop, profile of students so job listings can be sent matching interests, Career Day for students/alumni, career awareness workshop with university placement personnel, individual counseling, postings); Drexel (job search workshops; résumés, cover letters, interviewing; individual job counseling by appointment available to students and alumni); Emory (job strategy meeting each term; résumé assistance and job counseling); Florida State (individual consultation with faculty critiques of résumés, etc.); Hawaii (sessions on job searching, résumé writing, cover letters, interviewing; individual job counseling by appointment available to students and alumni); Illinois (résumé writing, interview role playing in library administration class, counseling/critiquing for individuals in library school placement office, computer-based placement profiles for students and alumni, job search workshops by university-wide placement service); Indiana (convocation on job search, seminar on résumé writing, interview role playing in course work, critique of individual résumés and letters); Iowa (job strategy and résumé writing session each term, individual counseling); Kent (annual placement workshops, résumé writing, interviewing strategies); Long Island (job hunting workshops); Maryland (placement colloquia; job search workshops and videotapes available); McGill (résumé writing, interview techniques, counseling for job hunting, reception for employers); Michigan (seminar sessions on job hunting, résumé writing, interviewing, and search strategies); Minnesota (résumé writing, individual counseling, interview techniques); Mississippi (résumé writing, letters, and interviewing); Missouri (student seminars, individual counseling); and Montreal (discussion on placement with speakers representing a certain type of library; résumé writing and interview techniques in administration course).

The following schools also offer additional programs: North Carolina (workshop on résumé preparation, job seeking strategy, interview techniques; students may do mock interview on videotape with critique); North Carolina–Greensboro (job hunting, résumé workshops); North Carolina Central (seminars, counseling); Oklahoma (seminars and workshops on résumé writing and interviewing, paperbag lunchtime panel discussions on job availability and placement); Peabody/Vanderbilt (regular seminars on library marketplace, résumé preparation, interviews, etc.); Pittsburgh (individual counseling, pre-conference strategy sessions, placement colloquium sessions, two-day-long workshops covering search strategy, résumés, and other means of access, interview techniques, interaction with recent graduates and other alumni, employers' open house); Pratt (job clinics throughout the year, book of résumés sent to employers); Rhode Island (résumés critiqued in library administration course, jobs seminar annually); Rutgers (seminars on job search and résumé writing, individual advising, interview role playing by video in Contemporary Issues class, paperbag lunchtime panel discussions, postings); San Jose (two-day workshops on alternative careers, twice a year; one-day session on résumé writing, interviews, and strategies); Simmons (series of 4 programs each semester); South Carolina (seminars on job search and résumé writing offered as part of curriculum); South Florida (résumé writing and interview sessions); Southern Mississippi (placement seminar); Syracuse (job search strategy workshops, career possibilities colloquium series, résumé critiques, career counseling); Tennessee (placement colloquium; assistance in résumé writing); Texas–Austin (job postings, individual counseling and job leads for students and alumni; seminars on job hunting, résumé writing and critiquing, interview strategies); Toronto (résumé writing, job search workshops, individual job counseling by appointment); UCLA (compiles *Job Hunting Handbook;* colloquia on job search strategy, résumé writing, and interviewing); Washington (job search strategy and interviewing discussions, postings); Western Michigan (résumé writing, individual counseling, interview techniques); Western Ontario (job search strategy workshops); Wisconsin–Madison (job finding programs, résumé writing, interview role playing, and career day); and Wisconsin–Milwaukee (Job Fair with interview role playing and résumé writing).

Employers will often list jobs with schools only in their particular geographical area; some library schools will give information to non-alumni regarding their specific locales, but are *not* staffed to handle mail requests and advice is usually given in person. Schools that will allow librarians in their areas to view listings include Alabama, Albany, Alberta, Arizona, Ball State, Brigham Young, British Columbia, Buffalo, Case Western, Catholic, Chicago, Dalhousie, Denver, Drexel, Emory, Florida State, Geneseo, Illinois, Indiana, Iowa, Kent, Kentucky, Louisiana, Maryland, McGill, Michigan, Minnesota, Missouri, Montreal, North Carolina, North Carolina–Greensboro, North Texas, Northern Illinois, Peabody/Vanderbilt, Pittsburgh, Pratt, Queens, Rhode Island, Rutgers, St. John's, San Jose, South Carolina, Southern California, Southern Connecticut, Southern Mississippi, Syracuse, Tennessee, Texas–Austin, Texas Woman's, Toronto, UCLA, Washington, Wayne State, Western Michigan, Western Ontario, Wisconsin–Madison, and Wisconsin–Milwaukee.

An up-to-date list of ALA-accredited programs is included in Part 3 of this edition of *The Bowker Annual*. Individuals interested in placement services of other library education programs should contact the schools directly.

FEDERAL LIBRARY JOBS

The first step in obtaining employment in a federal library is to become listed on the Librarian's Register, which is a subset of files maintained by the U.S. Office of Personnel Management (OPM) in order to match federal job applicants with federal job vacancies (Washington Area Office [SSS], P.O. Box 52, Washington, DC 20044). Applicants should obtain a Qualifications Information Statement for Professional Librarian Positions (QI-1410), a Federal Employment Application Instructions and Forms Pamphlet (OPM Form 1282), and an Occupational Supplement for Professional Librarian Positions (OPM Form 1203-B) from any Federal Job Information Center. (Federal Job Centers are located in many cities across the country. They are listed under "U.S. Government" in major metropolitan area telephone directories. A *Federal Job Information Centers Directory* is available from OPM.)

Job applicants are considered for all grades for which they are qualified and which they are willing to accept. As vacancies occur, applications will be evaluated in relation to an agency's specific requirements, and the best qualified candidates are referred for consideration. Eligibility will remain in effect for one year; after this time an applicant must submit updated information to remain eligible.

Although federal job examiners do not select those to be hired, they do play a crucial role in weighing the relative experience of those on the register. When selecting the most qualified candidates for referral to the hiring agency, the examiner must consider many factors simultaneously: work experience, education (formal and informal), geographical preference, etc. Any information that should be considered must be on these forms and must not be left for someone to discover during the interview stage. Chances are that the applicant may never reach the interview stage if pertinent experience or education is not explained at the outset.

Applications are accepted only when the register is "open." The frequency with which (and the length of time) the register is open depends on the size of the inventory. The inventory is judged to be too low when a significant proportion of applicants who are qualified for positions decline them. This so-called declination rate is reversed by opening the register, thereby expanding the applicant pool.

In recent years the register has been opened once each year, generally only for several weeks at a time. Advance notice goes to all local Federal Job Information Centers, so it is important to check frequently in order to be alerted to the registration period.

However, the Librarian's Register is open on a continuing basis for persons with training and experience in the fields of medical and law librarianship, engineering, the sciences, and computerized library systems.

In addition to filing the appropriate forms, applicants can attempt to make personal contact directly with federal agencies in which they are interested. Over half the vacancies occur in the Washington area. Most positions for librarians are in three agencies—Army, Navy, and Veterans Administration. The *Federal Times* and the Sunday *Washington Post* sometimes list federal library openings. There are some "excepted" agencies which are not required to hire through the usual OPM channels. While these agencies may require the standard forms, they maintain their own employee selection policies and procedures. Government establishments with positions outside the competitive civil service include Energy Research and Development Administration; Board of Governors of the Federal Reserve System; Central Intelligence Agency; Department of Medicine and Surgery; Federal Bureau of Investigation; Foreign Service of the United States; National Science Foundation; National Security Agency; Central Examining Office; Tennessee Valley Authority; U.S. Nuclear Regulatory Commission; U.S. Postal Service; Judicial Branch of the Government; Legislative Branch of the Government; U.S. Mission to the United Nations; World Bank and IFC; International Monetary Fund; Organization of American States; Pan American Health Organization; and United Nations Secretariat.

In addition, the Library of Congress operates its own independent merit selection system. Thus, applicants for positions at the library should submit an SF-171, Personal Qualifications Statement, to the Library of Congress, Employment Office, 101 Independence Ave. S.E., Room LM 107, Washington, DC 20540. Persons who apply for specific vacancies by Posting Number enhance their prospects for consideration.

ADDITIONAL GENERAL AND SPECIALIZED JOB SOURCES

Affirmative Action Register, 8356 Olive Blvd., St. Louis, MO 63132. The goal of this organization is to "provide female, minority, and handicapped candidates with an opportunity to learn of professional and managerial positions throughout the nation and to assist employers in implementing their Affirmative Action Programs." Free distribution of monthly bulletin is made to leading businesses, industrial, and academic institutions and over 4,000 agencies that recruit qualified minorities and women, as well as to all known female, minority, and handicapped professional organizations, placement offices, newspapers, magazines, rehabilitation facilities and over 8,000 federal, state, and local governmental employment units with a total readership in excess of 3.5 million (audited). Individual mail subscriptions are available for $15 per year. Library listings are in most every issue. Sent free to libraries on request.

The Chronicle of Higher Education (published weekly, except for one week each in August and December), 1333 New Hampshire Ave. N.W., Washington, DC 20036. Receives more classified ads for library openings now than previously, although many are at the administrative level. *Academe* (bulletin of the *American Association of University Professors*), One DuPont Circle, Washington, DC 20036, also lists librarian jobs at times.

Education Information Service, P.O. Box 662, Newton Lower Falls, MA 02162. Instant Alert service for $29 will send individual 12 notices of domestic or overseas openings on same day EIS learns of opening. Also publishes periodic list of educational openings, which includes openings for librarians worldwide, although library jobs are a small portion of the list. Cost $5.95.

School Libraries. School librarians often find that the channels for locating positions in education (e.g., contacting county or city school superintendent offices) are of more value than the usual ones for library positions. The *School Library Media Quarterly* 11 (Fall 1982):63-65 contains a discussion under the "Readers' Queries" column on recommended strategies for seeking a position in a school library media center. Primary sources include university placement offices which carry listings for a variety of school system jobs and *local* information networks among teachers and library media specialists. A list of commercial teacher agencies may be obtained from the *National Association of Teachers' Agencies*, 50 E. Wynnewood, Suite 210, Wynnewood, PA 19096, 215-642-1248.

OVERSEAS

Opportunities for employment in foreign countries are limited and immigration policies of individual countries should be investigated. Employment for Americans is virtually limited to U.S. government libraries, libraries of U.S. firms doing worldwide business, and American schools abroad. Library journals from other countries will sometimes list vacancy notices (e.g., *Quidunc* [Australia], *British Columbia Library Association Reporter, Canadian Library Journal, Feliciter*, and *Library Association Record, Times Literary Supplement, Ontario Library Review*, and *Times Higher Education Supplement*). Some persons have obtained jobs by contacting foreign publishers or vendors directly. Non-U.S. government jobs usually call for foreign language fluency.

Although they do not specifically discuss librarian positions, several general brochures may be of help in providing further addresses: *American Students and Teachers Abroad: Sources of Information about Overseas Study, Teaching, Work, Travel* and *Federal Jobs Overseas:* from Superintendent of Documents, U.S. Government Printing Office, Washington, DC 20402, for $1 and 30¢ respectively.

Action, P305, Washington, DC 20525. An umbrella agency which includes the Peace Corps and Vista. Will sometimes need librarians in developing nations and host communities in the United States. For further information, call toll-free 800-424-8580 ask for Recruitment. There are recruiting offices in many large cities.

Council for International Exchange of Scholars, Suite 300, 11 DuPont Circle, Washington, DC 20036, 202-833-4950. Administers U.S. government Fulbright awards for university lecturing and advanced research abroad; usually six to eight awards per year are made to specialists in library science. In addition, many countries offer awards in any specialization of research or lecturing for which specialists in library and information science may apply. Open to U.S. citizens with university or college teaching experience. Request registration forms to receive spring announcement for academic year to start 12 to 18 months later. Applications and information may be obtained, beginning in April each year, from the office of the graduate dean, chief academic officer, or international programs on U.S. college and university campuses, or directly from CIES.

Department of Defense, c/o Director, Department of Defense Dependent Schools, 2461 Eisenhower Ave., Alexandria, VA 22331. Overall management and operational responsibilities for the education of dependent children of active duty U.S. military personnel and DOD civilians who are stationed in foreign areas. Also responsible for teacher recruitment. For complete application brochure, write to above address.

Home Country Employment Registry, National Association for Foreign Student Affairs, 1860 19th St. N.W., Washington, DC 20009. Services are offered to U.S.-educated foreign students to assist them in locating employment in their home countries following completion of their studies.

International Association of School Librarianship, c/o School of Librarianship,

Western Michigan University, Kalamazoo, MI 49008. Informal contacts might be established through this group.

International School Services, P.O. Box 5910, Princeton, NJ 08540. Private, nonprofit organization established to provide educational services for American schools overseas, other than Department of Defense schools. These are American elementary and secondary schools enrolling children of business and diplomatic families living away from their homeland. ISS seeks to register men and women interested in working abroad in education who meet basic professional standards of training and experience. Specialist, guidance counselors, department heads, librarians, supervisors, and administrators normally will need one or more advanced degrees in the appropriate field as well as professional experience commensurate with positions sought. ISS also publishes a comprehensive directory of overseas schools. Information regarding this publication and other services may be obtained by writing to the above address.

U.S. Information Agency (U.S. Information Service overseas) occasionally will seek librarians with MLS and four years experience for Regional Library Consultant positions. (U.S. citizenship for 5 years also is required.) Candidates must have proven administrative ability and skills to coordinate the overseas USIS library program with other information functions of USIS in various cities worldwide. Relevant experience might include cooperative library program development, community outreach, public affairs, project management, and personnel training. USIA maintains more than 125 libraries in over 76 countries, with one million books and 400 local library staff worldwide. Libraries provide reference service and material on the United States for foreign audiences. Overseas allowances and differentials where applicable, vacation leave, term life insurance, medical and retirement programs. Send standard U.S. Government Form 171 to Employment Branch, USIA, Washington, DC 20547. All types of jobs within USIA are announced through a recording (202-724-9864 or 9865). However, chances are slim for a library position to be available.

OVERSEAS—SPECIAL PROGRAMS

International Exchanges. Most exchanges are handled by direct negotiation between interested parties. A few libraries, such as the Chicago Public Library, have established exchange programs for their own staff. In order to facilitate exchange arrangements, the *IFLA Journal* (issued February, May, August, and November) provides a listing of persons wishing to exchange their position for one *outside* their own country. All listings must include the following information: full name, address, present position, qualifications (with year of obtaining), language, abilities, preferred country/city/library and type of position. Send to International Federation of Library Associations and Institutions (IFLA) Secretariat, P.O. Box 95312, 2509 CH, The Hague, Netherlands.

A Librarian's Directory of Exchange Programs/Study Tours/Funding Sources and Job Opportunities Outside of the U.S. by Diane Stine lists additional information on groups that sponsor exchanges and contacts for possible positions abroad. Order from OLPR/ALA, 50 E. Huron, Chicago, IL 60611 for $1.50 *prepaid*.

USING INFORMATION SKILLS IN NON-LIBRARY SETTINGS

A great deal of interest has been shown in "alternative careers" or in using information skills in a variety of ways in non-library settings. These jobs are not usually found through the regular library placement sources, although many library schools are trying to generate such listings for their students and alumni. Job listings that do exist may not call specifically for "librarians" by that title so that ingenuity may be needed to search out jobs where information management skills are needed.

Some librarians are working on a free-lance basis by offering services to businesses, alternative schools, community agencies, legislators, etc.; these opportunities are usually not found in advertisements but created by developing contacts and publicity over a period of time. (A number of information brokering business firms have developed from individual free-lance experiences.) Small companies or other organizations often need "one-time" service for organizing files or collections, bibliographic research for special projects, indexing or abstracting, compilation of directories, and consulting services. Bibliographic networks and online data base companies are using librarians as information managers, trainers, researchers, systems and data base analysts, online services managers, etc. (Jobs in this area are sometimes found in library network newsletters or other data processing journals. Classifieds in *Publishers Weekly* may lead to information-related positions.) Librarians can be found working in law firms as litigation case supervisors (organizing and analyzing records needed for specific legal cases); with publishers as sales representatives, marketing directors, editors, and computer services experts; with community agencies as adult education coordinators, volunteer administrators, grants writers, etc.

Information on existing information services or methods for using information skills in non-library settings can be found in: *Wilson Library Bulletin* 49 (February 1975): 440–445; *Special Libraries* 67 (May/June 1976):243–250; *ASIS Bulletin* 2 (February 1976):10–20; *RQ* 18 (Winter 1978):177–179; *New York Times*, December 12, 1979 "Careers" section; *Show-Me Libraries* 31 (May 1980):5–8; *Bay State Librarian* 69 (Winter 1980):9–11; and *Savvy* (January 1981), pp. 20–23. The *Canadian Library Journal* 34, no. 2 (April 1977) has a whole issue on alternative librarianship. Syracuse University School of Information Studies, 113 Euclid Ave., Syracuse, NY 13210 has available *Proceedings of the Information Broker/Free-Lance Librarian Workshop*, April 1976 for $5 and *Alternative Careers in Information/Library Services: Summary of Proceedings of a Workshop*, July 1977 for $5.50.

The Directory of Fee-Based Information Services lists information brokers, freelance librarians, independent information specialists, and institutions that provide services for a fee. Individuals do not need to pay to have listings; directory is available for $12.95 prepaid plus $2.50 postage and handling from Information Alternative, P.O. Box 5571, Chicago, IL 60680 (312-461-0890). It is supplemented by *The Journal of Fee-Based Information Services* ($20 per year for 10 issues). Issues include new listings, changes of address, announcements, feature articles, exchange column, etc. Another Information Alternative publication is *So You Want to Be an Information Broker?*, proceedings of a May 1–2, 1981 workshop at SUNY-Albany School of Library and Information Sciences ($29.50 plus $1.50 postage).

A selected bibliography on "The Changing Role of the Information Professional" prepared for a 1980 workshop of the D.C. Law Librarians' Society is available for $1.50 from Sheryl Segal, 2144 California St. N.W., Washington, DC 20008. *What Else Can You Do With a Library Degree*, edited by Betty-Carol Sellen, is published by Neal-Schuman Publishers, Inc. and Gaylord Brothers, Inc. (P.O. Box 4901, Syracuse, NY 13221) for $14.95 plus 25¢ postage. Other publications include: *Fee-Based Information Services: A Study of a Growing Industry* by Lorig Maranjian and Richard W. Boss (New York, Bowker, 1980, $24.95); *The Information Brokers: How to Start and Operate Your Own Fee-Based Service* by Kelly Warnken (New York, Bowker, 1981, $24.95); and *Information Brokering: A State-of-the-Art Report* by Gary M. Kaplan (Emerald Valley Publishing Co., 2715 Terrace View Drive, Eugene, OR 97405. Write for current list of other titles in The Business of Information series.) Directories such as *Information Sources: The Membership Directory of the Information Industry Association; Library Resources Market Place;* and *Information Industry Market Place* might provide leads of possible organizations in which information skills can be applied. "Information Resource(s) Management—IRM" in the *Annual Review of Information Science and Technology*, v. 17 (1982), pp. 228-266, provides a listing of associations and journals involved with IRM, as well as an extensive bibliography on the topic.

"A National Profile of Information Professionals" by Donald W. King et al. [*Bulletin of the American Society for Information Science* 6 (August 1980):18-22] gives the results of a 1980 study funded by the National Science Foundation and carried out by the University of Pittsburgh School of Library and Information Science and King Research, Inc. *The Information Professional: Survey of an Emerging Field* is based on the study and was published in 1981 by Marcel Dekker.

Careers in Information, edited by Jane F. Spivack (White Plains, N.Y.: Knowledge Industry Publications, 1982) includes chapters on the work of information specialists, entrepreneurship in the information industry, and information professionals in the federal government, as well as guidance on finding a job, placements and salaries for the broader information field as well as librarianship. Anticipated for publication in 1983 by Neal-Schuman Publishers, Inc., is *New Career Options for Librarians*, edited by Dimi Berkner and Betty-Carol Sellen.

JOB HUNTING IN GENERAL

Wherever information needs to be organized and presented to patrons in an effective, efficient, and service-oriented fashion, the skills of professional librarians can be applied, whether or not they are in traditional library settings. However, it will take considerable investment of time, energy, imagination, and money on the part of an individual before a satisfying position is created or obtained, in a conventional library or another setting for information service. Usually, no one method of job-hunting or of job sources can be used alone.

Public and school library certification requirements often vary from state to state; contact the state library agency for such information. Certification requirements are summarized in *Certification of Public Libraries in the U.S.* (3rd ed., 1979) available from the ALA Library Administration and Management Association ($3). A summary of school library/media certification requirements by state is found in *School Library Journal* 24 (April 1978):38-50 or *Requirements for Certification*, edited by Elizabeth H. Woellner and published annually by the University of Chicago Press. State supervisors of school library media services may also be contacted for information on specific states; the *Bowker Annual* contains a list of these contact persons in Part 7.

Civil service requirements either on a local, county, or state level often add another layer of procedures to the job search. Some civil service jurisdictions require written and/or oral examinations; others assign a ranking based on a review of credentials. Jobs are usually filled from the top candidates on a qualified list of applicants. Since the exams are held only at certain time periods and a variety of jobs can be filled from a single list of applicants (e.g., all Librarian I positions regardless of type of function), it is important to find out whether a particular library falls under civil service procedures.

If one wishes a position in a specific subject area or in a particular geographical location, remember those reference skills to ferret information from directories and other tools regarding local industries, schools, subject collections, etc. Directories such as the *American Library Directory, Subject Collections, Directory of Special Libraries and Information Centers, Directory of Health Sciences Libraries*, as well as state directories or other special subject areas, can provide a wealth of information for job seekers. Some students have pooled resources to hire a clipping service for a specific time period in order to get classified ads for library openings in a particular geographical area. Working as a substitute librarian or in temporary positions while looking for a regular job can provide valuable contacts and experience. A description of a corps of temporary library workers who tackle all types of jobs through a business called Pro Libra Associates, Inc. (Box 707, Maplewood, NJ 07040, 201-762-0070) can be found in *American Libraries* 12 (October 1981):540-541. Similar agencies which hire library workers for part-time or temporary jobs might be found in other geographical areas, such as C. Berger and Company, O-North 469 Purnell St., Wheaton, IL 60187 (312-653-1115) in the Chicago area. Part-time jobs are not always advertised, but often found by canvassing local libraries and leaving applications.

For information on other job-hunting and personnel matters, please request a checklist of personnel materials available from the ALA Office for Library Personnel Resources, 50 E. Huron St., Chicago, IL 60611.

PLACEMENTS AND SALARIES, 1981: STILL HOLDING

Carol L. Learmont

Associate Dean, School of Library Service, Columbia University, New York

Stephen Van Houten

PHILSOM Librarian, Medical Library Center of New York

For this 31st annual report on placements and salaries of graduates of ALA-accredited library school programs, 65 of the 69 eligible schools responded to all or part of the questionnaire. Two schools in Canada, one in western, and one in southwestern United States were unable to respond.

In 1981 the average beginning level salary of both men and women was $15,633, based on 1,725 known full-time professional salaries obtained from 4,512 graduates of 65 library school programs. No dramatic increases, decreases, or other changes were noted in comparing the 1981 graduates with the class of 1980. The 1981 job market seemed very much like the 1980 market, and the number of new graduates in the market was almost the same. Forty-eight placement officers reported no major difficulty in placing graduates in 1981, two reported some difficulty, and four reported major difficulty. This was somewhat better than in 1980. There continues to be a severe shortage of people with science, math, and engineering backgrounds. There continues to be a need for people with an interest in cataloging and in children's work. There were at least 255 temporary professional placements reported in 1981 compared with 201 in 1980, and 189 in 1979. Temporary appointments continue to be on the increase. Once again this year, the Canadian salaries are given in U.S. dollars. The two categories, "Special Libraries" and "Other Information Specialties" appear as separate categories for the second year. This arrangement provides a place in which to place nontraditional positions.

Salaries for 1981 improved over those for 1980, but once again fell below the increase in cost of living. The 1981 salaries increased at the rate of 9.9 percent compared to 8.4 percent in 1980, and 4.8 percent in 1979. In 1981, the average (mean) beginning salary for women was $15,478, a 10 percent increase from 1980; and for men $16,516, a

Note: Adapted from *Library Journal*, October 1, 1982.

10.7 percent increase. Median salaries were $15,000 for all graduates, $15,000 for women, and $15,500 for men (Table 8). Table 13 shows that, for new graduates with relevant prior experience, the average beginning salary was $17,014, up from $15,570 in 1980; without experience, $14,385, up from $13,310 in 1980. Please note that in Table 8, the mean of low salaries for the total population should be less than the means of low salaries for the women and men populations because the values for the total populations include the minimum low salary values for each population.

Similarly, the mean of high salaries for the total population should be greater than the means of high salaries for women and men populations separately.

PLACEMENTS

First professional degrees were awarded to 4,512 graduates by the 65 schools reporting in 1981 (Table 1). In 1980, the 63 reporting schools awarded 4,396 first professional degrees; in 1979, 61 reporting schools awarded 5,139 degrees. In 1977, the average number of graduates of schools reporting was 103; in 1978 it was 88; in 1979, 84; in 1980, 70; in 1981, 69. The trend toward a continuing decline in the numbers of graduates noted in previous years may be slowing.

Table 1 shows permanent and temporary professional placements, as well as nonprofessional library placements and totals for the three. These are library or information-related positions. Table 1 also shows the number of graduates reported who were not in library positions or whose employment status was unknown at the beginning of April 1982. Thirteen percent were known not to be in library positions compared to 15 percent in 1980 and 13 percent in 1979. In April 1982 the whereabouts of 23 percent were unknown compared to 19 percent in April 1981 and 21 percent in April 1980. Sixty-four percent of the 1981 graduates were known to be employed either in professional or nonprofessional positions in libraries or information-related work, as were 66 percent of the 1980 graduates and 66 percent of the 1979 graduates. Fifty-four percent of the 1981 graduates were known to be employed in permanent professional positions, compared to 57 percent of the 1980 graduates and 58 percent of the 1979 graduates. Employment distribution for 2,442 of the 4,512 graduates is shown in Table 4, and Table 12 compares salaries by type of library for the 2,353 full-time professional placements. Of the 2,442 people reporting on how long they actively sought professional employment after getting their degrees, 732 (30 percent) reported searching for less than 90 days. There were 140 (6 percent) people who looked for three or four months; 74 (3 percent) who looked for four to six months; and 54 (2 percent) who looked for more than six months. Five hundred thirty-nine (22 percent) people went back to their previous positions, and 569 (23 percent) found jobs before graduation. Nothing is known about 334 (14 percent) others.

In 1981, 4 percent of known library and related placements were nonprofessional (Table 1). In 1980 and in 1979 these placements also represented 4 percent of the total. About 4 percent of the women and 4 percent of the men were in nonprofessional jobs. In 1980, it was 4 percent of the women and 6 percent of the men; in 1979, it was 4 percent for each. The percentage of graduates who have nonprofessional library positions has been almost unchanged in recent years.

The percentage of placements by type of library in 1981 was remarkably similar to the percentages in 1980 and there were not dramatic decreases in the numbers of people employed as there were between 1979 and 1980 (Table 5). College and university library placements dropped by 54 individuals, school libraries by 22, and public libraries by 17. The "Other Library Agencies" category increased by 17. This category, which includes special libraries and other information-related specialties, continues to grow.

Comparisons of U.S. and Canadian placements appear in Table 6. Table 7, show-

TABLE 1 STATUS OF 1981 GRADUATES, SPRING 1982

	No. of Graduates			Not in Library Positions			Empl. Not Known			Permanent Prof. Placements			Temp. Prof. Placements			Nonprof. Library Placements			Total In Library Positions		
	Women	Men	Total	Women	Men	Total	Women	Men	Total	Women	Men	Total	Women	Men	Total	Women	Men	Total	Women	Men	Total
United States	3,239	665	4,105	422	112	536	692	135	1,016	1837	358	2,204	157	28	185	131	32	164	2,125	418	2,553
Northeast	1,249	229	1,516	120	25	146	332	55	422	701	133	836	69	8	77	27	8	35	797	149	948
Southeast	543	82	662	47	10	57	144	25	202	331	43	377	12	1	13	9	3	13	352	47	403
Midwest	902	232	1,157	141	55	197	126	38	183	534	119	656	39	11	50	62	9	71	635	139	777
Southwest	243	41	297	36	4	40	33	10	55	150	23	174	11	3	14	13	1	14	174	27	202
West	302	81	473	78	18	96	57	7	154	121	40	161	26	5	31	20	11	31	167	56	223
Canada	306	97	407	35	19	54	36	7	43	173	62	238	61	8	70	1	1	2	235	71	310
All Schools	3,545	762	4,512	457	131	590	728	142	1,059	2,010	420	2,442	218	36	255	132	33	166	2,360	489	2,863

TABLE 2 PLACEMENTS AND SALARIES OF 1981 GRADUATES—SUMMARY BY REGION*

	Place- ments	Salaries			Low Salary			High Salary			Average Salary			Median Salary		
		Women	Men	Total	Women	Men	Total	Women	Men	Total	Women	Men	Total	Women	Men	Total
United States	2,204	1,350	244	1,602	5,000	8,000	5,000	37,000	35,000	37,000	15,441	16,522	15,597	15,000	15,500	15,000
Northeast	836	533	84	619	7,500	8,000	7,500	34,012	35,000	35,000	15,344	16,349	15,476	15,000	15,239	15,000
Southeast	377	239	30	271	7,200	11,000	7,200	37,000	28,000	37,000	15,081	15,122	15,076	14,400	14,500	14,400
Midwest	656	361	76	440	5,000	9,000	5,000	30,200	27,000	30,200	15,028	16,559	15,280	14,500	14,500	14,600
Southwest	174	115	20	136	10,320	10,000	10,000	24,000	34,300	34,300	15,985	16,634	16,073	15,192	16,000	14,500
West	161	102	34	136	10,800	11,149	10,800	35,000	30,000	35,000	17,644	18,040	17,743	16,500	17,000	15,500
Canada	238	93	29	123	10,009	12,511	10,009	30,627	29,193	30,627	16,011	16,462	16,096	15,847	15,847	15,847
All Schools	2,442	1,443	273	1,725	5,000	8,000	5,000	37,000	35,000	37,000	15,478	16,516	15,633	15,000	15,500	15,000

*Totals may include placements and salaries undifferentiated by type of library or by sex.

TABLE 3 PLACEMENTS AND SALARIES OF 1981 GRADUATES (BY INSTITUTION)*

Schools	Place-ments	Salaries Women	Salaries Men	Salaries Total	Low Salary Women	Low Salary Men	Low Salary Total	High Salary Women	High Salary Men	High Salary Total	Average Salary Women	Average Salary Men	Average Salary Total	Median Salary Women	Median Salary Men	Median Salary Total
Alabama	43	25	3	28	11876	12750	11876	20176	15500	20176	14898	14083	14811	15000	14000	14592
Albany	50	28	6	34	11000	10700	10700	21000	26203	26203	14483	15728	14703	14200	13000	14200
Arizona	14	9	3	12	11500	10000	10000	19000	21200	21200	14979	16400	15335	14800	18000	14800
Atlanta	19	11	4	15	12000	11000	11000	23400	15000	23400	16868	12750	15770	16000	11000	15000
Ball	14	10	1	11	6800	24200	6800	19900	24200	24200	12820	24200	13855	13000	24200	14000
Brigham Young	27	13	8	21	11500	11149	11149	25266	24300	25266	18960	16411	17989	19500	13860	17000
British Columbia	35	3	2	5	13664	15013	13664	16682	20435	20435	15676	17724	16495	16682	15013	16682
Buffalo	31	17	9	26	9300	13925	9300	20200	19000	20200	14888	14933	14904	15000	14500	14500
California (Berk.)	27	20	6	26	12000	14592	12000	25380	21000	25380	16889	18088	17166	16800	17976	16800
California (L.A.)	23	18	4	22	13000	13800	13000	21288	24000	24000	16030	17316	16263	16000	15000	16000
Case Western	40	5	3	8	11300	12000	11300	18966	18000	18966	14219	14000	14137	14400	12000	12000
Catholic	24	20	2	22	13000	26710	13000	34012	32013	34012	18585	29362	19565	17666	26710	18000
Chicago	30	12	5	18	13000	15000	13000	17500	22300	22300	14897	18603	15826	15000	8600	15000
Clarion	18	13	1	14	11300	14750	11300	25000	14750	25000	15199	14750	15167	15000	14750	14750
Columbia	43	22	4	26	10000	14200	10000	25000	16000	25000	15694	14925	15576	14756	14500	14756
Dalhousie	14	8	3	12	13257	13570	13257	24188	17265	24188	18003	14909	16841	17420	13892	16590
Denver	27	16	6	22	12000	16000	12000	23000	28000	28000	16954	19397	17620	16000	17000	17000
Drexel	80	61	14	75	10000	8000	8000	24000	35000	35000	15482	16896	15746	15000	15500	15000
Emory	31	26	4	30	13008	12266	12266	20605	14802	20605	15441	13567	15192	14900	13200	14500
Emporia	39	22	5	27	10600	11175	10600	19000	19132	19132	14674	15236	14778	14000	14500	14375
Florida State	43	26	4	31	10000	12000	10000	26600	15500	26600	15556	13631	15257	13900	13000	14000
Geneseo	37	14	2	16	7500	11500	7500	24000	14800	24000	14021	13150	13912	12650	11500	12650
Hawaii	15	10	2	12	11400	15000	11400	35000	22500	35000	19881	22500	20317	17200	15000	17200
Illinois	55	28	8	36	8500	14000	8500	30000	25000	30000	16645	17388	16810	17200	15500	15000
Indiana	78	43	8	52	5000	12000	5000	30000	27000	30000	14035	16217	14363	14000	15500	15000
Iowa	29	16	5	21	11000	15000	11000	21335	24000	24000	14443	18198	15337	13500	14400	14000
Kent State	65	41	7	49	8000	9000	8000	23088	16000	23088	14677	12959	14391	14200	16992	13700
Kentucky	36	14	1	15	10165	15900	10165	20000	15900	20000	14281	15900	14389	14000	13510	14000
Long Island	46	20	5	26	9919	12000	9919	16888	16000	16888	13749	14062	13726	13500	14560	13500
Louisiana State	34	16	2	18	12500	17000	12500	17500	17500	17500	14791	17250	15064	15000	17000	15000
Maryland	37	24	1	25	10000	16000	10000	28600	16000	28600	16656	16000	16630	16000	16000	16000

Michigan	77	58	11	69	9000	14150	9000	29289	22000	29289	15095	16295	15286	14500	15997	14610
Minnesota	20	15	2	17	12925	15750	12925	30200	21500	30200	17781	18625	17881	16641	15750	16641
Mississippi	9	9	0	9	10000	0	10000	15100	0	15100	13346	0	13346	14114	14114	
Missouri	36	26	9	35	10000	13666	10000	20300	26000	26000	15388	18938	16301	15000	16608	15575
Montreal	53	0	0	0									0			
North Carolina	28	20	6	26	10800	14700	10800	17600	19000	19000	14507	16387	14940	14800	15922	15000
North Carolina Central	14	4	0	4	11000	0	11000	19000	0	19000	14263	0	14263	13500	13500	
Northern Illinois	12	5	2	7	12000	15000	12000	27825	15600	27825	18365	15300	17489	19000	15000	15600
North Texas State	35	19	6	25	10320	10500	10320	23316	17844	23316	15938	14807	15666	16161	14500	15600
Peabody	34	22	1	23	7200	14500	7200	34200	14500	34200	15050	14500	15026	13350	14500	13500
Pittsburgh	69	29	7	36	9500	13008	9500	18500	17000	18500	14067	15200	14287	14000	15890	14000
Pratt	24	17	5	22	13000	14900	13000	25560	20000	25560	17323	17024	17231	16000	15200	16000
Queens	11	6	1	7	10650	13000	10650	16700	28738	28738	14518	28738	16549	15000	28738	15000
Rhode Island	33	29	2	31	7500	19477	7500	18258	21000	21000	12975	20239	13444	13000	19477	13000
Rosary	43	30	2	32	7388	12880	7388	29986	16008	29986	14683	14444	14668	13500	12880	13500
Rutgers	106	92	8	100	11000	15500	11000	25000	23000	25000	16249	18000	16389	15500	16500	15500
St. Johns	19	17	1	18	12000	14000	12000	20500	14000	20500	16700	14000	16550	18000	14000	16000
San Jose	13	11	0	11	13500	0	13500	35000	0	35000	2053	0	22053	18000	18000	
Simmons	136	85	12	97	10500	11000	10500	25000	19182	25000	14726	14524	14701	14700	13500	14600
South Carolina	21	18	2	21	8000	13000	8000	24000	16000	24000	14558	14500	14502	14000	13000	14000
Southern Connecticut	28	24	1	25	10500	12000	10500	20000	12000	20000	14235	12000	14145	13636	12000	13636
South Florida	40	34	2	36	11000	19500	11000	21000	24000	24000	15593	21750	15935	14900	19500	15000
Southern Mississippi	24	23	1	24	7550	11000	7550	37000	11000	37000	14662	11000	14509	13000	11000	12600
Syracuse	44	15	4	19	9500	16500	9500	22500	21500	22500	16774	18550	17148	18000	18000	18000
Tennessee	35	7	2	9	14000	11382	14000	22000	28000	28000	16100	19691	16898	15200	11382	15200
Texas	53	36	8	44	12000	12000	12000	24000	21000	24000	17011	15729	16778	15444	15444	16000
Texas Woman's	38	35	1	37	11268	34300	11268	21500	34300	34300	15760	34300	16240	15000	34300	15000
Toronto	52	41	9	50	12094	12511	12094	30627	29193	30627	15903	16385	15990	15430	14950	15013
Washington	29	14	8	22	10800	11820	10800	18000	29000	30000	15305	17864	16235	15028	17000	16000
Wayne	28	0	0	0									0			
Western Michigan	37	17	2	19	10500	13750	10500	24774	21000	24774	15276	17375	15497	14610	13750	14610
Western Ontario	84	41	15	56	10009	12928	10009	20018	22881	22881	15754	16651	15994	16265	16682	16682
Wisconsin (Madison)	37	22	3	25	12000	14000	12000	18000	15060	18000	14292	14620	14331	14200	14800	14700
Wisconsin (Milwaukee)	16	11	3	14	9000	12500	9000	23500	20500	23500	15727	15833	15750	14500	14500	14500

*Includes placements and salaries undifferentiated by type of library or by sex.

TABLE 4 PLACEMENTS BY TYPE OF LIBRARY*

Schools	Public Women	Public Men	Public Total	Elementary & Secondary Women	Elementary & Secondary Men	Elementary & Secondary Total	College & University Women	College & University Men	College & University Total	Special Women	Special Men	Special Total	Other Info. Specialties Women	Other Info. Specialties Men	Other Info. Specialties Total	Total Women	Total Men	Total
Alabama	13	0	13	13	1	14	10	5	15	0	0	0	1	0	1	37	6	43
Albany	8	4	12	12	2	14	9	1	10	8	1	9	1	3	4	39	11	50
Arizona	5	1	6	1	0	1	4	1	5	1	1	2	0	0	0	11	3	14
Atlanta	1	0	1	5	0	5	2	4	6	5	1	6	0	0	0	13	6	19
Ball	5	0	5	5	1	6	1	0	1	1	0	1	0	0	0	13	1	14
Brigham Young	3	2	5	6	2	8	2	5	7	5	2	7	0	0	0	16	11	27
British Columbia	7	4	11	2	3	5	9	0	9	6	4	10	3	1	3	26	8	35
Buffalo	6	4	10	4	1	5	3	2	5	6	4	8	1	0	1	20	11	31
California (Berk.)	8	1	9	0	0	0	4	2	6	4	4	8	4	0	4	20	7	27
California (LA)	7	2	9	0	0	0	6	1	7	4	1	5	2	1	2	19	4	23
Case Western	5	3	8	2	0	2	6	4	10	9	4	13	4	3	7	26	14	40
Catholic	5	3	8	4	0	4	3	0	3	10	2	12	0	0	0	22	2	24
Chicago	2	0	2	0	0	0	6	4	10	8	3	12	5	0	7	20	9	30
Clarion	4	0	4	10	1	11	2	0	2	1	0	1	0	1	0	17	1	18
Columbia	13	2	15	3	1	4	8	3	11	9	1	10	2	3	3	35	8	43
Dalhousie	2	0	2	1	0	1	5	2	8	2	1	3	0	0	0	10	3	14
Denver	4	1	5	3	1	4	5	2	7	8	1	9	1	0	1	21	6	27
Drexel	18	3	21	5	1	6	10	3	13	17	3	20	11	5	16	65	15	80
Emory	8	0	8	4	0	4	6	3	9	8	1	9	0	0	0	27	4	31
Emporia	5	2	7	19	3	22	5	2	7	1	0	1	0	0	0	32	7	39
Florida State	8	2	10	16	0	17	5	2	8	4	1	5	0	1	1	37	4	43
Geneseo	6	1	7	13	0	13	5	2	7	4	0	4	0	0	0	31	4	37
Hawaii	2	0	2	1	0	1	2	1	3	3	0	3	0	1	1	13	2	15
Illinois	14	3	17	6	0	6	12	7	19	8	3	11	2	0	2	42	13	55
Indiana	13	3	16	16	0	16	16	7	24	9	3	12	2	1	2	63	14	78
Iowa	11	1	12	3	3	6	7	2	9	2	0	2	0	0	0	23	6	29
Kent State	20	5	26	7	0	7	9	2	11	2	0	2	0	0	0	56	8	65
Kentucky	9	0	9	8	0	8	14	2	16	3	0	3	0	1	1	34	2	36
Long Island	16	5	22	5	1	6	6	3	9	5	1	6	0	0	0	34	11	46
Louisiana State	10	1	11	8	1	9	3	0	3	9	2	11	0	0	0	30	4	34

School												
Maryland	3	0	3	8	0	3	3	17	1	5	18	36	1	37
Michigan	19	7	26	10	0	24	29	8	0	2	8	65	12	77
Minnesota	6	1	7	2	0	2	2	6	0	0	7	18	2	20
Mississippi	2	0	2	4	0	2	2	1	1	0	0	9	0	9
Missouri	5	1	6	8	2	9	12	5	3	0	1	27	9	36
Montreal	6	2	8	0	0	7	14	19	5	3	8	33	20	53
North Carolina	5	2	7	0	0	7	12	2	2	1	28	21	7	28
North Carolina Central	2	0	2	3	0	3	4	0	1	3	3	13	1	14
Northern Illinois	5	1	6	4	0	3	4	0	0	0	0	10	2	12
North Texas State	9	4	13	8	1	2	2	6	1	0	1	28	7	35
Peabody	5	0	5	4	0	5	6	8	1	5	7	33	1	34
Pittsburgh	12	2	14	6	1	15	16	8	0	4	8	52	17	69
Pratt	3	2	5	1	1	14	22	15	5	0	20	19	5	24
Queens	1	0	1	1	1	7	2	10	1	0	11	8	3	11
Rhode Island	13	0	13	8	1	2	2	2	0	0	2	31	2	33
Rosary	15	1	16	7	1	6	6	2	2	0	3	38	5	43
Rutgers	28	2	30	16	3	3	7	10	1	0	10	98	8	106
St. Johns	5	1	6	2	0	18	18	33	0	2	36	18	1	19
San Jose	3	0	3	6	0	9	0	9	3	2	9	13	0	13
Simmons	27	4	31	9	1	7	0	2	0	2	2	117	19	136
South Carolina	3	0	3	8	1	10	35	43	5	10	48	18	2	21
Southern Connecticut	10	1	11	3	1	3	4	2	0	0	3	26	2	28
South Florida	12	1	13	19	0	5	6	7	0	1	7	38	2	40
Southern Mississippi	4	1	5	11	1	2	2	3	0	0	3	23	1	24
Syracuse	3	2	5	9	0	3	0	4	0	0	4	33	11	44
Tennessee	7	4	11	9	0	6	10	7	1	8	8	28	7	35
Texas	6	4	10	5	1	9	10	2	2	6	3	45	8	53
Texas Woman's	6	0	6	14	0	11	13	9	1	4	10	36	1	38
Toronto	12	5	17	16	1	7	8	6	1	0	6	41	10	52
Washington	7	3	10	1	1	4	5	14	4	8	18	19	10	29
Wayne	4	3	7	0	0	2	9	4	3	2	7	22	6	28
Western Michigan	12	0	12	4	0	4	2	12	3	1	15	34	3	37
Western Ontario	20	4	24	2	2	2	4	0	0	1	1	63	21	84
Wisconsin (Madison)	11	2	13	8	0	10	5	21	7	3	28	32	5	37
Wisconsin (Milwaukee)	1	0	1	5	1	6	2	4	0	0	6	13	3	16
Total	**528**	**110**	**642**	**407**	**42**	**417**	**556**	**470**	**92**	**107**	**565**	**2,010**	**420**	**2,442**

*From 1951 through 1966 these tabulations were for "special and other placements" in all kinds of libraries. From 1967 to 1979 these figures include only placements in library agencies that do not clearly belong to one of the other three groups; in the 1980 and 1981 report these figures include the sum of responses to placements in special libraries and in other information specialties.

TABLE 5 PLACEMENTS BY TYPE OF LIBRARY, 1951-1981

Year	Public	School	College & Universities	Other Library Agencies*	Total
1951–1955**	2,076 (33%)	1,424 (23%)	1,774 (28%)	1,000 (16%)	6,264
1956–1960**	2,057 (33)	1,287 (20)	1,878 (30)	1,105 (17)	6,327
1961–1965	2,876 (30)	1,979 (20)	3,167 (33)	1,600 (17)	9,622
1966–1970	4,773 (28)	3,969 (23)	5,834 (34)	2,456 (15)	17,032
1971	999 (29)	924 (26)	1,067 (30)	513 (15)	3,503
1972	1,117 (30)	987 (26)	1,073 (29)	574 (15)	3,751
1973	1,180 (31)	969 (25)	1,017 (26)	712 (18)	3,878
1974	1,132 (31)	893 (24)	952 (26)	691 (19)	3,668
1975	994 (30)	813 (24)	847 (25)	714 (21)	3,368
1976	764 (27.1)	655 (23.2)	741 (26.3)	657 (23.2)	2,817
1977	846 (28.4)	673 (22.6)	771 (25.9)	687 (23.1)	2,977
1978	779 (26.1)	590 (19.8)	819 (27.4)	798 (26.7)	2,986
1979	778 (27.4)	508 (17.9)	716 (25.3)	835 (29.4)	2,837
1980	659 (27.1)	473 (19.5)	610 (25.1)	687 (28.3)	2,429
1981	642 (27.3)	451 (19.2)	556 (23.6)	704 (20.9)	2,353

*From 1951 through 1966 these tabulations were for "special and other placements" in all kinds of libraries. From 1967 to 1979 these figures include only placements in library agencies that do not clearly belong to one of the other three groups; in the 1980 and 1981 report these figures include the sum of responses to placements in special libraries and in other information specialties.
**Figures for individual years are reported in preceding articles in this series.

ing special placements, is self-explanatory. However, it is becoming increasingly difficult to categorize some of the jobs that are reported. The table remains in hopes that it will give a rough picture of what specialties are currently hiring.

DEMAND AND SUPPLY

Fifty-six schools reported that a total of 55,677 positions were listed with them. These listings were for jobs at all levels and the same positions were no doubt listed in several places. In 1980, 50 schools reported 51,617 vacancies. The average number reported per school in 1981 was 994 compared to 1,032 in 1980, and 965 in 1979.

Eighteen schools reported increases in position listings in 1981 over 1980 ranging from 5 to 100 percent; the median was 12 percent. Twenty-three schools reported no significant changes from 1980. Twelve schools reported a decline, ranging from 9 to 66 percent; the median was 15 percent. Four placement officers reported major difficulty in placing 1981 graduates; two reported some difficulty; 48 reported no major difficulty. Seven placement officers felt that they had more difficulty placing graduates in 1981 than in 1980; 10 felt they had less difficulty; and 43 felt they had about the same amount of difficulty both years.

TABLE 6 U.S. AND CANADIAN PLACEMENTS COMPARED
(Percents May Not Add to 100 Because of Rounding)

	Placements	Public Libraries	School Libraries	College & University Libraries	Special Libraries	Other Info. Specialties
All Schools*	2353	642 (27.3%)	451 (19.2%)	556 (23.6%)	565 (24%)	139 (5.9%)
Women	1929	528 (27.4)	407 (21.1)	417 (21.6)	470 (24.4)	107 (5.5)
Men	412	110 (26.7)	42 (10.2)	136 (33.0)	92 (22.3)	32 (7.8)
U.S. Schools*	2117	579 (27.4)	433 (20.5)	508 (24.0)	482 (22.8)	115 (5.4)
Women	1758	481 (27.4)	395 (22.5)	385 (21.9)	408 (23.2)	89 (5.1)
Men	350	95 (27.1)	36 (10.3)	121 (34.6)	72 (20.6)	26 (7.4)
Canadian Schools*	236	63 (26.7)	18 (7.6)	48 (20.3)	83 (35.2)	24 (10.2)
Women	171	47 (27.5)	12 (7.0)	32 (18.7)	62 (36.3)	18 (10.5)
Men	62	15 (24.2)	6 (9.7)	15 (24.2)	20 (32.3)	6 (9.7)

*Includes individuals undifferentiated by sex.

TABLE 7 SPECIAL PLACEMENTS*

	Women	Men	Total
Government jurisdiction (U.S. and Canada)			
Other government agencies (except USVA hospitals)	52	16	68
State and provincial libraries	31	8	39
National libraries	26	11	37
Armed Services libraries (domestic)	5	2	7
Overseas agencies (incl. Armed Services)	4	—	4
Total government jurisdiction	118	37	155
Library science			
Advanced study	11	10	21
Teaching	10	5	15
Total library science	21	15	36
Children's services—school libraries	214	15	229
Children's services—public libraries	130	5	135
Business, finance, industrial, corporate	117	10	127
Youth Services—school libraries	102	15	117
Law	84	17	101
Science and technology	78	9	87
Medical	75	7	82
Audio-visual and media centers	66	12	78
Systems analysis; automation	38	16	54
Research and development	40	5	45
Rare books, manuscripts, archives	30	11	41
Social sciences	33	7	40
Information services (non-library)	34	4	38
Hospitals (incl. USVA hospitals)	31	2	33
Communications industry (advertising, newspaper, publishing, radio, TV, etc.)	25	6	31
Art and museum	24	6	30
Youth services (public libraries)	28	2	30
Music	14	3	17
Outreach activities and services	11	3	14
Religion (seminars, theological school)	6	7	13
Historical agencies	9	2	11
Records management	8	3	11
Blind, deaf, other disabled	8	2	10
Architecture	4	5	9
Genealogical	5	4	9
Maps	6	2	8
Networks and consortia	7	1	8
Pharmaceutical	7	1	8
Professional associations	6	2	8
International relations	5	2	7
Free lance	4	2	6
Information industry	3	3	6
Energy	5	—	5
International agencies	3	1	4
Spanish-speaking centers	3	1	4
Children's services (other)	4	—	4
Youth services (other)	3	1	4
Bookstore	2	1	3
Correctional institutions	1	2	3
Database publishing	3	—	3
Library consultant	3	—	3
Management consultant	2	1	3
Programmer (systems design)	2	1	3
Subscription library	1	2	3
Education	2	—	2
Indexing	1	1	2
Library subscription agency	—	2	2
Theater and dance	2	—	2
User documentation	—	2	2
ADI and online search	—	1	1
Career resources center	1	—	1
Conservation center	1	—	1
Gerontology	—	1	1
Personnel	1	—	1
Preservation and conservation	1	—	1
Total Special Placements	**1,433**	**259**	**1,692**

*Includes special placements in all types of libraries, not limited to the "special" or "other information specialties" categories shown in Table 4.

Two of the placement officers queried felt that there was no question that the number of vacancies is increasing because of the decline in the number of graduates and the retirements or career changing of previous graduates. Both these people represent large urban schools.

SALARIES

The salary statistics reported here include only full-time annual salaries and exclude such variables as vacations and other fringe benefits, which may be part of the total compensation. They do not reflect differences in hours worked per week. Such information might provide more precise comparability, but such data is probably beyond the needs of most library schools and of the profession. In any case, the validity of this analysis rests on comparable statistics collected since 1951.

Of the 65 schools reporting, 62 supplied some salary data. Not all schools could provide all the information requested, nor could they supply it for all employed graduates. Schools were asked to exclude data for graduates in irregular placements such as those for graduates from abroad returning to posts in their homelands; appointments in religious orders or elsewhere where remuneration is in the form of some combination of salary plus living, and all salaries for part-time employment. With these exclusions added to the number of salaries not known or not reported, there is known salary information for 1,725 of the 1981 graduates (1,443 women, 273 men, and 9 undifferentiated by sex). This represents 71 percent of the known placements and 38 percent of all graduates reported. In 1980, there was salary information on 69 percent of known placements representing 40 percent of the number of graduates reported. Salary data as reported by the 63 schools are contained in Tables 2 and 3 and summarized in Table 8 in U.S. dollars.

Average (Mean) Salaries

The 1981 average salary for all graduates was $15,633, an increase of $1,410 (9.9 percent) over the 1980 average of $14,223. For women, the average was $15,478, and for men the average was $16,516. Annual changes in average salaries since 1967 are shown in Table 9, which also includes a beginning salary index figure that may be compared with the Annual Cost of Living Index (COL) reports issued by the government.

The COL index for 1981 was 272.4, an increase of 25.4 points over the 1980 figure of 247, a gain of 10.3 percent. The comparable increase in the beginning salary index is 19 points, 6.4 points below the increase in the cost of living.

In 1981, the range in the category of average salaries is from a low of $12,820 to a high of $22,053, a difference of $9,233; for men the range was $11,000 to $34,300, a $23,300 difference. In the 60 schools that reported average salaries for both men and women, the women's average was highest in 23 schools, while the men's average was highest in 37 schools.

Table 12 summarizes the salaries offered to men and women in different types of libraries and in other information specialties. The average salary is higher for men

TABLE 8 SALARY DATA SUMMARIZED

	Women	Men	Total
Average (Mean) Salary	$15,478	$16,516	$15,633
Median Salary	15,000	15,500	15,000
Individual Salary Range	5,000–37,000	8,000–35,000	5,000–37,000

TABLE 9 AVERAGE SALARY INDEX FOR STARTING LIBRARY POSITIONS, 1967-1981

Year	Library Schools	Fifth-Year Graduates	Average Beginning Salary	Increase in Average	Beginning Index
1967	40	4,030	$ 7,305	—	—
1968	42	4,625	7,650	$ 355	105
1969	45	4,970	8,161	501	112
1970	48	5,569	8,611	450	118
1971	47	5,670	8,846	235	121
1972	48	6,079	9,248	402	127
1973	53	6,336	9,423	175	129
1974	52	6,370	10,000	617	137
1975	51	6,010	10,594	554	145
1976	53	5,415	11,149	555	153
1977	53	5,467	11,894	745	163
1978	62	5,442	12,527	633	171
1979	61	5,139	13,127	600	180
1980	63	4,396	14,223	1,096	195
1981	65	4,512	15,633	1,410	214

(the difference ranging from $773 to $3,518) in every category except "Other Information Specialties," where the average salary for women is higher by $853.

Median Salaries

In 1981, the median for all graduates was $15,000, an increase of $1,315 over the 1980 median of $13,685. The median for women was $15,000; for men, $15,500. In 30 of the 60 schools reporting both men and women, the median salary for women was higher than that for men; in 27 schools, it was lower. In three schools it was the same.

Salary Ranges

The 1981 range of individual salaries again shows a wide range between the high and low salaries. Women place both higher and lower than men. Table 13 shows the effects of experience and of no experience on salary levels. For the survey purposes, prior experience, if known, consisted of work of a professional and/or subject nature of a year or more, or a civil service rating. The range in 1981 (Table 8) was from a low of $5,000 to a high of $37,000, a difference of $32,000. The low salary was in a school library; the high salary was also in a school library, one of several over $30,000 in Alaska.

In 1981, the range of high salaries was from $11,000 to $37,000, a difference of $26,000. Eleven schools showed highs of $30,000 or more (8 women, 5 men). The median high salary for all graduates was $24,200; for women, it was $22,500; for men, $20,467. For the eighth year, women showed the highest median. The median high salary was $21,000 in 1980, with a range of salary from $20,000 to $32,500. Fifty-five salaries were $20,000 or more (36 women, 19 men) in 1980. Distribution of high salaries by type of library is outlined in Table 10 and in different context in Table 12.

In 1981, the category "Special Libraries" accounted for 30 percent of the 63 high salaries reported while the category "Other Information Specialties" accounted for 8 percent. In 1980, "Special Libraries" accounted for 28 percent of the 61 high salaries reported, and "Other Information Specialties" accounted for 8 percent. School libraries accounted for 44 percent, up from 30 percent in 1980; academic libraries accounted for 13 percent, down from 26 percent in 1980; public libraries had a 5 percent share, a drop from the 8 percent share in 1980. Many of these salaries were said to have been affected significantly by prior experience. The positions were scattered geographically and included 24 states and the District of Columbia, three Canadian provinces, Venezuela, Switzerland, and Guam. These last were presumably Americans going to school and

TABLE 10 HIGH SALARIES BY TYPE OF LIBRARY

	Public Women	Public Men	Public Total	School Women	School Men	School Total	College & Univ. Women	College & Univ. Men	College & Univ. Total	Special Women	Special Men	Special Total	Other Women	Other Men	Other Total
$ 9,000	2		2	1		1									
10,000							1		1	1		1			
11,000	1	3	4	1		1	1		1	2		2		1	1
12,000	1	2	3		1	1	1		1		2	2		1	1
13,000	5	3	8	3		3	5	5	10	2		2	5	2	7
14,000	7	7	14	1	3	4	5	9	14	2	2	4	1		1
15,000	7	3	10	3	2	5	8	3	11	6	4	10	3	2	5
16,000	9	4	13	6	4	10	8	8	16	2	4	6	1	1	2
17,000	7	6	13	3	1	4	8	3	11	4	6	10	3		3
18,000	10	5	15	4		4	11	3	14	7	1	8	2		2
19,000	2		2	7	2	9	1	3	4	8	3	11		1	1
20,000	3		3	7	2	9	2	1	3	7	2	9	2		2
21,000	3	2	5	3	3	6	4	1	5	2		2		2	2
22,000				2		2	1	2	3	4	1	5	3		3
23,000	1		1	3	2	5		1	1	3		3			
24,000		1	1	3	2	5		1	1	1	1	2	2		2
25,000	1		1	1		1	2	1	3	3	1	4	2		2
26,000	1		1	1	1	2				1		1			
27,000							1	1	2						
28,000				1		1				2		2	3		3
29,000				2	1	3									
30,000	1		1	1	2	3				2		2			
31,000										1		1			
32,000										1		1			
33,000															
34,000							1	1	2			2			
35,000				2		2								1	1
36,000															
37,000				1		1									

special libraries overseas. This pattern was similar to 1980. New York provided eleven of the high salaried positions, Texas and Ohio five each, Illinois four, and Alaska three.

The lowest beginning level salaries offered to 1981 graduates ranged from $5,000 to $13,664, with the median low salary of $10,700 for all graduates. Of the 60 schools reporting low salaries for both men and women, seven reported higher low salaries for women, 52 reported higher low salaries for men, and one school reported the same.

Based on reports from 58 schools, public libraries once again accounted for the majority of low salaries, 50 percent, up from 33 percent in 1980. Academic libraries accounted for 17 percent, down from 25 percent in 1980. School libraries accounted for 14 percent, down from 23 percent. Special libraries accounted for 14 percent and other information specialties for 5 percent. These two together accounted for 20 percent in 1980.

There was no significant pattern in the geographical location of the 27 states and two Canadian provinces represented. New York led with seven low-salaried placements; Ohio had six; and Alabama, Illinois, and Texas each had three. Distribution of low salaries is shown in Table 11 and Table 12.

This was the second year that most of the calculations shown in the tables were taken directly from data received about each graduate, rather than from an aggregate report from each school. A worrisome problem seems to be arising. In 1979, we had information on the salaries of 41.2 percent of the professional placements; in 1980, it was 39.5 percent; in 1981, it was 38.2 percent. In April 1982, the status of only 77 percent of the 1981 graduates was known; in April 1981, the status of 81 percent was known. It seems that with increased student participation in filling out the questionnaires used there is less complete information being given. It may also reflect cuts or other changes in placement operations, perhaps not as much attention is being paid to a followup of graduate placements.

TABLE 11 LOW SALARIES BY TYPE OF LIBRARY

	Public			School			College & Univ.			Special			Other		
	Women	Men	Total	Women	Men	Total	Women	Men	Total	Women	Men	Total	Women	Men	Total
$ 5,000				1		1									
6,000				1		1									
7,000	3		3	2		2									
8,000	2	1	3	1		1	1		1						
9,000	5	1	6	2		2	2		2						
10,000	12	2	14	6		6	6		6	6	1	7			
11,000	14	5	19	4		4	6	1	7	5		5	1	2	3
12,000	8	6	14	9	1	10	17	8	25	12	3	15	4	2	6
13,000	8	3	11	11		11	12	10	22	13	4	17	9	2	11
14,000	6	8	14	7	4	11	7	9	16	8	6	14	1		1
15,000		4	4	3	3	6	4	4	8	4	6	10	4	2	6
16,000	2	1	3	2	4	6	3	3	6	4	3	7			
17,000	1		1	1		1	1	2	3	3	2	5	3		3
18,000		2	2	1		1		3	3		1	1	1	1	2
19,000				2	1	3				1	1	2		1	1
20,000				1	2	3					1	1			
21,000		2	2	3		3	1		1	1		1		1	1
22,000													1		1
23,000				1		1									
24,000	1		1	2	1	3				1	1	2			
25,000													2		2
26,000				1		1				1		1			
27,000							1		1						
28,000					1	1	1		1		2	2	1		1
29,000					1	1	1		1						
30,000				1	2	3									

NEXT YEAR?

Twenty-seven placement officers see no change in the number of job vacancies reported so far in 1982 compared to 1981. Fourteen predict an increase; 12 think that there will be a decrease. Twenty-eight schools expect that 1982 graduates will have the same difficulty in finding professional positions as did the 1981 graduates; eight expect less difficulty; and 25 expect more difficulty.

The responses to a question about types of libraries which are noticeably increasing or decreasing in the number of positions to be filled are summarized as follows by number of schools reporting.

	Increasing	*Decreasing*
Public libraries	5	8
School libraries	7	16
Academic libraries	11	13
Special libraries	21	5

Thirty schools reported that salaries seem stronger for the 1982 graduates. Estimates ranged from $150 to $2,500 with most guesses in the $500 to $1,000 range. Twenty-three think there will be no change in salaries, and three think they will remain about the same.

There continues to be a very serious shortage of graduates with strong undergraduate backgrounds in all areas of the sciences. Forty-six schools (as against 23 in 1981) reported difficulty in filling positions requiring science majors, or at least some background in science. In each of the following categories, five or more schools reported that people with appropriate backgrounds were also in short supply: business, languages, mathematics, and engineering. These are the same backgrounds that have been in short supply for years. Other special majors mentioned were computer science, computer programming, law, and elementary education. These appear to reflect regional needs.

292 / LIBRARY EDUCATION, PLACEMENT, AND SALARIES

TABLE 12   COMPARISON OF SALARIES BY TYPE OF LIBRARY

	Place-ments	Salaries Known			Low Salary			High Salary			Average Salary			Median Salary		
		Women	Men	Total	Women	Men	Total	Women	Men	Total	Women	Men	Total	Women	Men	Total
Public Libraries																	
United States	579	382	66	451	7,200	8,000	7,200	30,200	24,000	30,200	14,020	14,804	14,132	14,000	14,610	14,100
Northeast	215	147	20	169	7,500	8,000	7,500	20,000	18,500	20,000	13,602	14,216	13,680	13,900	14,300	14,000
Southeast	89	61	7	68	7,200	11,000	7,200	26,600	24,000	26,600	14,328	15,212	14,419	13,500	14,800	13,500
Midwest	186	117	21	139	7,388	9,000	7,388	30,200	21,500	30,200	13,637	14,756	13,799	13,500	14,610	13,700
Southwest	46	30	9	39	10,320	10,500	10,320	23,316	21,200	23,316	15,144	15,392	15,201	15,000	15,600	15,000
West	43	27	9	36	11,500	11,149	11,149	25,464	18,060	25,464	16,013	15,321	15,840	15,948	16,400	15,948
Canada	63	30	7	37	10,009	12,511	10,009	20,852	17,516	20,852	14,931	15,386	15,017	15,013	15,597	15,430
All	642	412	73	488	7,200	8,000	7,200	30,200	24,000	30,200	14,087	14,860	14,199	14,000	14,800	14,200
School Libraries																	
United States	433	293	32	326	5,000	12,750	5,000	37,000	30,000	37,000	16,191	19,469	16,509	15,004	18,500	15,500
Northeast	134	87	13	100	7,500	12,750	7,500	22,500	28,738	28,738	16,928	18,642	15,411	15,000	16,500	15,000
Southeast	108	80	3	83	7,550	15,500	7,550	37,000	19,500	37,000	15,410	17,000	15,467	14,500	16,000	14,500
Midwest	114	73	10	83	5,000	14,375	5,000	29,986	24,200	29,986	16,808	18,671	17,032	16,200	17,000	16,500
Southwest	51	35	3	38	12,000	17,500	12,000	24,000	21,000	24,000	16,587	19,250	16,685	15,000	17,500	15,000
West	26	18	4	22	14,245	21,000	14,245	35,000	30,000	35,000	22,499	26,117	23,157	22,755	23,467	23,000
Canada	18	3	2	5	15,847	20,435	15,847	30,627	29,193	30,627	23,554	24,814	24,058	24,188	20,435	24,188
All	451	296	34	331	5,000	12,750	5,000	37,000	30,000	37,000	16,266	19,784	16,623	15,100	19,132	15,750
College/Univ. Libraries																	
United States	508	278	80	360	8,000	11,000	8,000	27,825	34,300	34,300	14,741	16,023	15,021	14,500	15,000	14,592
Northeast	162	90	18	108	10,000	12,000	10,000	25,000	19,182	25,000	14,892	15,738	15,033	14,500	16,000	14,700
Southeast	107	55	16	72	8,000	11,000	8,000	21,500	19,000	21,500	14,320	14,124	14,272	14,000	14,000	14,000
Midwest	165	89	31	121	9,000	12,000	9,000	27,825	27,000	27,825	14,397	16,443	14,916	14,500	15,000	14,500
Southwest	35	22	5	27	12,000	14,400	12,000	22,010	34,300	34,300	15,057	19,629	15,904	14,500	16,000	14,520
West	39	22	10	32	12,000	12,360	12,000	23,000	24,300	24,300	16,252	16,469	16,320	16,000	15,500	16,000
Canada	48	12	6	19	12,511	12,928	12,511	18,767	16,682	18,767	15,242	14,614	14,944	14,513	13,892	14,013
All	556	290	86	379	8,000	11,000	8,000	27,825	34,300	34,300	14,762	15,925	15,017	14,500	15,000	14,520
Special Libraries																	
United States	482	320	49	371	10,000	10,000	10,000	34,200	32,013	34,200	16,636	17,615	16,748	16,000	16,000	16,000
Northeast	233	169	20	189	10,000	12,000	10,000	34,012	32,013	34,012	16,717	17,333	16,782	16,000	15,890	16,000
Southeast	47	34	4	39	12,000	12,266	12,000	34,200	28,000	34,200	16,512	17,547	16,541	15,000	14,000	15,000
Midwest	125	67	11	79	10,500	13,800	10,500	30,000	26,000	30,000	16,400	18,135	16,600	15,200	15,750	15,300
Southwest	36	24	4	28	12,500	10,000	10,000	20,000	17,000	20,000	16,561	14,375	16,248	16,500	14,500	16,000
West	41	26	10	36	10,800	13,650	10,800	31,000	28,000	31,000	16,957	18,932	17,505	17,976	16,000
Canada	83	32	10	42	12,511	13,512	12,511	22,270	22,881	22,881	16,339	17,067	16,512	16,265	16,682	16,285
All	565	352	59	413	10,000	10,000	10,000	34,200	32,013	34,200	16,609	17,522	16,724	16,000	16,000	16,000

Other Information Specialties													
United States	115	57	15	72	11,500	11,000	11,000	28,600	35,000	35,000	17,662	16,959	17,515	16,700	15,000	16,500
Northeast	69	36	12	48	12,000	11,000	11,000	28,600	35,000	35,000	17,892	16,808	17,621	17,000	14,000	17,000
Southeast	11	4	0	4	11,500	0	11,500	22,000	22,000	0	15,175	0	15,175	13,200	0	13,200
Midwest	23	7	3	10	12,500	12,000	12,000	28,175	28,175	21,000	16,155	17,560	16,577	15,000	19,680	15,000
Southwest	4	4	0	4	15,000	0	15,000	24,000	24,000	0	18,675	0	18,675	16,700	0	16,700
West	8	6	0	6	13,146	0	13,146	28,000	28,000	0	19,021	0	19,021	16,500	0	16,500
Canada	24	14	4	18	13,664	13,345	13,345	20,852	20,852	16,682	16,791	15,431	16,489	15,847	15,013	15,847
All	139	71	19	90	11,500	11,000	11,000	28,600	35,000	35,000	17,490	16,637	17,310	16,700	15,013	16,500

TABLE 13 EFFECTS OF EXPERIENCE ON SALARIES

	Salaries Without Previous Experience (59 Schools)			Salaries With Previous Experience (59 Schools)		
	Women	Men	Total	Women	Men	Total
Number of Positions	548	108	658	647	113	762
Range of Low Salaries	$5,000–22,000	$9,000–19,477	$5,000–22,000	$7,200–21,335	$8,000–34,300	$7,200–20,000
Mean (Average)	11,629	13,773	11,628	13,242	17,671	13,148
Median	14,110	13,800	14,110	10,507	15,900	10,507
Range of High Salaries	12,000–31,000	11,000–21,500	11,000–31,000	15,100–37,000	13,892–35,000	15,100–37,000
Mean (Average)	18,145	16,077	18,275	23,251	21,647	24,879
Median	25,000	15,970	25,000	28,600	15,900	28,600
Range of Average Salaries	11,217–11,875	11,000–13,500	11,000–12,417	13,236–17,929	13,578–20,500	13,236–18,250
Mean (Average)	14,308	14,798	14,385	16,762	18,484	17,014
Median	17,937	14,723	17,937	17,837	15,900	17,684

The course work specializations for which there clearly seem to be an increasing demand and a short supply of qualified applicants are cataloging (ten mentions), information science and technology (nine mentions), and children's and young adult services (nine mentions). Other areas mentioned once or twice were records management, serials, law, information management, data processing, systems, chemical information, science, reference, and medical. Schools with strong information science components appear to be experiencing less difficulty in placing graduates than many other schools. In some schools, recruiters are reappearing after many years. At the same time, some placement officers note a reluctance on the part of recent graduates and those seeking mid-level positions to leave the geographical area where friends, families, spouses, and significant others are living.

The growing strength seen in the field of Special Libraries and Other Information Agencies is attributed to special efforts made by schools to generate interest in using graduates and to a "gradual enlightenment of business and industry." Many placement officers believe that children's work is perceived by students as a dead end but see a shortage ahead in this field. Many mention that the long- and short-range effect on all types of placements of budget cuts, falling enrollments at all levels, and the impact of the depressed economy will be to decrease the number of beginning and middle-level positions.

The trend which became clear last year continues. Schools are paying more attention to nontraditional placements and many are successfully seeking new markets for graduates. Despite the impact of the recession, prospects for the future appear to be good for the well-prepared, creative, and carefully advised new graduate.

The authors wish to thank all of the reporting schools for their continuing cooperation in making this report possible.

SEX, SALARIES, AND LIBRARY SUPPORT, 1981

Kathleen M. Heim

Assistant Professor, Graduate School of Library and Information Science, University of Illinois at Urbana-Champaign

Carolyn Kacena

Associate University Librarian, California State University at Fullerton

This report continues and updates the analyses of relationships between sex of director and per capita support in large public libraries and library systems initiated in 1972 by Carpenter and Shearer.[1] The data in this report are from the 1981 survey of public libraries conducted by the Allen County Public Library of Indiana.[2] The preface

Note: Adapted from *Library Journal*, September 15, 1981.

The authors wish to thank Raymond L. Carpenter and Kenneth D. Shearer for initiating this series of reports; Marsha Kraus Fulton who coded and helped to clean the data; Thressa Todd and Sally Eakin who formatted tables and typed the final report; and librarians at the University of Arizona—Robert Mitchell, Craig Hawbaker, and Margo Gutierrez—for help in tracking down appropriate economic indicators.

from this survey by Allen County Director, Rick J. Ashton, provides the background for data collection procedures:

> Our third decade of collection and dissemination of public library statistics begins with this publication. As a service to library administrators and governing authorities throughout North America, the Public Library of Fort Wayne and Allen County carried on the survey for 20 years. Now the Allen County Public Library, its successor institution, continues the tradition. This publication contains the findings of a survey conducted in February 1981.
>
> From the *American Library Directory* (33d ed., Bowker, 1980) we selected all public library agencies whose entries indicated their membership in the appropriate population group. In many cases we could not determine whether an agency was a public library performing direct service or the headquarters of a library cooperative or system. We did not exclude any of the doubtful cases from the survey. We mailed 501 questionnaires. Three hundred and sixteen libraries returned usable responses.
>
> Abla M. Shaheen, Deborah N. O'Neill, and Cathleen M. Arnoldy conducted the survey, tabulated the data, and prepared the copy for the press. Earlean C. Brooks typed the tables and Don B. Rust printed them.

The raw data from the Allen County survey have again been analyzed with the *SPSS (Statistical Package for the Social Sciences)* and similar analyses made as in the five prior reports.

The separation of U.S. and Canadian data is made here for the first time due to the current differential in the rate of exchange. (Throughout this report Canadian dollars are indicated by the designation "C" after the amount.) Since the previous ten years' statistics combined Canada into the total, we cannot calculate the change in mean total growth for the United States between 1981 and earlier reports.

Tables 1 and 2 are provided so that readers will have information regarding the response to the survey against which to measure our interpretations and comparisons.

CURRENT LIBRARY SUPPORT

In general library support kept better pace with inflation over the 1979–1980 period than in previous years. Trends noted in the five earlier reports vis-à-vis sex of administrator, however, have continued: women are not represented in director positions in proportion to their presence in the library work force; those women who *do* become administrators generally earn less than men; and lower per capita support and compensation of beginners is generated by libraries with female directors.

At the start of 1981, per capita support for large public libraries and library systems (Table 3) in the United States was up to $8.51 and in Canada, to $11.90C.

General U.S. inflation in 1979 was 11.5 percent; in 1980, 13.5 percent; and there was, at the time of this writing, no comparable inflation projection for 1981.[3] Since our data (collected in February 1981) carry us through 1980, for growth in the inflation rate we combined 1979 and 1980 in the United States for a 25 percent rate for the two-year period. Most of the regional growth in per capita expenditure appears to have come close to or exceeded this rate of inflation.

The Canadian inflation rate for the same period was 19.3 percent (1979, 9.1 percent; and 1980, 10.2 percent).[4] Per capita support for major public libraries and library systems in Canada did well against inflation with a 26 percent increase; the per capita funding level rose from $9.48C in 1979 to $11.90C at the start of 1981.

REGIONAL SUPPORT

The 1981 data continue to show regional differences in the growth of per capita support and in the percentage of growth as well. In Table 3, the increases in per capita support from 1979 to 1981 ranged from a low of 22 percent in the West to a high of 30

TABLE 1 DISTRIBUTION OF RESPONSES BY GEOGRAPHIC REGIONS, 1971–1981

U.S. Regions & Canada	1971 No. of Responses	1971 % of Total	1973 No. of Responses	1973 % of Total	1975 No. of Responses	1975 % of Total	1977 No. of Responses	1977 % of Total	1979 No. of Responses	1979 % of Total	1981 No. of Responses	1981 % of Total
Northeast	43	16%	43	16%	31	13%	40	14%	47	15%	46	14.2%
South	93	34%	93	34%	78	32%	98	34%	116	37%	118	36.5%
North Central	65	24%	63	23%	65	27%	69	24%	73	23%	73	22.6%
West	56	20%	58	21%	51	21%	62	21%	57	18%	62	19.2%
Canada	18	6%	19	7%	17	7%	21	7%	24	8%	24	7.4%
TOTAL	275	100%	276	101%*	242	100%	290	100%	317	101%*	323	100%

*Total is greater than 100% because of rounding.

TABLE 2 DISTRIBUTION OF RESPONSES BY SIZE OF POPULATION SERVED, 1971–1981

Size of Population Served	1971 No. of Responses	1971 % of Total	1973 No. of Responses	1973 % of Total	1975 No. of Responses	1975 % of Total	1977 No. of Responses	1977 % of Total	1979 No. of Responses	1979 % of Total	1981 No. of Responses	1981 % of Total
100,000–199,999	131	48%	139	50%	107	44%	152	52%	171	54%	168	52%
200,000–399,999	80	29%	79	29%	72	30%	78	27%	81	26%	77	23.8%
400,000–749,999	43	16%	37	13%	41	17%	41	14%	46	14%	51	15.8%
750,000 & over	20	7%	21	8%	22	9%	19	7%	19	6%	27	8.4%
TOTAL	274*	100%	276	100%	242	100%	290	100%	317	100%	323	100%

*One respondent did not report population size. Since this library offers service by contract, the size of the population is unknown to us.

TABLE 3 CHANGES IN THE MEAN PER CAPITA PUBLIC LIBRARY EXPENDITURE, BY REGION, 1979-1981

U.S. Regions & Canada	Per Capita Support (No. of Reporting Libraries)				Change: 1979-1981 (Percent)	
	1979		1981			
Northeast	$6.61	(47)	$8.61	(46)	$2.00	(30%)
South	$5.32	(116)	$6.64	(118)	$1.32	(25%)
North Central	$7.76	(73)	$9.89	(73)	$2.13	(27%)
West	$8.48	(57)	$10.37	(62)	$1.89	(22%)
All U.S.	*		$8.51	(299)	*	
Range of Means	*		$6.64 to 10.37		*	
Canada	$9.48C	(24)	$11.90C	(24)	$2.42C	(26%)

*1979 used both U.S. and Canada for "All." Due to differential in rate of exchange, they are separated for 1981. Comparison of 1979 and 1981 "All" data would be misleading.

percent in the Northeast. Comparable changes in 1979 ranged form a 3 percent low in the Northeast to a 14 percent high in the North Central region of the United States.[5] Compared to the losses sustained in the battle against inflation from the 1977-1979 period, libraries appeared to be catching up during 1979-1980. Per capita expenditure for all U.S. regions except the West, which lagged 3 percent behind, matched or exceeded the U.S. inflation rate of 25 percent. Canadian libraries with a 26 percent per capita increase stayed well ahead of their 19.3 percent inflation rate over the two-year period. We will have a better opportunity to verify this when the 1983 data are broken out the same way as 1981 and the overall total mean per capita figure for the United States can be compared as well as the Canadian one.

During the ten years that these data have been analyzed, rates of growth ranged from 121 percent in the Northeast to 155 percent in the South, although the South in real dollar support showed only a $4.04 growth over the decade while the West showed dollar per capita growth of $5.77 (Table 4). During the same time period, Canadians added 170 percent to their per capita support of libraries, raising their support from $4.40C in 1971 to $11.90C at the start of 1981.

TABLE 4 CHANGES IN THE MEAN PER CAPITA PUBLIC LIBRARY EXPENDITURE, BY REGION, 1971-1981

U.S. Regions & Canada	Per Capita Support (No. of Responses)				Change: 1971-1981 (Percent)	
	1971		1981			
Northeast	$3.90	(40)	$8.61	(46)	$4.71	(121%)
South	$2.60	(92)	$6.64	(118)	$4.04	(155%)
North Central	$4.40	(61)	$9.89	(73)	$5.49	(125%)
West	$4.60	(55)	$10.37	(62)	$5.77	(125%)
All U.S.	*		$8.51	(299)	*	
Range of Means	*		$6.64 to 10.37		*	
Canada	$4.40C	(18)	$11.90C	(24)	$7.50C	(170%)

*1971 used both U.S. and Canada for "All." Due to differential in rate of exchange, they are separated for 1981. Comparison of 1971 and 1981 "All" data would be misleading.

SUPPORT BY POPULATION

Looking first at Canadian support by population (Table 5), we see that overall growth (26 percent) beat inflation by 6.7 percent. While the largest reporting system showed no growth at all, or a real loss of 19.3 percent, those libraries in the 200,000–399,999 population size made major advances: a 49 percent increase.

In the United States, per capita increases were also varied although, on the whole, libraries and systems serving populations 200,000–399,999 still did the best—except in the West. In the Northeast, this group raised per capita support 46 percent; in the South, 25 percent; in the North Central region, 37 percent; and in the West, 15 percent. In the West, it was the system serving 100,000 to 200,000 people that stayed well ahead of inflation at 37 percent. Remember, the general inflationary change in the 1978–1980 time period was 25 percent.[6] From that standpoint, smaller libraries in the South kept

TABLE 5 CHANGES IN THE MEAN PER CAPITA PUBLIC LIBRARY EXPENDITURES, BY REGION AND SIZE OF POPULATION SERVED, 1979–1981*

	Per Capita Support 1979		Per Capita Support 1981		Change: 1979–1981 $	Change: 1979–1981 %
Northeast						
100,000–199,999	$7.42	(27)	$9.74	(23)	$2.32	(31%)
200,000–399,999	$4.14	(12)	$6.05	(10)	$1.91	(46%)
400,000–749,999	$5.67	(6)	$5.90	(8)	$0.23	(4%)
750,000+	$13.40	(2)	$12.86	(5)	−$0.54	(−4%)
South						
100,000–199,999	$4.54	(58)	$5.67	(58)	$1.13	(25%)
200,000–399,999	$5.33	(38)	$6.67	(33)	$1.34	(25%)
400,000–749,999	$7.42	(14)	$8.75	(20)	$1.33	(18%)
750,000+	$7.98	(6)	$8.53	(7)	$0.55	(7%)
North Central						
100,000–199,999	$7.39	(43)	$9.66	(43)	$2.27	(31%)
200,000–399,999	$7.08	(13)	$9.72	(14)	$2.64	(37%)
400,000–749,999	$9.52	(11)	$12.73	(8)	$3.21	(34%)
750,000+	$8.65	(6)	$ 8.60	(8)	−$0.05	(−.6%)
West						
100,000–199,999	$8.10	(29)	$11.09	(28)	$2.29	(37%)
200,000–399,999	$9.00	(13)	$10.34	(15)	$1.34	(15%)
400,000–749,999	$9.21	(11)	$9.83	(13)	$0.62	(7%)
750,000+	$7.63	(4)	$8.23	(6)	$0.60	(8%)
All U.S.						
100,000–199,999		*	$8.41	(152)		*
200,000–399,999		*	$7.93	(72)		*
400,000–749,999		*	$9.21	(49)		*
750,000+		*	$9.32	(26)		*
ALL		*	$8.51	(299)		*
Canada						
100,000–199,999	$9.71C	(14)	$11.46C	(16)	$1.75C	(18%)
200,000–399,999	$9.54C	(5)	$14.18C	(5)	$4.64C	(49%)
400,000–749,999	$9.80C	(4)	$13.30C	(2)	$3.50C	(36%)
750,000+	$4.70C	(1)	$4.70C	(1)	0	(0%)
ALL	$9.48C	(24)	$11.90C	(24)	$2.42C	(26%)

*Due to the change in exchange rate, comparison of 1979 and 1981 "All" data would be misleading; therefore, we do not have "All U.S." for 1979. The comparison will be made in 1983.

up with inflation and North Central libraries serving populations of 400,000-749,999 beat inflation strongly at 34 percent growth. Largest libraries again took the brunt of slow growth, with two regions actually showing negative results: the Northeast at −4 percent and North Central at −0.6 percent. Obviously everyone below 25 percent lost ground as well.

SEX OF DIRECTORS AND SUPPORT

Males held approximately two-thirds of the directorships of the libraries surveyed, a figure that has stayed fairly consistent over the last decade (Table 6).

Female directors continued to receive less per capita support than male directors, reversing some promising signs in the 1979 data (Table 7). The Canadians still show an advantage to their female directors, of 16 percent, but this is down from the 29 percent female advantage of two years ago.[7] Two U.S. regions, North Central and West, showed slight female advantages last time,[8] but are back to male advantage of some size (20 percent and 16 percent, respectively). The South and Northeast decreased the male director advantage somewhat but the male advantage is still well above the U.S. inflationary rate at 36 percent and 33 percent, respectively. Overall, the advantage to the male directors grew from 22 percent last year (which included the phenomenal Canadian female advantage) to 27 percent in the United States as a whole this time out—again, a larger than inflationary differential.

DIRECTORS' SALARIES: UNITED STATES

The median salary for all directors in 1981 was $33,330, with lack of data on two of the directors. This contrasts with $27,540 in 1979; $24,620 in 1977; $23,000 in 1975; $18,999 in 1973; and $17,160 in 1971. The lowest director's salary was $13,910 and the highest was $63,580 (Table 8).

The adequacy of all directors' compensation may be tested comparing the autumn 1980 U.S. Department of Labor's "Higher Living Standard" (Table 9) for an urban family of four ($34,409), with directors' median salary, which finds that while the directors have gained 21 percent (Table 10) from the previous survey in salary, they lost to inflation from 1978 to 1980, when measured by this standard; and for the first time since we have compared these statistics, they did not maintain a median salary above the "Higher Living Standard."

Table 11 compares median and ranges of directors' salaries by sex and region; Table 12 compares median salaries by population served and by sex; Table 13 compares mean (average) length of tenure by sex of director and population size; Table 14 and 15 relate tenure in position to sex by region, and Table 16 shows salary ranges by sex.

The median salary for U.S. male directors was $34,505 and for female directors, $29,220—an overall differential of 18 percent in favor of men (Table 11). This figure is interesting to compare with the findings of the recent ALA Office of Library Personnel Resources (OLPR) study, *The Racial, Ethnic, and Sexual Composition of Library Staffs in Academic and Public Libraries*, which found that the median salary for all female public library directors in 1980 was $18,554 compared to $28,250 for men—a differential of 52 percent.[9] When compared to male directors of *all* U.S. public libraries, women directors of large libraries and library systems fare better than women directors at large.

In comparison to the U.S. Department of Labor's "Higher Living Standard" (Table 9), male directors earn slightly more than the well-off urban family of four: the median male directors' salary of $34,505 is almost $100 above the higher living standard. However, the median salary for women directors at $29,220 is far below the higher liv-

TABLE 6 DISTRIBUTION OF RESPONSES, BY SEX OF DIRECTOR, 1973–1981

Sex of Director	1973* No. of Respondents	1973* % of Total	1975 No. of Respondents	1975 % of Total	1977 No. of Respondents	1977 % of Total	1979 No. of Respondents	1979 % of Total	1981 No. of Respondents	1981 % of Total
Male	175	66%	166	72%	199	69%	204	66%	215	66.8%
Female	89	34%	63	28%	88	31%	105	34%	107	33.2%
TOTAL**	264	100%	229	100%	287	100%	309	100%	322	100%

*Table was not provided for 1971 data.
**Totals differ from those in Tables 1 and 2 because some directorships were vacant.

TABLE 7 FINANCIAL ADVANTAGE OF MEN TO WOMEN IN PER CAPITA SUPPORT, BY REGION, 1981

U.S. Regions & Canada	Female (No. of Responses)	Male (No. of Responses)	% of Advantage* to Males
Northeast	$7.05 (13)	$9.22 (33)	33%
South	$5.43 (44)	$7.36 (74)	36%
North Central	$8.54 (16)	$10.27 (57)	20%
West	$9.47 (26)	$11.02 (36)	16%
All U.S.	$7.21 (99)	$9.16 (200)	27%
Canada	$13.59C (8)	$11.48C (15)	−16%

*Advantage figure by $\frac{\text{Men} - \text{Women}}{\text{Women}}$ as in earlier articles.

TABLE 8 DIRECTORS' SALARY, BY REGION, 1981

U.S. Regions & Canada	Median	(No. of Responses)	Minimum–Maximum
Northeast	$31,500	(45)	$18,000–57,000
South	$29,585	(118)	$13,910–62,640
North Central	$33,680	(73)	$18,000–62,040
West	$37,492	(61)	$26,180–63,580
All U.S.	$33,330	(297)	$13,910–63,580
Canada	$40,670C	(22)	$26,000–50,650C

ing standard. While males stayed almost even with the higher living standard, women directors were further behind than they were in 1979.

As in earlier reports, we looked at the range of salaries for 1981 (Table 9) and compared them to the lower, intermediate, and higher living standards (Table 9). Male directors' salaries ranged from $20,000–$63,580, so that *all* male directors were above the lower living standard of $14,044. Female directors still fall below the lower living standard figure with $13,910 for their minimum salary. At least this time, the median beginners' salary is below the minimum female director's salary, not that that is particularly heartening news.

REGIONAL CHANGES: UNITED STATES

Only the West continues the promising trends of equalization that seemed to occur in the late seventies.[10] The differential between male and female directors' median salaries dropped from 9 percent in 1979 to 7 percent in the West in the 1981 survey (Table 11). Everywhere else in the country the trend was to reverse: the Northeast increased the differential from 13 percent to 15 percent; the South from 31 percent to 32 percent, and North Central female librarians lost the most ground, going from 8 percent differential to 15 percent in two years. As we cannot directly compare the totals for 1979 and 1981, we will simply re-state that the all-U.S. differential in this survey was 18 percent and the 1983 data will be the first time we will be able to provide a direct comparison which excludes Canadian data.

SEX, POPULATION, AND SALARY

Although based on a relatively small sample size (7 responses) for female directors, the 2:1 ratio of male directors to female directors for the largest systems parallels the other population sizes (Table 12). However, this group of seven is unique in being the *only* U.S. group of female directors with median salary level higher than their male counterparts: the median difference was $1,420 or 3 percent higher than the male median salary level. The worst differential in the 1981 results was the population size 200,000–

TABLE 9 ANNUAL COST OF LOWER, INTERMEDIATE, AND HIGHER LIVING STANDARDS FOR AN URBAN FAMILY OF FOUR: AUTUMN 1980

Lower	Intermediate	Higher
$14,044	$23,134	$34,409

Source: U.S. Department of Labor, Bureau of Labor Statistics, *News*, "Autumn 1980 Urban Family Budgets and Comparative Indexes for Selected Urban Areas," April 22, 1981, p. 2.

TABLE 10 COMPARISON OF DIRECTORS' MEDIAN SALARY AND "HIGHER LIVING STANDARD," 1972–1981

	Year	Directors' Median Salary (increase from previous year)	Dept. of Labor Standard (increase from previous year)
U.S.	1972/73	$18,900	$16,558
	1974/75	$23,000 (+21%)	$20,777 (+25%)
	1976/77	$24,620 (+7%)	$23,759 (+14%)
	1978/79	$27,540 (+12%)	$27,420 (+15%)
	1980/81	$33,330 (+21%)	$34,409 (+25%)
Canada	1980/81	$40,670C	

TABLE 11 MEDIAN, MINIMUM, AND MAXIMUM OF DIRECTORS' SALARY, BY SEX AND BY REGION, 1981

U.S. Regions & Canada	Median	Male: Minimum-Maximum (No. of Responses)	Median (No. of Responses)	Female: Minimum-Maximum	Difference (Male-Female)
Northeast	$32,400 (32)	$20,000–57,000	$28,230 (32)	$18,000–48,000	$4,170 (15%)
South	32,955 (74)	20,000–62,640	24,990 (44)	13,910–55,560	$7,965 (32%)
North Central	34,500 (57)	22,000–62,040	30,020 (16)	18,000–52,520	$4,480 (15%)
West	38,750 (35)	28,500–63,580	36,360 (26)	26,180–45,700	$2,390 (7%)
All U.S.	34,505 (198)	20,000–63,580	29,220 (99)	13,910–55,560	$5,285 (18%)
Canada	$43,180C (14)	$26,000–50,650C	$33,595C (8)	$27,580–46,500C	$9,585C (29%)

TABLE 12 DIRECTORS' MEDIAN SALARIES, BY SEX OF DIRECTOR AND SIZE OF POPULATION SERVED, 1981

Population Served	Male	(No. of Responses)	Female	(No. of Responses)	Difference (Male-Female)	
U.S.:						
100,000–199,999	$30,505	(96)	$27,900	(54)	$2,605	(9%)
200,000–399,999	36,650	(48)	27,390	(24)	$9,260	(25%)
400,000–749,999	40,240	(35)	36,370	(14)	$3,870	(10%)
750,000+	42,580	(14)	44,000	(7)	−$1,420	(−3%)
ALL	34,505	(198)	29,220	(99)	$5,285	(18%)
Canada:						
100,000–199,999	38,590C	(8)	33,400C	(7)	$5,190C	(16%)
200,000–399,999	44,885C	(4)	46,500C	(1)	−$1,615C	(−3%)
400,000–749,999	49,575C	(2)	—			
750,000+		(0)	—	(0)		
ALL	$43,180C	(14)	$33,595C	(8)	$9,585C	(29%)

TABLE 13 MEAN TENURE OF DIRECTORS, BY SEX AND POPULATION SERVED, 1981

	Director Tenure in Years			
Size of Population Served	Male	(No. of Responses)	Female	(No. of Responses)
100,000–199,999	7.53	(107)	8.19	(60)
200,000–399,999	8.84	(52)	6.67	(24)
400,000–749,999	8.84	(36)	3.80	(14)
750,000+	9.99	(19)	5.82	(7)
ALL	8.29	(214)	7.10	(105)

TABLE 14 MEAN TENURE OF DIRECTORS, BY SEX AND REGION, 1981

	Director Tenure in Years			
U.S. Regions & Canada	Male	(No. of Responses)	Female	(No. of Responses)
Northeast	8.64	(33)	5.73	(12)
South	8.18	(74)	8.05	(43)
North Central	7.97	(57)	3.20	(16)
West	9.11	(35)	8.71	(26)
All U.S.	8.36	(199)	7.09	(97)
Canada	7.33	(15)	7.28	(8)
All	8.29	(214)	7.10	(105)

TABLE 15   CHANGES IN TENURE RANGE BY SEX, 1979-1981

	Male 1979	Male 1981	Female 1979	Female 1981
3 or less	29.7%	29.0%	30.8%	41.0%
4–10	39.6	38.3	44.2	35.2
11–15	19.3	16.8	11.5	12.4
16–20	8.4	9.3	6.7	7.6
20 or more	3.0	6.5	6.7	3.8

399,999: 25 percent differential between the salaries. The smallest systems (those serving 100,000-199,999) showed a differential of 9 percent. The 1981 survey results appear to support female directorships of both small and relatively large systems, since the differential is least startling in these cases, but the 200,000-399,999 populations appear to be considerably less willing to support female directors. However, as we can observe from the ALA-OLPR study cited earlier, women do far less well than men when the total directors' salary picture is taken into account.[11]

Comparing length of tenure in the position against these population figures (Table 13), it should be noted that in the smallest systems the mean tenure of the female library directors was longer than their male counterparts, while all other population groups had had female directors for shorter average tenures than male directors. While staying longer does not confer equity in pay or more pay for these female directors, this could be a contributing factor in the other population levels.

DIRECTORS' SALARIES: CANADA

The data gathered include a sufficient sampling of Canadian libraries to warrant segregating Canadian and U.S. data. Since the inflationary rates, exchange rate, and standard of living indicators for the two countries do not necessarily equate, we felt it was important to start the second decade of analysis with this change in reporting structure.

As indicated earlier, rather than convert all of the reported salaries, tables reflect Canadian dollars, not U.S. currency. This is particularly tricky in Table 16, for example, where the reader may feel we are doing a direct comparison of salaries. We are *not*. Using the December 30, 1980, effective exchange rate of 1.190,[12] the low range would result in $21,008 to $25,209 U.S.; the high of $50,000C would actually be $42,017 U.S.

To demonstrate exchange rate effect: Table 3 shows per capita support in Canada in 1979 at $9.48 Canadian which, at the effective exchange rate of 1.186 for December

TABLE 16   DISTRIBUTION OF DIRECTORS' SALARIES BY SEX OF DIRECTOR, 1981

	U.S. Male	U.S. Female	Canada Male	Canada Female
Under $20,000	0.0%	12.1%	0.0%	0.0%
$20,000–24,999	8.6	15.2	0.0	0.0
25,000–29,999	18.7	24.2	14.3	12.5
30,000–34,999	25.8	15.2	7.1	37.5
35,000–39,999	22.7	19.2	7.1	25.0
40,000–49,999	16.7	12.1	64.3	25.0
50,000–+	7.6	2.0	7.1	0.0

*For the Canadian portion of the table, treat the salaries on the left as Canadian dollars, not U.S. dollars.

31, 1978, was the same as $7.99 U.S.[13] Likewise, the median Canadian directors' salary of $34,957 in 1979 would equate at that time to a U.S. salary of $29,475.

The closest Canadian economic indication we could identify to compare with the U.S. Department of Labor's "Higher Living Standard" was the "household effective buying income projection to 1983" which is projected as $31,346C.[14] Using this to measure current compensation of Canadian public library directors of large library systems, the 1981 median salary of $40,670C is well above the projected 1983 average living standard. The low end of the scale at $26,000C is 21 percent below this living standard (Table 8). Table 12 demonstrates that all median directors' salaries are well above this standard, i.e., more than half of the directors reporting exceeded the effective buying income projected for two years from now. More critical is that the sexual differential on the median salaries for Canada is 29 percent up from the 23 percent differential of 1979. Tenure appears to be no explanation since the mean tenure of male librarians was 7.33 years and female directors, 7.28 years (Table 14). The population size of 200,000–399,999 shows a negative differential, or female advantage, of −3 percent (Table 12), but this is comparing one female director to four male directors and so the median salary has little meaning here.

BEGINNERS' COMPENSATION

Beginning librarians continue to lose the battle against inflation: with U.S. general inflation for 1979–1980 at 25 percent, gains in entry level professional salaries of 15–20 percent are not very impressive. The median U.S. beginning salary in large public libraries and systems at the outset of 1981 was $13,609. This is only slightly higher than the median beginning salary reported in the ALA-OLPR study (for April 1980), which found beginning salaries for *all* public libraries was $13,294;[15] and $1,463 higher than the most recent median salary for new placements as reported by Learmont in November 1980.[16] As we look at the regional statistics (Table 17), in relation to the 25 percent inflation rate, the West was the strongest gainer, at 20 percent (5 percent below inflation for the period); and beginning North Central librarians were the greatest losers, with salaries lagging 10 percent behind inflation.

When compared to the U.S. Department of Labor "Lower Living Standard" (Table 9) of $14,044, only in the West was the median beginning 1981 salary above this standard. In the Northeast, beginning librarians in large public libraries and systems were 13 percent below this standard; the Southern median beginners' salary was 7.6 percent below the standard; and in the North Central region, 3 percent below the standard. The U.S. total median was 3 percent below the lower living standard.

The Canadian beginners' median salary grew 19 percent, very close to the Cana-

TABLE 17   INCREASE IN 1981 MEDIAN BEGINNING PROFESSIONAL SALARIES OVER 1979, BY REGION

U.S. Regions & Canada	Median Salary 1979	Median Salary 1981	(No. of Responses)	1981 Minimum	1981 Maximum	Change: 1979–1981 $	Change: 1979–1981 %
Northeast	$10,650	$12,453	(46)	$ 9,000	$16,653	$1,803	(17%)
South	10,982	13,040	(118)	8,090	17,888	$2,058	(19%)
No. Central	11,825	13,576	(72)	9,000	19,440	$1,751	(15%)
West	12,480	14,915	(62)	10,848	18,276	$2,435	(20%)
All U.S.	*	13,609	(298)	8,090	19,440	*	
Canada	14,265C	16,991C	(24)	14,799C	21,502C	$2,726C	(19%)

TABLE 18 MEDIAN BEGINNING PROFESSIONAL SALARIES, BY SIZE OF POPULATION SERVED, 1981

	Median (No. of Responses)		Minimum	Maximum
U.S.:				
100,000–199,999	$13,068	(151)	$ 8,090	$19,440
200,000–399,999	13,896	(72)	9,500	17,892
400,000–749,999	13,920	(44)	10,000	18,276
750,000– +	14,485	(26)	11,130	17,226
Canada:				
100,000–199,999	16,734C	(16)	14,799C	20,000C
200,000–399,999	16,983C	(5)	15,317C	17,950C
400,000–749,999	19,333C	(2)	17,165C	21,502C
750,000– +	17,308C	(1)	17,308C	17,308C

dian inflation rate of 19.3 percent and much better than new librarians in the United States were able to do.

The size of population served (Table 18) appears to assist U.S. beginners to some degree at the median of the salary range and at the minimum level: the larger the library or system, the better the pay. The median range increased $1,417 from the smallest to the largest libraries analyzed. Whether or not this amount is sufficient to make up the difference for more expensive living in the largest cities, the largest cities were the only ones with the median beginning salary above the lower living standard. The minimum starting salaries range of $3,040 from smallest to largest libraries and systems is somewhat an improvement over the last report, but since all were below the lower living standard for an urban family of four, this is probably little comfort.

The maximum salaries fluctuated somewhat out of direct relationship, but it is probably not surprising that the effort here was to pay the higher priced beginner better in the smaller city to attract them away from the lures of the largest metropolitan areas.

For Canadian libraries, the sample sizes outside the smallest cities are so small that generalizing is difficult.

BEGINNERS AND SEX OF DIRECTOR

Table 19 shows the distribution of beginning salaries based on the sex of the directors: in the United States, beginners starting under female directors earned less than $14,000 in 64.7 percent of the cases reported; while under male directors 55.3 percent of the beginners' salaries were below $14,000.

Ignoring the effective exchange rate (December 31, 1980: 1.19) which would alter the lower Canadian salaries to the range of $11,765 to $12,604 and higher salaries to the range $12,605 and up, the women directors at least seem to have a slight edge over the men in compensating their entry-level professional.

The U.S. male directors' median beginners' salary is 5 percent higher than for the female directors. They are now $650 apart as shown in Table 20. This is an improvement in percentage differential although real dollar difference is slightly above the last surveys' results of $625. The range is tight in the United States—.1 percent to 11 percent differential with the minimum salaries closest together. The Canadians also had a 5 percent differential at the midpoint although a larger Canadian dollar differential in actual cash. The range was almost twice as big, however, from −2 percent (female advantage)

TABLE 19 DISTRIBUTION OF BEGINNING PROFESSIONAL SALARIES BY SEX OF DIRECTOR, 1981

	U.S. Male	U.S. Female	Canada* Male	Canada* Female
Less than $9,000	.5%	2.0%	—	—
$9,000– 9,999	1.5	6.1	—	—
10,000–10,999	8.5	6.1	—	—
11,000–11,999	10.6	21.2	—	—
12,000–12,999	13.6	13.1	—	—
13,000–13,999	20.6	16.2	—	—
14,000–14,999	18.6	17.2	6.7	—
15,000– and up	26.1	18.2	93.3	100

*For the Canadian portion of the table, treat the salaries on the left as Canadian dollars, not U.S. dollars.

at the minimum starting salary based on sex of director paying it, but 17 percent (male) advantage at the maximum beginners' compensation.

SUMMARY

In both countries overall, the libraries appear to be doing well in relation to general inflation in per capita support; but directors' compensation and beginners' compensation lost to inflation in the 1978–1980 period.

There were slight gains for the female directors. The West again lowered the differential between male and female directors' median salaries; and U.S. female directors of the largest systems (in terms of population served) had a slight salary advantage of 3 percent this year. Female directors in Canada were able to compensate their beginners a little better than their male counterparts (in 6.7 percent of the cases) and the overall range of beginners' salaries, at least in the United States, appears to be tightening, and in the process eliminating some of the male advantage in hiring entry-level librarians.

Two recent items may provide a broader context for the consideration of some of the issues pointed out here:

"Salaries of Municipal Officials for 1980" [Shirley Alsop Dorrington in *The Municipal Year Book 1981* (Washington, D.C.: International City Management Association, 1981), pp. 59–84] provides salaries of 24 municipal positions, including librar-

TABLE 20 RANGE OF MEDIAN BEGINNING PROFESSIONAL SALARIES BY SEX OF DIRECTOR, 1981

Sex of Director	Median Beginning Salary	Minimum/Maximum Beginning Salary
U.S.: Female	$13,164	$ 8,090–17,550
Male	13,814	8,100–19,440
Differential	$650 (5%)	$10–$1,890 (0.1%–11%)
Canada: Female	$16,293C	$15,175–18,348C
Male	17,165C	14,799–21,502C
Differential	$872C (5%)	–$376C to $3,154C (–2%) (17%)

ian, broken out by size of municipality. Comparisons for comparable pay studies may be made.

"Women in Municipal Management" (*Urban Data Service Report 2/80* available from the Center for the American Woman and Politics, Eagleton Institute of Politics, Rutgers—The State University, New Brunswick, NJ 08901) compares male and female municipal managers.

NOTES

1. Raymond L. Carpenter and Kenneth D. Shearer, "Sex and Salary Survey: Selected Statistics of Large Public Libraries in the United States and Canada," *Library Journal*, November 15, 1972, pp. 3682-3685. (Reprinted in *The Bowker Annual of Library and Book Trade Information, 1973*. Bowker, 1973, pp. 406-414.)

   _____. "Sex and Salary Update," *Library Journal*, January 15, 1974, pp. 101-107. (Reprinted in *The Bowker Annual of Library and Book Trade Information, 1974*. Bowker, 1974, pp. 310-322.)

   _____. "Public Library Support and Salaries in the Seventies," *Library Journal*, March 15, 1976, pp. 777-783. (Reprinted in *The Bowker Annual of Library and Book Trade Information, 1976*. Bowker, 1976, pp. 360-370.)

   Kathleen M. Heim and Carolyn Kacena, "Sex, Salaries, and Library Support," *Library Journal*, March 15, 1979, pp. 675-680.

   _____. "Sex, Salaries, and Library Support, 1979," *Library Journal*, January 1, 1980, pp. 17-22. (Reprinted in *The Bowker Annual of Library and Book Trade Information, 1980*. Bowker, 1980, pp. 334-344.)

2. *Statistics of Public Libraries in the United States and Canada Serving 100,000 Population or More*. Allen County Public Library, Indiana, June 1981.
3. "Consumer Price Index for Urban Wage Earners and Clerical Workers: Annual Averages and Changes, 1967-1980," *Monthly Labor Review*, May 1981, p. 43.
4. "Consumer Prices," *International Economic Indicators*, March 1981, p. 43.
5. Heim and Kacena, *LJ*, January 1, 1980, p. 19, Table 4.
6. "Consumer Price Index."
7. Heim and Kacena, *LJ*, January 1, 1980, p. 20, Table 7.
8. *Ibid.*
9. American Library Association, Office for Personnel Resources, *The Racial, Ethnic, and Sexual Composition of Library Staff in Academic and Public Libraries* (ALA-OLPR, 1981), p. 14; calculated from Table 9.
10. Heim and Kacena, *LJ*, January 1, 1980, p. 20, Table 10.
11. ALA-OLPR, p. 14.
12. Thayer C. Taylor, "S & MM's Canadian Metropolitan Market Projections to 1983," *Sales and Marketing Management*, October 29, 1979, p. 162.
13. "Free Market Rates of U.S. Dollars and/or Transfers Abroad (in Canadian Dollars per U.S. Dollar at end of month)" in *1977-1979 Pick's Currency Yearbook* (New York: Pick Publishing), p. 128.
14. "Foreign Exchange," *Wall Street Journal*, December 31, 1980, p. 15.
15. ALA-OLPR, p. 31.
16. Carol L. Learmont, "Placements & Salaries 1979: Wider Horizons," *Library Journal*, November 1, 1980, p. 2277, Table XI.

ACCREDITED LIBRARY SCHOOLS

This list of graduate schools accredited by the American Library Association was issued in October 1982. A list of more than 400 institutions offering both accredited and nonaccredited programs in librarianship appears in the thirty-fifth edition of the *American Library Directory* (Bowker, 1982).

NORTHEAST: CONN., D.C., MASS., MD., N.J., N.Y., PA., R.I.

Catholic University of America, School of Lib. and Info. Science, Washington, DC 20064. Elizabeth W. Stone, Dean. 202-635-5085.

Clarion State College, School of Lib. Science, Clarion, PA 16214. Elizabeth A. Rupert, Dean. 814-226-2271.

Columbia University, School of Lib. Service, New York, NY 10027. Richard L. Darling, Dean. 212-280-2291.

Drexel University, School of Lib. and Info. Science, Philadelphia, PA 19104. Guy Garrison, Dean. 215-895-2474.

Long Island University, C. W. Post Center, Palmer School of Lib. and Info. Science, Greenvale, NY 11548. Ralph J. Folcarelli, Dean. 516-299-2855, 2856.

Pratt Institute, Grad. School of Lib. and Info. Science, Brooklyn, NY 11205. Nasser Sharify, Dean. 212-636-3702.

Queens College, City University of New York, Grad. School of Lib. and Info. Studies, Flushing, NY 11367. Richard J. Hyman, Dir. 212-520-7194.

Rutgers University, School of Communication, Info., and Lib. Studies, New Brunswick, NJ 08903. William A. Stuart, Acting Dean. 201-932-7500.

St. John's University, Div. of Lib. and Info. Science, Jamaica, NY 11439. Mildred Lowe, Dir. 212-990-6161, ext. 6200.

Simmons College, Grad. School of Lib. and Info. Science, Boston, MA 20115. Robert D. Stueart, Dean. 617-738-2225.

Southern Connecticut State College, School of Lib. Science and Instructional Technology, New Haven, CT 06515. Emanuel T. Prostano, Acting Dean. 203-397-4532.

State University of New York at Albany, School of Lib. and Info. Science, Albany, NY 12222. Richard S. Halsey, Dean. 518-455-6288.

State University of New York at Buffalo, School of Info. and Lib. Studies, Buffalo, NY 14260. George S. Bobinski, Dean. 716-636-2411.

State University of New York, College of Arts and Science, Geneseo, School of Lib. and Info. Science, Geneseo, NY 14454. Douglas J. Harke, Acting Dean. 716-245-5546.

Syracuse University, School of Info. Studies, Syracuse, NY 13210. Evelyn H. Daniel, Dean. 315-423-2911.

University of Maryland, College of Lib. and Info. Services, College Park, MD 20742. Anne S. MacLeod, Acting Dean. 301-454-5441.

University of Pittsburgh, School of Lib. and Info. Science, Pittsburgh, PA 15260. Thomas J. Galvin, Dean. 412-624-5230.

University of Rhode Island, Grad. Lib. School, Kingston, RI 02881. Bernard S. Schlessinger, Dean. 401-792-2878, 2947.

SOUTHEAST: ALA., FLA., GA., KY., MISS., N.C., S.C., TENN.

Atlanta University, School of Lib. and Info. Studies, Atlanta, GA 30314. Lorene B. Brown, Dean. 404-681-0251, ext. 230.

Emory University, Div. of Lib. and Info. Management, Atlanta, GA 30322. A. Venable Lawson, Dir. 404-329-6840.

Florida State University, School of Lib. and Info. Studies, Tallahassee, FL 32306. Harold Goldstein, Dean. 904-644-5775.

North Carolina Central University, School of Lib. Science, Durham, NC 27707. Annette L. Phinazee, Dean. 919-683-6485.

University of Alabama, Grad. School of Lib. Service, University, AL 35486. James D. Ramer, Dean. 205-348-4610.

University of Kentucky, College of Lib. and Info. Science, Lexington, KY 40506. Timothy W. Sineath, Dean. 606-258-8876.

University of Mississippi, Grad. School of Lib. and Info. Science, University, MS 38677. Steven B. Schoenly, Acting Dir. 601-232-7440.

University of North Carolina, School of Lib. Science, Chapel Hill, NC 27514. Edward G. Holley, Dean. 919-962-8366.

University of North Carolina at Greensboro, Dept. of Lib. Science/Educational Technology, Greensboro, NC 27412. Keith C. Wright, Chairpn. 919-379-5710.

University of South Carolina, College of Libnshp., Columbia, SC 29208. F. William Summers, Dean. 803-777-3858.

University of South Florida, Grad. Dept. of Lib., Media and Info. Studies, Tampa, FL 33620. John A. McCrossan, Chpn. 813-974-3520.

University of Southern Mississippi, School of Lib. Service, Hattiesburg, MS 39406. Onva K. Boshears, Jr., Dean. 601-266-4228.

University of Tennessee, Knoxville, Grad. School of Lib. and Info. Science, Knoxville, TN 37996-4330. Ann E. Prentice, Dir. 615-974-2148.

Vanderbilt University, George Peabody College for Teachers, Dept. of Lib. and Info. Science, Nashville, TN 37203. Edwin S. Gleaves, Chpn. 615-322-8050.

MIDWEST: IOWA, ILL., IND., KANS., MICH., MINN., MO., OHIO, WIS.

Ball State University, Dept. of Lib. Science, Muncie, IN 47306. Ray R. Suput, Acting Chpn. 317-285-7180, 7189.

Case Western Reserve University, Matthew A. Baxter School of Info. and Lib. Science, Cleveland, OH 44106. Phyllis A. Richmond, Acting Dean. 216-368-3500.

Indiana University, School of Lib. and Info. Science, Bloomington, IN 47405. Herbert S. White, Dean. 812-335-2848.

Kent State University, School of Lib. Science, Kent, OH 44242. A. Robert Rogers, Dean. 216-672-2782.

Northern Illinois University, Dept. of Lib. Science, DeKalb, IL 60115. Henry C. Dequin, Interim Chpn. 815-753-1733.

Rosary College, Grad. School of Lib. and Info. Science, River Forest, IL 60305. Richard Tze-chung Li, Dean. 312-366-2490.

University of Chicago, Grad. Lib. School, Chicago, IL 60637. W. Boyd Rayward, Dean. 312-962-8272.

University of Illinois, Grad. School of Lib. and Info. Science, 1407 W. Gregory, 410 DKH, Urbana, IL 61801. Charles H. Davis, Dean. 217-333-3280.

Univesity of Iowa, School of Lib. Science, Iowa City, IA 52242. Carl F. Orgren, Dir. 319-353-3644.

University of Michigan, School of Lib. Science, Ann Arbor, MI 48109. Russell E. Bidlack, Dean. 313-764-9376.

University of Minnesota, Lib. School, 117 Pleasant St. S.E., Minneapolis, MN 55455. George D'Elia, Dir. 612-373-3100.

University of Missouri, Columbia, School of Lib. and Info. Science, Columbia, MO 65211. Edward P. Miller, Dean. 314-882-4546.

University of Wisconsin-Madison, Lib. School, Madison, WI 53706. Jane B. Robbins-Carter, Dir. 608-263-2900.

University of Wisconsin-Milwaukee, School of Lib. and Info. Science, Milwaukee, WI 53201. Mohammed M. Aman, Dean. 414-963-4707.

Wayne State University, Div. of Lib. Science, Detroit, MI 48202. Robert E. Booth, Dir. 313-577-1825.

Western Michigan University, School of Libnshp., Kalamazoo, MI 49008. Laurel A. Grotziner, Interim Dir. 616-383-1849.

SOUTHWEST: ARIZ., LA., OKLA., TEX.

Louisiana State University, School of Lib. and Info. Science, Baton Rouge, LA 70803. Sr. Marie L. Cairns, Acting Dean. 504-388-3158.

North Texas State University, School of Lib. and Info. Sciences, Denton, TX 76203. Dewey E. Carroll, Dean. 817-565-2445.

Texas Woman's University, School of Lib. Science, Denton, TX 76204. Brooke E. Sheldon, Dean. 817-387-2418.

University of Arizona, Grad. Lib. School, Tucson, AZ 85721. Ellen Altman, Dir. 602-626-3565.

University of Oklahoma, School of Lib. Science, Norman, OK 73019. Sylvia G. Faibisoff, Dir. 405-325-3921.

University of Texas at Austin, Grad. School of Lib. and Info. Science, Austin, TX 78712. Ronald E. Wyllys, Acting Dean. 512-471-3821.

WEST: CALIF., COLO., HAWAII, UTAH, WASH.

Brigham Young University, School of Lib. and Info. Sciences, Provo, UT 84602. Nathan M. Smith, Dir. 801-378-2977.

San Jose State University, Div. of Lib. Science, San Jose, CA 95192. Guy A. Marco, Dir. 408-277-2292.

University of California-Berkeley, School of Lib. and Info. Studies, Berkeley, CA 94720. Michael K. Buckland, Dean. 415-642-1464.

University of California-Los Angeles, Grad. School of Lib. and Info. Science, Los Angeles, CA 90024. Robert M. Hayes, Dean. 213-825-4351.

University of Denver, Grad. School of Libnshp. and Info. Management, Denver, CO 80208. Bernard M. Franckowiak, Dean. 303-753-2557.

University of Hawaii, Grad. School of Lib. Studies, Honolulu, HI 96822. Ira W. Harris, Dean. 808-948-7321.

University of Southern California, School of Lib. and Info. Management, University Park, Los Angeles, CA 90007. Roger C. Greer, Dean. 213-743-2548.

University of Washington, School of Libnshp., Seattle, WA 98195. Margaret Chisholm, Acting Dir. 206-543-1794.

CANADA

Dalhousie University, School of Lib. Service, Halifax, N.S. B3H 4H8. Norman Horrocks, Dir. 902-424-3656.

McGill University, Grad. School of Lib. Science, Montreal, P.Q. H3A 1Y1. Hans Möller, Dir. 514-392-5947.

Université de Montréal, Ecole de bibliothéconomie, Montréal, P.Q. H3C 3J7. Marcel Lajeunesse, Interim Dir. 514-343-6044.

University of Alberta, Faculty of Lib. Science, Edmonton, Alta. T6G 2J4. William Kurmey, Dean. 403-432-4578.

University of British Columbia, School of Libnshp., Vancouver, B.C. V6T 1W5. Basil Stuart-Stubbs, Dir. 604-228-2404.

University of Toronto, Faculty of Lib. and Info. Science, Toronto, Ont. M5S 1A1. Katherine H. Packer, Dean. 416-978-3234.

University of Western Ontario, School of Lib. and Info. Science, London, Ont. N6G 1H1. William J. Cameron, Dean. 519-679-3542.

LIBRARY SCHOLARSHIP SOURCES

For a more complete list of the scholarships, fellowships, and assistantships offered for library study, see *Financial Assistance for Library Education* published annually by the American Library Association.

American Library Association. (1) The David H. Clift Scholarship of $3,000 is given to a varying number of U.S. or Canadian citizens who have been admitted to accredited library schools. For information, write to: Staff Liaison, David H. Clift Scholarship Jury, ALA, 50 E. Huron St., Chicago, IL 60611; (2) the Louise Giles Minority Scholarship of $3,000 is given to a varying number of minority students who are U.S. or Canadian citizens and have been admitted to accredited library schools. For information, write to: Staff Liaison, Louise Giles Minority Scholarship Jury, ALA, 50 E. Huron St., Chicago, IL 60611; (3) the F. W. Faxon Scholarship of $3,000 is given to a U.S., Canadian, or foreign student who has been admitted to an accredited library school. Scholarship includes ten-week expenses-paid internship at F. W. Faxon in Westwood, Massachusetts. For information, write to: Staff Liaison, F. W. Faxon Scholarship, ALA, 50 E. Huron St., Chicago, IL 60611.

American-Scandinavian Foundation. Fellowships and grants for 25 to 30 students, in amounts from $500 to $7,500, for advanced study in Denmark, Finland, Iceland, Norway, or Sweden. For information, write to: Exchange Div., American-Scandinavian Foundation, 127 E. 73 St., New York, NY 10021.

Association of Jewish Libraries. A grant of $250 for graduate study. For information, write to: A. Metz, Braude Lib., Temple Beth EL, 70 Orchard Ave., Providence, RI 02906.

Beta Phi Mu. (1) The Sarah Rebecca Reed Scholarship of $1,500 each for a varying number of persons accepted in an ALA-accredited library program; (2) the Frank B. Sessa Scholarship for Continuing Education of $750 each for a varying number of Beta Phi Mu members for continuing education; (3) the Harold Lancour Scholarship for Foreign Study of $1,000 each for a varying number of students for graduate study in a foreign country related to the applicant's work or schooling. For information, write to: Exec. Secy., Beta Phi Mu, Grad. School of Lib. and Info. Science, Univ. of Pittsburgh, Pittsburgh, PA 15260.

Canadian Library Association. (1) The Howard V. Phalin-World Book Graduate Scholarship in Library Science of $2,500 (maximum); (2) the H. W. Wilson Scholarship of $2,000; and (3) the Elizabeth Dafoe Scholarship of $1,750 are given to a Canadian citizen or landed immigrant to attend an accredited Canadian library school. For information, write to: Scholarships and Awards Committee, Canadian Lib. Assn., 151 Sparks St., Ottawa, Ont. K1P 5E3, Canada.

Catholic Library Association. (1) Rev. Andrew L. Bouwhuis Scholarship of $1,500 for a person with a B.A. degree who has been accepted in an accredited library school. (Award based on financial need and proficiency.) (2) World Book-Childcraft Awards: one scholarship of a total of $1,000 to be distributed among no more than four recipients for a program of continuing education. Open to CLA members only. For information, write to: Scholarship Committee, Catholic Lib. Assn., 461 W. Lancaster Ave., Haverford, PA 19401.

Information Exchange System for Minority Personnel. Scholarship of $500, intended for minority students, for graduate study. For information, write to: Dorothy M. Haith, Chpn., Clara Stanton Jones School, Box 668, Fort Valley, GA 31030.

Medical Library Association. (1) Varying number of scholarships of $2,000 each for minority students, for graduate study in medical librarianship. (2) Grants of varying amounts for continuing education for medical librarians with an MLS and two years' professional experience. Open to MLA members only. For information, write to: Scholarship Committee, Medical Lib. Assn., Suite 3208, 919 N. Michigan Ave., Chicago, IL 60611.

The Frederic G. Melcher Scholarship (administered by Association of Library Service to Children, ALA). Two scholarships of $4,000 each for a U.S. or Canadian citizen admitted to an accredited library school who plans to work with children in school or public libraries. For information, write to: Exec. Secy., Assn. of Lib. Service to Children, ALA, 50 E. Huron St., Chicago, IL 60611.

Mountain Plains Library Association. Ten grants of $500 (maximum) each for residents of the association area. Open only to MPLA members with at least two years of membership. For information, write to: Joseph R. Edelen, Jr., MPLA Exec. Secy., Univ. of South Dakota Lib., Vermillion, SD 57069.

Natural Sciences and Engineering Research Council. (1) A varying number of scholarships of $10,500 each and (2) a varying number of scholarships of varying amounts for postgraduate study in science librarianship and documentation for a Canadian citizen or landed immigrant with a bachelor's degree in science or engineering. For information, write to: J. H. Danis, Scholarships Officer, Programs Branch, Natural Sciences and Engineering Research Council, Ottawa, Ont. K1A OR6, Canada.

New England Library Association. A scholarship of $500 for graduate study. For information, write to: Ronald B. Hunte, Exec. Secy., NELA, 292 Great Neck Rd., Acton, MA 01720.

Special Libraries Association. (1) Two $5,000 scholarships for U.S. or Canadian citizens, accepted by an ALA-accredited library education program, who show an aptitude for and interest in special libraries. (2) One $1,000 scholarship for a U.S. or Canadian citizen with an MLS and an interest in special libraries who has been accepted in an ALA-accredited Ph.D. program. (3) One $1,000 scholarship for a U.S. or foreign student with an MLS and an interest in special libraries who has been accepted in an ALA-accredited Ph.D. program. For information, write to: Scholarship Committee, SLA, 235 Park Ave. S., New York, NY 10003. (4) Three scholarships of $2,000 each for minority students with an interest in special libraries. Open to U.S. or Canadian citizens only. For information, write to: Positive Action Program for Minority Groups, c/o SLA.

LIBRARY SCHOLARSHIP AND AWARD RECIPIENTS, 1982

AALS Doctor Forum Award. For an outstanding doctoral dissertation. *Offered by:* Association of American Library Schools. *Winners:* Barbara Moran, Univ. of Buffalo, for "Career Progression of Male and Female Academic Library Administrators"; Edith H. Anselmo, Rutgers Univ., for "Productivity Impact and the Library Information Science Doctorate: A Methodological and Quantitative Study of Publications, Citers, and Citations"; and Julie M. Neway, Univ. of Illinois, for "The Role of the Information Specialist in Academic Research."

AALS Research Grant Award—$1,500–$2,500. For a project that reflects the goals and objectives of the Association of American Library Schools (AALS). *Offered by:* AALS. *Winners:* Rosemary DuMont and Robert Swisher (Univ. of Oklahoma), for "A Sex Structuring in Libraries: A Search for Explanations"; and Maurice P. Marchant and Nathan M. Smith (Brigham Young Univ.), for "The Public Library Director's View of Library Education."

AALS Research Paper Competition—$500. For a research paper concerning any aspect of librarianship or information studies by a member of AALS. *Offered by:* Association of American Library Schools. *Winners:* Alvin M. Schrader (Univ. of Alberta, Canada), for "In Search of a Name: Information Science and Its Antecedents"; and Charles McClure (Univ. of Oklahoma) and Peter Hernon (Simmons College), for "Assessing the Quality of Reference Service for Government Publications."

AASL Distinguished Library Service Award for School Administrators. For a unique and sustained contribution toward furthering the role of the library and its development in elementary and/or secondary education. *Offered by:* ALA American Association of School Librarians. *Winner:* James R. Trost.

AASL/Encyclopaedia Britannica School Library Media Program of the Year Award—$5,000. For outstanding school media programs. *Offered by:* ALA American Association of School Librarians and the Encyclopaedia Britannica Co. *Winner:* Shaker Heights City School District, Shaker Heights, Ohio.

AASL President's Award—$2,000. For demonstrating excellence and providing an outstanding national or international contribution to school librarianship and school library development. *Offered by:* ALA, American Association of School Librarians. *Donor:* Baker & Taylor. *Winner:* D. Philip Baker.

ACRL Academic/Research Librarian of the Year Award—$2,000. For an outstanding national or international contribution to academic and research librarianship and library development. *Offered by:* ALA, Association of College and Research Libraries. *Donor:* Baker & Taylor. *Winner:* William Budington.

ALA Honorary Life Membership Award. *Offered by:* American Library Association. *Winners:* George David Aiken, Carl Atwood Elliott, Virginia Haviland, and Frederick Kilgour.

ALTA Literacy Award. For an outstanding contribution to the extirpation of illiteracy. *Offered by:* ALA American Library Trustee Association. *Winner:* Lucretia Lupher.

ASCLA Exceptional Achievement Award. For recognition of leadership and achievement in the areas of library cooperation and state library development. *Offered by:* Association of Specialized & Cooperative Library Agencies. *Winner:* Robert R. McClarren.

ASCLA Exceptional Service Award. For exceptional service to ASCLA or any of its component areas of service, namely, services to patients, the homebound, medical, nursing, and other professional staff in hospitals, and inmates; demonstrating professional leadership, effective interpretation of program, pioneering activity, or significant research or experimental projects. *Offered by:* Association of Specialized & Cooperative Library Agencies. *Winner:* Harris McClaskey.

Joseph L. Andrews Bibliographic Award. For a significant contribution to legal bibliographical literature. *Offered by:* American Association of Law Libraries (AALL). *Winners:* Carol Boast and Lynn Foster for *Subject Compilations of State Laws: Research Guide and Annotated Bibliography;* and Kathryn Swanson for *Affirmative Action and Preferential Admissions in Higher Education: An Annotated Bibliography.*

Armed Forces Librarians Achievement Citation. For significant contributions to the development of armed forces library service and to organizations encouraging an interest in libraries and reading. *Offered by:* Armed Forces Librarians Section, ALA Public Library Association. *Winner:* Nellie B. Strickland.

Beta Phi Mu Award—$500. For distinguished service to education for librarianship. *Offered by:* ALA Awards Committee. *Donor:* Beta Phi Mu Library Science Honorary Association. *Winner:* David K. Berninghausen.

Beta Phi Mu Memorial Award. *Offered by:* ALA Awards Committee. *Donor:* Beta Phi Mu Library Science Honorary Association. *Winner:* Harold Lancour.

Blackwell North America Resources Section Scholarship Award (formerly National Library Service Resources Section Publication Award). Presented to the author/authors of an outstanding monograph, published article, or original paper on acquisitions pertaining to college or university libraries. *Offered by:* ALA Resources and Technical Services Division, Resources Section. *Donor:* Blackwell North America. *Winner:* Richard K. Gardner, for *Library Collections: Their Origin, Selection and Development.*

Rev. Andrew L. Bouwhuis Scholarship—$1,500. For a person with a B.A. degree who has been accepted in an accredited library school. (Award is based on financial need and proficiency.) *Offered by:* Catholic Library Association. *Winner:* To be announced.

CALA Distinguished Service Award. For outstanding leadership and achievement in library and information services at the national and/or international level. *Offered by:* Chinese-American Librarians Association. *Winner:* Ching-chih Chen, professor and associate dean, Graduate School of Library and Information Science, Simmons College, Boston, Mass.

CASLIS Award for Special Librarianship in Canada. *Offered by:* Canadian Assn. of Special Libraries and Information Services. *Winner:* Susan Klement.

CIS/GODORT/ALA Documents to the People Award—$1,000. For effectively encouraging the use of federal documents in support of library services. *Offered by:* ALA Government Documents Round Table. *Donor:* Congressional Information Service, Inc. *Winner:* Arne Richards.

CLA Dafoe Scholarship—$1,750. For a Canadian citizen or landed immigrant to attend an accredited Canadian library school. *Offered by:* Canadian Library Association. *Winner:* Patricia Bellamy, Vancouver, B.C., Canada.

CLA Outstanding Service to Librarianship Award. *Offered by:* Canadian Library Association. *Winners:* Bruce Peel, former librarian, Univ. of Alberta; and Robert Blackburn, former chief librarian, Univ. of Toronto.

CLR Fellowships. For a list of the recipients for the 1981–1982 academic year, see the report from the Council on Library Resources, Inc., in Part 2 of this *Bowker Annual.*

CSLA Award for Outstanding Congregational Librarian. For distinguished service to the congregation and/or community through devotion to the congregational library. *Offered by:* Church and Synagogue Library Association. *Winner:* Naomi Kauffman, librarian, Perkasie Mennonite Church, Perkasie, Pennsylvania.

CSLA Award for Outstanding Congregational Library. For responding in creative and innovative ways to the library's mission of reaching and serving the congregation and/or the wider community. *Offered by:* Church and Synagogue Library Association. *Winner:* Joseph and Elizabeth Schwartz Library, Beth Sholom Congregation, Elkins Park, Pa.

CSLA Award for Outstanding Contribution to Librarianship. For providing inspiration, guidance, leadership, or resources to enrich the field of church or synagogue librarianship. *Offered by:* Church and Synagogue Library Association. *Winner:* G. Martin Ruoss, Albuquerque, N. Mex.

Francis Joseph Campbell Citation. For an outstanding contribution to the advancement of library service to the blind. *Offered by:* Section on Library Service to the Blind and Physically Handicapped of the Association of Specialized and Cooperative Library Agencies. *Winner:* Frank Kurt Cylke.

James Bennett Childs Award. For a distinguished contribution to documents librarianship. *Offered by:* ALA Government Documents Round Table. *Winner:* James Adler.

David H. Clift Scholarship—$3,000. For a worthy student to begin a program of library education at the graduate level. *Offered by:* ALA Awards Committee, Standing Committee on Library Education. *Winners:* Carol Gates and Mary Margaret Case.

Cunningham Fellowship. A six-month grant and travel expenses in the United States and Canada for a foreign librarian. *Offered by:* Medical Library Association. *Winner:* Yan Zong Lin (People's Republic of China).

John Cotton Dana Award. For exceptional support and encouragement of special librarianship. *Offered by:* Special Libraries Association. *Winner:* James Humphry III.

Dartmouth Medal. For achievement in creating reference works of outstanding quality and significance. *Offered by:* ALA Reference and Adult Services Division. *Winner: The New Grove's Dictionary of Music and Musicians* (Grove).

Melvil Dewey Medal. For recent creative professional achievement of a high order, particularly in library management, library training, cataloging and classification, and the tools and techniques of librarianship. *Offered by:* ALA Awards Committee. *Donor:* Forest Press. *Winner:* Sarah K. Vann.

Janet Doe Lectureship. *Offered by:* Medical Library Association. *Winner:* Ursula Poland, Schaffer Library of Health Sciences, Albany Medical College, N.Y.

Ida and George Eliot Prize—$100. For an essay published in any journal in the preceding calendar year that has been judged most effective in furthering medical librarianship. *Offered by:* Medical Library Association. *Winners:* Joan Gard Marshall and Victor Neufeld (McMaster Univ. Health Science Library, Hamilton, Ont., Canada).

Facts on File Award—$1,000. For an individual who has made current affairs more meaningful to adults. *Winner:* Arthur S. Meyers.

Frederick Winthrop Faxon Scholarship—$3,000. *Offered by:* American Library Association. *Winner:* Sharon Vaughn Shirasawa.

Louise Giles Minority Scholarship—$3,000. For a worthy student who is a U.S. or Canadian citizen and is also a member of a principal minority group. *Offered by:* ALA Awards Committee, Office for Library Personnel Resources Advisory Committee. *Winners:* Maria Camarillo-Jones and Lisa Mitten.

Murray Gottlieb Prize—$100. For the best unpublished essay submitted by a medical librarian on the history of some aspect of health sciences or a detailed description of a library exhibit. *Offered by:* Medical Library Association. *Winner:* Lisa Dunkel, Langley Porter Psychiatric Institute, San Francisco, Calif.

Grolier Foundation Award—$1,000. For an unusual contribution to the stimulation and guidance of reading by children and young people through high school age, for continuing service, or one particular contribution of lasting value. *Offered by:* ALA Awards Committee. *Donor:* Grolier Foundation. *Winner:* Spencer Shaw.

Grolier National Library Week Award—$1,000. For the best plan for a public relations program. *Awarded by:* National Library Week Committee of the American Library Association. *Donor:* Grolier Educational Corp. *Winner:* Maine Library Association.

Bailey K. Howard–World Book Encyclopedia–ALA Goal Award—$5,000. To support programs that recognize, advance, and implement the goals and objectives of the American Library Association. *Donor:* World Book-Childcraft International, Inc. *Winner:* Committee on the Status of Women in Librarianship, for "Women Librarians Reentering the Work Force."

John Phillip Imroth Memorial Award for Intellectual Freedom—$500. For a notable contribution to intellectual freedom and remarkable personal courage. *Offered by:* ALA Intellectual Freedom Round Table. *Donor:* Intellectual Freedom Round Table. *Winner:* Steven Pico.

Information Industry Association Distinguished Service Award. For a unique contribution to the information industry. *Offered by:* Information Industry Association. *Winners:* Herbert R. Brinberg, president, Aspen Systems Corp.; J. Christopher Burns, former senior vice president, *Minneapolis Star & Tribune;* Peter Marx; and Daniel Sullivan.

Information Industry Association Hall of Fame Award. For leadership and innovation in furthering the progress of the information industry. *Offered by:* Information Industry Association. *Winner:* Roger K. Summit, president, Dialog Information Services, Inc.

Information Industry Association Honorary Professional Member Award. For long-term services to the information industry. *Offered by:* Information Industry Association. *Winners:* Ben H. Weil, formerly of Exxon Research Corp., and Morton David Goldberg, Esq., Schwab, Goldberg, Price & Dannay.

JMRT Professional Development Grant. *See* 3M Company Professional Development Grant.

J. Morris Jones–World Book Encyclopedia–ALA Goal Award—$5,000. To support programs that recognize, advance, and implement the goals and objectives of the American Library Association. *Donor:* World Book-Childcraft International, Inc. *Winner:* Association of College and Research Libraries, Bibliographic Instruction Section, for "Bringing Workshops to Members."

William T. Knox Outstanding Information Manager Award. For excellence in managing information resources or for a distinctive contribution to the information management field. *Offered by:* Associated Information Managers. *Winner:* Dr. Craig M. Cook, former principal, Arthur Young & Co., Washington, D.C.

LITA Award for Achievement in Library and Information Technology. For distinguished leadership, notable development or application of technology, superior accomplishments in research or education or original contributions to the literature of the field. *Offered by:* Library and Information Technology Association. *Winner:* Philip L. Long.

LRRT Research Award—$500. To encourage excellence in library research. *Offered by:* ALA Library Research Round Table. *Winners:* George D'Elia and Sandra Walsh, for "User Satisfaction with Library Service—A Measure of Public Library Performance."

Joseph W. Lippincott Award—$1,000. For distinguished service to the profession of librarianship, such service to include outstanding participation in the activities of professional library associations, notable published professional writing, or other significant activity on behalf of the profession and its aims. *Offered by:* ALA Awards Committee. *Donor:* Joseph W. Lippincott. *Winner:* Keith Doms.

MLA Minority Scholarship—$2,000. For a minority student entering an ALA-accredited library school. *Offered by:* Medical Library Association. *Winner:* Maimie McCain Doss, Univ. of Missouri School of Library and Information Science.

MLA President's Award. For an outstanding contribution to medical librarianship. *Offered by:* Medical Library Association. *Winner:* Scott Adams.

Margaret Mann Citation. For outstanding professional achievement in the area of cataloging and classification. *Offered by:* ALA Resources and Technical Services Division/Cataloging and Classification Section. *Winner:* Elizabeth Baughman.

Allie Beth Martin Award—$2,000. For an outstanding librarian. *Offered by:* ALA Public Library Association. *Donor:* Baker & Taylor. *Winner:* Murray L. Bob.

Frederic G. Melcher Scholarship—$4,000. For young people who wish to enter the field of library service to children. *Offered by:* ALA Association for Library Service to Children. *Winners:* Mary Kay Riedl and Janice L. Sevy.

Isadore Gilbert Mudge Citation. For a distinguished contribution to reference librarianship. *Offered by:* Reference and Adult Services Division of American Library Association. *Winner:* Robert L. Collison.

Gerd Muehsam Award—$70. For the best paper by a graduate student in library or information science on a topic dealing with art librarianship or visual resource curatorship. *Offered by:* Art Libraries Society of North America. *Winner:* Matthew Hogan.

Noyes Award—$250 and travel expenses to MLA annual meeting. For an outstanding contribution to medical librarianship. *Offered by:* Medical Library Association. *Winner:* Samuel Hitt, Univ. of North Carolina Health Sciences Library, Chapel Hill, N.C.

Shirley Olofson Memorial Award. For individuals to attend their second annual conference of ALA. *Offered by:* ALA Junior Members Round Table. *Winners:* Mollie Fein, Jeanette Larson, and Ann Lowman.

Helen Keating Ott Award. Presented to an individual or institution for a significant contribution to children's literature. *Offered by:* Church and Synagogue Library Association. *Winner:* Not awarded in 1982.

Howard V. Phalin-World Book Graduate Scholarship in Library Science—$2,500 (maximum). For a Canadian citizen or landed immigrant to attend an accredited library school in Canada or the United States. *Offered by:* Canadian Library Association. *Winner:* Margaret Taylor, Ottawa, Ont., Canada.

Esther J. Piercy Award. For contribution to librarianship in the field of technical services by younger members of the profession. *Offered by:* ALA Resources and Technical Services Division. *Winner:* Nancy R. John.

Plenum Scholarship Award—$1,000. For graduate study leading to a doctorate in library or information science. *Offered by:* Special Libraries Association. *Winner:* Sydney Keaveney.

Rittenhouse Award—$200. For the best unpublished paper on medical librarianship submitted by a student enrolled in, or having been enrolled in, a course for credit in an ALA-accredited library school, or a trainee in an internship program in medical librarianship. *Offered by:* Medical Library Association. *Winner:* Jane Loftin, Louisiana State Univ., School of Library and Information Science.

SLA Hall of Fame. For an extended and sustained period of distinguished service to the Special Libraries Association in all spheres of its activities. *Offered by:* Special Libraries Association. *Winner:* Alleen Thompson.

SLA Minority Stipends—$2,000. For students with financial need who show potential for special librarianship. *Offered by:* Special Libraries Association. *Winners:* Elois Moore, Warren Christian, and Velma Haley.

SLA Scholarships—$5,000. For students with financial need who show potential for special librarianship. *Offered by:* Special Libraries Association. *Winners:* Agnes Ann Fitzgibbons and Magdaline Quinlan.

Charles Scribner's Sons Award—$325. To attend ALA's annual conference. *Offered by:* ALA Association for Library Service to Children. *Donor:* Charles Scribner's Sons. *Winners:* Robin A. Branslator, Jeanette D. Newsom, Susan Melcher, and Judy G. Mizik.

John Sessions Memorial Award. For significant efforts to work with the labor community. *Offered by:* ALA Reference and Adult Services Division. *Winner:* The Robert F. Wagner Archives of the Tamiment Institute Library, New York Univ.

Ralph R. Shaw Award for Library Literature—$500. For an outstanding contribution to library literature issued during the three years preceding the presentation. *Offered by:* ALA Awards Committee. *Donor:* Scarecrow Press. *Winner:* Sheila A. Egoff, for *Thursday's Child* (ALA).

3M Company Professional Development Grant. To encourage professional development and participation of new librarians in ALA and JMRT activities. To cover expenses for recipients to attend ALA conference. *Offered by:* ALA Junior Members Round Table. *Winners:* Laureen Carol Bowman, Victoria Lee Steele, and P. Steven Thomas.

Trustee Citations. For distinguished service to library development whether on the local, state, or national level. *Offered by:* ALA American Library Trustee Association. *Donor:* ALA. *Winners:* Esther Lopato and Wilda Marston.

H. W. Wilson Co. Award—$500. For the best paper published in *Special Libraries* in 1981. *Offered by:* Special Libraries Association. *Winner:* Barbara Robinson, for "The Role of Special Libraries in the Emerging National Network" (January 1981).

H. W. Wilson Foundation Award—$2,000. Available to Canadian citizen or landed immigrant for pursuit of studies at an accredited Canadian library school. *Offered by:* Canadian Library Association. *Winner:* Gloria Anderson, Ottawa, Ont., Canada.

H. W. Wilson Library Periodical Award—$500. To a periodical published by a local, state, or regional library, library group, or library association in the United States or Canada that has made an outstanding contribution to librarianship. *Offered by:* ALA Awards Committee. *Donor:* H. W. Wilson Co. *Winner: Show-Me Libraries* (Missouri State Library), ed. by Madeline Matson.

H. W. Wilson Library Staff Development Grant—$250. *Offered by:* ALA Awards Committee. *Winner:* Rhode Island Dept. of State Library Services.

Justin Windsor Essay Prize—$500. For excellence in research in library history. *Offered by:* ALA Library History Round Table. *Winners:* Pamela Spence Richards, for "Aryan Librarianship: Academic and Research Libraries under Hitler"; and Wayne A. Wiegand, for "British Propaganda in American Public Libraries, 1914-1917."

George Wittenborn Memorial Award. For excellence of content and physical design of an art book, exhibition catalog, and/or periodical published in North America. *Offered by:* Art Libraries Society of North America. *Winners:* Brown Univ., Dept. of Art; Abbeville Press; Yale Univ. Press; National Gallery of Art; and Yale Univ. Gallery.

World Book-Childcraft Awards—$1,000. For continuing education program, distributed to no more than four recipients (candidates must be members of Catholic Library Association). *Offered by:* Catholic Library Association. *Winner:* To be announced.

Part 4
Research and Statistics

Library Research and Statistics

RESEARCH ON LIBRARIES AND LIBRARIANSHIP IN 1982

Mary Jo Lynch
Director, American Library Association Office for Research

Financial retrenchment definitely affected research on libraries and librarianship in 1982. Funds for such activities were cut back in three federal agencies—the Department of Education, the National Library of Medicine, and the National Science Foundation. The American Library Association considered closing its Office for Research (OFR) at the Annual Conference in Philadelphia. OFR survived at that time, although secretarial staff was cut in the fall.

At the same time, several organizations in the library community made funds available for research, albeit in small amounts. ALA's Association of College and Research Libraries (ACRL) established two annual awards made possible by the Institute for Scientific Information (ISI) in Philadelphia. The Samuel Lazerow Fellowship for Outstanding Contributions to Acquisitions or Technical Services in an Academic or Research Library supplies $1,000 to foster advances in acquisitions or technical services by providing a practicing librarian with funds for research, travel, or writing. The second award, the ACRL Doctoral Dissertation Fellowship, provides an award of $1,000 to a doctoral student working on a dissertation in the area of academic librarianship. The Young Adult Services Division (YASD) also established an annual award for research in cooperation with the periodical *VOYA (Voice of Youth Advocates)*. The YASD/VOYA Research Grant of $500 provides seed money for small-scale projects in order to "encourage significant research that will have an influence on library service to young adults."

Another research-related award was established in 1982 by the Association of American Library Schools. This organization has had a research grant award for several years which supported research related to education for library and information science. Now it also sponsors a "Research Paper Competition" open only to members of the organization but available to recognize excellence in papers concerning research on any aspect of librarianship or information studies. Up to two willing papers will be selected each year with an honorarium of $500 awarded to each paper. [For additional information on these AALS awards, see the AALS report in Part 1—*Ed.*]

TECHNICAL SERVICES

The most exciting research news of the year was previewed in January just before ALA's Midwinter Meeting in Denver. Participants in the online public access catalog (OPAC) evaluation project presented results of the pretest for their study of online catalog user behavior and needs. This project, sponsored by the Council on Library Resources (CLR) involves five participants—OCLC (Online Computer Library Center), the Research Libraries Group (RLG), the Library of Congress, Joseph Matthews and Associates, and the University of California Division of Library Automation. During 1982, 7,000 users of online catalogs at research, college, community college, public and government libraries and 3,000 people who had not used the online catalog at these institutions were asked to respond to questions about their attitudes toward online catalogs and their recent experiences with them. Seventeen different online catalogs were included in the study. In general, users are enthusiastic about online catalogs but do have trouble with some aspects of some systems. A final report of the study will be published early in 1983.

Already available is Charles Hildreth's *Online Public Access Catalogs: The User Interface* (OCLC, 1982), which was based on part of OCLC's April 1982 report to CLR on all aspects of OCLC's work on the project. The Hildreth monograph summarizes results of OCLC's effort to establish "some basic understanding of ten operating online public access catalogs"—a task made difficult by the fact that not only were the ten systems quite different from one another, but all were in the process of changing as the study was in progress. The report includes state-of-the-art reviews of both "The User-System Interface" and "Human Communication with Computers," as well as substantial information on the major components of the user-system interface in online catalogs at ten project sites, an overview of the hardware and software architecture and file structures at three sites, and a 24-page "Project Glossary" developed "because no uniform terminology exists for describing and analyzing the properties and behavior of online catalogs."

Online catalogs are only one aspect of library technical services that has inspired research. Many others were considered at an all day Conference-within-a-Conference on "Research By, For and About Librarians" in Philadelphia. The day-long program included plenary sessions featuring papers by Michael Buckland, Joseph Hewitt, and Jane Robbins-Carter, and smaller sessions organized by each of the five sections of ALA's Resources and Technical Services Division (RTSD)—Cataloging and Classification, Preservation of Library Materials, Reproduction of Library Materials, Resources, and Serials. Audiotapes of this meeting are available from ALA and some of the papers will be published in *Library Resources and Technical Services* and elsewhere.

COPYRIGHT

When the Copyright Law of 1976 was passed Congress was concerned that it achieve a balancing of the needs of users and the rights of owners of copyrighted materials. To ensure that this happens, the law directs the Register of Copyrights to report on the intended balancing every five years. In order to help the Register conduct the first of these five-year reviews in 1983, the Copyright Office contracted with King Research, Inc. (KRI) for "the gathering and analyzing of data which will help to assess whether or not section 108 of the Copyright Act of 1976 has achieved the intended statutory balancing between the rights of creators and the needs of users of copyrighted works." The results of that effort were published as *Libraries, Publishers, and Photocopying: Final Report of Surveys Conducted for the United States Copyright Office* (King Research, Inc., 1982).

Six data collection efforts were part of the study—three involving libraries, two involving library users, and one involving publishers. In phase one of the "Library Photocopying Survey," 790 libraries were asked for general information about such things as photocopying machines in or near the library, interlibrary loan requests, photocopy permission requests and computerized searches of bibliographic data bases. In phase two, a smaller sample of libraries were asked to provide detailed information about interlibrary loan requests and about photocopy transactions. Two user surveys were conducted—one of all patrons entering 21 different libraries and one of 823 library patrons making photocopies in 19 different libraries. Finally, serial and book publishers were asked to provide information on such topics as number of titles published, prices, revenue, photocopy permission requests and sales of reprints and article copies. Reaction to this extensive and carefully done report varied widely. In response to the Register of Copyright's request for comment on *Libraries, Publishers, and Photocopying*, ALA noted that the report supported its contention that the law is working effectively. The American Association of Publishers (AAP) took a different perspective. AAP believes that the study supports their request for several changes in the statute and the development of additional guidelines. It remains to be seen what opinion will be expressed in the Register's report to Congress, which is due January 1983.

See the five-year review of the new copyright law in the Special Reports section of Part 1; also see the annual report from the Copyright Office in the Federal Agencies section of Part 1—*Ed.*

SALARIES

In response to many requests for information about the compensation of librarians, the ALA Office for Research and Office for Library Personnel Resources designed a survey of librarian salaries. The survey, conducted in January 1982 with assistance from the Library Research Center of the Graduate School of Library and Information Science of the University of Illinois, requested information from public and academic libraries regarding salaries scheduled and paid to librarians in thirteen different professional positions. Tables in the report show results for five types of libraries in each of the four regions of the United States. The report also includes several appendixes, among which are an annotated bibliography of "Salary Surveys Providing Information on Library Workers" and a comprehensive essay on "Employee Compensation and the Library Manager." ALA intends to conduct such surveys regularly.

Another source of information on salaries became available for the first time in 1982. *Library Compensation Review* is "A Quarterly Survey of Salaries and Benefits Offered by Employers of Librarians and Information Specialists." This periodical presents, for 23 library positions, the salaries offered in advertisements in ten different periodicals during the previous quarter. Salaries for school librarians are not shown, but salaries offered to librarians in ten other types of library groups (e.g., academic library, law library, special library) are analyzed by type of position. Another set of tables shows salaries by type of library and position in the nine major zip code regions of the United States.

[See the reports in Part 3, "Placements and Salaries, 1981: Still Holding" and "Sex, Salaries, and Library Support, 1981"—*Ed.*]

THE AMERICAN LIBRARY ASSOCIATION

The Association of College and Research Libraries (ACRL) established three task forces with implications for research. An Ad Hoc Task Force on the Research Needs of Academic/Research Libraries was charged to "develop recommendations of appropriate mechanisms within ACRL by which the Association can establish and maintain on a continuing basis a short agenda of research priorities for academic and research libraries and to recommend the means by which these priorities may be made known to key funding entities." This task force was established partly because of dissatisfaction with "A Library and Information Science Research Agenda for the 1980's," which was rejected by some ACRL leaders as not responsive to the needs of academic libraries. That agenda had been developed in the summer of 1981 by a carefully selected group of prominent researchers and practitioners working with Cuadra Associates under contract to the Department of Education.

ACRL's Task Force on Performance Measures is charged "to determine whether ACRL should undertake to develop performance measures for academic libraries; and if so, to develop a plan of action for doing so for consideration by the ACRL Board." The Task Force on Library Statistics is charged to "define the statistical needs of academic libraries; examine whether or how these needs are being currently met; suggest ways ACRL could aid academic libraries and the profession by generating and/or disseminating these statistics and the concomitant costs of each." All three task forces will begin work at Midwinter 1983.

The American Association of School Librarians devoted considerable space to research in their journal, *School Library Media Quarterly*. The Winter and Spring 1982 issues (vol. 10, nos. 2 and 3) featured a thorough review of research in that field of librarianship. David Loertscher, who edited this series, also led a panel discussion at AASL's Houston conference in October on the subject of what should be done to improve the research base for the school library media field.

At the Philadelphia conference, "Research Forums" were sponsored by several ALA units. The American Association of School Librarians scheduled one on its own and another was sponsored jointly by the Association of Library Service to Children, the Young Adult Services Division, and the Public Library Association. The Library Research Round Table (LRRT) continued its policy of sponsoring both formal "Research Forums" for the presentation of research results and an Information Exchange Suite for informal discussion of research in progress. LRRT's annual Research Award was given to a paper on "User Satisfaction with Library Service—A Measure of Public Library Performance?" which was the work of George D'Elia of the University of Minnesota and Sandra Walsh of Ramsey County (Minnesota) Public Library.

The Philadelphia conference also featured ALA's first annual Poster Session, borrowing a concept that is popular at meetings of other professional associations. Typically, poster sessions present research findings, innovative programs, or solutions to problems. A reading of the abstracts led this writer to conclude that at least 25 percent of the 100 entries in Philadelphia could be described as research. This program innovation was successful and will be repeated in 1983.

LIBRARY AND INFORMATION SCIENCE EDUCATION

The Department of Education issued only one Request for Proposal (RFP) in fiscal 1982—a long-awaited RFP to study "New Directions for Library and Information Science Education." According to the RFP, this 18-month project will "identify the present and future competencies needed by library and information science professionals" and "examine the education requirements necessary to achieve those competencies." In late September a contract was awarded to King Research, Inc. (KRI) to conduct the study. A press release from KRI indicates that their work will promote communication among the participants in the process of educating and employing library and information science professionals. In the "New Directions" study "a planning process will be established to identify, define, describe and validate competencies; define education and training requirements; design and implement curricula; establish and validate measures of competency attainment; and evaluate curricula." KRI will take the planning process through one complete cycle during the course of this project and will "document the process so that it can be repeated as desired by the profession."

NATIONAL CENTER FOR EDUCATION STATISTICS

Several sources of numerical data to support research and development efforts in the library field were released by the National Center for Education Statistics (NCES) in 1982. *Statistics of Public Libraries 1977-78* continues the series of public library surveys conducted every four years. [For a report on the results of the 1977-1978 survey, see the 1982 edition of the *Bowker Annual*, pp. 329-338—*Ed.*] *Statistics of Library Networks and Cooperative Organizations 1977-78* is an initial effort at presenting summary data about this increasingly important area of library service. The survey which produced data for this publication also gathered data for a directory of these organizations which was published by NCES in 1980. [See the 1982 edition of the *Bowker Annual*, pp. 344-351, for a report on the results of the survey—*Ed.*] Continuing a series published approximately every two years is *Library Statistics of Colleges and Universities 1979, Institutional Data*. [See the 1981 edition of the *Bowker Annual*, pp. 287-303—*Ed.*] Summary data to accompany this publication was prepared by NCES and published by the Association of College and Research Libraries as *Library Statistics of Colleges and Universities, Summary Data, 1979*.

U.S. PUBLIC LIBRARY STATISTICS IN SERIES: A BIBLIOGRAPHY AND SUBJECT INDEX

Herbert Goldhor

Director, Library Research Center, Graduate School of Library and Information Science, University of Illinois, Urbana, IL

This report is a bibliography and subject index to public library statistics from 34 publications that appeared at least once between 1977 and 1982 and at least twice between 1973 and 1982, and are expected to appear again in the future on a more or less regular basis. Also indexed are some of the one-time counts or surveys. [For an analysis of the public library statistics compiled by state (and provincial) library agencies for the year 1974, see the 1978 edition of the *Bowker Annual*, pp. 215-234—*Ed.*]

The focus of this report is U.S. public libraries; compilations of data on other countries are included only when they are useful for comparison. For example, several sources that include data for a number of countries, one of which is the United States, are included, as well as one compilation dealing exclusively with Canadian public libraries and another on public libraries in the United Kingdom. By the same token, some series indexed here are of data relating to book prices, book title production, and other topics closely related to the work of public libraries.

The bibliography includes the latest edition of each statistics compilation (as of 1982). Earlier editions of a compilation may or may not have had the same exact title or publisher or cover exactly the same subjects, and changes in future editions are to be expected. (Measurable differences have occurred between the state library agency statistical compilations produced in 1974—referred to earlier in this report—and those that are currently being produced.) To better handle such changes in the future, all relevant data (not just state library agency data and compilations in series) will be indexed in the computerized data base known as the *Fact Book of the American Public Library*, which has been developed at the University of Illinois Library Research Center over the last few years.

A preliminary version of the *Fact Book* appeared in 1981 [Herbert Goldhor, comp., *Fact Book of the American Public Library*. Occasional Papers no. 150 (Urbana:

University of Illinois Graduate School of Library and Information Science, August 1981), 79 pp.]. The computerized online version is essentially the same—a subject index to statistical data relevant to any aspect of public library operation, with a brief summary of those data and a bibliographical reference to the original source—e.g., a journal article, a book, an annual report of a library, the report of a survey or other research. The computerized data bank uses a controlled vocabulary and can be interrogated by subject. Access to the data base is free (for the present); inquiries are invited by phone (217-333-1980) or mail (410 David Kinley Hall, University of Illinois, 1407 W. Gregory Dr., Urbana, IL 61801-3680), and a printout of the requested information will be sent promptly.

Readers are invited to send us notices of omissions and errors, suggestions for the future, and other comments. Compilers of any statistical publications relating to public libraries are requested to send a copy of each edition to the Library Research Center for inclusion in the *Fact Book* data base.

BIBLIOGRAPHY

The compilations that are represented in this list are arranged into four groups (there is no significance to the other of listing within each of the groups):

A. Compilations that cover all of the United States.
B. Those that cover only a part of the United States (usually two or more states).
C. Those that cover one or more countries, but not the United States.
D. Those that cover one or more countries, including the United States.

The symbol "I" (following the slash in a reference number) indicates that the data are given solely for "individual" libraries; "T" (following the slash) indicates that "totals, subtotals, averages, or other measures" are given in addition to figures for individual libraries. If no letter follows the reference number, no data are given for individual institutions.

A1/T   Helen M. Eckard, *Statistics of Public Libraries, 1977-1978*, NCES 82-204. (Washington, D.C., National Center for Education Statistics, 1982). 132 pp. (A summary appears in *Bowker Annual, 1982*, pp. 329-338.) Some data are given for each of 334 U.S. public libraries (by name), which served more than 100,000 people in 1978, arranged alphabetically by state and then by city. Other data are given for FY 1977 or for 1978 for all U.S. public libraries, for each of six population size groups (and for other categories), in regard to service outlets, staff, income by source, expenditures by category, collections, circulation, hours and days open, and buildings. A previous compilation was done in 1978 with 1974 data.

A2   Chandler B. Grannis, "Statistical Report: 1981 Domestic Title Output and Price Averages," *Publishers Weekly*, October 1, 1982, pp. 40-41. Preliminary figures appeared in *Publishers Weekly*, March 12, 1982, pp. 42-46, and were reprinted in the *Bowker Annual of Library and Book Trade Information*, 27th ed. (New York: R. R. Bowker Co., 1982), pp. 383-391. Published annually. For each of about 25 subjects, gives the number of hardcover books and of trade paperbacks published in the United States and their average list price.

A3   "Indexes of American Public Library Circulation and Expenditures," *American Libraries* 13 (July/August 1982): 458. Based on data from a random sample of 50 libraries, each serving more than 25,000 people.

A4 "Book Review Media Statistics," in the *Bowker Annual of Library and Book Trade Information*, 27th ed. (New York: R. R. Bowker Co., 1982), p. 414. Published annually. For each of 11 journals, gives the number of adult, juvenile, young adult, and total titles reviewed for each of the last two years.

A5 International Personnel Management Association, *Pay Rates in the Public Service: Survey of 62 Common Job Classes in the Public Sector* (Washington, D.C., 1982), pp. 39–40. Has salary data (minimum, maximum, median, and quartiles) for 1,600 to 1,800 positions in more than 200 jurisdictions at five levels of government, including junior librarian and librarian (second-level professional position). Also shown are the number of steps to the maximum, the number of hours of work per week, and four regional subtotals for each of the five levels. This survey has been conducted (and the results published) annually for more than 12 years.

A6 "Public and Academic Library Acquisition Expenditures," in the *Bowker Annual of Library and Book Trade Information*, 27th ed. (New York: R. R. Bowker Co., 1982), pp. 316–318. Published annually. Gives data for each state (with U.S. total) on number of libraries for which acquisition expenditures were supplied for the *American Library Directory*, the dollar total and the subtotals for books, periodicals, audiovisuals, microforms, binding, and "unspecified."

A7/I Joseph Green, "Urban-Suburban Public Library Statistics," in *Bowker Annual of Library and Book Trade Information*, 27th ed. (New York: R. R. Bowker Co., 1982), pp. 321-328. Published annually. For each of 50 large public libraries gives data on finances, services, staff, and work load, for each of the last two years.

A8 Urban Libraries Council, *Pocket Facts about Public Libraries* (Chicago, 1982), 9 pp. Published annually for at least four years. For each state, gives total appropriation for direct aid to public libraries, for public and multitype library systems and networks, for buildings, total state aid, and per capita.

A9 Norman B. Brown and Jane Phillips, "Price Indexes for 1982 U.S. Periodicals and Serial Services," *Library Journal*, August 1982, pp. 1379-1382. Published annually. Has data on prices of periodicals in up to 24 different subject fields.

A10/I ALA Association of Specialized and Cooperative Library Agencies, *Salary Data-State Library Agencies* (Chicago, 1981), 4 pp. For each of the 50 states, gives salary (or salary range) of each of eight positions or position groups. Also published in 1979 and 1980.

A11 U.S. Bureau of the Census, *Public Employment in 1979*. GE 79, no. 1 (Washington, D.C.: GPO, 1980). Other titles in this series, all published in 1980, are:
———. *City Employment in 1979*. GE 79, no. 2.
———. *Local Government Employment in Selected Metropolitan Areas and Large Counties: 1979*. GE 79, no. 3.
———. *County Government Employment in 1979*. GE 79, no. 4.

A12 U.S. Bureau of the Census, *State Government Finances in 1979*. GF 79, no. 3. (Washington, D.C.: GPO, 1980). Other titles in this series, all published in 1980, are:
———. *City Government Finances in 1978-79*. GF 79, no. 4.
———. *Governmental Finances in 1978-79*. GF 79, no. 5.

_____. *Local Government Finances in Selected Metropolitan Areas and Large Counties: 1978–79.* GF 79, no. 6.

_____. *County Government Finances in 1978–79.* GF 79, no. 8.

A13 U.S. Bureau of the Census, *Employment of Major Local Governments.* Vol. 3, no. 1 of 1977 Census of Governments (Washington, D.C.: GPO, 1979).

_____. *Compendium of Public Employment.* Vol. 3, no. 2.

_____. *Local Government in Metropolitan Areas.* Vol. 5. The Census of Governments is done every five years.

A14/I Minneapolis (Minn.) Public Library and Information Center, *1981 City Public Library Circulation and Central Library Attendance Survey: Summary* (Minneapolis, 1982), 3 pp. Published annually since at least 1976. Includes data on each of up to 59 of the largest U.S. municipal public libraries.

A15 University of Arizona Graduate Library School, *Library Compensation Review: A Quarterly Survey of Salaries and Benefits Offered by Employers of Librarians and Information Specialists* 1 (Winter 1982): 1–29. To be published quarterly. Has data on the number of position vacancies in U.S. public libraries that were advertised in previous calendar quarter, distributed by a dozen or so job categories and ten regions of the United States, with average high and low salaries offered.

A16 John P. Dessauer, "Book Industry Markets, 1976–1985," in *Book Industry Trends, 1981,* Research Report no. 11. (New York: Book Industry Study Group, 1981). Published annually since 1977. Tables 4, 4A, 5, and 5A have data on U.S. public library acquisitions of eight types of materials (including binding).

A17 Anita W. Heard, "Fringe Benefits in Large Public Libraries of the United States—The Professional's Guide," *Public Libraries* 21 (Fall 1982): 83–87. Based on responses from 74 libraries with annual budgets of more than $1 million each. Also published in 1980 and 1981.

B1/T Carl R. Sandstedt, comp., *1982 Salary Survey: West-North-Central States* (St. Peters, Mo.; St. Charles City-County Library, 1982), 4 pp. Published annually since 1977. Data for each of about 90 public libraries, 12 systems, and the state library agencies in 6 states in regard to (a) salaries for 7 positions, and (b) 7 budget items; plus range and mean salary of each position for each of 6 budget size groups.

B2/I Memphis and Shelby County (Tenn.) Public Library and Information Center, *1982 Statistics of Southern Public Libraries* (Memphis, 1982), 3 pp. Issued for several years at least. Data given for each of about 100 public libraries (with budgets of more than $300,000) in regard to beginning or actual salary paid each of six professional positions, plus total salaries, expenditures for materials, total budget, total circulation, and population served.

B3/I Library Administrators Conference of Northern Illinois, *LACONI Salary Survey: 1981* (Bellwood, Ill., LACONI, 1981) unpaged. Published annually. For each of 168 public libraries in northern Illinois, has various miscellaneous data (size of building, hours open, etc.) and for each position or group of positions has salary or salary range, full or part time, education of incumbent, years of experience, number of persons supervised, etc.

B4/I   Iowa State Office for Planning and Programming, Division of Local Government Affairs, Local Government Personnel Services Center, *Iowa Local Government Salary and Benefit Survey: 1982*, 10th ed. (Des Moines, 1982), 128 pp. Since 1972. For each of 134 Iowa municipalities (serving more than 2,000 people), gives the salary of up to 131 classes of positions in 16 city departments, including library director, supervising librarian, librarian, and library aide. The number of positions in each class is shown.

B5/T   Illinois Municipal League, *1981 Municipal Compensation Survey* (Springfield, Ill., 1981), 298 pp. Has minimum and maximum salary for "librarian," along with the number of such employees, for each of up to 227 municipalities of more than 5,000 population. For towns under and over 10,000 population, the mean and median salaries are shown for five geographic subdivisions of the state and for all cities. This survey has been published for each of the last several years.

B6   Metropolitan Washington Council of Governments, Metropolitan Washington Library Council, *Annual Statistical Data for Public Libraries in Metropolitan Washington: Fiscal Year 1981* (Washington, D.C., n.d.), 55 pp. For each of nine public libraries in Maryland, the District of Columbia, and Virginia, gives data on services (number of branches, number of bookmobiles, and number of reference questions), statistical information (population served, receipts by source, holdings by type of material, circulation, interlibrary loans, and expenditures by category), fringe benefits (insurance, retirement, hours of work, sick leave, and vacation allowance), and salary ranges (for clerical, paraprofessional, and junior professional employees, associate director, and director).

B7/T   Edward A. Howard, comp. "Larger Public Libraries in Indiana," (Evansville: Evansville-Vanderburgh County [Ind.] Public Library, August 1982), 2 pp. Has salary data for each of 24 libraries (by name), with median and average for the group, in regard to current year's salary for a beginning clerk and for a new library school graduate. Fringe benefit data include the number of paid holidays, the number of paid sick days, and percentage of hospital insurance premium paid by employer. The adjusted hourly rate of pay for a beginning clerk is calculated by subtracting holidays and vacation allowance from official work year. Also shown are population served, assessed valuation, next year's anticipated expenditures, and this year's budget distribution for salaries, materials, and all other expenses. There was at least one earlier edition.

C1/T   Chartered Institute of Public Finance and Accountancy, *Public Library Statistics, 1980-81 Actuals* (London, 1982), 27 pp. Published annually. For all 166 public library authorities in the United Kingdom, has data on income and expenditures, staff, service points, book stock, circulation, interlibrary loans, etc.

C2   *The Book Report* (London, Euromonitor Publications, 1981). Includes the annual Euromonitor Book Readership Survey, which had appeared separately in five earlier years. The 1981 survey was not seen, but the 1980 edition (88 pp.) had interview responses of 2,000 adults in the United Kingdom and data on U.K. book production.

C3/T   Statistics Canada, *Culture Statistics: Public Libraries in Canada*, no. 87-651 (Ottawa, 1981), 45 pp. Published annually. Has data for all of Canada, for each of 12 provinces, and for each of about 20 census metropolitan areas and about 30 large census urban centers by name.

D1/T Jaques Cattell Press, ed., *American Library Directory*, 35th ed. (New York: R. R. Bowker Co., 1982), 1,917 pp. Published annually. Lists more than 9,500 public libraries in the United States and Canada with data on each (obtained by questionnaire) on income and expenditures, population served, holdings, circulation, etc.; includes some state and national totals. Summary data on the number of public libraries and branches are reprinted each year in *Bowker Annual*.

D2/T "Public Library Buildings," *Library Journal*, December 1, 1982, pp. 2222-2228. Published annually and reprinted in *Bowker Annual of Library and Book Trade Information* in the following year. Detailed data are given by state (or province) and then by city for the United States and Canada for new buildings, additions, and remodeling; also includes a cost summary over the last several years.

D3 Nelson A. Piper, "Prices of U.S. and Foreign Published Materials," in *Bowker Annual of Library and Book Trade Information*, 27th ed. (New York: R. R. Bowker Co., 1982), pp. 396-405. Published annually. Has average prices and number of titles in each of the last four years for 25 subject areas for several media (including periodicals, hard- and softcover books, and microfilm).

D4/I Allen County (Ind.) Public Library, *Statistics of Public Libraries in the United States and Canada Serving 100,000 Population or More* (Ft. Wayne, 1981), 9 pp. Published biennially. For more than 300 public libraries, gives four expenditures figures and the salaries of the director, the assistant director, and beginning professional librarian. For a summary and analyses of these data, see item D5.

D5 Kathleen M. Heim and Carolyn Kacena, "Sex, Salaries and Library Support, 1981," *Library Journal*, September 15, 1981, pp. 1692-1699. Usually reprinted in *Bowker Annual of Library and Book Trade Information*. Fifth of a series, based on item D4.

D6 Carol L. Learmont and Stephen Van Houton, "Placements and Salaries 1981: Still Holding," *Library Journal*, October 1, 1982, pp. 1821-1827. Published annually since 1951. Number of new graduates from accredited library schools in the United States and Canada; placement and salary data by type of library and by sex. Usually reprinted in *Bowker Annual*.

D7/T International City Management Association, "Salaries of Municipal Officials for 1981," in *The Municipal Year Book: 1982* (Washington, D.C., 1982), pp. 73-87, 91-93. Published annually. Has mean and quartiles of salaries of head librarians of about 1,500 U.S. cities in each of several population size groups and by geographic region, city type, and form of government. The head librarian's salary is shown for over half of all 200 Canadian public libraries serving more than 10,000 people each. Also published in *Urban Data Service Report*.

SUBJECT INDEX

The subject index includes some 61 subject headings (with definitions in parentheses), followed by the corresponding reference numbers from the bibliography. (Some cross-references also are included.) There are 278 references in the subject index to the 34 compilations of data in the bibliography. This is an arithmetic average of 8.2 references (and a median of 4) per compilation, with a range from 1 to 34. The four compilations with the largest number of references (A1, B6, C1, C3), with 25 to 34 references each, account for 42% of all index references, while 17, with 1 to 4 references each, account for only 15%.

When we divide the 61 subject headings into related groups and compare the results with those of the 1974 study conducted by the state library agencies, we find the following:

	References		
	Goldhor Study		1974 Study
Group	No.	%	(%)
Finances	88	32	40
Staff and salaries	80	29	5
Library materials	49	17	21
Public services	38	14	19
Miscellaneous	23	8	15
	278	100%	100%

Finances, the group with the largest number of references, had a stronger representation in the 1974 analysis of state library agency statistics. The staff and salaries category represents 29% of the 278 index references, compared with only 5% for the 1974 compilations; clearly, repeat compilations are compensating for the minimal attention given to this subject in the state library agency statistics. Data on library materials are 17% of all references in this study and 21% of the 1974 study; public services 14% (vs. 19%); and miscellaneous topics 8% (vs. 15%).

Agencies (number of various kinds; population served per agency): A1, C1, C3

Audiovisual materials (number held or number added—not separated out by specific type and regardless of method of counting): A1, C3, D1. *See also* Materials, miscellaneous library

Audiovisual materials price index: A16, D3

Binding price index: A16
See also Finances-Expenditures for Library Materials—Binding and Rebinding

Book collection, annual additions to (titles or volumes; ratio to volumes held; or separately for various subdivisions, with percentages of total and per capita): A1, A16, C1, C2, C3

Book collection, composition of (separately for lending and reference books, adult fiction, adult nonfiction, and juvenile; by title or by volume; by language; by hardback or paperback; and per capita): C1, C3

Book collection—number of titles/volumes held (per capita): A1, B3, B6, C3, D1

Book price index (hardback; quality and mass market paperbacks; British books; adult and juvenile; trade and reference/subscription books; and breakdown by subject): A2, A16, C2, D3

Book reviews (number of reviews of adult, young adult, and juvenile books): A4

Bookmobiles (number; number of stops; expenditures for): A1, B6, C1, C3, D1

Branch libraries (number and circulation): A1, B6, D1, D4
See also Buildings

Buildings (number of square feet; linear feet of shelving; number of reader seats; costs and sources of funds; new buildings, additions, remodeling, and leased space for central libraries or branches): A1, B3, C3, D2

Central library data (circulation; visitors; book stock; and hours open): A14
See also Buildings

Circulation (annual totals per capita, per FTE staff; composition by adult and juvenile, fiction, and nonfiction; annual index value): A1, A3, A7, A14, B2, B3, B6, C1, C2, C3, D1, D4

Directors (sex; number of years on job; similar data for assistant directors): B3, D4, D5
  See also Salaries of directors

Employees, nonprofessional (clerical or building employees; per capita; FET; extent of formal education): A1, B3, C3

Employees, professional (per capita; FTE; position vacancies; number of new library school graduates added per year; sex; full-time or part-time status; ratio to nonprofessional employees; number of persons supervised; extent of formal education): A1, A7, A15, B3, C1, C3, D6

Employees, total number of (per capita; FTE; by size of population served; by different types of local government units): A1, A7, A11, A13, A17, B1, B3, C1, C3, D1

Films (number held and number added per year, 8mm or 16mm): A1, B6, C3

Finances-expenditures, capital: A1, B6, C1, C3

Finances-expenditures for equipment (separately for audiovisual and other equipment): A1, B6

Finances-expenditures for library materials (undistributed by type of material, or with data for multiple types—may or may not include binding; per capita and per circulation): A1, A3, A6, A7, A16, B1, B2, B7, C1, C3, D4

Finances-expenditures for library materials—audiovisuals (undistributed by type of material, or with data for multiple types): A1, A6, A16, B6, C3, D1

Finances-expenditures for library materials—binding and rebinding: A1, A6, A16, B6, C1, D1

Finances-expenditures for library materials—books: A1, A6, A16, B6, C1, C3

Finances-expenditures for library materials—microforms: A1, A6, A16, B6

Finances-expenditures for library materials—periodicals and newspapers: A1, A6, A16, B6, C1

Finances-expenditures for library materials—sound recordings: B6, C1

Finances-expenditures for plant operation and maintenance: A1, B6, C3

Finances-expenditures for salaries (for professional librarians, nonprofessional employees or both; for library employees in different types of local government units; may or may not include retirement fund contributions): A1, A3, A11, A13, B1, B2, B3, B6, B7, C1, C3, D4

Finances-expenditures, total (capital outlay plus operating expenditures; as percent of total city expenditures; by population size): A1, A12, A13, B2, B6, C1, C3

Finances-expenditures, total current operating (per capita; per FTE staff; sometimes with expenditure subdivisions and in annual index form): A1, A3, A7, A12, A13, B1, B7, C3, D1, D4, D5

Finances-income—state and federal aid: A1, A7, A8, A12, C3, D1

Finance-income, total (per capita and with analysis by sources): A1, B6, C1, C3, D1

Fringe benefits (paid holidays; vacations; sick leave; retirement; health insurance; etc.): A17, B6, B7

Geographic region, distribution by: D5

Government (number of municipal, county, and special district libraries): A12, A13, D1

Hours of work (overtime pay, flextime, and work on Sundays): A5, A17, B3, B6

Hours open per week (Sunday opening and number of days open per week): A1, A17, B3, C1, C3

Interlibrary loans (either loans sent or loans received; geographic distribution of sources of loans; number of loans per agency): A1, B6, C1, C3

Materials, miscellaneous library (number added or number held; flat pictures, study prints, charts, games, maps, manuscripts, framed pictures, and vertical file drawers): A1, C1

See also Films; Microforms; Slides; Sound recordings

Microforms (number added or number held and titles or physical pieces): A1, B6, C1, C3
  See also Finances-expenditures for library materials—microforms

Microforms price index: A16, D3

Order work (percent of materials ordered direct, from wholesalers and from local bookstores): A16, C2

Periodicals (newspapers and serials: number held and number added; titles, copies, and bound volumes): A1, B6, C1, C3, D1
  See also Finances-expenditures for library materials—periodicals and newspapers

Periodicals price index (newspapers price index and serials price index): A9, A16, D3
  See also Book price index

Photocopies (from coin-operated machines and provided by libraries): C1

Population served: A1, A7, B1, B2, B6, B7, C1, D1, D4, D5

Public libraries, number of (by size of area served): A1, C1, C3, D1
  See also Government

Reference questions (per capita and per agency): A7, B6, C3

Salaries of clerical employees (pages and other hourly paid employees; starting clerical position): A17, B1, B2, B3, B4, B6, B7

Salaries of subprofessional employees: B1, B2, B3, B6

Salaries of beginning professional librarians (by sex; by regions of the country): A5, A10, A15, A17, B1, B2, B6, B7, D4, D5, D6

Salaries of professional librarians (by sex): A5, A10, A15, B3, B4

Salaries of assistant/associate directors and of department heads: A10, A15, B1, B2, B3, B4, B6, D4

Salaries of directors: A5, A10, A15, B1, B2, B3, B4, B5, B6, D4, D5, D7

Slides (number held or added): C3

Sound recordings (discs; tapes or cassettes; number added and number held): A1, B6, C1, C3
  See also Circulation; Finances-expenditures for library materials—sound recordings

Unions of library employees: A17, B1

Users/nonusers, public library (age; sex; social class; subject of book currently being read; source of that book; number of books bought on last purchase and whether hardback or paper, for whom, and on what subject): C2

Volunteers: B3

CHARACTERISTICS OF THE U.S. POPULATION SERVED BY LIBRARIES, 1982

W. Vance Grant

Head, Statistical Information Office, NCES

	Number	Percent
Total U.S. population (July 1, 1982)[a]	231,990,000	100.0
Resident population of 50 states and D.C.	231,479,000	99.8
Armed forces overseas	511,000	0.2
Resident population of U.S. outlying areas (July 1, 1981)[b]	3,629,000	—
U.S. population, five years and over, including armed forces abroad (July 1, 1982)[c]	214,627,000	100.0
5–9 years	15,945,000	7.4

CHARACTERISTICS OF THE U.S. POPULATION SERVED BY LIBRARIES, 1982 (cont.)

	Number	Percent
10–14 years	18,014,000	8.4
15–19 years	19,829,000	9.2
20–24 years	21,920,000	10.2
25–64 years	112,087,000	52.2
Age 65 and over	26,833,000	12.5
Public and private school enrollment (fall 1982)	57,178,000	100.0
Kindergarten through grade 8[d]	30,945,000	54.1
Grades 9–12[d]	13,875,000	24.3
Higher education, total enrollment[e]	12,358,000	21.6
Private school enrollment[f]	7,744,000	13.5
Kindergarten through grade 8[d]	3,625,000	11.7
Grades 9–12[d]	1,435,000	10.3
Higher education, total enrollment[e]	2,684,000	21.7
Educational status of population aged 25 and over		
Total aged 25 and over (March 1980)[g,h]	127,882,000	100.0
With four or more years of college	21,740,000	17.0
With one to three years of college	18,927,000	14.8
With four years of high school or more	87,727,000	68.6
With less than four years of high school	40,155,000	31.4
Residence in and outside metropolitan areas[g]		
Total noninstitutional population (April 1, 1980)[g]	226,500,000	100.0
Nonmetropolitan areas	57,100,000	25.2
Metropolitan areas	169,400,000	74.8
In central cities	67,900,000	30.0
Outside central cities	101,500,000	44.8
Employment status[i]		
Total noninstitutional population 16 years old and over (October 1982)	175,069,000	—
Civilian labor force, total[j]	110,644,000	100.0
Employed[j]	99,093,000	89.6
Unemployed[j]	11,551,000	10.4
Total faculty and students served by college and university libraries (fall 1982)[k]	13,228,000	100.0
Faculty[d]	870,000	6.6
Students[e]	12,358,000	93.4

[a] Estimates of the Bureau of the Census, *Current Population Reports*, Series P-25, No. 923.
[b] Estimates of the Bureau of the Census, *Current Population Reports*, Series P-25, No. 919.
[c] Unpublished projections of the Bureau of the Census (October 1982).
[d] Estimates of the National Center for Education Statistics, *Back-to-School* press release, September 5, 1982.
[e] Preliminary data from the National Center for Education Statistics survey of fall enrollment in higher education.
[f] A segment of public and private school enrollment reported above. Percentages for private school enrollment are based on the total figures for public and private school enrollment at each level.
[g] Data from the Bureau of the Census, *Statistical Abstract of the United States, 1981*.
[h] Numbers, derived from percentages, are approximations only.
[i] Data from the Bureau of Labor Statistics, published in *Economic Indicators*, November 1982.
[j] Seasonally adjusted.
[k] Includes full-time and part-time instructional staff and students.

NUMBER OF LIBRARIES IN THE UNITED STATES AND CANADA

Statistics are from the thirty-fifth edition of the *American Library Directory* (*ALD*) edited by Jaques Cattell Press (R. R. Bowker, 1982). In addition to listing and describing some 32,100 individual libraries, the thirty-fifth edition of *ALD* lists over 300 library consortia, including processing and purchasing centers and other specialized organizations. Data are exclusive of elementary and secondary school libraries. The directory does not list small public libraries. Law libraries with fewer than 10,000 volumes are included only if they specialize in a specific field.

LIBRARIES IN THE UNITED STATES

A. Public libraries 8,768
   Public libraries with branches 1,298
   Public library branches .. 6,056
   Total public libraries (including branches) 14,824*

B. Junior college libraries ... 1,263
   Departmental 18
   Departmental medicine 7
   Departmental religious 3
   University and college ... 1,915
   Departmental 1,728
   Departmental law ... 182
   Departmental medicine 240
   Departmental religious 116
   Total academic libraries .. 4,924*

C. Armed forces
   Air Force 126
   Medical 16
   Army 178
   Law 3
   Medical 28
   Navy 161
   Medical 20
   Total armed forces libraries 465*

D. Government libraries 1,565
   Law 420
   Medical 247
   Total government libraries 1,565*

E. Special libraries 4,291*

F. Law libraries 417*

G. Medical libraries 1,625*

H. Religious libraries 838*
   Total law (including academic, armed forces and government) 1,022
   Total medical (including academic, armed forces and government) 2,183
   Total religious (including academic) 957
   Total special (including all law, medical and religious) 8,453
   Total libraries counted (*) 28,949

LIBRARIES IN REGIONS ADMINISTERED BY THE UNITED STATES

A. Public libraries 12
   Public libraries with branches 4
   Public library branches .. 23
   Total public libraries (including branches) ... 35*

B. Junior college libraries ... 9
   University and college libraries 27
   Departmental 19
   Departmental law ... 3
   Total academic libraries .. 55*

C. Armed forces
    Air Force 1
    Army 1
    Navy 4
    Total armed forces 6*
D. Government libraries 10
    Law 6
    Medical 1
    Total government libraries 10*
E. Special libraries 9*
F. Medical libraries 3*
    Total libraries counted (*) 118

LIBRARIES IN CANADA

A. Public libraries 738
    Public libraries with branches 128
    Public library branches .. 900
    Total public libraries (including branches) ... 1,638*
B. Junior college libraries ... 119
    Departmental 7
    Departmental medicine 2
    Departmental religious 1
    University and college ... 145
    Departmental 226
    Departmental law ... 18
    Departmental medicine 30
    Departmental religious 18
    Total academic libraries .. 497*
C. Government libraries 262*
    Law 19
    Medical 4
D. Special libraries 475*
E. Law libraries 27*
F. Medical libraries 127*
G. Religious libraries 43*
    Total libraries counted (*) 3,069

SUMMARY

Total U.S. libraries 28,949
Total libraries administered by the United States 118
Total Canadian libraries 3,069
Grand total libraries listed ... 32,136

*Note: Numbers followed by an asterisk are added to find "Total libraries counted" for each of the three geographic areas (United States, U.S.-administered regions, and Canada). The sum of the three totals is the "Grand total of libraries listed" in the *ALD* (shown in the Summary). For details on the count of libraries, see the preface to the thirty-fifth edition of the *ALD—Ed.*

PUBLIC AND ACADEMIC LIBRARY ACQUISITION EXPENDITURES

Every two years the R. R. Bowker Company compiles statistics on library acquisition expenditures from information reported in the American Library Directory (*ALD*). The statistics given here are based on information from the 35th edition of the directory (1982). In most cases, the statistics reflect expenditures for the 1981–1982 period. The total number of public libraries listed in the 35th edition of *ALD* is 8,768; the total number of academic libraries is 4,924.

UNDERSTANDING THE TABLES

Number of libraries includes only those libraries in *ALD* that reported annual acquisition expenditures (7,500 public libraries; 2,795 academic libraries). This year, libraries that reported annual income but not expenditures are not included in the count. Academic libraries include university, college, and junior college libraries. Special academic libraries, such as law and medical libraries, that reported acquisition expenditures separately from the institution's main library are counted as independent libraries.

Total acquisition expenditures for a given state is almost always greater than (in a few cases equal to) the sum of the categories of expenditure. This is because the total acquisition expenditures amount also includes the expenditures of libraries that did not itemize by category.

Figures in *categories of expenditure* columns represent only those libraries that itemized expenditures. Libraries that reported a total acquisition expenditure amount but did not itemize are only represented in the total acquisition expenditures column.

Unspecified includes monies reported as not specifically for books, periodicals, audiovisual, microform, or binding (e.g., library materials). This column also includes monies reported for categories in combination, for example, audiovisual *and* microform. When libraries report only total acquisition expenditures without itemizing by category, the total amount is not reflected as unspecified.

Estimated percent of acquisitions is based on a comparison of the total expenditures for each of the categories and the total of all of the categories, that is, the total amount spent on books in the United States was compared with the sum of all of the categories of expenditure. The reader should note, therefore, that the percentages are not based on the figures in the total acquisition expenditures column.

340 / LIBRARY RESEARCH AND STATISTICS

TABLE 1 PUBLIC LIBRARY ACQUISITION EXPENDITURES, 1981–1982

State	Number of Libraries	Total Acquisition Expenditures	Books	Periodicals	Audiovisual	Microform	Binding	Unspecified
Alabama	126	$ 3,498,120	$ 1,742,551	$ 403,011	$ 317,020	$ 199,979	$ 28,802	$ 182,149
Alaska	24	1,563,039	489,802	62,718	206,565	212,800	25,330	30,000
Arizona	64	3,412,625	2,210,864	232,379	126,049	19,281	78,200	129,291
Arkansas	37	1,409,807	702,406	97,199	33,219	39,247	12,730	13,569
California	178	36,008,065	19,663,527	2,549,607	1,331,749	446,881	268,525	1,030,053
Colorado	114	4,766,720	3,207,843	365,736	122,115	27,408	63,235	324,300
Connecticut	138	5,843,839	2,561,612	295,229	237,901	27,695	56,412	86,585
Delaware	25	1,039,328	616,348	140,663	87,312	5,100	—	3,500
District of Columbia	1	803,700	679,022	92,220	32,458	—	—	—
Florida	125	12,358,031	6,369,008	785,355	732,097	192,755	116,264	140,070
Georgia	50	4,954,232	1,312,437	158,065	132,050	91,762	29,826	175,147
Hawaii	2	1,702,487	—	—	—	—	—	—
Idaho	91	1,086,983	587,453	40,986	37,744	8,239	3,700	7,991
Illinois	508	23,727,334	9,644,981	1,447,511	1,374,177	374,668	245,805	436,054
Indiana	207	7,827,976	3,792,346	367,435	403,324	38,787	129,044	269,781
Iowa	468	4,980,507	2,319,757	341,158	157,923	32,548	23,301	°384
Kansas	285	4,113,605	2,515,855	344,057	82,457	23,015	32,586	18,088
Kentucky	110	8,924,269	3,681,509	161,173	254,956	32,763	31,654	27,050
Louisiana	64	6,026,844	1,924,077	358,417	185,124	1,083	60,680	510,123
Maine	169	7,630,797	793,405	93,296	21,372	12,731	16,239	15,080
Maryland	28	8,818,627	5,502,358	347,445	558,855	24,419	82,328	46,000
Massachusetts	311	14,751,250	5,367,606	541,901	281,317	149,361	107,395	1,790,138
Michigan	349	13,349,483	7,438,378	642,516	697,615	52,907	138,495	505,496
Minnesota	107	6,996,964	3,582,928	480,336	502,836	99,834	88,651	1,041,101
Mississippi	52	2,350,984	1,001,322	160,982	70,347	25,589	15,351	36,343
Missouri	126	8,349,138	3,624,512	385,771	397,506	117,209	80,275	354,129
Montana	73	965,537	533,489	82,219	6,477	2,981	4,455	59,121
Nebraska	183	2,235,574	594,091	61,359	65,124	40,374	24,033	303,261
Nevada	20	1,129,609	303,456	30,651	22,780	—	3,375	560,316
New Hampshire	216	1,798,898	886,808	41,543	24,887	6,984	9,998	570,125
New Jersey	289	14,951,705	7,648,186	1,153,020	479,491	150,284	84,179	673,471
New Mexico	39	1,245,955	610,690	90,000	36,457	3,519	6,000	950

New York	688	41,972,168	25,958,617	2,339,684	869,605	240,354	275,269	2,929,170
North Carolina	121	7,521,724	3,596,443	542,760	384,210	40,245	57,909	125,214
North Dakota	43	880,354	495,922	34,323	71,231	9,172	2,200	9,158
Ohio	236	21,533,745	13,103,657	1,767,801	1,359,728	195,468	297,500	295,708
Oklahoma	80	2,818,009	1,735,238	336,869	138,223	44,210	41,436	1,044
Oregon	90	2,865,991	1,469,451	155,301	60,484	3,000	7,850	81,629
Pennsylvania	430	10,854,471	4,189,661	969,942	267,617	169,116	60,309	3,906,565
Rhode Island	39	1,586,868	646,139	81,688	17,019	13,500	19,776	22,629
South Carolina	39	2,673,484	865,947	76,074	129,356	3,900	22,865	382,417
South Dakota	62	1,983,243	413,529	83,883	78,509	27,532	10,636	3,179
Tennessee	103	3,380,436	1,776,973	296,667	290,938	39,437	30,993	319,989
Texas	360	17,414,366	9,939,002	1,744,816	1,055,382	70,262	330,144	2,079,492
Utah	36	1,931,263	515,863	28,780	42,365	2,300	28,846	2,780
Vermont	120	985,343	448,205	45,966	27,310	16,229	4,371	13,328
Virginia	81	7,877,912	4,304,891	558,094	226,492	76,409	103,195	870,880
Washington	61	7,993,475	3,709,219	642,221	489,772	36,771	20,629	358,506
West Virginia	71	2,234,203	1,071,537	64,901	355,528	3,789	16,283	167,237
Wisconsin	235	7,424,388	2,594,840	351,951	393,751	49,516	59,513	119,640
Wyoming	22	1,000,763	415,880	42,199	34,190	2,500	9,350	
Pacific Islands	2	213,448	130,578	36,074	45,346	1,000	450	
Puerto Rico	1	141,262						
Virgin Islands	1	150,000						
Total U.S.	7,500	$358,032,104	$179,290,219	$22,553,952	$15,356,360	$3,504,807	$3,266,392	$21,036,781
Estimated % of Acquisitions			73.2	9.2	6.3	1.4	1.3	8.6

TABLE 2 COLLEGE AND UNIVERSITY LIBRARY ACQUISITION EXPENDITURES, 1981–1982

State	Number of Libraries	Total Acquisition Expenditures	Books	Periodicals	Audiovisual	Microform	Binding	Unspecified
Alabama	49	$ 6,710,115	$ 3,588,035	$ 1,683,833	$ 102,693	$ 135,474	$ 187,872	$ 27,375
Alaska	11	1,670,003	671,007	303,722	45,000	65,743	41,000	24,000
Arizona	27	8,762,982	1,756,572	1,416,446	87,584	41,427	197,151	—
Arkansas	30	4,787,518	1,216,544	875,380	21,947	148,293	89,478	418,339
California	222	60,645,726	21,530,979	16,686,677	1,066,131	1,252,957	3,288,633	6,580,404
Colorado	38	6,120,629	2,409,798	2,012,122	267,476	61,006	178,830	28,191
Connecticut	45	10,185,430	2,417,273	2,309,501	126,568	91,601	385,645	73,397
Delaware	7	2,167,259	925,386	792,273	3,800	2,200	141,600	—
District of Columbia	24	8,577,068	2,804,026	2,358,429	116,498	126,285	215,854	784,620
Florida	85	19,640,720	8,082,344	5,964,428	547,805	371,619	935,966	1,044,089
Georgia	68	10,755,641	3,852,084	4,461,021	160,475	240,921	532,660	494,892
Hawaii	15	2,569,079	1,226,557	172,061	66,932	66,238	139,200	972,372
Idaho	10	2,065,769	578,906	562,754	51,427	26,482	43,479	—
Illinois	122	27,595,917	7,927,717	7,447,501	726,221	239,543	1,142,555	1,370,769
Indiana	49	11,935,904	3,286,489	2,785,022	117,057	106,484	459,470	2,750,309
Iowa	52	8,406,025	1,633,702	3,806,562	81,009	130,000	392,937	174,350
Kansas	51	6,374,407	2,921,957	2,401,098	113,898	59,758	264,727	5,000
Kentucky	39	6,750,685	2,438,167	2,536,497	76,197	51,720	298,031	87,194
Louisiana	33	7,691,621	2,085,267	2,063,444	87,495	179,406	371,687	1,405,533
Maine	26	2,321,729	833,885	831,435	35,582	29,287	49,920	10,000
Maryland	37	4,417,659	1,623,016	1,044,456	123,023	153,215	78,397	500
Massachusetts	125	28,132,704	7,038,319	5,230,696	273,122	245,072	1,642,444	11,271,943
Michigan	83	20,797,283	3,529,547	3,847,346	291,015	187,226	705,740	4,062,918
Minnesota	51	8,334,077	3,062,346	3,188,978	124,860	67,592	420,267	122,997
Mississippi	46	6,014,768	1,954,744	1,225,313	106,999	164,705	—	29,585
Missouri	73	9,864,669	3,040,497	3,975,976	221,115	211,496	429,328	193,194

Montana	12	1,265,117		666,180	16,500	3,560	20,100	
Nebraska	32	5,030,823	1,740,697	2,032,698	96,153	31,983	231,007	155,040
Nevada	6	1,195,277	398,765	540,745	19,120		53,984	16,600
New Hampshire	24	3,554,015	1,176,462	629,078	41,650	202,557	106,406	958,333
New Jersey	53	10,327,674	4,201,817	2,787,063	451,314	246,600	353,160	53,853
New Mexico	23	3,484,766	1,055,290	973,777	43,365	24,704	193,212	79,866
New York	202	43,964,396	16,344,702	11,496,574	591,649	936,524	1,577,929	2,178,076
North Carolina	110	19,405,597	4,952,616	5,299,972	378,792	221,572	739,368	3,349,246
North Dakota	13	1,038,801	414,945	502,400	31,513	5,600	31,250	36,200
Ohio	121	18,617,813	6,335,789	6,269,576	434,407	310,372	791,482	1,670,610
Oklahoma	45	8,692,375	1,747,891	1,659,807	68,669	92,781	178,187	1,348,480
Oregon	40	6,241,932	1,731,219	2,493,047	106,623	107,983	203,850	604,951
Pennsylvania	149	23,738,710	8,205,025	7,384,197	379,259	580,750	1,380,131	835,291
Rhode Island	11	2,150,313	572,200	286,698	20,222	27,216	40,249	75,228
South Carolina	50	7,060,282	2,311,720	2,662,680	69,309	107,823	320,343	317,725
South Dakota	17	1,825,408	525,055	567,798	38,293	15,259	44,450	36,950
Tennessee	59	10,240,024	3,753,662	3,819,979	218,045	186,896	461,227	692,865
Texas	140	27,419,936	11,064,523	7,171,146	680,022	411,200	1,141,471	2,366,012
Utah	12	1,796,405	562,700	861,100	76,380	27,700	61,700	2,000
Vermont	18	2,328,105	1,040,228	989,300	29,793	43,207	116,760	
Virginia	71	14,473,162	4,328,373	4,346,558	296,266	227,311	458,005	42,900
Washington	45	10,173,002	3,083,943	4,494,670	229,846	92,294	449,045	437,438
West Virginia	29	3,587,060	652,942	640,476	114,441	70,813	40,022	37,300
Wisconsin	61	10,772,330	4,094,662	4,596,369	337,236	180,475	370,014	248,777
Wyoming	8	1,467,935	462,833	751,362	33,765	2,600	49,400	2,475
Pacific Islands	2	94,000	6,000	3,000				
Puerto Rico	22	1,982,047	881,970	611,773	86,961	40,830	61,463	159,000
Virgin Islands	2	166,000	91,000	30,000			5,000	
Total U.S.	2,795	$535,388,692	$174,600,443	$154,550,994	$9,931,522	$8,654,360	$22,112,086	$47,637,187
Estimated % of Acquisitions			41.8	37.0	2.4	2.1	5.3	11.4

URBAN-SUBURBAN PUBLIC LIBRARY STATISTICS, 1980-1981

Joseph Green
Director, Atlantic County Library, Egg Harbor City, New Jersey 08215

Beginning in 1969, and for each year since 1972, data have been collected from urban and suburban public library systems around the United States for the primary purpose of comparing urban libraries with the suburban libraries around them. This report reprints the survey results for the years 1980 and 1981, which were originally published in the 1982 *Bowker Annual*. (No survey was done in 1982.) Data for earlier years can be found in earlier editions of the *Bowker Annual*. The next survey is planned for 1983.

A library system is defined as one that is centrally funded and uses a common policy for controlling the basic operation of public libraries within a particular jurisdiction. This strict definition makes it difficult to survey many suburban libraries that are either cooperatives or federations, among them those in the suburbs of New York, Chicago, and Philadelphia.

Of the 50 libraries questioned, 36 answered the 1980-1981 survey for a 72 percent response rate. Although some earlier respondents did not participate in the survey, other former nonparticipants did send information. This situation, of course, causes inconsistency in the survey.

In Tables 1 through 6, the libraries are arranged by reported population, largest to smallest. The following abbreviations are used in the tables: "C" for calendar year, "F" for fiscal year, "U" for urban libraries, "S" for suburban libraries, and "U/S" for urban-suburban libraries.

Once again, we issue our annual caveat to anyone using the data in budget work. Although the survey does allow for comparisons of urban libraries on a national basis, survey participants use statistics to meet local priorities, and it is difficult to make comparisons between libraries in different areas of the country.

TABLE 1 TOTAL LIBRARY SERVICE AREA POPULATION AND TOTAL OPERATING EXPENSES, 1980–1981

Library	Population 1980	Population 1981	Total Operating Expenses 1980	Total Operating Expenses 1981
Chicago Public Lib., IL (U) (C)	3,369,359	3,005,072	$27,273,792	$25,273,441
Los Angeles Public Lib., CA (U) (F)	2,817,800	2,966,763	15,110,324	16,587,592
Brooklyn Public Lib., NY (U) (F)	2,230,936	2,230,936	16,013,365	19,141,636
Philadelphia Public Lib., PA (U) (C)	1,950,098	1,950,098	17,255,960	17,070,653
Houston Public Lib., TX (U) (C)	1,232,802	1,573,847	1,935,414	10,781,107
Detroit Public Lib., MI (U) (C)	1,203,339	1,203,339	14,138,129	14,012,771
Buffalo/Erie County Public Lib., NY (U/S) (C)	1,113,491	1,113,491	11,680,265	11,945,950
Orange County Public Lib., CA (S) (F)	940,025	972,625	8,219,793	11,336,135
Milwaukee Public Lib., WI (U) (C)	981,362	971,646	9,291,000	9,923,000
San Antonio Public Lib., TX (U) (F)	926,000	924,207	2,770,203	3,294,691
San Diego Public Lib., CA (U) (F)	842,200	887,700	5,528,336	5,836,437
Cincinnati/Hamilton County Public Lib., OH (U/S) (C)	924,000	873,000	8,763,052	9,619,890
St. Louis County Public Lib., MO (S) (C)	767,937	816,672	5,890,779	6,779,443
Enoch Pratt Free Lib., Baltimore, MD (U) (F)	783,320	783,320	9,621,808	10,240,185
Memphis/Shelby County Public Lib., TX (U/S) (F)	756,800	777,113	6,196,212	6,871,578
King County Lib. System, WA (S) (C)	712,000	751,680	5,697,821	6,610,612
Columbus/Franklin County Public Lib., OH (U/S) (C)	700,000	700,000	6,677,029	7,575,804
Louisville Public Lib., KY (U/S) (F)	695,055	684,793	5,196,670	5,055,587
San Francisco Public Lib., CA (U) (F)	642,900	680,700	8,207,207	8,041,271
Prince George's County Memorial Lib., MD (S) (F)	666,603	665,071	8,301,104	8,657,185
Baltimore County Public Lib., MD (S) (F)	655,615	655,615	9,683,882	10,395,986
Fairfax County Public Lib., VA (S) (F)	614,800	641,800	6,256,526	7,172,821
Cuyahoga County Public Lib., OH (S) (C)	620,000	620,000	11,371,272	11,715,339
Jacksonville Public Lib. System, FL (U/S) (F)	598,218	603,785	3,574,660	3,717,883
Contra Costa County Lib. System, CA (S) (F)	574,500	590,500	5,016,178	5,134,318
Hennepin County Lib. System, MN (S) (C)	573,246	576,508	7,828,431	8,909,656
Cleveland Public Lib., OH (U) (C)	625,000	572,000	12,153,389	13,827,652
New Orleans Public Lib., LA (U) (C)	599,129	569,125	3,061,308	3,361,246
Dayton/Montgomery County Public Lib., OH (U/S) (C)	568,353	568,353	4,293,040	5,147,457
Denver Public Lib., CO (U) (C)	515,000	515,000	7,499,200	8,682,400
Fresno County Public Lib., CA (U/S) (F)	479,850	507,875	3,492,871	3,682,375
St. Louis Public Lib., MO (U) (C)	525,000	465,000	4,868,085	4,938,720
Tulsa City/County Lib., OK (U/S) (F)	450,000	460,000	4,068,354	4,304,875
Pittsburgh Public Lib., PA (U) (C)	520,117	423,960	6,930,578	7,370,093
Annapolis/Anne Arundel County Public Lib., MD (U/S) (F)	368,000	372,800	3,531,312	4,062,803
Omaha Public Lib., NE (U) (C)	314,255	314,255	2,435,953	2,576,101

TABLE 2 TOTAL PUBLIC LIBRARY STATE AND FEDERAL AID, 1980–1981

Library	Total State Aid 1980	Total State Aid 1981	Total Federal Aid 1980	Total Federal Aid 1981
Chicago Public Lib., IL (U) (C)	$4,875,876	$4,463,387	$401,723	$508,241
Los Angeles Public Lib., CA (U) (F)	92,053	11,995	0	0
Brooklyn Public Lib., NY (U) (F)	2,227,495	2,181,761	1,511,875	1,121,017
Philadelphia Public Lib., PA (U) (C)	2,341,147	2,458,262	242,673	136,351
Houston Public Lib., TX (U) (C)	0	0	0	0
Detroit Public Lib., MI (U) (C)	1,047,995	1,017,796	58,075	88,538
Buffalo/Erie County Public Lib., NY (U)(S) (C)	1,768,428	1,549,462	254,802	313,091
Orange County Public Lib., CA (S)(F)	3,070,451	2,734,407	0	0
Milwaukee Public Lib., WI (U) (C)	0	0	0	0
San Antonio Public Lib., TX (U) (F)	72,913	91,063	155,495	72,913
San Diego Public Lib., CA (U) (F)	1,153	492	607,900	624,914
Cincinnati/Hamilton County Public Lib., OH (U/S) (C)	243,414	181,286	0	0
St. Louis County Public Lib., MO (S) (C)	271,112	291,183	50,000	50,000
Enoch Pratt Free Lib., Baltimore, MD (U) (F)	4,920,039	5,253,277	772,960	879,552
Memphis/Shelby County Public Lib., TX (U/S) (F)	376,592	333,815	257,957	212,197
King County Lib. System, WA (S) (C)	0	0	0	0
Columbus/Franklin County Public Lib., OH (U/S) (C)	0	0	0	0
Louisville Public Lib., KY (U/S) (F)	125,230	106,523	138,257	168,934
San Francisco Public Lib., CA (U) (F)	28,636	23,987	995,057	338,742
Prince George's County Memorial Lib., MD (S) (F)	1,350,982	1,350,697	156,031	190,184
Baltimore County Public Lib., MD (S) (F)	1,026,853	1,020,965	0	0
Fairfax County Public Lib., VA (S)(F)	148,911	249,673	2,538	0
Cuyahoga County Public Lib., OH (S) (C)	0	0	0	0
Jacksonville Public Lib. System, FL (U/S) (F)	248,398	298,057	211,423	219,643
Contra Costa County Lib. System, CA (S) (F)	13,849	12,759	19,471	22,520
Hennepin County Lib. System, MN (S) (C)	258,083	326,996	n/a	n/a
Cleveland Public Lib., OH (U) (C)	551,747	255,445	0	0
New Orleans Public Lib., LA (U) (C)	232,275	233,043	116,102	113,558
Dayton/Montgomery County Public Lib., OH (U/S) (C)	3,006	2,139	40,910	9,405
Denver Public Lib., CO (U) (C)	488,000	492,000	0	0
Fresno County Public Lib., CA (U/S) (F)	672,771	1,061	574,525	703,610
St. Louis Public Lib., MO (U) (C)	223,251	179,230	138,923	169,606
Tulsa City-County Lib., OK (U/S)(F)	124,671	158,942	0	0
Pittsburgh Public Lib., PA (U) (C)	1,491,280	1,530,762	2,333,463	2,864,370
Annapolis/Anne Arundel County Public Lib., MD (U/S) (F)	734,931	762,680	66,548	52,192
Omaha Public Lib., NE (U) (C)	34,474	35,839	12,000	12,000

TABLE 3   PUBLIC LIBRARY SALARY AND OTHER EXPENDITURES, 1980-1981

Library	Salary Expenditures 1980	1981	Other Expenditures 1980	1981
Chicago Public Lib., IL (U)(C)	$17,062,903	$17,366,636	$8,027,320	$11,354,360
Los Angeles Public Lib., CA (U)(F)	14,482,057	16,587,306	628,267	843,286
Brooklyn Public Lib., NY (U)(F)	12,899,693	13,768,676	5,439,846	7,855,836
Philadelphia Public Lib., PA (U)(C)	14,116,551	13,979,575	555,589	496,465
Houston Public Lib., TX (U)(C)	5,744,271	6,819,894	340,863	498,838
Detroit Public Lib., MI (U)(C)	10,950,300	10,691,314	3,547,829	3,321,457
Buffalo/Erie County Public Lib., NY (U/S)(C)	8,992,079	9,393,914	2,688,187	2,552,035
Orange County Public Lib., CA (S)(F)	3,937,773	4,397,878	4,282,020	6,938,257
Milwaukee Public Lib., WI (U)(C)	7,532,000	8,082,000	1,759,000	1,841,000
San Antonio Public Lib., TX (U)(F)	1,597,210	1,842,536	1,172,993	2,201,155
San Diego Public Lib., CA (U)(F)	3,546,220	3,909,840	1,982,116	1,926,597
Cincinnati/Hamilton County Public Lib., OH (U/S)(C)	5,489,130	5,897,909	3,273,922	3,721,981
St. Louis County Public Lib., MO (S)(C)	3,850,086	4,676,222	2,040,693	2,103,191
Enoch Pratt Free Lib., Baltimore, MD (U)(F)	6,619,495	7,280,083	1,866,279	1,681,389
Memphis/Shelby County Public Lib., TX (U/S)(F)	4,522,677	5,109,609	1,673,535	1,761,969
King County Lib. System, WA (S)(C)	3,627,834	4,299,032	2,069,987	2,311,580
Columbus/Franklin County Public Lib., OH (U/S)(C)	3,593,338	4,035,732	3,083,691	3,538,072
Louisville Public Lib., KY (U/S)(F)	2,712,405	2,823,957	2,484,266	2,231,630
San Francisco Public Lib., CA (U)(F)	6,823,769	6,387,424	1,374,931	1,624,972
Prince George's County Memorial Lib., MD (S)(F)	5,713,921	5,882,765	2,460,199	2,626,060
Baltimore County Public Lib., MD (S)(F)	6,278,418	6,870,533	3,405,464	3,525,453
Fairfax County Public Lib., VA (S)(F)	4,501,449	5,060,212	1,755,077	2,112,609
Cuyahoga County Public Lib., OH (S)(C)	6,096,497	6,025,185	4,932,017	5,421,233
Jacksonville Public Lib. System, FL (U/S)(F)	2,323,467	2,509,071	1,251,193	1,208,811
Contra Costa County Lib. System, CA (S)(F)	3,308,041	3,513,536	1,629,973	1,595,973
Hennepin County Lib. System, MN (S)(C)	5,370,392	6,044,254	2,458,039	2,865,402
Cleveland Public Lib., OH (U)(C)	7,608,107	8,380,545	4,545,282	5,447,107
New Orleans Public Lib., LA (U)(C)	1,614,544	1,588,516	1,446,764	1,772,730

TABLE 3   PUBLIC LIBRARY SALARY AND OTHER EXPENDITURES, 1980-1981
(cont.)

	Salary Expenditures		Other Expenditures	
Library	1980	1981	1980	1981
Dayton/Montgomery County Public Lib., OH (U/S) (C)	2,548,011	2,758,391	1,745,029	1,839,943
Denver Public Lib., CO (U) (C)	5,959,025	6,243,300	1,540,175	2,439,200
Fresno County Public Lib., CA (U/S) (F)	2,565,710	2,699,751	927,161	982,624
St. Louis Public Lib., MO (U) (C)	3,649,087	3,579,273	1,218,998	1,359,447
Tulsa City-County Lib., OK (U/S) (F)	2,381,942	2,762,783	1,090,138	1,273,940
Pittsburgh Public Lib., PA (U) (C)	5,121,149	5,619,078	1,809,429	1,751,015
Annapolis/Anne Arundel County Public Lib., MD (U/S) (F)	2,327,085	2,563,607	1,204,228	1,499,197
Omaha Public Lib., NE (U) (C)	1,626,753	1,864,604	809,201	711,497

TABLE 4 PUBLIC LIBRARY CIRCULATION, REFERENCE FIGURES, AND SERVICE OUTLETS, 1980–1981

Library	Circulation 1980	Circulation 1981	Reference Figures 1980	Reference Figures 1981	Service Outlets 1980	Service Outlets 1981
Chicago Public Lib., IL (U) (C)	6,608,290	7,229,063	4,007,780	5,257,749	88	88
Los Angeles Public Lib., CA (U) (F)	10,836,108	10,842,753	16,872,038	12,314,960	141	141
Brooklyn Public Lib., NY (U) (F)	6,983,217	6,667,318	2,706,754	2,534,443	59	59
Philadelphia Public Lib., PA (U) (C)	4,903,301	5,003,398	1,457,908	2,016,733	52	52
Houston Public Lib., TX (U) (C)	5,503,313	5,753,205	2,086,893	2,222,110	30	30
Detroit Public Lib., MI (U) (C)	1,921,921	1,719,039	2,508,367	2,345,429	32	32
Buffalo/Erie County Public Lib., NY (U/S) (C)	5,454,117	5,671,596	—	—	63	63
Orange County Public Lib., CA (S) (F)	5,821,330	6,604,297	634,210	826,358	116	79
Milwaukee Public Lib., WI (U) (C)	3,287,607	3,073,243	1,300,142	1,385,533	13	13
San Antonio Public Lib., TX (U) (F)	2,244,943	2,197,592	—	—	16	16
San Diego Public Lib., CA (U) (F)	4,102,386	4,235,888	1,149,268	1,237,632	31	31
Cincinnati/Hamilton County Public Lib., OH (U/S) (C)	5,654,005	5,845,093	1,750,047	1,826,696	92	88
St. Louis County Public Lib., MO (S) (C)	7,269,432	7,521,921	91,944	93,455	337	323
Enoch Pratt Free Lib., Baltimore, MD (U) (F)	2,214,845	2,318,562	371,907	373,036	36	36
Memphis/Shelby County Public Lib., TX (U/S) (F)	2,575,171	2,572,297	315,155	349,252	34	34
King County Lib. System, WA (S) (C)	3,833,681	4,150,036	96,000	103,000	44	44
Columbus/Franklin County Public Lib., OH (U/S) (C)	3,084,857	3,307,731	680,838	721,233	24	23
Louisville Public Lib., KY (U/S) (F)	2,214,707	2,371,199	418,665	548,195	28	24
San Francisco Public Lib., CA (U) (F)	2,304,102	2,435,234	987,795	929,950	29	29
Prince George's County Memorial Lib., MD (S) (F)	3,706,766	3,794,615	946,562	1,059,190	21	21
Baltimore County Public Lib., MD (S) (F)	8,141,262	8,418,223	373,162	431,491	22	22
Fairfax County Public Lib., VA (S) (F)	5,080,099	5,333,638	1,660,625	1,886,625	21	22
Cuyahoga County Public Lib., OH (S) (C)	4,196,055	4,543,226	n/a	1,525,125	26	26
Jacksonville Public Lib. System, FL (U/S) (F)	2,177,556	2,157,906	520,902	514,517	12	12
Contra Costa County Lib. System, CA (S) (F)	2,986,812	3,016,631	362,781	363,781	21	21
Hennepin County Lib. System, MN (S) (C)	4,528,641	4,612,062	646,864	665,467	25	25
Cleveland Public Lib., OH (U) (C)	2,929,777	3,118,006	2,347,053	2,555,435	35	34
New Orleans Public Lib., LA (U) (C)	1,099,425	1,143,420	816,183	393,177	12	12
Dayton/Montgomery County Public Lib., OH (U/S) (C)	4,441,967	4,598,334	517,097	523,494	21	21
Denver Public Lib., CO (U) (C)	2,862,488	2,922,046	806,904	839,051	23	23
Fresno County Public Lib., CA (U/S) (F)	2,021,585	2,028,773	510,179	535,536	72	72
St. Louis Public Lib., MO (U) (C)	1,540,820	1,429,294	448,677	458,384	26	23
Tulsa City-County Public Lib., OK (U/S) (F)	1,695,987	1,753,570	617,251	674,380	21	21
Pittsburgh Public Lib., PA (U) (C)	2,942,141	2,908,157	513,679	536,616	28	28
Annapolis/Anne Arundel County Public Lib., MD (U/S) (F)	3,420,672	3,605,009	125,702	129,469	14	14
Omaha Public Lib., NE (U) (C)	1,651,365	1,735,235	243,545	268,857	11	10

URBAN-SUBURBAN PUBLIC LIBRARY STATISTICS / 349

TABLE 5 PUBLIC LIBRARY TOTAL FULL-TIME EQUIVALENT (FTE) PROFESSIONAL AND NONPROFESSIONAL STAFF, 1980–1981

Library	Total Staff 1980	Total Staff 1981	Professional Staff 1980	Professional Staff 1981
Chicago Public Lib., IL (U) (C)	1,885	1,457	717	572
Los Angeles Public Lib., CA (U) (F)	1,126.5	1,141.5	392.5	399
Brooklyn Public Lib., NY (U) (F)	663	638	252	261
Philadelphia Public Lib., PA (U) (C)	—	—	247	245
Houston Public Lib., TX (U) (C)	550	552	154	154
Detroit Public Lib., MI (U) (C)	450	434	214	200
Buffalo/Erie County Public Lib., NY (U/S) (C)	528.31	548.96	171.5	176.5
Orange County Public Lib., CA (S) (F)	288	292	79	82
Milwaukee Public Lib., WI (U) (C)	335	345.5	13	13
San Antonio Public Lib., TX (U) (F)	185	185	22	22
San Diego Public Lib., CA (U) (F)	220.77	235.19	84.38	84.88
Cincinnati/Hamilton County Public Lib., OH (U/S) (C)	389.8	386	126.5	121
St. Louis County Public Lib., MO (S) (C)	376	370	45	38
Enoch Pratt Free Lib., Baltimore, MD (U) (F)	425.5	447	148.5	160
Memphis/Shelby County Public Lib., TX (U/S) (F)	258.8	258.8	141	141
King County Lib. System, WA (S) (C)	228	241	68	69.5
Columbus/Franklin County Public Lib., OH (U/S) (C)	233.5	251.5	100	100
Louisville Public Lib., KY (U/S) (F)	199.41	192.80	41.57	41
San Francisco Public Lib., CA (U) (F)	284.5	292	143	140
Prince George's County Memorial Lib., MD (S) (F)	353	344	104	98
Baltimore County Public Lib., MD (S) (F)	478	479	93	93
Fairfax County Public Lib., VA (S) (F)	320	323	89.5	89.5
Cuyahoga County Public Lib., OH (S) (C)	491	478	177	170
Jacksonville Public Lib. System, FL (U/S) (F)	181	157	53	51
Contra Costa County Lib. System, CA (S) (F)	183.6	151.8	63	53.2
Hennepin County Lib. System, MN (S) (C)	312.9	347.8	102.7	112.4
Cleveland Public Lib., OH (U) (C)	417	395	35	34
New Orleans Public Lib., LA (U) (C)	169.41	161.44	41.75	37.75
Dayton/Montgomery County Public Lib., OH (U/S) (C)	216	218	43.7	43.3
Denver Public Lib., CO (U) (C)	355	345	120	110
Fresno County Public Lib., CA (U/S) (F)	136.6	136.6	38.8	38.8
St. Louis Public Lib., MO (U) (C)	240.70	226.5	61	54
Tulsa City-County Lib., OK (U/S) (F)	181.5	184.5	48	48
Pittsburgh Public Lib., PA (U) (C)	362	368	103	110
Annapolis/Anne Arundel County Public Lib., MD (U/S) (F)	223	204.5	45	41
Omaha Public Lib., NE (U) (C)	117.74	113.72	37	35

TABLE 6 PUBLIC LIBRARY PER CAPITA SUPPORT AND CIRCULATION, AND WORKLOAD PER STAFF MEMBER (RANK BY VOLUME), 1980–1981

Library	Per capita support 1980	Per capita support 1981	Per capita circulation 1980	Per capita circulation 1981	Workload per staff member 1980	Workload per staff member 1981
Chicago Public Lib., IL (U)(C)	$ 8.09 (23)	$ 8.41 (26)	1.9 (31)	2.4 (26a)	3506 (35)	4962 (34)
Los Angeles Public Lib., CA (U)(F)	5.14 (34)	5.59 (35)	3.8 (20)	3.6 (20b)	9619 (24)	9499 (25)
Brooklyn Public Lib., NY (U)(F)	7.18 (31)	8.58 (25)	3.1 (26)	3.0 (24a)	10533 (19)	10450 (20)
Philadelphia Public Lib., PA (U)(C)	8.85 (19)	8.75 (23)	2.5 (29)	2.6 (27)		
Houston Public Lib., TX (U)(C)	7.25 (30)	6.85 (31)	4.5 (17)	3.7 (19)	10006 (21)	10422 (21)
Detroit Public Lib., MI (U)(C)	11.75 (10)	11.64 (11)	1.6 (33)	1.4 (29)	4271 (34)	3961 (35)
Buffalo/Erie County Public Lib., NY (U/S)(C)	10.49 (11)	10.73 (16)	4.9 (15a)	5.1 (14a)	10326 (20)	10332 (19)
Orange County Public Lib., CA (S)(F)	8.74 (20)	11.66 (10)	6.2 (8)	6.8 (19)	20213 (23)	22617 (1)
Milwaukee Public Lib., WI (U)(C)	9.47 (16)	9.50 (18)	3.3 (24)	3.2 (23)	9814 (23)	8895 (26)
San Antonio Public Lib., TX (U)(F)	2.99 (36)	3.56 (36)	2.4 (30)	2.4 (26)	12135 (15)	11879 (17)
San Diego Public Lib., CA (U)(F)	6.56 (32)	6.57 (32)	4.9 (15b)	4.8 (15)	18582 (4)	18010 (5)
Cincinnati/Hamilton County Public Lib., OH (U/S)(C)	9.48 (15)	11.02 (13)	6.1 (9)	6.7 (10)	14505 (11)	15143 (11)
St. Louis County Public Lib., MO (S)(C)	7.67 (26)	8.30 (27)	9.5 (2)	9.2 (3)	19334 (3)	20330 (3)
Enoch Pratt Free Lib., Baltimore, MD (U)(F)	12.28 (9)	13.07 (7)	2.8 (28)	3.0 (24)	5205 (33)	5187 (33)
Memphis/Shelby County Public Lib., TX (U/S)(F)	8.19 (22)	8.84 (21)	3.4 (23)	3.3 (22)	9950 (22)	9939 (22)
King County Lib. System, WA (S)(C)	8.00 (24)	8.79 (22)	5.4 (12)	5.5 (13)	16814 (6)	17220 (8)
Columbus/Franklin County Public Lib., OH (U/S)(C)	9.54 (14)	10.82 (15)	4.4 (18)	4.7 (16)	13211 (14)	13152 (15)
Louisville Public Lib., KY (U/S)(F)	7.48 (28)	7.38 (29)	3.2 (25)	3.5 (21)	11106 (17)	12299 (16)
San Francisco Public Lib., CA (U)(F)	12.77 (7)	11.81 (9)	3.6 (22a)	3.6 (20a)	8099 (28)	8340 (28)
Prince George's County Memorial Lib., MD (S)(F)	12.45 (8)	13.02 (8)	5.6 (11a)	5.6 (12)	10501 (18)	10769 (18)
Baltimore County Public Lib., MD (S)(F)	14.77 (3)	15.86 (5)	12.4 (1)	12.8 (1)	17032 (5)	17575 (7)
Fairfax County Public Lib., VA (S)(F)	10.18 (12)	11.18 (12)	8.3 (4)	8.3 (4)	15875 (8)	16513 (9)
Cuyahoga County Public Lib., OH (S)(C)	18.34 (2)	18.90 (2)	6.8 (7)	7.3 (7)	8546 (26)	9505 (23)
Jacksonville Public Lib. System, FL (U/S)(F)	5.98 (33)	6.16 (34)	3.6 (22b)	3.6 (20a)	12031 (16)	13745 (13)
Contra Costa County Lib. System, CA (S)(F)	8.73 (21)	8.69 (24)	5.2 (14)	5.1 (14)	16268 (7)	19872 (4)
Hennepin County Lib. System, MN (S)(C)	13.66 (5)	15.45 (6)	7.9 (5)	8.0 (6)	14473 (12)	13261 (14)
Cleveland Public Lib., OH (U)(C)	19.45 (1)	24.17 (1)	4.7 (16)	5.5 (13a)	7026 (30)	7894 (30)
New Orleans Public Lib., LA (U)(C)	5.11 (35)	5.91 (33)	1.8 (32)	2.0 (28)	6490 (31)	7083 (31)
Dayton/Montgomery County Public Lib., OH (U/S)(C)	7.55 (27)	9.06 (20)	7.8 (6)	8.1 (5)	20565 (1)	21093 (2)
Denver Public Lib., CO (U)(C)	14.56 (4)	16.86 (4)	5.6 (11b)	5.7 (11)	8063 (29)	8470 (27)
Fresno County Public Lib., CA (U/S)(F)	7.28 (29)	7.25 (30)	4.2 (19)	4.0 (17)	14799 (10)	14852 (12)
St. Louis Public Lib., MO (U)(C)	9.27 (17)	10.62 (17)	2.9 (27)	3.1 (25)	6401 (32)	6310 (33)
Tulsa City-County Lib., OK (U/S)(F)	9.04 (18)	9.36 (19)	3.8 (21)	3.8 (18)	9344 (25)	9504 (24)
Pittsburgh Public Lib., PA (U)(C)	13.33 (6)	17.38 (3)	5.7 (10)	6.9 (8)	8127 (27)	7903 (29)
Annapolis/Anne Arundel County Public Lib., MD (U/S)(F)	9.60 (13)	10.90 (14)	9.3 (3)	9.7 (2)	15339 (9)	17628 (6)
Omaha Public Lib., NE (U)(C)	7.75 (25)	8.20 (28)	5.3 (13)	5.5 (13a)	14026 (13)	15259 (10)

NCES SURVEY OF PRIVATE SCHOOL LIBRARY MEDIA CENTERS, 1979

Milbrey L. Jones

Planning and Budget Officer
Libraries and Learning Technologies Programs

This report is a brief overview of the 1979 NCES survey of private school library media centers, including some of the data from the survey. The final published report, which will be available in early 1983, will include more comprehensive data on library media collections, staff, and expenditures in private schools, together with some analysis and comparisons of the private school data with that collected for public schools.

The statistics collected in the survey of private elementary and secondary school media centers are estimates for the year 1979, based on the weighted responses of a survey of 1,505 of the approximately 17,000 private schools in the 50 states and the District of Columbia. The sample design was a one-stage stratified simple random sample. Strata were by affiliation (Catholic, other religious affiliation, or not affiliated), school level, and pupil membership.

RESULTS OF THE SURVEY

In 1979, 83 percent of private schools (14,242 of a total of 17,204) had school library media centers. (This figure compares roughly with the 85 percent of the public schools with library media centers.) The only previous figures that could be located on private school libraries were collected by either the Office of Education or Department of Education for 1962, when only 44 percent of private schools (8,329 of the total of 18,891) had a centralized school library facility.)[1]

Private secondary schools and all schools enrolling 300 pupils or more were more likely to have a school library media center than were elementary and combined schools (those that are administered as a single unit serving both elementary and secondary school children) or small schools regardless of grade level (Table 1). The percentage of schools with library media centers was greatest among Catholic schools, and the smallest percentage was among schools without religious affiliation.

The National Center for Education Statistics estimates that 4,290,074 students

TABLE 1 PRIVATE SCHOOLS WITH LIBRARY MEDIA CENTERS (LMC), BY AFFILIATION, LEVEL, AND ENROLLMENT, 1979

Level and Enrollment	All Private Schools	Number w/LMC	Percent w/LMC	Catholic	Other Affiliations	Unaffiliated
All schools	17,204	14,242	83	97	68	62
300 or more	5,505	5,184	94	96	89	88
Under 300	11,699	9,058	77	97	64	53
Secondary only	2,538	2,424	96	100	96	81
300 or more	1,362	1,362	100	100	100	100
Under 300	1,176	1,062	90	100	95	73
Elementary/combined	14,666	11,818	81	96	65	58
300 or more	4,143	3,822	92	95	87	85
Under 300	10,523	7,966	76	97	61	49

TABLE 2 EXPENDITURES FOR LIBRARY MEDIA CENTERS
IN PRIVATE SCHOOLS, 1979

	All Schools		Secondary		Elementary/Combined	
Expenditures	Total	Mean per Pupil	Total	Mean per Pupil	Total	Mean per Pupil
Total	$93,441,773	21.78	$36,094,675	11.28	$57,347,098	52.65
Salaries and wages	48,089,613	11.21	22,606,111	7.06	25,483,502	23.39
Library books	23,834,746	5.56	6,213,985	1.94	17,620,761	16.18
All other instructional materials	11,711,537	2.73	4,027,694	1.26	7,683,843	7.05
Equipment	6,983,231	1.61	1,965,449	0.61	5,017,782	4.61
Other	2,822,646	0.66	1,281,436	0.40	1,541,210	1.41

in private elementary or secondary schools were served by the 14,242 school library media centers—about 86 percent of the nation's population of private school children in 1979.

Expenditures

As shown in Table 2, expenditures for salaries were the highest percentage of the total expenditures by private school library media centers in 1979, with expenditures for books ranking significantly higher than the remaining categories. The figures for salaries exclude substantial amounts (more than $37 million) for contributed services and volunteer services. The amounts for contributed services and volunteer services were the estimated equivalent salaries or wages that would be paid to these staff members if they were determined on the same basis as paid employees.

The mean per pupil expenditure for library books and for all other types of library media resources will not add many items to a library media center's collections. For example, an annual expenditure of $5.56 per pupil for library books in a school of 1,000 students would add fewer than 300 books to a library media center collection.

Personnel

There were 28,937 individuals employed in private school libraries in 1979, the majority on a part-time basis (Table 3). About half of the paid professional staff were

TABLE 3 PRIVATE SCHOOL LIBRARY MEDIA
CENTER EMPLOYEES, 1979

	Number of Staff		
Type of Staff	Total	Secondary	Elementary
Total employees	28,937	6,518	12,419
Full time	7,245	2,483	4,762
Part time	21,692	4,035	17,657
Paid staff, full-time equivalents	6,822	2,526	4,296
Library media specialists	3,729	1,560	2,169
Teachers	1,246	196	1,050
Other	1,847	770	1,077
Unpaid staff, full-time equivalents	15,548	1,332	14,215
Library media specialists	1,006	257	749
Teachers	710	91	619
Other	13,832	985	12,847

professional school library media specialists. Although not shown in the tables, approximately 90 percent of the professional staff working in private school library media centers held at least a bachelor's degree, and women staff members outnumbered men to a considerable degree.

The ratio of full-time equivalent paid and unpaid professional library media center employees in private schools to the number of students enrolled was one staff member to about 906 students. The AASL/AECT media standard calls for a full-time library specialist for every 250 students or major fraction thereof.[2] The exceedingly favorable ratio of all paid and unpaid library media center staff—both professional and nonprofessional—to students (1 to 192) is accounted for by the large number of volunteer and contributed services personnel, most of whom were neither library media specialists nor teachers.

Library Materials

The average number of books and audiovisual titles held by private school library media centers—about 4,198 and 531 per school, respectively—indicates very small collections (Table 4). An average of 340 books per school and about 57 audiovisual titles per school were added in 1978-1979, showing very marginal additions to collections. Whether looking at book collections or audiovisual collections or number of periodical subscriptions held at the end of the 1978-1979 school year, the collections of most private school library media centers are far below the standards recommended by the American Association of School Librarians (AASL) and the Association for Educational Communications and Technology (AECT).[3]

Financial Needs

The reports provided by private school library media centers on their degree of need for financial assistance in acquiring resources appear to indicate only modest needs in any of the four areas surveyed—library books, periodical subscriptions, audiovisual materials, and audiovisual equipment (Table 5). Only slightly more than half of the schools reported a moderate need for library books. More than 40 percent of the schools indicated moderate need for audiovisual materials and audiovisual equipment. These expressed needs should be examined in relation to the size of collections, expenditures, and additions to collections over a one-year period. (Tables 2 and 4).

TABLE 4   LIBRARY MATERIALS IN PRIVATE SCHOOL LIBRARY MEDIA CENTERS, 1979

	Number of Items per School		
Level	Books	Periodicals	Audiovisual Titles
Acquisitions during school year			
All schools	340	—	57
Secondary only	613	—	78
Elementary/combined	273	—	51
Holdings at end of school year			
All schools	5,461	24	854
Secondary only	9,149	56	1,156
Elementary/combined	4,566	16	781

TABLE 5 NEED FOR FINANCIAL ASSISTANCE AMONG PRIVATE SCHOOLS TO ACQUIRE LIBRARY RESOURCES, 1979

Degree of Need	Library Books	Periodical Subscriptions	Audiovisual Materials	Audiovisual Equipment
No need	10.7	10.9	23.1	20.3
Moderate need	50.7	39.8	42.9	40.5
Strong need	26.3	27.0	22.3	22.4
Very strong need	12.3	22.3	12.7	16.8

NOTES

1. *National Inventory of School Facilities and Personnel* (OE-21026) (U.S. Department of Health, Education, and Welfare, Office of Education, Spring 1962), Table 5D and Table 18.
2. American Association of School Librarians and Association for Educational Communications and Technology, *Media Programs: District and School* (Chicago and Washington, D.C.: ALA and AECT), 1975, p. 33.
3. Ibid.

LIBRARY BUILDINGS IN 1982

Bette-Lee Fox
Associate Editor, *Library Journal*

Ann Burns
Assistant Editor, *Library Journal*

Deborah Waithe
Assistant Editor, *Library Journal*

New library buildings for fiscal 1982—new construction and addition/renovation projects—are reported in this issue. The bottom line reveals that more money went into new public library facilities than in any of the past six years except for 1979. [See Tables 1–5.] Most of this money was locally raised; state funding for construction was at a disappointing low, and federal funding continued at a figure that seems surprising since it must come, from the most part, from libraries tapping into Appalachian or Community Development funds. Gift funds were at an all-time high for recent years.

There is some indication that some of the growing local funding was from building mortgages taken out by libraries and evidently lumped with other "local" funding. Additional trends seen in the present crop of buildings: a continued emphasis on energy conservation, including solar projects; greater attention to security; a lot of adaptive reuse of nonlibrary structures; sharing of space with other agencies; and unusual efforts to achieve economies in other ways, such as construction by volunteer or prison labor, the use of prefabricated buildings, and design-build construction approaches.

The year's crop of new and remodeled academic libraries has the $22,471,000 University of North Carolina structure leading the parade of 20 new buildings; the lead renovation project, at the University of Kansas, was unusually thorough, rebuilding all but the outside shell; and the number of academic library projects maturing in fiscal 1982 is a respectable one when compared to the record of past years. [See Tables 6–9.]

Note: Adapted from *Library Journal*, December 1, 1982.

TABLE 1 NEW PUBLIC LIBRARY BUILDINGS
(Year Ending June 30, 1982)

Community	Pop. in M	Code	Project Cost	Gross Sq. Ft.	Const. Cost	Sq. Ft. Cost	Equip. Cost	Site Cost	Other Costs	Vols.	Reader Seats	Fed. Funds	State Funds	Local Funds	Gift Funds	Architect
ALABAMA																
Birmingham	30	B	1,207,290	15,100	1,030,061	66.42	104,229	100,000	80,244	77,000	139	522,000	0	765,534	0	Kidd
Lincoln[1]	4	M	75,452	2,000	62,000	31.00	7,452	owned	6,000	10,000	11	62,000	0	13,452	0	Dean
ARIZONA																
Mesa	180	M	4,478,232	102,673	3,892,198	37.90	314,079	owned	271,955	154,000	333	0	0	4,478,232	0	Horlbeck
Prescott Valley	4	B	19,750	1,000	19,750	19.75	0	owned	0	6,000	4	0	0	19,750	0	not reported
CALIFORNIA																
Anaheim	30	B	1,515,586	18,000	1,240,000	67.22	116,086	owned	159,500	90,000	122	988,178	411,511	115,887	0	Blurock
COLORADO																
Aurora[2]	180	M	4,000,000	55,000	3,300,000	60.00	350,000	owned	350,000	300,000	275	0	0	4,000,000	0	Warner...Brooks
Palmer Lake[3]	1	B	120,071	3,400	94,351	27.75	9,411	owned	6,309	9,300	20	35,000	0	15,571	69,500	Wood, P.
CONNECTICUT																
Granby[4]	8	M	880,000	8,021	577,500	71.99	133,300	owned	169,200	40,000	34	0	100,000	680,000	100,000	Galliher
Portland	8	M	1,900,000	17,500	1,423,653	81.35	150,000	owned	326,347	134,000	120	0	100,000	1,800,000	0	Jeter
Stratford[5]	50	M	2,800,000	35,890	1,900,000	52.94	434,000	owned	466,000	140,000	n/a	0	100,000	2,700,000	0	Galliher
DELAWARE																
Delmar	8	M	194,683	3,100	161,200	52.00	n/a	23,743	9,740	18,000	30	0	0	0	194,683	Clendaniel, R. C.
FLORIDA																
Coral Springs	42	B	1,202,001	13,680	876,859	64.10	56,928	184,358	83,356	55,000	115	0	0	1,202,001	0	Schieff & Assoc.
GEORGIA																
Blakely	18	M	600,000	9,000	400,000	44.44	120,000	12,000	68,000	40,000	32	0	400,000	200,000	0	Thomson, C.
Claxton	9	B	472,260	6,517	337,438	51.78	60,185	40,000	34,637	24,500	50	0	288,667	85,000	98,593	Akins, E.
Dalton	69	MS	1,987,500	40,000	1,327,613	33.19	401,000	108,000	150,886	125,000	188	450,000	637,500	700,000	200,000	Kirkman Assoc.
Eastman[6]	56	MS	715,000	13,400	564,569	42.00	115,029	owned	35,402	81,000	118	0	452,000	125,688	137,312	Tuten & Assoc.
ILLINOIS																
Alsip	21	M	2,286,933	24,000	1,589,089	66.21	244,473	181,500	271,871	87,500	158	0	0	0	2,286,933	Kleb, O.
Batavia	15	M	489,713	10,077	360,035	26.18	96,213	owned	33,465	60,000	82	0	0	489,713	0	Hestrup & Assoc.
Bloomingdale	13	M	1,374,475	21,725	1,077,665	49.60	103,147	owned	193,663	100,000	100	0	0	1,371,975	2,500	Jaki & Assoc.
Cahokia	19	M	373,985	6,000	312,380	52.06	15,800	19,000	26,805	40,000	55	0	0	343,745	30,240	Weisenstein
Channahon	8	M	714,493	9,200	534,941	58.15	63,770	39,970	75,812	42,000	57	0	17,000	697,493	0	Carlson, H. J.
Hazel Crest	28	M	1,400,000	16,700	1,116,930	66.88	124,084	owned	159,833	50,000	50	0	0	1,400,000	0	Ventsch, L.
Lake Zurich	16	M	775,000	11,800	642,000	54.00	65,000	owned	68,000	60,000	56	0	0	705,000	70,000	O'Donnell
Morton[7]	14	M	756,604	9,500	443,552	46.69	72,000	225,000	16,052	34,060	62	0	0	661,604	95,000	Westlake, D.
Palos Park	3	M	149,886	2,256	102,681	45.51	19,913	11,323	15,969	15,000	22	0	0	119,658	30,228	Bailey & Assoc.
Zion[8]	31	M	897,550	12,864	740,260	57.55	85,800	owned	71,490	100,000	88	0	0	889,550	8,000	Hunter, R.

TABLE 1 NEW PUBLIC LIBRARY BUILDINGS
(Year Ending June 30, 1982) (cont.)

Community	Pop. in M	Code	Project Cost	Gross Sq. Ft.	Const. Cost	Sq. Ft. Cost	Equip. Cost	Site Cost	Other Costs	Vols.	Reader Seats	Fed. Funds	State Funds	Local Funds	Gift Funds	Architect
INDIANA																
Brownsburg	18	M	2,400,000	25,035	1,716,995	68.58	246,783	55,146	381,076	72,000	121	0	0	2,400,000	0	Randall, J.P.
KANSAS																
Ashland	1	M	490,000	6,000	410,000	68.33	40,000	0	30,000	30,000	45	0	0	0	490,000	Fisher, W.I.
Dodge City[9]	18	MS	1,748,467	36,000	1,255,796	34.88	200,747	45,000	246,924	97,400	116	0	0	1,695,855	52,612	Williams.
LOUISIANA																
Bayou Pigeon	1	B	94,180	1,365	71,835	53.30	4,910	10,000	7,435	6,000	10	94,180	0	0	0	Schwing & Assoc.
Lockport	6	B	728,304	1,819	592,450	66.21	34,860	33,000	67,994	14,000	24	500,000	217,000	2,629	8,675	Gulf South.
Marrero	30	B	293,099	5,738	206,694	36.02	70,000	owned	16,405	40,000	83	0	0	293,099	0	Saunders & Assoc.
Tioga	20	B	128,935	3,600	120,500	33.47	35,000	owned	8,435	n/a	23	0	0	128,935	0	Yeager.
MARYLAND																
Cockeysville	150	B	1,839,997	26,000	1,415,914	53.48	173,035	owned	170,379	80,000	104	0	0	1,990,340	0	Downing & Assoc.
Frederick	118	MS	2,456,000	29,000	n/a	84.69	n/a	350,000	n/a	136,000	111	0	332	2,295,668	160,000	Wening, R.W.
Olney	n/a	B	1,881,814	16,540	1,189,225	71.90	296,680	214,035	181,874	65,000	200	0	118,000	1,763,814	0	VVKR Inc.
Pikesville	80	B	1,150,018	18,500	873,337	46.26	181,089	owned	95,592	61,000	62	0	0	1,241,255	0	Myers & D'Aleo
Waldorf	26	B	621,000	8,000	407,200	50.90	44,800	150,000	19,000	50,000	56	0	90,407	361,593	169,000	Ward, G. T.
MICHIGAN																
Fremont	11	M	660,401	11,998	522,938	43.59	67,463	owned	70,000	57,000	90	0	0	0	660,401	Holmes & Black
MINNESOTA																
Brooklyn Center	155	n/a	3,663,517	32,155	2,406,908	74.85	257,007	359,724	638,878	110,000	n/a	0	0	3,663,517	0	Stageberg.
Jackson	6	M	608,417	6,100	422,943	69.33	61,721	61,283	62,470	24,000	30	0	0	0	610,500	InterDesign, Inc.
Monticello	12	B	551,000	6,000	336,000	56.00	75,000	73,000	67,000	30,000	48	0	0	551,000	0	McEnary.
MISSISSIPPI																
Crawford[10]	1	B	16,551	936	13,125	14.02	3,426	owned	0	3,800	20	4,551	0	12,000	0	Simmons.
Mt. Olive	1	B	33,349	1,750	33,049	18.89	300	owned	0	8,500	29	0	0	33,049	0	not reported
Newhebron[11]	1	B	1,550	480	1,500	3.23	0	owned	50	2,000	8	1,500	0	50	0	not reported
Sunflower[12]	1	B	55,025	504	47,857	94.95	5,313	owned	1,855	3,000	10	51,368	0	2,460	1,196	Weilenman & Assoc.
MONTANA																
Bozeman[13]	30	MS	1,528,717	20,733	1,048,616	50.58	161,329	191,250	127,522	40,000	96	0	0	1,463,217	65,500	Matson.
NEVADA																
Beatty[14]	4	M	111,932	2,991	103,424	37.42	4,387	owned	4,121	14,000	15	0	0	0	111,932	Goodwin.
Boulder City	10	M	933,639	10,000	761,081	76.10	120,347	owned	52,211	35,000	73	0	0	0	933,639	Tates & Assoc.
NEW JERSEY																
Hopatcong[15]	27	B	971,800	7,600	684,200	90.03	105,000	8,100	174,500	34,040	102	0	0	963,700	8,100	Houghton, W.I.
Piscataway	15	B	947,600	12,296	735,432	59.81	92,924	30,000	89,244	30,000	65	597,600	100,000	250,000	0	Bolen, J.
Vernon	16	B	935,500	7,600	660,800	86.95	105,000	owned	169,700	31,275	97	0	0	935,500	0	Young, A.

358 / LIBRARY RESEARCH AND STATISTICS

NEW YORK													
Flushing	23	B	690,000	7,500	500,000	67.00	90,000	25,000	75,000	40,000	104	0	0	0	Kaminsky & Shipper
Flushing	15	B	715,001	7,500	550,000	73.00	90,000	1	75,000	40,000	104	0	0	0	Gueron ....
Shirley	35	M	1,727,260	19,600	1,235,226	63.02	185,081	150,000	156,953	110,000	156	0	0	150,000	Bentel & Bentel
NORTH CAROLINA														
Columbia[16]	4	n/a	181,227	5,000	140,336	28.00	19,500	21,391	0	13,500	34	79,369	55,200	46,658	not reported
Hillsborough[17]	45	M	490,880	11,600	405,880	35.00	85,000	owned	n/a	60,000	76	0	39,500	0	Nassif, J.
Mt. Airy	25	B	1,676,413	13,570	1,307,800	96.37	81,089	97,500	190,024	90,000	108	784,663	30,150	0	Pease...&Mazria
Rural Hall[18]	23	B	674,515	8,500	558,515	65.71	40,000	30,000	46,000	40,000	40	265,000	0	0	Kirby & Assoc.
Waynesville	46	M	1,516,912	26,454	1,263,777	47.77	159,790	owned	93,345	80,000	145	634,370	90,300	116,472	Foy & Lee Assoc.
OHIO														
Cleveland	17	B	908,004	9,000	727,317	80.81	49,350	40,000	91,337	25,000	81		0	0	Gaede, R.C.
Cleveland	16	B	1,145,785	9,800	918,181	93.69	51,317	93,127	83,160	20,000	60		0	0	Collins & Rimer
St.Marys	10	M	540,934	8,911	464,029	52.07	76,905	owned	39,217	50,000	70		0	0	Strong....
OKLAHOMA														
Cordell	4	B	323,000	5,500	263,000	47.81	35,000	owned	25,000	20,000	40	0	2,630	165,000	Nausbaum & Thomas
Tulsa	18	B	728,290	9,545	577,054	60.45	47,595	53,358	40,283	40,000	47	533,500	0	0	Imel & Graber
OREGON														
Reedsport	10	B	517,850	6,000	390,342	65.06	21,001	66,000	40,507	22,000	58	387,337	13,259	99,454	Miller, V.
PENNSYLVANIA														
Bensalem	52	B	988,598	15,322	674,071	43.99	204,527	owned	110,000	50,000	99	0	0	0	Kramer, W. E.
SOUTH CAROLINA														
North Myrtle Bch	10	B	235,830	7,000	161,603	23.09	29,229	40,000	4,998	20,000	48	0	0	99,718	Connor, W. K.
Rock Hill	107	MS	2,195,516	33,250	1,580,865	47.54	317,548	150,000	147,103	180,000	221	0	0	110,000	Gaulden, E.
SOUTH DAKOTA														
Custer[19]	6	M	550,000	8,730	333,420	38.19	0	80,000	136,580	14,000	35	0	0	550,000	Randall, Steve
TENNESSEE														
Ashland City[20]	2	M	57,800	1,440	n/a	n/a	0	0	0	8,000	15	0	0	0	not reported
Memphis	4	B	427,000	6,000	270,000	45.00	33,000	owned	124,000	30,000	40	0	0	285,000	Thompson, H. F.
Milan[21]	12	n/a	623,457	7,500	n/a	n/a	30,379	50,000	30,444	50,000	60	0	0	15,231	Thomas....
Mt. Juliet	10	B	117,800	3,040	73,400	38.75	15,000	25,000	4,400	25,000	16	59,000	0	47,000	Conley & Co.
Portland	4	n/a	150,000	3,500	142,500	40.71	7,500	owned	0	10,000	24	0	0	70,000	Utley, T.
TEXAS														
Dallas	904	MS	41,700,000	646,000	34,600,000	53.56	3,300,000	owned	3,800,000	2,500,000	1300	4,900,000	0	25,800,000	11,000,000 Fisher & Spillman
Fairfield	5	M	250,000	5,310	180,176	33.93	36,880	21,000	9,944	26,750	46	0	0	104,000	146,000 Stripling. L.
Fort Stockton	12	M	717,385	12,200	551,385	45.20	100,000	owned	66,000	50,000	118	0	0	594,000	123,385 Huckabee & Donham
Groesbeck[22]	16	M	55,000	4,200	54,000	12.16	1,000	owned	0	40,000	26	0	0	15,000	40,000 not reported
Sour Lake	5	M	46,235	2,400	45,583	18.99	652	owned	0	20,000	16	46,235	0	0	46,235 Corbet, L.
UTAH														
St. George[23]	30	MS	1,378,478	21,548	1,062,108	49.29	241,872	owned	69,928	75,000	172	0	0	1,378,478	0 Stoker, L.A.

LIBRARY BUILDINGS IN 1982 / 359

TABLE 1 NEW PUBLIC LIBRARY BUILDINGS
(Year Ending June 30, 1982) (cont.)

Community	Pop. in M	Code	Project Cost	Gross Sq. Ft.	Const. Cost	Sq. Ft. Cost	Equip. Cost	Site Cost	Other Costs	Vols.	Reader Seats	Fed. Funds	State Funds	Local Funds	Gift Funds	Architect
VIRGINIA																
Fairfax[24]	10	M	258,150	1,600	247,650	161.34	4,000	owned	6,500	10,000	32	0	0	258,150	0	not reported
WASHINGTON																
Bonney Lake	12	B	355,200	3,400	240,107	70.62	22,039	29,000	64,054	16,000	27	0	0	355,220	0	Tsang, J. C.
King County	25	B	581,868	6,400	427,589	66.81	47,245	owned	107,035	25,000	48	0	0	581,868	0	Lewis-Nelson Assoc.
Orting[25]	4	B	285,085	2,967	208,058	70.12	6,000	51,000	20,027	11,100	25	259,385	0	25,700	0	Moore, G.
Tonasket	3	n/a	421,000	5,074	381,407	75.17	14,000	8,300	17,293	7,000	22	391,100	0	20,000	10,000	Tan . . .
WYOMING																
Green River	42	MS	1,282,145	15,000	1,136,454	75.76	60,295	owned	85,396	100,000	79	0	0	1,282,145	0	Richardson, Assoc.
VIRGIN ISLANDS																
St. Croix[26]	10	B	75,000	170	75,000	382.35	0	owned	0	5,000	0	70,000	n/a	5,000	0	not reported

TABLE 2 STATE LIBRARY AGENCY BUILDINGS
(Year Ending June 30, 1982)

	Pop. in M	Code	Project Cost	Gross Sq. Ft.	Const. Cost	Sq. Ft. Cost	Equip. Cost	Site Cost	Other Costs	Vols.	Reader Seats	Fed. Funds	State Funds	Local Funds	Gift Funds	Architect
KENTUCKY																
Frankfort, Dept.[27a] for Libs. & Archives	4	MS	10,500,000	134,000	8,591,910	64.12	850,000	owned	1,058,090	31,000	112	0	10,500,000	0	0	Peck . . .
NEW JERSEY																
Ewing Twp., NJ[27b] Records & Storage Ctr./Lib. for Blind & Physically Handicapped	60	M	9,750,000	105,292	6,717,251	63.80	2,521,164	owned	511,585	1,657,427	46	0	9,750,000	0	0	Mahony . . . & Davis Brody

TABLE 3 PUBLIC LIBRARY BUILDINGS: ADDITIONS, REMODELINGS, AND RENOVATIONS
(Year Ending June 30, 1982)

Community	Pop in M	Code	Project Cost	Gross Sq. Ft.	Const. Cost	Sq. Ft. Cost	Equipt. Cost	Site Cost	Other Costs	Vols.	Reader Seats	Fed. Funds	State Funds	Local Funds	Gift Funds	Architect
ARIZONA																
Tucson[27]	65	B	138,121	1,400	108,508	77.50	18,000	owned	11,613	40,000	40	n/a	0	138,121	0	Noggle, McCarthy
CALIFORNIA																
Palo Alto	56	M	674,000	20,368	554,000	27.20	n/a	owned	0	117,000	165	0	0	674,000	0	Spencer Assocs.
CONNECTICUT																
Norwalk	76	M	3,480,000	47,730	2,685,900	56.30	320,000	210,000	264,100	170,000	180	1,307,000	72,000	1,891,000	210,000	John Gaydosh
Salisbury	4	M	695,700	13,151	504,980	38.39	51,400	owned	139,320	50,000	60	143,700	100,000	57,000	395,000	Huygens & DeMella
Stamford	102	B	6,914,000	96,000	5,767,000	72.02	572,000	owned	575,000	250,000	400	n/a	72,000	6,692,000	150,000	Warner ...
DELAWARE																
Frankford	3	M	165,000	2,080	24,500	11.78	14,000	125,000	1,500	10,000	20	40,000	0	0	125,000	not reported
FLORIDA																
Arcadia	20	M	22,898	995	17,574	17.96	4,624	owned	700	7,000	24	0	0	0	22,898	Carl Cool
Ft. Lauderdale	300	B	1,082,951	34,460	744,347	21.60	261,985	n/a	76,619	180,000	270	0	0	1,082,951	0	Haack ...
Hollywood	121	B	364,764	10,800	266,667	24.69	70,840	owned	27,257	70,000	106	0	0	364,764	0	Shiff & Assocs.
Royal Palm Bch	10	B	19,500	1,000	3,500	3.50	16,000	leased	0	6,000	14	0	0	19,500	0	not reported
Tamarac	31	B	545,632	9,750	8,553	.88	33,816	500,000	3,263	45,000	75	0	0	545,632	0	not reported
GEORGIA																
Forsyth	16	B	622,347	10,400	475,000	45.67	87,347	owned	60,000	36,000	68	0	350,000	272,347	0	Brittain ...
Perry	78	MS	437,645	5,247	304,618	58.06	46,511	60,000	26,516	50,000	72	0	180,249	238,764	18,632	Holliday ...
ILLINOIS																
Champaign	435	S	125,910	10,350	56,722	5.48	57,279	owned	11,909	15,600	n/a	0	125,910	0	0	Bob Gruber
*Joliet	2	M	n/a	3,200	14,672	4.60	n/a	leased	n/a	8,000	60	n/a	n/a	n/a	n/a	not reported
Lena	4	M	88,829	2,190	78,017	34.79	3,205	owned	7,607	26,000	24	0	0	84,129	4,700	J. E. Anderson
Oswego	18	M	903,295	14,800	680,667	45.99	119,247	25,000	78,381	70,000	102	0	0	893,674	9,621	Kleb Associates
Quincy	42	M	20,000	3,500	9,700	2.77	10,300	owned	0	24,000	13	n/a	n/a	n/a	20,000	not reported
Rushville	3	M	9,074	726	0	n/a	9,074	0	0	4,770	16	3,000	0	6,074	0	not reported
Tinley Park	26	M	389,717	12,500	318,918	25.00	46,429	owned	24,370	27,000	47	0	0	389,717	0	Hammond ...
INDIANA																
Evansville	138	M	162,000	2,391	132,797	55.54	18,703	owned	10,500	n/a	n/a	20,000	0	0	142,000	Gaisser ...
IOWA																
Keystone	618	M	37,414	1,000	36,970	36.97	444	owned	0	5,000	36	0	0	1,414	36,000	not reported
Schleswig	2	M	22,438	1,440	9,397	6.52	11,834	owned	1,206	14,000	11	1,000	0	7,248	14,190	not reported
KANSAS																
Hesston	3	M	100,000	3,553	71,719	28.15	16,889	owned	11,392	15,000	30	0	0	100,000	0	Bishop Architects
Sterling	3	M	140,000	3,700	130,000	48.00	5,000	owned	10,000	2,500	30	0	0	0	140,000	Mann & Company

TABLE 3 PUBLIC LIBRARY BUILDINGS: ADDITIONS, REMODELINGS, AND RENOVATIONS
(Year Ending June 30, 1982) (cont.)

Community	Pop. in M	Code	Project Cost	Gross Sq. Ft.	Const. Cost	Sq. Ft. Cost	Equip. Cost	Site Cost	Other Costs	Vols.	Reader Seats	Fed. Funds	State Funds	Local Funds	Gift Funds	Architect
LOUISIANA																
Eunice	30	B	135,070	4,556	69,994	15.36	17,683	40,000	7,393	40,000	56	0	0	135,070	0	not reported
Lafitte	1	B	86,500	1,600	9,500	5.94	27,000	n/a	0	10,000	25	0	0	36,500	50,000	not reported
New Iberia	50	BS	381,612	24,811	294,500	11.86	63,552	owned	23,560	100,000	97	0	0	381,612	0	Gerald Gesser
New Orleans	10	B	121,841	1,700	108,041	63.55	4,262	owned	9,538	15,000	16	114,281	0	6,760	800	Hayden & Assocs.
MARYLAND																
Chaneyville	8	B	151,522	3,625	112,435	31.02	39,087	0	0	n/a	n/a	0	0	0	0	not reported
Ocean City[28]	7	B	62,308	5,000	3,000	12.46	59,308	owned	0	20,200	38	0	0	62,308	0	not reported
MASSACHUSETTS																
Danvers	25	M	2,248,085	30,000	1,947,861	65.92	113,774	owned	186,450	135,000	200	0	0	2,208,000	40,085	Padjen Architects
Medfield	10	M	412,000	7,000	200,000	58.00	25,000	160,000	27,000	60,000	50	0	0	14,000	3,000	CityDesign
Medway[29]	7	M	282,446	12,870	161,817	12.57	42,486	owned	78,143	32,000	57	395,000	18,390	264,056	0	Whitman & Howard
Plymouth	32	M	231,584	3,500	185,832	61.30	28,752	owned	17,000	80,000	75	0	0	231,584	0	Nicholas Filla
MICHIGAN																
Howard City	4	M	66,094	1,500	35,220	23.48	5,874	25,000	n/a	n/a	n/a	0	0	66,094	0	not reported
MINNESOTA																
Blaine	40	M	361,774	18,578	262,594	14.13	60,685	owned	38,495	100,000	135	0	0	361,774	0	G. L. Lindberg
Jordan	6	B	93,797	4,149	12,387	22.61	11,410	70,000	0	25,000	20	0	0	38,797	55,000	not reported
Roseville	190	M	411,179	20,700	301,824	14.58	55,206	n/a	54,149	100,000	71	0	0	411,179	0	Buetow & Assocs.
MISSISSIPPI																
Houston	5	B	141,332	6,100	118,954	19.50	15,000	owned	7,378	14,450	32	30,000	66,244	45,088	0	Marion M. Fox
NEVADA																
Gabbs	1	M	83,400	1,494	83,400	55.82	n/a	owned	n/a	30,000	40	0	0	0	83,400	Habitat, Inc.
NEW JERSEY																
Succasunna	20	M	387,000	4,100	267,000	65.13	50,000	owned	70,000	80,000	118	0	0	187,000	200,000	John Bolen
NEW MEXICO																
Albuquerque	130	B	918,600	16,000	768,100	48.00	90,000	owned	60,500	125,000	135	0	0	918,600	0	G. Sanders
NEW YORK																
Oceanside	39	M	107,216	760	78,625	103.45	16,763	owned	11,828	6,684	16	n/a	n/a	n/a	n/a	R. Euker
Setauket[30]	40	M	1,250,153	15,000	822,357	54.82	199,891	owned	227,905	300,000	114	0	0	0	0	Arelt & Lorio
Suffern	25	M	54,015	3,888	54,015	13.89	n/a	owned	0	70,000	65	0	0	54,015	0	not reported
Syracuse	18	M	33,000	600	26,000	43.33	0	owned	7,000	n/a	n/a	33,000	0	0	0	C. Croom
West Hempstead	16	M	225,658	9,000	169,258	18.81	38,900	owned	17,500	160,000	110	53,000	0	159,658	13,000	R. Miller
NORTH CAROLINA																
Burlington[31]	99	M	584,994	15,597	492,334	32.00	42,086	owned	50,574	75,000	76	512,295	60,300	11,399	1,000	Alley

LIBRARY BUILDINGS IN 1982 / 363

NORTH DAKOTA														
Bismarck	635	M	2,500,000	47,000	n/a	n/a	n/a	n/a	150,000	75	0	n/a	0	Tvenge-Larson
OHIO														
Cleveland	9	B	575,951	6,124	494,726	80.78	35,612	owned	45,613	20,000	54	0	0	575,951	0	Blunden Barclay
OKLAHOMA														
Skiatook	4	B	330,703	5,400	253,922	47.02	1,236	50,000	25,545	20,000	32	115,000	0	164,629	28,074	Olsen & Coffey
PENNSYLVANIA														
Bethel	6	M	85,280	1,620	21,100	13.64	16,280	44,000	3,900	n/a	12	85,280	0	0	0	Spotts ....
Carmichaels	8	M	107,850	2,500	97,075	43.14	1,675	owned	9,100	6,000	20	0	0	106,280	1,570	J. Pellis
TENNESSEE														
Hendersonville	26	B	240,000	5,800	180,000	31.03	40,000	owned	20,000	24,000	60	0	0	200,000	40,000	Thomas & Miller
Old Hickory[32]	9	B	283,135	6,700	241,625	40.00	22,260	6,500	12,750	25,000	50	250,125	0	33,010	0	Swaney & Vogt
TEXAS														
Diboll	5	M	171,127	1,260	155,556	48.79	2,757	owned	12,814	36,000	41	0	0	30,000	141,127	Temple Assocs.
Grand Saline	3	M	30,000	2,964	30,000	10.12	0	leased	0	n/a	22	0	0	0	30,000	not reported
Johnson City	2	M	41,359	1,704	29,343	17.22	6,016	6,000	0	18,000	15	0	0	788	40,571	N. Harp
Odessa	115	M	1,813,177	47,398	911,343	34.52	50,341	756,000	95,493	238,200	170	1,608,321	0	85,856	119,000	Covington
Plano	82	S	247,140	13,000	165,481	12.73	52,159	owned	29,500	22,000	0	0	0	247,140	0	B. Burgesser
Quitman	5	M	126,000	6,000	n/a	n/a	15,000	111,000	n/a	12,000	25	0	0	25,000	101,000	not reported
UTAH														
Nephi	4	M	60,000	3,000	48,000	16.00	10,000	owned	2,000	10,500	25	50,000	0	10,000	0	D. Ashworth
VIRGINIA														
Danville	6	B	10,000	1,200	3,600	3.00	6,400	0	0	7,800	10	0	4,400	5,600	0	not reported
Mathews	8	M	86,890	3,276	77,920	24.00	7,058	owned	1,912	18,000	40	0	0	84,890	2,000	Planning ....
Williamsburg	33	M	1,286,909	n/a	1,086,550	70.10	75,000	owned	125,359	30,000	80	0	0	1,286,900	0	Shriver ....
WASHINGTON														
Tacoma	22	B	116,594	3,500	91,361	26.10	17,299	owned	7,934	20,000	45	0	0	109,312	7,282	J. Kinkella
WISCONSIN														
Baraboo	12	M	717,535	15,200	600,110	39.48	61,231	owned	56,194	45,000	75	0	0	617,535	100,000	Strang Partners
Fontana[33]	2	B	156,543	2,610	124,309	47.63	19,387	owned	12,847	24,000	25	0	0	0	156,543	not reported
Lancaster	4	M	250,000	5,000	193,416	38.68	35,178	owned	21,406	35,000	60	0	0	50,000	200,000	Rose/Orr
VIRGIN ISLANDS														
St. John	5	B	450,000	n/a	350,000	143.44	40,000	owned	60,000	10,000	30	297,000	0	153,000	0	T. Fults
Frederiksted	15	B	656,000	7,656	621,000	85.68	n/a	owned	35,000	n/a	n/a	439,520	0	216,480	0	J. Coughlin

*Note: The figures for the remodeling project in Joliet, Illinois refer to the Joliet Correctional Center Library.

TABLE 4   PUBLIC LIBRARY BUILDINGS, 1979–1981 (Not Previously Reported)

Community	Pop in M	Code	Project Cost	Gross Sq.Ft.	Const. Cost	Sq.Ft. Cost	Equip. Cost	Site Cost	Others Costs	Volumes	Reader Seats	Fed. Funds	State Funds	Local Funds	Gift Funds	Architect
Atmore, AL (1980)	20	B	$14,151	728	$14,151	$19.43	0	0	0	35,000	27	0	0	$14,151	0	not reported
Blountsville, AL (1981)	2	M	9,000	400	9,000	22.50	$35	owned	0	n/a	10	0	0	9,000	0	not reported
Calera, AL (1981)	2	M	7,942	1,560	7,942	5.09	53	owned	0	25,000	15	0	0	7,942	0	not reported
Hartselle, AL (1981)	9	B	140,000	2,652	90,700	34.20	20,000	owned	$29,300	16,346	n/a	$120,000	0	6,000	$22,000	Underwood...
Helena, AL (1981)	2	M	1,017	908	1,017	1.12	53	leased	0	10,000	9	0	0	1,017	0	not reported
Lyme, CT (1981)	2	M	61,630	1,200	41,433	55.65	15,230	owned	4,967	28,000	32	0	0	0	61,630	Elliot, T.
Clearwater, FL (1980)	89	M	1,354,748	36,000	1,156,900	32.14	102,933	owned	94,915	n/a	200	0	$200,000	654,748	500,000	Watson & Co.
Hallandale, FL (1981)	37	B	1,257,346	14,700	1,112,348	75.67	82,132	owned	62,866	55,000	100	0	0	1,257,346	0	Miller &...
Lauderdale Lks., FL (1981)	25	M	419,010	7,900	337,174	42.68	49,186	leased	32,650	n/a	n/a	0	0	419,010	0	Schiff...
Zephyrhills, FL (1981)	24	M	57,163	2,050	57,163	27.86	n/a	owned	0	12,000	24	0	0	11,163	46,000	none
Glennville, GA (1980)	9	B	203,563	4,250	155,089	36.49	32,586	owned	15,888	15,000	27	0	105,000	94,000	4,156	Tuten, J.A.
Glen Ellyn, IL (1980)	25	M	929,016	28,000	797,016	28.47	65,000	owned	67,000	300,000	65	0	0	929,016	0	O'Donnell...
Lisle, IL (1981)	21	M	1,035,111	13,500	799,400	59.22	115,974	owned	119,737	60,000	64	0	0	1,035,111	0	Kleb Assocs.
Richton Park, IL (1981)	9	M	33,212	2,700	24,347	9.02	7,616	leased	1,249	15,000	17	20,000	0	13,212	0	O'Donnell...
Sidell, IL (1981)	1	M	65,000	2,000	45,000	22.50	0	20,000	0	6,000	20	0	689	17,728	0	none
Sugar Grove, IL[34] (1980)	3	M	291,479	4,650	257,231	56.00	11,448	owned	19,600	30,000	21	0	0	81,048	3,200	Emma, T.A.
Baton Rouge, LA (1979)	n/a	B	1,971,462	30,000	1,743,000	58.10	228,462	owned	n/a	100,000	176	1,971,462	0	0	0	Desmond...
Columbia, MD (1981)	120	MS	3,300,000	46,000	2,825,000	61.41	300,000	owned	175,000	250,000	200	0	0	3,300,000	0	VVKR...

LIBRARY BUILDINGS IN 1982 / 365

Gaithersburg, MD (1981)	n/a	B	2,895,678	36,000	53.76	494,906	236,907	228,518	150,000	250	0	118,000	2,777,678	0	McLeod...
Chanhassen, MN (1981)	9	B	291,261	3,200	85.00	19,581	owned	0	31,000	0	0	0	291,261	0	Boarman, J.
Minneapolis, MN (1981)	30	B	2,289,721	18,500	80.55	1,490,224	382,772	146,047	45,000	115	0	0	2,289,721	0	Myers...
Kosciusko, MS (1980)	7	MS	284,953	7,808	28.35	221,425	owned	17,558	54,500	70	0	284,953	0	0	Godfrey...
Cape Girardeau, MO (1980)	34	M	1,076,324	18,900	41.23	779,269	47,500	82,628	109,000	102	0	0	909,324	167,000	Hoener, T.
Cleveland, OH (1980)	22	B	937,616	9,900	69.27	685,862	97,334	102,899	25,000	76	0	0	342,000	0	Myers, R.C.
Cleveland, OH (1980)	33	B	1,403,599	10,900	108.65	1,184,267	56,000	105,020	25,000	55	0	0	937,616	0	Ceruti, J.
Cleveland, OH (1979)	25	B	814,949	7,800	86.24	672,700	33,000	66,095	25,000	46	0	0	1,403,599	0	Zung, T.T.K.
Cleveland, OH (1981)	28	B	416,340	8,200	40.52	332,302	owned	49,400	20,000	51	0	0	814,949	0	Whitley...
Cleveland, OH (1980)	26	B	448,860	8,094	44.36	359,120	owned	49,270	20,000	61	0	0	416,340	0	Payer, E.
Philadelphia, PA (1981)	20	B	342,000	1,225	71.85	315,000	owned	22,500	41,000	72	0	0	448,860	0	Payer, E.
Nederland, TX (1981)	20	M	130,000	2,000	54.00	108,117	owned	15,386	40,000	32	0	0	130,000	0	Moore...
Sealy, TX (1981)	10	M	542,017	7,800	48.46	378,000	50,116	73,918	20,000	44	0	0	0	542,017	Rieniets, J.H.
Burlington, VT (1981)	38	M	2,402,000	40,000	51.14	2,045,400	owned	142,600	120,000	150	0	0	2,400,000	2,000	Anderson...
Charlottesville, VA (1981)	62	MS	2,250,000	25,259	66.12	1,670,000	owned	160,000	150,000	130	0	0	2,025,000	225,000	Rinehart, J.
Bellevue, Alberta (1981)	2	M	75,800	1,260	49.21	62,000	owned	6,100	10,000	16	0	34,950	39,950	0	Matson...
Ft. Saskatchewan, Alberta (1979)	12	M	1,400,000	20,000	66.00	1,320,000	owned	80,000	50,000	95	0	570,000	870,000	0	MacPherson, D.

REFERENCES

1. Preengineered building: old brick and rock exterior.
2. Cable TV studio; drive-in checkout; CLSI cataloging for staff and patrons.

3. Shares facility with the historical society.
4. Shares facility with senior center.
5. Preserved nineteenth-century exterior; computer check-out system.
6. Sun utilized for lighting, heating, and cooling.
7. Used Design-Build method of bidding; unique financing including mortgage.
8. Free-standing garage for bookmobile and van; mortgage sold to public.
9. Energy efficient; complete access to handicapped.
10. Shares building with city hall and fire department.
11. Portable library; pilot project for state.
12. Trailer is first library in town; preliminary plans begun for permanent building.
13. Passive solar features—extensive use of glass on south side with sun screens; water tube trombe wall.
14. Geodesic dome with balcony; electric chair-lift to balcony.
15. Passive solar design; library staff had input in exterior design and made all decisions about interior design; circulating art prints.
16. Preengineered structure, planned and designed by the building committee.
17. Housed in converted school building.
18. Passive solar design; solar atrium; salt storage trays; trombe walls.
19. Located in community center; passive solar system.
20. Purchased completed building and property.
21. Community building housing senior citizens center and health department.
22. Townspeople donated most services and equipment.
23. Won Utah state "Illuminating Engineer Society Award" 1982 for outstanding lighting and energy management.
24. Prefabricated structure.
25. Library occupies half of HUD-funded community center.
26. Prefabricated structure.
27. Tucson Public Library's first branch library dedicated in June 1961.
27a. State Library and State Archives, providing additional storage for 112,000 cubic ft. of archives and records.
27b. See "News Section," *Library Journal*, December 1, 1982.
28. Construction work done by County Maintenance Dept. and work-release program prisoners. Project cost only about 10 percent of original projected cost as a result.
29. Originally built as elementary school in 1940.
30. Project financed through mortgage monies; no government funds used.
31. Originally built in 1916, the building was a U.S. post office until 1938.
32. Original building was a gift of the Dupont Co. in 1937.
33. Building was a Depression project and constructed for under $15,000. It opened debt free on February 12, 1934, one-hundred twenty-fifth anniversary of Lincoln's birth.
34. Project was financed by mortgage monies, on present tax base.

TABLE 5 PUBLIC LIBRARY BUILDINGS: SIX-YEAR COST SUMMARY

	Fiscal 1977	Fiscal 1978	Fiscal 1979	Fiscal 1980	Fiscal 1981	Fiscal 1982
Number of new bldgs.	142	135	168	100	82	90
Number of ARR's (1)	69	85	112	65	76	72
Sq. ft. new bldgs.	2,100,016	1,355,130	2,898,585	1,662,699	1,134,748	2,037,543
Sq. ft. ARR's	585,635	663,915	912,567	488,528	954,106	712,771
New bldgs.						
Construction cost	$85,986,538	$54,508,361	$96,010,260	$79,984,894	$64,658,453	$107,220,538
Equipment cost	10,727,160	7,433,541	13,336,842	9,712,822	9,059,027	14,487,981
Site cost	8,401,254	5,508,018	3,233,751	3,234,525	3,265,157	3,556,109
Other costs	9,442,938	6,712,240	8,523,617	9,602,584	7,167,009	13,162,904
Total—Project cost	114,557,890	74,162,160	121,109,470	102,538,025	86,019,599	141,074,894
ARR's—Project cost	17,144,009	18,891,111	29,930,142	20,398,544	55,388,161	36,334,608
New & ARR Project cost	$131,701,899	$93,053,271	$151,039,612	$122,936,569	$141,407,760	$177,409,502
Fund Sources						
Federal, new bldgs.	$19,226,511	$13,304,652	$63,354,045	$29,005,800	$18,269,728	$11,716,336
Federal, ARR's	1,149,718	4,046,901	18,414,336	4,253,080	4,105,877	5,497,522
Federal, total	$20,376,229	$17,351,553	$81,768,381	$33,258,880	$22,375,605	$17,213,858
State, new bldgs.	$5,757,047	$5,803,920	$13,897,410	$1,394,677	$3,537,248	$23,513,456
State, ARR's	1,381,725	2,658,733	1,404,067	3,367,304	1,343,174	1,049,493
State, total	$7,138,772	$8,462,653	$15,301,477	$4,761,981	$4,880,422	$24,562,949
Local, new bldgs.	$82,266,956	$47,193,528	$73,994,629	$63,348,408	$57,099,210	$86,662,313
Local, ARR's	13,286,234	10,371,229	9,854,905	9,190,767	43,598,892	23,054,200
Local, total	$95,553,190	$57,564,757	$83,849,534	$72,539,175	$100,698,102	$109,716,513
Gift, new bldgs.	$7,307,376	$7,860,060	$11,398,318	$5,506,812	$5,699,152	$19,808,877
Gift, ARR's	1,326,332	1,658,467	1,352,053	3,560,915	6,366,551	2,701,493
Gift, total	$8,633,708	$9,518,527	$12,750,371	$9,067,727	$12,065,703	$22,510,370
Total funds used	$131,701,899	$92,897,490	$193,669,763	$119,627,763	$140,109,832	$174,003,690

(1) Additions, Remodelings and Renovations

TABLE 6 ACADEMIC LIBRARIES, 1972–1982

	1972	1973	1974	1975	1976	1977	1978–1979	1980	1981	1982
New Libraries	17	17	21	18	15	6	38	14	19	20
Additions	2	1	9	2	5	5	8	2	0	9
Additions plus Renovation	3	3	10	5	8	7	22	11	11	6
TOTALS	22	21	40	25	25	18	66	27	30	35
Combined Additions and Addition plus Renovation	5	4	19	7	13	12	30	13	11	15
Percentage of Combined A & R	22.72	19.04	47.50	28.00	46.42	66.63	45.45	48.15	36.66	42.85

TABLE 7 NEW ACADEMIC LIBRARY BUILDINGS
(Year Ending June 30, 1982)

Name of Institution	Project Cost	Gross Area	Assignable	Non-Assignable	Sq.Ft. Cost	Building Cost	Equipment Cost	Book Capacity	Seating Capacity	Architect
Univ. of North Carolina, Chapel Hill	$22,471,718	436,600	305,200	131,400	$41.00	$17,888,964	2,200,000	1,500,000	3,300	Boney, L.N.
Memorial Univ. of Newfoundland, St. John's[1]	14,000,000	207,000	175,000	32,000	62.80	13,000,000	1,000,000	1,500,000	2,000	Architects Guild
Univ. of Oklahoma, Norman	13,100,000	152,619	103,734	48,885	70.64	10,780,215	1,225,000	700,000	1,100	Hellmuth
The Atlanta Univ., Ga.	12,500,000	219,414	176,514	42,900	52.41	11,500,000	1,000,000	1,000,000	2,700	Toombs
Univ. of Hawaii at Hilo	10,118,822	95,853	73,096	22,757	91.23	8,744,427	859,484	450,000	900	Chapman
Purdue Univ., W. Lafayette, Ind.	9,370,000	99,850	70,000	29,850	69.43	6,932,920	1,777,172	1,200,000	1,340	Scholer, W.
Suffolk Univ., Boston, Mass.	8,950,000	41,000	23,970	17,030	70.73	2,900,000	282,000	122,000	400	Knight
SUNY, Coll. at Old Westbury	8,086,342	84,435	53,440	30,995	89.84	7,586,342	500,000	300,000	800	Kouzmanoff, A.
Arizona State Univ., Science & Engineering Lib. Tempe	8,061,800	98,000	89,000	9,000	64.00	6,229,400	1,832,400	325,000	1,050	Drover
Univ. of Nevada, Las Vegas	7,000,000	91,000	67,875	23,125	65.93	6,000,000	1,000,000	250,000	800	Miller, J.
Yale Univ., New Haven, Ct.	6,700,000	80,000	71,500	8,500	53.00	4,200,000	100,000	1,800,000	80	Roth & Moore
St. Mary's Coll., Notre Dame, Ind.	6,435,000	78,000	72,767	5,233	66.41	5,810,000	625,000	250,000	540	Woollen
Kennesaw Coll., Marietta, Ga.	4,357,400	101,593	72,705	28,888	31.74	3,224,858	266,155	300,000	1,000	Hall
Le Moyne Coll., Syracuse, N.Y.	3,940,600	58,670	56,000	2,670	52.85	3,100,500	288,887	225,000	700	Quinlivan

Name of Institution	Project Cost	Gross Area	Assignable	Non-Assignable	Sq. Ft. Cost	Building Cost	Equipment Cost	Book Capacity	Seating Capacity	Architect
Pennsylvania State Univ., Media (Del. Cty. Campus)	n/a	50,330	35,591	14,739	49.43	2,488,112	299,000	100,000	625	Geddes . . .
Northern Montana Coll., Havre	2,322,000	33,440	24,610	8,830	51.13	1,709,800	413,600	126,000	228	Whirry, G.
Mercer Univ., Sch. of Medicine Lib., Macon, Ga.	987,100	18,300	18,300	0	42.86	784,300	202,800	83,000	142	not reported
Southwest Missouri State Univ., Springfield	841,380	26,465	10,000	16,465	30.13	797,088	371	200,000	12	Rich, Paul
John Wesley Coll., High Point, N.C.	160,000	2,961	2,808	153	42.84	126,850	35,000	28,000	40	Spinks, D.
Southwestern Adventist Coll., Keene, Tex.	14,400	380	377	3	13.57	5,157	1,725	750	14	none

TABLE 8 ACADEMIC LIBRARY BUILDINGS: ADDITION AND RENOVATION
(Year Ending June 30, 1982)

Name of Institution		Project Cost	Gross Area	Assignable	Non-Assignable	Sq. Ft. Cost	Building Cost	Equipment Cost	Book Capacity	Seating Capacity	Architect
Univ. of Maryland, Engineering & Sci. Lib., College Park	Total	n/a	355,000	252,000	103,000	65.00	23,000,000	n/a	189,000	264	M F E Inc.
	New	n/a	150,900	n/a	n/a	80.00	11,900,000	n/a	n/a	164	
	Renovated	n/a	204,500	n/a	n/a	34.00	6,950,000	n/a	n/a	100	
Wittenberg Univ., Springfield, Ohio	Total	5,569,650	91,810	73,488	18,322	43.63	5,145,251	424,399	482,150	779	Glaser & Myers
	New	4,477,471	59,061	47,249	11,812	54.52	n/a	n/a	276,550	453	
	Renovated	1,092,179	32,249	26,199	6,050	23.98	n/a	n/a	205,600	326	
Denison Univ. Libs. Granville, Ohio	Total	4,608,000	93,862	75,104	18,758	n/a	4,313,000	295,000	360,000	650	Warner . . .
	New	4,406,000	40,180	32,144	8,036	109.65	4,131,000	275,000	33,900	222	
	Renovated	202,000	53,682	42,960	10,722	3.76	182,000	20,000	326,100	428	
Colgate Univ., Hamilton, N.Y.	Total	4,146,392	111,000	94,350	16,650	28.32	3,144,015	521,882	688,000	985	Newman, H.S.
	New	3,466,747	36,000	30,600	5,400	70.45	2,536,406	467,630	180,000	470	
	Renovated	679,645	75,000	63,750	11,250	8.10	607,609	54,252	508,000	515	
St. Joseph's Univ., Philadelphia, Pa.	Total	3,349,000	66,000	53,000	13,000	50.74	2,960,600	231,105	350,000	600	Sabatino, J.S.
	New	n/a	41,000	31,000	10,000	n/a	n/a	n/a	n/a	n/a	
	Renovated	n/a	25,000	22,000	3,000	n/a	n/a	n/a	n/a	n/a	
St. Edward's Univ., Austin, Tex.	Total	2,500,000	35,000	n/a	n/a	71.43	2,050,000	450,000	250,000	400	Johnson, B.
	New	n/a	20,000	n/a	n/a	n/a	n/a	n/a	180,000	224	
	Renovated	n/a	15,000	n/a	n/a	n/a	n/a	n/a	70,000	176	

TABLE 9 ACADEMIC LIBRARY BUILDINGS: RENOVATION ONLY
(Year Ending June 30, 1982)

Name of Institution	Project Cost	Gross Area	Assignable	Non-Assignable	Sq.Ft. Cost	Building Cost	Equipment Cost	Book Capacity	Seating Capacity	Architect
Univ. of Kansas, Lawrence	6,220,000	189,304	153,500	35,804	30.28	5,731,699	488,301	1,300,000	1,172	Hollis & Miller
Brown Univ., Providence, R.I.	4,500,000	70,000	56,000	14,000	49.60	3,471,000	115,000	500,000	100	Shepley...
Union Theological Seminary, New York, N.Y.	2,855,000	52,120	47,380	4,740	60.00	2,775,000	80,000	500,000	168	Mitchell...
St. Francis Coll., Brooklyn, N.Y.	1,847,150	23,297	15,000	8,297	53.35	1,243,000	300,000	117,000	298	Warner...
Stanford Univ., Cal.	2,215,000	n/a	47,000	n/a	47.13	1,463,100	309,400	n/a	n/a	Hellmuth...
Hawaii Loa Coll. LRC., Kaneohe	765,000	22,000	n/a	n/a	n/a	n/a	n/a	100,000	300	Aotani...
Louisiana State Univ. in Shreveport	750,000	34,000	30,000	4,000	7.88	268,000	480,000	150,000	300	Wilson, Wm.
Bates Coll., Lewiston, Me.	710,776	40,000	1,614	8,3860	15.69	627,518	58,200	255,570	300	Architect's Collab.
Colgate Univ., Science Lib., Hamilton, N.Y.	456,417	10,074	9,374	700	45.31	311,437	144,980	50,000	136	Grant, R.

Book Trade Research and Statistics

BOOK TITLE OUTPUT AND AVERAGE PRICES: 1982 PRELIMINARY FIGURES

Chandler B. Grannis
Contributing Editor, *Publishers Weekly*

Close to 50,000 books were published in 1982 in the United States, according to preliminary title production figures compiled for *Publishers Weekly* by the R. R. Bowker Company's Data Services Division presented in Tables 1–3 with this article. Whether or not there were substantial increases or declines from 1981 output in any of the 23 subject categories reported, or in the total, will be seen when the final compilations are completed in summer 1982. However, the totals will probably include approximately 4,500 mass market paperbound titles and 12,000 or more other paperbacks.

According to the preliminary figures shown in Table 4, hardcover books of all kinds, at all price ranges, have risen approximately 14.9%. In many areas, the averages are raised by the presence of some very high-priced books. This factor is dealt with, in part, in Table 5: Preliminary figures suggest an overall decline of approximately 4.9% (1982 vs. 1981) after eliminating volumes priced at $81 or more. Yet, in categories where comparisons are possible, increases, not declines, are indicated by Table 5.

In this report, Table 5 covers all 23 Dewey subject categories for the first time; formerly only a few of the broad Dewey "century" classifications were covered. It may be interesting to compare the 1982 figures in the column headed "Total volumes" in Table 4 with those under the same heading in Table 5 to see how many or how few $81-plus volumes there were in one category or another and in which fields the higher prices most affected the averages.

Another improvement in these annual statistics concerns the mass market paperback count. Before 1980 the counting of all U.S. title output was based on entries in the *Weekly Record* (also referred to as the *Book Publishing Record* (*BPR*) database), employing Library of Congress data that omit mass market paperbacks. The latter obviously were being undercounted. To obtain more accurate figures, the mass market paperback count, beginning in 1981, has been taken from entries in Bowker's *Paperbound Books in Print*. Therefore, although the hardcover and trade paperbound figures in Table 1 come from the *BPR* base, the overall book output totals in the last column at the right also include the *PBIP* mass market paperback totals.

Table 2 shows the total mass market paperback output in all 23 categories, but at this time the figures concerning new books and new editions are not available. Table 3 covers paperbacks other than mass market; here, new books and new editions are counted,

---

Note: Adapted from *Publishers Weekly*, March 11, 1983, where the article was entitled "Title Output and Average Prices: 1982 Preliminary Figures." Table 8 is reprinted from "Title Output and Price Averages," *Publishers Weekly*, October 1, 1982.

TABLE 1 AMERICAN BOOK TITLE PRODUCTION, 1980–1982

Hardbound and paperbound books, domestic and imported, from listings in Bowker's *Weekly Record* and *Paperbound Books in Print*

Categories with Dewey Decimal Numbers	1980 titles (final)			1981 titles (final)			1982 titles (preliminary)			
	\-All hardbound and all paperbound-			\-All hardbound and all paperbound-			\-Hardbound & trade paperbound only-			All hard- & paper- bound
	New Books	New Editions	Totals	New Books	New Editions	Totals	New Books	New Editions	Totals	Totals
Agriculture (630–639: 712–719)	382	79	461	398	76	474	268	77	345	347
Art (700–711; 720–779)	1,437	254	1,691	1,458	235	1,693	1,131	214	1,345	1,354
*Biography	1,399	492	1,891	1,481	379	1,860	1,169	195	1,364	1,430
Business (650–659)	935	250	1,185	1,040	302	1,342	807	282	1,089	1,101
Education (370–379)	876	135	1,011	1,020	152	1,172	733	129	862	872
Fiction	1,918	917	2,835	5,003	652	5,655	1,709	363	2,072	4,768
General Works (000–099)	1,428	215	1,643	1,514	229	1,743	1,635	231	1,866	1,918
History (900–909; 930–999)	1,569	651	2,220	1,856	465	2,321	1,400	350	1,750	1,787
Home Economics (640–649)	767	112	879	957	151	1,108	705	110	815	883
Juveniles	2,585	274	2,859	2,901	201	3,102	2,252	123	2,375	2,576
Language (400–499)	433	96	529	649	112	761	351	103	454	464
Law (340–349)	816	286	1,102	1,132	316	1,448	817	326	1,143	1,144

372 / BOOK TRADE RESEARCH AND STATISTICS

Category									
Literature (800–810; 813–820; 823–899)	1,317	369	1,686	1,521	256	1,777	1,211	212	1,423	1,459
Medicine (610–619)	2,667	625	3,292	3,163	625	3,788	2,218	408	2,626	2,652
Music (780–789)	236	121	357	297	101	398	213	67	280	284
Philosophy, Psychology (100–199)	1,097	332	1,429	1,221	244	1,465	941	204	1,145	1,199
Poetry, Drama (811; 812; 821; 822)	962	217	1,179	1,063	120	1,183	752	78	830	845
Religion (200–299)	1,635	420	2,055	1,931	347	2,278	1,452	242	1,694	1,708
Science (500–599)	2,551	556	3,109	2,798	577	3,375	2,086	427	2,513	2,526
Sociology, Economics (300–339; 350–369; 380–399)	5,876	1,276	7,152	6,679	1,122	7,801	5,051	879	5,930	5,980
Sports, Recreation (790–799)	808	163	971	1,099	165	1,264	657	122	779	966
Technology (600–609; 620–629; 660–699)	1,923	414	2,337	1,877	436	2,313	1,528	325	1,853	1,865
Travel (910–919)	413	91	504	376	96	472	286	91	377	398
TOTAL	34,030	8,347	42,377	41,434	7,359	48,793	29,372	5,558	34,930	38,526

*Dewey Decimal Numbers omitted because biographies counted here come from many Dewey classifications.

Note: In all tables, figures for mass market paperbound book production for 1981 and 1982 are based on entries in *Paperbound Books in Print*. All other figures are from the *Weekly Record* (*American Book Publishing Record*) database.

TABLE 2 MASS MARKET PAPERBOUND TITLES, 1981-1982

	1981 final	1982 prelim.
Agriculture	5	2
Art	8	9
Biography	74	66
Business	9	12
Education	14	10
Fiction	3,097	2,696
General works	86	52
History	43	37
Home Economics	109	68
Juveniles	240	201
Language	20	10
Law	4	1
Literature	44	36
Medicine	35	26
Music	1	4
Philosophy, Psychology	80	54
Poetry, Drama	16	15
Religion	26	14
Science	17	13
Sociology, Economics	52	50
Sports Recreation	178	187
Technology	11	12
Travel	4	21
TOTAL	**4,175**	**3,596**

SOURCE: Paperbound Books in Print (R. R. Bowker Co.)

Note: Final report for 1982 will include about 750 additional titles not yet classified.

but without breakdown by categories. Table 4 covers average hardcover prices per volume.

Table 6 deals with per-volume averages in the mass market paperback field, showing for the first time a truly comprehensive two-year comparison by categories. Table 7 presents per-volume averages in the trade paperback field, also by category. Table 8 shows per-volume price comparisons from a different but highly significant source—the hardcover novels, biographies, and books of history cited in publishers' advertisements in the Fall Announcement issues of *Publishers Weekly*.

TABLE 3 PAPERBACKS OTHER THAN MASS MARKET, 1980-1982
(From *Weekly Record* listings of domestic and imported books)

	1980 titles (final)			1981 titles (final) Totals	1982 titles (preliminary)		
Categories	New Bks.	New Eds.	Totals		New Bks.	New Eds.	Totals
Fiction	271	156	427	399	195	59	254
Nonfiction	8,535	1,857	10,392	12,011	8,247	1,682	9,929
Total	8,806	2,013	10,819	12,410	8,442	1,741	10,183

TABLE 4 AVERAGE PER-VOLUME PRICES OF HARDCOVER BOOKS, 1977-1982
(From *Weekly Record* listings of domestic and imported books)

Categories with Dewey Decimal Numbers	1977 vols. (final) Average prices	1979 volumes (final) Total volumes	1979 Average prices	1980 volumes (final) Total volumes	1980 Average prices	1981 volumes (final) Total volumes	1981 Average prices	1982 volumes (preliminary) Total volumes	1982 Total prices	1982 Average prices
Agriculture (630–639; 712–719)	$16.24	419	$20.94	360	$27.55	390	$31.88	236	$7,731.77	$32.76
Art (700–711; 720–779)	21.24	1,399	21.95	1,132	27.70	1,094	31.87	783	24,761.20	31.62
*Biography	15.34	1,675	17.52	1,508	19.77	1,348	21.85	992	21,022.95	21.19
Business (650–659)	18.00	1,077	23.11	898	22.45	1,045	23.09	815	20,535.44	25.19
Education (370–379)	12.95	706	15.10	626	17.01	697	18.77	524	11,005.70	21.00
Fiction	10.09	2,027	11.99	2,100	12.46	1,855	15.49	1,658	22,759.53	13.72
General Works (000–099)	30.99	989	28.56	1,190	29.84	1,295	35.02	948	34,467.68	36.35
History (900–909; 930–999)	17.12	1,685	19.79	1,743	22.78	1,761	23.15	1,285	34,687.53	26.99
Home Economics (640–649)	11.16	552	11.95	517	13.31	584	16.07	469	7,900.93	16.84
Juveniles	6.65	3,002	7.14	2,742	8.16	2,660	8.31	1,922	17,055.48	8.87
Language (400–499)	14.96	356	18.25	318	22.16	328	22.95	279	6,266.64	22.46
Law (340–349)	25.04	891	29.44	759	33.25	1,175	36.30	829	29,539.97	35.63
Literature (800–810; 813–820; 823–899)	15.78	1,290	17.64	1,266	18.70	1,190	19.79	987	20,333.33	21.10
Medicine (610–619)	24.00	2,554	29.27	2,596	34.28	3,065	36.47	2,095	81,100.67	38.71
Music (780–789)	20.13	289	18.93	273	21.79	284	25.82	190	5,098.02	26.83
Philosophy, Psychology (100–199)	14.43	1,024	17.98	1,045	21.70	982	22.41	810	18,859.10	23.28
Poetry, Drama (811; 812; 821; 822)	13.63	868	15.83	753	17.85	699	19.34	467	9,086.57	19.45
Religion (200–299)	12.26	1,286	14.83	1,109	17.61	1,147	18.54	827	14,694.37	17.76
Science (500–599)	24.88	2,525	30.59	2,481	37.45	2,778	40.63	1,971	85,516.97	43.38
Sociology, Economics (300–339; 350–369; 380–399)	29.88	5,656	43.57†	5,138	31.76	5,616	29.28	4,145	201,522.02	48.61
Sports, Recreation (790–799)	12.28	750	13.88	644	15.92	738	18.82	468	9,159.99	19.57
Technology (600–609; 620–629; 660–699)	23.61	1,838	27.82	1,742	33.64	1,864	36.76	1,264	51,171.87	40.48
Travel (910–919)	18.44	342	15.02	253	16.80	234	19.55	181	3,947.25	21.80
Total	$19.22	33,200	$23.96	31,234	$24.64	32,829	26.63	24,145	$738,724.98	$30.59

*Dewey Decimal Numbers omitted because biographies counted here come from many Dewey classifications. †See Table 5.

The computer procedures and programs for producing the statistics in this report have come increasingly under review, and further improvements are being pursued. Among them are translated titles and imported titles, not available for the past couple of years, mass market breakdowns of originals vs. new editions; and data on schoolbooks.

TABLE 5 AVERAGE PER-VOLUME PRICES OF HARDCOVER BOOKS, ELIMINATING ALL VOLUMES PRICED AT $81 OR MORE, 1977-1982
(Compare indicated classifications with Table 4)

Dewey Classifications	1977 (final)	1979 (final)	1980 (final)	1981 (prelim. only)	1982 (preliminary) Total volumes	1982 (preliminary) Total prices	1982 (preliminary) Average prices
Agriculture (630–639; 712–719)					224	$ 6,490.12	$28.97
Art (700–711; 720–779)					753	20,028.50	26.59
Biography					973	18,716.45	19.23
Business (650–659)					808	19,017.19	23.53
Education (370–379)					521	10,736.45	20.60
Fiction					1,654	22,343.58	13.50
General Works (000–099)	$22.45	$21.06	$23.34	$25.15	891	24,113.43	27.06
History (900–909; 930–999)					1,266	30,325.67	23.95
Home Economics (640–649)					466	7,496.43	16.08
Juveniles					1,921	16,968.48	8.83
Language (400–499)	$14.55	$18.07	$20.14	$20.65	276	5,936.14	21.50
Law (340–349)					789	22,829.52	28.93
Literature (800–810; 813–820; 823–899)					980	19,811.33	20.21
Medicine (610–619)					1,930	63,533.00	32.91
Music (780–789)					187	4,774.07	25.52
Philosophy, Psychology (100–199)	$14.17	$17.50	$20.18	$21.61	806	18,256.60	22.65
Poetry, Drama (811; 812; 821; 822)					461	8,172.57	17.72
Religion (200–299)	11.98	13.01	15.55	16.58	821	13,684.37	16.66
Science (500–599)	23.78	27.77	32.67	33.97	1,779	62,413.70	35.08
Sociology, Economics (300–399; 350–369; 380–399)					4,027	96,111.87	23.86
Sports, Recreation (790–799)					465	8,575.41	18.44
Technology, (600–609; 620–629; 660–699)					1,165	36,335.87	31.18
Travel (910–999)					177	3,347.25	18.91
Total	$17.32	$19.63	$22.48	$24.33	23,340	$540,018.00	$23.13

TABLE 6 AVERAGE PER-VOLUME PRICES OF MASS MARKET PAPERBACKS, 1981-1982
(From *Paperbound Books in Print*)

	1981 volumes (final) Average prices	1982 volumes (preliminary) Total volumes	1982 volumes (preliminary) Total prices	1982 volumes (preliminary) Average prices
Agriculture	$2.54	2	$ 7.90	$3.95
Art	5.49	9	76.10	8.45
Biography	3.82	66	244.75	3.70
Business	4.63	12	46.70	3.89
Education	3.96	10	44.85	4.48
Fiction	2.47	2,696	7,423.99	2.75
General Works	3.62	52	193.90	3.72
History	3.53	37	154.25	4.16
Home Economics	4.34	68	333.68	4.90
Juveniles	1.79	201	407.65	2.02
Language	3.41	10	30.35	3.03
Law	3.08	1	3.50	3.50
Literature	3.41	36	129.40	3.59
Medicine	3.66	26	132.35	5.09
Music	—	4	22.70	5.67
Philosophy, Psychology	2.83	54	205.55	3.80
Poetry, Drama	3.21	15	49.00	3.26
Religion	2.70	14	53.40	3.81
Science	4.45	13	67.80	5.21
Sociology, Economics	3.43	50	218.10	4.36
Sports, Recreation	3.04	187	549.25	2.93
Technology	4.20	12	43.75	3.64
Travel	3.22	21	166.80	7.94
Total	**$2.65**	**3,596**	**$10,605.72**	**$2.95**

TABLE 7 AVERAGE PER-VOLUME PRICES OF TRADE PAPERBACKS, 1977-1982
(From Weekly Record listings of domestic and imported books)

Categories	1977 volumes (final) Average prices	1979 volumes (final) Total volumes	1979 Average prices	1980 volumes (final) Total volumes	1980 Average prices	1981 volumes (final) Total volumes	1981 Average prices	1982 volumes (preliminary) Total volumes	1982 Total prices	1982 Average prices
Agriculture	$ 5.01	117	$ 6.80	104	$ 8.54	96	$ 9.74	95	$ 1,064.69	$11.20
Art	6.27	634	8.33	563	9.09	651	10.07	507	5,396.02	10.64
Biography	4.91	314	5.64	363	6.57	444	7.33	336	2,813.00	8.37
Business	7.09	277	8.94	285	9.90	309	10.10	246	3,136.83	12.75
Education	5.72	404	6.91	382	8.42	484	9.54	315	3,227.20	10.24
Fiction	4.20	388	4.42	432	5.71	479	5.81	388	2,564.64	6.60
General Works	6.18	480	6.47	544	8.00	578	10.90	879	7,711.95	8.77
History	5.81	474	6.67	478	7.57	634	9.10	426	4,419.20	10.37
Home Economics	4.77	337	5.48	360	6.33	465	7.01	326	2,585.33	7.93
Juveniles	2.68	413	3.23	460	3.50	504	3.35	402	1,579.10	3.92
Language	7.79	205	7.53	215	8.59	252	8.56	165	1,636.33	9.91
Law	10.66	361	11.68	317	11.33	307	12.34	273	3,261.19	11.94
Literature	5.18	447	6.50	424	7.26	477	8.14	410	3,673.83	8.96
Medicine	7.63	667	9.55	682	11.46	814	12.35	478	6,192.34	12.95
Music	6.36	97	9.17	83	9.36	126	10.12	83	837.19	10.08
Philosophy, Psychology	5.57	340	6.56	382	7.57	415	9.66	314	3,454.32	11.00
Poetry, Drama	4.71	504	4.21	442	5.09	525	6.00	341	2,308.29	6.76
Religion	3.68	1,038	4.59	937	6.15	1,142	6.81	822	6,235.25	7.58
Science	8.81	614	11.48	630	13.46	648	14.75	494	6,856.66	13.87
Sociology, Economics	6.03	2,036	8.07	2,016	9.75	2,275	11.56	1,659	34,320.86	20.68
Sports, Recreation	4.87	360	6.12	326	7.11	414	7.86	291	2,726.58	9.36
Technology	7.97	556	9.24	601	13.52	918	14.60	528	8,914.73	16.88
Travel	5.21	294	5.97	247	6.73	263	8.20	187	1,500.07	8.02
Total	$ 5.93	11,357	$ 7.21	11,279	$ 8.60	13,220	$ 9.76	9,965	$116,415.60	$11.68

TABLE 8 AVERAGE AND MEDIAN PRICES, THREE CATEGORIES, PW FALL ANNOUNCEMENT ADS, 1972-1982

Novels, Except Mystery, Western, SF, Gothic: Average & Median Prices			Biography Memoirs, Letters: Average & Median Prices			History, Including Pictorial, but Not Art Books: Average & Median Prices		
	Avg.	Med.		Avg.	Med.		Avg.	Med.
1982—177 vols./41 pubs.	$14.75	$14.95	1982—140 vols./62 pubs.	$20.43	$18.95	1982—152 vols./64 pubs.	$22.88	$19.50
1981—243 vols./45 pubs.	$12.61	$13.50	1981—116 vols./54 pubs.	$18.09	$16.95	1981—188 vols./70 pubs.	$20.35	$19.00
1980—317 vols./42 pubs.	$11.73	$11.50	1980—130 vols./56 pubs.	$17.05	$15.00	1980—154 vols./57 pubs.	$19.85	$18.50
1979—291 vols./43 pubs.	$10.42	$ 9.95	1979—160 vols./67 pubs.	$15.92	$13.95	1979—219 vols./67 pubs.	$16.88	$15.95
1978—282 vols./43 pubs.	$ 9.63	$ 8.95	1978—213 vols./73 pubs.	$13.54	$12.95	1978—207 vols./85 pubs.	$15.59	$15.00
1977—233 vols./37 pubs.	$ 9.18	$ 8.95	1977—169 vols./62 pubs.	$13.12	$12.50	1977—241 vols./72 pubs.	$15.83	$15.00
1976—174 vols./34 pubs.	$ 8.74	$ 8.95	1976—130 vols./61 pubs.	$12.87	$11.95	1976—151 vols./63 pubs.	$13.96	$14.95
1975—150 vols./35 pubs.	$ 8.51	$ 7.95	1975—128 vols./53 pubs.	$12.50	$10.95	1975—178 vols./74 pubs.	$15.32	$13.95
1974—212 vols./38 pubs.	$ 7.68	$ 7.95	1974—190 vols./80 pubs.	$12.31	$10.95	1974—219 vols./74 pubs.	$12.91	$12.50
1973—225 vols./40 pubs.	$ 7.34	$ 6.95	1973—190 vols./78 pubs.	$10.67	$ 8.95	1973—228 vols./73 pubs.	$13.38	$12.50
1972—171 vols./37 pubs.	$ 6.95	$ 6.95	1972—170 vols./61 pubs.	$10.12	$ 8.95	1972—262 vols./89 pubs.	$12.30	$12.30

BOOK SALES STATISTICS: HIGHLIGHTS FROM AAP ANNUAL SURVEY, 1981

Chandler B. Grannis

American book publishers' estimated net receipts from sales in 1981 amounted to more than $7.665 billion, according to the annual statistical report of the Association of American Publishers (AAP), compiled by Touche, Ross & Company. The total reflected the lowest rate of dollar increase in several years. Sales in 1980 had been 11.2% over those of 1979; 1979 sales had increased 9.3% over 1978; and 1978 sales were 12.7% over 1977.

Table 1 includes the percentage changes in receipts from 1980 to 1981 in the various divisions of book publishing. Modest increases can be seen in the categories of trade, elementary and secondary, book clubs, and university presses; there were, however, only slight dollar increases in the religious and subscription reference categories and sharp declines in sales of standardized tests and college nontext materials. The most noteworthy increases were in the professional, juvenile hardbound, mail order, mass market, and college text areas and in "other sales" (sales of sheets except to prebinders, also "miscellaneous merchandise").

Early reports for 1982, from *Publishers Weekly* and the AAP's newly instituted *Monthly Sales Trends Indicator*, suggested a generally less favorable picture for the year than for 1981. The publishers' total receipts differ, of course, from the consumer expenditure figures, which are estimated by John P. Dessauer, along with unit sales (number of copies sold) in the article immediately following this one.

U.S. book export and import data are also reviewed in this volume in the International Statistics section of Part 5. Exports account for an average of 8% or more of U.S. publishers' total sales. The largest foreign market is Canada, with about 33% of foreign sales of U.S. books, followed by the United Kingdom, Australia, and Japan.

Several notes accompany the AAP table. First, the figures for adult paperbound books include sales of "nonrack-size" books by mass market publishers, which amounted to $85.9 million in 1980 and $92.9 million in 1981. Second, in the line for professional medical books, some 35% of the sales in each column (except 1972) should probably be transferred to the college textbook line. Third, the basis of the sales figures is the final 1977 Census of Manufactures (Bureau of the Census, Department of Commerce) survey of book publishing, issued in 1980 and augmented from year to year by information from the participating publishers. Some figures from AAP and the census have not yet been reconciled, especially in the area of college texts.

Other points noted by AAP are that the census does not cover most university press and other nonprofit or institutional publishing, nor does it cover audiovisual and other nonbook materials—areas that AAP does cover; and that AAP omits Sunday school materials, and "certain pamphlets." AAP also does not report sales abroad of U.S. publishers' foreign subsidiaries.

TABLE 1 ESTIMATED BOOK PUBLISHING INDUSTRY SALES 1972, 1977, 1980, and 1981
(Millions of Dollars)

	1972 $	1977 $	1977 % Change from 1972	1980 $	1980 % Change from 1977	1980 % Change from 1972	1981 $	1981 % Change from 1980	1981 % Change from 1972
Trade (Total)	444.8	887.2	99.5	1271.3	43.3	185.8	1353.7	6.5	204.3
Adult hardbound	251.5	501.3	99.3	695.9	38.8	176.7	735.6	5.7	192.5
Adult paperbound	82.4	223.7	171.5	364.6	63.0	342.5	384.7	5.5	366.8
Juvenile hardbound	106.5	136.1	27.8	168.5	23.8	58.2	190.2	12.9	78.6
Juvenile paperbound	4.4	26.1	493.2	42.3	62.1	861.4	43.2	2.2	882.5
Religious (Total)	117.5	250.6	113.3	351.4	40.2	199.1	360.1	2.5	206.5
Bibles, testaments, hymnals and prayerbooks	61.6	116.3	88.8	168.3	44.7	173.2	171.1	1.7	177.9
Other religious	55.9	134.3	140.3	183.1	36.3	227.5	189.0	3.2	238.0
Professional (Total)	381.0	698.2	83.3	999.1	43.1	162.2	1140.7	14.2	199.4
Technical and scientific	131.8	249.3	89.2	334.8	34.3	154.0	391.1	16.8	196.7
Business and other professional	192.2	286.3	49.0	424.4	48.2	120.8	492.7	16.1	156.4
Medical	57.0	162.6	185.3	239.9	47.5	320.9	256.9	7.1	350.8
Book clubs	240.5	406.7	69.1	538.3	32.4	123.8	571.1	6.1	137.5
Mail order publications	198.9	396.4	99.3	566.9	43.0	185.0	653.6	15.3	228.6
Mass market paperback Rack-sized	250.0	487.7	95.1	653.3	34.0	161.3	735.6	12.6	194.3
University presses	41.4	56.1	35.5	80.7	43.9	94.9	86.0	6.6	107.8
Elementary and secondary text	497.6	755.9	51.9	940.3	24.4	89.0	998.6	6.2	100.7
College text	375.3	649.7	73.1	952.7	46.6	153.9	1074.7	12.8	186.3
Standardized tests	26.5	44.6	68.3	67.2	50.7	153.6	62.6	−6.9	175.7
Subscription reference	278.9	294.4	5.6	384.7	30.7	37.9	386.2	0.4	38.5
AV and other media (Total)	116.2	151.3	30.2	166.7	10.2	43.5	166.8	0.1	43.5
Elhi	101.2	131.4	29.8	147.9	12.6	46.1	148.9	0.7	47.2
College	9.2	11.6	26.1	8.7	−25.0	−5.4	6.7	−23.2	−27.4
Other	5.8	8.3	43.1	10.1	21.7	74.1	11.2	10.3	92.1
Other sales	49.2	63.4	28.9	66.8	5.4	35.8	75.4	12.8	53.2
Total	3017.8	5142.2	70.4	7039.4	36.9	133.3	7665.1	8.9	154.0

Source: *AAP Industry Statistics, 1981* (New York: Association of American Publishers, 1982).

U.S. CONSUMER EXPENDITURES ON BOOKS, 1981

John P. Dessauer
Book Industry Statistician

American consumers, individuals as well as institutions, spent an estimated $9.1 billion in 1981 in acquiring 1.7 billion books. This represented an increase of 10.7% in dollars and 0.5% in units over such expenditures in 1980, but constituted a slackening of growth, particularly in units, from the prior year, when the increases had been 12.5% and 3.0%, respectively.

These data emerge from my estimates in *Book Industry Trends, 1982*—as revised in the December 1982, issue of *Trends Update*—published by the Book Industry Study Group. As in previous years, the estimates cover the major book categories (Table 1) and principal distribution channels (Table 2). In addition, average dollar-per-unit expenditures are shown in Table 1, providing some indication of the inflation to which consumer purchases were subjected.

The big surprise, and disappointment, of 1981 was the abysmal unit performance of adult trade paperbounds. At a time when this category was hailed by many observers as the most promising in the consumer field, it posted a 10.5% decline in unit sales, contributing significantly (along with religious paperbounds) to the flatness of the industry's overall unit record. One need not look far for an explanation of this phenomenon: Trade paperbacks experienced the largest increase of any category in dollars per unit—a whopping 24.5%!

Although price inflation alone did not account for this jump—the trade paperbound title mix has grown consistently in complexity, quality, and richness of content and illustration, thus justifying higher cover prices—purely inflationary hikes undoubtedly played a role in generating the unit erosion. The phenomenon is particularly noteworthy because dollar-per-unit rates of increase in most other categories were below those of 1980, despite the fact that 1981 was a year of substantial general inflation.

Among distribution channels, the growth of retailers' and institutional acquisitions slowed in 1981, while that of direct-to-consumer sales quickened somewhat. "Other" sales, which include remainders, gained substantially in dollars but declined in units. In general, the year was an encouraging one for books, considering that the recession was already in full bloom. When comparing it to 1982, which appears to have established a much more dismal record, we may yet view 1981 with nostalgia.

Note: At press time, preliminary data on 1982 estimated consumer expenditures, by principal distribution channels, became available and was added to Table 2 of this report. For an analysis of the 1982 data, see "Estimated Book Industry Sales, 1981-1982: Sluggish—But Booksellers Are Still Doing Well," *Publishers Weekly*, February 18, 1983.

TABLE 1 ESTIMATED U.S. CONSUMER EXPENDITURES ON BOOKS, 1980 AND 1981
Millions of Dollars and Units

	1980 Dollars	1980 Units	1981 Dollars	1981 Units	% Change Dollars	% Change Units	Dollars per Unit 1980	Dollars per Unit 1981	Percent Change
Trade	1,966.4	387.43	2,185.0	390.99	11.1	.9	5.08	5.59	10.0
Adult hardbound	1,160.8	151.79	1,286.4	161.61	10.8	6.5	7.65	7.96	4.0
Adult paperbound	478.8	116.35	534.2	104.11	11.6	10.5−	4.12	5.13	24.5
Juvenile hardbound	233.1	62.88	263.3	70.18	13.0	11.6	3.71	3.75	1.1
Juvenile paperbound	93.7	56.41	101.1	55.07	7.9	2.4−	1.66	1.84	10.8
Religious	516.4	99.54	574.7	96.29	11.3	3.3−	5.19	5.97	15.0
Hardbound	346.0	37.02	403.6	39.23	16.6	6.0	9.35	10.29	10.0
Paperbound	170.4	62.52	171.1	57.06	.4−	8.7−	2.73	3.00	9.9
Professional	998.1	51.82	1,099.4	51.94	10.1	4.6	19.26	21.17	9.9
Hardbound	792.1	29.30	869.9	28.95	9.8	1.2−	27.03	30.05	11.2
Paperbound	202.4	22.52	229.5	22.99	13.4	2.1	8.99	9.98	11.0
Book Clubs	524.0	211.08	555.1	210.49	5.9	.3−	2.48	2.63	6.0
Hardbound	404.5	66.53	431.4	65.07	6.6	2.2−	6.08	6.63	9.0
Paperbound	119.5	144.55	123.7	145.42	3.5	.6	.83	.85	2.4
Mail order Publications	577.8	51.43	675.2	59.85	16.9	16.4	11.23	11.28	.5
Mass market paperbound	1,207.9	533.64	1,397.6	563.68	15.7	5.6	2.26	2.48	9.7
University Presses	82.5	9.12	86.6	9.64	5.0	5.7	9.05	8.98	.8−
Hardbound	60.5	4.01	60.5	3.94	.0	1.7−	15.09	15.36	1.8
Paperbound	22.3	5.11	26.1	5.70	17.0	11.5	4.36	4.58	5.0
Elhi text	936.2	250.69	996.0	252.75	6.4	.8	3.73	3.94	5.6
Hardbound	503.8	95.38	558.5	102.13	10.9	7.1	5.28	5.47	3.6
Paperbound	432.3	155.31	437.5	150.62	1.2	3.0−	2.78	2.90	4.3
College text	1,075.0	96.48	1,209.7	98.04	12.5	1.6	11.14	12.34	10.8
Hardbound	805.4	62.65	908.9	63.50	12.9	1.4	12.86	14.31	11.3
Paperbound	269.5	33.83	300.8	34.54	11.6	2.1	7.97	8.71	9.3
Subscription reference	321.9	.98	328.5	1.00	2.1	2.0	328.47	328.50	.0
Total	8,224.3	1,693.79	9,107.8	1,734.65	10.7	.5	4.86	5.25	8.0

Source: Book Industry Trends, 1982.

TABLE 2 CHANNELS OF U.S. BOOK DISTRIBUTION—ESTIMATED CONSUMER EXPENDITURES, 1980–1982
Millions of Dollars and Units

	1980 Dollars	1980 Units	1981 Dollars	1981 Units	Percent Change 1980–1981 Dollars	Percent Change 1980–1981 Units	1982 Dollars	1982 Units	Percent Change 1981–1982 Dollars	Percent Change 1981–1982 Units
General retailers	3,028.4	736.50	3,447.5	777.34	13.8	2.5	3,764.7	806.29	9.2	3.7
College stores	1,437.1	197.33	1,623.2	200.77	12.9	1.7	1,738.4	205.04	7.1	2.1
Libraries and institutions	659.9	73.49	687.1	64.13	4.1	12.7–	702.2	55.65	2.2	–13.2
Schools	1,221.7	308.02	1,268.7	293.41	3.9	4.7–	1,334.7	285.54	5.2	–2.7
Direct to consumer	1,796.2	315.26	1,948.5	325.08	10.1	3.1	1,876.4	269.67	–3.7	–17.4
Other	108.0	63.19	132.7	73.92	23.9	23.0–	137.2	77.39	3.4	4.7
Total	8,224.3	1,693.79	9,107.8	1,734.65	10.7	.5	9,553.6	1,699.58	4.9	–2.0

Source: Data for 1980 and 1981 are from *Book Industry Trends, 1982;* figures for 1982 and the 1981–1982 percent changes are from "Estimated Book Industry Sales, 1981–1982; Sluggish—But Booksellers Are Still Doing Well," *Publishers Weekly,* February 18, 1983.

PRICES OF U.S. AND FOREIGN PUBLISHED MATERIALS

Nelson A. Piper

*Assistant University Librarian, Collections, The General Library,
University of California, Davis, CA 95616
916-752-2110*

In spite of the realization of single-digit inflation rates for the Consumer Price Index and the Producer Price Index during late 1982 and in early 1983, double-digit cost increases continue to be the norm for U.S. published materials and for most materials published abroad. The 15.7 percent overall increase in the cost of periodicals included in Norman Brown's "Preliminary Survey of 1983 Subscription Prices of U.S. Periodicals" released on February 5, 1983 indicates that the double-digit trend in the cost of U.S. published materials still has not been reversed. The overall rates of increase for U.S. periodicals and books were remarkably parallel in 1982. The rise in the cost of library materials published abroad was again mitigated by the continued rise in value of the U.S. dollar in the international money market.

U.S. PUBLISHED MATERIALS

The cost of library materials in the U.S. marketplace in 1982 (see Tables 1–8) continued the substantial upward trends of 1980 and 1981. The changes in the indexes for the principal categories of U.S. published materials are as follows:

Materials	Index Change	Percent Change
Periodicals	23.1	14.5
Serial services	17.4	11.3
Hardcover books	20.6	14.9
(Higher priced) paperbacks	32.4	19.7
Mass market paperbacks	11.3	11.3

For the first time, an actual price index broken down by subject class is available for mass market paperbacks (Table 4). Users of the table should note, however, that several of the subject classes that make up the survey are still quite limited in size, e.g., "Agriculture," with the highest rate of increase (155.5 points), consists of only two books, and "Business" and "Technology", which recorded declines of 16.00 and 13.30 index points, respectively, consist of only 12 titles each.

Libraries using the various U.S. price indexes, or any other indexes, should again be careful not to be misled by overall, or general, rates of increase. The rates of increase for specific subject classes within each index must be analyzed with an individual library's purchasing pattern clearly in mind. Moreover, the capacity of a single component of an index to skew the general rate of change must be understood by all users. Last year's article noted that a sharp drop in the price of 4,649 sociology/economics titles included in the 27,007 hardcover books making up the 1981 preliminary survey was largely responsible for the small 3.5 percent rise in the cost of U.S. hardcover books in 1981. Conversely, an analysis of the 1982 preliminary data for U.S. hardcover books, reveals that a sharp rise in the cost of the 4,145 sociology/economics books included in the 24,145 books making up the 1982 preliminary survey is largely responsible for the 14.9 percent rise in the cost of hardcover books in 1982. A close look at the 1982 survey reveals that the only other hardcover book subject class recording a higher than aver-

TABLE 1 U.S. PERIODICALS: AVERAGE PRICES AND PRICE INDEXES, 1979–1982*
(Index Base: 1977 = 100)

Subject Area	1977 Average Price	1979 Average Price	1979 Index	1980 Average Price	1980 Index	1981 Average Price	1981 Index	1982 Average Price	1982 Index
ALL U.S. PERIODICALS[†]	$24.59	$30.37	123.5	$34.54	140.5	$39.13	159.1	$44.80	182.2
Agriculture	11.58	14.16	122.3	15.24	131.6	17.24	148.9	19.76	170.6
Business and economics	18.62	22.97	123.4	25.42	136.5	28.88	155.1	32.67	175.5
Chemistry and physics	93.76	118.33	126.2	137.45	146.6	156.30	166.7	177.94	189.8
Children's periodicals	5.82	6.70	115.1	7.85	134.9	8.56	147.1	9.90	170.1
Education	17.54	21.61	123.2	23.45	133.7	25.18	143.6	28.18	160.7
Engineering	35.77	42.95	120.1	49.15	137.4	54.55	152.5	61.54	172.0
Fine and applied arts	13.72	17.42	127.0	18.67	136.1	20.51	149.5	23.35	170.2
General interest periodicals	16.19	18.28	112.9	19.87	122.7	21.83	134.8	23.93	147.8
History	12.64	14.67	116.1	15.77	124.8	17.96	142.1	20.37	161.2
Home economics	18.73	23.21	123.9	24.63	131.5	27.34	146.0	34.27	183.0
Industrial arts	14.37	17.65	122.8	20.70	144.1	22.62	157.4	27.13	188.8
Journalism and communications	16.97	23.86	140.6	27.34	161.1	29.80	175.6	33.91	199.8
Labor and industrial relations	11.24	15.74	140.0	18.84	167.6	21.68	192.9	24.72	219.9
Law	17.36	20.98	120.9	23.00	132.5	24.80	142.9	27.53	158.6
Library Science	16.97	20.82	122.7	23.25	137.0	28.47	167.8	33.52	197.5
Literature and language	11.82	13.84	117.1	15.30	129.4	17.30	146.4	19.39	164.0
Math, botany, geology, and general science	47.13	58.84	124.8	67.54	143.3	75.62	160.4	87.99	186.7
Medicine	51.31	63.31	123.4	73.37	143.0	86.38	168.3	102.87	200.5
Philosophy and religion	10.89	13.25	121.7	14.73	135.3	15.40	141.4	17.92	164.6
Physical education and recreation	10.00	12.27	122.7	13.83	138.3	15.42	154.2	16.91	169.1
Political science	14.83	17.47	117.8	19.30	130.1	22.69	153.0	25.89	174.6
Psychology	31.74	38.10	120.0	41.95	132.2	47.27	148.9	54.21	170.8
Sociology and anthropology	19.68	23.70	120.4	27.56	140.0	31.37	159.4	36.38	184.9
Zoology	33.69	40.15	119.2	44.58	132.3	48.32	143.4	61.07	181.3
Total number of periodicals	3,218	3,314		3,358		3,425		3,544	

*Compiled by Norman B. Brown and Jane Phillips. For further comments see *Library Journal*, August 1982, "Price Indexes for 1982: U.S. Periodicals and Serial Services," by Norman B. Brown and Jane Phillips. Note that this table uses a one-year (1977) rather than a three-year (1977–1979) base, conforming to the practice of the Bureau of Labor Statistics and making these price indexes comparable to the consumer price indexes. For average prices for years prior to 1979, see previous editions of the *Bowker Annual*.
[†]Based on the total group of titles included in this table.

TABLE 2 U.S. SERIAL SERVICES: AVERAGE PRICES AND PRICE INDEXES, 1979-1982*†
(Index Base: 1977 = 100)

	1977 Average Price	1979 Average Price	1979 Index	1980 Average Price	1980 Index	1981 Average Price	1981 Index	1982 Average Price	1982 Index
Business	$216.28	$249.05	115.2	$294.00	135.9	$343.29	158.7	$371.03	171.6
General and humanities	90.44	118.83	131.4	124.28	137.4	142.04	157.1	160.03	176.9
Law	126.74	158.65	125.2	184.38	145.5	212.85	167.9	232.61	183.5
Science and technology	141.16	173.96	123.2	191.35	135.6	214.01	151.6	229.98	162.9
Social sciences (excluding business and law)	145.50	169.55	116.5	190.07	130.6	215.12	147.8	249.03	171.2
Soviet translations	175.41	201.89	115.1	229.68	130.9	253.79	144.7	298.22	170.0
U.S. documents	62.88	75.87	120.7	78.87	125.4	84.48	134.4	99.05	157.5
"Wilson Index"	438.00	487.75	111.4	541.92	123.7	600.58	137.1	583.83	133.3
All services combined‡	$142.27	$171.06	120.2	$194.21	136.5	$219.75	154.5	$244.52	171.9
Total number of services	1,432	1,450		1,470		1,477		1,494	

*Compiled by Norman B. Brown and Jane Phillips. For further comments see *Library Journal*, August 1982, "Price Indexes for 1982: U.S. Periodicals and Serial Services," by Norman B. Brown and Jane Phillips. Note that this table uses a one-year (1977) rather than a three-year (1977–1979) base, conforming to the practice of the Bureau of Labor Statistics and making these price indexes comparable to the consumer price indexes. For average prices for years prior to 1979, see previous editions of the *Bowker Annual*.
†The definition of a serial service has been taken from the *American National Standard Criteria for Price Indexes for Library Materials* (ANSI Z39.20-1974).
‡Excludes "Wilson Index."

TABLE 3 U.S. HARDCOVER BOOKS: AVERAGE PRICES AND PRICE INDEXES, 1979–1982*
(Index Base: 1977 = 100)

Categories with Dewey Decimal Numbers	1977 Average Price	1979 (Final) Vols.	1979 Average Price	1979 Index	1980 (Final) Vols.	1980 Average Price	1980 Index	1981 (Final) Vols.	1981 Average Price	1981 Index	1982 (Preliminary) Vols.	1982 Average Price	1982 Index
Agriculture (630–639; 712–719)	$16.24	419	$20.94	128.9	360	$27.55	169.6	390	$31.88	196.3	236	$32.76	201.8
Art (700–711; 720–779)	21.24	1,399	21.95	103.3	1,132	27.70	130.4	1,094	31.87	150.0	783	31.62	148.9
Biography[1]	15.34	1,675	17.52	114.2	1,508	19.77	128.9	1,348	21.85	142.4	992	21.19	138.1
Business (650–659)	18.00	1,077	23.11	128.4	898	22.45	124.7	1,045	23.09	128.3	815	25.19	139.9
Education (370–379)	12.95	706	15.10	116.6	626	17.01	131.4	697	18.77	144.9	524	21.00	162.2
Fiction	10.09	2,027	11.99	118.8	2,100	12.46	123.5	1,855	15.49	153.5	1,658	13.72	136.0
General Works (000–099)	30.99	989	28.56	92.2	1,190	29.84	96.3	1,295	35.02	113.0	948	36.35	117.3
History (900–909; 930–999)	17.12	1,685	19.79	115.6	1,743	22.78	133.1	1,761	23.15	135.2	1,285	26.99	157.6
Home Economics (640–649)	11.16	552	11.95	107.1	517	13.31	119.3	584	16.07	144.0	469	16.84	150.9
Juveniles	6.65	3,002	7.14	107.4	2,742	8.16	122.7	2,660	8.31	125.0	1,922	8.87	133.4
Language (400–499)	14.96	356	18.25	122.0	318	22.16	148.2	328	22.95	153.4	279	22.46	150.1
Law (340–349)	25.04	891	29.44	117.6	759	33.25	132.8	1,175	36.30	145.0	829	35.63	142.3
Literature (800–810; 813–820; 823–89)	15.78	1,290	17.64	111.8	1,266	18.70	118.5	1,190	19.79	125.4	987	21.10	133.7

Category										
Medicine (610–619)	24.00	2,554	29.27	122.0	2,596	34.28	142.8	3,065	36.47	152.0	2,095	38.71	161.3
Music (780–789)	20.13	289	18.93	94.0	273	21.79	108.2	284	25.82	128.3	190	26.83	133.3
Philosophy, Psychology (100–199)	14.43	1,024	17.98	124.6	1,045	21.70	150.4	982	22.41	155.3	810	23.28	161.3
Poetry, Drama (811; 812; 821; 822)	13.63	868	15.83	116.1	753	17.85	130.1	699	19.34	141.9	467	19.45	142.7
Religion (200–299)	12.26	1,286	14.83	121.0	1,109	17.61	143.6	1,147	18.54	151.2	827	17.76	144.9
Science (500–599)	24.88	2,525	30.59	123.0	2,481	37.45	150.5	2,778	40.63	163.3	1,971	43.38	174.4
Sociology, Economics (300–339; 350–369; 380–399)	29.88	5,656	43.57	145.8	5,138	31.76	106.3	5,616	29.28	98.0	4,145	48.61	162.7
Sports, Recreation (790–799)	12.28	750	13.88	113.0	644	15.92	129.6	738	18.82	153.3	468	19.57	159.4
Technology (600–609; 620–629; 660–699)	23.61	1,838	27.82	117.8	1,742	33.64	142.5	1,864	36.76	155.7	1,264	40.48	172.8
Travel (910–919)	18.44	342	15.02	81.4	253	16.80	91.1	234	19.55	106.0	181	21.88	118.2
Total	$19.22	33,200	$23.96	124.7	31,234	$24.64	128.2	32,829	26.63	138.6	24,145	30.59	159.2

*Compiled by Nelson A. Piper from data supplied by the R. R. Bowker Company. Price indexes on Tables 3 and 5 are based on books recorded in the R. R. Bowker Company's *Weekly Record* (cumulated in the *American Book Publishing Record*). The 1982 preliminary figures include items listed during 1982 with an imprint date of 1982. Final data for 1981 include items listed between January 1981 and June 1982 with an imprint date of 1981; final data for 1980 include items listed between January 1980 and June 1981 with an imprint date of 1980; final data for 1979 include items listed between January 1979 and June 1980 with an imprint date of 1979; final data for 1978 include items listed between January 1978 and June 1979 with an imprint date of 1978; data for 1977 include items listed between January 1977 and June 1978 with an imprint date of 1977. (See the report "Book Title Output and Average Prices, 1982 Preliminary Figures" by Chandler B. Grannis, earlier in this section—*Ed.*)

TABLE 4 U.S. MASS MARKET PAPERBACKS AVERAGE PRICES AND INDEXES, 1981–1982*
(Index Base: 1981 = 100)

	1981			1982			
	Total Volumes	Total Prices	Average Prices	Total Volumes	Total Prices	Average Prices	Index
Agriculture	5	$12.70	$2.54	2	$7.90	$3.95	155.5
Art	7	38.45	5.49	9	76.10	8.45	153.9
Biography	72	275.30	3.82	66	244.75	3.70	96.9
Business	12	55.60	4.63	12	46.70	3.89	84.0
Education	9	35.65	3.96	10	44.85	4.48	131.2
Fiction	2,782	6,879.15	2.47	2,696	7,423.99	2.75	113.4
General works	77	279.30	3.62	52	193.90	3.72	102.8
History	45	158.90	3.53	37	154.25	4.16	117.8
Home economics	99	430.35	4.34	68	333.68	4.90	112.9
Juvenile	223	400.20	1.79	201	407.65	2.07	112.8
Language	18	61.50	3.41	10	30.35	3.03	88.9
Law	4	12.35	3.08	1	3.50	3.50	113.6
Literature	43	146.90	3.41	36	129.40	3.59	105.3
Medicine	33	120.85	3.66	26	132.35	5.09	139.1
Music	—	—	—	4	22.70	5.67	—
Philosophy, psychology	77	218.35	2.83	54	205.55	3.80	134.3
Poetry, drama	16	51.45	3.21	15	49.00	3.26	101.6
Religion	26	70.20	2.70	14	53.40	3.81	141.1
Science	17	75.65	4.45	13	67.80	5.21	117.1
Sociology, economics	50	171.65	3.43	50	218.10	4.36	127.1
Sports, recreation	145	441.85	3.04	187	549.25	2.93	96.4
Technology	11	46.20	4.20	12	43.95	3.64	86.7
Travel	4	12.90	3.22	21	166.80	7.94	246.6
Total	3,775	$9,995.45	$2.65	3,596	$10,605.72	$2.95	111.3

*Compiled by Nelson A. Piper from data supplied by the R. R. Bowker Company. Average prices of mass market paperbacks published in 1981 and 1982 shown in this table are based on listings of 1981 and 1982 mass market titles in *Paperbound Books in Print*. Comparable figures for earlier years are not available. See also Table 5.

TABLE 5 U.S. TRADE (HIGHER PRICED) PAPERBACK BOOKS: AVERAGE PRICES AND PRICE INDEXES, 1979–1982
(Index Base: 1977 = 100)*

	1977 Average Price	1979 (Final) No. of Books	1979 (Final) Average Price	1979 (Final) Index	1980 (Final) No. of Books	1980 (Final) Average Price	1980 (Final) Index	1981 (Final) No. of Books	1981 (Final) Average Price	1981 (Final) Index	1982 (Preliminary) No. of Books	1982 (Preliminary) Average Price	1982 (Preliminary) Index
Agriculture	$5.01	117	$6.80	135.7	104	$8.54	170.5	96	$9.74	194.4	95	$11.20	223.6
Art	6.27	634	8.33	132.8	563	9.09	145.0	651	10.07	160.6	507	10.64	169.7
Biography	4.91	314	5.64	114.9	363	6.57	133.8	444	7.33	149.3	336	8.37	170.5
Business	7.09	277	8.94	126.1	285	9.90	139.6	309	10.10	142.4	246	12.75	179.8
Education	5.72	404	6.91	120.8	382	8.42	147.2	484	9.54	166.8	315	10.24	179.0
Fiction	4.20	388	4.42	105.2	432	5.71	136.0	479	5.81	138.3	388	6.60	157.1
General works	6.18	480	6.47	104.7	544	8.00	129.4	578	10.90	176.4	879	8.77	141.9
History	5.81	474	6.67	114.8	478	7.57	130.3	634	9.10	156.6	426	10.37	178.5
Home economics	4.77	337	5.48	114.9	360	6.33	132.7	465	7.01	147.0	326	7.93	166.2
Juveniles	2.68	413	3.23	120.5	460	3.50	130.6	504	3.35	125.0	402	3.92	146.3
Language	7.79	205	7.53	96.7	215	8.59	110.3	252	8.50	109.1	165	9.91	127.2
Law	10.66	361	11.68	109.6	317	11.33	106.3	307	12.34	115.8	273	11.94	112.0
Literature	5.18	447	6.50	125.5	424	7.26	140.2	477	8.14	157.1	410	8.96	173.0
Medicine	7.63	667	9.55	125.2	682	11.46	150.2	814	12.35	161.9	478	12.95	169.7
Music	6.36	97	9.17	144.2	83	9.36	147.2	126	10.12	159.1	83	10.08	158.5
Philosophy, psychology	5.57	340	6.56	117.8	382	7.57	135.9	415	9.66	173.4	314	11.00	197.5
Poetry, drama	4.71	504	4.21	89.4	442	5.09	108.1	525	6.00	127.4	341	6.76	143.5
Religion	3.68	1,038	4.59	124.7	937	6.15	167.1	1,142	6.81	185.0	822	7.58	206.0
Science	8.81	614	11.48	130.3	630	13.46	152.8	648	14.75	167.4	494	13.87	157.4
Sociology, economics	6.03	2,036	8.07	133.8	2,016	9.75	161.7	2,275	11.56	191.7	1,659	20.68	343.0
Sports, recreation	4.87	360	6.12	125.7	326	7.11	146.0	414	7.86	161.4	291	9.36	192.2
Technology	7.97	556	9.24	115.9	601	13.52	169.6	918	14.60	183.2	528	16.88	211.8
Travel	5.21	294	5.97	114.6	247	6.73	129.2	263	8.20	157.4	187	8.02	153.9
Total	$5.93	11,357	$7.21	121.6	11,279	$8.60	145.0	13,220	$9.76	164.6	9,965	$11.68	197.0

*See footnote to Table 3.

TABLE 6 U.S. NONPRINT MEDIA: AVERAGE PRICES AND PRICE INDEXES, 1978–1982*
(Index Base: 1972 = 100)

Category	1972 Average Price	1978 Average Quantity	1978 Index	1979 Average Price	1979 Index	1980 Average Price	1980 Index	1981 Average Price	1981 Index	1982 Average Price	1982 Index
16mm Films											
Average rental cost per minute	$ 1.15	$ 1.22	106.1	$ 1.35	117.3	$ 1.41	122.6	$ 1.65	143.4	$ 1.61	140.0
Average color purchase cost per minute	11.95	12.56	105.1	13.62	113.9	12.03	100.6	16.09	133.7	15.01	125.6
Average cost of color film	241.39	350.42	145.1	328.24	135.9	279.09	115.6	343.79	123.1	432.35	179.1
Average length per film (min.)	20.2	27.9	—	24.1	—	23.2	—	21.4	—	28.7	—
Videocassettes											
Average purchase cost per minute	—	—	—	—	—	7.58	100.0	14.87	196.1	10.47	138.1
Average purchase cost	—	—	—	—	—	271.93	100.0	322.54	118.6	337.40	124.1
Filmstrips											
Average cost of filmstrip	12.95	17.43	134.6	21.42	165.4	21.74	167.8	25.40	196.1	29.14	225.0
Average cost of filmstrip set (cassette)	37.56	62.31	165.9	65.97	175.6	67.39	179.4	71.12	189.3	81.62	217.3
Average number of filmstrips per set	2.9	3.6	—	3.08	—	3.1	—	2.8	—	2.8	—
Average number of frames per filmstrip	63.3	58.0	—	71.8	—	67.9	—	71.4	—	67.8	—
Multimedia Kits											
Average cost per kit	51.33	117.38	228.7	85.70	166.9	92.71	180.6	46.99	91.5	57.52	112.1
Sound Recordings											
Average cost per disc	6.10	7.06	115.8	7.21	118.2	7.75	127.0	9.00	147.5	—	—
Average cost per cassette	7.81	12.57	161.1	12.58	161.1	9.34	119.5	12.48	159.7	10.74	137.5

*Compiled by David B. Walch from listings in the following journals: *Booklist*, *Choice*, and *School Library Journal*.

TABLE 7 U.S. LIBRARY MICROFILM: AVERAGE RATES
AND INDEX VALUES, 1981–1982*
(Index Base: 1978 = 100)

| | Negative Microfilm (35mm) ||| Positive Microfilm (35mm) |||
Year	Average Rate/ Exposure	Index Value	Change in Index	Average Rate/ Foot	Index Value	Change in Index
1978	$.0836	100	0	$.1612	100	0
1981	.0998	132.8	+32.8	.2021	142.5	+42.5
1982	.1067	142.0	+ 9.3	.2184	154.0	+11.5

*Compiled by Imre T. Jármy, National Preservation Program Office, The Library of Congress, consultant to the Library Materials Price Index Committee, Resources Section, Resources and Technical Services Division, American Library Association, from data secured by correspondence and by telephone interviews with the staff of the 50 indexed libraries. The complete list will be published in a pertinent journal of American librarianship. The title of the journal was not available at press time.

age rise in average costs was "History" with a 16.6 percent increase in cost—all other subject classes comprising the 1982 hardcover survey recorded substantially lower rates of increase or actual declines in their average costs. The preliminary cost increase data also should be used with considerable care. As an example, the overall average cost for hardcover books resulting from the 1981 preliminary survey was $25.48 per volume compared to the $26.63 per volume cost resulting from the final 1981 survey, a difference of $1.15 per volume.

The U.S. Nonprint Media Index (Table 6) is now based on the considerably more comprehensive combination of media listings from *Booklist* and *Choice*, as well as the listings from *School Library Journal*. The compiler believes that this increase in coverage will result in much more reliable price indexes for media materials in the future.

TABLE 8 SELECTED U.S. DAILY NEWSPAPERS:
AVERAGE SUBSCRIPTION RATES AND INDEX
VALUES, 1981–1982*
(Index Base: 1978 = 100)

Year	Average Rate	Index Value	Change in Index
1978	$ 76.4391	100.0	0
1981	98.5521	164.7	64.7
1982	103.6382	173.2	+8.5

*Compiled by Imre T. Jármy, National Preservation Program Office, The Library of Congress, consultant to the Library Materials Price Index Committee, Resource Section, Resources and Technical Services Division, American Library Association, from data secured by correspondence and by telephone interviews with the circulation managers and publishers of the indexed newspapers and, when necessary, by examining the final issue of a title for the year. Data were compiled for the 133 titles surveyed in the continental United States, and Alaska and Hawaii. The complete list will be published in a pertinent journal of American librarianship. The title of the journal was not available at press time.

An analysis of the index for 1982 reveals several interesting developments in the cost of media materials. The average cost per minute of 16mm film is down 8.1 index points (or 6.7 percent). In spite of this decline in cost, the average cost of an entire 16mm film in 1982 increased by 56.0 index points (or 25.8 percent) over the 1981 average cost. The reason for this seeming anomaly is simply that the average length of 16mm films in 1982 increased by over seven minutes when compared to the average length of films in 1981.

The price indexes for U.S. library microfilm (Table 7) and selected U.S. daily newspapers (Table 8) recorded moderate increases between 1981 and 1982. Negative microfilm increased by $.0069 per exposure, and positive microfilm increased $.0163 per foot. The average subscription rate for U.S. daily newspapers increased from $98.5521 to $103.6382, or 5.2 percent.

FOREIGN PUBLISHED MATERIALS

The increased utility to U.S. libraries of international price information (Tables 9-15) reported in last year's article has been considerably reduced in 1982. The compilation of Table 9 (British Books by Major Categories) and Table 10 (British Adult Nonfiction Books) has been suspended with the data collected for the period covering January through August 1981. The suspension is due to the difficulties experienced by the (British) Library Association in securing the financial support required to collate and analyze the raw data obtained from the *British National Bibliography*. The Library Association is presently seeking special funding from other sources to continue its valuable work sometime in the future.

In the meantime, U.S. academic and research libraries will undoubtedly find that Table 11 (British Academic Books) is a very useful substitute for the two suspended indexes. The new index is based on price information, published under the auspices of the Centre for Library and Information Management of Loughborough University of Technology, for copyright books deposited in the Cambridge University Library. A comparison of the new British index with the index for German hardcover/scholarly paperback books (Table 14) will give U.S. libraries reliable price information on the British and German books that they are most likely to buy.

The extension of the original 1981 preliminary data for British books through August of 1981 illustrates that the preliminary price information for the 8,819 books comprising Table 9 (British Books by Major Categories) in the 1982 *Bowker Annual* can be extended to cover the 17,087 books included in the January through August 1981 survey; the rate of change in the overall unit cost for 1980 over 1981 increases to 10.2 index points (or 7.3 percent) compared to the original increase of 3.1 index points (or 2.2 percent). An analysis of Table 9 reveals that the cost of British books generally rose as the size of the 1981 preliminary statistical base increased. The pattern of Table 10 reveals a similar trend with all categories except General Works (000) increasing in average cost.

The overall rate of increase in average cost for British academic books (Table 11) based on 1981 final data and 1982 preliminary data is 16.4 index points, or 14.6 percent. The majority of the subject classes making up the new index recorded significant price index increases in 1982, with two exceptions, 200 (Religion) and 400 (Language). Users of this new index should also note that the base year for the index is 1979, rather than 1977, and that beginning in 1982 books on public safety have been shifted from the 600s to the 300s. Evidence of the change is seen in the following name changes of subjects included in the 300s: Social Sciences becomes Sociology, Social Welfare becomes Social Problems and Services. It is much too early to predict the long-term effect of the above changes on the indexes.

TABLE 9 BRITISH BOOKS BY MAJOR CATEGORIES: AVERAGE PRICES AND PRICE INDEXES, 1979–1981*
(Index Base: 1977 = 100)†

	1977	1979			1980			1981 (Preliminary)		
	Average Price £ p	No. of Books	Average Price £ p	Index	No. of Books	Average Price £ p	Index	No. of Books	Average Price £ p	Index
Adult fiction	2.55	4,039	3.20	125.5	5,628	3.68	144.3	3,153	4.11	161.2
Adult nonfiction[1]	6.40	25,038	7.70	120.3	37,340	8.83	138.0	13,371	9.70	151.6
Reference books[2]	7.30	2,326	9.15	125.3	3,818	11.32	155.1	211	15.02	205.8
Children's fiction	1.44	1,441	1.86	129.2	1,822	1.99	138.2	726	2.54	176.4
Children's nonfiction	1.19	1,242	1.37	115.1	1,916	1.81	152.1	557	2.40	201.7
All categories combined	5.49	31,760	6.62	120.6	46,706	7.65	139.3	17,087	8.21	149.5

*Data compiled by Richard Hume Werking from the *Library Association Record*, July and November 1981.
†The index year 1977 has been adopted to conform to the year used in the U.S. Government's Consumer Price Index.
[1] See Table 10 for breakdown by Dewey classes.
[2] Reference books are included in the total for nonfiction.

TABLE 10   BRITISH ADULT NONFICTION BOOKS: AVERAGE PRICES AND PRICE INDEXES, 1979–1981*
(Index Base: 1977 = 100)†

Classes	1977 Average Price £ p	1979 No. of Books	1979 Average Price £ p	1979 Index	1980 No. of Books	1980 Average Price £ p	1980 Index	1981 (Preliminary) No. of Books	1981 Average Price £ p	1981 Index
000	8.18	986	12.70	155.3	1,282	14.39	175.9	437	11.05	135.1
100	5.61	716	7.45	132.8	987	8.70	155.1	402	8.79	156.7
200	3.18	1,035	4.60	144.7	1,499	3.88	122.0	569	4.13	129.9
300	6.28	7,114	7.03	111.9	10,517	8.95	142.5	3,326	10.23	162.9
400	3.63	781	2.74	75.5	881	4.11	113.2	294	5.62	154.8
500	10.95	2,163	13.78	125.8	3,142	14.03	128.1	1,104	14.91	136.2
600	7.94	4,965	9.99	125.8	8,626	10.18	128.2	2,882	12.35	155.5
700	5.57	2,516	6.19	111.1	3,686	8.27	148.5	1,460	8.40	150.8
800	3.44	2,181	4.78	139.0	3,188	4.99	145.1	1,438	5.85	170.1
900	4.54	2,581	4.91	108.1	3,532	5.83	128.4	1,473	7.27	160.1

*Data compiled by Richard Hume Werking from the *Library Association Record*, July and November 1981.
†The index year 1977 has been adopted to conform to the year used in the U.S. Government's Consumer Price Index.
‡000 General works; Bibliographies; Librarianship
 100 Philosophy; Psychology; Occultism, etc.
 200 Not subdivided
 300 Sociology; Politics; Economics; Law; Public Administration; Social Problems and Services; Education; Social Customs, etc.
 400 Language; School Readers
 500 General Science; Mathematics; Astronomy; Physics; Chemistry; Geology; Meterology; Pre-history; Anthropology
 600 Medicine; Public Safety; Engineering/Technology; Agriculture; Domestic Economy; Business Management; Printing and Book Trade; Manufacturers; Chemical Technology; Building
 700 Architecture; Fine Arts; Photography; Music; Entertainment; Sports, Amusements
 800 General and Foreign Literature; English Literature
 900 Geography; Travel; Biography; History

TABLE 11 BRITISH ACADEMIC BOOKS: AVERAGE PRICES AND COST INDEXES, 1980–1982*
(Index Base: 1979 = 100)

Dewey Classes[†]	1979 Average Price £ p	1980 No. of Books	1980 Average Price £ p	1980 Index	1981 No. of Books	1981 Average Price £ p	1981 Index	1982 (Preliminary)[‡] No. of Books	1982 Average Price £ p	1982 Index
000	14.17	896	15.16	107.0	507	12.10	85.4	247	14.48	102.2
100	8.89	642	9.78	110.1	409	10.29	115.8	148	13.39	150.6
200	5.47	818	5.59	103.5	481	5.97	109.1	244	5.83	106.6
300	9.15	5,146	10.17	111.2	3,687	10.69	116.8	1,481	12.09	132.1
400	7.62	255	8.33	109.3	147	11.09	145.4	89	10.28	134.9
500	16.67	1,793	16.75	100.5	1,225	18.51	110.4	511	22.26	133.5
600	14.32	4,253	13.12	91.6	2,460	16.78	117.2	976	19.51	136.2
700	9.57	1,423	13.57	141.8	949	11.83	123.6	425	12.53	130.9
800	7.19	1,484	8.10	112.7	1,163	7.37	102.5	443	9.08	126.3
900	7.78	1,513	8.45	108.6	1,256	9.04	116.2	485	9.81	126.1
Total	10.81	18,223	11.46	106.0	12,284	12.16	112.5	5,049	13.93	128.9

*Data compiled by Richard Hume Werking from *CLAIM* (Report numbers 2, 12, and 21) published under the auspices of the Centre for Library and Information Management, Loughborough University of Technology.
[†]See Table 10 for breakdown of Dewey classes.
[‡]The preliminary data for 1982 cover the period from January through June 1982.

TABLE 12 GERMAN BOOKS: AVERAGE PRICES AND PRICE INDEXES, 1979–1981*
(Index Base: 1977 = 100)

	1977	1979		1980		1981	
	Average Price	Average Price	Index	Average Price	Index	Average Price	Index
General, library science, college level textbooks	DM68.47	DM67.57	98.7	DM75.23	109.9	DM66.45	97.0
Religion, theology	23.21	26.08	112.4	24.06	103.7	23.00	99.1
Philosophy, psychology	26.67	24.43	91.6	27.81	104.3	30.15	113.0
Law, administration	33.92	46.28	136.4	47.04	138.7	62.65	184.7
Social sciences, economics, statistics	25.97	31.73	122.2	32.98	127.0	32.30	124.4
Political and military science	22.91	27.44	119.8	25.50	111.3	24.90	108.7
Literature and linguistics	27.79	27.03	97.3	27.71	99.7	30.63	110.2
Belles lettres	6.57	7.47	113.7	7.20	109.6	8.15	124.0
Juveniles	9.07	7.85	86.5	10.29	113.5	9.47	104.4
Education	16.50	17.96	108.8	18.20	110.3	20.69	125.4
School textbooks	10.88	11.51	105.8	11.58	106.4	13.61	125.1
Fine arts	49.70	49.09	98.8	51.76	104.1	54.30	109.3
Music, dance, theatre, film, radio	28.04	25.84	92.2	26.38	94.1	29.20	104.1
History, folklore	38.79	37.29	96.1	39.78	102.6	39.63	102.2
Geography, anthropology, travel	32.20	30.49	94.7	31.14	96.7	29.83	92.6
Medicine	50.29	58.10	115.5	59.91	119.1	65.57	130.4
Natural sciences	93.45	101.75	108.9	99.60	106.6	122.81	131.4
Mathematics	28.98	34.82	120.2	36.48	125.9	42.06	145.1
Technology	42.45	55.13	129.9	62.40	147.0	57.11	134.5
Touring guides and directories	21.78	30.09	138.2	31.02	142.4	29.03	133.3
Home economics and agriculture	25.10	22.36	89.1	24.09	96.0	25.70	102.4
Sports and recreation	18.99	19.01	100.1	20.26	106.7	21.45	113.0
Miscellaneous	11.30	8.39	74.2	13.60	120.4	11.69	103.5
Total.	DM21.87	DM23.62	108.0	DM25.23	115.4	DM26.60	121.6

*This is a combined index for numbered paperback books (Taschenbucher) and for bound volumes and scholarly paperbacks (andere Titel). The indexes are tentative and based on average prices unadjusted for title production. Figures for 1981 were compiled by Peter Graham and Paul Peters from *Buch und Buchhandel in Zahlen* (Frankfurt, 1981). The index year 1977 has been adopted to conform to the year used in the U.S. Government's Consumer Price Index.

Information note: The average annual market exchange rate for 1981 was 2.2600 Deutsche Marks per U.S. dollar, as reported by the Bureau of Statistics, International Monetary Fund in its periodical *International Financial Statistics.*

TABLE 13 GERMAN PAPERBACK BOOKS: AVERAGE PRICES AND PRICE INDEXES, 1979–1981*
(Index Base: 1977 = 100)

	1977 Average Price	1979 Average Price	1979 Index	1980 Average Price	1980 Index	1981 Average Price	1981 Index
General, library science, college level textbooks	DM6.47	DM5.01	77.4	DM8.71	134.6	DM13.04	201.5
Religion, theology	7.03	7.84	111.5	7.29	103.7	8.92	126.9
Philosophy, psychology	8.06	8.99	111.5	9.44	117.1	9.18	113.9
Law, administration	8.95	10.58	118.2	13.41	149.8	10.42	116.4
Social sciences, economics, statistics	10.02	10.27	102.5	10.75	107.3	11.06	110.4
Political and military science	8.24	8.85	107.4	9.34	113.3	10.08	122.3
Literature and linguistics	8.36	9.01	107.8	10.21	122.1	10.02	119.9
Belle lettres	4.89	5.75	117.6	5.70	116.6	6.21	127.0
Juvenile	4.77	5.16	108.2	5.51	115.5	5.59	117.2
Education	10.88	11.01	101.2	11.63	106.9	10.70	98.3
School textbooks	2.52	3.62	143.7	3.12	123.8	3.05	121.0
Fine arts	10.28	8.80	85.6	11.77	114.5	11.11	108.1
Music, dance, theater, film, radio	8.11	7.47	92.1	8.60	106.0	9.64	118.9
History, folklore	8.35	9.01	107.9	9.22	110.4	10.75	128.7
Geography, anthropology, travel	6.82	7.74	113.5	9.09	133.3	9.90	145.2
Medicine	10.42	10.96	105.2	12.15	116.6	10.58	101.5
Natural sciences	10.85	13.49	124.3	12.31	113.5	12.86	118.5
Mathematics	15.00	15.32	102.1	16.21	108.1	17.53	116.9
Technology	20.63	26.04	126.2	28.22	136.8	36.72	178.0
Touring guides and directories	7.11	7.69	108.2	10.46	147.1	9.93	139.7
Home economics and agriculture	6.77	6.89	101.8	7.38	109.0	8.25	121.9
Sports and recreation	6.81	7.83	115.0	7.69	112.9	8.24	121.0
Miscellaneous	5.00	5.90	118.0	8.87	177.4	8.73	174.7
Total	DM6.69	DM7.27	108.7	DM7.76	116.0	DM8.13	121.5

*Indexes are tentative and based on average prices unadjusted for title production for numbered paperback books (Taschenbucher). Figures for 1981 were compiled by Peter Graham and Paul Peters from *Buch und Buchhandel in Zahlen* (Frankfurt, 1982). The index year 1977 has been adopted to conform to the year used in the U.S. Government's Consumer Price Index.

Information note: The average annual market exchange rate for 1981 was 2.2600 Deutsche Marks per U.S. dollar, as reported by the Bureau of Statistics, International Monetary Fund in its periodical *International Financial Statistics*.

TABLE 14 GERMAN HARDCOVER AND SCHOLARLY PAPERBACK BOOKS: AVERAGE PRICES AND PRICE INDEXES, 1979–1981*
(Index Base: 1977 = 100)

	1977 Average Price	1979 Average Price	1979 Index	1980 Average Price	1980 Index	1981 Average Price	1981 Index
General, library science, college level textbooks	DM82.28	DM80.56	98.0	DM86.93	105.7	DM73.66	89.5
Religion, theology	27.67	29.97	108.3	28.63	103.5	26.24	94.8
Philosophy, psychology	40.38	33.55	83.1	38.14	94.5	44.68	110.6
Law, administration	37.50	50.46	134.6	50.79	135.4	70.32	187.5
Social sciences, economics, statistics	32.20	40.38	125.4	39.71	123.3	39.90	124.0
Political and military science	27.85	34.36	123.4	32.52	116.8	33.07	118.7
Literature and linguistics	40.90	36.62	89.5	36.06	88.2	42.57	104.1
Belle lettres	7.48	8.75	117.0	8.20	109.6	9.82	131.3
Juvenile	12.86	9.60	74.7	12.69	98.7	11.54	89.7
Education	18.19	19.28	106.0	19.40	106.7	23.07	126.8
School textbooks	10.98	11.60	105.6	11.79	107.4	13.80	125.7
Fine arts	58.51	56.96	97.4	63.70	108.9	65.08	111.2
Music, dance, theater, film, radio	37.89	37.00	97.7	38.73	102.2	46.13	121.7
History, folklore	49.82	49.92	100.2	53.43	107.2	54.73	109.9
Geography, anthropology, travel	34.76	33.10	95.2	34.05	98.0	35.19	101.2
Medicine	61.55	69.13	112.3	68.47	111.2	76.41	124.1
Natural sciences	131.28	122.87	93.6	118.89	90.6	143.29	109.1
Mathematics	32.83	39.10	119.1	41.55	126.6	46.60	142.0
Technology	45.39	59.25	130.5	67.79	149.4	60.87	134.1
Touring guides and directories	22.94	32.42	141.3	34.08	148.6	33.80	147.3
Home economics and agriculture	31.49	38.78	91.4	31.38	99.7	33.90	107.7
Sports and recreation	24.55	25.96	105.7	28.51	116.1	29.97	122.1
Miscellaneous	11.71	9.05	77.3	14.32	122.3	12.63	107.9
Total	DM27.68	DM30.37	109.8	DM32.18	116.3	DM35.39	127.9

*Indexes are tentative and based on average prices unadjusted for title production for bound volumes and scholarly paperbacks (andere Titel). Figures for 1981 were compiled by Peter Graham and Paul Peters from *Buch und Buchhandel in Zahlen* (Frankfurt, 1982). The index year 1977 has been adopted to conform to the year used in the U.S. Government's Consumer Price Index.

Information note: The average annual market exchange rate for 1981 was 2.2600 Deutsche Marks per U.S. dollar, as reported by the Bureau of Statistics, International Monetary Fund in its periodical *International Financial Statistics*.

TABLE 15 LATIN AMERICAN BOOKS: NUMBER OF COPIES AND
AVERAGE COST, FY 1981 AND 1982*

	Number of Books FY 1981	Number of Books FY 1982	Average Cost FY 1981	Average Cost FY 1982	%(+ or −) over 1981
Argentina	4,025	4,839†	$12.49†	$10.52	−15.7
Bolivia	1,552	1,603†	12.64†	10.89	−13.8
Brazil	8,341	9,094	8.63†	7.68	−11.0
Chile	1,040	1,165	15.24†	19.07	+25.1
Colombia	2,122	1,786	12.67†	13.18	+4.0
Costa Rica	73	592	7.60	7.70	+1.3
Cuba	225	119	9.73	9.83	+1.0
Dominican Republic	600	575	10.10	10.02	−.8
Ecuador	659	586†	7.51	8.95	+19.2
El Salvador	109	172	10.36	17.55	+69.4
Guatemala	246	280	8.78	9.14	+4.1
Guyana	190	46	5.74	16.54	+188.1
Haiti	293	176	8.75	9.44	+7.9
Honduras	194	342	7.89	4.70	−40.4
Jamaica	294	150	4.42	7.62	+72.4
Mexico	3,975	3,673	9.34†	9.02	−3.4
Nicaragua	323	227	8.34	8.82	+5.7
Panama	40	66	5.69†	8.64	+51.8
Paraguay	281	195	12.71†	12.30	−3.2
Peru	2,923	2,515†	7.67†	9.34	+21.7
Puerto Rico	390	366	8.82	8.04	−8.8
Surinam‡	139	26	8.58	—	—
Trinidad	159	32	7.72	6.94	−10.1
Uruguay	1,921	1,606†	10.13	14.93	+47.4
Venezuela	835	710	10.50	10.96	+4.4
Other Caribbean	871	1,654	4.70	8.95	+90.4

*Compiled by Peter J. de la Garza, Seminars on the Acquisition of Latin American Library Materials (SALALM), Acquisition Committee, from reports on the number and cost of current monographs purchased by eight selected U.S. libraries. The participants include the libraries of Cornell University, University of Florida, University of Illinois, Library of Congress, University of Minnesota, New York Public Library, University of Texas, and University of Wisconsin.
†Includes some binding costs.
‡Data for FY 1982 are insufficient for meaningful comparison.

Two of the three German book price indexes recorded moderate increases in 1981. The combined index for both hardcover and all paperback books (Table 12) increased by 6.2 index points (or 5.3 percent), and the German paperback books index (Table 13) increased by 5.5 index points (or 4.8 percent). The hardcover/scholarly paperback book index (Table 14) just managed to reach the double-digit inflation rate by increasing 11.6 index points (or 10 percent).

Users of the three German indexes should also pay careful attention to their library's acquisitions profile. In the case of Table 12, the increases and decreases in price levels are almost equally balanced between the various subject classifications (13 increases, 10 decreases); Table 13 records substantially more increases than decreases (14 increases, 9 decreases). The hardcover/scholarly paperback index (Table 14), most likely to be of value to the majority of U.S. libraries purchasing German books, recorded 17 increases and 6 decreases in the subject classes comprising the index. The largest increase was the 52.1 index point increase (or 38.4 percent) recorded by law and administration books. The biggest decrease in index points was the 16.2 index point decline (or 15.3 percent) recorded by general library science and college-level textbooks.

The price information included in Table 15 (Latin American Books) again reveals an extremely wide variation in the average cost of Latin American books purchased by eight U.S. libraries in 1982. There is also an extremely wide variation in the rates of change in the price indexes for library materials. The lowest rate of change is a decrease of 40.4 percent for books published in Honduras. The highest rate of change is an increase of 188.1 percent for books published in Guyana. The cost of books from 16 of the 26 countries included in the survey increased in 1982, and books from 9 of the countries decreased in cost. Information from one country, Surinam, proved to be insufficient for meaningful comparison.

As reported in last year's article, U.S. libraries that expend a significant portion of their book budget for materials published in foreign countries will benefit substantially from the continued rise in 1982 of the value of the dollar against the value of the currencies of other nations. A comparison of the value of the currencies of a representative group of countries with the U.S. dollar at the beginning and close of 1982 (Bank of America. Foreign Exchange Trading Section. *Foreign checks drafts & remittance orders.* Jan. 6, 1982, and Dec. 28, 1982) illustrates the dramatic gain of U.S. purchasing power abroad during 1982. (Percent changes within parentheses indicate a negative change.)

Country	Jan. 6, 1982	Dec. 28, 1982	% Change
Canada	.85500	.81800	(4.3)
France	.18100	.15200	(16.6)
England	1.94000	1.63500	(16.0)
Germany	.45100	.42400	(6.6)
Japan	.00465	.00421	(9.5)
Netherlands	.41000	.38400	(7.3)
Spain	.01050	.00810	(22.9)

USING THE PRICE INDEXES

In planning future budgets, libraries should bear in mind that the favorable trend in U.S. purchasing power noted above can easily be reversed. It is for this reason that the ALA/RTSD/RS Library Materials Price Index Committee has sponsored the preparation and publication of the tables that accompany this article.

The price indexes, which were designed to measure the rate of price change of newly published materials against those of earlier years on the national level, are useful for comparing with local purchasing patterns. They reflect retail prices, not the cost to a particular library, and were never intended to be a substitute for information that a library might collect about its own purchases. The prices on which the indexes are based do not include discounts, vendor service charges, or other service charges. These variables naturally affect the average price for library materials paid by a particular library; however, as recent studies have shown, this does not necessarily mean that the rate of increase in prices paid by a particular library is significantly different from the rate of increase shown by the price indexes. The Library Materials Price Index Committee is very interested in pursuing correlations of individual library's prices with national prices and would like to be informed of any studies undertaken.

It is also important to remember that in anticipation of the revision of ANSI Z39.20-1974, the three-year base period on which the price indexes have been calculated in the past is being changed to a one-year base period. Moreover, 1977 has been adopted as the new base year in most instances. These changes will make it easier to compare with the U.S. government Consumer Price Index, which also has a one-year base of 1977. It is expected that conversion to the 1977 base will be completed for all tables, for which sufficient historical cost information is available, in the 1984 edition of the *Bowker Annual*.

As always, users are cautioned to use the indexes with care, noting the particulars of each index. For example, in comparing the categories of preliminary and final in the U.S. and British book price tables, users should compare like categories only and not make the mistake of comparing preliminary figures with final figures.

In addition to the indexes presented here, there are at least two other published price indexes: "Price Indexes, Foreign and Domestic Music," which appears in the *Music Library Association Notes*, and "Price Index for Legal Publications," which appears in the *Law Library Journal*. Also, timely updates of several of the Library Materials Price Index Committee's sponsored indexes are published in the *RTSD Newsletter*.

The current members of the Library Materials Price Index Committee are Nelson A. Piper, chairperson, Mary Elizabeth Clack, Peter Graham, Dennis E. Smith, and Richard Hume Werking. Consultants to the committee are Noreen G. Alldredge, Norman B. Brown, Imre Jármy, Jane Phillips, David B. Walch, and Sally F. Williams.

NUMBER OF BOOK OUTLETS IN THE UNITED STATES AND CANADA

The *American Book Trade Directory* has been published by the R. R. Bowker Company since 1915. Revised annually, it features lists of booksellers, publishers, wholesalers, periodicals, reference tools, and other information about the U.S. book market as well as markets in Great Britain and Canada. The data provided in Tables 1 and 2 for the

TABLE 1 BOOKSTORES IN THE UNITED STATES (AND CANADA)*

Antiquarian	1,048 (69)	Museum store and art gallery	245 (14)
Mail order—antiquarian	625 (21)	Newsdealer	132 (6)
College	2,718 (136)	Office supply	56 (2)
Department store	1,167 (108)	Paperback**	733 (38)
Drugstore	20 (3)	Religious	3,490 (184)
Educational	98 (16)	Remainder	19 (2)
Exporter-importer	32 (1)	Rental	2 (0)
Foreign language	81 (35)	Science-technology	57 (8)
General	5,603 (1,015)	Special***	1,472 (187)
Gift shop	109 (10)	Stationer	140 (26)
Juvenile	141 (19)	Used	561 (25)
Law	61 (3)	Total listed in the United States	19,049
Mail order (general)	326 (13)		
Medical	113 (3)	Total listed in Canada	1,944

*In Tables 1 and 2, the Canadian figure for each category is in parentheses following the U.S. figure.

**This figure does not include paperback departments of general bookstores, department stores, stationers, drugstores, or wholesalers handling paperbacks.

***"Special" includes stores specializing in subjects other than those specifically given in the list.

TABLE 2 WHOLESALERS IN THE UNITED STATES (AND CANADA)

General wholesalers	742 (116)	Total listed in the United States	1024
Paperback wholesalers	282 (17)	Total listed in Canada	113

United States and Canada, the most current available, are from the 1982 edition of the directory.

The 20,993 stores of various types shown in Table 1 are located in approximately 6,300 cities in the United States, Canada, and regions administered by the United States. All "general" bookstores are assumed to carry hardbound (trade) books, paperbacks, and children's books; special effort has been made to apply this category only to bookstores for which this term can properly be applied. All "college" stores are assumed to carry college-level textbooks. The term "educational" is used for outlets handling school textbooks up to and including the high school level. The category "mail order" has been confined to those outlets that sell general trade books by mail and are not book clubs; all others operating by mail have been classified according to the kinds of books carried. The term "antiquarian" covers dealers in old and rare books. Stores handling only secondhand books are classified by the category "used." The category "paperbacks" represents stores with stock consisting of more than an 80% holding of paperbound books. Other stores with paperback departments are listed under the major classification ("general," "department store," "stationers," etc.), with the fact that paperbacks are carried given in the entry. A bookstore that specializes in a subject to the extent of 50% of its stock has that subject designated as its major category.

BOOK REVIEW MEDIA STATISTICS

NUMBER OF BOOKS REVIEWED BY MAJOR BOOK-REVIEWING PUBLICATIONS, 1981 AND 1982

	Adult 1981	Adult 1982	Juvenile 1981	Juvenile 1982	Young Adult 1981	Young Adult 1982	Total 1981	Total 1982
Booklist[1]	3,022	3,387	1,270	1,540	1,139	1,225	5,872	6,584
Bulletin of the Center for Children's Books	—	—	480	490	408	418	888	908
Choice[2]	6,462	6,929	—	—	—	—	6,462	6,929
Horn Book	50	59	292	318	98	111	440	488
Kirkus Services	3,996	3,536	903	869	—	—	4,899	4,405
Library Journal	5,878	5,100	—	—	—	—	5,878	5,100
New York Review of Books	400	400	—	—	—	—	400	400
New York Times Sunday Book Review[3]	2,000	2,266	224	234	—	—	2,224	2,500
Publishers Weekly[4]	4,346	4,515	560	585	—	—	4,906	5,100
School Library Journal[5]	—	30	2,291	2,295	306	250	2,597	2,575
Washington Post Book World	1,910	1,870	102	121	—	—	2,012	1,991

[1] All figures are for a 12-month period from September 1 to August 31, e.g., 1981 figures are for September 1, 1980–August 31, 1981. Totals include reference and subscription books. In addition, *Booklist* publishes reviews of nonprint materials—1,501 in 1981 and 1,297 in 1982 (including 216 special nonprint lists)—and of special bibliographies—4,000 in 1982 (not counted in 1981).

[2] All figures are for a 12-month period beginning in September and ending in July/August, e.g., 1981 figures are for September 1980–July/August 1981. Totals do not include nonprint materials.

[3] Adult figure includes paperbacks reviewed in "New and Noteworthy" column.

[4] Includes reviews of paperback originals and reprints.

[5] Adult figure for 1982 represents professional reading titles, which were not counted in 1981.

Part 5
International Reports and Statistics

International Reports

FRANKFURT BOOK FAIR, 1982

Herbert R. Lottman
International Correspondent, *Publishers Weekly*

Looking up at one more dim Frankfurt sky, publisher Paul Brinkman of Amsterdam's Ploegsma exclaimed: "Rain is the best weather for publishers! That's when people *read*." Inside Hall 5, where the world's trade had gathered for the 34th Frankfurt Book Fair, Thérèse de Saint Phalle, a 16-year fair veteran from Paris's Flammarion, carried an appointment book listing an average of 18 meetings per day; adding the people she saw at two or more parties and a dinner each evening, and chance encounters in the aisles, she estimated that she had exchanged rights information with 250 to 300 heads of houses, editors-in-chief or subsidiary rights managers, in the 5½ day run of the show. She didn't have to mourn the absence of any of her regular publishing partners at this year's fair (which ran from October 6 to October 11); despite the recession that wouldn't go away in every major publishing country—and some acute crises in a couple of minor ones—nearly all the world's logos, and most familiar faces, were visible once again. Participants filled every hotel room in the city and spilled over to towns and villages within a 50-mile radius of the fairgrounds. Perhaps they had to spend more time than previously adapting to new conditions, but the news is that they were doing it successfully; a random sampling of visitors to Hall 5 turned up more positive than negative reactions.

Observing that the exhibit halls were "fairly crowded this year," Book Fair director Peter Weidhaas explained at an opening ceremony: "It is only seemingly a paradox to attribute the crush to changes in economic and social conditions to which major events in other lines of business have paid tribute in the form of stagnating or declining numbers of participants. I gather only one thing clearly from these figures: Fewer and fewer publishers can afford *not* to attend the Frankfurt Book Fair!" There were an even 100 new foreign exhibitors this time; room was found for them by reducing the size of as many existing stands, and 40 other companies on the waiting list never made it. In numbers: there were 5,866 exhibitors, against 5,534 last year; 4,169 were non-German (against 4,069). More significantly, individual exhibitors were up from 3,924 to 4,076 (including the hundred non-Germans already referred to). There were more books on the racks, from more countries (88 against last year's 86). And the fair was girding itself to get still bigger: one could hardly fail to notice the construction going on. In a year or possibly two, the fair won't have to turn down or scale down exhibiting space any more.

It was being said that there were fewer American visitors, but that was hard to prove. The weathervane of U.S. participation has always been the collective exhibit of exporter Feffer & Simons, which helps staff the booths of its client houses. Publishers or other key personnel are usually present at the booths, and the impression is of a shopping mall with designer boutiques. This year 34 houses occupied 350 square meters; there were as many publishing people as ever, including Roger W. Straus, Jr. of Farrar, Straus

Note: Adapted from *Publishers Weekly*, November 5, 1982, where the article was entitled "Frankfurt 1982: Adjusting to a Leaner Publishing World."

& Giroux, Seymour Lawrence (who had just switched his imprint to Dutton), Werner Mark Linz of Crossroad, Mildred Hird and Alun Davies of Bantam, Betty Prashker and Allan Eady of Crown. Combined Book Exhibit showed 57 publishing imprints, up 15 from 1981, with new stands ingeniously carved out of the existing space allotment. Academia Book Exhibits of Fairfax, Virginia, showed for 30 publishers, a rise over last year in imprints and in people who actually made the trip. Most American paperback houses were grouped in collective areas staffed by their overseas distributors. And some of the larger American houses had double or triple or even bigger stands of their own—Simon & Schuster, Doubleday, McGraw-Hill, the Random House group, Harper & Row, Holt, Rinehart and Winston, Harcourt Brace Jovanovich, John Wiley, and Prentice-Hall among them.

THE BRITISH IN FORCE

The British could say once more that they were the largest non-German exhibiting nation, with 573 individual exhibitors (the United States was runner-up with 476). There were impressive compounds for some of them (like the Heinemann group, Penguin, Macmillan, Granada), and the Publishers Association staffed an information booth; across the aisle the British Council ran a large culturally oriented display, with books chosen not by publishers but by the council. Most European countries did collective displays, often to exhibit smaller houses which couldn't afford individual booths. The French made a particular effort this year, with a larger-than-ever collective stand run by the Office de Promotion de l'Edition Française. A formal invitation was sent out to 1,200 foreign colleagues, booksellers, local cultural institutions, and teachers for a reception on the stand on October 6. Earlier that day the French Minister of Culture Jack Lang put in a personal appearance, flying to the fair in a military plane with TV and print journalists; the junket included two Goncourt Prize novelists. The obvious intent was to show the flag, but Lang's press conference proved to be a non-event. When he was challenged about his remarks on American cultural imperialism made at a meeting of UNESCO in Mexico, Lang denied anti-American intentions, but added that "certain industrial realities" couldn't be ignored.

Obviously this fair was going to be a microcosm of the great world outside, and veterans watched nervously for signs. One seasoned international publisher had told *PW*'s correspondent on opening day: "It isn't true that publishing is in crisis. Some publishers are, and others are doing quite well." Another publisher, successful in a tough Latin American market, expressed disappointment at what he saw as sluggish behavior on the part of his fellows. "When things don't go well in our part of the world we look for ways to make them go better, we don't just sit on our hands. Maybe it's because we have 100 percent inflation; we have to grow 125 percent to make any money." Charles Pick of Heinemann admitted that his group had trimmed its sails—reorganized, cut lists—and the year was going "according to plan." His comment was typical of those expressed by UK publishers. Meanwhile the host country's book business was in its second year of recession. "But we've all done a lot to adjust," Bertelsmann's Olaf Paeschke reported. "We reduced personnel and numbers of books published, so next year should show improvement." He noted that mass market paperbacks continued to live an economic life of their own in Germany; growth hadn't peaked yet. But it *would* peak, and then they'd have to cope with problems of saturation and overproduction. Both trade and paperback people were looking to the Christmas season, waiting to see if buyers have turned away from books to video. Paeschke thinks they haven't.

Japan, Kodansha president Toshiyuki Hattori told *PW*, continues to suffer zero growth. Since there has been a rise in the number of booksellers, each bookseller's share of the market is down; title output is up, copies sold down; the return to happier times will be gradual.

"Italian publishing has been slow, but not as slow as some will tell you," a leading Italian book person confided. "Some publishers are still making good money." He spoke in full knowledge of the crisis then unraveling in Milan, where Rizzoli was offering itself to court receivers. The effect of its failure on the rest of the market would be serious, but it was still too early to say whether the group and its book division will survive in their present form or anything resembling it (*PW,* October 12). Two Latin American countries had assumed low profiles: Mexico, where publishing assets had suddenly dropped to zilch in world currencies, not only restricting that country's ability to pay for rights or books, but wiping out assets owned by foreign groups. Post-Falklands Argentina was the other country with payments problems. At Frankfurt, publishers from both countries, and agents selling into them, sought to behave as if the worst would soon be over.

To try to add up the results of a Frankfurt fair is complicated by the way publishers do business. It is possible to get a fairly accurate picture of the bookselling side, for that is almost immediately apparent in the form of orders. But rights negotiations go on before, during, and after the fair; an option given at the fair may or may not be taken up. Fewer publishers than ever commit themselves in the febrile atmosphere of Frankfurt, the exceptions being the seekers of blockbuster-type bestsellers, often acquired according to auction rules; those who refuse to play the game lose the opportunity to get a book that might become a list leader. Book sales—sales of actual copies—were going well—or great, according to Lee Selverne of the U.S. World Media Service, exporter of trade books and paperbacks. The situation was mixed for scientific and technical publishers, who exhibit in a hall of their own. "It's quieter, but it's not shell shock," Charles R. Ellis of New York's Elsevier Science Publishing explained. Publishers who publish books only, and mainly for library sales, were worst off; those who also aim at professional book buyers, and publishers of journals, were doing better. But Ellis found bookseller attendance down for the second year running, particularly from the Middle East, Far East, and Eastern Europe; Elsevier people didn't have to schedule appointments at 15-minute intervals. (Elsevier's science division, representing about a third of the turnover of the Dutch publishing-printing giant, is having a good year; Ellis' U.S. operations are "in a growth pattern," and indeed Elsevier considers the United States as its growth area.)

RIGHTS DULL—BUT REWARDING

As for rights: one publisher after the other, one agent after the next, reported that the fair was "dull" yet rewarding. The sellers of rights were not experiencing miracles, but doing business according to plan. Thus Roslyn Targ of New York, who said as she was checking out of the Frankfurt Intercontinental that she'd had as good a fair as she could have, without a new book available from her star author Harold Robbins. Lionel Leventhal of London's Arms & Armour Press admitted that publishers had arrived in Frankfurt with lower expectations and, in these limits, were doing well. (The specialized nature of his own list lent itself less to licensing than to book sales, and sales were "excellent.") "It's our best year ever," declared another London man, André Deutsch —but he was talking about rights and co-editions. He had sold over 100,000 copies of a co-published children's book to several countries, and had placed rights to a novel on the Booker Award short list (Britain's annual prize excitement was evidently transferable to foreign climes). Expensive projects, books involving the participation of publishers in countries with varying inflation rates and in varying stages of crisis, were certainly harder to do, but the experienced packagers came prepared. David Campbell of Mitchell Beazley admitted that his firm had brought fewer projects, and more conservative ones, and had made do with fewer people on the stand. But on these new terms, he added, "We got what we were looking for." In another area of publishing Jean-Loup Chiflet, new foreign rights director at France's Larousse, observed that "security is in reference books"; he was sure that "if we all do more essential books we'll have fewer troubles." Still, there was gloom among the French, who were depressed by recently released trade statistics which seemed to confirm their fears. "Publishers are like peasants," countered Hachette's Jean-Claude Lattès. "They can't get themselves to say that things are going well." His own firm, after restructuring, was going to be in the black this year for the first time in a long time.

One Frankfurt tradition, the wonder book, dies hard. Some were saying that *Princess Daisy* was the last. "They are plugging B-level authors at A-level prices, and sometimes getting away with it," complained Albin Michel's American foreign editor Ivan Nabokov. Sure enough, there were a number of potential world bestsellers, with Morton Janklow and Ed Victor in person to usher them in. Some of the auctions simply took the form of a walk around the books by the chief agents; the action could have been visible only to the most experienced eye. And while most negotiations involved foreign rights, American publishers and agents were also peddling U.S. rights—paperback rights—at Frankfurt, simply because, as Doubleday's Sam Vaughan told *PW*, all the principals usually involved in these negotiations had temporarily transferred their operations to Frankfurt. A book Doubleday had acquired before the fair from Janklow, Barbara Taylor Bradford's *Voice of the Heart*, was being offered to U.S. mass marketers by Janklow with an assist from Doubleday's Jacqueline Everly for foreign rights. It was reported that Doubleday had paid $3 million for rights, in this book and another by the same author. American, German, French, Italian, Spanish publishers left the fairgrounds at night weighed down by manuscripts to be read after a couple of parties and a dinner, to be able to say yes or no next morning. The ultimate Frankfurt story, reported by Ivan Nabokov about himself, was that by the time he had gotten to the third or fourth manuscript the night before he found the reading slow and the book dull; only when he was ready to put it away did he realize it was written in Spanish, a language he doesn't know.

Alfred Knopf staged another Frankfurt special: the secret manuscript. Each foreign publisher who wished to read it had to sign a letter agreeing that only that person and one other in the house could see it; if an outside reader had to be brought in to authenticate the material Knopf would have to ratify the choice; and of course the readers were sworn to secrecy. The subject was the apparent murder, in the form of an accident, of Mao's aide Lin Piao in 1971. Readers were given a deadline for decision, but even the decisions were kept secret by Knopf's Carol Janeway.

The Frankfurt-based Russian-language publisher Possev was showing another potential shocker in the form of a detective novel: "Murder in Red Square," based on known scandals in the entourage of Leonid Brezhnev. The émigré authors, Fridrikh Nezansky, former attorney in the office of Moscow's public prosecutor, and screenwriter and director Edward Topol, created a Starsky and Hutch fictional team to solve the case. In another vein, Germany's Severin & Siedler was doing "Eichman Interrogated," edited text of the pretrial interrogations of the Nazi officer brought back to Israel by Israeli agents, and Farrar, Straus & Giroux was readying a translation by Ralph Manheim. Sam Summerlin and Paul Gendelman of the New York Times Syndication Sales Corporation did half a million dollars of business off their stand in press and book rights for Richard Nixon's *Leaders* (from Warner Books); Nixon is still big in Europe, they observed. They did less well with Jimmy Carter's *Keeping Faith*.

A French house, Mazarine, was showing a 300,000-word report on *Les Américains*, by veteran New York-based French correspondent Léo Sauvage; it was being touted as iconoclastic and myth-busting, a European view of Americans in the manner of previous books on the British, the Italians, the Russians.

The fair's fastest book seemed to be *Grace: Story of a Princess*, with full text and photo coverage of her whole career, and a photo report on the funeral in Monaco. The book had been produced in soft covers (for St. Martin's Press and a Collins imprint) in 18 days from conception to printing, by London packager Michael Balfour. A previous Balfour fastie, *A Royal Baby Book*, done for Pan in hardback, came out 18 days after the announcement that Princess Diana was pregnant. Balfour and projects coordinator Belinda Davies were in Frankfurt to show the book to the rest of the world; they had soon closed with a Finnish house and were negotiating in France and Italy.

If there was no *Princess Daisy* at this Frankfurt fair, there was no Fritz Molden either. The absence of that bull of a publisher may have contributed to the calmer atmosphere. It was also true that the kind of publishing for which Molden was known was on its way out. The Germans were saying that his overbidding had brought him down; the clubs and the mass market houses simply stopped following his lead. Molden himself had put an ocean between himself and the fair; on his return to Europe he would take up new responsibilities on the staff of the Stuttgart house of Seewald, which had set up a Molden Verlag imprint, although all the goodies on Molden's own list had been taken over by C. Bertelsmann Verlag.

But more than one publisher was changing jobs. Germans are calling the present wave of job-switching "musical chairs," and the "Who's Who at The Frankfurt Book Fair" issued for this year's event was more appreciated than ever. A party which was also an explanation was held on the eve of the fair in the offices of S. Fischer Verlag. Just seven years ago at a Frankfurt fair, *PW*'s correspondent happened to be standing in a hotel corridor when Fischer's managing director Wolfgang Mertz emerged from a meeting of the house's senior staff. New owner Georg von Holtzbrinck had introduced his daughter, and it seemed to the editors as if a rich man had handed over that venerable literary imprint (Kafka, Freud, Mann) as a gift to this young woman. Mertz went on to other firms, but as time went on it became evident that Monika Schoeller wasn't wasting a heritage but caring for it, having introduced a frontlist worthy of the backlist. Now Mertz was back (having recently left Bertelsmann over a "policy disagreement"); Arnulf Conradi, formerly editor-in-chief at Claassen, had also joined the staff. A dinner party for Fischer's favorite trading partners in Europe and America seemed the way "to get to know them or to renew your acquaintance with them," in the words of the invitation.

In other publishing news, the prestigious Israel Museum in Jerusalem and New York's Macmillan signed an agreement during the fair—in the presence of Jerusalem's mayor Teddy Kollek—under which Macmillan becomes worldwide distributor and co-publisher of Israel Museum publications starting January 1. The arrangement was negotiated on the Israeli side by publisher Asher Weill, consultant to the museum, and for Macmillan by president Jeremiah Kaplan and Charles E. Smith, vice-president of the firm's professional books division. The Israel Museum has won design awards for several of its monographs and catalogues; there are some 20 new titles annually.

McGraw-Hill had brought software to its Frankfurt stands for the first time: 15 different programs in all, shown via an Apple II operating on the stand. William P. Orr, manager for foreign rights, reported "an exciting year" for the house. Nearby, Robert

Maxwell in person conducted a press conference on the Pergamon stand to stress the "broad range of publishing services" now offered by the Pergamon/British Printing and Communication Corporation group: electronic database publishing had been added to a product list that already included Walt Disney books and something called "Sport Goofy Encyclopedia."

A PEACE PRIZE FOR KENNAN

A formal event, directed not to the international trade but to the German public, is the annual award of the German book trade's Peace Prize. This year's winner (of DM 25,000) was former ambassador George F. Kennan, whose reputation has remained alive in Germany, where he is known as one "who repeatedly raised his voice in warning against the irrationality of the arms race." He addressed a Sunday morning audience in historic Paulskirche, speaking in German, calling for an end to economic sanctions against the Soviet Union and to Western rearmament, both of which he felt encouraged hostility instead of protecting against it. Pantheon Books was showing and selling Kennan's forthcoming *The Nuclear Delusion* to a dozen countries. The official fair opening ceremony had been addressed by Helmut Schmidt, who remarked that the invitation had been sent to the chancellor, "but you have to be satisfied with Mr. Schmidt." He made some pessimistic remarks about the attraction of the youngest generation to electronic media; on another plane, he expressed fear that the new German government majority will permit mergers of press groups that anti-trust vigilance had prevented under the Social Democrats.

When publishers from all over meet only once a year, even a cocktail party is an event; those in the first hours, like the Fischer dinner already referred to or Harper & Row's traditional opening nighter for international publishing's beautiful people, are usually the first and best opportunities for making contact, jotting down appointments. Sometimes the party itself, because of its sponsorship, is news, and is discourteously utilized to take the host's temperature. Everyone was talking about Bertelsmann—for when Bertelsmann sneezes, Germany, and many other countries too, catch cold, and here was Bertelsmann throwing a big one in a grand ballroom. The gossip went this way: hadn't they cut the guest list from 1,500 to 600? (Didn't seem so.) Wasn't the spread less elegant, weren't the quantities down? (Alas, yes.) The next rumor was that Bertelsmann's worldwide Spanish club organization was giving its last party, for it was an anniversary; at the next Frankfurt fair Spanish and Spanish American and Portuguese and Portuguese American publishers would have time on their hands on Wednesday evening.

VISITING PUBLISHERS' PARTIES

For its 175th anniversary, John Wiley has been giving itself birthday parties around the world—New York, London, New Delhi, Tokyo, Mexico City, Brisbane, and Sydney. During the fair the firm bused its bookseller and publisher guests to a top-of-the-market castle hotel outside town. Harcourt Brace Jovanovich took over a ballroom to receive its colleagues, Dutch publishers Kluwer and Meulenhoff threw receptions, and Reader's Digest book program entertained foreign publishing partners (Americans get a separate party in New York). The Japanese house Shueisha unveiled a major "Gallery of World Photography" project at a party, with an assist from the people responsible for its materialization, Dai Nippon Printing Company. "We want to get closer to our American publishing partners," Frankfurt fair director Peter Weidhaas told a lunchtime gathering of American and German publishers, unveiling details of next March's German Book Fair in New York. (Weidhaas told *PW* that Americans never have time to visit German-language exhibition halls at the fair; they always intend to do so, but get stopped too often by friends in the aisles and never make it; the New York event is designed to bridge the distance between the two countries' industries.)

The International Book Committee used a fairgrounds site to honor one of its members, Sigfred Taubert, who had presided over the phenomenal growth of the fair during the early postwar years.

A regular Frankfurt event, the general assembly of the International Group of Scientific, Technical and Medical Publishers (STM) is scheduled for the morning before the fair opens in a Frankfurt Intercontinental salon. This year's was coupled with the first annual general meeting of the International Electronic Publishing Research Center (IEPRC), and the latter sponsored a reception for both groups following their meetings. The reasoning was that both STM and IEPRC are concerned with new techniques in information transmission (IEPRC, with 50 members, is engaged in technical and economic research in information publishing), and it is hoped that by supporting the new center, STM publishers will increase the practical applications of its findings. STM's assembly heard reports from its chairman Robert H. Craven (F.A. Davis) and from its standing committees, W. Bradford Wiley for copyright, Charles Ellis for marketing, Stanley A. Lewis (Taylor & Francis) on scientific journals, Robert Campbell (Blackwell Scientific) on innovations. In his annual report STM secretary Paul Nijhoff Asser pointed out that the Amsterdam-based group had suffered a decline in membership, though new applications for membership had brought the total back to the previous figure, 134. He warned that in time of stress professionals needed to stick together, and offered as one good reason for doing so the continuing trend toward erosion of copyright, and "by the very organizations we have appointed to uphold it." It meant that "STM should be as political an animal as we can be, in UNESCO as well as in . . . the Berne convention." STM represents its sector of the publishing community in conferences of international governmental and non-governmental organizations, and sponsors a number of events on its own. One was to take place soon after Frankfurt, a New York seminar run jointly by the marketing and journals committees on November 11 and 12.

The STMers manifested a certain degree of regret that American publishers were not as internationally oriented as, say, their British counterparts; it was said that the AAP had not been interested in attending a copyright meeting in Paris although such meetings dealt with matters of vital concern to their trade. A matter of insufficient funds? "But aren't you the richest people in the world?" a member teased. Meanwhile the British Publishers Association's Book Development Council distributed "fight piracy" stickers and flyers inviting publishers from outside Britain "who share our determination" to join the fight. "Have you seen the examples of book piracy on our stand?" the leaflet concluded.

Another annual event is the international meeting of education publishers sponsored by one of their leaders, the Stuttgart house of Ernst Klett Verlag. One common concern is diversification, especially in countries that share Germany's declining school population. The subject this time was microcomputers in schools, with formal presentations by Alan Hill of Heinemann Computers in Education Ltd., and by similarly inspired executives of France's Fernand Nathan and Sweden's Esselte Studium.

One of the publishing community's most unusual institutions is the Motovun group, named for the Yugoslav village where its annual business meetings are held. This is an informal grouping of publishers of large-format illustrated projects, and books like the McGraw-Hill photo report on China have come out of it. At a breakfast meeting it was announced that the 1983 meeting would take place June 25 to 29. There would be formal reports (the main speaker at this year's session was Harper & Row's Art Stiles), although the chief business as always will be informal presentations in village cafés, on bathing beaches, or in sailing vessels. The group's acting chairman is Edward Booher, formerly of McGraw-Hill; its guiding spirit is Nebojša Tomašević of Jugoslovenska Revija in Belgrade.

To provide a handle on the fair for the non-professional press and broadcast media, Frankfurt sets a theme every second year. This time the subject was religion. The German book-buying public could visit special exhibits in the German-language area tied to the theme, with the participation of 650 publishers from 33 countries, who provided 6,000 titles; there were daily round-table discussions, and a media highlight was the visit of the Dalai Lama, on a European tour. Two Hopi priests from the Pueblo Indian tribe were also present, and fair officials proudly noted that this was the first encounter of the two religious bodies. Fair director Weidhaas gave the theme a trade emphasis in his opening remarks: "It would be disastrous for the book trade not to view the readers and purchasers of religious literature as the reading public per se. The Bible was and is the longest selling book on the market. . . . So why did we select religion as focal topic of the fair? Because, among other reasons, we wanted to sharpen the book producers' and distributors' awareness of these connections."

Next year the fair will take place a week later, into rainy weather: October 12 to 17. But it will be a year without a theme.

THE IFLA CONFERENCE, 1982

Russell Shank

Director, University of California Library, Los Angeles

Jean E. Lowrie

Professor, School of Librarianship, Western Michigan University

The forty-eighth General Conference of the International Federation of Library Associations and Institutions (IFLA) was held in Montreal, Canada, from August 22 to 28, 1982, with the Association pour l'avancement des sciences et des techniques de la documentation (ASTED) as its host. The conference theme was "Networks," a most appropriate choice because of the need for library cooperation in troubled economic times worldwide. Furthermore, networking is closely allied with IFLA's major concerns: Universal Bibliographic Control (UBC) and Universal Availability of Publications (UAP). With extensive work being done everywhere on networks, it was not difficult for all segments of the IFLA constituency to produce papers directly related to the theme.

PLENARY SESSIONS

During the official opening, presentations were made by the mayor of Montreal, the Quebec minister of affaires culturelles, and the Canadian minister of communications. Harrison Bryan of Australia led the plenary sessions throughout the conference, which in general highlighted experiences in Canada, the Federal Republic of Germany, China, and the socialist countries. The first plenary session featured a paper by Célène R. Cartier, directeur des bibliothèques, Université Laval, Quebec, Canada, on the importance of networks within the context of the present world of information, emphasizing the need and the challenge to eliminate all forms of isolation in all countries without racial, political, religious, or territorial restrictions.

Perhaps because of the conference location, the Canadian experiment called Telidon was featured, both in various papers and in the exhibits. Telidon was seen as a generic example of the tying together of computers and television distribution systems for delivery of information to meet users' demands and needs. This, however, was merely one of the many discussions based on the emerging communication revolution and the growth of computer-based information service. Conference-goers also heard about the LIBRIS system in Sweden, the multinational experience in EURONET, MEDLARS in Australia and the Western Pacific, and the MEDINFORM network in the German Democratic Republic, among others. Although national approaches differ, the importance of new communication and computer technologies to the future of network services formed a common thread in each of the presentations.

Also featured were the Japanese, the Canadian, and the Australian approaches to networking in library service for the blind, and school, research, public, special, and national library representatives made presentations throughout the week to show how they had been included in networks in various countries. The large tasks involved in bringing these various kinds of libraries together into multitype networks was most apparent in the papers in the plenary sessions.

The final plenary session was divided into two sections, the "Networks of the 80's: Realizations," at which five national presentations were described, and "Toward the Network of Tomorrow." Among the highlights of the session were papers by delegates from Colombia and the China Society of Library Science. A presentation by E. Cornish of the World Future Society on "Electronic Networks and Human Concerns" prognosticated computer programs in the year 2002, the changes in home use as well as in libraries. "Books will be more relevant to practical every day areas.... Libraries will add a lot of new information products" and adopt the new electronic products.

THE PRESESSION MEETINGS

The presession seminar was of particular interest this year, since it was designed specifically for Latin American and Caribbean library school educators. The seminar was sponsored by the International Development Research Center and IFLA, planned jointly by American, Canadian, and Latin American educators, and chaired by William Cameron (Canada) and R. Horowitz (Venezuela). The theme was "Education for Research: Research for Education" with Spanish as the official language for the first time. Among the many recommendations that were forthcoming, of immediate interest is the current effort being made to establish an international bibliography of research studies in library education. A pilot project is being implemented among the library schools in Canada. It is expected that this will be expanded to include translations from around the world.

Other presessions included a meeting of the Art Libraries Society of North America and the Computer Communications Group. The U.S. National Commission of Libraries and Information Science held its first meeting outside the United States, which enabled its members to attend many of the IFLA sessions and to reemphasize their interest in international sharing.

THE ISSUES ADDRESSED

One of the strong program elements of the conference pertained to the impact of the field of information science on library education. All of the presentations in these topical areas suggested a dynamism that belies the notion that any nation has found satisfactory solutions to the problems of attracting and educating people with sufficient intellectual power to address the ever-increasing sophisticated tasks in the new information environment.

Some of the most troublesome issues raised in the new age received major attention. Many new data bases are required to sustain online information services: the attempts to create them in art, medicine, technology, and the social sciences were reported. There was a description of the findings of the IFLA international study of copyright of bibliographical records. Although the laws of various nations allow copyright and many data bases are covered by legal protections, there is, nevertheless, a vagueness among government officials and producers of data bases as to the value of this protection. The uneasiness occasioned by what is called transborder data flow also raises many vital issues for the concept of the sharing of library resources (which were delineated in one of the conference's major sessions). Many of the budding legal ideas concerning the need to control the flow of information derive from parochial views about the invasion of the privacy of individuals and the economic, political, and military values of local proprietary information in many countries. Attempts to control access to such information for nationalistic reasons runs counter to the sharing of bibliographic information which is central to international library cooperation.

Nevertheless, work progresses apace on a number of IFLA programs that are important to networking among nations. Chief among these are Universal Bibliographic Control (UBC) and Universal Access to Publications (UAP). Each of these programs aims to provide either protocols for the arrangements for the exchange of information or the infrastructure that is necessary for the collection, the preservation, and the free flow of publications among nations. Progress on these programs is the subject of numerous publications, articles, and papers, as well as presentations at IFLA conferences.

Increased interaction among libraries also heightens the need for standards and measurements of service to assure a universal understanding of the utility of the relationships. Statistics, management information, and user satisfaction measures were featured in a number of programs, including a description of a statistical model for data analysis and networks and standard identification numbers for libraries, library materials, and patrons. Additionally, the need for research in both the historical and the planning perspectives was covered.

Presentations from the representatives of the People's Republic of China showed the signs of the new and increasing participation by representatives of that country. The developments of library services of the Chinese Academy of Sciences and the National Library, as well as a description of the acquisitions procedures of the National Library and of library architecture in the PRC drew much attention.

FUTURE CONFERENCES

Since this was not a council year, no elections were held and no general resolutions were presented. The emphasis was placed on the programs for the sections and divisions as outlined in the new Medium Term Program for 1981–1985. At the 1983 conference and council meeting, which will be held in Munich, Federal Republic of Germany, August 21 to 27, on the university campus, many new members will be nominated

to section committees, and the president and five other persons will be elected to the executive board. The theme of the conference will be "Libraries in a Technological World."
The calendar of future conferences is as follows:

1984, Nairobi, Kenya, August 19–25 (conference only)

1985, New York City, August 18–24 (conference and council)

1986, Tokyo, Japan (conference only)

1987, United Kingdom (conference and council)

THE VATICAN LIBRARY AND ARCHIVES

Silvio A. Bedini

Keeper of the Rare Books, Smithsonian Institution, Washington, DC 20560

Among the several contenders to the claim of being the greatest library in the world, the Biblioteca Apostolica Vaticana, or Vatican Library, ranks extremely high. On the basis of its holdings, it is among the top three (along with the Bibliothèque Nationale in Paris and the British Library in London). At present, the Vatican Library contains more than 100,000 manuscripts (of which approximately 70,000 are codices or manuscript books), 100,000 separate autograph items, 100,000 maps and engravings, and between 700,000 and 1 million printed books. Of the latter, more than 7,000 are incunabula, or books printed before 1500. Housed in a magnificent sixteenth-century edifice, the library has a staff of 80.

THE VATICAN LIBRARY

During the Middle Ages, important collections of books were generally owned by churches, monasteries, and highly placed ecclesiastics; those owned by the popes were particularly prominent. Throughout the history of the papacy, the pontiffs of Avignon and Rome collected and preserved written materials, not only those useful to the discharge of their office but other materials as well in an effort to safeguard the civilization of classical antiquity for succeeding generations.

In 1295, the Vatican Library was known to have contained 443 volumes, but after 1345 many of them were dispersed, and others were transported to Avignon when it became the site of the Holy See. Thereafter, serious efforts were made by a number of the popes to build the collections. John XXII made a good beginning by purchasing books and having manuscripts copied. Gifts of manuscripts came from many sources, and the pontiffs supplemented them by exercising the traditional papal right of the inheritance of prelates—*ius spolii*—by means of which all the possessions of a deceased member of the Curia became the property of the Apostolic Camera, or papal exchequer. As a consequence of the practice, important acquisitions were made. Clement VI continued the book-building program, and the growing collections were housed in the Turris Angelorum, or Tower of the Angels, at Avignon.

Although the collection of juridical literature at the Sorbonne was unrivaled in the fourteenth century, that of the papal library eventually surpassed it. However, the papal holdings suffered repeated misfortunes, and when the popes eventually returned to Rome after the Council of Constance, few of the library materials were brought with them. (A large number of the manuscripts, which found their way into the Borghese family library, were returned to the Vatican Library in 1891, when Leo XIII purchased the Borghese collection.)

In the fifteenth century, Martin V and Eugene IV resumed the building of the library's collections, which at this time were restricted to the private use of the popes and the Curia. But it was Nicholas V who first conceived of having a great papal library for public use. Although the present Vatican Library owes much of its richness to the energy and foresight of several pontiffs, Nicholas V was chiefly responsible for assembling the classical masterpieces. During his eighteen-year reign, the library's holdings increased from 340 to 1,200 volumes. He was the first pope to give papal recognition to printing (in 1454), with his issuance of the *Thirty Line Indulgence* and the *Thirty-one Line Indulgence* on behalf of the king of Cyprus. (His establishment of the library coincided almost simultaneously with the development of movable type in Europe.)

Nicholas V inherited 340 manuscripts from Eugene IV, which he added to his own collection; later he donated 5,000 manuscripts to the papal library, initiating the first important division of its collections. He systematically increased its holdings by sending experienced men to other countries, including Germany, England, and Denmark, to locate and purchase manuscripts. Following the fall of Constantinople, when the Turks dispersed the valuable imperial library, Nicholas commissioned special agents to acquire all important manuscripts from this resource that were for sale. He also employed skilled copyists at fixed salaries to copy the originals that he was unable to purchase. At the same time, he invited exiled Byzantine scholars, as well as competent Italian scholars, to Rome to translate Greek classics into Latin for his library. By the time of his death in 1455, he had amassed 1,500 manuscripts, thus substantially increasing the papal library's importance.

Whereas Nicholas V concerned himself primarily with an acquisition program, it was one of his successors, Sixtus IV, who first directed his attention to the library's housing and maintenance. Determined to find room for the books and manuscripts in the Vatican Palace, he had them placed in rooms on the first floor of the Cortile del Pappagallo under the Borgia Apartments, where they remained for more than a century. The rooms were dark and damp and unsuitable for the maintenance of books and manuscripts, but it was nonetheless an attractive location, with the walls decorated by prominent artists of the period. The collections were divided within its four halls, with one each for Greek and Latin works, another for the most important codices, and a separate hall for the papal archives and registers. A fifth hall was provided for the use of the librarian, his three deputies, and a bookbinder; it also was used as a reading room. In this period books were loaned from the library, and readers were allowed limited use of the facilities. In 1475, Giovanni Tortelli was named director of the library, and Platina (Bartolommeo de Sacchi), the celebrated scholar, was appointed its librarian and became its first cataloger.

Probably more than any other research resource, the Vatican Library and Archives have been ravaged by vandals and usurpers throughout the centuries. Each time they left a heavy toll on the world of learning. Among the first of the invaders was Alaric, who in 410 sacked and partially destroyed the Lateran in which the major part of the archives was held. Within a half century Attila the Hun plundered Rome and sailed away with enslaved Romans and most of the city's treasure. For centuries thereafter, the Vatican searched in vain for copies of papal decrees of the reign of Leo I.

One of the most devastating invasions was in 1527, resulting in the sack of Rome by Constable Charles de Bourbon. Although the church's most precious documents and its collection of golden seals were safely stored in Castel Sant' Angelo, where Clement VII and a few of his cardinals had found refuge, and Philibert, Prince of Orange, had made his headquarters in the halls of the library during the occupation, the library and archives suffered serious losses. Manuscripts and papal documents were scattered in the streets and used for litter in the horse stalls. The registers of the Apostolic Camera were used to make wadding for cannon, and the acts of the sacred Chancellery fell into the hands of soldiers. Although the library presently contains more than 7,000 fifteenth-century works, it might in fact have contained a full set of incunabula had it not been for the destruction wrought upon the library during the sack of Rome by Constable Charles de Bourbon.

After Rome had recovered from this devastation, a major change occurred in the Vatican Library, with the appointment of the first cardinal librarian to supervise its operation. Marcello Cervini, the first to occupy this position, added 240 manuscripts and many printed books to the collection. In 1555, he was elected Pope Marcellus II, but he died 22 days later.

Although Gregory XIII visualized the erection of a separate building to house the burgeoning library and archives, it remained for his successor, Pius V, to bring it to reality. The building Pius had constructed divided the gigantic quadrangle of the Cortile del Belvedere and was designed by Domenico Fontana. It was erected between 1587 and 1589, over a period of 13 months, at a cost of approximately $25,850, which rose to $42,075 by the time the building was furnished. To the Sistine Hall, named after its founder, were brought the greatest treasures of the collection, which was formally named the Biblioteca Apostolica Vaticana, or Vatican Library.

During the seventeenth century the library continued to grow, augmented by the numerous acquisitions of successive popes and by the absorption of other libraries. In 1621, Gregory XV received from Duke Maximilian of Bavaria the Biblioteca Palatina, which one of his generals had captured at the fall of Heidelberg during the Thirty Years' War. In 1658, Alexander VII purchased the Biblioteca Urbina, which had been founded by Duke Federico da Montefeltro; he also acquired a large number of the famous palimpsests from the Benedictine abbey at Bobbio. In 1690, the Biblioteca Alexandrina was bequeathed to the Ottoboni Library by Queen Christina of Sweden. This important collection included the famous manuscripts of the Abbey of Fleury, among others, and books taken from Prague, Würzburg, and Bremen by her father, King Gustavus Adolphus, totaling more than 2,000 Latin and almost 200 Greek manuscripts.

In the next century other great acquisitions were made. In 1746, Benedict XIV added the Biblioteca Ottoboniana, which in turn included the famous Altemps Library of some 900 Greek and Latin manuscripts collected by the Ottoboni pope Alexander VIII. It was in the same period that Marchese Alessandro Capponi bequeathed his manuscripts, and other important benefactions came from succeeding pontiffs, from Clement XIII in 1758, Clement XIV in 1769, and Pius VI in 1775.

Then, as the century neared its end, there came a major reversal. In 1798, the French carried off nearly 500 of the most artistically important manuscripts. It was not until a few years later that these were restored, except for a few from the Palatine collection, which were returned to Heidelberg. Then two years later the pope acceded to the request of the king of Prussia to restore 848 German manuscripts to Heidelberg.

In the nineteenth century, other important additions were made, beginning with the library of Cardinal Zelada in 1800 and the collection of fine arts literature of Count Cignogara in 1823. Gregory XVI made numerous purchases, and in 1856 Pius IX acquired more than 40,000 volumes formerly owned by the late Cardinal Angelo Mai. In

1891 Leo XIII purchased the great Borghese library containing many of the stolen Avignon manuscripts, and in 1902 he purchased the celebrated Barberini library.

Prior to the pontificate of Leo XIII, the Vatican Library had remained a restricted private institution operating primarily for the use of the state. A few scholars were admitted, but lack of space and absence of modern bibliographic tools necessitated limited access. In 1881, Leo XIII took the unprecedented action of opening the archives to researchers. He also brought about many other changes in the library. He added a large reference room stocked with some 60,000 works of reference in 1892, provided metal shelving for manuscripts, and initiated a restoration laboratory.

In the nineteenth century, a number of important scholars served as prefect or as cardinal librarian of the Vatican Library, each adding significantly to its development. Cardinal Giuseppe Mezzofanti, who became prefect in 1833 and was made cardinal in 1838, was famous for his extraordinary command of languages; he wrote and spoke about 50 languages and dialects and understood some 20 others. The numerous published learned works and treatises of Cardinal Librarian Mariano Rampolla, Marchese del Tindaro, established him among the greatest scholars of his time. He continued to work in the library's interests even after he became papal secretary of state in 1887. But the most conspicuous of the nineteenth-century cardinal librarians was probably Mai, who served as prefect from 1819 to 1825. He discovered a great number of unknown religious and secular texts on the sciences, as well as Greek and Latin literature, which filled some 50 stout volumes. He also discovered a remarkable number of palimpsests, which he succeeded in deciphering and restoring. Most notable among them was Cicero's *De Re Republica*, which he found in 1820. Others of importance were Dionysius's *Roman Antiquities*, Plautus's *Vidularia*, Eusebius of Caesarea's *Chronicon*, and Fronto's letters.

It was during this period of its history that the library undertook publication of scientifically prepared catalogs, as well as a series of facsimile reproductions of holdings of particular interest. Much of this new enterprise was due to Franz Ehrle, S.J., who served as director of the library from 1895 to 1914. He was succeeded by another equally passionate librarian, Achille Ratti, who was elected Pope Pius XI in 1922, and to whom is due the major credit for modernization of the library facilities. He installed six-tiered metal shelving, remodeled the reference room to provide better accommodations, and provided a new entrance from the Cortile del Belvedere, among other changes. During his reign as pope, he succeeded in increasing the collections enormously. Later prefects instituted a photographic facility and expanded the publications program.

Since 1928, printed books have been progressively recataloged by means of a system adapted from the Library of Congress. This project was begun with funding provided by the Carnegie Endowment for International Peace and with the assistance of a group of American librarians, who also recommended card indexing of the manuscripts. In 1934, a school of library science was formed as part of the Vatican Library.

THE SECRET ARCHIVES

The Archivio Segreto Vaticano, or "Secret" Archives, must be considered together with the Vatican Library, although at present they are separate. In effect, they are twin organizations, closely connected and under the supervision of the same cardinal librarian, but occasionally in rivalry. Much material has been exchanged between them, particularly while Cardinal Giovanni Mercati was prefect of the library and his brother, Monsignor Angelo Mercati, was prefect of the archives.

The archives are designated as "secret," because they are the personal and state archives of the popes, who for centuries reigned as sovereigns of the Christian world and whose files were as confidential as the diplomatic archives of any nation. Furthermore, they include the archives of the various congregations and of the Sacred Rota, containing processes for beatification and canonization, annulments of marriages, and other extremely confidential information that cannot be made available to the public. The archives exist primarily for the use of the Vatican officialdom, and consequently access by others has been prohibited.

In the year 1881, Leo XIII startled the world by throwing the archives open to the public with the statement "The Church needs nothing but the truth." Nevertheless, he restricted the use of the archival materials of the past century, making available only those to 1781. The "hundred years' rule" has been maintained, so that documents relating to the immediate past century are unaccessible, as well as those confidential items already mentioned.

The opportunity to conduct research in the archives is considered a special privilege, and not a right. A researcher must provide a letter of introduction from an important cultural organization, the head of a major library or archive, or a highly placed diplomat. This requirement may be waived for an eminent scholar. After the letter has been presented, the candidate is interviewed by the prefect or his delegate, and the research to be undertaken is discussed. If approved, the applicant is provided with a form letter addressed to His Holiness the Pope, which he must copy in his own hand. In due course, if approval is given, the applicant must provide two prints of a photographic portrait, one of which is attached to the precious permit and the other filed. The permit is issued for a limited period and must be presented each time the facilities are used. A sign-in/sign-out procedure is another precautionary measure to protect the collections. Applicants for permits are carefully screened, and not more than about 200 are issued each year. The primary reason for this limitation is the small size of the staff and the limited seating facilities in the study room. Separate permits must be obtained for the library and the archives.

Systematic storage of the papal archives can be traced to the fourth century to Pope S. Damasus, who maintained his records in the Cancelleria. They were moved afterward to St. John Lateran for greater convenience. Beginning in the seventh century, the archives were contained in the library, then known as the Scrinium. According to accounts of the council held at Rome in 649, the library was then well cataloged and arranged under the supervision of a papal librarian, Theophylactus. It was the departure of the popes for Avignon that led to the dispersal of the library and archives in the Lateran. The books and documents were taken first to Assisi for safekeeping; then, in 1339, Benedict XII had the thirteenth-century registers brought to Avignon. The remainder of the materials contained in the convent at Assisi were subsequently dispersed and lost.

In the fifteenth century, Sixtus IV transferred the most important documents of the Holy See to Castel Sant' Angelo, and several decades later Leo X selected others from the Biblioteca Segreta and stored them in the same stronghold, maintained in silk bags. They constituted only a small part of the Vatican's records, however.

In the sixteenth century, Pius IV and Pius V contemplated the desirability of collecting all the Vatican records in a single repository, but it was not until the reign of Clement VIII that a suitable place was found for them. Clement had a fine circular hall built at the top of the Castel and had the walls fitted with handsome wooden presses, which were elaborately decorated. Into these presses he brought together all the scattered collections of documents and transferred many others from the library. In the center of the room were kept the great iron safes of the Vatican treasury. The room, with its presses and safes now empty, is open to the public.

Urban VIII enlarged the archives by adding to it the bulls from the time of Sixtus

IV and Pius V, which had been marked *par Voie secreto*, the registers and minutes of the papal briefs from about 1500 to 1567, a number of volumes of records returned from Avignon, and the correspondence of nuncios of the sixteenth century. Later, Alexander VII added the papers of the secretariat of state and subsequently the correspondence of cardinals and princes, the series entitled *Varia Politicorum*, and 500 more volumes of records from Avignon to swell the archival collections.

The materials remained at Castel Sant' Angelo until 1798, when French troops ordered the prefect, Gaetano Marini, to yield the keys to the castle. In doing so, he ventured to request permission to transfer all documents still preserved there to the Vatican Archives, and permission was granted. This was the first time that all of the Vatican's archival materials were brought together.

This achievement was nullified, however, in 1810, when Napoleon I ordered the transfer of the Vatican Archives to Paris, where he planned to form an international library with them and those already removed from Spain and Vienna, which would provide a source of revenue for the government. He sent France's chief archivist to Rome to select all documents and registers relating to public rights, legislation, general administration, and political history. In particular, he sought the records of the trials of Giordano Bruno and Galileo Galilei, the trial of the Templars, and the bull of excommunication against Napoleon himself. More than 3,000 cases of papers were shipped from Rome to Paris by means of multiple teams of mules and oxen over the Alps. Contained in this vast cargo were not only the archives of the Vatican but also of monasteries and churches. The Vatican archivists were required to accompany the wagons on their journey and to assist in the arrangement of the materials in Paris. There a search was begun for documents that would reveal the ambitions of the papal court and abuses committed by the popes throughout history against sovereign authority. These Napoleon planned to use in self-justification.

During the period that the archives remained in Paris, they were neither sought nor used by scholars. Following Napoleon's defeat in 1814, the allies entering Paris issued a decree ordering the restoration of all its properties to the Vatican. However, the Vatican now lacked financial resources to return the materials to Rome, and the contents of the countless packing cases presented a serious problem. While the archives remained in Paris, there was a considerable amount of pilferage, and other materials that had been distributed were never returned. Because of their inability to return all the materials, in 1816 the Vatican archivists sold large quantities of the papers that were judged to be of lesser importance to the papier-mâché makers and for use as wrapping paper. Some 700 volumes of registers of the bulls of the papal Dataria were found to be used in Parisian butcher shops for wrapping meat. Some of the dispersed materials eventually came to light in other repositories, including the Bibliothèque Nationale.

After the archives had been returned to Rome from France, a new plan was devised for their organization, into two sets of *fondi*, or deposits—foreign and internal. But the archives were to suffer yet further dispersal. When, in 1848, Pius IX was forced to flee the Quirinal Palace, he left behind documents not only in the Quirinal but in several other palaces, which were taken over by the new Italian government. These materials dealt chiefly with the Vatican's administrative, judicial, and financial matters and were reassembled in the State Archives, or Archivio di Stato di Roma, where they are available for study.

When Leo XIII turned his attention to the archives as part of his plan to reorganize the Vatican, he made extensive changes. He provided more space for the housing and use of the materials and made substantial additions, including 2,000 volumes of papal briefs and all the archives of the Dataria, or Vatican bursar.

THE CHRISTIAN MUSEUM

In 1756, Benedict XIV established the Museo Sacro, or Christian Museum, as an adjunct of the Vatican Library, for the purpose of housing and displaying objects of liturgical art and historical relics and curiosities formerly in the Lateran, artifacts of paleolithic, medieval, and Renaissance minor arts, in addition to paintings of the Roman era, all of which had been collected through the centuries by popes and princes of the church.

In 1952, Cardinal Francis Spellman presented the library with a copy of the *Index of Christian Art*, which had been prepared by C. E. Morey at Princeton University. In 1960, this valuable tool was transferred to the Christian Museum; the section in which it was placed (renamed the *Indici di Iconografia Cristiana*) also comprised the inventory of the Christian Museum and that of the illuminations contained in Vatican manuscripts.

Included in the collections of the Christian Museum are items from the catacombs ranging from rings, lamps, crosses, bas-reliefs in ivory, wood, and metal, twelfth- and thirteenth-century diptyches and triptyches, and Roman mosaics and frescoes.

THE SECULAR MUSEUM

Adjacent to, but apart from, the Christian Museum is the Museo Profano, or Secular Museum, which was formed in 1767 by Clement XIII and which is likewise administered by the library. Prior to the establishment of a formal Vatican museum complex—the Museo Pio-Clementino established by Clement XIV in the 1770s, the Museo Chiaramonti e Braccio Nuovo added at the beginning of the nineteenth century by Pius VI, and the later museums and galleries that are now combined under the Monumenti, Musei e Gallerie Pontificie—gifts from heads of state to reigning popes and papal acquisitions of art and other precious objects were added to the library's collections.

In time, the growth of these collections of objects led to the creation of a special facility for their display in the northern end of a long gallery of the library. Among objects presently on display are enormous vases from French and German potteries, including Sèvres vases presented to Pius IX by Mareschal McMahon, Berlin vases from Prussia's Wilhelm I, and others from Charles X, President Grévy, and President Carnot of France. Interspersed throughout the hall is the silver baptismal font in which the Prince Imperial of France was baptized, a large oriental alabaster vase from the Khedive Ibrahim Pasha, two granite tables supported on bronze figures of Hercules, a malachite cross from Prince Demidoff, a malachite vase from Czar Nicholas I, two notable vases of red quartz from Czar Alexander, a basin of Scottish granite presented to Cardinal Giacomo Antonelli by the Duke of Northumberland, a Sèvres candlestick given by Napoleon to his erstwhile prisoner, Pius VII, and not the least is a huge block of virgin malachite from the Grand Duke Constantine.

The hall in which these auspicious gifts are displayed is more than 200 feet long, nearly 50 feet wide, and 30 feet high. Constructed for Sixtus V and completed in the year of the Spanish Armada, the pillars and ceiling are decorated in the Pompeiian style and the walls are frescoed, providing an appropriate setting for the state gifts. Of particular historical interest are a few scientific objects, including a large globe owned by Julius II, a few other globes and mathematical instruments, and the Sferologio Farnese, a planisferic planetarium made for Dorotea Sofia, Duchess of Parma, and presented to Leo XIII on his golden jubilee by the Count of Caserta. Decorated wooden presses lining the walls contain collections of manuscripts and papal family archives, and a number of glass-topped exhibit cases display some of the library's greatest treasures. Among them are the palimpsest of Cicero's *De Re Republica*, the fourth-century *Codex Vaticanus*, a fourth-century *Vatican Virgil*, a ninth-century Terence, the breviary of Matthias Corvinus, the 30-foot long parchment scroll of *The Book of Joshua*, and numerous other unique items.

NUMISMATIC CABINET

Yet another adjunct of the library is the Gabinetto Numismatico, or Medaleria, maintained in an annex. Established in 1738, it contains the extensive collection of papal coins and medals.

SCHOOL OF PALEOGRAPHY

An important facility that forms part of the archives is the restoration laboratory established in the late nineteenth century under Leo XIII for the conservation of the Vatican's holdings in papyrus, parchment, paper editions, and bindings. Now designated the Scuola di Paleografia, Diplomatica e Archivistica, it is supplemented with a photographic facility having the most up-to-date techniques for photographic reproduction.

PUBLICATIONS

The Vatican Library has always cooperated with others in the publication of learned works from or about its collections. Since the reign of Leo XIII, in particular, it has developed outstanding editorial activity in various fields, including history, philology, and the humanities.

The *Codices manuscripti recensiti*, the main series of catalogs of manuscripts issued by the library, now number some 40 volumes. In addition to the series, separate catalogs have been published of its collections of Egyptian and Latin papyri, as well as of seven or eight other collections. Under the rubic of *Studi e Testi*, which includes editions and scholarly studies of materials in the library and archives collections, more than 300 volumes have been published since the series was initiated in 1900.

Facsimile editions of notable manuscripts are produced in the series entitled *Codices e Vaticanis selecti quam simillime expressi*. Approximately 40 volumes have been issued, ranging from the *Bibbia graeca, cod. B* (Vat. gr. 1209), to the book of designs of Giuliano da Sangallo (Barb. lat. 4424). A great number of monumental editions have also been undertaken by the library, including the *Pontificum Romanorum diplomata papyracea quae supersunt*, the *Mappamondo cinese*, the *Monumenta cartografica Vaticana*, the *Documenti cartografici dello Stato Pontificio*, and a series of the most important plans of the city of Rome of the sixteenth, seventeenth, and eighteenth centuries. The series *Collectanea Archivi Vaticani* is a publication of the archives.

Recently, under the aegis of its present prefect, Monsignor Alfons M. Stickler, the library has ventured upon a new program of facsimile reproduction, in cooperation with an American and a German publisher. The project had its genesis at a conference on the conservation of books and manuscripts sponsored by the Vatican Library in 1975, in which it was recommended that libraries seek means of reproducing the most irreplaceable holdings of the library in the highest quality possible. The first work produced in the new series is the Vatican's *Codex Benedictus*, also known as the *Lectionary for the Feast of St. Benedict, St. Maur, and St. Scholastica*, the original of which was produced by the monks of Monte Cassino in the eleventh century. The edition of this costly work is limited to 600 copies. Each of the facsimiles will be accompanied by a companion volume having the same format that will consist of transcriptions and translations by the foremost scholars of the world.

Other titles scheduled for reproduction are the fifteenth-century atlas based on Ptolemy's *Cosmographia* (which had been commissioned for the Duke of Urbino in the fifteenth century), Sandro Botticelli's drawings for Dante's *Divina Commedia* (undertaken for Lorenzo de' Medici), the poems, letters, and sketches of Michelangelo Buonarotti, King Henry VIII's *Defense of the Seven Sacraments against Luther*, and equivalent treasures.

Meanwhile, a considerable portion of the contents of the Vatican Library and Archives has already been microfilmed in a continuing program with assistance from the Knights of Columbus, including thousands of color slides of illuminated manuscripts, and deposited at St. Louis, Missouri, in the Pius XII Library of St. Louis University, for the use of scholars and students.

THE VATICAN AS REPOSITORY

In addition to its own holdings, the Vatican Library has many other collections of manuscripts on deposit. Included are those from the Casa of the Neophytes, the Stefano Borgia collection from the Congregation of the Propaganda Fide, the Rossiano, Casimiri, and Boncompagni-Ludovisi collections, the Sistine Chapel volumes of the Chamberlains (and numerous other journals), the Archives of Saint Peter, and those of the Capella Giulia. Also on deposit are collections from six of Rome's most ancient churches.

The Vatican Library and Archives played an important role during World War II in providing a refuge for libraries throughout the Italian peninsula, made possible by the Vatican's neutral status. Shortly before the Chigi palace at Ariccia was damaged by bombs, the Chigi family archives, which contained the papers of Alexander VII and the Chigi cardinals, were removed and sent to the Vatican. The Roman municipal libraries housed in Benedict's old Subiaco were also transferred before that shelter was destroyed. Other collections that found a temporary home at the Vatican were the library founded at Grottaferrata by Abbot Nilo and the library of the Duke of York at Frascati, both of which had suffered from bombing. The books were rescued and placed for safekeeping in the Vatican, together with the bronzes of Nero's pleasure barges at Nemi, vessels which were subsequently burned by the Germans. Perhaps the most important collection to find a haven at the Vatican during the war was the great library of the Benedictine monastery at Monte Cassino. The books and manuscripts were hurriedly loaded on trucks and taken first to Spoleto and then to Castel Sant' Angelo, finally reaching safety within the walls of the Vatican before the monastery was destroyed.

LIBRARY AND INFORMATION SERVICES IN CYPRUS

John F. Harvey

*International Library and Information Science Consultant,
Box 122, Lyndonville, VT 05851; and 603 Chanteclair House,
2 Sophoulis St., Nicosia 136, Cyprus*

Cyprus, the birthplace of Aphrodite, the goddess of love, is located in the eastern Mediterranean Sea; it has 3,572 square miles (somewhat smaller than Connecticut) and a population of 719,000 people.[1] The island's history of invasion and turmoil extends back at least to 7000 BC, and it has been a natural intersection point for West Asian, North African, and southeast European people and culture. Since 1963 (later revised), a "Green Line" and other designations have separated the island into four discrete and inviolable political and military zones: Turkish Cypriots and others in the so-called Turkish Federated State of Kibris (Cyprus) in the north and northeast; Greek Cypriots and others in the Republic of Cyprus in the south and southwest; the United Nations force in Cyprus patrolling a narrow buffer zone separating them; and British sovereign military bases in an area subdivided into four sections on the southern coast and the central plain.

Because Cyprus can be divided into two zones for library purposes, this paper also will be so divided. Unless otherwise indicated, all locations are Nicosia or Lefkosia (Nicosia in Turkish). Most library volume numbers represent accession number totals, not current shelf counts. Unless otherwise indicated, the word "ministry" refers to the Ministry of Education in the Greek sector or to the so-called Ministry of Education, Culture and Sport in the Turkish sector. This paper is in no way political, evaluative, or prescriptive; however, it does follow U.S. Embassy, Nicosia, policy when referring to government agencies in the generally unrecognized Turkish Federated State of Kibris. Table 1 shows summary data on each sector.

GREEK SECTOR

In 1965 and 1978, the 1887 legal depository law was revised under the auspices of the Ministry to the President. A comprehensive school and public library development plan has been proposed, and public, school, and community library regulations have been approved. The Cyprus Library Association represents Cyprus in the International Federation of Library Associations and Institutions and the Commonwealth Library Association.

In 1980, Greek Cyprus had 1.57 library volumes per person, one library staff member for every 2,045 persons, and spent C£0.212 (U.S.$0.57) per person on library material annually. The literacy level was 90 to 95 percent.

Most Cypriot library personnel are classified and paid at the clerical level, but a few school and several public, college, and special library personnel have college degrees or diplomas. Several have completed a Greek paraprofessional diploma program; four have graduate library school degrees. Savvas Petrides, a Loughborough University MLS graduate, established the Office of the Ministry inspector of libraries in 1967, which now provides a variety of services.

Note: The author would like to thank Eleni Mavridou, Savvas Petrides, and Suhayla Yashar for assistance in preparing this paper.

TABLE 1 CYPRIOT LIBRARY STATISTICS, 1980*

	Public Libraries	School Libraries	College Libraries	Special Libraries	Total
		Greek Sector			
Libraries	106	66	10	34	214
Staff members†					
Full time	20	61	7	30	121
Part time	95	7	8	25	135
Volumes	186,000	325,000	46,800	260,100	817,900
Total expenditures					
C£	39,500	24,200[a]	6,600	37,685	107,985
$U.S.	104,850	65,340[a]	17,820	101,750	289,760
		Turkish Sector			
Libraries	14	27	2	4	47
Staff members†					
Full time	21	4	2	3	31
Part time	6	60	0	2	69
Volumes	83,859	84,678	3,000	8,003	179,540
Total expenditures					
TL	550,000	203,860	120,000	500,000	1,373,860
$U.S.	7,012	2,525	1,490	6,191	17,218

*Exchange rate: C£2.7 = U.S.$1.00; U.S. $1.00 = 80.7 Turkish lira.
†Not included in this table are the Ministry Office staff: 3 full-time staff members in the Greek sector and 2 staff members (1 full-time and 1 part-time) in the Turkish sector.
[a]Greek Cypriot school library materials expenditures include ministry subsidy of C£6,000, the exact expenditures of 12 schools, and an estimated mean of C£200 for 54 additional public secondary school libraries, or C£10,800.

School Libraries

Since 1962, public elementary schools have been responsible for maintaining their own book collections, always in classrooms. Many schools also have small teachers' collections. Three central elementary libraries have been identified. The private (British) English-language Junior School has served K-7 grades on a spacious campus since 1948. From a 5,000-volume collection, 400 volumes are charged out weekly to the 250 students. Since 1896, the private Nareg Armenian Elementary School has served K-6 grade students. Its teacher-librarian charges out 300 volumes weekly in this 100-pupil Armenian-language school with a 1,400-volume collection. St. Barnabas School for the Blind, supported by the national government directly, serves grades K-9 with a braille library.

A ministry regulation requires each secondary school of general or technical education to maintain a central library; schools with more than 500 students must have a full-time librarian. Libraries are financed by the local school board and by ministry book fund contributions for the neediest on a matching basis and providing an approved book list is used. In 1982, public school libraries served 50,000 students, had 5.5 volumes per student, and received C£25,000 (U.S.$50,000) in government contributions (for collections and one new library construction) plus C£1 (U.S.$2) per student in technical schools. School libraries are now encouraged to become resource centers combining media and books on the shelves and in the catalogs.

Founded in 1830, the public Pancyprian Gymnasium's Severios Library serves grades 7-12. This Greek-language school, located within the medieval walls, houses most books in glass-doored bookcases but does not loan them. The three staff members work with a book per pupil ratio of 16.8 and a 1980 material budget of C£1 (U.S.$2.70) per pupil annually for 2,300 students. The public Technical School, near the Cyprus Hilton, seats 60 and charges out 600 volumes per week to 1,800 students. Its library contains a varied collection, half each in English and Greek, the former more useful for technology and the latter for literature.

On a wooded campus, the private English School, dating from 1900, prepares 750 grade 6-12 students in English for British higher education. Its library contains 9,000 well-selected books. Circulation is 500 volumes per week, and the annual 1980 book budget was C£4 (U.S.$10.80) per student. Founded in 1922, the American Academy, Nicosia, Library serves a private school teaching 500 students in English. It has a new library room, new foreign graduate librarian, and new shelving and furniture.[2] The Melkonian Institute Library maintains a private, endowed international Armenian-language research collection of 25,000 volumes.

Public Libraries

There are five types of public libraries in the Greek sector. First is Nicosia's (150,000 population) public library administered by a board of directors appointed by the ministry. Second are three libraries in the second, third, and fourth largest towns—Limassol (110,000), Larnaca (35,000), and Paphos (12,000)—controlled by the municipalities. Third are community libraries with control shared by the village government and the ministry. Fourth, the ministry controls mobile libraries; and last, foreign cultural centers control and finance their own libraries.

For 1982, the ministry's public library fund was C£5,500 (U.S.$11,000). The Nicosia library is totally financed by the ministry. In Limassol, Larnaca, and Paphos, the municipality pays for salaries and books and the ministry contributes annual 1982 book fund amounts up to C£1,400 (U.S.$2,800) each. Community libraries are financed on a matching basis by village and ministry, and the ministry finances mobile libraries. Public libraries must select books for purchase with Ministry funds from a list published by the Ministry Inspector.

The Ministry of Education Library, serving both as Nicosia's public library and as the ministry's education library, is housed in (a) an independent, centrally located Eleftheria Square building seating 14, (b) a 2,500-volume children's branch near St. Anthony's School, and (c) a small education branch in suburban Strovolos. With 50,000 volumes, the library is Cyprus's largest; it dates from 1927. The collection, supported in 1980 by a C£3,000 (U.S.$8,100) materials budget, consists primarily of English- and other foreign-language materials.

The Limassol Municipal Library is handsomely housed in a fine old mansion. It provides reference and loan service from a 10,000-volume collection and a 1982 C£2,000 (U.S.$4,000) materials budget; card cataloging and classification have just been started. The Larnaca Municipal Library is housed in an attractive new building in the Municipal Garden; it has one staff member and 9,500 cataloged books. The Paphos Municipal Library circulates books and has a good downtown location in an independent building.

Since 1963, public library service in community libraries has been based on a plan to make services readily available to every citizen. Each library is supervised by a volunteer and is open a few hours per week. An advisory board submits an annual budget, and the ministry keeps book fund accounts, provides guidance, and maintains a union catalog. In 1980, 96 libraries had 67,000 volumes, served 125,000 people, and spent C£20,000 (U.S.$54,000) on material. Among the better village libraries are those in Agros, Aradippou, Avgorou, Astromeritis, Athienou, Klirou, and Polis Chrysochous. Since 1970, bookmobiles have provided triweekly service. In 1982, four bookmobiles with 20,000 volumes loaned 1,200 volumes per week in 173 small villages.

Five foreign cultural centers operate libraries. Largest among them is the British Council Library, dating from 1940 and having 30,000 British volumes, including the best collection of bibliographic material. The American Center Library has 8,000 American books, periodicals, newspapers, records, and films. From its own building, the Goethe Institute Library provides Federal Republic of Germany material. The French Cultural Center offers 8,000 French volumes, films, and records. The new Soviet Cultural Center provides a library with Russian and English books, periodicals, records, newspapers, and pamphlets.

Academic Libraries

Cyprus University has been in the planning stages for several years; in the meantime, most college-bound students go abroad—and some stay, causing a "brain drain." Seven public tertiary level institutions in the Greek sector do offer diplomas but they do not offer degrees. In addition, Kykkos St. Barnabas Seminary School educates priests under the Cypriot Orthodox Church, and several small proprietary colleges operate without a library. Altogether, in 1980, six public institutional libraries served 2,370 students.

The Pedagogical Academy provides a three-year Greek-language program for 130 elementary education students. Founded in 1935, its library has two full-time staff members and 25,000 volumes and seats 100. Half the books are in English, half in Greek. The Pedagogical Institute provides Greek-language workshops for public elementary and secondary school teachers and sponsors annual library workshops in cooperation with foreign agencies. In addition to journal subscriptions and 15,000 volumes, in 1980 the library had an annual materials budget of C£5,000 (U.S.$13,500).

The Higher Technical Institute offers a three-year English-language engineering assistant diploma curriculum, and its library has 2,000 volumes for 450 students. Providing a two-year English-language program, the Hotel and Catering Institute's Loizou Library seats a third of the student body and has map cases and display shelves for its 3,000 volumes. The School of Nursing and Midwifery operates a three-year curriculum in Greek and English for 250 students. This is a registered nurse preparatory program under the Ministry of Health served by an 800-volume library.

Special Libraries and Information Centers

Cyprus is recognized by scholars internationally as a major archeological study site, and the strongest study centers and collections are found in the fields of archeology and history. Since 1933, the Phaneromeni Library has concentrated on Cypriot medieval and Byzantine history. This is an interesting private reference library that serves the public with a 40,000-volume collection. The Department of Antiquities archeological library contains 15,000 volumes and in 1980 had a C£3,500 (U.S.$9,450) annual materials budget. There is also the fast-growing Cyprus American Archeological Research Institute Library, 700 volumes, with hostel facilities. The Archbishopric Library, the island's oldest, dating from 1821, contains church and island history, including much rare manuscript and book material.

Most government ministries sponsor libraries, some of which are very useful. The overcrowded 10,000-volume Ministry of Foreign Affairs Library has difficulty in coping with the new foreign material flow. This UN document depository uses the UDC classification. The Ministry of Commerce and Industry Library was established with UNIDO assistance. It has several pieces of foreign library equipment, edge notched card files and microfiche, and routes new periodical issues to users, all unusual in Cyprus. A keyword punched card index has been started. Two hundred serial titles are received, plus industrial standards and UN documents.

Ministry of Agriculture and Natural Resources department libraries exchange annual reports and new accession lists. Combined, these five libraries have seven staff members and hold 13,000 volumes. They exchange material with FAO in Rome and NAL in Beltsville, Maryland. The Ministry Department of Fisheries Library has a 1981 computer printout of its holdings by author, title, and accession number, unique in Cyprus. Since 1976, P. Orphanos, the Cyprus AGRIS center head, has sent to FAO coded indexing information for each Cypriot agricultural research publication—30 a year. This, too, is unique in Cyprus.

The British Royal Air Force Base near Akrotiri and the Royal Army bases near Dhekelia and Episkopi maintain military recreational reading libraries in Ayios Nicholaos, Pergamos, Berengaria, and Nicosia. In addition, the British maintain school libraries for children of military personnel—St. John Comprehensive School, Episkopi, and King Richard Comprehensive School, Dhekelia. These libraries form Cyprus's only library networks—a total of 17 staff members, 134,900 volumes, and annual materials expenditures of C£27,635 (U.S.$74,605).

The government Public Record Office and the National Struggle Museum contain archive collections. The former, started in 1978, collects government records for safekeeping, and an archive retirement, calendaring, storage, and service program has been started. By 1980, four staff members had collected 4,000 boxes of material. The National Struggle Museum contains material on the 1950's union with Greece campaign and the struggle for freedom from Great Britain through a large photo, clipping, newspaper, and artifact collection.

In addition, there is also the Parliament Library, which contains 8,000 Cypriot and foreign volumes in closed stacks and locked bookcases.

Library Materials and Equipment

Most libraries in the Greek sector have either a classified or dictionary card catalog, an accession record, and a shelf list. Cataloging is carried out in brief form on cards typed by the librarian. Almost all use a simple DDC classification and some use short author numbers. Most libraries have open access, though locked glass-door bookcases are not uncommon. They use the Browne or Newark charging system to circulate books for home use.

Material collections, 95 percent of which are of foreign origin, emphasize bound books. History, philosophy, archeology, architecture, classical literature, and fiction are prominent in most school and public libraries. A few libraries contain old manuscripts and rare books.

Material selection is based on bookstore visits, advertisements, staff recommendations, and textbook bibliographies—foreign bibliographies are available in foreign cultural centers. Libraries order most material through local bookstores or direct from the publisher. (Some material, especially journals, is received by gift or exchange from abroad.) Books generally are ordered from Greece and the United Kingdom. (Few books are published in Cyprus; there are no full-time publishers, only printers.) Leading bookstores include Bridge House, Philippides, Hellas and Moufflon, Estoa in Larnaca, and Ioannides in Limassol. MAM Cyprus Publications provides dealer service.

Most commercial office items are adapted, and card forms printed, locally; there are no library supply and equipment companies, as such. Local carpenters have made most of the furniture, and special library equipment—even photocopiers and electric typewriters—is rare. In contrast, there are several commercial binders who do acceptable work.

TURKISH SECTOR

In 1980, the Turkish sector had approximately 1.16 library volumes per citizen and one library staff member for every 1,611 citizens; it spent TL8.2 (U.S.$0.10) annually per person on library materials. The literacy level was 90 to 95 percent.

According to approved ministry library regulations, in the Turkish sector any 5,000-volume library must have a full-time librarian and each secondary, technical school, or lycee must maintain a central library. Mobile service must be provided for elementary schools. Library fines must be kept low and membership fees eliminated; most books must be replaced with the same or a similar title. An accession record is required, and, with ministry approval, books may be discarded. All libraries must use the DDC classification. The Ministry Library Inspectorate started a union library catalog in 1980, and a library association also has been started.

There are 11 professional librarians in the Turkish sector, all bachelor's-level Turkish university library science graduates. Four work in public libraries, two in college libraries, one in a special library, two in mobile elementary school libraries, one in the ministry, and one is awaiting a position. A typical monthly Turkish Cypriot professional salary equalled TL16,000 (U.S.$198) in 1980. Librarians are classified at a bachelor's degree-level just below that of a teacher. Ata Sami, an Ankara University Department of Library Science graduate, is the ministry inspector of libraries. He started the inspectorate in 1972 and ranks as an assistant director or headmaster.

School Libraries

Ninety-five elementary schools serving refugees outside Lefkosia receive library service from two bookmobiles, and others have classroom collections. The bookmobiles reach each school weekly. Secondary and technical school libraries are financed by the ministry. A total of 12,800 students were served in 1980 in 25 schools, per school materials expenditures were TL4,000 (U.S.$50), and per student expenditures were TL7.8 (U.S.$0.10). The 25 libraries contained 55,655 volumes—2,226 volumes per school, or 4.3 volumes per student. In each school, one to four full-time teachers carry out part-time library duties for five to six hours two days per week, though a student assistant committee may do much of the work. The inspector visits each library semiannually.

Lycee Twentieth of July, facing the old city's Girne Gate, founded in 1891, serves grades 7-12, teaches in Turkish, and has the largest school enrollment (1,207) and collection (7,200 volumes). Books are separated into Turkish and English sections. A well-typed card catalog exists, and the school is now starting to classify its collection. Lycee Turkish, founded in 1891, serves grades 7-12, has 6,500 volumes, and teaches 660 students in Turkish. Founded in 1964, Lycee Mariff serves 777 students, teaches mostly in English, and has sent many graduates to universities abroad. Many of the 4,610 books were American and British cultural center gifts.

Public Libraries

In addition to the National (Public) Library there are three other types of public libraries in Lefkosia (population 36,730). First are the municipal libraries supervised by the ministry and located in the six largest towns. Second are the community libraries in villages under ministry supervision. Third are the foreign cultural centers, which control and finance their own libraries. Municipal libraries are financed entirely by the ministry; community libraries have no financial support but may receive gifts. For the 1980 fiscal year, total public library support for personnel was TL2,100,047 (U.S.$26,009). Gifts were received from several foreign governments.

The National Library, serving as the Lefkosia public library, was opened in 1960 and is housed in an independent building near Ataturk Square. (Construction has started on a new building near the Girne Gate.) It seats 20 in three reading rooms, and Fatma Ismail is the Ankara graduate librarian. The 34,000-volume collection contains Turkish-language material and is supported by an annual TL250,000 (U.S.$3,094) budget. The seven staff members provide loan and reference service. A plan exists to make the National Library a "national" depository, with six copies of each new Turkish/Cypriot publication to be deposited there.

Founded in 1953, the Magosa (Famagusta) Public Library is housed inside the city walls in a remodeled, high ceilinged medieval structure. It seats 40 and has 3 staff members. The library has a multilingual collection of 26,000 volumes and serves 17,180 people. The Girne (Kyrenia) Public Library is located in a second floor business area suite of reading, reference, and periodical rooms and stacks. It contains 5,460 Turkish books that circulate heavily to 4,760 citizens. Its annual materials expenditure is TL60,000 (U.S.$743). The Guzelyurt (Morphu) Public Library provides both public and school library service, and the 6,331-volume collection serves 7,660 people. Public librarians meet monthly for discussion under the inspector's supervision.

Two foreign cultural centers operate libraries. Outside the city walls, the American Center maintains a library of 300 books. The British Council occupies the former High Commissioner's large, walled, and shaded compound and contains 600 books. Each center has access to the materials and services in its Greek zone headquarters.

Academic Libraries

The Turkish sector has two colleges, which are under ministry supervision and operate with ministry financial support: The new Higher Technical Institute, Magosa, provides a three-year English-language program leading to an engineering assistant diploma, and the Teachers Training College, Girne, provides a three-year Turkish-language program for 130 elementary education students. The library of the two colleges, which seats 25 (but whose circulation is small) has a neatly typed card catalog, and most of the 3,000 books are in English. The Ankara graduate librarian, Ahmet Yildrin, is also an instructor. (A plan is being considered to combine the two colleges with new educational units to form a Turkish Cypriot University.)

Special Libraries and Information Centers

The Court Library, which contains 3,000 continuations and monographs on British and Turkish Cypriot law, occupies a modest room on Ataturk Square. Its annual materials budget is TL300,000 (U.S.$3,720), and Makbule Otuken is the Ankara-educated librarian. The Sultan Mahmud II Library is a bibliographic museum containing illuminated manuscripts, fine bindings, and rare old books. It was donated to the island's Turkish government in 1829 and operates today under the auspices of the Department of Antiquities. The impressive Parliament Building also contains a library, and most government ministries have book collections that will soon be organized into libraries.

In 1971, the National Archive and Research Center was established in a Girne mansion under Mustafa Hasim Altan. Half a million pieces are available, mostly records and publications from Cyprus's Ottoman, British, and Republic periods. A government materials selection and retirement program has been approved, but a space shortage has inhibited its implementation to date. Also interesting to history scholars is the Evkaf Dairesi in Lefkosia, which houses extensive court, school, religious, and commercial records for the past four centuries.

Library Materials and Equipment

Most libraries in the Turkish sector have dictionary catalogs and detailed accession records. Cataloging is brief, on cards typed by the librarian. DDC is used extensively in simple form with short author numbers. Most libraries have open access, use the Newark charging system, and circulate books for home use.

Material collections, 99 percent of which are of foreign origin (primarily Turkish) emphasize bound monographs. History, religion, and literature dominate most school and public library stock; social science, art, and science and technology are not well represented, and both young adult and children's material are in short supply.

Library selection is based on bookstore visits, publishers' advertisements, and staff recommendations. (Bibliographies are available in foreign cultural centers.) Public libraries send their recommendations to the ministry for the inspector's approval; for school libraries, teachers select for ministry committee approval.

Public and school library book orders are placed with the Lefkosia branch bookstore of the Republic of Turkey National Education Ministry Press, or direct with Turkish or British publishers, or with a local bookshop. Rustem's Bookshop, the leading retailer and also publisher of an occasional book, will accept any kind of book or serial order. There are no publishing companies, as such (only printers); however, the Turkish National Education Ministry Press does publish a large number of school and library books.

In Lefkosia, as in Nikosia, most commercial office items are adapted, and card forms printed, locally, since there are no library and equipment companies. Most furniture has been made by local carpenters. In contrast, the National Library does employ a full-time book binder to serve all ministry libraries.

NOTES

1. The reader interested in additional Cypriot library and bibliographic information may wish to consult these recent publications:

    John F. Harvey, "Cypriot Libraries," *International Library Review* 14 (April 1982); 107–134. A comprehensive survey containing numerous current statistical tables and citations to previous titles. The present paper leans heavily on information collected for that one.

    John F. Harvey, "A Researcher's Guide to Cypriot Libraries," 1981, unpublished, 5 pp.

    C. D. Stephanou, "Cyprus," *ALA World Encyclopedia of Library and Information Services* (Chicago: American Library Association, 1980), pp. 170–172.

    John F. Harvey, "Current Cypriot Serials," *Serials Librarian* 8 (1983), in preparation. A comprehensive bibliography of all types of serials with introduction.

2. John F. Harvey, "American Academy, Nicosia, Library Report," 1982, unpublished, 40 pp.

International Statistics

INTERNATIONAL STANDARD CRITERIA FOR PRICE INDEXES FOR LIBRARY MATERIALS

Frederick C. Lynden
*Assistant University Librarian for Technical Services,
Brown University Library
Providence, RI 02912*

What is the need for international data on the prices of library materials? No one has to be reminded of the economic conditions in the world today. Funds are scarce and library materials are costly. According to a recent study by the Association of Research Libraries, "from 1968/69 to 1978/79, ARL member libraries spent 91% more for library materials, yet added 22.5% fewer books to their collections."[1] Clearly American librarians are worried about rising costs and shrinking budgets. An article from the *European Studies Newsletter* (1981), entitled "Will American Libraries Continue to Have European Books?" reflects the pessimistic outlook for building strong European collections:

> To summarize: libraries are in the grip of a profound and deep seated inflationary period which ravages attempts to build European collections since the countries of Western Europe are not those most drastically affected. To cope with the situation libraries need 1) more information sharing about such topics as prices and sources.[2]

Price indexes for library materials can be of great value to librarians: (1) they can be used to prepare and justify library materials budgets; (2) they can be used for resource allocation by subject categories; (3) they can be used to analyze cost trends and aid in planning future budgets; (4) they can assist library administrators in interpreting the costs of their programs to those who control their funds; and (5) they can be used to calculate the effects of materials cost increases on other parts of the library's budget. The quantitative information on publishing that goes hand in hand with price information can also be extremely helpful in indicating coverage of foreign output and related costs. In short, price indexes are an excellent management tool.

Statistics on the average prices of books and periodicals in other countries also can be useful. Such data are a good measure of the ability of the average citizen to obtain these materials, when compared with figures on average income, for example. Comparisons with other educational materials are also helpful: Is the average price of a book more or less expensive than the cost of admission to a movie? Ultimately, it would be hoped that prices for the whole range of library materials, including media, would be available.

EARLY EFFORTS TOWARD AN INTERNATIONAL STANDARD

Much of the credit for encouraging the development of an international standard for price indexes of library materials must go to William H. Kurth, who, in the October 1955 issue of *College and Research Libraries*, first proposed U.S. book and periodical cost indexes. Kurth also was the first librarian to present a plan to the International Federation of Library Associations and Institutions for the development of international price indexes. In 1972, he spoke to the IFLA Committee on Statistics and Standards on "Price Indexes for Library Materials: The Need on an International Basis." Two years later, he chaired the ANSI Z-39 subcommittee that created the American National Standard.

In November 1974, Kurth again spoke to the IFLA Committee on Statistics and Standards on "A Strategy for Developing Price Indexes for Library Materials," explaining how price indexes work and why they are needed and outlining his recommendations. He suggested that the ANSI standard be used as a model by other national groups and that librarians work closely with their national standards agencies, national library associations, national statistical bureaus, and publishers associations to develop price indexes. At this IFLA meeting, the Committee on Statistics and Standards passed the following resolution:

> The Committee endorses the ANSI (American National Standards Institute) Standard on Price Indexes entitled "Criteria for Price Indexes for Library Materials" for consideration by ISO/TC 46 (The International Organization for Standardization, Technical Committee 46).[3]

Unfortunately, William Kurth did not live to see his dream realized. He died in 1977 without seeing an international standard created.

Kurth's legacy to the library world was the 1974 ANSI standard, which had a number of features of value for international comparisons. First, the standard gave preference to definitions from the UNESCO 1964 *Recommendation Concerning the International Standardization of Statistics Relating to Book Production and Periodicals*. Second, for subject classification, the standard offered the option of translating the Dewey Classification into the Universal Decimal Classification (UDC) and its 23 groups as set forth in the UNESCO recommendation. Third, the country of publication definition encouraged national indexes. It was Kurth's intent that "an agency in each country prepare the price index information solely for its own output of library materials as a natural extension of its regular book and periodical statistics reporting."[4] As he pointed out, this arrangement would avoid endless duplication.

Despite Kurth's pleas and the resolutions of the IFLA Committee, no international standard was under development in 1977. However, several events in 1977 called attention to the need for an international standard. In spring 1977, LIBER (Ligue des Bibliothèques Européennes de Recherche) held a seminar at the University of Leiden, where members heard a plan from their Working Group on Management "to create an index on academic book prices and production for each European country."[5] After discussion, it was agreed that price indexes from four countries (Great Britain, Germany, France, and the Netherlands) would be produced. The LIBER concerns were reinforced in summer 1977 by Alexander Allardyce, who urged that IFLA's Division of Collections and Services work on international coordination of price information. He pointed out:

> One of the most important practical fact-finding tasks now being carried on systematically in some countries and piece-meal in others is on book prices. IFLA has hitherto merely touched on it. It is now of far more than academic importance. Not only have book prices escalated through inflation, but in some countries inflation has been compounded by devaluation. . . . The librarian's presentation to administrative authorities has to depend more upon induction and persuasion than on general information. Modern fiscal management requires a higher ratio of fact to opinion, and so the need for external evidence is great.[6]

At the IFLA meeting in September 1977 in Brussels, Jane Pulis, of the Library Materials Price Index Committee, addressed the Section on Statistics on the need for an international standard. She reported on developments in the United States and overseas, including the appointment of an ISO ad hoc working group. At the same IFLA meeting, the Section on Exchange of Publications offered the following resolution:

> IFLA is requested to take note of the Section's interest in book price indexes for various kinds of acquisition, to review their availability and relevance for the output of major publishing countries, and to take steps to have more complete, reliable, and prompt statistics made available.[7]

The ISO ad hoc working group met in November 1977, with Karl Neubauer as IFLA representative and with members from Great Britain, Germany, the United States, and the International Organization for Standardization in attendance. The group agreed upon five points:

1. A price index for budgeting of libraries for resource allocation is necessary.
2. A price index must be internationally compatible.
3. The ANSI Price Index Standard (ANSI Z-39.20) should be used as a starting base for the development of an international standard.
4. There should be established a working group of ISO to prepare an international standard of price indexes for library materials in close cooperation with IFLA.
5. Germany and IFLA will make proposals for some changes of the ANSI standard for international use.[8]

Unfortunately, because of other pressing issues, ISO/TC-46 did not establish the working group.

DEVELOPMENTS SINCE 1977

IFLA Section on Statistics Preconference, 1982

In 1981, Robert Frase, executive director of the American National Standards Committee Z-39, raised the issue of a standard for price indexes for library materials at the spring plenary meeting of ISO/TC-46 in Nanjing. A decision to poll members regarding the formation of a working group led to the appointment of the working group at the 1982 IFLA Section on Statistics preconference in Montreal, Canada.

Two central themes were considered by the Section on Statistics at the preconference: 1) further cooperation between IFLA and UNESCO and 2) cooperation between IFLA and the ISO. The section, chaired by Karl W. Neubauer (State Library, Berlin), heard reports from Karl J. W. Hochgesand, UNESCO program specialist, and Johanna Eggert (Secretariat of ISO/Technical Committee 46). Section members discussed a proposed short questionnaire for gathering UNESCO statistics; statistics on book production and periodicals; a clearinghouse for library statistics in developing countries; the Australian Census of Library Services; and price indexes for library materials. Two principal approaches were recommended in considering price indexes for library materials: (1) development of an international standard and (2) reporting of price data in UNESCO statistics. ISO Working Group 8 was established to create International Standard Criteria for Price Indexes for Library Materials, headed by Morton Hein (Bibliotekskonsulent, Bibliotekstilsynet in Copenhagen). Hein was asked to call a first constituent meeting, in which Canada, Germany, the Netherlands, Sweden, the United Kingdom, and the United States would participate.

Toward a Model International Standard

During the five years between the time of peak interest in international price indexes in 1977 and the 1982 decision to establish an ISO working group, there were a number of changes and improvements in the price index situation, in response to criticisms of the existing price indexes. In 1977, Jane Pulis voiced the contention of U.S. librarians that national indexes did not reflect local conditions. Alexander Allardyce pointed out that existing indexes lacked timeliness and did not reflect the actual materials in libraries, dealer discounts, or markups for foreign sales. He suggested three steps for dealing with these problems: (1) the establishment of international criteria with agreed-upon subject categories; (2) the creation of publishing price indexes by the major publishing countries; and (3) the creation of selected indexes according to type and size of library.

The response of the Library Materials Price Index Committee (LMPIC) of the American Library Association to the criticism of national indexes as not being reflective of local conditions was that national and local indexes are mutually exclusive, but they also are complementary. Libraries buy subsets of national production, and it is not possible to show discounts or markups due to the great variance from library to library. The LMPIC recommends that libraries do local studies and then compare them with national data. To improve the timeliness of the indexes, the Price Index Committee now publishes data in the bimonthly *RTSD Newsletter* (Resources and Technical Services Division of the American Library Association) as soon as it is available. As for the exclusion of nonbook materials, the LMPIC has now begun to index newspapers and media. The Price Index Committee is also working on the development of an academic book price index for the United States.

The *American National Standard Criteria for Price Indexes for Library Materials* came up for revision in 1979, and the ANSI revision subcommittee began meeting then to deal with some of the concerns noted previously and other issues. If approved, the revised standard will have sections on a U.S. newspaper index and a media index. The revision will also respond to complaints about the lack of detail in the Dewey Classification subject coverage, the size of the sample, and the three-year base period of the 1974 index criteria. The revision permits three different classifications (LC, Dewey, or UDC) and is flexible on narrower subject breakdowns, with the caution that compilers remember historical comparability. According to the revised standard, "when there is a sizeable discrepancy between the total population and the index population, a sample drawn by currently existing statistical standards is preferred."[9] It also permits a base period of one year, retains international definitions as far as possible, and uses ALA and AACR2 definitions for newer publication formats. The revision recommends using one currency, preferably the currency of the country of publication. Thus, the proposed revised standard continues the work of William Kurth to create a model for an international standard.

One feature of the proposed revision is designed to make it more valuable for the user. The revision requires that all future indexes contain statements on the materials included in the index, with appropriate definitions; the country or countries of their publication; the time span covered; the subject classification; the method of compilation, including the source of data; and the estimated total population and the index population of materials covered. The revision committee has called these provisions the "truth in indexing" statements. It is hoped that these statements will allow the user to evaluate the index. All indexes must still include list price, number of volumes (or in the case of periodicals, number of titles), and average price by subject categories. The previous price index formula (the average price for the current year, divided by the average price in the base year, multiplied by 100) is still in use as well.

IN CONCLUSION

Progress has been made toward the goal of providing more reliable international information on the costs of library materials. The first of two steps has been taken. A working group has been appointed to produce International Standard Criteria for Price Indexes for Library Materials. The IFLA preconference offered its support to this effort to create a standard that will ultimately permit comparability of publishing costs from country to country. The next step for IFLA will be to encourage the publication in the *UNESCO Statistical Yearbook* of national average price information for library materials. This information can become the raw material for indexes and provide a measure of the costs of materials on an international level for librarians, publishers, and booksellers. With the advent of improved computerized control of cost data, better bibliographic control of the publishing output of the nations of the world, and continuing support from IFLA, the efforts to create international standard criteria for price indexes and international reporting of price data are bound to succeed.

NOTES

1. *The Economics and Financial Management of Research Libraries: A Report on an Exploratory Meeting* (Washington, D.C.: Council on Library Resources, 1981), p. 1.
2. Erwin K. Welsch, "Will American Libraries Continue to Have European Books?" *European Studies Newsletter* 10 (March 1981): 7.
3. "Price Index Resolution," *IFLA Annual, 1974* (Munich: Verlag Dokumentation, 1975), p. 41.
4. William H. Kurth, "A Strategy for Developing Price Indexes for Library Materials," prepared for the IFLA Committee on Statistics and Standards, November 1974, p. 5.
5. "Academic Book Prices Discussion Paper, Lieber Meeting, 27 April 1977," *Lieber Bulletin* 9/10 (1978): 113.
6. Alexander Allardyce, "Some Opportunities for IFLA's Division of Collections and Services," *IFLA Journal* 3 (1977): 243.
7. "Resolution from the Section on the Exchange of Publications," *IFLA Annual, 1977* (Munich: K. G. Sauer, 1978), p. 35.
8. "Price Indexes for Library Materials," *IFLA Journal* 4 (1978): 60.
9. Draft revision of ANSI Z-39.20-1974, *American National Standard Criteria for Price Indexes for Library Materials*, May 1982, 23 pp.

U.S. BOOK EXPORTS AND IMPORTS AND INTERNATIONAL TITLE OUTPUT

Chandler B. Grannis

Contributing Editor, *Publishers Weekly*

U.S. book exports increased substantially in dollar value in 1981, and book imports declined a little, both by comparison with 1980. That is the gist of figures selected and arranged by *PW* from data that the Department of Commerce no longer has funds to organize and publish, but which it has gathered and has supplied for industry use at our request.

Exports—those, that is, that are recorded by the Department of Commerce—exceeded $603.2 million in 1981, a sum 17.9% above the reported figure for 1980 (Table 1). Book imports—also subject to limitations in recording—came to over $294.8 million in 1981, which was 3.8% below the 1980 report (Table 2). The excess of exports over imports, in dollar value, widened dramatically in 1981; it should be noted, however, that the ratio tends to fluctuate from year to year.

Note: Adapted from *Publishers Weekly*, September 17, 1982, where the article was entitled "U.S. Book Exports and Imports: The UNESCO Reports."

TABLE 1 U.S. BOOK EXPORTS, 1979-1981
Shipments Valued at $500 or More Only

	TO ALL COUNTRIES, Dollar Values				TO ALL COUNTRIES, Units				TO CANADA ONLY, Dollar Values		
	1979	1980	1981	% Change 1980–1981	1979	1980	1981	% Change 1980–1981	1979	1980	1981
Bibles, Testaments & Other Religious Books (2703020)	$23,943,939	$31,867,260	$33,894,757	+ 6.4	39,090,837	43,501,521	35,871,584	−17.5	$6,399,153	$6,848,742	$7,710,272
Dictionaries & Thesauruses (2703040)	5,735,680	6,018,536	7,098,264	+17.9	1,562,092	1,726,792	2,689,611	+55.8	1,273,275	1,312,839	1,557,846
Encyclopedias (2703060)	29,878,607	27,944,503	25,819,529	− 7.6	6,840,325	6,462,048	4,619,219	−28.5	9,199,365	9,340,069	7,011,290
Textbooks, Workbooks & Standardized Tests (2703070)	83,550,838	99,657,783	118,716,052	+19.1					38,064,696	37,395,796	41,283,009
Technical, Scientific & Professional Books (2703080)	51,577,922	53,927,278	79,637,779	+47.7	14,846,886	15,807,469	21,678,179	+37.1	12,385,527	11,816,779	15,745,842
Books Not Elsewhere Classified & Pamphlets (2704000)	237,891,882	284,159,654	327,185,497	+15.1	180,163,203	199,852,375	215,360,345	+ 7.8	107,881,787	121,136,963	143,059,209
Children's Picture & Coloring Books (7375200)	6,666,452	8,049,807	10,848,562	+34.8					2,914,796	3,451,007	4,718,255
Total Domestic Merchandise, Omitting Shipments Under $500	$439,245,220	$511,622,823	$603,200,440	+17.9					$178,118,599	$191,302,195	$221,085,723

SOURCE: U.S. Department of Commerce, *Printing and Publishing*, issues of April 1979 and Spring–Summer 1980, and *P&P* editors; 1981 figures compiled from data supplied to *PW* by U.S. Department of Commerce, Bureau of Industrial Economics (William S. Lofquist, Printing and Publishing Industry Specialist).

TABLE 2 U.S. BOOK IMPORTS, 1979-1981
Shipments Valued at $250 or More Only

	Dollar Values 1979	1980	1981	% Change from 1980	Units 1979	1980	1981	% Change from 1980
Bibles and Prayerbooks (2702520)	$ 6,082,482	$ 5,912,777	5,363,579	− 9.3	3,388,872	1,513,528	2,234,254	+ 47.6
Books, Foreign Language (2702540)	25,456,683	30,100,817	27,021,249	−10.2	17,373,156	17,953,146	18,297,425	+ 1.9
Books Not Specially Provided for, wholly or in part the work of an author who is a U.S. national or domiciliary (2702560)	3,454,528	4,152,073	7,178,346	+72.9	1,228,169	1,148,225	15,202,787	+1224.2*
Other Books (2702580)	229,713,246	257,041,783	246,895,088	− 3.9	183,092,783	196,199,815	202,306,063	+ 3.1
Toy Books and Coloring Books (7375200)	3,978,548	9,303,476	8,406,121	− 9.6	—	—	—	—
Total Imports, Omitting Shipments Under $250	**$268,685,497**	**$306,510,936**	**$294,862,383**	**− 3.8**	—	—	—	—

SOURCE: U.S. Department of Commerce, *Printing & Publishing*, issues of April 1979 and Spring–Summer 1980, and *P&P* editors; 1981 figures compiled from data supplied to *PW* by U.S. Department of Commerce, Bureau of Industrial Economics (William S. Lofquist, Printing and Publishing Industry Specialist).
*See accompanying article.

Canada, the United Kingdom, and Australia accounted in 1981 for roughly 63% of the U.S. book export market, to judge from the Department of Commerce tally; and in the same year the United Kingdom, Japan, and Canada together supplied about 58% of U.S. book imports.

As we point out every year, the figures presented here do not account for the full amount of the U.S. international book trade. The export figures specifically exclude shipments valued under $500 "and low-valued exports by mail." The import figures exclude shipments valued under $250 "and low-valued nondutiable imports by mail."

Because of these limitations, the reported totals fall short of actuality by unknown and possibly significant amounts. The exclusions apply not only to books but to other industries as well; and to the extent that an industry's international activity includes thousands of small shipments, the Department of Commerce reports are bound to be incomplete.

Until the spring of 1982, nevertheless, the world of print was benefited by a Department of Commerce publication, *Printing and Publishing*, a modest, low-budget quarterly that presented the available data in useful arrangements along with analytical reviews. Under a directive from the Office of Management and Budget, that valuable service to a major industry was canceled as an "economy" move in the spring of 1982, just before year-end 1981 data could be organized for publication. The former editor of the quarterly, William S. Lofquist, is designated Printing and Publishing Industry Specialist, Bureau of Industrial Economics, U.S. Department of Commerce, Washington, D.C. 20230. He has generously answered queries regarding the Department of Commerce's data, which are still assembled and computerized.

A word should be said about an apparently surprising figure in Table 2, at the far right, under "Units," showing that more than 15.2 million units—an increase from 1980 of about 14.1 million—were imported in the "author . . . U.S. national or domiciliary" category. The computer data show that of the 15.2 million units, over 13.7 million

TABLE 3 U.S. BOOK EXPORTS AND IMPORTS: PRINCIPAL COUNTRIES, 1981

	Dollars 1981	% Change 1980–81		Dollars 1981	% Change 1980–81
U.S. Exports (over $500 shipments only)			**U.S. Imports (Over $250 shipments only)**		
Canada	$221,085,723	+ 15.6	United Kingdom	$90,840,357	− 13.7
United Kingdom	90,109,326	− 4.4	Japan	44,585,307	+ 20.2
Australia	53,348,172	+ 36.7	Canada	39,252,863	− 1.5
Nigeria	22,177,822	+131.6	Germany, W.	16,442,051	− 4.5
Mexico	21,695,165	+ 47.9	Hong Kong	15,520,380	− 11.7
Japan	21,343,698	+ 5.1	Spain	15,157,382	+ 2.6
Netherlands	14,654,782	+ 31.9	Italy	14,108,956	− 15.7
Rep. S. Africa	10,621,634	+ 74.6	Netherlands	8,795,091	− 6.2
Brazil	9,795,851	− 25.2	Switzerland	7,861,061	+ 8.1
Germany, W.	9,638,096	+ 13.7	France	5,946,085	− 6.5
Saudi Arabia	8,442,042	+ 87.9	Mexico	5,578,452	− 30.5
Singapore	8,255,662	+ 21.2	Singapore	5,115,987	+ 7.7
All others	$112,032,467	———	All others	$25,658,411	———
Total, all countries	**$603,200,440**	**+ 17.9**	**Total, all countries**	**$294,862,383**	**− 3.8**

Source: Figures supplied to *PW* by U.S. Department of Commerce, Bureau of Industrial Economics (William S. Lofquist, Printing and Publishing Industry Specialist).

Note: U.S. export data do not include individual shipments valued under $500 and low-valued exports shipped by mail. U.S. import data do not include individual shipments valued under $250 and low-valued imports shipped by mail.

TABLE 4 TITLE OUTPUT: PRINCIPAL BOOK-PRODUCING COUNTRIES, 1977-1979

	1977	1978	1979		1977	1978	1979
AFRICA				**EUROPE**			
Egypt	1,472	—	—	Austria	6,800	6,439	6,783
Nigeria	—	1,175	—	Belgium	5,964	9,012	10,040
				Bulgaria	4,088	4,234	4,600
NORTH AMERICA				Czechoslovakia	9,568	9,588	10,089
Canada	17,868	22,168	—	Denmark	8,021	8,642	9,415
Cuba	1,039	—	—	Finland	3,679	3,367	4,834
*U.S.A.	87,780	87,569	88,721	France	31,673	21,225	25,019
				Germany (E.)	5,844	6,680	5,816
SOUTH AMERICA				Germany (W.)	48,736	50,950	59,668
Argentina	5,285	4,627	4,541	Greece	4,981	—	4,664
Brazil	17,984	18,102	—	Hungary	9,048	9,579	9,120
Peru	910	968	857	Italy	10,116	10,679	11,162
Uruguay	—	—	1,012	Netherlands	13,111	13,393	13,429
				Norway	4,823	4,407	5,405
ASIA				Poland	11,552	11,849	11,191
Bangladesh	—	1,229	—	Portugal	6,122	6,274	5,726
China	—	12,493	14,738	Romania	7,218	7,562	7,288
Cyprus	570	1,054	1,325	Spain	24,896	23,231	24,569
Hong Kong	1,735	—	—	Sweden	6,009	5,256	5,396
India	12,885	12,932	11,087	Switzerland	9,894	10,077	10,765
Indonesia	2,265	—	2,402	United Kingdom	36,196	38,641	41,564
Iran	3,027	2,657	—	Yugoslavia	10,418	10,609	12,061
Iraq	1,758	1,618	—				
Israel	2,214	—	2,397				
Japan	40,905	43,973	44,392	**OCEANIA**			
Rep. Korea	13,081	16,364	16,081				
Malaysia	1,341	1,328	2,037	Australia	6,375	7,658	8,391
Pakistan	1,331	1,317	1,184	New Zealand	1,939	2,079	2,496
Philippines	1,753	—	—				
Singapore	1,207	1,306	1,087				
Sri Lanka	1,201	1,405	1,582				
Thailand	3,390	—	—	**U.S.S.R.**	**85,395**	**84,727**	**80,560**
Turkey	6,830	—	5,071	Byeloruss S.S.R.	2,330	2,618	2,806
Vietnam	1,504	1,721	—	Ukraine S.S.R.	8,430	8,259	9,032

Sources: UNESCO Statistical Yearbook 1981, Table 8.2 (New York, Unipub, 1982); for U.S.A. figures, R. R. Bowker Co. Data Services and University Microfilms.
*Includes books and pamphlets issued through U.S. Government Printing Office (in 1977, est. 15,000; in 1978, 14,814; in 1979, 13,506); also university theses (in 1977, est. 31,000; in 1978, 31,529; in 1979, 30,035). *Not* included in the U.S. figures are publications of state and local governments, publications of numerous institutions, and many reports, proceedings, lab manuals, and workbooks.

came from Canada; and that these were valued at a little over $2.3 million, an average of about 16 cents per unit. Presumably this represents a special situation, not yet identified, involving very-low-cost items.

Table 3 shows dollar values of U.S. book exports and imports, for the top dozen countries in each group, in 1981. These figures also are extracted by *PW* from the Department of Commerce computer data.

Tables 4 and 5 offer excerpts from basic international publishing tabulations compiled by UNESCO. These are extracted by *PW* from *UNESCO Statistical Yearbook, 1981*, published in 1982 and available from Unipub, New York. The most recent book industry figures in this edition of the bulky annual are for 1979. Table 4 covers total book title output of leading book-producing countries. Table 5 reports numbers of translations, by original language, for the top 20 languages for 1975-1977.

TABLE 5 TRANSLATIONS BY ORIGINAL
LANGUAGE: TOP 20 LANGUAGES,
1975–1977

	1975	1976	1977
English	19,020	19,264	19,577
Russian	6,563	6,994	6,771
French	5,298	6,105	6,054
German	4,338	4,665	4,656
Italian	1,045	1,323	1,260
Swedish	1,043	1,166	1,158
Czech	516	663	715
Hungarian	696	682	685
Spanish	935	751	649
Danish	512	589	577
Polish	676	570	539
Dutch	329	367	448
Serbo-Croatian	307	463	437
Latin	443	479	432
Classical Greek	478	496	387
Romanian	480	376	383
Bulgarian	247	284	289
Norwegian	224	235	279
Arabic	192	260	227
Hebrew	161	232	215
Subtotal, top-20 languages	43,588	45,964	44,738
Total All Languages	**47,775**	**50,381**	**50,047**

SOURCE: UNESCO Statistical Yearbook 1981, Table 8.12.

BRITISH BOOK PRODUCTION, 1982

British publishers established a new record last year—one that will not be generally welcomed. In 1982, they issued an all-time record total of 48,307 titles, of which 37,947 were new books and 10,360 were reprints and new editions. The output of new books and new editions according to category is given in detail in Table 1. The figures have been compiled from the book lists that have appeared week by week in *The Bookseller*.

This 1982 total represents an increase of 5,224, or 12.1 percent, on last year's total of 43,083 (Table 2). The number of new books rose by 4,251, or 12.6 percent; of new editions by 973, or 19.4 percent. The total is 149 up on the previous record, set in 1980, when 48,158 books were issued: The increase against that year is in new books, the new editions total showing a small fall.

Once again, it is hard to find any clear cause for the rise. It contrasts with 1981's 10.5 percent fall from the 1980 level: *The Bookseller* then recorded an immediate comment that the publishers must be "going sane." Many may feel that a contrary comment should be made on 1982's sharp rise. The suggestion that imported English-language

Note: Adapted from *The Bookseller* (12 Dyott Street, London WC1A 1DR, England), January 1 and 8, 1983, where the article was entitled "An Unwelcome Record."

446 / INTERNATIONAL STATISTICS

TABLE 1 BOOK TITLE OUTPUT, 1982

Classification	December 1982 Total	December 1982 Reprints and New Editions	December 1982 Trans.	December 1982 Limited Editions	January–December 1982 Total	January–December 1982 Reprints and New Editions	January–December 1982 Trans.	January–December 1982 Limited Editions
Aeronautics	17	2	—	—	238	39	—	—
Agriculture and forestry	37	2	—	—	512	90	7	1
Architecture	31	8	2	—	384	74	6	3
Art	96	16	1	—	1,279	176	36	10
Astronomy	10	1	—	—	155	39	3	—
Bibliography and library economy	114	29	1	—	776	151	2	—
Biography	110	30	6	—	1,491	314	67	2
Chemistry and physics	76	6	—	—	754	121	26	—
Children's books	154	54	5	—	2,917	535	100	7
Commerce	90	18	—	—	1,493	384	3	1
Customs, costumes, folklore	17	2	—	—	172	30	8	—
Domestic science	54	34	—	—	776	190	8	—
Education	115	17	9	—	1,175	181	5	—
Engineering	166	33	5	—	1,662	382	27	—
Entertainment	91	5	9	—	717	102	29	—
Fiction	351	146	9	—	4,879	2,033	178	3
General	81	8	1	—	777	104	7	1
Geography and archaeology	57	9	—	—	683	109	9	3
Geology and meteorology	46	6	—	1	418	65	7	—
History	149	28	17	—	1,503	310	70	4
Humour	16	1	—	—	215	29	2	—
Industry	55	11	—	—	569	113	4	—
Language	77	42	—	—	664	138	10	1

Law and public administration	182	58	—	1,464	387	—
Literature	161	18	1	1,612	217	6
Mathematics	77	8	7	924	180	—
Medical science	391	91	1	3,274	583	2
Military science	15	—	2	143	21	—
Music	77	6	1	498	95	1
Natural sciences	108	14	2	1,507	178	1
Occultism	15	1	1	193	41	—
Philosophy	32	6	1	521	104	50
Photography	36	7	—	268	44	—
Plays	15	3	3	253	77	—
Poetry	79	7	4	794	90	49
Political science and economy	475	80	25	4,263	849	146
Psychology	93	15	1	834	161	20
Religion and theology	114	14	8	1,856	452	157
School textbooks	172	31	2	1,807	312	7
Science, general	4	1	—	58	14	12
Sociology	99	9	3	1,174	137	8
Sports and outdoor games	34	9	—	541	120	34
Stockbreeding	17	8	—	297	53	6
Trade	82	9	—	606	125	2
Travel and guidebooks	111	75	8	869	348	28
Wireless and television	23	3	1	342	66	3
Total	4,422	981	127	48,307	10,360	1,391	105

Note: This table shows the books recorded in December and the total for January–December with the numbers of new editions, translations, and limited editions.

TABLE 2 TITLE OUTPUT, 1947–1982

Year	Total	Reprints and New Editions
1947	13,046	2,441
1948	14,686	3,924
1949	17,034	5,110
1950	17,072	5,334
1951	18,066	4,938
1952	18,741	5,428
1953	18,257	5,523
1954	18,188	4,846
1955	19,962	5,770
1956	19,107	5,302
1957	20,719	5,921
1958	22,143	5,971
1959	20,690	5,522
1960	23,783	4,989
1961	24,893	6,406
1962	25,079	6,104
1963	26,023	5,656
1964	26,154	5,260
1965	26,358	5,313
1966	28,883	5,919
1967	29,619	7,060
1968	31,470	8,778
1969	32,393	9,106
1970	33,489	9,977
1971	32,538	8,975
1972	33,140	8,486
1973	35,254	9,556
1974	32,194	7,852
1975	35,608	8,361
1976	34,434	8,227
1977	36,322	8,638
1978	38,766	9,236
1979	41,940	9,086
1980	48,158	10,776
1981	43,083	9,387
1982	48,307	10,360

books handled through British distributors have inflated the figures will not stand; in years past the proportion of imported titles has remained virtually constant.

As Table 3 shows, there was measured output in all the main categories, with large increases in political science, religion, literature, and medical science. Children's books fell, but as they have been having a hard time since 1980, it is surprising that they fell by only 17, to 2,917. Fiction, which (except for the small minority of top bestseller writers or specially hyped titles) is always regarded as having a hard time, nevertheless managed a rise of 132, to 4,879 titles, for the year.

TABLE 3 COMPARISON OF BOOK PRODUCTION
BY SUBJECT, 1981 AND 1982

	1981	1982	+ or −
New books	33,696	37,947	+4,251
New editions	9,387	10,360	+973
Totals	43,083	48,307	
Art	1,383	1,279	−104
Biography	1,243	1,491	+248
Chemistry and physics	682	754	+72
Children's books	2,934	2,917	−17
Commerce	1,213	1,493	+280
Education	1,040	1,175	+135
Engineering	1,488	1,662	+174
Fiction	4,747	4,879	+132
History	1,432	1,503	+71
Industry	492	569	+77
Law and public administration	1,399	1,464	+65
Literature	1,151	1,612	+461
Medical science	2,838	3,274	+436
Natural sciences	1,234	1,507	+273
Political science	3,764	4,263	+499
Religion	1,363	1,856	+493
School textbooks	1,991	1,807	−184
Sociology	1,031	1,174	+143
Travel and guidebooks	677	869	+192

Part 6
Reference Information

Bibliographies

THE LIBRARIAN'S BOOKSHELF

Jo-Ann Michalak

Former Librarian, School of Library Service, Columbia University Libraries, New York

This bibliography is intended as a buying and reading guide for individual librarians and library collections. A few of the titles listed are core titles that any staff development collection might contain, but most are recently published titles with an emphasis on continuing education. Bibliographic tools that most libraries are likely to have for day-to-day operations have been excluded from this list.

BOOKS

General Works

ALA World Encyclopedia of Library and Information Services, ed. by Robert Wedgeworth. Chicago: American Library Association, 1980. $95.

The ALA Yearbook 1982: A Review of Library Events, Chicago: American Library Association, 1982. $60.

Advances in Librarianship, ed. by Michael Harris. New York: Academic Press, 1970- . Vol. 12, 1982. $30.

American Library Directory, 1982. 35th ed. New York: R. R. Bowker, 1982. $89.95.

Bowker Annual of Library and Book Trade Information 1983. 28th ed. New York: R. R. Bowker, 1983. $55.

Directory of Special Libraries and Information Centers. 7th ed. Detroit: Gale, 1982. Vols. 1-3. Vol. 1 $225; Vol. 2 $200; Vol. 3 $210.

Encyclopedia of Library and Information Science. New York: Marcel Dekker, 1968-1981. Vols. 1-33. $55 per vol.

Fang, Josephine Riss, and Songe, Alice H. *International Guide to Library, Archival, and Information Science Associations*. 2nd ed. New York: R. R. Bowker, 1980. $32.50.

Ladenson, Alex. *Library Law and Legislation in the United States*. Metuchen, NJ: Scarecrow, 1982. $14.50.

Libraries in the Political Process, ed. by E. J. Josey. Phoenix, AZ: Oryx Press, 1980. $24.50.

Lilley, Dorothy, and Badough, Rose Marie. *Library and Information Science: A Guide to Information Sources*. Detroit: Gale, 1982. $40.

Vaillancourt, Pauline M. *International Directory of Acronyms in Library, Information and Computer Sciences*. New York: R. R. Bowker, 1980. $50.

Who's Who in Library and Information Services, ed. by Joel Lee. Chicago: American Library Association, 1982. $150.

Administration and Personnel

Advances in Library Administration and Organization, Vol. 1, ed. by Gerald B. McCabe, B. Kriessman, and W. Carl Jackson. Greenwich, CT: JAI Press, 1982. $34.50.

Alley, Brian, and Cargill, Jennifer. *Keeping Track of What You Spend: The Librarian's Guide to Simple Bookkeeping*. Phoenix, AZ: Oryx Press, 1982. $25.

453

Bailey, Martha. *Supervisory and Middle Managers in Libraries.* Metuchen, NJ: Scarecrow, 1981. $12.

Blagden, John. *Do We Really Need Libraries: An Assessment of Approaches to Evaluation of the Performances of Libraries.* Hamden, CT: Shoe String, 1980. $18.95.

Bommer, Michael R. W., and Chorba, Ronald W. *Decision Making for Library Management.* White Plains, NY: Knowledge Industry, 1982. $27.50.

Boss, Richard W. *Grant Money and How to Get It: A Handbook for Librarians.* New York: R. R. Bowker, 1980. $19.95.

Breivik, Patricia, and Gibson, E. Burr. *Funding Alternatives for Libraries.* Chicago: American Library Association, 1979. $10.

Chen, Ching-Chih. *Library Management Without Bias.* Greenwich, CT: JAI Press, 1981. $32.50.

―――. *Zero-Base Budgeting in Library Management: A Manual for Librarians.* Phoenix, AZ: Oryx Press, 1980. $35.

Corry, Emmett. *Grants for Libraries: A Guide to Public and Private Funding Programs and Proposal Writing Techniques.* Littleton, CO: Libraries Unlimited, 1982. $22.50.

De Hart, Florence E. *Librarian's Psychological Commitments: Human Relations in Librarianship.* Westport, CT: Greenwood Press, 1979. $19.95.

Edsall, Marian S. *Library Promotion Handbook.* Phoenix, AZ: Oryx Press, 1980. $32.50.

Garvey, Mona. *Library Public Relations.* New York: H. W. Wilson, 1980. $14.

Kohn, Rita, and Teppler, K. *You Can Do It: A PR Skills Manual for Librarians.* Metuchen, NJ: Scarecrow, 1981. $12.50.

Lancaster, F. W. *The Measurement and Evaluation of Library Services.* Washington, DC: Information Resources Press, 1977. $29.95.

Martin, Murray S. *Issues in Personnel Management.* Greenwich, CT: JAI Press, 1981. $32.50.

O'Connor, M. J. *Research in Library Management.* Boston Spa, England: The British Library, Lending Division, 1980. £8. (BLR & D Report, no. 5550).

O'Reilly, Robert C., and O'Reilly, Marjorie I. *Librarians and Labor Relations: Employment Under Union Contracts.* Westport, CT: Greenwood Press, 1981. $25.

Personnel Administration in Libraries, ed. by Sheila Creth and Frederick Duda. New York: Neal-Schuman, 1981. $24.95.

Personnel Policies and Procedures in Libraries, ed. by Nancy Van Zant. New York: Neal-Schuman, 1980. $24.95.

Reeves, William Joseph. *Librarians as Professionals: The Occupation's Impact on Library Work Arrangements.* Lexington, MA: Lexington Books, 1980. $21.95.

Rizzo, John. *Management for Librarians.* Westport, CT: Greenwood Press, 1980. $35.

Rowley, Jennifer E., and Rowley, P. J. *Operations Research: A Tool for Library Management.* Chicago: American Library Association, 1981. $10.

Sherman, Steve. *ABC's of Library Promotion.* 2nd ed. Metuchen, NJ: Scarecrow, 1980. $13.

Smith, David. *Systems Thinking in Library and Information Management.* Hamden, CT: Shoe String, 1981. $16.

Strategies for Library Administration: Concepts and Approaches, ed. by Charles R. McClure and A. R. Samuels. Littleton, CO: Libraries Unlimited, 1982. $28.50.

Stueart, Robert. *Library Management.* 2nd ed. Littleton, CO: Libraries Unlimited, 1981. $25.

Archives, Conservation, and Special Collections

Archivists and Machine-Readable Records: Proceedings of a Conference . . . , ed. by Carolyn Geda et al. Chicago: Society of American Archivists, 1980. $10.

Automating the Archives: Issues and Problems in Computer Applications, ed. by Lawrence J. Crank. White Plains, NY: Knowledge Industry, 1980. $34.50.

Banks, Paul Noble. *A Selective Bibliography on the Conservation of Research Libraries Materials.* Chicago: Newberry Library, 1981. $10.

Clinton, Alan. *Printed Ephemera: Collection, Organization and Access.* Hamden, CT: Shoe String, 1981. $15.

Cook, Michael. *Archives and the Computer.* Woburn, MA: Butterworths, 1980. $34.95.

Friends of the Libraries Sourcebook, ed. by Sandy Dolnick. Chicago: American Library Association, 1980. $7.

Gracy, David B. *An Introduction to Archives and Manuscripts.* New York: Special Libraries Association, 1981. $7.25.

Morrow, Carolyn Clark. *Conservation Treatment Procedures: A Manual of Step-by-Step Procedures for the Maintenance and Repair of Library Materials.* Littleton, CO: Libraries Unlimited, 1982. $18.50.

Preservation of Library Materials, ed. by Joyce R. Russell. New York: Special Libraries Association, 1980. $9.50.

Society of American Archivists. Basic Manual Series, unnumbered series. $4.00 for members, $5.00 for nonmembers. (Most recent title is Hickerson, H. Thomas. *Archives and Manuscripts: An Introduction to Automated Access.* Chicago: SAA, 1981.)

Swartzburg, Susan. *Preserving Library Materials: A Manual.* Metuchen, NJ: Scarecrow, 1980. $12.50.

Young, Laura S. *Bookbinding and Conservation by Hand.* New York: R. R. Bowker, 1981. $35.

Audiovisual

Audio-Visual Equipment Directory 1982-83. 28th ed. Fairfax, VA: National Audio-Visual Association, 1982. $23.

Audiovisual Market Place, 1983: A Multimedia Guide, 13th ed. New York: R. R. Bowker, 1982. $39.95.

Educational Media Yearbook 1982, ed. by James W. Brown. Littleton, CO: Libraries Unlimited, 1982. $37.50.

Spirt, Diana L. *Library Media Manual.* New York: H. W. Wilson, 1979. $6.

Video and Cable Guidelines, ed. by Leslie C. Burk and R. Esteves. Chicago: American Library Association, Library and Information Technology Association, 1980. $9.75.

Video Involvement for Libraries, ed. by Susan Spaeth Cherry. Chicago: American Library Association, 1981. $6.

Automation, Information Retrieval, and Information Technology

Annual Review of Information Science and Technology. Washington, DC: American Society for Information Science. White Plains, NY: Knowledge Industry. Vols. 3-5 (1968-1970) and Vols. 7-11 (1972-1976). $35 per vol. Vols. 12-17 (1977-1982). $42.50 per vol.

Boss, Richard, W. *The Library Manager's Guide to Automation.* White Plains, NY: Knowledge Industry, 1979. $29.50.

Clinic on Library Applications of Data Processing. University of Illinois Proceedings. Champaign, IL: University of Illinois, Grad. School of Lib. Science, Publications Office, 1963-1981. 1968-74/$7 per vol. 1975-76/$8 per vol. 1977-79/$9 per vol. 1980-81/$10 per vol.

Corbin, John. *Developing Computer and Network Based Library Systems.* Phoenix, AZ: Oryx Press, 1981. $30.

Fedida, Sam, and Malik, Rex. *The Viewdata Revolution.* New York: Wiley, 1980. $38.95.

Fosdick, Howard. *Computer Basics for Librarians and Information Specialists.* Arlington, VA: Information Resources, 1981. $17.50.

Grosch, Audrey N. *Minicomputers in Libraries 1981-82*. White Plains, NY: Knowledge Industry, 1981. $34.50.

Hildreth, Charles R. *Online Public Access Catalogs: The User Interface*. Dublin, OH: OCLC, 1982. $18.

International On-Line Information Meeting. 1st-5th (1977-1981). Oxford: Learned Information. $30.

Lancaster, F. Wilfrid. *Libraries and Librarians in an Age of Electronics*. Arlington, VA: Information Resources Press, 1982. $22.50.

Library Technology Reports. Chicago: American Library Association, 1965- . $135 per year. Recent issues have been on such topics as Movable Compact Shelving, On-line Acquisitions Systems for Libraries, and CRT terminals.

Professional Librarian's Reader in Library Automation and Technology, ed. by Susan K. Martin. New York: Knowledge Industry, 1980. $24.50.

Rorvig, Mark E. *Microcomputers and Libraries: A Guide to Technology, Products and Applications*. White Plains, NY: Knowledge Industry, 1981. $27.50.

Sigel, Efrem et al. *The Future of Videotext*. White Plains, NY: Knowledge Industry, 1982. $32.95.

―――. *Video Discs: The Technology, the Applications, and the Future*. White Plains, NY: Knowledge Industry, 1981. $29.95.

Wood, R. Kent, and Woolley, R. D. *An Overview of Videodisc Technology and Some Potential Applications in the Library, Information and Instructional Sciences*. Syracuse, NY: ERIC, 1980. $7. (1R-50.)

Woolfe, Roger. *Videotex: The New Television-Telephone Information Services*. London: Heyden, 1980. $16.

Buildings, Furniture, Equipment

Lushington, Nolan, and Mills, Willis N., Jr. *Libraries Designed for Users*. Hamden, CT: Shoe String, 1980. $24.50.

Mallery, Mary S., and DeVore, Ralph E. *A Sign System for Libraries*. Chicago: American Library Association, 1982. $5.

Mason, Ellsworth. *Mason on Library Buildings*. Metuchen, NJ: Scarecrow, 1980. $29.50.

Pierce, William S. *Furnishing the Library Interior*. New York: Marcel Dekker, 1980. $46.25.

Reynolds, Linda, and Barrett, S. *Library Signs and Guiding: A Practical Guide to Design and Production*. Hamden, CT: Shoe String, 1981. $32.50.

Children's and Young Adults' Services and Materials

The Arbuthnot Lectures, 1970-79. Association for Library Service to Children. Chicago: American Library Association, 1980. $12.50.

Bernstein, Joanne E. *Books to Help Children Cope with Separation and Loss*. 2nd ed. New York: R. R. Bowker, 1983. $27.50 (tent.).

Celebrating Children's Books: Essays on Children's Literature in Honor of Zena Sutherland, ed. by Betsy Hearne and Marilyn Kaye. New York: Lothrop, Lee & Shepard Books, 1981. $12.95.

Children and Books. 6th ed. Glenview, IL: Scott, Foresman, 1981. $21.95.

Children and Libraries: Patterns of Access to Materials and Services in School and Public Libraries, ed. by Zena Sutherland. Chicago: Univ. of Chicago Press, 1981. $10.

Children's Media Market Place, 1982. 2nd ed. New York: Neal-Schuman, 1982. $24.95.

Cianciolo, Patricia A. *Picture Books for Children*. 2nd ed. Chicago: American Library Association, 1981. $12.50.

Donelson, Kenneth L., and Nilsen, Alleen Pace. *Literature for Today's Young Adults*. Glenview, IL: Scott, Foresman, 1980. $13.95.

Dreyer, Sharon. *The Bookfinder: A Guide to Children's Literature about the Needs and Problems of Youth*. Circle Pines, MN: American Guidance Service, 1977-1981. 2 vols. $69.50.

Egoff, Sheila. *Thursday's Child: Trends and Patterns in Contemporary Children's Literature*. Chicago: American Library Association, 1981. $15.

Haviland, Virginia, ed. *Children's Literature: A Guide to Reference Sources*. Washington, DC: Library of Congress, 1966. $12. 1st supplement, 1972. $12. 2nd supplement, 1978. $12. 3rd supplement, 1980. $11.

Lima, Carolyn W. *A to Zoo: Subject Access to Children's Picture Books*. New York: R. R. Bowker, 1982. $29.95.

Lukens, Rebecca J. *A Critical Handbook of Children's Literature*. 2nd ed. Glenview, IL: Scott, Foresman, 1982. $8.95.

Rohrlick, Paula. *Exploring the Arts: Films and Video Programs for Young Viewers*. New York: R. R. Bowker, 1982. $24.95 (pap.).

Vandergrift, Kay E. *Child and Story: The Literary Connection*. New York: Neal-Schuman, 1981. $15.95.

Young Adult Literature: Background and Criticism, ed. by Millicent Lenz and Ramona Mahood. Chicago: American Library Association, 1980. $30.

Circulation

Bahr, Alice H. *Book Theft and Library Security Systems, 1981-82*. 2nd ed. White Plains, NY: Knowledge Industry, 1980. $24.50.

Hubbard, William J. *Stack Management: A Practical Guide to Shelving and Maintaining Library Collections*. Chicago: American Library Association, 1981. $7.

Matthews, Joseph R. *Comparative Information for Automated Circulation Systems: Turnkey and Other Systems*. 2nd ed. Grass Valley, CA: J. Matthews and Associates, Inc., 1981. $20.

Collection Development

Alternative Materials in Libraries, ed. by James P. Danky and E. Shore. Metuchen, NJ: Scarecrow, 1982. $16.

American Library Association. Collection Development Committee. *Guidelines for Collection Development*, ed. by David L. Perkins. Chicago: American Library Association, 1979. $5.

Collection Development and Acquisitions, 1970-1980: An Annotated, Critical Bibliography, comp. by Irene P. Godden, K. W. Fachan, and P. A. Smith. Metuchen, NJ: Scarecrow, 1982. $11.

Collection Development in Libraries: A Treatise, ed. by Robert D. Stueart and George B. Miller, Jr. Greenwich, CT: JAI Press, 1980. 2 vols. $60.

Gardner, Richard K. *Library Collections: Their Origin, Selection and Development*. New York: McGraw-Hill, 1981. $15.95.

Katz, William A. *Collection Development: The Selection of Materials for Libraries*. New York: Holt, 1980. $18.95.

Shaping Library Collections for the 1980's, ed. by Peter Spyers-Duran and Thomas Mann, Jr. Phoenix, AZ: Oryx Press, 1981. $24.50.

Weeding Library Collections—II, ed. by Stanley J. Slote. 2nd, rev. ed. Littleton, CO: Libraries Unlimited, 1982. $21.50.

College and University Libraries

Academic Librarianship: Yesterday, Today and Tomorrow, ed. by Robert Stueart. New York: Neal-Schuman, 1982. $24.95.

Association of Research Libraries. *Minutes*. Washington, DC: ARL, 1932- 98th meeting entitled Resources for Research Libraries, 1981. $12.50.

Bender, David R. *Learning Resources and the Instructional Program in Community Colleges*. Hamden, CT: Shoe String, 1980. $19.50.

Cline, Hugh, and Sinnott, L. T. *Building Library Collections: Policies and Practices in Academic Libraries*. Toronto: Lexington Books, 1981. $16.95.

College Librarianship, ed. by William Miller and D. S. Rockwood. Metuchen, NJ: Scarecrow, 1981. $15.

Johnson, Edward R. *Organization Development for Academic Libraries*. Westport, CT: Greenwood Press, 1980. $22.50.

McClure, Charles R. *Information for Academic Library Decision Making*. Westport, CT: Greenwood Press, 1980. $23.95.

Priorities for Academic Libraries, ed. by Thomas J. Galvin and Beverly P. Lynch. San Francisco, CA: Jossey-Bass, 1982. $7.95.

SPEC Kits. Washington, DC: Association of Research Libraries. 1973- . Nos. 1- . $7.50 for members, $15 for nonmembers. (Recent kits have been on such topics as Approval Plans, Public Service Goals and Objectives, and Personnel Classification Systems.)

Shiflett, Orvin Lee. *Origins of American Academic Librarianship*. Norwood, NJ: Ablex, 1981. $22.50.

University Library History: An International Review, ed by. James Thompson. Hamden, CT: Shoe String, 1980. $35.

Comparative and International Librarianship

Amadi, Adolphe A. *African Libraries: Western Tradition and Colonial Brainwashing*. Metuchen, NJ: Scarecrow, 1981. $14.

Andersen, Axel, Friis-Hansen, J. B., and Kajberg, L. *Library and Information Services in the Soviet Union*. Copenhagen: Royal School of Librarianship, 1981. No price given.

Foskett, Douglas J. *Introduction to Comparative Librarianship*. Bangalore, India: Sarada Kangarathan Endowment for Library Science, 1979. $8.

Indian Librarianship, ed. by Ravindra N. Sharma. New Delhi: Kalyani Publishers, 1981. RS 80.

International Handbook of Contemporary Developments in Librarianship, ed. by Miles M. Jackson. Westport, CT: Greenwood Press, 1981. $65.

Maack, Mary Niles. *Libraries in Senegal: Continuity and Change in an Emerging Nation*. Chicago: American Library Association, 1981. $20.

Simsova, Sylva. *A Primer of Comparative Librarianship*. Hamden, CT: Shoe String, 1982. $14.50.

Copyright

Johnston, Donald. *Copyright Handbook*. 2nd ed. New York: R. R. Bowker, 1982. $27.50.

Miller, Jerome K. *Applying the New Copyright Law: A Guide for Education and Librarians*. Chicago: American Library Association, 1979. $11.

―――. *U.S. Copyright Documents: An Annotated Collection for Use by Educators and Librarians*. Littleton, CO: Libraries Unlimited, 1981. $25.

Education for Librarianship

Bramley, Gerald. *History of Library Education*. 2nd. ed. Hamden, CT: Shoe String, 1980. $13.50.

Coburn, Louis. *Classroom and Field: The Internship in American Library Education*. Flushing, NY: Queens College Press, 1981. $7.50.

Conant, Ralph Wendell. *The Conant Report: A Study of the Education of Librarians*. Cambridge, MA: MIT Press, 1980. $20.

Dale, Doris C. *Career Patterns of Women Librarians with Doctorates*. Urbana, IL: Univ. of Illinois, GSLS, 1980. $3. (Occasional Papers, no. 147.)

Debons, Anthony et al. *The Information Professional: Survey of an Emerging Field*. New York: Marcel Dekker, 1981. $35.

Extended Library Education Programs: Proceedings of a Conference . . . , ed. by Richard L. Darling and T. Belanger. New York: Columbia University School of Library Service, 1980. $6.

Financial Assistance for Library Education: Academic Year 1982-83. Chicago: American Library Association, 1981. 75¢.

Morehead, Joe. Theory and Practice in Library Education. Littleton, CO: Libraries Unlimited, 1980. $25.

What Else You Can Do with a Library Degree, ed. by Betty-Carol Sellen. Syracuse, NY: Gaylord, 1980. $14.75.

World Guide to Library Schools and Training Courses in Documentation. 2nd ed. Paris: Unesco, 1981. $50. (U.S. dist. by Shoe String, Hamden, CT.)

Information and Society

The Federal Role in the Federal System: The Dynamics of Growth. Federal Involvement in Libraries. Washington, DC: Advisory Commission on Intergovernmental relations, 1980. $2.50.

The Future of the Printed Word: The Impact and Implications of the New Communications Technology. Westport, CT: Greenwood Press, 1980. $25.

An Information Agenda for the 1980s: Proceedings of a Colloquium June 17-18, 1980, ed. by Carlton Rochell. Chicago: American Library Association, 1981. $7.50.

Information Industry Association. Membership Directory, 1981-82. Bethesda, MD: Information Industry Association, 1981. $21.

Information Industry Market Place, 1983. An International Directory of Information Products and Services. New York: R. R. Bowker, 1982. $39.95.

Strategies for Meeting the Information Needs of Society in the Year 2000, ed. by Martha Boaz. Littleton, CO: Libraries Unlimited, 1981. $22.50.

Warnken, Kelly. The Information Brokers: How to Start and Operate Your Own Fee-Based Service. New York: R. R. Bowker, 1981. $24.95.

Intellectual Freedom

Censorship, Libraries and the Law, ed. by Haig A. Bosmajian. New York: Neal-Schuman, 1982. $22.95.

de Grazia, Edward, and Newman, Roger K. Banned Films: Movies, Censors and the First Amendment. New York: R. R. Bowker, 1982. $24.95. pap. $14.95.

Obler, Eli M. Defending Intellectual Freedom: The Library and the Censor. Westport, CT: Greenwood Press, 1980. $22.95.

Library History

Dictionary of American Library Biography. Littleton, CO: Libraries Unlimited, 1978. $85.

Goodrum, Charles A., and Dalrumple, H. W. The Library of Congress. Boulder, CO: Westview, 1982. $25.

Hamlin, Arthur T. The University Library in the United States: Its Origins and Development. Philadelphia: University of Pennsylvania Press, 1981. $25.

Harris, Michael H., and Davis, Donald G., Jr. American Library History: A Bibliography. Austin, TX: University of Texas Press, 1978. $22.50.

Hilker, Helen-Anne. Ten First Street Southeast: Congress Builds a Library, 1886-1897. Washington, DC: Library of Congress, 1980. $5.50.

McCrimmon, Barbara. Power, Politics and Print: The Publication of the British Museum Catalogue, 1881-1900. Hamden, CT: Shoe String, 1981. $17.50.

Weibel, Kathleen, and Heim, Kathleen M. The Role of Women in Librarianship 1876-1976: The Entry, Advancement, and Struggle for Equalization in One Profession. Phoenix, AZ: Oryx Press, 1979. $27.50.

Microforms and Computer Output Microforms

Folcarelli, Ralph J., Tannenbaum, A. C., and Ferragamo, R. C. *The Microform Connection: A Basic Guide for Libraries.* New York: R. R. Bowker, 1982. $35.

Gabriel, Michael R. *The Microform Revolution in Libraries.* Greenwich, CT: JAI Press, 1980. $32.50.

Networks, Interlibrary Cooperation, and Resource Sharing

Jones, C. Lee. *Linking Bibliographic Data Bases: A Discussion of the Battelle Technical Report.* Arlington, VA: ERIC Document Reproduction Service, 1981. ED 195 274. $3.65 + postage. MF $.91.

Martin, Susan K. *Library Networks, 1981-82.* 4th ed. White Plains, NY: Knowledge Industry, 1980. $29.50.

Maruskin, Albert F. *OCLC: Its Governance, Function, Financing, and Technology.* New York: Marcel Dekker, 1980. $22.75.

Networks for Networkers: Critical Issues in Cooperative Library Development, ed. by Barbara Markuson and Blanche Woolls. New York: Neal-Schuman, 1980. $17.95.

Rouse, William, and Rouse, S. H. *Management of Library Networks: Policy Analyses, Implementation, and Control.* New York: Wiley, 1980. $32.95.

Smalley, Donald A. et al. *Technical Report on Linking the Bibliographic Utilities: Benefits and Costs.* Submitted to the Council on Library Resources, September 15, 1980. Columbus, OH: Battelle, 1980. $9.

Periodicals and Serials

Brown, Clara D. *Serials: Past, Present, Future.* 2nd rev. ed. Birmingham: Ebsco Industries Inc., 1980. $19.50.

Osborn, Andrew D. *Serial Publications: Their Place and Treatment in Libraries.* 3rd ed. Chicago: American Library Association, 1980. $20.

Serials Automation for Acquisitions and Inventory Control, ed. by William G. Potter and A. F. Sirkin. Chicago: American Library Association, 1981. $12.50.

The Serials Collection: Organization and Administration, ed. by Nancy Jean Melin. Ann Arbor, MI: Pierian, 1982, $16.95.

Serials Collection Development: Choices and Strategies, ed. by Sul H. Lee. Ann Arbor, MI: Pierian, 1981. $16.95.

Serials Management in an Automated Age. Annual Serial Conference. Vol. 1. Westport, CT: Meckler Publishing, 1982. $35.

Public Libraries

Fact Book of the American Public Library, comp. by Herbert Goldhor. Urbana, IL: University of Illinois, GSLIS, 1981. $3. (Occasional Papers, no. 150.)

Getz, Malcolm. *Public Libraries: An Economic View.* Baltimore, MD: Johns Hopkins, 1980. $15.

Jenkins, Harold R. *Management of a Public Library.* Greenwich, CT: JAI Press, 1980. $32.50.

Leerburger, Benedict A. *Marketing the Library.* White Plains, NY: Knowledge Industry, 1981. $24.50.

Local Public Library Administration, completely revised by Ellen Altman. 2nd ed. Chicago: American Library Association, 1980. $20.

Palmour, Vernon E. *Planning Process for Public Libraries.* Chicago: American Library Association, 1980. $12.

Public Librarianship: A Reader, ed. by Jane Robbins-Carter. Littleton, CO: Libraries Unlimited, 1982. $35.

Public Library Association. *Output Measures for Public Libraries: A Manual of Standardized Procedures,* by Douglas Zweizig and Eleanor Jo Rodger. Chicago: American Library Association, 1982. $8.

Role of the Humanities in the Public Library, ed. by R. Broadus. Chicago:

American Library Association, 1980. $20.

Wheeler and Goldhor's Practical Administration of Public Libraries, completely revised by Carlton Rochell. New York: Harper & Row, 1981. $27.50.

Reference Services, Online Searching, and Bibliographic Instruction

Beaubien, Ann K. et al. *Learning the Library: Concepts and Methods for Effective Bibliographic Instruction.* New York: R. R. Bowker, 1982. $35.

Breivik, Patricia Senn. *Planning the Library Instruction Program.* Chicago: American Library Association, 1982. $10.

Drake, Miriam A. *User Fees: A Practical Perspective.* Littleton, CO: Libraries Unlimited, 1981. $17.50.

Jahoda, Gerald. *Librarian and Reference Queries: A Systematic Approach.* New York: Academic Press, 1980. $12.

Library and Information Manager's Guide to Online Services, ed. by Ryan Hoover. White Plains, NY: Knowledge Industry, 1980. $29.50.

Library Orientation Series. 1–12; 1972–1981. Ann Arbor, MI: Pierian Press. 1, 5, 9 o.p.; 2–12 $14.95. Recent vols. have been on Reform and Renewal in Higher Education: Implementation for Library Administration; Library Instruction and Faculty Development; Directions for the Decade: Teaching Library Use Competence.

Meadow, Charles T., and Cockrane, P. A. *Basics of Online Searching.* New York: Wiley, 1981. $18.95.

Online Searching: An Introduction, ed. by W. M. Henry et al. Woburn, MA: Butterworths, 1980. $31.95.

Reference and Online Services Handbook: Guidelines, Policies and Procedures for Libraries, ed. by Bill Katz. New York: Neal-Schuman, 1982. $29.95.

Renford, Beverly. *Bibliographic Instruction: A Handbook.* New York: Neal-Schuman, 1980. $17.95.

Rice, James, Jr. *Teaching Library Use: A Guide for Library Instruction.* Westport, CT: Greenwood Press, 1981. $25.

Sheehy, Eugene, P. *Guide to Reference Books.* 9th ed. Chicago: American Library Association, 1976. $30. 1st supplement, 1980. $15.

Theories of Bibliographic Education: Designs for Teaching, ed. by Cerise Oberman and K. Strauch. New York: R. R. Bowker, 1982. $35.

Research

Busha, Charles H. *Research Methods in Librarianship: Techniques and Interpretation.* New York: Academic Press, 1980. $19.50.

Library Science Research Reader and Bibliographic Guide, ed. by Charles H. Busha. Littleton, CO: Libraries Unlimited, 1981. $23.50.

Martyn, John, and Lancaster, F. Wilfrid. *Investigative Methods in Library and Information Science: An Introduction.* Arlington, VA: Information Resources, 1981. $30.50.

School Libraries/Media Centers

American Association of School Librarians. *Evaluating the School Library Media Program: A Working Bibliography Prepared for the Building-Level Media Specialist.* Chicago: AASL, 1980. $1.

Baker, D. Philip, and Bender, D. R. *Library Media Programs and the Special Learner.* Hamden, CT: Shoe String, 1981. $19.50.

Billings, Rolland G., and Goldman, Errol. *Professional Negotiations for Media/ Library Professionals: District and School.* Washington, DC: Association for Educational Communication and Technology, 1980. $8.50.

Carroll, Frances. *Recent Advances in School Librarianship.* New York: Pergamon, 1981. $30.

Galvin, Thomas J. *Excellence in School Media Programs.* Chicago: American Library Association, 1980. $12.50.

Gillespie, John T., and Spirt, Diane L. *Administering the School Library Media Program.* New York: R. R. Bowker, 1983. $27.50 (tent.).

Hicks, Warren. *Managing the Building-level School Media Program.* Chicago: American Library Association, 1981. $4.50 (School Media Centers: Focus on Trends and Issues, no. 7)

The Library Media Specialist in Curriculum Development, ed. by Nevada Wallis Thomason. Metuchen, NJ: Scarecrow, 1981. $15.

Microcomputers in the Schools, ed. by James L. Thomas. Phoenix, AZ: Oryx Press, 1981. $25.

Nonprint in the Secondary Curriculum: Readings for Reference, ed. by James L. Thomas. Littleton, CO: Libraries Unlimited, 1982. $19.50.

Schmid, William T. *Media Center Management: A Practical Guide.* New York: Hastings House, 1980. $16.95.

Taggart, Dorothy. *Management and Administration of the School Library Media Program.* Hamden, CT: Shoe String, 1980. $17.50.

Taylor, Mary M. *School Library and Media Center Acquisitions: Policies and Procedures.* Phoenix, AZ: Oryx Press, 1981. $27.50.

Van Orden, Phyllis J. *The Collection Program in Elementary and Middle Schools: Concepts, Practices, and Information Sources.* Littleton, CO: Libraries Unlimited, 1982. $18.50.

Services for Special Groups

Bell, Lorna J. *The Large Print Book and Its User.* Phoenix, AZ: Oryx Press, 1980. $37.95.

Books for the Gifted Child, ed. by Barbara H. Baskin and Karen H. Harris. New York: R. R. Bowker, 1980. $17.95; $10.95 (pap.).

Clendening, Corinne P. and Davies, Ruth Ann. *Challenging the Gifted: Curriculum Enrichment and Acceleration Models.* New York: R. R. Bowker, 1983. $32.50 (tent.).

———. *Creating Programs for the Gifted: A Guide for Teachers, Librarians, and Students.* New York: R. R. Bowker, 1980. $24.95.

High/Low Handbook: Books, Materials and Services for the Teenage Problem Reader, ed. by Ellen V. LiBretto. New York: R. R. Bowker, 1981. $19.95.

Jail Library Service: A Guide for Librarians and Jail Administrators, ed. by Linda Bayley and others. Chicago: American Library Association, 1981. $16.

Jones, Edward V., III. *Reading Instruction for the Adult Illiterate.* Chicago: American Library Association, 1981. $12.50.

Library Services for the Handicapped Adult, ed. by James L. Thomas and Carol H. Thomas. Phoenix, AZ: Oryx Press, 1982. $18.50.

Marshall, Margaret Richardson. *Libraries and the Handicapped Child.* Lexington, MA: Lexington Books, 1981. $26.50.

Meeting the Needs of the Handicapped: A Resource for Teachers and Librarians, ed. by Carol H. Thomas and James L. Thomas. Phoenix, AZ: Oryx Press, 1980. $27.50.

Pearlman, Della. *No Choice: Library Services for the Mentally Handicapped.* Phoenix, AZ: Oryx Press, 1981. $17.25.

Turock, Betty J. *Serving the Older Adult: A Guide to Library Programs and Information Sources.* New York: R. R. Bowker, 1983. $29.95.

Using Bibliotherapy: A Guide to Theory and Technique, ed. by Rhea Joyce Rubin. Phoenix, AZ: Oryx Press, 1978. $17.95.

Velleman, Ruth A. *Serving Physically Disabled People: An Information Handbook for All Libraries.* New York: R. R. Bowker, 1979. $17.50.

Wright, Keith. *Library and Information Services for Handicapped Individuals.*

Littleton, CO: Libraries Unlimited, 1979. $19.50.

Special Libraries

Ahrensfeld, Janet L., Christianson, E. B., and King, D. E. *Special Libraries: A Guide for Management.* 2nd ed. New York: Special Libraries Association, 1981. $17.

Blunt, Adrian. *Law Librarianship.* Hamden, CT: Shoe String, 1980. $12.

Closurdo, Janette S. *Library Management.* vol. 1. New York: Special Libraries Association, 1980. $8.50.

Larsgaard, Mary. *Map Librarianship.* Littleton, CO: Libraries Unlimited, 1978. $18.50.

Picture Librarianship, ed. by Helen P. Harrison. Phoenix, AZ: Oryx Press, 1981. $37.50.

Report on Library Cooperation, 1982, ed. by Nancy L. Wareham, 4th ed. Chicago: Association of Specialized and Cooperative Library Agencies, 1982. $10.

Ristow, Walter W. *The Emergence of Maps in Libraries.* Hamden, CT: Shoe String, 1980. $27.50.

Special Librarianship: A New Reader. Metuchen, NJ: Scarecrow, 1980. $27.50.

Special Library Role in Networks: Proceedings of a Conference . . . New York: Special Libraries Association, 1980. $10.50.

Van Halm, Johan. *The Development of Special Libraries as an International Phenomenon.* New York: Special Libraries Association, 1978. $19.50.

State Libraries

The ASLA Report on Interlibrary Cooperation. Chicago: Association of State Library Agencies (ALA), 1980. $15.

The State Library Agencies: A Survey Project Report, 1981, comp. and ed. by Ann B. Walker. Chicago: Association of Specialized and Cooperative Library Agencies, 1981. $25.

Technical Services

Bernhardt, Frances Simonsen. *Introduction to Library Technical Services.* New York: H. W. Wilson, 1979. $15.

Technical Services: Acquisitions

Boss, Richard W. *Automating Library Acquisitions: Issues and Outlook.* White Plains, NY: Knowledge Industry, 1982. $27.50.

Technical Services: Cataloging and Classification

AACR2 Decisions and Rule Interpretations: A Consolidation of the Decisions and Rule Interpretations . . . made by the Library of Congress, the National Library of Canada, the British Library and the National Library of Australia. Ottawa: Canadian Library Association, 1981. $25.

American Library Association. Filing Committee. *ALA Filing Rules.* Chicago: American Library Association, 1980. $3.50.

Berman, Sanford. *Joy of Cataloging. Essays, Letters, Reviews and Other Explosions.* Phoenix, AZ: Oryx Press, 1981. $32.50.

The Card Catalog—Current Issues, Readings and Selected Bibliography, ed. by Cynthia C. Ryans. Metuchen, NJ: Scarecrow, 1981. $16.

Chan, Lois Mai. *Cataloging and Classification: An Introduction.* New York: McGraw-Hill, 1980. $18.95.

Clack, Doris Hargrett. *The Making of a Code: Issues Underlying AACR2.* Chicago: American Library Association, 1980. $15.

Closing the Catalog, ed. by Kaye Gapen. Phoenix, AZ: Oryx Press, 1980. $27.50.

Foster, Donald L. *Managing the Catalog Department.* 2nd ed. Metuchen, NJ: Scarecrow, 1982. $15.

Gorman, Michael. *Concise AACR2.* Chicago: American Library Association, 1981. $7.50.

Immroth's *Guide to the Library of Congress Classification*. 3rd ed. Littleton, CO: Libraries Unlimited, 1980. $27.50.

Lehnus, Donald J. *Book Numbers: History, Principles and Application*. Chicago: American Library Association, 1980. $7.50.

Malinconico, S. Michael, and Fasana, Paul. *The Future of the Catalog: The Library's Choices*. White Plains, NY: Knowledge Industry, 1979. $24.50.

Rather, John Carson. *Library of Congress Filing Rules*. Washington, DC: Library of Congress, 1980. $5.

Wellisch, Hans H. *Indexing and Abstracting: A Guide to International Sources*. Santa Barbara, CA: ABC-Clio, 1980. $32.50.

Wiederkehr, Robert R. V. *Alternatives for Future Library Catalogs: A Cost Model; Final Report of the Library Catalog Cost Model Project*. Rockville, MD: King Research for the Association of Research Libraries, 1980. $12.

Wynar, Bohdan, et al. *Introduction to Cataloging and Classification*. 6th ed. Metuchen, NJ: Libraries Unlimited, 1980. $30.

PERIODICALS

A new guide to over 200 library/information periodicals has been published:

Stevens, Norman D., and Stevens, Nora B. *Author's Guide to Journals in Library and Information Science*. New York: Haworth Press, 1982. $19.95.

The journals in the list that follows might normally be purchased as part of a continuing education program in a library or as subscriptions for individual librarians. Titles used primarily for selection have been excluded.

ALA Washington Newsletter
American Libraries
American Society for Information Science Journal
CABLIS (Current Awareness for Librarianship and Information Scientists)
Cataloging and Classification Quarterly
Collection Management
College and Research Libraries
Conservation Administration News
Drexel Library Quarterly
IFLA Journal
International Library Review
Journal of Academic Librarianship
Journal of Education for Librarianship
Journal of Library Administration
Journal of Library Automation
Journal of Library History, Philosophy, and Comparative Librarianship
Library Journal
Library of Congress Information Bulletin
Library Quarterly
Library Research
Library Resources and Technical Services
Library Trends
Newsletter on Intellectual Freedom
On Line
Online Review
Public Library Quarterly
RQ
RSR (Reference Services Review)
School Library Journal
School Media Quarterly
Serials Librarian
Serials Review
Special Libraries
Top of the News

BASIC PUBLICATIONS FOR THE PUBLISHER AND THE BOOK TRADE

Margaret M. Spier

Librarian, R. R. Bowker Company

BIBLIOGRAPHIES OF BOOKS ABOUT BOOKS AND THE BOOK TRADE

These six books contain extensive bibliographies.

Gottlieb, Robin. *Publishing Children's Books in America, 1919–1976: An Annotated Bibliography.* New York: Children's Book Council, 1978. $15.

Lee, Marshall. *Bookmaking: The Illustrated Guide to Design/Production/Editing.* New York: R. R. Bowker, 1980. $32.50. Bibliography is divided into four parts: Part 1 covers books and includes a general bibliography as well as extensive coverage of books on all technical aspects of bookmaking; Part 2 lists periodicals; Part 3 lists films, filmstrips, etc.; Part 4 lists other sources.

Lehmann-Haupt, Hellmut, Wroth, Lawrence C., and Silver, Rollo. *The Book in America.* 2nd ed. New York: R. R. Bowker, 1951, o.p. Bibliography covers cultural history, bibliography, printing and bookmaking, book illustration, bookselling, and publishing.

Melcher, Daniel, and Larrick, Nancy. *Printing and Promotion Handbook.* 3rd ed. New York: McGraw-Hill, 1966. $24.95. Bibliography covers general reference, advertising, artwork, book publishing, color, copyright, copywriting, direct mail, displays, editing and proofreading, layout and design, lettering, magazine publishing, newspaper publishing, packaging, paper, photography, printing, publicity, radio and TV, shipping, typography, and visual aids.

The Reader's Adviser: A Layman's Guide to Literature. 12th ed. 3 vols. New York: R. R. Bowker, 1974–1977. $75 (3-vol. set); $29.95 (ea. vol.). Vol. 1. *The Best in American and British Fiction, Poetry, Essays, Literary Biography, Bibliography, and Reference,* edited by Sarah L. Prakken. 1974. Chapters "Books about Books" and "Bibliography" cover history of publishing and bookselling, practice of publishing, bookmaking, rare book collecting, trade and specialized bibliographies, book selection tools, best books, etc. Vol. 2. *The Best in American and British Drama and World Literature in English Translation,* edited by F. J. Sypher. 1977. Vol. 3. *The Best in the Reference Literature of the World,* edited by Jack A. Clarke. 1977.

Tanselle, G. Thomas. *Guide to the Study of United States Imprints.* 2 vols. Cambridge, Mass.: Belknap Press of Harvard University Press, 1971. $65. Includes sections on general studies of American printing and publishing as well as studies of individual printers and publishers.

TRADE BIBLIOGRAPHIES

American Book Publishing Record Cumulative, 1876–1949: An American National Bibliography. 15 vols. New York: R. R. Bowker, 1980. $1,975.

American Book Publishing Record Cumulative, 1950–1977: An American National Bibliography. 15 vols. New York: R. R. Bowker, 1979. $1,975.

American Book Publishing Record Five-Year Cumulatives. New York: R. R. Bowker, 1960–1964 Cumulative. 5 vols. $150. 1965–1969 Cumulative. 5 vols. $150. 1970–1974 Cumulative. 4 vols.

$150. 1975–1979 Cumulative. 5 vols. $175. Annual vols.: 1978, $53; 1979, $53; 1980, $59; 1981, $68; 1982, $76.50.

Book Publishers Directory: An Information Service Covering New and Established, Private and Special Interest, Avant-Garde and Alternative, Organization and Association, Government and Institution Presses, edited by Elizabeth Geiser and Annie Brewer. Detroit: Gale, 1981. $180. Supplement, 1980. $80.

Books in Print. 6 vols. New York: R. R. Bowker, ann. $149.50.

Books in Print Supplement. New York: R. R. Bowker, ann. $75.50.

Books in Series 1876–1949. 3 vols. New York: R. R. Bowker, 1982. $150.

Books in Series in the United States. 3rd ed. New York: R. R. Bowker, 1980. $175.

British Books in Print: The Reference Catalog of Current Literature. New York: R. R. Bowker, 1982. $150. (plus duty where applicable).

Canadian Books in Print, edited by Marian Butler. Toronto: University of Toronto Press, ann. $50.

Canadian Books in Print: Subject Index, edited by Marian Butler. Toronto: University of Toronto Press, ann. $50.

Cumulative Book Index. New York: H. W. Wilson. Monthly with bound semiannual and larger cumulations. Service basis.

El-Hi Textbooks in Print. New York: R. R. Bowker, ann. $49.50.

Forthcoming Books. New York: R. R. Bowker, $67.50 a year. $15 single copy. Bimonthly supplement to *Books in Print.*

Large Type Books in Print. New York: R. R. Bowker, 1982. $35.

Paperbound Books in Print. New York: R. R. Bowker. 3 vols. $55.

Publishers' Trade List Annual. New York: R. R. Bowker, ann. 5 vols. $85.

Robert, Reginald, and Burgess, M. R. *Cumulative Paperback Index, 1939–59.* Detroit: Gale, 1973. $38.

Small Press Record of Books in Print, edited by Len Fulton. Paradise, Calif.: Dustbooks, 1982. $23.95.

Subject Guide to Books in Print. 3 vols. New York: R. R. Bowker, ann. $99.50.

Subject Guide to Forthcoming Books. New York: R. R. Bowker. $39.50 a year. $95 in combination with *Forthcoming Books.*

Turner, Mary C., ed. *Libros en Venta.* Supplement, 1978. New York: R. R. Bowker, 1980. $42.50.

⸻. Supplement 1979/1980; 1981; Supplement 1981; 1982. San Juan, P.R.: Melcher Ediciones. $50 each. Distributed by Gale Research. A Spanish-language "Books in Print/Subject Guide."

BOOK PUBLISHING

Education and Practice

Association of American University Presses. *One Book—Five Ways: The Publishing Procedures of Five University Presses.* Los Altos, Calif.: William Kaufmann, 1978. $19.95. pap. $11.95.

Bailey, Herbert S., Jr. *The Art and Science of Book Publishing.* Austin: University of Texas Press, 1980. pap. $7.95.

Bodian, Nat G. *Book Marketing Handbook: Tips and Techniques for the Sale and Promotion of Scientific, Technical, Professional, and Scholarly Books and Journals.* New York: R. R. Bowker, 1980. $45.

⸻. *Book Marketing Handbook, Volume Two: 1,000 More Tips and Techniques for the Sale and Promotion of Scientific, Technical, Professional, and Scholarly Books and Journals.* New York: R. R. Bowker, 1983. $49.50.

Bohne, Harald, and Van Ierssel, Harry. *Publishing: The Creative Business.* Toronto: Association of Canadian Publishers, 1973. pap. $7.50.

Brownstone, David M. *The Dictionary of Publishing.* New York: Van Nostrand Reinhold, 1982. $18.95.

Crutchley, Brooke. *To Be a Printer.* New York: Cambridge University Press, 1980. $19.95.

Dessauer, John P. *Book Publishing: What It Is, What It Does.* New York: R. R. Bowker, 1981. $23.95. pap. $13.95.

Glaister, Geoffrey. *Glaister's Glossary of the Book: Terms Used in Paper-Making, Printing, Bookbinding, and Publishing.* 2nd ed., completely rev. Berkeley: University of California Press, 1979. $75.

Grannis, Chandler B. *Getting into Book Publishing.* New York: R. R. Bowker, 1979. Pamphlet, one free; in bulk 75¢ each.

Grannis, Chandler B., ed. *What Happens in Book Publishing.* 2nd ed. New York: Columbia University Press, 1967. $27.50.

Greenfeld, Howard. *Books: From Writer to Reader.* New York: Crown, 1976. $8.95. pap. $4.95.

Hackett, Alice Payne, and Burke, James Henry. *Eighty Years of Best Sellers, 1895-1975.* New York: R. R. Bowker, 1977. $18.95.

Peters, Jean, ed. *Bookman's Glossary.* 6th ed. New York: R. R. Bowker, 1983. $21.95.

Smith, Datus C., Jr. *A Guide to Book Publishing.* New York: R. R. Bowker, 1966. $14.25.

To Be a Publisher: A Handbook on Some Principles and Programs in Publishing Education. Prepared by the Association of American Publishers Education for Publishing Program. New York: Association of American Publishers, 1979. $10.

Analysis, Statistics, Surveys

ANSI Standards Committee Z-39. *American National Standard for Compiling Book Publishing Statistics, Z-39.8.* New York: American National Standards Institute. 1978. $4.

Altbach, Philip G., and Rathgeber, Eva-Marie. *Publishing in the Third World: Trend Report and Bibliography.* New York: Praeger, 1980. $27.95.

Arthur Andersen & Co. *Book Distribution in the U.S.: Issues and Perceptions.* New York: Book Industry Study Group, 1982. $60.

Association of American Publishers 1981 Industry Statistics. New York: Association of American Publishers, 1982. Nonmemb. $250.

Association of American Publishers. *1982 Survey of Compensation and Personnel Practices in the Publishing Industry.* Prepared and Conducted by Sibson & Company, Inc. New York: Association of American Publishers, 1982. Participant $45. Non-part. $90.

Benjamin, Curtis G. *A Candid Critique of Book Publishing.* New York: R. R. Bowker, 1977. $16.50.

Book Industry Study Group, Inc. *Special Reports.* New York: Book Industry Study Group. Vol. 1, No. 1. Lambert, Douglas M. *Physical Distribution: A Profit Opportunity for Printers, Publishers, and Their Customers.* August, 1982. $25. Distributed to nonmembers by R. R. Bowker.

Bowker Annual of Library and Book Trade Information. New York: R. R. Bowker, ann. $55.

Bowker Lectures on Book Publishing. New York: R. R. Bowker, 1957. o.p.

Bowker Lectures on Book Publishing, New Series. New York: R. R. Bowker. 10 vols. 1973-1982. $3 each. No. 1. Pilpel, Harriet F. *Obscenity and the Constitution.* 1973. No. 2. Ringer, Barbara A. *The Demonology of Copyright.* 1974. No. 3. Henne, Frances E. *The Library World and the Publishing of Children's Books.* 1975. No. 4. Vaughan, Samuel S. *Medium Rare: A Look at the Book and Its People.* 1976. No. 5. Bailey,

Herbert S. *The Traditional Book in the Electronic Age.* 1977. No. 6. Mayer, Peter. *The Spirit of the Enterprise.* 1978. No. 7. De Gennaro, Richard. *Research Libraries Enter the Information Age.* 1979. No. 8. Dystel, Oscar. *Mass Market Publishing: More Observations, Speculations and Provocations.* 1980. No. 9. Giroux, Robert. *The Education of an Editor.* 1981. No. 10. Martin, Lowell. *The Public Library: Middle Age Crisis or Old Age?* 1982.

The Business of Publishing: A PW Anthology. New York: R. R. Bowker, 1976. $18.50.

Cheney, O. H. *Economic Survey of the Book Industry, 1930-31.* The Cheney Report. Reprinted. New York: R. R. Bowker, 1960. o.p.

Compaine, Benjamin. *The Book Industry in Transition: An Economic Analysis of Book Distribution and Marketing.* White Plains, N.Y.: Knowledge Industry Publications, 1978. $24.95.

Coser, Lewis A., Kadushin, Charles, and Powell, Walter W. *Books: The Culture and Commerce of Publishing.* New York: Basic Books, 1982. $19.

Dessauer, John P. *Book Industry Trends, 1982.* New York: Book Industry Study Group, 1982. $150. *Book Industry Trends, 1979, Book Industry Trends, 1980,* and *Book Industry Trends, 1981* still available from the Book Industry Study Group.

———. *Trends Update* (monthly). Expands upon statistics in the annual compilation and explains forecasting techniques. $240 a year. $25 single copy. Both publications distributed to nonmembers by R. R. Bowker.

Fitzgerald, Frances. *America Revised: History Schoolbooks in the Twentieth Century.* Boston: Little, Brown, 1979. $11.95.

Gedin, Per. *Literature in the Marketplace.* Translated by George Bisset. Woodstock, N.Y.: Overlook, 1977. $12.95.

Machlup, Fritz, and Leeson, Kenneth W. *Information through the Printed Word: The Dissemination of Scholarly, Scientific, and Intellectual Knowledge.* 4 vols. Vol. 1. *Book Publishing.* Vol. 2. *Journals.* Vol. 3. *Libraries.* Vol. 4. *Books, Journals, and Bibliographic Services.* New York: Praeger, 1978. Vol. 1, $33.95; Vol. 2, $35.95; Vol. 3, $31.95; Vol. 4, $34.95.

Shatzkin, Leonard. *In Cold Type: Overcoming the Book Crisis.* Boston: Houghton Mifflin, 1982. $17.95.

Smith, Roger H., ed. *The American Reading Public: A Symposium.* New York: R. R. Bowker, 1964. o.p.

Whiteside, Thomas. *The Blockbuster Complex.* Middletown, Conn.: Wesleyan University Press. Distributed by Columbia University Press, 1981. $12.95.

Yankelovich, Skelly, and White, Inc. *The 1978 Consumer Research Study on Reading and Book Purchasing.* New York: Book Industry Study Group, 1978. Apply for price scale.

History

Bonn, Thomas L. *Under Cover: An Illustrated History of American Mass-Market Paperbacks.* New York: Penguin Books, 1982. $12.95.

Briggs, Asa, ed. *Essays in the History of Publishing: In Celebration of the 250th Anniversary of the House of Longman, 1724-1974.* New York: Longman, 1974. $15.

Cerf, Bennett. *At Random: The Reminiscences of Bennett Cerf.* New York: Random House, 1977. $12.95.

Crider, Allen Billy. *Mass Market Publishing in America.* Boston: G. K. Hall, 1982. $35.

Haydn, Hiram. *Words & Faces.* New York: Harcourt Brace Jovanovich, 1974. $8.95.

Hodges, Sheila. *Golancz: The Story of a Publishing House*. London: Golancz, 1978. £7.50.

Kurian, George. *Directory of American Book Publishing: From Founding Fathers to Today's Conglomerates*. New York: Monarch, 1975. $25.

Lehmann-Haupt, Hellmut. *The Book in America*. 2nd ed. New York: R. R. Bowker, 1951. o.p.

Madison, Charles. *Jewish Publishing in America*. New York: Hebrew Publishing Co., 1976. $11.95.

Morpurgo, J. E. *Allen Lane: King Penguin*. New York: Methuen, 1979. $25.

Mott, Frank Luther. *Golden Multitudes: The Story of Best Sellers in the United States (1662-1945)*. Reprint ed. New York: R. R. Bowker, 1960. o.p.

Norrie, Ian. *Mumby's Publishing and Bookselling in the Twentieth Century*. 6th ed. London: Bell & Hyman Ltd., 1982. Distributed by R. R. Bowker. $35.

O'Brien, Geoffrey. *Hardboiled America: The Lurid Years of Paperbacks*. New York: Van Nostrand Reinhold, 1981. $16.95.

Regnery, Henry. *Memoirs of a Dissident Publisher*. New York: Harcourt Brace Jovanovich, 1979. $12.95.

Schick, Frank L. *The Paperbound Book in America: The History of Paperbacks and Their European Background*. New York: R. R. Bowker, 1958. o.p.

Schreuders, Piet. *Paperbacks U.S.A.: A Graphic History, 1939-1959*. Translated from the Dutch by Josh Pachter. San Diego: Blue Dolphin Enterprises, 1981. $10.95.

Stern, Madeleine B. *Books and Book People in 19th-Century America*. New York: R. R. Bowker, 1978. $28.50.

———. *Publishers for Mass Entertainment in Nineteenth Century America*. Boston: G. K. Hall, 1980. $28.

Tebbel, John. *A History of Book Publishing in the United States*. 4 vols. Vol. 1. *The Creation of an Industry, 1630-1865*. Vol. 2. *The Expansion of an Industry, 1865-1919*. Vol. 3. *The Golden Age between Two Wars, 1920-1940*. Vol. 4. *The Great Change, 1940-1980*. New York: R. R. Bowker, 1972, 1975, 1978, 1981. $37.50 each.

SCHOLARLY BOOKS

Gaskell, Philip. *From Writer to Reader: Studies in Editorial Method*. New York: Oxford University Press, 1978. $29.50.

Harman, Eleanor, and Montagnes, Ian, eds. *The Thesis and the Book*. Toronto: University of Toronto Press, 1976. $10. pap. $6.

Horne, David. *Boards and Buckram: Writings from "Scholarly Books in America," 1962-1969*. Hanover, N.H.: University Press of New England, 1980. Distributed by American University Press Services, Inc., New York. $10.

Nemeyer, Carol A. *Scholarly Reprint Publishing in the United States*. New York: R. R. Bowker, 1972. o.p.

Scholarly Communication: The Report of the National Enquiry. Baltimore: Johns Hopkins University Press, 1979. $14. pap. $4.95.

EDITORS, AGENTS, AUTHORS

Applebaum, Judith, and Evans, Nancy. *How to Get Happily Published*. New York: Harper & Row, 1978. $11.95.

Berg, A. Scott. *Max Perkins: Editor of Genius*. New York: Pocket Books. pap. $2.95.

Commins, Dorothy Berliner. *What Is an Editor? Saxe Commins at Work*. Chicago: University of Chicago Press, 1978. $5.95.

Henderson, Bill, ed. *The Art of Literary Publishing: Editors on Their Craft*. Yonkers, N.Y.: Pushcart, 1980. $15.

Madison, Charles. *Irving to Irving: Author-Publisher Relations: 1800–1974.* New York: R. R. Bowker, 1974. $15.95.

Reynolds, Paul R. *The Middle Man: The Adventures of a Literary Agent.* New York: Morrow, 1972. $6.95.

Unseld, Siegfried. *The Author and His Publisher.* Chicago: University of Chicago Press, 1980. $12.50.

Watson, Graham. *Book Society: Reminiscences of a Literary Agent.* New York: Atheneum, 1980. $10.95.

BOOK DESIGN AND PRODUCTION

Grannis, Chandler B. *The Heritage of the Graphic Arts.* New York: R. R. Bowker, 1972. $24.95.

Lee, Marshall. *Bookmaking: The Illustrated Guide to Design and Production.* 2nd ed. New York: R. R. Bowker, 1980. $32.50.

Mintz, Patricia Barnes. *Dictionary of Graphic Arts Terms: A Communication Tool for People Who Buy Type & Printing.* New York: Van Nostrand Reinhold, 1981. $17.95.

Rice, Stanley. *Book Design: Systematic Aspects.* New York: R. R. Bowker, 1978. $18.95.

———. *Book Design: Text Format Models.* New York: R. R. Bowker, 1978. $18.95.

Roberts, Matt T., and Etherington, Don. *Bookbinding and the Conservation of Books: A Dictionary of Descriptive Terminology.* Washington, D.C.: Library of Congress. For sale by the Supt. of Docs., U.S. G.P.O., 1982. $27.

Strauss, Victor. *The Printing Industry: An Introduction to Its Many Branches, Processes and Products.* New York: R. R. Bowker, 1967. $32.50.

White, Jan. *Editing by Design.* 2nd ed. New York: R. R. Bowker, 1982. pap. $24.95.

Wilson, Adrian. *The Design of Books.* Layton, Utah: Peregrine Smith, 1974. pap. $9.95.

BOOKSELLING

Anderson, Charles B., ed. *Bookselling in America and the World: A Souvenir Book Celebrating the 75th Anniversary of the American Booksellers Association.* New York: Times Books, 1975. $9.50.

Bliven, Bruce. *Book Traveller.* New York: Dodd, Mead, 1975. $4.95. o.p.

Manual on Bookselling: How to Open and Run Your Own Bookstore. 3rd ed. New York: American Booksellers Association, 1980. Distributed by Harmony Books. $15.95. pap. $8.95.

White, Ken. *Bookstore Planning and Design.* New York: McGraw-Hill, 1982. $39.50.

CENSORSHIP

de Grazia, Edward, comp. *Censorship Landmarks.* New York: R. R. Bowker, 1969. $29.50.

Ernst, Morris L., and Schwartz, Alan U. *Censorship.* New York: Macmillan, 1964. $6.95.

Haight, Anne Lyon. *Banned Books.* 4th ed., updated and enlarged by Chandler B. Grannis. New York: R. R. Bowker, 1978. $14.95.

Hentoff, Nat. *The First Freedom: The Tumultuous History of Free Speech in America.* New York: Delacorte, 1980. $11.95. pap. $2.50.

Jenkinson, Edward B. *Censors in the Classroom: The Mind Benders.* Carbondale, Ill.: Southern Illinois University Press, 1979. $13.95.

Moon, Eric, ed. *Book Selection and Censorship in the Sixties.* New York: R. R. Bowker, 1969. $18.95.

COPYRIGHT

Bogsch, Arpad. *The Law of Copyright under the Universal Convention.* 3rd ed. New York: R. R. Bowker, 1969. o.p.

Cambridge Research Institute. *Omnibus Copyright Revision: Comparative Anal-*

ysis of the Issues. Washington, D.C.: American Society for Information Science, 1973. $48.

Copyright Revision Act of 1976: Law, Explanation, Committee Reports. Chicago: Commerce Clearing House, 1976. $12.50.

Johnston, Donald F. *Copyright Handbook.* 2nd ed. New York: R. R. Bowker, 1982. $27.50.

McDonald, Dennis D., and Bush, Colleen G. *Libraries, Publishers and Photocopying: Final Report of Surveys Conducted for the United States Copyright Office.* Rockville, Md: King Research, Inc., 1982. $25.

Wittenberg, Philip. *Protection of Literary Property.* Boston: The Writer, Inc., 1978. $12.95.

BOOK TRADE DIRECTORIES AND YEARBOOKS

American and Canadian

American Book Trade Directory, 1982. 28th ed. New York: R. R. Bowker, ann. $89.95.

Chernofsky, Jacob L., ed. *AB Bookman's Yearbook.* 2 vols. Clifton, N.J.: AB Bookman's Weekly, ann. $10; free to subscribers to *AB Bookman's Weekly.*

Congrat-Butlar, Stefan, ed. *Translation & Translators: An International Directory and Guide.* New York: R. R. Bowker, 1979. $35.

Kim, Ung Chon. *Policies of Publishers.* Metuchen, N.J.: Scarecrow, 1982. pap. $15.

Literary Market Place, 1983, with Names & Numbers. New York: R. R. Bowker, ann. $37.50. The business directory of American book publishing.

Publishers, Distributors, & Wholesalers of the United States: A Directory. New York: R. R. Bowker, 1982. pap. $28.50.

U.S. Book Publishing Yearbook and Directory, 1981/82. White Plains, N.Y.: Knowledge Industry Publications, 1982. $65.

Foreign and International

International ISBN Publishers Directory. New York: R. R. Bowker, 1981. $95.

International Literary Market Place 1982-83. New York: R. R. Bowker, 1982. $52.50.

Publishers' International Directory. 2 vols. New York: K. G. Saur. Distributed by Gale Research, 1982. $175.

Taubert, Sigfred, ed. *The Book Trade of the World.* Vol. I. *Europe and International Sections.* Vol. II. *U.S.A., Canada, Central and South America, Australia and New Zealand.* Vol. III. *Africa, Asia.* New York: R. R. Bowker. Vol. I, 1972, $70; Vol. II, 1976, $70; Vol. III, 1980, $70.

UNESCO Statistical Yearbook, 1981. New York: Unipub, 1982. $104.

Who Distributes What and Where: An International Directory of Publishers, Imprints, Agents, and Distributors. New York: R. R. Bowker, 1981. $44.

Newspapers and Periodicals

Directory of Newspapers and Periodicals. Philadelphia: N. W. Ayer, ann. $79.

Editor and Publisher International Year Book. New York: Editor and Publisher, ann. $40.

Irregular Serials and Annuals: An International Directory. New York: R. R. Bowker, 1982. $85.

Magazine Industry Market Place: The Directory of American Periodical Publishing. New York: R. R. Bowker, 1982. $39.95.

New Serial Titles 1950-1970. New York: R. R. Bowker, 1973. 4 vols. o.p. Available on microfilm, $100; or xerographic reprint, $250.

New Serial Titles 1950-1970, Subject Guide. New York: R. R. Bowker, 1975. 2 vols. $138.50.

Sources of Serials: An International Publisher and Corporate Author Directory to Ulrich's and Irregular Serials. New York: R. R. Bowker, 1981. $65.

Ulrich's International Periodicals Directory. 21st ed. 2 vols. New York: R. R. Bowker, 1982. $89.50.

Working Press of the Nation: Newspapers, Magazines, Radio and TV, and Internal Publications. Chicago: National Research Bureau, ann. 5 vols. $241.

EDITING

Barzun, Jacques. *Simple and Direct: A Rhetoric for Writers.* New York: Harper & Row, 1976. $11.95.

Bernstein, Theodore. *The Careful Writer.* New York: Atheneum, 1965. $14.95. pap. $9.95.

The Chicago Manual of Style. 13th rev. ed. Chicago: University of Chicago Press, 1982. $25.

Fowler, H. W. *Dictionary of Modern English Usage.* 2nd rev. ed. New York: Oxford University Press, 1965. $15.

Jordan, Lewis. *The New York Times Manual of Style and Usage.* New York: Times Books, 1976. $10.

Skillin, Marjorie E., and Gay, Robert M. *Words into Type.* Rev. ed. Englewood Cliffs, N.J.: Prentice-Hall, 1974. $22.95.

Strunk, William, Jr., and White, E. B. *Elements of Style.* 3rd ed. New York: Macmillan, 1978. $6.95. pap. $2.95.

Zinsser, William. *On Writing Well: An Informal Guide to Writing Nonfiction.* 2nd ed. New York: Harper & Row, 1980. $11.50.

PERIODICALS

AB Bookman's Weekly (weekly including yearbook). Clifton, N.J.: AB Bookman's Weekly. $50.

American Book Publishing Record (monthly). New York: R. R. Bowker. $38.50.

The American Bookseller (monthly). New York: American Booksellers Association. $12.

BP Report: On the Business of Book Publishing (weekly). White Plains, N.Y.: Knowledge Industry Publications. $215.

Publishers Weekly. New York: R. R. Bowker. $59.

Scholarly Publishing: A Journal for Authors & Publishers (quarterly). Toronto: University of Toronto Press. $25.

Weekly Record. New York: R. R. Bowker. $32.50. A weekly listing of current American book publications, providing complete cataloging information.

For a list of periodicals reviewing books, see *Literary Market Place.*

DISTINGUISHED BOOKS

LITERARY PRIZES, 1982

ASCAP-Deems Taylor Awards. *Offered by:* American Society of Composers, Authors, and Publishers. *Winners:* Norm Cohen for *Long Steel Rail* (Univ. of Illinois); Arthur Cohn for *Recorded Classical Music* (Schirmer Books); David King Dunaway for *How Can I Keep from Singing: Pete Seeger* (McGraw-Hill); Joseph Kerman for *The Masses and Motets of William Byrd* (Univ. of California); Robert Palmer for *Deep Blues* (Viking); Harvey Rachlin for *The Encyclopedia of the Music Business* (Harper); Steven Stucky for *Lutoslawski and His Music* (Cambridge Univ.); and Virgil Thomson for *A Virgil Thomson Reader* (Houghton Mifflin).

Academy of American Poets Fellowship Award. For distinguished poetic achievement. *Winners:* John Ashbery and John Frederick Nims.

Jane Addams Children's Book Award. For a book promoting the cause of peace, social justice, and world community. *Offered by:* Women's International League for Peace and Freedom and the Jane Addams Peace Association. *Winner:* Athena V. Lord for *A Spirit to Ride the Whirlwind* (Macmillan).

American Academy and Institute of Arts and Letters Award for Distinguished Service to the Arts. *Winner:* Alfred A. Knopf.

American Academy and Institute of Arts and Letters Awards in Literature. *Winners:* David Bradley, Jr., Frederick Buechner, MacDonald Harris, Daryl Hine, Josephine Jacobsen, Donald Keene, Berton Roueché, and Robert Stone.

American Academy in Rome Fellowship in Creative Writing. *Offered by:* American Academy and Institute of Arts and Letters. *Winner:* Mark Helprin.

American Book Awards. *Winners:* (national medal for literature) John Cheever; (autobiography/biography—hardcover) David McCullough for *Mornings on Horseback* (Simon & Schuster); (autobiography/biography—paperback) Ronald Steel for *Walter Lippmann and the American Century* (Vintage/Random House); (fiction—hardcover) John Updike for *Rabbit Is Rich* (Knopf); (fiction—paperback) William Maxwell for *So Long, See You Tomorrow* (Ballantine); (first novel) Robb Forman Dew for *Dale Loves Sophie to Death* (Farrar, Straus); (general nonfiction—hardcover) Tracy Kidder for *The Soul of a New Machine* (Atlantic/Little, Brown); (general nonfiction—paperback) Victor S. Navasky for *Naming Names* (Penguin); (history—hardcover) Peter John Powell for *People of the Sacred Mountain: A History of the Northern Cheyenne Chiefs and Warrior Societies* (Harper); (history—paperback) Robert Wohl for *The Generation of 1914* (Harvard Univ.); (poetry) William Bronk for *Life Supports* (North Point Press); (science—hardcover) Donald C. Johanson and Maitland A. Edey for *Lucy: The Beginnings of Humankind* (Simon & Schuster); (science—paperback) Fred Alan Wolf for *Taking the Quantum Leap: The New Physics for Nonscientists* (Harper); (translation) Robert Lyons Danly for *In the Shade of Spring Leaves* (Yale Univ.) and Ian

Hideo Levy for *The Ten Thousand Leaves* (Princeton Univ.).

American Book Awards—Children's Books. *Winners:* (fiction—hardcover) Lloyd Alexander for *Westmark* (Dutton); (fiction—paperback) Ouida Sebestyen for *Words by Heart* (Bantam); (nonfiction) Susan Bonners for *A Penguin Year* (Delacorte); (picture books—hardcover) Maurice Sendak for *Outside Over There* (Harper); (picture books—paperback) Peter Spier for *Noah's Ark* (Zephyr Books/Doubleday).

American Printing History Association Award. For a distinguished contribution to the study of the history of publishing and printing. *Winner:* John W. Tebbel for *A History of Book Publishing in the United States* (Bowker).

American-Scandinavian Foundation/PEN Translation Prizes. For previously unpublished translations of poetry and fiction by Scandinavian writers born in the last century. *Winners:* (fiction) Kjersti Danielson Board for *The Plough and the Sword* by Theodor Kallifatides; (poetry) Susanna C. Nied for *alfabet* by Inger Christensen.

Hans Christian Andersen Medals. For the entire body of work of one author and one illustrator. *Offered by:* International Board on Books for Young People. *Winners:* Lygia Bojunga Nunes (Brazil) and Zbigniew Rychlicki (Poland).

Joseph L. Andrews Bibliographical Award. For a significant contribution to legal bibliographical literature. *Offered by:* American Association of Law Libraries. *Winners:* Carol Boast and Lynn Foster for *Subject Compilations of State Laws: Research Guide and Annotated Bibliography* and Kathryn Swanson for *Affirmative Action & Preferential Admissions in Higher Education: An Annotated Bibliography*.

Anisfield-Wolf Awards. For contributions to the improvement of racial or ethnic understanding. *Offered by:* Cleveland Foundation. *Winners:* Peter John Powell for *People of the Sacred Mountain: A History of the Northern Cheyenne Chiefs and Warrior Societies* (Harper) and Geoffrey G. Field for *Evangelist of Race: The Germanic Vision of Houston Stewart Chamberlain* (Columbia Univ.).

Associated Writing Programs Awards. For book-length manuscripts to be published by university presses. *Winners:* (poetry) Alice Fulton for "Dance Script with Electric Ballerina" and Jonathan Holden for "Leverage" (publishers to be announced); (short fiction) Alvin Greenberg for *Delta Q* (Univ. of Missouri); (novel) John Solensten for *Good Thunder* (SUNY Press).

Association of Jewish Libraries Book Awards. For outstanding contributions in the field of Jewish literature for children. *Winners:* (children's book) Barbara Cohen for *Yussel's Prayer* (Lothrop, Lee & Shepard); (older children's book) Kathryn Lasky for *The Night Journey* (Frederick Warne); (body of work) Barbara Cohen.

Association of Logos Bookstores Book Awards. For excellence in religious publishing. *Winners:* (best creative book) Morris West for *The Clowns of God* (Morrow); (best inspirational book) Tom Sine for *The Mustard Seed Conspiracy* (Word Books); (best scholarly book) *The New Bible Dictionary*, rev. ed. (Tyndale House); (best children's book) Elspeth Campbell Murphy for *David and I Talked with God* (David C. Cook); (most significant author) Frederick Buechner (Harper); (most significant new publisher) Crossroad/Continuum; (publisher with best overall content) Inter-Varsity Press.

Australian Children's Book Awards. For literary merit, but with attention to the quality and design of the book as whole. *Winners:* (book of the year) Colin Thiele for *The Valley Between* (Rigby); (picture book of the year) Jan Ormerod for *Sunshine* (Kestrel); (medal for junior readers) Christobel Mattingley for *Rum-*

mage, illustrated by Patricia Mullins (Angus & Robertson).

Bancroft Prizes—$4,000 each. For books of exceptional merit and distinction in American history, American diplomacy, and the international relations of the United States. *Offered by:* Columbia University. *Winners:* Edward Countryman for *A People in Revolution: The American Revolution and Political Society in New York, 1760-1790* (Johns Hopkins Univ.) and Mary P. Ryan for *Cradle of the Middle Class: The Family in Oneida County, New York, 1780-1865* (Cambridge Univ.).

Banta Award. For literary achievement by a Wisconsin author. *Offered by:* Wisconsin Library Association. *Winner:* Chad Walsh for *Hang Me Up My Begging Bowl* (Swallow Press).

Alice Hunt Bartlett Award (Great Britain). *Offered by:* Poetry Society. *Winners:* Thomas McCarthy for *The Sorrow Garden* (Anvil Press) and Carol Rumens for *Unplayed Music* (Secker & Warburg).

Mildred L. Batchelder Award. For an American publisher of a children's book originally published in a foreign language in a foreign country and subsequently published in English in the United States. *Winner:* Bradbury Press for *The Battle Horse* by Harry Kullman.

Beefeater Club Prize for Literature. For works of true literary merit, having significance for both England and the United States. *Winner:* Pierre Berton for *The Invasion of Canada, 1812-1813* (Little, Brown) and *Flames Across the Border: The Canadian-American Tragedy, 1813-1814* (Little, Brown).

Before Columbus Foundation American Book Awards. For literary achievement by people of various ethnic backgrounds. *Winners:* Russell Banks for *The Book of Jamaica* (Houghton); Lorna Dee Cervantes for *Emplumada* (Univ. of Pittsburgh); Frank Chin for *Chickencoop Chinaman* and *Year of the Dragon* (Univ. of Washington); Tato Laviera for *Enclave* (Arte Publico Press/Revista Chicano Riquena); E. L. Mayo for *Collected Poems* (New Letters/Swallow Press); Duane Niatum for *Songs for the Harvester of Dreams* (Univ. of Washington); Hilton Obenzinger for *This Passover or Next I Will Never Be in Jerusalem* (Momo's Press); Leroy Quintana for *Sangre* (Prima Agua Press); Jerome Rothenberg for *Pre-Faces and Other Writing* (New Directions); Ronald Tanaka for *Shino Suite* (Greenfield Review); Joyce Carol Thomas for *Marked by Fire* (Avon); Al Young for *Bodies and Soul* (Creative Arts). *Special Anthology Award:* Him Mark Lai, Genny Lim, Judy Yung, eds., *Island: Poetry and History of Chinese Immigrants on Angel Island, 1910-1949* (HOC DOI Project). *Special Lifetime Achievement Award:* Chester Himes.

Curtis G. Benjamin Award for Creative Publishing. *Winner:* Ian Ballantine.

Bennett Award. For a writer who has not received full recognition, or a writer at a critical stage of creative development. *Offered by:* Hudson Review. *Winner:* Seamus Heaney.

Gerard and Ella Berman Award. For a book of Jewish history. *Offered by:* Jewish Book Council of the National Jewish Welfare Board. *Winner:* David Ruderman for *The World of a Renaissance Jew* (Hebrew Union College).

Irma Simonton Black Award. For unified excellence of story line, language and illustration in a published work for young children. *Offered by:* Bank Street College of Education. *Winner:* Ann Cameron for *The Stories Julian Tells*, illus. by Ann Strugnell (Pantheon).

James Tait Black Memorial Prizes (Great Britain). For the best biography and the best novel of the year. *Offered by:* University of Edinburgh. *Winners:* (biography) Victoria Glendinning for *Edith Sitwell: Unicorn Among Lions* (Weidenfeld and Nicolson); (novel) Salman Rushdie for *Midnight's Children* (Jonathan Cape) and Paul Theroux for *The Mosquito Coast* (Hamish Hamilton).

Bologna Children's Book Fair Prizes (Italy). *Offered by:* Bologna Trade Fair Promotion Agency. *Winners:* (younger children) Les Secrets de l'Image Series (Gallimard); (young adults) Peter Dickinson and Michael Foreman for *City of Gold and Other Stories from the Old Testament* (Gollancz and Pantheon); (budding critics) T. Nakamura for *The Pixies' Invitation* (Kaisei-sha, Japan).

Booker McConnell Prize (Great Britain). For a full-length novel in English by a citizen of Britain or the British Commonwealth, Republic of Ireland or South Africa. *Offered by:* National Book League. *Winner:* Thomas Keneally for *Schindler's Ark* (Hodder & Stoughton).

Books in Canada Award (Canada). For literary achievement by a first novelist. *Winner:* Joy Kogawa for *Obasan* (Lester & Orpen Dennys).

Boston Globe–Horn Book Awards. For excellence in text and illustration. *Winners:* (fiction) Ruth Park for *Playing Beatie Bow* (Atheneum); (nonfiction) Aranka Siegal for *Upon the Head of the Goat: A Childhood in Hungary, 1939–1944* (Farrar, Straus); (illustration) Alice and Martin Provensen for *A Visit to William Blake's Inn: Poems for Innocent and Experienced Travelers*, by Nancy Willard (Harcourt).

Brandeis University Creative Arts Award in Fiction. *Winner:* C. Vann Woodward.

John Nicholas Brown Prize. *Offered by:* Mediaeval Academy of America. *Winner:* John J. Contreni for *The Cathedral School of Laon from 850 to 930: Its Manuscripts and Masters* (Arbeo-Gesellschaft).

John Burroughs Medal. *Winner:* Peter Matthiessen for *Sand Rivers* (Viking).

Witter Bynner Foundation Prize for Poetry. *Offered by:* American Academy and Institute of Arts and Letters. *Winner:* William Heyen.

Caldecott Medal. For the artist of the most distinguished picture book. *Offered by:* R. R. Bowker Company. *Winner:* Chris Van Allsburg for *Jumanji* (Houghton).

John W. Campbell Award. For an author whose first professional story was published in the preceding two years. *Offered by:* World Science Fiction Convention. *Winner:* Alexis Gilliland.

John W. Campbell Memorial Award. For an outstanding science fiction novel. *Offered by:* Science Fiction Research Association. *Winner:* Russell Hoban for *Riddley Walker* (Summit/Washington Square Press).

Canada Council Children's Literature Prizes. For an outstanding author and illustrator. *Winners:* (English-language book) Monica Hughes for *The Guardian of Isis* (Hamish Hamilton); Heather Woodall, illus., for *Ytek and the Arctic Orchid* (Douglas & McIntyre); (French-language book) Suzanne Martel for *Nos Amis Robots* (Editions Heritage) and Joanne Ouellet, illus., for *Les Papinachois* (Hurtubise HMH).

Canada Council Translation Prizes. For the best translation in English and in French. *Winners:* (French into English) Ray Ellenwood for *The Entrails* by Claude Gauvreau (Coach House Press); (English into French) Ivan Steenhout for *The Biography of John A. MacDonald: The Young Politician*, Vol. 1, and *The Old Chieftain*, Vol. 2, by Donald Creighton (Les Editions de l'Homme).

Canadian Association of Children's Librarians Book of the Year. *Winner:* Janet Lunn for *The Root Cellar* (Lester & Orpen Dennys).

Canadian Authors Association Literary Awards. For literary excellence without sacrificing popular appeal. *Winners:* (novel) Joy Kogawa for *Obasan* (Lester & Orpen Dennys); (nonfiction) Claude Bissell for *The Young Vincent Massey* (Univ. of Toronto); (poetry) Gary Geddes for *The Acid Test* (Turnstone

Press); (drama) Allan Stratton for *Rexy!* (Playwrights Canada).

Melville Cane Award. For an outstanding book of poems and a book on poetry or a poet. *Offered by:* Poetry Society of America. *Winner:* Gerald Stern for *The Red Coal* (Houghton).

Carey-Thomas Awards. For a distinguished project of book publishing. *Offered by:* R. R. Bowker Company. *Winner:* University of Chicago Press for *The Lisle Letters*, edited by Muriel St. Clare Byrne. *Honor Citations:* North Point Press and Vintage Books. *Special Citations:* Random House for the new translation of Marcel Proust's *Remembrance of Things Past* and Shorewood Fine Art Books for *The Small Paintings of the Masters.*

Carnegie Medal (Great Britain). For an outstanding book for children. *Offered by:* British Library Association. *Winner:* Robert Westall for *The Scarecrows* (Chatto & Windus).

Children's Book Guild Award. For a total body of work of nonfiction. *Winner:* Tana Hoban.

Cholmondeley Award (Great Britain). For contributions to poetry. *Offered by:* Society of Authors. *Winners:* Basil Bunting; Herbert Lomas; and William Scammell.

Christopher Book Awards. For books that affirm the highest values of the human spirit. *Winners:* (adult books) Mark Ya. Asbel for *Refusenik: Trapped in the Soviet Union* (Houghton Mifflin); John Bierman for *Righteous Gentile: The Story of Raoul Wallenberg* (Viking); Eugenia Ginzburg for *Within the Whirlwind* (Helen and Kurt Wolff/ Harcourt); Barry Neil Kaufman for *A Miracle to Believe In* (Doubleday); Karen Burton Mains for *The Fragile Curtain* (David C. Cook); Joanna L. Stratton for *Pioneer Women: Voices from the Kansas Frontier* (Simon & Schuster); Donald Woods for *Asking for Trouble: The Autobiography of a Banned Journalist* (Atheneum); (children's books) Caroline Feller Bauer for *My Mom Travels a Lot*, illus. by Nancy Winslow Parker (Warne); Barbara Shook Hazen for *Even if I Did Something Awful*, illus. by Nancy Kincade (Atheneum); Malcolm MacCloud for *A Gift of Mirrorvax* (Atheneum); John Rowe Townsend for *The Islanders* (Lippincott).

Frank and Ethel Cohen Award. For a book of Jewish thought. *Offered by:* Jewish Book Council. *Winner:* Robert Alter for *The Art of Biblical Narrative* (Basic Books).

Carr P. Collins Award. For an outstanding book of nonfiction. *Offered by:* Texas Institute of Letters. *Winner:* Phillip Lopate for *Bachelorhood: Tales of the Metropolis* (Little, Brown).

Columbia University Translation Awards. For excellence in translation. *Winners:* Melvin Elberger for poems by the Yiddish author Jacob Glatstein; Raphael Rudnik for poems by the Dutch author Martinus Nijhoff.

Common Wealth Award. For distinguished service in literature. *Winner:* Wright Morris.

Commonwealth Poetry Prize (Great Britain). For a first published book of poetry in English by an author from a Commonwealth country other than Great Britain. *Offered by:* Commonwealth Institute and the National Book League. *Winner:* Peter Goldsworthy for *Readings from Ecclesiastes* (Angus & Robertson—Australia).

Thomas Cook Travel Book Awards (Great Britain). For the best travel book and the best guide book. *Offered by:* National Book League. *Winner:* Tim Severin for *The Sindbad Voyage* (Hutchinson) and *India: A Travel Survival Kit* (Lonely Planet).

Alice Fay Di Castagnola Award. *Offered by:* Poetry Society of America. *Winner:* Robert Peters for "Hawker of Morwenstone: Eccentric Cornish Vicar" (ms.).

Dutton First Novel Award. *Winner:* Albert Haley for *Exotic* (Dutton).

Ralph Waldo Emerson Award. *Offered by:* Phi Beta Kappa. *Winner:* Robert Nozick for *Philosophical Explanations* (Belknap/Harvard Univ.).

Kurt Maschler Emil Award. For a work of the imagination in which text and illustration are of excellence. *Winners:* Angela Carter and Michael Foreman for *The Sleeping Beauty and Other Favourite Fairy Tales* (Gollancz).

English-Speaking Union Awards: For books of outstanding merit sent to English-speaking countries abroad to serve as interpreters of American life and culture. *Winners:* (adult books) Sandra Brant and Elissa Cullman for *Small Folk: A Celebration of Childhood in America* (Dutton); William S. Cohen for *Roll Call: One Year in the United States Senate* (Simon & Schuster); Hope Cooke for *Time Change: An Autobiography* (Simon & Schuster); William O. Douglas for *The Court Years: 1939–1975* (Random); Ellen Carol DuBois for *Elizabeth Cady Stanton/Susan B. Anthony: Correspondence, Writings, Speeches* (Schocken Books); David McCullough for *Mornings on Horseback* (Simon & Schuster); Linda O. McMurry for *George Washington Carver: Scientist and Symbol* (Oxford Univ. Press); Mary E. Mebane for *Mary: An Autobiography* (Viking); Marianne Moore for *The Complete Poems of Marianne Moore* (Viking); S. J. Perelman for *The Last Laugh* (Simon & Schuster); Milton Rugoff for *The Beechers: An American Family in the Nineteenth Century* (Harper); Harold C. Schonberg for *Facing the Music* (Summit Books); Suzanne Shelton for *Divine Dancer: A Biography of Ruth St. Denis* (Doubleday); Elizabeth Spencer for *The Stories of Elizabeth Spencer* (Doubleday); Studs Terkel for *American Dreams: Lost and Found* (Pantheon); Eudora Welty for *The Collected Stories of Eudora Welty* (Harcourt); Leslie Wheeler for *Loving Warriors: Selected Letters of Lucy Stone and Henry Blackwell* (Dial); Lynne Withey for *Dearest Friend: A Life of Abigail Adams* (Free Press); (children's books) Byrd Taylor and Peter Parnall for *Desert Voices* (Scribners); Carol Carrick for *Ben and the Porcupine* (Houghton Mifflin); Paul Goble for *The Gift of the Sacred Dog* (Bradbury Press); Carol Lerner for *Seasons of the Tallgrass Prairie* (William Morrow); David Macaulay for *Unbuilding* (Houghton Mifflin).

William and Janice Epstein Award. For a book of Jewish fiction. *Winner:* Mark Helprin for *Ellis Island and Other Stories* (Delacorte/Seymour Lawrence).

Christopher Ewart-Biggs Memorial Prize (Great Britain). For writing in English or French that contributes to peace and understanding. *Winner: Fortnight Magazine* (Irish Independent).

Geoffrey Faber Memorial Prize (Great Britain). *Offered by:* Faber & Faber Ltd. *Winners:* Paul Muldoon for *Why Brownlee Left* (Faber) and Tom Paulin for *The Strange Museum* (Faber).

Eleanor Farjeon Award (Great Britain). For distinguished services to children's books. *Offered by:* Children's Book Circle. *Winners:* Nancy and Aidan Chambers.

Dorothy Canfield Fisher Children's Book Award. For a children's book by a distinguished Vermont author selected by Vermont school children. *Offered by:* Vermont Dept. of Libraries and Vermont Congress of Parents and Teachers. *Winner:* Francine Pascal for *The Hand-Me-Down Kid* (Viking).

William Frank Memorial Award. To promote an appreciation of Jewish children's literature. *Offered by:* Jewish Book Council. *Winner:* Kathryn Lasky for *The Night Journey* (Warne).

George Freedley Memorial Award. *Offered by:* Theatre Library Association. *Winner:* Margaret Brenman-Gibson for *Clifford Odets: American Play-*

wright, the Years from 1906 to 1940 (Atheneum).

R. T. French Tastemaker Awards. For the outstanding cookbooks of the year. *Offered by:* R. T. French Company. *Winners:* (American) Bert Greene for *Honest American Fare* (Contemporary Books); (best cookbook and basic/general) James Beard for *The New James Beard* (Knopf); (international) Anne Willan and L'Ecole de Cuisine la Varenne for *French Regional Cooking* (Morrow); (natural foods and special diets) Madhur Jaffrey for *Madhur Jaffrey's World-of-the-East Vegetarian Cooking* (Knopf); (original softcover—international) Barbara Kafka for *American Food & California Wine* (Irene Chalmers Cookbooks); (original softcover—single subject) Mable Hoffman for *Appetizers* (HP Books); (original softcover—specialty) Lorna J. Sass for *Christmas Feasts from History* (Irene Chalmers Cookbooks); (single subject) Bernard Clayton, Jr. for *The Complete Book of Pastry—Sweet and Savory* (Simon & Schuster); (specialty) Judith Olney for *Judith Olney's Entertainments* (Barron's Educational Series); (time conscious) Pierre Franey for *The New York Times More 60-Minute Gourmet* (Times Books).

Friends of American Writers. *Winners:* Jane Smiley for *At Paradise Gate* (Simon & Schuster); Barry Holstun Lopez for *Winter Count* (Scribner's); Emily Crofford for *A Matter of Pride* (Carolrhoda Books); David Kherdian for *Beyond Two Rivers* (Greenwillow).

Friends of the Dallas Public Library Award. For a book that makes an important contribution to knowledge. *Winner:* John Ettling for *The Germ of Laziness* (Harvard Univ.).

Garden State Children's Book Awards. For children's books with literary merit that are popular with readers. *Offered by:* New Jersey Library Association. *Winners:* (easy-to-read) Wilson Gage for *Mrs. Gaddy and the Ghost*, illus. by Marylin Hafner (Greenwillow); (younger fiction) Beverly Cleary for *Ramona and Her Mother*, illus. by Alan Tiegreen (Morrow); (younger nonfiction) Aliki for *Mummies Made in Egypt* (Harper).

Christian Gauss Award. For an outstanding book in the field of literary scholarship or criticism. *Offered by:* Phi Beta Kappa. *Winner:* Lawrence Lipking for *The Life of the Poet: Beginning and Ending Poetic Careers* (Univ. of Chicago Press).

Georgia Children's Book Awards. *Offered by:* Univ. of Georgia College of Education. *Winners:* (children's book) Willo Davis Roberts for *Don't Hurt Laurie!* (Atheneum); (children's picture book) Steven Kellogg for *Pinkerton, Behave!* (Dial).

Leon L. Gildesgame Award. For excellence in visual arts. *Winners:* Janet Blatter and Sybil Milton for *Art of the Holocaust* (Rutledge/Layla Productions).

Tony Godwin Award. For an American or British editor (in alternate years) to spend six weeks working at a publishing house in the other's country. *Offered by:* Harcourt Brace Jovanovich. *Winner:* Ileene Smith (Summit Books).

Golden Kite Awards. *See* Society of Children's Book Writers.

Golden Spur Awards. *See* Western Writers of America.

Governor General's Literary Awards. To honor literary excellence. *Offered by:* Canada Council. *Winners—English-language works:* (fiction) Mavis Gallant for *Home Truths: Selected Canadian Stories* (Macmillan-Gage); (poetry) F. R. Scott for *The Collected Poems of F. R. Scott* (McClelland and Stewart); (drama) Sharon Pollock for *Blood Relations* (NeWest Press); (nonfiction) George Calef for *Caribou and the Barren-lands* (Canadian Arctic Resources Committee/Firefly Books). *French-language works:* (fiction) Denys Chabot for *La Province Lunaire* (Hurtubise HMH); (poetry) Michel Beaulieu for

Visages (Éditions du Noroît); (drama) Marie Laberge for *C'etait avant la Guerre a l'Anse à Gilles* (VLB Editeur); (nonfiction) Madeleine Oellette-Michalska for *L'Échappée des Discours de L'Oeil* (Nouvelle Optique).

Great Lakes Colleges Association Awards. For literary merit in a first book of fiction and a first book of poetry. *Winners:* (fiction) Annabel Thomas for The *Phototropic Woman* (Univ. of Iowa); (poetry) Jared Carter for *Work, for the Night Is Coming* (Macmillan).

Kate Greenaway Medal (Great Britain). For distinguished illustration of a book for children. *Offered by:* British Library Association. *Winner:* Charles Keeping for *The Highwayman* (Oxford Univ.).

Eric Gregory Trust Awards (Great Britain). For poets under the age of 30. *Offered by:* Society of Authors. *Winners:* Steve Ellis; Jeremy Reed; Alison Brackenbury; Neil Astley; Chris O'Neil; Joseph Britow; John Gibbens; James Lasdun.

Guardian Fiction Prize (Great Britain). For a novel of originality and promise by a British or Commonwealth writer. *Offered by:* Manchester *Guardian*. *Winners:* (adult) Glyn Hughes for *Where I Used to Play on the Green* (Gollancz); (children's book) Michelle Magorian for *Good Night, Mr. Tom* (Kestrel).

Garavi Gujarat Book Award (Great Britain). For a book of fiction or nonfiction that promotes racial harmony. *Offered by:* National Book League. *Winners:* Rukshana Smith for *Sumitra's Story* (Bodley Head) and Brian Thompson for *The Story of Prince Rama* (Kestrel).

Alice and Edith Hamilton Prize. For the best original, scholarly book-length manuscript on women. *Offered by:* University of Michigan Rackham School of Graduate Studies. *Winner:* Sally Price for *Co-wives and Calabashes: The Social and Artistic Life of Saramaka Women*.

John L. Haney Fund Prizes. For distinguished works of scholarship in the humanities and social sciences. *Offered by:* University of Pennsylvania Press. *Winners:* (humanities) A. C. Elias for *Swift at Moor Park* (Univ. of Pennsylvania); (social sciences) Henry Glassie for *Passing the Time in Ballymenone* (Univ. of Pennsylvania).

Haskins Medal. For a distinguished book in the field of medieval studies by a scholar in the United States or Canada. *Winner:* Richard Krautheimer for *Rome: Profile of a City, 312-1308* (Princeton Univ.).

R. R. Hawkins Award. For the most outstanding book of the year from the fields of science, medicine, technology, and business. *Offered by:* Association of American Publishers Professional and Scholarly Publishing Division. *Winner:* Architectural History Foundation, ed., for *Le Corbusier Sketchbooks, I & II* (MIT Press).

Hawthornden Prize (Great Britain). For a work of imaginative literature by an English writer under the age of 41. *Offered by:* Society of Authors. *Winner:* Douglas Dunn for *St. Kilda's Parliament* (Faber).

Florence Roberts Head Memorial Award. For an outstanding book about the Ohio scene. *Offered by:* Ohioana Library Association. *Winner:* Carrie Young for *Green Broke* (Dodd).

Hugh Hefner First Amendment Award. For a work that contributes to protect the First Amendment. *Offered by:* Playboy Foundation. *Winner:* Franklyn S. Haiman for *Speech and Law in a Free Society* (Univ. of Chicago).

Heinemann Award (Great Britain). For a genuine contribution to literature. *Offered by:* Royal Society of Literature. *Winners:* James Lees-Milne for *Harold Nicolson*, Vol. II. (Chatto & Windus) and Jonathan Raban for *Old Glory* (Collins).

Heinz Literature Prize. For an outstanding collection of unpublished short fiction. *Offered by:* University of Pittsburgh Press and the Howard Heinz Endowment. *Winner:* Robley Wilson, Jr. for *Dancing for Men* (Univ. of Pittsburgh).

Ernest Hemingway Foundation Award. For a work of first fiction by an American. *Winner:* Marilynne Robinson for *Housekeeping* (Farrar).

David Higham Prize (Great Britain). For a first novel or book of short stories. *Winner:* Glyn Hughes for *Where I Used to Play on the Green* (Gollancz).

Winifred Holtby Prize (Great Britain). For the best regional novel. *Winner:* Alan Judd for *A Breed of Heroes* (Hodder & Stoughton).

Clarence L. Holte Prize. For a contribution by a living writer to the public understanding of the cultural heritage of Africa and the African diaspora. *Winner:* Ivan Van Sertima for *They Came Before Columbus: The African Presence in Ancient America* (Random).

Amelia Frances Howard-Gibbon Award (Canada). For the illustrator of an outstanding book. *Offered by:* Canadian Library Association, Canadian Association of Children's Librarians. *Winner:* Heather Woodall for *Ytek and the Arctic Orchid* (Douglas & McIntyre).

Hugo Awards. *See* World Science Fiction Convention.

International Reading Association Children's Book Award. For a first or second book of fiction or nonfiction by an author of promise. *Winner:* Michelle Magorian for *Good Night, Mr. Tom* (Kestrel/ Penguin—UK/ Harper—US).

Iowa School of Letters Award. For short fiction. *Offered by:* Iowa Arts Council Writers Workshop and the University of Iowa Press. *Winner:* Dianne Benedict for *Shiny Objects* (Univ. of Iowa).

Joseph Henry Jackson Award. For an unpublished work of fiction, nonfictional prose, or poetry. *Offered by:* San Francisco Foundation. *Winner:* Lucille Lang Day for "Self-Portrait with Hand Microscope" (poetry).

Leon Jolson Award. For a book on the holocaust. *Winner:* Michael Marrus and Robert O. Paxton for *Vichy France and the Jews* (Basic Books).

Jesse Jones Award. For an outstanding book of fiction. *Winner:* Beverly Lowry for *Daddy's Girl* (Viking).

Juniper Prize. For an outstanding manuscript of original English poetry. *Offered by:* University of Massachusetts Press. *Winner:* Jane Flanders for *Students of Snow* (Univ. of Massachusetts).

Jane Heidinger Kafka Prize. For an outstanding work of fiction by an American woman. *Offered by:* University of Rochester English Department and Writers' Workshop. *Winner:* Mary Gordon for *The Company of Women* (Random).

Sue Kaufman Prize. For a first work of fiction. *Offered by:* American Academy and Institute of Arts and Letters. *Winner:* Ted Mooney for *Easy Travel to Other Planets* (Farrar).

Robert F. Kennedy Book Awards. For works that reflect Robert Kennedy's purposes. *Winners:* Janet Sharp Hermann for *The Pursuit of a Dream* (Oxford Univ.) and Peter S. Prescott for *The Child Savers: Juvenile Justice Observed* (Knopf).

Irvin Kerlan Award. For singular attainments in the creation of children's literature. *Offered by:* University of Minnesota Kerland Collection Committee. *Winner:* Jean Craighead George.

Robert Kirsch Award. For an outstanding body of work by an author from the West or featuring the West. *Offered by:* Los Angeles Times. *Winner:* Kenneth Millar (Ross Macdonald, pseud.).

Roger Klein Award. For an outstanding editor. *Offered by:* PEN American Center. *Winner:* Pat Strachan, exec. editor, Farrar, Straus & Giroux.

Janusz Korczak Award. For a book about the welfare and nurturing of children. *Offered by:* Anti-Defamation League of B'nai B'rith. *Winners:* Gilbert W. Kliman and Albert Rosenfeld for *Responsible Parenthood: The Child's Psyche Through the Six-Year Pregnancy* (Holt) and Aranka Siegal for *Upon the Head of the Goat: A Childhood in Hungary, 1939-1944* (Farrar).

Evelyn Sibley Lampman Award. For a significant contribution to children's literature in the Pacific Northwest area. *Offered by:* Oregon Library Association. *Winner:* Walt Morey.

Harold Morton Landon Prize. For a published translation of poetry from any language into English. *Winner:* Rika Lesser for *Guide to the Underworld* from the Swedish of Gunnar Ekelof (Univ. of Massachusetts).

Jules F. Landry Award. For the best manuscript in southern history, biography, or literature. *Offered by:* Louisiana State University Press. *Winner:* Drew Gilpin Faust for *James Henry Hammond and the Old South: A Design for Mastery* (Louisiana State Univ.).

Abraham Lincoln Literary Award. For an outstanding contribution to American literature. *Offered by:* Union League Club. *Winner:* John Updike.

Locus Awards. *Offered by:* Locus Publications. *Winners:* (anthology) Robert Lynn Asprin, ed., for *Shadows of Sanctuary* (Ace); (artist) Michael Whelan; (fantasy novel) Gene Wolfe for *The Claw of the Conciliator* (Simon & Schuster); (first novel) Somtow Sucharitkul for *Starship and Haiku* (Pocket Books/Timescape); (magazine) *The Magazine of Fantasy and Science Fiction*; (novelette) George R. R. Martin for *Guardians* (Analog); (novella) John Varley for *Blue Champagne* (New Voices 4); (publisher) Pocket Books/Timescape; (related nonfiction book) Stephen King for *Danse Macabre* (Everest); (science fiction novel) Julian May for *The Many-Colored Land* (Houghton Mifflin); (short story) John Varley for *The Pusher* (Fantasy and Science Fiction); (single-author collection) George R. R. Martin for *Sandkings* (Pocket Books/Timescape).

Los Angeles Times Book Awards. To honor literary excellence. *Winners:* (biography) Gay Wilson Allen for *Waldo Emerson: A Biography* (Viking); (current interest) Jonathan Schell for *The Fate of the Earth* (Knopf); (fiction) Robert Stone for *A Flag for Sunrise* (Knopf); (history) Jonathan Spence for *The Gate of Heavenly Peace: The Chinese and Their Revolution, 1895-1980* (Viking); (poetry) Allen Ginsberg for *Plutonium Ode* (City Lights).

James Russell Lowell Prize. For an outstanding literary or linguistic study, a critical edition, or a critical biography. *Offered by:* Modern Language Association of America. *Winner:* Gay Wilson Allen for *Waldo Emerson: A Biography* (Viking).

Howard R. Marraro Prize. For a distinguished scholarly study on any phase of Italian literature or comparative literature involving Italy. *Winners:* Rebecca J. West for *Eugenio Montale: Poet on the Edge* (Harvard Univ.) and John W. Boyer for *Political Radicalism in Late Imperial Vienna: Origins of the Christian Social Movement, 1848-1897* (Univ. of Chicago).

Lenore Marshall/Nation Prize. For an outstanding book of poems published in the United States. *Offered by:* The Nation and the New Hope Foundation. *Winner:* John Logan for *Only the Dreamer Can Change the Dream* (Ecco Press) and *The Bridge of Change: Poems, 1974-80* (BOA Editions).

Somerset Maugham Awards (Great Britain). For young British authors to gain experience in foreign countries. *Offered by:* Society of Authors. *Winners:* William Boyd for *A Good Man in Africa* (Hamish Hamilton) and Adam Mars-Jones for *Lantern Lecture* (Faber).

Frederic G. Melcher Award. For a work that makes a significant contribution to religious liberalism. *Offered by:* Unitarian Universalist Association. *Winner:* Anthony Dunbar for *Against the Grain* (Univ. of Virginia).

Kenneth W. Mildenberger Medal. For an outstanding research publication in the field of teaching foreign languages and literature. *Winner:* Stephen D. Krashen for *Second Language Acquisition and Second Language Learning* (Pergamon).

Mother Goose Award (Great Britain). For children's book illustration. *Offered by:* Books for Your Children Booksellers. *Winner:* Jan Ormerod for *Sunshine* (Kestrel).

Frank Luther Mott-Kappa Tau Alpha Award. For the best-researched book dealing with the media. *Offered by:* National Journalism Scholarship Society. *Winner:* Edwin R. Bayley for *Joe McCarthy and the Press* (Univ. of Wisconsin/Pantheon).

National Arts Club Gold Medal of Honor for Literature. *Winner:* Barabara W. Tuchman.

National Book Critics Circle Awards. *Winners:* (Criticism) Gore Vidal for *The Second American Revolution and Other Essays, 1976-1982* (Random); (Fiction) Stanley Elkin for *George Mills* (Dutton); (Nonfiction) Robert A. Caro for *The Path to Power, Vol. I: The Years of Lyndon Johnson* (Knopf); (Poetry) Katha Pollitt for *Anarctic Traveller* (Knopf); (Ivan Sandrof/Board Award) Leslie A. Marchand for *Byron's Letters and Journals* (Belknap Press).

National Council of Teachers of English Awards. *Winners:* (Alan Award) Robert Cormier for *The Chocolate War* (Pantheon/Dell); (poetry for children) John Ciardi; (scientific and technical writing—book) Devendra Sahal for *Patterns of Technological Innovations* (Addison-Wesley); (collection of essays) Dwight W. Stevenson, Renee R. Betz, David L. Carson, Donald H. Cunningham, and Thomas M. Sawyer, eds., for *Courses, Components, and Exercises in Technical Communication* (National Council of Teachers of English).

Nebula Awards. For outstanding works of science fiction. *Offered by:* Science Fiction Writers of America. *Winners:* (novel) Gene Wolfe for *The Claw of the Conciliator* (Timescape); (novella) Poul Anderson for *The Saturn Game* (Analog); (novelette) Michael Bishop for *The Quickening* (Universe 11); (short story) Lisa Tuttle for *The Bone Flute* (Fantasy and Science Fiction).

Nene Award. For an outstanding children's book selected by Hawaii's school children. *Offered by:* Hawaii Association of School Librarians and the Hawaii Library Association Children's and Youth Section. *Winner:* Judy Blume for *Superfudge* (Dutton).

Neustadt International Prize for Literature. For distinguished and continuing artistic achievement in poetry, drama, or fiction. *Offered by:* University of Oklahoma. *Winner:* Octavio Paz, Mexican poet and essayist.

New York Academy of Sciences Awards. For quality books about science for children. *Winners:* (younger category) Bernie Zubrowski for *Messing Around with Water Pumps and Siphons*, illus. by Steve Lindblom (Little, Brown); (older category) John C. McLoughlin for *The Tree of Animal Life* (Dodd).

New York Times Best Illustrated Children's Book Awards. *Winners:* Mitsumasa Anno for *Anno's Britain* (Philomel Books); Guy Billout for *Squid & Spider: A Look at the Animal Kingdom* (Prentice-Hall); Oscar de Mejo for *The Tiny Visitor* (Pantheon); Henrik Drescher for *The Strange Appearance of Howard Cranebill, Jr.* (Lothrop, Lee & Shepard); Fritz Eichenberg for *Rainbows Are Made: Poems by Carl Sandburg*, ed. by Lee Bennett Hopkins (Harcourt); John S. Goodall for *Paddy Goes Traveling* (Atheneum/McElderry); Jenny Thorne for *My Uncle* (Atheneum/McElderry); Chris Van Allsburg for *Ben's Dream* (Houghton); Gabrielle Vincent for *Smile, Ernest and Celestine* (Greenwillow); Lisbeth Zwerger for *The*

Gift of the Magi by O. Henry, lettering by Michael Neugebauer (Alphabet Press/Neugebauer).

John Newbery Medal. For the most distinguished contribution to literature for children. *Donor:* ALA Association for Library Service to Children. *Medal contributed by:* Daniel Melcher. *Winner:* Nancy Willard for *A Visit to William Blake's Inn: Poems for Innocent and Experienced Travelers* (Harcourt).

Nobel Prize for Literature. For the total literary output of a distinguished writer. *Offered by:* Swedish Academy. *Winner:* Gabriel García Márquez (Colombia).

Noma Award for Publishing in Africa (Japan). To encourage publication in Africa of books by African writers. *Winner:* Meshack Asare for *The Brassman's Secret* (Educational Press, Ghana).

Flannery O'Connor Short Fiction Awards. *Offered by:* University of Georgia Press. *Winners:* David Walton for *Evening Out* (Univ. of Georgia) and Allison Wilson for *From the Bottom Up* (Univ. of Georgia).

Ohioana Book Awards. To honor Ohio authors. *Offered by:* Ohioana Library Association. *Winners:* (fiction) Thomas Berger for *Reinhart's Women* (Delacorte/Seymour Lawrence); (biography) Milton Rugoff for *The Beechers: An American Family in the Nineteenth Century* (Harper); (history) Jacob Rader Marcus for *The American Jewish Woman* (KTAV/American Jewish Archive).

George Orwell Award. *Offered by:* National Council of Teachers of English. *Winners:* Stephen Hilgartner, Richard C. Bell, and Rory O'Connor for *Nukespeak: Nuclear Language, Visions and Mindset* (Sierra Club).

Pegasus Prize for Literature. For an important foreign work from a country whose literature is rarely translated into English. *Offered by:* Mobil Corporation. *Winner: Rituals* by Cees Nooteboom, translated from the Dutch by Adrienne Dixon (published in Amsterdam by Uitgeverij de Arbeiderspers; English translation to be published in the U.S. by Louisiana State Univ. Press).

PEN American Center and PEN South PEN/Faulkner Award. For outstanding fiction by an American author. *Winner:* David Bradley for *The Chaneysville Incident* (Harper).

PEN American Center Awards. *Winners:* (publisher citation) Morris Philipson, director, University of Chicago Press; (translation prize) Hiroaki Sato and Burton Watson for *From the Country of Eight Islands* (Anchor Press); (medal for translation) Gregory Rabassa, translator of Spanish and Portuguese literature; (writing awards for prisoners—fiction) William T. Stirewalt for *Lieutenant Beezlefat*; (nonfiction) John Ruzas for *The Day the Kept Lost Their Keeper*; (poetry) Thomas G. Nickens for *5:00 P.M.*

PEN Los Angeles Center Awards. For writing that exemplifies the principles of freedom of expression. *Winners:* (body of work) Neil Simon; (fiction) Ann Nietzke for *Windowlight* (Capra Press).

Maxwell Perkins Editors Award. *Offered by:* PEN Los Angeles Center. *Winner:* Jean Stone, editor of Irving Stone.

Maxwell Perkins Prize. For a first work of fiction about the American experience. *Offered by:* Charles Scribner's Sons. *Winner:* Margaret Mitchell Dukore for *A Novel Called Heritage* (Scribner's).

James D. Phelan Award. For an unpublished work of fiction, nonfictional prose, poetry, or drama. *Offered by:* San Francisco Foundation. *Winner:* Melissa Brown-Pritchard for *Curtain Calls* (Scribner's).

Phi Beta Kappa Science Award. *Winner:* Bernard Lovell for *Emerging Cosmology* (Columbia Univ.).

Pilgrim Award. For a work of outstanding scholarship in science fiction. *Offered by:* Science Fiction Research Association. *Winner:* Neil Barron for *Anatomy of Wonder* (Bowker).

Edgar Allan Poe Awards. For outstanding mystery, crime, and suspense writing. *Offered by:* Mystery Writers of America. *Winners:* (critical/biographical study) Jon L. Breen for *What about Murder?* (Scarecrow); (fact crime) Robert W. Greene for *The Sting Man: Inside Abscam* (Dutton); (first novel) Stuart Woods for *Chiefs* (Norton); (novel) William Bayer for *Peregrine* (Congdon & Lattés); (paperback) L. A. Morse for *The Old Dick* (Avon); (short story) Jack Richie for *The Absence of Emily* (*Ellery Queen's Mystery Magazine*); (children's mystery) Norma Fox Mazer for *Taking Terri Mueller* (Avon).

George Polk Memorial Awards. For outstanding achievement in journalism. *Offered by:* Long Island University Dept. of Journalism. *Winner:* Edwin R. Bayley for *Joe McCarthy and the Press* (Univ. of Wisconsin/Pantheon).

Prix Fémina (France). For an outstanding novel. *Winner:* Anne Hebert for *Les Fous de Bassan* (Seuil).

Prix Goncourt (France). For a work of imagination in prose, preferably a novel, exemplifying youth, originality, *esprit*, and form. *Winner:* Dominique Fernandez for *Dans la Main de l'Ange* (Grasset).

Prix Interallié (France). For a distinguished novel. *Winner:* Eric Ollivier for *L'Orphelin de Mer* (Denoël).

Prix Médicis (France). To honor experimental fiction written in French. *Winner:* Jean-François Josselin for *L'Enfer et Cie* (Grasset).

Prix Médicis Étranger (France). For the best foreign novel translated into French. *Winner:* Humberto Eco for *The Name of the Rose* (Grasset).

Prix Renaudot (France). For a distinguished novel. *Winner:* Georges-Olivier Chateaureynaud for *La Faculté des Songes* (Grasset).

PSP Awards. For the most outstanding books in the fields of science, medicine, technology, and business. *Offered by:* Professional and Scholarly Publishing Division, Association of American Publishers. *Winners:* (architecture and urban planning) Underground Space Center, University of Minnesota for *Earth Sheltered Community Design* (Van Nostrand Reinhold); (book design and production) Michael E. Doyle for *Color Drawing* (Van Nostrand Reinhold); (engineering) Virgil J. Lunardini for *Heat Transfer in Cold Climates* (Van Nostrand Reinhold); (health sciences) Ruth Ochroch for *The Diagnosis and Treatment of Minimal Brain Dysfunction in Children: A Clinical Approach* (Human Sciences Press); (humanities) Lynne Withey for *Dearest Friend: A Life of Abigail Adams* (Free Press); (life sciences) Clifford Grobstein for *From Chance to Purpose: An Appraisal of External Human Fertilization* (Addison-Wesley); (most creative and innovative new project) Louis J. Girard for *Corneal Surgery, Vol. II* (C. V. Mosby); (physical and earth sciences) Michael H. Carr for *The Surface of Mars* (Yale Univ.); (social and behavioral sciences) Samuel P. Huntington for *American Politics: The Promise of Disharmony* (Harvard Univ.); (technology) Henry R. Bungay for *Energy: The Biomass Options* (Wiley).

Pulitzer Prizes in Letters. To honor distinguished works by American writers, dealing preferably with American themes. *Winners:* (biography) William S. McFeely for *Grant: A Biography* (Norton); (fiction) John Updike for *Rabbit Is Rich* (Knopf); (general nonfiction) Tracy Kidder for *The Soul of a New Machine* (Atlantic/Little, Brown); (history) C. Vann Woodward, ed., for *Mary Chesnut's Civil War* (Yale Univ.); (poetry) Sylvia Plath for *The Collected Poems* (Harper).

Pushcart Press Editors' Book Award. For an unpublished book of exceptional quality. *Winner:* Paul T. Rogers for *Saul's Book* (Pushcart).

Trevor Reese Memorial Prize (Great Britain). For the best scholarly book published in Great Britain in the field of British Imperial and Commonwealth history. *Offered by:* University of London Institute of Commonwealth Studies. *Winner:* M. E. Yapp for *Strategies of British India: Britain, Iran, and Afghanistan, 1798-1850* (Clarendon).

Regina Medal. For excellence in the writing of literature for children. *Offered by:* Catholic Library Association. *Winner:* Theodor Seuss Geisel (Dr. Seuss).

Richard and Hilda Rosenthal Foundation Award. For a work of fiction that is a considerable literary achievement though not necessarily a commercial success. *Offered by:* American Academy and Institute of Arts and Letters. *Winner:* Marilynne Robinson for *Housekeeping* (Farrar).

David H. Russell Award. *Offered by:* National Council of Teachers of English. *Winner:* Donald H. Graves for *Balance the Basics: Let Them Write* (Ford Foundation).

John Llewelyn Rhys Memorial Prize (Great Britain). *Winner:* William Boyd for *An Ice-Cream War* (Hamish Hamilton).

Carl Sandburg Awards. For exceptional achievement in literature by Chicago-area writers. *Offered by:* Friends of the Chicago Public Library. *Winners:* (fiction) Eugene Kennedy for *Father's Day* (Doubleday); (nonfiction) Studs Terkel for *American Dreams: Lost and Found* (Atheneum); (poetry) Mary Swander for *Succession* (Univ. of Georgia); (children's books) Jamie Gilson for *Do Bananas Chew Gum?* (Lothrop, Lee).

Delmore Schwartz Memorial Poetry Award. *Offered by:* New York University College of Arts and Science. *Winner:* Sherod Santos for *Accidental Weather* (Doubleday).

Scribner's Crime Novel Award. *Winner:* Carol Clemeau Esler for *The Ariadne Clue* (Scribner's).

Seal Books Award (Canada). For an outstanding first novel. *Winner:* Janette Turner Hospital for *The Ivory Swing* (McClelland & Stewart).

Mina P. Shaughnessy Medal. For an outstanding research publication in the field of teaching English language and literature. *Winner:* John Hollander for *Rhyme's Reason: A Guide to English Verse* (Yale Univ.).

John Gilmary Shea Prize. For the most distinguished contribution to the history of the Catholic Church. *Winner:* Felix Gilbert for *The Pope, His Banker, and Venice* (Harvard Univ.).

Shelley Memorial Award for Poetry. *Offered by:* Poetry Society of America. *Winner:* Alan Dugan.

Kenneth B. Smilen/Present Tense Literary Awards. To honor authors and translators of works that have intrinsic value and lasting quality, and reflect humane Jewish values. *Offered by:* American Jewish Committee. *Winners:* (biography and autobiography) Jacobo Timerman for *Prisoner Without a Name, Cell Without a Number* (Knopf); (fiction) Jay Neugeboren for *The Stolen Jew* (Holt); (history) Jonathan Frankel for *Prophecy and Politics* (Cambridge Univ.); (religious thought) James L. Kugel for *The Idea of Biblical Poetry* (Yale Univ.); (social/political analysis) Shlomo Avineri for *The Making of Modern Zionism* (Basic Books); (translation) T. Carmi for *The Penguin Book of Hebrew Verse* (Viking/Penguin).

W. H. Smith & Son Literary Award (Great Britain). For a book that makes a significant contribution to literature. *Winner:* George Clare for *Last Waltz in Vienna: The Destruction of a Family, 1842-1942* (Macmillan).

John Ben Snow Prize. For an outstanding nonfiction manuscript dealing with some aspect of New York State. *Offered by:* Syracuse University Press. *Winner:* Roger M. Haydon, ed., for "Upstate

Travels: British Views of 19th Century New York."

Society of Children's Book Writers Golden Kite Awards. *Winners:* (fiction) M. E. Kerr for *Little Little* (Harper); (nonfiction) Elizabeth Helfman for *Blissymbolics* (Lodestar).

Society of Midland Authors Awards. For outstanding books about the Midwest or by Midwest authors. *Winners:* (fiction) Eugene Kennedy for *Father's Day* (Doubleday); (biography) Dempsey Travis for *An Autobiography of Black Chicago* (Urban Research, Inc.); (history) Melvin Holli and Peter d'Jones for *Ethnic Chicago* (Eerdmans) and James P. Barry for *Wrecks and Rescues of the Great Lakes* (Oaktree); (nonfiction, sociology/psychology) Jonathan Raban for *Old Glory: An American Voyage* (Simon & Schuster); (nonfiction, politics/economics) James R. Millar for *ABC's of Soviet Socialism* (Univ. of Illinois); (poetry) Sonia Gernes for *Brief Lives* (Univ. of Notre Dame); (children's book) Annabelle Irwin and Lee Hadley (Hadley Irwin, pseud.) for *Moon and Me* (Atheneum).

Southern California Council on Literature for Children and Young People Award. *Winners:* (fiction) Eiveen Weiman for *Which Way Courage* (Atheneum); (series) Malka Drucker for Jewish Holidays Series (Holiday House); (body of work) Julia Cunningham.

Agnes Lynch Starrett Poetry Prize. *Offered by:* University of Pittsburgh Press. *Winner:* Lawrence Joseph for *Shouting at No One* (Univ. of Pittsburgh).

Sydney Taylor Award. For a body of work with general literary merit and a definite positive Jewish focus. *Offered by:* Association of Jewish Libraries. *Winner:* Barbara Cohen.

Texas Bluebonnet Award. *Offered by:* Texas Association of School Librarians and Children's Round Table of the Texas Library Association. *Winner:* Judy Blume for *Superfudge* (Dutton).

Theatre Library Association Award. For the outstanding book in the field of motion pictures and broadcasting. *Winner:* William Alexander for *Film on the Left: American Documentary Film from 1931 to 1942* (Princeton Univ.).

Travelling Scholarships (Great Britain). To enable British writers to travel. *Winners:* Douglas Dunn and Mervyn Jones.

University of Southern Mississippi Silver Medallion. *Winner:* Beverly Cleary.

Utah Children's Book Award. For a book chosen by Utah school children. *Offered by:* Children's Literature Association of Utah. *Winner:* Judy Blume for *Superfudge* (Dutton).

Voertman's Poetry Award. *Winner:* Pattiann Rogers for *The Expectation of Light* (Princeton Univ.).

Harold D. Vursell Memorial Award. *Offered by:* American Academy and Institute of Arts and Letters. *Winner:* Eleanor Perenyi for *Green Thoughts* (Random).

Marjorie Peabody Waite Award. *Offered by:* American Academy and Institute of Arts and Letters. *Winner:* Edouard Roditi.

Western Writers of America Golden Spur Awards. To promote excellence in the writing of Western literature. *Winners:* (cover art) Wayne Baize for *A Touch of Winter* (*The Quarter Horse Journal*); (historical novel) Loren D. Estleman for *Aces and Eights* (Doubleday); (nonfiction) David Dary for *Cowboy Culture* (Knopf); (novel) Lee McElroy for *Eyes of the Hawk* (Doubleday); Lee Head for *Horizon* (Putnam); (short subjects—fiction) Carla Kelly for *Kathleen Flaherty's Long Winter* (*Far West Magazine*); (nonfiction) Alice J. Hall for *Buffalo Bill and the Enduring West* (National Geographic); (children's fiction) Mark J. Harris for *The Last Run* (Lothrop, Lee & Shepard).

Whitbread Literary Awards (Great Britain). For literature of merit that is readable on a wide scale. *Offered by:* Booksellers Association of Great Britain. *Winners:* (novel) John Wain for *Young Shoulders* (Macmillan); (biography) Edward Crankshaw for *Bismark* (Macmillan); (first novel) Bruce Chatwin for *On the Black Hill* (Jonathan Cape); (children's novel) W. J. Corbett for *The Song of Pentecost* (Methuen).

William Allen White Children's Book Award. *Winner:* Carole S. Adler for *The Magic of the Glits* (Macmillan).

Walt Whitman Award. For an American poet who has not yet published a book of poems. *Winner:* Anthony Petrosky for *Jurgis Petraskas* (Louisiana Univ.).

Walt Whitman Citation of Merit for Poetry. *Offered by:* New York State Council on the Arts. *Winner:* Isabella Gardner (posthumously).

Thornton Wilder Prize. For a distinguished translation of contemporary American literature into foreign languages. *Offered by:* Columbia University Translation Center. *Winner:* Ihsan Abbas, chairman of the Dept. of Arabic and Near Eastern Languages at the American University of Beirut.

William Carlos Williams Award. For a book of poetry published by a small press, nonprofit press, or university press. *Offered by:* Poetry Society of America. *Winner:* John Logan for *Only the Dreamer Can Change the Dream: Selected Poems* (Ecco Press).

H. W. Wilson Indexing Award. *Offered by:* American Society of Indexers. *Winner:* Catherine Fix for index to *Diagnosis of Bone and Joint Disorders* by Donald Resnick and Gen Niwayama (W. B. Saunders).

H. W. Wingate Awards (Great Britain). For fiction or nonfiction that stimulates an awareness of Jewish interest. *Winners:* Mordecai Richler for *Joshua Then and Now* (Macmillan) and Jerry White for *Rothschild Buildings* (Routledge & Kegan Paul).

Laurence L. Winship Book Award. For a book having some relation to New England. *Offered by:* Boston Globe. *Winner:* William Sargent for *Shallow Waters: A Year on Cape Cod's Pleasant Bay* (Houghton Mifflin).

Workmen's Circle Award for Yiddish Literature. *Winner:* Joshua A. Fishman for *Never Say Die!* (Mouton Publishers).

World Fantasy Convention Awards. *Winners:* (novel) John Crowley for *Little, Big* (Bantam); (novella) Parke Godwin for *The Fire When It Comes* (Fantasy and Science Fiction); (short story) Dennis Etchison for *The Dark Country* (Fantasy Tales) and Stephen King for *Do the Dead Sing* (Yankee); (anthology) Terri Windling and Mark Alan Arnold for *Elsewhere* (Ace); (life achievement award) Italo Calvino.

World Science Fiction Convention Hugo Awards. For outstanding science fiction writing. *Winners:* (novel) C. J. Cherryh for *Downbelow Station* (DAW Books); (novella) Poul Anderson for *The Saturn Game* (Analog); (novelette) Roger Zelazny for *Unicorn Variation* (Isaac Asimov's Science Fiction Magazine); (short story) John Varley for *The Pusher* (Fantasy and Science Fiction).

Yale Series of Younger Poets Award. *Winner:* Cathy Song for *From the White Place* (Yale Univ.).

Young Hoosier Book Award. *Offered by:* Association for Indiana Media Educators. *Winner:* Eth Clifford for *Help! I'm a Prisoner in the Library* (Houghton Mifflin).

Morton Dauwen Zabel Award. *Offered by:* American Academy and Institute of Arts and Letters. *Winner:* Harold Bloom.

NOTABLE BOOKS OF 1982

This is the thirty-sixth year in which this list of distinguished books has been issued by the Notable Books Council of Reference and Adult Services Division of the American Library Association.

Anderson, Jervis. *This Was Harlem: A Cultural Portrait, 1900-1950.* Farrar.
The Auschwitz Album: A Book Based upon an Album Discovered by a Concentration Camp Survivor, Lili Meier. Random.
Baker, Russell. *Growing Up.* Congdon and Weed.
Ballantyne, Sheila. *Imaginary Crimes.* Viking.
Berriault, Gina. *The Infinite Passion of Expectation: Twenty-five Stories.* North Point Press.
Braudel, Fernand. *The Structures of Everyday Life: The Limits of the Possible* (Civilization and Capitalism, 15th-18th Century, Vol. 1). Harper.
Brown, Bruce. *Mountain in the Clouds: A Search for the Wild Salmon.* Simon and Schuster.
Campbell, Jeremy. *Grammatical Man: Information, Entropy, Language, and Life.* Simon and Schuster.
Caro, Robert A. *The Path to Power* (The Years of Lyndon Johnson, Vol. 1). Knopf.
DeLillo, Don. *The Names.* Knopf.
Del Vecchio, John M. *The 13th Valley: A Novel.* Bantam.
Eckholm, Erik P. *Down to Earth: Environment and Human Needs.* Norton.
Fisher, M. F. K. *As They Were.* Knopf.
Forché, Carolyn. *The Country Between Us.* Harper.
Gernes, Sonia. *The Way to St. Ives.* Scribner.
Hoffman, Alice. *White Horses.* Putnam.
Hoffman, Ethan. *Concrete Mama: Prison Profiles from Walla Walla.* Univ. of Missouri Press.
Holliday, J. S. *The World Rushed In: The California Gold Rush Experience.* Simon and Schuster.

Ishiguro, Kazuo. *A Pale View of Hills.* Putnam.
Keegan, John. *Six Armies in Normandy: From D-day to the Liberation of Paris, June 16th-August 25th, 1944.* Viking.
Kogawa, Joy. *Obasan.* Godine.
Lacey, Robert. *The Kingdom.* Harcourt.
Madson, John. *Where the Sky Began: Land of the Tallgrass Prairie.* Houghton Mifflin.
Mason, Bobbie Ann. *Shiloh and Other Stories.* Harper.
Millgate, Michael. *Thomas Hardy: A Biography.* Random.
Murray, William. *Italy: The Fatal Gift.* Dodd, Mead.
Noël Hume, Ivor. *Martin's Hundred.* Knopf.
Nye, Naomi Shihab. *Hugging the Jukebox.* Dutton.
Ondaatje, Michael. *Running in the Family.* Norton.
Pais, Abraham. *'Subtle Is the Lord . . .': The Science and the Life of Albert Einstein.* Oxford Univ. Press.
Piercy, Marge. *Circles on the Water: Selected Poems of Marge Piercy.* Knopf.
Plowden, David. *An American Chronology.* Viking.
Rodriguez, Richard. *Hunger of Memory: The Education of Richard Rodriguez, an Autobiography.* Godine.
Schell, Jonathan. *The Fate of the Earth.* Knopf.
Simpson, Eileen. *Poets in Their Youth: A Memoir.* Random.
Singer, Isaac Bashevis. *The Collected Stories of Isaac Bashevis Singer.* Farrar.
Soyinka, Wole. *Aké: The Years of Childhood.* Random.
Thurman, Judith. *Isak Dinesen: The Life of a Storyteller.* St. Martin's.

Tyler, Anne. *Dinner at the Homesick Restaurant.* Knopf.
Updike, John. *Bech Is Back.* Knopf.
Vargas Llosa, Mario. *Aunt Julia and the Scriptwriter.* Farrar.
Wongar, B. *Babaru: Stories.* Univ. of Illinois Press.

BEST YOUNG ADULT BOOKS OF 1982

Each year a committee of the Young Adult Services Division of the American Library Association compiles a list of best books for young adults selected on the basis of young adult appeal. These titles must meet acceptable standards of library merit and provide a variety of subjects for different tastes and a broad range of reading levels. *School Library Journal* (*SLJ*) also provides a list of best books for young adults. This year the list was compiled by *SLJ*'s young adult review committee, which is chaired by Ron Brown, young adult specialist at Boston Public Library, and made up of public and school librarians in the greater Boston Area. The *SLJ* list was published in the December 1982 issue of the journal. The following list combines the titles selected for both lists. The notation ALA or *SLJ* following the price indicates the source of titles chosen.

Alexander, Lloyd. *The Kestrel.* Dutton. $10.95. ALA.
Anderson, Jervis. *This Was Harlem: A Cultural Portrait, 1900–1950.* Farrar. $17.95. *SLJ.*
Bane, Michael. *White Boy Singin' the Blues: The Black Roots of White Rock.* Penguin. $5.95. *SLJ.*
Banks, Lynne Reid. *The Writing on the Wall.* Harper. $9.89. ALA.
Bradley, Marion Zimmer. *Hawkmistress.* DAW. $2.95. ALA.
Bradshaw, Gillian. *In Winter's Shadow.* Simon and Schuster. $16.50. *SLJ.*
Brancato, Robin F. *Sweet Bells Jangled out of Tune.* Knopf. $9.95. ALA.
Brooks, Terry. *The Elfstones of Shannara.* Ballantine. $15.95; pap. $7.95. *SLJ.*
Butterworth, Emma Macalik. *As the Waltz Was Ending.* Four Winds. $9.95. ALA.
Clapp, Patricia. *Witches' Children.* Lothrop, Lee & Shepard. $9.50. ALA.
Cohen, Barbara, and Bahija Lovejoy. *Seven Daughters and Seven Sons.* Atheneum. $10.95. ALA.
Davis, Daniel S. *Behind Barbed Wire: The Imprisonment of Japanese Americans during World War II.* Dutton. $12.95. ALA.
Davis-Gardner, Angela. *Felice.* Random. $13.50. *SLJ.*
Dragonwagon, Crescent, and Paul Zindel. *To Take a Dare.* Harper. $9.89. ALA.
Duffy, Maureen. *Gor Saga.* Viking. $13.95. *SLJ.*
Duncan, Lois. *Chapters: My Growth as a Writer.* Little, Brown. $10.95. ALA.
Earle, Peter. *The Sack of Panama: Sir Henry Morgan's Adventures on the Spanish Main.* Viking. $16.95. *SLJ.*
Epstein, Sam, and Beryl Epstein. *Kids in Court.* Four Winds. $9.95. ALA.
Farris, Jack. *Me and Gallagher.* Simon and Schuster. $13.95. *SLJ.*
Ferrigno, Lou, and Douglas Kent Hall. *The Incredible Lou Ferrigno.* Simon and Schuster. $14.95. *SLJ.*
Ford, Richard. *Quest for the Faradawn.* Delacorte. $14.95. ALA.
Garden, Nancy. *Annie on My Mind.* Farrar. $10.95. ALA.
Girion, Barbara. *A Handful of Stars.* Scribners. $10.95. ALA.
Glenn, Mel. *Class Dismissed! High School Poems.* Clarion (Houghton). $10.95. ALA.
Goldston, Robert. *Sinister Touches.* Dial. $11.95. ALA.

Guest, Judith. *Second Heaven.* Viking. $14.95. *SLJ.*

Hamilton, Virginia. *Sweet Whispers, Brother Rush.* Philomel. $10.95. ALA.

Handlin, Oscar, and Lilian Handlin. *A Restless People: Americans in Rebellion, 1770-1787.* Anchor (dist. by Doubleday). $14.95. *SLJ.*

Heinlein, Robert A. *Friday.* Holt. $14.95. *SLJ.*

Hellman, Peter, and Lili Meier. *Auschwitz Album: A Book Based upon an Album Discovered by a Concentration Camp Survivor, Lili Meier.* Random. $23. ALA.

Howe, Irving, and Ilana Wiener Howe, eds. *Short Shorts: An Anthology of the Shortest Stories.* Godine. $12.95. *SLJ.*

Irwin, Hadley. *What about Grandma?* Atheneum. $8.95. ALA.

Jones, Douglas C. *The Barefoot Brigade.* Holt. $15. *SLJ.*

Jordan, Teresa. *Cowgirls: Women of the American West.* Doubleday. $19.95. *SLJ.*

Kazimiroff, Theodore L. *The Last Algonquin.* Walker. $12.95. ALA, *SLJ.*

Kinsella, W. P. *Shoeless Joe.* Houghton. $11.95 *SLJ.*

Lawrence, Louise, *Calling B for Butterfly.* Harper. $11.50. ALA.

Lehrman, Robert. *Juggling.* Harper. $11.89. ALA.

Lester, Julius. *This Strange New Feeling.* Dial. $10.95. ALA.

Llywelyn, Morgan. *The Horse Goddess.* Houghton. $15.95. ALA, *SLJ.*

Lynn, Elizabeth A. *The Sardonyx Net.* Berkley. $2.75. ALA.

McCaffrey, Anne. *Crystal Singer.* Ballantine/Del Rey. $2.95. *SLJ.*

McKinley, Robin. *The Blue Sword.* Greenwillow. $11.50. ALA.

Magorian, Michelle. *Good Night, Mr. Tom.* Harper. $10.89. ALA.

Magubane, Peter. *Black Child.* Knopf. $16.50, pap. $8.95. ALA.

Murphy, Jim. *Death Run.* Clarion (Houghton). $9.95. ALA.

Naylor, Phyllis R. *A String of Chances.* Atheneum. $10.95. ALA.

Oneal, Zibby. *A Formal Feeling.* Viking. $10.95. ALA.

Park, Ruth. *Playing Beatie Bow.* Atheneum. $9.95. ALA.

Petersen, P. J. *Nobody Else Can Walk It for You.* Delacorte. $10.95. ALA.

Pierce, Meredith Ann. *The Darkangel.* Atlantic/Little, Brown. $11.95. ALA.

Riley, Jocelyn. *Only My Mouth Is Smiling.* Morrow. $9.50. ALA.

Robeson, Susan. *The Whole World in His Hands.* Citadel Press. $17.95. ALA.

Robinson, Spider. *Mindkiller.* Holt. $14.50. *SLJ.*

Schell, Jonathan. *The Fate of the Earth.* Knopf. $11.95. ALA.

Searls, Hank. *Sounding.* Ballantine/Random. $13.50; pap. $6.95. ALA.

Sebestyen, Ouida. *I O U's.* Atlantic/Little, Brown. $10.95. ALA.

Simon, Nissa. *Don't Worry, You're Normal: A Teenager's Guide to Self Health.* Crowell. $8.89. ALA.

Stachow, Hasso G. *If This Be Glory.* Tr. from German by J. Maxwell Brownjohn. Doubleday. $14.95. *SLJ.*

Steiner, George. *The Portage to San Cristobal of A.H.* Simon and Schuster. $13.50. *SLJ.*

Strasser, Todd. *Rock 'n Roll Nights.* Delacorte. $10.95. ALA.

Terry, Douglas. *The Last Texas Hero.* Doubleday. $14.95. ALA, *SLJ.*

Thomas, Joyce Carol. *Marked by Fire.* Avon. $2.25. ALA.

Tyler, Anne. *Dinner at the Homesick Restaurant.* Knopf. $13.50. *SLJ.*

Vinge, Joan D. *Psion.* Delacorte. $12.95. ALA.

Voigt, Cynthia. *Tell Me if the Lovers Are Losers.* Atheneum. $10.95. ALA.

Wernert, Susan, ed. *Reader's Digest North American Wildlife.* Reader's Digest (dist. by Random). $20.50. *SLJ.*

Wersba, Barbara. *The Carnival in My Mind.* Harper. $10.50. ALA.

Wharton, William. *A Midnight Clear.* Knopf. $12.95. ALA, *SLJ.*

Wolitzer, Meg. *Sleepwalking.* Random. $12.50. *SLJ.*

Yolen, Jane. *Dragon's Blood.* Delacorte. $11.95. ALA.

BEST CHILDREN'S BOOKS OF 1982

A list of notable children's books is selected each year by the Notable Children's Books Committee of the Association for Library Service to Children of the American Library Association (ALA). The committee is aided by suggestions from school and public children's librarians throughout the United States. The book review editors of *School Library Journal* (*SLJ*) also compile a list each year, with full annotations, of best books for children. The following list is a combination of ALA's Notable Children's Books of 1982 and *SLJ*'s selection of "Best Books 1982," published in the December 1982 issue of *SLJ*. The source of each selection is indicated by the notation ALA or *SLJ* following each entry. [See the article "Literary Prizes" for Newbery, Caldecott, and other award winners—*Ed.*]

Adoff, Arnold. *All the Colors of the Race.* Illus. by John Steptoe. Lothrop. $9.50. ALA.

Alexander, Lloyd. *The Kestrel.* Dutton. $10.95. ALA.

Anno, Mitsumasa. *Anno's Counting House.* Philomel. $12.95. ALA.

Arnosky, Jim. *Drawing from Nature.* Lothrop. $10.50. ALA.

Barton, Byron. *Airport.* Crowell. $9.89. ALA, *SLJ.*

Bawden, Nina. *Kept in the Dark.* Lothrop. $9.50. ALA.

Bennett, Jill. *Tiny Tim: Verses for Children.* Illus. by Helen Oxenbury. Delacorte. $10.95 *SLJ.*

Bierhorst, John, ed. *The Whistling Skeleton: American Tales of the Supernatural.* Collected by George Bird Grinnell. Illus. by Robert Andrew Parker. Four Winds. $12.95. ALA.

Brown, Marc, and Stephen Krensky. *Dinosaurs Beware: A Safety Guide.* Atlantic Monthly Press. $10.95. ALA.

Bryan, Ashley. *I'm Going to Sing: Black American Spirituals.* Volume Two. Atheneum. $10.95. ALA.

Buchwald, Emile. *Floramel and Esteban.* Illus. by Charles Robinson. Harcourt. $9.95. ALA.

Butterworth, Emma M. *As the Waltz Was Ending.* Four Winds. $9.95. ALA.

Byars, Betsy. *The Animal, the Vegetable, & John D. Jones.* Illus. by Ruth Sanderson. Delacorte. $9.95. *SLJ.*

———. *The Two-Thousand-Pound Goldfish.* Harper. $9.89. ALA.

Cameron, Eleanor. *That Julia Redfern.* Illus. by Gail Owens. Dutton. $9.95. ALA, *SLJ.*

Cendrars, Blaise. *Shadow.* Trans. and illus. by Marcia Brown. Scribners. $12.95. ALA.

Cleary, Beverly. *Ralph S. Mouse.* Illus. by Paul O. Zelinsky. Morrow. $8. *SLJ.*

Cohen, Barbara. *Gooseberries to Oranges.* Pictures by Beverly Brodsky. Lothrop. $10.50. ALA.

Cohen, Barbara, and Bahija Lovejoy. *Seven Daughters and Seven Sons.* Atheneum. $10.95. ALA.

Connor, Patrick. *People at Home (Looking at Art).* Atheneum. $11.95. ALA.

Courlander, Harold. *The Crest and the Hide and Other African Stories, Heroes, Chiefs, Bards, Hunters, Sorcerers and Common People.* Illus. by Monica Vachula. Coward. $11.95. ALA.

Crews, Donald. *Carousel.* Greenwillow. $9.50. ALA.

Crowell, Robert L. *The Lore and Legend of Flowers*. Illus. by Anne Ophelia Dowden. Crowell. $13.89. ALA.
de Paola, Tomie. *Francis, the Poor Man of Assisi*. Holiday. $14.95. ALA.
———. *Giorgio's Village*. Putnam. $11.95. ALA.
DePauw, Linda Grant. *Seafaring Women*. Houghton. $10.45. ALA, SLJ.
Donnelly, Elfie. *Offbeat Friends*. Trans. by Anthea Bell. Crown. $8.95. ALA.
Fisher, Leonard Everett. *Number Art: Thirteen 1 2 3s from around the World*. Four Winds. $10.95. ALA.
Fleischman, Paul. *Graven Images*. Illus. by Andrew Glass. Harper. $9.89. ALA, SLJ.
Fritz, Jean. *The Good Giants and the Bad Pukwudgies*. Illus. by Tomie de Paola. Putnam. $10.95. ALA.
———. *Homesick: My Own Story*. Illus. by Margot Tomes. Putnam. $9.95. ALA, SLJ.
Gardam, Jane. *The Hollow Land*. Illus. by Janet Rawlins. Greenwillow. $9.50. ALA.
Giblin, James C. *Chimney Sweeps: Yesterday and Today*. Illus. by Margot Tomes. Crowell. $10.89. ALA.
Ginsburg, Mirra. *Across the Stream*. Pictures by Nancy Tafuri. Greenwillow. $9.50. ALA.
Goldston, Robert. *Sinister Touches: The Secret War against Hitler*. Dial. $11.95. ALA, SLJ.
Goor, Ron, and Nancy Goor. *In the Driver's Seat*. Crowell. $10.95. SLJ.
Greenberg, Harvey R. *Hanging In: What You Should Know about Psychotherapy*. Four Winds/Scholastic. $12.95. SLJ.
Greene, Carol. *Hinny Winny Bunco*. Pictures by Jeanette Winter. Harper. $8.89. ALA.
Grimm Brothers, The. *Rapunzel*. Retold by Barbara Rogasky with illus. by Trina Scharf Hyman. Holiday. $12.95. ALA.
———. *The Six Swans*. Retold by Wanda Gag. Illus. by Margot Tomes. Coward. $8.95. SLJ.

Gundersheimer, Karen. *Happy Winter*. Harper. $9.89. ALA.
Hamilton, Virginia. *Sweet Whispers, Brother Rush*. Philomel. $10.95. ALA, SLJ.
Hart, Jane, comp. *Singing Bee: A Collection of Favorite Children's Songs*. Pictures by Anita Lobel. Lothrop. $16. ALA, SLJ.
Haugen, Tormod. *The Night Birds*. Trans. from the Norwegian by Sheila La Farge. Delacorte. $9.95. SLJ.
Heide, Florence Parry. *Time's Up*. Drawings by Marilyn Hafner. Holiday. $8.95. ALA.
Hill, Eric. *Spot's Birthday Party*. Putnam. $8.95. ALA.
Holmes, Anita. *Cactus, the All-American Plant*. Illus. by Joyce Ann Polvsyk. Four Winds. $14.95. ALA.
Horwitz, Elinor L. *How to Wreck a Building*. Photos by Joshua Horwitz. Pantheon. $9.95. ALA.
Hughes, Shirley. *Alfie Gets in First*. Lothrop. $8.50. ALA.
Hurwitz, Johanna. *The Rabbi's Girls*. Illus. by Pamela Johnson. Morrow. $8.50. ALA.
Hutchins, Pat. *1 Hunter*. Greenwillow. $9.50. ALA, SLJ.
Huynh, Quang-Nhuong. *The Land I Lost: Adventures of a Boy in Vietnam*. Pictures by Vo-Dinh Mai. Harper. $9.89. ALA.
Jones, Diana Wynne. *Witch Week*. Greenwillow. $9. SLJ.
Kennedy, X. J., and Dorothy M. Kennedy. *Knock at a Star: A Child's Introduction to Poetry*. Illus. by Karen Ann Weinhaus. Little, Brown. $12.95. SLJ.
Kerr, M. E. *What I Really Think of You*. Harper. $10. SLJ.
Kilgore, Kathleen. *The Wolfman of Beacon Hill*. Little, Brown. $10.95. SLJ.
King-Smith, Dick. *Pigs Might Fly*. Drawings by Mary Rayner. Viking. $10.95. ALA.
Krementz, Jill. *How It Feels to Be Adopted*. Knopf. $11.95. ALA.
Kuskin, Karla. *The Philharmonic Gets*

Dressed. Illus. by Marc Simont. Harper. $10.50. ALA.

Lauber, Patricia. *Journey to the Planets.* Crown. $11.95. ALA, *SLJ.*

Lawrence, D. H. *Birds, Beasts and the Third Thing: Poems by D. H. Lawrence.* Selected and illus. by Alice Martin Provensen. Viking. $12.95. ALA.

Lens, Sidney. *The Bomb.* Lodestar. $11.50. *SLJ.*

Lerner, Carol. *A Biblical Garden.* Trans. from the Hebrew Bible by Ralph Lerner. Morrow. $10.95. ALA.

Livingston, Myra Cohn. *A Circle of Seasons.* Illus. by Leonard Everett Fisher. Holiday. $12.95. ALA.

Lobel, Arnold. *Ming Lo Moves the Mountain.* Greenwillow. $9.50. ALA.

Louie, Ai-Ling. *Yeh-Shen: A Cinderella Story from China.* Illus. by Ed Young. Philomel. $10.95. ALA, *SLJ.*

McKinley, Robin. *The Blue Sword.* Greenwillow. $11.50. ALA.

McPhail, David. *Pig Pig Rides.* Unicorn/Dutton. $8.69. *SLJ.*

Magorian, Michelle. *Good Night, Mr. Tom.* Harper. $10.89. ALA.

Mahy, Margaret. *The Haunting.* Atheneum. $8.95. *SLJ.*

Mark, Jan. *Nothing to Be Afraid Of.* Harper. $8.95. *SLJ.*

Maruki, Toshi. *Horoshima No Pika.* Lothrop. $12. ALA.

Meltzer, Milton, ed. *The Jewish Americans: A History in Their Own Words.* Crowell. $10.89. ALA.

Moore, Lilian. *Something New Begins: New and Selected Poems.* Illus. by Mary Jane Dunton. Atheneum. $10.95. ALA.

Morgan, Alison. *Paul's Kite.* Atheneum. $8.95. *SLJ.*

Naylor, Phyllis R. *A String of Chances.* Atheneum. $10.95. ALA.

Norton, Mary. *The Borrowers Avenged.* Illus. by Beth and Joe Krush. Harcourt. $12.95. ALA, *SLJ.*

Nostlinger, Christine. *Marrying Off Mother.* Trans. from the German by Anthea Bell. Harcourt. $8.95. *SLJ.*

Oneal, Zibby. *A Formal Feeling.* Viking. $10.95. ALA.

Ormerod, Jan. *Moonlight.* Lothrop. $9.50. ALA.

Park, Ruth. *Playing Beatie Bow.* Atheneum. $9.95. ALA, *SLJ.*

Patent, Dorothy Hinshaw. *Spider Magic.* Holiday. $8.95. ALA.

Phipson, Joan. *The Watcher in the Garden.* Atheneum. $10.95. *SLJ.*

Radin, Ruth Yaffe. *A Winter Place.* Paintings by Mattie Lou O'Kelley. Atlantic/Little, Brown. $11.95. ALA.

Robinson, Barbara. *Temporary Times, Temporary Places.* Harper. $7.95. ALA, *SLJ.*

Rodgers, Mary. *Summer Switch.* Harper. $9.95. *SLJ.*

Rylant, Cynthia. *When I Was Young In The Mountains.* Illus. by Diane Goode. Dutton. $9.95. ALA.

St. George, Judith. *The Brooklyn Bridge: They Said It Couldn't Be Built.* Putnam. $10.95. ALA.

Sandburg, Carl. *Rainbows Are Made: Poems by Carl Sandburg.* Selected by Lee Bennett Hopkins. Wood engravings by Fritz Eichenberg. Harcourt. $12.95. ALA.

Say, Allen. *The Bicycle Man.* Parnassus/Houghton. $12.45. ALA.

Schlee, Ann. *Ask Me No Questions.* Holt. $13.95. *SLJ.*

Schwartz, Alvin. *The Cat's Elbow and Other Secret Languages.* Pictures by Margot Zemach. Farrar. $9.95. ALA.

Schwartz, Amy. *Bea and Mr. Jones.* Bradbury. $8.95. *SLJ.*

Shub, Elizabeth. *The White Stallion.* Pictures by Rachel Isadora. Greenwillow. $7.50. ALA, *SLJ.*

Simon, Seymour. *The Long Journey from Space.* Crown. $9.95. ALA.

Singer, Isaac Bashevis. *The Golem.* Illus. by Uri Shulevitz. Farrar. $9.95. ALA, *SLJ.*

Spier, Peter. *Peter Spier's Rain.* Doubleday. $10.95. ALA.

Steig, William. *Doctor De Soto.* Farrar. $11.95. ALA.

Sutcliff, Rosemary. *The Road to Camlann.* Illus. by Shirley Felts. Dutton. $11.50. ALA.

Testa, Fulvio. *If You Take a Pencil*. Dial. $10.95. *SLJ*.

Thrasher, Crysta. *End of a Dark Road*. Atheneum. $10.95. *SLJ*.

Tinkelman, Murray. *Rodeo: The Great American Sport*. Greenwillow. $8.59; pap. $7. ALA.

Van Leeuwen, Jean. *Amanda Pig and Her Big Brother Oliver*. Pictures by Ann Schweninger. Dial. $8.89. ALA.

Vincent, Gabrielle. *Ernest and Celestine*. Greenwillow. $9. *SLJ*.

———. *Ernest and Celestine's Picnic*. Greenwillow. $9. ALA, *SLJ*.

———. *Smile, Ernest and Celestine*. Greenwillow. $9. *SLJ*.

Voigt, Cynthia. *Dicey's Song*. Atheneum. $10.95. ALA.

Walker, Lester. *Carpentry for Children*. Overlook. $14.95. ALA.

Walsh, Jill Paton. *The Green Book*. Illus. by Lloyd Bloom. Farrar. $9.95. *SLJ*.

Weiss, Ann E. *God and Government: The Separation of Church and State*. Houghton. $8.95. *SLJ*.

Williams, Vera B. *A Chair for My Mother*. Greenwillow. $9.50. ALA.

Wiseman, David. *Thimbles*. Houghton. $7.95. ALA.

Yep, Laurence. *Dragon of the Lost Sea*. Harper. $10.50. ALA.

BEST SELLERS OF 1982: HARDCOVER FICTION AND NONFICTION

Daisy Maryles

Senior Editor, *Publishers Weekly*

A look at the 1982 annual hardcover bestsellers reaffirms trends that have become more prevalent in these end-of-the-year lists (a preponderance of veteran novelists and how-to books) and reveals some surprises (higher unit sales for fiction best sellers).

The following specific observations can be made:

1. The fiction list was dominated by veterans of *Publishers Weekly*'s Annual Summary Bestseller lists—17 of the top 25 novels were by authors who have enjoyed spots on these lists in previous years. Even the two first novels were by writers who had made their reputations with nonfiction best sellers.

2. Sequels and science fiction were favored novels this year. Five of the top 15 fiction books were sequels, and one was the first book in a projected historical trilogy. Three science fiction titles were among the year's top sellers; last year we noted how unusual it was for even one science fiction novel to hit these lists.

3. Unit sales of the top 25 novels were higher than ever; for the first time, a few fiction titles with reported sales over 100,000 didn't even make the top 25 list. Last year only 21 of the top 25 sold more than 100,000 copies, down from 1980 when 24 out of the 25 fiction titles went over the 100,000-copy mark.

4. In nonfiction, self-help and how-to ruled the list. Including cookbooks, 10 of the top 25 nonfiction titles were giving consumers all manner of advice from an

Note: Adapted from *Publishers Weekly*, March 11, 1983, where the article was entitled "Hardcover Top Sellers."

exercise program to calorie-wise cooking recipes, from how to train a dog to how to increase sexual pleasure. Previously, a media superstar got a spot on these lists via a tell-all biography or autobiography; nowadays, a chance at a spot on the list is more likely via a book on exercise and diet.

5. Nonfiction unit sales also broke a record; for the first time, all the top 15 titles went over the 200,000 mark (actually 17 books had reported sales of 200,000 copies or more). Last year, only nine nonfiction books had sales of more than 200,000 books.

The books on *PW*'s annual bestseller lists, including runners-up, are ranked on the basis of sales figures supplied by publishers. These figures, according to the respective firms, reflect only 1982 U.S. trade sales—that is, sales to bookstores, wholesalers, and libraries only. Not included, claim publishers, are book club, overseas, and direct mail transactions. Some books appear in the listings without accompanying sales figures. These were submitted to *PW* in confidence, for use only in placing the titles in their correct positions on a specific list.

"Sales" as used on these lists refer to books shipped and billed in calendar year 1982. Publishers were asked to reflect returns made in 1981 in their numbers. Still, in many cases, the 1982 sales figures include books on bookstore and wholesaler shelves and/or books on the way back to the publishers' warehouses as well as books already stacking up on returns piles.

Since the two national bookstore chains—B. Dalton and Waldenbooks—have their own end-of-the-year bestseller lists, based on actual sales to customers as registered on the chains' computers, *PW* thought it might be interesting to compare the ranking of books on its annual list with the two compiled by the retailers. In fiction, 14 of the top 15 books on *PW*'s list placed among the top 15 of B. Dalton and Waldenbooks. In nonfiction, the duplication was lower; 10 nonfiction highrollers at B. Dalton and nine at Waldenbooks were also among *PW*'s top 15. This year, the *New York Times* compiled an annual bestseller list, based on the data gathered for its weekly lists. Comparisons with that list showed that 10 of the top 15 fiction and nonfiction books on the *Times* list ranked among *PW*'s top sellers.

THE FICTION BEST SELLERS

A new Michener novel usually guarantees the veteran writer the lead spot on these bestseller charts. In his latest magnum opus, the prolific writer ventures into a new frontier—*Space*—providing his readers with 622 pages of prodigious research on America's exploration of space, with stories and lectures on such issues as evolutionism vs. Creationism and the possibility of extraterrestrial life. Certainly, 1982 sales of 572,565 garnered the book the number 1 spot on our weekly national bestseller list through almost all of the busy fall and holiday selling season; but the sales earned Michener only the number 2 place on the annual list.

In fact, one of those extraterrestrial creatures captured the number 1 spot on the *PW* annual list—*E.T. The Extra-Terrestrial Storybook* by William Kotzwinkle, based on a screenplay by Melissa Mathison, with color stills from the popular film, had sales of about 665,800 last year, more than enough to make it the bestselling fiction book. Still, at $6.95 and some 56 pages (including pictures), the book's classification as a novel does raise some questions. In fact, B. Dalton never listed the book among its fiction bestseller titles and instead ranked it throughout the year among the chain's bestselling children's books, specifically since it was bought and merchandised as a book for children. But the appeal of *E.T.* transcended that youthful categorization, and the book became one of the few titles that breaks out of the children's area to be counted alongside books for adults. Both *PW* and the *Times*, as well as most retailers, considered it an adult fiction book on their weekly bestseller charts.

In addition to the popularity of outer space frontiers and characters, 1982 was a banner year for science fiction and fantasy. Three veteran writers of the genre placed on the fiction bestseller list. Isaac Asimov returned to science fiction, after over a decade of writing on other subjects, with the fourth novel in the Foundation series. In the number 12 spot, with sales of 213,297, the book is Asimov's two hundred and sixty-first book and first best seller. The series had already won the author a Hugo for "best all-time science fiction series." Taking the number 9 spot is Arthur C. Clarke's *2010: Odyssey Two*, the long-awaited sequel to the 1968 *2001: A Space Odyssey*. So far, Clarke's *2010* was the only book able to nudge *Space* off its top perch on *PW*'s weekly list (only for a week or two). Fantasy fiction enjoyed a notch on the annual top seller list with *The One Tree: Book Two, The Second Chronicles of Thomas Covenant*. Sales of 186,000 copies and a 22-week run on the weekly charts earned Stephen R. Donaldson the number 14 spot on the list.

Sequels also figured in three other novels in the top 15 grouping. In the number 6 position, with sales of 288,756, is *The Valley of Horses*, Jean Auel's sequel to her bestselling first novel, *The Clan of the Cave Bear*. Both books are installments in Auel's continuing sequence of The Earth Children™. *The Clan . . .* was a runner-up on the 1980 list with sales of 119,000 copies in its first year of publication. Jeffrey Archer earns the number 11 position with sales of 224,600 copies of *The Prodigal Daughter*. The book continues the tale begun in *Kane & Abel*, a 1980 runner-up best seller with sales of 121,000 books. And if the trend exhibited by this year's collection of bestselling sequels continues—stronger sales than the earlier installments—then *North and South* by John Jakes is off to a flying start. First of a projected historical trilogy dealing with events before, during, and after the American Civil War, Jakes's first hardcover took the number 8 spot with sales of 262,000. Previously, all eight volumes in his Kent Family Chronicles earned top spots on paperback bestseller charts.

Authors of the remaining novels making up the 1982 top 15 list—Ludlum, Sheldon, Krantz, King, Follett, Steel and Robbins—are synonymous with bestsellerdom. In the number 3 spot, Robert Ludlum changed publishers for his latest thriller, *The Parsifal Mosaic*, and enjoyed his highest sales ever—497,245 books. It was *PW*'s longest-running hardcover best seller in 1982 with 38 appearances on the weekly list. Interestingly, annual sales of 250,000 copies were enough to snag the number 1 spot on the 1979 end-of-the-year list; that was Ludlum's *The Matarese Circle*. Sidney Sheldon also had his highest hardcover sales with *Master of the Game*, number 4 on the 1982 list; in 1980 *Rage of Angels* made number 3, and in 1978, *Bloodline* hit number 4. *Mistral's Daughter* marks Judith Krantz's third time on an annual list—a perfect score considering that she has only published three books. Her first novel, *Scruples*, made the number 5 spot in 1978 with sales of 210,000 copies; in 1980, *Princess Daisy* sold about 300,000 titles and made number 4; and in 1982, sales of 295,045 secured the number 5 spot for *Mistral's Daughter*.

Bestselling author Stephen King (he made these lists in 1979, 1980, and 1981), tried something a bit different in 1982—instead of a full-length, horror-suspense novel, he offered his readers a quartet of novels with some of the elements that made him famous. The results—yet another best seller with sales of 270,264 and the number 7 spot on the annual list. Ken Follett's new thriller, *The Man from St. Petersburg*, added more elements of sentiment and romance than found in his previous books; the change only increased his readership, and sales of over 220,000 gave him the number 10 spot. In 1980, Follett's *The Key to Rebecca* made number 6; in 1979, he was the number 11 spot with *Triple;* and in 1978 *The Eye of the Needle* made number 10. Danielle Steel scored her biggest hardcover hit with *Crossings*, taking the number 13 position with sales of 198,833. She was the first runner-up in 1981 with sales of 127,571 for *Remembrance*.

Rounding out the top 15 is Harold Robbins's *Spellbinder* with sales of 163,000. The author's first appearance on these lists was in 1961 with *The Carpetbaggers* (number 5 with sales of 105,000) and his most recent one was in 1981 for *Goodbye, Janette* (number 7 with sales of 202,000 copies).

THE FICTION RUNNERS-UP

As noted earlier, a much wider spread of fiction titles achieved sales of 100,000 copies or more than ever before. And again in the second tier of fiction best sellers, the surest way to gain a spot was to have already published a best seller; six of the 10 books are by authors who have had novels on earlier end-of-the-year bestseller lists, and the two first novels *Lace* and *Celebrity*, were by authors with established records in nonfiction. Science fiction popularity continued with two books making the runners-up roster.

In ranked order, the 10 fiction runners-up are: *The Case of Lucy Bending* by Lawrence Sanders (Putnam, 8/82; 144,000 copies sold in 1982); *Eden Burning* by Belva Plain (Delacorte, 6/14/82; 135,224); *Second Heaven* by Judith Guest (Viking, 10/4/82; 127,993); *Cinnamon Skin* by John D. MacDonald (Harper & Row, 6/82; 125,162); *Friday* by Robert Heinlein (Holt, Rinehart and Winston, 6/1/82; 125,000); *Lace* by Shirley Conran (Simon & Schuster, 8/16/82; 124,000); *Thy Brother's Wife* by Andrew M. Greeley (Warner/Bernard Geis, 4/12/82; 120,181); *Life, the Universe and Everything* by Douglas Adams (Harmony, 10/19/82; 117,098); *Celebrity* by Thomas Thompson (Doubleday, 4/8/82; 113,334); and *Max* by Howard Fast (Houghton Mifflin, 9/21/82; 110,432).

THE NONFICTION LEADERS

Fitness and diet books continued to obsess American readers, and these books fattened the purses of otherwise figure-watching authors. The 1982 nonfiction top 15 list includes three books with calorie-conscious recipes and is headed by one of the most popular workout books to have ever been published—*Jane Fonda's Workout Book*. Its 1982 sales topped 692,000 copies: it was the longest-running hardcover best seller on *PW*'s weekly list with a total of 48 appearances, 27 in the number 1 position; and it was the leading hardcover seller in 1982 at both B. Dalton and Waldenbooks.

Richard Simmons scored another impressive hit with his *Never-Say-Diet Cookbook*, number 9 with sales of 294,576. His *Never-Say-Diet Book* was number 3 in 1981 with sales of 570,000 copies. Weight Watchers followers had two new recipe books to choose from in the bestselling stack: *The Weight Watchers Food Plan Diet Cookbook*, number 8 with sales of 300,000, and *Weight Watchers 365-Day Menu Cookbook*, number 11 with sales of 265,000. The latter enjoys a repeat performance; in its first year of publication (1981) it took the number 8 spot on the annual bestseller list with sales of 230,000 copies sold.

Even cookbooks with caloric recipes racked up hefty sales, and *Better Homes & Gardens New Cookbook* also makes a reappearance on these lists, this time in the number 4 spot with sales of 445,950 books sold in 1982. Last year, sales of over 465,000 copies garnered it the number 6 spot. It's the ninth edition of this perennial best seller, and it qualified for consideration as a new book since it was the first revision since 1964 (about 75 percent of the book was completely revised).

Two authors—Leo Buscaglia and Andrew A. Rooney—can relish the not-so-common distinction of having more than one of their books appear on the same end-of-the-year list. Leo Buscaglia takes the number 2 and number 12 spots for *Living, Loving and Learning* and *The Fall of Freddie the Leaf*, respectively. During 1982, Buscaglia also had two earlier books appear on the mass market and trade paperback lists. Known as "Dr. Love," Buscaglia writes books that offer an inspirational message aimed at helping people share in a better understanding of life and love. *Living, Loving and Learning* is a collection of lectures delivered worldwide by the author, an effective lecturer, between 1970 and 1981. *The Fall of Freddie the Leaf*, reminiscent of *Jonathan Livingston Seagull*, is an allegorical tale of the short life of a leaf illustrating the delicate balance between life and death.

Rooney's new book, *And More by Andy Rooney*, sold 510,714 copies in 1982, giving it the number 3 spot for the year; it was the runaway nonfiction best seller at Christmas time. His earlier book, *A Few Minutes with Andy Rooney*, makes a second appearance on these lists; its sales of 306,000 gives it the number 7 spot for 1982 (it was number 10 in 1981 with sales of 200,000 books). In both books the author's essays explore everyday life much in the same way Rooney does weekly on "60 Minutes" and three times a week in a syndicated column appearing in over 225 newspapers.

It was only two years ago that *PW* noted the growing trend in publishing—mass market firms entering the hardcover mainstream. It's not difficult to make note of yet another trend—that mass market firms are taking more and more spots on these annual end-of-the-year lists. The most impressive performance in this direction was by Warner Books, which has three of the top 15 nonfiction best sellers. In addition to the Richard Simmons book—which has the advantage of being written by the host of a nationally syndicated show on one of the major networks—Warner has two other top sellers (both of which made it to the lead position on national weekly bestseller charts)—*Life Extension*, number 5 with sales of 352,270 in 1982 and *Megatrends*, with 1982 sales of 210,708 giving it the number 15 position for the year. Billed as "a scientific approach" to gaining longevity, the authors, Durk Pearson and Sandy Shaw, appeared on many network talk shows; the publisher claims that one appearance by Pearson on "The Merv Griffin Show" drew the largest mail in the history of the program—over 100,000 letters. For *Megatrends*, the author had research teams studying 600 newspapers throughout America every month for 10 years. As part of the marketing plan, the publisher sent copies of *Megatrends* with a letter from Steve Ross, president of Warner Communications, to all presidents of the *Fortune* 500 companies as well as to the Washington press corps. Both actions certainly helped propel the book to bestsellerdom.

The eclecticism of the subjects that can make a nonfiction bestseller list is certainly obvious from the rest of the books on the top 15 nonfiction top sellers.

In the number 6 position with 1982 sales of about 332,000 is *When Bad Things Happen to Good People*, an inspirational book of faith by Boston-based rabbi Harold S. Kushner; the book was on *PW*'s 1982 bestseller list for 41 weeks and stayed on until a paperback edition appeared in mid-February. A book on training dogs takes the number 10 spot with sales of about 267,000 copies. The publisher attributes the phenomenal success of *No Bad Dogs: The Woodhouse Way* to the author's many appearances on television. Viewers were able to see Barbara Woodhouse train an untutored dog in six minutes in her 10-week syndicated program. A veteran English trainer, she estimates that she has trained about 17,000 dogs (and owners) over the past 30 years. Charles Paul Conn's third book on the Amway Corporation, *An Uncommon Freedom*, makes the list in the number 14 position with sales of 233,052 books. His first book on Amway was number 6 in 1977 with sales of 211,000 copies; in 1979, *The Winner's Circle* got the number 10 spot with sales of 210,000 copies. A good bit of controversy surrounded the publishing of number 13, *The G Spot*, but neither its rank nor criticism was unlucky for the book, which sold about 242,000 copies in 1982. The book offered women advice on attaining yet another new kind of orgasm by finding the so-called Grafenberg Spot.

THE NONFICTION RUNNERS-UP

The second tier of nonfiction best sellers offered a number of interesting books: an inspirational business manual, the memoirs of a former U.S. president; fitness advice for the pregnant woman; power advice for the ambitious woman; a personal memoir of a Pulitzer prize-winning columnist (the publisher claims the book owes its success almost entirely to early support by the independent booksellers across the country); the first of three volumes on another U.S. president's life by a Pulitzer Prize-winning author; and a sleeper best seller about well-run American businesses (the publisher's sales advance by early November was about 8,100 copies; by Christmas those numbers swelled to over 122,000 copies).

In ranked order, the 10 nonfiction runners-up are: *The One-Minute Manager* by Kenneth Blanchard and Spencer Johnson (Morrow, published 9/1/82); *Keeping Faith: Memoirs of a President* by Jimmy Carter (Bantam, 11/2/82; 200,000 copies sold in 1982); *Jane Fonda's Workout Book for Pregnancy, Birth and Recovery* by Femmy DeLyser (Simon & Schuster, 8/31/82; 172,200); *Having It All, Love, Success, Sex, Money* by Helen Gurley Brown (Simon & Schuster, 10/29/82; 171,400); *Growing Up* by Russell Baker (Congdon & Weed, 10/5/82; 154,582); *The Path to Power: Volume I of the Years of Lyndon Johnson* by Robert A. Caro (Knopf, 11/29/82; 153,398); *Betty Crocker's Microwave Cookbook* by General Mills (Random House, 9/25/82; 141,942); *Indecent Exposure: A True Story of Hollywood and Wall Street* by David McClintick (Morrow, 8/1/82); *Princess* by Robert Lacey (Times Books, 7/1/82; 125,000); and *In Search of Excellence: Lessons from America's Best-Run Companies* by Thomas J. Peters and Robert H. Waterman, Jr. (Harper & Row, 11/82; 122,218).

PUBLISHERS WEEKLY HARDCOVER TOP SELLERS

Fiction

1. *E.T. The Extra-Terrestrial Storybook* by William Kotzwinkle (published June 1982) Putnam; 665,800 copies sold in 1982
2. *Space* by James A. Michener (October 12, 1982) Random House; 572,565
3. *The Parsifal Mosaic* by Robert Ludlum (March 19, 1982) Random House; 497,245
*4. *Master of the Game* by Sidney Sheldon (September 1, 1982) Morrow
5. *Mistral's Daughter* by Judith Krantz (January 9, 1983; shipped on October 22, 1982) Crown; 295,045
6. *The Valley of Horses* by Jean M. Auel (September 10, 1982) Crown; 288,756
7. *Different Seasons* by Stephen King (August 27, 1982) Viking; 270,264
8. *North and South* by John Jakes (February 12, 1982) Harcourt Brace Jovanovich; 262,000
9. *2010: Odyssey Two* by Arthur C. Clarke (December 1, 1982) A Del Rey Book/Ballantine; 260,000
*10. *The Man from St. Petersburg* by Ken Follett (May 1, 1982) Morrow
11. *The Prodigal Daughter* by Jeffrey Archer (June 14, 1982) Linden Press; 224,600
12. *Foundation's Edge* by Isaac Asimov (October 8, 1982) Doubleday; 213,297
13. *Crossings* by Danielle Steel (September 7, 1982) Delacorte; 198,833
14. *The One Tree: Book Two of the Second Chronicles of Thomas Covenant* by Stephen R. Donaldson (April 12, 1982) A Del Rey Book/Ballantine; 186,000
15. *Spellbinder* by Harold Robbins (September 24, 1982) Simon & Schuster; 163,800

Note: Rankings on this list are determined by sales figures provided by publishers; the numbers reflect reports of copies "shipped and billed" only and should not be regarded as net sales figures since publishers do not yet know what their final returns will be.

*Sales figures were submitted to *PW* in confidence, for use only in placing the titles in their correct positions on a specific list.

Nonfiction

1. *Jane Fonda's Workout Book* by Jane Fonda (November 16, 1981) Simon & Schuster; 692,800
2. *Living, Loving and Learning* by Leo Buscaglia (April 15, 1982) Charles B. Slack/Holt, Rinehart and Winston; 550,000
3. *And More by Andy Rooney* by Andrew A. Rooney (October 25, 1982) Atheneum; 510,714
4. *Better Homes & Gardens New Cookbook* (August 1981) Meredith; 445,950
5. *Life Extension: Adding Years to Your Life and Life to Your Years—A Practical Scientific Approach* by Durk Pearson and Sandy Shaw (June 28, 1982) Warner; 352,270
6. *When Bad Things Happen to Good People* by Harold S. Kushner (October 5, 1981) Schocken; 332,000
7. *A Few Minutes with Andy Rooney* by Andrew A. Rooney (October 28, 1981) Atheneum; 306,000
8. *The Weight Watchers Food Plan Diet Cookbook* by Jean Nidetch (September 1982) NAL Books; 300,000
9. *Richard Simmons' Never-Say-Diet Cookbook* by Richard Simmons (June 28, 1982) Warner; 294,576
10. *No Bad Dogs: The Woodhouse Way* by Barbara Woodhouse (January 10, 1982) Summit Books; 267,000
11. *Weight Watchers 365-Day Menu Cookbook* by Weight Watchers International (October 1981) NAL Books; 265,000
12. *The Fall of Freddie the Leaf* by Leo Buscaglia (October 14, 1982) Charles B. Slack/Holt, Rinehart and Winston; 250,000
13. *The G Spot and Other Recent Discoveries about Human Sexuality* by Alice Kahn Ladas, Beverly Whipple and John D. Perry (September 15, 1982) Holt, Rinehart and Winston; 242,000
14. *An Uncommon Freedom* by Charles Paul Conn (April 15, 1982) Revell; 233,052
15. *Megatrends: Ten New Directions Transforming Our Lives* by John Naisbitt (October 18, 1982) Warner; 210,708

Part 7
Directory of Organizations

Directory of Library and Related Organizations

NATIONAL LIBRARY AND INFORMATION-INDUSTRY ASSOCIATIONS, UNITED STATES AND CANADA

AMERICAN ASSOCIATION OF LAW LIBRARIES
53 W. Jackson Blvd., Chicago, IL 60604
312-939-4764

OBJECT

"To promote librarianship, to develop and increase the usefulness of law libraries, to cultivate the science of law librarianship and to foster a spirit of cooperation among members of the profession." Established 1906. Memb. 2,850. Dues (Active) $65; (Inst.) $65; (Assoc.) $65 & $125; (Student) $10. Year. June 1 to May 31.

MEMBERSHIP

Persons officially connected with a law library or with a law section of a state or general library, separately maintained; and institutions. Associate membership available for others.

OFFICERS (JUNE 1982-1983)

Pres. Leah F. Chanin, Mercer Univ., Law Lib., Macon, GA 31207; *V.P./Pres.-Elect.* M. Kathleen Price, Univ. of Minnesota, Law Lib., 229 19 Ave. S., Minneapolis, MN 55455; *Secy.* Shirley Raissi Bysiewicz, Univ. of Connecticut, School of Law Lib., 1800 Asylum Ave., West Hartford, CT 06117; *Treas.* Joyce Malden, Municipal Reference Lib., 1004 City Hall, Chicago, IL 60602; *Immed. Past Pres.* Roger F. Jacobs, U.S. Supreme Court Law Lib., One First St., NE, Washington, DC 20543.

EXECUTIVE BOARD (1982-1983)

Officers; Anthony P. Grech; Marcia Koslov; Betty W. Taylor; Sarah K. Wiant; Maureen M. Moore; Harry S. Martin, III.

COMMITTEE CHAIRPERSONS (1982-1983)

Awards. Sue Wood, Supreme Court of New York, 500 Court House, Syracuse, NY 13202.

Certification Board. Edgar J. Bellefontaine, Social Law Lib., 1200 Court House, Boston, MA 02108.

CONELL. Sara Sonet, Supreme Court of the United States, Lib., One First St., Washington, DC 20543.

CONELL Co-Chair. Mickie A. Voges, Univ. of Texas, Tarlton Law Lib., 727 E. 26 St., Austin, TX 78705.

Constitution and Bylaws. Peter Schanck, Univ. of Detroit School of Law Lib., 651 E. Jefferson Ave., Detroit MI 48226.

Copyright. James S. Heller, U.S. Dept. of Justice Lib., 10 St. & Constitution Ave., Washington, DC 20530.

Education. Dan J. Freehling, Univ. of Maine School of Law, 246 Deering, Portland, ME 04102.

Elections. Francis Doyle, Loyola Univ. Law Lib., One E. Pearson St., Chicago, IL 60611.

Exchange of Duplicates. Margaret A. Lundahl, Isham, Lincoln & Beale, One 1st National Plaza, 42nd fl., Chicago, IL 60603.

Foreign, Comparative, and International Law. Claire M. Germain, Law School Lib., Duke Univ. School of Law, Durham, NC 27706.

Index to Foreign Legal Periodicals. Jan Stepan, Harvard Law School Lib., Langdell Hall, Cambridge MA 02138.

Indexing of Periodical Literature. George Grossman, Northwestern Univ., School of Law Lib., 357 E. Chicago Ave., Chicago, IL 60611.

Law Library Journal. Kenneth Zick, Wake Forest Univ., School of Law Lib., Winston-Salem, NC 27109.

Legislation & Legal Developments. Johanna Thompson, Delaware Law School Law Lib., Box 7475, Concord Pike, Wilmington, DE 19803.

Membership/Recruitment. Donald G. Ziegenfuss, Carlton, Fields, Ward, Emmanuel, Smith & Cutler, P.A. Lib., 20th fl., The Exchange National Bank Bldg., 610 N. Florida Ave., Tampa, FL 33602.

Memorials. George Skinner, Univ. of Arkansas, School of Law Lib., Fayetteville, AR 72701.

Nominations. John A. Sigel, California State Supreme Court Law Lib., 4241 State Bldg. Annex, 455 Golden Gate Ave., San Francisco, CA 94102.

Placement. Larry B. Wenger, Univ. of Virginia, Law Lib., North Grounds, Charlottesville, VA 22901.

Public Relations. Anne Haward Butler, Alston & Bird, 35 Broad St., 1200 C&S National Bank Bldg., Atlanta GA 30335.

Relations with Publishers & Dealers. Andrew R. Brann, Ohio State Univ., College of Law Lib., 1659 N. High St., Columbus, OH 43210.

Scholarships & Grants. William Benemann, Golden Gate Univ., School of Law, 536 Mission St., San Francisco, CA 94105.

Standards. Reynold J. Kosek, Mercer Univ., Walter F. George School of Law, 1021 Georgia Ave., Macon, GA 31201.

Statistics. David Thomas, Brigham Young Univ., Law Lib., Provo, UT 84602.

SPECIAL-INTEREST SECTION CHAIRPERSONS

Academic Law Libraries. Fannie S. Fishlyn, Univ. of Southern California Law Lib., University Park, Los Angeles, CA 90089.

Automation & Scientific Development. Duncan Webb, Michigan State Law Lib., Box 30012, Lansing MI 48909.

Contemporary Social Problems. David Bridgman, Santa Clara County Law Lib., 191 N. First St., San Jose, CA 95113.

Government Documents. Judy Gecas, Univ. of Chicago Law Lib., 1121 E. 60 St., Chicago, IL 60637.

Micrographics & Audio-Visual. Bethany Ochal, Orange County Law Lib., 515 N. Flower St., Santa Ana, CA 92703.

On-Line Bibliographic Services. Ermina Hahn, Rutgers Law Lib., 15 Washington St., Newark, NJ 07102.

Private Law Libraries. Margaret Shediac, Howard, Rice, Nemerovski, Canady & Pollak, 650 California St., Suite 2900, San Francisco, CA 94108.

Readers' Services. Chet Bunnell, Univ. of Mississippi Law Lib., Jackson MS 38677.

State, Court & County Law Libraries. Edgar Bellefontaine, Social Law

Lib., 1200 Court House, Boston, MA 02108.
Technical Services. Gayle S. Edelman, Univ. of Chicago Law Lib., 1121 E. 60 St., Chicago, IL 60637.

REPRESENTATIVES

ABA (American Bar Association). Robert F. Jacobs.
American Correctional Association. E. Ann Puckett.
American Library Association. Phyllis C. Marion.
American Library Association. Adult Services Committee, Inter-Library Loan Code Revision Committee. Randall Peterson.
American National Standards Institute. Committee PH-5. Larry Wenger.
American National Standards Institute. Committee Z-39. Robert L. Oakley.
American Society for Information Science. Jill Mubarak.
Association of American Law Schools. Bernard D. Reams, Jr.
British-Irish Association of Law Libraries. Muriel Anderson.
CLENE. Dennis J. Stone.
Canadian Association of Law Libraries. Lillian McPherson.
Council of National Library and Information Associations. Ad Hoc Committee on Copyright. Jack S. Ellenberger, William H. Jepson.
International Association of Law Libraries. Arno Liivak.
Library of Congress. Patrick E. Kehoe.
Special Libraries Association. Frances H. Hall.
U.S. Copyright Office. James S. Heller.

AMERICAN LIBRARY ASSOCIATION
Executive Director, Robert Wedgeworth
50 E. Huron St., Chicago, IL 60611
312-944-6780

OBJECT

The American Library Association is an organization for librarians and libraries with the overarching objective of promoting and improving library service and librarianship. Memb. (Indiv.) 33,888; (Inst.) 3,260. Dues (Indiv.) 1st year, $25; 2nd and 3rd years, $35; 4th year and beyond, $50; (Nonsalaried Libns.) $15; (Trustee & Assoc. Membs.) $20; (Student) $10; (Foreign Indiv.) $30; (Inst.) $50 & up (depending upon operating expenses of institution).

MEMBERSHIP

Any person, library, or other organization interested in library service and librarians.

OFFICERS

Pres. Carol A. Nemeyer, Assoc. Libn. for National Programs, Lib. of Congress, Washington, DC 20540; *V.P./Pres.-Elect.* Brooke E. Sheldon, Dir., School of Lib. Science, Texas Women's Univ., Denton TX 76204; *Treas.* Herbert Biblo, Dir., Long

Island Lib. Resources Council, Inc., Box 31, Bellport, NY 11713; *Exec. Dir. (Ex officio)* Robert Wedgeworth, ALA Headquarters, 50 E. Huron St., Chicago, IL 60611.

Address general correspondence to the executive director.

EXECUTIVE BOARD

Officers; *Immediate Past Pres.* Elizabeth (Betty) W. Stone (1983); E. J. Josey (1983); Ella G. Yates-Edwards (1983); Jane Anne Hannigan (1984); vacant (1984); Judith R. Farley (1985); Regina Minudri (1985); David Snider (1986); F. William Summers (1986).

ENDOWMENT TRUSTEES

William V. Jackson (1983); John Juergensmeyer (1984); John E. Velde (1982).

DIVISIONS

See the separate entries that follow: American Assn. of School Libns.; American Lib. Trustee Assn.; Assn. for Lib. Service to Children; Assn. of College and Research Libs.; Assn. of Specialized and Cooperative Lib. Agencies; Lib. Admin. and Management Assn.; Lib. and Info. Technology Assn.; Public Lib. Assn.; Reference and Adult Services Div.; Resources and Technical Services Div.; Young Adult Services Div.

PUBLICATIONS

American Libraries (11 per year; memb.).

ALA Handbook of Organizations and Membership Directory 1982-1983 (ann.).

ALA Yearbook (ann.; $60 hardbound, $25 paper).

Booklist (22 issues; $40).

Choice (11 issues; $75).

ROUND TABLE CHAIRPERSONS

(ALA staff liaison is given in parentheses.)

Exhibits. Larry Block, Univ. Microfilms International, 300 N. Zeeb Rd., Ann Arbor, MI 48106 (Chris J. Hoy).

Federal Librarians. Ellen Cook, 8510 Montpelier Dr., Laurel MD 20708 (Anne A. Heanue).

Government Documents. Barbara Kile, Government Documents & Microforms Dept., Fondren Lib., Rice Univ., Box 1892, Houston, TX 77251 (Bill Drewett).

Intellectual Freedom. Susan Kamm, Box 26467, Los Angeles, CA 90026 (Judith F. Krug).

International Relations. Edwin S. Holmgren, Dir., Branch Lib. Systems, New York Public Lib., New York, NY 10016.

Junior Members. June Breland, Mitchell Memorial Lib., Box 5408, Mississippi State Univ., MS 39762 (Patricia Scarry).

Library History. Anna Lous Ashby, Pierpont Morgan Lib., 29 E. 36 St., New York, NY 10017 (Joel M. Lee).

Library Instruction. May Brottman, Emerson Jr. H.S., 7101 N. Cumberland Ave., Niles, IL 60648 (Jeneice Guy).

Library Research. Ann Prentice, Dean, Grad. School of Lib. & Info. Science, Univ. of Tennessee, 804 Volunteer Blvd., Knoxville, TN 37916 (Mary Jo Lynch).

Map and Geography. Alice C. Hudson, Map Div., Public Lib., New York, New York 10018 (Celeste Lavelli).

Social Responsibilities. Linda Pierce, 3634 Edwards Rd., No. 27, Cincinnati, OH 45208 (Jean E. Coleman).

Staff Organizations. Kathleen Prendergast, Public Lib., 425 N. Michigan Ave., Chicago, Il 60611 (John Katzenberger).

COMMITTEE CHAIRPERSONS

Accreditation (Standing). Eleanor Montague, Univ. of Calif., Riverside, CA 92521 (Elinor Yungmeyer).

"American Libraries," Editorial Advisory Committee for (Standing). James Thompson, 7950 N. Stadium Dr., No. 166, Houston, TX 77030 (Arthur Plotnik).

Awards (Standing). Fred Lynden, 31 Ferry Lane, Barrington, RI 02806 (Peggy Barber).

Chapter Relations (Standing). Josette Lyders, 4322 Waycross, Houston, 77035 (Patricia Scarry).

Conference Program (Standing). William A. Gosling, Dorothy Pollet Gray, John A. Humphrey (Ruth R. Frame).

Constitution and Bylaws (Standing). Frances V. Sedney, Harford County Lib., 100 Pennsylvania Ave., Bel Air, MD 21014 (Miriam L. Hornback).

Council Orientation (Special). Joseph Kimbrough, Minneapolis Public Lib. & Info. Center, 300 Nicollet Mall, Minneapolis, MN 55401 (Miriam L. Hornback).

Instruction in the Use of Libraries (Standing). Joseph A. Boisse, Samuel Paley Lib., Temple Univ., Philadelphia, PA 19122 (Andrew M. Hansen).

Intellectual Freedom (Standing, Council). J. Dennis Day, Dir., Public Lib., 209 E. Fifth St. S., Salt Lake City, UT 84111 (Judith F. Krug).

International Relations (Standing, Council). Russell Shank, Univ. Libn., Univ. of California, Los Angeles, CA 90024.

Legislation (Standing, Council). Susan Brynteson, Dir. of Lib. Services, Univ. of Delaware, Newark DE 19711 (Eileen D. Cooke).

Library Education (Standing, Council). Evelyn H. Daniel, School of Info. Studies, Syracuse Univ., Syracuse, NY 13210 (Margaret Myers).

Library Personnel Resources, Office for (Standing, Advisory). Patricia Pond, School of Lib. & Info. Science, Univ. of Pittsburgh, PA 15260 (Margaret Myers).

Mediation, Arbitration, and Inquiry, Staff Committee on (Standing). Jeneice Guy, ALA Headquarters, 50 E. Huron St., Chicago, IL 60611.

Membership (Standing). Joseph Mika, Univ. of Southern Mississippi School of Lib. Services, Box 5146, Southern Sta., Hattiesburg, MS 39401.

National Library Week (Standing). Carole Cushmore, R. R. Bowker Co., 1180 Ave. of the Americas, New York, NY 10036 (Peggy Barber).

Organization (Standing, Council). Robert Rohlf, Hennepin County Lib., Edina, MN 55435 (Ruth R. Frame).

Outreach Services, Office for Library (Standing, Advisory). William D. Cunningham, 3806 V. St., SE, Washington, DC 20020 (Jean E. Coleman).

Planning (Standing, Council). Patricia Senn Breivik, Auraria Lib., Lawrence at 11 St., Denver, CO 80204 (Ruth R. Frame).

Professional Ethics (Standing, Council). Ann E. Prentice, Grad. School of Lib. Info. Science, Univ. of Tennessee, 804 Volunteer Blvd., Knoxville, TN 37916 (Judith F. Krug).

Program Evaluation and Support (Standing, Council). Beverly P. Lynch, Univ. of Illinois at Chicago Circle, Box 8198, Chicago, IL 60680 (Sheldon I. Landman).

Publishing (Standing, Council). John Y. Cole, Center for the Book, Lib. of Congress, Washington, DC 20540.

Reference and Subscription Books Review (Standing). Stuart W. Miller, International Assn. of Assessing Officers, 1313 E. 60 St., Chicago, IL 60637 (Helen K. Wright).

Research (Standing). Charles Davis, Dean, Grad. School of Lib. & Info.

Science, Univ. of Illinois, 410 David Kinley Hall, 1401 W. Gregory Dr., Urbana, IL 61801 (Mary Jo Lynch).

Resolutions (Standing, Council). Monteria Hightower, Public Lib., Seattle, WA 98104 (Miriam L. Hornback).

Standards (Standing). Jasper G. Schad, Box 68, Wichita State Univ., Wichita, KS 67208 (Ruth R. Frame).

Women in Librarianship, Status of (Standing, Council). Cynthia Johanson, Collection Management Div., Lib. of Congress, Washington, DC 20540 (Margaret Myers).

JOINT COMMITTEE CHAIRPERSONS

American Correctional Association—ASCLA Committee on Institution Libraries. Connie House, Box 6164, Arlington, VA 22206.

American Federation of Labor/Congress of Industrial Organizations-ALA, Library Service to Labor Groups, RASD. ALA Chpn. Arthur S. Meyers, 2105 Concord, Muncie, IN 47304; AFL/CIO Co-Chpn. Jim Auerback, AFL/CIO, Dept. of Educ., 815 16 St. N.W., Rm. 407, Washington, DC 20006.

Anglo-American Cataloguing Rules Common Revision Fund. ALA Rep. to be appointed; CLA Rep. Laurie Bowes, Canadian Lib. Assn., 151 Sparks St., Ottawa, Ont. K1P 5E3 Canada; (British) Lib. Assn. Rep. Joel C. Dowling, c/o Lib. Assn., 7 Ridgmount St., London, WC 1E 7AE, England.

Anglo-American Cataloguing Rules, Joint Steering Committee for Revision of. ALA Chpn. Frances Hinton, 105 W. Walnut Lane, Philadelphia, PA 19144.

Association for Educational Communications and Technology—AASL. AASL and AECT chpns. to be appointed.

Association of American Publishers—ALA. ALA Pres. Carol A. Nemeyer, Assoc. Libn. for National Programs, Lib. of Congress, Washington, DC 20540; AAP chpn. to be appointed.

Association of American Publishers—RTSD. ALA Chpn. Juanita S. Doares, Collection Management & Development, Rm. 105, Public Lib., Fifth Ave. & 42 St., New York, NY 10018; AAP Chpn. Judith Garodnick, One Wall St., Fort Lee, NJ 07024.

Children's Book Council—ALA. ALA Co-Chpn. Amy Kellman, Carnegie Lib., Pittsburgh, PA 15213; CBC Co-Chpn. Patricia Ross, Pantheon-Knopf Jr. Books, 201 E. 50 St., New York, NY 10022.

Society of American Archivists—ALA Joint Committee on Library-Archives Relationships. SAA Chpn. Peter Parker, Historical Society of Pennsylvania, 1300 Locust St., Philadelphia, PA 19107.

U.S. National Park Service—ALSC Joint Committee. ALSC Co-Chpn. Susan H. Galloway, 522 N. Rockwell, Apt. 15E, Oklahoma City, OK 73127; U.S. National Park Service Co-Chpn. Patricia M. Stanek, Cowpens National Battlefield, Box 335, Chesnee, SC 29323.

AMERICAN LIBRARY ASSOCIATION
AMERICAN ASSOCIATION OF SCHOOL LIBRARIANS
Executive Director, Alice E. Fite
Program Officer, Ruth E. Feathers
50 E. Huron St., Chicago, IL 60611
312-944-6780

OBJECT

The American Association of School Librarians is interested in the general improvement and extension of library media services for children and young people. AASL has specific responsibility for planning programs of study and service for the improvement and extension of library media services in elementary and secondary schools as a means of strengthening the educational program; evaluation, selection, interpretation, and utilization of media as they are used in the context of the school program; stimulation of continuous study and research in the library field and to establish criteria of evaluation; synthesis of the activities of all units of the American Library Association in areas of mutual concern; representation and interpretation of the need for the function of school libraries to other educational and lay groups; stimulation of professional growth, improvement of the status of school librarians, and encouragement of participation by members in appropriate type-of-activity divisions; and conduct activities and projects beyond the scope of type-of-activity divisions, after specific approval by the ALA Council. Established in 1951 as a separate division of ALA. Memb. 7,000.

MEMBERSHIP

Open to all libraries, school library media specialists, interested individuals and business firms with requisite membership in the ALA.

OFFICERS

Pres. Dorothy W. Blake, Atlanta Public Schools, 2930 Forrest Hill Dr. S.W., Atlanta, GA 30315; *1st V.P. Pres.-Elect.* Judith M. King, 333 University Blvd. W., #201, Kensington, MD 20895; *2nd V.P.* Glenn E. Estes; *Rec. Secy.* Winifred E. Duncan; *Past Pres.* Betty Jo Buckingham; *Exec Dir.* Alice E. Fite.

BOARD OF DIRECTORS

Regional Dirs. Edna M. Bayliss, Region I (1985); Rosa L. Presberry, Region II (1983); Richard J. Sorensen, Region III (1984); E. Louise Dial, Region IV (1985); Thomas L. Hart, Region V (1984); Lotsee P. Smith, Region VI (1983); Elizabeth B. Day, Region VII (l985); *Regional Dirs. from Affiliate Assembly.* Hugh A. Durbin (1984); Carolyn L. Cain (1983); *Affiliate Assembly Chpn.* Karen A. Whitney; *NPSS Chpn.* Jeanette M. Smith; *SS Chpn.* Elfrieda B. McCauley; *Ex officio Ed. School Library Media Quarterly.* Jack R. Luskay.

PUBLICATION

School Library Media Quarterly (q.; memb.; nonmemb. $20). *Ed.* Jack R. Luskay, John Jay Senior H.S., Katonah, NY l0536.

SECTION COMMITTEES— CHAIRPERSONS

Nonpublic Schools Section (NPSS)

Executive. Jeannette M. Smith, Forsyth Country Day School, 5501 Shallowford Rd., Lewisville NC 27023.

Bylaws. Walter E. DeMelle, Jr. Edsel Ford Memorial Lib., Hotchkiss School, Lakeville, CT 06039.
International and Domestic Exchanges (Ad Hoc). Elva A. Harmon, 1315 E. 26 Place, Tulsa, OK 74114.
Nominating—1983 Election. Mary Lou S. Treat, Winchester Rd, Northfield, MA 03160.
Program—Los Angeles, 1983. Stephen L. Matthews, Box 1233, Middleburg, VA 22117.

Supervisors Section (SS)

Executive. Elfrieda B. McCauley, Greenwich Public Schools, Havemeyer Bldg., 290 Greenwich Ave., Greenwich, CT 06830.
Bylaws. Ellen M. Stepanian, Shaker Heights City School Dist., 15600 Parkland Dr., Shaker Heights, OH 44120.
Nominating—1983 Election. James G. Maxwell, Lane Educational Service Dist., Box 2680, Eugene, OR 97401.
Publications (Ad Hoc). Mary Oppman, 7740 Oak Ave., Gary, IN 46403.
Program—Los Angeles, 1983. Constance J. Champlin, West Maple IMC, 8800 Maple St., Omaha NE 68104.
Critical Issues Facing School Library Media Supervisors (Discussion Group). Constance J. Champlin, 2051 N. 54 St., Omaha, NE 68104.

AASL COMMITTEE CHAIRPERSONS

Program Coordinating. Betty Jo Buckingham, State Dept. of Public Instruction, Grimes State Office Bldg., Des Moines, IA 50319.

Unit Group I—Organizational Maintenance

Unit Head. Marie V. Haley, Sioux City Community Schools, 1221 Pierce St., Sioux City, IA 51105.
Bylaws. Jean D. Battey, Dept. of Education, State Office Bldg., Montpelier, VT 05602.
Conference Program Planning—Los Angeles, 1983. Rosalind E. Miller, 404 University Lib., Georgia State Univ., University Plaza, Atlanta, GA 30303.
Local Arrangements—Los Angeles, 1983. Margaret H. Miller, 4321 Matilija Ave., Sherman Oaks, CA 91423.
Nominating—1983 Election. D. Philip Baker, c/o IMC, 21 Burdick St., Stamford, CT 06905.
Resolutions. Glenn E Estes, GLSIS, Univ. of Tennessee, 804 Volunteer Blvd, Knoxville, TN 37916.

Unit Group II—Organizational Relationships

Unit Head. Diane A. Ball, 2410 Fairmont Ave., Dayton, OH 45419.
American Association of School Administrators (Liaison). To be announced.
American University Press Services, Inc. (Advisory). Diane A. Ball, 2410 Fairmont Ave., Dayton, OH 45419.
Association for Educational Communications and Technology (Joint). To be announced.
Association for Supervision and Curriculum Development (Liaison). Karen A. Dowling, Professional Lib., Rm. 50, Montgomery County Public Schools, 850 Hungerford Rd., Rockville, MD 20850.
International Reading Association (Liaison). Virginia Mathews, 17 Overshore Dr. W., Hamden, CT 06514.
National Association of Secondary School Principals (Liaison). Edward W. Barth, 13802 Loree Lane, Rockville, MD 20853.
National Congress of Parents and Teachers (Liaison). Doris Masek, 6815 N. Algonquin Ave., Chicago, IL 60646.
National Council for the Social Studies (Liaison). Margaret B. Lefever, 7106 Beechwood Dr. Chevy Chase, MD 20815.

National Council of Teachers of English (Liaison). W. Duane Johnson, Lib. Science Dept, Univ. of Northern Iowa, Cedar Falls, IA 50613.
National Council of Teachers of Mathematics (Liaison). Edward W. Barth, 13802 Loree Lane, Rockville, MD 20853.

Unit Group III—Media Personal Development

Unit Head. Jill M. Sienola, 253 College St. S.W., Apt. 3-A, Valley City, ND 58072.
Library Education. Leah Hiland, Dept. of Lib. Science, Univ. of Northern Iowa, Cedar Falls, IA 50613.
Networking—Interconnection of Learning Resources. Donald C. Adcock, School Dist. No. 41, 793 N. Main St., Glen Ellyn, IL 60137.
Professional Development. Geraldine W. Bell, Public Schools, 2015 Park Place, Birmingham, AL 35202.
Research. Milbrey L. Jones, 201 Eye St. S.W., Apt. 819, Washington, DC 20024.
Video Communications. Joan E. Griffis, 4752 S.W. 39 Dr., Portland, OR 97221.

Unit Group IV—Media Program Development

Unit Head. Wanna M. Ernst, 16 Brisbane Dr., Charleston, SC 29407.
Early Childhood Education. Chow Loy Tom, 2101 E. Harvard Ave., Apt. 405, Denver, CO 80210.
Elementary School Materials Selection (Ad Hoc). Helen E. Williams, 9883 Good Luck Rd., Lanham, MD 20801.
Evaluation of School Media Programs. Linda S. York, 6031 Pineland Dr., Apt. 2008, Dallas, TX 75231.
Facilities, Media Center. Rebecca T. Bingham, Dir. of Lib. Media Services, Burrett Center, 4409 Preston Hwy., Louisville, KY 40213.
Library Media Skills Instruction (Ad Hoc). Patricia L. Meier, 2230 1/2 Ripley, Davenport, IA 52083.
School Faculty Materials Selection (Ad Hoc). Joan Myers, Dir. of Libs., School Dist. of Philadelphia, 21 St., S. of the Pkwy., Philadelphia, PA 19103.
School Library Media Sevices to Children with Special Needs. Jeannine L. Laughlin, School of Lib. Science, Univ. of Southern Mississippi, Box 5146, Southern Sta., Hattiesburg, MS 39401.
Secondary School Materials Selection (Ad Hoc). Margaret Lefever, 7106 Beechwood Dr. Chevy Chase, MD 20815.
Standards Program and Implementation. Donald A. Colberg, SEMBCS, 3301 S. Monaco, Denver, Co 80222.
Student Involvement in the Media Center Program. Doris W. Cox, Homestead Apts. #314, 808 W. Riverside, Muncie, IN 47303.
Vocational/Technical Materials Selection (Ad Hoc). Myran L. Slick, R.D. 2, Box 226, Holsopple, PA 15935.

Unit Group V—Public Information

Unit Head. David A. Russell, College of Education, Univ. of Wyoming, Laramie, WY 82071.
AASL Distinguished Library Service Award for School Administrators. Paula K. Montgomery, #32, 5842 Stevens Forest Rd., Columbia, MD 21045.
Intellectual Freedom Award/ AASL SIRS. Glenn E. Estes, SLIS, Univ. of Tennessee, 804 Volunteer Blvd., Knoxville, TX 37916.
Intellectual Freedom Representation and Information. To be announced.
International Relations. Lucille C. Thomas, 1184 Union St., Brooklyn, NY 11225.
Legislation. Paula M. Short, 302

Colony Woods Dr., Chapel Hill, NC 27514.

President's Award Selection. AASL/Baker & Taylor. Ellen M. Stepanian, Shaker Heights City School Dist., 15600 Parkland Dr., Shaker Heights, OH 44120.

School Library Media Program of the Year Award Selection, AASL/Encyclopaedia Britannica. Donald A. Colberg, SEMBCS, 3301 Monaco, Denver, CO 30222.

COMMITTEES (SPECIAL)

AASL General Conference—Houston, 1982. Albert H. Saley, R.D. 1, Box 111, Blairstown, NJ 07028.

Publications Advisory. Helen Lloyd Snoke, School of Lib. Science, Univ. of Michigan, 580 Union Dr., Ann Arbor, MI 48109.

REPRESENTATIVES

ALA Legislation Assembly. Paula M. Short.

ALA Membership Promotion Task Force. Anne C. Ansley.

Associated Organizations for Professionals in Education. Leah Hiland.

Education U.S.A. Advisory Board. Alice E. Fite.

Educational Media Council. Alice E. Fite.

Freedom to Read Foundation. To be appointed.

Library Education Assembly. Leah Hiland.

RTSD/CCS/AASL Cataloging of Children's Materials. Winifred E. Duncan.

AFFILIATE ASSEMBLY

The Affiliate Assembly is composed of the representatives and delegates of the organizations affiliated with the American Association of School Librarians. The specific purpose of this assembly is to provide a channel for communication for reporting concerns of the affiliate organizations and their membership and for reporting the actions of the American Association of School Librarians to the affiliates.

Executive Committee

Karen A. Whitney, 8247 W. Vale Dr., Phoenix, AZ 85033.

Bylaws

Carol Diehl, School Dist., 901 W. Washington St., New London, WI 54961.

Nominating Committee—1983 Election

Barbara J. Nemer, 3449 Yates Ave. N., Crystal, MN 55422.

Affiliate Assembly Recommendations Committee

Bernice L. Yesner, 16 Sunbrook Rd., Woodbridge CT 06525.

Affiliates

Region I. Connecticut Educational Media Assn.; Massachusetts Assn. for Educational Media; Maine Educational Media Assn.; New England Educational Media Assn.; Rhode Island Educational Media Assn.; Vermont Educational Media Assn.

Region II. Delaware Learning Resources Assn.; District of Columbia Assn. of School Libns.; Maryland Educational Media Organization; Educational Media Assn. of New Jersey; Pennsylvania School Libns. Assn.; School Lib. Media Sec., New York Lib. Assn.

Region III. Assn. for Indiana Media Educators; Illinois Assn. for Media in Education; Iowa Educational Media Assn.; Michigan Assn. for Media in Education; Minnesota Educational Media Organization; Missouri Assn. of School Libns.; Ohio Educational Lib. Media Assn.; Wisconsin School

Lib. Media Assn.; School Div., Michigan Lib. Assn.

Region IV. Mountain Plains Lib. Assn., Children's & School Sec.; Colorado Educational Media Assn.; Kansas Assn. of School Libns.; Nebraska Educational Media Assn.; Nebraska Lib. Assn. School, Children's & Young People's Sec.; North Dakota Assn. of School Libns.; South Dakota School Lib./Media Assn.; Wyoming School Lib. Media Assn.

Region V. Alabama Instructional Media Assn.; Children & School Libns. Div., Alabama Lib. Assn.; Florida Assn. for Media in Education, Inc.; Georgia Lib. Media Dept.; School & Children's Sec., Georgia Lib. Assn.; Kentucky School Media Dept.; North Carolina Assn. of School Libns.; School & Children's Sec., Southeastern Lib. Assn.; South Carolina Assn. of School Libns.; School Lib. Sec., Tennessee Education Assn.; Virginia Educational Media Assn.

Region VI. Louisiana Assn. of School Libns.; School Libs., Children, Young Adult Services, New Mexico Lib. Assn.; Oklahoma Assn. of School Lib. Media Specialists; School Libs. Div., Arizona State Lib. Assn.; School Libs. Div., Arkansas Lib. Assn.; Texas Assn. of School Libs.

Region VII. AASL-Alaska; California Media & Lib. Educators Assn.; Hawaii Assn. of School Libs.; Oregon Educational Media Assn.; School Lib./Media Div., Montana Lib. Assn.; Washington State Assn. of School Libns.

AMERICAN LIBRARY ASSOCIATION
AMERICAN LIBRARY TRUSTEE ASSOCIATION
ALTA Program Officer, Sharon L. Jordan
50 E. Huron St., Chicago, IL 60611
312-944-6780

OBJECT

The development of effective library service for all people in all types of communities and in all types of libraries; it follows that its members are concerned as policymakers with organizational patterns of service, with the development of competent personnel, the provision of adequate financing, the passage of suitable legislation, and the encouragement of citizen support for libraries. Open to all interested persons and organizations. Organized 1890. Became an ALA division 1961. Memb. 1,710. (For dues and membership year, see ALA entry.)

OFFICERS (1982-1983)

Pres. M. Don Surratt, 3717 N. Pine Grove, Chicago, IL 60613; *1st V.P./Pres. Elect.* Barbara Cooper, 936 Intracoastal Dr., #6-D, Fort Lauderdale, FL 33304; *2nd V.P.* Joanne Wisener; *Secy.* Herbert Davis; *Council Rep./Parliamentarian.* Jean M. Coleman.

BOARD OF DIRECTORS

Officers; *Council Administrators,* Jeanne Davies (1982); Gloria Glaser (1982); Jo Anne Thorbeck (1982); Esther Lopato (1983); Norma Buzan (l983); *Reg. V.Ps.* Kay Vowvalidis (1983); Schuyler Mott (1983); Athalie

Solloway (1982); Nell Henry (1983); Mildred King (1983); Lila Milford (1983); Eugene Harple (1983); Aileen Schrader (1984); Ione Simek (1984); James Voyles (1984); *Past Pres.* Jeanne Davies; *PLA Past Pres. Ex officio.* Agnes Griffen (1983); Ed. *The ALTA Newsletter.* Nancy Stiegemeyer.

PUBLICATION

The ALTA Newsletter. Ed. Nancy Stiegemeyer, 215 Camellia Dr., Cape Girardeau, MO 63701.

COMMITTEE CHAIRPERSONS

Action Development. Charles Reid, 620 West Dr., Paramus, NJ 07652.

ALTA Foundation Committee. Herbert Davis, Box 108, Brooklandville, MD 21022.

Awards. Lila Milford, 1225 Northwood Ct., Marion, IN 46952.

Budget. Barbara Cooper, 936 Intracoastal Dr., #6-D, Fort Lauderdale, FL 33304.

Committee on Service to Specialized Clientele. Marguerite W. Yates, 190 Windemere Rd., Lockport NY 14094; Arthur Kirschenbaum, Washington, DC.

Conference Program and Evaluation. Norma Buzan, 3057 Betsy Ross Dr., Bloomfield Hills, MI 48013.

Education of Trustees. Jerome Brill, 38 McElroy St., West Islip, NY 11795; Robert Manley, 816 Union Blvd., West Islip, NY 11795.

Intellectual Freedom. Patricia Turner, 3419 Redman Rd., Balitmore MD 21207.

Jury on Trustee Citations. Virginia Young, 10 E. Parkway Dr., Columbia, MO 65201; Minnie-Lou Lynch, 404 E. Sixth St., Oakdale, LA 71463.

Legislation. Sylvia Shorstein, 6908 LaLoma Dr., Jacksonville FL 32217; Norma Mihalevich, Box 287, Crocker, MO 65452.

Nominating. Jeanne Davies, Box 159, Deer Trail, CO 80105.

Publications. James A. Hess, 91 Farms Rd. Circle, East Brunswick, NJ 08816.

Publicity. Nancy Bray, 801 North St., #5, Cape Girardeau, MO 63701; Mary Anne Heaphy, 43 Oswego St., Baldwinsville, NY 13027.

Resolutions Committee. John Parsons, One Scott Circle, Apt. 112, Washington DC 20036.

Speakers Bureau. Mardy Dane, 21380 Edgecliff Dr., Euclid, OH 44123.

State Associations. Joanne Wisener, 860 19 Place, Yuma, AZ 85364.

Task Force on Liaison with Leagues of Municipalities. Theodore Wenzl, 83 Jordan Blvd., Delmar, NY 12054.

Task Force on Membership. John Parsons, One Scott Circle, Apt. 112, Washington, DC 20036.

AMERICAN LIBRARY ASSOCIATION
ASSOCIATION FOR LIBRARY SERVICE TO CHILDREN
Executive Director, Ann Carlson Weeks
50 E. Huron St., Chicago, IL 60611
312-944-6780

OBJECT

"Interested in the improvement and extension of library services to children in all types of libraries. Responsible for the evaluation and selection of book and nonbook materials for, and the improvement of techniques of, library services to children from preschool through the eighth grade or junior high school age, when such materials or techniques are intended for use in more than one type of library." Founded 1900. Memb. 4,978. (For information on dues see ALA entry.)

MEMBERSHIP

Open to anyone interested in library services to children.

OFFICERS (JULY 1982-JULY 1983)

Pres. Margaret M. Kimmel, School of Lib. & Info. Science, Univ. of Pittsburgh, 135 N. Bellefield, Pittsburgh, PA 19103; *V.P.* Phyllis Van Orden, 2009 Ted Hines, Tallahassee, FL 32308; *Exec. Dir.* Ann Carlson Weeks, ALSC/ALA, 50 E. Huron St., Chicago, IL 60611; *Past Pres.* Helen Mullen, Office of Work with Children, Free Lib. of Philadelphia, Logan Sq., Philadelphia, PA 19103.

(Address general correspondence to the executive director.)

DIRECTORS

Officers; Margaret Bush (ALA Councilor); Adele M. Fasick; Linda R. Silver; Elizabeth Huntoon; Mary R. Somerville; Caroline Ward; Marianne Carus; Ruth I. Gordon; Virginia McKee.

PUBLICATIONS

Top of the News (q.; memb.; $20 nonmemb.).

COMMITTEE CHAIRPERSONS

Priority Group I—Child Advocacy

Coord. Marilyn Iarusso, Office of Children's Services, New York Public Lib., 455 Fifth Ave., New York, NY 10016.
Boy Scouts of America (Advisory).

Andrea L. Hynes, 7208 Zircon Dr. S.W., Tacoma, WA 98498.
Legislation. Susan Collier, 76 Whitman Dr., New Providence, NJ 07974.
Mass Media (Liaison with). Sara L. Miller, 52-6 Foxwood Dr., Pleasantville, NY 10570.
Organizations Serving the Child (Liaison with). Jeanette A. Studley, 2622 Garfield St. NW, Washington, DC 20008.
U.S. National Park Service/ALS (Joint). Susan H. Galloway, 522 N. Rockwell, Apt. 15E, Oklahoma City, OK 73127.

Priority Group II—Evaluation of Media

Coord. Gertrude B. Herman, 1425 Skyline Dr., Madison, WI 53705.
Mildred L. Batchelder Award Selection—1983. Patricia J. Cianciola, 4206 Wabaningo Rd., Okemos, MI 48864.
Mildred L. Batchelder Award Selection—1984. M. Jean Greenlaw, North Texas State Univ., Box 13857, Denton TX 76203.
Caldecott Award—1983. Marilyn B. Iarusso, Office of Children's Services, New York Public Lib., 8 E. 40 St., New York, NY 10016.
Caldecott Award—1984. Ellin Greene, Graduate Lib. School, Univ. of Chicago, 1100 E. 57 St., Chicago, IL 60637.
Film Evaluation. Robert J. Grover, 1725 Trowman Way, Emporia, KS 66801.
Filmstrip Evaluation. Maria Salvadore, Children's Services, D.C. Public Lib. System, 901 G. St. NW, Washington, DC 20001.
"Multimedia Approach to Children's Literature" Revision (Ad Hoc). Lynne R. Pickens, 1481 Hampton Ct., Decatur, GA 30033.
Newbery Award—1983. Margaret N. Coughlan, Children's Literature Center, Lib. of Congress, Washington, DC 20540.

Newbery Award—1984. Elizabeth M. Greggs, King County Lib. System, 300 Eighth Ave. N., Seattle, WA 98109.

Notable Children's Books. Marilyn Kaye, Div. of Lib. and Info. Science, St. John's Univ., Jamaica, NY 11439.

Notable Children's Books 1976—1980 Reevaluation (ad hoc). Amy Kellman, 211 Castlegate Rd., Pittsburgh, PA 15221.

Recording Evaluation. Sharon Gunn, 2678 Briarlake Woods Way, Atlanta, GA 30345.

Selection of Children's Books from Various Cultures. Grace Ruth, 859 42 Ave., San Francisco, CA 94121.

Toys, Games and Realia Evaluation. Janet J. Gilles, 35730 Timberlane Dr.; Solon, OH 44139.

Laura Ingalls Wilder Award—1983. Spencer Shaw, School of Libnshp., Suzzalo Lib., FM-30, Univ. of Washington, Seattle, WA 98195.

Priority Group III—Professional Development

Coord. Barbara M. Barstow, Berea Public Lib., 7 Berea Commons, Berea, OH 44017.

Arbuthnot Honor Lecture. Phillis M. Wilson, 4806 Carriage Park Rd., Fairfax, VA 22032.

Continuing Education. Lois Winkel, 1113 Hill St., Greensboro, NC 27408.

Managing Children's Services (Discussion Group). Mary Bauer, 10216 Edgewood Ave., Silver Spring, MD 20901.

Media Evaluation: The Group Process, Implementation (Ad Hoc). Bridget L. Lamont, Illinois State Lib., Development Group, Centennial Bldg., Rm. 011, Springfield, IL 62756.

Melcher Scholarship. Deborah Weilerstein, Arlington County Dept. of Libs., 1015 N. Quincy St., Arlington, VA 22201.

Charles Scribner Award Selection. BettyJo Peterson, Children's Literature Specialist, Henry Madden Lib., California State Univ., Fresno, CA 93740.

State and Regional Leadership (Discussion Group). Margo Daniels, 7400 Old Dominion Dr., McLean, VA 22101.

Teachers of Children's Literature (Discussion Group). Judith Weedman, 1950 W. Liberty, #7, Ann Arbor, MI 48103.

Priority Group IV—Social Responsibilities

Coord. Kathleen S. Reif, 1020 St. Albans Rd., Baltimore, MD 21239.

Children with Special Needs (Library Services to). Judith F. Davie, 2515A Patriot Way, Greensboro, NC 27408.

Intellectual Freedom. Mae Benne, 331 N.W. 53, Seattle, WA 98107.

International Relations. Mary Lou White, 2530 Brookdale Dr., Springfield, OH 45502.

Preschool Services and Parent Education. Kathy A. East, 7011 Rock Woods Place, Worthington, OH 43085.

Program Support Publications (Ad Hoc). Beth Babikow, Baltimore County Public Lib., 320 York Rd., Towson, MD 21204.

Social Issues in Relation to Library Materials and Services for Children (Discussion Group). Anitra T. Steele, Mid-Continent Public Lib., 15616 E. 24 Hwy., Independence, MO 64050.

Priority Group V—Planning, Research,and Development

Coord. Neel Parikh, 2136 Byron St., Berkeley, CA 94702.

Collection of Children's Books for Adult Research (Discussion Group). Henrietta Smith, 1202 N.W. Second St., Delray Beach, FL 33444.

Local Arrangements—Los Angeles

1983. Priscilla Moxom, 2924 Angus St., Los Angeles, CA 90039.
Membership. Jill L. Locke, Farmington Community Lib., 32737 W. 12 Mile Rd., Farmington Hills, MI 48018.
Nominating—1983. Gail Sage, 1721 Laguna Rd., Santa Rosa, CA 95401.
Organization and Bylaws. Ethel B. Manheimer, 2373 Woolsey St., Berkeley, CA 94705.
Program Evaluation and Support. Hellen Mullen, Office of Work with Children, Free Lib. of Philadelphia, Logan Sq., Philadelphia PA 19103.
Publications. Marjorie Jones, The Junior Literary Guild, 245 Park Ave., New York, NY 10167.
Research and Development. Ellin Greene, Univ. of Chicago, Grad. Lib. School, 1100 E. 57 St., Chicago, IL 60637.
Special Collections (National Planning of). Mary E. Bogan, Box 891, Emporia, KS 66801.
"Top of the News" (Joint ALSC/YASD Editorial). Marilyn J. Kaye, Div. of Lib. & Info. Science, St. John's Univ., Jamaica, NY 11439.

REPRESENTATIVES

ALA Appointments. Phyllis Van Orden.
ALA Budget Assembly. Phyllis Van Orden.
ALA Legislation Assembly. Susan Collier.
ALA Library Education Assembly. Lois Winkel.
ALA Dallas Conference (1984) Conference Program. Phyllis Van Orden.
ALA Membership Promotion Task Force. Jill L. Locke.
Caroline M. Hewins Scholarship. Priscilla Moulton.
International Board on Books for Young People, U.S. Section, Executive Board. Margaret Kimmel, Ann Carlson Weeks, Mary Lou White.

RTSD/CCS Cataloging of Children's Materials. Helen P. Gregory; Marilyn Karrenbrock.

LIAISON WITH OTHER NATIONAL ORGANIZATIONS

American Association for Gifted Children. Naomi Noyes.
American National Red Cross. Red Cross Youth. Barbara Shumer.
Association for Children and Adults with Learning Disabilities. Clara Bohrer.
Big Brothers and Big Sisters of America. Helen Mullen.
Boys Clubs of America. Jane Kunstsler.
Camp Fire Inc. Anitra T. Steele.
Child Welfare League of America. Ethel Ambrose.
Children's Defense Fund. Effie Lee Morris.
Children's Theatre Association. Amy E. Spaulding.
Day Care and Child Development Council of America. Margaret Bush.
Four-H Programs, Extension Service. Elizabeth Simmons.
Girls Clubs of America. Karen Breen.
Girl Scouts of America. To be announced.
National Association for the Education of Young Children. Jeanette Studley.
National Story League. Linda Hansford.
Parents Without Partners. To be announced.
Puppeteers of America. Darrell Hildebrandt.
Salvation Army. Margaret Malm.
Society of American Magicians. Marion Peck.
Young Men's Christian Association. Jill L. Locke.
Young Women's Christian Association. Elizabeth Simmons.

AMERICAN LIBRARY ASSOCIATION
ASSOCIATION OF COLLEGE AND RESEARCH LIBRARIES
Executive Director, Julie A. Carroll Virgo
50 E. Huron St., Chicago, IL 60611
312-944-6780

OBJECT

"Represents research and special libraries and libraries in institutions of postsecondary education, including those of community and junior colleges, colleges, and universities." Founded 1938. Memb. 9,000. (For information on dues, see ALA entry.)

OFFICERS (JULY 1982-JULY 1983)

Pres. Carla J. Stoffle, Univ. of Wisconsin-Parkside, Kenosha, WI 53141; *V.P./Pres.-Elect.* Joyce Ball, California State Univ., Sacramento, CA 95819; *Past Pres.* David C. Weber, Stanford Univ., Stanford, CA 94305.

BOARD OF DIRECTORS

Officers; section chairs and vice-chairs; *Dirs.-at-Large.* George M. Bailey (1983); Imogene I. Book (1984); Sara Lou Whildin (1984); Barbara Collinsworth (1985); Betty L. Hacker (1985); Willis M. Hubbard (1985); Donald F. Jay (1983); Jean Major (1986).

PUBLICATIONS

ACRL Nonprint Media Publications (occasional). *Ed.* Jean W. Farrington, 221 Martroy Lane, Wallingford, PA 19086.

ACRL Publications in Librarianship (formerly *ACRL Monograph Series*) (occasional). *Ed.* Arthur P. Young, Univ. of Rhode Island, Kingston, RI 02881.

Choice (11 per year; $75); *Choice Reviews on Cards* ($150). *Ed.* Rebecca D. Dixon, 100 Riverside Center, Middletown, CT 06457.

College & Research Libraries (6 per year; memb.; nonmemb. $35). *Ed.* C. James Schmidt, Research Library Group, Jordan Quad, Stanford, CA 94305.

College & Research Libraries (11 per year; memb.; nonmemb.; $10). *Ed.* George M. Eberhart, ACRL Headquarters.

SECTION CHAIRPERSONS

Anthropology. Pamela Haas, American Museum of Natural History Lib., Central Park W. at 79 St., New York, NY 10024.

Art. Shirley Solvick, 630 Merrick, No. 202, Detroit, MI 48202.

Asian and African. Merry Burlingham, 309 E. 33 St., Apt. B, Austin, TX 78705.

Bibliographic Instruction. Anne Roberts, State Univ. of New York, Lib. 104, 1400 Washington Ave., Albany, NY 12222.

College Libraries. Thomas Kirk, Berea College, Berea, KY 40404.

Community and Junior College Libraries. Joseph Linderfeld, 491 N. Highland St., Apt. 12, Memphis, TN 38122.

Education and Behavioral Science. Hannelore Rader, Lib. Learning Center, Univ. of Wisconsin-Parkside, Kenosha, WI 53141.

Law and Political Science. Robert Goehlert, Indiana Univ. Lib., Bloomington, IN 47405.

Rare Books and Manuscripts. Joan M. Friedman, 178 Linden St., New Haven, CT 06511.

Science and Technology. Charles L. Gilreath, Texas A & M Univ. Lib., College Station, TX 77843.

Slavic and East European. Tatjana Lorkovic, Univ. of Iowa Lib., Iowa City, IA 52242.
University Libraries. Kenneth G. Peterson, Morris Lib., Southern Illinois Univ., Carbondale, IL 62901.
Western European Specialists. Charles Fineman, Univ. of California, Santa Cruz, CA 95064.

DISCUSSION GROUPS

Black Studies Librarianship. Jeff Jackson, Reference Dept., Univ. of Wisconsin-Parkside, Wood Rd., Kenosha, WI 53141.
Cinema Librarians. Nancy H. Allen, Community Lib., Univ. of Illinois, 122 Gregory HL, Urbana, IL 61501.
Librarians of Library Science Collections. Jean L. Loup, Lib., Univ. of Michigan, Ann Arbor, MI 48109 (1983).
Staff Development in Academic Research Libraries. Nancy Kranich, New York, NY 10012.
Undergraduate Librarians. Lynne Brody, Academic Center 101, Univ. of Texas, Austin, TX 78712.

COMMITTEE CHAIRPERSONS

ACRL Academic or Research Librarian of the Year Award. Patricia Oyler, Simmons College, School of Lib. Science, Boston, MA 02115.
"ACRL Nonprint Media Publications" Editorial Bd. Ed. Jean W. Farrington, 221 Martroy Lane, Wallingford, PA 19086 (1984).
"ACRL Publications in Librarianship" Editorial Bd. Ed. Arthur P. Young, Univ. of Rhode Island, Kingston, RI 02881 (1987).
Academic Status. D. Kaye Gapen, Gorgas Lib., Univ. of Alabama, University, AL 35486 (1983).
Appointments (1982) and Nominations (1983). P. Grady Morein, Univ. of Evansville, Evansville, IN 47702.

Audiovisual. Linda Piele, Univ. of Wisconsin-Parkside, Kenosha, WI 53141 (1984).
Budget and Finance. Sherrie Bergman, Wheaton College, Norton, MA 02766 (1984).
Chapters Council. Wendy Culotta, 2120 Florida Ave., Long Beach, CA 90814.
"Choice" Editorial Bd. Dwight F. Burlingame, Bowling Green State Univ., Bowling Green, OH 43403 (1983).
"College & Research Libraries" Editorial Bd. Ed. C. James Schmidt, Research Libs. Group, Jordan Quad, Stanford, CA 94305.
"College & Research Libraries News" Editorial Bd. Jean Whalen, State Univ. of New York, 1400 Washington Ave., Albany, NY 12222 (1984).
College Library Standards (Ad Hoc). Jacquelyn Morris, Univ. of the Pacific, Irving Martin Lib., Stockton, CA 95211.
Conference Program Planning—Los Angeles, 1983. Carla J. Stoffle, Univ. of Wisconsin-Parkside, Wood Rd., Kenosha, WI 53141.
Conference Program Planning—Dallas, 1984. Joyce Ball, California State Univ., 200 Jed Smith Dr., Sacramento, CA 95819.
Constitution and Bylaws. Karen Wittenborg, Stanford Univ., Stanford, CA 94305 (1984).
Continuing Education. Keith Cottam, 1211 Gen. MacArthur Dr., Brentwood, TX 37027.
Copyright Committee (Ad Hoc). Mary Williamson, Univ. of Wisconsin Memorial Lib., Madison, WI 53706.
Legislation. Elaine Sloan, Indiana Univ. Lib., Bloomington, IN 47401 (1984).
Membership. O. Gene Norman, 2417 Morton St., Terre Haute, IN 47802 (1983).

Planning. David C. Weber, Stanford Univ., Stanford, CA 94305 (1983).
Publications. Joanne R. Euster, J. Paul Leonard Lib., San Francisco State Univ., San Francisco, CA 94132 (1984),
Standards and Accreditation. Patricia Ann Sacks, 2997 Fairfield Dr., Allentown, PA 18103 (1984).
Supplemental Funds. To be announced.

REPRESENTATIVES

ALA Interdivisional Committee on Catalog Form, Function and Use. Sue Martin.
American Association for the Advancement of Science. Jacqueline Morris.
American Council on Education. Joseph Boisse.
ALA Committee on Appointments. Joyce Ball.
ALA Conference Program Planning Committee (Los Angeles, 1983). Carla Stoffle.
ALA Conference Program Planning Committee (Dallas, 1984). Joyce Ball.
ALA Legislation Assembly. Elaine Sloan.
ALA Membership Promotion Task Force. O. Gene Norman.
ALA Planning and Budget Assembly. Joyce Ball.
ALA Resources and Technical Services Division, Committee on Cataloging: Description and Access. LeRoy D. Ortopan.
ALA Standing Committee on Library Education (SCOLE). Keith Cottam; D. Kaye Gapen; Jean L. Loup.
Association for Asian Studies, Committee on East Asian Libraries. Warren Rsuneishi.
Freedom to Read Foundation. Tom G. Watson.
LC Cataloging in Publication Advisory Group. Richard C. Pollard.

AMERICAN LIBRARY ASSOCIATION
ASSOCIATION OF SPECIALIZED AND COOPERATIVE LIBRARY AGENCIES
Executive Director, Sandra M. Cooper
50 E. Huron St., Chicago, IL 60611
312-944-6780

OBJECT

To represent state library agencies, specialized library agencies, and multitype library cooperatives. Within the interest of these types of library organizations, the Association of Specialized and Cooperative Library Agencies has specific responsibility for:

1. Development and evaluation of goals and plans for state library agencies, specialized library agencies, and multitype library cooperatives to facilitate the implementation, improvement, and extension of library activities designed to foster improved user services, coordinating such activities with other appropriate ALA units.

2. Representation and interpretation of the role, functions, and services of state library agencies, specialized library agencies, and multitype library cooperatives within and outside the profession, including contact with national organizations and government agencies.

3. Development of policies, studies, and activities in matters affecting state library agencies, specialized library agencies, and multitype library cooperatives relating to (a) state and local library legislation, (b) state grants-in-aid and appropriations, and (c) relationships among state, federal, regional, and local governments, coordinating such activities with other appropriate ALA units.

4. Establishment, evaluation, and promotion of standards and service guidelines relating to the concerns of this association.

5. Identifying the interests and needs of all persons, encouraging the creation of services to meet these needs within the areas of concern of the association, and promoting the use of these services provided by state library agencies, specialized library agencies, and multitype library cooperatives.

6. Stimulating the professional growth and promoting the specialized training and continuing education of library personnel at all levels in the areas of concern of this association and encouraging membership participation in appropriate type-of-activity divisions within ALA.

7. Assisting in the coordination of activities of other units within ALA that have a bearing on the concerns of this association.

8. Granting recognition for outstanding library service within the areas of concern of this association.

9. Acting as a clearinghouse for the exchange of information and encouraging the development of materials, publications, and research within the areas of concern of this association.

BOARD OF DIRECTORS

Pres. Nancy L. Wareham, Exec. Dir., Cleveland Area Metropolitan Lib. System, 11000 Euclid Ave., Rm. 309, Cleveland, OH 44106; *V.P./Pres.-Elect.* Christine L. Kirby, Cons. for Service to the Disadvantaged, Massachusetts Board of Lib. Commissioners, 648 Beacon St., Boston, MA 02215; *Past. Pres.* Anne Marie F. Falsone, Asst. Commissioner of Education, State Lib., 1362 Lincoln St., Denver, CO 80203; *Div. Councillor.* Barratt Wilkins (1985). *Dirs.-at-Large.* Marcia Lowell (1983); S. Stephen Prine, Jr. (1983); John D. Christensen (1984); Rhea J. Rubin (1984). *Sec. Reps.* Larry D. Weitkemper, HCLS Chpn (1983); Jan L. Ames, LSBPH Chpn. (1983); Karen L. Hopkins, LSDS Chpn (1983); Grace J. Lyons, LSIES Chpn. (1983); Priscilla K. Linsley, LSPS Chpn. (1983); Sara Ann Parker, MLCS Chpn. (1983); Richard M. Cheski, SLAS Chpn. (1983). *Ex officio* (Nonvoting). *Interface Ed.* Edward Seidenberg; *Planning, Organization, and Bylaws Committee Chpn.* Patricia H. Smith; *Exec. Dir.* Sandra M. Cooper.

PUBLICATION

Interface (q.; memb.; nonmemb. $10). *Ed.* Edward Seidenberg, Texas State Lib., Box 12927, Capitol Sta., Austin, TX 78711.

COMMITTEES

American Correctional Association—ASCLA Committee on Institutional Libraries (Joint). Connie House, Box 6164, Arlington, VA 22206.

Awards. Patricia M. Hogan, Administrative Libn., Community Lib., 500 W. Irving Park Rd., Itasca, IL 60143.

Awards—Exceptional Achievement Award Jury. Bonnie B. Mitchell, 325 Berger Alley, Columbus, OH 43206.

Bibliotherapy. Frank L. Turner, Jr., Box 1024, Lake Dallas, TX 75065.

Budget and Finance. Christine L. Kirby, Cons. for Service to the Disadvantaged, Massachusetts Board of Lib. Commissioners, 648 Beacon St., Boston, MA 02215.

Conference Program. Barbara L. Perkis, Asst. Dir., Illinois Regional Lib. for the Blind & Physically Handicapped, 1055 W. Roosevelt Rd., Chicago, IL 60608.

Continuing Education. Suzanne Mahmoodi, Continuing Education & Lib. Research Specialist, OPLIC, 301 Hanover Bldg., 480 Cedar St., St. Paul, MN 55101.

Guidelines for Library Service to Small Residential Institutions (Ad Hoc, Subcommittee). Sandra F. Reuben, Los Angeles County Public Lib., 320 W. Temple St., Los Angeles, CA 90012.

"Interface" Advisory. Alphonse F. Trezza, Associate Prof., School of Lib. & Info. Science, Florida State Univ., Tallahassee, FL 32306.

International Year of Disabled Persons (Ad Hoc). Phyllis I. Dalton, 850 E. Desert Inn Rd., No. 1101, Las Vegas, NV 89109.

Legislation. Barbara F. Weaver, State Libn., New Jersey State Lib., CN 520, Trenton, NJ 08625.

Membership Promotion. Beverly A. Jones, Chief Planning Officer, Oklahoma Dept. of Libnshp., 200 N.E. 18 St., Oklahoma City, OK 73105.

Nominating. Bridget Later Lamont, Dept. Dir., State Lib., Centennial Bldg., Springfield, IL 62756.

Planning, Organization, and Bylaws. Patricia H. Smith, Mgr., Systems Development, Lib. Development Div., Texas State Lib., Box 12927, Capitol Sta., Austin, TX 78711.

Publications. Donna O. Dziedzic, 2124 N. Sedgwick, Chicago, IL 60614.

Research. Rosemary Du Mont, School of Lib. Science, Univ. of Oklahoma, 401 W. Brooks St., Rm. 116, Norman, OK 73019.

Standards for the Library Functions at the State Level (Ad Hoc, Subcommittee). Denny R. Stephens, Asst. Dir., Oklahoma Dept. of Libnshp., 200 N.E. 18 St., Oklahoma city, OK 73105.

Standards Review. Janet L. Blumberg, Chief, Lib. Development, Washington State Lib., AJ-11, Olympia, WA 98504.

Standards Review for Library Service to the Blind and Physically Handicapped (Ad Hoc, Subcommittee). To be announced.

REPRESENTATIVES

ALA Government Documents Round Table (GODORT). Cynthia R. Ansell (1983).

ALA International Relations Assembly. Blane K. Dessy (1983).

ALA Legislation Assembly. Barbara F. Weaver (1983).

ALA Library Education Assembly. Suzanne Mahmoodi (1983).

ALA Membership Promotion Task Force. Beverly A. Jones (1984).

ALA/LAMA/BES Committees for Facilities for Specialized Library Services. Kieth C. Wright (1983).

ALA/RASD Interlibrary Loan Committee. Theresa A. Trucksis (1984).

ALA/RTSD/CCS Cataloging: Description & Access Committee. To be announced.

ALA/RTSD Catalog Form, Function & Use Committee. Jane Y. Kelly (1984).

American Correctional Association (ACA). Connie House.

Association for Radio Reading Services, Inc. Barbara L. Wilson (1983).

Chief Officers of State Library Agencies (COSLA). Exec. Dir., Sandra M. Cooper.

Freedom to Read Foundation. William R. Murray, Jr. (1983).

Interagency Council on Library Resources for Nursing. To be announced.

SECTION CHAIRPERSONS

Health Care Libraries Section (HCLS). Larry D. Weitkemper, Chief, Lib. Services (142D), V.A. Medical Center, Middleville Rd., Northport, NY 11768.

Library Service to the Blind and Physically Handicapped (LSBPH). Jan L. Ames, Dir., Washington Regional Lib. for the Blind & Physically Handicapped. 811 Harrison, Seattle, WA 98129.

Library Service to the Deaf Section (LSDS). Karen Ann Hopkins, Mgr., Training & Media Services, National Technical Inst. for the Deaf, Rochester Inst. of Technology, One Lomb Memorial Dr., Rochester, NY 14623.

Library Service to the Impaired Elderly Section. Grace J. Lyons, Libn., Lib. for the Blind & Physically Handicapped, District of Columbia Public Lib., 901 G St N.W., Washington, DC 20001.

Library Service to Prisoners Section (LSPS). Priscilla K. Linsley, Two Cleveland Rd. W., Princeton, NJ 08540.

Multitype Library Cooperation Section (MLCS). Sara Ann Parker, State Libn., State Lib., 930 E. Lyndale Ave., Helena, MT 59601.

State Library Agency Section (SLAS). Richard M. Cheski, State Libn., State Lib., 65 S. Front St., Columbus, OH 43215.

AMERICAN LIBRARY ASSOCIATION
LIBRARY ADMINISTRATION AND MANAGEMENT ASSOCIATION
Executive Director, Roger H. Parent
50 E. Huron St., Chicago, IL 60611
312-944-6780

OBJECT

"The Library Administration and Management Association provides an organizational framework for encouraging the study of administrative theory, for improving the practice of administration in libraries, and for identifying and fostering administrative skill. Toward these ends, the division is responsible for all elements of general administration which are common to more than one type of library. These may include organizational structure, financial administration, personnel management and training, buildings and equipment, and public relations. LAMA meets this responsibility in the following ways:

1. Study and review of activities assigned to the division with due regard for changing developments in these activities.

2. Initiating and overseeing activities and projects appropriate to the division, including activities involving bibliography compilation, publication, study, and review of professional literature within the scope of the division.

3. Synthesis of those activities of other ALA units which have a bearing upon the responsibilities or work of the division.

4. Representation and interpretation of library administrative activities in contacts outside the library profession.

5. Aiding the professional development of librarians engaged in administration and encouragement of their

participation in appropriate type-of-library divisions.

6. Planning and development of those programs of study and research in library administrative problems which are most needed by the profession." Established 1957.

OFFICERS

Pres. David R. Smith, Hennepin County Lib., Edina, MN 55435; *V.P./Pres.-Elect.* Nancy McAdams; *Past Pres.* Carolyn Snyder; *Exec. Dir.* Roger H. Parent.

(Address correspondence to the executive director.)

BOARD OF DIRECTORS

Dirs.: Bob Carmack; Gloria Stockton; Anne Marie Allison; David Dowell; Ann Heidbreder Eastman; Betty Turock. *Dirs.-at-Large.* Sue Fontaine; Ronald Leach; *Councillor.* Dale Canelas; *Ex officio. Sec. V.-chpns.*, B. Franklin Hemphill; Laurence Miller; Dale Montanelli; Mary Jordan Coe; Sally Brickman; Louise P. Berry. *Committee Organizer.* Betty Bender.

PUBLICATIONS

LAMA Newsletter (q.; memb.) *Ed.* Edward D. Garten, Tennessee Technical Univ., Box 5066, Cookeville, TN 38501.

COMMITTEE CHAIRPERSONS

Budget and Finance. Gary M. Shirk, 3741 20 Ave., Minneapolis, MN 55407.
Membership. Eugene T. Neely, Rutgers Univ. Lib., 185 University Ave., Newark, NJ 07102.
Nominating. Evelyn King, Box 206, College Station, TX 77841.
Organization. Betty Bender, Spokane Public Lib., W906 Main, Spokane, WA 99201.
Orientation. Stella Bentley, Indiana Univ. Libs., Bloomington, IN 47405.
Program. Susan Stroyan, 2013 Taylor St., Bloomington, IL 61701.
Publications. Ross Stephen, Franklin Moore Lib., Rider College, 2083 Lawrenceville Rd., Lawrenceville, NJ 08648.
Small Libraries Publications. Kay Cassell, Huntington Public Lib., 338 Main St., Huntington, NY 11743.
Task Force on Extra-Conference Programs. Donald Kelsey, 499 Wilson Lib., 309 19 Ave. S., Minneapolis, MN 55455.

DISCUSSION GROUP CHAIRPERSONS

Asst.-to-the-Dir. Bart Lessin, Central Michigan Univ. Lib., Mt. Pleasant, MI 48859.
Fund Raising. Pamela Bonnell, 8630 Spring Valley, #101, Dallas, TX 75240.
Middle Management. Matthew Simon, Queens College Lib., Flushing, NY 11367.
Racism Sexism Awareness. Honore Francois, Prince George's County Memorial Lib., 6532 Adelphi Rd., Hyattsville, MD 20782.
Women Administrators. Carol N. Derner, Lake County Public Lib., Merrillville, IN 47410; Bessie K. Hahn, The Goldfarb Lib., Brandeis Univ., Waltham, MA 02154.

SECTION CHAIRPERSONS

ALA Poster Session Committee. Elizabeth Salzer.
Buildings and Equipment Section. Bob Carmack, I.D. Weeks Lib., Univ. of South Dakota, Vermillion, SD 57069.
Catalog Form, Function, and Use Committee. Mary Frances Collins.
Circulation Services Section. Gloria Stockton, Northern Regional Lib. Facility, Univ. of California, Bldg. 400, Richmond Field Sta., Richmond, CA 94804.

Library Education Assembly. Ruth Person.

Library Organization and Management Section. Anne Marie Allison, Wayne State Univ. Lib., Detroit, MI 48202.

Medical Library Association. Faith Van Toll.

Personnel Administration Section. Davil Dowell, Illinois Institute of Technology, Chicago, IL 60616.

Public Relations Section. Ann Heidbreder Eastman, College of Arts and Sciences, VA Polytechnic Institute/State Univ., Blacksburg, VA 24601.

Statistics Section. Betty Turock, 11 Undercliff Rd., Montclair, NJ 07042.

AMERICAN LIBRARY ASSOCIATION
LIBRARY AND INFORMATION TECHNOLOGY ASSOCIATION
Executive Director, Donald P. Hammer
50 E. Huron St., Chicago, IL 60611
312-944-6780

OBJECT

"The Library and Information Technology Association provides its members and, to a lesser extent, the information dissemination field as a whole, with a forum for discussion, an environment for learning, and a program for action on all phases of the development and application of automated and technological systems in the library and information sciences. Since its activities and interests are derived as responses to the needs and demands of its members, its program is flexible, varied, and encompasses many aspects of the field. Its primary concern is the design, development, and implementation of technological systems in the library and information science fields. Within that general precept, the interests of the division include such varied activities as systems development, electronic data processing, mechanized information retrieval, operations research, standards development, telecommunications, networks and collaborative efforts, management techniques, information technology and other aspects of audiovisual and video cable communications activities, and hardware applications related to all of these areas. Although it has no facilities to carry out research, it attempts to encourage its members in that activity.

Information about all of these activities is disseminated through the division's publishing program, seminars and institutes, exhibits, conference programs, and committee work. The division provides an advisory and consultative function when called upon to do so.

It regards continuing education as one of its major responsibilities and through the above channels it attempts to inform its members of current activities and trends, and it also provides retrospective information for those new to the field."

OFFICERS

Pres. Carolyn M. Gray, Asst. Dir. for Technical Services & Automation, Brandeis Univ. Goldfarb Lib., 415 South St., Waltham, MA 02254; *V.P./Pres.-Elect.* Kenneth E. Dowlin, Dir., Pikes Peak Regional Lib. Dist., 20 N. Cascade Ave., Colorado

Springs, CO 80901; *Past Pres.* Brigitte L. Kenney, Infocon, Inc., 400 Plateau Pkwy., Golden, CO 80401.

DIRECTORS

Officers; Hugh Atkinson (1984); Mary Margaret Diebler (l983); Lois M. Kershner (1985); Barbara Feldman (1983); James C. Thompson (1983); *Councillor.* Bonnie K. Juergens (1985); *Ex officio. Bylaws and Organization Committee Chpn.* Heike Kordish (1984); *Exec Dir.* Donald P. Hammer.

PUBLICATIONS

Information Technology and Libraries (ITAL, formerly *JOLA)* (q.; memb.; nonmemb. $20). *Ed.* Brian Aveney, Blackwell North America, 10300 S.W. Allen Blvd., Beaverton, OR 97005. For information or to send manuscripts, contact the editor.

LITA Newsletter (3 issues.; memb.). *Ed.* Carol A. Parkhurst, Systems Libn., Univ. of Nevada Lib., Reno, NV 89557.

COMMITTEE CHAIRPERSONS

Awards. Mary Fisher Ghikas, Asst. Commissioner, Public Lib., 425 N. Michigan Ave., Chicago, IL 60611.

Bylaws and Organization. Heike Kordish, Columbia Univ. Libs., 322 Butler Lib., New York, NY 10027.

Education. Walter J. Fraser, Systems & Automation Dept., Shields Lib., Univ. of California, Davis, CA 95616.

Goals and Long-Range Planning. Joseph R. Matthews, Joseph R. Matthews & Associates, 213 Hill St., Grass Valley, CA 95945.

ITAL Editorial Board. Brian Aveney, Blackwell North America, 10300 S.W. Allen Blvd., Beaverton, OR 97005.

Legislation and Regulation. David H. Brunell, FLC/FEDLINK, Lib. of Congress, Washington, DC 20540.

Membership. Frances Carducci, 12 Blackwatch Terr., Apt. 9, Fairport, NY 14450.

National Conference-Baltimore, 1983. Berna L. Heyman, E. G. Swem Lib., College of William & Mary, Williamsburg, VA 32185.

Nominating. Lois M. Kershner, 10690 Stokes Ave., Cupertino, CA 95014.

Oral History. To be announced.

Program Planning. Sue Tyner, Asst. Univ. Libn. for Technical Services, Univ. of Arizona Lib., Tucson, AZ 85721.

Publications. Michael J. Gorman, 246A Lib., Univ. of Illinois, 1408 W. Gregory Dr., Urbana, IL 61801.

Representation in Machine-Readable Form of Bibliographic Information, RTSD/LITA/RASD (MARBI). Dorothy Gregor, Head Tech. Services, Univ. of California Lib., Berkeley, CA 94720.

Technical Standards for Library Automation (TESLA). Paul B. Lagueux, Council on Library Resources, 1785 Massachusetts Ave. N.W., Washington, DC 20036.

Telecommunications. Joan M. Maier, Chief, Lib. Services, Lib., Rm. 51, National Oceanic and Atmospheric Admin., 325 Broadway, Boulder, CO 80303.

DISCUSSION GROUP CHAIRPERSON

Automation Vendor/User Discussion Group. Richard R. Rowe, Pres., F. W. Faxon, 15 Southwest Pk., Westwood, MA 02090.

Information & Referral. Diana deNoyelles, Special Asst., Los Angeles County Public Lib., 320 W. Temple St., Los Angeles, CA 90012.

Library & Information Technology. Diane Mayo, 2775 Mesa Verde, Apt. P-213, Costa Mesa, CA 92626.

Microprocessor. Walter J. Fraser, Systems & Automation Dept., Shields Lib., Univ. of California, Davis, CA 95616.

On-line Catalogs. William G. Potter, 214 Lib., Univ. of Illinois, 1408 W. Gregory Dr., Urbana, IL 61801.

Programmers. Walter Crawford, Program Analyst, Research Libs. Group, Jordan Quad., Stanford, CA 94305.

Retrospective Conversion. Anne G. Adler, Fondren Lib., Tech. Services, Rice Univ., Houston, TX 77001.

SECTION CHAIRPERSONS

Audio-Visual Section (AVS). Barbara Ortiz Feldman, 7 Bahama Rd., Morris Plains, NJ 07950.

Information Science & Automation Section (ISAS). James C. Thompson, 7950 N. Stadium Dr., #207, Houston, TX 77030.

Video and Cable Communications Section (VCCS). Mary Margaret Diebler, 5743-220 Harwich Ct., Alexandria, VA 22311.

AMERICAN LIBRARY ASSOCIATION
PUBLIC LIBRARY ASSOCIATION
Executive Director, Shirley Mills-Fischer
50 E. Huron St., Chicago, IL 60611
312-944-6780

OBJECT

To advance the development, effectiveness, and financial support of public library service to the American people; to speak for the library profession at the national level on matters pertaining to public libraries; and to enrich the professional competence and opportunities of public librarians. In order to accomplish this mission, the Public Library Association has adopted the following goals:

1. Conducting and sponsoring research about how the public library can respond to changing social needs and technological developments.

2. Developing and disseminating materials useful to public libraries in interpreting public library services and needs.

3. Conducting continuing education for public librarians by programming at national and regional conferences, by publications such as the journal, and by other delivery methods.

4. Establishing, evaluating, and promoting goals, guidelines, and standards for public libraries.

5. Maintaining liaison with relevant national agencies and organizations engaged in public administration and human services such as National Association of Counties, Municipal League, Commission on Post-Secondary Education.

6. Maintaining liaison with other divisions and units of ALA and other library organizations such as the Association of American Library Schools and the Urban Libraries Council.

7. Defining the role of the public library in service to a wide range of user and potential user groups.

8. Promoting and interpreting the public library to a changing society

through legislative programs and other appropriate means.

9. Identifying legislation to improve and to equalize support of public libraries.

Organized 1951. Memb. 5,000.

MEMBERSHIP

Open to all ALA members interested in the improvement and expansion of public library services to all ages in various types of communities.

OFFICERS (1982-1983)

Pres. Donald J. Sager, Elmhurst Public Lib., 211 Prospect, Elmhurst, IL 60126; *V.P.* Nancy M. Bolt, 1088 Fox Run Rd., Milford, OH 45150; *Past Pres.* Agnes M. Griffen, Montgomery Dept. of Public Libs., 99 Maryland Ave., Rockville, MD 20850.

BOARD OF DIRECTORS (1982-1983)

Officers; Nina S. Ladof; Jerome G. Pennington; Mildred K. Smock; Charles M. Brown; Melissa Forinash Buckingham; Albert V. Tweedy. *Sec. Reps.* AEPS *Pres.* Jane C. Heiser; AFLS *Pres.* Dorothy A. Cross; CIS *Pres.* Dorothy S. Puryear; MLS *Pres.* Lelia C. White; PLSS *Pres.* Janice S. Farley; SMLS *Pres.* Claudia Sumler; *Ex officio.* PLA-ALA Membership *Rep.* Patricia Olsen Wilson; *Past Pres.* ALTA. Jeanne Davies; *Councillor.* Kathleen Mehaffey Balcom; *Exec. Dir.* Shirley Mills-Fischer.

PUBLICATIONS

Public Libraries (q.; memb.; nonmemb. $10). *Ed.* Kenneth D. Shearer, Jr., 1205 LeClair St., Chapel Hill, NC 27514.

Public Library Reporter (occas.). Ed. varies. Standing orders or single order available from Order Dept., ALA, 50 E. Huron St., Chicago, IL 60611.

SECTION HEADS

Alternative Education Programs (AEPS). Jane C. Heiser.

Armed Forces Librarians (AFLS). Dorothy A. Cross.

Community Information (CIS). Dorothy S. Puryear.

Metropolitan Libraries (MLS). Lelia C. White.

Public Library Systems (PLSS). Janice S. Farley.

Small & Medium Sized Libraries Section (SMLS). Claudia Sumler.

COMMITTEE AND TASK FORCE CHAIRPERSONS

Accreditation (Task Force). R. Kathleen Molz, Columbia Univ. School of Lib. Science, 516 Butler Lib., New York, NY 10027.

Audiovisual. Victor Frank Kralisz, Dallas Public Lib., 1515 Young St., Dallas, TX 75201.

Bylaws. Pat Woodrum, Tulsa City-County Lib., 400 Civic Center, Tulsa, OK 74103.

Cataloging Needs of Public Libraries. Maurice Freedman, Westchester Lib. System, 8 Winchester Plaza, Elmsford, NY 10523.

Children, Service to. Ethel N. Ambrose, Central Arkansas Lib. System, 700 Louisiana St., Little Rock, AR 72201.

Conference Program Coordinating. Jon Scheer, Audelia Rd., Branch Lib., 10045 Audelia Rd., Dallas, TX 75238.

Division Program—Dallas, 1984. Sandra Stephan, Maryland State Dept. of Educ., 200 W. Baltimore St., Baltimore, MD 21201.

Division Program—Los Angeles, 1983. Linda F. Crismond, Los Angeles County Public Lib., Box 111, Los Angeles, CA 90053.

Education of Public Librarians. Suzanne Mahmoodi, OPLIC, 301 Hanover Bldg., 480 Cedar St., St. Paul, MN 55101.

Goals, Guidelines, and Standards for Public Libraries. Ronald A. Dubberly, Seattle Public Lib., 1000 Fourth St., Seattle, WA 98104.
Legislation. Nettie Barcroft Taylor, State Dept. of Educ., Lib. Development Div., Baltimore, MD 21201.
Membership. Patricia Olsen Wilson, Avon Township Public Lib., 210 W. University Dr., Rochester, MI 48063.
Allie Beth Martin Award. George R. Steward, Birmingham Public Lib., 2020 Park Place, Birmingham, AL 35203.
Multilingual Library Service. Patrick Valentine, North Carolina Foreign Language Lib., 328 Gillespie St., Fayetteville, NC 28301.
National Conference (1983). Charles W. Robinson, Baltimore County Public Lib., 320 York Rd., Towson, MD 21204.
National Conference (1983) Evaluation. Henry E. Bates, Jr., Milwaukee Public Lib., 814 W. Wisconsin Ave., Milwaukee, WI 53233.
National Conference (1983) Exhibits. Milton E. Dutcher, Baltimore County Public Lib., North Point Area Branch, 1716 Merritt Blvd., Baltimore, MD 21222.
National Conference (1983) Local Arrangements. Anna A. Curry, Enoch Pratt Free Lib., 400 Cathedral St., Baltimore, MD 21201.
National Conference (1983) Program Committee. Robert H. Rohlf, Hennepin County Lib., Minnetonka, MN 55343.
National Conference (1983) Public Relations. Barbara Webb, Fairfax County Public Lib., 5502 Port Royal Rd., Springfield, VA 22151.
National Conference (1983) Registration. Betty M. Ragsdale, Blue Ridge Regional Lib., Box 5264, Martinsville, VA 24115.
Network Relations (Task Force). Betty Turock, Rutgers Univ. Grad. School of Lib. & Info. Studies, 4 Huntington St., New Brunswick, NJ 08903.
Nominating—1983. William W. Sannwald, City Libn., City of San Diego, 202 C St., Mail Sta. 99B, San Diego, CA 92102.
Nominating—1984. Robert H. Rohlf, Hennepin County Lib., Ridgedale Dr. at Plymouth Rd., Minnetonka, MN 55343.
Organization. David M. Henington, Houston Public Lib., 500 McKinney, Houston, TX 77002.
Orientation. Jerome Penningon, Appleton Public Lib., 121 S. Oneida St., Appleton, WI 54911.
Planning. Thomas C. Phelps, National Endowment for the Humanities, 806 15 St. N.W., MS 406, Washington, DC 20506.
Planning Process Discussion Group. Suzanne LeBarron, Dept. of Lib. & Archives, Box 537, Frankfort, KY 40601.
Planning Process Financial Development (Task Force). Barratt Wilkins, State Lib. Div. of Lib. Services, R. A. Gray Bldg., Tallahassee, FL 32301.
Preconference—Los Angeles, 1983. William Sannwald, San Diego Public Lib., 202 St., MS 9B, San Diego, CA 92101; Kevin Hegarty, Tacoma Public Lib., 1102 Tacoma Ave. S., Tacoma, WA 98402.
Public Library Data Base. Karen Krueger, 6809 Donna Dr., Middleton, WI 53562.
Public Library Heritage. Donald D. Food, Lib. & Info. Science Programs, Univ. of Arkansas, Little Rock, AR 72204.
Public Library Use of CATV, Radio & Television. Ronald Kozlowski, Louisville Free Public Lib., Fourth & York Sts., Louisville, KY 40203.
Public Relations Marketing. Joyce McMullin, Cattahoochee Valley Regional Lib., 1120 Bradley Dr., Columbus, GA 31995.

Publications. Peter Hiatt, Grad. School of Lib. Science, Univ. of Washington, 133 Suzzallo Lib., FM-30, Seattle, WA 98195.
"Public Libraries" Editorial Board. Barbara Webb, Fairfax County Public Lib., 5502 Port Royal Rd., Springfield, VA 22151.
"Public Library Reporter" Subcommittee. W. Bernard Lukenbill, Univ. of Texas, GSLS, Box 7576, Austin, TX 78712.
Research. Kenneth Dowlin, Pikes Peak Lib. Dist., Box 1579, Colorado Springs, CO 80901.
State and Regional Affiliates (Task Force). Sarah Ann Long, Dauphin County Lib. System, 101 Walnut St., Harrisburg, PA 17101.
Use of Microcomputers in Public Libraries. Russell E. Walker, Upper Arlington Public Lib., 2800 Tremont Rd., Columbus, OH 43221.
Videotex. Kevin Hegarty, Tacoma Public Lib., 1102 Tacoma Ave. S., Tacoma, WA 98402.

AMERICAN LIBRARY ASSOCIATION
REFERENCE AND ADULT SERVICES DIVISION
Executive Director, Andrew M. Hansen
50 E. Huron St., Chicago, IL 60611
312-944-6780

OBJECT

The Reference and Adult Services Division is responsible for stimulating and supporting in every type of library the delivery of reference/information services to all groups, regardless of age, and of general library services and materials to adults. This involves facilitating the development and conduct of direct service to library users, the development of programs and guidelines for service to meet the needs of these users, and assisting libraries in reaching potential users.

The specific responsibilities of RASD are:

1. Conduct of activities and projects within the division's areas of responsibility.
2. Encouragement of the development of librarians engaged in these activities, and stimulation of participation by members of appropriate type-of-library divisions.
3. Synthesis of the activities of all units within the American Library Association that have a bearing on the type of activities represented by the division.
4. Representation and interpretation of the division's activities in contacts outside the profession.
5. Planning and development of programs of study and research in these areas for the total profession.
6. Continuous study and review of the division's activities.

Formed by merger of Adult Sevices Division and Reference Services Division, 1972. Memb. 5,496. (For information on dues, see ALA entry.)

OFFICERS (1982-1983)

Pres. Danuta A. Nitecki, 804 S. Lincoln Ave., Urbana, IL 61801; *V.P./Pres.-Elect.* Kay A. Cassell, Huntington Public Lib., 338 Main St., Huntington, NY 11743; *Secy.* Jean A. Coberly, History Dept., Seattle Public

Lib., 100 Fourth Ave., Seattle, WA 98104.

DIRECTORS

Officers; Jeanne Gelinas; James Rettig; Susan DiMattia; Sharon Anne Hogan; Tina Roose; Margaret L. Thrasher; *Councillor.* Ruth M. Katz; *Past Pres.* Geraldine B. King; *Ex officio, History Sec. Chpn.* Arthur H. Miller, Jr.; *Machine-Assisted Reference Sec.* James H. Sweetland; *Ed. RASD Update.* Della L. Giblon; *Ed. RQ.* Kathleen M. Heim; *Council of State and Regional Groups Chpn.* Glenda S. Neely, Univ. of Louisville, Louisville, KY 40208; *Exec. Dir.* Andrew M. Hansen.

(Address general correspondence to the executive director.)

PUBLICATIONS

RQ (q.; memb.; nonmemb. $20). Kathleen M. Heim, Grad. School of Lib. & Info Science, 410 David Kinley Hall, Univ. of Illinois, 1407 W. Gregory Dr., Urbana, IL 61801.

RASD Update (periodic; memb.; nonmemb. $6). *Ed.* Della L. Giblon, Leon County Public Lib., 1940 N. Monroe St., Suite 81, Tallahassee, FL 32303.

SECTION CHAIRPERSONS

History. Arthur H. Miller, Jr., Donnelley Lib., Lake Forest College, Sheridan & College Rds., Lake Forest, IL 60045.

Machine-Assisted Reference (MARS). James H. Sweetland, 147 Lakewood Gardens Lane, Madison, WI 53704.

COMMITTEE CHAIRPERSONS

Adult Library Materials. Catherine Smith, 388 Pattie Dr., Berea, OH 44017.

Adults, Library Services to. Neysa Eberhard, Newton Public Lib., 720 North Oak, Newton, KS 67114.

AFL/CIO-ALA Library Service to Labor Groups. Arthur S. Meyers, 2105 Concord, Muncie, IN 47304.

Aging Population, Library Service to an. Nancy Clare Bolin, Maryland State Dept. of Educ., Div. of Lib. Development, 200 W. Baltimore St., Baltimore, MD 21201.

Audio-Visual Subcommittee. Janice A. Kubiak, Free Lib. of Philadelphia, Logan Sq., Philadelphia, PA 19103.

Basic Buying List for the Spanish-Speaking. Fabio Restrepo, Box 1321, Denton, TX 76202.

Bibliography. Judith B. Quinlan, Perkins Lib., Reference Dept., Duke Univ., Durham, NC 27706.

Business Reference Services. Linda J. Piele, Library/Learning Center, Univ. of Wisconsin-Parkside, Box 2000, Kenosha, WI 53141.

Catalog Use. Douglas Ferguson, 1801 Rose St., Berkeley, CA 94703.

Conference Program. Marilyn H. Boria, General Info Services Div., The Chicago Public Lib., 425 N. Michigan Ave., Chicago, IL 60611.

Cooperative Reference Services. Ellen Zabel Hahn, General Reading Rms. Div., LJ 144, Lib. of Congress, Washington, DC 20540.

Dartmouth Medal. Thomas M. Gaughan, Box 916, Bard College, Annandale-on-Hudson, NY 12504.

Evaluation of Reference and Adult Services. Charles A. Bunge, Lib. School, Univ. of Wisconsin, 600 N. Park St., Madison, WI 53706.

Executive. Danuta A. Nitecki, 804 S. Lincoln Ave., Urbana, IL 61801.

Facts on File Award. Phyllis Massar, Ferguson Lib., Stamford, CT 06901.

Interlibrary Loan. Mary U. Hardin, 1501 Locust St., Norman, OK 73069.

Legislation. Marvin W. Mounce,

3104 Huntington Woods Blvd., Tallahassee, FL 32303.
Membership. Judith A. Tuttle, Circulation Dept., Memorial Lib., Univ. of Wisconsin, 728 State St., Madison, WI 53706.
Multilingual Subcommittee. William E. McElwain, Foreign Language Section, Chicago Public Lib., 78 E. Washington, Chicago, IL 60602.
Isadore Gilbert Mudge Citation. Joyce Duncan Falk, 164 Esplanade, Irvine, CA 92715.
Nominating. Cynthia B. Duncan, Univ. Lib., Old Dominion Univ., Norfolk, VA 23508.
Notable Books Council. Kenneth L. Ferstl, Box 13256, North Texas State Univ., Denton, TX 76203.
Organization. Margaret L. Thrasher, Prince George's County Memorial Lib. System, 6532 Adelphi Rd., Hyattsville, MD 20782.
Performance Standards ad hoc. Mary Canada, Reference Dept., Perkins Lib., Duke Univ., Durham, NC 27706.
Planning. Peter G. Watson, Box 1543, Paradise, CA 95969.
Professional Development. George M. Bailey, 2129 Villa Maria Rd., Claremont, CA 91711.
Publications. Peggy Glover, Free Lib. of Philadelphia, Logan Sq., Philadelphia, PA 19103.
Reference Services to Children and Young Adults. Neel Parikh, 2136 Byron St., Berkeley, CA 94702.
Reference Sources. Kevin M. Rosswurm, Akron-Summit County Public Lib., 55 S. Main St., Akron, OH 44326.
Reference Sources for Small and Medium-sized Libraries (4th Ed.) ad hoc. Deborah C. Masters, B16 Univ. Lib., State Univ. of New York, 1400 Washington Ave., Albany, NY 12222.
Reference Tools Advisory. Sandra Leach, Main Lib., Reference Rm., Univ. of Tennessee Lib., Knoxville, TN 37996.
RQ Editorial Advisory Board. Kathleen M. Heim, Grad. School of Lib. & Info. Science, 410 David Kinley, Univ. of Illinois, 1407 W. Gregory Dr., Urbana, IL 61801.
John Sessions Memorial Award. Mark Leggett, 902 N. Pennsylvania, The Plaza, Apt. 312, Indianapolis, IN 46204.
Spanish-Speaking, Library Services to. Nathan A. Josel, Jr., El Paso Public Lib., 501 N. Oregon St., El Paso, TX 79901.
Standards and Guidelines. Winston Tabb, 11303 Handlebar Rd., Reston, VA 22091.
Wilson Indexes. Larry Earl Bone, Mercy College Libs., 555 Broadway, Dobbs Ferry, NY 10522.

DISCUSSION GROUP CHAIRPERSONS

Adult Materials and Services. Nancy Fisher, Cuyahoga Public Lib., 4510 Memphis Ave., Cleveland, OH 44144.
Interlibrary Loan. Mary Jackson, Interlibrary Loan, Univ. of Pennsylvania Libs., 4320 Walnut St., Philadelphia, PA 19104.
Library Services to an Aging Population. Allan Kleiman, Service to the Aging/SAGE Program, Brooklyn Public Lib., Brooklyn, NY 11229.
Multilingual Services and Materials. William E. McElwain, Foreign Language Sec., Chicago Public Lib., Chicago, IL 60602.
Reference Service in Large Research Libraries. Brian Nielsen, Reference Dept., Northwestern Univ., Evanston, IL 60201.
Reference Services in Medium-sized Research Libraries. Barbara B. Brand, Reference Dept., Main Lib., State Univ. of New York, Stony Brook, NY 11794.
Women's Materials and Women Library Users. Gurley Turner, Cata-

lyst, 14 E. 60 St., New York, NY 10022.

REPRESENTATIVES

ALA Legislation Assembly. Marvin W. Mounce, 3104 Huntington Woods Blvd., Tallahassee, FL 32303.
ALA Legislation Committee (Ad Hoc Copyright Subcommittee). Mary U. Hardin, Oklahoma Dept. of Libs., 200 N.E. 18 St., Oklahoma City, OK 73105.
ALA Library Instruction Round Table. Sheila Laidlaw, Sigmund Samuel Lib., Univ, of Toronto, Ont. M5S 1A5, Canada.
ALA Membership Promotion Task Force. Judith A. Tuttle, Univ. of Wisconsin Lib., Madison, WI 53705.
Coalition of Adult Education Organization. Andrew M. Hansen, ALA, 50 E. Huron St., Chicago, IL 60611. One to be appointed.
Freedom to Read Foundation. Deborah Ellis Dennis, Univ. of Maryland Libs., College Park, MD 20742.

AMERICAN LIBRARY ASSOCIATION RESOURCES AND TECHNICAL SERVICES DIVISION
Executive Director, William I. Bunnell
50 E. Huron St., Chicago, IL 60611
312-944-6780

OBJECT

"Responsibilities for the following activities: acquisition, identification, cataloging, classification, reproduction, and preservation of library materials; the development and coordination of the country's library resources; and those areas of selection and evaluation involved in the acquisition of library materials and pertinent to the development of library resources. Any member of the American Library Association may elect membership in this division according to the provisions of the bylaws." Established 1957. Memb. 6,351. (For information on dues, see ALA entry.)

OFFICERS (JUNE 1982-JUNE 1983)

Pres. Norman J. Shaffer, 11505 Soward Dr., Silver Spring, MD 20902; *V Pl Pres.-Elect.* Susan Brynteson, Univ. of Delaware Lib., Newark, DE 19711; *Chpn. Council of Regional Groups.* Doris H. Clack, 1115 Frazier Ave., Tallahassee, FL 19711; *Past Pres.* Charlotte C. Hensley, 1385 Edinboro Dr., Boulder, CO 80303. (Address correspondence to the executive secretary.)

DIRECTORS

Officers. *Section chairpersons:* Judith P. Cannan (CCS); R. Gay Walker (PLMS); John Webb (RLMS); Marion T. Reid (RS); Dorothy J. Glasby (SS). *Dirs.-at-Large.* Joe A. Hewitt (1985); Robin N. Downes (1983). *Council of Regional Groups vice-chpn./chpn.* Lois Upham (1984). *Ex officio: Lib. of Congress liaison.* Joseph Howard. *LRTS ed.* Elizabeth Tate (1985). *Parliamentarian.* Edward Swanson (1983). *RTSD Newsletter ed.* Arnold Hirshon (1985). *RTSD Planning Committee chpn.* Susan H. Vita (1983).

PUBLICATIONS

Library Resources & Technical Services (q.; memb. or $20). *Ed.* Elizabeth Tate, 11415 Farmland Dr., Rockville, MD 20852.

RTSD Newsletter (bi-mo.; memb. or *LRTS* subscription, or $8 yearly). *Ed.* Arnold Hirshon, Box 9184, Duke Sta., Durham, NC 27706.

SECTION CHAIRPERSONS

Cataloging and Classification. Judith P. Cannan, 4106 Duvawn St., Alexandria, VA 22310.

Preservation of Library Materials. R. Gay Walker, Yale Univ. Lib., 120 High St., New Haven, CT 06520.

Reproduction of Library Materials. John Webb, Administrator, Technical Services Div., State Lib., Salem, OR 97310.

Resources. Marion T. Reid, c/o Technical Services Div., Milton S. Eisenhower Lib., John Hopkins Univ., Baltimore, MD 21218.

Serials. Dorothy J. Glasby, 3612 Thornapple St., Chevy Chase, MD 20815.

COMMITTEE CHAIRPERSONS

Association of American Publishers/RTSD Joint Committee. Juanita S. Doares, Collection Management & Development, Rm. 105, New York Public Lib., Fifth Ave. & 42 St., New York, NY 10018.

Audiovisual. Sheila Intner, Asst. Professor, School of Lib. Service, Columbia Univ., New York, NY 10027.

Catalog, Form, Function & Use. Dorothy McGarry, Physical Science & Technical Libs., 8251 Boelter Hall, Univ. of California, Los Angeles, CA 90024.

Commercial Technical Services Committee. Mary Fischer Ghikas, 1520 W. Touhy Ave., Chicago, IL 60626.

Conference Program. Norman J. Shaffer, 11505 Soward Dr., Silver Spring, MD 20902.

Duplicates Exchange Union. Christina L. Feick, Serials Div., Princeton Univ. Lib., Princeton, NJ 08544.

Education. Carolyn Frost, School of Lib. Science, Univ. of Michigan, 580 Union Dr., Ann Arbor, MI 48109.

International Relations. E. Dale Cluff, R.R.1, Box 37B, Makanda, IL 62958.

Membership. Murray S. Martin, Univ. Libn., Wessell Lib., Tufts Univ., Medford, MA 02155.

Nominating. Robert C. Sullivan, Chief, Order Dept., Lib. of Congress, Washington, DC 20540.

Organization and Bylaws. Charlotta C. Hensley, 1385 Edinboro Dr., Boulder, CO 80303.

Piercy Award Jury. Marcia Tuttle, Serials Dept., Wilson Lib., 024-A, Univ. of North Carolina, Chapel Hill, NC 27514.

Planning and Research. Susan H. Vita, 3711 Taylor St., Chevy Chase, MD 20815.

Preservation Microfilming. Francis F. Spreitzer, 4415 W. 62 St., Los Angeles, CA 90043.

Program Evaluation and Support. Susan Brynteson, Univ. of Delaware Lib., Newark, DE 19711.

Representation in Machine-Readable Form of Bibliographic Information, RTSD/LITA/RASD (MARBI). Dorothy Gregor, Head, Technical Services, Univ. of California Lib., Berkeley, CA 94720.

Representation in Machine-Readable Form of Bibliographic Information (MARBI), Character Set Task Force (Ad Hoc). Charles Payne, 5807 Blackstone, Chicago, IL 60637.

Technical Services Costs. Charles Renner, Technical Services, 168 Lib., Iowa State Univ., Ames, IA 50011.

REPRESENTATIVES

ALA Freedom to Read Foundation. Paul Cors.

ALA Government Documents Round Table. Gail M. Nichols.
ALA Legislation Assembly. Ann H. Eastman; William A. Gosling, Alternate.
ALA Library and Information Technology Association. Susan Brynteson & Judith N. Kharbas.
ALA Membership Promotion Task Force. Murray S. Martin.
American National Standards Institute, Inc. (ANSI), Standards Committee Z39 on Library Work, Documentation and Related Publishing Practices. Susan H. Vita; Janice E. Anderson, Alternate.
CONSER Advisory Group. Jean Cook.
Joint Advisory Committee on Nonbook Materials. Sheila Inter & Nancy B. Olson.
Joint Steering Committee for Revision of AACR. Frances Hinton.
National Institute for Conservation. John P. Baker.
Universal Serials and Book Exchange Inc. Pamela M. Bluh.
National Conservation Advisory Council. Pamela W. Darling.

DISCUSSION GROUPS

Acquisition of Library Materials. Jana K. Stevens, Acquisitions Dept., Bobst Lib., New York Univ., New York, NY 10012.
Automated Acquisitions/In-Process Control Systems. Amira Lefkowitz, Technical Services Dept., Univ. Research Lib., Univ. of California, Los Angeles, CA 90024; Harold D. Neikirk, Libn., Acquisitions Dept., Univ. Lib., Univ. of Delaware, Newark, DE 19711.
Booksellers. Donald B. Satisky, Sr., V.P., Blackwell/North America, 6024 S.W. Jean Rd., Bldg. G., Lake Oswego, OR 97034.
Cataloging Maintenance. Dennis Hamilton, Catalog Dept., Univ. of California Lib., Santa Barbara, CA 93106.
Cataloging Norms. Roberta Engleman, Rare Book Collection, Wilson Lib., Univ. of North Carolina, Chapel Hill, NC 27514.
Chief Collection Development Officers of Large Research Libraries. Florence Blakely, Asst. Libn. for Collection Development, Duke Univ. Lib., Durham, NC 27706.
Commercial Automation, Support of Technical Services in Medium-Sized Research Libraries. Richard Van Arden, Head of Online Cataloging, Marriott Lib., Univ. of Utah, Salt Lake City, UT 84112.
Copy Cataloging. Susan Jacobson, Univ. of Pennsylvania Lib., Philadelphia, PA 19104.
Head of Cataloging Departments. Susan Rhee, Head, Cataloging Dept., Univ. of California Lib., San Diego, CA 92903.
Pre-order & Pre-catalog Searching. Marcia Anderson, Michigan State Univ. Lib., East Lansing, MI 48824.
Preservation of Library Materials. Robert L. DeCandido, New York Public Lib., Fifth Ave. & 42 St., New York, NY 10018.
Reproduction of Library Materials. Bohdan Yasinsky, 925 Schindler Dr., Silver Spring, MD 20903.
Research Libraries. Diane Harkins, Head, Serials Cataloging Sec., Duke Univ. Lib., Durham, NC 27706.
Retrospective Conversion. Roberta F. Kirby, Univ. of South Alabama, Mobile, AL 36688.
Role of the Professional in Academic Research Technical Services Departments. Lawrence R. Keating, M.D. Anderson Lib., Univ. of Houston Central Campus, 4800 Calhoun Blvd., Houston, TX 77004.
Technical Services Administrators of Large Public Libraries. Mariko Kaya, Chief of Technical Services, Los

Angeles County Public Lib., 320 W. Temple St., Box 111, Los Angeles, CA 90053.

Technical Services Administrators of Medium-Sized Research Libraries. Irene Godden, Asst. Dir. for Technical Services, Colorado State Univ. Libs., Fort Collins, CO 80523.

Technical Services Administrators of Smaller Research Libraries. Thomas J. Crage, 519 E. 86 St., #3E, New York, NY 10028.

Technical Services Directors of Large Research Libraries. James N. Myers, Asst. Dir. for Technical Services, Green Lib., Stanford, CA 94305.

Technical Services Directors of Processing Centers. Dallas Shawkey, Public Lib., 109 Montgomery St., Brooklyn, NY 11225.

AMERICAN LIBRARY ASSOCIATION
YOUNG ADULT SERVICES DIVISION
Executive Director, Evelyn Shaevel
50 E. Huron St., Chicago, IL 60611
312-944-6780

OBJECT

"Interested in the improvement and extension of services to young people in all types of libraries; has specific responsibility for the evaluation, selection, interrelation and use of books and nonbook materials for young adults except when such materials are intended for only one type of library." Established 1957. Memb. 3,000. (For information on dues, see ALA entry.)

MEMBERSHIP

Open to anyone interested in library services to young adults.

OFFICERS (JULY 1982-JULY 1983)

Pres. Barbara Newmark, 11 Lake St., #3G White Plains, NY 10603; *V.P.* Penelope S. Jeffrey, 4733 Morningside Dr., Cleveland, OH 44109; *Past Pres.* Evie Wilson, 8602 Champlain Ct., Tampa, FL 33614; *Division Councillor.* Bruce Daniels, Dept. of State Lib. Services, 95 Davis St., Providence, RI 02908.

DIRECTORS

Joan Atkinson; Jack Forman; Lydia LaFleur; Ellen LiBretto; Larry Rakow; Suzanne Sullivan.

COMMITTEE CHAIRPERSONS

Best Books for Young Adults. Jacqueline Brown Woody, Prince George's County Lib., Glenarden Branch, 8724 Glenarden Pkwy., Glenarden, MD 20706.

Education. Mary K. Biagini, 740 W. Main St., Kent, OH 44240.

High-Interest, Low-Literacy Level Materials Evaluation. Elizabeth Acerra, 1097 E. 95 St., Brooklyn, NY 11236.

Ideas and Activities. Rhonna A. Goodman, New York Public Lib., Staten Island Borough Office, 10 Hyatt St., Staten Island, NY 10301.

Intellectual Freedom. Judith Flum, 302 Euclid Ave., Apt. 204, Oakland, CA 94610.

Leadership Training. Penelope S. Jeffrey, 4733 Morningside Dr., Cleveland, OH 44109.

Legislation Committee. Catherine Monnin, Cuyahoga County Public Lib., Maple Heights, Regional Branch, 5225 Library Lane, Maple Heights, OH 44137.

Library of Congress, YASD Advisory Committee to the Collection and Development Section and the National Library Service for the Blind and Physically Handicapped of the Library of Congress. Linda Lapides, Enoch Pratt Free Lib., 400 Cathedral St., Baltimore, MD 21201.

Media Selection and Usage. Nancy Baker Colberg, Edwin A. Bemis, Littleton Public Lib., 6014 S. Datura St., Denver, CO 80201.

Membership Promotion. Jo Ann Kingston, 614 Bedford Place, Grand Blanc, MI 48439.

National Organization Serving the Young Adult Liaison. Ricki Fifer, 82-24 135 St., #3A, Kew Gardens, NY 11435.

Nominating 1982. Eleanor Pourron, Arlington County Public Lib., 1015 Quincy St., Arlington, VA 22201.

Organization and Bylaws. Roberta Gellert, Lewis Rd., Irvington, NY 10533.

Program Planning Clearinghouse. Evie Wilson, 8602 Champlain Ct., Apt. 85, Tampa, FL 33614.

Public Relations. Elizabeth Talbot, 4008 Loma Vista Ave., Oakland, CA 94619.

Publications. Patsy Perritt, 226 Middleton Lib., Louisiana State Univ., Baton Rouge, LA 70803.

Publishers Liaison. Neal Porter, Scribner Book Companies, 597 Fifth Ave., New York, NY 10017.

Research. Henry C. Dequin, Northern Illinois Univ., DeKalb, IL 60115.

Selected Films for Young Adults. Vivian Wynn, Mayfield Regional Lib., 6080 Wilson Mills Rd., Mayfield Village, OH 44404.

Spanish Speaking Youth Committee, Library Service to. John W. Cunningham, 979 N. Fifth St., Philadelphia, PA 19123.

"Survival Kit Revisions." Rosemary Kneale, 7020 Hunting Lane, Chagrin Falls, OH 44022.

Television. Sylvie A. Tupacz, Dallas Public Lib., 1515 Young St., Dallas, TX 75201.

Top of the News Editorial. Marilyn Kaye, Div. of Lib. & Info. Services, St. John's Univ., Grand Central & Utopia Pkwys., Jamaica, NY 11439.

Young Adults with Special Needs. Jeri C. Baker, Community Services Libn., Dallas Public Lib., 9495 Marsh Lane, Dallas, TX 75220.

Youth Participation. Jana Varlejs, 101A Hill St., Highland Park, NJ 08904.

AMERICAN MERCHANT MARINE LIBRARY ASSOCIATION
(Affiliated with United Seamen's Service)
Executive Director, Mace Mavroleon
One World Trade Center, Suite 2601, New York, NY 10048

OBJECT

Provides ship and shore library service for American-flag merchant vessels, the Military Sealift Command, the Coast Guard, and other waterborne operations of the U.S. government.

OFFICERS

Chpn. of the Bd. RADM Bruce Keener, III; *Pres.* Thomas J. Smith; *Treas.* Hubert Carr; *Secy.* Capt. Franklin K. Riley.

TRUSTEES

Mr. W. J. Amoss; Ralph R. Bagley; Vice Adm. W. E. Caldwell; Nicholas Cretan; Rebekah T. Dallas; Maj. Gen. H.R. DelMar; John I. Dugan; Arthur W. Friedberg; Capt. Robert E. Hart; RADM Thomas A. King; George F. Lowman; Frank X. McNerney; Capt. Howard E. Miniter, USN; Andrew Rich; George J. Ryan; Richard T. Soper; Anthony J. Tozzoli; Rev. James R. Whittemore.

AMERICAN SOCIETY FOR INFORMATION SCIENCE
Executive Director, Samuel B. Beatty
1010 16 St. N.W., Washington, DC 20036
202-659-3644

OBJECT

"The American Society for Information Science provides a forum for the discussion, publication, and critical analysis of work dealing with the design, management, and use of information systems and technology." Memb. (Indiv.) 4,700; (Student) 480; (Inst.) 100. Dues (Indiv.) $75; (Student) $15; (Inst.) $300; (Sustaining Sponsor) $600.

OFFICERS

Pres. Charles Davis, Univ. of Illinois, Champaign/Urbana, Champaign, IL 61820; *Pres.-Elect.* Donald W. King; King Research Inc., Rockville, MD 20852; *Treas.* Frank Slater, Univ. of Pittsburgh, G-33 Hillman Lib., Pittsburgh, PA 15260; *Past Pres.* Mary C. Berger, Cuadra Assocs., 1523 Sixth St., Santa Monica, CA 90401.
(Address correspondence to the executive director)

BOARD OF DIRECTORS

Officers; *Chapter Assembly Dir.* Joe Ann Clifton; *SIG Cabinet Dir.* George Abbott; *Dirs.-at-Large.* Ching Chih Chen; Ward Shaw; Carol Johnson; Darlene Myers; David Penniman; Stephanie Normann.

PUBLICATIONS

Note: Unless otherwise indicated, publications are available from Knowledge Industry Publications, 2 Corporate Park Dr., White Plains, NY 10604.

Annual Review of Information Science and Technology (vol. 3, 1968-vol. 10, 1975, $35 each, memb. $28; vol. 11, 1976-vol. 17, 1982, $42.50 each, memb. $34).

Bulletin of the American Society for Information Science ($6 per year, memb. or $35 domestic, $42.50 foreign). Available directly from ASIS.

Collective Index to the Journal of the American Society for Information Science (vol. 1, 1950-vol. 25, 1974, $60 each, memb. $42). Available from John Wiley & Sons, 605 Third Ave., New York, NY 10016.

Computer-Readable Data Bases: A Directory and Data Sourcebook 1982 ($120, memb. $96).

Cumulative Index to the Annual Review of Information Science and

Technology (vols. 1-10, $35 each, memb. $28).

Journal of the American Society for Information Science; formerly *American Documentation* (bi-mo.; memb. or $55 domestic, $60 foreign). Available from John Wiley & Sons, 605 Third Ave., New York, NY 10016.

Key Papers in the Design and Evaluation of Information Systems. Ed. Donald W. King ($25, memb. $20).

Library and Reference Facilities in the Area of the District of Columbia (10th ed., 1979, $19.50, memb. $15.60).

Proceedings of the ASIS Annual Meetings (vol. 5, 1968-vol. 9, 1972, $15 each, memb. $12; vol. 10, 1973-vol. 19, 1982, $19.50 each, memb. $15.60).

COMMITTEE CHAIRPERSONS

Awards and Honors. Mauro Pittaro, Engineering Information, Inc., 345 E. 47 St., New York, NY 10017.

Budget and Finance. Frank Slater, Univ. of Pittsburgh, G-33 Hillman Lib., Pittsburgh, PA 15260.

Conferences and Meetings. Edward J. Kazlauskas, School of Lib. & Info. Management, Univ. of Southern California, Los Angeles, CA 90007.

Constitution and Bylaws. Barbara Sandulik, Imperial Clevite Inc., 540 E. 105 St., Cleveland, OH 44108.

Education. Carol Tenopir, Univ. of Illinois, Urbana, IL 61801.

Executive. Charles H. Davis, Univ. of Illinois, Urbana, IL 61801.

International Relations. Baja el-Hadidy, Catholic Univ. of America, Washington, DC 20004.

Marketing. Patricia Earnest, 2775 Mesa Verde Dr., Costa Mesa, CA 92626.

Membership. Judith L. Krone, Washington, DC 20037.

Nominations. Mary C. Berger, Cuadra Associates, 1523 Sixth St., Santa Monica, CA 90401.

Professionalism. Pamela Cibbarelli, Cibbarelli Associates, 18652 Florida, Huntington Beach, CA 92648.

Public Affairs. Jeffrey Davidson, 2708 Fenimore Rd., Wheaton, MD 20902.

Publications. Bonnie C. Carroll, Dept. of Energy, Technical Info. Center, Box 62, Oak Ridge, TN 37830.

Research. Manfred Kochin, Mental Health Research Institute, Univ. of Michigan, Ann Arbor, MI 48104.

Standards. David Liston, King Research, 6000 Executive Blvd., Rockville, MD 20852.

AMERICAN THEOLOGICAL LIBRARY ASSOCIATION
Executive Secretary, Albert E. Hurd
5600 S. Woodlawn Ave., Chicago, IL 60637

OBJECT

"To bring its members into closer working relationships with each other, to support theological and religious librarianship, to improve theological libraries, and to interpret the role of such libraries in theological education, developing and implementing standards of library service, promoting research and experimental projects, encouraging cooperative programs that make resources more available, publishing and disseminating literature and research tools and aids, cooperating with organizations having similar aims and otherwise supporting and aiding theological education." Founded 1947. Memb. (Inst.) 160; (Indiv.) 460. Dues (Inst.) $50-$300, based on total library expenditure; (Indiv.) $10-$55, based on salary scale. Year. May 1-April 30.

ATLA is a member of the Council of National Library and Information Associations.

MEMBERSHIP

Persons engaged in professional library or bibliographical work in theological or religious fields and others who are interested in the work of theological librarianship.

OFFICERS (JUNE 1982-JUNE 1983)

Pres. Robert Dvorak, Gordon Conwell Theological Seminary, South Hamilton, MA 01982; *V.P./Pres.-Elect.* Martha Aycock, Union Theological Seminary, Richmond, VA 23227; *Past. Pres.* Jerry Campbell, Perkins School of Theology, Southern Methodist Univ., Dallas, TX 75275; *Treas.* Robert A. Olsen, Jr., Libn., Brite Divinity School, Texas Christian Univ., Fort Worth, TX 76129; *Newsletter Ed.* Donn Michael Farris, Divinity School Lib., Duke Univ., Durham, NC 27706.

BOARD OF DIRECTORS

James Dunkly; Roberta Hamburger; Dorothy Ruth Parks; Richard D. Spoor; Betty O'Brien; Lawrence H. Hill; *ATS Rep.* David Schuller.

PUBLICATIONS

Newsletter (q.; memb. or $10).
Proceedings (ann.; memb. or $20).
Religion Index One (formerly *Index to Religious Periodical Literature, 1949-date*).
Religion Index Two: Multi-Author Works.

COMMITTEE CHAIRPERSONS

ATLA Newsletter. Donn Michael Farris, Ed., Divinity School Lib., Duke Univ., Durham, NC 27706.

ATLA Representative to ANSI Z39. Warren Kissinger, 6309 Queen's Chapel Rd., Hyattsville, MD 20782.

ATLA Representative to the Council of National Library and Information Associations. James Irvine, Princeton Theological Seminary, Box 111, Princeton, NJ 08540.

Archivist. Gerald W. Gillette, Presbyterian Historical Society, 425 Lombard St., Philadelphia, PA 19147.

Bibliographic Systems. Elizabeth Flynn, Graduate Theological Union, 2400 Ridge Rd., Berkeley, CA 94709.

Collection Evaluation and Development. Donald Vorp, McCormick Theological Seminary, 1100 E. 55 St., Chicago, IL 60615.

Microtext Reproduction Board. Charles Willard, Exec. Secy., Princeton Theological Seminary, Princeton, NJ 08540; Maria Grossmann, Andover-Harvard Lib., 45 Francis Ave., Cambridge, MA 02138.

Nominating. John Sayre, Grad. Seminary, Enid, OK 73701.

Periodical Indexing Board. R. Grant Bracewell, Emmanuel College Lib., 75 Queen's Pk., Toronto, Ont. M5S 1K7, Canada.

Program. Erich Schultz, Wilfrid Laurier Univ., Waterloo, Ont. N2L 3C5, Canada.

Publication. Betty O'Brien, St. Leonard College, Dayton, OH 45459.

Reader Services. Norman Desmarais, 3104 Harview Ave., Baltimore, MD 21234.

Relationships with Learned Societ-

ies. Andrew Scrimgeour, Iliff School of Theology Lib., 2201 S. University, Denver, CO 80210.
Statistician and Liaison with ALA Statistics Coordinating Committee. David Green, General Theological Seminary, 175 Ninth Ave., New York, NY 10011.
Systems and Standards. Doralyn Hickey, Reporter, School of Lib. & Info. Sciences, North Texas State Univ., Denton, TX 76203.

ART LIBRARIES SOCIETY OF NORTH AMERICA (ARLIS/NA)
Executive Secretary, Pamela J. Parry
3775 Bear Creek Circle, Tucson, AZ 85749
602-749-9112

OBJECT
"To promote art librarianship and visual resources curatorship, particularly by acting as a forum for the interchange of information and materials on the visual arts." Established 1972. Memb. 1,100. Dues (Inst.) $60; (Indiv.) $35; (Business Affiliate) $60; (Student) $20; (Retired/unemployed) $25; (Sustaining) $150; (Sponsor) $500. Year. Jan.-Dec. 31.

MEMBERSHIP
Open and encouraged for all those interested in visual librarianship, whether they be professional librarians, students, library assistants, art book publishers, art book dealers, art historians, archivists, architects, slide and photograph curators, or retired associates in these fields.

OFFICERS (FEB. 1983-FEB. 1984)
Chpn. Nancy Allen, Museum of Fine Arts Lib., Boston, MA 02115; *Past. Chpn.* Caroline Backlund, National Gallery of Art Lib., Washington, DC 20565; *Treas.* Jeffrey Horrell, Dartmouth College, Sherman Art Lib., Hanover, NH 03755.
(Address correspondence to the executive secretary.)

COMMITTEES
(Direct correspondence to headquarters.)
Cataloging Advisory.
Conference.
Education.
Fund Raising.
International Relations.
Membership.
Gerd Muehsam Award.
Nominating.
Publications.
Standards.
Wittenborn Award.

EXECUTIVE BOARD
The chairperson, past chairperson, chairperson-elect, secretary, treasurer, and four regional representatives (East, Midwest, West, and Canada).

PUBLICATIONS
Art Documentation (bi-mo.; memb.)
Handbook and List of Members (ann.; memb.)
Occasional Papers (price varies).
Miscellaneous others (request current list from headquarters).

CHAPTERS
Allegheny; Arizona; DC-Maryland-Virginia; Delaware Valley; Kansas-

Missouri; Kentucky-Tennessee; Michigan; Mid-States; New England; New Jersey; New York; Northern California; Northwest; Ohio; Southeast; Southern California; Texas; Twin Cities; Western New York.

ASSOCIATED INFORMATION MANAGERS
Executive Director, Rita Lombardo
316 Pennsylvania Ave. S.E., Suite 400,
Washington, DC 20003
202-544-2892

OBJECT

To advance information management as a profession and to promote information management as an executive function by improving recognition of its applicability as a strategic and tactical tool in achieving organizational and executive effectiveness. AIM provides the meeting ground for the professionals responsible for meeting the present and future information needs of their organizations within the information management context. Established January 1981. Membership. 1,000 (reg.).

MEMBERSHIP

Data processing, telecommunications, librarianship, records management, office automation, and management information systems (MIS) personnel. Its primary focus is on the management of these information activities and on making the total information base supportive of management and the decision making process. Board of Directors made up of leading information professionals in industry, academia, and government. Dues (regular) $60; (foreign) $95; (student) $25.

BOARD OF DIRECTORS

Herbert R. Brinberg, Pres. & CEO, Aspen Systems Corp.; J. William Doolittle, Sr. Partner, Prather, Seeger, Doolittle & Farmer; Sarah T. Kadec, Special Asst. to the Dir., Science & Education Management Staff, U.S. Dept. of Agriculture; James G. Kollegger, Pres., EIC/Intelligence, Inc.; Rhoda R. Mancher, Deputy Asst. Attorney General, Office of Info. Technology, Dept. of Justice; Donald A. Marchand, Inst. of Info. Management, Technology & Policy, Univ. of South Carolina; Herbert N. McCauley, V.P., Management Info. Systems, Harris Corp.; Morton F. Meltzer, Info. Mgr., Martin Marietta Corp.; Deanna C. Nash, Sr. Consultant, Systemhouse Ltd. (Canada); John J. Walsh, Founder & Pres., Office Technology Group, Inc.

EXECUTIVE COMMITTEE

Herbert R. Brinberg, Pres. & CEO, Aspen Systems Corp.; Roberta Gardner, Dir., Info. Services, Moody's Investors Service, Inc.; Andrew P. Garvin, Chpn. & Chief Exec., FIND/SVP; Joseph H. Kuney, V.P., Informatics, Inc.; Joan Maier McKean,

Chief, Lib. Services, National Oceanic & Atmospheric Admin.; Michael D. Majcher, Mgr., Info. Resources, Xerox Corp.; Morton F. Meltzer, Info. Mgr., Martin Marietta Corp. Co.-Chpns. Sarah T. Kadec, Special Asst. to the Dir., Science & Education Management Staff, U.S. Dept. of Agriculture, and James G. Kollegger, Pres., Environment Information Center, Inc.

PUBLICATIONS

AIM Membership Roster. Annual directory.

AIM Network (bi-weekly). Newsletter.

Marketing Yourself in Your Organization, by Morton Meltzer. (memb. $9.95; nonmemb. $14.95).

Partners in Fact: Information Managers/Information Company Executives Talk. (memb. $14.95; nonmemb. $19.95).

Who's Who in Information Management. (ann.; nonmemb. $25).

ASSOCIATION OF ACADEMIC HEALTH SCIENCES LIBRARY DIRECTORS
Executive Secretary, Elizabeth J. Sawyers, Health Sciences Library, Ohio State University, 376 W. Tenth Ave., Columbus, OH 43210

OBJECT

"To promote, in cooperation with educational institutions, other educational associations, government agencies, and other non-profit organizations, the common interests of academic health sciences libraries located in the United States and elsewhere, through publications, research, and discussion of problems of mutual interest and concern, and to advance the efficient and effective operation of academic health sciences libraries for the benefit of faculty, students, administrators, and practitioners."

MEMBERSHIP

Regular membership is available to nonprofit educational institutions operating a school of health sciences that has full or provisional accreditation by the Association of American Medical Colleges. Annual dues $50. Regular members shall be represented by the chief administrative officer of the member institution's health sciences library.

Associate membership (and nonvoting representation) is available to organizations having an interest in the purposes and activities of the association.

OFFICERS (JUNE 1982-JUNE 1983)

Pres. Richard Lyders, Texas Medical Center Lib., Houston Academy of Medicine, Jesse H. Jones Lib. Bldg., Houston, TX 77030; *Pres.-Elect.* Glenn L. Brudvig, Biomedical Lib., 325A Diehl Hall 505 Essex St., S.E., Univ. of Minnesota Minneapolis, MN 55455; *Past Pres.* Virginia H. Holtz, Middleton Health Sciences Lib., 1305 Linden Dr., Madison, WI 53706.

Secy.-Treas. Elizabeth J. Sawyers, Health Sciences Lib., Ohio State Univ., 376 W. Tenth Ave., Columbus, OH 43210.

BOARD OF DIRECTORS
(JUNE 1982-JUNE 1983)

Officers; Nelson J. Gilman, Norris Medical Lib., Univ. of Southern California, 2025 Zonal Ave., Los Angeles, CA 90033; Gloria Werner, UCLA Biomedical Lib., Center for Health Sciences, Univ. of California, Los Angeles, CA 90024; L. Yvonne Wulff, Alfred Taubman Medical Lib., Univ. of Michigan, 1135 E. Catherine, Ann Arbor, MI 48109.

COMMITTEE CHAIRPERSONS

Audit Committee. Betty Feeney.
Bylaws Committee. Doris Bolef.
Committee on Information Control and Technology. Thomas Lange.
Committee on the Development of Standards and Guidelines. Erika Love.
Medical Education Committee. Jo Ann Bell.
Newsletter Advisory Committee. Richard Frederickson.
Nominating Committee. Jean Miller.
Program Committee. Virginia Algermissen.
Statistics: Annual Statistics of Medical Libraries in the U.S. and Canada. Editorial Board. Richard Lyders.

MEETINGS

An annual business meeting is held in conjunction with the annual meeting of the Medical Library Association in June. Annual membership meeting and program is held in conjunction with the annual meeting of the Association of American Medical Colleges in October.

ASSOCIATION OF AMERICAN LIBRARY SCHOOLS
Executive Secretary, Janet Phillips
471 Park Lane, State College, PA 16801
814-238-0254

OBJECT

"To advance education for librarianship." Founded 1915. Memb. 790. Dues (Inst.) $125; (Assoc. Inst.) $75; (Indiv.) $25; (Assoc. Indiv.) $20. Year. Sept. 1982-1983.

MEMBERSHIP

Any library school with a program accredited by the ALA Committee on Accreditation may become an institutional member; any educator who is employed full time for a full academic year in a library school with an accredited program may become a personal member.

Any school that offers a graduate degree in librarianship or a cognate field but whose program is not accredited by the ALA Committee on Accreditation may become an associate institutional member; any part-time faculty member or doctoral student of a library school with an accredited program or any full-time faculty member employed for a full academic year at other schools that offer graduate degrees in librarianship or cognate fields may become an associate personal member.

OFFICERS (FEB. 1983-JAN. 1984)

Pres. Robert D. Stueart, Grad. School of Lib. & Info. Science, Simmons College, Boston, MA 02115; *Past Pres.* F. William Summers, College of Libnshp., Univ. of South Carolina, Columbia, SC 29208. (Address correspondence to the executive secretary.)

DIRECTORS

Marcy Murphy (Indiana); Shirley Fitzgibbons (Indiana); Annette Phinazee (North Carolina Central).

PUBLICATION

Journal of Education for Librarianship (5 per year; $20).

COMMITTEE CHAIRPERSONS

Conference. Jane B. Robbins-Carter, Dir., Lib. School, Univ. of Wisconsin-Madison, Madison, WI 53706.
Continuing Education. Joan C. Durrance, School of Lib. Science, Univ. of Michigan, Ann Arbor, MI 48109.
Editorial Board. Charles D. Patterson, School of Lib. & Info. Science, Louisiana State Univ., Baton Rouge, LA 70803.
Governmental Relations. Herbert White, Dean, School of Lib. & Info. Science, Indiana Univ., Bloomington, IN 47405.
Nominating. Joseph J. Mika, Asst. Dean, School of Lib. Service, Univ. of Southern Mississippi, Hattiesburg, MS 39406.
Research. Charles McClure, School of Lib. Science, Univ. of Oklahoma, Norman, OK 73019.

REPRESENTATIVES

ALA SCOLE. Shirley Fitzgibbons (Indiana).
Council of Communication Societies. Guy Garrision (Drexel).
IFLA. Robert D. Stueart (Simmons); Josephine Fang (Simmons).
Organization of American States. Margaret Goggin (Denver).

ASSOCIATION OF JEWISH LIBRARIES
c/o National Foundation for Jewish Culture
122 E. 42 St., Rm. 408, New York, NY 10017

OBJECT

"To promote and improve library services and professional standards in all Jewish libraries and collections of Judaica; to serve as a center of dissemination of Jewish library information and guidance; to encourage the establishment of Jewish libraries and collections of Judaica; to promote publication of literature which will be of assistance to Jewish librarianship; to encourage people to enter the field of librarianship." Organized 1966 from the merger of the Jewish Librarians Association and the Jewish Library Association. Memb. 600. Dues (Inst.) $18; (Student/retired) $10. Year. Calendar.

OFFICERS (JUNE 1982-JUNE 1984)

Pres. Philip E. Miller, Klau Lib., Hebrew Union College-Jewish Institute of Religion, New York, NY 10012; *Treas.* Debra Reed, Klau Lib., Hebrew Union College-Jewish Institute of Religion, New York, NY 10012; *Corres. Secy.* Edith Lubetski, Hedi Steinberg Lib., Yeshiva Univ., 245 Lexington Ave., New York, NY 10016; *Rec. Secy.* Ralph R. Simon, Temple Emanu El, 2200 S. Green Rd., University Heights, OH 44121.

(Address correspondence to the president.)

PUBLICATIONS

AJL Newsletter (bienn.) *Ed.* Irene S. Levin, 48 Georgia St., Valley Stream, NY 11580.
AJL Bulletin (2 per year).
Proceedings.

DIVISIONS

Research and Special Libraries. Charles Cutter, Brandeis Univ. Lib., Waltham, MA 02154.
Synagogue School and Center Libraries. Hazel B. Karp, Hebrew Academy of Atlanta Lib., 1892 N. Druid Hills Rd. N.E., Atlanta, GA 30319.

ASSOCIATION OF RESEARCH LIBRARIES
Executive Director, Shirley Echelman
1527 New Hampshire Ave. N.W., Washington, DC 20036
202-232-2466

OBJECT

"To initiate and develop plans for strengthening research library resources and services in support of higher education and research." Established 1932 by the chief librarians of 43 research libraries. Memb. (Inst.) 113. Dues (ann.) $3,850. Year. Jan.-Dec.

MEMBERSHIP

Membership is institutional.

OFFICERS (OCT. 1982-OCT. 1983)

Pres. James F. Govan, Dir., Univ. of North Carolina Libs., Chapel Hill, NC 27515; *V.P.* Eldred Smith, Dir., Univ. of Minnesota Libs., Minneapolis, MN 55455; *Past Pres.* Millicent D. Abell, Libn., Univ. of California, San Diego Lib., La Jolla, CA 92037.

BOARD OF DIRECTORS

Sterling J. Albrecht, Brigham Young Univ. Lib.; Hugh C. Atkinson, Univ. of Illinois Lib.; Patricia Battin, Columbia Univ. Libs.; John McDonald, Univ. of Connecticut Lib.; William J. Studer, Ohio State Univ. Libs.; Richard J. Talbot, Univ. of Massachusetts Libs.; Paul Vassallo, Univ. of New Mexico Libs.; Anne Woodsworth, York Univ. Libs.

PUBLICATIONS

ARL Annual Salary Survey (ann.; memb. or $10).
The ARL Library Index and Quantitative Relationships in the ARL. Kendon Stubbs ($5).
ARL Statistics (ann.; memb. or $10).
ARL Minutes (s. ann.; memb. or $12.50 each).
ARL Newsletter (approx. 6 per year; memb. or $15).
Cumulated ARL University Library Statistics, 1962-63 through 1978-79. Compiled by Kendon Stubbs and David Buxton ($15).
Our Cultural Heritage: Whence Salvation? Louis B. Wright; The Uses of the Past, Gordon N. Ray; remarks to the 89th membership meeting of the association ($3).
76 United Statesiana. Seventy-six works of American Scholarship relating to America as published during two centuries from the Revolutionary era of the United States through the nation's bicentennial year. Ed. by

Edward C. Lathem ($7.50; $5.75 paper to nonmembs.).
13 Colonial Americana. Ed. by Edward C. Lathem ($7.50).
(The above two titles are distributed by the Univ. of Virginia Press.)

COMMITTEE CHAIRPERSONS

ARL/CRL Joint Committee on Expanded Access to Journal Collections. John P. McDonald, Univ. of Connecticut Lib., Storrs, CT 06268.

ARL Statistics. Richard J. Talbot, Univ. of Massachusetts Libs., Amherst, MA 01002.

Center for Chinese Research Materials. Philip McNiff, Boston Public Lib., Boston, MA 02117.

Federal Relations. Carlton C. Rochell, New York Univ. Libs., New York, NY 10003.

Interlibrary Loan. Sterling Albrecht, Brigham Young Univ., Provo, Utah 84602.

Membership Committee on Nonuniversity Libraries. Roy L. Kidman, Univ. of Southern California Libs., Los Angeles, CA 90007.

Nominations. ARL Vice-President.

Office of Management Studies. Jay Lucker, Massachusetts Institute of Technology, Cambridge, MA 02139.

Preservation of Research Library Materials. David Stam, New York Public Lib., New York, NY 10018.

TASK FORCE CHAIRPERSONS

Bibliographic Control. James Govan, Univ. of North Carolina Libs., Chapel Hill, NC 27515.

Collection Development. Joseph H. Treyz, Univ. of Wisconsin Libs., Madison, WI 53706.

Library Education. Margot B. McBurney, Queen's Univ. Lib., Kingston, Ont. K7L 5C4, Canada.

National Library Network Development. William J. Studer, Ohio State Univ. Libs., Columbus, OH 43210.

ARL MEMBERSHIP IN 1982

Nonuniversity Libraries

Boston Public Lib.; Center for Research Libs.; John Crerar Lib.; Lib. of Congress; Linda Hall Lib.; National Agricultural Lib.; National Lib. of Canada; National Lib. of Medicine; New York Public Lib.; New York State Lib.; Newberry Lib.; Smithsonian Institution Libs.

University Libraries

Alabama; Alberta; Arizona; Arizona State; Boston; Brigham Young; British Columbia; Brown; California (Berkeley); California (Davis); California (Irvine); California (Los Angeles); California (Riverside); California (San Diego); California (Santa Barbara); Case Western Reserve; Chicago; Cincinnati; Colorado; Colorado State; Columbia; Connecticut; Cornell; Dartmouth; Duke; Emory; Florida; Florida State; Georgetown; Georgia; Guelph; Harvard; Hawaii; Houston; Howard; Illinois; Indiana; Iowa; Iowa State; Johns Hopkins; Kansas; Kent State; Kentucky; Louisiana State; McGill; McMaster; Manitoba; Maryland; Massachusetts; Massachusetts Institute of Technology; Miami; Michigan; Michigan State; Minnesota; Missouri; Nebraska; New Mexico; New York; North Carolina; Northwestern; Notre Dame; Ohio State; Oklahoma; Oklahoma State; Oregon; Pennsylvania; Pennsylvania State; Pittsburgh; Princeton; Purdue; Queen's (Kingston, Canada); Rice; Rochester; Rutgers; Saskatchewan; South Carolina; Southern California; Southern Illinois; Stanford; SUNY (Albany); SUNY (Buffalo); SUNY (Stony Brook); Syracuse; Temple; Tennessee; Texas; Texas A & M; Toronto; Tulane; Utah; Vanderbilt; Virginia; Virginia Polytechnic; Washington; Washington (St. Louis); Washington State; Wayne State; Western Ontario; Wisconsin; Yale; York.

ASSOCIATION OF VISUAL SCIENCE LIBRARIANS
c/o Pat Carlson, Librarian
Southern California College of Optometry
2001 Associated Rd., Fullerton, CA 92631

OBJECT

"To foster collective and individual acquisition and dissemination of visual science information, to improve services for all persons seeking such information, and to develop standards for libraries to which members are attached." Founded 1968. Memb. (U.S.) 51; (foreign) 13. Annual meeting held in December in connection with the American Academy of Optometry; Houston, Texas (1983); St. Louis, Missouri (1984).

OFFICERS

Chpn. Pat Carlson, Libn., Southern California College of Optometry, 2001 Associated Rd., Fullerton, CA 92631; *Chpn. Elect.* Suzanne Ferimer, Libn., Univ. of Houston, College of Optometry, Cullen Blvd., Houston, TX 77004.

PUBLICATIONS

Opening Day Book Collection—Visual Science.
PhD Theses in Physiological Optics (irreg.).
Standards for Vision Science Libraries.
Union List of Vision-Related Serials (irreg.).

BETA PHI MU
(International Library Science Honor Society)
Executive Secretary, Blanche Woolls
School of Library and Information Science
University of Pittsburgh, Pittsburgh, PA 15260

OBJECT

"To recognize high scholarship in the study of librarianship, and to sponsor appropriate professional and scholarly projects." Founded at the University of Illinois in 1948. Memb. 18,500.

MEMBERSHIP

Open to graduates of library school programs accredited by the American Library Association who fulfill the following requirements: complete the course requirements leading to a fifth-year or other advanced degree in librarianship with a scholastic average of A- (e.g., 4.83 where A equals 5 points, 3.83 where A equals 4 points, etc.)—this provision shall also apply to planned programs of advanced study beyond the fifth year that do not culminate in a degree but that require full-time study for one or more academic years; receive a letter of recommendation from their respective library schools attesting to their demonstrated fitness of successful professional careers. Former graduates of accredited library schools are also eligible on the same basis.

OFFICERS

Pres. Robert D. Stueart, Dean, Grad. School of Lib. & Info. Science, Simmons College, Boston, MA 02115; *V.P./Pres.-Elect.* H. Joanne Harrar, Dir. of Libs., Univ. of Maryland, College Park, MD 20742; *Past Pres.* Mary Alice Hunt, Assoc. Prof., School of Lib. Science, Florida State Univ., Tallahassee, FL 32306; *Treas.* Marilyn P. Whitmore, Univ. Archivist, Hillman Lib., Univ. of Pittsburgh, Pittsburgh, PA 15260; *Exec. Secy.* Blanche Woolls, Prof., School of Lib. & Info. Science, Univ. of Pittsburgh, Pittsburgh, PA 15260; *Admin. Secy.* Mary Y. Tomaino, School of Lib. & Info. Science, Univ. of Pittsburgh, Pittsburgh, PA 15260.

DIRECTORS

Carol Penka, 200 Main Lib., Univ. of Illinois, Urbana, IL 61801 (Alpha Chapter—Univ. of Illinois/1983); Mary Jane Kahao, Grad. School of Lib. Science Lib., Louisiana State Univ., Baton Rouge, LA 70803 (Beta Zeta Chapter—Louisiana State Univ./1983); David L. Searcy, 703 Durant Place N.E., Apt. 1, Atlanta, GA 30308 (Zeta Chapter—Atlanta Univ./1984); Dorothy M. Shields, Asst. Prof., School of Lib. and Info. Sciences, Brigham Young Univ., Provo, UT 84602 (Beta Theta Chapter—Brigham Young Univ./1984); Trudi Bellardo, College of Lib. & Info. Science, Univ. of Kentucky, Lexington, KY 40506 (Upsilon Chapter—Univ. of Kentucky/1985); Gordon Eriksen, 220 S. Kendall, #13, Kalamazoo, MI 49007 (Kappa Chapter—Western Michigan Univ./1985); *Directors-at-Large.* Edward Holley, Dean, Grad. School of Lib. Science, Univ. of North Carolina, Chapel Hill, NC 27514 (1984); Charles D. Patterson, Prof., School of Lib & Info. Sciences, Louisiana State Univ., Baton Rouge, LA 70803 (1985).

PUBLICATIONS

Newsletter (bienn.).

Beta Phi Mu sponsors a modern Chapbook series. These small volumes, issued in limited editions, are intended to create a beautiful combination of text and format in the interest of the graphic arts and are available to members only. In January 1980, the 14th in the Chapbook series was published by the society, *A Book for a Sixpence: The Circulating Library in America* by David Kaser.

CHAPTERS

Alpha. Univ. of Illinois, Grad. School of Lib. & Info. Science, Urbana, IL 61801; *Beta.* Univ. of Southern California, School of Lib. Science, University Park, Los Angeles, CA 90007; *Gamma.* Florida State Univ., School of Lib. Science, Tallahassee, FL 32306; *Delta* (Inactive). Loughborough College of Further Education, School of Libnshp., Loughborough, England; *Epsilon.* Univ. of North Carolina, School of Lib. Science, Chapel Hill, NC 27514; *Zeta.* Atlanta Univ., School of Lib. & Info. Studies, Atlanta, GA 30314; *Theta.* Pratt Institute, Grad. School of Lib. & Info. Science, Brooklyn, NY 11205; *Iota.* Catholic Univ. of America, School of Lib. & Info. Science, Washington, DC 20064, and Univ. of Maryland, College of Lib. & Info. Services, College Park, MD 20742; *Kappa.* Western Michigan Univ., School of Libnshp., Kalamazoo, MI 49008; *Lambda.* Univ. of Oklahoma, School of Lib Science, Norman, OK 73019; *Mu.* Univ. of Michigan, School of Lib. Science, Ann Arbor, MI 48109; *Nu.* Columbia Univ., School of Lib. Service, New York, NY 10027;

Xi. Univ. of Hawaii, Grad. School of Lib. Studies, Honolulu, HI 96822; *Omicron.* Rutgers Univ., Grad. School of Lib. & Info. Studies, New Brunswick, NJ 08903; *Pi.* Univ. of Pittsburgh, School of Lib. & Info. Science, Pittsburgh, PA 15260; *Rho.* Kent State Univ., School of Lib. Science, Kent, OH 44242; *Sigma.* Drexel Univ., School of Lib. & Info. Science, Philadelphia, PA 19104; *Tau.* State Univ. of New York at Geneseo, School of Lib. & Info. Science, College of Arts and Science, Geneseo, NY 14454; *Upsilon.* Univ. of Kentucky, College of Lib. Science, Lexington, KY 40506; *Phi.* Univ. of Denver, Grad. School of Libnshp. and Info Mgmt., Denver, CO 80208; *Pi Lambda Sigma.* Syracuse Univ., School of Info. Studies, Syracuse, NY 13210; *Chi.* Indiana Univ. School of Lib. & Info. Science, Bloomington, IN 47401; *Psi.* Univ. of Missouri, Columbia, School of Lib. & Info. Science, Columbia, MO 65211; *Omega.* San Jose State Univ., Div. of Lib. Science, San Jose, CA 95192; *Beta Alpha.* Queens College, City College of New York, Grad. School of Lib. & Info. Studies, Flushing, NY 11367; *Beta Beta.* Simmons College, Grad. School of Lib. & Info. Science, Boston, MA 02115; *Beta Delta.* State Univ. of New York-Buffalo, School of Info. & Lib. Studies, Buffalo, NY 14260; *Beta Epsilon.* Emporia State Univ., School of Lib. Science, Emporia, KS 66801; *Beta Zeta.* Louisiana State Univ., Grad. School of Lib. Science, Baton Rouge, LA 70803; *Beta Eta.* Univ. of Texas at Austin, Grad. School of Lib. and Info. Science, Austin, TX 78712; *Beta Theta.* Brigham Young Univ., School of Lib. & Info. Science, Provo, UT 84602; *Beta Iota.* Univ. of Rhode Island, Grad. Lib. School, Kingston, RI 02881; *Beta Kappa.* Univ. of Alabama, Grad. School of Lib. Service, University, AL 35486; *Beta Lambda.* North Texas State Univ., School of Lib. & Info. Science, Denton, TX 76203, and Texas Woman's Univ., School of Lib. Science, Denton, TX 76204; *Beta Mu.* Long Island Univ., Palmer Grad. Lib. School, C.W. Post Center, Greenvale, NY 11548; *Beta Nu.* St. John's Univ., Div. of Lib. & Info. Science, Jamaica, NY 11439; *Beta Xi.* North Carolina Central Univ., School of Lib. Science, Durham, NC 27707; *Beta Omicron.* Univ. of Tennessee, Knoxville, Grad. School of Lib. & Info. Science, Knoxville, TN 37916; *Beta Pi.* Univ. of Arizona, Grad. Lib. School, Tucson, AZ 85721; *Beta Rho.* Univ. of Wisconsin-Milwaukee, School of Lib. Science, Milwaukee, WI 53201; *Beta Sigma.* Clarion State College, School of Lib. Science, Clarion, PA 16214; *Beta Tau.* Wayne State Univ., Div. of Lib. Science, Detroit, MI 48202; *Beta Upsilon.* Alabama A & M Univ., School of Lib. Media, Normal, AL 35762; *Beta Phi.* Univ. of South Florida, Grad. Dept. of Lib., Media & Info. Studies, Tampa, FL 33620.

BIBLIOGRAPHICAL SOCIETY OF AMERICA
Executive Director, Deirdre C. Stam
Box 397, Grand Central Sta., New York, NY 10017

OBJECT

"To promote bibliographical research and to issue bibliographical publications." Organized 1904. Memb. 1,400. Dues. $20. Year. Calendar.

OFFICERS (JAN. 1982-JAN. 1984)

Pres. Marcus A. McCorison, American Antiquarian Society, Salisbury St. & Park Ave., Worcester, MA 01609; *1st V.P.* G. Thomas Tanselle, Guggenheim Memorial Foundation, 90 Park Ave., New York, NY 10016; *Treas.* Frank S. Streeter, 141 E. 72 St., New York, NY 10021; *Secy.* Peter VanWingen, Rare Book Rm., Lib. of Congress, Washington, DC 20540.

COUNCIL

Officers; John Bidwell; Joan M. Friedman; Roland Folter; William Matheson; Katharine F. Pantzer; Paul Needham; Richard G. Landon; Bernard M. Rosenthal; Roger E. Stoddard; Elizabeth A. Swaim; G. Thomas Tanselle; W. Thomas Taylor.

PUBLICATIONS

Papers (q.; memb.). *Eds.* John Lancaster and Ruth Martimer, Box 467, Williamsburg, MA 01096.

Book Review Eds. John Lancaster and Ruth Martimer, Box 467, Williamsburg, MA 01096.

COMMITTEE CHAIRPERSON

Publications. G. Thomas Tanselle, Guggenheim Memorial Foundation, 90 Park Ave., New York, NY 10016.

CANADIAN ASSOCIATION FOR INFORMATION SCIENCE (ASSOCIATION CANADIENNE DES SCIENCES DE L'INFORMATION)
Secretariat/Secrétariat, c/o Robert Leitch, 47 Gore St. E., Perth Ont. K7H 1H6, Canada
613-267-3499

OBJECT

Brings together individuals and organizations concerned with the production, manipulation, storage, retrieval, and dissemination of information with emphasis on the application of modern technologies in these areas. CAIS is dedicated to enhancing the activity of the information transfer process, utilizing the vehicles of research, development, application, and education, and serves as a forum for dialogue and exchange of ideas concerned with the theory and practice of all factors involved in the communication of information. Dues (Inst.) $75; (Regular) $25; (Student) $10.

MEMBERSHIP

Institutions and all individuals interested in information science and who are involved in the gathering, the organization, and the dissemination of information (computer scientists, documentalists, information scientists, librarians, journalists, sociologists, psychologists, linguists, administrators, etc.) can become members of the Canadian Association for Information Science.

PUBLICATIONS

CAIS Bulletin (irreg.; free with membership).

The Canadian Conference of Information Science: Proceedings (ann.; ninth ann., 1981, $16.50).

The Canadian Journal of Information Science (ann.; nonmemb. $12).

CANADIAN LIBRARY ASSOCIATION
Executive Director, Paul Kitchen
151 Sparks St., Ottawa, Ont. K1P 5E3, Canada
613-232-9625

OBJECT

To develop high standards of librarianship and of library and information service. CLA develops standards for public, university, school, and college libraries and library technician programs; offers library school scholarships and book awards; carries on international liaison with other library associations; and makes representation to government and official commissions. Founded in Hamilton in 1946, CLA is a nonprofit voluntary organization governed by an elected council and board of directors. Memb. (Indiv.) 4,100; (Inst.) 1,000. Dues (Indiv.) $49 & $77, depending on salary; (Inst.) $45 & $77, depending on budget. Year. July 1-June 30.

MEMBERSHIP

Open to individuals, institutions, and groups interested in librarianship and in library and information services.

OFFICERS (1982-1983)

Pres. Pearce Penney, Chief Provincial Libn., Nfld. Public Lib. Services, St. John's, Nfld. A1B 3A3; *1st V.P./Pres.-Elect.* Prof. Lois M. Bewley, School of Libnshp., Univ. of British Columbia, Vancouver, B.C. V6T 1W5; *2nd V.P.* Hazel Fry, Area Head, Environment-Science-Technology Lib., Univ. of Calgary, Calgary, Alta. T2N 1N4; *Treas.* Vivienne Monty, Government and Business Lib., York Univ., Downsview, Ont. M3J 2R6; *Past Pres.* Marianne F. Scott, Dir. of Libs., McGill Univ. Lib., Montréal, P.Q. H3A 1Y1. (Address general correspondence to the executive director.)

BOARD OF DIRECTORS

Officers, division presidents.

COUNCIL

Officers; division presidents; councillors, including representatives of ASTED and provincial/regional library associations.

COUNCILLORS-AT-LARGE

To June 30, 1983: Marie Zielinska, Gordon Ray.

To June 30, 1984: Madge Mac Gown, Donald Mills.

To June 30, 1985: Claire Coté, Donald Harvey.

PUBLICATIONS

Canadian Library Journal (6 issues; memb. or nonmemb. subscribers, Canada $20, U.S. $24 [Can.], international $30 [Can.]).

CM: Canadian Materials for Schools and Libraries (4 per year, $20).

DIVISION CHAIRPERSONS

Canadian Association of College and University Libraries. Ann Nevill, Health Sciences Libn., W.K. Kellogg Health Sciences Lib., Dalhousie Lib., Halifax, N.S. B3H 4H7.

Canadian Association of Public Libraries. Don Miller, Dir., Greater Victoria Public Lib., Victoria, B.C. V8W 3H2.

Canadian Association of Special Libraries and Information Services. Nancy Brydges, Libn., Canadian Wheat Board, Winnipeg, Man. R3C 2P5.

Canadian Library Trustees Association. Anne Hart, Centre for Newfoundland Studies, Memorial Univ. Lib., St. John's, Nfld. A1B 3Y1.

Canadian School Library Association. John Tooth, Chief Libn., Manitoba Dept. of Educ., Winnipeg, Man R3G 0T3.

ASSOCIATION REPRESENTATIVES

Association pour l'Avancement des Sciences et des Techniques de la Documentation (ASTED). Lise Brousseau, Dir.-Gen. ASTED, 7243 rue Saint-Denis, Montréal, P.Q. H2R 2E3.

Atlantic Provinces Library Association. Barbara Eddy, Education Libn., Memorial Univ., St. John's, Nfld. A1C 5S7.

British Columbia Library Association. Maureen Willison, Greater Vancouver Lib. Federation, Vancouver, B.C. V5L 3X3.

Library Association of Alberta. John R. Gishler, Social Sciences Dept., Calgary Public Lib., Calgary, Alta. T2G 2M2.

Manitoba Library Association. Eileen McFadden, Univ. Archivist, Brandon Univ., Brandon, Man. R7A 6A9.

Ontario Library Association. Barbara Smith, Coord. of Media Services, Peel Bd. of Educ., Media Centre, Mississauga, Ont. L5G 1Z3.

Québec Library Association. Donna Duncan, Asst. Area Libn. (Technical Services), Technical Services Office, McLennan Lib., McGill Univ., Montréal, P.Q. H3A 1Y1.

Saskatchewan Library Association. Bryan Foran, Libn., Carlyle King Branch, Saskatoon Public Lib., Saskatoon, Sask. S7K 5J7.

CATHOLIC LIBRARY ASSOCIATION
Executive Director, Matthew R. Wilt
461 W. Lancaster Ave., Haverford, PA 19041
215-649-5250

OBJECT

"The promotion and encouragement of Catholic literature and library work through cooperation, publications, education and information." Founded 1921. Memb. 3,280. Dues $20-$500.

OFFICERS (APRIL 1981-APRIL 1983)

Pres. Kelly Fitzpatrick, Mt. St. Mary's College, Emmitsburg, MD 21727; *V.P.* Sister M. Dennis Lynch, SHCJ, Rosemont College, Rosemont, PA 19010; *Past Pres.* Sister Franz

Lang, OP, Barry College Lib., Miami, FL 33161. (Address general correspondence to the executive director.)

EXECUTIVE BOARD

Officers; Mary A. Grant, St. John's Univ., Jamaica, NY 11439; Brother Emmett Corry, OSF, St. John's Univ., Jamaica, NY 11439; Sister Teresa Rigel, CSJ, Red Cloud Indian School, Pine Ridge, SD 57770; Irma C. Godfrey, 6247 Westway Place, St. Louis, MO 63109; Sister Chrysantha Rudnik, CSSF, Felician College, Chicago, IL 60659; Gayle E. Salvatore, Brother Martin H.S., New Orleans, LA 70122.

PUBLICATIONS

Catholic Library World (10 issues; memb. or $30).
The Catholic Periodical and Literature Index (subscription).

COMMITTEE CHAIRPERSONS

Advisory Council. Sister M. Dennis Lynch, SHCJ, Rosemont College, Rosemont, PA 19010.
Catholic Library World Editorial. Sister Marie Melton, RSM, St. John's Univ., Jamaica, NY 11439.
The Catholic Periodical and Literature Index. Sister Thérèse Marie Gaudreau, SND, Trinity College, Washington, DC 20017.
Constitution and Bylaws. Sister Margaret Huyck, CSJ, Lib. Consultant, New Orleans, LA 70122.
Continuing Education. Sister Kathryn Dobbs, CSFN, Holy Family College, Philadelphia, PA 19114.
Elections. Sister Rose Anthony Moos, CSJ, Sacred Heart Convent, Salina, KS 67401.
Finance. Arnold M. Rzepecki, Sacred Heart Seminary College, Detroit, MI 48206.

Membership. Membership Development Committee.
Nominations. Sister Mary Arthur Hoagland, IHM, Office of the Superintendent of Schools, Philadelphia, PA 19103.
Program Coordinator. John T. Corrigan, CFX, CLA Headquarters, 461 W. Lancaster Ave., Haverford, PA 19041.
Public Relations. Sister Mary Margaret Cribben, RSM, Villanova College, Villanova, PA 19085.
Publications. Brother Emmett Corry, OSF, St. John's Univ., Jamaica, NY 11439.
Regina Medal. Sister Rita Ann Bert, OSF, Oak Lawn Public Lib., Oak Lawn, IL 60453.
Scholarship. Rev. Joseph P. Browne, CSC, Univ. of Portland, Portland, OR 97203.

ORGANIZATIONS TO WHICH CLA HAS REPRESENTATION

Catholic Press Association. John T. Corrigan, CFX, CLA Headquarters, 461 W. Lancaster Ave., Haverford, PA 19041.
Continuing Library Education Network Exchange (CLENE). Sister Kathryn Dobbs, CSFN, Holy Family College, Philadelphia, PA 19114.
Council of National Library and Information Association (CNLIA). Matthew R. Wilt, Exec. Dir., CLA Headquarters, 461 W. Lancaster Ave., Haverford, PA 19041; Brother Emmett Corry, OSF, St. John's Univ., Jamaica, NY 11439.
Special Libraries Association. Mary-Jo DiMuccio, Sunnyvale Public Lib., Sunnyvale, CA 94087.

OTHER REPRESENTED ORGANIZATIONS

AASL Standards Committee.
American National Standards Committee: Library and Information Sci-

ence and Related Publishing Practices (ANSC Z39).
Catholic Health Association.
National Catholic Educational Association.
Universal Serials and Book Exchange (USBE).

SECTION CHAIRPERSONS

Archives. Sister Martin Joseph Jones, SSMN, State Univ. College at Buffalo, Buffalo, NY 14222.

Children's Libraries. Sister Barbara Anne Kilpatrick, RSM, St. Vincent de Paul School, Nashville, TN 37208.

College, University, Seminary Libraries. Brother Paul J. Ostendorf, FSC, St. Mary's College, Winona, MN 55987.

High School Libraries. Sister Jean Bostley, SSJ, St. Joseph Central H.S., Pittsfield, MA 01201.

Library Education. Sister M. Lauretta McCusker, OP, Rosary College, River Forest, IL 60305.

Parish/Community Libraries. Sister Mary Agnes Sullivan, OP, St. Catherine, KY 40061.

Public Libraries. Margaret Long, Public Lib. of Cincinnati, Cincinnati, OH 45202.

ROUND TABLE CHAIRPERSON

Cataloging and Classification Round Table. Tina-Karen Weiner, La Salle College, Philadelphia, PA 19141.

CHIEF OFFICERS OF STATE LIBRARY AGENCIES
Robert L. Clark, State Librarian,
Oklahoma Department of Libraries
200 N. E. 18 St., Oklahoma City, OK 73105

OBJECT

The object of COSLA is to provide "a means for cooperative action among its state and territorial members to strengthen the work of the respective state and territorial agencies. Its purpose is to provide a continuing mechanism for dealing with the problems faced by the heads of these agencies which are responsible for state and territorial library development."

MEMBERSHIP

The Chief Officers of State Library Agencies is an independent organization of the men and women who head the state and territorial agencies responsible for library development. Its membership consists solely of the top library officers of the 50 states and one territory, variously designated as state librarian, director, commissioner, or executive secretary.

OFFICERS (NOV. 1982-NOV. 1984)

Chpn. Robert L. Clark, State Libn., Oklahoma Dept. of Libs., c/o 200 N. E. 18 St., Oklahoma City, OK 73105; *V. Chpn.* Gary Strong, State Libn., California State Lib., Box 2037, Sacramento, CA 95809; *Secy.* John L. Kopischke, Dir., Nebraska Lib. Commission, 1420 P, Lincoln, NE 68508; *Treas.* Barbara Weaver, Asst. Commissioner & State Libn., State Dept. of Educ., Div. of State Libs., Archives & History, 185 W. State St., CN520, Trenton, NJ 08625; *ALA*

Affiliation. Sandra Cooper, ALA, Exec. Secy. ASCLA.

DIRECTORS

Officers; immediate past chpn.: Patricia Klinck, State Libn., Vermont Dept. of Libs., c/o State Office Bldg., Montpelier, VT 05602; two elected members: Elliot L. Shelkrot, State Libn., State Lib. of Pennsylvania, Harrisburg, PA 17120; David M. Woodburn, Dir., Mississippi Lib. Commission, Box 3260, Jackson, MS 39207.

COMMITTEE CHAIRPERSONS

Legislation. Bill Asp, Dir., Office of Public Libs. & Interlibrary Cooperation, Minnesota.

Liaison with ALA and Other National Library-Related Organizations. Ray Ewick, Dir., Indiana State Lib.

Liaison with Library of Congress. John Kopischke, Dir., Nebraska Lib. Commission.

Liaison with Library of Congress, Division for Blind and Physically Handicapped. Russell Davis, Utah State Lib. Commission.

Liaison with National Commission on Libraries and Information Science. Elliot Shelkrot, Pennsylvania State Lib.

Liaison with U.S. Department of Education. Barratt Wilkins, State Libn., Florida State Lib.

CHINESE-AMERICAN LIBRARIANS ASSOCIATION
Executive Director, John Yung-hsiang Lai
Harvard-Yenching Library, Harvard University
2 Divinity Ave., Cambridge, MA 02138

OBJECT

"(1) To enhance communication among Chinese-American librarians as well as between Chinese-American librarians and other librarians; (2) to serve as a forum for discussion of mutual problems and professional concerns among Chinese-American librarians; (3) to promote Sino-American librarianship and library services; and (4) to provide a vehicle whereby Chinese-American librarians may cooperate with other associations and organizations having similar or allied interest."

MEMBERSHIP

Membership is open to everyone who is interested in the association's goals and activities. Memb. 360. Dues (Regular) $15; (Student and Nonsalaried) $7.50; (Inst.) $45; (Permanent) $150.

OFFICERS (JULY 1982-JUNE 1983)

Pres. Bessie Hahn, Dir. of Lib. Services, Brandeis Univ., Waltham, MA 02254; *V.P./Pres.-Elect.* Norma Yueh, Dir., Ramapo College Lib., Mahwah, NJ 07430; *Exec. Dir.* John Yung-hsiang Lai, Associate Lib., Harvard-Yenching Lib., Harvard Univ., Cambridge, MA 02138; *Secy.* Marjorie H. Li, Rutgers Univ. Lib., New Brunswick, NJ 08903; *Treas.* Cecilia Chen, Educational Resources Center, California State Univ. Dominguez Hills, Carson, CA 90747.

PUBLICATIONS

Journal of Library and Information Science (2 per year; memb. or $15).

Membership Directory, 1982 (*memb.*).
Newsletter (3 per year; memb.).

COMMITTEE CHAIRPERSONS

Annual Program. Norma Yueh, Ramapo College Lib., Mahwah, NJ 07430.
Awards. Shirley L. Chang, Lock Haven State College Lib., Lock Haven, PA 17745.
Books to China, James K. M. Cheng, Far Eastern Lib., Univ. of Chicago, Chicago, IL 60637.
Membership. Eunice Ting, UCLA Biomedical Lib., UCLA, Los Angeles, CA 90024.
Nominating. David T. Liu, Pharr Memorial Lib., Pharr, TX 78577.
Publications. Chiou-sen Chen, Rutgers Univ., New Brunswick, NJ 08903.
Foundation. Hwa-wei Lee, Ohio Univ. Lib., Athens, OH 45701.

CHAPTER CHAIRPERSONS

California. Sally Tseng, Univ. Lib., Univ. of California at Irvine, Irvine, CA 92713.
Mid-Atlantic. Peter C. Ku, Learning Resources Center, Howard Community College, Columbia, MD 21044.
Mid-West. Peter S. Wang, Morton Arboretum Lib., Lisle, IL 60532.
Northeast. Nelson Chou, East Asia Lib., Rutgers Univ., New Brunswick, NJ 08903.
Southwest. Cecilia Tung, Libn., Texas Instruments, Garland, TX 75042.

JOURNAL OFFICER

John Yung-hsiang Lai, Harvard-Yenching Lib., Cambridge, MA 02138.

DISTINGUISHED SERVICE AWARDS

The 1982 distinguished service award was presented to Dr. Ching-chih Chen, Simmons College Grad. School of Lib. & Info. Science on July 14, 1982.

CHURCH AND SYNAGOGUE LIBRARY ASSOCIATION
Executive Secretary, Dorothy J. Rodda
Box 1130, Bryn Mawr, PA 19010

OBJECT

"To act as a unifying core for the many existing church and synagogue libraries; to provide the opportunity for a mutual sharing of practices and problems; to inspire and encourage a sense of purpose and mission among church and synagogue librarians; to study and guide the development of church and synagogue librarianship toward recognition as a formal branch of the library profession." Founded 1967. Memb. 1,600. Dues (Contributing) $100; (Inst.) $75; (Affiliated) $35; (Church or Synagogue) $20; (Indiv.) $10. Year. July 1982-June 1983.

OFFICERS (JULY 1982-JUNE 1983)

Pres. Anita Dalton, 41 Aberdeen Rd. N., Galt, Cambridge, Ont., N1S 2X1 Canada; *1st V.P./Pres.-Elect.* Ruth Sawner, 2826 San Gabriel, Austin, TX 78705; *2nd V.P.* Sally Bruce McClatchey, 3355 Ridgewood Road N.W., Atlanta, GA 30327; *Treas.* Patricia W. Tabler, Box 116, Keedysville, MD 21756; *Past Pres.* Elsie E. Lehman, 1051 College Ave.,

Harrisonburg, VA 22801; *Publns. Dir. and Bulletin Ed.* William H. Gentz, 300 E. 34 St., Apt. 9C, New York, NY 10016.

EXECUTIVE BOARD

Officers; committee chairpersons.

PUBLICATIONS

Church and Synagogue Libraries (bi-mo.; memb. or $15, Can. $18). Ed. William H. Gentz. Book reviews, ads, $145 for full-page, camera-ready ad, one-time rate.

CSLA Guide No. 1. Setting Up a Library: How to Begin or Begin Again ($2.50).

CSLA Guide No. 2, rev. 2nd ed. *Promotion Planning All Year 'Round* ($4.50).

CSLA Guide No. 3, rev. ed. *Workshop Planning* ($6.50).

CSLA Guide No. 4, rev. ed. *Selecting Library Materials* ($2.50).

CSLA Guide No. 5, Cataloging Books Step by Step (2.50).

CSLA Guide No. 6. Standards for Church and Synagogue Libraries ($3.75).

CSLA Guide No. 7. Classifying Church or Synagogue Library Materials ($2.50).

CSLA Guide No. 8. Subject Headings for Church or Synagogue Libraries ($3.50).

CSLA Guide No. 9. A Policy and Procedure Manual for Church and Synagogue Libraries ($3.75).

CSLA Guide No. 10. Archives in the Church or Synagogue Library ($4.50).

Church and Synagogue Library Resources: Annotated Bibliography ($2.50).

A Basic Book List for Church Libraries: Annotated Bibliography ($1.75).

Helping Children Through Books: Annotated Bibliography ($3.75).

The Family Uses the Library. Leaflet (5¢; $3.75/100).

The Teacher and the Library —Partners in Religious Education. Leaflet (10¢; $7/100).

Setting Up a Library: How to Begin or Begin Again. Slide set with reading script ($75; rental fee $10).

COMMITTEE CHAIRPERSONS

Awards. Jean Van Esch.
Chapters. Fay W. Grosse.
Continuing Education. Joyce L. White.
Finance and Fund Raising. Robert Dvorak.
Library Services. Judith Stromdahl.
Membership. Lois Seyfrit.
Nominations and Elections. Elsie E. Lehman.
Public Relations. Maryanne J. Dotts.
Sites. Ruth Roth.

CONTINUING LIBRARY EDUCATION NETWORK AND EXCHANGE (CLENE), INC.

Executive Director, Patsy Haley Stann
620 Michigan Ave. N.E., Washington, DC 20064
202-635-5825

OBJECT

The basic missions of CLENE, Inc., are (1) to provide equal access to continuing education opportunities, available in sufficient quantity and quality over a substantial period of time to ensure library and information science personnel and organizations the competency to deliver quality library and information services to all; (2) to create an awareness and a sense of need for continuing education of library personnel on the part of employers and individuals as a means of responding to societal and technological change. Founded 1975. Memb. 260. Dues (Indiv.) $25; (Inst. assoc.) $50-$150; (State agency) $750-$3,000 according to population. Year. Twelve months from date of entry.

MEMBERSHIP

CLENE, Inc., welcomes as members institutions—libraries, information centers, data banks, schools and departments of library, media, and information science—any organization concerned with continuing education; professional associations in library, media, information science, and allied disciplines; local, state, regional, and national associations; individuals; state library and educational agencies; consortia.

OFFICERS (JUNE 1982-JUNE 1983)

Pres. Alphonse F. Trezza, Assoc. Prof., School of Lib. & Info. Studies, Florida State Univ., Tallahassee, FL 32306; *Pres.-Elect.* John Hinkle, Continuing Education Coord., Oklahoma Dept. of Libs., 200 N.E. 18 St., Oklahoma City, OK 25202; *Exec. Dir.* Patsy Haley Stann, 620 Michigan Ave. N.E., Washington, DC 20064; *Treas.* Sydelle Popinsky, Continuing Education Consultant, Texas State Lib., 1004 Eason, Austin, TX 78703; *Past Pres.* Janet L. Blumberg, Chief, Lib. Development Div., Washington State Lib., Olympia, WA 98504. (Address correspondence to the executive director.)

BOARD OF DIRECTORS

Officers; Ann Armbrister, Assoc. Dir. for Lib. Services, AMIGOS Bibliographic Council, Inc., 11300 N. Central Expressway, Suite 321, Dallas, TX 75243; Evalyn Clough, Asst. to the Dean, School of Lib. & Info. Science, Univ. of Pittsburgh, Pittsburgh, PA 15260; Joan C. Durrance, Coord. of Continuing Education, School of Lib. Science, Univ. of Michigan, Ann Arbor, MI 48109; Vee Friesner, Dir of Lib. Development, Kansas State Lib., Box 7, Rte. 1, St. George, KS 66535; Donald Haynes, State Libn., Virginia State Lib., Richmond, VA 23219; Sandra S. Stephan, Specialist in Staff Development & Continuing Education, Div. of Lib. Development & Services, Maryland State Dept. of Educ., 200 W. Baltimore St., Baltimore, MD 21201; Sharon A. Sullivan, Personnel Libn., Ohio State Univ. Libs., 1858 Neil Ave. Mall, Columbus, OH.

PUBLICATIONS

CLENExchange. (4/year). Newsletter $10.

Continuing Education Communicator (mo.). $10 (Indiv.); $15 (Institutional nonmemb.).

Directory of Continuing Education Opportunities (1979). $22.80.

Model Continuing Education Recognition System in Library and Information Science 1979. $29.80.

Proceedings of CLENE Assembly I: Self-Assessment (January 1976). $4.25 (memb.); $5 (nonmemb.).

Who's Who in Continuing Education: Human Resources in Continuing Library, Information, Media Education (1979). $30.

Concept Papers

#1. *Developing CE Learning Materials.* Sheldon & Woolls (1977). $4.25 (memb.); $5 (nonmemb.).

#2. *Guide to Planning and Teaching CE Courses.* Washtien (1975). $4.25 (memb.); $5 (nonmemb.).

#3. *Planning & Evaluating Library*

Training Programs. Sheldon (1976). $4.25 (memb.); $5 (nonmemb.).
#4. *Helping Adults to Learn.* Knox (1976) (out of print).
#5. *Continuing Library Education: Needs Assessment & Model Programs.* Virgo, Dunkel, Angione (1977). $10.20 (memb.); $12 (nonmemb.).
#6. *Recognition for Your Continuing Education Accomplishments.* James Nelson (June 1979).
#7. *Planning Coordinated Systems of Continuing Library Education, A Workbook and Discussion Guide.* Kathleen Weibel (1982). $6 (memb.); $6.90 (nonmemb.).
Annotated Bibliography of Recent Continuing Education Literature (1976). $4.25 (memb.); $5 (nonmemb.).
Continuing Education Resource Book (1977). $2.55 (memb.); $3 (nonmemb.).
Continuing Education Planning Inventory: A Self-Evaluation Checklist (1977). $1.70 (memb.); $2 (nonmemb.).
Guidelines for Relevant Groups Involved in Home Study Programs (1977). $4.25 (memb.); $5 (nonmemb.).

For more information or to order publications, write to CLENE, Inc., 620 Michigan Ave. N.E., Washington, DC 20064. (202-635-5825)

COMMITTEES

Finance.
Long Range Planning.
Membership Promotion.
Membership Services.
Publications Advisory.
Research & Development.
Voluntary Recognition.

COUNCIL OF NATIONAL LIBRARY AND INFORMATION ASSOCIATIONS, INC.
461 W. Lancaster Ave., Haverford, PA 19041
215-649-5251

OBJECT

To provide a central agency for cooperation among library/information associations and other professional organizations of the United States and Canada in promoting matters of common interest.

MEMBERSHIP

Open to national library/information associations and organizations with related interests of the United States and Canada. American Assn. of Law Libs.; American Lib. Assn.; American Society of Indexers; American Theological Lib. Assn.; Art Libs. Society/North America; Assn. of Christian Libs., Inc.; Assn. of Jewish Libs.; Catholic Lib. Assn.; Chinese-American Libns. Assn.; Church and Synagogue Lib. Assn.; Council of Planning Libns.; Lib. Binding Institute; Lib. Public Relations Council; Lutheran Lib. Assn.; Medical Lib. Assn.; Music Lib. Assn.; National Federation of Abstracting and Indexing Services; National Lib. Assn.; Society of American Archivists; Special Libs. Assn.; Theatre Lib. Assn.

OFFICERS (JULY 1982-JUNE 1983)

Chpn. David Bender, Exec. Dir., Special Libs. Assn., 235 Park Ave.

S., New York, NY 10003; *V. Chpn.* John T. Corrigan, CFX, Catholic Lib. Assn., 461 W. Lancaster Ave., Haverford, PA 19041; *Secy.-Treas.* Emmet Corry, OSF, Div. of Lib. & Info. Science, St. John's Univ., Grand Central & Utopia Pkwys., Jamaica, NY 11439. (Address correspondence to chairperson at 461 W. Lancaster Ave., Haverford, PA 19041.)

DIRECTORS

Robert DeCandido, New York Public Lib., Research Lib., Fifth Ave. & 42 St., New York, NY 10018 (July 1980-June 1983); James Irvine, Princeton Theological Seminary, Box 111, Princeton, NJ 08540 (July 1981-1984); D. Sherman Clarke, Olin Lib., Rm. 110, Cornell Univ., Ithaca, NY 14853 (July 1982-June 1985).

COUNCIL OF PLANNING LIBRARIANS, PUBLICATIONS OFFICE
1313 E. 60 St., Chicago, IL 60637

OBJECT

To provide a special interest group in the field of city and regional planning for libraries and librarians, faculty, professional planners, university, government, and private planning organizations; to provide an opportunity for exchange among those interested in problems of library organization and research and in the dissemination of information about city and regional planning; to sponsor programs of service to the planning profession and librarianship; to advise on library organization for new planning programs; to aid and support administrators, faculty, and librarians in their efforts to educate the public and their appointed or elected representatives to the necessity for strong library programs in support of planning. Founded 1960. Memb. 150. Dues. $35 (Inst.); $15 (Indiv.). Year. July 1-June 30.

MEMBERSHIP

Open to any individual or institution that supports the purpose of the council, upon written application and payment of dues to the treasurer.

OFFICERS (1982-1983)

Pres. Gretchen Beal, Knoxville-Knox County Metropolitan Planning Commission, City/County Bldg., Suite 403, Knoxville, TN 37902; *V.P./Pres.-Elect.* Marilyn Meyers, Wichita State Univ. Lib., Campus Box 68, Wichita, KS 67208; *Secy.* Rona Gregory, Rotch Lib. of Architecture & Planning, M.I.T., 77 Massachusetts Ave., Cambridge, MA 02139; *Treas.* Jon Greene, Architecture & Planning Lib., Univ. of California, Los Angeles, CA 90024; *Member-at-Large.* Lynne De-Merritt, Municipal Research & Services Center, 4719 Brooklyn Ave. N.E., Seattle, WA 98105; *Editor, Publications Program.* James Hecimovich, 1313 E. 60 St., Chicago, IL 60637.

PUBLICATIONS

CPL Bibliographies (approx. 30 bibliographies published per year). May be purchased on standing order subscription or by individual issue. Free catalog on request.

#84. *A Bibliography on Natural Resources and Environmental Conflict: Management Strategies and Pro-*

cesses. John R. Ehrmann & Patricia A. Bidol ($10).

#85. *Health Care Cost Containment Strategies: A Bibliography.* Robert J. Juster & Joyce A. Lanning ($10).

#86. *Industrial Development of Urban Space: A Selected and Annotated Bibliography.* Rosalind G. Bauchum ($4).

#87. *The Sociology of Range Management: A Bibliography.* Jere Lee Gilles ($8).

#88. *Women in Suburbia: A Bibliography.* Hugh Wilson & Sally Ridgeway ($6).

#89. *Shopping Centers: A Bibliography.* John A. Dawson ($10).

#90. *National Parks in Urban Areas: An Annotated Bibliography.* Kathleen Fahey ($10).

#91. *Hazardous Substances in Canada: A Selected Bibliography.* John J. Miletich ($5).

#92. *Revenue and Expenditure Forecasting in State and Local Government: A Selective, Annotated Bibliography.* Margaret B. Guss & David R. Brink ($6).

#93. *Studies Relating Automobile Design and Vehicle Safety: An Annotated Bibliography.* Margaret E. Shepard ($15).

COUNCIL ON LIBRARY RESOURCES, INC.
Secretary-Treasurer, Mary Agnes Thompson
1785 Massachusetts Ave. N.W., Washington, DC 20036
202-296-4757

OBJECT

A private operating foundation, the council seeks to assist in finding solutions to the problems of libraries, particularly academic and research libraries. In pursuit of this aim, the council makes grants to and contracts with other organizations and individuals, and calls upon many others for advice and assistance with its work. The council was established in 1956 by the Ford Foundation, and it continues to receive support from Ford and other foundations as well; the Andrew W. Mellon Foundation, the Carnegie Corporation of New York, the Pew Memorial Trust, the Alfred P. Sloan Foundation, and the Lilly Endowment. The council's current program includes establishment of a computerized system of national bibliographic control, professional education, library resources and their preservation, international programs, and library operations and services.

MEMBERSHIP

The council's membership and board of directors is limited to 20.

OFFICERS

Chpn. Whitney North Seymour; *V. Chpn.* Louis B. Wright; *Pres.* Warren J. Haas; *Secy.-Treas.* Mary Agnes Thompson. (Address correspondence to headquarters.)

PUBLICATIONS

Annual Report.
CLR Recent Developments.

EDUCATIONAL FILM LIBRARY ASSOCIATION
Executive Director, Nadine Covert
43 W. 61 St., New York, NY 10023
212-246-4533

OBJECT
"To promote the production, distribution and utilization of educational films and other audio-visual materials." Incorporated 1943. Memb. 1,800. Dues (Inst.) $85-$180; (Commercial organizations) $200; (Indiv.) $35. Year. July-June.

OFFICERS
Pres. Clifford Ehlinger (1980-1983), Dir., Div. of Media, Grant Wood Area Education Agency, 4401 Sixth St. S.W., Cedar Rapids, IA 52404; *V.P./Past Pres.* Stephen Hess (1982-1983), Dir., Educational Media Center, Univ. of Utah, 207 Milton Bennion Hall, Salt Lake City, UT 84112; *Pres.-Elect.* Catherine Egan (1981-1984), Audiovisual Services, Pennsylvania State Univ., Foxhill Rd., University Park, PA 16802; *Treas.* Nadine Covert (Ex officio), Exec. Dir., EFLA, 43 W. 61 St., New York, NY 10023; *Secy.* Gerald Rogers (1982-1985), Dir., Media & Technology, Education Service Center, Region XVII, 4000 22 Place, Lubbock, TX 79410.

BOARD OF DIRECTORS
Officers; Carol Doolittle (1982-1985), Dir., Media Services, Audio Visual Resource Center, Cornell Univ., 8 Research Park, Ithaca, NY 14850; Lillian Katz (1981-1984), Port Washington Public Lib., 245 Main St., Port Washington, NY 11050; Angie Leclercq (1980-1983), Head, Undergraduate Lib., Univ. of Tennessee, 1015 Volunteer Blvd., Knoxville, TN 37916; Lilly Loo (1980-1983), Regional Headquarters, Los Angeles County Lib., 12348 E. Imperial Hwy., Norwalk, CA 90650; Elfrieda McCauley (1981-1984), Coord., Media Services, Greenwich Public Schools, Box 292, Havemeyer Bldg., Greenwich, CT 06830; Michael Miller (1982-1985), Head, Audio Visual Services, Mid-Hudson Lib. System, 103 Market St., Poughkeepsie, NY 12601.

PUBLICATIONS
American Film Festival Program Guide (ann.).
EFLA Bulletin (q.). *Ed.* Maryann Chach.
EFLA Evaluations (5 per year). *Ed.* Judith Trojan.
Sightlines (q.). *Ed.* Nadine Covert.
Write for list of other books and pamphlets.

FEDERAL LIBRARY COMMITTEE
Executive Director, James P. Riley
Library of Congress, Washington, DC 20540
202-287-6055

OBJECT
"For the purpose of concentrating the intellectual resources present in the federal library and library related information community: To achieve better utilization of library resources and facilities; to provide more effective planning, development, and oper-

ation of federal libraries; to promote an optimum exchange of experience, skill, and resources; to promote more effective service to the nation at large. Secretariat efforts and the work groups are organized to: consider policies and problems relating to federal libraries; evaluate existing federal library programs and resources; determine priorities among library issues requiring attention; examine the organization and policies for acquiring, preserving, and making information available; study the need for a potential of technological innovation in library practices; and study library budgeting and staffing problems, including the recruiting, education, training, and remuneration of librarians." Founded 1965. Memb. (Federal libs.) 2,200; (Federal libns.) 3,300. Year. Oct. 1-Sept. 30.

MEMBERSHIP

Libn. of Congress, Dir. of the National Agricultural Lib., Dir. of the National Lib. of Medicine, representatives from each of the other executive departments, and delegates from the National Aeronautics and Space Admin., the National Science Foundation, the Smithsonian Institution, the U.S. Supreme Court, U.S. Information Agency, the Veterans Admin., and the National Archives. Six members will be selected on a rotation basis by the permanent members of the committee from independent agencies, boards, committees, and commissions. These rotating members will serve two-year terms. Ten regional members shall be selected on a rotating basis by the permanent members of the committee to represent federal libraries following the geographic pattern developed by the Federal Regional Councils. These rotating regional members will serve two-year terms. The ten regional members, one from each of the ten federal regions, shall be voting members. In addition to the permanent representative of DOD, one nonvoting member shall be selected from each of the three services (U.S. Army, U.S. Navy, U.S. Air Force). These service members, who will serve for two years, will be selected by the permanent Department of Defense member from a slate provided by the Federal Library Committee. The membership in each service shall be rotated equitably among the special service, technical, and academic and school libraries in that service. DOD shall continue to have one voting member in the committee. The DOD representative may poll the three service members for their opinions before reaching a decision concerning the vote. A representative of the Office of Management and Budget, designated by the budget director and others appointed by the chairperson, will meet with the committee as observers.

OFFICERS

Chpn. Carol Nemeyer, Assoc. Libn. for National Programs, Lib. of Congress, Washington, DC 20540; *Exec. Dir.* James P. Riley, Federal Library Committee, Library of Congress, Washington, DC 20540. (Address correspondence to the executive director.)

PUBLICATIONS

Annual Report (Oct.).
FLC Newsletter (irreg.).

FEDLINK NETWORK OFFICE
Federal Library Committee, Library of Congress,
Washington, DC 20540
202-287-6454

OBJECT

The Federal Library and Information Network (FEDLINK) is an FLC operating cooperative program, established to minimize costs and enhance services through the use of on-line data base services for shared cataloging, interlibrary loan, acquisitions, and information retrieval. FEDLINK was established to:

1. Expedite and facilitate on-line data base services among federal libraries and information centers.
2. Develop plans for the expansion of such services to federal libraries and information centers.
3. Promote cooperation and utilization of the full potential of networks and technologies to institutions and provide for formal relationships between library and information networks and the FEDLINK membership.
4. To serve as the major federal library and information cooperative system in the emerging national library and information service network.
5. Promote education, research, and training in network services and new library and information technology for the benefit of federal libraries and information centers.

MEMBERSHIP

FEDLINK membership is nationwide and is made up of over 400 libraries, information centers, and systems that participate in automated systems and services sponsored and coordinated by FLC.

OFFICERS

Dir. James P. Riley.

INFORMATION INDUSTRY ASSOCIATION
President, Paul G. Zurkowski
316 Pennsylvania Ave. S.E., Suite 400,
Washington, DC 20003
202-544-1969

MEMBERSHIP

For details on membership and dues, write to the association headquarters. Memb. Over 170.

STAFF

Pres. Paul G. Zurkowski; *V.P., Government Relations.* Robert S. Willard; *Mgr., Finance & Admin.* Frank Martins; *Mgr., Marketing & Publications.* Fred Rosenau; *Mgr., Meetings.* Karen MacArthur.

BOARD OF DIRECTORS

Chpn. Roy K. Campbell, Dun & Bradstreet; *V. Chpn.* Norman M. Wellen, Business International Corp.; *Secy.* Peter Marx, Chase Econometrics/Interactive Data Corp.; *Treas.* Robert November, ITT Communications Operations & Information Services; *Past Chpn.* Thomas A. Grogan, McGraw-Hill; Robert F. Asleson, International Thomson Information, Inc.; William A. Beltz, Bureau of National Affairs; Elizabeth B. Eddison, Warner-Eddison Assocs.; Peter Genereaux, DTSS Inc.; Lois Granick, PsycINFO; James G. Kollegger, EIC/Intelligence, Inc.; James Holly, Times Mirror Videotex Services; Paul Massa, Congressional Information Service; Jerome S. Rubin; William J. Senter, Xerox Publishing Group.

PUBLICATIONS

The Business of Information Report (1983).
Information Sources (1983-1984).
Planning Product Innovation (1981).
Understanding U.S. Information Policy (1982).

LUTHERAN CHURCH LIBRARY ASSOCIATION
122 W. Franklin Ave., Minneapolis, MN 55404
612-870-3623
Executive Secretary, Wilma Jensen
(Home address: 3620 Fairlawn Dr., Minnetonka, MN 55404
612-473-5965)

OBJECT

"To promote the growth of church libraries by publishing a quarterly journal, *Lutheran Libraries;* furnishing booklists; assisting member libraries with technical problems; providing meetings for mutual encouragement, assistance, and exchange of ideas among members." Founded 1958. Memb. 1,800. Dues. $15, $25, $100, $500, $1,000. Year. Jan.-Jan.

OFFICERS (JAN. 1983-JAN. 1985)

Pres. Marlys Johnson, Libn. Fluidyne Engineering Corp. & Elim Lutheran Lib., 4709 Oregon Ave. N., Minneapolis, MN 55428; *V.P.* Mary Egdahl, Libn., Our Saviors Lutheran Lib., 3165 Maryola Court, Lafayette, CA 94549; *Secy.* Vivian Thoreson, American Lutheran Church Women, 422 S. Fifth St., Minneapolis, MN 55415; *Treas.* Mrs. G. Frank (Jane) Johnson, 2930 S. Hwy. 101, Wayzata, MN 55391. (Address correspondence to the executive secretary.)

EXECUTIVE BOARD

Ruby Forlan; Elaine Hanson; Mary Jordan; Charles Mann; Solveig Bartz; Astrid Wang.

ADVISORY BOARD

Chpn. Gary Klammer; Rev. Rolf Aaseng; Mrs. H. O. Egertson; Mrs. Donald Gauerke; Mrs. Harold Groff; Rev. James Gunther; Rev. A. B. Hanson; Malvin Lundeen; Mary Egdahl; Rev. A. C. Paul; Don Rosenberg; Stanley Sandberg; Les Schmidt; Aron Valleskey; Daniel Brumm.

PUBLICATION

Lutheran Libraries (q.; memb., nonmemb. $8). *Ed.* Erwin E. John, 6450 Warren St., Minneapolis, MN 55435.

COMMITTEE CHAIRPERSONS

Budget. Rev. Carl Manfred, 5227 Oaklawn Ave., Minneapolis, MN 55436.

Finance. Mrs. Lloyd (Betty) LeDell, Libn., Grace Lutheran of Deephaven, 15800 Sunset D., Minnetonka, MN 55343.
Library Services Board. Mrs. Forrest (Juanita) Carpenter, Libn., Rte. 1, Prior Lake, MN 55372.
Publications Board. Rev. Carl Weller, Augsburg Publishing House, 426 S. Fifth St., Minneapolis, MN 55415.
Council of National Library & Info. Assn. Wilma W. Jensen, Exec. Secy; Mary A. Huebner, Libn., Concordia College, 171 White Plains Rd., Bronxville, NY 10708.

MEDICAL LIBRARY ASSOCIATION
Executive Director, Raymond A. Palmer
919 N. Michigan Ave., Chicago, IL 60611
312-266-2456

OBJECT

Founded in 1898 and incorporated in 1934, its major purpose is to foster medical and allied scientific libraries, to promote the educational and professional growth of health sciences librarians, and to exchange medical literature among the members. Through its programs and publications, MLA encourages professional development of its membership, whose foremost concern is for the dissemination of health sciences information for those in research, education, and patient care. Memb. (Inst.) 1,350. (Indiv.) 3,680. Dues (Inst.) Subscriptions up to 199 $100, 200-299 $135, 300-599 $165, 600-999 $200, 1,000+ $235; (Indiv.) $60. Year. From month of payment.

MEMBERSHIP

Open to those working in or interested in medical libraries.

OFFICERS

Pres. Nancy M. Lorenzi, Univ. of Cincinnati, Medical Center Libs., Cincinnati, OH 45267; *Pres.-Elect.* Nina W. Matheson, Planning Office, National Lib. of Medicine, Bethesda, MD 20209; *Past Pres.* Charles W. Sargent, Lib. of the Health Sciences, Texas Tech Univ. Health Sciences Center, Lubbock, TX 79430.

DIRECTORS

Eloise C. Foster; Lucretia McClure; Jana Bradley; Judith Messerle; Ruth W. Wender; Alison Bunting; Mary Horres.

PUBLICATIONS

Bulletin (q.; $65).
Current Catalog Proof Sheets (w.; $58).
Index to Audiovisual Serials in the Health Sciences (4 per year; $27).
MLA News (mo. $25/year).

STANDING COMMITTEE CHAIRPERSONS

Audiovisual Standards and Practices Committee. Frances Bischoff, Wishard Memorial Hospital, 100 W. 10 St., Indianapolis, IN 46202.
Bulletin Consulting Editors Panel. Susan Crawford, Washington Univ. School of Medicine, The Library, 4580 Scott Ave., St. Louis, MO 63110.
By-laws Committee. Aletha Kowitz,

American Dental Assn. Lib., 211 E. Chicago Ave., Chicago, IL 60611.
Certification & Recertification Appeals Panel. Lucretia McClure, Univ. of Rochester, School of Medicine/Dentistry, Edward G. Miner Lib., 601 Elmwood Ave., Rochester, NY 14642.
Certification Eligibility Committee. Audrey J. Kidder, Southern Illinois Univ., School of Medicine, 801 N. Rutledge St., Springfield, IL 62708.
Certification Examination Review Committee. Susan J. Feinglos, Duke Medical Center, Medical Lib., Durham, NC 27710.
Committee on Committees. Nina W. Matheson, Planning Office, National Lib. of Medicine, 8600 Rockville Pike, Bethesda, MD 20209.
Continuing Education Committee. Susan E. Hill, Cleveland Health Lib., 2119 Abington Rd., Cleveland, OH 44108.
Copyright Committee. Wayne J. Peay, Eccles Health Sciences Lib., Univ. of Utah, Salt Lake City, UT 84112.
Editorial Committee for the Bulletin. Joanne C. Callard, Health Sciences Center Lib., Univ. of Oklahoma, Box 26901, Oklahoma City, OK 73109.
Editorial Committee for the MLA News. Anne M. Pascarelli, New York Academy of Medicine Lib., 2 E. 103 St., New York, NY 10029.
Elections Committee. Nina W. Matheson, Planning Office, National Lib. of Medicine, 8600 Rockville Pike, Bethesda, MD 20209.
Exchange Committee. R. Thomas Lange, Univ. of South Carolina, School of Medicine Lib., Columbia, GA 29208.
Executive Committee. Nancy M. Lorenzi, Univ. of Cincinnati, Medical Center Libs., 231 Bethesda Ave., Cincinnati, OH 45267.
Finance. Lucretia McClure, Univ. of Rochester, School of Medicine/Dentistry, Edward G. Miner Lib., 601 Elmwood Ave., Rochester, NY 14642.
Health Sciences Library Technicians Committee. Alice J. Hurlebaus, Univ. of Cincinnati, Medical Center Libs., 231 Bethesda Ave., Cincinnati, OH 45267.
Honors and Awards Committee. Gwendolyn Cruzat, Univ. of Michigan, School of Lib. Science, Ann Arbor, MI 48109.
Janet Doe Lectureship Subcommittee. Gwendolyn Cruzat, Univ. of Michigan, School of Lib. Science, Ann Arbor, MI 48109.
Eliot Prize Subcommitte. Sheldon Kotzin, National Lib. of Medicine, 8600 Rockville Pike, Bethesda, MD 20209.
ISI Award. Erich Meyerhoff, Cornell Univ. Medical College, S. J. Wood Lib., 1300 York Ave., New York, NY 10021.
Gottlieb Prize Subcommitter. Jeanette C. McCray, Univ. of Arizona, Health Sciences Center Lib., Tucson, AZ 85724.
Hospital Library Standards & Practices Committee. Rosalind F. Dudden, Lib. & Media Resources Dept., Mercy Medical Center, 1619 Milwaukee St., Denver, CO 80206.
Interlibrary Loan & Resource Sharing Standards & Practices Committee. M. Sandra Wood, Hershey Medical Lib., George T. Harrell Lib., Pennsylvania State Univ., Hershey, PA 17033.
International Cooperation Committee. Beverlee A. French, Univ. of California-San Diego, Sciences & Engineering Lib, C-075E, La Jolla, CA 92093.
Legislation Committee. Lucile S. Stark, Western Psychiatric Institute & Clinic Lib., 3811 O'Hara St., Pittsburgh, PA 15261.
Library Standards and Pratices

Committee. Katherine J. Hoffman, Houston Academy of Medicine, Texas Medical Center Lib., 1133 M. D. Anderson Blvd., Houston, TX 77030.

MLA HeSCA Joint Committee to Develop Guidelines for Audiovisual Facilities in Health Sciences Libraries. Gloria Holland, Veterans Admin. Medical Center (14A), 700 S. 19 St., Birmingham, AL 35233.

MLA/NLM Liaison. Eloise C. Foster, Lib. of the American Hospital Assn., 840 N. Lake Shore Dr., Chicago, IL 60611.

Membership Committee. Timothy D. Mason, Texas College of Osteopathic Medicine, Camp Bowie at Montgomery, Fort Worth, TX 76107

National Issues Advisory Council. Nancy M. Lorenzi, Univ. of Cincinnati, Medical Center Lib., Cincinnati, OH 45267.

1983 National Program Committee. Richard Lyders, HAM-TMC Lib., 1133 M. D. Anderson Blvd., Houston, TX 77030.

1984 National Program Committee. Charles R. Bandy, Medical Center Lib., Univ. of Colorado, 4200 E. Ninth Ave., Denver, CO 80220.

1985 National Program Committee. Rachael K. Goldstein, Columbia Univ., Health Sciences Lib., 701 W. 168 St., New York, NY 10032.

Nominating Committee. Nina W. Matheson, Planning Office, National Lib. of Medicine, 8600 Rockville Pike, Bethesda, MD 20209.

Oral History Committee. Suzanne Grefsheim, George Washington Univ., Himmelfarb Lib., 2300 Eye St. N.W., Washington, DC 20037.

Program and Convention Committee. D. A. Thomas, Univ. of Kansas Medical Center, Clendening Lib., College of Health Sciences & Hospital, 39 & Rainbow Blvd., Kansas City, KS 66103.

Publication Panel. Frances Groen, McGill Univ., Medical Lib., 3655 Drummond St., Montreal, PQ H3G 1Y6, Canada.

Publication & Information Industries Relations Committee. David C. Anderson, Univ. of California-Davis, Health Sciences Lib., Davis, CA 95616.

Recertification Committee. Penny Coppernoll-Blach, Dialog Information Services, 3460 Hillview Ave., Palo Alto, CA 94304.

Research Committee. Erika Love, Univ. of New Mexico, Medical Center Lib., Albuquerque, NM 87109.

Rittenhouse Award Subcommittee. Elaine A. Tate, Medical Lib., Martin Army Community Hospital, Fort Benning, GA 31905.

Scholarship & Grants Committee. Elaine Russon Martin, Apt. 1237-S, Crystal Towers, 1600 S. Eads St., Arlington, VA 22202.

Status & Economic Interests of Health Sciences Library Personnel Committee. Jill Golrick, Health Sciences Central Lib., Univ. of Arizona, Tucson, AZ 85724.

Surveys & Statistics Committee. Faith Van Toll, Wayne State Univ., Vera Shiffman Medical Lib., 4325 Brush St., Detroit, MI 48201.

Ad Hoc Committees

Ad Hoc Committee on Automating the Exchange. Raymond A. Palmer, Medical Lib. Assn., 919 N. Michigan Ave., #3208, Chicago, IL 60611.

Ad Hoc Committee on Consumer Health Information. Ellen Gartenfeld, Mount Auburn Hospital, 330 Mount Auburn St., Cambridge, MA 02138.

Ad Hoc Committee for the International Exchange & Redistribution of Library Materials. Janis Apted, Houston Academy of Medicine-Texas Medical Center Lib., 1133 M. D. Anderson Blvd., Houston, TX 77030.

MUSIC LIBRARY ASSOCIATION
2017 Walnut St., Philadelphia, PA 19103
215-569-3948

OBJECT

"To promote the establishment, growth, and use of music libraries; to encourage the collection of music and musical literature in libraries; to further studies in musical bibliography; to increase efficiency in music library service and administration." Founded 1931. Memb. about 1,700. Dues (Inst.) $31; (Indiv.) $24; (Student) $12. Year. Sept. 1-Aug. 31.

OFFICERS

Pres. Donald W. Krummel, Grad. Lib. School, Univ. of Illinois, Urbana, IL 61801; *V.P./Pres.-Elect.* Mary W. Davidson, Music Lib., Wellesley College, Wellesley, MA 02181; *Secy.* George R. Hill, Music Dept., Baruch College/CUNY, 17 Lexington Ave., New York, NY 10010; *Treas.* Harold J. Diamond, Music Lib., Lehman College/CUNY, Bedford Park Blvd. W., Bronx, NY 10468; *Ed. of "Notes."* Susan T. Sommer, Special Collections-Music, New York Public Lib., 111 Amsterdam Ave., New York, NY 10023; *Exec. Secy.* Suzanne Thorin, Research Facilities Section, General Reading Rooms Div., Lib. of Congress, Washington, DC 20540.

DIRECTORS

Officers; Olga Buth; Margaret F. Lospinuso; Charles W. Simpson; Gillian Anderson; Neil M. Ratliff; Annie Thompson.

PUBLICATIONS

MLA Index Series (irreg.; price varies according to size).
MLA Newsletter (q.; free to memb.).
MLA Technical Reports (irreg.; price varies according to size).
Music Cataloging Bulletin (mo.; $12).
Notes (q.; inst. subscription $31; nonmemb. subscription $21).

COMMITTEE CHAIRPERSONS

Administration. Brenda C. Goldman, Music Lib., Tufts Univ., Medford, MA 02155.
Audio-Visual. Philip Youngholm, Connecticut College Lib., New London, CT 06320.
Automation. Garrett H. Bowles, Music Lib., Univ. of California at San Diego, La Jolla, CA 92093.
Awards. Geraldine Ostrove, New England Conservatory of Music, 33 Gainsborough St., Boston, MA 02115;
Cataloging. Judith Kaufman, Music Lib., State Univ. of New York, Stony Brook, NY 11794.
Conservation. Jean Geil, Music Lib., Univ. of Illinois, Urbana, IL 61801.
Constitutional Revision. Geraldine Ostrove, Lib., New England Conservatory of Music, Boston, MA 02115.
Education. Ruth Tucker, Cornell Univ., Ithaca, NY.
Legislation. Carolyn O. Hunter, 5472 Bradford Court, Alexandria, VA 22311.
Microforms. Stuart Milligan, Sibley Music Lib., Eastman School of Music, Rochester, NY 14604.
Public Library. Donna Mendro, Dallas Public Lib., Dallas, TX 75201.
Publications. Kathryn P. Logan, Music Library, Univ. of North Carolina, Chapel Hill, NC 27514.

NATIONAL LIBRARIANS ASSOCIATION
Secretary-Treasurer, Donna Hanson
Drawer B, College Station, Pullman, WA 99163
509-334-3167

OBJECT

"To promote librarianship, to develop and increase the usefulness of libraries, to cultivate the science of librarianship, to protect the interest of professionally qualified librarians, and to perform other functions necessary for the betterment of the profession of librarianship. It functions as an association of librarians, rather than as an association of libraries." Established 1975. Memb. 450. Dues. $20 per year; $35 for 2 years; (Students and Retired and Unemployed Librarians) $10. Year. July 1-June 30.

MEMBERSHIP

Any person interested in librarianship and libraries who holds a graduate degree in library science may become a member upon election by the executive board and payment of the annual dues. The executive board may authorize exceptions to the degree requirements to applicants who present evidence of outstanding contributions to the profession. Student membership is available to those graduate students enrolled full time at any accredited library school.

OFFICERS (JULY 1, 1982-JUNE 30, 1983)

Pres. Indra David, Oakland Univ. Lib., Rochester, MI; *V.P.* David Bernstein, Bloomfield Hills Township Public Lib., MI; *Immed. Past Pres.* Ellis Hodgin, Univ. of Baltimore Lib. (Address all correspondence to the current president.)

PUBLICATION

NLA Newsletter: The National Librarian (q.; 1 year $15, 2 years $28, 3 years $39).

COMMITTEE CHAIRPERSONS

Certification Standards. David Perkins, California State Univ., Northridge, CA 91330.

Professional Education. John Colson, 813 Somonauk St., Sycamore, IL 60178.

Professional Welfare. Chair, Gerald Johns, San Diego State Univ. Lib., San Diego, CA 92181

NATIONAL MICROGRAPHICS ASSOCIATION
Executive Director, O. Gordon Banks
8719 Colesville Rd., Silver Spring, MD 20910
301-587-8202

OBJECT

The National Micrographics Association (NMA) is the trade and professional association that represents the manufacturers, vendors, and professional users of micrographic equipment and software. The purpose of the association is to promote the lawful interests of the micrographic industry in the direction of good business ethics; the liberal discussion of subjects pertaining to the industry and its relationship to other information management technologies, technological improvement, and research; standardization; the methods of manufacturing and marketing; and the education of the consumer in the use of information management systems. Founded 1943. Memb. 10,000. Dues. (Indiv.) $60. Year. July 1, 1982-June 30, 1983.

OFFICERS

Pres. William J. McGlone, Jr., Microfilm Products Div., 3M Co., 3M Center-Bldg. 220-9E, St. Paul, MN 55144; *V.P.* John P. Luke, Marketing Research & Admin., BSMD-Eastman Kodak Co., 343 State St., Rochester, NY 14650; *Treas.* Roger E. Blue, Total Information Management Corp., 1545 Park Ave., Emeryville, CA 94608. (Address general correspondence to the executive director.)

PUBLICATION

Journal of Micrographics (mo.; memb. subscriptions). *Ed.* Ellen T. Meyer. Book reviews included; product review included. Ads accepted.

SOCIETY OF AMERICAN ARCHIVISTS
Executive Director, Ann Morgan Campbell
330 S. Wells St., Suite 810, Chicago, IL 60606
312-922-0140

OBJECT

"To promote sound principles of archival economy and to facilitate cooperation among archivists and archival agencies." Founded 1936. Memb. 4,000. Dues (Indiv.) $45-$75, graduated according to salary; (Associate) $40, domestic; (Student) $30 with a two-year maximum on student membership; (Inst.) $50; (Sustaining) $100.

OFFICERS (1982-1983)

Pres. J. Frank Cook, B134 Memorial Lib., Univ. of Wisconsin-Madison, Madison, WI 53706; *V.P.* David B. Gracy II, Texas State Archives, Capitol Station, Box 12927, Austin, TX 78711; *Treas.* Paul H. McCarthy, Univ. of Alaska, Box 80687, College Sta., Fairbanks, AK 99708.

COUNCIL

Lynn A. Bonfield; Meyer H. Fishbein; Robert S. Gordon; Larry J. Hackman; Edie Hedlin; Sue E. Holbert; William L. Joyce; Richard Lytle; Virginia C. Purdy.

STAFF

Exec. Dir. Ann Morgan Campbell; *Dir. Administrative Services.* Joyce E. Gianatasio; *Membership Asst.* Bernice Brack; *Bookkeeper.* Andrea Giannattasio; *Publications Asst.* Suzanne Fulton; *Administrative Aide.* Antonia Pedroza; *Program Officer.* Mary Lynn Ritzenthaler; *Managing Ed.* Deborah Risteen; *Projects Ed.* Terry Abraham; *Ed, The American Archivist.* Charles Schultz; *Program Asst.* Linda Ziemer, Sylvia Burck.

PUBLICATIONS

The American Archivist (q.; $30). *Ed.* Charles Schultz; *Managing Ed.* Deborah Risteen, 330 S. Wells, Suite 810, Chicago, IL 60606. Book for review and related correspondence should be addressed to the editor. Rates for B/W ads: full-page, $200;

half-page, $125; outside back cover, $300; half-page minimum insertion; 10% discount for four consecutive insertions; 15% agency commission.

SAA Newsletter. (6 per year; memb.) *Ed.* Deborah Risteen, SAA, 330 S. Wells, Suite 810, Chicago, IL 60606. Rates for B/W ads: full-page, $300; half-page, $175; quarter-page, $90; eighth-page, $50. 10% discount for six consecutive insertions; 15% agency commission.

PROFESSIONAL AFFINITY GROUPS (PAGs) AND CHAIRS

Acquisition. Carolyn Wallace, Univ. of North Carolina, 024-A Wilson Lib., Chapel Hill, NC 27514.

Aural & Graphic Records. Gerald J. Munoff, Kentucky Dept. of Lib. & Archives, Box 537, Frankfort, KY 40602.

Business Archives. Linda Edgerly, 103 W. 75 St., Apt. 3B, New York, NY 10023.

Conservation. Howard P. Lowell, 2530 N.W. 11 St., Oklahoma City, OK 73107.

College & University Archives. Patrick Quinn, University Archives, Northwestern Univ. Lib., Evanston, IL 60201.

Description. Victoria Irons Walch, 9927 Capperton Dr., Oakton, VA 22124.

Government Records. Lewis Bellardo, Kentucky Dept. of Lib. & Archives, Box 537, Frankfort, KY 40602.

Manuscript Repositories. Robert Byrd, Duke Univ., Perkins Lib., Manuscript Dept., Durham, NC 27706.

Oral History. Marjorie Fletcher, American College Archives & Oral History Center, 270 Bryn Mawr Ave., Bryn Mawr, PA 19010.

Reference, Access, Outreach. Alexia Helsley, South Carolina Dept. of Archives & History, Box 11669, Capitol St., Columbia, SC 29211.

Religious. Thomas Wilsted, Salvation Army Archives, 145 W. 15 St., New York, NY 10011.

Theme Collections. Frederic Miller, Temple Univ., Paley Lib.-Urban Archives Center, Philadelphia, PA 19122.

SPECIAL LIBRARIES ASSOCIATION
Executive Director, David R. Bender
235 Park Ave. S., New York, NY 10003
212-477-9250

OBJECT

"To provide an association of individuals and organizations having a professional, scientific or technical interest in library and information science, especially as these are applied in the recording, retrieval, and dissemination of knowledge and information in areas such as the physical, biological, technical and social sciences and the humanities; and to promote and improve the communication, dissemination, and use of such information and knowledge for the benefit of libraries or other educational organizations." Organized 1909. Memb. 11,500. Dues. (Sustaining) $250; (Indiv.) $55; (Student) $12. Year. Jan.-Dec. and July-June.

OFFICERS (JUNE 1982-JUNE 1983)

Pres. Janet Rigney, Council on Foreign Relations, Lib., 58 E. 68 St., New York, NY 10021; *Pres.-Elect.*

Pat Molholt, Rensselaer Polytechnic Inst., Folsom Lib., Troy, NY 12181; *Div. Cabinet Chpn.* Valerie Noble, Upjohn Co., Business Lib. 88-91, Kalamazoo, MI 49001; *Div. Cabinet Chpn.-Elect.* Jean K. Martin, Molycorp. Inc., Box 54945, Los Angeles, CA 90054; *Chapter Cabinet Chpn.* Vivian J. Arterbery, Rand Corp., Lib., 1700 Main St., Santa Monica, CA 90406; *Chapter Cabinet Chpn.-Elect.* Marilyn K. Johnson, Shell Oil Co., Info. & Lib. Services, Box 587, Houston, TX 77001; *Treas.* Muriel Regan, Gossage Regan Assocs., 15 W. 44 St., New York, NY 10036; *Past. Pres.* George H. Ginader, International Creative Management, Inc., 40 W. 57 St., New York, NY 10019.

DIRECTORS

Jack Leister (1981-1984); Jacqueline J. Desoer (1980-1983); Ruth S. Smith (1980-1983); M. Elizabeth Moore (1981-1984). Frank H. Spaulding (1982-1985); Mary Lou Stursa (1982-1985).

PUBLICATIONS

Special Libraries (q.) and *Specia-List* (mo.). Cannot be ordered separately ($36 for both; add $5 postage outside the U.S., including Canada). *Ed.* Nancy M. Viggiano.

COMMITTEE CHAIRPERSONS

Awards. James B. Dodd, Georgia Inst. of Technology, Price Gilbert Memorial Lib., Atlanta, GA 30332.

Consultation Service. Gerri L. Hilt, Russell Reynolds Assn., Inc., Research Dept., 200 S. Wacker Dr., Suite 3600, Chicago, IL 60606.

Copyright Law Implementation. Efren W. Gonzalez, Bristol-Myers Products, 1350 Liberty Ave., Hillside, NJ 07207.

Education. Miriam H. Tees, McGill Univ., Grad. School of Lib. Science, 3459 McTavish St., Montreal, P.Q. H3A 1Y1, Canada.

Government Information Services. John F. Kane, Aluminum Co. of America, Alcoa Technical Center, Info. Dept., Alcoa Center, PA 15069.

Networking. Edythe Moore, Aerospace Corp., Box 92957, Los Angeles, CA 90009.

Nominating. Vivian D. Hewitt, Carnegie Endowment for International Peace, 30 Rockefeller Plaza, New York, NY 10020.

Positive Action Program for Minority Groups. Thomasina Capel, Institute for Defense Analyses, Technical Info. Services, 1801 N. Beauregard St., Alexandria, VA 22202.

Publications. Del Sweeney, Pennsylvania State Univ., Pennsylvania Transportation Inst., Research Bldg. B, University Park, PA 16802.

Publisher Relations. John Patton, Suffolk Cooperative Lib. System, 627 N. Sunrise Service Rd., Bellport, NY 11713.

Scholarship. Ellen Todd Hanks, Univ. of Texas-San Antonio, Health Science Center Lib., 7703 Floyd Curl Dr., San Antonio, TX 78284.

Standards. Audrey N. Grosch, Univ. of Minnesota, Lib. Systems Dept., S-34 Wilson Lib., Minneapolis, MN 55455.

Statistics. Beth G. Ansley, Georgia Power Co., Lib., Box 4545, Atlanta, GA 30302.

Student Relations Officer. Julie H. Bichteler, Univ. of Texas at Austin, Grad. School of Lib. Science, Box 7576, Univ. Sta., Austin, TX 78712.

H. W. Wilson Co. Award. Ronald R. Sommer, Head, Reader's Services, Univ. of Tennessee, Center for Health Sciences, Lib., 800 Madison Ave., Memphis, TN 38163.

THEATRE LIBRARY ASSOCIATION
Secretary-Treasurer, Richard M. Buck
111 Amsterdam Ave., New York, NY 10023

OBJECT

"To further the interests of collecting, preserving, and using theatre, cinema, and performing arts materials in libraries, museums, and private collections." Founded 1937. Memb. 500. Dues. (Indiv.) $20; (Inst.) $25. Year. Jan. 1-Dec. 31, 1983.

OFFICERS (1982-1983)

Pres. Louis A. Rachow, Hampden-Edwin Booth Theatre Collection and Lib., The Players, 16 Gramercy Pk., New York, NY 10003; *V.P.* Don B. Wilmeth, Chairman, Dept. of Theatre Arts, Brown Univ., Providence, RI 02912; *Secy.-Treas.* Richard M. Buck, Asst. to the Chief, Performing Arts Research Center, New York Public Lib. at Lincoln Center, 111 Amsterdam Ave., New York, NY 10023; *Rec. Secy.* Birgitte Kueppers, Archivist, Shubert Archive, Lyceum Theatre, 149 W. 45 St., New York, NY 10036. (Address correspondence, except *Broadside* & *Par*, to the secretary-treasurer. Address *Broadside* & *Par* correspondence to Ginine Cocuzza, 115 Willow St., Brooklyn, NY 11201.)

EXECUTIVE BOARD

Officers; William Appleton; Lee Ash; Mary Ashe; Laraine Correll; Geraldine Duclow; Mary Ann Jensen; Margaret Mahard; Julian Mates, Robert L. Parkinson, Anne G. Schlosser, Alan L. Woods. *Ex officio.* Ginine Cocuzza; Barbara Naomi Cohen; Dorothy L. Swerdlove; *Honorary.* Rosamond Gilder, Paul Myers.

COMMITTEE CHAIRPERSONS

Awards. Don B. Wilmeth.
Nominations. Mary Ann Jensen.
Program and Special Events. Richard M. Buck.
Publications. To be announced.

PUBLICATIONS

Broadside (q.; memb.).
Performing Arts Resources (ann.; memb.).

UNIVERSAL SERIALS AND BOOK EXCHANGE, INC.
Executive Director, Alice Dulany Ball
3335 V St. N.E., Washington, DC 20018
202-529-2555

OBJECT

"To promote the distribution and interchange of books, periodicals, and other scholarly materials among libraries and other educational and scientific institutions of the United States, and between them and libraries and institutions of other countries." Organized 1948. Memb. year—libraries: Jan. 1-Dec. 31. Memb. year—associations: Jan. 1-Dec. 31.

MEMBERSHIP

Membership in USBE is open to any library that serves a constituency and is an institution or part of an institution or organization. The USBE corporation includes a representative from each member library and from each of a group of sponsoring organizations listed below.

BOARD OF DIRECTORS

Pres. Juanita S. Doares, Assoc. Dir., Collection Management and Development, New York Public Lib., New York, NY 10017; *V.P./Pres.-Elect.* Susan K. Martin, Dir., Milton S. Eisenhower Lib., Johns Hopkins Univ.; *Secy.* Virginia Boucher, Head, Interlibrary Cooperation, Univ. of Colorado, Boulder, CO 80309; *Treas.* Murray S. Martin, Libn., Wessell Lib., Tufts Univ., Medford, MA 02155; *Past Pres.* H. Joanne Harrar, Dir. of Libs., Univ. of Maryland, College Park, MD 20742.

MEMBERS OF THE BOARD

Executive director; Alice D. Ball; Patricia W. Berger, Chief, Lib. & Info. Services, National Bureau of Standards; Helen Citron, Assoc. Dir. of Lib., Georgia Institute of Technology; Richard DeGennaro, Dir. of Libs., Univ. of Pennsylvania, Philadelphia, PA 19104; Joyce Gartrell, Head, Serials Cataloging, Columbia Univ. Libs., New York, NY 10027; Nancy Marshall, Assoc. Dir. of Libs. for Public Services, Univ. of Wisconsin-Madison; Benita M. Weber, Head, Serials Dept., Univ. of New Mexico.

SPONSORING MEMBERS

Alabama Lib. Assn.; Alaska Lib. Assn.; American Assn. of Law Libs.; American Council of Learned Societies; American Society for Info. Science; American Lib. Assn.; American Theological Lib. Assn.; Arizona State Lib. Assn.; Assn. of American Lib. Schools; Assn. of Jewish Libs.; Assn. of Research Libs.; Assn. of Special Libs. of the Philippines; Associazione Italiano Biblioteche; British Columbia Lib. Assn.; California Lib. Assn.; Catholic Lib. Assn.; Colorado Lib. Assn.; District of Columbia Lib. Assn; Ethiopian Lib. Assn.; Federal Lib. Committee; Federation of Indian Lib. Assns.; Florida Lib. Assn.; Idaho Lib. Assn.; Interamerican Assn. of Agricultural Libns. and Documentalists; Jordan Lib. Assn.; Kenya Lib. Assn.; Lib. of Congress; Maryland Lib. Assn.; Medical Lib. Assn.; Michigan Lib. Assn.; Music Lib. Assn.; National Academy of Sciences; National Agricultural Lib.; National Lib. of Medicine; New Jersey Lib. Assn.; North Carolina Lib. Assn.; Pennsylvania Lib. Assn.; Philippine Lib. Assn.; Smithsonian Institution; Social Science Research Council; South African Lib. Assn.; Southeastern Lib. Assn.; Special Libs. Assn.; Special Libs. Assn. of Japan; Theatre Lib. Assn.; Uganda Lib. Assn.; Vereinigung Osterreichischer Bibliothekare.

STATE, PROVINCIAL, AND REGIONAL LIBRARY ASSOCIATIONS

The associations in this section are organized under three headings: United States, Canada, and Regional Associations. Both the United States and Canada are represented under Regional Associations. Unless otherwise specified, correspondence is to be addressed to the secretary or executive secretary name in the entry.

UNITED STATES

Alabama

Memb. 1,400. Founded 1904. Term of Office. Apr. 1982-Apr. 1983. Publication. *The Alabama Librarian* (10 per year).

Ed. Joe Acker, Carl Elliott Regional Lib., 20 E. 18 St., Jasper 35501; *Pres.* Jane McRae, 4608 Scenic View Dr., Bessemer 35020; *1st V.P./Pres.-Elect.* Pat Moore, 613 Winwood Dr., Birmingham 35226; *2nd V.P.* Donna Barrett, 9014 C Mahogany Row, Huntsville 35802; *Secy.* Ann Hamilton, Box A-20, Birmingham Southern College, 35204; *Treas.* Cherrell Bunkett, Rte. 2, Box 112B, Morris 35116; *ALA Chapter Councillor.* James Ramer, Dean, Grad. School of Lib. Service, Univ. of Alabama, Box 6242, University 35486; *Past Pres.* Julia Rotenberry, 249 Highland St. N., Montevallo 35115.

Address correspondence to the executive secretary, Alabama Lib. Assn., Box BY, University 35486.

Alaska

Memb. (Indiv.) 276; (Inst.) 27. Term of Office. Mar. 1983-Mar. 1984. Publications. *Sourdough* (q.); *Newspoke* (bi-mo.).

Pres. Pat Wilson, 9215 Gee St., Juneau 99801; *V.P./Pres.-Elect.* To be announced; *Secy.* To be announced; *Treas.* Judy Monroe, 5240 E. 42, Anchorage 99504.

Arizona

Memb. 1,050. Term of Office. Oct. 1, 1982-Oct. 1, 1983. Publication. *ASLA Newsletter* (mo.).

Ed. Caryl Major, 3213 W. Sunnyside Ave., Phoenix 85029; *Pres.* Sandra Steffey Lobeck, Yuma Elementary School Dist., 450 Sixth St., Yuma 85364; *Pres.-Elect.* Donald Riggs, Arizona State Univ. Lib., Tempe 85287; *Secy.* Hazel Robinson, Flagstaff Unified School Dist., 701 N. Kendrick, Flagstaff 86001; *Treas.* Jeannette Daane, 2123 S. Paseo Loma, Mesa 85202.

Arkansas

Memb. 1,150. Term of Office. Sept. 1982-Sept. 1983. Publication. *Arkansas Libraries* (q.).

Pres. Jay Ziolko, Mississippi County Lib. System, 200 N. Fifth, Blytheville 72315; *Exec. Dir.* Ruth Williams, Box 2275, Little Rock 72203.

Address correspondence to the executive director.

California

Memb. (Indiv.) 3,050; (Inst.) 178; (Business) 70. Term of Office. Jan. 1-Dec. 31, 1983. Publication. *The CLA Newsletter* (mo.).

Pres. Carol Aronoff, Santa Monica Public Lib., 1343 Sixth St., Santa Monica 90401; *V.P./Pres.-Elect.* Josephine R. Terry, County Libn., Butte County Lib., 1820 Mitchell Ave., Oroville 95965; *Treas.* Wm. F. McCoy, Univ. of California Lib., Davis 95616; *ALA Chapter Councillor.* Gilbert W. McNamee, San Francisco Public Lib., Business Branch, 530 Kearny St., San Francisco 94108.

Address correspondence to Stefan B. Moses, Exec. Dir., California Lib. Assn., 717 K St., Suite 300, Sacramento 95814.

Colorado

Term of Office. Nov. 1982-Oct. 1983. Publication. *Colorado Libraries* (q.). *Ed.* Johannah Sherrer, Michener Lib., Univ. of Northern Colorado, Greeley 80639.

Pres. Irene Godden, Univ. Libs., Colorado State Univ., Fort Collins 80523; *1st V.P./Pres.-Elect.* John Campbell, Pathfinder RLSS, S. First & Uncompahgre, Montrose 81401; *2nd V.P.* Natalia Greer, Villa Regional Lib., 455 S. Pierce, Lakewood 80226; *Exec. Secy.* Theresa Sentman, Box 8028, Colorado Springs 80933; *Past Pres.* Michael Herbison, Univ. of Colorado at Colorado Springs, Box 7150, Colorado Springs 80933.

Connecticut

Memb. 750. Term of Office. July 1, 1982-July 30, 1983. Publication. *Connecticut Libraries* (11 per year). *Ed.* Gretchen Swackhammer, 74C River Bend Rd., Stratford 06497.

Pres. Leslie Berman Burger, Connecticut State Lib., 231 Capitol Ave., Hartford 06106; *V.P./Pres.-Elect.* Mary Dymek, Prosser Public Lib., One Tunxis Ave., Bloomfield 06002; *Treas.* Carol Hutchinson, Sherwood Dr., Southport 06490; *Secy.* Jeanne Simpson, Connecticut Lib. Assn., State Lib., 231 Capitol Ave., Hartford 06106.

Delaware

Memb. (Indiv.) 224; (Inst.) 22. Term of Office. May 1982-May 1983. Publication. *DLA Bulletin.* (3 per year).

Pres. Judith Roberts, Cape Henlopen H.S., Cape Henlopen 19958; *V.P./Pres.-Elect.* David Burdash, Wilmington Inst., Tenth & Market St., Wilmington 19801; *Secy.* Emily McKnatt Dreshfield, 7 Cartier Ct., Drummond Ridge, Newark 19711; *Treas.* Margaret Wang, Univ. of Delaware Lib., Newark 19711.

Address correspondence to the Delaware Lib. Assn., Box 1843, Wilmington 19899.

District of Columbia

Memb. 900. Term of Office. May 1982-May 1983. Publication. *Intercom* (mo.). *Co-Eds.* Mary Feldman, National Center for Family Studies, The Catholic Univ. of America, Washington, DC 20064; Jacque-Lynne Schulman, Pergamon Press, International, 1340 Old Chain Bridge Rd., McLean, VA 22101.

Pres. Judith A. Sessions, George Washington Univ. Lib., 2130 H St. N.W., Washington, DC 20052; *Pres.-Elect.* Darrell Lemke, Consortium of Universities, 1356 Connecticut Ave. N.W., Washington, DC 20036; *Treas.* Melinda Renner, Atomic Industrial Forum, 7101 Wisconsin Ave. N.W., 12 fl., Washington, DC 20014; *Secy.* Susan M. Fifer, National Geographic Lib., 17 & M Sts. N.W., Washington, DC 20036.

Florida

Memb. (Indiv.) 800; (In-state Inst.) 50; (Out-of-state Inst.) 30. Term of Office. July 1, 1982-June 30, 1983.

Pres. Harold Goldstein, Florida State Univ., School of Lib. & Info. Studies, Tallahassee 32306; *V.P./Pres.-Elect.* Jean F. Rhein, Seminole County Public Lib., 101 E. First St., 3rd fl., Sanford 32771; *Secy.* Anne G. Keeler, Extension Div., Orlando Public Lib., 10 N. Rosalind Ave., Orlando 32801; *Treas.* Thomas L. Reitz, 1333 Gunnison Ave., Orlando 32804.

Georgia

Memb. 850. Term of Office. Oct. 1981-Oct. 1983. Publication. *Georgia Librarian* (q.). *Ed.* Wanda J. Calhoun, Augusta Regional Lib., Augusta 30902.

Pres. Charles E. Beard, Dir. of Libs., West Georgia College, Carrollton 30117; *1st V.P.* Jane R. Morgan, Materials Specialist, Fulton County Schools, 3121 Norman Berry Dr., East Point 30344; *2nd V.P.* Sara June McDavid, Media Specialist, Parkview H.S., Liburn 30247; *Treas.* Gayle McKinney, Online Search Services Coord., Reference Dept., Pullen Lib., Georgia State Univ., University Plaza,

Atlanta 30303; *Secy.* Virginia L. Rutherford, Coord., Southern Forestry Info. Network, Science Lib., Univ. of Georgia, Athens 30602; *Exec. Secy.* Ann W. Morton, Box 833, Tucker 30084.

Hawaii

Memb. 425. Term of Office. Mar. 1982-Mar. 1983. Publications. *Hawaii Library Association Journal* (ann.); *Hawaii Library Association Newsletter* (5 per year); *HLA Membership Directory* (ann.); *Directory of Libraries & Information Sources in Hawaii & the Pacific Islands* (irreg.).

Pres. Edna Hurd, Kamehameha School; *V.P.* Cynthia Timberlake, Libn., Bishop Museum, Honolulu; *Secy.* Florianna Cofman, Waianae Lib., Waianae; *Treas.* Marilyn Martam, Hawaii Medical Lib.

Address correspondence to the president.

Idaho

Memb. 364. Term of Office. June 1, 1982-Oct 31, 1983. Publication. *The Idaho Librarian* (q.). *Ed.* Jeanne Lipscomb.

Pres. John Hartung, Kootenai County Lib., Coeur d'Alene 83814; *Pres.-Elect.* Anna Green, Portneuf District Lib., Chubbuck 83202; *Secy.* Dorothy Goodrich, Kootenai County Lib., Coeur d'Alene 83814.

Illinois

Memb. 3,300. Term of Office. Jan. 1983-Dec. 1983. Publication. *ILA Reporter* (4 per year).

Pres. Judith Prescher; *V.P./Pres.-Elect.* Valerie Wilford; *Treas.* Kathleen Heim; *Exec. Dir.* Willine C. Mahony.

Address correspondence to the executive director, ILA, 425 N. Michigan Ave., Suite 1304, Chicago 60611.

Indiana

Memb. (Indiv.) 1,130; (Inst.) 241. Term of Office. Nov. 1982-May 1983. Publications. *Focus on Indiana Libraries* (10 per year). *Ed.* Beth Steele, ILA/ILTA Exec. Office, 1100 W. 42 St., Indianapolis 46208; *Indiana Libraries*. (q.). *Ed.* Dr. Ray Trevis, Dept. of Lib. Science, Ball State Univ., Muncie 47306.

Pres. Robert Y. Coward, Franklin College Lib., Franklin 46131; *V.P./Pres.-Elect.* Linda Robertson, Wabash Public Lib., 188 W. Hill, Wabash 46992; *Secy.* David Cooper, Noblesville Public Lib., 16 S. Tenth St., Noblesville 46060; *Treas.* Leslie R. Galbraith, Christian Theological Seminary, 1000 W. 42 St., Indianapolis 46208; *Exec. Dir.* Ann Moreau, ILA, 1100 W. 42 St., Indianapolis 46208.

Address correspondence to the executive director.

Iowa

Memb. 1,608. Term of Office. Jan. 1983-Jan. 1984. Publication. *The Catalyst* (bi-mo.).

Ed. Naomi Stovall, 921 Insurance Exchange Bldg., Des Moines 50309.

Pres. Kay Runge, Scott County Lib., 215 N. Second St., Eldridge 52748.

Kansas

Memb. 1,000. Term of Office. July 1982-June 1983. Publications. *KLA Newsletter* (q.); *KLA Membership Directory* (ann.).

Pres. Richard J. Rademacher, Wichita Public Lib., 223 S. Main St., Wichita 67208; *V.P./Pres.-Elect.* Arnita Graber, 200 W. Broadway, Newton 67114; *Secy.* Karyl Buffington, Coffeyville Public Lib., 311 W. Tenth, Coffeyville 67337; *Treas.* Rowena Olsen, McPherson College Lib., McPherson 67460.

Kentucky

Memb. 962. Term of Office. Jan. 1982-Dec. 1983. Publication. *Kentucky Libraries* (q.).
Pres. Betty Delius, Dir., Bellarmine College, Louisville 40205; *V.P.* Margaret Trevathian, Libn., Calloway County, Public Lib., Murray 42071; *Secy.* Sara Chumbler, Libn., D. T. Cooper Elementary School, Paducah 42001.

Louisiana

Memb. (Indiv.) 1,475; (Inst.) 83. Term of Office. July 1982-July 1983. Publication. *LLA Bulletin* (q.).
Pres. Dolores Owen, 218 Antigua Dr., Lafayette 70503; *1st V.P./Pres.-Elect.* Joy Lowe, Rte. 5, Box 331, Ruston 71270; *2nd V.P.* Sr. Marie Cairns, School of Lib. & Info. Science, Louisiana State Univ., Baton Rouge 70803; *Secy.* Cynthia Phillips, 556 Octavia St., New Orleans 70115; *Parliamentarian.* Anthony Benoit, 4265 Hyacinth Ave., Baton Rouge 70808; *Exec. Dir.* Chris Thomas, Box 131, Baton Rouge 70821.

Address correspondence to the executive director.

Maine

Memb. 700. Term of Office. *(Pres. & V.P.).* Spring 1982-Spring 1984. Publication. *Downeast Libraries* (4 per year); *Monthly Memo* (mo.).
Pres. Schuyler Mott, Paris Hill, Paris 04271; *V.P.* Glenna Nowell, Gardiner Public Lib., Gardiner 04345; *Secy.* Catherine H. Cocks, Miller Lib., Colby College, Waterville 04901; *Treas.* J. Michael Francescki, Merrill Memorial Lib., Yarmouth 04096.

Address correspondence to Maine Lib. Assn., c/o Maine Municipal Assn., Local Government Center, Community Dr., Augusta 04330.

Maryland

Memb. Approx. 900. Term of Office. June 1, 1982-June 1, 1983.
Pres. Jo Ann Pinder, Anne Arundel County Public Libs., 5 Harry S. Truman Pkwy., Annapolis, 21401; *1st V.P.* Anne Shaw Burgan, Network Services Div., Enoch Pratt Free Lib., 400 Cathedral St., Baltimore 21202; *2nd V.P.* Cathy O'Connell, Washington County Free Lib., 100 S. Potomac St., Hagerstown 21740; *Treas.* George Sands, Caroline County Public Lib., 100 Market St., Denton 21629.

Address correspondence to the president.

Massachusetts

Memb. (Indiv.) 1,000; (Inst.) 200. Term of Office. July 1981-June 1983. Publication. *Bay State Librarian* (2 per year). *Ed.* Robin Robinson-Sorkin, 33 Chilton St., Cambridge 02138.
Pres. Robert Maier, Bedford Public Lib., Bedford 01730; *V.P.* Constance Clancy, South Hadley Public Lib., South Hadley 01075; *Rec. Secy.* Ann Reynolds, Wellesley Free Lib., Wellesley 02181; *Treas.* Claudia Morner, Cape Cod Community College, West Barnstable 02668; *Exec. Secy.* Pat Demit, Box 7, Nahant 01908.

Address correspondence to the executive secretary.

Michigan

Memb. (Indiv.) 2,200; (Inst.) 150. Term of Office. Nov. 1, 1982-Oct. 31, 1983. Publication. *Michigan Librarian Newsletter* (10 per year).
Pres. Margaret Thomas, Farmington Branch Lib., 23500 Liberty, Farmington 48024; *1st V.P./Pres.-Elect.* Eleanor Pinkham, Kalamazoo College, Kalamazoo, 49001; *Treas.* Carol Goodwin, Lib. Cooperative of Ma-

comb, Mt. Clemens 48044; *Exec. Dir.* Marianne Gessner, Michigan Lib. Assn., 226 W. Washtenaw Ave., Lansing 48933.

Address correspondence to the executive director.

Minnesota

Memb. 900. Term of Office. *(Pres. & V.P.).* Nov. 1, 1982-Oct. 31, 1983; *(Secy.)* Nov. 1, 1982-Oct. 31, 1984; *(Treas.)* Nov. 1, 1981-Oct. 31, 1983. Publication. *MLA Newsletter* (10 per year).

Pres. Marlys O'Brien, Kitchigami Regional Lib., Box 84, Pine River 56474; *V.P./Pres.-Elect.* Michael Kathman, 414 Eighth Ave. N., Cold Spring 56320; *ALA Chapter Councilor.* Edward Swanson, 1065 Portland Ave., St. Paul 55104; *Secy.* Darlene Arnold, OPLIC, 301 Hanover Bldg., 480 Cedar St., St. Paul 55101; *Treas.* Bruce Willms, 1653 Hague Ave., St. Paul 55104; *Exec. Dir.* Adele Panzer Morris, Minnesota Lib. Assn., Box 484, Rosemount 55068.

Address correspondence to the executive director.

Mississippi

Memb. 1,000. Term of Office. Jan. 1982-Dec. 1983. Publication. *Mississippi Libraries* (q.).

Pres. Jo Wilson, W. B. Roberts Lib., Delta State Univ., Cleveland 38733; *V.P./Pres.-Elect.* Anice C. Powell, Sunflower County Lib., 201 Cypress Dr., Indianola 38751.; *Secy.* Ollie V. Sykes, 2600 Tenth Ave., Meridian 29301; *Treas.* Rachel Smith, Box 127, Mississippi College, Clinton 39056; *Exec. Secy.* Kay V. Mitchell, Box 470, Jackson 39056.

Address correspondence to the executive secretary.

Missouri

Memb. 1,349. Term of Office. Sept. 24, 1982-Oct. 21, 1983. Publication. *Missouri Library Association Newsletter* (6 per year).

Pres. Paul White, Dir., Kinderhook Regional Lib., 104 E. Commercial, Lebanon 65536; *V.P./Pres.-Elect.* Martha Maxwell, Dir., Cape Girardeau Public Lib., 711 N. Clark, Cape Girardeau 63701; *Treas.* Beth Eckles, Dir., Boonslick Regional Lib., Sixth and Lamine, Sedalia 65301; *Secy.* Marsha Parker, St. Charles City-County Lib., Box 529, St. Peters 63376.

Montana

Memb. 560. Term of Office. June 1, 1982-May 31, 1983. Publication. *MLA President's Newsletter* (4-6 per year).

Pres. Karen Everett, Box 66, Shepherd 59079; *V.P./Pres.-Elect.* Rita Schmidt, 3721 Seventh Ave. N., Great Falls 59405; *Secy.* Michael Ober, Flathead Valley Community College, One First St. E., Kalispell 59901.

Nebraska

Memb. 760. Term of Office. Oct. 1982-Oct. 1983. Publication. *NLA Quarterly.*

Pres. Thomas Boyle, 2050 Hazel St., Fremont 68025; *V.P./Pres.-Elect.* Robert Trautwein, 2512 26 St., Columbus 68601; *Secy.* Margaret S. Mills, 660 N. State St., Box 427, Osceola 68651; *Treas.* Morel Fry, Nebraska Lib. Commission, 1420 P St., Lincoln 68508; *Exec. Secy.* Ray Means, Dir., Alumni Memorial Lib., Creighton Univ., 2500 California St., Omaha 68178.

Address correspondence to the executive secretary.

Nevada

Memb. 300. Term of Office. Jan. 1, 1983-Dec. 31, 1983. Publication. *Highroller* (4 per year).
Pres. Dean A. Allen, Dir., Learning Resources Center, Western Nevada Community College, Carson City 89701; *V.P./Pres.-Elect.* To be announced; *Exec. Secy.* Carol Parkhurst, Systems Lib., Getchell Lib., Univ. of Nevada, Reno 89557; *Treas.* To be announced; *Past Pres.* Dean A. Allen, S. Nevada Vo-Tech. Center Lib., 5710 Mountain Vista, Las Vegas 89120.

New Hampshire

Memb. 353. Term of Office. May 1982-May 1983. Publication *NHLA Newsletter* (bi-mo.).
Pres. Cheryl Stockman, West Manchester Community Lib., 76 N. Main St., Manchester 03102; *1st V.P.* Andrew Carnegie, 5 Robin Lane, Exeter 03833; *2nd V.P.* John Courtney, Concord Public Lib., 35 Green St., Concord 03301; *Secy.* Carol Sykes, Laconia Public Lib., 695 Main St., Laconia 03246; *Treas.* Barry Hennessey, Dimond Lib., Univ. of New Hampshire, Durham 03824.

New Jersey

Memb. 1,600. Term of Office. May 1982-May 1983. Publication. *New Jersey Libraries* (q.).
Pres. Dorothy E. Johnson, Asst. Dir., Bloomfield Public Lib., 90 Broad St., Bloomfield 07003; *V.P./Pres.-Elect.* Elaine McConnell, Dir., Piscataway Township Libs., 500 Hoes Lane, Piscataway 08854; *2nd V.P.* Eleanor Brome, Dir., Cranford Public Lib., 224 Walnut Ave., Cranford 07016; *Past Pres.* June Adams, Dir., Somerset County Lib., Box 6700, Bridgewater 08807; *Rec. Secy.* Barbara Irwin, Dir., NJ Historical Society, 230 Broadway, Newark 07104; *Corres. Secy.* Alyce Bowers, Dir., Rockaway Township Lib., 61 Mount Hope Rd., Rockaway 07866; *Treas.* Rowland Bennett, Dir., Maplewood Memorial Lib., 51 Baker St., Maplewood 07040; *Exec. Dir.* Abigail Studdiford, New Jersey Lib. Assn., 116 W. State St., Trenton 08608.
Address correspondence to the executive director.

New Mexico

Memb. 661. Term of Office. Apr. 1982-Apr. 1983. Publication. *New Mexico Library Association Newsletter.* Ed. Rebecca Phillips, Univ. of New Mexico, 214 Carlisle Blvd. N.E., Albuquerque 87106.
Pres. Benjamin T. Wakashige, Univ. of Albuquerque, St. Joseph Place N.W., Albuquerque 87140; *1st. V.P./Pres.-Elect.* Linda J. Erickson, Sandia National Laboratory, 1001 Santa Ana S.E., Albuquerue 87123; *2nd V.P.* Cheryl Wilson, New Mexico State Univ., 1109 Skyway, Las Cruces 88001; *Secy.* Cherrill M. Whitlow, Rio Grande H.S., 2702 Morrow Rd. N.E., Albuquerque 87106; *Treas.* Eleanor A. Noble, Univ. of Albuquerque, 4401 Roxbury N.E., Albuquerque 87111.

New York

Memb. 3,500. Term of Office. Oct. 1982-Oct. 1983. Publication. *NYLA Bulletin* (10 per year). *Ed.* Diana J. Dean.
Pres. Gerald R. Shields, Asst. Dean, School of Info. & Lib. Studies, SUNY Buffalo, Buffalo 14260; *1st V.P.* Carol A. Kearney, Dir. of Libs., Buffalo City Schools, City Hall, Rm. 408, Buffalo 14202; *2nd V.P.* Robert E. Barron, School-Lib. Liaison, State Educ. Dept., Cultural Education Center, Empire State Plaza, Albany 12230; *Exec. Dir.* Nancy W. Lian,

CAE, New York Lib. Assn., 15 Park Row, Suite 434, New York City 10038.
Address correspondence to the executive director.

North Carolina

Memb. 2,000. Term of Office. Oct. 1981-Oct. 1983. Publication. *North Carolina Libraries* (q.). *Ed.* Jonathan A. Lindsey, Carlyle Campbell Lib., Meredith College, Raleigh 27611.
Pres. Mertys W. Bell, Dean of Learning Resources, Guilford Technical Institute, Box 309, Jamestown 27282; *1st V.P./Pres.-Elect.* Leland M. Park, Davidson College Lib., Davidson 28036; *2nd V.P.* Carol Southerland, Box 1046, Elizabethtown 28337; *Secy.* Mary Jo Godwin, Edgecombe County Memorial Lib., 909 Main St., Tarboro 27886; *Treas.* W. Robert Pollard, Head of Reference, D.H. Hill Lib., North Carolina State Univ., Raleigh 27607.

North Dakota

Memb. (Indiv.) 350; (Inst.) 30. Term of Office. *(Pres., V.P., and Pres.-Elect.).* Oct. 1981-Oct. 1983. Publication. *The Good Stuff.* (q.).
Pres. Ron Rudser, Minot State College Lib., Minot 58701; *V.P./Pres.-Elect.* Jerry Kaup, Dir., Minot Public Lib., Minot 58701; *Secy.* Connie Strand, Harley French Medical Lib., Univ. of North Dakota Lib., Grand Forks 58202; *Treas.* Cheryl Bailey, Mary College Lib., Bismarck 58501.

Ohio

Memb. (Indiv.) 1904; (Inst.) 226. Term of Office. Oct. 1982-Oct. 1983. Publications. *Ohio Library Association Bulletin* (3 per year); *Ohio Libraries: Newsletter of the Ohio Library Association* (9 per year).
Pres. Wallace White, Flesh Public Lib., Piqua 45356; *V.P./Pres.-Elect.* Rachel Nelson, Cleveland Heights-Univ. Heights Public Lib., Cleveland Heights 44118; *Secy.* Linda Harfst, OVAL, Wellston 45692; *Exec. Dir.* A. Chapman Parsons, 40 S. Third St., Suite 409, Columbus 43215.
Address correspondence to the executive director.

Oklahoma

Memb. (Indiv.) 950; (Inst.) 50. Term of Office. July 1, 1982-June 30, 1983. Publication. *Oklahoma Librarian* (bi-mo.).
Pres. Mary Sherman, Pioneer Multi-County Lib. System, 225 N. Webster, Norman 73069; *V.P./Pres.-Elect.* Frances Alsworth, Central State Univ. Lib., 100 N. University Dr., Edmond 73034; *Secy.* Susan McVey, Dulaney-Browne Lib., Oklahoma City Univ., 2501 N. Blackwelder, Oklahoma City 73106; *Treas.* Ray Lau, Northwestern Oklahoma State Univ., Alva 73717; *Exec. Secy.* Dorothy Gaither, 1747 W. Virgin, Tulsa 74127.
Address correspondence to the executive secretary.

Oregon

Memb. (Indiv.) 675; (Inst.) 50. Term of Office. April 1982-April 1983. Publication. *Oregon Library News* (mo.). *Ed.* James Lockwood, OSSHE Council, Kerr Lib., Oregon State Univ. Corvallis 97331.
Pres. Martin W. Stephenson, Corvallis Public Lib., 645 N.W. Monroe, Corvallis 97330; *V.P./Pres.-Elect.* Stanley Ruckman, Linn-Benton Community College, Learning Resources Center, Albany 97321; *Secy.* Willa Ralphs, St. Helens Public Lib., 21 Plaza, St. Helens 97051; *Treas.* Janet Irwin, Lib. Assn. of Portland, 801 S.W. Tenth Ave., Portland 97205.

Pennsylvania

Memb. 2,000. Term of Office. Oct. 1982-Oct. 1983. Publication. *PLA Bulletin* (mo.).
Pres. Jack M. Berk, Bethlehem Public Lib., 11 W. Church St., Bethlehem 18018; *Exec. Dir.* Diane D. Ward, Pennsylvania Lib. Assn., 126 Locust St., Harrisburg 17101.

Puerto Rico

Memb. 300. Term of Office. April 1982-March 1984. Publications. *Boletín* (s. ann.); *Cuadernos Bibliotecológicos* (irreg.); *Informa* (mo.); *Cuadernos Bibliográficos* (irreg.).
Pres. Luisa Vigo.
Address correspondence to the Sociedad de Bibliotecarios de Puerto Rico, Apdo. 22898, U.P.R. Sta., Río Piedras 00931.

Rhode Island

Memb. (Indiv.) 560; (Inst.) 33. Term of Office. Nov. 1982-Oct. 1983. Publication. *Rhode Island Library Association Bulletin* (mo.). *Ed.* Deborah Barchi.
Pres. Howard Boksenbaum, Barrington Public Lib., Barrington 02806; *V.P.* Frances Farrell, Providence Public Lib., Providence 02903; *Secy.* Frank P. Iacono, Rhode Island Dept. of State Lib. Services, Providence 02908; *Treas.* Charles Moore, Woonsocket-Harris Public Lib., Woonsocket 02895; *Mem.-at-Large.* Mary Ellen Hardiman, North Providence Union Free Lib., North Providence 02890; *N.E.L.A. Councillor.* Jacquelyn Toy, Rocham-Branch, Providence Public Lib., Providence 02906; *ALA Councillor.* Margaret A. Bush, Providence Public Lib., Providence 02903.
Address correspondence to the secretary.

St. Croix

Memb. 48. Term of Office. Apr. 1982-May 1983. Publications. *SCLA Newsletter* (q.); *Studies in Virgin Islands Librarianship* (irreg.).
Pres. Wallace Williams; *V.P.* Helen Tompkins; *Secy.* Liane Forbes; *Treas.* Nancy Fisk; *Bd. Membs.* Marty Ammerman, Avi Whitney.

South Carolina

Memb. 750. Term of Office. Oct. 1982-Oct. 1983. Publication. *The South Carolina Librarian* (s. ann.). *Ed.* Laurance Mitlin, Dacus Lib., Winthrop College, Rock Hill 29733; *News and Views of South Carolina Library Association* (bi.-mo.). *Ed.* John Sukovich, Wessels Lib., Newberry College, Newberry 29108.
Pres. H. Paul Dove, Jr., Francis Marion College Lib., Florence 29501; *V.P./Pres.-Elect.* Drucilla G. Reeves, Brookland-Cayce 29033; *2nd V.P.* Margie E. Herron, South Carolina State Lib., Box 11469, Columbia 29211; *Treas.* Donna Nance, Thomas Cooper Lib., Univ. of South Carolina, Columbia 29208; *Secy.* Anne K. Middleton, South Carolina State Lib., Box 11469, Columbia 29211; *Exec. Secy.* Louise Whitmore, Box 25, Edisto Island 29438.

South Dakota

Memb. (Indiv.) 415; (Inst.) 52. Term of Office. Oct. 1982-Oct. 1983/84. Publications. *Bookmarks* (bi-mo.); *Newsletter.*
Ed. Phil Brown, H. M. Briggs Lib., South Dakota State Univ., Brookings 57006; *Co.-Ed.* Tina Cunningham, Brookings Public Lib., Brookings 57006; *Pres.* Carol Davis, Sturgis Public Lib., 1040 Second St., Sturgis 57785; *Pres.-Elect.* Susan Sandness, Minnehaha County Lib., Hartford

57033; *Secy.* Nancy Sabbe, Madison Public Lib., 209 E. Center, Madison 57042; *Treas.* Sandra Norlin, Brookings Public Lib., Brookings 57006.

Tennessee

Memb. 1,215. Term of Office. May 1982-May 1983. Publication. *Tennessee Librarian* (q.).

Pres. Diane N. Baird, Senior Lib., Warioto Regional Lib. Center, Clarksville 37040; *Pres.-Elect.* Janet S. Fiahser, Asst. Dean, East Tennessee State Univ. Medical Lib., Johnson City 37614; *Treas.* Marion Kimbrough, Assoc. Professor, Dept. of Lib./Info. Science, Peabody College of Vanderbilt Univ., Nashville 37203; *Exec. Secy.* Betty Nance, Box 120085, Nashville 37212.

Texas

Term of Office. Apr. 1982-Apr. 1983.

Pres. Elizabeth Crab, Dir., N.E. Texas Lib. System, 15523 El Estado, Dallas 75248; *Pres.-Elect.* James O. Wallace, Dir., San Antonio College Lib., 1001 Howard, San Antonio 78284; *Continuing Exec. Dir.* Jerre Hetherington, TLA Office, 8989 Westherimer, Suite 108, Houston 77063.

Address correspondence to the executive director.

Utah

Memb. 550. Term of Office *(Pres. & V.P.)* Mar. 1982-Mar. 1983. Publication. *ULA Newsletter* (irreg.).

Pres. Brenda Branyan, Utah State Univ., UNC 30, Logan 84322; *1st V.P.* Craige Hall, Weber State College, 3750 Harrison Blvd., Ogden 84408; *2nd V.P.* Lynnda Waingsgard, Weber County Lib., 2464 Jefferson Ave., Ogden 84401; *Exec. Secy.* Gerald A. Buttars, Utah State Lib. Commission, 2150 S. 300 W., Salt Lake City 84115.

Vermont

Memb. 450. Term of Office. Jan. 1983-Dec. 1983. Publication. *VLA News* (10/yr.).

Pres. Dewey Patterson, Librarian, Vermont Technical College, Randolph Center 05061; *V.P./Pres. Elect.* Jean Marcy, St. Johnsbury Atheneum, 30 Main St., St. Johnsbury 05819; *Secy.* Anita Danigelis, 470 S. Willard, Burlington 05401; *Treas.* Laurel Stanley, Lyndon State College Lib., Lyndonville 05851.

Virginia

Memb. 1,100. Term of Office. Oct. 1982-Nov. 1983. Publication. *Virginia Librarian Newsletter* (6 per year).

Pres. Dean Burgess, Dir., Portsmouth Public Lib., 601 Court St., Portsmouth 23704; *V.P./Pres.-Elect.* Tim Byrne, Cabell Lib., Virginia Commonwealth Univ., 901 Park Ave., Richmond 23284; *Secy.* John Stewart, Asst. Dir., Virginia Beach Dept. of Public Lib., Administrative Offices, Municipal Center, Virginia Beach 23456; *Treas.* Rene Perez-Lopez, Norfolk Public Lib., 301 E. City Hall Ave., Norfolk 23510; *Exec. Dir.* Deborah M. Trocchi, Publishers' Services, 80 S. Early St., Alexandria 22304.

Address correspondence to the executive director.

Washington

Memb. (Indiv.) 1,000; (Inst.) 31. Term of Office. Aug. 1981-July 1983. Publications. *Highlights* (bi-mo.); *Password* (bi-mo.).

Pres. Anthony M. Wilson, Highline College Lib., Midway 98031; *1st V.P./Pres.-Elect.* Anne Haley, Walla Walla Public Lib., Walla Walla 99362;

2nd V.P. Charlotte Jones, Spokane Public Lib., W. 906 Main, Spokane 99201; *Secy.* Makiko Doi, Central Washington University Lib., Ellensburg 98926; *Treas.* June Perrin, Spokane Public Lib., Spokane 99207; *Legislative Consultant.* Melanie Stewart, Box 1075, Olympia 98507; *Corresponding Secy.* Marjorie Burns, 1232 143 Ave. S.E., Bellevue, WA 98007.

West Virginia

Memb. (Indiv.). 642; (Inst.) 23. Term of Office. Dec. 1982-Nov. 1983. Publication. *West Virginia Libraries* (q.).

Pres. Karen Goff, Reference Lib., West Virginia Lib. Commission, Science & Cultural Center, Charleston 25305; *1st V.P./Pres.-Elect.* Jeanne Mollendeck, Parkersburg H.S., 2101 Dudley Ave., Parkersburg 26101; *2nd V.P.* Charles A. Julian, Robert F. Kidd Lib., Glenville State College, Glenville 26305; *Treas.* Dave Childers, West Virginia Lib. Commission, Science & Cultural Center, Charleston 25305; *ALA Councillor.* Jo Ellen Flagg, Kanawha County Public Lib., 123 Capitol St., Charleston 25301.

Address correspondence to the president.

Wisconsin

Memb. 2,000. Term of Office. Jan. 1983-Dec. 1983. Publication. *WLA Newsletter* (bi-mo.).

Pres. Daniel Bradbury, Janesville Public Lib., 316 S. Main St., Janesville 53545; *V.P.* Dennis Ribbens, Lawrence Univ. Lib., Appleton 54912.

Address correspondence to the president.

Wyoming

Memb. (Indiv.) 440; (Inst.) 12; (Subscribers) 24. Term of Office. Apr. 1981-Apr. 1982. Publication. *Wyoming Library Roundup* (tri-mo.)

Ed. Linn Rounds, Wyoming State Lib., Cheyenne 82002; *Pres.* Linda Goolsby, 1228 Ritter, Rawlins 82301; *V.P.* Barbara Fraley, Johnson Co. Lib., 90 N. Main St., Buffalo 82834; *Exec. Secy.* Lucie P. Osborn, Laramie County Lib. System, 2800 Central Ave., Cheyenne 82001.

CANADA

Alberta

Memb. (Indiv.) 309; (Inst.) 79; (Trustee) 36. Term of Office. May 1982-May 1983. Publication. *Letter of the L.A.A.* (mo.).

Pres. John Gishler, Head, Social Sciences Dept., Calgary Public Lib., 616 MacLeod Trail S.E., Calgary T2G 2M2; *1st V.P./Pres.-Elect.* Nora Robinson, Alberta Vocational Centre Lib. 332 Sixth Ave. S.E., Calgary T2G 4S6; *2nd V.P.* Jan Macdonald, MacLeod Dixon, 1500 Home Oil Tower, 324 Eighth Ave. S.W., Calgary T2P 2Z2; *Treas.* Pat Garneau, Lib., Edmonton Journal, Box 2421, Edmonton T5J 2S6.

Address correspondence to the president, Box 1357, Edmonton T5J 2N2.

British Columbia

Memb. 584. Term of Office. Apr. 1, 1982-May 31, 1983. Publication. *The Reporter* (6 per year). *Ed.* Gael Blackhall.

Pres. Harry Newsom; *V.P.* Margaret Friesen; *Secy.* Pia Christiansen; *Treas.* Jim Looney.

Address correspondence to BCLA, Box 46378 Sta. G., Vancouver V6R 4G6.

Manitoba

Memb. 300. Term of Office. Sept. 1982-Sept. 1983. Publication. *Manitoba Library Association Bulletin* (q.).

Pres. Eileen McFadden, John E. Robbins Lib., Brandon Univ., Brandon R7A 6A9; *Past Pres.* Doreen Shanks, D. S. Woods Education Lib., Univ. of Manitoba, Winnipeg R3T 2N2; *1st V.P.* Don Mills, Winnipeg Public Lib., 251 Donald St., Winnipeg R3C 3P5; *Secy.* Beth Marshall, Elizabeth Dafoe Lib., Univ. of Manitoba, Winnipeg R3T 2N2; *Treas.* Harold Drake, St. Paul's College Lib., 430 Dysart Rd., Winnipeg R3T 2M6.

Address correspondence to E. MacMillan, 6 Fermor Ave., Winnipeg R2M 0Y2.

Ontario

Memb. 2,200. Term of Office. Nov. 1, 1982-Oct. 31, 1983. Publications. *Focus* (bi-mo.); *The Reviewing Librarian* (q.).

Pres. Beth Miller; *1st V.P.* Elizabeth Cummings; *2nd V.P.* Eva Martin; *Past Pres.* Barbara J. Smith; *Treas.* George Court; *Exec. Dir.* Diane Wheatley.

Address correspondence to Ontario Lib. Assn., Suite 402, 73 Richmond St. W., Toronto M5H 1Z4.

Quebec

Memb. (Indiv.) 160; (Inst.) 67; (Commercial) 6. Term of Office. May 1982-May 1983. Publication. *ABQ/QLA Bulletin*.

Pres. Anne Galler, Concordia Univ., Lib. Sci. Programme, 7141 Sherbrooke St. W., Rm. VL 125, Montreal H4B 1R6; *V.P.* Donna Duncan, McGill Univ., McLennan Lib., 3459 McTavish St., Montreal H3A 1Y1; *Treas.* Francoise Brais, Editions Heritage, 300 rue Arran, St. Lambert; *English Secy.* Sharon Huffman, Reginald J. P. Dawson Lib., 1967 Graham Blvd., Mount Royal H3R 1G9; *French Secy.* Agnes Lassonde, 1680 Barre St., St. Laurent H4L 4M9.

Saskatchewan

Memb. 250. Term of Office. *(Pres., 1st V.P./Pres.-Elect., Past Pres.)* July 1, 1982-June 30, 1983; *(2nd V.P., Secy.)* July 1, 1981-June 30, 1983. *(Treas.)* July 1, 1982-June 30, 1984. Publication. *Saskatchewan Library Forum* (5 per year).

Pres. Alan Ball, BCD Lib. and Automation Consultants, 2268 Osler, Regina S4P 1W8; *1st V.P./Pres.-Elect.* Anne Smart, Frances Morrison Lib., 311 23 St. E. Saskatoon S7K 0J6; *2nd V.P.* Bryan Foran, Carlyle King Lib., 3130 Laurier Dr., Saskatoon S7L 5J7; *Past Pres.* Ken Sagal, STI Lib., Box 1420, Moose Jaw S6H 4R4; *Secy.* Linda Fritz, Native Law Centre Lib., Univ. of Saskatchewan, Diefenbaker Centre, Saskatoon S7M 0W0; *Treas.* Ved Arora, Provincial Lib., 1352 Winnipeg St., Regina S4P 3V7.

REGIONAL

Atlantic Provinces: N.B., Nfld. N.S., P.E.I.

Memb. (Indiv.) 310; (Inst.) 185. Term of Office. May 1982-Apr. 1983. Publication. *APLA Bulletin* (bi-mo.).

Pres. Anna Oxley; *Pres.-Elect.* André Guay; *V.P. Nova Scotia.* Margot Schenk; *V.P. Prince Edward Island.* Frances Dindial; *V.P. Newfoundland.* Patricia M. Wilson; *V.P. New Brunswick.* Ruth Cunningham; *Secy.* Susan Svetlik; *Treas.* Linda Harvey.

Address correspondence to Atlantic Provinces Lib. Assn., c/o School of Lib. Service, Dalhousie Univ., Halifax B3H 4H8, N.S.

Middle Atlantic: Del., Md., N.J., Pa., Va.

Term of Office. July 1982-March 1983.

Pres. Jane E. Hukill, Brandywine College Lib., Box 7139, Concord Pike, Wilmington, DE 19803; *V.P.*

Nicholas Winowich, Kanawha County Public Lib., 123 Capitol St., Charleston, WV 25301; Secy.-Treas. Richard Parsons, Baltimore County Public Lib., 320 York Rd., Towson, MD 21204.

Midwest: Ill., Ind., Mich., Minn., Ohio, Wis.

Term of Office. Oct. 1979-Oct. 1983.

Pres. Robert H. Donahugh, Dir., Public Lib. of Youngstown and Mahoning County, 305 Wick Ave., Youngstown, OH 44503; V.P. Walter D. Morrill, Box 287, Duggan Lib., Hanover College, Hanover, IN 47243; Secy. Joseph Kimbrough, Dir., Minneapolis Public Lib. & Info. Center, 300 Nicollet Mall, Minneapolis, MN 55401.

Address correspondence to the president, Midwest Federation of Lib. Assns.

Mountain Plains: Colo., Kans., Nebr., Nev., N. Dak., S. Dak., Utah, Wyo.

Publication. *MPLA Newsletter* (bi-mo.).

Pres. Dorothy Middleton, East H.S., 2800 E. Pershing Blvd., Cheyenne, WY 82001; V.P./Pres.-Elect. Donna Jones Colby Public Lib., Colby, KS 67701; Secy. Jerry Kaup, Minot Public Lib., Minot, ND 58701; Exec. Secy. Joe Edelen, Technical Services, I. D. Weeks Lib., Univ. of South Dakota, Vermillion, SD 57069.

New England: Conn., Mass., Maine, N.H., R.I., Vt.

Term of Office. Oct. 1982-Oct. 1983. Publications. *NELA Newsletter* (6 per year). Ed. Brenda Claflin, 45 Arlington Rd., West Hartford, CT 06107; *A Guide to Newspaper Indexes in New England*; *The Genealogists' Handbook for New England Research*.

Pres. Peggy Wargo, Fairfield Public Lib., Fairfield, CT 06430; V.P./Pres.-Elect. Janice F. Sieburth, Univ. of Rhode Island Lib., Kingston, RI 02881; Treas. David S. Ferriero, Humanities Libn., M.I.T., Cambridge, 02139; Secy. Ruth Rothman, Portland Public Lib., Portland, ME 04103; Dirs. Diane R. Tebbets, University of New Hampshire Lib., Durham, NH 03824; Margo Brown-Crist, Central Massachusetts Regional Lib. System, Worcester, MA; Past Pres. Stanley Brown, Dartmouth College Lib., Hanover, NH 03755; Exec. Secy. Ex officio. Ronald B. Hunte, CAE, New England Lib. Assn., 292 Great Rd., Acton, MA 01720.

Address correspondence to the executive secretary.

Pacific Northwest: Alaska, Idaho, Mont., Oreg., Wash., Alta., B.C.

Memb. 950 (Active); 320 (Subscribers). Term of Office. (Pres./1st V.P.) Oct. 1982-1983. Publication. *PNLA Quarterly*.

Pres. Richard Moore, Dir. of the Lib., Southern Oregon State College, 1250 Siskiyou Blvd., Ashland, OR 97520; 1st V.P. Vicki Kreimeyer, Lewis & Clark College, 11661 S.W. Boones Bend Dr., Beaverton, OR 97005; 2nd V.P. Barbara Tolliver, School of Libnshp., 133 Suzzalo Lib., FM-30, Univ. of Washington, Seattle, WA 98195; Secy. George Smith, Woodburn Public Lib., 280 Garfield St., Woodburn, OR 97071; Treas. Audrey Kolb, Alaska State Lib., 1215 Cowles St., Fairbanks, AK 99701.

Southeastern: Ala., Fla., Ga., Ky., La., Miss., N.C., S.C., Tenn., Va., W.Va.

Memb. 2,500. Term of Office. Nov. 1982-Nov. 1984. Publication. *The Southeastern Librarian* (q.).

Pres. Barratt Wilkins, Pres., State Lib. of Florida, R. A. Gray Bldg., Tallahassee, FL 32301; V.P./Pres.-

Elect. Rebecca T. Bingham, Dir. of Library Media Services, Jefferson County Public Schools, Durrett Education Center, 4409 Preston Hwy., Louisville, KY 40213; *Secy.* David L. Ince, The Library, Valdosta State College, Valdosta, GA 31698; *Treas.* Arial A. Stephens, Public Lib. of Charlotte & Mecklenburg County, 310 N. Tryon St., Charlotte, NC 28202; *Exec. Secy.* Ann W. Morton, Box 987, Tucker, GA 30084.

Address correspondence to the executive secretary.

Southwestern: Ariz., Ark., La., N. Mex., Okla., Tex.

Memb. 869. Term of Office. Oct. 1982-Oct. 1984. Publication. *SWLA Newsletter* (q.).

Pres. Doralyn J. Hickey, School of Lib. & Info. Sciences, North Texas State Univ., Denton, TX 76204; *V.P./Pres. Elect.* James B. Stewart, Victoria Public Lib., Victoria, TX 77901; *Exec. Secy.* Judy Stanley, SWLA, Box 23713 TWU Sta., Denton, TX 76204.

STATE LIBRARY AGENCIES

The State library administrative agency in each of the states has the latest information on state plans for the use of federal funds under the Library Services and Construction Act. The directors, addresses, and telephone numbers of the state agencies are listed below.

Alabama

Anthony W. Miele, Dir., Alabama Public Lib. Services, 6030 Monticello Dr., Montgomery 36130. Tel: 205-277-7330.

Alaska

Richard B. Engen, Dir. of Libs. & Museums, Dept. of Educ., Pouch G., State Office Bldg., Juneau 99811. Tel: 907-465-2910.

Arizona

Sharon G. Womack, Dir., Dept. of Lib., Archives & Public Records, State Capitol, 3rd fl., Phoenix 85007. Tel: 602-255-4035.

Arkansas

John A. (Pat) Murphy, Jr., State Libn., Arkansas State Lib., One Capitol Mall, Little Rock 72201. Tel: 501-371-1526.

California

Gary E. Strong, State Libn., California State Lib., Box 2037, Sacramento 95809. Tel: 916-445-2585 or 4027.

Colorado

Anne Marie Falsone, Deputy State Libn., Colorado State Lib., 1326 Lincoln St., Denver 80203. Tel: 303-866-3695.

Connecticut

Clarence R. Walters, State Libn., Connecticut State Lib., 231 Capitol Ave., Hartford 06115. Tel: 203-566-4192 or 4301.

Delaware

Sylvia Short, Dir., Delaware Division of Libs., Box 639, Dover 19901. Tel: 302-736-4748.

District of Columbia

Hardy R. Franklin, Dir., Dist. of Columbia Public Lib., 901 G St. N.W., Washington 20001. Tel: 202-727-1101.

Florida

Barratt Wilkins, State Libn., State Lib. of Florida, R. A. Gray Bldg., Tallahassee 32304. Tel: 904-487-2651.

Georgia

Joe B. Forsee, State Libn., Div. of Public Lib. Services, 156 Trinity Ave. S.W., Atlanta 30303. Tel: 404-656-2461.

Hawaii

Bartholomew A. Kane, Asst. Superintendent/State Libn., Div. of Lib. Services, Dept. of Educ., Box 2360, Honolulu 96804. Tel: 808-735-5510.

Idaho

Charles M. Bolles, State Libn., Idaho State Lib., 325 W. State St., Boise 83702. Tel: 208-334-2150.

Illinois

Kathryn J. Gesterfield, Dir., Illinois State Lib., Centennial Memorial Bldg., Springfield 62756. Tel: 217-782-2994.

Indiana

C. Ray Ewick, Dir., Indiana State Lib., 140 N. Senate Ave., Indianapolis 46204. Tel: 317-232-3692.

Iowa

Barry L. Porter, Dir., State Lib. of Iowa, Historical Bldg., Des Moines 50319. Tel: 515-281-4105.

Kansas

Dwayne Johnson, State Libn., Kansas State Lib., 3rd fl., State Capitol, Topeka 66612. Tel: 913-296-3296.

Kentucky

James A. Nelson, State Libn. & Commissioner, Kentucky Dept. of Libs. & Archives, Box 537, Frankfort 40602. Tel: 502-875-7000.

Louisiana

Thomas F. Jaques, State Libn., Louisiana State Lib., Box 131, Baton Rouge 70821. Tel: 504-342-4923.

Maine

J. Gary Nichols, State Libn., Maine State Lib., Cultural Bldg., State House Station 64, Augusta 04333. Tel: 207-289-3561.

Maryland

Nettie B. Taylor, Asst. State Superintendent for Libs., Div. of Lib. Development & Services, State Dept. of Educ., 200 W. Baltimore St., Baltimore 21201. Tel: 301-659-2000.

Massachusetts

Ronald Piggford, Dir., Massachusetts Board of Lib. Commissioners, 648 Beacon St., Boston 02215. Tel: 617-267-9400.

Michigan

Frances X. Scannell, State Libn., Box 30007, Lansing 48909. Tel: 517-373-1580.

Minnesota

William Asp, Dir., Lib. Div., Dept. of Educ., 301 Hanover Bldg., 480 Cedar St., St. Paul 55101. Tel: 612-296-2821.

Mississippi

David M. Woodburn, Dir., Mississippi Lib. Commission, 1100 State Office Bldg., Box 3260, Jackson 39207. Tel: 601-354-6369.

Missouri

Charles O'Halloran, State Libn., Missouri State Lib., Box 387, Jefferson City 65102. Tel: 314-751-2751.

Montana

Sarah Parker, State Libn., Montana State Lib., 930 E. Lyndale Ave., Helena 59601. Tel: 406-449-3004.

Nebraska

John L. Kopischke, Dir., Nebraska Lib. Commission, Lincoln 68509. Tel: 402-471-2045.

Nevada

Joseph J. Anderson, State Libn., Nevada State Lib., Capitol Complex, Carson City 89710. Tel: 702-885-5130.

New Hampshire

Shirley Adamovich, State Libn., New Hampshire State Lib., 20 Park St., Concord 03301. Tel: 603-271-2392.

New Jersey

Barbara F. Weaver, Asst. Commissioner for Education/State Libn., Div. of State Lib., Archives & History, 185 W. State St., Trenton 08625. Tel: 609-292-6200.

New Mexico

Paul Agriesti, Acting Dir., New Mexico State Lib., 325 Don Gaspar St., Santa Fe 87503. Tel: 505-827-3804.

New York

Joseph F. Shubert, State Libn./Asst. Commissioner for Libs., Rm. 10C34, C.E.C., Empire State Plaza, Albany 12230. Tel: 518-474-5930.

North Carolina

David Neil McKay, Dir./State Libn., Dept. of Cultural Resources, Div. of State Lib., 109 E. Jones St., Raleigh 27611. Tel: 919-733-2570.

North Dakota

Ruth Mahan, State Libn., North Dakota State Lib., Liberty Memorial Bldg., Capitol Grounds, Bismarck 58505. Tel: 701-224-2492.

Ohio

Richard M. Cheski, Dir., State Lib. of Ohio, 65 S. Front St., Columbus 43215. Tel: 614-462-6843.

Oklahoma

Robert L. Clark, Jr., Dir., Oklahoma Dept. of Libs., 200 N.E. 18 St., Oklahoma City 73105. Tel: 405-521-2502.

Oregon

Kay Grasing, Acting State Libn., Oregon State Lib., Salem 97310. Tel: 503-378-4367.

Pennsylvania

Elliot L. Shelkrot, State Libn., State Lib. of Pennsylvania, Box 1601, Harrisburg 17105. Tel: 717-787-2646.

Rhode Island

Fay Zipkowitz, Dir., Dept. of State Lib. Services, 95 Davis St., Providence 02908. Tel: 401-277-2726.

South Carolina

Betty E. Callaham, State Libn., South Carolina State Lib., 1500 Senate St., Box 11469, Columbia 29211. Tel: 803-758-3181.

South Dakota

Clarence Coffindaffer, State Libn., South Dakota State Lib., State Lib. Bldg., Pierre 57501. Tel: 605-773-3131.

Tennessee

Olivia K. Young, State Libn. & Archivist, Tennessee State Lib. &

Archives, 403 Seventh Ave. N., Nashville 37219. Tel: 615-741-2451.

Texas

Dorman H. Winfrey, Dir.-Libn., Texas State Lib., Box 12927, Capitol Sta., Austin 78711. Tel: 512-475-2166.

Utah

Russell L. Davis, Dir., Utah State Lib., 2150 S. 300 W., Suite 16, Salt Lake City 84115. Tel: 801-533-5875.

Vermont

Patricia E. Klinck, State Libn., State of Vermont, Dept. of Libs., c/o State Office Bldg. Post Office, Montpelier 05602. Tel: 802-828-3261 ext. 3265.

Virginia

Donald R. Haynes, State Libn., Virginia State Lib., Richmond 23219. Tel: 804-786-2332.

Washington

Roderick G. Swartz, State Libn., Washington State Lib., Olympia 98504. Tel: 206-753-5592.

West Virginia

Frederic J. Glazer, Exec. Secy., Science & Cultural Center, West Virginia Lib. Commission, Charleston 25305. Tel: 304-348-2041.

Wisconsin

Leslyn Shires, Asst. Superintendent, Div. for Lib. Services, Dept. of Public Instruction, 125 S. Webster St., Madison 53702. Tel: 608-266-2205.

Wyoming

Wayne H. Johnson, State Libn., Wyoming State Lib., Barnett Bldg., Cheyenne 82002. Tel: 307-777-7281.

American Samoa

Sailautusi Avegalio, Federal Grants Mgr., Dept. of Educ., Box 1329, Pago Pago 96799. Tel: 633-5237.

Guam

Magdalena S. Taitano, Libn., Nieves M. Flores Memorial Lib., Box 652, Agana 96910. Tel: 472-6417.

Northern Mariana Islands

Ruth Tighe, Dir. of Lib. Services, Commonwealth of the Northern Mariana Islands, Saipan 96950. Tel: 6534.

Pacific Islands (Trust Territory of)

Harold Crouch, Chief of Federal Programs, Dept. of Educ., Trust Territory of the Pacific Islands, Saipan 96950. Tel: 9448.

Puerto Rico

Blanca N. Rivera de Ponce, Dir., Public Lib. Div., Dept. of Educ., Apartado 859, Hato Rey 00919. Tel: 809-753-9191 or 754-0750.

Virgin Islands

Henry C. Chang, Dir., Libs. & Museums, Dept. of Conservation & Cultural Affairs, Government of the Virgin Islands, Box 390, Charlotte Amalie, St. Thomas 00801. Tel: 809-744-3407.

STATE SCHOOL LIBRARY MEDIA ASSOCIATIONS

Unless otherwise specified, correspondence to an association listed in this section is to be addressed to the secretary or executive secretary named in the entry.

Alabama

Alabama Lib. Assn., Div. of Children's and School Libns. Memb. 405. Term of Office. Apr. 1982-Apr. 1983. Publication. *Alabama Librarian*.

Chpn. Betty Ruth Goodwyn, Box 405-U, Rte. One, Helena 35080; *Chpn.-Elect.* Vicky Dennis, 589 S. Forest Dr., Birmingham 35209; *Secy.* Mary Maude McCain, 548 Collette St., Birmingham 35204.

Alaska

[See entry under State, Provincial, and Regional Library Associations—*Ed.*]

Arizona

School Lib. Div. Arizona State Lib. Assn. Memb. 400. Term of Office. Nov. 1982-Sept. 1983. Publication. *ASLA Newsletter*.

Pres. Bettie Herron, Rte. 3, Box 864, Cottonwood 86326; *Pres.-Elect.* Caryl Major, 3213 W. Sunnyside Ave., Phoenix 85029; *Secy.* Diane Cole, 7919 N. Zarragoza, Tucson 85704; *Treas.* Jerry Wilson, 4148 N. 23 Dr., Phoenix 85015.

Arkansas

School Lib. Div., Arkansas Lib. Assn. Memb. 294. Term of Office. Jan. 1983-Dec. 1983.

Chpn. Frankie Halt, North Little Rock, AR.

California

California Media and Lib. Educators Assn. (CMLEA), Suite 204, 1575 Old Bayshore Hwy., Burlingame 94010. Tel. 415-692-2350. Job Hotline. 415-697-8832. Memb. 1,500. Term of Office. June 1982-May 1983. Publication. *CMLEA Journal* (ann.).

Pres. Jay Monfort, Mgr., Educational Media Center, Santa Clara County Office of Education, 100 Skyport Dr., San Jose 95115; *Pres.-Elect.* Jack Stolz, Dir., Instructional Media Services, Santa Barbara County Schools, 4400 Cathedral Oaks Rd., Santa Barbara 93111; *Past Pres.* Marian D. Copeland, Coord. Instruction Materials Center, Rialto Unified School Dist., 182 E. Walnut Ave., Rialto 92376; *Secy.* Norma Dick, Dir., Support Services, Clovis Unified School Dist., 5545 E. Herndon Ave., Clovis 93716; *Treas.* Mel Nickerson, Coord., Instructional Media Center, California State College, Stanislaus, 801 Monte Vista Ave., Turlock 95380. *Business Office Secy.* Nancy Kohn, CMLEA, 1575 Old Bayshore Hwy., Burlingame 94010.

Colorado

Colorado Educational Media Assn. Memb. 680. Term of Office. Feb. 1982-Feb. 1983. Publication. *The Medium* (mo.).

Pres. Robert Card, Colorado Springs Schools, 1036 N. Franklin, Colorado Springs 80903; *Exec. Secy.* Terry Walljasper, Colorado Educational Media Assn., Box 22814, Wellshire Sta., Denver 80222.

Connecticut

Connecticut Educational Media Assn. Term of Office. May 1982-May 1983.

Officers to be elected.

Address correspondence to Anne Weimann, Administrative Secy., 25 Elmwood Ave., Trumbull 06611. Tel. 203-372-2260.

Delaware

Delaware School Lib. Media Assn. Memb. 116. Term of Office. June 1982-June 1983. Publication. *DSLMA Newsletter.*

Pres. Cindy Hesseltine, Stokes Elementary School, 11 E. Camden-Wyoming Ave., Camden-Wyoming 19934; *V. P./Pres.-Elect.* Patricia Robertson, Conrad Jr. H.S., Jackson Ave. & Boxwood Rd., Wilmington 19804. *Secy.* Nancy Stewart, Sanford School, Hochessin 19707; *Treas.* Susan Menson, Sanford School, Hochessin 19707.

District of Columbia

D.C. Assn. of Schools Libns. Memb. 150. Term of Office. Aug. 1982-Aug. 1983. Publication. *Newsletter* (3 per year).

Pres. Etrula Williams, Shadd Elementary School, 5601 E. Capitol St. S.E., Washington 20019; *V.P./Pres.-Elect.* Patricia Copelin, Brookland School, Michigan Ave. & Randolph St. N.E., Washington 20017; *Rec. Secy.* Nathalia Ramsundar, Reed Learning Center, 2200 Champlain St. N.W., Washington 20009; *Corresp. Secy.* Dorothea Hunter, Sousa Jr. H.S., 37 St. & Ely Place S.E., Washington 20019; *Treas.* Ellevia Smith, Burroughs Elementary School, 18 & Monroe Sts. N.E., Washington 20019; *Immediate Past Pres.* Gwendolyn Cogdell, Jefferson Jr. H.S., Eight & H Sts. S.W., Washington 20024.

Florida

Florida Assn. for Media in Education, Inc. Memb. 1,400. Term of Office. Oct. 1982-Oct. 1983. Publication. *Florida Media Quarterly* (q.).

Pres. Winona Jones, 911 Manning Rd., Palm Harbor 33563; *V.P.* Ron Slawson, 4720 N.W. 16 Place, Gainesville 32601; *Pres.-Elect.* Ruth Flintom, 444 N.E. 36 St., Boca Raton 33431; *Secy.* Frances Hamilton, 4158 Kent Ave., Lake Worth 33461; *Treas.* Henrietta Smith, 1202 N.W. Second St., Delray Beach 33444.

Address correspondence to the president.

Georgia

School and Children's Lib. Div. of the Georgia Lib. Assn. Term of Office. Nov. 1981-Nov. 1983.

Chpn. Beth Johnson, Head, Children's Dept., Ida Williams Branch, Atlanta Public Lib., 269 Buckhead Ave. N.E., Atlanta 30309.

Hawaii

Hawaii Assn. of School Libns. Memb. 225. Term of Office. June 1, 1982-May 31, 1983. Publications. *The Golden Key* (ann.); *HASL Newsletter* (q.), c/o HASL, Box 23019, Honolulu 96822.

Pres. Harry Y. Uyehara; *1st V.P.* Irene Zane; *2nd V.P.* Karen Muronaga; *Rec. Secy.* Francine Grudzias; *Corres. Secy.* Lucy Fujinaka; *Treas.* Ginger Enomoto; *Dirs.* May C. Chun; Beverly Fujita.

Idaho

School Libs. Div. of the Idaho Lib. Assn. Term of Office. May 1982-May 1983. Publication. Column in *The Idaho Librarian* (q.).

Chpn. Vaughn Overlie, Libn., Genesee Public Schools, Genesee 83832; *Chpn. Elect.* Barbara Gessner, Libn., Lapwai Public School, Lapwai 83540.

Illinois

Illinois Assn. for Media in Education (IAME). (Formerly Illinois Assn. of School Libns.) Memb. 700. Term of Office. Jan. 1983-Dec. 1983. Publication. *IAME News for You* (q.). *Ed.* Charles Rusiewski, 207 E. Chester, Nashville 62263.

Pres. Ray Bouma, Media Center, Park Ridge School Dist. #64, 400 South Western Ave., Park Ridge 60068.

Indiana

Assn. for Indiana Media Educators. Memb. 950. Term of Office. *(Pres.).* Apr. 30, 1982-Apr. 30, 1983. Publication. *Indiana Media Journal.*

Pres. Gloria Haycock, Northwestern Consolidated Schools, Box 79Y, Rte. 1, Fairland 46126; *Exec. Secy.* Lawrence Reck, School of Education, Indiana State Univ., Terre Haute 47809.

Iowa

Iowa Educational Media Assn. Memb. 500. Term of Office. Apr. 1982-Apr. 1983. Publication. *Iowa Media Message* (q.). *Ed.* Donald Rieck, 121 Pearson Hall, Iowa State Univ., Ames 50011.

Pres. Charles Ruebling, 804 Gaskill, Ames 50010; *V.P./Pres.-Elect.* Pat Severson, 2406 North Shore Dr., Clear Lake 50428; *Past Pres.* Eleanor Blanks, 635-46 St., Des Moines 50312; *Secy.* Paula Behrendt, 2306 Sixth, Harlan 51537; *Treas.* Marjean Wegner, 7019 N.W. Beaver, Des Moines 50323; *Dirs.* (1983) Connie Maxson; Lee Meyer; Loretta Moon.

Kansas

Kansas Assn. of School Libns. Memb. 800. Term of Office. July 1982-June 1983. Publication. *KASL Newsletter* (s. ann.).

Pres. Martha Dirks, 332 N. Tenth, WaKeeney 67672; *V.P./Pres. Elect.* Phyllis Monyakula, 5807 W. 99, Overland Park 66207; *Treas.* Janice Ostrom, 519 Garden, Salina 67401; *Secy.* Joyce Funk, 916 S.E. Croco Rd., Topeka 66605.

Kentucky

Kentucky School Media Assn. Memb. 650. Term of Office. Oct. 1982-Oct. 1983. Publication. *KSMA Newsletter.*

Pres. James R. Connor, Rte. 12, Box 7, London 40741; *Pres.-Elect.* Jacqueline VanWilligen, 657 Montclair Dr., Lexington 40502; *Secy.* Debra L. Nimmo, 212 S. Broadway, Providence 42450; *Treas.* Sara A. Brady, 190 Breckinridge Sq., Louisville 40220.

Louisiana

Louisiana Assn. of School Libns., c/o Louisiana Lib. Assn., Box 131, Baton Rouge 70821. Memb. 415. Term of Office. July 1, 1982-June 30, 1983.

Pres. Genevieve Wheeler, 12987 N. Lake Carmel Dr., New Orleans 70128; *1st V.P./Pres.-Elect.* Kathleen C. Simms, 250 Clara Dr., Baton Rouge 70808; *2nd V.P.* Sue Hill, 6780 Nellie Ave., Baton Rouge 70805; *Secy.* Florence Brumfield, 2041 Betty Blvd., Morrero 70072; *Treas.* Marvene Dearman, 1471 Chevelle Dr., Baton Rouge 70806.

Maine

Maine Educational Media Assn. Memb. 200. Term of Office. Oct. 1982-Sept. 1983. Publication. *Mediacy* (q.).

Pres. Edna Mae Bayliss, Maranacook Community School, Readfield 04355; *Pres.-Elect.* Jean Labrecque, Bonny Eagle H.S., R.F.D. 1, West Buxton 04093; *V.P.* Marcia McGee, Sumner H.S., Sullivan; *Secy.* Thomas Peterson, Windham H.S., R.F.D. 1, South Windham 04082; *Treas.* Bruce White, Univ. of Maine at Augusta, Augusta 04330.

Maryland

Maryland Educational Media Organization. Memb. 600. Term of Office.

Oct. 1982-Oct. 1983. Publication. *MEMO-Random* (newsletter, q.).

Pres. Margaret Denman-West, Box 056, Westminster 21157; *Pres.-Elect.* Gary Ambridge, 1603 Deborah Ct., Forest Hill 21050; *Secy.* Peter Shambarger, 1286 Graff Ct., Apt. 2D, Annapolis 21403; *Treas.* Charlie O. Waggoner, Jr., 39 James Ave., Littlestown, PA 17340; *Past Pres.* Walker Jung, 235 Coldbrook Rd., Baltimore 21093.

Massachusetts

Massachusetts Assn. for Educational Media. Memb. 450. Term of Office. June 1, 1982-May 31, 1983. Publication. *Media Forum* (q.).

Pres. Edna Kotomski, 28 Strathmore Rd., Worcester 01610; *Pres.-Elect.* Garrett Mitchell, Jr., 40 Longfellow Rd., Worcester 01602; *Secy.* Connie Schlotterbeck, 5 Valley View Rd., Wayland 01778; *Treas.* Vivian Robb, 15 Beach St., Marion 02738.

Address correspondence to the president.

Michigan

Michigan Assn. for Media in Education (MAME), Univ. of Michigan, 3338 School of Education Bldg., Ann Arbor 48109. Memb. 900. Term of Office. One year. Publication. *Media Spectrum* (q.).

Pres. Mary Ann Paulin, 1205 Joliet, Marquette; *Pres.-Elect.* Jeannine Cronkhite, 19182 Lancashire, Detroit 48223; *Secy.* Cathy Marine, 4036 Hill Dr., Apt. 201, Utica 48087; *Treas.* Deborah Anthony, 1415 John R Rd., Rochester 48063; *Past Pres.* Frank Bommarito, 3167 Maumee Trail, Port Huron 48040; *Coord. of Special Interest Div.* Gayle DeEtte Harmer, 4546 Meadowlawn Dr., Port Huron 48060; *Coord. of Regions.* Katherine Walsh, 2889 E. River Rd., Mt. Pleasant 48858.

Minnesota

Minnesota Educational Media Organization. Memb. 1,200. Term of Office. May 1982-May 1983. Publication. *Minnesota Media.*

Pres. Larry Gifford, 1415 10 St. N.E., Rochester 55901; *Secy.* Norma Dickau, 114 S.E. Fourth St., Joseph 56374; *Past Pres.* Donald E. Overlie, Owatonna H.S., Owatonna 55060.

Mississippi

Mississippi Assn. of Media Educators. Memb. 70. Term of Office. Mar. 1982-Mar. 1983. Publication. *MAME* (newsletter, bi-ann.). *Ed.* Barbara Carroon, Hinds County Schools.

Pres. Joseph L. Ellison, Media Center, Jackson State Univ., Jackson 39217; *V.P./Pres.-Elect.* Edward Garcia, Univ. of Southern Mississippi; *V.P.(Membership).* Dale Sellers, Mississippi Gulf Coast Jr. College, Perkinston Campus; *Secy.* Carroll K. Cagle, Greenwood Public Schools; *Past Pres.* Joan P. Haynie, Mississippi Authority for Educational Television.

Missouri

Missouri Assn. of School Libns. Memb. 600. Term of Office. Sept. 1, 1982-Aug. 31, 1983. Publication. *MASL Newsletter* (4 per year). *Ed.* Mary Reinert, Rte. 3, Nevada 64772.

Pres. Maureen Taliaferro, Box 41, Columbia 65205; *V.P./Pres.-Elect.* Aileen Helmick, 318 Johnson, Warrensburg 64093; *Secy.* Joan Young, 1860 E. Meadow Dr., Springfield 65804; *Treas.* Dorothy Phoenix, 28 W. Winthrope Rd., Kansas City 64113.

Address correspondence to the president.

Montana

Montana School Lib. Media, Div. of Montana Lib. Assn. Memb. 170.

Term of Office. May 1982-May 1983. Publication. *Newsletter* (q.).
Chpn. Sally Mortier, Western Montana College, Dillon 59725.
Address general correspondence to MSL/MA, c/o Montana Lib. Assn., Montana State Lib., 1515 E. Sixth Ave., Helena 59620.

Nebraska

Nebraska Educational Media Assn. Memb. 400. Term of Office. July 1, l982-June 30, 1983. Publication. *NEMA Newsletter* (4 per year). *Eds.* Cliff Lowell, Box 485, E.S.U. #11, Holdrege 68949; Carol Truett, UNL Dept. of Education Admin., 200 A Teachers College, Univ. of N. Lincoln, Lincoln 68588.
Pres. Sonya Collison, Roseland Public Schools, Box 8, Roseland 68973; *Pres.-Elect.* Jean Lienemann, Sutton Public Schools, Box 590, Sutton 68979.

Nevada

Nevada Assn. of School Libns. Memb. 55. Term of Office. Jan. 1, 1983-Dec. 31, 1983.
Chpn. Merilyn Grosshans, Las Vegas H.S., 315 S. Seventh St., Las Vegas 89101.

New Hampshire

New Hampshire Educational Media Assn. Memb. 185. Term of Office. June 1982-June 1983. Publication. *Online* (irreg.).
Pres. Shelley Lochhead, Hopkinton H.S., Contoocook 03229; *Pres.-Elect.* Janet Zeller, Maple St. School, Contoocook 03229; *Treas.* Jane McKersie, Pelham H.S., Marsh Rd., Pelham 03076; *Rec. Secy.* Alice Getchell, Sanborn Regional Middle School, Newton Junction 03859; *Corres. Secy.* Marcia Burch, Jr. H.S., Claremont 03743.

Address correspondence to the president.

New Jersey

Educational Media Assn. of New Jersey (EMAnj). (Organized Apr. 1977 through merger of New Jersey School Media Assn. and New Jersey Assn. of Educational Communication and Technology.) Memb. 1,000. Term of Office. June 1982-June 1983. Publications. *Signal Tab* (newsletter, mo.); *Emanations* (journal, q.).
Pres. Mary Jane McNally, 249 Belleville Ave., Apt. 43A, Bloomfield 07003; *Pres.-Elect.* Ellie Brainard, 100B Cedar Lane, Highland Park 09804; *V.P.* Ruth Toor, 61 Greenbriar Dr., Berkeley Heights 07922; *Rec. Secy.* Leah Karpen, 9 John Circle, Norwood 07648; *Corres. Secy.* Jean Montgomery, 61 Galway Dr., Mendham 07945; *Treas.* Rosemary Skeele, 22 Winding Way, Parsippany 07054.

New Mexico

New Mexico Lib. Assn., School Libs., Young Adult Services Div. Memb. 237. Term of Office. Apr. 1982-Apr. 1983.
Chpn. Allison Almquist, 10320 San Luis Rey N.E., Albuquerque 87111.

New York

School Lib. Media Sec., New York Lib. Assn., 15 Park Row, Suite 434, New York 10038. Memb. 875. Term of Office. Nov. 1982-Nov. 1983. Publications. Participates in *NYLA Bulletin* (mo. except July and Aug.); *SLMS Gram* (s. ann.).
Pres. Margaret Johnson, Dir. of School Libs., City School Dist. of Albany, Academy Park, Elk St., Albany 12207; *1st V.P.* Helen Flowers, Lib. Media Specialist, Bay Shore H.S., 155 Third Ave., Bay Shore 11706; *2nd V.P. & SLMS Publications.* Shirley Rappaport, Lib. Media

Specialist, John Dewey H.S., 50 Ave. X, Brooklyn 11223; *Secy.* Jean Bewley, Lib. Media Specialist, Main St. Elementary School, North Syracuse Central Schools, North Syracuse 13212; *Treas.* Barbara Jones, Lib. Media Specialist, Sandy Creek Central Schools, Sandy Creek 13145.

North Carolina

North Carolina Assn. of School Libns. Memb. 900. Term of Office. Oct. 1981-Oct. 1983.

Chpn. Paula M. Fennell, 302 Colony Woods Dr., Chapel Hill 27514; *Chpn.-Elect.* Judie Davie, Dept. of Lib. Science/Educational Technology, Univ. of North Carolina at Greensboro, Greensboro 27402; *Secy.-Treas.* Connie Hull, Media Coord., Tarboro H.S., Tarboro 27886.

North Dakota

North Dakota Lib. Assn., School Lib. Media Sec. Memb. 85. Term of Office. One year. Publication. *The Good Stuff* (q.).

Pres. Neil V. Price, Box 8174, UND Sta., Grand Forks 58202; *Secy.* Maureen P. Halvorson, 319 Fifth St. S.W., Jamestown 58401.

Address correspondence to the president.

Ohio

Ohio Educational Lib. Media Assn. Memb. 1,700. Term of Office. Oct. 1983-Jan. 1984. Publication. *Ohio Media Spectrum* (q.).

Pres. Anne Hyland, Northeastern Local Schools, 1414 Bowman, Springfield 45502.

Address correspondence to the president.

Oklahoma

Oklahoma Assn. of School Lib. Media Specialists. Memb. 150. Term of Office. July 1, 1982-June 30, 1983. Publications. *School Library News* column in *Oklahoma Librarian* (q.). "Library Resources" section in *Oklahoma Educator* (mo.).

Chpn. Donnice Cochinour, 911 W. Main, Norman H.S., Norman 73069; *Chpn.-Elect.* Sybil Connelly, Windsor Hills Elementary School, 2909 Ann Arbour, Oklahoma City 73127; *Secy.* Patsy Loomis, Allen Bowden School, Box 371A, Rte. 13, Tulsa 74107; *Treas.* La Vonne Sanborn, Westwood Elementary School, 502 S. Kings Hwy., Stillwater 74074. *Past Chpn.* Letty Rains, Jefferson School, Norman 73071.

Oregon

Oregon Educational Media Assn. Memb. 800. Term of Office. Oct. 1, 1982-Sept. 30, 1983. Publication. *Interchange.*

Pres. Jim Heath, I.M.C. Director, Douglas County ESD, 1871 N.E. Stephens, Roseburg 97470; *Pres.-Elect.* Allan Quick, Supv. Lib. Services, West Linn School Dist., West Linn 97068; *Exec. Secy.* Sherry Hevland, 16695 S.W. Rosa Rd., Beaverton 97007.

Pennsylvania

Pennsylvania School Libns. Assn. Memb. 1,300. Term of Office. July 1, 1982-June 30, 1984. Publications. *Learning and Media* (4 per year); *027.8* (4 per year).

Pres. Anna Harkins, 5630 Glen Hill Dr., Bethel Park 15102; *V.P./Pres.-Elect.* Sharon Nardelli, Baldwin School, Morris & Montgomery, Bryn Mawr 19010; *Secy.* Judith B. Palmer, 28 Oxford Ct., Pittsburgh 15237; *Treas.* Hope Sebring, Box 74, Delmont 15626; *Past Pres.* Sue A. Walker, 6065 Parkridge Dr., East Petersburg 17520.

Rhode Island

Rhode Island Educational Media Assn. Memb. 225. Term of Office. June 1981-June 1983. Publications. *RIEMA* (newsletter, 9 per year).

Pres. Lillian Desrosiers, Lib. Reference Asst., Bristol Community College, 777 Elsbree St., Fall River 02720; *Pres.-Elect.* Raymond Argamache, Regional Mgr., United Camera, 155 Slade St., Tiverton 02878; *V.P.* Michael W. Mello, Dir. of Instruction, Portsmouth School Dept., Middle Rd., Portsmouth 02871; *Secy.* Arlene Luber, Media Specialist, E. Providence School Dept., 2 Jackson Walkway, Apt. 1012, Providence 02903; *Treas.* Alice Reinhardt, School Libn., Slater Jr. H.S., 55 E. Knowlton, East Providence 02915.

South Carolina

South Carolina Assn. of School Libns. Memb. 600. Term of Office. Apr. 1982-Apr. 1983. Publication. *Media Messenger* (5 per year).

Pres. Drucilla Reeves, 1500 Bradley Dr., Columbia 29204; *V.P./Pres.-Elect.* A'LaPerle Hickman, 582 Lincoln Ave. N.W., Box 2602, Aiken 29801.

South Dakota

South Dakota School Lib. Media Assn., Sec. of the South Dakota Lib. Assn. and South Dakota Education Assn. Term of Office. Oct. 1982-Oct. 1983.

Pres. Kathryn Brill, Lead H.S., Lead 57754; *Secy.* Kitty Brewer, Madison Senior H.S., Madison 57042; *Treas.* Jean Hirning, West Jr. High, Rapid City 57701.

Tennessee

Tennessee Education Assn., School Lib. Sec., 598 James Robertson Pkwy., Nashville 37219. Term of Office. June 1982-June 1983.

Chpn. Carolyn C. Daniel, 1309 Clearview Dr., Mount Juliet 37122.

Texas

Texas Assn. of School Libns. Memb. 1,800. Term of Office. Apr. 1982-Apr. 1983. Publication. *Media Matters* (2 per year).

Chpn. Carol Bramlett, 3205 41 St., Lubbock 79413; *Chpn.-Elect.* Kathryn Meharg, 2631 Pittsburg, Houston 77005; *Secy.* Mayenell Mason, 1606 Ave. R., Huntsville 77340; *Treas.* Marybeth Green, 7912 Merchant, Amarillo 79121; *Councillor.* Jo Ann Bell, Arapaho Bldg., 1300 Cypress, Richardson 75080.

Utah

Utah Educational Lib. Media Assn. Memb. 180. Term of Office. Mar. 1982-Mar. 1983. Publication. *UELMA Journal* (q.).

Pres. Sheilah Hoffman, Weber School District, 1122 Washington Blvd., Ogden 84404; *V.P./Pres.-Elect.* Marilyn Taylor, Dee Elementary School, 550 22 St., Ogden 84404; *Secy.-Treas.* Paula Zsiray, 342 N. 500 E., Logan 84321.

Utah Library Assn., Children's and Young Adult's Section. Memb. 60. Publications. *Horsefeathers* (mo.); *HATU* (q.). Term of office. March 1983-March 1984.

Chpn. protem. Marcia LeClair-Marzolf, Salt Lake City, UT 84121.

Vermont

Vermont Educational Media Assn. Memb. 114. Term of Office. May 1982-May 1983. Publication. *VEMA News* (q.).

Pres. Judith Davison, St. Albans City Elementary School, St. Albans 05478; *V.P./Pres.-Elect/Proj. Dir.* Nancy Hunt, Orchard School, South Burlington 05401; *Secy.* Tom Karlen,

Randolph Union H.S., Randolph 05060; *Treas.* Richard Hurd, RD 2, Granview Dr., Barre 05641.

Virginia

Virginia Educational Media Assn. (VEMA). Term of Office. Nov. 1982-Nov. 1983.
Pres. Gary Ellerman, Radford Univ., Box 5820, Radford 24142; *V.P./Pres.-Elect.* Mary B. Mather, 1005 Fleming Dr., #1, Virginia Beach 23451; *Secy.* Inez L. Ramsey, 282 Franklin St., Harrisonburg 22801; *Treas.* Vykuntapathi Thota, Box 5002N, Virginia State Univ., Petersburg 23808.

Washington

Washington Lib. Media Assn. Memb. 700. Term of Office. Jan. 1, 1983-Dec. 31, 1983. Publication. *The Medium* (q.); *The Newsletter* (irreg.).
Pres. Cathy McLeod, 2111 N. Walnut St., Ellensburg 98926; *Pres.-Elect.* Shirley Painter, 118 W. 23 Place, Kennewick 99336; *V.P.* Bob D. Johnson, 2511 Holly Lane, Olympia 98501; *Secy.* Nancy Graff, 1815 W. 17 Ave., Kennewick 99336; *Treas.* Barbara Baker, 18645 101 Ave. N.E., Bothell 98011.

Address correspondence to the president.

West Virginia

West Virginia Educational Assn. Memb. 350. Term of Office. Nov. 1982-Nov. 1983. Publication. *WVEMA Newsletter* (mo.).

Pres. Robert Moore, Dir. of Educational Media Services, West Virginia Wesleyan College, Buckhannon 26201; *V.P./Pres. Elect.* Tom Blevins, Bluefield State College, Bluefield 24701; *Treas.* Julia Dillinger, Kanawha County Schools, Charleston 25300; *Secy.* Lin Wilson, West Virginia Univ., Morgantown 26505; *Memb. Secy.* Trudy Berkey, West Virginia Northern Community College, New Martinsville 26155; *Past Pres.* Richard Hudson, Alderson Broaddus College, Philippi 26461.

Wisconsin

Wisconsin School Lib. Media Assn., Div. of Wisconsin Lib. Assn. Term of Office. Jan. 1983-Dec. 1983. Publication. *WLA Newsletter* (6 per year). *Ed.* Don Johnson.
Pres. Vonna Pitel, Cedarburg H.S., W63N611 Evergreen Blvd., Cedarburg 53012; *V.P./Pres.-Elect.* Roger Krentz, Platteville Public Schools, 1205 Camp St., Platteville 53818; *Secy.* Leora McGee, Milwaukee Public Schools, Milwaukee 53201; *Financial Adviser.* Neah Lohr, Reedsburg School Dist., Reedsburg 53959.

Wyoming

Wyoming School Lib. Media Assn. Memb. 25. Term of Office. May 1982-Apr. 1983.
Chpn. Frank Zielke, Box 442, Greybull 82426; *Vice-Chpn.* Sharlye Good, Box 392, Midwest 82643; *Secy.* Georgia Teske, Box 2826, Gillette 82716.

STATE SUPERVISORS OF SCHOOL LIBRARY MEDIA SERVICES

Alabama

Hallie A. Jordan, Educational Specialist, Lib. Media Services, 111 Coliseum Blvd., Montgomery 36193. Tel: 205-832-5810.

Alaska

Jo Morse, Alaska State Lib., School Lib. Media Coord., 650 International Airport Rd., Anchorage 99502. Tel: 907-274-6625.

Arizona

Mary Choncoff, Education Program Specialist, State Dept. of Educ., 1535 W. Jefferson, Phoenix 85007. Tel: 602-255-5961.

Arkansas

Betty J. Morgan, Specialist, Lib. Services, Arkansas Dept. of Educ., State Educ. Bldg., Rm. 301B, Little Rock 72201. Tel: 501-371-1861.

California

Gerald W. Hamrin, ECIA Chapter 2 Program Administrator, State Dept. of Educ., 721 Capitol Mall, Sacramento 95814. Tel: 916-445-7458.

Colorado

Boyd Dressler, Consultant, ESEA Title IV, State Dept. of Educ., 201 E. Colfax, Denver 80203. Tel: 303-866-5714.

Connecticut

Robert G. Hale, Sr. Coord., Learning Resources & Technology Unit, and Instructional Television Consultant; Betty B. Billman, Lib. Media Consultant; Elizabeth M. Glass, Computer Technology Consultant; Dorothy W. Headspeth, Info. Specialist; and Brenda H. White, Lib. Media Consultant, Learning Resources and Technology Unit, State Dept. of Educ., Box 2219, Hartford 06145. Tel: 203-566-5409.

Delaware

Richard L. Krueger, Lib. Specialist, State Dept. of Public Instruction, John G. Townsend Bldg., Box 1402, Dover 19901. Tel: 302-736-4692.

District of Columbia

Marie Haris, Asst. Dir., Dept. of Lib. Science, Public Schools of the District of Columbia, 801 Seventh St. S.W., Washington 20024. Tel: 202-724-4952.

Florida

Sandra W. Ulm, Administrator, School Lib. Media Services, State Dept. of Educ., Knott Bldg., Tallahassee 32301. Tel: 904-488-0095.

Georgia

Nancy P. Hove, Dir., Instructional Media Services, State Dept. of Educ., Suite 2054 Twin Towers E., Atlanta 30334. Tel: 404-656-2418.

Hawaii

Patsy Izumo, Dir., Multimedia Services Branch, State Dept. of Educ., 641 18 Ave., Honolulu 96816. Tel: 808-732-5535.

Idaho

Rudy H. Leverett, Coord., Educational Media Services, State Dept. of Educ., Len B. Jordan Bldg., 650 State St., Boise 83720. Tel: 208-334-2281.

Illinois

Marie Rose Sivak, Program Consultant, Lib. Media Services & Gifted Education, State Bd. of Educ., 100 N. First St., Springfield 62777. Tel: 217-782-3810.

Indiana

Phyllis Land, Dir., Div. of Federal Resources & School Improvement, State Dept. of Public Instruction, Indianapolis 46204. Tel: 317-927-0296.

Iowa

Betty Jo Buckingham, Consultant, Education Media, State Dept. of Public Instruction, Resource Center, Grimes State Office Bldg., Des Moines 50319. Tel: 515-281-3707.

Kansas

June Saine Level, Lib. Media Consultant, Educational Assistance Sec., Kansas State Dept. of Educ., 110 E. Tenth St., Topeka 66612. Tel: 913-296-3434.

Kentucky

Judy L. Cooper, Program Mgr. for School Media Services, State Dept. of Educ., 1830 Capital Plaza Tower, Frankfort 40601. Tel: 502-564-2672.

Louisiana

James S. Cookston, State Supv. of School Lib., State Dept. of Educ., Box 44064, Education Bldg., Rm. 408, Baton Rouge 70804. Tel: 504-342-3399.

Maine

John W. Boynton, Coord., Media Services, Maine State Lib., LMA Bldg., State House Sta. 64, Augusta 04333. Tel: 207-289-2956.

Maryland

Paula Montgomery, Chief, School Media Services Branch, Div. of Lib. Development & Services, State Dept. of Educ., 200 W. Baltimore St., Baltimore 21201. Tel: 301-659-2125.

Massachusetts

Position vacant. Write to: Department of Education, 1385 Hancock St., Quincy 02169. Tel. 617-770-7500.

Michigan

Francis Scannell, State Dept. of Educ., State Lib. Services, Box 30007, Lansing 48909. Tel: 517-373-1580.

Minnesota

Robert H. Miller, Supv., Educational Media Unit, State Dept. of Educ., Capitol Square Bldg., St. Paul 55101. Tel: 612-296-6114.

Mississippi

John Barlow, State Dept. of Educ., Educational Media Services, Box 771, Jackson 39205. Tel: 601-354-6864.

Missouri

Position vacant. Write to: Dept. of Elementary & Secondary Educ., Box 480, Jefferson City 65102. Tel: 314-751-4445.

Montana

Sheila Cates, Lib. Media Specialist, Office of Public Instruction, Resource Center, Capitol Bldg., 1300 11 Ave., Helena 59620. Tel: 406-449-3126.

Nebraska

Jack Baillie, Administrative Asst., State Dept. of Educ., Box 94987, 301 Centennial Mall S., Lincoln 68509. Tel: 402-471-2783.

Nevada

William F. Arensdorf, Chpn., Instructional Materials and Equipment, State Dept. of Educ., Capitol Complex, Carson City 89710. Tel: 702-885-3136.

New Hampshire

Horace L. Roberts, Educational Consultant, Libs. and Learning Resources Program, State Dept. of Educ., Div. of Instruction, 64 N. Main St., Concord 03301. Tel: 603-271-2401.

New Jersey

Anne Voss, Coord., School and College Media Services, State Dept. of Educ., State Lib., CN 520, Trenton 08625. Tel: 609-292-6256.

New Mexico

Jack McCoy, Lib. Media Specialist, State Dept. of Educ., Santa Fe 87501-2786. Tel: 505-827-6646.

New York

Beatrice Griggs, Administrator, Bur. of School Lib. Media Programs, State Educ. Dept., Albany 12234. Tel: 518-474-2468.

North Carolina

Elsie L. Brumback, Deputy Asst. State Superintendent, Dept. of Public Instruction, Raleigh 27611. Tel: 919-733-3170.

North Dakota

Patricia Herbel, Coord. of Curriculum, Dept. of Public Instruction, State Capitol, Bismarck 58505. Tel: 701-224-2281.

Ohio

Theresa M. Fredericka, Lib. Media Consultant, State Dept. of Educ., 65 S. Front St., Rm. 1005, Columbus 43215. Tel: 614-466-2761.

Oklahoma

Barbara Spriestersbach, Asst. Administrator; Pam Allen, Betty Riley, and Clarice Roads, Coords.; Lib. & Learning Resources Div., State Dept. of Educ., 2500 N. Lincoln Blvd., Oklahoma City 73105. Tel: 405-521-2956.

Oregon

George Katagiri, Coord., Instructional Technology, Oregon Dept. of Educ., 700 Pringle Pkwy. S.E., Salem 97310. Tel: 503-378-4974.

Pennsylvania

Doris M. Epler, Div. of School Lib. Media and Educational Resource Services, State Dept. of Educ., Box 911, 333 Market St., Harrisburg 17108. Tel: 717-787-6704.

Rhode Island

Richard Harrington, Coord. Consolidated Grant Programs, State Dept. of Educ. 22 Hayes St., Providence 02908. Tel: 401-277-2617.

South Carolina

Margaret W. Ehrhardt, Lib./Media Consultant, State Dept. of Educ., Rutledge Bldg., Rm. 803, Columbia 29201. Tel: 803-758-2652.

South Dakota

James O. Hansen, State Superintendent, Div. of Elementary & Secondary Education, Richard F. Kneip Bldg., Pierre 57501. Tel: 605-773-3243.

Tennessee

Christine Brown, Dir., School Lib. Resources, 111 Cordell Hull Bldg., Nashville 37219. Tel: 615-741-7856.

Texas

Mary R. Boyvey, Learning Resources Program Dir., Instructional Resources Div., Texas Education Agency, 201 E. 11 St., Austin 78701. Tel: 512-834-4081.

Utah

Bruce Griffin, Assoc. Supt., Curriculum and Instruction Div., State Office of Educ., 250 E. Fifth S., Salt Lake City 84111. Tel: 801-533-5431.

Kenneth Neal, Media Services Coord., Curriculum and Instruction Div., State Office of Educ., 250 E. Fifth S., Salt Lake City 84111. Tel: 801-533-5573.

Dorothy Wardrop, Coord., Curriculum Development, Curriculum and Instruction Div., State Office of Educ., 250 E. Fifth S., Salt Lake City 84111. Tel: 801-533-5572.

Vermont

Jean D. Battey, School Lib./Media Coord., Vermont Dept. of Educ., Montpelier 05602-2703. Tel: 802-828-3124.

Virginia

Mary Stuart Mason, Supv., School Libs. and Textbooks, State Dept. of Educ., Box 6Q, Richmond 23216. Tel: 804-225-2855.

Washington

Nancy Motomatsu, Supv., Learning Resources Services, Office of State Superintendent of Public Instruction, 7510 Armstrong St. S.W., FG-11, Tumwater 98504. Tel: 206-753-6723.

West Virginia

Carolyn R. Skidmore, Dir., ECIA Chapter 2, and Lib. Media & Learning Resources, 1900 Washington St. E., B-346, Charleston 25305. Tel: 304-348-3925.

Wisconsin

Dianne McAfee Williams, Dir., Bur. of Instructional Media and Technology, State Dept. of Public Instruction, Box 7841, Madison 53707. Tel: 608-266-1965.

Wyoming

Jack Prince, Coord., Instructional Resources, Wyoming Dept. of Educ., Hathaway Bldg., Cheyenne 82002. Tel: 302-777-6252.

American Samoa

Emma S. Fung Chen Pen, Program Dir., Office of Lib. Services, Dept. of Educ., Box 1329, Pago Pago 96799. Tel: 633-1181/1182.

Northern Mariana Islands (Commonwealth of the)

Ruth L. Tighe, Acting Head, Office of Lib. Services, CNMI Dept. of Educ., Saipan, CM 96950.

Pacific Islands (Trust Territory of)

Tamar Jordan, Supv., Lib. Services, Dept. of Educ., Majuor, Marshall Islands 96960.

Tomokichy Aisek, Supv., Lib. Services, Dept. of Educ., Truk, Caroline Islands 96942.

Puerto Rico

Blanca N. Rivera de Ponce, Dir, Public Lib. Div., Dept. of Educ., Box 759, Hato Rey 00919. Tel: 809-753-9191; 754-0750.

Virgin Islands

Fiolina B. Mills, Dir., L.S.I.M. Dept. of Educ., Box 6640, St. Thomas 00801.

INTERNATIONAL LIBRARY ASSOCIATIONS

INTER-AMERICAN ASSOCIATION OF AGRICULTURAL LIBRARIANS AND DOCUMENTALISTS
IICA-CIDIA, 7170 Turrialba, Costa Rica

OBJECT
"To serve as liaison among the agricultural librarians and documentalists of the Americas and other parts of the world; to promote the exchange of information and experiences through technical publications and meetings; to promote the improvement of library services in the field of agriculture and related sciences; to encourage the improvement of the professional level of the librarians and documentalists in the field of agriculture in Latin America."

OFFICERS
Pres. Orlando Arboleda, Info. Specialist, IICA-CIDIA, San José, Costa Rica; *V.P.* Ubaldino Dantas Machado, EMBRAPA/DID, Brasilia, Brazil; *Exec. Secy.* Ana Maria Paz de Erickson, IICA-CIDIA, 7170 Turrialba, Costa Rica. (Address correspondence to the executive secretary.)

PUBLICATIONS
AIBDA Actualidades (irreg., 5 per year).
Boletín Informativo (q.).
Boletín Especial (irreg.).
Revista AIBDA (2 per year).
Páginas de Contenido: Ciencias de la Información (3 per year).
Proceedings. Tercera Reunión Interamericana de Bibliotecarios y Documentalistas Agrícolas, Buenos Aires, Argentina, April 10-14, 1972 (U.S. price: $10 including postage). Out of print. Available in Microfiche. (Price U.S. $10).
Proceedings. Cuarta Reunión Interamericana de Bibliotecarios y Documentalistas Agrícolas, Mexico, D.F., April 8-11, 1975 (U.S. price: Memb. $5 including postage; nonmemb. $10 including postage).
Proceedings. Quinta Reunión Interamericana de Bibliotecarios y Documentalistas Agrícolas, San José, Costa Rica, April 10-14, 1978 (U.S. price: Memb. $10 plus postage; nonmemb. $15 plus postage).

INTERNATIONAL ASSOCIATION OF AGRICULTURAL LIBRARIANS AND DOCUMENTALISTS
c/o P. J. Wortley, Secy.-Treas.,
Centre for Overseas Pest Research
College House, Wrights Lane, London, England W8 5SJ

OBJECT
"The Association shall, internationally and nationally, promote agricultural library science and documentation as well as the professional interest of agricultural librarians and

documentalists." Founded 1955. Memb. 525. Dues (Inst.) $26; (Indiv.) $13.

OFFICERS (1980-1985)

Pres. E. J. Mann, England; *V.Ps.* H. Haendler, Germany; G. Paez, USA; *Secy.-Treas.* P. J. Wortley, England; *Ed.* V. Howe, England.

EXECUTIVE COMMITTEE

M. Bonnichon, France; A. d'Ambroso, Italy; L. Gregorio, Philippines; J. Hansen, Denmark; W. Laux, Germany; A. Lebowitz, Italy; A. Rutgers, Netherlands; A. G. Yaikova, USSR; representatives of national associations of agricultural librarians and documentalists.

PUBLICATION

Quarterly Bulletin of the IAALD (memb.).

INTERNATIONAL ASSOCIATION OF LAW LIBRARIES
Vanderbilt Law Library, Nashville, TN 37240, USA

OBJECT

"To promote on a cooperative, non-profit, and fraternal basis the work of individuals, libraries, and other institutions and agencies concerned with the acquisition and bibliographic processing of legal materials collected on a multinational basis, and to facilitate the research and other uses of such materials on a worldwide basis." Founded 1959. Memb. over 600 in 64 countries.

OFFICERS (1983-1986)

Pres. Igor I. Kavass, Vanderbilt Univ., Law School Lib., Nashville, TN 37240, USA; *1st V.P.* Klaus Menzinger, Bibliothek für Rechtswissenschaft der Universität Freiburg, D-7800 Freiburg, Fed. Rep. of Germany; *2nd V. P.* Ivan Sipkov, Lib. of Congress, Washington, DC 20540, USA; *Secy.* Adolf Sprudzs, Law School Lib., Univ. of Chicago, 1121 E. 60 St., Chicago, IL 60637, USA; *Treas.* Arno Liivak, Rutgers Univ., Law Lib., Camden, NJ 08102, USA.

BOARD MEMBERS (1983-1986)

Officers: Robert F. Brian, Australia; Myrna Feliciano, Philippines; Eric Gaskell, Belgium; Lajos Nagy, Hungary; Fernando de Trazegnies, Peru; Yoshiro Tsuno, Japan; Christian Wiktor, Canada; Shaikha Zakaria, Malaysia.

SERVICES

1. The dissemination of professional information through the *International Journal of Legal Information* through continuous contacts with the affiliated national groups of law librarians and through work within other international organizations, such as IFLA and FID.
2. Continuing education through the one-week IALL Seminars in International Law Librarianship annually.
3. The preparation of special literature for law librarians, such as the *European Law Libraries Guide,* and of introductions to basic foreign legal literature.
4. Direct personal contacts and exchanges between IALL members.

IALL REPRESENTATIVES

A liaison between the law librarians of their regions and the IALL administration is being appointed for every country or major area.

PUBLICATION

International Journal of Legal Information (6 per year). *Ed.-in-Chief.* Arno Liivak, Rutgers Univ. Law Lib., Camden, NJ 08120, USA; *Assoc. Ed.* Igor I. Kavass, Vanderbilt Law Lib., Nashville, TN 37240, USA; Klaus Menzinger, Bibl. für Rechtswissenschaft der Universität Freiburg, Werthmannplatz 1, 7800 Freiburg i. Br., Fed. Rep. of Germany; Ivan Sipkov, Law Lib., Lib. of Congress, Washington, DC 20540, USA; Adolf Sprudzs, Univ. of Chicago Law School, 1121 E. 60 St., Chicago, IL 60637, USA.

INTERNATIONAL ASSOCIATION OF METROPOLITAN CITY LIBRARIES
c/o P. J. Th. Schoots, Director, Gemeentebibliothek Rotterdam, Nieŭwe Markt 1, NL-3001 Rotterdam, Netherlands

OBJECT

"The Association was founded to assist the worldwide flow of information and knowledge by promoting practical collaboration in the exchange of books, exhibitions, staff, and information." Memb. 97.

OFFICERS

Pres. Pieter J. van Swigchem, Openbare Bibliothek, Bilderdijkstraat 1-7, The Hague, Netherlands; *Secy.-Treas.* Piet J. Th. Schoots, Gemeentebibliothek, Nieŭwe Markt 1, NL-3001 Rotterdam, Netherlands; *Past Pres.* Juergen Eyssen, Stadtbibliothek Hildesheimer Str. 12, D-3000 Hannover 1, Fed. Rep. of Germany. (Address correspondence to the secretary-treasurer.)

PROGRAM

A research team and correspondents are engaged in drawing up a practical code of recommended practice in international city library cooperation and in formulating objectives, standards, and performance measures for metropolitan city libraries.

PUBLICATIONS

Review of the Three Year Research and Exchange Programme 1968-1971.
Annual International Statistics of City Libraries (INTAMEL).

INTERNATIONAL ASSOCIATION OF MUSIC LIBRARIES, ARCHIVES AND DOCUMENTATION CENTRES (IAML)
Musikaliska akademiens bibliotek
Box 16 326, S-103 26, Stockholm, Sweden

OBJECT

To promote the activities of music libraries, archives, and documentation centers and to strengthen the cooperation among them, to promote the availability of all publications and documents relating to music and further their bibliographical control, to encourage the development of standards in all areas that concern the association, and to support the protection and preservation of musical documents of the past and the present. Memb. 1,800.

OFFICERS

Pres. Brian Redfern, 15 Tudor St., Canning Hanson Pk., Birmingham B18 4DG, England; *Past Pres.* Barry S. Brook, City Univ. of New York, 33 W. 42 St., New York, NY 10036, USA; *V.P.s.* Maria Calderisi, National Lib., Music Div., Ottawa K1A ON4, Canada; Janos Kárpáti, Lib. of the Liszt Ferenc Academy of Music, Box 206, H-1391 Budapest, Hungary; Nanna Schiodt, Svanevaenget 20, DK-2100 Kobenhavn O, Denmark; Heinz Werner, Berliner Stadtbibliothek, Breite Strasse 32-34, DDR-102 Berlin, German Democratic Rep.; *Secy.-Gen.* Anders Lonn, Musikaliska akademiens bibliotek, Box 16 326, S-103 26, Stockholm, Sweden; *Treas.* Wolfgang Rehm, Schiffmanngasse 18, A-5020 Salzburg, Austria.

PUBLICATION

Fontes Artis Musicae (4 per year, memb.).

COMMISSION CHAIRPERSONS

Bibliography. Maria Calderisi, National Lib., Music Div., Ottawa K1A ON4, Canada.

Broadcasting Music Libraries. Lucas van Dijck, Nederlandse Omroep Stichting, P.O.B. 10, NL-1200 JB Hilversum, Netherlands.

Cataloging. Brian Redfern, 15 Tudor St., Canning Hanson Pk., Birmingham B18 4DG, England.

International Inventory of Musical Sources. Kurt von Fischer, Laubholzstr. 46, CH-8703 Erlebach ZH, Switzerland.

International Repertory of Music Literature. Barry S. Brook, RILM Center City Univ. of New York, 33 W. 42 St., New York, NY 10036, USA.

International Repertory of Musical Iconography. Barry S. Brook, Research Center for Musical Iconography, Research Center for Musical Iconography, City Univ. of New York, 33 W. 42 St., New York, NY 10036, USA.

Libraries in Music Teaching Institutions. Anthony Hodges, Royal Northern College of Music, 124 Oxford Rd., Manchester M13 9RD, England.

Music Information Center. William Elias, Israel Music Institute, P.O.B. 11253, Tel-Aviv 61112, Israel.

Public Music Libraries. Eric Cooper, London Borough of Enfield, Music Dept., Town Hall, Green Lanes, Palmers Green, London N13 4XD, England.

Record Libraries, Claes Cnattingius, Sveriges Riksradio, Grammofonarkivet, S-10510 Stockholm, Sweden.

Research Music Libraries. Richard Andrewes, Pendlebury Lib., Univ. Music School, West Road, Cambridge CB3 9DP, England.
Service and Training. Don L. Roberts, Music Lib., Northwestern Univ., Evanston, IL 60201, USA.

US BRANCH

Pres. Geraldine Ostrove, New England Conservatory of Music, Spaulding Lib., 33 Gainsborough St., Boston, MA 02115; *Secy.-Treas.* Don L. Roberts, Music Lib., Northwestern Univ., Evanston, IL 60201.

UK BRANCH

Pres. John May, 5 Hotham Rd., London SW15 1QN; *Gen. Secy.* Susan M. Clegg, Birmingham School of Music, Paradise Circus, Birmingham B3 3HG; *Hon. Treas.* Pam Thompson, Royal College of Music Lib., Prince Consort Rd., London SW7 2BS.

PUBLICATION

BRIO. Ed. Clifford Bartlett, BBC Music Lib., Yalding House, London WIN 6AJ (2 per year; memb.).

INTERNATIONAL ASSOCIATON OF ORIENTALIST LIBRARIANS (IALO)
c/o Secretary/Treasurer, Rosa M. Vallejo
The National Library Building, Rm. 405,
T. M. Kalaw St., Manila, Philippines 2801

OBJECT

"To promote better communication among Orientalist librarians and libraries, and others in related fields, throughout the world; to provide a forum for the discussion of problems of common interest; to improve international cooperation among institutions holding research resources for Oriental Studies." The term Orient here specifies the Middle East, East Asia, and the South and Southeast Asia regions.
Founded in 1967 at the 27th International Congress of Orientalists in Ann Arbor, Michigan. Affiliated with the International Federation of Library Associations and Institutions (IFLA).

OFFICERS

Pres. Serafin D. Quiason; *Secy.-Treas.* Rosa M. Vallejo, Rm 405, The National Lib. Building, T. M. Kalaw St., Manila, Philippines 2801; *Ed.* Eloise Van Niel, 3888 Monterey Dr., Honolulu, HI 96816.

PUBLICATION

International Association of Orientalist Librarians Bulletin (s. ann., memb.).

INTERNATIONAL ASSOCIATION OF SCHOOL LIBRARIANSHIP
School of Librarianship, Western Michigan Univ., Kalamazoo, MI 49008

OBJECT

"To encourage the development of school libraries and library programs throughout all countries; to promote the professional preparation of school librarians; to bring about close collaboration among school libraries in all countries, including the loan and exchange of literature; to initiate and coordinate activities, conferences and other projects in the field of school librarianship." Founded 1971. Memb. (Indiv.) 600; 19 (Assn.).

OFFICERS & EXECUTIVE BOARD

Pres. Amy Robertson, Jamaica, West Indies; *V.P.* Michael Cooke, Aberystwyth, Wales; *Treas.* Anne Shafer, Evanston, IL, U.S.A.; *Exec. Secy.* Jean Lowrie, Kalamazoo, MI, U.S.A.; *Dirs.* David Elaturoti, Nigeria, Africa; Valerie Packer, Artarmon, Australia; John G. Wright, Alberta, Canada; Axel Wisbom, Hellerup, Denmark; Mieko Nagajura, Kanagawa, Japan; Rosario de Horowitz, Berkeley, CA, U.S.A./Caracas, Venezuela.

PUBLICATIONS

IASL Newsletter (q.).
IASL Conference Proceedings (ann.).
IASL Monograph Series.
Directory of Nationalk School Library Associations.
Persons to Contact for Visiting School Libraries/Media Centers

AMERICAN MEMBERSHIPS

American Assn. of School Libs.; Hawaii School Lib. Assn.; Maryland Educational Media Organization; Oregon Educational Media Assn.

INTERNATIONAL ASSOCIATION OF SOUND ARCHIVES
c/o Helen Harrison, Media Librarian, Open University Library, Walton Hall, Milton Keynes, MK7 6AA, England

OBJECT

IASA is a UNESCO-affiliated organization established in 1969 to function as a medium for international cooperation between archives and other institutions that preserve recorded sound documents. This association is involved with the preservation, organization, and use of sound recordings; techniques of recordings and methods of reproducing sound; the international exchange of literature and information; and in all subjects relating to the professional work of sound archives.

MEMBERSHIP

Open to all categories of archives, institutions, and individuals who preserve sound recordings or have a serious interest in the purposes or welfare of IASA.

OFFICERS (1981-1984)

Pres. David G. Lance, Keeper of the Dept. of Sound Records, Imperial War Museum, Lambeth Rd., London SE1 6HZ, England; *V.P.s.* Peter Burgis, National Lib. of Australia, Sound Recordings Lib., Canberra City, A.C.T. 2600, Australia; Dietrich

Schüller, Phonogrammarchiv der Österreichischen Akademie der Wissenshaften, Liebiggasse 5, A-1010 Vienna, Austria; Rolf Schuursma, Erasmus Universiteit, Universiteitsbibliotheek, Burg. Oudlaan 50, NL-3062 PA Rotterdam, Netherlands; *Ed.* Ann Briegleb, Music Dept. Univ. of California, Los Angeles, CA 90024, USA; *Secy.* Helen P. Harrison, Media Libn., Open Univ. Lib., Walton Hall, Milton Keynes MK7 6AA, England; *Treas.* Ulf Scharlau, Süddeutscher Rundfunk, Schallarchiv/Bandaustausch, Neckarstr. 230, D-7000 Stuttgart 1, Fed. Rep. of Germany.

PUBLICATIONS

An Archive Approach to Oral History.
Directory of IASA Member Archives, 2nd Ed., 1982.
Phonographic Bulletin (3 per year, memb. or subscription).

INTERNATIONAL COUNCIL ON ARCHIVES
Secretariat, 60 rue des Francs-Burgeois
F-75003 Paris, France

OBJECT

"To establish, maintain, and strengthen relations among archivists of all lands, and among all professional and other agencies or institutions concerned with the custody, organization, or administration of archives, public or private, wherever located." Established 1948. Memb. 690 (representing 109 countries). Dues (Indiv.) $25; (Inst.) $50; (Archives Assns.) $50 or $100 (Central Archives Directorates) $200 minimum, computed on the basis of GNP and GNO per capita.

OFFICERS

Pres. Alfred W. Mabbs; *V.P.s.* Dagfinn Mannsaker, Ms. Soemartini; *Exec. Secy.* C. Kescketméti; *Treas.* Alfred Wagner.
(Address all correspondence to the executive secretary.)

PUBLICATIONS

Archivium (ann.; memb. or subscription to Verlag Dokumentation München, Possenbacker Str. 2, Postfach 71 1009, D-8 Munich 71, Fed. Rep. of Germany).
ICA Bulletin (s. ann.; memb., or U.S. $5).
Microfilm Bulletin (subscriptions to Centro Nacional de Microfilm, serrano 15, Madrid 6, Spain).
ADPA—Archives and Automation (ann. 250 FB or U.S. $9 memb.; subscriptions to M. Jean Pieyns, Archives de l'Etat, rue Pouplin, 8, B-4000 Liege, Belgium).
Guides to the Sources of the History of Nations (Latin American Series, 10 vols. pub.; African Series, 9 vols. pub.; Asian Series, 3 vols. pub.).
Archival Handbooks (8 vols. pub.).

INTERNATIONAL FEDERATION FOR DOCUMENTATION
Box G0402, 2509 LK The Hague, Netherlands

OBJECT

To group internationally organizations and individuals interested in the problems of documentation and to coordinate their efforts; to promote the study, organization, and practice of documentation in all its forms, and to contribute to the creation of an international network of information systems.

PROGRAM

The program of the federation includes activities for which the following committees have been established: Central Classification Committee (for UDC); Research on the Theoretical Basis of Information; Linguistics in Documentation; Information for Industry; Education and Training; Classification Research; Terminology of Information and Docmentation; Patent Information and Docmentation; Social Sciences Documention; Informetrics. It also includes the BSO Panel (Broad System of Ordering).

OFFICERS

Pres. Ricardo A. Gietz, CAICYT, Moreno 431/33, 1091 Buenos Aires, Argentina; *V.P.s.* S. Fujiwara, Dept. of Chemistry, Chiba Univ., Yoyoi-cho 1-3, Chiba, Japan; M. W. Hill, Science Reference Libn., British Lib., 25 Southhampton Bldgs., Chancery Lane, London, England; A. I. Mikhailov, VINITI, Baltijskaja ul. 14, Moscow A219, USSR; *Treas.* Margarita Almada de Ascencio, Mexico City, Mexico; *Councillors.* Yone Sepulveda Chastinet, Brasilia, Brazil; Emilia Currás, Madrid, Spain; I. Essaid, Baghdad, Iraq; Peggy Wai Chee Hochstadt, Singapore; A. van der Laan, The Hague, Netherlands; P. Lázár, Budapest, Hungary; E.-J. von Ledebur, Bonn, Fed. Rep. of Germany; S. S. Ljungberg, Södertälje, Sweden; Elmer V. Smith, Ottawa, Canada; Marcel Thomas, Paris, France; Neva Tudor-Silović, Azgreb, Yugoslavia; Mu'azu H. Wali, Lagos, Nigeria; *Belgian Member.* Monique Jucquois-Delpierre, La Hulpe, Belgium; *Secy.-Gen.* K. R. Brown, The Hague, Netherlands; *Pres., FID/CLA.* A. L. Carvalho de Miranda, Brasilia, Brazil; *Pres., FID/CAO.* B. L. Burton, Hong Kong.

(Address all correspondence to the secretary-general.)

PUBLICATIONS

FID News Bulletin (mo.) with supplements on document reproduction (q.).
Newsletter on Education and Training Programmes for Information Personnel (q.).
International Forum on Information and Documentation (q.).
R & D Projects in Documentation and Librarianship (bi-mo.).
FID Directory (bienn.).
FID Publications (ann.).
FID Annual Report (ann.).
Proceedings of congresses; Universal Decimal Classification editions; manuals; directories; bibliographies on information science, documentation, reproduction, mechanization, linguistics, training, and classification.

MEMBERSHIP

Approved by the FID Council; ratification by the FID General Assembly.

AMERICAN MEMBERSHIP

U.S. Interim National Committee for FID.

INTERNATIONAL FEDERATION OF FILM ARCHIVES
Secretariat, Coudenberg 70, B-1000 Brussels, Belgium

OBJECT

"To facilitate communication and cooperation between its members, and to promote the exchange of films and information; to maintain a code of archive practice calculated to satisfy all national film industries, and to encourage industries to assist in the work of the Federation's members; to advise its members on all matters of interest to them, especially the preservation and study of films; to give every possible assistance and encouragement to new film archives and to those interested in creating them." Founded in Paris, 1938. 69 members in 50 countries.

EXECUTIVE COMMITTEE
(JUNE 1981-JUNE 1983)

Pres. Wolfgang Klaue, DDR; *V.Ps.* Eileen Bowser, USA; David Francis, UK; Raymond Borde, France; *Secy.-Gen.* Robert Daudelin, Canada; *Treas.* Jan de Vaal, Netherlands. (Address correspondence to B. Van der Elst, executive secretary, at headquarters address.)

COMMITTEE MEMBERS

Todor Andreykov, Bulgaria; Guido Cincotti, Italy; M. Gonzalez-Casanova, Mexico; Eva Orbanz, Fed. Rep. of Germany; Anna-Lena Wibom, Sweden.

PUBLICATIONS

Film Preservation (available in English or French).
The Preservation and Restoration of Colour and Sound in Films.
Film Cataloging.
Handbook for Film Archives (available in English or French).
International Directory to Film & TV Documentation Sources.
International Index to Film and Television Periodicals (cards service).
International Index to Film Periodicals (cumulative volumes).
Guidelines for Describing Unpublished Script Materials.
Annual Bibliography of FIAF Members' Publications.
Proceedings of the FIAF Symposiums: 1977: L'Influence du Cinema Sovietique Muet Sur le Cinema Mondial/The Influence of Silent Soviet Cinema on World Cinema; 1978: Cinema 1900-1906; 1980: Problems of Selection in Film Archives.

INTERNATIONAL FEDERATION OF LIBRARY ASSOCIATIONS AND INSTITUTIONS (IFLA)
c/o The Royal Library, Box 95312,
2509 CH The Hague, Netherlands

OBJECT

"To promote international understanding, cooperation, discussion, research, and development in all fields of library activity, including bibliography, information services, and the education of library personnel, and to provide a body through which librarianship can be represented in matters of international interest." Founded 1927. Memb. (Lib. Assns.) 155; (Insti.) 762; (Aff.) 101; 115 countries.

OFFICERS AND EXECUTIVE BOARD

Pres. Else Granheim, Dir., Norwegian Directorate for Public and School Libs., Oslo, Norway; *1st V.P.* Ljudmila Gvishiani, Dir., State Lib. of Foreign Literature, Moscow, USSR; *2nd V.P.* Hans-Peter Geh, Dir., Württembergische Landsbibliothek, Stuttgart, Fed. Rep. of Germany; *Treas.* Marie-Louise Bossuat, Dir., Bibliographical Center of the National Lib., Paris, France; *Exec. Bd.* G. Rückl, Dir., Central Lib. Institute, Berlin, DDR; E. R. S. Fifoot, Pres., Three Rivers Books, Ltd., Oxford, UK; Jean Lowrie, Prof., School of Libnshp., Western Michigan Univ., Kalamazoo, Mich,. USA; J. S. Soosai, Rubber Research Institute of Malaysia, Kuala Lumpur, Malaysia; *Ex officio Members.* Henriette Avram, Chirman, Professional Bd., Dir. for Processing System, Networks, and Automation Planning, Lib. of Congress, Washington D.C., USA; Rutherford D. Rogers, Chairman, Programme Management Committee, Dir., Yale Univ. Lib., New Haven, Conn., USA; *Secy.-Gen.* Margareet Wijnstroom, IFLA Headquarters; *Dir.,* *IFLA International Office for Universal Bibliographic Control.* D. Anderson, c/o Reference Div., British Lib., London, UK; *Dir., IFLA Office for International Lending.* M. B. Line, c/o British Lib. Lending Div., Boston Spa, Wetherby, West Yorkshire, UK; *Publications Officer.* W. R. H. Koops, Univ. Libn., Groningen, Netherlands; *Professional Coord.* A. L. van Wesemael, IFLA headquarters.

PUBLICATIONS

IFLA Annual.
IFLA Journal (q.).
IFLA Directory (biennial).
IFLA Publications Series.
International Cataloguing (q.).

AMERICAN MEMBERSHIP

American Lib. Assn.; Art Libs. Society of North America; Assn. of American Lib. Schols.; Assn. of Research Libs.; International Assn. of Law Libs.; International Assn. of Orientalist Libns.; International Assn. of School Libns.; Medical Lib. Assn.; Special Libs. Assn. *Institutional Members:* There are 134 libraries and related institutions that are institutional members or affiliates of IFLA in the United States (out of a total of 903), and 37 Personal Affiliates (out of a total of 87).

INTERNATIONAL INSTITUTE FOR CHILDREN'S LITERATURE AND READING RESEARCH
Mayerhofg. 6, A-1040 Vienna, Austria

OBJECT

"To create an international center of work and coordination; to take over the tasks of a documentations center of juvenile literature and reading education; to mediate between the individual countries and circles dealing with children's books and reading." Established Apr. 7, 1965. Dues. Austrian schillings 250 (with a subscription to *Bookbird);* Austrian schillings 270 (with a subscription of *Bookbird* and *Jugend und Buch).*

PROGRAM

Promotion of international research in field and collection and evaluation of results of such research; international bibliography of technical literature on juvenile reading; meetings and exhibitions; compilation and publication of recommendation lists; advisory service; concrete studies on juvenile literature; collaboration with publishers; reading research.

OFFICERS

Pres. Adolf März; *Hon. Pres.* Josef Stummvoll; *V.P.* Otwald Kropatsch; *Dir.* Lucia Binder; *V.-Dir.* Viktor Böhm. (Address all inquiries to director at headquarters address.)

PUBLICATIONS

Bookbird (q.; memb. or Austrian schillings 250 [approx. $14]).
Jugend und Buch (memb. or Austrian schillings 120 [approx. $7]).
Schriften zur Jugendlekture (series of books and brochures dealing with questions on juvenile literature and literary education in German).

INTERNATIONAL ORGANIZATION FOR STANDARDIZATION
ISO Central Secretariat
1 r. de Varembé, Case postale 56, CH-1211 Geneva 20, Switzerland

OBJECT

To promote the development of standards in the world in order to facilitate the international exchange of goods and services and to develop mutual coperation in the spheres of intellectual, scientific, technological, and economic activity.

OFFICERS

Pres. D. C. Kothari, India; *V.P.* Jan Ollner, Sweden; *Secy.-Gen.* Olle Sturen, Sweden.

TECHNICAL WORK

The technical work of ISO is carried out by over 160 technical committees. These include:

TC 46-Documentation (Secretariat, DIN Deutsches Institut fur Normung, 4-10, Burggrafenstr., Postfach 1107, D-1000 Berlin 30). Scope: Standardization of practices relating to libraries, documentation and information centers, indexing and abstracting services, archives, information science, and publishing.

TC 37—Terminology (Principles & Coordination) (Secretariat, Osterreisches Normungsinstitut, Leopoldgasse 4, A-1020 Vienna, Austria). Scope: Standardization of methods for setting up and coordinating national and international standardized terminologies.

TC 97—Computers & Information Processing (Secretariat, American National Standards Institute ANSI, 1430 Broadway, New York, NY 10018, USA). Scope: Standardization in the area of computers and associated information processing systems and peripheral equipment, devices, and media related thereto.

PUBLICATIONS

Catalogue (ann.).
Memento (ann.).
Bulletin (mo.).
Liaisons
Member Bodies.

FOREIGN LIBRARY ASSOCIATIONS

The following list of regional and national foreign library associations is a selective one. For a more complete list with detailed information, see *International Guide to Library, Archival, and Information Science Associations* by Josephine Riss Fang and Alice H. Songe (R. R. Bowker, 1980). The *Guide* also provides information on international associations, some of which are described in detail under "International Library Associations" (immediately preceding this section). A more complete list of foreign and international library associations also can be found in *International Literary Market Place* (R. R. Bowker), an annual publication.

REGIONAL

Africa

International Assn. for the Development of Documentation, Libs. & Archives in Africa, *Secy.* Zacheus Sunday Ali, Box 375, Dakar, Senegal.

Standing Conference of African Lib. Schools, c/o School of Libns., Archivists & Documentalists, Univ. of Dakar, B. P. 3252, Dakar, Senegal.

Standing Conference of African Univ. Libs., Eastern Area (SCAULEA), c/o Univ. Libn., Univ. of Nairobi, Kenya.

Standing Conference of African Univ. Libs., Western Area (SCAULWA), c/o M. Jean Aboghe-Obyan, Bibliotheque Universitaire, Univ. Omar Bongo, Libreville., Gabon.

Standing Conference of East African Libns., c/o Tanzania Lib. Assn., Box 2645, Dar-es-Salaam, Tanzania.

The Americas

Asociación de Bibliotecas Universitarias, de Investigación e Institucionales del Caribe (Assn. of Caribbean Univ., Research & Institutional Libs.), *Gen. Secy.* Oneida R. Ortiz, Apdo. Postal S. Estación de la Universidad, San Juan, PR 00931.

Asociación Latinoamericana de Escuelas de Bibliotecologia y Ciencias de la Información (Latin American Assn. of Schools of Lib. and Info. Science), Colegio de Bibliotecologia, Universidad Nacional Autónoma de México, México 20, D. F., Mexico.

Seminar on the Acquisition of Latin American Lib. Materials, SALALM Secretariat, *Exec. Secy.* Suzanne Hodgman. Memorial Lib., Univ. of Wisconsin-Madison, Madison, WI 53706.

Asia

Congress of Southeast Asian Libns. (CONSAL), *Chpn.* Patricia Lim, c/o Singapore Lib. Assn., National Lib., Stamford Rd., Singapore 6, Republic of Singapore.

British Commonwealth of Nations

Commmonwealth Lib. Assn., c/o The Library Assn., 7 Ridgmount St., London WC1E 7AE.

Standing Conference on Lib. Materials on Africa (SCOLMA), c/o *Secy.* P. M. Larby, Institute of Commonwealth Studies, 27 Russell Sq., London WC1B 5DS, England.

Europe

LIBER (Ligue des Bibliothèques Européenes de Recherche), Assn. of European Research Lib., c/o R. Mathys, Zentralbibliothek Zürich,

Zahringerplatz 6, Postfach 8025, Zürich, Switzerland.

Nordiska Vetenskapliga Bibliotekarieförbundet (Scandinavian Assn. of Research Libns.), c/o Chefbibliotekarie Tor Holm, Svenska Handelshögskolans bibliotek, Arkadiagatan 22, SF-00100 Helsingfors 10, Finland.

NATIONAL

Afghanistan

Anjuman Kitab-Khana-l (Afghan Lib. Assn.), *Exec. Secy.* Eidi M. Khoursand, Box 3142, Kabul.

Argentina

Asociación Argentina de Bibliotecas y Centros de Información Científicos y Técnicos (Argentine Assn. of Scientific & Technical Libs. & Info. Centers), Santa Fe 1145, Buenos Aires. Exec. Secy. Olga E. Veronelli.

Australia

Australian School Lib. Assn., c/o *Secy.* Box 80, Balmain N.S.W. 2041.

Lib. Assn. of Australia, *Exec. Dir.* Susan Acutt, 376 Jones St., Ultimo, NSW 2007.

Lib. Automated Systems Info. Exchange (LASIE), *Pres.* Dorothy Peake, Box 602, Lane Cove, N.S.W. 2066

The School Lib. Assn. of New South Wales, c/o *Secy.*, Box 80, Balmain N.S.W. 2041.

State Libns.' Council of Australia, *Chpn.* W. L. Brown, State Lib. of Tasmania, 91 Murray St., Hobart, Tasmania 7000.

Austria

Österreichische Gesellschaft für Dokumentation und Information—ÖGDI (Austrian Society for Documentation and Info.), *Exec. Secy.* Bruno Hofer, c/o ON, Österreichisches Normungsinstitut, Leopoldsgasse 4, POB 130, A-1021 Vienna.

Verband Österreichischer Volksbüchereien und Volksbibliothekare (Assn. of Austrian Public Libs. & Libns.), *Exec. Secy.* Rudolf Müller, Langegasse 37, A-1080 Vienna.

Vereinigung Österreichischer Bibliothekare—VÖB (Assn. of Austrian Libns.), *Pres.* Ferdinand Baumgartner, c/o Österreichische Nationalbibliothek, Josefsplatz 1, A-1015 Vienna.

Belgium

Association Belge de Documentation-ABD/Belgische Vereniging voor Documentatie-BVD (Belgian Assn. for Documentation), PB 110, 1040 Brussels 26. *Pres.* De Backer Roger.

Association des Archivistes et Bibliothécaires de Belgique/Vereniging van Archivarissen en Bibliothecarissen van België (Belgian Assn. of Archivists & Libns.) *Exec. Secy.* T. Verschaffel, Bibliothèque Royale Albert I, 4 bd. de l'Empereur, B-1000 Brussels.

Association des Bibliothécaries–Documentalistes de l'Institute d'Etudes Sociales de l'Etat (Assn. of Libns. & Documentalists of the State Institute of Social Studies). *Secy.* Claire Gerard, 24 rue de l'Abbaye, B-1050 Brussels.

Vereniging van Religieus-Wetenschappelijke Bibliothécarissen (Assn. of Theological Libns.) Minderbroederstr. 5, B-3800 St. Truiden. *Exec. Secy.* K. Van de Casteele, Spoorweglaan 237, B-2610 Wilrijk.

Vlaamse Vereniging voor Bibliotheek, Archief, en Documentatiewezen—VVBAD (Flemish Assn. of Libns., Archivists, & Documentalists) *Pres.* E. Heidbuchel; *Secy.* F. Franssens; Goudbloemstraat 10, 2000 Antwerpen.

Bolivia

Asocicación Boliviana de Bibliotecarios (Bolivian Lib. Assn.), *Pres.* Efraín Virreira Sánchez, Casilla 992, Cochabamba.

Brazil

Associação dos Arquivistas Brasileiros (Assn. of Brazilian Archivists), Praia de Botafogo 186, Sala B-217, CEP 22253 Rio do Janeiro, RJ. *Pres.* Lia Temporal Malcher.

Federaçáo Brasiliera de Associações de Bibliotecários (Brazilian Federation of Lib. Assns.), c/o *Pres.* Elizabeth Maria Ramos de Carvalho, rua Humberto de Campos 366, ap. 1302, 22430 Rio de Janeiro, R.J.

Bulgaria

Bulgarian Union of Public Libraries, ul. Alabin, Sofia.

Sekciylna na Bibliotechnite Rabotnitsi pri Zentrainija Komitet na Profesionalniya Suyuz na Rabotnicite ot Poligrafičeskata Promišlenost i Kulturnite Instituti (Lib. Sec. at the Trade Union of the Workers in the Polygraphic Industry & Cultural Institutions), c/o Cyril and Methodius National Lib. blvd., Tolbuhin. *Pres.* Stefan Kancev.

Canada

Association Canadienne des Écoles des Bibliothecaires (Canadian Assn. of Lib. Schools), *Pres.* Samuel Rothstein, School of Libnshp., Univ. of British Columbia, Vancouver, B.C. V6T 1WS.

Association pour l'avancement des sciences et des techniques de la documentation (ASTED, Inc.), *Dir.-Gen.* Lise Brousseau, 7243 rue Saint-Denis, Montréal, P.Q. H2R 2E3.

Canadian Lib. Assn., *Exec. Dir.* Paul Kitchen, 151 Sparks St., Ottawa, Ont. K1P 5E3. (For detailed information on the Canadian Lib. Assn. and its divisions, see "National Library and Information Industry Associations, U.S. and Canada"; for information on the library associations of the provinces of Canada, see "State, Provincial, and Regional Library Associations.")

Conseil Canadien des Écoles Bibliothéconomie (CCLS/CCEB) (Canadian Council of Lib. Schools), *Pres.* William J. Cameron, Dean, School of Lib. & Info. Science, Univ. of Western Ontario, London, Ont. N6A 5B9, Canada.

Association Canadienne de Science de l'Information (Canadian Assn. for Info. Science), c/o Robert Leitch, 47 Gore St. E., Perth, Ont. K7H 1H6.

La Société Bibliographique du Canada (Bibliographical Society of Canada), *Secy.-Treas.* Eleanor E. Magee, Box 1110, Sta. B, London, Ont. N6A 5K2.

Chile

Colegio de Bibliotecarios de Chile, A. G. (Chilean Lib Assn.) *Pres.* Ursula Schadich Schonhals; *Secy. Gen.* Eliana Bazán del Campo, Casilla 3741, Santiago.

China, People's Republic of

Library Assn. of China, c/o National Central Lib., 43 Nan Hai Rd., Taipei. *Exec. Dir.* Karl M. Ku.

Zhongguo Tushuguan Xuehui (China Society of Lib. Science [CSLS]), *Secy.-Gen.* Tan Xiangjin; 7 Wenjinjie, Beijing (Peking).

Colombia

Asociación Colombiana de Bibliotecarios—ASCOLBI (Colombian Assn. of Libns.), Apdo. Aéreo 30883, Bogotá, D.E.

Colegio Colombiana de Bibliotecarios—CCB (Colombian Academy of Libns.), Apdo. Aéreo 1307, Medellin.

Costa Rica

Asociación Costarricense de Bibliotecarios (Assn. of Costa Rican Libns.), Apdo. Postal 3308, San José.

Cyprus

Kypriakos Synthesmos Vivliothicarion (Lib. Assn. of Cyprus), c/o Pedagogical Academy, Box 1039, Nikosia. *Secy.* Paris G. Rossos.

Czechoslovakia

Ústřední knihovnická rada CSR (Central Lib. Council of the Czechoslovak Socialist Republic), *Chief, Dept. of Libs.* Marie Sedláčková, c/o Ministry of Culture of CSR, Valdštejnská 10, Prague 1-Malá Strana.

Zväz slovenských knihovníkov a informatikov (Assn. of Slovak Libns. & Documentalists), *Pres.* Vít Rak; *Exec. Secy.* Štefan Kimlička, Michalská 1, 814 17 Bratislava.

Denmark

Arkivforeningen (The Archives Society), *Exec. Secy.* Erik Gobel, Rigsarkivet, Regsdagsgarden 9, DK-1218 Copenhagen K.

Danmarks Biblioteksforening (Danish Lib. Assn.), *Pres.* K. J. Mortensen, Trekronergade 15, DK-2500 Valby-Copenhagen.

Danmarks Forskningsbiblioteksforening (Danish Research Lib. Assn.), *Pres.* M. Laursen Vig, c/o Roskilde Universitetsbibliotek, Box 258, DK-4000, Roskilde.

Danmarks Skolebiblioteksforening (Assn. of Danish School Libs.), *Exec. Secy.* Niels Jacobsen, Frankrigsgade 4, 2300 Kobenham S.

Dansk Musikbiblioteksforening, Dansk sektion of AIBM (Danish Assn. of Music Libs., Danish Sec. of AIBM) c/o *Secy.*, Irlandsvej 90, DK-2300 Copenhagen K.

Dominican Republic

Asociación Dominicana de Bibliotecarios—ASODOBI (Dominican Lib. Assn.), c/o Biblioteca Nacional, Plaza de la Cultura, Santo Domingo. *Pres.* Prospero J. Mella Chavier; *Secy. Gen.* Hipólito González C.

Ecuador

Asociación Ecuatoriana de Bibliotecarios—AEB (Ecuadorian Lib. Assn.), *Exec. Secy.* Elizabeth Carrion, Casa de la Cultura Ecuatoriana, Casilla 87, Quito.

Egypt

See United Arab Republic.

El Salvador

Asociación de Bibliotecarios de El Salvador (El Salvador Lib. Assn.), c/o *Secy.-Gen.* Edgar Antonio Pérez Borja, Urbanización Gerardo Barrios Polígono, "B" No. 5, San Salvador, C.A.

Ethiopia

Ye Ethiopia Betemetsahft Serategnot Mahber (Ethiopian Lib. Assn. [ELA]) *Exec. Secy.* Asrat Tilahun, Box 30530, Addis Ababa.

Finland

Kirjastonhoitajaliitto-Bibliotekarieförbundet r.y. (Finnish Libns. Assn.), *Exec. Secy.* Anna-Maija Hintikka, Temppelikatu 1 A 12, SF-00100 Helsinki 10.

Suomen Kirjastoseura-Finlands Biblioteksförening (Finnish Lib. Assn.), *Exec. Secy.* Hilkka M. Kauppi, Museokatu 18, SF-00100 Helsinki 10.

Tieteellisten Kirjastojen Virkailijat-Vetenskapliga Bibliotekens Tjänstemannaförening ry (Assn. of Research & Univ. Libns.), *Exec. Secy.* Kirsti Janhunen, Temppelikatu 1 A 12, 00100 Helsinki 10.

Tietopalveluseura-Samfundet för Informationstjänst i Finland (Finnish Society for Information Services), c/o *Pres.* Ritva Launo, The State Alcohol Monopoly of Finland (ALKO), Helsinki.

France

Association des archivistes français (Assn. of French Archivists), *Pres.* M. Charnier; *Exec. Secys.* Mme. Rey-Courtel and Mlle. Etienne, 60 r. des Francs-Bourgeois, F-75141 Paris, CEDEX 03.

Association des Bibliothèques ecclésiastiques de France (Assn. of French Theological Libs.), *Exec. Secy.* Paul-Marie Guillaume, 6 rue du Regard, F-75006 Paris.

Association des Bibliothécaires Français (Assn. of French Libns.), *Exec. Secy.* Jean-Marc Léri, 65 rue de Richelieu, F-75002 Paris.

Association Française des Documentalistes et des Bibliotécaires Spécialisés—ADBS (Assn. of France Info. Scientists & Special Libns.), *Exec. Secy.* R. Maes, 5, av. Franco russe, 75007 Paris.

German Democratic Republic

Bibliotheksverband der Deutschen Demokratischen Republik (Lib. Assn. of the German Democratic Republic), c/o *Exec. Secy.* Hermann-Matern-Str. 57, DDR-1040 Berlin.

Germany, Federal Republic of

Arbeitsgemeinschaft der Hochschulbibliotheken (Working Group of Univ. Libs.), *Chpn.* H. Sontag, c/o Universitätsbibliothek der Technischen Universität Berlin, Strasse des 17. Juni 135, D-1000 Berlin 12.

Arbeitsgemeinschaft der Kunstbibliotheken (Working Group of Art Libs.), *Exec. Secy.* Jürgen Zimmer, Bibliothek des Zentralinstituts für Kungstgeschichte in München, Meiserstr. 10, D-8000 München 2.

Arbeitsgemeinschaft der Spezialbibliotheken (Assn. of Special Libs.), *Chpn.* Walter Manz, Zentralbibliothek der Kernforschungsanlage Jülich GmbH, Postfach 1913, D-5170 Jülich 1.

Deutsche Gesellschaft für Dokumentation, e.V.—DGD (German Society for Documentation), *Scientific Secy.* Hilde Strohl-Goebel, Westendstr. 19, D6000 Frankfurt am Main 1.

Deutscher Bibliotheksverband (German Lib. Assn.), *Secy.* Victoria Scherzberg. Bundesallee 184/185, 1000 Berlin 31.

Verband der Bibliotheken des Landes Nordrhein-Westfalen (Assn. of Libs. in the Federal State of North Rhine-Westphalia), *Chpn.* Johannes Schultheis, Direktor, Stadtbücherei Bochum, Vorsitzender, Rathausplatz 2-6, 4630 Bochum.

Verein der Bibliothekare an Öffentlichen Bibliotheken (Assn. of Libns. at Public Libs.), *Secy.* Roonstr. 57, 2800 Bremen 1.

Verein der Diplom-Bibliothekare an Wissenschaftlichen Bibliotheken (Assn. of Graduated Libns. at Academic Libs.). *Chpn.* Ulla Usemann-Keller, c/o Deutsches Bibliotheksinstitut, Bundesallee 184/185, D-1000 Berlin 31.

Verein Deutscher Archivare—VDA (Assn. of German Archivists), *Chpn.* Eckhart Franz, Hessisches Staatsarchiv, Schloss, D-6100 Darmstadt.

Verein Deutscher Bibliothekare e.V.—VDB (Assn. of German Libns.), *Pres.* Ltd. Bibliotheksdirektor Jürgen Hering; *Secy.* Robert K. Jopp, Universitätsbibliothek Stuttgart, Postfach 506, Holzgartenstrasse 16, D-7000 Stuttgart 1.

Ghana

Ghana Lib. Assn., *Exec. Secy.* P. Amonoo, Box 4105, Accra, Ghana.

Greece

Enosis Ellenon Bibliothakarion (Greek Lib. Assn.), Box 2118, Athens-124.

Guatemala

Asociación Bibliotecológica Guatemalteca (Lib. Assn. of Guatemala), c/o *Dir.*, 18 Avenida "A," 4-04 Zona 15 V.H.I., Guatemala, C.A.

Guyana

Guyana Lib. Assn. (GLA), *Secy.* Wenda Stephenson, c/o National Lib., Box 10240, 76/77 Main St., Georgetown.

Honduras

Asociación de Bibliotecarios y Archivistas de Honduras (Assn. of Libns. & Archivists of Honduras), *Secy.-Gen.* Juan Angel Ayes R., 3 Av. 4y5C., no. 416, Comayagüela, DC, Tegucigalpa.

Hong Kong

Hong Kong Lib. Assn., *Pres.* R. W. Frenier, c/o Lib., Univ. of Hong Kong, Pofulam Rd., Hong Kong.

Hungary

Magyar Könyvtárosok Egyesülete (Assn. of Hungarian Libns.), *Secy.* D. Kovács, Box 244, H-1368 Budapest. Tájékoztatási Tudományos Társaság—MTESZ/TTT (Info. Science Society), c/o Pál Gágyor, Kossuth ter 6-8, Budapest 1055.

Iceland

Bókavarðafélag Islands (Icelandic Lib. Assn.), *Pres.* Eiríkur Th. Einarsson, Box 7050, 127 Reykjavík.

India

Indian Assn. of Special Libs. & Info. Centres (IASLIC), *Exec. Secy* S. K. Kapoor, P-291. CIT Scheme 6M, Kankurgachi, Calcutta 700 054.

Indian Lib. Assn. (ILA), *Pres.* P. B. Mangla; *Secy.* O. P. Trikha, A/40-41, No. 201, Ansal Bldgs., Dr. Mukerjee Nagar, Delhi 110009.

Indonesia

Ikatan Pustakawan Indonesia—IPI (Indonesian Lib. Assn.), *Pres.* Mastini Hardjo Prakoso; *Secy.* Soemarno HS, Jalan Merdeka Selatan 11, Jakarta-Pusat.

Iran

Iranian Lib. Assn., *Exec. Secy.* M. Niknam Vazifeh, Box 11-1391, Tehran.

Iraq

Iraqi Lib. Assn., *Exec. Secy.* N. Kamal-al-Deen, Box 4081, Baghdad-Adhamya.

Ireland

Cumann Leahbharlann Na h-Éireann (Lib. Assn. of Ireland), *Pres.* S. Bohan; *Hon. Secy.* N. Hardiman, Thomas Prior House, Merrion Rd., Dublin 4.

Cumann Leabharlannaith Scoile—CLS (Irish Assn. of School Libns.), Headquarters: The Lib., Univ. College, Dublin 4. *Exec. Secy.* Sister Mary Columban, Loreto Convent, Foxrock Co., Dublin.

Italy

Associazione Italiana Biblioteche—AIB (Italian Libs. Assn.), *Secy.* A. M. Caproni, c/o Istituto di Patologia del Libro, Via Milano 76, 00184 Rome.

Associazione Nazionale Archivistica Italiana—ANAI (National Assn. of Italian Archivists), *Secy.* Antonio Dentoni-Litta, Via di Ponziano 15, 00152 Rome.

Ente Nazionale per le Biblioteche Popolari e Scholastiche (National Assn. for Public & Academic Libs.), Via Michele Mercati 4, 1-00197 Rome.

Federazione Italiana delle Biblioteche Popolari—FIBP (Federation of Italian Public Libs.) c/o La Società Umanitaria, Via Davario 7, Cap. N., 1-20122 Milan.

Ivory Coast

Association pour le Développement de la Documentation, des Bibliothèques et Archives de las Côte d'Ivoire (Assn. for the Devolopment of Documentation, Libs. & Archives of the Ivory Coast), c/o Bibliothèque Nationale, B.P. 20915 Abidjan.

Jamaica

Jamaica Lib. Assn. (JLA), *Secy.* Hermine C. Salmon, Box 58, Kingston 5.

Japan

Nihon Toshokan Kyôkai (Japan Lib. Assn. [JLA]) *Secy.-Gen.* Hitoshi Kurihara, 1-10, Taishido 1-chome, Setagaya-ku, Tokyo 154.

Nippon Dokumentêsyon Kyôkai—NIPDOK (Japan Doucumentation Society) *Exec. Secy.* Tsunetaka Ueda, Sasaki Bldg., 5-7 Koisikawa 2-chome, Bunkyô-ku, Tokyo 112.

Senmon Toshokan Kyôgikai—SENTOKYO (Japan Special Lib. Assn.), *Exec. Dir.* Kenjiro Okamura, c/o National Diet Lib., 1-10-1 Nagata-cho, Chiyoda-ku, Tokyo 100.

Jordan

Jordan Lib. Assn. (JLA), *Pres.* Anwar Akroush; *Secy.* Medhat Mar'ei; *Treas.* Butros Hashweh, Box 6289, Amman.

Korea, Democratic People's Republic of

Lib. Assn. of the Democratic People's Republic of Korea, *Secy.* Li Geug, Central Lib., Box 109, Pyongyang.

Korea, Republic of

Hanguk Tosogwan Hyophoe (Korean Lib. Assn.), *Exec. Secy.* Dae Kwon Park, 100-177, 1-Ka, Hoehyun-Dong, Choong-Ku, CPO Box 2041, Seoul.

Laos

Association des Bibliothécaires Laotiens (Laos Lib. Assn.), Direction de la Bibliothèque Nationale, Ministry of Education, Box 704, Vientiane.

Lebanon

Lebanese Lib. Assn. (LLA), V.P. L. Hanhan, Saab Medical Lib., AUB, Beirut.

Malaysia

Persatuan Perpustakaan Malaysia—PPM (Lib. Assn. of Malaysia), *Secy.* Aizan Mohd. Ali, Box 2545, Kuala Lumpur.

Mauritania

Association Mauritanienne des Bibliothécaires, des Archivistes et des Documentalistes—AMBAD (Mauritanian Assn. of Libns., Archivists & Documentalists), c/o *Pres.* Oumar Diouwara, Dir., National Lib., Nouakchott.

Mexico

Asociación de Bibliotecarios de Instituciónes de Enseñanza Superior e Investigación—ABIESI (Assn. of Libns. of Higher Education & Research Institutions), *Pres.* Elsa Barberena, Apdo. Postal 5-611, México 5, D.F.

Asociación Mexicana de Bibliotecarios, A.C. (Mexican Assn. of Libns.), *Pres.* Adolfo Rodriquez, Apdo. 27-102, Mexico 7, D.F.

Colegio Nacional de Bibliotecarios—CNB (Mexico National College of Librariana), *Pres.* Estela Morales,

Apdo. Postal 20-697, 01000 Mexico, D.F.

Netherlands

Nederlandse Vereniging van Bedrijfsarchivarissen—NVBA (Netherlands Assn. of Business Archivists), *Secy.* C. L. Groenland, Aalsburg 25 26-6602 WD Wijchen.

Nederlandse Vereniging van Bibliothecarissen, Documentalisten en Literatuuronderzoekers—NVB (Dutch Lib. Assn.), p/a Mw. H. J. Krikke-Scholten, Nolweg 13 d, 4209 AW Schelluinen.

UKB-Samenwerkingsverband van de Universiteits- en Hogeschoolbibliotheken en de Koninklijke Bibliotheek (Assn. of Univ. Libs. & the Royal Lib.), *Exec. Secy.* J. L. M. van Dijk, c/o Bibliotheek Rijksuniversiteit Limburg, Postbus 616, 6200 MD Maastricht.

Vereniging va Archivarissen in Nederland—VAN (Assn. of Archivists in the Netherlands), *Exec. Secy.* A. W. M. Koolen, Postbus 897, 8901 BR Leeuwarden.

Vereniging voor het Theologisch Bibliothecariaat (Assn. of Theological Libns.), *Exec. Secy.* R. T. M. Van Dijk, Postbus 289, 6500 AG Nijmegen.

New Zealand

New Zealand Lib. Assn. (NZLA), *Pres.* J. D. MacLean; *Exec. Officer* H. Stephen-Smith, 20 Brandon St., Box 12-212, Wellington 1.

Nicaragua

Asociación de Bibliotecas Universitarias 6 Especializadas de Nicaragua—ABUEN (Assn. of Univ. & Special Libs. of Nicaragua), *Secy.* Cecilie Aguilar Briceño, Biblioteca Central, Universidad Nacional Autónoma de Nicaragua, Apdo. No. 68, León.

Nigeria

Nigerian Lib. Assn. (NLA), c/o *Hon. Secy.* E. O. Ejiko, P.M.B. 12655, Lagos.

Norway

Arkivarforeningen (Assn. of Archivists), *Secy.-Treas.* Atle Steinar Nilsen, Postboks 10, Kringsja, Oslo 8.

Norsk Bibliothekforening—NBF (Norwegian Lib. Assn.), *Secy.-Treas.* G. Langland, Malerhaugveien 20, Oslo 6.

Norske Forskningebibliotekarers Forening—NFF (Assn. of Norwegian Research Libns.). *Secy.* G. Langland, Malerhaugveien 20, Oslo 6.

Pakistan

Pakistan Lib. Assn. (PLA), *Exec. Secy.* A. H. Siddiqui, c/o Pakistan Institute of Development Economics, Univ. Campus, Box 1091, Islamabad.

Society for the Promotion & Improvement of Libs. (SPIL), *Pres.* Hakim Mohammed Said, Al-Majeed, Hamdard Centre, Nazimabad, Karachi-18.

Panama

Asociación Panameña de Bibliotecarios (Panama Assn. of Libns.), c/o Apdo. 6991, Panama 5, Republic of Panama.

Papua New Guinea

Papua New Guinea Lib. Assn. (PNGLA), *Secy.* Rhonda Eva, Box 5368, Boroko, PNG.

Paraguay

Asociación de Bibliotecarios Universitarios del Paraguay—ABUP (Paraguayan Assn. of Univ. Libns.), c/o Zayda Caballero, Head, Escuela de Bibliotecología, Universidad Nacional de Asunción, Casilla de Correo, 1408 Asunción, Paraguay.

Peru

Agrupación de Bibliotecas para la Integración de la Información Socio-Económica—ABIISE (Lib. Group for the Integration of Socio-Economic Info.), *Dir.* Isabel Olivera Rivarola, Apdo. 2874, Lima 100.

Asociación Peruana de Archiveros (Assn. of Peruvian Archivists), Archivo General de la Nación, C. Manuel Cuadros s/n., Palacio de Justicia, Apdo. 3124, Lima 100.

Asociación Peruana de Bibliotecarios (Assn. of Peruvian Libns.), *Exec. Secy.* Amparo Geraldino de Orban, Apdo. 3760, Lima.

Philippines

Assn. of Special Libs. of the Philippines (ASLP), *Pres.* Susima Lazo Gonzales, Box 4118, Manila.

Philippine Lib. Assn. Inc. (PLAI), *Pres.* Filomena M. Tann, c/o National Lib., Teodoro M. Kalaw St., Manila.

Poland

Stowarzyszenie Bibliotekarzy, Polskich—SBP (Polish Libns. Assn.), *Pres.* Stefan Kubów; *Gen. Secy.* Wladyslawa Wasilewska, ul. Konopczyńskiego 5/7, 00953 Warsaw.

Portugal

Associação Portuguesa de Bibliotecários, Arquivistas e Documentalistas—BAD (Portuguese Assn. of Libns., Archivists & Documentalists), *Exec. Secy.* José Garcia Sottomayor, Rua Ocidental ao Campo Grande 83, 1751 Lisboa.

Rhodesia

See Zimbabwe.

Romania, Socialist Republic of

Asociatia Bibliotecarilor din Republica Socialista Romania/Association des Bibliothecaires de la République Socialiste de Roumanie), *Pres.* G. Botez, Biblioteca Centrala de Stat, Strada Ion Ghica 4, 7001 8 Bucharest.

Scotland

See United Kingdom

Senegal

Commission des Bibliothèques de l'ASDBAM, Association Sénégalaise pour le Développement de la Documentation, des Bibliothèques, des Archives et des Musées (Senegal Assn. for the Development of Documentation, Libs., Archives & Museums), *Gen. Secy.* Miss Aïssatou Wade, B.P. 375, Dakar.

Sierra Leone

Sierra Leone Lib. Assn. (SLLA), c/o *Secy.* F. Thorpe, Sierra Leone Lib. Bd., Rokell St., Freetown.

Singapore

Congress of Southeast Asian Libns. (CONSAL), *Chpn.* Mrs. Hedwig Anuar, c/o National Lib., Stamford Rd., Singapore 0617.

Lib. Assn. of Singapore (LAS), *Hon. Secy.*, c/o National Lib., Stamford Rd., Singapore 0617.

South Africa

South African Lib. Assn., c/o Lib., Univ. of the North, Private Bag X5090, Pietersburg 0700.

Spain

Asociación Nacional de Bibliotecarios, Archiveros, Arqueólogos y Documentalists (National Assn. of Libns., Archivists & Archeologists), *Exec. Secy.* C. Iniguez, Paseo de Calvo Sotelo 22, Apdo. 14281, Madrid 1.

Sri Lanka (Ceylon)

Sri Lanka Lib. Assn. (SLLA). *Exec. Secy.* N. A. T. de Silva, c/o

Univ. of Colombo, Race Course, Reid Ave., Colombo 7.

Sudan
Sudan Lib. Assn. (SLA), *Exec. Secy.* Mohamed Omar, Box 1361, Khartoum.

Sweden
Svenska Arkivasamfundet (Swedish Assn. of Archivists), Rijksarkivet, Fack, S-100, 26 Stockholm.
Svenska Bibliotekariesamfundet—SBS (Swedish Assn. of Univ. & Research Libs.), c/o *Secy.* Birgit Antonsson, Uppsala universitets-bibliotek, Box 510, S-75120 Uppsala.
Sveriges Allmänna Biblioteksförening—SAB (Swedish Lib. Assn.), *Pres.* B. Martinsson, Box 1706, S-221 01 Lund.
Sveriges Vetenskapliga Specialbiblioteks Förening—SVSF, (Assn. of Special Research Libs.), *Pres.* W. Odelberg; *Secy.* Ingrid Björkman, c/o Statens Psykologisk-Pedagogiska Bibliothek, Box 50063, 104 05 Stockholm.
Tekniska Litteratursällskapet—TLS (Swedish Society for Technical Documentation), *Secy.* Birgitta Levin, Box 5073, S-10242 Stockholm 5.
Vetenskapliga Bibliotekens Tjänstemannaförening—VBT (Union of Univ. & Research Libs.), *Pres.* Lillemor Lundström, The Royal Lib., Box 5039, S-102 41 Stockholm.

Switzerland
Schweizerische Vereingung für Dokumentation/Association Suisse de Documentation—SVD/ASD (Swiss Assn. of Documentation), *Secy.-Treas.* W. Bruderer, BID GD PTT 3030 Berne.
Vereinigung Schweizerischer Archivare—VSA (Assn. of Swiss Archivists), c/o *Pres.* Walter Lendi, Staatsarchivar, Staatsarchiv St. Gallen, Regierungsgebäude, CH 9901, St. Gallen.
Vereinigung Schweizerischer Bibliothkare/Association des Bibliothécaires Suisses/Associazione dei Bibliotecari Svizzeri—VSB/ABS (Assn. of Swiss Libns.), *Exec. Secy.* W. Treichler, Hallwylstrasse 15, CH-3003 Bern.

Tanzania
Tanzania Lib. Assn., *Exec. Secy.* T. E. Mlaki, Box 2645, Dar-es-Salaam.

Trinidad and Tobago
Lib. Assn. of Trinidad & Tobago (LATT), *Secy.* L. Marcelle, Box 1177, Port of Spain, Trinidad.

Tunisia
Tunisian Assn. of Docmentalists, Libns. & Archivists (Association Tunisienne des Documentalistes, Bibliothécaires et Archivistes), *Exec. Secy.* Rudha Tlili, 43 rue de la Liberté, Le Bardo.

Turkey
Türk Kütüphaneciler Derneği—TKD (Turkish Libns. Assn.), *Exec. Secy.* Nejat Sefercioglu, Necatibey Caddesi 19/22, P.K. 175, Yenisehir, Ankara.

Uganda
Uganda Lib. Assn. (ULA), *Chpn.* P. Birungi; *Secy.* J. N. Kiyimba, Box 5894, Kampala.
Uganda Schools Lib. Assn. (USLA), *Exec. Secy.* J. W. Nabembezi, Box 7014, Kampala.

Union of Soviet Socialist Republics
USSR Lib. Council, *Pres.* N. S. Kartashov, Lenin State Lib., 3 Prospect Kalinina, 101 000 Moscow.

United Arab Republic
Egyptian Lib. and Archives Assn. (ELAA), *Exec. Secy.* Ahmed M.

Mansour, c/o Lib. of Fine Arts, 24 El-Matbáa, Al-Ahlia, Boulaq, Cairo. Egyptian School Lib. Assn. (ESLA), *Exec. Secy.* M. Alabasiri, 35 Algalaa St., Cairo.

United Kingdom

ASLIB (Association of Special Libraries & Information Bureaux), *Dir.* Dr. D. A. Lewis, 3 Belgrave Sq., London SW1 X8PL.

Assn. of British Theological and Philosophical Libs. (ABTAPL), *Hon. Secy.* Mary Elliott, King's College Lib., Strand, London WC2R 2LS.

Bibliographical Society, *Hon. Secy.* M. M. Foot, British Lib., Reference Div., Great Russell St., London WC1B 3DG.

British & Irish Assn. Of Law Libns. (BIALL), *Hon. Secy.* D. M. Blake, Libn., Harding Law Lib., Univ. of Birmingham, Box 363, Birmingham B15 2TT.

The Lib. Assn., *Exec. Secy.* Keith Lawrey, 7 Ridgmount St., London WCIE 7AE.

Private Libs. Assn. (PLA), *Exec. Secy.* Frank Broomhead, Ravelston, South View Rd., Pinner, Middlesex.

School Lib. Assn. (SLA), *Chpn.* Elizabeth King; *Exec. Secy.* Miriam Curtis. Victoria House, 29-31 George St., Oxford OX1 2AY.

Scottish Lib. Assn. (SLA), *Hon. Secy.* Robert Craig, Dept. of Libnshp., Univ. of Strathclyde, Livingstone Tower, Glasgow G1 1XH.

Society of Archivists (SA), *Exec. Secy.* C. M. Short, South Yorkshire County Record Office, Cultural Activities Centre, 56 Ellin St., Sheffield S1 4PL.

The Standing Conference of National & Univ. Libs. (SCONUL), *Exec. Secy.* A. J. Loveday, Secretariat & Registered Office, 102 Euston St., London NW1 2HA.

Welsh Lib. Assn.., *Exec. Secy.*, c/o County Lib. Headquarters, County Civic Centre, Mold, Clwyd CH7 6NW.

Uruguay

Agrupación Bibliotecológica del Uruguay—ABU (Lib. & Archive Science Assn. of Uruguay), *Pres.* Luis Alberto Musso, Cerro Largo 1666, Montevideo.

Venezuela

Colegio de Bibliotecólogos y Archivólogos de Venezuela—COL-BAV (Assn. of Venezuelan Libns. & Archivists), *Exec. Secy.* M. Hermoso, Apdo. 6283, Caracas 101.

Wales

See United Kingdom.

Yugoslavia

Društvo Bibliotekara Bosne i Hercegovine—DB BiH (Lib. Assn. of Bosnia & Herzegovina), *Exec. Secy.* Fahrudin Kalender, Obala 42, YU-71000 Sarajevo.

Društvo Bibliotekarjev Slovenije—DBS (Society of Libns. in Slovenia), *Exec. Secy.* Ana Martelanc, Turjaška 1, YU-61000 Ljubljana.

Hrvatsko bibliotekarsko društvo—HBD (Croatian Lib. Assn.), *Pres.* Mira Mikačić; *Exec. Secy.* Irina Pažameta, National & Univ. Lib., Marulićev trg 21, YU-41000 Zagreb.

Savez Bibliotečkih Radnika Srbije (Union of Lib. Workers of Serbia), *Exec. Secy.* Branka Popović, Skerlićeva 1, YU-11000 Belgrade.

Sojuz na društvata na bibliotekarite na SR Makedonija (Union of Librarians Association of Macedonia), Bul. "Goce Delčev" br. 6, Box 566, YU-91000 Skopje.

Savez Društava Bibliotekara Jugoslavije (Union of Libns. Assns. of Yugoslavia), 21000 Novi Sad. *Pres.* R. Vukoslavović; *Secy.* D. Bajić.

Zaire

Association Zairoise des Archivistes, Bibliothecaires, et Documentalistes—AZABDO (Zairian Assn. of Archivists, Libns. & Documentalists), *Exec. Secy.* Mulamba Mukunya, Box 805, Kinshasa XI.

Zambia

Zambia Lib. Assn. (ZLA), Box 32839, Lusaka.

Zimbabwe

Zimbabwe Lib. Assn.—ZLA, *Hon. Secy.* R. Molam, Box 3133, Harare.

Directory of Book Trade and Related Organizations

BOOK TRADE ASSOCIATIONS, UNITED STATES AND CANADA

For more extensive information on the associations listed in this section, see the annual issues of the *Literary Market Place* (Bowker).

Advertising Typographers Assn. of America, Inc., 461 Eighth Ave., New York, NY 10001. 212-594-0685.

American Booksellers Assn., Inc., 122 E. 42 St., New York, NY 10168. 212-867-9060. *Pres.* Donald Laing; *Exec. Dir.* G. Roysce Smith.

American Institute of Graphic Arts, 1059 Third Ave., New York, NY 10021. 212-752-0813. *Pres.* David Brown; *Exec. Dir.* Caroline W. Hightower.

American Medical Publishers Assn. *Pres.* Albert E. Meier, W. B. Saunders, W. Washingtion Sq., Philadelphia, PA 19105. 215-574-4700; *Pres. Elect.* Mercedes Bierman, Wiley Medical, John Wiley & Sons, Inc., 605 Third Ave., New York, NY 10158. 212-850-6000; *Secy.-Treas.* Lewis Reines, Churchill-Livingstone, Inc., 1560 Broadway, New York, NY 10036. 212-819-5400.

American Printing History Assn., Box 4922, Grand Central Sta., New York, NY 10163. *Pres.* Morris A. Gelfand; *V.P.s* Marie Korey, John Hench, Terry Belanger; *Secy.* Anna Lou Ashby; *Treas.* Philip Sperling; *Ed., Printing History.* Susan O. Thompson; *Ed. & Asst. Ed., The*

Apha Letter. Catherine T. Brody, Philip Sperling.
Address correspondence to APHA, Box 4922.

American Society for Information Science (ASIS), 1010 16 St. N.W., Washington, DC 20036. 202-659-3644.

American Society of Indexers, 235 Park Ave. S., 8 fl., New York, NY 10003. *Pres.* Mauro Pittaro, Jr., Engineering Info. Inc., 345 E. 47 St., New York, NY 10017. 212-705-7603.

American Society of Journalists & Authors, 1501 Broadway, Suite 1907, New York, NY 10036. *Pres.* June Roth; *Exec. V.P.* John Ingersoll; *V.P.s* Dodi Schultz, Ruth Winter; *Secy.* Evelyn Kaye; *Treas.* Alden Todd. 212-997-0947.

American Society of Magazine Photographers (ASMP), 205 Lexington Ave., New York, NY 10016. 212-889-9144. *Dir.* Stuart Kahan.

American Society of Picture Professionals, Inc., Box 5283, Grand Central Sta., New York, NY 10017. *Pres.* Roberta Groves, 212-682-6626; *Secy.* Alice Lundoff, 212-888-3595.

American Translators Assn., 109 Croton Ave., Ossining, NY 10562.

630

914-941-1500. *Pres.* Ben Teague; *Staff Administrator.* Rosemary Malia.

Antiquarian Booksellers Assn. of America, Inc., 50 Rockefeller Plaza, New York, NY 10020. 212-757-9395. *Pres.* E. Woodburn; *V.P.* L. Weinstein; *Secy.* J. Lowe; *Treas.* R. Wapner; *Admin. Asst.* Janice M. Farina.

Assn. of American Publishers, One Park Ave., New York, NY 10016. 212-689-8920. *Pres.* Townsend Hoopes; *V.P.s* Thomas D. McKee, Donald A. Eklund; *Dirs.* Phyllis Ball, Joan Cunliffe, Parker B. Ladd, Mary E. McNulty, Saundra L. Smith; *Washington Office.* 1707 L St. N.W., Washington, DC 20336. 202-293-2585; *V.P.* Richard P. Kleeman; *Dirs.* Roy H. Millenson, Diane G. Rennert, Carol A. Risher; *Chpn.* Alexander J. Burke, Jr., McGraw-Hill International; *V. Chpn.* Brooks Thomas, Harper & Row; *Secy.* David R. Godine, David R. Godine Publisher; *Treas.* Donald A. Schaefer, Prentice-Hall.

Assn. of American Univ. Presses, One Park Ave., New York, NY 10016. 212-889-6040. *Pres.* David H. Gilbert; *Dir.*, Univ. of Nebraska Press; *Exec. Dir.* Richard Koffler.

Address correspondence to the executive director.

Assn. of Book Travelers, c/o *Pres.* Edward Ponger, 21 Colingwood Rd., Marlboro, NJ 07746; *Treas.* Vicki Brooks, Cerberus Group; *Secy.* Conrad Heintzelman.

Address correspondence to the president.

Assn. of Canadian Publishers, 70 The Esplanade, Toronto, Ont., M5E IR2 Canada. 416-361-1408. *Pres.* Denis Deneau; *V.P.* Rob Sanders; *Treas.* Harry Van Ierssel; *Secy.* D. Rogosin. *Exec. Dir.* Phyllis Yaffe.

Address correspondence to the secretary.

Assn. of Jewish Book Publishers, House of Living Judaism, 838 Fifth Ave., New York, NY 10021. *Pres.* Sol Scharfstein.

Address correspondence to the president.

Bibliographical Society of America. *See* National Library & Information-Industry Associations, United States and Canada, earlier in Part 7, for more detailed information—*Ed.*

Book Industry Study Group, Inc., 160 Fifth Ave., New York, NY 10010. 212-929-1393. *Chpn.* DeWitt C. Baker; *V. Chpn.* Howard Willets, Jr.; *Treas.* George Q. Nichols; *Secy.* Hendrik Edelman; *Managing Agent.* SKP Associates.

Address correspondence to Sandra K. Paul.

Book League of New York. *Pres.* Alfred H. Lane, Columbia Univ. Lib., New York, NY 10027. 212-280-3532; *Treas.* A. C. Frasca, Jr., Freshet Press Inc., 90 Hamilton Rd., Rockville Centre, NY 11570. 506-766-3011.

Book Manufacturers Institute, 111 Prospect St., Stamford, CT 06901. 203-324-9670. *Pres.* B. Carl Jones, Pres., Haddon Craftsmen, Inc., Ash Street & Wyoming Ave., Scranton, PA 18509; *Exec. V.P.* Douglas E. Horner.

Book Publicists of Southern California, 6430 Sunset Blvd., Suite 503, Hollywood, CA 90028. 213-461-3921. *Pres.* Irwin Zucker; *V.P.* Sol Marshall; *Secy.* Elsie Rogers; *Treas.* Steven Jay Rubin.

Book Week Headquarters, Children's Book Council, Inc., 67 Irving Place, New York, NY 10003. 212-254-2666. *Exec. Dir.* John Donovan;

Chpn. 1983. Phyllis Larkin, Macmillan Publishing Co., 866 Third Ave, New York, NY 10022. 212-935-2000.

The Bookbinders' Guild of New York, c/o *Secy.* Joel Moss, A. Horowitz and Sons, 300 Fairfield Rd., Fairfield, NJ 07006. 201-575-7070; *Pres.* Sam Green, Murray Printing Co., 60 E. 42 St., New York, NY 10017; *V.P.* Thomas R. Snyder, Dikeman Laminating, 181 Sargeant Ave., Clifton, NJ 07013; *Treas.* Eugene Sanchez, William Morrow & Co., 105 Madison Ave., New York, NY 10016. *Asst. Secy.* Hank Perrine, John Wiley & Sons Inc., 605 Third Ave., New York, NY 10158.

Bookbuilders of Boston, Inc., c/o *Pres.* Richard O. Sales, Houghton Mifflin Co., One Beacon St., Boston, MA 02108. 617-725-5580; *1st V.P.* Martin B. Sweeney, The Alpine Press, 100 Alpine Circle, Stoughton, MA 02072. 617-341-1800.

Bookbuilders of Southern California, 5225 Wilshire Blvd., Suite 316, Los Angeles, CA 90036. *Pres.* Bert Johnson, Graphics Two, 6090 W. Pico Blvd., Los Angeles, CA 90035; *V.P.* Mike Downa, Arcata Book Group, 7120 Hayvenhurst, Van Nuys, CA 91406; *Secy.-Treas.* Joan Valentine, Knapp Communications, Inc., 5900 Wilshire Blvd., Los Angeles, CA 90036.

Bookbuilders West, 170 Ninth St., San Francisco, CA 94103. *Pres.* Sharon Hawkes Grant, 90 Wilson Dr., Framingham, MA. 617-875-7585; *V.P.* Pam Smith, Carpenter/Offutt Paper Co., 333 Oyster Point Blvd., S. San Francisco, CA 94080. 415-873-1383; *Secy.* Alan Sarles, Color Tech Corp., 780 Broadway, Redwood City, CA 94063. 415-365-8788; *Treas.* Bob Odell, University of California Press, 2223 Fulton St., 4th fl., Berkeley, CA 94720. 415-642-5394. (Address correspondence to the secretary.)

Canadian Book Publishers' Council, 45 Charles St. E., 7 fl., Toronto, ON M4Y 1S2, Canada. 416-964-7231. *Pres.* Geoffrey Dean, John Wiley & Sons Canada Ltd.; *1st V.P.* Alan Cobham, Nelson, Canada; *Exec. Dir.* Jacqueline Hushion; *Member Organizations.* The School Group, The College Group, The Trade Group, The Paperback Group.

Canadian Booksellers Assn., 49 Laing St., Toronto, Ont. M4L 2N4, Canada. 416-469-5976. *Exec. Dir.* Bernard E. Rath; *Convention Mgr.* Irene Read.

Chicago Book Clinic, 664 N. Michigan Ave., Suite 720, Chicago, IL 60611. 312-951-8254. *Pres.* Stuart J. Murphy, Ligature Publishing Services, Inc.; *Exec. V.P.* Trudi Jenny, Follett Publishing Co.; *Treas.* Brad Heywood, John F. Cuneo Co.

Chicago Publishers Assn., c/o *Pres.* Robert J. R. Follett, Follett Corp., 1000 W. Washington Blvd., Chicago, IL 60607. 312-666-4300.

The Children's Book Council, 67 Irving Place, New York, NY 10003. 212-254-2666. *Exec. Dir.* John Donovan; *Assoc. Dir.* Paula Quint; *Asst. Dir.* Christine Stawicki; *Pres.* Janet Schulman, V.P & Ed.-in-Chief, Juvenile Books, Random House, 201 E. 50 St., New York, NY 10022. 212-751-2600.

Christian Booksellers Assn., Box 200, 2620 Venetucci Blvd., Colorado Springs, CO 80901. 303-576-7880. *Exec. V.P.* John T. Bass

Connecticut Book Publishers Assn., c/o *Pres.* Alex M. Yudkin, Associated Booksellers, 147 McKinley Ave., Bridgeport, CT 06606; *V.P.* Richard Dunn; *Treas.* John Atkin.

The Copyright Society of the U.S.A., New York Univ. School of Law, 40 Washington Sq. S., New York, NY 10012. 212-598-2280/2210. *Pres.* Alan J. Hartnick; *Secy.* Raymond D. Weisbond; *Exec. Dir.* Alan Latman; *Asst.* Kate McKay.

Council on Interracial Books for Children, Inc., 1841 Broadway, New York, NY 10023. 212-757-5339. *Dir.* Bradford Chambers; *Pres.* Beryl Banfield; *V.P.s* Albert V. Schwartz, Frieda Zames, Irma Garcia, Marylou Byler; *Managing Ed., Interracial Books for Children Bulletin.* Ruth Charnes; *Book Review Coord.* Lyla Hoffman; *Dir., CIBC Racism & Sexism Resource Center for Educators.* Robert B. Moore; *Secy.* Elsa Velasquez.

Edition Bookbinders of New York, Inc., Box 124, Fort Lee, NJ 07024. 201-947-7289. *Pres.* Martin Blumberg, American Book-Stratford Press; *Exec. Secy.* Morton Windman; *Treas.* Sam Goldman, Publishers Book Bindery.

Educational Paperback Assn., c/o *Pres.* John Michel, Florida Educational Paperbacks, 5405 Boran Place, Tampa, FL 33610.

Evangelical Christian Publishers Assn., Box 2439, Vista, CA 92083. 619-941-1636. *Exec. Dir.* C. E. (Ted) Andrew.

Fourth Avenue Booksellers, *Perm. Secy.* Stanley Gilman, Box 456,New York, NY 10276.

Graphic Artists Guild, 30 E. 20 St., Rm. 405, New York, NY 10003. 212-777-7353. *Pres.* Diane Dillon.

Guild of Book Workers, 663 Fifth Ave., New York, NY 10022. 212-757-6454. *Pres.* Caroline F. Schimmel.

Information Industry Assn. See "National Library and Information Industry Associations" earlier in Part 7—*Ed.*

International Assn. of Book Publishing Consultants, c/o Joseph Marks, 485 Fifth Ave., New York, NY 10017. 212-867-6341.

International Assn. of Printing House Craftsmen, Inc., 7599 Kenwood Rd., Cincinnati, OH 45236. 513-891-0611. *Pres.* J. Redmond Collins; *Exec. V.P.* John A. Davies.

International Copyright Information Center (INCINC), Assn. of American Publishers, 2005 Massachusetts Ave. N.W., Washington, DC 20036. 202-232-3335. *Dir.* Carol A. Risher.

International Standard Book Numbering Agency (ISBN) and Standard Address Number Agency (SAN), 1180 Ave. of the Americas, New York, NY 10036. 212-764-3390/3391. *Dir.* Emery I. Koltay; *Officers.* Beatrice Jacobson, Leigh C. Yuster, Scott MacFarland, Frank Zirpolo, Lucy Iervasi.

JWB Jewish Book Council, 15 E. 26 St., New York, NY 10010. 212-532-4949. *Pres.* Robert Gordis. *Dir.* Ruth S. Frank.

Library Binding Institute, Box 217, Accord, MA 02018. 617-740-1592. *Exec. Dir.* Albert L. Leitschuh; *Communications Specialist* Lana Shanbar; *General Counsel* Dudley A. Weiss; *Technical Consultant* Werner Rebsamen.

Address correspondence to Lana Shanbar.

Magazine & Paperback Marketing Institute (MPMI), 344 Main St., Suite 205, Mount Kisco, NY 10549. 914-666-6788. *Exec. V.P.* Woodford Bankson, Jr.

Metropolitan Lithographers Assn., 21 E. 73 St., New York, NY 10021.

212-772-1027. *Pres.* Stephen S. Gerson; *Exec. Dir.* Albert N. Greco.

Midwest Book Travelers Assn., c/o *Pres.* Ted Heinecken, Heinecken Assocs., 1733 N. Mohawk St., Chicago, IL 60614. 312-649-9181; *V.P.* Peter Muehr; *Treas.* Robert Rainer; *Secy.* Pat Friedlander.

Minnesota Book Publishers Roundtable, c/o *Pres.* Norton Stillman, Nodin Press, Inc., 519 N. Third St., Minneapolis, MN 55401; *V.P.* Dave Bender, Greenhaven Press, 577 Shoreview Park Rd., St. Paul, MN 55112; *Secy.-Treas.* Eric Rohmann, Winston Press, 430 Oak Grove St., Minneapolis, MN 55403.

National Assn. of College Stores, 528 E. Lorain St., Box 58, Oberlin, OH 44074. 216-775-7777. *Pres.* Eldon Speed, Stanford Bookstore, Stanford, CA 94305; *Exec. Dir.* Garis F. Distelhorst.

National Council of Churches of Christ in the U.S.A., Div. of Education & Ministry, 475 Riverside Dr., New York, NY 10115. 212-870-2271/2272. *Assoc. General Secy.* David Ng.

National Micrographics Assn. See National Library & Information-Industry Associations, United States and Canada, earlier in Part 7, for more detailed information—*Ed.*

New Mexico Book League, 8532 Horacio Place N.E., Albuquerque, NM 87111. 505-299-8940. *Exec. Dir.* Dwight A. Myers; *Pres.* Jack D. Rittenhouse; *V.P.* Concha Encinias; *Treas.* Frank N. Skinner; *Ed.* Carol A. Myers.

New York Rights & Permissions Group, c/o *Chpn.* Dorothy McKittrick Harris, Reader's Digest General Books, 750 Third Ave., New York, NY 10017. 212-850-7009.

New York State Small Press Assn., 198 1/2 Main St., Nyack, NY 10960. 914-358-1190. *Exec. Dir.* Janey Tannenbaum.

Northern California Booksellers Assn., c/o *Pres.* Andy Ross, Cody's Books, 2454 Telegraph Ave., Berkeley, CA 94701.

Periodical & Book Assn. of America, Inc., 313 W. 53 St., New York, NY 10019. 212-307-6182.

Periodical Distributors of Canada. c/o *Pres.* Jim Neal, 120 Sinnot Rd., Scarborough, Ont. M1L 4N1, Canada. 705-567-3318; *Secy.* Cliff Connelly, 5 Kirkland St., Box 488, Kirkland Lake, Ont., Canada.

Philadelphia Book Clinic, *Secy.-Treas.* Thomas Colaiezzi, Lea & Febiger, 600 Washington Sq., Philadelphia, PA 19106. 215-925-8700.

Pi Beta Alpha (formerly Professional Bookmen of America, Inc.), 1215 Farwell Dr., Madison, WI 53704. *Pres.* Donald J. Brennan; *Exec. Sec.* Charles L. Schmalbach.

Printing Industries of Metropolitan New York, Inc., 461 Eighth Ave., New York, NY 10001. 212-279-2100. *Pres.* James J. Conner III; *Dir., Industrial Relations.* James E. Horne; *Dir., Government Affairs.* Stuart L. Litvin; *Dir., Industry Activities.* Gary J. Miller.

Proofreaders Club of New York, c/o *Pres.* Allan Treshan, 38-15 149 St., Flushing, NY 11354. 212-461-8509.

Publishers' Ad Club, c/o *Secy.* Caroline Barnett, Denhard & Stewart, 122 E. 42 St., New York, NY 10017. 212-986-1900; *Pres.* Peter Minichiello, Pocket Books, 1230 Ave. of the Americas, New York, NY 10020. 212-246-2121; *V.P.* Susan Ball, William

Morrow & Co., 105 Madison Ave., New York, NY 10016. 212-899-3050; *Treas.* Polly Scarvalone, The New York Review of Books, 250 W. 57 St., New York, NY 10019. 212-757-8070.

Publishers' Alliance, c/o James W. Millar, Box 3, Glen Ridge, NJ 07028. 201-429-0169.

Publishers' Library Marketing Group, *Pres.* Marjorie Naughton, Clarion Books, 52 Vanderbilt Ave., New York, NY 10017. 212-972-1192; *V.P.* John Mason, The Putnam Publishing Group. 51 Madison, New York, NY. 212-689-9200; *Treas.* Susan Kalkbrenner, William Morrow & Co., 105 Madison Ave., New York, NY 10016. 212-889-3050.

Publishers' Publicity Assn., c/o *Pres.* Julie Knickerbocker, Simon & Schuster, 1230 Ave. of the Americas, New York, NY 10020. 212-245-6400; *V.P.* Jill Danzig, Pantheon Books, 201 E. 50 St., New York, NY 10022. 212-751-2600; *Secy.* Marcia Burch, Penguin Books, 625 Madison Ave., New York, NY 10022. 212-755-4330; *Treas.* Harriet Blacker, Putnam Publishing Group, 200 Madison Ave., New York, NY 10016. 212-576-8900.

The Religion Publishing Group, c/o Marilyn M. Jensen, Guideposts, 747 Third Ave., New York, NY 10017. 212-754-0726; *Pres.* Peter Hewitt, 5537 Pulaski Ave., Philadelphia, PA 19144; *Secy.-Treas.* Marilyn M. Jensen.

Research & Engineering Council of the Graphic Arts Industry, Inc., Box 2740, Landover Hills, MD 20784. 301-577-5400. *Pres.* Donald H. Laux; *1st V.P.-Secy.* George Kaplan; *2nd V.P.-Treas.* William O. Krenkler; *Managing Dir.* Harold A. Molz.

Société de Developpement du Livre et du Périodique, 1151 r. Alexandre-DeSève, Montreal, PQ H2L 2T7, Canada. 514-524-7528. *Prés.* Guy Saint-Jean; *Directeur Général.* Louise Rochon; Association des Editeurs Canadiens, *Prés.* M. René Bonenfant; Association des Libraries du Québec, *Pres.* Hélène Chassé; Société Canadienne Française de Protection du Droit d'Auteur, *Prés.* Pierre Tisseyre; Societe des Editeurs de Manuels Scolaires du Québec, *Prés.* Pierre Tisseyre.

Society of Author's Representatives, Inc., Box 650, Old Chelsea Sta., New York, NY 10113. 212-741-1356. *Pres.* Carl Brandt; *Exec. Secy.* Susan Bell.

Society of Photographer & Artist Representatives, Inc. (SPAR), Box 845, New York, NY 10150. 212-490-5895. *Pres.* Anthony Andriulli.

Society of Photographers in Communication. See American Society of Magazine Photographers (ASMP).

Southern California Booksellers Assn., c/o *Pres.* Glenn Goldman, c/o Book Soup, 8868 Sunset Blvd., Los Angeles, CA 90069. 213-659-3110; *V.P.* Lori Flores, c/o Children's Book & Music Center, 2500 Santa Monica, CA 90404. 213-829-0215; *Secy.* Betty Gaskill, Publisher's Rep., 18560 Van Owen St., Reseda, CA 91335. 213-996-4038; *Treas.* Fran Chaplin, Bookseller, 1235 S. Hipoint St., Los Angeles, CA 90035. 213-276-1904.

Standard Address Number (SAN) Agency. See International Standard Book Numbering Agency.

Technical Assn. of the Pulp & Paper Industry (TAPPI), One Dunwoody Pk., Atlanta, GA 30338. 404-394-6130. *Pres.* Sherwood G. Holt; *V.P.* Terry O. Norris; *Exec. Dir.-Treas.* W. L. Cullison; *Vice Chpn. Bd. of Dirs.* Philip E. Nethercut.

West Coast Bookmen's Assn., 27 McNear Dr., San Rafael, CA 94901. *Secy.* Frank G. Goodall.

Western Book Publishers Assn., Box 4242, San Francisco, CA 94101. *Pres.* Hal Siverman.

Women's National Book Assn., c/o *National Pres.* Sylvia H. Cross, 19824 Septo St., Chatsworth, CA 91311. 213-886-8448 (home); *V.P./Pres.-Elect.* Sandra K. Paul, SKP Associates, 160 Fifth Ave., New York, NY 10010. 212-675-7804 (office); *Secy.* Cathy Rentschler, H. W. Wilson Co., 950 University Ave., Bronx, NY 10452. 212-588-8400, ext. 257 (office); *Treas.* Sandra J. Souza, 1606 Stafford Rd., Fall River, MA 02721. 617-678-4179; *Past Pres.* Mary Glenn Hearne, Public Library of Nashville and Davidson Counties, Eighth Ave., North and Union, Nashville, TN 37203. 615-244-4700, ext. 68 (office). *NATIONAL COMMITTEE CHAIRS: Pannell Chpn.* Ann Heidbreder Eastman, College of Arts and Sciences, Virginia Polytechnic Institute & State Univ., Blacksburg, VA 24061. 703-961-6390 (office). *Publicity.* Joann Breslin, 115 Fairview Ave., Jersey City, NJ 07304. 201-432-6967; *Status of Women.* Claire Friedland, 36 E. 36 St., New York, NY 10016. 212-685-6205; *Ed. The Bookwoman.* Jean K. Crawford, Abingdon Press, 201 Eighth Ave. S., Nashville, TN 37202. 615-749-6422 (office); *Book Review Ed.,* *The Bookwoman.* Mary V. Gaver, 300 Virginia Ave., Danville, VA 24541. 804-799-6746; *Membership Chpn.* Anne J. Richter, 55 N. Mountain Ave., A-2, Mountclair, NJ 07042. 201-746-5166 (home); *UN/NGO Rep.* Sally Wecksler, 170 West End Ave., New York, NY 10023. 212-787-2239 (office); *Finance Chpn.* Sandra K. Paul, SKP Associates, 160 Fifth Ave., New York, NY 10010. 212-675-7804 (office). *CHAPTER PRESIDENTS: Binghamton.* L. Jeanette Clarke Lee, 8 Pine St., Binghamton, NY 13901. 607-723-6626; *Boston.* Gaylyn Fullington, 225 Mass. Ave., Apt. 914, Boston, MA 02115. 617-247-2823; *Cleveland.* Billie Joy Reinhart, 2856 Fairfax, Cleveland Heights, OH 44118. 216-371-0459; *Detroit.* Olga Pobutsky, 16815 Parkside, Detroit, MI 48221. 313-863-1389; *Los Angeles.* Elin Guthrie, 1295 S. Cloverdale Ave., Los Angeles, CA 90019. 213-935-0558 (home); *Nashville.* Cosette Kies, 2116 Hobbs Rd., C-1, Nashville, TN 37215. 615-297-7995; *New York.* Barbara J. Meredith, Dir., Center for Publishing, New York University, 2 University Place, New York, NY 10003. 212-598-2371; *San Francisco.* Elizabeth Pomada, 1029 Jones St., San Francisco, CA 94109. 415-673-0939 (office); *Washington, DC/Baltimore, MD.* Kevin Maricle, Office of the General Counsel, U.S. Copyright Office, Lib. of Congress, Washington, DC 20559. 202-287-8380.

INTERNATIONAL AND FOREIGN BOOK TRADE ASSOCIATIONS

For Canadian book trade associations, see the preceding section, "Book Trade Associations, United States and Canada." For a more extensive list of book trade organizations outside the United States and Canada, with more detailed information, consult *International Literary Market Place* (R. R.

Bowker), an annual publication, which also provides extensive lists of major bookstores and publishers in each country.

INTERNATIONAL

Antiquarian Booksellers Assn. (International), 45 E. Hill, London SW18 2QZ, England.

International Booksellers Federation (IBF), Grunangergasse 4, A-1010 Vienna 1, Austria. *Secy.-Gen.* Gerhard Prosser.

International League of Antiquarian Booksellers, c/o *Pres.* Bob de Graaf, Zuideinde 40, NL-2479 Nieuwkoop, Netherlands.

International Publishers Assn., 3 av. de Miremont, CH-1206 Geneva, Switzerland. *Secy.-Gen.* J. Alexis Koutchoumow.

NATIONAL

Argentina

Cámara Argentina de Editores de Libros (Council of Argentine Book Publishers), Talcahuano 374, p. 3, Of. 7, Buenos Aires 1013.

Cámara Argentina de Publicaciones (Argentine Publications Assn.), Reconquista 1011, p. 6, 1003 Buenos Aires. *Pres.* Manuel Rodriguez.

Cámara Argentina del Libro (Argentine Book Assn.), Av. Belgrano 1580, p. 6, 1093 Buenos Aires. *Pres.* Jaime Rodriguez.

Federación Argentina de Librerías, Papelerías y Actividades Afines (Federation of Bookstores, Stationers and Related Activites), Balcarce 179/83, Rosario, Santa Fe. *Pres.* Isaac Kostzer.

Australia

Assn. of Australian Univ. Presses, c/o Univ. of Queensland Press, Box 42, St. Lucia, Qld. 4068. *Pres.* Frank W. Thompson.

Australian Book Publishers Assn., 161 Clarence St., Sydney, N.S.W. 2000. *Dir.* Sandra Forbes.

Australian Booksellers Assn., Box 3254, Sydney, N.S.W. 2001.

Austria

Hauptverband der graphischen Unternehmungen Österreichs (Austrian Graphical Assn.), Grünangergasse 4, A-1010 Vienna 1. *Pres.* Komm.-Rat Dr. Dkfm. Willi Maiwald; *Gen. Secy.* Dr. Hans Inmann.

Hauptverband des österreichischen Buchhandels (Austrian Publishers and Booksellers Assn.), Grünangergasse 4, A-1010 Vienna. *Secy.* Gerhard Prosser.

Osterreichischer Verlegerverband (Assn. of Austrian Publishers), Grünangergasse 4, A-1010 Vienna. *Secy.* Gerhard Prosser.

Verband der Antiquare Österreichs (Austrian Antiquarian Booksellers Assn.), Grünangergasse 4, A-1010 Vienna. *Secy.* Gerhard Prosser.

Belguim

Association des Editeurs Belges (Belgian Publishers Assn.), 111 av. du Parc. B-1060 Brussels. *Dir.* J. De Raeymaeker.

Cercle Belge de la Librairie (Belgian Booksellers Assn.), r. du Luxembourg 5, bte. 1, B-1040 Brussels.

Syndicat Belge de la Librairie Ancienne et Moderne (Belgian Assn. of Antiquarian and Modern Booksellers), r. du Chêne 21, B-1000 Brussels.

Vereniging ter Bevordering van het Vlaamse Boekwezen (Assn. for the Promotion of Flemish Books), Frankrijklei 93, B-2000 Antwerp. *Secy.* A. Wouters. Member organizations: Algemene Vlaamse Boekverkopersbond; Uitgeversbond-Vereniging van Uitgevers van Nederlandstalige Boeken at the same address; and Bond-Alleenverkopers van Nederlandstalige Boeken (Book importers), De Smethlaan 4, B-1980 Tervuren. *Secy.* J. van den Berg.

Bolivia

Cámara Boliviana del Libro (Bolivian Booksellers Assn.), Box 682, La Paz. *Pres. Lic.* Javier Gisbert.

Brazil

Associação Brasileira de Livreiros Antiquarios (Brazilian Assn. of Antiquarian Booksellers), Rua do Rosario 135-137, 20000 Rio de Janeiro RJ.

Associação Brasileira do Livro (Brazilian Booksellers Assn.), Av. 13 de Maio 23, andar 16, Rio de Janeiro. *Dir.* Alberjano Torres.

Cámara Brasileira do Livro (Brazilian Book Assn.), Av. Ipiranga 1267, andar 10, São Paulo. *Secy.* Jose Gorayeb.

Sindicato Nacional dos Editores de Livros (Brazilian Book Publishers Assn.), Av. Rio Branco 37, 15 andar, Salas 1503/6 e 1510/12, 20097 Rio de Janeiro. *Gen. Secy.* Berta Ribeiro.

Bulgaria

Drzavno Obedinenie Bulgarska Kniga (State Bulgarian Book Assn.), pl. Slavejkov 11, Sofia.

Soyuz Knigoizdatelite i Knizharite (Union of Publishers and Booksellers), vu Solum 4, Sofia.

Burma

Burmese Publishers Union, 146 Bogyoke Market, Rangoon.

Chile

Cámara Chilena del Libro, Av. Bulnes 188, Santiago. *Secy.* A. Newman.

Colombia

Cámara Colombiana de la Industria Editorial (Colombian Publishers Council), Cr. 7a, No. 17-51, Of. 409-410, Apdo. áereo 8998, Bogotá. *Exec. Secy.* Hipólito Hincapié.

Czechoslovakia

Ministerstvo Kultury CSR, Odbor Knižni Kultury (Ministry of Culture CSR, Dept. for Publishing and Book Trade), Staré Mésto, námesti Perštynĕ 1, 117 65 Prague 1.

Denmark

Danske Antikvarboghandlerforening (Danish Antiquarian Booksellers Assn.), Box 2184, DK-1017 Copenhagen.

Danske Boghandlerforening (Danish Booksellers Assn.), Boghandlernes Hus, Siljangade 6, DK-2300 Copenhagen S. *Secy.* Elisabeth Brodersen.

Danske Forlaeggerforening (Danish Publishers Assn.), Kobmagergade 11, DK-1150 Copenhagen K. *Dir.* Erik V. Krustrup.

Ecuador

Sociedad de Libreros del Ecuador (Booksellers Society of Ecuador), C. Bolivar 268 y Venezuela, Of. 501, p. 5, Quito. *Secy.* Eduardo Ruiz G.

Finland

Kirja-ja Paperikauppojen Liitto ry (Finnish Booksellers & Stationers Assn.), Pieni Roobertinkatu 13 B 26, SF-00130 Helsinki 13. *Secy.* Olli Eräkivi.

Suomen Antikvariaattiyhdistys Finska Antikvariatforeningen (Finnish Antiquarian Booksellers Assn.), P. Makasiininkatu 6, Helsinki 13.

Suomen Kustannusyhdistys (Publishers Assn. of Finland), Merimiehenkatu 12 A-6, SF-00150, Helsinki 15. *Secy.-Gen.* Unto Lappi.

France

Cercle de la Librairie (Booksellers Circle), 35 rue Grégoire-de-Tours, F-

75279 Paris, Cedex 06. *Dir.* Claude Boislève.

Fédération française des Syndicats de Libraires (French Booksellers Assn.), 259 rue St.-Honoré, F-75001 Paris.

Office de Promotion de l'Edition Française (Promotion Office of French Publishing), 117 bd. St.-Germain, F-75279 Paris, Cedex 06. *Managing Dir.* Gustave Girardot; *Secy.-Gen.* Marc Franconie; *Asst. Dir.* Pierre-Dominique Parent.

Syndicat du Livre Ancien et des Métiers annexes (Assn. of Antiquarian Books), 117 bd. St.-Germain, F-75006, Paris. *Pres.* Pierre Berès.

Syndicat National de l'Edition (French Publishers Assn.), 35 rue Grégoire de Tours, 75279 Paris, Cedex 06. *Secy.* Pierre Fredet.

Syndicat National des Importateurs et Exportateurs de Livres (National French Assn. of Book Importers and Exporters), 35 rue Grégoire de Tours 75279 Paris, Cedex 06.

German Democratic Republic

Börsenverein der Deutschen Buchhändler zu Leipzig (Assn. of GDR Publishers and Booksellers in Leipzig), Gerichtsweg 26, 7010 Leipzig.

Germany (Federal Republic of)

Börsenverein des deutschen Buchhandels (German Publishers and Booksellers Assn.), Grosser Hirschgraben 17-21, Box 2404, D-6000 Frankfurt am Main 1. *Secy.* Dr. Hans-Karl von Kupsch.

Bundeverband der Deutschen Versandbuchhändler e.V. (National Federation of German Mail-Order Booksellers), An der Ringkirche 6, D-6200 Wiesbaden. *Dirs.* Dr. Stefan Rutkowsky; Kornelia Wahl.

Landesverband der Buchhändler und Verleger in Niedersachsen e.V. (Provincial Federation of Booksellers & Publishers in Lower Saxony), Hausmannstr. 2, D-3000 Hannover 1. *Managing Dir.* Wolfgang Grimpe.

Presse-Grosso—Verband Deutscher Buch-, Zeitungs-und Zeitschriften-Grossisten e.V. (Federation of German Wholesalers of Books, Newspapers & Periodicals), Classen-Kappelmann-Str. 24, D-5000 Cologne 41.

Verband Bayerischer Verlage und Buchhandlungen e.V. (Bavarian Publishers & Booksellers Federation), Thierschstr. 17, D-8000 Munich 22. *Secy.* F. Nosske.

Verband deutscher Antiquare e.V. (German Antiquarian Booksellers Assn.), Sofienstr. 5, 6900 Heidelberg 1.

Verband Deutscher Bühnenverleger e.V. (Federation of German Theatrical Publishers & Drama Agencies), Bismarckstr. 17, D-1000 Berlin 12.

Ghana

Ghana Booksellers Assn., Box 7869, Accra.

Great Britain

See United Kingdom.

Greece

Syllogos Ekdoton Vivliopolon (Greek Publishers & Booksellers Assn.), 54 Themistocleus St., Athens 145.

Hong Kong

Hong Kong Booksellers & Stationers Assn., Man Wah House, Kowloon.

Hungary

Magyar Könyvkiadók és Könyvterjesztök Egyesülése (Hungarian Publishers & Booksellers Assn.), Vörösmarty tér 1, 1051 Budapest, *Pres.* György Bernát; *Secy. Gen.* Ferenc Zöld.

Iceland

Iceland Publishers Assn., Laufasvegi 12, 101 Reykjavik. *Pres.* Oliver Steinn Jóhannesson, Strandgötu 31, 220 Hafnarfjördur. *Gen. Mgr.* Björn Gíslason.

India

All-India Booksellers & Publishers Assn., 17L Connaught Circus, Box 328, New Delhi 110001. *Pres.* A. N. Varma.

Bombay Booksellers & Publishers Assn., c/o Bhadkamkar Marg, Navjivan Cooperative Housing Society, Bldg. 3, 6th fl., Office 25, Bombay 400 008.

Booksellers & Publishers Assn. of South India, c/o Higginbothams, Ltd., 814, Anna Salai, Mount Rd., Madras 600 002.

Delhi State Booksellers & Publishers Assn., c/o The Students' Stores, Box 1511, 100 006 Delhi. *Pres.* Devendra Sharma.

Federation of Indian Publishers, 18/I-C Institutional Area; New Delhi 110 067. *Pres.* Narendrakumar; *Exec. Secy.* R. K. Dhingra.

Indian Assn. of Univ. Presses, Calcutta Univ. Press, Calcutta. *Secy.* Salil Kumar Chakrabarti.

Indonesia

Ikatan Penerbit Indonesia (IKAPI) (Assn. of Indonesian Book Publishers), Jalan Kalipasir 32, Jakarta Pusat. *Pres.* Ismid Hadad.

Ireland (Republic of)

CLE/Irish Book Publishers Assn., 55 Dame St., Dublin 2. *Secy.* Hilary Kennedy.

Israel

Book & Printing Center of the Israel Export Institute, Box 29732, 29 Hamered St., 68 125 Tel Aviv. *Dir.* Baruch Schaefer.

Book Publishers Assn. of Israel, Box 20123, 29 Carlebach St., Tel Aviv. *Pres.* Mordechai Bernstein; *Exec. Dir.* Benjamin Sella; *International Promotion & Literary Rights Dept. Dir.* Lorna Soifer.

Italy

Associazione Italiana Editori (Italian Publishers Assn.), Via delle Erbe 2, I-20121 Milan. *Secy.* Archille Ormezzano.

Associazione Librai Antiquari d'Italia (Antiquarian Booksellers Assn. of Italy), Via Jacopo Nardi 6, I-50132 Florence. *Pres.* Renzo Rizzi.

Associazione Librai Italiani (Italian Booksellers Assn.), Piazza G. G. Belli 2, I-00153 Rome.

Jamaica

Booksellers Assn. of Jamaica, c/o B. A. Sangster, Sangster's Book Stores, Ltd., Box 366, 97 Harbour St., Kingston.

Japan

Antiquarian Booksellers Assn. of Japan, 29 San-ei-cho, Shinjuku-ku, Tokyo 160.

Books-on-Japan-in-English Club, Shinnichibo Bldg., 2-1 Sarugaku-cho 1-chome, Chiyoda-ku, Tokyo 101.

Japan Book Importers Assn., Rm. 603, Aizawa Bldg., 20-3, Nihonbashi, 1-chome, Chuo-ku, Tokyo 103. *Secy.* Mitsuo Shibata.

Japan Book Publishers Assn., 6 Fukuromachi, Shinjuku-ku, Tokyo 162. *Secy.* S. Sasaki.

Japan Booksellers Federation, 1-2 Surugadai, Kanda, Chiyoda-ku, Tokyo 101.

Textbook Publishers Assn. of Japan (Kyokasho Kyokai), 20-2 Honshiocho Shinjuku-ku, Tokyo 160. *Secy.* Masae Kusaka.

Kenya

Kenya Publishers Assn., Box 72532, Nairobi. *Secy.* G. P. Lewis.

Korea (Republic of)

Korean Publishers Assn., 105-2 Sagan-dong, Chongno-ku, Seoul 110. *Pres.* Young-Bin Min; *V.P.s* Jong-Sung Moon; Yun-Hee Hong; Young-Hwan Kim; *Secy.* Doo-Young Lee.

Luxembourg

Confédération du Commerce Luxembourgeois-Groupement Papetiers-Libraires (Confederation of Retailers, Group for Stationers & Booksellers), 23, Centre Allée-Scheffer, Luxembourg. *Pres.* Pierre Ernster; *Secy.* Fernand Kass.

Malaysia

Malaysian Book Publishers Assn., 48A Jalan SS 2/67, Petaling Jaya. *Hon. Secy.* Johnny Ong.

Mexico

Instituto Mexicano del Libro A.C. (Mexican Book Institute), Paseo de la Reforma 95, Dept. 1024, México 4 D.F. *Secy.-Gen.* Isabel Ruiz González.

Morocco

Syndicat des Libraires du Maroc (Assn. of Booksellers of Morocco), 10 av. Dar el Maghzen, Rabat.

Netherlands

Koninklijke Nederlandse Uitgeversbond (Royal Dutch Publishers Assn.), Keizersgracht 391, 1016 EJ Amsterdam. *Secy.* R. M. Vrij; *Managing Dir.* A. Th. Hulskamp.

Nederlandsche Vereeniging van Antiquaren (Antiquarian Booksellers Assn. of the Netherlands), Nieuwe Spiegelstra. 33-35, 1017-DC Amsterdam. *Pres.* A. Gerits.

Nederlandse Boekverkopersbond (Booksellers Assn. of the Netherlands), Waalsdorperweg 119, 2597-HS The Hague. *Chpn* H. J. M. Nelissen

Vereeniging ter bevordering van de belangen des Boekhandels (Dutch Book Trade Assn.), Lassusstraat 9, Box 5475, 1007 AL Amsterdam. *Secy.* M. van Vollenhoven-Nagel.

New Zealand

Book Publishers Assn. of New Zealand, Box 78071, Grey Lynn, Auckland 2. *Pres.* B. D. Phillips; *Dir.* Gerard Reid.

Booksellers Assn. of New Zealand, Inc., Box 11-377, Wellington. *Dir.* Kate Fortune.

Nigeria

Nigerian Booksellers Assn. Box 3168, Ibadan. *Pres.* W. Adegbonmire.

Nigerian Publishers Assn., c/o P.M.B. 5164, Ibadan. *Pres.* Bankole O. Bolodeoku.

Norway

Norsk Antikvarbokhandlerforening (Norwegian Antiquarian Booksellers Assn.), Ullevalsveien 1, Oslo 1.

Norske Bokhandlerforening (Norwegian Booksellers Assn.), Øvre Vollgate 15, Oslo 1.

Norsk Bokhandler-Medhjelper-Forening (Norwegian Book Trade Employees Assn.), Øvre Vollgate 15, Oslo 1.

Norske Forleggerforening (Norwegian Publishers Assn.), Øvre Vollgate 15, Oslo 1. *Dir.* Paul M. Rothe.

Norsk Musikkforleggerforening (Norwegian Music Publishers Assn.), Box 1499 Vika, Oslo 1.

Pakistan

Pakistan Publishers and Booksellers Assn., YMCA Bldg., Shahra-e-Quaid-e-Azam, Lahore.

Paraguay

Cámara Paraguaya del Libro (Paraguayan Publishers Assn.), Casilla de Correo 1705, Asunción.

Peru

Cámara Peruana del Libro (Peruvian Publishers Assn.), Jirón Washington 1206, of. 507-508, Lima 100. *Pres.* Andrés Carbone O.

Philippines

Philippine Book Dealers Assn., MCC Box 1103, Makati Commerical Centre, Makati, Metro Manila. *Pres.* Jose C. Benedicto.

Philippine Educational Publishers Assn., 927 Quezon Ave., Quezon City 3008, Metro Manila. *Pres.* Jesus Ernesto R. Sibal.

Poland

Polskie Towarzystwo Wydawców Ksiazek (Polish Publishers Assn.), ul. Mazowiecka 2/4, 00-048 Warsaw.

Stowarzyszenie Ksiegarzy Polskich (Assn. of Polish Booksellers), ul. Mokotowska 4/6,00-641 Warsaw. *Pres.* Tadeusz Hussak.

Portugal

Associação Portuguesa de Editores e Livreiros (Portuguese Assn. of Publishers and Booksellers), Largo de Andaluz 16, 1, Esq., 1000 Lisboa.

Romania

Centrala editorială (Romanian Publishing Center), Piata Scînteii 1, R-79715 Bucharest. *Gen. Dir.* Gheorghe Trandafir.

Singapore

Singapore Book Publishers Assn., Box 846, Colombo Court Post Office, Singapore 0617. *Secy.* Charles Cher.

South Africa (Republic of)

Associated Booksellers of Southern Africa, One Meerendal, Nightingale Way, Pinelands 7405. *Secy.* P. G. van Rooyen.

Book Trade Assn. of South Africa, Box 105, Parow 7500. *Contact:* W. R. van der Vyver.

South African Publishers Assn., One Meerendal, Nightingale Way, Pinelands 7405. *Secy.* P. G. van Rooyen.

Spain

Federacion de Gremios de Editores de España (Spanish Federation of Publishers Assn.), Paseo Castellana, 82 Madrid 6. *Pres.* Francisco Pérez González; *Secy.-Gen.* Jaime Brull.

Gremi d'Editors de Catalunya (Assn. of Catalonian Publishers), Mallorca, 272-274, Barcelona 37. *Pres.* Josep Lluis Monreal.

Gremi de Libreters de Barcelona i Catalunya (Assn. of Barcelona and Catalunya Booksellers), c. Mallorca 272-276, Barcelona 37.

Instituto Nacional del Libro Español (Spanish Publishers & Booksellers Institute), Santiago Rusiñol 8-10, Madrid 3. *Dir.* José M. Béthencourt.

Sri Lanka

Booksellers Assn. of Sri Lanka, Box 244, Colombo 2. *Secy.* W. L. Mendis.

Sri Lanka Publishers Assn., 61 Sangaraja Mawatha, Colombo 10. *Secy.-Gen.* Eamon Kariyakarawana.

Sweden

Svenska Antikvariatföreningen, Box 22549, S-104 22 Stockholm.

Svenska Bokförläggareföreningen (Swedish Publishers Assn.), Sveavägen 52, S-111 34 Stockholm. *Managing Dir.* Lars Bergman.

Svenska Bokhandlareföreningen,

Div. of Bok-, Pappers- och Kontorsvaruförbundet (Swedish Booksellers Assn., Div. of the Swedish Federation of Book, Stationery & Office Supplies Dealers), Skeppargatan 27, S-114 52 Stockholm. *Secy.* Per Nordenson.

Svenska Tryckeriföreningen (Swedish Printing Industries Federation), Blasieholmsgatan 4A, Box 16383, S-10327 Stockholm. *Managing Dir.* Per Galmark.

Switzerland

Schweizerischer Buchhändler-und Verleger-Verband (Swiss German-Language Booksellers & Publishers Assn.), Bellerivestr. 3, CH-8034 Zurich. *Managing Dir.* Peter Oprecht.

Società Editori della Svizzera Italiana (Publishers Assn. for the Italian-Speaking Part of Switzerland), Box 282, Viale Portone 4, CH-6501 Bellinzona.

Société des Libraires et Editeurs de la Suisse Romande (Assn. of Swiss French-Language Booksellers & Publishers), 2 av. Agassiz, CH-1001 Lausanne. *Secy.* Robert Junod.

Vereinigung der Buchantiquare und Kupferstichhändler der Schweiz (Assn. of Swiss Antiquarians & Print Dealers), c/o Markus Krebser, Bälliz 64, CH-3601 Thun.

Thailand

Publishers and Booksellers Assn. of Thailand, 25 Sukhumvit Soi 56, Bangkok. *Secy.* W. Tantinirandr.

Tunisia

Syndicat des Libraires de Tunisie (Tunisian Booksellers Assn.), 10 av. de France, Tunis.

Turkey

Türk Editörler Derneği (Turkish Publishers Assn.), Ankara Caddesi 60, Istanbul.

United Kingdom

Assn. of Learned & Professional Society Publishers, R. J. Millson, 30 Austenwood Close, Chalfont St., Peter Gerrards Cross, Bucks., SL9 9DE.

Booksellers Assn. of Great Britain & Ireland, 154 Buckingham Palace Rd., London SW1W 9TZ. *Dir.* T. E. Godfray.

Educational Publishers Council, 19 Bedford Sq., London WC1B 3HJ. *Dir.* John R. M. Davies.

National Book League, Book House, 45 E. Hill, London SW18 2QZ. *Dir.* Martyn Goff, O.B.E.

National Federation of Retail Newsagents, 2 Bridewell Place, London EC4V 6AR.

Publishers Assn., 19 Bedford Sq., London WC1B 3HJ. *Secy/Chief Exec.* Clive Bradley.

Uruguay

Cámara Uruguaya del Libro (Uruguayan Publishing Council), Carlos Roxlo 1446, p. 1, Apdo. 2, Montevideo. *Secy.* Arnaldo Medone.

Yugoslavia

Association of Yugoslav Publishers & Booksellers, Kneza Miloša str. 25, Box 883, Belgrade. *Pres.* Vidak Perić.

Zambia

Booksellers & Publishers Assn. of Zambia, Box 35961, Lusaka.

Zimbabwe

Booksellers Assn. of Zimbabwe, Box 1934, Salisbury. *Secy.* A. Muchaziwepi.

Calendar, 1983–1984

The list below contains information (as of February 1983) regarding place and date of association meetings or promotional events that are, for the most part, national or international in scope. State and regional library association meetings also are included. For those who wish to contact the association directly, addresses of library and book trade associations are listed in Part 7 of this *Bowker Annual*. For information on additional book trade and promotional events, see the *1982 Exhibits Directory*, published by the Association of American Publishers; *Chase's Calendar of Annual Events*, published by the Apple Tree Press, Box 1012, Flint, MI 49501; *Literary Market Place* and *International Literary Market Place*, published by R. R. Bowker; *Publishers Weekly* "Calendar," appearing in each issue; and *Library Journal's* "Calendar" feature, appearing in each semimonthly issue.

1983

May

2–6	International Reading Association	Anaheim, CA
4–6	Delaware Library Association	Sussex Co., DE
4–7	Association of Research Libraries	Banff, Alta., Canada
5–7	Pennsylvania School Libraries Association	Seven Springs, PA
5–7	Indiana Library Association	Indianapolis, IN
6	Council of National Library and Information Associations	New York, NY
8–13	Association for Educational Data Systems	Portland, OR
12–14	Minnesota Library Association	St. Paul, MN
15–17	Massachusetts Library Association	Worcester, MA
16–18	Information Industry Association	Chicago, IL
16–19	National Computer Conference	*
19–20	Maryland Library Association	Frederick, MD
18–23	Warsaw International Book Fair	Warsaw, Poland
22–25	American Society for Information Science	Lexington, KY
5/28–6/2	Medical Library Association	Houston, TX

June

4–6	Special Libraries Association	New Orleans, LA
4–7	American Booksellers Association	Dallas, TX
12–15	Association of American University Presses	Minneapolis, MN
16–21	Canadian Library Association	Winnipeg, Man., Canada
18–22	Association of Jewish Libraries	Los Angeles, CA
19–21	Church and Synagogue Library Association	Atlanta, GA
20–24	American Theological Library Association	Richmond, VA
26–29	American Association of Law Libraries	Houston, TX

*To be announced.

6/26-7/1	American Library Association	Los Angeles, CA
6/26-7/1	Theatre Library Association	Los Angeles, CA
*	Association of Christian Librarians	Wheaton, IL
6/30-7/5	National Education Association	Philadelphia, PA

July

16-19	Canadian Booksellers Association	Toronto, Ont., Canada
25-29	Association for Computing Machinery/SIGGRAPH	Detroit, MI
*	Christian Booksellers Association	Washington, DC

August

21-27	International Federation of Library Associations and Institutions	Munich, FRG
23-27	Pacific Northwest Library Association	Sun Valley, ID

September

6-12	Moscow International Book Fair	Moscow, USSR
18-20	Association of Information and Dissemination Centers (ASIDIC)	Philadelphia, PA
18-21	Library Information and Technology Association	Baltimore, MD
9/29-10/2	Oral History Association	Seattle, WA

October

2-6	American Society for Information Science	Washington, DC
4-8	North Carolina Library Association	Winston-Salem, NC
4-6	European Association of Information Services (EUSIDIC)	Nice, France
5-7	Iowa Library Association	Waterloo, IA
5-8	Arizona Library Association	Tucson, AZ
5-8	Society of American Archivists	Minneapolis, MN
6-8	Idaho Library Association	Couer d'Alene, ID
12-14	Kentucky Library Association	Louisville, KY
12-14	Nebraska Library Association	Omaha, NE
12-17	Frankfurt Book Fair	Frankfurt, FRG
13-15	Missouri Library Association	Springfield, MO
13-15	South Carolina Library Association	Greenville, SC
15-19	Colorado Library Association	Colorado Springs, CO
18-20	Association of Research Libraries	Chapel Hill, NC
19-23	New York Library Association	Buffalo, NY
20-22	West Virginia Library Association	Wheeling, WV
24-26	Association for Computing Machinery	New York, NY
26-29	Georgia Library Association	Jekyll Island, GA
10/26-11/1	World Telecommunications and Electronics Book Fair	Geneva, Switzerland
10/30-11/2	Book Manufacturers Institute	Boca Raton, FL
10/30-11/2	Pennsylvania Library Association	Pittsburgh, PA
10/30-11/2	New England Library Association	Hyannis, MA

*To be announced.

November

7-9	Information Industry Association	New York, NY
9-11	Mississippi Library Association	Jackson, MS
14-20	National Children's Book Week	United States
17-20	Virginia Library Association	Hot Springs, VA

December

2	Council of National Library and Information Associations	New York, NY
3-7	California Library Association	Oakland, CA
27-30	Modern Language Association	New York, NY
*	International Online Information Meeting	London, England

1984

January

7-10	American Library Association	Colorado Springs, CO
25-27	Special Libraries Association	*
*	Canadian Book Publishers Council	Niagara-on-the Lake, Canada

February

7-9	National Micrographics Association (Exec. Conf.)	Marco Island, FL
14-17	ACM Computer Science Conference	Philadelphia, PA

March

4-10	Music Library Association	Boulder, CO
11-18	Leipzig International Book Fair	Leipzig, GDR
*	Association of American Publishers	West Palm Beach, FL

April

2-7	Texas Library Association	Corpus Christi, TX
4-6	Louisiana Library Association	Baton Rouge, LA
4-7	Association of College and Research Libraries	*
9-12	National Micrographics Association	Chicago, IL
23-27	National Association of College Stores	New Orleans, LA
23-26	Catholic Library Association	Boston, MA
*	Alabama Library Association	Birmingham, AL
*	Bologna Book Fair	Bologna, Italy

May

2-4	Wyoming Library Association	*
7-11	International Reading Association	Atlanta, GA
25-31	Medical Library Association	Denver, CO
23-28	Warsaw International Book Fair	Warsaw, Poland
26-29	American Booksellers Association	Washington, DC

*To be announced.

June

9-14	Special Libraries Association	New York, NY
19-23	American Theological Library Association	Holland, MI
23-28	American Library Association	Dallas, TX
24-26	Church and Synagogue Library Association	Indianapolis, IN
*	Association of American University Presses	Spring Lake, NJ
*	Canadian Library Association	Toronto, Ont., Canada

July

1-4	American Association of Law Libraries	San Diego, CA
23-27	Association for Computing Machinery/SIGGRAPH	Minneapolis, MN
*	Christian Booksellers Association	Anaheim, CA

August

19-25	International Federation of Library Associations and Institutions	Nairobi, Kenya
8/30-9/2	Society of American Archivists	Washington, DC

October

10-15	Frankfurt Book Fair	Frankfurt, FRG
21-26	American Society for Information Science	Philadelphia, PA
24-26	Wisconsin Library Association	LaCrosse, WI
*	Association of Research Libraries	Washington, DC

November

1-4	Book Manufacturers' Institute	Southampton, Bermuda

December

1-5	California Library Association	Los Angeles, CA
27-30	Modern Language Association	Washington, DC

*To be announced.

Index

A

AALS, *see* Association of American Library Schools
AAP, *see* Association of American Publishers
AAP College Textbook Publishers Fiche Service, 146
AAP Copyright Circle, 148
AAP Exhibits Directory, 151
AAP Industry Statistics, 1981, 381
AAP Newsletter, 151
AAP Student Service, 145
AASL, *see* American Library Association, American Association of School Librarians
AAU, *see* Association of American Universities
A&I Services, 50
ABA, *see* American Booksellers Association
ABA Basic Book List, 125
ABA Book Buyer's Handbook, 124
ABA Evaluation of Computer Hardware & Software Vendors, 125
ABA Newswire, 124–125
ABA Sidelines Directory, 125
ACRL, *see* American Library Association, Association of College and Research Libraries
ACRL Doctoral Dissertation Fellowships, 323
ADAPSO, *see* Association of Data Processing Service Organizations
ADONIS, 75
AECT, *see* Association for Educational Communications and Technology
AFLI, *see* Association for Library Information
AGRICOLA, 118, 119
AGRIS data base, 119
AIM, *see* Associated Information Managers
AIM Career Clearinghouse, 267
ALA, *see* American Library Association
ALA Intellectual Freedom Manual, 130
ALA Librarians Copyright Kit, 130
ALA Survey of Librarian Salaries, 132
ALAI, *see* Association Litteraire et Artistique Internationale
ALIS, *see* National Oceanic and Atmospheric Administration, Automated Library and Information System
ALSC, *see* American Library Association, Association for Library Service to Children
ALTA, *see* American Library Association, American Library Trustee Association
AMIGOS, 9–10
ANSI Committee Z39, *see* American National Standards Committee Z39
ANSI Price Index Standard, 438–439
ANSI Technical Report Numbers, 96
ARL, *see* Association of Research Libraries
ARLIS/NA, *see* Art Libraries Society/North America
ASCLA, *see* American Library Association, Association of Specialized and Cooperative Library Agencies
ASIS, *see* American Society for Information Science
ASIS JOBLINE, 267
AT&T, *see* American Telephone & Telegraph
ATLA, *see* American Theological Library Association
Abbreviations of Titles and Periodicals, 139
Abstracting & indexing services, public sector support, 50
Academic libraries, *see* College and university libraries
Academic Library Management Intern Program, 198
Access, to information, *see* Information access
Acquisitions, *see* Library acquisitions
Action, 275
Adult literacy programs, 128–129
Affirmative Action Register, 274
Agents, literary, 469
Aging, library services for, 208
Agricultural libraries, *see* National Agricultural Library
Alabama, LSCA library cooperation projects, 211–212
Allardyce, Alexander, 439

Allen County (Ind.) Public Library, 294–295
Alternative Careers in Information/Library Services: Summary of Proceedings of a Workshop, 277
Americans, Les, 413
American Academy (Nicosia) Library, 430
American Archivist, 157
American Association of Law Libraries, 505–507
  placement service, 266
American Association of School Librarians (AASL), *see* American Library Association, American Association of School Librarians
American Book Awards, 35, 125, 144, 150
American Book Trade Directory, 403
American Bookseller, 124
American Booksellers Association (ABA), 124–127, 145
  book promotion activities, 125–126
  Category Paperback Bestseller Program, 145
  censorship and book-banning issues, 126–127
  conventions and regional meetings, 126
  legal activities, 34
  Mass Paperback Fiche Service, 145
  publications, 124–125
  workshops and seminars, 125
American Center Library (Cyprus), 431
American Cyanamid Company, 66
"American Federation of Library Associations: The Time Has Come," 22
American Indian Libraries Newsletter, 266
American Libraries
  Career LEADS EXPRESS service, 133, 266
  Consultants Keyword Clearinghouse, 266
  continuing education activities, 133
American Library Association (ALA), 29–30, 127–135, 507–510
  Accreditation Committee, 134
  American Association of School Librarians, 30, 129, 134, 326, 511–515
    research activities, 326
    second national conference, 134
  American Indian Libraries Newsletter, 266
  American Library Trustee Association, 133, 515–516
  annual conference, 127
  Association for Library Service to Children, 30, 516–519
    Notable Children's Books Committee, 492
  Association of College and Research Libraries, 132–133, 266, 323, 325–326, 520–522
    continuing education courses, 132–133
    library research task forces, 325–326
    placement service, 266
    research awards, 323
  Association of Specialized and Cooperative Library Agencies, 128, 133, 522–525
    Bibliotherapy Committee, 133
    Continuing Education Committee, 133
  Black Caucus, 267
  budget issues, 128
  Catalog Form, Function, and Use Committee, 129
  censorship activities, 130–131
  Committee on the Status of Women in Librarianship, 132
  continuing education activities, 132–134
  copyright concerns, 30–31
  copyright law and, 56, 58, 59–60, 62, 64–65
    Betamax copyright case, 172
  Diversity in Collection Development policy, 130
  financial status, 22
  information access activities, 128–129
  Information Service and Database Development Project, 134
  Intellectual Freedom Committee, 130–131
  legislative and funding activities, 129–130
  legislative program, 22
  Library Administration and Management Association, 525–527
  Library and Information Technology Association, 133, 527–529
  library awareness activities, 127, 131–132
  Library Materials Price Index Committee, 439
  Library Research Round Table, 326
  Library Symbol Implementation Group, 127
  National Library Week, 131
  Notable Books Council of Reference and Adult Services, 489–490
  Notable Children's Books Committee, 492

Office for Intellectual Freedom, 130
Office for Library Personnel Resources, 132, 266
  salary surveys, 132, 325
  workshops, 133
Office of Library Outreach Services, 128–129
organizational structure, 21–22
placement services, 266–267
poster session, 326
Public Information Office, 131
Public Library Association, 133, 529–532
public library support, 134
Publishing Services, 130
  Books and Pamphlets unit, 134
Reference and Adult Services Division, 56, 532–535
Reference and Subscription Books Review Committee, 129
Resources and Technical Services Division, 133, 535–538
scholarships, 312
Social Responsibilities Round Table, 267
staff changes, 134–135
Standing Committee on Library Education, 133–134
Young Adult Services Division, 30, 129, 133, 490, 538–539
VOYA Research Grant, 323
American Library Directory, 332
American Library Trustee Association (ALTA), *see* American Library Association, American Library Trustee Association
American Merchant Marine Library Association, 539–540
American National Standard Criteria for Price Indexes for Library Materials, 439
American National Standards Committee Z39, 135–139
  CLR grants, 195
  funding, 138
  membership, 136
  officers and committees, 136–137
  organizational changes, 136
  publicity and exhibits, 138
  status of published standards, 137–138
American National Standards Technical Report Numbers, 96
American-Scandinavian Foundation, scholarships, 312
American Society for Information Science (ASIS), 540–541
  placement services, 267
American Telephone & Telegraph (AT&T), divestiture and legislative activities, 175, 189
American Theological Library Association (ATLA), 541–543
Amway organization, public library support, 7
Anderson, Mary Jane, 134
Annual Statistical Data for Public Libraries in Metropolitan Washington, 331
Apple bill, 179, 192
Aquaculture information services, 119
Archeological libraries, in Cyprus, 431
Archives
  bibliography, 454–455
  in China, 160
  CLR-supported project, 199
  conservation training, 261
  in Cyprus, 432, 434–435
  evaluation of, 159
  funding, 4, 158
  legislation, 159
  NHPRC grants, 241–242
  national information system for, 159
  presidential libraries, 120–123
  tribal, 159–160
  U.S. economy and, 158
  of Vatican Library, 422–424
  see also Library materials, conservation and preservation
Archivists, *see* Society of American Archivists
Arizona, LSCA MURL program, 209
Arkansas, funding of library construction, 6
Arms, William and Carolyn, 8
Art librarians, placement service, 267
Art Libraries Society/North America (ARLIS/NA), 267, 543–544
Assets of the Information Society, 153
Associated Information Managers (AIM), 267, 544–545
Association Canadienne des Sciences de l'Information, 553–554
Association for Educational Communications and Technology (AECT), 29, 267
Association for Library and Information Science Education, 143
Association for Library Information (AFLI), 73

Association for Library Service to Children, *see* American Library Association, Association for Library Service to Children
Association Litteraire et Artistique Internationale (ALAI), symposium on cable television, 88
Association of Academic Health Sciences Library Directors, 545-546
Association of American Library Schools (AALS), 140-143, 546-547
  conferences and workshops, 140-141
  goals of, 140
  interorganizational relations, 142-143
  library and information science research grant, 323
  organizational structure and membership, 140
  proposed name change, 143
  publications, 141-142
  research activities, 142
  Research Paper Competition, 323
Association of American Publishers (AAP), 143-151
  awards, 150-151
  Book Distribution Task Force, 149-150
  book promotion activities, 125-126
  book sales survey, 380-381
  College Division, 145-146
    Marketing Committee, 146
  copyright activities, 31, 34, 56, 61, 144
    King Research/Copyright Office surveys, 325
  Copyright Committee, 148
  Direct Marketing/Book Club Division, 147
  Education for Publishing Program, 150
  Freedom to Read Committee, 148
  General Publishing Division, 144-145
  International Division, 147
  International Freedom to Publish Committee, 149
  legislative activities, 178-184
    education & library funding programs, 178-180
    first amendment, 183-184
    postal rates and services, 180-181
  liaison activities, 151
  Mass Market Paperback Division, 145
  New Technology Committee, 148
  organizational structure, 144
  photocopying lawsuits (1982), 66-67
  Postal Committee, 149
  Professional and Scholarly Publishing Division, 146
  publications, 151

Publishing Education Information Service, 150
School Division, 146-147
see also American Book Awards
Association of American Universities (AAU), cooperative project with CLR, 199
Association of College and Research Libraries (ACRL), *see* American Library Association, Association of College and Research Libraries
Association of Data Processing Service Organizations (ADAPSO), software protection bill, 188
Association of Jewish Libraries, 547-548
  graduate study grant, 312
Association of Research Libraries (ARL), 548-549
  microform project, 197
  Office of Management Studies, CLR support, 199
  staff development survey, 19
Association of Specialized and Cooperative Library Agencies (ASCLA), *see* American Library Association, Association of Specialized and Cooperative Library Agencies
Association of Visual Science Librarians, 550
Audiovisual materials
  bibliography, 455
  LC's talking book program, 107-108
  NLM, 115, 116
Author/publisher relations, 33
Authors, reference books for, 469
Authors' League of America, 56, 182
Automation, *see* Library automation
Awards, information industry, 154
Awards, library, 314-320
  ARCL, 323
Awards, literary, 473-488
  AAP, 150-151
  American Book Awards, 35, 125, 144, 150
Awards, publishing, 150-151

B

BCH, *see* Booksellers Clearing House
BCR, *see* Bibliographic Center for Research
BOCES, *see* Board of Cooperative Educational Services
BSDP, *see* Council on Library Resources,

INDEX / 653

Bibliographic Service Development Program
Banned Book Week, 126
Basic Books, Inc. v. Gnomon Corporation, 61
Battelle Institutes, online bibliographic services study, 71
Battin, Pat, 72
Baxter (Matthew A.) School of Information and Library Science, 25
Beckman, Margaret, 13
Beltway Project (Washington, D.C.), 77
Benedictine Monastery at Monte Cassino, library of, 427
Benjamin (Curtis G.) Award for Creative Publishing, 150–151
Berger (C.) and Company, 279
Best books, *see* Books, best books
Best sellers, 495–501
  ABA Category Paperback Bestseller List Program, 125
Beta Phi Mu, 550–552
  scholarships, 312
Betamax case, 62, 172, 182
Bibliographic Center for Research (BCR), 9, 10
  interlibrary loan services development, 75
Bibliographic control
  ERIC objectives, 98
  HEA funding, 225, 226
Bibliographic data bases
  AGRIS, 119
  CLR development program, 195–197
  ERIC, 103
  FLC services, 89–90
  NTIS, 94–95
  for serial publications, 197
Bibliographic exchange, CLR project, 195–196, 201
Bibliographic Information Interchange on Magnetic Tape, 139
Bibliographic Service Development Program, *see under* Council on Library Resources
Bibliographical Society of America, 553
  for librarians and library collection development, 453–464
Bibliographies
  microcomputer-generated, 79
  for publishers and book trade, 465–472
  of public library statistical data, 328–332
Bibliotherapy, 133
Biographies, average and median prices (1972–1982), 379
Biomedical literature, 115–116

Blind, library services for, 107–108, 128
Board of Cooperative Educational Services (BOCES)
  off-air taping copyright case, 59, 67
  use of microcomputers by, 80
Book clubs, 147
Book deacidification, LC tests, 22, 105–106
Book design and production
  bibliography, 470
  British book production (1982), 445–449
Book detection systems, 3–4
Book distribution, AAP activities, 149–150
Book Distribution in the United States: Issues and Perceptions, 150
Book editing, bibliography, 472
Book editors, reference books for, 469
Book exports and imports, U.S., 380, 440–445
Book fairs, 151
  Frankfurt Book Fair, 409–416
  Moscow Book Fair Reception in Exile, 149
Book imports, *see* Book exports and imports
"Book Industry Markets, 1976–1985," 330
Book Industry Trends, 1982, statistics from, 383, 384
Book preservation and conservation, *see* Library materials, conservation and preservation
Book prices, *see* Books, prices
Book programs, Center for the Book, 108–109
Book promotion
  AAP activities, 145
  ABA activities, 125–126
Book Report, 331
Book review media, statistics, 405
Book rights, 411
Book sales, 8, 31
  fiction and nonfiction, 495–496
  international, 411
  statistics, AAP survey, 380–381
Book trade
  bibliographies, 465–466
  directories and yearbooks, 471–472
  international, *see* International book trade
Book trade associations
  foreign, 637–643
  international, 637
  U.S. and Canada, 630–636
Book wholesalers, 404
Book banning
  Baileyville (Maine) case, 25
  booksellers and, 126

Book banning (Cont.)
  Island Trees (N.Y.) Union Free School Board case, 27, 130–131, 149
  legislation, 28
  school libraries, 26–28
Bookbinding, CLR report on, 200
Bookbinding and the Conservation of Books, 106
Booklist/RSBR, 134
Bookplate (San Francisco, Calif.), and the Hearst Books antitrust suit, 126
Books
  about books, bibliography, 465
  best books, 489–490
    children's, 492–495
    young adults', 490–491
  best sellers, 125, 495–501
  bibliotherapy, 133
  for blind and physically handicapped, 107–108
  censorship, *see* Censorship
  Consumer expenditures, U.S., 382–384
  direct marketing, 147
  exports and imports, U.S., 380, 440–445
  hardcover, 32
  paperback, *see* Paperback books
  preservation and conservation, *see* Library materials, conservation and preservation
  prices, 4, 371–379
    British books, 394, 395, 396, 397
    German books, 398–400
    hardcover, 375, 376, 388–389
    Latin American books, 401, 402
    U.S., 385
  pricing, discriminatory practices, 126
  purchase of, state funding, 5–6
  sales, *see* Book sales
  scholarly, 146
    bibliography, 469
  textbooks, *see* Textbooks
  title output, 371–379
    British, 445–449
    international, 444
  translations by original language, 445
"Books on Trial" (PBS program), 25
Bookseller, British book production statistics from, 445–449
Booksellers
  AAP activities for, 145
  continuing education for, 125
  see also American Booksellers Association
Booksellers Clearing House (BCH), 35
Booksellers School, 125

Bookselling, 34–35
  bibliography, 470
  critical issues, 126–127
  manual of, 125
  professional and scholarly books, 146
Bookstores
  college bookstores, 145–146
  number in U.S. and Canada, 403–404
  U.S. consumer expenditures, 384
Boss, Richard, 17
Boston Library Consortium, 213
Boulder (Colo.) Public Library, 73
Boxes for the Protection of Rare Books: Their Design and Construction, 106
Braille books, 107
British and Irish Library Resources, 200
British Council Library (Cyprus), 431
Brown, Marvin, 33
Brown, Roland, 72
Buffalo & Erie County (N.Y.) Library, 29
Buildings, *see* Library buildings
Burgess, Dean, 6
Burke (Theresa M.) Employment Agency, 268
Burress, Lee, book censorship report, 26
Buscaglia, Leo, 498–499
Business of Information Report, 1983, 152–153
Bynum, Raymond, 27

C

CAPCON, 73
CCC, *see* Copyright Clearance Center
CDS, *see* Library of Congress, Catalog Distribution Service
CIES, *see* Council for International Exchange of Scholars
CIJE, *see* Current Index to Journals in Education
CIP, *see* Library of Congress, Cataloging in Publication Division
CIP Survey Final Report, 197
CIS, *see* Congressional Information Service
CKC, *see* Consultants Keyword Clearinghouse
CLA, *see* Catholic Library Association
CLASS, *see* California Library Authority for Systems and Services
CLENE, *see* Continuing Library Education Network and Exchange
CLR, *see* Council on Library Resources
CLSI, *see* Computer Library Services, Inc.

CNLIA, *see* Council of National Library and Information Associations
COM publications, 110-111
  see also Computer Output Microforms
CONSER, *see* Conversion of Serials
CONTU, *see* National Commission on New Technological Uses of Copyrighted Works
CRL, *see* Center for Research Libraries
CRS, *see* Congressional Research Service
CUFT, *see* Center for the Utilization of Federal Technology
C/W MARS, *see* Central/Western Massachusetts Automated Resource Sharing Network
Cable television
  copyright and, 87, 88
  legislation, 175, 188
Cable Television Copyright Act, amendments, 188
California, LSCA library cooperation project, 212
California Library Authority for Systems and Services (CLASS), 11
Campbell, David, 412
Canada
  book trade, bibliography, 471
  book trade associations, 630-636
  bookstores, 403-404
  libraries, 338
  library director, sex of, and library support, 299
  library directors' salaries, 300, 301, 302-305
  library placements, 286
  national library and information-industry associations, 505-578
  per capita library support, 295, 297
  provincial library associations, 588-591
  Telidon experiment, 417
Canadian Association for Information Science, 553-554
Canadian Library Association, 554-555
  scholarships, 312
Capital Letter, 151
Careers in Information, 278
Carter Presidential Materials Project, 121
Case Western Reserve University, Matthew A. Baxter School of Information and Library Science, 25
Cassette books, 107
Cataloging and classification
  automated, private professional services, 51, 52
  bibliography, 463-464
  CLR research project, 323-324
  continuing education institutes, 133
  FLC/OCLC database services, 89-90
  LC, 110-111
  MARC tapes, 50
  NLM, 115
  see also Online catalogs
Cataloging-in-Publication data, 197
Category Paperback Bestseller List program, 125
Catholic Library Association (CLA), 555-557
  placement service, 267
  scholarships, 312
Censorship
  AAP activities, 148
  ALA activities, 130-131
  bibliography, 459, 470
  legislation, and booksellers, 126
  see also Book banning
Censorship or Selection: Choosing Books for Public Schools (videotape), 130
Census Bureau, U.S., public employment statistical publications, 329-330
Center for Applied Linguistics, 129
Center for Research Libraries (CRL), electronic document transmission, 75
Center for the Book, 108-109
Center for the Utilization of Federal Technology (CUFT), 96
Central Massachusetts Library System, 213
Central/Western Massachusetts Automated Resource Sharing (C/W MARS) Network, 73
Certification, of librarians, 278
Certification of Public Libraries in the U.S., 278
"Changing Role of the Information Professional," 277
Charlotte and Mecklenburg County (N.C.) Public Library, 210
Cheap CE—Providing Continuing Education with Limited Resources: A Practical Guide, 133
Chicago Graduate Library School, CLR support, 198
Chief Officers of State Library Agencies, 557-558
Chiflet, Jean-Loup, 412
Child pornography legislation, 131
  AAP activities, 149, 183-184
Children of the Heav'nly King: Religious Expression in the Central Blue Ridge, 109
Children's books, 492-495
Children's services, bibliography, 456-457

656 / INDEX

China, People's Republic of, library services, 418
Chinese-American Librarians Association, 558-559
Christian Museum, of the Vatican Library, 425
Chronicle of Higher Education, library placement listings, 274
Church and Synagogue Library Association, 559-560
Civil service requirements, for librarians, 278
Coalition Building, 130
Coalition for Literacy, 128-129
Codex Benedictus, 426
Codices e Vaticanis selecti quam simillime expressi, 426
Codices manuscripti recensiti, 426
Cody's Books (Berkeley, Cal.), and Hearst Books antitrust suit, 126
Collection development
  bibliography, 453-464
  HEA grants, 226
College and university libraries, 3
  ACRL research activities, 325-326
  acquisitions expenditures, 342-343
  acquisitions research award, 323
  bibliography, 457-458
  buildings, 368-370
  in Cyprus, 431, 434
  fund raising activities, 7-8
  HEA funding, 214-216
  placements, 284-285
  salary ranges, 289, 290, 292
College bookstores, AAP activities and services, 145-146
College Library Program, 199
College Library Resources Program, HEA, 214-216
College textbooks, AAP activities, 145-146
Colorado, state library networking activities, 10
Committee Z39, *see* American National Standards Committee Z39
Commemorative stamps, honoring U.S. libraries, 174
Communications legislation, 188-190
Computer Equipment Contribution Act (Apple bill), 179, 192
Computer Library Services, Inc. (CLSI), DataPhase, 10, 13
Computer literacy, 14, 77, 192
Computer Output Microforms
  bibliography, 460
  see also COM publications

Computer software, legislation affecting use of, 60-61, 88, 187, 188
Computers
  education and training, 192
  in U.S. public schools, 24
  see also Library automation; Microcomputers
Conant Report, 17
Conference Employment Clearing House, 268
Conferences
  AALS, 140-141
  AASL, 134
  ALA, 127
  IFLA, 416-419
  IIA, 152
  LC, "Preservation and New Technology," 68, 106
  NCLIS, 44
  presidential library programs, 123
  "Research By, For and About Librarians," 324
  UCLA Graduate School of Library and Information Science, 198
  Universal Postal Union Conference, 180
  Video Recording for Educational Uses, 59
  WHCOLIS, 82-83
  White House Conference on Aging, 222-223
Congressional Information Service (CIS), 50
Congressional Research Service (CRS), 108
Connecticut, state library networking activities, 10
Conservation and preservation, *see* Library materials, conservation and preservation
Consortium for Native American Archives, 159
Consultants, library, 17
Consultants Keyword Clearinghouse (CKC), 266
Continuing education
  ALA activities, 132-134
  in conservation and preservation, 261-263
  in librarianship, 258
  Wyoming librarians, 213
Continuing Library Education Network and Exchange (CLENE), 560-562
Conversion of Serials (CONSER), 197
Cookbooks, 498
Copyright, 3
  AAP activities, 34, 144, 148

ALA concerns, 30-31
  bibliography, 458, 470-471
  Cable television and, 88
  computer use and, 88
  IFLA studies, 200, 201
  international developments, 87-88
  OCLC database, 74
  SLA activities, 163-164
  works-for-hire, 88
  see also Copyright law; Copyright Office, U.S.
Copyright and Library Materials for the Handicapped, 201
Copyright Clearance Center (CCC), 56, 62
  AAP photocopying lawsuits and, 66
  Annual Authorizations Service, 62
  Document Delivery Awareness Program, 62
  Large Industrial Users Assistance Program, 62
Copyright law, 55-70, 171-172, 181-183
  CONTU report, 57
  computer software and, 60-61
  court cases, 61-62, 66-67
  five-year review, 57-58, 182-183, 324
  manufacturing clause, 34, 85-86, 178, 181-182, 187-188
  new technologies and, 68
  off-air taping and, 58-59
  preparation for, 56-57
  work-for-hire provisions, 183
Copyright Office, U.S., 63-65, 84-88
  Conference on Video Recording for Educational Uses, 59
  copyright law and, 63-65, 67-68
  Deposits and Acquisitions Section, 84
  formalities study, 182
  Information and Reference Division, 85
  King Research surveys, 324-325
  Licensing Division, 84
  Photocopying Discussion Group, 68
  registration, 84
  regulations, 86-87
  renewal claims, 86
  Section 108(i) Report, 85
Copyright Royalty Tribunal, 84
Council for International Exchange of Scholars (CIES), as source of library teaching and research awards, 275
Council of Library/Media Technical Assistants, placement service, 267
Council of National Library and Information Associations (CNLIA), 562-563
  Ad Hoc Committee on Copyright Law Practice and Implementation, 56, 66
Council of Planning Librarians, Publications Office, 563-564
Council on Library Resources (CLR), 194-203, 564
  Academic Library Management Intern Program, 198
  Battelle study, 71
  Bibliographic Service Development Program, 71, 194-197
  Committee on Production Guidelines for Book Longevity, 200
  international programs, 200-201
  library operations and services support, 198-200
  Name Authority File Service task force, 195-196
  online catalog user study, 71-72
  Online public access catalog (OPAC) evaluation project, 323-324
  preservation activities support, 200
  Professional Education and Training for Research Librarianship, 197-198
Court Library (Cyprus), 434
Coyne, James, 28
Criteria for Price Indexes for Library Materials, 139
Cultural Conservation Report, 109
Culture Statistics: Public Libraries in Canada, 331
Cunha, George, 261
Current awareness services, NTIS, 95
Current Index to Journals in Education (CIJE), 101-104
Cyprus, library and information services in, 428-435
Cyprus Library Association, 428
Cyprus Ministry of Education Library, 430
Cyprus Public Record Office, archives of, 432

D

DEMAND System, 74
DEZ (diethyl zinc) deacidification test, at the Library of Congress, 105-106
Dalton (B.) Booksellers, 496
Data bases
  bibliographic, see Bibliographic data bases
  ERIC, 103

Data bases (Cont.)
  government documentation, 96
  OCLC, 74
  online, see Online headings
  toxicology, 116
Data Phase, 10, 13, 73
de Gennaro, Richard, 12
Deaf, library services for, 128
Debt Collection Act, 191
Department of Agriculture, U.S., Interagency Panel for the Assessment of the National Agricultural Library, 92
Department of Commerce, U.S. book export/import data, 440–443
  NTIS, see National Technical Information Service
Department of Defense, U.S., as source of library positions abroad, 275
Department of Education, U.S., 29
  federal funding, 178–179
  library and information science education study, 326
Diet books, 498
Direct marketing, of books, 147
Directories, as library placement sources, 278
Directory of ERIC Microfiche Collections, 103
Directory of ERIC Search Services, 103
Directory of Fee-Based Information Services, 277
Disposition of Government Records, 201
Dixon, Rebecca, 135
Document delivery, 51
  ERIC, 102
  LC future planning, 75
  NTIS, 95
  SUNY/OCLC SOLID Service, 75
Documentation, Inc., 49
Durham County (N.C.) Library, 210

E

ECIA-2, see Education Consolidation and Improvement Act, Chapter 2
EDRS, see Educational Resources Information Center, Document Reproduction Services
EIS, see Education Information Service
ERIC, see Educational Resources Information Center
E.T. The Extraterrestrial Storybook, 496–497
East, John R., 186

Economics of Research Libraries, 199
Editors, reference books for, 469
Education
  funding legislation, 178–180
  future of, 28
Education Consolidation and Improvement Act (ECIA), 179
Education Consolidation and Improvement Act, Chapter 2 (ECIA-2), 231–236
  allocations by state, 233
  appropriations (1981), 234
  school block grant, 170, 172
  state spending patterns, 235
Education for librarianship, 18–19, 257–260
  ALA activities, 132–134
  accredited programs, 257
  areas of increased concentration, 257–258
  bibliography, 458–459
  CLR support, 197–198
  conservation of library materials, 260–263
  doctoral programs, 259
  impact of information science on, 418
  impact of new technology on, 24–25
  library educators and, 259–260
  NEH grants, 237
  periodicals list, 464
  research, 326
  scholarships and fellowships
    see also Library scholarships and fellowships
  undergraduate programs, 259
  see also Higher Education Act; Library schools
Education for publishing
  AAP activities, 150
  bibliography, 466–467
  information service, 150
Education Information Service (EIS), library placement listings, 274
Educational associations, and the new copyright law, 59–60, 65–66
Educational Film Library Association, 565
Educational Resources Information Center (ERIC), 98–104
  current status, 104
  Document Reproduction Service, 102
  mission and objectives, 98–99
  organizational structure, 99–100
  products and services, 101–104
    document delivery, 102
    information analysis, 104

microfiche, 102-103
online retrieval and search, 103
question/answer service, 103
"Eichman Interrogated," 412
Eisenhower (Dwight D.) Library, 120, 122, 123
Electronic and Computer Technician Vocational Education Incentive Grants Act, 192
Electronic publishing, 415
Elementary and Secondary Education Act, 23
Elementary and Secondary Education Bloc Grant, 231
Elementary school libraries, see School libraries
Elements of a National Library and Information Services Program, 83
Ellis, Charles R., 411
Employment opportunities, see Library placement sources
Encyclopaedia Britannica Educational Corporation v. Board of Cooperative Educational Services (BOCES) of Erie County, New York, 59, 67
English, Glenn, 186
English School (Cyprus), library of, 430
Enoch Pratt Free Library, 209
Ethnic Recordings in American: A Neglected Heritage, 109
Evaluation of Archival Institutions: Services, Principles and Guide to Self-Study, 159
Exhibits
AAP publications, 151
ANSI Committee Z39, 138
"The American Cowboy," 109
LC, 112
"Braille, Bebop, and Bach," 108
Export, of books, see Book exports and imports, U.S.

F

FAUL, 72
FEDLINK, see Federal Library and Information Network
FEDLINK Network Office, 567
FID, see International Federation for Documentation
FLC, see Federal Library Committee
FRF, see Freedom to Read Foundation
Facente, Gary, 134
Facilities Funding Finesse, 130
Fact Book of the American Public Library, 327-328
Family Opportunity Act, 192
Federal Cylinder Project, 109
Federal Job Information Centers Directory, 273
Federal librarians
placement services, 273-274
standards for, 91-92, 175
OMB Circular A-76 and OPM personnel standards, 36-41, 132, 163
Federal libraries
FLC survey, 92
see also names of national libraries, e.g., Library of Congress, etc.
Federal Library and Information Network (FEDLINK), 89-90
Federal Library Committee (FLC), 89-92, 565-566
Automated Library and Information System for NOAA library system, 91
Consultation Service, 90-91
federal libraries' survey, 92
Interagency Panel for the Assessment of the National Agricultural Library, 92
Intergovernmental Library Cooperation Project, 92
microcomputer project, 91
OPM standards for federal librarians and, 91-92
Fee-Based Information Services: A Study of a Growing Industry, 277
Fellowships, see Library scholarships and fellowships
Fellowships at Centers for Advanced Study, 238
Ferber case, 131, 183
Ferraro, Geraldine, 15, 39
Fiction
best sellers, 496-498
novels, average and median prices, 379
unit sales, 495
Financial Assistance for Library Education directory, 133-134
Financing Online Search Services in Publicly Supported Libraries, 129
First amendment legislation, 183-184, 190-191
see also Censorship
Florence Agreement on the Importation of Educational, Scientific and Cultural Materials, 172-173
Folklore, 87
Ford Foundation, conference, 59

Ford (Gerald R.) Library and Museum, 121, 123
Foreign exchange programs, 276
Frankfurt Book Fair, 409-416
Freedom of Information Act, 178
  Copyright office amendments, 87
Freedom of Information Reform Act, 187
Freedom to publish, AAP activities, 149
Freedom to read, AAP activities, 148
Freedom to Read Founation (FRF), 25, 130-131
"Freight pass-through" policy, 126
French Cultural Center (Cyprus), 431
Freund, Alfred, 18
"Friends of the Library" groups, 16-17
"Fringe Benefits in Large Public Libraries of the United States—The Professional's Guide," 330

G

GAO, see General Accounting Office, U.S.
GEPA, see General Education Provisions Act
GPO, see Government Printing Office
General Accounting Office (GAO), U.S., MEDLARS report, 113
General Consultants Discussion Group, 17
General Education Provisions Act (GEPA), 172, 179, 232
General Electric and Computer Sciences Corporation, 49
Germany
  book prices, 398-400, 401
  Frankfurt Book Fair, 409-416
  International Distribution Specialists meeting, 150
Girne (Kyrenia) Public Library, 434
Give-A-Book Certificate program, 125
Go Ask Alice, 26
Goethe Institute Library (Cyprus), 431
Goldberg, Morton David, 154
Goldhor, Herbert, 327
Gonzalez, Efren, 164
Government, role in library and information services, 42-47
Government competition, in information marketplace, 185-187
Government documents and publications
  CLR-supported manual, 201
  distribution, funding of, 171
  FLC services, 89-90
  OMB cutbacks, 173
Government Printing Office (GPO)
  financial problems, 4
  Superintendent of Documents, funding, 171
Government-sponsored research, NTIS, 93-97
Gnomon Corporation, 61
Grace: Story of a Princess, 413
Grants, historical publications and records, 240-243
Grants, library
  AALS grants, 323
  ACRL grants, 323
  AJL grant, 312
  CLR grants, 195, 197, 201-203
  ECIA block grants, 170, 172, 231
  HEA grants, 214-216, 224-231
  MPLA grants, 313
  NEH grants, 236-239
  NLM grants, 116
  see also Library funding
Grapes of Wrath, banning of, 26
Great Britain
  book prices, 394, 395, 396, 397
  book production, 445-449
Greene (Stephen) Memorial Library, 150
Greensboro (N.C.) Public Library, 210
Guide to CCC-Participating Document Delivery Services, 62
Guide to Sources of Agricultural and Biological Research, 118
Guidelines for Off-Air Recording of Broadcast Programming for Educational Purposes, 60, 67
"Guidelines for Off-Air Taping of Copyrighted Programs for Educational Use," 171
Guinzburg, Thomas, 33
Guzelyurt (Morphu) Public Library, 434

H

HEA, see Higher Education Act
HSIN, see Health Sciences Information Network
Handicapped, library services for, 107-108, 128, 206, 462-463
Harcourt Brace Jovanovich, 33
Hardcover books, 32, 375, 376
  best sellers, 495-501
  prices, 388-389
    Germany, 400
Harper & Row, 33
Hashim, Elinor, 83
Hatch, Orrin, 187
Hattori, Toshiyuki, 410-411

Hazardous Substances Information Services, 116
Health Sciences Information Network (HSIN), 213-214
Hearing impaired, library services for, 128
Hearst Books antitrust suit, 126
Hechinger, Fred M., 23-24
Herner and Company, 49
Higher Education Act (HEA)
  Title II-A, College Library Resources, 214-216
  Title II-B, Library Career Training, 216-221
  Title II-B, Library Research and Demonstration Program, 221-223
  Title II-C, Strengthening Research Library Resources, 215, 224-231
  preservation microfilming, 22
Hildreth, Charles, 324
Historical publications and records, funding, 240-243
History of the National Library of Medicine: The Nation's Treasury of Medical Knowledge, 115
Home Country Employment Registry, as source of library positions, 275
Home videotaping legislation, 182, 187
Hoover (Herbert) Presidential Library, 121, 122
Horton, Forest Woody, 46
"How to" books, 495-496
Huckleberry Finn, banning of, 26

I

IAML, *see* International Association of Music Libraries, Archives and Documentation Centres
IAOL, *see* International Association of Orientalist Librarians
IBM/NCLIS projects, 84
IEPRC, *see* International Electronic Publishing Research Center
IESMP, *see* Information Exchange System for Minority Personnel
IFLA, *see* International Federation of Library Associations and Institutions
IFLA International Study of Copyright of Bibliographic Records in Machine Readable Form, 200
IFLA Journal, foreign exchange listings, 276
IIA, *see* Information Industry Association
ILL, *see* Interlibrary loan
ILLINET, 11
ILS, *see* Integrated Library System
INCOLSA, 75, 213
IOWANET, 11
ISBN, *see* International Standard Book Number
ISI, *see* Institute for Scientific Information
ISO, *see* International Organization for Standardization
ISO Standards Handbook I—Information Transfer, 139
ISO/TC46, *see* International Organization for Standardization, Technical Committee 46: Documentation
Illinois
  library volunteer programs, 15-16
  public libraries, survey, 20
Illinois Department of Education, support for microcomputer technology in schools, 77
Import, of books, *see* Book exports and imports
Index of Christian Art, 425
Indexes, public library statistical data, 332-335
"Indexes of American Public Library Circulation and Expenditures," 328
Indiana, LSCA library cooperation activities, 212-213
Indiana University School of Library and Information Science, dual masters program, 24
Information
  definition and characteristics, 42-44
  as resource or commodity, 43
  and society, bibliography, 459
Information access
  ALA activities, 128-129
  legislation, 188
Information Agency, U.S., 192, 276
Information brokering, 53, 277
Information Brokering: A State-of-the-Art Report, 277
Information Brokers: How to Start and Operate Your Own Fee-Based Service, 277
Information centers
  in Cyprus, 431-432, 434-435
  private sector professional services for, 48-55
  see also Educational Resources Information Center (ERIC)
Information clearinghouses, ERIC, 100
"Information Controllability Explosion," 12
Information distributors, 152
Information Dynamics Corporation, 49

Information exchange
  archival, 159
  NTIS, 97
Information Exchange System for Minority Personnel (IESMP)
  placement service, 267-268
  scholarship for graduate study, 313
Information flow, 418
Information industry
  awards, 154
  legislation, 184-193
  survey, 152
Information Industry Association (IIA), 56, 151-156, 567-568
  annual conferences, 152
  awards, 154
  Business of Information Report, 1983, 152-153
  government competition in information marketplace, 185
  local chapter activities, 155
  organizational structure and new officers, 153-154
  President's midyear report, 155-156
  proprietary rights legislation and, 187
  publications, 153
  seminars and workshops, 155
Information-industry associations, 505-578
Information Industry Market Place, 277-278
Information Institute of the International Academy, conference on information management education, 142-143
Information managers, 152
Information marketing, 155
Information on Microfiche Headings, 139
Information Organization Heads, 142
Information Policy Primer, 153
Information processors, 152
Information producers, 152
Information Professional: Survey of an Emerging Field, 278
"Information Resource(s) Management—IRM," 278
Information retailers, 152
Information retrieval, bibliography, 455-456
Information science, and library education, 418
Information Science and Technology Act, 191
Information science research, NSF support, 244-253

Information services
  for blind and physically handicapped, 128
  in Cyprus, 428-435
  ERIC, 98-104
  FLC, 90
  history, 48-49
  NAL, 119
  NLM's Toxicology Information Program, 116
  NTIS, 93-97
  pricing and costs, 43
  pricing policies & cost recovery, 46-47
  public sector/private sector interaction in, 42-47
  publishing education, 150
  for rural areas, 82, 117-118
  standards, *see* American National Standards Committee Z39
  U.S. Copyright Office, 85
  value of, 43
Information society, 42
Information Sources: The Membership Directory of the Information Industry Association, 153
Information technology
  bibliography, 455-456
  HEA grants, 221-222
  legislation affecting, 191-192
  NSF support, 244, 246-253
Information users, 44
Institute for Scientific Information (ISI), 50
  research awards, 323
Instructional materials, ECIA funding, 231-236
Integrated Library System (ILS), 116
Integrated library systems, 13-14
Intellectual freedom
  bibliography, 459
  see also Book banning; Censorship
Intelligence Identities Act, 190
Intelligence reporting, 183-184
Inter-American Association of Agricultural Librarians and Documentalists, 607
Intergovernmental Library Cooperation Project, 92
Interlibrary cooperation, *see* Library Cooperation; Library networks and networking
Interlibrary loan (ILL)
  message system proposal, 73
  microcomputer-based networking, 74
  NLM, 114
  national and regional network development, 75

International Association of Agricultural Librarians and Documentalists, 607–608
International Association of Law Libraries, 608–609
International Association of Metropolitan City Libraries, 609
International Association of Music Libraries, Archives and Documentation Centres (IAML), 610–611
International Association of Orientalist Librarians (IAOL), 611
International Association of School Librarianship, 275–276, 612
International Association of Sound Archives, 612–613
International book trade
 AAP activities, 147
 bibliography, 471
 Frankfurt Book Fair, 409–416
 U.S. exports and imports, 440–445
International Communication Agency, 192
International Communications Industries Association (NAVA), 24
International copyright, 87–88
International Council on Archives, 613
International Distribution Specialists, meeting (1982), 150
International Electronic Publishing Research Center (IEPRC), 415
International exchange programs, for library personnel, 276
International Federation for Documentation (FID), 614
International Federation of Film Archives, 615
International Federation of Library Associations and Institutions (IFLA), 615–616
 AALS and, 142
 CLR-supported studies, 200–201
 General Conference (1982), 416–419
 standard criteria for price indexes for library materials, 437–438
 UBC and UAP programs, 418
International Group of Scientific, Technical and Medical Publishers (STM), 415
International Institute for Children's Literature and Reading Research, 616–617
International library associations, 607–617
International Organization for Standardization (ISO), 438, 617
 CLR support, 195

International Organization for Standardization, Technical Committee 46: Documentation (ISO/TC46), 139
International School Services, as source of library positions abroad, 276
International Standard Book Number (ISBN), 139
International standards
 ISO Technical Committee 46: Documentation, 139
 for library materials' price indexes, 436–440
International Telecommunications Competition and Deregulation Act, 190
Iowa Local Government Salary and Benefit Survey: 1982, 331
Island Trees Union Free School District No. 26, et al. v. Pico, et. al., 27, 130–131, 149
Israel Museum, 413

J

Jane Fonda's Workout Book, 498
Job "hotlines," *see* Library joblines
Job Partnership Training Act, 179–180
Jobs, *see* Library placement sources
Johns Hopkins University, study to develop preservation strategies for U.S. libraries, 22–23
Johns Hopkins University Center for Social Organization of Schools, study on instructional uses of microcomputers, 78
Johnson (Lyndon B.) Library, 121, 122
Johnson, Richard D., 135
Journal of Education for Librarianship, 141
Journal of Fee-Based Information Services, 277
Journals, *see* Periodicals and serials

K

KRI, *see* King Research, Inc.
Kanon, Joseph, 33
Kennan, George F., German book trade Peace Prize, 414
Kennedy (John F.) Library, 121, 123
King, Donald W., 278
King Research, Inc. (KRI)
 copyright studies, 3, 30–31, 63, 67, 85, 172, 182–183, 324–325

King Research, Inc. (KRI) (Cont.)
  library and information science education study, 326
  library consulting activities, 17
  OCLC study, 73
  OLLT contract on future competencies of information science professionals, 223
King Research Report on Photocopying in Libraries, 30-31
Koenig, Michael E. D., 12
Kotzwinkle, William, 496
Krug, Judith, 25
Kurth, William H., 436-437

L

LACONI Salary Survey: 1981, 330
LAMA, *see* American Library Association, Library Administration and Management Association
LAMBDA Patron Access Module (PAM), 10, 73-74
LASP, *see* Linked Authority System Project
LC, *see* Library of Congress
LIBER, *see* Ligue des Bibliothèques Européennes de Recherche
LITA, *see* American Library Association, Library and Information Technology Association
LLS, *see* OCLC, Local Library System
LRRT, *see* Library Research Round Table
LSCA, *see* Library Services and Construction Act
LSP, *see* Linked System Project
Land Tenure Center, international collection of, 118
Lang, Jack, 410
"Larger Public Libraries in Indiana," 331
Larnaca (Cyprus) Municipal Library, 430
Lattès, Jean-Claude, 412
Lazerow (Samuel) Fellowship, 323
Learning Resources Corporation of America, 8
Lectionary for the Feast of St. Benedict, St. Maur, and St. Scholastica, 426
Legislation affecting librarianship, 28, 167-177
  ALA activities, 22, 129-130
  archives, 159
  copyright, 85-86, 171-172
    see also Copyright law
  ECIA, Chapter 2, 170, 172, 231-236
  funding legislation, 178-180
  library postal rates, 174
  library programs, 170-171
  medical libraries, 174
  NCLIS, 81, 174
  Nairobi Protocol, 172-173
  OPM standards for federal library positions, 175
  Presidential Libraries Act, 120
  telecommunications, 74
  see also Higher Education Act; Library Services and Construction Act
Legislation affecting publishing, 28, 178-184
  copyright, 85-86, 181-183
    see also Copyright law
  education and library funding programs, 178-180
  first amendment, 183
  Northern California Booksellers Association suit, 34
  postal rates and service, 180-181
Legislation affecting the information industry, 184-193
  First Amendment freedoms, 190-191
  government competition in information marketplace, 185-187
  information flows and information technology, 191-192
  proprietary rights, 187-188
  telecommunications, 188-190
Legislative Policy and General Guide to Legislative Action, 130
Letters of Delegates to Congress, 112
Librarians
  alternate careers, 17-18
  certification requirements, 278
  civil service requirements, 278
  contractor, 39
  in Cyprus, 433
  federal, *see* Federal librarians
  "free-lance," 277
  international exchange programs, 276
  minority, 266, 267
  OMB's Circular A-76 and, 38-41
  OPM proposal on qualifications and job classification, 105
  placement sources, *see* Library placement sources
  placements, *see* Library placements
  professional status, 15-16
  salaries, entry-level, 305-307
  salary surveys, 132, 325
  staff development programs, 19-20
  training, HEA assistance, 216-221
  in U.S., statistics, 48

INDEX / 665

Librarian's Copyright Kit: What You Must Know Now, 56
Librarian's Directory of Exchange Programs/Study Tours/Funding Sources and Job Opportunities Outside the U.S., 276
Librarian's Register, 273-274
Librarianship
  comparative and international, bibliography, 458
  see also Education for librarianship; Legislation affecting librarianship
Libraries
  acquisitions, *see* Library acquisitions
  administration and management, *see* Library management
  "America's Libraries," commemorative stamp, 174
  automation, *see* Library automation
  book detection systems, 3-4
  buildings, *see* Library buildings
  circulation, bibliography, 457
  collection development
    bibliography, 453-464
    HEA grants, 226
  Cypriot, 428-435
  facilities management, 53-54
  "friends" groups, 16-17
  funding, *see* Grants, library; Library funding
  history, bibliography, 459
  private sector professional services, 48-55
  in U.S., statistics, 337-338
  U.S. population served by, characteristics of, 335-336
  see also types of libraries, e.g. Public libraries, School libraries, etc.
Libraries, Publishers and Photocopying: Final Report of Surveys Conducted for the U.S. Copyright Office, 67, 172, 324
"Libraries, Technology, and the Information Marketplace," 12
"Libraries Are Nobody's Little Sister," 6
Library acquisitions, 463
  Cypriot libraries, 432, 435
  expenditures, 339-343
  FLC services, 90
  LC, 109-110
  private sector professional services, 51
  research fellowship award, 323
Library administration, *see* Library management
Library Administration and Management Association, *see* American Library Association, Library Administration and Management Association
Library agencies, state, 591-594
"Library and Information Science Research Agenda for the 1980's," 325
Library and Information Technology Association (LITA), *see* American Library Association, Library and Information Technology Association
Library associations, 21-22
  copyright law and, 59-60, 65-66
  foreign, 618-629
  international, 607-617
  as job placement sources, 266-268
  national, 505-578
  response to NCLIS Public/Private Sectors Task Force report, 45-46
  state and regional, 578-591
    placement services, 269-270
  see also names of specific associations, e.g., American Library Association, etc.
Library automation, 12-14
  bibliography, 455-456
  integrated library systems, 13-14
  online databases, 13
  see also Online *headings*
  see also Computers; Microcomputers
Library awards, 314-320, 323
Library awareness, ALA activities, 127, 131-132
Library buildings, 3, 356-370
  bibliography, 456
  college and university libraries, 368-370
  James Madison Memorial Building, 106-107
  LSCA construction projects, 210, 211
  public libraries, 357-368
Library Career Training Program, 216-221
Library Careers, *see* Library placement sources
Library collections, European, 436
Library Compensation Review, 325, 330
Library consultants, 17
Library cooperation, 12
  federal/nonfederal libraries, 92
  LSCA funding, 210-214
  see also Library networks and networking
Library directors
  salaries, 301-303, 304, 305
  sex and salaries, 294-308
  tenure, 303-304
Library education, *see* Education for librarianship

Library Education Fellowship/Traineeship Program, 217-219, 220
Library educators, 259-260
Library funding, 4-8
  ALA activities, 129-130
  bibliographic services, 194-197
  CLR, 194-203
  in Canada and U.S., per capita support, 295
    regional differences, 295, 297
  college and university libraries, HEA, 214-216
  ECIA provisions, 231-236
  federal, 4-5
  legislation, 178-180
    FY 82, 167, 169
    FY 83, 168, 169-171
  library career training, HEA, 216-221
  local, 6-8
  NEH support, 236-239
  Professional Education and Training for Research Librarianship Program, 197-198
  public libraries, 29
    construction, 210, 211
    services, 204-210
    sex of director and per capita support, 294-308
  research and demonstration projects, 221-223
  research libraries, HEA support, 224-231
  state, 5-6
  urban libraries, 208-209
  see also Library Services and Construction Act
Library grants, *see* Grants, library
Library Issues, 199
Library joblines, 264-266
Library literature, as source of job placements, 264
Library management
  bibliography, 453-454
  private sector support services, 49
  training programs, 19
  use of microcomputers for, 79-80
  see also Library directors
Library materials
  acquisitions expenditures, 339-343
  audiovisuals, *see* Audiovisual materials
  books, *see* Books
  conservation and preservation, 22-23
    bibliography, 454-455
    CLR-supported activities, 200
    continuing education programs, 261-262
  education and training, 260-263
  HEA grants, 226
  LC, 105-106
  presidential libraries, 120-123
  in Cypriot libraries, 432-433, 435
  microfilm, 393
  nonprint media, 392
  periodicals, *see* Periodicals
  photocopying, copyright issues, 30-31
  price indexes, international standard criteria for, 436-440
  prices, U.S. and foreign, 385-403
  school library media centers, 354
Library media centers, *see* School library media centers
Library media specialists, 354
Library networks and networking, 8-12
  automated, 13-14
  bibliography, 460
  IFLA conference, 416-419
  interlibrary loan networks, 75
  LC activities, 75, 110-111
  Linked System Project, 195-196
  local resource sharing, *13*
  microcomputer-based systems, 73-74
  NLM, 114
  online catalogs, 71-72
  optical-disk systems development, 74
  personnel changes, 72
  regional, 9-10, 72-73, 75
  SLA-NCLIS task force, 82
  Standard Network Interconnection for library computer systems, 195
  statewide, 10-11, 72-73, 75
  telecommunications legislation and, 74
  in U.S., 70-76
  see also names of specific networks, e.g. FEDLINK, SOLINET etc.
Library of Congress (LC), 105-112
  acquisitions, 109-110
  book deacidification tests, 22
  budget, 108
  CLR Linked System Project, 195-196
  Catalog Distribution Service DEMAND System, 74
  cataloging and networking, 110-111
  Cataloging in Publication Division, CLR funding, 197
  Center for the Book, 108-109
  collections, 109-110
  Copyright office regulations and, 86
  cultural services, 108-109
  government library resources study, 75
  James Madison Memorial Building, 106-107
  legislation affecting, 170-171

Manuscript Division, 110
Music Division, 110
Name Authority Cooperative (NACO) Project, 75
National Library Service for the Blind and Physically Handicapped, 107–108
National Library Services, 206
Network Advisory Committee, 74–75
Network Development Office, 75
Nitrate Film Control System, 110
OPAC evaluation project, 323
placement service, 274
preservation activities, 105–106
publications and exhibits, 111–112
reference services, 108
staff, 108–109
use of new technologies, 68
Library personnel, 3, 14–20
ALA activities, 132
appointments, 20–21
archivists, 158
consultants, 17
Cypriot libraries, 428, 433
directors, *see* Library directors
international exchange programs, 276
librarians, *see* Librarians
network leadership changes, 72
OLPR workshops, 133
OPM proposal on qualificiations and job classification, 105
OPM standards, 36–38, 39–41
placement sources, *see* Library placement sources
placements, *see* Library placements
retirements & resignations, 21
salaries, 20, 288–293
average (mean), 288–289
and experience, 293
high salaries, 290
low salaries, 291
median, 289
by region, 281
research surveys, 325
salary ranges, 289–290
by type of library, 284–285
school library media centers, 353
staff development programs, 19–20
training, HEA assistance, 216–221
unions, 20
volunteers, 15
Library placement sources, 264–279
American Libraries, 133
directories, 278
federal, 273–274
foreign countries, 275–276

joblines, 264–266
library associations and groups, 266–268
library education programs, 270–273
non-library settings, 276–278
state and regional library associations, 269–270
state library agencies, 269
Library placements, 20, 279–293
demand and supply, 286, 288
by name of library school, 282–283
nonprofessional, 280, 281
professional, 280, 281
by region, 281
"specialty," 287
by type of library, 284–285, 286
U.S. *v.* Canada, 286
Library postal rates, 174
Library research, 323–327
ALA, 325–326
bibliography, 461
CLR support, 197–198
HEA funding, 215, 221–223, 224–231
King Research/Copyright Office surveys, 324–325
librarians' salaries, 325
in library and information science education, 326
NEH grants, 238
National Center for Education Research, 326–327
technical services, 323–324
Library Research and Demonstration Program, 221–223
Library Research Round Table (LRRT), 326
Library Resources Corporation of America, 54
Library Resources Market Place, 277–278
Library salaries, *see under* Library personnel
Library scholarships and fellowships, 312–320
acquisitions, 323
library career training, 217–219, 220
NEH, 238
technical services, 323
Library schools
accreditation, 134
accredited programs, 257, 309–311
student body character, changes in, 258–259
declining enrollments, 257
degrees awarded (1981), 280, 281
graduates, placements and salaries, 20, 279–293
by institution, 282–283

Library schools (Cont.)
   by region, 281
   by type of library, 284–285, 286
   placement services, 270–273
   self-studies, 19
   see also Association of American Library Schools; Education for Librarianship
Library security, 3–4
Library Services and Construction Act (LSCA), 4, 5, 6, 167, 203–214
   ALA activities, 129, 130
   funds impoundment, 173–174
   MURL program, 208–210
   Title I, Public Library Services, 204–210
   Title II, Public Library Construction, 210, 211
   Title III, Interlibrary Cooperation, 210–214
Library Services and Construction Act: An Historical Overview from the Viewpoint of Major Participants, 203
Library services and programs
   adult literacy, 128–129
   for adults, 3
   appropriations, FY 83, 168
   in Cyprus, 428–435
   federal funding, 4–5
   funding legislation, 167–171, 178–180
   for gifted, 462
   history, 48–49
   local funding, 6–8
   NEH funding, 236–239
   public sector/private sector interaction, 42–47
   of school library media centers, 461–462
   standards, *see* American National Standards Committee Z39
   state funding, 5–6
   see also Interlibrary loan; Library Services and Construction Act; Reference services
Library services for children, 456–457
Library services for persons of limited English-speaking ability, LSCA funding, 207–208
Library services for rural areas, 117–118
Library services for the aging, LSCA funding, 208
Library services for the blind
   ALA activities, 128
   LC, 107–108
Library services for the deaf and hearing impaired, 128

Library services for the disadvantaged, LSCA funding, 204–206
Library services for the handicapped
   ALA activities, 128
   bibliography, 462–463
   LC, 107–108
   LSCA funding, 206
Library services for the institutionalized, LSCA funding, 207
Library services for young adults
   ALA activities, 30, 129, 133, 323, 490, 538–539
   bibliography, 456–457
Library standards
   CLR activities, 195
   for federal librarians, 91–92, 163, 175
   see also American National Standards Committee Z39; International standards
Library statistics
   ACRL Task Force on Library Statistics, 326
   academic library acquisitions expenditures, 342–343
   Cypriot libraries, 429
   library construction and additional renovation projects, 356–370
   of National Center for Education Statistics, 326–327
   placements and salaries (1981), 279–293
   public libraries, 327–335
      acquisitions expenditures, 339–341
   school library media centers, NCES survey, 352–355
   sex, salaries, and library support, 294–308
   urban-suburban libraries, 344–351
   U.S. and Canadian libraries, 337–338
   U.S. librarians, 48
   U.S. population served by libraries, characteristics of, 335–336
   see also Library surveys
Library Statistics of Colleges and Universities 1979, Institutional Data, 327
Library Statistics of College and Universities, Summary Data, 1979, 327
Library surveys
   archival institutions, 159
   archival profession, 158
   copyright and photocopying, 63, 67, 85
   copyright law, 324
   federal libraries, 92
   National Center for Education Statistics, 326–327
   online searching, 129

by private sector organizations, 50
salaries, 132
  librarians', 325
  sex, salaries and library support, 294–308
  urban-suburban library systems, 344–357
  see also Library statistics
Library systems
  automated, 13–14, 51, 52
  LSCA projects, 213
  development, 53
Library Training Institute Program, 219–221
Library trustees, workshop for, 133
Library unions, 20
Ligue des Bibliothèques Européennes de Recherche (LIBER), 437
Limassol (Cyprus) Municipal Library, 430
Lincoln City (Neb.) Libraries, 209
Linked Authority System Project (LASP), 75
Linked System Project (LSP), 75, 195–196
Lister Hill National Center for Biomedical Communications, 115–116
Literacy programs, 128–129
Literary agents, 469
Literary awards, see Awards, literary
Local Government Records: An Introduction to Their Management, Preservation and Use, 242
Loertscher, David, 326
Lofquist, William S., 443
Longevity in Book Binding, 200
Loving Sex for Both Sexes, 27
Lutheran Church Library Association, 568–569
Lycee Twentieth of July (Cyprus), 433

M

MARC information exchange, at LC, 111
MARC tapes, 50
MECC, see Minnesota Educational Computing Consortium
"MEDLARS and Health Information Policy," 112
MEDLARS/MEDLINE, 113, 114
MEDLARS III, 115
MIDLNET, 9, 72, 73
MLA, see Medical Library Association; Music Library Association
MLA's Role in the Educational Process for Health Sciences Librarians, 198

MLAA, see Medical Library Assistance Act
MPLA, see Mountain Plains Library Association
MS Union Catalog, 213
MURL program, see Major Urban Resource Libraries (MURL) program
McCormick, Thomas, 28
McCoy, Richard, 9, 72
McGraw-Hill, 413
Macmillan/Israel Museum publishing agreement, 413
Madison (James) Memorial Building, 106–107
Magosa (Famagusta) Public Library, 434
Mail Fraud bill, 180–181
Major Urban Resource Libraries (MURL) program, 208–210
Manual on Bookselling, 125
Manuscript collections, 419–420, 426, 427
  national information system, 159
Martin, Lowell, 3, 17
Maryland, LSCA MURL program, 209
Mass market paperbacks, 374, 377
  prices, 390
Massachusetts
  LSCA library cooperative activities, 213
  state library networking activities, 111
Matthews (Joseph) and Associates, OPAC evaluation project, 323
Matting and Hinging of Works of Art on Paper, 106
Media, nonprint, prices, 392
Media centers, see School library media centers
Media specialists, 354
Medical librarians, placement service, 268
Medical libraries
  legislation affecting, 174
  see also National Library of Medicine
Medical Library Assistance Act (MLAA), 171, 174
Medical Library Association (MLA), 569–571
  MLA's Role in the Education Process for Health Sciences Librarians, 198
  placement service, 268
Medical publications, 146
Megatrends, 499
Melcher (Frederic G.) Scholarship, 313
Melkonian Institute Library, 430
Mertz, Wolfgang, 413
Michener, James, 496
Microcomputer-based networks, 73–74
Microcomputers, 14

Microcomputers (Cont.)
  administrative uses, 79–80
  FLC project, 91
  instructional uses, 78
  in libraries, LITA institute, 133
  limitations of, 80
  purchase of, legislation affecting, 192
  in school libraries, 76–80
    state financial support, 77–78
  in school library media centers, 79–80
  in the schools, 24
  training for use of, 80
Microfiche services
  AAP, 146
  ERIC, 102–103
Microfilm, U.S. library, price indexes, 393, 394
Microfilming
  HEA funding, 22
  Vatican Library holdings, 427
Microforms
  ARL Microform Project, 197
  bibliography, 460
  LC cataloging of, 111
Midwest Region Library Network, *see* MIDLNET
Minnesota Educational Computing Consortium (MECC), 77
Minnesota Library Trustees Association, 133
Minnesota Office of Public Libraries and Interlibrary Cooperation, 133
Minorities
  graduate study scholarship, 313
  library placement services, 266
  library placement sources, 274
Missing Children Act, 191
Mississippi, LSCA library cooperation activities, 213
Missouri State Library, placement service, 269
"Model Policy Concerning College and University Photocopying for Classroom, Research and Library Reserve Use," 65
Molden, Fritz, 413
Monte Cassino, Benedictine Monastery at, 427
Montgomery County (Pa.) Community College, library media technology program, 25
Moscow Book Fair Reception in Exile, 149
Motovun Group, 415
Mountain Plains Library Association (MPLA), grants, 313

"Murder in Red Square," 412
Museums
  Cyprus' National Struggle Museum, 432
  of Vatican Library, 425–426
Music, LC acquisitions, 110
Music librarians, placement service, 268
Music Library Association (MLA), 572
  placement service, 268
Musical Instruments in the Dayton C. Miller Flute Collection at the Library of Congress, A Catalog, 112

N

NACO, *see* Name Authority Cooperative Project
NACS, *see* National Association of College Stores
NAL, *see* National Agricultural Library
NARS, *see* National Archives and Records Service
NAVA, *see* International Communications Industries Association
NCES, *see* National Center for Education Statistics
NCLIS, *see* National Commission on Libraries and Information Science
NEA, *see* National Endowment for the Arts
NEBASE, 209
NEDCC, *see* Northeast Document Conservation Center
NEH, *see* National Endowment for the Humanities
NELINET, 9
NHPRC, *see* National Historical Publications and Records Commission
NLM, *see* National Library of Medicine
NLS, *see* Library of Congress, National Library Services
NLS/BPH, *see* National Library Service for the Blind and Physically Handicapped
NMAC, *see* National Medical Audiovisual Center
NOAA, *see* National Oceanic and Atmospheric Administration
NTIS, *see* National Technical Information Service
NUC, see *National Union Catalog*
Nairobi Protocol, 172–173
Name Authority Cooperative (NACO) Project, 75
Napa City-County (Calif.) Library, 212

INDEX / 671

National Agricultural Library (NAL), 117–119
 aquaculture information service, 119
 distribution of AGRIS tapes, 119
 education and training programs, 118–119
 federal funding, 171, 179
 Interagency Panel for the Assessment of the NAL, 92
 land tenure and tropical soils information files, 118
 officers, 119
 rural library information services, 117–118
 science symposium, 117
 state extension publications, 118
 telecommunications and computerized systems and equipment, 117
 tours, 119
National Archive and Research Center (Cyprus), 434
National Archives and Records Service (NARS), 158
 funding, 171
 funding legislation (1982), 169
 legislation for independence of, 159
 presidential libraries, 120–123
National Association of College Stores (NACS)
 The Booksellers Store, 125
 College Division Liaison Committee, 146
National Audio-Visual Association, *see* International Communications Industries Association
National Book Awards, *see* American Book Awards
National Center for Education Statistics (NCES)
 library surveys, 326–327
 report on use of microcomputers in the schools, 77, 78
 school library media centers survey, 352–355
National Commission on Excellence in Education, 28
National Commission on Libraries and Information Science (NCLIS), 81–84
 annual report, 83
 appointments, 174
 Community Information and Referral task force, 82
 Conference on Resolution of Copyright Issues, 44
 Cultural Minorities task force, 82
 government library resources study, 75
 international activities, 83
 legislative activities, 81
 NCLIS/IBM projects, 84
 National Rural Information Services Development Program, 82
 1975 program document, quoted, 42
 Public/Private Sectors Task Force, 44–47, 81, 113
 SLA/NCLIS task force, 82
 WHCOLIS-related activities, 82–83
National Commission on New Technological Uses of Copyrighted Works (CONTU), report, 57
National Driver Registration Act, 191
National Endowment for the Arts (NEA), federal funding, 171
National Endowment for the Humanities (NEH), 236–240
 challenge grants, 238
 federal funding, 171
 funding for archival projects, 158
 funding for development of tribal archives, 159–160
 Research Resources Programs, 238
 state humanities councils, 239–240
National Historical Publications and Records Commission (NHPRC), 240–243
 funding, 171
 funding of archival projects, 158
 publications program, 241, 243
National Institute of Education (NIE), ERIC, *see* Educational Resources Information Center
National Librarians Association, 573
National libraries, *see* names of specific libraries, e.g. Library of Congress, etc.
National Library (Lefkosia, Cyprus), 434
National Library of Medicine (NLM), 112–116
 CITE/ILS study on online catalog systems, 115
 federal support of, 5, 171, 179
 grant programs, 116
 interlibrary loans, 114
 Lister Hill Center for Biomedical Communications, 115–116
 MEDLARS/MEDLINE pricing policy reports, 113
 MEDLARS III system, 115
 National Medical Audiovisual Center, 116
 network services, 114

National Library of Medicine (NLM) (Cont.)
 Regional Medical Library Network, 114
 Toxicology Information Program, 116
"National Library of Medicine's Medical Literature Analysis and Retrieval System," 112
National Library Service for the Blind and Physically Handicapped (NLS/BPH), 107–108
National Library Week, 131
National Medal for Literature, 150
National Medical Audiovisual Center (NMAC), 116
National Micrographics Association, 573–574
National Oceanic and Atmospheric Administration (NOAA), Automated Library and Information System, 91
"National Profile of Information Professionals," 278
National Registry for Librarians, 268
National Rural Information Services Development Program, 82
National Science Foundation (NSF), 244–253
 awards, FY 82, 246–253
 dissemination of research results, 245
 federal funding, 179
 Information Impact Program, 244
 Information Science Program, 244
 Information Technology Program, 244, 246–253
 proposal submission and review, 245
National security information, 183–184
National Struggle Museum (Cyprus), 432
National Technical Information Service (NTIS), 56, 93–97
 American National Standard Technical Report Numbers, 96
 bibliographic database, 94–95
 Center for the Utilization of Federal Technology, 96
 federal support of, 5
 history, 93–94
 marketing services, 96–97
 patent information, 96
 purpose, 94
 role in international information exchange, 97
 scope, 94
National Union Catalog (NUC), 105, 110

Natural Sciences and Engineering Research Council, scholarships, 313
Nebraska, LSCA MURL program, 209
Nevler, Leona, 32
New Career Options for Librarians, 278
"New Directions for Library and Information Science Education," 326
New England Library Association, scholarship, 313
New England Library Network, *see* NELINET
"New Growth in a 'No growth' Era," 7
New technology
 AAP activities, 148
 copyright and use of, 68
 for libraries, 51
New York City Board of Education, book banning, 28
New York (state)
 library networking activities, 11
 LSCA-supported union serial lists projects, 213
Newark (N.J.) Public Library, 29
Newspapers
 directories of, 471–472
 as sources of library job placements, 264
 U.S., subscription rates, 393
Nezansky, Fridrikh, 412
Nicosia Public Library, 430
1981 City Public Library Circulation and Central Library Attendance Survey: Summary, 330
1981 Municipal Compensation Survey, 331
1982 Salary Survey: West-North-Central States, 330
1982 Statistics of Southern Public Libraries, 330
Nixon Presidential Materials Project, 121
Nonfiction
 best sellers, 498–500
 British, 396
 unit sales, 496
Nonprint media, prices, 392
North Carolina, LSCA MURL program, 210
Northeast Document Conservation Center (NEDCC), course in conservation, 261
Northern California Booksellers Association, 34
 and Hearst Books antitrust suit, 126
Notable Books Council of Reference and Adult Services, notable books list, 489–490

Novels
  average and median prices (1972-1982), 379
  sequels, 495, 497
  see also Fiction

O

OCLC, 8, 50, 51
  database copyright, 74
  distributed systems development, 73
  in Indiana libraries, 212
  interlibrary loan systems, 9, 75
  Local Library System, 9, 73
  new user categories, 71
  OPAC evaluation project, 323
  online catalog user study, 71-72
  operations, 70-71
  regional and statewide networks, 72-73
  shared cataloging service, 89-90
  Total Library System, 9, 73
OHIONET, Library Machine System, 75
OIF, *see* American Library Association, Office for Intellectual Freedom
OLLT, *see* Office of Libraries and Learning Technologies, U.S.
OLOS, *see* American Library Association, Office of Library Outreach Services
OLPR, *see* American Library Association, Office for Library Personnel Resources
OMB, *see* Office of Management and Budget, U.S.
OPAC, *see* Online public access catalog evaluation project
OPM, *see* Office of Personnel Management, U.S.
OTA, *see* Office of Technology Assessment, U.S.
Occasional Paper No. 1: Library Services to Developmentally Disabled Children and Adults, 128
Office of Libraries and Learning Technologies (OLLT), U.S.
  Library Research and Demonstration Program, 221-223
  School Media Resources Branch, 29
Office of Management and Budget (OMB), U.S., Circular A-76, 36, 38-41
Office of Personnel Management (OPM), U.S.
  library personnel standards, 36-38, 39-41, 175

  librarians, 15, 91-92, 132, 163
  library placement services, 273
Office of Technology Assessment (OTA), U.S.
  MEDLARS report, 113
  support of federal initiatives in education, 4
Omaha (Neb.) Public Library, 209
Omnibus Budget Reconciliation Act, 231
Online, Inc., 268
Online catalogs, 71-72
  ALA activities, 129
  CLR evaluation, 71-72, 196, 323-324
  Mississippi libraries, 213
"Online Catalogs and Library Users," 13
Online Computer Library Center, *see* OCLC
Online databases, 13
Online public access catalog (OPAC) evaluation project, 323-324
Online Public Access Catalogs: The User Interface, 72, 196, 324
Online searching
  bibliography, 461
  fees, ALA survey, 129
Online services
  ERIC, 103
  FLC, 89-90
  NTIS, 94-95
Openers (library newspaper), 134
Optical-disk systems, 74
  LC preservation and retrieval system, 106
Oral histories, LC acquisitions, 110
Output Measures for Public Libraries: A Manual of Standardized Procedures, 134
Outreach services, ALA activities, 128-129

P

PAM, *see* LAMBDA Patron Access Module
PDE, *see* Pennsylvania Department of Education
PETREL, *see* Professional Education and Training for Research Librarianship
PIO, *see* American Library Association, Public Information Office
PLA, *see* American Library Association, Public Library Association
PNBC, *see* Pacific Northwest Bibliographic Center

Pacific Northwest Bibliographic Center (PNBC), 9
Paeschke, Olaf, 410
Pancyprian Gymnasium's Severios Library, 429-430
Pankake, Marcia, 7
Papal archives, 422-424
Paperback books
　AAP activities, 145
　ABA activities, 145
　　Category Paperback Bestseller List program, 125
　microcomputer-based collection control, 79
　prices
　　Germany, 399, 400
　　mass market, 377, 390
　　trade, 378, 391
　sales (1982), 31
　title output, 374
　U.S. consumer expenditures, 382, 383
Paperback houses, 32
Paperback rights, 412
Paphos (Cyprus) Municipal Library, 430
Participants in the Information Marketplace, 153
Patents
　legislation, 187
　NTIS, 96
Pay Rates in the Public Service: Survey of 62 Common Job Classes in the Public Sector, 329
Pearson, Durk, 499
Pedagogical Academy (Cyprus), 431
Pennsylvania Department of Education (PDE), and microcomputer technology in the schools, 77
Periodicals and serials
　bibliography, 460
　CONSER database, 197
　control systems, 14
　directories, 471-472
　library/information field, 464
　photocopying and, 67
　publishing industry, 472
　reprint services, 102
　U.S., prices, 385, 386, 387
Peters, Jean, 18
Phoenix (Ariz.) Public Library, 209
Photocopying
　ALA concerns, 30-31, 34
　in colleges and universities, 65-66
　in for-profit organizations, 163-164
　new copyright law and, 57
Photocopying by Academic, Public and Non-Profit Research Libraries, 148

Pick, Charles, 410
Pickaxe and Pencil: References for the Study of the WPA, 111
Pocket Facts About Public Libraries, 329
Pornography, *see* Child pornography legislation
Postal rates and service, 174
　AAP activities, 149
　legislation, 180-181
Postal Service, U.S.
　"America's Libraries" commemorative stamp, 127
　federal funding, 180
　legislation, 180-181
Prashker, Betty, 32-33
Preservation, *see* Library materials, conservation and preservation
Preservation Education Directory, 260
Presidential libraries, 120-123
　development of U.S. system, 120-121
　educational programs and conferences, 123
　holdings, 121-122
　use of, 122
Presidential Libraries Act, 120
Presidential library museums, 122-123
Presidential Recordings and Materials Preservation Act of 1974, 121
Presidential Records Act of 1978, 120
Price indexes, for library materials, 436-440
"Price Indexes for Library Materials: The Need on an International Basis," 437
"Price Indexes for 1982 U.S. Periodicals and Serial Services," 329
"Prices of U.S. and Foreign Published Materials," 332
Printing and Publishing, 443
Privacy Act, 191
　Copyright Office amendments, 87
Private school library media centers, NCES survey, 352-355
Private sector, role in library and information services, 42-55
Prizes, *see* Awards
Pro Libra Associates, 279
Proceedings of the Information Broker/Free-lance Librarian Workshop, 277
Professional Education and Training for Research in Librarianship (PETREL), 197-198
Professional publications, AAP activities, 146
Profiles of International Book Fairs, 151

"Public and Academic Library Acquisition Expenditures," 329
Public Libraries, 133
Public libraries, 3
  ALA activities, 134
  adult programming, 3
  bibliography, 460–461
  book censorship cases, 26
  buildings, 357–368
    additions, remodelings, and renovations, 361–363
    new buildings, 357–360
  certification requirements, 278
  in Cyprus, 430–431, 433–434
  expenditures, 297, 298
    acquisitions, 339–341
  fund raising, 8
  funding, 29
  interlibrary loan message system proposal for, 73
  LSCA construction projects, 210, 211
  LSCA-funded services, 204–214
  placements, 284–285
  salaries, sex of director, and library support, survey, 294–308
  salary ranges, 289, 290, 292
  statistics, bibliography and subject index, 327–335
  use statistics, urban *v.* suburban, 344–351
Public Library Association (PLA), *see* American Library Association, Public Library Association
"Public Library Buildings," 332
"Public Library: Democracy's Resource—A Statement of Principles," 134
Public Library Statistics, 1980–81 Actuals, 331
Public school libraries, *see* School libraries
Public schools
  microcomputers in, 23–24
  projected enrollment (1990), 28
Public sector, in library and information services, 42–47
Public Sector/Private Sector Interaction in Providing Information Services, 81, 113
Publisher/author relations, 33
Publishing awards, of AAP, 150–151
Publishing industry
  bibliography, 466–469
  copyright activities, 34
  cost-cutting activities, 33
  education, *see* Education for publishing
  hardcover publishing, 32
  legislation, *see* Legislation affecting publishing
  paperback houses, 32
  personnel changes, 32–33
  pricing policies, freight-pass-through practice, 4
  statistics, *see* Publishing statistics
  surveys, *see* Publishing surveys
  see also Association of American Publishers
Publishing statistics, 31
  bibliography, 467–468
  book exports and imports, 440–445
  book review media, 405
  book sales, 380–381, 411
  book title output and prices, 371–379
  British book production, 445–449
  U.S. and Canadian bookstores, 403–404
  U.S. and foreign published materials, prices, 385–403
  U.S. consumer book expenditures, 382–384
Publishing surveys, bibliography, 467–468
Pulis, Jane, 437–438

R

RASD, *see* American Library Association, Reference and Adult Services Division
RCC, *see* Rack Clearance Center
RIE, see Resources in Education
RLG, *see* Research Libraries Group
RLIN, *see* Research Libraries Information Network
RSBRC, *see* American Library Association, Reference and Subscription Books Review Committee
RTSD, *see* American Library Association, Resources and Technical Services Division
Rack Clearance Center (RCC), 145
"Read More About It" TV announcements, 108
Ready reference services, ERIC, 103
Recorded books, 107
Records management, CLR-supported project, 201
Reference books, ALA Review Committee activities, 129, 134
Reference services
  bibliography, 461
  LC, 108
  online databases for, 13
Reforma, placement service, 268

Regional library associations, 589–591
Regional Medical Library Network, 114
Regional networks, 72–73, 75
  NLM, 114
Religious art and artifacts, Vatican Library collections, 425
Requirements for Certification, 278
"Research By, For and About Librarians," 324
Research in librarianship, *see* Library research
Research libraries
  HEA funding, 22, 215, 224–231
  see also Association of College and Research Libraries; Association of Research Libraries; Research Libraries Group
Research Libraries Group (RLG)
  CLR Linked System Project, 195–196
  distributed systems development, 73
  OPAC evaluation project, 323
  online catalog user study, 71–72
  operations, 70–71
Research Libraries Information Network (RLIN), 8–9
  Battelle study, 71
  operations, 70–71
Resolution on Data Needed for the Copyright Five-Year Review, 59
Resource sharing
  Federal Library Committee, 89–92
  see also Library networks and networking
Resources for the Information Economy, 153
Resources in Education (RIE), 101–104
Ringer, Barbara, 16
Rochelle, Carleton, 8, 12
Rooney, Andrew, 498, 499
Roosevelt (Franklin D.) Library, 120, 122, 123
Royal Baby Book, 413
Rural libraries, 117–118
Rush (James E.) Associates, Inc., 213
  interlibrary loan message system proposal, 73

S

SAA, *see* Society of American Archivists
SAA Newsletter, 157
SCOLE, *see* American Library Association, Standing Committee on Library Education
SLA, *see* Special Libraries Association
SNI, *see* Standard Network Interconnection
SOLID Service, 75
SOLINET, 10, 73–74
SONY Betamax case, 62, 172, 182
SONY Video Communications Products Company, 106
SRIM, *see* Selected Research in Microfiche service
SRRT, *see* Social Responsibilities Round Table
STM, *see* International Group of Scientific, Technical and Medical Publishers
STRN, *see* Standard Technical Report Numbers
SUNY/Geneseo School of Library and Information Science, 25
SUNY/OCLC, 10
  SOLID service, 75
St. Martin's Press, *Show Me!* publication, 28
Salaries, *see under* Library personnel
"Salaries of Municipal Officials for 1981," 332
Salary Data-State Library Agencies, 329
San Francisco (Calif.) Public Library, 29
Santa Clara County (Calif.) Public Library, 24
Sauvage, Léo, 413
Scheck, Michael, 25
Scholarly books and journals, AAP activities, 146
"Scholarly Journal Publishing and Library Photocopying: Economic Issues Bearing on Copyright," 67
Scholarships, *see* Library scholarships and fellowships
School boards, book banning and, 27
School libraries
  book censorship in, 26, 148
  in Cyprus, 429–430, 433
  microcomputers in, 76–80
  placements, 284–285
  salary ranges, 289, 290, 292
  as source for library positions, 274
  see also School library media centers
School Library Journal, best book lists, 490–491, 492–495
School library media associations, 595–602
School library media centers
  certification requirements, 278
  expenditures, 353
  financial needs, 354–355
  funding legislation, ECIA, 231–236
  library materials, 354

microcomputers in, 79-80
NCES survey, 352-355
personnel, 353-354
programs and services, bibliography, 461-462
state supervisors of services, 603-606
School Library Media Quarterly, as source of library positions, 274
Science fiction, 495
  best sellers, 497
Scientific and technical information
  NAL's science symposium, 117
  NTIS, 93-97
Scientific and technical publications, AAP activities, 146
Secondary school libraries, *see* School libraries
Secular Museum, of the Vatican Library, 425-426
Selected Research in Microfiche (SRIM) service, 95
Self-help books, 495-496
Sellen, Betty Carol, 18
Seminars, *see* Workshops and seminars
Serial control systems, 14
Serials, *see* Periodicals and serials
Services Industries Development Act, 192
Shared cataloging, FLC/OCLC database service, 89-90
Shaw, Edward, 8, 72
Shaw, Sandy, 499
Shinn, James, 3
Show me!, 28
Simmons, Richard, 498
Simmons College Graduate School of Library and Information Science, course in conservation, 261-262
68 Great Ideas: The Library Awareness Handbook, 127
Slaughterhouse-Five, banning of, 26
Small Business Innovation Research Awards, 251
So You Want to Be an Information Broker?, 277
Social Responsibilities Round Table (SRRT), jobline, 267
Society of American Archivists (SAA), 156-160, 574-575
  CLR support, 199
  conservation training sessions, 262
  history and mission, 156-157
  Institution Evaluation program, 159
  meetings, 157
  National Information System task force, 159
  placement service, 268
  publications program, 157
  study tour in China, 160
  volunteer groups (Professional Affinity Groups), 157-158
Softcover books, *see* Paperback books
Software, *see* Computer software
Southeastern Library Network, *see* SOLINET
Soviet Cultural Center (Cyprus), 431
Space, 496
Special collections, bibliography, 454-455
Special libraries
  bibliography, 463
  placements, 284-285
  salary ranges, 289, 290, 292
Special Libraries Association (SLA), 160-164, 575-576
  building program, 162
  copyright activities, 163-164
  in Cyprus, 431-432, 434-435
  long-range planning effort, 161
  OPM standards for federal librarians and, 163
  placement service, 268
  public relations program, 161-162
  SLA-NCLIS task force, 82
  scholarships, 313
  75th anniversary celebration, 164
Special Research Initiation Awards for New Investigators, 244-245, 250-251
SpeciaLine, 268
SpeciaList, 268
Spivak, Jane F., 278
Squibb (E.R.) & Sons, Inc., 66
Standard Network Interconnection (SNI), funding for, 195
Standard Technical Report Numbers (STRN), 96
Standards, *see* American National Standards Committee Z39; International standards; Library standards
State Department Authorization Act, 192
State Historical Records Advisory Boards, 242
State libraries, bibliography, 463
State library agencies, 591-594
  buildings, 360
  placement services, 269
State library associations, 579-588
State school library media associations, 595-602
Statewide networks, 10-11, 72-73, 75
"Statistical Report: 1981 Domestic Title Output and Price Averages," 328

Statistics of Library Networks and Cooperative Organizations 1977-78, 327
Statistics of Public Libraries in the United States and Canada Serving 100,000 Population or More, 332
Statistics of Public Libraries 1977-78, 327, 328
Stevenson-Wydler Technology Innovation Act of 1980, 96
Stewart, Donald E., 134
Stroke of the Pen, 123
Structure for the Identification of Countries of the World for Information Interchange, 139
Student services, of AAP, 145
Suburban libraries, v. urban libraries, use statistics, 344-351
Sultan Mahmud II Library (Cyprus), 434
Summit, Roger K., 154
Superintendent of Documents, funding, 171

T

TIP, *see* Toxicology Information Program
T.I.P. kits, 132
TLS, *see* OCLC, Total Library System
Tampa-Hillsborough County (Fla.) Public Library System, book censorship, 27
Technical services
  bibliographies, 463-464
  research and development, 323-324
  research fellowship award, 323
  see also Cataloging and classification
Technology, *see* Information technology; New technology
Technology Education Act, 179, 192
Technology transfer, NTIS, 97
Teknekron Controls, Inc., 106
Telecommunications Competition and Deregulation Act of 1981, 74
Telecommunications legislation, 175, 188-190
"Telematics—2001 A.D.," 8
Telidon experiment, 417
Temkin, Victor, 33
Texas, library networking activities, 11
Texas Woman's University, 19
Textbook Questions and Answers, 146
Textbooks
  banning of, 27-28
  college, 145-146
  K-12, 146-147
Theatre Library Association, 577

Thesauri, of scientific and technical terms, 94-95
365 Days, 25
Tiffany, Connie, 12
Topics in Personnel (T.I.P.) kits, 132
Topol, Edward, 412
Tours, NAL, 119
Toward a Federal Library and Information Services Network: A Proposal, 75
Toxicology Information Program (TIP), 116
Trade books
  paperbacks, 378, 391
  sales (1982), 31
Transborder information flow, 418
Translations, of books, 445
Tribal archives, 159-160
"Tribal Archives: An Introduction," 160
Tri-State Library Cooperative, 10
Tropical soils information, 118
Truman (Harry S.) Library, 120, 123
Tucson (Ariz.) Public Library, 209

U

UAP, *see* Universal Access to Publications
UBC, *see* Universal Bibliographic Control
UCC, *see* Universal Copyright Convention
UNESCO, 88, 192
UNESCO Statistical Yearbook, 1981, book trade data from, 444, 445
USBE, *see* Universal Serials and Book Exchange
USIA, *see* Information Agency, U.S.
UTLAS, *see* University of Toronto Library Automation System
Understanding U.S. Information Policy: The Infostructure Handbook, 153
Union serial lists
  microcomputer-generated, 80
  New York State libraries, 213
Unions, *see* Library unions
United States
  book exports and imports, 440-445
  book sales statistics, 380-381
  book stores, 403-404
  book trade, bibliography, 471
  book trade associations, 630-636
  consumer book expenditures, 382-384
  as information society, 42
  libraries, 337-338
  library and information-related associations, 505-578

library directors' salaries, 299-304
library materials, prices, 385-403
library networking in, 70-76
library placements, 286
per capita library support, 295, 297
population served by libraries, characteristics of, 335-336
school library media associations, 595-602
state and regional library associations, 578-588, 589-591
state library agencies, 591-594
Universal Access to Publications (UAP), 418
Universal Bibliographic Control (UBC), 418
Universal City Studios v. SONY Corporation of America, see **Betamax case**
Universal Copyright Convention (UCC), Intergovernmental Copyright Committee, 87
Universal Postal Union Conference, 180
Universal Serials and Book Exchange (USBE), 75, 577-578
University libraries, *see* College and university libraries
University of California (Berkeley) General Library, preservation activities, 23
University of California (Los Angeles) Graduate School of Library and Information Science, CLR support, 198
University of Michigan School of Library Science, CLR support, 197
University of Texas (Austin), preservation activities, 23
University of Toronto Library Automation system (UTLAS), 9
Urban libraries
  LSCA funding, 208-209
  v. suburban libraries, use statistics, 344-351
"Urban-Suburban Public Library Statistics," 329
"User Satisfaction with Library Service—A Measure of Public Library Performance?," 326

V

VIM project, 77
VOYA, *see* Voice of Youth Advocates
VTLS, *see* Virginia Tech Library System
Vatican Library & Archives, 419-427

Christian Museum, 425
facsimile reproduction program, 426-427
history, 419-422
holdings, 419
Numismatic Cabinet, 426
publications, 426-427
as repository, 427
School of Paleography, 426
"secret" archives, 422-424
Secular Museum, 425-426
Videodisc and Microcomputers (VIM) project, 77
Videodisc systems, in the schools, 77
Videotaping, of copyrighted material, 182, 187
Virginia, state library networking activities, 11
Virginia Tech Library System (VTLS), 11
Voice of the Heart, 412
Voice of Youth Advocates (VOYA), YASD/VOYA Research Grant, 323
Volunteer programs, in libraries, 15, 157-158
Volunteers in Libraries II, 15

W

WANG VS minicomputer system, 89
WHCOLIS, *see* White House Conference on Library and Information Services
WILS, *see* Wisconsin Interlibrary Services
WIPO, *see* World Intellectual Property Organization
WLN, *see* Washington Library Network
Waldenbooks, 496
Wankesha County (Wisc.) Library System, 74
Warner, Alice Sizer, 15
Warner Books, 499
Washington Library Network (WLN), 8
  CLR Linked System Project, 195-196
Wedgeworth, Robert, 22, 61
Weeks, Ann Carlson, 134
Weidhaas, Peter, 409, 416
Weil, Ben H., 154
West Virginia, library networking activities, 11
Westat, 49
  see also King Research, Inc.
Western Massachusetts Library System, 213

What Else You Can Do With A Library Degree, 18, 277
White, Herbert, 22
White House Conference on Aging, 222–223
White House Conference on Library and Information Services (WHCOLIS), 82–83
Wirth bill, and AT&T, 189
Wisconsin Interlibrary Services (WILS), 75
Women in librarianship, 16
 ALA activities, 132
 directors' salaries and library support, survey of, 294–308
 sex discrimination, 39, 40
Woodland High School Library (Bailyville, Me.), book-banning case, 25
Worcester Area (Mass.) Cooperating Libraries, 213
Workshops and seminars AALS, 140–141
 for archivists, 157
 for booksellers, 125
 IIA, 155
 for library personnel, 133
 for library trustees, 133
World Book-Childcraft Awards, 312

World Intellectual Property Organization (WIPO), 88
Wyatt, Robert, 32
Wyoming
 LSCA library cooperation activities, 213–214
 state library funding, 5–6

Y

YASD, *see* American Library Association, Young Adult Services Division
Young, Richard, 33
Young adult books, 490–491
Young adult services
 ALA activities, 30, 129, 133, 323, 490, 538–539
 bibliography, 456–457

Z

Z39 Committee, *see* American National Standards Committee Z39
Zurkowski, Paul G., 155–156

Directory of U.S. and Canadian Libraries

This directory has been compiled for ready reference. For libraries not listed, see the *American Library Directory* (R. R. Bowker, 1982).

UNITED STATES

Univ. of Alabama
Amelia Gayle Gorgas Lib., Box S, University, AL 35486
Tel: 205-348-5298

Alameda County Library
3121 Diablo, Hayward, CA 94545
Tel: 415-881-6337

Annapolis & Anne Arundel County Public Library
5 Harry S. Truman Pkwy., Annapolis, MD 21401
Tel: 301-224-7371

Arizona State Univ. Library
Tempe, AZ 85281
Tel: 602-965-3417

Atlanta Public Library
One Margaret Mitchell Sq. N.W., Carnegie Way & Forsyth St., Atlanta, GA 30303
Tel: 404-688-4636

Baltimore County Public Library
320 York Rd., Towson, MD 21204
Tel: 301-296-8500

Boston Athenaeum
10½ Beacon St., Boston, MA 02108
Tel: 617-227-0270

Boston Public Library
666 Boylston St., Box 286, Boston, MA 02117
Tel: 617-536-5400

Boston Univ.
Mugar Memorial Lib., 771 Commonwealth Ave., Boston, MA 02115
Tel: 617-353-3710

Brigham Young Univ.
Harold B. Lee Lib., University Hill, Provo, UT 84602
Tel: 801-378-2905

Brooklyn Public Library
Grand Army Plaza, Brooklyn, NY 11238
Tel: 212-780-7712

Broward County Libraries
Box 5463, Fort Lauderdale, FL 33310
Tel: 305-765-4063

Brown Univ. Library
Providence, RI 02912
Tel: 401-863-2167

Buffalo and Erie County Public Library
Lafayette Sq., Buffalo, NY 14203
Tel: 716-856-7525

Univ. of California, Berkeley
Univ. Lib., Berkeley, CA 94720
Tel: 415-642-3773

Univ. of California, Davis
General Lib., Davis, CA 95616
Tel: 916-752-2110

Univ. of California, Los Angeles
Univ. Lib., 405 Hilgard Ave., Los Angeles, CA 90024
Tel: 213-825-1201

Univ. of California, San Diego
Univ. Libs., Mail Code C-075, La Jolla, CA 92093
Tel: 619-452-3336

Univ. of California, Santa Barbara
Campus Lib., Santa Barbara, CA 93106
Tel: 805-961-2741

Carnegie Library of Pittsburgh
4400 Forbes Ave., Pittsburgh, PA 15213
Tel: 412-622-3100

Case Western Reserve
Univ. Libs., 2040 Adelbert Rd., Cleveland, OH 44106
Tel: 216-368-3530

Univ. of Chicago
Joseph Regenstein Lib., 1100 E. 57 St., Chicago, IL 60637
Tel: 312-962-7874

Chicago Public Library
425 N. Michigan Ave., Chicago, IL 60611
Tel: 312-269-2900

Univ. of Cincinnati
Central Lib., University & Woodside, Cincinnati, OH 45221
Tel: 513-475-2218

Cincinnati-Hamilton County Public Library
800 Vine St., Cincinnati, OH 45202
Tel: 513-369-6000

Cleveland Public Library
325 Superior Ave., Cleveland, OH 44114
Tel: 216-623-2800

Univ. of Colorado at Boulder
Norlin Lib., Campus Box 184, Boulder, CO 80309
Tel: 303-492-7511

Colorado State Univ.
William E. Morgan Lib., Fort Collins, CO 80523
Tel: 303-491-5911

Columbia Univ. Libraries
535 W. 114 St., New York, NY 10027
Tel: 212-280-2271

Univ. of Connecticut Library
Storrs, CT 06268
Tel: 203-486-2219

Contra Costa County Library
1750 Oak Park Blvd., Pleasant Hill, CA 94523
Tel: 415-944-3423

Cornell Univ. Libraries
Ithaca, NY 14853
Tel: 607-256-3689

Cuyahoga County Public Library
4510 Memphis Ave., Cleveland, OH 44144
Tel: 216-398-1800

John Crerar Library
35 W. 33 St., Chicago, IL 60616
Tel: 312-225-2526

Dallas Public Library
1515 Young St., Dallas, TX 75201
Tel: 214-749-4100

Dartmouth College
Baker Memorial Lib., Hanover, NH 03755
Tel: 603-646-2235

Dayton-Montgomery County Public Library
215 E. Third St., Dayton, OH 45402
Tel: 513-224-1651

Denver Public Library
1357 Broadway, Denver, CO 80203
Tel: 303-573-5152, ext. 271

Detroit Public Library
5201 Woodward Ave., Detroit, MI 48202
Tel: 313-833-1000

District of Columbia Public Library
Martin Luther King Memorial Lib., 901 G St. N.W., Washington, DC 20001
Tel: 202-727-1101

Duke Univ.
William R. Perkins Lib., Durham, NC 27706
Tel: 919-684-2034

Emory Univ. Libraries
Atlanta, GA 30322
Tel: 404-329-6861

Enoch Pratt Free Library
400 Cathedral St., Baltimore, MD 21201
Tel: 301-396-5430

Fairfax County Public Library
5502 Port Royal Rd., Springfield, VA 22151
Tel: 703-321-9810

Univ. of Florida Libraries
210 Library W., Gainesville, FL 32611
Tel: 904-392-0341

Florida State Univ.
Robert Manning Strozier Lib., Tallahassee, FL 32306
Tel: 904-644-5211

Fort Worth Public Library
300 Taylor St., Fort Worth, TX 76102
Tel: 817-870-7700

Fresno County Free Library
2420 Mariposa St., Fresno, CA 93721
Tel: 209-488-3191

Georgetown Univ.
Joseph Mark Lauinger Lib., Box 37445, Washington, DC 20013
Tel: 202-625-4095

Univ. of Georgia Libraries
Athens, GA 30602
Tel: 404-542-2716

Harvard Univ. Library
Cambridge, MA 02138
Tel: 617-495-3650

Univ. of Hawaii
Thomas Hale Hamilton Lib., 2550 The Mall, Honolulu, HI 96822
Tel: 808-948-7205

Hennepin County Library
York Ave. S. at 70, Edina, MN 55435
Tel: 612-830-4944

Univ. of Houston
M. D. Anderson Memorial Lib., 4800 Calhoun Blvd., Houston, TX 77004
Tel: 713-749-4241

Houston Public Library
500 McKinney Ave., Houston, TX 77002
Tel: 713-224-5441

Howard Univ.
Founders Lib., 2400 Sixth St. N.W., Washington, DC 20059
Tel: 202-636-7253

Univ. of Illinois at Urbana-Champaign
Univ. Lib., Wright St., 230 Lib. UIUC, Urbana, IL 61801
Tel: 217-333-0790

Indiana Univ. Libraries
Tenth St. & Jordan Ave., Bloomington, IN 47405
Tel: 812-335-3403

Indianapolis-Marion County Public Library
Box 211, 40 E. Saint Clair St., Indianapolis, IN 46206
Tel: 317-269-1700

Univ. of Iowa Libraries
Iowa City, IA 52242
Tel: 319-353-4450

Iowa State Univ. Library
Ames, IA 50011
Tel: 515-294-1442

Jacksonville Public Library System
Haydon Burns Lib., 122 N. Ocean St., Jacksonville, FL 32202
Tel: 904-633-6870

Jefferson Parish Library
Box 7490, 3420 N. Causeway Blvd. at Melvil Dewey Dr., Metairie, LA 70010
Tel: 504-834-5850

Johns Hopkins Univ.
Milton S. Eisenhower Lib., Baltimore, MD 21218
Tel: 301-338-8000

Joint Univ. Libraries
See Vanderbilt Univ. Library

Kansas City Public Library
311 E. 12 St., Kansas City, MO 64106
Tel: 816-221-2685

Univ. of Kansas
Watson Lib., Lawrence, KS 66045
Tel: 913-864-3601

Kent State Univ. Libraries
Kent, OH 44242
Tel: 216-672-2962

Univ. of Kentucky
Margaret I. King Lib., Lexington, KY 40506
Tel: 606-257-3801

King County Library System
300 Eighth Ave. N., Seattle, WA 98109
Tel: 206-344-7465

Library of Congress
Washington, DC 20540
Tel: 202-287-5000

Los Angeles County Public Library System
Box 111, 320 W. Temple St., Los Angeles, CA 90053
Tel: 213-974-6501

Los Angeles Public Library System
630 W. Fifth St., Los Angeles, CA 90071
Tel: 213-626-7555

Louisiana State Univ.
Troy H. Middleton Lib., Baton Rouge, LA 70803
Tel: 504-388-2217

Louisville Free Public Library
Fourth & York Sts., Louisville, KY 40203
Tel: 502-584-4154

Maricopa County Library
3375 W. Durango, Phoenix, AZ 85009
Tel: 602-269-2535

Univ. of Maryland at College Park
Univ. Libs., College Park, MD 20742
Tel: 301-454-3011

Univ. of Massachusetts at Amherst
Univ. Lib., Amherst, MA 01003
Tel: 413-545-0284

Massachusetts Institute of Technology Libraries
Rm. 14 S-216, Cambridge, MA 02139
Tel: 617-253-5651

Memphis-Shelby County Public Library
1850 Peabody Ave., Memphis, TN 38104
Tel: 901-528-2950

Univ. of Miami
Otto G. Richter Lib., Box 248214, Memorial Dr., Coral Gables, FL 33124
Tel: 305-284-3551

Miami-Dade Public Library System
One Biscayne Blvd., Miami, FL 33132
Tel: 305-579-5001

Univ. of Michigan
Univ. Libs., Ann Arbor, MI 48109
Tel: 313-764-9356

Michigan State Univ. Library
East Lansing, MI 48824
Tel: 517-355-2344

Milwaukee Public Library
814 W. Wisconsin Ave., Milwaukee, WI 53233
Tel: 414-278-3000

Minneapolis Public Library
300 Nicollet Mall, Minneapolis, MN 55401
Tel: 612-372-6500

Univ. of Minnesota
O. Meredith Wilson Lib., 309 19 Ave. S., Minneapolis, MN 55455
Tel: 612-373-3097

Univ. of Missouri-Kansas City Libraries
5100 Rockhill Rd., Kansas City, MO 64110
Tel: 816-276-1531

Montgomery County Department of Public Libraries
99 Maryland Ave., Rockville, MD 20850
Tel: 301-279-1401

Nassau Library System
900 Jerusalem Ave., Uniondale, NY 11553
Tel: 516-292-8920

National Agricultural Library
U.S. Dept. of Agriculture, 10301 Baltimore Blvd., Beltsville, MD 20705
Tel: 301-344-3755

National Library of Medicine
8600 Rockville Pike, Bethesda, MD 20209
Tel: 301-496-4000

Univ. of Nebraska-Lincoln
Univ. Libs., Lincoln, NE 68588
Tel: 402-472-2526

State Univ. of New York at Albany
Univ. Lib., 1400 Washington Ave., Albany, NY 12222
Tel: 518-457-8542

State Univ. of New York at Buffalo
Univ. Libs., 432 Capen Hall, Buffalo, NY 14260
Tel: 716-636-2965

State Univ. of New York at Stony Brook
Frank Melville Jr. Memorial Lib., Stony Brook, NY 11794
Tel: 516-246-5650

New York Public Library
Astor, Lenox and Tilden Foundations Lib., Fifth Ave. & 42 St., New York, NY 10018
Tel: 212-930-0800

New York Univ.
Elmer Holmes Bobst Lib., 70 Washington Sq. S., New York, NY 10012
Tel: 212-598-2484

Newberry Library
60 W. Walton St., Chicago, IL 60610
Tel: 312-943-9090

Univ. of North Carolina at Greensboro
Walter Clinton Jackson Lib., 1000 Spring Garden St., Greensboro, NC 27412
Tel: 919-379-5880

Northwestern Univ. Library
1935 Sheridan Rd., Evanston, IL 60201
Tel: 312-492-7658

Univ. of Notre Dame Library
221 Memorial Lib., Notre Dame, IN 46556
Tel: 219-239-5252

Ohio State Univ.
William Oxley Thompson Memorial Lib., 1858 Neil Ave. Mall, Columbus, OH 43210
Tel: 614-422-6151

Univ. of Oklahoma
Univ. Lib., 401 W. Brooks, Norman, OK 73019
Tel: 405-325-2611

Oklahoma State Univ. Library
Stillwater, OK 74078
Tel: 405-624-6313

Omaha Public Library
W. Dale Clark Lib., 215 S. 15 St., Omaha, NE 68102
Tel: 402-444-4800

Orange County Library System
Orlando Public Lib., 10 N. Rosalind Ave., Orlando, FL 32801

Orange County Public Library
431 City Drive S., Orange, CA 92668
Tel: 714-634-7841

Univ. of Oregon Library
Eugene, OR 97403
Tel: 503-686-3056

Univ. of Pennsylvania
Van Pelt Lib., 3420 Walnut St., Philadelphia, PA 19104
Tel: 215-243-7091

Pennsylvania State Univ.
Fred Lewis Pattee Lib., University Park, PA 16802
Tel: 814-865-0401

Free Library of Philadelphia
Logan Sq., Philadelphia, PA 19103
Tel: 215-686-5322

Phoenix Public Library
12 E. McDowell Rd., Phoenix, AZ 85004
Tel: 602-262-6451

Univ. of Pittsburgh
Hillman Lib., Pittsburgh, PA 15260
Tel: 412-624-4400

Prince George's County Memorial Library System
6532 Adelphi Rd., Hyattsville, MD 20782
Tel: 301-699-3500

Princeton Univ. Library
Princeton, NJ 08540
Tel: 609-452-3180

Purdue Univ. Libraries
Stewart Center, West Lafayette, IN 47907
Tel: 317-494-2900

Queens Borough Public Library
89-11 Merrick Blvd., Jamaica, NY 11432
Tel: 212-990-0700

Univ. of Rochester
Rush Rhees Lib., Rochester, NY 14627
Tel: 716-275-4461

Rutgers Univ. Libraries
College Ave., New Brunswick, NJ 08901
Tel: 201-932-7505

Sacramento Public Library
7000 Franklin Blvd., Suite 540, Sacramento, CA 95823
Tel: 916-440-5926

Saint Louis County Library
1640 S. Lindbergh Blvd., Saint Louis, MO 63131
Tel: 314-994-3300

Saint Louis Public Library
1301 Olive St., Saint Louis, MO 63103
Tel: 314-241-2288

San Antonio Public Library
203 S. St. Mary's, San Antonio, TX 78205
Tel: 512-299-7790

San Bernardino County Library
104 W. Fourth St., San Bernardino, CA 92415
Tel: 714-383-1734

San Diego County Public Library
5555 Overland Ave., Bldg. 15, San Diego, CA 92123
Tel: 714-565-5100

San Diego Public Library
820 E St., San Diego, CA 92101
Tel: 619-236-5800

San Francisco Public Library
Civic Center, San Francisco, CA 94102
Tel: 415-558-4235

San Jose Public Library
180 W. San Carlos St., San Jose, CA 95113
Tel: 408-277-4822

San Mateo County Public Library
25 Tower Rd., Belmont, CA 94002
Tel: 415-573-2056

Seattle Public Library
1000 Fourth Ave., Seattle, WA 98104
Tel: 206-625-2665

Smithsonian Institution Libraries
Constitution Ave. at Tenth St. N.W., Washington, DC 20560
Tel: 202-357-2240

Univ. of South Carolina
Thomas Cooper Lib., Columbia, SC 29208
Tel: 803-777-3142

Univ. of Southern California
Edward L. Doheny Memorial Lib., University Park, Los Angeles, CA 90007
Tel: 213-743-6050

Stanford Univ. Libraries
Stanford, CA 94305
Tel: 415-497-9108

Syracuse Univ.
Ernst S. Bird Lib., 222 Waverly Ave., Syracuse, NY 13210
Tel: 315-423-2575

Tampa-Hillsborough County Public Library System
900 N. Ashley, Tampa, FL 33602
Tel: 813-223-8947

Temple Univ.
Samuel Paley Lib., Berks & 13 Sts., Philadelphia, PA 19122
Tel: 215-787-8231

Univ. of Tennessee, Knoxville
James D. Hoskins Lib., Knoxville, TN 37916
Tel: 615-974-0111

Univ. of Texas at Austin
General Libs., Box P, Austin, TX 78712
Tel: 512-471-3811

Texas A & M Univ.
Sterling C. Evans Lib., College Station, TX 77843
Tel: 713-845-8111

Tulane Univ. of Louisiana
Howard-Tilton Memorial Lib., New Orleans, LA 70118
Tel: 504-865-5131

Tulsa City-County Public Library
400 Civic Center, Tulsa, OK 74103
Tel: 918-581-5221

Univ. of Utah
Marriott Lib., Salt Lake City, UT 84112
Tel: 801-581-8558

Vanderbilt Univ. Library
419 21 Ave. S., Nashville, TN 37203
Tel: 615-322-2834

Univ. of Virginia
Alderman Lib., Charlottesville, VA 22904
Tel: 804-924-3026

Virginia Polytechnic Institute & State Univ.
Univ. Libs., Blacksburg, VA 24061
Tel: 703-961-5593

Univ. of Washington Libraries
FM-25, Seattle, WA 98195
Tel: 206-543-1760

Washington State Univ. Library
Pullman, WA 99164
Tel: 509-335-4557

Washington Univ. Libraries
Skinker & Lindell Blvds., Saint Louis, MO 63130
Tel: 314-889-5400

Wayne State Univ. Libraries
Detroit, MI 48202
Tel: 313-557-4020

Univ. of Wisconsin-Milwaukee
Golda Meir Lib., Box 604, 2311 E. Hartford Ave., Milwaukee, WI 53201
Tel: 414-963-4785

Yale Univ. Library
Box 1603A, Yale Sta., 120 High St., New Haven, CT 06520
Tel: 203-436-8335

CANADA

Univ. of Alberta Libraries
Edmonton, Alta. T6G 2J8
Tel: 403-432-3790

Bibliothèque de Québec
37 r. Ste-Angele, Quebec, P.Q. G1R 4G5
Tel: 418-694-6356

Univ. of British Columbia Library
1956 Main Mall, Vancouver, B.C. V6T 1Y3
Tel: 604-228-3871

London Public Libraries & Museums
305 Queens Ave., London, Ont. N6B 3L7
Tel: 519-432-7166

McGill Univ. Libraries
3459 McTavish St., Montreal, P.Q. H3A 1Y1
Tel: 514-392-4948

McMaster Univ. Library
1280 Main St. W., Hamilton, Ont. L8S 4L6
Tel: 416-525-9140

Montreal City Library (Bibliothéque de la Ville de Montreal)
1210 Sherbrooke E., Montreal, P.Q. H2L 1L9
Tel: 514-872-5923

National Library of Canada (Bibliothéque Nationale du Canada)
395 Wellington St., Ottawa, Ont. K1A 0N4
Tel: 613-995-9481

Queen's Univ. at Kingston
Douglas Lib., Kingston, Ont. K7L 5C4
Tel: 613-547-5950

Regina Public Library
2311 12 Ave., Regina, Sask. S4P 0N3
Tel: 306-569-7615

Saint Catharines Public Library
54 Church St., Saint Catharines, Ont. L2R 7K2
Tel: 416-688-6103

Saskatoon Public Library
311 23 St. E., Saskatoon, Sask. S7K 0J6
Tel: 306-664-9555

Scarborough Public Library
1076 Ellesmere Rd., Scarborough, Ont. M1P 4P4
Tel: 416-291-1991

Toronto Public Library
40 Orchard View Blvd., Toronto, Ont. M4R 1B9
Tel: 416-484-8015

Univ. of Toronto Libraries
Toronto, Ont. M5S 1A5
Tel: 416-978-2294

Univ. of Western Ontario
D. B. Weldon Lib., 1151 Richmond St. N., London, Ont. N6A 3K7
Tel: 519-679-6191

Windsor Public Library
850 Ouellette Ave., Windsor, Ont. N9A 4M9
Tel: 519-255-6770